GOVERNORS STATE UNIVERSITY LIBRARY

SO-ARK-732
3 1611 00318 1119

3rd Edition

MEDIA TODAY

An INTRODUCTION *to* MASS COMMUNICATION

Praise for *Media Today*, 3rd Edition

"*Media Today* is the best textbook to understand the organization, economics, and emerging trends within the U.S. media sector. Its institutional focus and the level of detail and updated knowledge it provides in this regard makes it the best textbook for an introductory media course."

Gisela Gil-Egui, *Fairfield University*

"What makes *Media Today* especially stand out is the extra attention to the dynamics of the ever-changing media industries. Joe Turow's book offers a nuanced, comprehensive and accessible treatment of how economic incentives and current trends in media matter for us and our democracy."

Matt McAllister, *Pennsylvania State University*

"*Media Today* engages students and serves as a helpful guide to our new media-saturated world. The writing is lively and concise, and the colorful illustrations are full of zest. Turow's dry wit engages students in a conversational narrative that prompts them to connect what they read to their own experience of contemporary media trends."

Edward M. Clift, *Woodbury University*

"*Media Today* skillfully weaves together all the core components needed for an introductory media course: basics of media literacy and criticism, details about a wide range of the most current media, and an uncommonly thorough integration of the functioning of media industries. Accessible and smart in its writing style and full of useful illustrations and tables, *Media Today* is not only up-to-date in its information, but its perspective prepares the future of media studies."

Amanda Lotz, *University of Michigan*

3rd Edition

MEDIA TODAY

An INTRODUCTION *to* MASS COMMUNICATION

JOSEPH TUROW

GOVERNORS STATE UNIVERSITY
UNIVERSITY PARK
IL 60466

Routledge
Taylor & Francis Group

NEW YORK AND LONDON

P
90
.T874
2009

Senior Acquisitions Editor: Matt Byrnie
Development Editor: Nicole Solano
Freelance Development Editor: Kristen Desmond LeFevre
Senior Editorial Assistant: Stan Spring
Production Editor: Alf Symons
Project Manager: Alex Lazarou
Marketing Manager: Joon Won Moon
Text Design: Keystroke, Alf Symons and Alex Lazarou
Copy-editor: Rosalind Wall
Proofreader: Felicity Watts
Indexer: Jackie Butterley
Graphics: Integra and Laserwords
Cover Design: Pearl Chang and Christian Munoz
Composition: Refinecatch and SwalesWillis
Companion Website Designer: Leon Nolan
DVD Project Manager: Patrick Sutton, Lawrence Industrial Imaging

Published 2009
by Routledge
270 Madison Ave, New York, NY 10016

Simultaneously published in the UK
by Routledge
2 Park Square, Milton Park, Abingdon, Oxon OX14 4RN

First published in 1999 by Houghton Mifflin Company
Revised and reprinted in a Second Edition in 2003 by Houghton Mifflin Company

Routledge is an imprint of the Taylor & Francis Group, an informa business

© 2009 Taylor & Francis

Typeset in Frutiger and Sabon by RefineCatch
Printed and bound in Canada by Transcontinental Interglobe

All rights reserved. No part of this book may be reprinted or reproduced or utilised in any form or by any electronic, mechanical, or other means, now known or hereafter invented, including photocopying and recording, or in any information storage or retrieval system, without permission in writing from the publishers.

Trademark Notice: Product or corporate names may be trademarks or registered trademarks, and are used only for identification and explanation without intent to infringe.

The authors and publishers have taken care in the preparation of this book but make no expressed or implied warranty of any kind and assume no responsibility for errors or omissions. No liability is assumed for incidental or consequential damages in connection with or arising out of the use of the information or programs contained herein.

Library of Congress Cataloging-in-Publication Data
Turow, Joseph.
   Media today : an introduction to mass communication / Joseph Turow.—3rd ed.
      p. cm.
   Includes bibliographical references and index.
   1. Mass media. I. Title.
   P90.T874 2008
   302.23—dc22

                                                                                  2008021757

   ISBN10: 0-415-96058-4 (hbk)
   ISBN10: 0-415-96059-2 (pbk)
   ISBN10: 0-203-89534-7 (ebk)

   ISBN13: 978-0-415-96058-8 (hbk)
   ISBN13: 978-0-415-96059-5 (pbk)
   ISBN13: 978-0-203-89534-4 (ebk)

For Judy

About the Author

Joseph Turow is the Robert Lewis Shayon Professor of Communication and Associate Dean for Graduate Studies at the University of Pennsylvania's Annenberg School for Communication. He has been described by the *New York Times* as "probably the reigning academic expert on media fragmentation." He holds a Ph.D. in communication from the University of Pennsylvania, where he has taught since 1986. He has also served on the faculty at Purdue University and has lectured at many other universities in the United States and around the world.

Turow has published more than seventy articles in scholarly journals and ten books on mass media industries in addition to *Media Today*. Among those books are *Niche Envy: Marketing Discrimination in the Digital Age* (MIT Press), *Breaking Up America: Advertisers and the New Media World* (University of Chicago Press), *The Hyperlinked Society* (University of Michigan Press), and *Playing Doctor* (Oxford University Press). He has also written about media and advertising for the popular press, including *The Washington Post*, the *Los Angeles Times*, *The Boston Globe*, and the *San Francisco Chronicle*.

Turow has received two departmental Best Teaching Awards, along with numerous conference-paper awards. He served as elected Chair of the Mass Communication Division of the International Communication Association for four years. Turow edits "The New Media World" book series for the University of Michigan Press and currently serves on the editorial boards of the *Journal of Broadcasting and Electronic Media*, *Poetics*, and *New Media & Society*.

Brief Contents

Preface   *xx*
Acknowledgments   *xxvii*
A Visual Tour of Media Today   *xxviii*
To the Student   *xxxii*

Part One
Understanding the Nature of Mass Media   **2**

1   Understanding Mass Media and the Importance of Media Literacy 4
2   Making Sense of the Media Business 38
3   Formal and Informal Controls on Media Content: Government
        Regulation, Self-Regulation, and Ethics 80
4   Making Sense of Research on Media Effects and Media Culture 142

Part Two
Media Giants and Cross-Media Activities   **186**

5   A World of Blurred Media Boundaries 188
6   Understanding the Strategies of Media Giants 230

Part Three
The Print Media   **260**

7   The Book Industry 262
8   The Newspaper Industry 298
9   The Magazine Industry 342

Part Four
The Electronic Media   **378**

10   The Recording Industry 380
11   The Radio Industry 418
12   The Motion Picture Industry 462
13   The Television Industry 504
14   The Internet and Video Game Industries 546

Part Five
Advertising and Public Relations   **590**

15   The Advertising Industry 592
16   The Public Relations Industry 624

Epilogue   660
Notes   662
Photo Credits   667
Index   669

Detailed Contents

Part One
Understanding the Nature of Mass Media

1   UNDERSTANDING MASS MEDIA
    AND THE IMPORTANCE OF MEDIA
    LITERACY   4
Varieties of Communication   6
    Communication Defined   7
        Culture Today: Mediated Interpersonal
        Communication Breakdown   8
    From Communication to Mass
        Communication   12
    Mass Communication Defined   17
    Media Innovation   18
        Culture Today: Where Does the Term
        Media Come From?   20
Mass Media in our Personal Lives   20
    How People Use the Mass Media   21
        Culture Today: Catch Phrases as Social
        Currency   22
Mass Media, Culture, and Society   23
    What is Culture?   25
    Criticisms of Mass Media's Relation to
        Culture   28
Media Literacy   28
    Foundations of Media Literacy   29
    Media Literacy Skills   32
    Becoming a Media Literate Person   33
    Questioning Media Trends   33

2   MAKING SENSE OF THE MEDIA
    BUSINESS   38
The Economy of Mass Media   40
    The Role of the Audience   41
        Critical Consumer: How Much am
        I Worth?   47
The Primary Genres   47
    Entertainment   48
    News   52
        Culture Today: A Dramady Says
        Goodbye   53
    Information   57
    Education   58
    Advertisements   59
    Mixing Genres   61
The Business of Mass Media   61
Production of Mass Media Content   62
        Culture Today: Silicon Freelancers   63
        Media Production Firms   63
        Tech & Infrastructure: Increasing Pressures
        on Special Effects Shops   65
Distribution of Mass Media Content   66
        Culture Today: The Disappearance of the
        Record Store   68
Exhibition of Mass Media Content   69
Financing Mass Media Content   71
    Funding New Production   71
    Funding When Production is Already
        Complete   72
Media Literacy and the Business of Media   74

3   FORMAL AND INFORMAL CONTROLS
    ON MEDIA CONTENT: GOVERNMENT
    REGULATION, SELF-REGULATION,
    AND ETHICS   80
    **Government Regulation of the Media
    Marketplace   82**
       Approaches to Media Regulation   82
       Political, Economic, and Cultural Influences
          on Government Regulation of the
          Media   87
    **U.S. Media Regulation and the First
    Amendment   87**
       What Does the First Amendment Mean by
          "No Law," and Where Does it
          Apply?   88
       What Does the First Amendment Mean by
          "The Press"?   89
       What Does the First Amendment Mean by
          "Abridging"?   90
    Types of Media Regulation   92
       Regulating Content Before Distribution   92
          Culture Today: A Selection of Challenged
             or Banned Books in the 2000s   95
          Critical Consumer: Prior Restraint and
             Student Journalism on the Web   103
       Regulating Information After
          Distribution   104
          World View: U.S. Libel Laws Meet the
             Internet   106
          Is it Ethical? Self-regulation or Market
             Pressure: the Imus Case   109
          Critical Consumer: Web User Beware   113
       Economic Regulation   115
    **The Struggle with Government over
    Information Gathering   117**
       Gathering Information on Government
          Documents and Meetings   117
       Gathering Information on News
          Events   118
       Gathering Information from Confidential
          Sources   118
       Allowing Information Gathering   119
    Media Self-regulation   120
       External Pressures on Media Organizations
          to Self-regulate   121

    Internal Pressures on Media to
       Self-regulate   123
       World View: Video Game Ratings
          Systems   126
    Ethics   131
       Classical Ethics   131
       Making Ethical Decisions   133
       Ethical Duties to Various Constituencies
          134
    Media Literacy, Regulation, and Ethics   136
       Media Regulations and the Savvy
          Citizen   137

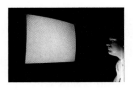

4   MAKING SENSE OF RESEARCH ON MEDIA
    EFFECTS AND MEDIA CULTURE   142
    The Nature of Mass Media Research   144
       Approaches to Mass Media Research   144
       Tools for Evaluating Mass Media
          Research   149
    **The Early Years of Mass Media Research in the
    United States   151**
       Searching for Community: Early Critical
          Studies Research   152
       Fearing Propaganda: Early Concerns About
          Persuasion   154
       Kids and Movies: Continuing Effects
          Research   157
       Social Relations and the Media   158
          Media Research: Could These Results Have
             Occurred by Chance?   161
       The Limits of Propaganda: Limited Effects
          Research   161
    **Consolidating the Mainstream
    Approach   163**
       Studying Opinion and Behavior
          Change   164
       Studying What People Learn from
          Media   164
          Is it Ethical? When Politics Meets Social
             Research   166
       Studying Why, When and How People Use
          the Media   167
          Media Research: A World Class Idea   168
          Culture Today: Bridging the Global Digital
             Divide   170

The Rise of Critical Approaches 170
  Moving from Mainstream to
    Critical 171
Cultural Studies 176
  Historical Approaches to Cultural
    Studies 177
  Anthropological Approaches to Cultural
    Studies 177

  Linguistic and Literary Approaches to
    Cultural Studies 178
**Using Media Research to Develop Media
Literacy Skills** 179
  Where Do You Stand with Respect to Media
    Effects? 179
  How to Make Sense of Discussions and
    Arguments About Media Effects 179

Part Two
Media Giants and Cross-Media Activities

**5 A WORLD OF BLURRED MEDIA
BOUNDARIES** 188
**Six Current Guiding Mass Media
Trends** 189
  Media Fragmentation 190
  Audience Erosion 190
Audience Segmentation 191
  Segmentation When Outlets are not
    Advertiser-Supported 193
  Segmentation When Outlets are Advertiser-
    Supported 194
**Distribution of Products Across Media
Boundaries** 196
  Reasons for Crossing Media Boundaries:
    Covering Costs 197
  Reasons for Crossing Media Boundaries:
    Achieving a Good Share of Mind 201
Globalization 202
  Worldwide Tastes in Media vs. American
    Media Tastes 204
  Local Media Organizations vs. Global
    Media Organizations 205
  World View: Viacom's Joint Venture
    in India 206
Conglomeration 207
  Synergy 209
  Culture Today: 7-Eleven Morphs into *The
    Simpsons* Version of Itself 212
Digital Convergence 213
  A Remarkable Development 213
  Encouraging Cross-media Distribution 214

  Encouraging Controversy 216
  Forcing New Models 217
**Media Literacy: Taking a Critical View
of Blurring Media Boundaries** 218
  Media Profile: Herbert Schiller 219
  Three Common Criticisms of the Growth
    of Conglomerates 220
  Determining Your Point of View
    as a Critical Consumer of
    Media 224

**6 UNDERSTANDING THE STRATEGIES
OF MEDIA GIANTS** 230
Three Contemporary Media Giants 232
The Walt Disney Company 232
  Critical Consumer: Does Mickey Mouse
    Have a Personality? 234
  Three Main Strategies 235
    World View: Disney to China: "It's a Small
      World After All" 238
News Corporation 239
  Media Profile: Rupert Murdoch 243
  Three Main Strategies 243
    Culture Today: Buying Space on MySpace
    244
Google 249
  Media Profile: Google Founders Sergey
    Brin and Larry Page 250
  Three Main Strategies 250
    World View: Globalizing Google 252
Media Literacy and Corporate Strategies 257

Part Three
The Print Media

7 THE BOOK INDUSTRY 262
The Meaning of a Book 264
The History of the Book 264
    Gutenberg and the Advent of Movable
        Type 265
The Impact of the Book on Society 266
    The Book in Britain 267
    The Book in the British Colonies 268
U.S. Book Publishing Becomes an
    Industry 268
    The Advent of Dime Novels and Domestic
        Novels 270
    Conglomerates Enter the Book
        Industry 270
        Critical Consumer: The Advent of
            the Serial 271
        Critical Consumer: Book
            Conglomerates 272
The Book Industry Today 272
    Educational and Training Books 272
        World View: The Scarcity of Textbooks 273
    Consumer Books 274
        Culture Today: Harry Potter Goes
            Green 276
Variety and Specialization in Book
    Publishing 278
    Financing Book Publishing 278
Production in the Book Publishing
    Industry 280
    Production in Trade Publishing 280
    Production at a University Press 281
        Tech & Infrastructure: Books on
            Demand 282
    Book Production and the Electronic
        Age 283
    Ethical Pitfalls in Book Production 284
        Critical Consumer: Plagiarism in the
            Twenty-first Century 285
    Reducing the Risks of Failure During the
        Production Process 286
        Critical Consumer: Targeting in the Book
            Industry 287

Distribution in the Book Industry 289
    The Role of Wholesalers in the Distribution
        Process 289
    Assessing a Title's Popularity 290
Exhibition in Book Publishing 291
    Exhibition in Textbook Publishing 291
    Exhibition Via Bookstores 293
    Exhibition Via the Web 294
Media Literacy and the Book Industry 294

8 THE NEWSPAPER INDUSTRY 298
The Development of the Newspaper 300
    The Rise of the Adversarial Press 300
    The Birth of the First Amendment 301
    Newspapers in Post-revolutionary
        America 301
Newspapers Become Mass Media 302
Changing Approaches to News 303
    Financing the Paper 304
    Defining News 304
    Organizing the News Process 305
A Revolution in Newspaper Publishing 306
    A Readership Revolution 306
    An Advertising Revolution 306
Print Journalism in the Early Twentieth
    Century 307
    The Era of Yellow Journalism 307
    The Newspaper Industry
        Consolidates 309
    The Rise of the Tabloids 309
    Newspaper Industry Woes 309
        Media Profile: Katharine Graham 310
An Overview of the Modern Newspaper
    Industry 312
    Daily Newspapers 312
    Weekly Newspapers 316
    Newspaper Niches 317
Financing the Newspaper Business 317
    Advertising 317
        World View: Ethnic Newspapers 318
    Advertising Challenges Facing
        Newspapers 320

Circulation Challenges Facing
Newspapers   321
**Production and the Newspaper
Industry   322**
Creating Newspaper Content   323
Critical Consumer: Project Censored   325
The Technology of Publishing the
Paper   326
Tech & Infrastructure: Printing: to
Outsource or Not to Outsource?   327
**Distribution and the Newspaper
Industry   327**
Determining Where to Market the
Newspaper   329
Tech & Infrastructure: Newsprint and
Recycling   330
A Critical View of Marketing and
Distribution Tactics in the Newspaper
Industry   330
Exhibition in the Newspaper Industry   331
Achieving Total Market Coverage   331
New Exhibition Strategies for
Newspapers   332
**A Key Industry Issue: Building
Readership   332**
Building Print Readership   333
Building Digital Newspapers   335
**Media Literacy and the Newspaper
Industry   337**

9   THE MAGAZINE INDUSTRY   342
The Development of Magazines   343
The Transformation of Magazines into
Mass Media   344
The Rise of Women's Magazines   344
Fundamental Changes in Magazine
Publishing   346

**New Roles for Mass-circulation
Magazines   347**
Sensational News: the Work of the
Muckrakers   347
Entertainment Roles: the *Ladies' Home
Journal* and the *Saturday Evening
Post*   348
Magazines Later in the Twentieth
Century   349
**An Overview of the Modern Magazine
Industry   350**
Five Major Types of Magazines   351
Business-to-business Magazines/Trade
Magazines   351
Consumer Magazines   352
Literary Reviews and Academic
Journals   353
Culture Today: Academic Journals and
Open Access   354
Newsletters   354
Comic Books   355
Financing Magazine Publishing   356
Controlled-circulation Magazines   356
Paid-circulation Magazines   358
Market Segmentation   359
World View: Magazines in China Come of
Age   360
Production and the Magazine Industry   360
Magazine Production Goals   360
Producing the Magazine as Brand   364
Culture Today: Pushing Time Ahead   365
Media Profile: Oprah Winfrey, Cross-media
Phenomenon   366
Distribution and the Magazine Industry   367
Exhibition and the Magazine Industry   369
Tech & Infrastructure: Cover Lines   370
**Media Literacy and the Magazine
Industry   371**
Conglomeration   371
Advertiser Influence on Content   372
Critical Consumer: Jean Kilbourne and
Magazines   373

Part Four
The Electronic Media

10   THE RECORDING INDUSTRY   380
The Rise of Records   381
   Minstrel Shows   382
   Vaudeville Shows   382
   Listening to Music at Home   383
   The Advent of the Record Player   383
   Records and the Rise of Radio   385
Rethinking Radio and Recordings,
1950–1980   387
   The Development of Formats   387
      Media Profile: Berry Gordy   388
   New Developments in Technology   389
   Toward a New Digital World: the 1980s
     and 1990s   389
An Overview of the Modern Recording
Industry   390
   International Ownership   390
   Fragmented Production   391
   Concentration of Distribution   391
Unique Features of the Recording
Industry   392
   U.S. Sales and Audiences   392
   Singles vs. Albums   392
   Diverse Recording Media Formats   393
   Diverse Music Genres   395
Production and the Recording Industry   396
   Artists Looking for Labels; Labels Looking
     for Artists   396
     World View: Latin Music   397
   Finding Music to Record   398
   Royalties   399
   Compensating Artists   399
   Producing a Record   399
   Self-producing CDs for Sale   400
     Tech & Infrastructure: Analog vs.
      Digital   401
Distribution in the Recording Industry   402
   The Importance of Promotion   403
   Video, Internet, and Movie
     Promotions   405
   Concert Tours   406

Exhibition in the Recording Industry   406
   Digital Downloads   406
     Is It Ethical? Corporate Sponsorship
      of Music Stars   407
   Traditional Record Stores   407
   Other Retail Stores   408
     Culture Today: Gold, Platinum, and
      Diamonds   408
   Internet Stores   409
   Record Clubs   409
   Direct Sales   409
Two Major Public Controversies   409
   Concerns Over Lyrics   410
   Concern About Access to Music   411
Media Literacy and the Recording
Industry   413

11   THE RADIO INDUSTRY   418
The Rise of Radio   419
   The Early Days of Radio   419
     Tech & Infrastructure: How the Radio
      Spectrum Works   421
   Determining the Use of Radio   421
   The Creation of the RCA   422
   Government Regulation of Radio   423
Radio in the 1920s, 1930s, and 1940s   425
   Network Programming   426
Rethinking Radio, 1950 to 1970   427
   Radio and the Rise of Television   428
   The Baby Boom, Radio, and
     Recordings   428
   Ethics and Payola   428
   FM Radio and the Fragmentation of Rock
     Music   430
Challenges of Fragmentation and
Digitalization, 1970 to the Present   430
An Overview of the Terrestrial Radio
Industry   432
   When and Where People Listen to
     the Radio   432
   AM vs. FM Technology   432

Commercial Radio Stations vs.
Noncommercial Radio Stations   433
Radio Market Size   433
Production in the Radio Industry   434
Radio Formats   435
Determining Listening Patterns   437
Working with Formats   440
Culture Today: Payola Radio   441
Producing the Playlist   442
Conducting Research to Compile the
Playlist   443
Maintaining the Format and Retaining the
Target Audience   443
**Distribution in the Broadcast Radio
Industry   445**
The Role of Networks and Syndicators   445
Format Networks vs. Traditional
Networks   446
**Exhibition in the Broadcast Radio
Industry   447**
Advertising's Role in Radio Exhibition   447
Placing and Scheduling Commercials   448
Learning Who Listens   448
Conducting Market Research to Determine
Station Ratings   449
When Stations Fare Poorly in the
Ratings   451
Broadcast Radio and Social Controversy   451
Radio Consolidation   451
The Radio Industry's Increasing Influence
over the Political Process   452
Radio and the New Digital World   453
Satellite Radio   453
Internet Radio   455
**Traditional Radio's Responses to Digital
Music   456**
Commercial Time   456
HD Radio   457
Internet Participation   457
Media Literacy and the Radio Industry   459

12   THE MOTION PICTURE INDUSTRY   462
The Rise of Motion Pictures   464
Using Photographic Images to Simulate
Motion   464

Films Become Mass Entertainment
Media   465
Vertical Integration and the Advent of the
Studio System   467
Self-regulation and the Film Industry   468
New Challenges for the Film Industry   469
Media Profile: Hattie McDaniel   470
Is It Ethical? Increasing the "Gross" at the
Box Office   472
Changes in Technology   473
**An Overview of the Modern Motion Picture
Industry   473**
**Production in the Motion Picture
Industry   476**
The Role of the Majors   477
Distinguishing Between Production and
Distribution   477
The Role of Independent Producers   477
The Process of Making a Movie   477
World View: Hollywood Meets
Bollywood   480
World View: Asian Film Trend   484
**Theatrical Distribution in the Motion Picture
Industry   485**
Finding Movies to Distribute   486
Releasing Movies   486
Marketing Movies   487
Is It Ethical? Who's the Critic?   489
**Theatrical Exhibition in the Motion Picture
Industry   490**
The Relationship Between Distributors and
Theater Chains   490
Digital Theaters   492
Tech & Infrastructure: Digital Film   493
**Non-theatrical Distribution and
Exhibition   493**
Traditional and Online Video Stores   494
Exhibition of Movies on Television   495
The Problem of Piracy   495
**Media Literacy and the Motion Picture
Industry   497**
Cultural Diversity and Cultural
Colonialism   497

13 THE TELEVISION INDUSTRY   504
  The Rise of Television   505
    Television in its Earliest Forms   505
    Television Gains Widespread Acceptance in
      the 1950s   506
    Television in the 1960s   507
  The Rise of Cable Television   509
    Government Regulation of the Cable
      Television Industry in the 1960s and
      1970s   510
  A Fragmented Television Era   511
    New Networks Emerge   511
    New Technologies Mean New Opportunities
      and New Challenges   511
    Consolidating Ownership   512
      Tech & Infrastructure: TV Ratings
        and Kids   513
  **An Overview of the Modern Television
    Industry   513**
    Television Broadcasting   514
      Culture Today: Digital TV Conversion   515
    Cable and Satellite Services   517
  Production in the Television Industry   519
    Producing Channel Lineups   520
    Producing Broadcast Channel Lineups   523
    Producing Individual Channels: Cable,
      Satellite, and Broadcast   525
      World View: Hispanic Television   527
      Culture Today: The Broadcast Networks
        and African Americans   530
  Distribution in the Television Industry   532
    Syndication   533
  **Challenges to Traditional TV Production
    and Distribution   535**
    New Avenues for Network
      Distribution   536
    New Avenues for Production Firms   537
  Exhibition in the Broadcast Industry   537
  Television and Media Literacy   538
    Audience Issues   539
    Content Issues   540
    Industry Control Issues   541

**14 THE INTERNET AND VIDEO GAME
  INDUSTRIES   546**
  An Industry Background   547
  The Rise of Computers and the Internet   549
    The Advent of the Personal Computer   550
    Online Capability   551
    The Hyperlink and the World Wide
      Web   552
  The Rise of Video Games   553
  **An Overview of the Modern Internet
    Industry   555**
    Production and Distribution in the Internet
      Industry   555
      World View: Google in China   559
    Exhibition in the Internet Industry   563
      Media Research: The Pew Internet and
        American Life Project   564
  **An Overview of the Modern Video Game
    Industry   568**
    Video Game Hardware   568
      World View: PlayStation Nation:
        Ireland?   570
    Video Game Software   572
    Advertising Content and Video Games   574
      Culture Today: Girl Games   575
      World View: Digital Resistance? Digital
        Terror?   577
    Distribution and Exhibition of Video
      Games   578
  **Media Literacy and the Internet and Video
    Game Industries   579**
    Blurring of Media Boundaries   580
    The Power of Conglomerates   580
    The Filtering of Content   582
    Privacy   583

Part Five
Advertising and Public Relations

15 THE ADVERTISING INDUSTRY 592
    The Rise of the Advertising Industry 593
    The Birth of the Advertising Agency 594
    The Advent of Radio Advertising 596
    Advertising, the Postwar Era, and
        Television 596
    Trends in the Second Half of the Twentieth
        Century 597
    **An Overview of the Modern Advertising
        Industry 598**
    Advertising Agencies 599
        Media Profile: Tom Burrell 602
    Production in the Advertising Industry 603
        Media Profile: Lionel Sosa 604
    Creating Portraits 606
        Culture Today: Dove's Contrary Approach
            to Beauty Ads 607
    Distribution in the Advertising Industry 608
    Exhibition in the Advertising Industry 611
        Culture Today: Advertising to Hispanics
            Outdoors 611
    Cross-platform Deals 612
    Determining an Advertisement's
        Success 613
    Threats to Traditional Advertising 613
    **Media Literacy and the Advertising
        Industry 615**
        Is It Ethical? Is it Ethical to Advertise? 615
    Advertising and Commercialism 616
        Culture Today: Ubiquitous Advertising 617
    Advertising and Democracy 618
    The Power of Conglomerates 619

16 THE PUBLIC RELATIONS INDUSTRY 624
    **Distinguishing Between Public Relations and
        Advertising 625**

    What is Public Relations? 625
    The Rise of Public Relations 627
    Early Pioneers in Advertising and Public
        Relations: Benjamin Franklin and P. T.
        Barnum 627
    The Public Relations Industry comes
        of Age 629
    Growth and Change in the PR
        Industry 632
    **An Overview of the Modern Public Relations
        Industry 633**
    Corporate Communication
        Departments 633
    Public Relations Agencies 634
    Major Public Relations Activities 635
    Corporate Communications 636
    Financial Communications 637
    Consumer and Business-to-business
        Communication 638
    Public Affairs 639
    Crisis Management 640
    Media Relations 642
    **Production in the Public Relations
        Industry 642**
    **Distribution in the Public Relations
        Industry 643**
        Culture Today: Buzz Marketing 644
    **Exhibition in the Public Relations
        Industry 645**
        Culture Today: Protecting Stars from
            Journalists 646
    **The Rise of Integrated Marketing
        Communication 647**
    Branded Entertainment 647
    Database Marketing 649
    Relationship Marketing 649
    Agency Holding Companies 649
    **Media Literacy and the Persuasion
        Industries 650**
    Truth and Hidden Influence in the
        Persuasion Industries 651
    Targeting and the Persuasion
        Industries 652
    Conglomerates and the Persuasion
        Industries 655

Feature Topics

CULTURE TODAY

Mediated Interpersonal Communication
  Breakdown 8
Where Does the Term *Media* Come From? 20
Catch Phrases as Social Currency 22
A Dramady Says Goodbye 53
Silicon Freelancers 63
The Disappearance of the Record Store 68
A Selection of Challenged or Banned Books in the
  2000s 95
Bridging the Global Digital Divide 170
7-Eleven Morphs into *The Simpsons* Version of
  Itself 212
Buying Space on MySpace 244
Harry Potter Goes Green 276
Academic Journals and Open Access 354
Pushing Time Ahead 365
Gold, Platinum, and Diamonds 408
Payola Radio 441
Digital TV Conversion 515
The Broadcast Networks and African
  Americans 530
Girl Games 575
Dove's Contrary Approach to Beauty Ads 607
Advertising to Hispanics Outdoors 611
Ubiquitous Advertising 617
Buzz Marketing 644
Protecting Stars from Journalists 646

CRITICAL CONSUMER

How Much am I Worth? 47
Prior Restraint and Student Journalism on
  the Web 103
Web User Beware 113
Does Mickey Mouse Have a Personality? 234
The Advent of the Serial 271
Book Conglomerates 272
Plagiarism in the Twenty-first Century 285
Targeting in the Book Industry 287
Project Censored 325
Jean Kilbourne and Magazines 373

TECH & INFRASTRUCTURE

Increasing Pressures on Special Effects Shops 65
Books on Demand 282
Printing: to Outsource or Not to Outsource? 327
Newsprint and Recycling 330
Cover Lines 370
Analog vs. Digital 401
How the Radio Spectrum Works 421
Digital Film 493
TV Ratings and Kids 513

WORLD VIEW

U.S. Libel Laws Meet the Internet   106
Video Game Ratings Systems   126
Viacom's Joint Venture in India   206
Disney to China: "It's a Small World After
   All"   238
Globalizing Google   252
The Scarcity of Textbooks   273
Ethnic Newspapers   318
Magazines in China Come of Age   360
Latin Music   397
Hollywood Meets Bollywood   480
Asian Film Trend   484
Hispanic Television   527
Google in China   559
PlayStation Nation: Ireland?   570
Digital Resistance? Digital Terror?   577

MEDIA RESEARCH

Could These Results Have Occurred by
   Chance?   161
A World Class Idea   168
The Pew Internet and American Life Project   564

MEDIA PROFILE

Herbert Schiller   219
Rupert Murdoch   243
Google Founders Sergey Brin and Larry Page   250
Katharine Graham   310
Oprah Winfrey, Cross-media Phenomenon   366
Berry Gordy   388
Hattie McDaniel   470
Tom Burrell   602
Lionel Sosa   604

IS IT ETHICAL?

Self-regulation or Market Pressure: the
   Imus Case   109
When Politics Meets Social Research   166
Corporate Sponsorship of Music Stars   407
Increasing the "Gross" at the Box Office   472
Who's the Critic?   489
Is it Ethical to Advertise?   615

Preface

Welcome to the third edition of *Media Today: An Introduction to Mass Communication*. *Media Today* stems from my concern that students in the introductory course need to be exposed to a fuller, more realistic view of the exciting, changing world of media in the new century. This innovative and up-to-date third edition reveals the forces that guide the creation, distribution, and exhibition of media systems; places the Internet and digital media as organic parts of those media systems; and actively challenges students to see and hear their favorite media products in genuinely new ways.

A Cutting-Edge, Real-World Approach to Studying Mass Communication

Media Today is the product of over three decades of teaching the introductory course, talking to colleagues around the country about course trends and issues, and writing about mass media industries and issues in the scholarly and popular press. The hope is that readers will become critical, media literate consumers of mass media and, if they go on to work in mass media industries, more alert, sensitive practitioners. The book presents a cutting-edge, real-world approach to the contemporary media system and its issues without wrenching the instructor from the familiar flow of topics in the basic course.

The third edition of *Media Today* is built around four distinct concepts:

- **A media systems approach**
- **Unique insights into media trends**
- **Emphasis on the centrality of digital convergence**
- **A media literacy goal**

Let's take a look at each:

A Media Systems Approach

Unlike other texts for the introductory course, the third edition of *Media Today* takes a media systems approach out of the conviction that the best way to engage students is to reveal the forces that guide the creation, distribution and exhibition of news, information, entertainment, education, and advertising with media systems. Then, once they begin to understand the ways these systems operate, students will be able to interact with the media around them in new ways.

The key to this unique approach is this: What fundamentally separates mass communication from other forms of communication is neither the size of the audience (it could be large or small) nor the use of technology (mediated communication can be mass or interpersonal). Rather, what distinguishes mass communication is the industrialized, or mass production, process that is involved in creating and circulating the material. It is this industrial process that generates the potential for reaching millions (even billions) of diverse anonymous people at around the same time (say, through televising the Olympic games). The third edition of *Media Today* uses this production-based approach to scrutinize the media, in order to show students how the industrial nature of the process is central to the definition of mass communication.

The text introduces the media as an interconnected system of industries—not as totally separate from one another. Of course, an introductory text can't begin with a sophisticated exploration of boundary blurring. Students have to first understand the nature of the mass communication process. They must become aware that taking a mass communication perspective on the world means learning to see the interconnected system of media products that surrounds them every day in new ways.

Chapters 1 through 4 introduce this notion of interconnected news as they explore the nature of the mass communication process, the business of media, society's formal and informal controls on media, and research on media effects and culture. Chapters 7 through 16 emphasize this industrial process, beginning with an overview of each industry, and then moving through production, distribution and exhibition, taking time to discuss relevant issues and controversies along the way.

Unique Insights Into Media Trends

Chapter 5: A World of Blurred Media Boundaries is unique among introductory media texts, and introduces students to the general media environment by taking a close look at the six trends that are guiding today's media environment:

- Media fragmentation
- Audience segmentation
- Distribution of products across media boundaries
- Globalization
- Conglomeration
- Digital convergence

Chapter 6: Understanding the Strategies of Media Giants builds upon students' new understanding of these six guiding trends through vivid case studies that examine how three of the largest media firms—News Corporation, Disney, and Google—are responding to these trends across media, and how their strategies are influencing all media industries. Students are then equipped with the media literacy skills and knowledge about the "big picture" to consider and explore ten individual media industries—from books (Chapter 7) to public relations (Chapter 16).

Emphasis on the Centrality of Digital Convergence

This edition of *Media Today* takes full account of one of the most important developments of our time: the rise of digital media, including the Internet, video games, MP3 players, and mobile phones, and their convergence—that is, their interconnection and blurring—with each other and with traditional mass media such as newspapers, magazines, and analog television. It used to be that an introductory mass communication text could nod to new-media developments by concentrating them in a chapter on the Internet and maybe one on video games. That is no longer enough.

It is today simply impossible to write about workings of the newspaper, television, magazine, recording, movie, television, advertising, and public relations industries without taking into account fundamental changes being wrought by websites, blogs, email, MP3 files, and multimedia streams. Consequently, the reader will find that every chapter incorporates digital-media developments into the main flow of the material.

Chapter 1: Understanding Mass Media and the Importance of Media Literacy announces from its very first line—"Your TV is ringing"—that this book will cover a wide variety of media in ways that highlight the clash between the new and the old. Chapter 2: Making Sense of the Media Business's introduction to the business aspects of the media shows how Internet activities—like those involved with broadcast television and newspapers—can be illuminated through the categories of production, distribution, and exhibition. Chapter 3: Formal and Informal Controls on Media Content's discussion of formal and informal controls on media content, and Chapter 4: Making Sense of Research on Media Effects and Media Culture's discussion of the history of media research on key social issues, cover topics related to the Internet and other digital vehicles alongside topics relating to traditional media. Chapter 5: A World of Blurred Media Boundaries' introduction to the blurring of media boundaries and Chapter 6: Understanding the Strategies of Media Giants's close examination of the cross-media strategies of major media firms place digital changes at the center of corporate activities—developments that Chapter 6 underscores with a section devoted to Google's activities on the web and across many other platforms.

This emphasis on the centrality of digital convergence is carried through each of the ten chapters on the individual media industries (Chapters 7 through 16). Chapter 8: The Newspaper Industry introduces students to the opportunities and challenges of the online, on-mobile, 24/7 organizational environment that has been emerging. Similarly, much of Chapter 10: The Recording Industry centers on the transformation that is taking place around digital music. Chapter 14: The Internet and Video Game Industries describes unique characteristics of the web domain and of the digital-gaming environment.

A Media Literacy Goal

The overarching goal of the third edition of *Media Today* is to help students become media literate members of society. Being media literate involves applying critical thinking skills to the mass media, and finding meanings beneath the surface of movies, ads, and other types of content. It also involves reasoning clearly about controversies that may involve the websites students use, the mobile devices they carry, the TV shows they watch, the music they hear, the magazines they read, and much more. It means becoming a more aware and responsible citizen—parent, voter, worker—in our media-driven society.

The aim of *Media Today*, third edition, is to help students become critical consumers who seriously examine the mass media's roles in their lives and in the greater culture, without making them totally cynical and distrustful of all mass media. The text helps students think in an educated manner about the forces that shape the media and their relationships with them so that they will become media literate citizens who are:

- Knowledgeable about the influences that guide media organizations
- Up-to-date on political issues relating to the media
- Sensitive to the ethical dimensions of media activities
- Knowledgeable about scholarship regarding media effects

Media Today encourages and develops these skills and attributes as it presents students with a realistic, cutting-edge picture of the changing media world in the new century. It reinforces and develops student media literacy skills in every chapter of the text, through unique chapter-ending sections applying media literacy to the issues of the chapter.

Media Today's Features

A number of valuable features—including boxes and end-of-chapter materials—appear in each chapter to enhance students' exploration and enjoyment of the third edition of *Media Today*.

Engaging, Up-to-Date Feature Boxes Provide Students Perspective and Interest

These 65 boxed features have been completely updated throughout the book to address the latest issues, trends, and developments in today's media environment. Topics include controversies in video game ratings systems (World View box, Chapter 3), advertising on social networking sites like MySpace.com and Facebook.com (Culture Today box, Chapter 6), digital television conversion (Culture Today box, Chapter 13), the rising tide of celebrity journalism (Culture Today box, Chapter 16), and much, much more.

New! Culture Today boxes: explore current, often controversial issues in today's media-rich environment. Boxes encourage a media literacy approach by asking students to consider the role that mass media play in shaping and reflecting our culture.

Updated! Critical Consumer boxes: challenge students to think critically about controversies they encounter in the films and TV shows they watch, the music they listen to, and the books, newspapers, and magazines they read. Boxes prompt students to explore the effects and implications of mass media on individuals and on society as a whole.

Updated! Tech & Infrastructure boxes: help students demystify mass media technologies by explaining how they work, helping students understand their role in the production, distribution, and exhibition of content across media outlets and around the world.

Updated! World View boxes: focus on the global aspects of mass media systems and provide an up-to-date, international perspective on the availability and social implications of media throughout the world.

Updated! Is It Ethical? boxes: use vivid, current, real-world examples to discuss issues of ethics in increasingly competitive industry environments.

Updated! Media Profile boxes: take an in-depth look at biographies of media people—both historical and current—with a special emphasis on diversity. Boxes feature profiles of media practitioners, critics, institutional leaders, and others.

Updated! Media Research boxes: introduce students to practical aspects of real-world media research and discuss the impact of research findings. Emphasis is placed on the importance and influence of historical and ongoing media research.

Rich and Diverse Chapter-Ending Materials and Exercises Give Students an Opportunity to Test and Explore What They've Learned

These valuable end-of-chapter materials are designed to challenge students to think critically and to build their media literacy skills.

Updated! Questions for Critical Thinking and Discussion: challenge students to consider the "big picture" impact of what they've learned in each chapter and to apply their knowledge to contemporary debates about the media.

New! Questions for Constructing Media Literacy: ask students to think about how THEY use the media.

New! Case Studies: ask students to research the media they consume regularly in their everyday lives (say, for instance a magazine of their choosing), exploring in depth how mass media move through the production, distribution, and exhibition processes.

Updated! Online Chapter Review and Study Guide: provides students with a way to recap what they've read in a chapter, or to review for an upcoming exam.

New! Internet Resources: connect students to relevant websites to guide them to learn more about the topics discussed in each chapter.

Updated! Key Terms: highlight the important terms introduced in each chapter, which can also be found in the marginal glossary, or reviewed through interactive flash cards on the *Media Today* student website.

Media Today's Ancillary Package

A full array of new ancillary materials supplementing these book-based features—including a companion DVD and rich online resources for instructors and students—make teaching the course, and being a student in it, especially rewarding.

For Students   Student Website at
www.routledge.com/textbooks/mediatoday

The student website features content-rich assets to help students expand their knowledge, update their text, study for exams, and more! Features include:

- **Dynamic self-quizzes for each book chapter:** help students test their knowledge and prepare for exams.
- **Interactive *Key Terms* flashcards:** provide students with a fun way to review important terms and definitions.

- **Chapter summaries and study guides:** recap the key points and themes of each chapter.
- *Study Podcasts* **audio chapter summaries:** allow students to recap each chapter and study *on the go!* These free podcasts can be downloaded directly from the *Media Today* website and are playable on any MP3 audio device.
- *Media Today* **internship and career guide:** offers students information and job listings to get started in a career in media.
- *Internet Resources:* direct students to key media websites for further study and the latest news on media industries.
- **Regularly updated author blog *Media Today and Tomorrow*:** connects students to the most recent developments, controversies, and trends in mass media, and offers a forum for critical discussion with the author.

For Instructors Instructors Website at
www.routledge.com/textbooks/mediatoday

The password-protected instructor provides complete instructor support in the form of:

- Complete, online, and downloadable Instructor's Manual: written by Harry Haines of Trinity University (both in PDF and Word formats) summarizes key learning objectives of each chapter and provides a rich selection of website features to help students expand their knowledge, update their text, study for exams, and more!
- Extensive test bank: provides multiple-choice, true–false, and fill-in-the-blank questions for exams for each chapter.
- PowerPoint presentations: offer lecture outlines for each chapter, along with a set of slides for every figure in the text.
- Regularly updated author blog *Media Today and Tomorrow*: suggests new lecture starters and classroom discussion topics pulled from today's media headlines.

Media Today Companion DVD

Packaged with every copy of *Media Today*, the companion DVD includes audio and video examples keyed to each chapter of the book. Historical clips—including early sound recordings, silent films, and television—provide rich background context and illuminate examples discussed in the text, while excerpts from critical documentaries about the media produced by the Media Education Foundation allow students to see media literacy in action.

Key Readings in Media Today (ISBN 13: 978-0-415-99205-3)

Edited by Brooke Erin Duffy and Joseph Turow, this exciting new student-friendly anthology brings together 31 of the most important historical and contemporary writings on media, technology, and culture to help students make sense of the rapidly changing media environment. Designed to supplement *Media Today* and enrich students' understanding of key issues and controversies in twenty-first-century media, *Key Readings in Media Today* presents works of media criticism drawn from the academic and popular press on each of the media industries profiled in *Media Today*. This anthology can be packaged with *Media Today* or purchased separately.

Acknowledgments

A book such as this is impossible to create alone, and so there are several people to thank. My wife Judy has been very supportive with her encouragement and smart advice. At the University of Pennsylvania's Annenberg School for Communication, a number of graduate students helped with research and editorial work. Special thanks go to Andrew Crocco, Brooke Erin Duffy, Joel Penney, and Alison Perelman for their work on this edition.

At Routledge, I'm indebted to Matt Byrnie, whose enthusiasm for the project and helpful suggestions were an important incentive. Kristen Desmond LeFevre, the supervisory editor, has been enormously influential to this project. Her terrific ideas and hard work shine through on every page. In addition, thanks go to the professional insights and efforts of development editor Nicole Solano, editorial assistant Stan Spring, marketing director Amy Lee, marketing manager Joon Won Moon, production editor Alf Symons, project manager Alex Lazarou, copy editor Rosalind Wall, and proofreader, Felicity Watts.

I would also like to thank the following academic reviewers whose (anonymous) suggestions during the reviewing process helped me greatly as I prepared the third edition:

Larry Burris, *Middle Tennessee State University*
Edward Clift, *Woodbury University*
John Couper, *Idaho State University*
Greg Downey, *University of Wisconsin-Madison*
Emily Erickson, *Louisiana State University*
Peter Galarneau, *West Virginia Wesleyan College*
Gisela Gil-Egui, *Fairfield University*
David Gudelunas, *Fairfield University*
Harry W. Haines, *Trinity University*
Sharon Hollenback, *Syracuse University*
Junhao Hong, *State University of New York at Buffalo*
Kelli Lammie, *State University of New York at Albany*
Deb Merskin, *University of Oregon*
Steve Miller, *Rutgers University*
David D. Perlmutter, *University of Kansas*
Elli Lester Roushanzamir, *University of Georgia, Athens*
Marshel Rossow, *Minnesota State University, Mankato*
Cathy Stablein, *College of DuPage*
Susan Weill, *Texas State University*

A Visual Tour of *Media Today*

Discussion quotes

Provocative quotes from media figures draw attention to key ideas and spark discussion.

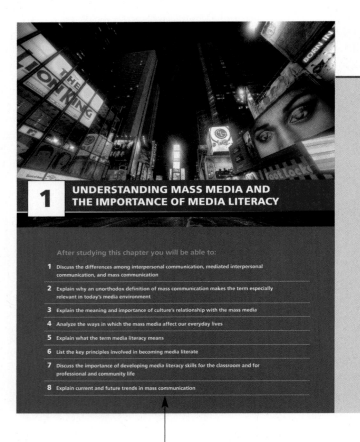

Learning objectives

Each chapter begins with a set of clearly defined goals to make the point of the chapter clear to the student from the outset.

Chapter openings

Engaging stories connect the student's daily interactions with media to key concepts introduced and issues raised in each chapter.

Informative boxed features

Boxed features enhance the student's exploration and enjoyment of every chapter by exploring current, and sometimes controversial, trends and issues in the media world today.

Catch Phrases as Social Currency

CULTURE TODAY

Have you ever considered why some phrases from movies, television shows, songs, and advertisements become *social currency*, phrases that people use with one another to show that they are "in"? Several years ago, conversations were frequently peppered with the quips, "You're fired!" and "That's hot," made popular by reality TV stars Donald Trump and Paris Hilton, respectively.

Catch phrases can come from a variety of media sources. During the 1984 presidential campaign, Walter Mondale asked his Democratic rival Gary Hart, "Where's the beef?" when he wanted to question his opponent's politic... rience. Although the expression has since died, at th... there was widespread use of this phrase, which ori... from a Wendy's hamburger chain television comme...

Other examples of catch phrases include Homer Sin... ubiquitous "D'oh"; "Bringing sexy back," from... Timberlake's hit single; "I'm kind of a big deal," a fam... from the 2004 comedy *Anchorman: The Legend*...

Prior Restraint and Student Journalism on the Web

CRITICAL CONSUMER

Freedom of the press, issues of security and concerns about school image are bumping into one another as more and more high school journalism classes publish their papers online. School administrators that have allowed their students a lot of leeway when producing paper-bound news work are having second thoughts when the students turn to cyber-journalism.

Most of the restrictions have to do with publishing the last names of students, or their names next to their photos. Administrators worry that the wide reach... means that some stalkers may collect the... tos with the intention to do harm. They also... Federal Education Records Privacy Act, enac... its what Web newspapers may reveal about... because of the Internet's reach far beyond...

Some champions of student journalism w... administrators will go beyond concerns abou... what Web newspapers can write about. Adi... quite aware that Web editions make student... to alumni and legislators who live away fro... nity. Worried about their image and the poli... administrators may use their right to exercis... as a way to keep students' critical comme... widely circulated.

Such was the case at California's La Serr... where in 2006, student journalists were ba...

lishing the June issue of their newspaper *The Freelancer*. According to students, the ban was as a form of retribution for their May issue, which included a feature on students' attitudes toward sex. Some students considered pursuing legal action under a California law protecting student journalists, yet nothing has been filed to date. In a similar vein, during the spring of 2007, the student newspaper at St Francis High School in Minnesota was taken offline after it published a photo of a student destroying an American flag. Administrators said they feared the photo might be offen...

Self-regulation or Market Pressure: the Imus Case

IS IT ETHICAL?

You may recall the controversy that surrounded radio talk-show host Don Imus in 2007, after he made disparaging comments about the Rutgers University women's basketball team. A week after the incident, MSNBC announced that it would drop its telecast of his *Imus in the Morning* radio program. The following day, CBS made public its decision to fire Imus.

Civil rights activist Reverend Jesse Jackson declared CBS's dismissal of Imus as "a victory for public decency." He continued, "No one should use the public airwaves to transmit racial or sexual degradation." Jackson's sentiment reflected a sense of faith in the self-regulatory powers of the media.

Yet not everyone was convinced that this self-regulation stemmed from the broadcasters' ethical consciousness. Instead, some believed that the broadcasters' decision to cancel Imus's radio program was prompted by disapproval from marketers.

At least eight advertisers—among them corporate behemoths like General Motors, Sprint Nextel, GlaxoSmithKline, Procter & Gamble, and American Express—immediately pulled their sponsorship of the show. As a representative from Sprint explained, "We do not want our advertising associated with content which we, our customers and the public find offensive."

Radio talk-show host Don Imus (left) speaks with Rev. Al Sharpton (right) during Sharpton's radio show in New York, where Imus apologized for insensitive remarks he made about the Rutgers women's basketball team.

Andrew Hampp, a columnist for trade magazine *Advertising Age*, argued that the loss of ad dollars was a driving force behind CBS and MSNBC's dismissal of Imus. In fact, MSNBC lost roughly $2.5 million in ad revenue. "If the whole Imus debacle tells us anything," Hampp noted, "it is that today the marketers are truly the reigning power in the fragmented media world."

While the upshot of the Imus controversy remains the same, this case raises important questions about who really controls media content—and for what reasons.

Sources: Andrew Hampp, "Imus Mess Makes Arbiters of Advertisers," *Advertising Age*, April 16, 2007, accessed 3/6/08, www.acage.com; "CBS Fires Don Imus Over Racial Slur," *CBS News*, April 12, 2007, accessed 3/6/08, http://www.cbsnews.com/stories/2007/04/12/national/main2876073.shtml

---

Marginal glossary

Provides key terms where students need them—next to their discussion in the text.

Government Regulation of the Media Marketplace

regulation with regard to mass media, laws and guidelines that influence the way media companies produce, distribute, or exhibit materials for audiences

When we talk about the **regulation** of mass media, we mean laws and guidelines that influence the way media companies produce, distribute or exhibit materials for audiences. Government regulation of mass media covers a wide range of territory. It can mean regulation by federal, state, county, or city government. Such regulation is carried out for different reasons, and in different ways, in different countries. Americans are often horrified by the extent of government control in other countries compared to that in their own country. Still, every government justifies its approach to regulation on the grounds that it is the best for that society. Sometimes many people in the society agree with the laws and guidelines, even though outsiders consider them unacceptable. Other times, people in the society believe that the laws are unfair and would like to see them change, but feel powerless.

Approaches to Media Regulation

Scholars who compare media systems around the world describe four different approaches to government regulation of the media. These approaches describe the amount of control government should have over the media, from high levels of control to low levels of control. (See Figure 3.1.) Those four approaches are:

- Authoritarian
- Communist
- Libertarian
- Social responsibility

Engaging images

Illuminating tables and figures give students a visual key
to unlock difficult concepts and theories, while vivid
photos and illustrations enrich students' understanding
of the ideas discussed in each chapter.

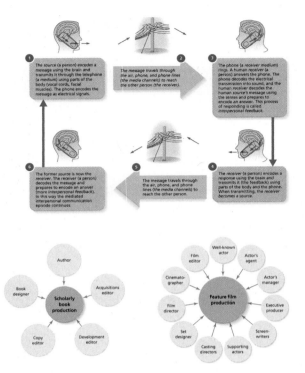

Table 1.1	Differences in Types of Communication		
	Interpersonal Communication	**Mediated Interpersonal Communication**	**Mass Communication**
Message	Uses all the senses	Typically verbal and/or visual	Typically verbal and/or visual
Source	An individual	An individual	One or more organizations
Encoding	By an individual's brain	By an individual's brain and technology	By an organization and technology
Channel	The air	The air, technology	The air, technology
Receiver	A few individuals in the same location	A few or many individuals in the same location	Typically, many people in different locations
Decoding	By an individual's brain	By technology and an individual's brain	By technology and an individual's brain
Feedback	Immediate and direct	Immediate or delayed; generally direct	Immediate or delayed; generally indirect
Noise	Environmental, mechanical, and semantic	Environmental mechanical, and semantic, with environmental sometimes caused by organizations	Environmental, mechanical, and semantic, sometimes caused by organizations

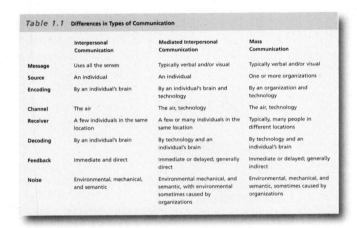

Meaningful end-of-chapter materials

These valuable end-of-chapter resources and exercises go
beyond standard chapter reviews to challenge students to
think critically and to build their media literacy skills.

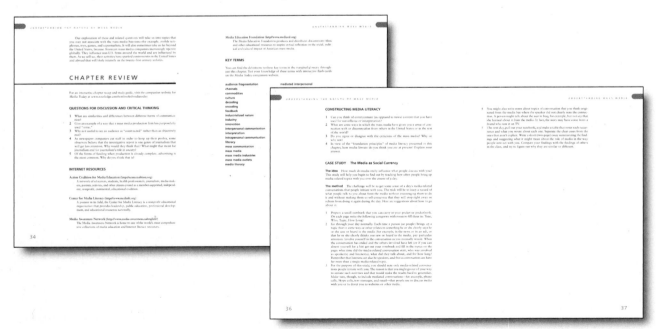

Companion website www.routledge.com/textbooks/mediatoday

The website features material to help students expand their knowledge, update their text, study for exams, and more! Features include:

- Dynamic self-quizzes for each chapter
- Interactive vocabulary flashcards
- Chapter summaries and study guides
- Downloadable chapter summary podcasts
- Author's blog *Media Today and Tomorrow* connects the text to the latest issues in the media

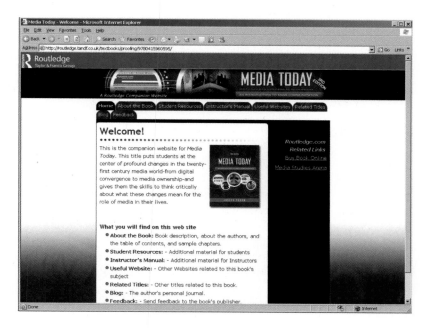

Media Today DVD

Packaged with every copy of *Media Today*, the companion DVD includes audio and video examples keyed to each chapter of the book.

- Historical clips—including early sound recordings, silent films, and television— provide rich context.
- Excerpts from documentaries about the media produced by the Media Education Foundation show students media literacy in action.

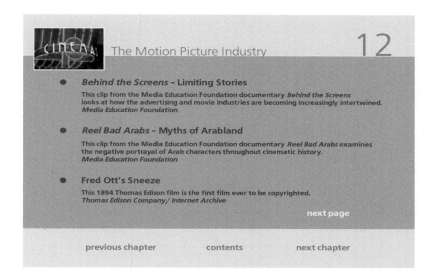

To the Student

I hope that you'll find *Media Today* fun to read, helpful for understanding the media-saturated world around you, and (if you're so inclined) useful for thinking about a future career in mass media. More likely than not, you've grown up with all or at least most of the media we cover in this book. Your family has probably had newspapers, books, magazines, CDs, radios, and a television set in your home from the time you were born. It's likely, too, that you have also had a computer and the Internet in your home from the time you were small. In one sense, then, you're already an "expert" at mass media: you've seen a lot of it, you know what you like, and you know what you don't like. At the same time, there's probably a lot about the content mass media present, the industries behind them, and their roles in society that you haven't considered yet.

The purpose of *Media Today* is to introduce you to these ideas, with the expectation that they will help you think about the media you think you already know in entirely new ways. To get the most out of this text, use all the bells and whistles that come with it. The chapter objectives, the marginal glossary, the art and photo selections, and the boxed features have all been created with an eye toward making the text itself as clear and relevant as possible. The companion website accessible at www.routledge.com/textbooks/mediatoday and the *Media Today* DVD packaged with this book will also be of enormous value for helping you learn more about book topics, studying for exams, learning about careers in mass media, quizzing yourself, and more. Get to know all these learning aids, and let us know what you think of them.

You'll notice that there is a quotation on the first page of every chapter. Please do not assume that I agree with the point or attitude expressed in the statement. Rather, the purpose of the quotations is to present yet another provocative springboard for discussion about one or more themes of the chapter. Think about the statement. Find out something about the person who said it. Try to relate it to issues in the chapter and the rest of *Media Today*. Consider why you might argue with it and why you might agree with it—and what difference that might make in the way you approach the industry the quotation mentions as well as the media at large.

MEDIA TODAY

chapters

1 UNDERSTANDING MASS MEDIA AND THE IMPORTANCE OF MEDIA LITERACY

2 MAKING SENSE OF THE MEDIA BUSINESS

3 FORMAL AND INFORMAL CONTROLS ON MEDIA CONTENT: GOVERNMENT REGULATION, SELF-REGULATION, AND ETHICS

4 MAKING SENSE OF RESEARCH ON MEDIA EFFECTS AND MEDIA CULTURE

Mass media circulate words, sounds, and images that surround us. Too often, we immerse ourselves in media materials without asking where they come from, what meanings they might have, and what their consequences might be.

This section introduces media literacy and applies it to some basic but crucial questions. What is mass communication and how does it work? What roles do governments, businesses, academic researchers, members of the public, advocacy organizations, and culture play in what we read, see and hear? This section—and the sections that follow—aim to help you become a critical consumer by encouraging you to ask questions—and get answers—about the media you use.

understanding the

part one

understanding the nature of mass media

nature of mass media

1

UNDERSTANDING MASS MEDIA AND THE IMPORTANCE OF MEDIA LITERACY

After studying this chapter, you will be able to:

1 Discuss the differences among interpersonal communication, mediated interpersonal communication, and mass communication

2 Explain why an unorthodox definition of mass communication makes the term especially relevant in today's media environment

3 Explain the meaning and importance of culture's relationship with the mass media

4 Analyze the ways in which the mass media affect our everyday lives

5 Explain what the term media literacy means

6 List the key principles involved in becoming media literate

7 Discuss the importance of developing media literacy skills for the classroom and for professional and community life

8 Explain current and future trends in mass communication

"Whoever controls the media controls the culture."

– ALLEN GINSBERG, POET

"Information is the oxygen of the modern age."

– RONALD REAGAN, US PRESIDENT

Media Today

"Your TV is ringing."

Maybe you saw the Verizon ad that shows a cellphone with a TV attached to it—pointing out that you can talk on the phone and watch TV at the same time, on one piece of equipment. If you saw it, you might have said, "cool," or "I want that," or "what a ridiculous thing to do." But Verizon could have gone further. The ad could have pointed out that some of the company's cellphones also let you watch movies, play video games, download and listen to music, and read a newspaper or magazine.

It's an exciting time to study mass communication. None of the activities described above could have been attempted on a cellphone (call it a mobile device) just a few years ago. They raise questions about the impact that these and other technologies will have on us, our society, and the content of TV, movies, video games, music, newspapers, magazines, and movie companies. In fact, the transformations are so great that you have the opportunity to know more than conventional experts, to challenge traditional thinking, and to encourage fresh public discussions about media and society.

Consider the mass media menu that Americans have today. Instead of three or four TV channels, most Americans receive more than fifty and a substantial number receive one hundred and fifty and more. Radio in urban areas delivers dozens of stations; satellite radio brings in hundreds more, and music streaming on the Web—sometimes called Internet radio—is carried out by countless broadcast and non-broadcast entities. The advent of home computers, VCRs, CD players, DVDs, and DBS has brought far more channels of sights and sounds into people's lives than ever before. So has the Internet and the World Wide Web, the computer network that Americans use to interact with information, news and entertainment from all over the nation and the world.

Research indicates that Americans typically spend an enormous amount of time with mass media.[1] Think about your own

media habits. How close do you come to the average 32 hours a week (about 4.5 hours a day) of television that Americans view on the traditional TV set as well as online? What about radio? Studies suggest that Americans listen to around 15 hours a week of radio in the regular broadcast mode, via satellite channels or from their online feeds. Do you do that, or do you instead listen to recorded music on your iPod or on your MP3 or CD player? Studies show that Americans spend an average of about 3.5 hours a week with recorded music, but college students undoubtedly do more of it. And what about your time reading books, newspapers and magazines? Data show that on average Americans spend about 8 hours a week with one or another of these, both their printed versions and their websites. Just a few years ago, media such as *television*, *radio, books* and *newspapers* seemed pretty separate. It was clear what content from each medium looked or sounded like, and it would have been foolish to suggest that newspaper articles and television programs would show up on the same channel. Today, with the rise of new computer technologies that we will explain in the coming pages, this "foolishness" is exactly what has happened. The access people have on the Internet to content from different types of media is part of a process called **convergence**. Convergence takes place when content that has traditionally been confined to one medium appears on multiple media channels.

The media of mass communication, then, are an integral part of our lives, occurring in a wide variety of settings. In this chapter, we will explore and define communication, media, and culture, and we will consider how the relationships among them affect us and the world in which we live. We will also consider why the term mass communication remains relevant in the twenty-first century, contrary to what some writers say. In fact, the changes taking place in the media system actually make a rethought and redefined version of the term more important than ever.

Varieties of Communication

convergence when content that has traditionally been confined to one medium appears on multiple media channels

audience fragmentation the process of dividing audience members into segments based on background and lifestyle in order to send them messages targeted to their specific characteristics

mass production process the industrial process that creates the potential for reaching millions, even billions, of diverse, anonymous people at around the same time

industrial nature what distinguishes mass communication from other forms of communication is the industrialized—or mass production—process that is involved in creating the message material. This industrial process creates the potential for reaching billions of diverse, anonymous people simultaneously.

The traditional notion of the audience as a large mass of anonymous individuals has given way beneath the fragmenting of audiences to reveal smaller, specially targeted media audiences made up of individuals who are segmented by any number of characteristics.

To understand why some writers suggest that the term *mass communication* doesn't connect to what's going on in today's world, we have to look at how the term has traditionally been used. Over the past one hundred years, people who wrote about mass communication tended to relate it to the size of the audience. That made a lot of sense back then. From the mid-nineteenth century onward, new technologies such as high-speed newspaper presses, radio, movies, and television provided access to the huge "masses" of people. Not only were those audiences very large, they were dispersed geographically, quite diverse (that is, made up of different types of people), and typically anonymous to the companies that created the material. The essential reason newspapers, radio, television, and other such media were considered different from other means of communication had to do with the size and composition of the audience.

This perspective on mass communication worked very well until the past couple of decades when the key aspects of the traditional definition of mass communication as reaching huge, diverse groups no longer fit. The reason is that the arrival of media channels—including the growing number of radio and TV stations, the rise of the VCR, the multiplication of cable networks, and the rise of the Web—led to **audience fragmentation** (see Figure 1.1). That is, as people watched or read these new channels, there were fewer people using any one of them. Because these new media channels do not necessarily individually reach large numbers of people—the "masses"—some writers suggested that we can abandon the term *mass communication*.

However, the view in this book is that mass communication is still a critically important part of society. In our view, what really separates mass communication from other forms of communication is not the size of the audience—it can be large or small. Rather, what makes mass communication special is the way the content of the communication message is created.

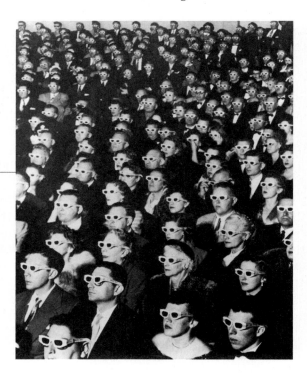

Mass communication is carried out by organizations working together in industries to produce and circulate a wide range of content—from entertainment to news to educational materials. It is this industrial, **mass production process** that creates the *potential* for reaching millions, even billions, of diverse, anonymous people at around the same time (say, through televising the Olympic games). And it is the **industrial nature** of the process—for example, the various companies that work together within the television or Internet industries—that makes mass communication different from other forms of communication even when

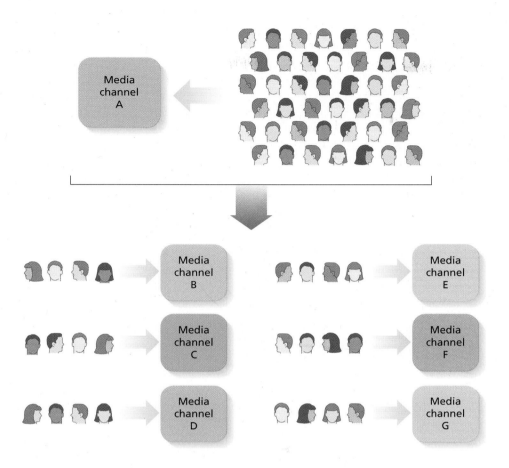

Figure 1.1

Audience Fragmentation
The arrival of the diverse array of media channels has had a fragmenting effect on audiences—as audience members move to watch, read, or listen to a new channel, fewer people use any single channel.

the audience is relatively small and even one-to-one. To help you understand how mass communication relates to other forms of communication, let's take a closer look.

Communication Defined

Different types of communication are a basic feature of human life. In general, the word **communication** refers to people interacting in ways that at least one of the parties involved understands as messages.

What are messages? **Messages** are collections of symbols that appear purposefully organized (meaningful) to those sending or receiving them. Think about the many ways that you signal to others what you want to do or how much you care about them. The signals are often verbal but they can also be through body language. When Jane shouts excitedly to her friend Jack and leaps with joy into his arms after she wins a tennis match, that's a form of communication. It's likely that Jack, whose arms she almost broke, realizes that she wants to tell him something. People who study communication would typically call the interaction just described **interpersonal communication,** a form that involves two or three individuals signaling to each other using their voices, facial and hand gestures, and other signs (even clothes) that they use to convey meaning. When you talk to your parents about your coursework, discuss a recent movie over dinner with friends, or converse with your professor during her office hours, you are participating in the interpersonal form of communication.

communication refers to people interacting in ways that at least one of the parties involved understands as messages

messages collections of symbols that appear purposefully organized (meaningful) to those sending or receiving them

interpersonal communication a form of communication that involves two or three individuals signaling to each other using their voices, facial, and hand gestures, and other signs (even clothes) that they use to convey meaning

Mediated Interpersonal Communication Breakdown

When tragedy strikes, it is not unusual for people to lose their sense of security in the world—at least temporarily. Yet large-scale crises may also prompt people to lose faith in the communication systems that they have come to depend on for information.

During the September 11, 2001 terrorist attacks on the World Trade Center and the Pentagon, many media channels were inaccessible. Phone lines were jammed for hours, and some local radio and television stations were knocked off the air. In addition, a number of websites crashed while others failed to provide information about the attacks, leading one reporter to declare that "the Internet failed miserably."

In 2007, during the shooting rampage at Virginia Tech, discussions resurfaced about communication during crises. This time, however, the focus was not on the technology but on the way people were using it, particularly new media formats such as mobile devices, blogs, and social networking sites.

As the attacks unfolded, many students used their Facebook and MySpace pages to let family and friends know they were okay. In fact, science reporter Alan Boyle remarked that "the media methods employed during [the] crisis broke new ground—and undoubtedly saved lives in the process."

Others, meanwhile, questioned why Virginia Tech authorities did not take advantage of communication technologies to immediately alert members of the campus community that they were in danger. Andrew Kantor, a technology reporter for *USA Today*, saw this event and its aftermath as evidence that people have yet to adapt fully to new types of communication.

Sources: Alan Boyle, "How Smart Mobs Coped with a Massacre," *MSNBC*, accessed on 6/11/07, http://www.msnbc.msn.com/id/18184075/; Andrew Kantor, "Virginia Tech Tragedy Highlights Differences between Old, New Media," *USA Today*, accessed on 6/11/07, www.usatoday.com; Jen Muehlbauer, "Reporting the Unthinkable," *The Industry Standard's Media Grok*, accessed on 9/12/01, http://www.nettime.org/Lists-Archives/nettime-bold-0109/msg00273.html.

---

mediated interpersonal communication a specialized type of interpersonal communication that is assisted by a device, such as a pen or pencil, a computer, or a telephone

intrapersonal communication an individual "talking" to himself or herself

small group communication communication among three or more individuals

organizational communication the interactions of individuals in a formal working environment

Mediated interpersonal communication, which is a specialized type of interpersonal communication, can be described as interpersonal communication that is assisted by a device, such as a pen, a computer, or a telephone. When you write a thank you note to your grandmother, send an email to your graduate teaching assistant, or call a friend on the phone, you are participating in the mediated form of interpersonal communication. In this form of communication, the people you are interacting with can't touch you and you can't touch them. You might even be thousands of miles from each other. The technology—the pen and paper, the computer, the telephone—becomes the vehicle (the medium) that allows you to interact with them.

Communication scholars also differentiate among other forms of communication. Some write about **intrapersonal communication,** which involves an individual "talking" to himself or herself—for example, an internal "conversation" that weighs the pros and cons of a decision.

Other researchers write about *small group communication, organizational communication,* or *public communication.* **Small group communication** involves communication among three or more individuals. Think of the deliberations of five friends who get together to plan a ski trip. **Organizational communication** involves the interaction of individuals in a formal working environment. When an executive sends messages down the chain of command, this is a form of organizational communication. **Public communication** involves one person who speaks to a large number of people—for instance, a professor speaking to students, or a candidate for public office talking to a crowd at a rally.

In communication, the source is the originator of a message.

Note that these forms of communication can each take place interpersonally or they can be mediated. A group planning a ski group can meet face-to-face or can interact through email. The boss could talk to her department heads in her office, or leave a message on their phone mail system. A professor can talk in front of the class, or leave a video of himself or herself for the students to watch.

public communication one person who speaks to a large number of people

While the types of communication described above have their differences, they have a central similarity: they involve *messages*. Seven major elements are involved in every interaction that involves messages. These elements are the *source, encoder, transmitter, channel, decoder, receiver, and feedback*. Let's take them one at a time.

Source   The **source** is the originator of the message. The source may be a person (when Jane speaks to Jack), or several people (a choir singing). But the source can also be an organization. For example, suppose you receive a notice in your mailbox from your bank. While individuals who work there created and sent the notice, from your standpoint, "the bank" was the source of the message. The source may or may not have knowledge about the intended receiver of the message, but it does have a thought or idea to transmit to some other person or organization.

source   the originator of the message which may be a person, several people or an organization

Encoding   **Encoding** is the process by which the source translates the thoughts and ideas so that they can be perceived by the human senses—these are primarily sight and sound, but may also include smell, taste, and touch. A source creates or encodes a message in anticipation of its transmission to a receiver. When the source is an individual, the encoding goes on in the individual's brain. When the source is an organization, encoding takes place when people in the organization create messages.

encoding   the process by which the source translates the thoughts and ideas so that they can be perceived by the human senses—primarily sight and sound, but may also include smell, taste, and touch

Transmitting   The **transmitter** performs the physical activity of actually sending out the message. Picture an employee apologizing to a supervisor for taking an unauthorized day off from work. The employee's vocal cords and face muscles—in fact, his entire body—will be involved in the transmission of the words, tone, and physical movements that the supervisor standing in front of him will understand as meaningful. Now, picture this same employee apologizing to his supervisor, not in person, but over the phone. In this case, a second type of transmitter operates along with the vocal cords. That second transmitter is the telephone, which turns sound waves from the vocal cords into electrical impulses that can travel across the phone lines.

transmitter   performs the physical activity of distributing the message

The telephone is an example of a mediating technology, or medium, of communication. A **medium** is part of a technical system that helps in the transmission,

medium   part of a technical system that helps in the transmission, distribution, or reception of messages

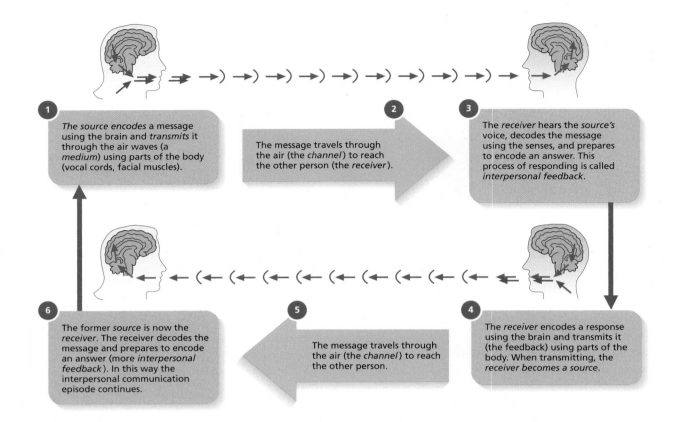

1 *The source encodes* a message using the brain and *transmits* it through the air waves (a *medium*) using parts of the body (vocal cords, facial muscles).

2 The message travels through the air (the *channel*) to reach the other person (the *receiver*).

3 The *receiver* hears the *source's* voice, decodes the message using the senses, and prepares to encode an answer. This process of responding is called *interpersonal feedback*.

4 The *receiver* encodes a response using the brain and transmits it (the feedback) using parts of the body. When transmitting, the *receiver becomes a source*.

5 The message travels through the air (the *channel*) to reach the other person.

6 The former *source* is now the *receiver*. The receiver decodes the message and prepares to encode an answer (more *interpersonal feedback*). In this way the interpersonal communication episode continues.

Figure 1.2

A Model of Interpersonal Communication

In this model of interpersonal communication, information moves from a starting point at the source, through the transmitter, via the channel, to the receiver for decoding.

channels the pathways through which the transmitter sends all features of the message, whether they involve sight, sound, smell, or touch

decoding the process by which the receiver translates the source's thoughts and ideas so that they have meaning

distribution, or reception of messages. It helps communication take place when senders and receivers are not face-to-face. The Internet is an example of a medium, as are the radio, CD, television, and DVD. (Note that the term *medium* is singular; it refers to one technological vehicle for communication. The plural is *media*.)

Channel All communication, whether mediated or not, takes place through channels. **Channels** are the pathways through which the transmitter sends all features of the message, whether they involve sight, sound, smell, or touch. When a man on the street walks up to you and shouts at you in a way that you can hardly understand, the *channel* is the air through which the sound waves move from the man's vocal cords. If your roommate yells at you through the phone, two channels are at work: one channel is the air that vibrates the phone mechanism, and the other is the wire through which the electrical impulses move toward you.

Decoding Before a receiver can hear (and make sense of) a source's message, the transmitted impulses must be converted to signs that the brain can perceive as meaningful. **Decoding** is the way in which this is done. It is the reverse of the encoding process—it is the process by which the receiver translates the source's thoughts and ideas so that they have meaning.

In the case of the interpersonal communication, the decoder is biological: the brain is the decoder. When the telephone is involved, the electrical impulses that traveled through the phone lines must be decoded into sound waves before they can be decoded by the brain. In fact, all media require this sort of decoding. When you play music on an MP3 player or iPod, it decodes the impulses that have been laid down on the disk so that you can hear the tunes. Similarly, the television is the

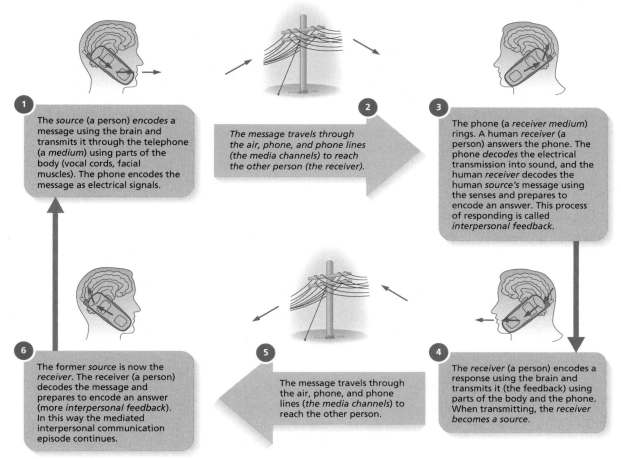

1. The *source* (a person) *encodes* a message using the brain and transmits it through the telephone (a *medium*) using parts of the body (vocal cords, facial muscles). The phone encodes the message as electrical signals.

2. *The message travels through the air, phone, and phone lines (the media channels) to reach the other person (the receiver).*

3. The phone (a *receiver medium*) rings. A human *receiver* (a person) answers the phone. The phone *decodes* the electrical transmission into sound, and the human *receiver* decodes the human *source's* message using the senses and prepares to encode an answer. This process of responding is called *interpersonal feedback*.

4. The *receiver* (a person) encodes a response using the brain and transmits it (the feedback) using parts of the body and the phone. When transmitting, the *receiver becomes a source.*

5. The message travels through the air, phone, and phone lines (*the media channels*) to reach the other person.

6. The former *source* is now the *receiver*. The receiver (a person) decodes the message and prepares to encode an answer (more *interpersonal feedback*). In this way the mediated interpersonal communication episode continues.

Figure 1.3

A Model of Mediated Interpersonal Communication
In this model of mediated interpersonal communication, information moves from a starting point to a source, who encodes a message. The message is transmitted through channels to the receiver, who decodes the message.

decoder that takes the electrical impulses from the air or cable and converts them into the programs you watch.

Receiver   As suggested above, the **receiver** is the person or organization that gets the message. Sometimes the source's message will reach its intended receiver; sometimes it reaches another receiver altogether. But even if someone other than the intended receiver receives the message, communication has still taken place. Say, for example, that you assume that your friend Brad is in the next room and, as a result, you shout your opinion about his new girlfriend, Keiko. Even if it turns out that Brad wasn't in the next room at all and did not hear (receive) the message you sent him, but instead his girlfriend, Keiko, was in the next room, the episode can still be considered interpersonal communication: your message was encoded, transmitted via your vocal cords, sent through the channel of the air, decoded by the receiver (although not the one you intended), and received.

Feedback   **Feedback** occurs when the receiver responds to the message with what the sender perceives as a message. When Keiko, your friend's girlfriend, tells you, "I never knew you felt that way about me, you jerk," that is feedback. In fact, this sort of feedback continues the interpersonal communication process. As Figure 1.2 shows, two people continue their communication by continually receiving and responding to each other's messages. The same thing happens with mediated interpersonal communication, as shown in Figure 1.3. The communication "episode"

receiver   the person or organization that gets the message

feedback   when the receiver responds to the message with what the sender perceives as a message

between the two ends when one of them sends no more feedback to the other (the person walks away, the parties hang up the phone).

Feedback doesn't always take place immediately, especially in mediated interpersonal communication. Say you send your friend an email. Keiko reads it, gets embarrassed by something you wrote and decides to write you a reply. You read the note and then, after thinking about it for a day, write back directly to her. Her email and your response are examples of delayed feedback.

noise is an environmental, mechanical, and semantic sound in the communication situation that interferes with the delivery of the message. Environmental noise comes from the setting where the source and receiver are communicating. Mechanical noise comes from the medium through which the communication is taking place. Semantic noise involves language that one or more of the participants doesn't understand.

Noise **Noise** is an environmental, mechanical, and semantic sound in the communication situation that interferes with the delivery of the message. Environmental noise comes from the setting where the source and receiver are communicating. In an interpersonal communication situation, Ahmed, the source, may be at a cricket match trying to talk on the phone, and Sally, the receiver, might be at an auction where people are screaming bids. Mechanical noise comes from the medium through which the communication is taking place. Say there is static on the phone—that would be mechanical noise that would add to the environmental noise. Semantic noise involves language that one or more of the participants doesn't understand. Let's say Ahmed tells Sally that "the bowler attempted a bouncer that turned into a beamer." Even when Ahmed repeats the words three times through the environmental and mechanical noise so that she hears them, Sally has no idea what Ahmed is talking about, since she knows little about the sport of cricket.

From Communication to Mass Communication

One way to understand mass communication is to show its similarities to and differences from other forms of communication. One similarity is that mass communication takes place through media. Small groups can come together in virtual chat rooms that are connected by wired networks, organizations can connect their far-flung employees via video conference facilities that are linked through cables and satellites, and professors who deliver public lectures can record them for projection from a computer server to different classes at different times. In other words, the channels used in mediated forms of interpersonal, group, organizational and public communication are sometimes similar to those used in mass communication.

Yet another similarity between these other forms of communication and mass communication is that we can describe mass communication using the same terms of source, encoder, transmitter, channel, decoder, receiver, feedback, and noise that are shown in Table 1.1. But here is also where we begin to see differences. The most important differences relate to the source of the message, its transmitter and the way feedback takes place.

Differences in the Source In the other forms of communication we've discussed, *individuals* are the source of the message that scholars study. In mass communication, by contrast, complex organizations, often companies, take responsibility for the activity. The source is an *organization* such as a company, not a single person.

To get a strong grasp of the difference, think of Jon Stewart delivering his version of the news on Comedy Central's *The Daily Show*. If Jon were in the same room as you telling you about what he just read in the paper, that would be a clear case of interpersonal communication and Stewart would be a source. If your friend were to record that conversation on his video camera and his brother were to watch

Table 1.1 **Differences in Types of Communication**

	Interpersonal Communication	Mediated Interpersonal Communication	Mass Communication
Message	Uses all the senses	Typically verbal and/or visual	Typically verbal and/or visual
Source	An individual	An individual	One or more organizations
Encoding	By an individual's brain	By an individual's brain and technology	By an organization and technology
Channel	The air	The air, technology	The air, technology
Receiver	A few individuals in the same location	A few or many individuals in the same location	Typically, many people in different locations
Decoding	By an individual's brain	By technology and an individual's brain	By technology and an individual's brain
Feedback	Immediate and direct	Immediate or delayed; generally direct	Immediate or delayed; generally indirect
Noise	Environmental, mechanical, and semantic	Environmental, mechanical, and semantic, with environmental sometimes caused by organizations	Environmental, mechanical, and semantic, sometimes caused by organizations

the video of Jon talking about the news, that is an example of mediated interpersonal communication where Jon is still the source.

The difference between these two examples of the source and Jon's appearance on *The Daily Show* is that behind Stewart is an organization that is creating the news satire for him to present. Sure, Jon is reading the messages, and so it may seem that he should be called "the source." But employees of *The Daily Show* helped him write his script, produced and edited the videos he introduces, and prepared his set for the broadcast. Moreover, the photos and clips he satirizes sometimes come from news firms, such as ABC News. So Jon is really just the most visible representative of an *organizational source*.

Differences in Transmission The critical role of organizations in mass communication compared to other communication forms also shows up in the transmission of the message. In interpersonal, small group, and public communication, an individual sender or a committee takes responsibility for transmittingthe message—perhaps using microphones when speaking to a crowd or telephones when speaking at a distance. In mass communication, however, transmission is too complex to be accomplished by an indi-

Mediated forms of interpersonal, group, organizational, and public communication may use channels similar to those used in mass communication.

13

Jon Stewart, host of *The Daily Show*, isn't a one-man band. It takes the entire Comedy Central organization—writers, producers, engineers, stage managers, sound technicians, camera people (to name a few)—to create each evening's program. Stewart is the most visible representative of the organizational source that creates *The Daily Show*.

vidual or even a few people. That is because transmission involves distributing the material to several locations and presenting the material (that is, exhibiting it) at those locations. Instead of a few individuals, a number of organizations (usually large ones) are typically involved in the process.

Think of our *Daily Show* example again. When Jon reads the script on *The Daily Show*, his vocal cords transmit the words into a microphone; the air and electric current are a channel for them. That may seem no different from mediated interpersonal communication, but it is only the beginning. Transmission of Jon on Comedy Central involves a number of further steps. First the show is sent to a satellite company that the network uses to send its programs to cable TV systems around the country. The cable systems, which themselves are complex organizations, receive those messages and send them to "head-end" transmission centers that they own. These centers send out the program through coaxial cables that eventually connect to television sets in locations (homes, bars, hotels) where subscribers have paid to receive the signal. In this way, millions of people around the country can watch *The Daily Show* at the same time.

Of course, individuals do work for production and distribution firms involved in mass communication. Unlike mediated communication activities, though, the creation and transmission of mass media messages—of news articles, television programs and recorded music, for example—are the result of decisions and activities by many people working together in companies that interact with other companies.

Differences in Feedback   The third major difference between mass communication and other communication forms relates to feedback. We can talk about

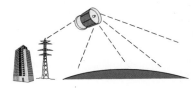

1 The *source*, a media organization, creates a *message* in words and/or images. Often working with other organizations in its industry, it encodes the image for *transmission* (that is, *distribution*) through a *medium*. Let's say that in this case the organization is a TV network news division, the message is a news report, and the media are both television and a website.

2 The electronic impulses travel from ground transmitters owned by the network to satellites (*media channels*) leased by it and from there to TV stations (*mass media outlets*) around the country and the world. The stations, in turn, send the impulses to other transmitters that broadcast them through the air (another media channel) to millions of televisions. After the TV transmission, a version of the report is placed on the TV network's website through high speed cable lines.

3 The *receivers* are millions of people who receive the electronic impulses on their TV sets (more media). The TV sets decode the impulses back into video and commentary, which the viewers themselves decode as messages.

6 Network employees—not those directly involved with the original news report or website discussions —receive the messages and send summaries of them to the news and marketing staff and to website designers. The marketing staff uses this *indirect feedback* to convince advetisers of the involvement of viewers in site. Web designers use some of the comments to alter the site's look. Encouraged by responses to the Web activity and by telephone surveys that reveal general audience interest in the topic, executives in the news organization decide to air more stories on the topic and expand their website discussions about it. In this way, the feedback influences the network's mass communication activities.

5 The responding individuals are now sources in mediated communication with an organization. Their individual messages are transmitted across phone and cable lines to reach the TV network's website.

4 In many cases, there is no response from viewers—no *feedback*. in this example, though, assume that several thousand of these viewers later go to the TV network's website to find out more about the report and participate in a poll. They are involved in feedback to the station on a *delayed basis.*

Figure 1.4

A Model of Mass Communication

In this model of mass communication, the elements (source, message, transmission, etc.) are all marked by the industrial production and multiple distribution by mass media organizations.

Where Does the Term *Media* Come From?

Until the "Roaring" 1920s, to most Americans a medium was a fortune teller or palm reader, not a publication, and as for media—well, there was no such thing. The term *media* was just an obscure Latin plural of the word *medium*.

Then came modern advertising and a sense of media that had nothing to do with psychics. Advertisers began to speak of placing ads in different media.

The original means of mass communication were print—magazines, journals, and newspapers—and their collective name was already in place: publications. Then radio and television were added to the mix, and the term *publications* would not stretch to fit. Needing a term that would encompass all these means of communication, writers borrowed *media* from the advertising people and have used it ever since to accommodate these and even newer means of communication, such as the Internet.

"Welcome to 'All About the Media,' where members of the media discuss the role of the media in media coverage of the media."

duction lines for decades. The manufacturer may make new products with the Ivory name, but an Ivory Soap bar that you bought on Tuesday will be the same as the one you will buy on Friday. But in mass media firms, both the R&D function and the basic production line for the same product must focus on change continually. For example, the *Wall Street Journal* must update its stories or people will stop buying the paper and subscribing to their website; Twentieth Century Fox cannot survive on only one film; executives at the MTV cable network realize that if they run only one music video or one reality program, viewers will catch on and tune out.

This need for constant innovation means constant risk. The next day's issue of a newspaper could turn off many readers. Fox's next film could fail. MTV's lineup of programs could lead people to reach for their remote controls. For this reason, media employees always look for ways to balance the need for continual, rapid innovation with a desire to control risk. As we will see in Chapter 2, they try to lower their chances of failure by relying on themes and plots and people that have done well in the past. The ways in which they solve these problems can influence much of what we see and hear.

Mass Media in our Personal Lives

Mass media materials speak to the most personal parts of our lives. They also connect us to the world beyond our private circumstances. As a result, mass media industries are a major force in society. To understand what this means, we have to dig a bit deeper into how people use the media and what they get out of them.

How People Use the Mass Media

Scholars have found that individuals adapt their use of mass media to their own particular needs.[2] Broadly speaking, we can say that people use the media in four ways: *enjoyment, companionship, surveillance,* and *interpretation.* Let's examine these uses one at a time.

Enjoyment   The desire for enjoyment, or personal pleasure, is a basic human urge. Watching a television program, studying the Bible, finishing a newspaper crossword puzzle, even reading an advertisement can bring this kind of gratification to many people.

News stories, daytime soap operas, sports, and primetime dramas can ignite everyday talk with friends, relatives, work colleagues, and even strangers. During the mid-1990s, for example, many local television stations around the United States were advertising their morning talk programs with the phrase "We give you something to talk about." This process of using media content for everyday interpersonal discussions is called using media materials as **social currency** or coins of exchange. "Did you hear Jay Leno's joke last night?" someone might ask around the water cooler at work. "No, I watched Letterman," might be one reply. That might trigger a chain of comments about TV comedy that bring a number of people into the conversation.

Of course, another way people can bring mass media material into friendly conversation is by experiencing the content together. If you have attended Super Bowl parties, you have an idea of how a televised event can energize friends in ways that have little to do with what is taking place on the screen. In this way, the media provide us with the enjoyment we seek as a basic human need.

Companionship   On a very different note, mass media bring pleasure to the lonely and the alone. A chronically ill hospital patient or a home-bound senior citizen may find companionship by viewing their favorite sports teams on TV, or listening to the music of days gone by on the radio.

Sometimes, media can even draw out people who feel troubled and in need of friends. The term **parasocial interaction** describes the psychological connections that some media users establish with celebrities they learn about through the mass media. People who are involved in a parasocial interaction typically enjoy a feeling of bonding with those celebrities. You might know someone who gets so involved with media images of rock or rap stars that they sometimes act as if they know them well. In a few publicized cases, this feeling has gotten out of control, leading individuals to stalk, and even harm, the media figures who were the objects of their adulation. In 1999, for example, actor Brad Pitt found himself with an unwanted visitor when a nineteen-year-old woman broke into his home. He was not there at the time, but a caretaker found this self-styled "Number one fan" wearing Pitt's clothes and asleep in his bed.[3]

Surveillance   Using media for **surveillance** means employing them to learn about what is happening in the world around us. We do this every day, often without realizing it. Do you turn on the radio or TV each morning to find out the weather? Do you check the stock listings to find out how your investments are

social currency   media content used as coins of exchange in everyday interpersonal discussions

parasocial interaction   the psychological connections that some media users establish with celebrities that they learn about through the mass media

surveillance   using the media to learn about what is happening in the world around us

21

Catch Phrases as Social Currency

Have you ever considered why some phrases from movies, television shows, songs, and advertisements become *social currency*, phrases that people use with one another to show that they are "in"? Several years ago, conversations were frequently peppered with the quips, "You're fired!" and "That's hot," made popular by reality TV stars Donald Trump and Paris Hilton, respectively.

Catch phrases can come from a variety of media sources. During the 1984 presidential campaign, Walter Mondale asked his Democratic rival Gary Hart, "Where's the beef?" when he wanted to question his opponent's political experience. Although the expression has since died, at the time there was widespread use of this phrase, which originated from a Wendy's hamburger chain television commercial.

Other examples of catch phrases include Homer Simpson's ubiquitous "D'oh"; "Bringing sexy back," from Justin Timberlake's hit single; "I'm kind of a big deal," a famous line from the 2004 comedy *Anchorman: The Legend of Ron Burgundy*; the Black Panthers' slogan "right on" during the

The catch phrases and comedy bits of comedians like Sacha Baron Cohen, here as Borat, are often a source of social currency we use everyday in our personal and professional conversations.

1960s; and "A-OK," which was originally used by astronauts during the early days of the space program. Many catch phrases disappear, but some become embedded in popular culture, particularly when they fill a void in the language.

Think about how many catch phrases you know and try to figure out their origin.

faring? Have you read classified ads online to look for a job, concert tickets, or previously owned furniture? Have you ever called or logged on to Fandango or Moviefone to find out where and when a film is playing? All these activities are illustrations of using the mass media for surveillance. Of course, our surveillance can be more global. Many people are interested in knowing what is going on in the world beyond their immediate neighborhood. *Did the flooding upstate destroy any houses? Will Congress raise taxes? What's going on with the negotiations for peace in the Middle East?*

Interpretation   Although surveillance through the mass media satisfies many people, it supplies only part of what they want to know about the world. They also want to find out *why* things are happening—who or what is the cause—and what to do about them. When people try to find reasons, they are looking for **interpretation**.

interpretation using the media to find out *why* things are happening—who or what is the cause—and what to do about them

Many of us turn to the media to learn not just what is going on, but also why and what, if any, actions to take. We may read newspaper editorials to understand the actions of national leaders and come to conclusions about whether or not we agree with these actions. We know that financial magazines such as *Money* and *Barron's* are written to appeal to people who want to understand how investment vehicles work and which ones to choose. And we are aware that libraries, bookstores, and some websites (howstuffworks.com comes to mind) specialize in "how to" topics ranging from raising children, to installing a retaining wall, to dying with dignity. Some people who are genuinely confused about some topics find mass media the most useful sources of answers. Pre-teens, for example, may want to understand why women and men behave romantically toward each other but they may feel embarrassed to ask their parents. They may be quite open to different opinions—in *Spiderman*, *Oprah*, Justin Timberlake's music, or *Mad* magazine—about where sexual attraction comes from and what the appropriate behavior is.

But how do people actually use the explanations they get from the mass media? Researchers have found that the credibility people place in the positions that mass media take depends on the extent to which the individuals agree with the values they find in that content.[4] For example, a person who is rooted in a religiously conservative approach to the Bible would not be likely to agree with a nature book that is based on the theory of evolution; a political liberal would probably not be persuaded by the interpretations that politically conservative magazines offer about ways to end poverty. Keep in mind, however, that in these examples, these people would probably not search out such media content to begin with. Unless people have a good reason to confront materials that go against their values (if they will be engaging in a debate on the ideas, for example), most people stay away from media that do not reflect (and reinforce) their own beliefs, values, or interests. And if they do come across materials that go against their values, they tend to dismiss them as biased.

Multiple Use of Mass Media Content The example of a pre-teen seeking interpretations of romance from four very different outlets—a movie series, a television talk show, a musical record, and a magazine—raises an important point about the four uses that people make of the mass media: the uses are not linked to any particular medium or genre. If we take television as an example, we might be tempted to suggest that enjoyment comes from certain sitcoms or adventure series, that companionship comes from soap operas, that surveillance is achieved through network and local news programs, and that interpretation can be found in Sunday morning political talk shows such as *Meet the Press*, as well as from daily talk fests such as *Jerry Springer* and *The View*. In fact, we may divide many kinds of content in these ways. Communication researchers point out, however, that individuals can get just about any gratification they are seeking from just about any program—or any kind of mass media materials.[5]

You might find, for example, that you use the *CBS Evening News* for enjoyment, surveillance, and interpretation. *Enjoyment* might come from the satisfaction of watching reporters' familiar faces day after day (is a little parasocial interaction working here?); *surveillance* might be satisfied by reports from different parts of the globe; and *interpretation* might flow from stray comments by the reporters and those they interview about what ought to be done to solve problems.

Mass Media, Culture, and Society

At the same time that mass media are fulfilling private desires for enjoyment, companionship, surveillance, and interpretation, they often lead us to share the materials we are reading and listening to with millions of people. This sharing is made possible, of course, because of the industrial nature of the activity and its technology of production and distribution. When complex organizations comprising of many workers join together to use the latest technology to produce media,

Millions of people around the world saw *Shrek* in theaters within a few months of its release thanks to global publicity campaigns by Dreamworks and Universal.

those organizations have the potential to distribute the same message to huge numbers of people.

Consider the typical television broadcast of the Grammy Awards, the ceremony in which the recording industry honors its most successful talent. It is transmitted via satellite from Los Angeles to broadcast television production facilities in New York, then distributed "live" to every corner of the United States, as well as to many parts of the world.

Or, consider a typical presidential news conference. It is covered by dozens of newspaper reporters and television and radio news crews. Snippets of the event will commonly end up confronting Americans around the country in many different forms during that day and the next on the national news, on the local news, in the morning paper, and throughout the day on hourly radio news reports.

As a third, and slightly different example, consider a mega-hit film such as one of the *Shrek* movies. Millions of people around the world saw it in theaters within a few months of its release. In addition, word of the movie's popularity sped around the globe as Dreamworks and Universal, its joint domestic distributors, and UIP, its distributor outside the United States, revved up a publicity and advertising machine. It peppered as many media outlets as possible with word of the high-octane action and head-lopping digital effects.

Shrek, the presidential news conference, and the Grammy Awards represent only three examples of activities that happen all the time in industrialized countries such as the United States. Linking large numbers of people to share the same materials virtually instantly has become standard practice for the broadcast television, Internet, radio, cable TV, and satellite television industries. Just as significant is the sharing that takes place relatively more slowly when newspapers, magazines, books, movies, billboards, and other mass media release their messages. Because of mass media industries and their abilities to mass produce media content, millions of people within the United States and around the world can receive the same messages within a fairly short time. Think about it: here are huge numbers of people who are physically separated from one another, have no obvious relationship with one another, and most often are unknown to one another. Yet on a daily basis they are watching the same news stories, listening to the same music, and reading the same magazine articles.

What is Culture?

We can understand why this large-scale sharing of messages is important by exploring the cultural context in which the mass media operate. **Culture** is a very broad term. When we use the term *culture*, we are talking about ways of life that are passed on to members of a society through time and that keep the society together. We typically use the word **society** to refer to large numbers of individuals, groups, and organizations that live in the same general area and consider themselves connected to one another through the sharing of a culture.

What is shared includes learned behaviors, beliefs, and values. A culture lays out guidelines about who belongs to the society and what rules apply to them. It provides guideposts about where and what to learn, where and how to work, how to eat and sleep. It tells us how we should act toward family members, friends, and strangers, and much, much more. In other words, a culture helps us make sense of ourselves and our place in the world.

A culture provides people with ideas about the kinds of arguments concerning particular subjects that are acceptable. In American culture, people would likely feel that on certain topics (vegetarianism, for example), all sorts of positions are acceptable, whereas on other topics (cannibalism, incest) the range of acceptable views is much narrower. Moreover, American culture allows for the existence of groups with habits that many people consider odd and unusual but not threatening to the more general way of life. Such group lifestyles are called **subcultures**. The Amish of Pennsylvania who live without modern appliances at home represent such a subculture, as do Catholic monks who lead a secluded existence devoted to God.

For small populations living close together, people use interpersonal communication to share an awareness of their culture and to pass on that way of life to the next generation. Consider campers and their counselors coming together in a summer camp as an example of a culture. The counselors establish their leadership over the campers by making sure everyone follows traditional rules. The counselors threaten them with extra chores if they violate rules, and give them rewards when they follow the rules. Traditional camp songs encourage campers to feel good about the camp, to see themselves as connected to each other, and to want to return year after year. Arguments over certain rules—like Friday night lights-out time—may be tolerated, but arguments over other rules (for example, daily bunk inspection) are not. Subcultures considered dangerous aren't tolerated. If campers decide that they wanted to live alone in the woods instead of in the bunks, for example, they would not be allowed to do that and would be punished if they disobeyed.

Mass Communication and Culture   The camp's culture provides the camp society's members with direct evidence of who belongs and what the rules are. In places with large numbers of people—cities or countries, for example—such notions cannot always be understood simply by looking around. The mass media allow us to view clearly the ideas that people have about their broad cultural connections with others, and where they stand in the larger society. When mass media encourage huge numbers of people who are dispersed and unrelated to share the same materials, they are focusing people's attention on what is culturally important to think about and to talk and argue with others about. In other words, mass media create people's common lived experiences, a sense of the common culture and the varieties of subcultures acceptable to it.

The mass media present ideas of the culture in three broad and related ways: (1) They direct people's attention toward codes of acceptable behavior within

culture   ways of life that are passed on to members of a society through time and that keep the society together

society   large numbers of individuals, groups, and organizations that live in the same general area and consider themselves connected to one another through the sharing of a culture

subcultures   groups with habits that many people consider odd and unusual but not threatening to the more general way of life

the society and how to talk about them, (2) they tell people what and who counts in their world and why, and (3) they tell people what others think of them, and what people "like themselves" think of others. Let's look at each of the ways separately.

The Mass Media Direct People's Attention Toward the Codes of Acceptable Behavior Within Society and How to Talk About Them
A culture provides individuals with notions about how to approach the entire spectrum of life's decisions, from waking to sleeping. It also gives people ideas about the arguments concerning all these subjects that are acceptable. If you think about the mass media from this standpoint, you'll realize that this is exactly what they do. Newspapers continually give us a look at how government works, as do Internet sites such as Wonkette and Huffington Post. TV's *CSI* series act out behavior the police consider unacceptable and open up issues where the rules of police and "criminal" behavior are contested or unclear. Magazine articles provide ideas, and a range of arguments, about what looks attractive, and how to act toward the opposite sex. We may personally disagree with many of these ideas. At the same time, we may well realize that these ideas are shared and possibly accepted broadly in society.

These cultural rules and arguments can be found in even the most sensational mass media materials. You may have heard of, or remember, the first trial of O. J. Simpson, the ex-football star and actor accused of murdering his wife and her friend. The criminal prosecution, covered live on Court TV and the Cable News Network (CNN), became *the* media event of the mid-1990s. Although some observers dismissed the trial as sensationalist trash, others pointed out how it paraded for viewers cultural rules and arguments about marriage, race, and violence. Years later, in 2006, anger erupted in many media outlets when Regan Books announced that it would release a memoir by Simpson that would discuss how he *might* have killed the two people. Commentators voiced the opinion that such a book was taboo, and public indignation seemed so intense that the book company's owner, News Corporation, decided not to release the title and recalled printed copies from stores.

The Mass Media Tell What and Who Counts in Their World and Why
Mass media tell us who is "famous"—from movie stars to scientists—and give us reasons why. They define the leaders to watch, from the U.S. president to religious ministers. News reports tell us who these people are in "real life." Fictional presentations such as books, movies, and TV dramas may tell us what they (or people like them) do and are like. Many of the presentations are angrily critical or bitingly satirical; American culture allows for this sort of argumentation. Through critical presentations or heroic ones, though, mass media presentations offer members of the society a sense of the qualities that we ought to expect in good leaders.

Fiction often shows us what leaders *ought* to be like—what values count in the society. Actor Denzel Washington excels at playing law enforcement officers who are courageous, smart, loyal, persevering, strong, and handsome; think, for example, of the movies *Déjà Vu* and *Inside Man*. Sometimes, mass media discussions of fiction and nonfiction merge in curious ways. During the election of 2000, for example, several mass media commentators noted that President Bartlett of the then-popular *West Wing* TV drama would be a better choice than any of the real candidates because of his better leadership qualities.

The mass media can connect us with people and events far beyond the confines of our own homes.

The Mass Media Help People to Understand Themselves and Their Connection With, or Disconnection From Others

Am I leadership material? Am I good-looking? Am I more or less religious than most people? Is what I like to eat what most people like to eat? Is my apartment as neat as most people's homes? How do I fit into the culture? Mass media allow us, and sometimes even encourage us, to ask questions such as these. When we read newspapers, listen to the radio, or watch TV we can't help but compare ourselves to the portrayals these media present. Sometimes we may shrug the comparisons off with the clear conviction that we simply don't care if we are different from people who are famous or considered "in." Other times we might feel that we ought to be more in tune with what's going on; this may lead us to buy new clothes or adopt a new hair style. Often, we might simply take in ideas of what the world is like outside our direct reach and try to figure out how we fit in.

At the same time that the mass media get us wondering how we fit in, they may also encourage feelings of connection with people whom we have never met. Newscasters, textbooks, and even advertisements tell us that we are part of a nation that extends far beyond what we can see. We may perceive that sense of connection differently depending on our personal interests. We may feel a bond of sympathy with people in a U.S. city that the news shows ravaged by floods. We may feel linked to people thousands of miles away that a website tells us share our political opinions. We may feel camaraderie with Super Bowl viewers around the country, especially those rooting for the team we are supporting.

Similarly, we may feel *dis*connected from people and nations that mass media tell us have belief systems that we do not share. U.S. news and entertainment are filled with portrayals of nations, individuals, and types of individuals who, we are told, do not subscribe to key values of American culture. Labels such as *rogue* *nation, Nazi, communists, terrorists,* and *Islamic extremists* suggest threats to an American sense of decency. When mass media attach these labels to countries or individuals, we may well see them as enemies of our way of life, unless we have personal reasons not to believe the media portrayals.

Criticisms of Mass Media's Relation to Culture

Some social observers have been critical of the way mass media have used their power as reflectors and creators of culture. One criticism is that mass media present unfortunate prejudices about the world by systematically using **stereotypes**—predictable depictions that reflect (and sometimes create) cultural prejudices—and **political ideologies**—beliefs about who should hold the greatest power within a culture, and why. Another is that mass media detract from the quality of American culture. A third criticism, related to the first two, is that the mass media's cultural presentations encourage political and economic manipulation of their audiences.

Criticisms such as these have made people think deeply about the role that mass media play in American culture. These criticisms do have *their* weak points. Some might note that it is too simplistic to say that mass media detract from the quality of American culture. Different parts of the U.S. population use the mass media differently and, as a result, may confront different kinds of images. Related to this point is the idea that people bring their own personalities to the materials they read and watch. They are not simply passive recipients of messages. They actively interpret, reshape, and even reject some of them.

Nevertheless, the observations about stereotypes, cultural quality and political ideology should make us think about the power of mass media over our lives. Many people—most people at one time or another—do seem to see the mass media as mirroring parts of the society and the world beyond it, especially parts they do not know first hand. Most people do accept what the mass media tell them in news—and even in entertainment—about what and who counts in their world and why. Many seem to believe that the mass media's codes of acceptable behavior accurately describe large numbers of people, even if the codes don't describe their own norms. And they accept the mass media's images as starting points for understanding where they fit in society in relation to others and their connection with, or disconnection from, others. They may disagree with these images, or think that they shouldn't exist. Nevertheless, the media images serve as starting points for their concerns about, and arguments over, reality. We will have more to say about critical views on the effects of media in Chapter 4.

stereotypes predictable depictions that reflect (and sometimes create) cultural prejudices

political ideologies beliefs about who should hold the greatest power within a culture

Media Literacy

It is no exaggeration to say that everyone is influenced in one way or another by mass media messages. Some people, though, have learned how to step back and seriously examine the mass media's role in their lives and in American life. The aim of this book is to help you to be one of those people. The goal is not to make you cynical and distrustful of all mass media. In the vast landscape of the media, there is much to enjoy and appreciate. Instead, the goal is to help you think in an educated manner about the forces that shape the media and your relationships with them so that you will better evaluate what you see and hear. The aim is to help you to be media literate.

There are very practical benefits to being media literate.

■ Consider your use of the Internet. Most Americans go online on a regular basis, but research shows that they have little understanding of the privacy policies of the websites they visit. As a media literate person—certainly as someone who has read this book—you would know about website privacy issues and how to take care not to give out private information about yourself.

■ Consider your use of the TV set. Do you know that the United States is going through a conversion to digital television that may make your TV obsolete? Did you know that Americans who have the obsolete television sets can apply for government funds to buy a special converter so that they can continue to receive over-the-air TV? As a media literate person, you would understand why all this is happening and how to save money as a result of the government program.

■ Consider that you are applying for a job working for a media firm, or a position that requires you to relate to media personnel. The person who interviews you may test your knowledge of the business by using industry terms and discussing new developments. Would you know how to engage in an energetic conversation on the present and future of new and traditional media industries? If you were media literate, you would.

More generally, being media literate can be satisfying and fun. For example, knowing movie history can make watching films fascinating because you will be able to notice historical and technical features of the films that you wouldn't have otherwise noticed. Having a comparative understanding of different forms of news can help you think more clearly about what you can expect from journalism today and how it is changing. Understanding the forces that shape formulas and genres, and the social controversies around stereotyping and violence, can make playing even the most predictable video games and watching even the most hackneyed television shows jumping-off points for thinking critically about yourself in relation to images of others in society. All these and other media activities can also start important conversations between you and your friends about the directions of our culture and your place in it. That, in turn, can help you become a more aware and responsible citizen—parent, voter, worker—in our media-driven society (see Figure 1.5).

Foundations of Media Literacy

When we speak about **literacy**, we mean the ability to effectively comprehend and use messages that are expressed in written or printed symbols, such as letters. When we speak about **media literacy**, however, we mean something broader. To quote the National Leadership Conference on Media Literacy, it is "the ability to access, analyze, evaluate and communicate messages in a variety of forms."[6]

There are many views of exactly what media literacy is and what it can do for people. It seems, however, that most scholars would accept the following six "foundation principles" for teaching people literacy skills.[7] We have already been building these principles in this chapter, so you will be familiar with the ideas behind them.

literacy the ability to effectively comprehend and use messages that are expressed in written or printed symbols, such as letters

media literacy the ablility to apply critical thinking skills to the mass media, thereby becoming a more aware and responsible citizen—parent, voter, worker—in our media-driven society

Figure 1.5
Constructing Media Literacy
Steps to becoming a media literate citizen.

Attributes
- Knowledgeable about the influences that guide media organizations.
- Up-to-date on political issues relating to the media.
- Sensitive to ways of seeing media content as a means of learning about culture.
- Knowledgeable about scholarship regarding media effects.
- Sensitive to the ethical dimensions of media activities.
- Able to enjoy media materials in a sophisticated manner.

Skills
- An understanding of the commercial forces behind media materials.
- An awareness of ways in which the public can influence the production and distribution of mass media materials.
- An ability to think through the ethical implications of media firms' activities.
- An awareness of political influences that shape media materials.
- An ability to examine media content for cultural, commercial, and political meanings.
- An understanding of research on the media's implications for the individual and society.

Foundational Principles
- Media materials are constructed.
- Media materials are created and distributed within a commercial environment.
- Media materials are created and distributed within a political environment.
- Mass media present ideas within primary genres of entertainment, news, information, education, and advertising.
- People are active recipients of media messages.
- Media representations play a role in the way society understands its reality.

Principle 1: Media Materials are Constructed
As we already know, when we read newspapers, watch TV, and surf the Web we should continually be aware that what we are seeing and hearing is not any kind of pure reality. Rather, it is a construction—that is, a human creation that presents a kind of script about the culture.

Principle 2: Media Materials are Created and Distributed Within a Commercial Environment
When we try to understand media materials as human-created cultural scripts, we must look at many considerations that surround and affect the humans who are involved in creating and releasing the media materials. We have already noted in this chapter that mass media materials are produced by organizations that exist in a commercial setting. The need to bring in revenues, often to sell advertising, is foremost in the minds of those who manage these organizations. In forthcoming chapters we will elaborate on what this means and how it affects the media products.

Principle 3: Media Materials are Created and Distributed Within a Political Environment
"Political" refers to the way a society is governed. When it comes to mass media, the term refers to a variety of activities. These range from the specific regulations that governments place on mass media, to decisions by courts about what restrictions the government can place on the media, to the struggle by various interest groups to change what media do (often using government leverage). For many media observers, being aware that media operate within a political environment leads to the idea that this environment deeply influences the media content itself. To them, it means being aware that the ideas in the media have political implications—that they are ideological.

*Principle 4: Mass Media Present Their Ideas Within Primary Genres
of Entertainment, News, Information, Education, and Advertising*
Media scholar Patricia Aufterheide and others note that every medium—the television, the movie, the magazine—has its own codes and conventions, its own ways of presenting cultural reality. Although you probably haven't thought about it, it's a good bet that you recognize the differences between the way these media do things. A report of a presidential press conference looks different depending on whether it was written for a newspaper or a magazine, presented on TV as news, described on a website's blog, or put together for the big screen. You probably also recognize, though, that mass media are similar in some of their approaches to presenting the world. The most important commonality is that they organize the world into a number of basic storytelling forms that we recognize as entertainment, news, information, education, and advertising.

Principle 5: People are Active Recipients of Media Messages
As we noted earlier, the process of meaning-making out of media forms consists of an interaction between the reader and the materials. People bring their own personalities to the materials they read and watch. They may get angry at some ideas and reject or change them. We also noted, though, that emphasizing the input of the individual does not take away from the broad social importance of the media. Because so many people share mass media materials, we might expect that large segments of the society see mass media as having cultural importance for the society as a whole. That realization points to the final foundation principle.

*Principle 6: Media Representations Play a Role in the Way Society Understands
its Reality*
People may like what they see about their society or they may complain about it. They may want people to view media images about themselves and others,

Media literacy allows you to examine the forces and influences behind the media you consume on a daily basis.

31

or they fear that others will be influenced by presentations (for example, stereotypes and violence) in ways that could cause problems. Even with an active audience, then, mass media hold crucial importance for society's visions of itself.

Media Literacy Skills

While it is important to understand the foundational principles of media literacy, there are skills you'll need to acquire if you are to make use of those elements in your daily life. They are presented below, along with some of the questions you should be able to answer if you have those skills:

An Understanding of the Commercial Forces Behind Media Materials
How do firms in various media industries make money? How exactly does advertising fit into that? What role does market research play in the activities of media producers and distributors? How do all these activities influence actual mass media materials and how do I know when they do?

An Awareness of Political Influences That Shape Media Materials
What are current political issues relating to the regulation of media industries? How is the federal government approaching the regulation of new media such as the Internet? What roles do states and local communities play in regulation of the mass media? What are ways to think about the ideological messages in mass media materials?

An Ability to Examine Media Content Systematically for Broadly Cultural as well as Specifically Commercial and Political Meanings
How do we systematically examine news, entertainment, and advertising from various critical perspectives? How, for example, can we see the popularity of the Fox TV show *American Idol* as a reflection of broad trends in American culture? To what extent can we see the show as a product of the network's particular commercial situation within the changing TV industry? And to what extent can we see it as an ideological statement about the American people's readiness to vote when they are enthusiastic about a person or topic?

An Ability to Think Through the Ethical Implications of Media Firms' Activities
How do we explore and analyze the moral dilemmas that might be created as a result of commercial or political pressures that weigh on mass media organizations? Consider sexist and racist gangsta rap as an example. The music can be very profitable. Some observers insist, however, that producing and distributing such music is immoral. Others argue that the music reflects a part of U.S. culture that should not be swept under the rug. What is an executive to do? How should firms systematically think about such issues? How should consumers respond to them?

An Understanding of Research on the Mass Media's Implications for the Individual and Society
What have scholars learned over the years about the effects of violent programming on children? How much do people really learn from news programs? What kinds of conversations do people have about what they watch and read? What can cultural historians tell us about the long-term effects of media such as the book and the television on society?

An Awareness of Ways the Public Can Influence the Production and Distribution of Mass Media Materials
How can a group concerned about certain media images complain effectively about that material? How can the group add its pressures to the many industrial and political pressures on media organizations in ways that will be make its arguments effective? What constitutional and moral issues might be relevant here?

Becoming a Media Literate Person

Once you understand the foundational elements of media literacy, and have developed key media literacy skills, you are on your way to becoming a media literate person. Based on what we have just discussed, you can see that a media literate person is:

- Knowledgeable about the influences that guide media organizations
- Up-to-date on political issues relating to the media
- Sensitive to ways of seeing media content as a means of learning about culture
- Sensitive to the ethical dimensions of media activities
- Knowledgeable about scholarship regarding media effects
- Able to enjoy media materials in a sophisticated manner

Questioning Media Trends

For executives and would-be executives, understanding the strategies of multimedia conglomerates can mean the difference between a successful career and failure. But changes in the media business affect more than just the fortunes of the people who work in the business. For members of the media literate public, the power held by the mass media raises a host of social issues. Here are just a few:

- Do media conglomerates have the ability to control what we receive over a variety of media channels? If so, do they use that ability?
- Are portrayals of sex and violence increasing in the new media environment, as some critics allege? Do media organizations have the power to lower the amount of sex and violence? Would they do it if they could?
- Does the segmentation of audiences by media companies lead to groups that those firms consider more attractive, getting better advertising discounts and greater diversity of content than groups that those firms consider less important? If so, what consequences will that have for social tensions and the ability of parts of society to share ideas with one another?
- What (if anything) should be done about the increasing ability of mass media firms to invade people's privacy by storing information they gain when they interact with them? Should the federal government pass laws that force companies to respect people's privacy, or should we leave it up to corporate self-regulation? What do we know about the history of corporate self-regulation that would lead us to believe that it would or wouldn't work in this situation?
- Should global media companies adapt to the cultural values of the nations in which they work, even if those values infringe upon free press and free speech?

Our exploration of these and related questions will take us into topics that you may not associate with the mass media business—for example, mobile telephones, toys, games, and supermarkets. It will also sometimes take us far beyond the United States, because American mass media companies increasingly operate globally. They influence non-U.S. firms around the world and are influenced by them. As we will see, their activities have sparked controversies in the United States and abroad that will likely intensify as the twenty-first century unfolds.

CHAPTER REVIEW

For an interactive chapter recap and study guide, visit the companion website for *Media Today* at www.routledge.com/textbooks/mediatoday

QUESTIONS FOR DISCUSSION AND CRITICAL THINKING

1 What are the similarities and differences between different forms of communication?
2 Give an example of a way that a mass media production firm has purposefully used "noise."
3 Why is it useful to see an audience as "constructed" rather than as objectively real?
4 As newspaper companies cut staff in order to keep up their profits, some observers believe that the investigative report is one genre of journalism that will get less attention. Why would they think that? What might that mean for journalism and for journalism's role in society?
5 Of the forms of funding when production is already complete, advertising is the most common. Why do you think that is?

INTERNET RESOURCES

Action Coalition for Media Education (http://acmecoalition.org)
A network of educators, students, health professionals, journalists, mediamakers, parents, activists, and other citizens joined as a member-supported, independent, nonprofit, continental, educational coalition.

Center for Media Literacy (http://www.medialit.org)
A pioneer in its field, the Center for Media Literacy is a nonprofit educational organization that provides leadership, public education, professional development, and educational resources nationally.

Media Awareness Network (http://www.media-awareness.ca/english/)
The Media Awareness Network is home to one of the world's most comprehensive collections of media education and Internet literacy resources.

Media Education Foundation (http//www.mediaed.org)

The Media Education Foundation produces and distributes documentary films and other educational resources to inspire critical reflection on the social, political and cultural impact of American mass media.

KEY TERMS

You can find the definitions to these key terms in the marginal glossary throughout this chapter. Test your knowledge of these terms with interactive flash cards on the Media Today companion website.

audience fragmentation

channels

commodities

convergence

culture

decoding

encoding

feedback

industrial nature

industry

innovation

interpersonal communication

interpretation

intrapersonal communication

literacy

mass media

mass media outlets

mass production process

media literate

mediated interpersonal communication

medium

messages

noise

organizational communication

parasocial interaction

political ideologies

public communication

receiver

research and development (R&D)

small group communication

social currency

society

source

stereotypes

subcultures

surveillance

transmitter

CONSTRUCTING MEDIA LITERACY

1 Can you think of entertainment (as opposed to news) content that you have used for surveillance or interpretation?

2 What are some ways in which the mass media have given you a sense of connection with or disconnection from others in the United States or in the rest of the world?

3 Do you agree or disagree with the criticisms of the mass media? Why or why not?

4 In view of the "foundation principles" of media literacy presented in this chapter, how media literate do you think you are at present? Explain your answer.

CASE STUDY   The Media as Social Currency

The idea   How much do media really influence what people discuss with you? This study will help you begin to find out by tracking how often people bring up media-related topics with you over the course of a day.

The method   The challenge will be to get some sense of a day's media-related conversations that people initiate with you. The trick will be to keep a record of what people talk to you about from the media, but without encouraging them to do it and without making them so self-conscious that they will stop right away or refrain from doing it again during the day. Here are suggestions about how to go about it:

1   Prepare a small notebook that you can carry in your pocket or pocketbook. On each page write the following categories with room to fill them in: Time, Who, Topic, How Long?

2   Go through your day normally. Each time a person (or people) brings up a topic that in some way or other relates to something they clearly say they saw or heard in the media (for example, in the news or in an ad), or that they clearly think *you* saw or heard in the media, pay particular attention. Involve yourself in the conversation as you normally would. When the conversation has ended and the others involved have left (or if you can absent yourself for a bit) get out your notebook and fill in the topics on the page: what time did the media-related conversation start, who was involved as speaker(s) and listener(s), what did they talk about, and for how long? Remember that listeners can also be speakers, and that a conversation can have far more than a single media-related topic.

3   For the purpose of this study, you should note only media-related conversations people initiate with you. The reason is that you might go out of your way to initiate such activities and that would make the results hard to generalize. Make sure, though, to include mediated conversations—for example, phone calls, Skype calls, text messages, and email—that people use to discuss media with you or to direct you to websites or other media.

4   You might also write notes about topics of conversation that you think origi-nated from the media but where the speaker did not clearly note the connec-tion. A person might talk about the war in Iraq, for example, but not say that she learned about it from the media. In fact, the story may have come from a friend who saw it on TV.

5   The next day, pull out your notebook, and make a table that notes each occur-rence and what you wrote about each one. Separate the clear cases from the ones that aren't explicit. Write a short (two-page) essay summarizing the find-ings. What might this mean about media's role in the way people interact with you? Compare your findings with the findings of others in the class, and try to figure out why they are similar or different.

2 MAKING SENSE OF THE MEDIA BUSINESS

After studying this chapter, you will be able to:

1 Recognize how mass media personnel consider the audience an integral part of business concerns

2 Describe the primary genres of the materials created by various mass media industries

3 Identify and discuss the processes of producing, distributing, and exhibiting materials in mass media industries

4 Explain the way media firms finance the production, distribution, and exhibition of media materials

5 Harness your media literacy skills to evaluate what this means to you as a media consumer

"If anyone said we were in the radio business, it wouldn't be someone from our company. We're not in the business of providing news and information. We're not in the business of providing well-researched music. We're simply in the business of selling our customers' products."

– LOWRY MAYS, CLEAR CHANNEL CEO

Media Today

As we discussed in Chapter 1, understanding the changing media system and the issues surrounding it can help us to be responsible citizens—parents, voters, workers—in our media-driven society. If you know how news is created, you might be able to read a paper or watch a TV news magazine with a much keener sense of what's going on. If you know how TV entertainment shows get on the air, and how and why the firms that produce them are changing, you may be able to come up with strategies for influencing those changes that will benefit social groups that you care about. If you are aware of the strategies of media conglomerates, you may have a better understanding of why certain companies want to move into certain businesses, and be able to decide whether the government officials you voted for are doing the right thing by allowing or not allowing them to do that.

The difficulty with getting up to speed on these topics is that understanding the mass media industry can be a bewildering experience. Let's say, for example, that community leaders in the neighborhood where you live have begun to complain about billboard advertising because of the overwhelming number of signs featuring sexual images or advertising beer. In order to help a community group petition billboard company executives to change their companies' ad policies, you decide you must learn about the billboard business. You quickly find that billboards are part of a large and growing "outdoor advertising" industry. Moreover, you learn that mass media conglomerates own some of the biggest companies in the industry. These conglomerates also run several radio stations and other media outlets in your city.

You are faced with a number of crucial questions here. First, how do you begin to get enough of a grasp on the outdoor advertising industry to learn about the factors that affect its policies for accepting ads and how those policies can be changed? Second, is the local radio business tied to some of the goals of the outdoor firms, and, if so, does that make it harder or easier to influence ad policies? Third, in terms of your interest in changing outdoor advertising policies, is it relevant that the mass media conglomerates own both the outdoor firms and radio stations? If so, how?

You want to learn as much as possible about the outdoor advertising industry to understand how its policies on beer and sex can be changed. But should you also learn about the radio industry and the conglomerates? If so, what should you learn? And where do you start? Must you conduct research on each industry separately, as if the activities in one industry cannot help you understand the activities in another? If that's the case, you may find yourself thinking that it's not worth the time and effort.

This chapter aims to assure you that becoming knowledgeable about the business of mass media is not as intimidating as it may sound. By learning a small number of general points about the mass media business, you will understand particular conglomerates and mass media industries much better than if you started from scratch every time.

The Economy of Mass Media

In its *2006 Communications Industry Forecast,* the highly regarded Veronis Suhler Stevenson (VSS) consulting firm estimated that 2005 spending on media had reached $896.94 billion.[1] That number will give you one sense of the large overall size of the media business. As we move through this book, we will see that the revenues of individual media industries come to tens of billions of dollars, and sometimes far more. Table 2.1 gives you another sense of the media economy by presenting the revenues of the five biggest media firms. As the table notes, those five companies alone brought in almost $97 billion in 2005.

How does one begin to examine such large industries and companies? Well, no matter what its size or what specific industry or industries it operates in, any mass media organization must be concerned with six primary activities:

- Production
- Exhibition
- Finance
- Distribution
- Audience research
- Government regulation

content the material that a mass media firm produces, distributes, or exhibits.

These six activities are related to five major genres of **content,** the material that a mass media firm produces, distributes, or exhibits. These five genres are:

- Entertainment
- Information
- Advertising
- News
- Education

Success with the right audience is crucial if a mass media organization is to continue operating. So let's look at the way mass media people think about, and conduct research on, the audiences for the content that their companies produce, distribute, exhibit, or finance.

Table 2.1 **The Top Five Largest U.S. Media Companies, by Revenue, 2005**

Rank	Company	Revenue
1	Time Warner	$33,728
2	Comcast Corp.	$22,078
3	Walt Disney Co.	$17,154
4	News Corp.	$12,563
5	NBC Universal (General Electric Co.)	$12,437

Notes: Dollars in millions. The revenues for the first four firms include all their subsidiaries. The revenues for the fifth just include the revenues for NBC Universal, which is the media subsidiary of the General Electric Company.

Source: Advertising Age. http://adage.com/datacenter/datapopup.php?article_id=112269

The Role of the Audience

No media business can exist without content that attracts consumers, or **audiences**. When mass media personnel speak of their audience, they mean the people to whom they are directing their products. **Media practitioners**—the people who select or create the material that a mass media firm produces, distributes, or exhibits— are keenly aware that the kinds of content they produce, distribute, and exhibit must be attractive to audiences if money is to flow their way instead of to their competitors.

But audiences pose enormous risks as well as great opportunities for success for media practitioners. There are three questions they must answer:

1   How should we think about our audience? How should we define our audience?
2   Will the material we are thinking of creating, distributing, or exhibiting to attract that audience generate adequate revenues?
3   Were the people we thought would be attracted to our products in fact attracted to our products? Why or why not?

Thinking About Audiences and Defining Target Audiences   Executives who are charting the direction of media firms do not think about the members of their audience in the same way that they think about themselves. Take, for example, Kaya. She thinks of herself in a number of ways—as a hard worker who juggles her communication studies major with her twenty-hour-a-week job at a local restaurant; as a caring daughter who visits her parents twice a week; as a moderate churchgoer (about two Sundays a month); as a girlfriend who tries to make time for her boyfriend, Omar, in her busy week; as a loyal friend who tries hard to keep up with high school classmates by using the phone and email.

Now consider how executives at a magazine that Kaya gets—say, *Time*—think of her. Of course, it's very unlikely that they would know her personally. In fact, they are not really thinking specifically about Kaya at all. Instead, the characteristics that describe Kaya for *Time* are those that *Time* executives can use when they parade clusters of readers in front of potential advertisers as types of people the advertisers can reach through their magazine. The magazine got some of its data from a questionnaire that Kaya filled out after she received a student discount to the periodical. Other data came from lists that the magazine bought from companies that bring together information about millions of people and sell that information to media firms.

To *Time*, Kaya is (among other things) in the 18–34 age group, female, a student, a small-car owner, unmarried, childless, an apartment renter, an earner of $30,000 a year, the possessor of two credit cards, an avid moviegoer, not a big TV watcher, and someone who has taken at least three airplane trips in the past two years. As you can see, *Time*'s way of characterizing Kaya is quite different from the way she describes herself. *Time* knows nothing about Kaya's loyalty to her friends, her parents, and her boyfriend. Nor does the company track her interest in communication studies or her churchgoing. Part of the reason is that *Time* simply doesn't have this information. But the major reason is that *Time* collected the information it *does* have about Kaya because these are some of the characteristics that major advertisers consider when they think about buying space in magazines. A car manufacturer who is thinking of advertising in the magazine doesn't care how many times a month Kaya goes to church or whether she visits her parents. The car manufacturer *does* care about her age, her gender, her income, and the kind of car she

audiences   the people to whom a media product is directed

media practitioners   the people who select or create the material that a mass media firm produces, distributes or exhibits

41

presently owns because it believes this information predicts the likelihood that she can be convinced to buy its brand. Kaya's age and student status make her attractive to advertisers like car manufacturers even though she doesn't make a lot of money; they believe these factors indicate that she will make a lot more some day.

Because *Time* magazine gets at least half of its revenue from advertising, its executives want to keep subscribers who are attractive to advertisers, so they use the information they have about Kaya and subscribers like her, and about other groups of subscribers that they have identified as being attractive to advertisers, to help them decide what kinds of materials in the magazine will keep these people as subscribers. These identified and selected population segments, then, become the desired audience for the media vehicle (in this case, the magazine). Once executives have identified the target segments, they try to learn things about them that will lead to increasing sales. That, in turn, leads to more research to understand the groups. Figure 2.1 illustrates this process by focusing on Kaya. The example assumes that *Time* marketers are attracted by what they know about Kaya and want her to be part of their audience. If they didn't find Kaya and people with characteristics like hers attractive as consumers, they would produce content that would speak to different interests and that might drive Kaya away, rather than encourage her to renew her subscription.

Thinking about the audience, then, means learning to think of people primarily as consumers of media materials and other products. For media professionals, thinking about people in this way requires a combination of intuition and solid knowledge of the marketplace. As the example of Kaya and *Time* magazine suggests, when advertisers contribute all or part of a firm's revenue stream, the firm's executives have two challenges: they have to create content that will attract audiences, and they must also make sure that the content and the audience it brings in will be attractive to advertisers so that money flows its way, instead of to its competitors. To do this, they need to decide whether enough advertisers want to reach that audience in order to provide **adequate revenue**—enough cash to allow the enterprise to pay for itself and give the owners or bankers who put up the money the desired return on their investment.

Sometimes, in fact, media executives reverse the order of the questions. They first ask which audiences advertisers want to reach, and then look for ways to attract those audiences. ABC television network executives know, for example, that advertisers covet viewers in the 18–34 age group from 8 to 11 p.m. That basic premise guides much of their thinking about the programming decisions. All the production firms that work with the network know that they must come up with ideas that will be a magnet to that age group. (Think *Grey's Anatomy* and the rest of ABC's Thursday night schedule to get a concrete sense of what this means.)

This can get quite complex, but the most important questions executives ask are often quite basic. Say, for example, a greeting card company president wants his firm to create a new **line**—a new assortment of products with a particular, predetermined format. Should the company aim the line at *everybody*? That plan probably wouldn't work out well, since in recent years the lines offered by greeting card companies have been quite **targeted**: they have been written and drawn to appeal to particular segments of society rather than to the population as a whole. Well, then, what segments should be the targets? Women or men; the rich, the middle class, or the poor; Asians, Latinos, whites, or blacks; people who live in the eastern United States or those who live in the Midwest—or some combination of these and other categories?

adequate revenue enough cash to allow the enterprise to pay for itself and give the owners or bankers who put up the money the desired return on their investment

line an assortment of products with a particular, predetermined format

targeted created to appeal to particular segments of society rather than the population as a whole

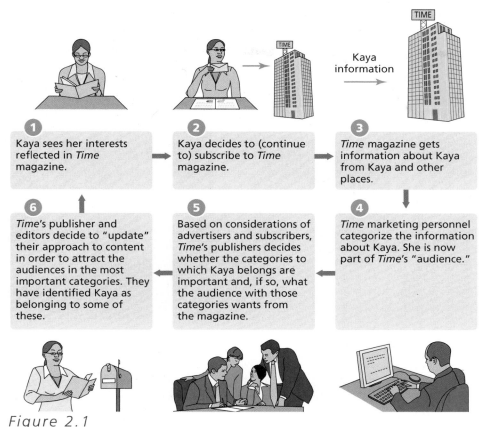

Kaya information

1 Kaya sees her interests reflected in *Time* magazine.

2 Kaya decides to (continue to) subscribe to *Time* magazine.

3 *Time* magazine gets information about Kaya from Kaya and other places.

4 *Time* marketing personnel categorize the information about Kaya. She is now part of *Time*'s "audience."

5 Based on considerations of advertisers and subscribers, *Time*'s publishers decides whether the categories to which Kaya belongs are important and, if so, what the audience with those categories wants from the magazine.

6 *Time*'s publisher and editors decide to "update" their approach to content in order to attract the audiences in the most important categories. They have identified Kaya as belonging to some of these.

Figure 2.1

Kaya and the Constructed Audience

The ways in which executives at *Time* view their readers and the way in which *Time*'s readers view themselves are very different.

Therefore, many companies spend a lot of energy deciding which audiences they should pursue, what those audiences' characteristics are, and what those audiences like and don't like. Executives try to verify their intuitions and control their risks with research. In conducting this research, they think about the types of people who make up their audience—that is, they construct their audience—in three broad ways: through demographics, psychographics, and lifestyle categories.

Demographics

The use of demographics is one of the simplest and most common ways to construct audiences. The term **demographics** refers to characteristics by which people are divided into particular social categories. Media executives focus on those characteristics, or factors, which they believe are most relevant to understanding how and why people use their medium. **Demographic indicators** include such factors as age, gender, occupation, ethnicity, race, and income (see Figure 2.2).

Psychographics

A second way to differentiate groups is by **psychographics**, or categorizing people on the basis of their attitudes, personality types, or motivations. Consider the management of an interior design magazine that wants advertisers to understand its readership beyond the familiar demographics of "high income," "age thirty and up," and "homeowners." The magazine executives hire a research firm to inter-

demographics
characteristics by which people are divided into particular social categories

demographic indicators
factors such as age, gender, occupation, ethnicity, race, and income

psychographics a way to differentiate among people or groups by categorizing them according to their attitudes, personality types, or motivations

43

Popular shows like ABC's
Grey's Anatomy attract key
audiences for advertisers.

view a large number of subscribers and create psychological profiles of them. The researchers find that the readers can be divided into three psychographic types: *comparers* (20 percent of subscribers), who like to read the magazine to see how their furniture stacks up against the pieces on the pages; *idea hunters* (40 percent of subscribers), who read it to help them with their own decorating; and *art lovers* (40 percent), who subscribe because they love the beautiful furniture that appears in the magazine each month. The researchers also find that the three psychographic categories differ in terms of the length of time people remain subscribers. Those

Figure 2.2

Demographic Indicators
Demographic indicators, like those shown in this figure, help media executives group individuals into categories that will be most attractive to their target advertisers.

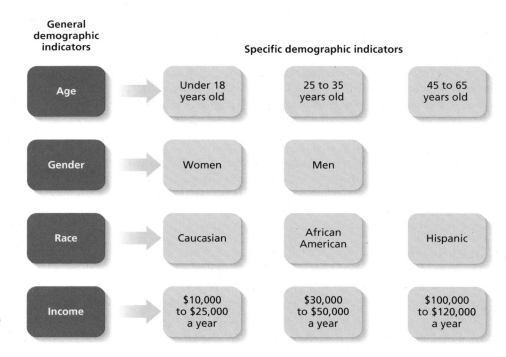

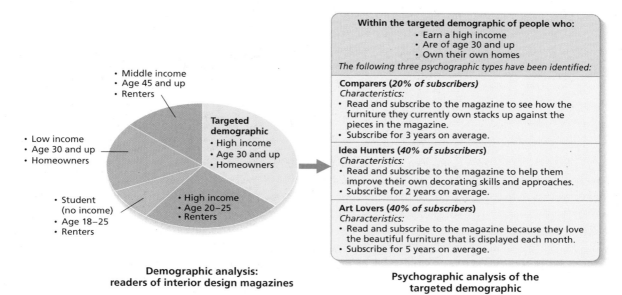

Demographic analysis:
readers of interior design magazines

Psychographic analysis of the
targeted demographic

Figure 2.3

Psychographic Indicators

Psychographic indicators can help media executives further shape their product to attract the audience members their advertisers seek.

readers who are classified as art lovers stay the longest time (an average of five years), while those classified as idea hunters stay the shortest time (two years), with the comparers in the middle (three years). The magazine executives can use this construction of the audience to shape their articles to appeal to the comparers and art lovers and to find advertisers that are interested in any of the groups (see Figure 2.3).

Lifestyle Categories

The third broad way to describe media audiences is by using **lifestyle categories**—finding activities in which potential audiences are involved that mark them as different from others in the audience or in the population at large. Suppose, for example, that the interior design magazine conducts another research study that finds that its readers go to restaurants, own expensive cars, and travel outside the United States far more than the average for the U.S. population. In this way, the magazine's employees are categorizing readers from a lifestyle point of view.

Keep in mind that what media professionals learn about their audiences through research is relevant only if it relates to making money by attracting advertisers or by keeping them as audience members. The lifestyle characteristics that our fictional interior design magazine found are terrific—just the sort that will attract major automobile, airline, hotel and restaurant advertisers. The demographics and psychographics are also useful for getting sponsors as well as for thinking about the kind of content that will keep particular groups as part of the audience.

Creating Content to Attract the Target Audience

A key challenge for many people who work in mass media industries is knowing what kind of content to present to their audiences, and how to present it. While this may seem straightforward, it actually involves quite a bit of selection, thought, and risk.

Suppose you are in charge of programming for CBS; that is, setting the television schedule for the coming year. Your job is to set up the menu of shows that

lifestyle categories
activities in which potential audiences are involved that mark them as different from others in the population at large

the owners of CBS hope will attract tens of millions of viewers to their airwaves every day. Quite a daunting task, isn't it? For one thing, you must try to get a thorough understanding of the audiences your company wants to attract—who they are and what they like. For another, you have to have a strong grasp of the kinds of materials that may be available to meet audience interests at different times of the day. What will grab people's attention? Who can create it? How do you even begin to determine whether the ideas that potential creators pitch to you will succeed?

Sometimes the answers to these questions are based on the intuitions and experiences of the executives in charge. To lower their risk, they may choose creators with good **track records**—that is, a history of successes. They may also choose to produce material that is similar to other material that has recently been successful. For example, if a comedy/horror movie aimed at young adults has recently been successful at the box office, executives might search for another film of the same type, hoping that lightning will strike twice.

When a lot of money is at stake (and it usually is), executives often turn to **research and development (R&D)** activities to systematically investigate potential sources of revenue. These activities involve learning about the leisure habits of different audiences through a number of tools, including surveys, focus groups, or the analysis of existing data.

In **surveys**, a certain number of carefully chosen people are asked the same questions individually over the phone or in person. A **focus group** is an assemblage of eight to ten carefully chosen people who are asked to discuss their habits and opinions about one or more topics. The **analysis of existing data** involves systematic investigation of the potential audience for certain kinds of content (who they are, where they are, how much they like the idea, how much they will pay for it) and the competitors (who they are, how similar their products are, how powerful they are). Based on these results, executives must decide what kinds of materials to create and how—and whether their proposed budget is adequate to create the product and market it successfully against the competition.

Black Entertainment Television (BET) provides an example. In the 1990s, executives of this cable service were aware that African-Americans tend to watch television substantially more than other Americans. They also learned that African-Americans accounted for about 20 percent of the audience for HBO, the major cable movie channel supported by monthly subscriber fees. African-Americans' presence in that audience was more than 7 percentage points higher than their presence in the general population. These figures were among the data that led BET to embark upon a new pay-cable service aimed specifically at the African-American audience.

Measuring the Content's Success with the Target Audience You might think that all of the questions about whether the mass media material will fly with audiences finally get answered when the material is created and released. Actually, determining whether or not the content that the company puts out is a success with the existing or desired audience can be simple or difficult, depending on the mass medium and the exact questions asked. The seemingly simple part may involve counting the sales—how many magazines or movie tickets were sold. In cases where sales are not involved, such as with radio, broadcast television, and the Web, ratings companies conduct regular surveys to count audiences in order to help executives determine how many people watched particular programs. As we will see later in the text, however, neither counting sales nor conducting ratings surveys is really a simple activity.

track record the previous successes or failures of a product, person, or organization

research and development (R&D) departments within companies that explore new ideas and generate new products and services, systematically investigating potential sources of revenue through surveys, focus groups, or the analysis of existing data

surveys a research tool that seeks to ask a certain number of carefully chosen people the same questions individually over the phone or in person

focus group an assemblage of eight to ten carefully chosen people who are asked to discuss their habits and opinions about one or more topics

analysis of existing data a systematic investigation into the potential audience for the material (who they are, where they are, how much they like the idea, how much they will pay for it) and the competitors (who they are, how similar their products are, how powerful they are)

How Much am I Worth?

Have you ever considered how much your name is worth? Of course, to us, our name is our identity; it's who we are and how people know us. When we meet someone new, we can freely give that person our name as a sign of friendship. But we can also withhold our name, or information about ourselves, if we don't want to talk to that person again.

Information about who you are is worth a lot of money to marketers. InfoUSA, a database marketing firm, has collected information on more than 210 million individuals. Customers can access infoUSA's databases online through their Sales Genie service, which costs between $75 and $180 per month. Another company, CAS Marketing Solutions, sells lists of consumer information for as little as $35 per thousand names.

For these database companies, your name, along with your accompanying information, is a commodity. These corporations have assembled massive databases to store knowledge about you from the purchases that you have made, information you have given out, or even which sites you visit on the Web.

CAS Marketing Solutions claims to have "psychographic data that defines the lifestyle characteristics, behavior and

product interests of individuals" based on social roles, interests, and hobbies. For example, they may classify you based on the type of music you like, the books you read, the pets you own, even the type of food you like to eat.

Information like this is valuable to a wide range of marketers for it can give them a strong idea of who you are and what you are likely to buy in the future.

Your name can be bought and sold, just as you buy and sell a CD or a car. Such transactions occur without your knowing that people are making money off your name.

Nevertheless, counting sales and audiences is a lot easier than determining why a media product succeeded or failed. There may be many reasons, only some of which have to do with the attractiveness of the content itself. Executives often try to find out what went wrong—or what went right—so that they can avoid future mistakes and/or repeat past successes. That sometimes involves conducting focus groups or surveys to gauge the intended audience's opinions. Often, though, executives discuss their failures and successes with one another. They try to figure out what elements led to success and which led to failure. This is not at all "scientific," but it's often the best that people whose business it is to select or create mass media content can do.

The Primary Genres

When media practitioners try to determine how to choose or produce content that is appropriate for the audiences they want to reach, they must do so with an understanding of the major categories of content from which they can build their

Some films like *Syriana* intend to entertain as well as make serious political points.

genres major categories of media content

material. Major categories of media content are called **genres**. A genre is a category of artistic composition, as in music or literature, marked by a distinctive style, form, or content.[2] The primary genres that media practitioners discuss are *entertainment, news, information, education,* and *advertising.* Let's first take a look at the primary genres.

Entertainment

entertainment material that grabs the audience's attention and leaves agreeable feelings, as opposed to challenging their views of themselves and the world

The word **entertainment** derives from the Latin *tenere*, which means "to hold or keep steady, busy, or amused." The notion of making money by keeping an audience steady, busy, or amused remains central to those in the business of entertainment. Media practitioners, then, define entertainment as material that grabs the audience's attention and leaves agreeable feelings, as opposed to challenging their views of themselves and the world. However, this doesn't mean that people who work in the entertainment business always stay away from informing or persuading. Many movies that are categorized under "entertainment" by their production firms have been written and produced with the intention of making a political point (think of *The Day After Tomorrow, Syriana,* or *Blood Diamond*) or an educational point (like *Schindler's List, Crash,* or *Letters from Iwo Jima*). When media practitioners label a product as "entertainment," though, they are signaling to their audiences that their primary concern should be with enjoyment, not with any other messages that may be included.

subgenres subcategories of media content genres

Subgenres of Entertainment One way to understand entertainment is to see it as consisting of four **subgenres**—festivals, gaming, drama, and comedy. We can see each of these subgenres, in turn, as having still more subcategories nested within it. Consider, for example, the subgenre *gaming*, which may include sports

Genre	ENTERTAINMENT			
Subgenre	**Festival**	**Drama**	**Gaming**	**Comedy**
Second-level subgenre	Parades	Workplace	Sports	Situation comedy
Third-level subgenre	Secular parades	Dramas about professionals	Professional sports	Work-based sitcoms
Fourth-level subgenre	Nonrecurring secular parades	Hospital dramas	NFL Football	Hospital-based sitcoms

(*Sunday Night NFL Football*), quiz shows (*Deal or No Deal*), and newspaper crossword puzzles, among other forms. Similarly, the subgenre *comedy* may include situation comedies (*Two and a Half Men*), standup comedy routines (Dane Cook) and their ancillary products (Cook's CD/DVD *Retaliation*), certain radio talk shows (*The Howard Stern Show*), and joke lists (Michael Kilgarriff's *1000 Knock-Knock Jokes for Kids*), among other forms. We can even go further and think of a more specific level—subgenres of these subgenres. We can break *situation comedies* into school sitcoms (*Everybody Hates Chris*), workplace sitcoms (*The Office*), family sitcoms (*Family Guy*) and buddy sitcoms (*My Name is Earl*). In turn, people who are specialists in sitcoms might be able to create still further subgenres of these categories. Workplace sitcoms might be divided into hospital sitcoms (*Scrubs*) and office sitcoms (*The Office, 30 Rock*). Take a look at Figure 2.4 for an illustration of these relationships.

Here, entertainment is divided into subgenres of festival, gaming, drama, and comedy. One subgenre under each is extended two levels to illustrate how these categories contain subcategories. You might be able to break these down into even

Figure 2.4

Entertainment Genres and Subgenres

Here, entertainment is divided into subgenres of festival, gaming, drama, and comedy. One subgenre under each is extended two levels to illustrate how these categories contain subcategories. You might be able to break these down into even more specific categories. For example, people who write hospital-based sitcoms might be able to describe various subgenres of these sitcoms.

The popularity of NBC's *The Office* may inspire other networks to produce more sitcoms set in the workplace.

more specific categories. For example, people who write hospital-based sitcoms might be able to describe various subgenres of these sitcoms.

Entertainment Formulas   You may have noticed that there are key elements that make up various subgenres: the family situation comedy, the hospital drama, the baseball broadcast, or any other subgenre. This specific combination of elements is called a **formula**—a patterned approach to creating content that is characterized by three major features:

formula a patterned approach to creating content that is characterized by the use of setting, typical characters, and patterns of action

- setting
- typical characters
- patterns of action[3]

setting the environment in which content takes place

The **setting** is the environment in which content takes place. A football program such as *Sunday Night NFL Football* takes place in a stadium and in an announcer's booth. A doctor show such as *Grey's Anatomy* takes place in a hospital.

typical characters those who appear regularly in the subgenre

The **typical characters** are those who appear regularly in the subgenre. In the football program, the announcers, the athletes, the referees and the coaches are typical characters. Doctor shows such as *Grey's Anatomy* are populated by (you guessed it) doctors, patients, nurses, and medical technicians.

patterns of action the predictable activities associated with the characters in the settings

The **patterns of action** are the predictable activities associated with the characters in the settings. The football program's patterns of action center on the rules of the game, which are bounded by the clock (sixty minutes plus time-outs and half time) and the field (the playing zones). The patterns of action in doctor shows aren't so clearly based on rules. Nevertheless, each episode does have its plot patterns, revolving around issues of life and death.

As the *Grey's Anatomy* example suggests, it is easiest to think of formulas in relation to the storytelling aspects of entertainment. But formulas also apply to non-storytelling entertainment. As the football example suggests, people who work

The hit reality show *Survivor* is based on a Swedish show *Expedition: Robinson.* There are numerous international adaptations of *Survivor* including Australia, Bulgaria, the Czech Republic, England, Israel, Pakistan, and South Africa.

on sports broadcasts recognize the types of settings, characters, and activity patterns that uniquely describe their business. The same holds for quiz shows, reality shows, and even computer games.

When it comes to reality shows, you can probably suggest different forms of the subgenre depending on whether you are discussing *Amazing Race*, *Dancing with the Stars*, or *Survivor*. *Survivor* would seem to be part of what might be called an "isolation" reality show subgenre, along with such series as *The Apprentice*, *The Biggest Loser*, and *Big Brother*. They contain similar formula elements:

- *Setting*: a location that isolates a group with minimal interference from the "outside" world
- *Typical characters*: good-looking individuals of diverse ethnic backgrounds who have certain expected character profiles, selfish or generous, gregarious or loner, crafty or naïve
- *Patterns of action*: challenges that the producers set up that often set members of the group against one another and lead to individuals being chosen to leave

Regardless of the subgenre, formulas can be quite complex and textured. We have already noted that television doctor shows have predictable characters and settings as well as plots. You might think that this formula would limit the number of interesting stories that can be told. Nevertheless, more than seventy television medical series and made-for-TV movies have aired in the United States since the mid-1950s. TV writers have found enormous variety in the kind of relationships they set up between doctors and patients, doctors and nurses, nurses and patients, nurses and nurses, and doctors and doctors. Add to these relationships the medical system's changing knowledge of diseases and the changing economic environment. Together, these factors have allowed doctor shows to thrive at several points in U.S. TV history.[4]

Keep in mind, too, that formulas can and do change. Media practitioners who use these formulas to create stories for movies, television, video games or other media are often steeped in their history. Interviews with writers of doctor shows, for instance, reveal that most of them were quite familiar with the programs that came before the ones they created. Writers and producers in all mass media often "borrow" plot elements, characters, and settings from previously successful stories. Their hope is that the basic elements of the formula will stay popular and that they can reshape these elements to fit what they believe are the interests of contemporary audiences.

Examples are all around us, but you have to know something about the history of a mass medium to notice them. Perhaps you've seen the remakes of classic horror movies that appeared in movie theaters over the past few years—for example, *The Hitcher* (2007), *Day of the Dead* (2007), *Halloween* (2007), *Wicker Man* (2006), and *Omen* (2006). If you go back to the originals, you will see how the writers borrowed settings, characters, and plot elements from the originals and then changed them to fit their idea of what audiences of the 2000s would like. More broadly, you can watch TV or movie westerns from various decades and see how the elements continue and change at the same time. Rent some old films and try it. Watching TV, going to the movies, reading novels, and even playing video games will take on a whole new dimension.

Apart from updating genres, writers and producers are also eager to find new ways to mix entertainment subgenres in ways that will entertain their target audi-

hybrid genres   a term used by some academic writers to describe mixed genres

hybridity   the process of mixing genres within a culture and across cultures

dramady   a subgenre that blends the rules associated with drama (serious) and comedy (funny)

ences. In fact, creators don't always use "pure" genres. They sometimes mix them in ways they hope will attract audiences and keep them coming back. The term **hybrid genres** can be used to describe mixed genres; the process of mixing genres within a culture and across cultures is called **hybridity**. Hybrid genres are all around us. One example of hybrid popular music is much of the work of T-Pain, which consciously blends rhythm-and-blues influences with sounds and sensibilities of rap. Hybridity can also take place across cultures. Think of attempts by U.S. producers and writers to mix plots, settings, and characters of Indian "Bollywood" films with traditional Hollywood plots, characters and settings. An obvious example is *Bride and Prejudice*, a 2004 movie that inserts an Indian family into the basic plot of the Jane Austen novel *Pride and Prejudice* and follows them through Indian, U.K. and U.S. locales. The advertising tagline for the movie, which was filmed in India, the United Kingdom and the United States, trumpeted this hybridity: "Bollywood meets Hollywood … and it's the perfect match."[5]

Apart from combining specific entertainment subgenres, some producers and writers try to get people's attention by blending the rules associated with drama (serious) and comedy (funny) into what some media practitioners call a **dramady**. A contemporary example of a dramady is *The Sopranos*, the HBO cable television series that completed its first-run episodes in 2007. Combining the tone of serious mob movies such as *The Godfather* and *Goodfellas* with the comedic sensibilities of films such as *Get Shorty, Analyze This,* and *The Crew*, the program centers on a New Jersey Mafia boss, Tony Soprano, who has problems involving his family as well as his criminal business. Tony's attempts to cope with his world, to do the right thing within the weird sense of morality in which he lives, lead the show to careen from screwball hilarity to dead-serious pathos. James Gandolfini, who plays the role, puts it this way:

> The writing was so bizarre … and such good writing. You'd be laughing and then five minutes later there's a violent scene. … [Tony Soprano's] a guy who always tries to do the right thing in his mind, which ends up screwing up everybody's life. He's always trying to do the right thing and it's never really the right thing—like blowing up his friend's restaurant to stop a hit. Nobody would think like that; he thinks it's doing the right thing, and instead it reverberates down the path and screws up everybody's lives.[6]

News

It would be unusual for someone to mistake *The Sopranos* for a news show. From the standpoint of its creation, though, the genre of news is similar to the genre of entertainment in a basic way: news, like entertainment, involves the telling of stories.

We often don't think of news in this way, but it is useful to pause and consider this point. When you watch the *ABC World News,* in one sense *ABC World News* anchor Charles Gibson is telling you a tale with a beginning, a middle, and an end. Of course, Gibson reads most of the story and shows short video clips of the accompanying action, whereas other storytelling media genres (like a sitcom) continuously illustrate the story through acting. The tales that Charles Gibson tells during his newscast, however, may not be that different from the sitcom you will be viewing just two hours later on the same network. In fact, many of the ideas for nonnews television programming are generated from news. Consider, for example,

A Dramady Says Goodbye

On June 10, 2007, after eight years of mobster melodrama, Tony Soprano and the rest of the cast of HBO's critically acclaimed series *The Sopranos* said goodbye to fans. The finale was watched by nearly 12 million viewers, none of whom, it seemed, could reach an agreement about the episode's final moments.

During the last scene, Mafia boss Tony sat with his family at a local diner as the camera panned the mysterious, unknown characters around them. Anticipation built as audiences wondered whether one of these individuals might "whack" Tony. Abruptly, the screen went black, causing some viewers to believe their cable went out. Instead, the fade-out was producer David Chase's deliberate attempt to leave the series open-ended.

In the hours and days after the episode aired, media critics voiced their opinion of what *Variety* described as "a finale without finality." Some lauded Chase's unorthodox ending, describing it as "genius," "brilliant," and "the perfect final note." Others, meanwhile, denounced Chase's "lack of creativity" and likened the conclusion to an ill-conceived prank at the audience's expense.

Fans of the show were perhaps more vehement in their opinions, and many of them turned to the Internet to voice their critiques. In fact, so many individuals attempted to post feedback on the HBO website that they ended up crashing the site. Blogs, too, became a hotbed for discussion and speculation about what the future would hold for *The Sopranos*. On her Deadline Hollywood blog, Nikki Finke

addressed rumors that the finale was created to generate interest in a future DVD and/or film that would pick up where the series left off. If so, she wrote, "That kind of commercialism shouldn't be tolerated."

Despite the mixed reviews of *The Sopranos'* finale, there was one recurring theme: the ending was consistent with what Chase had done with the series over the years. As *San Jose Mercury News* columnist Charlie McCollum explained, "In a world where resolution is expected, no previous great television series ever has gone out on such a high note of ambiguity, such a lack of denouement." In this respect, at least, *The Sopranos* achieved a fond farewell.

Sources: "Out of 'Whack': Critics Weigh in on *Sopranos* Finale." *Editor and Publisher*. Accessed 6/14/07. http://www.editorand publisher.com; Phil Gallo. "Review: *The Sopranos*." *Variety*. Accessed 6/11/07. www.variety.com

NBC's *Law and Order*, which boasts that its screenplays are "ripped from the headlines."

Reporters, directors, editors, producers, and other people who work in the news business are called **journalists**. A journalist is someone who is trained to report nonfiction events to an audience. Their reporting can be in print (newspapers, magazines) or electronic media (radio, TV, the Web). Historically, newspapers have been central to the circulation of news in America. But as we'll see in later chapters, big changes are taking place that are eroding the presence and power of newspapers in people's lives. Today's journalists are learning that they must present news in many media, including audio and video reports on the Web.

journalist an individual who is trained to report nonfiction events to an audience

How would these people explain the difference between what they produce and other storytelling genres, such as entertainment? They would undoubtedly argue that there is one clear distinction: news stories are constrained by facts, whereas entertainment stories are not. The writer of the screenplay for a TV show that is "based on a true story" or "ripped from the headlines" can decide whether a character who is accused of rape is guilty or innocent. The reporter of the real-life news event, however, should never make such a judgment. Building on this basic distinction, news workers divide news broadly into four subgenres:

- ▨ Hard news
- ▨ Investigative reports
- ▨ Editorials
- ▨ Soft news

Hard News **Hard news** is what most people probably think of as news. It is the firsthand reportage of a battle, the coverage of a congressional bill's passage, the details of a forest fire. News workers use four guidelines when they try to decide what is and what isn't hard news. An event that fits only one of these guidelines will probably not be considered hard news. Additionally, the more of these guidelines that apply to an event, the more likely news workers are to cover it.

▨ **Timeliness**
A hard news event must have happened recently—typically within the past day or so. A murder that happened yesterday might deserve coverage. A murder that happened last year would not, unless new information about it has been released or discovered.

▨ **Unusualness**
Hard news events are those that most people would consider unusual. To use the classic example, "Dog Bites Man" is not news, whereas "Man Bites Dog" is.

▨ **Conflict**
Conflicts—struggles between opposing forces—often lie at the center of hard news stories. Often these struggles are physical; they can be wars or bar-room brawls. Sometimes the conflicts involve wars of words, as between members of Congress. Other times they pit humans against nature (a fire or other natural disaster).

▨ **The closeness of the incident**
An event is more likely to be seen as hard news if it happens close by than if it takes place far away. Note, however, that *closeness* carries two meanings: it can mean geographically close (physically near to the audience), or it can mean psychologically close. An incident is psychologically close when members of the audience feel a connection to it even though it takes place far away. Because of Boston's large Irish population, for example, newspaper editors in Boston may consider certain happenings in Ireland to be hard news, whereas editors in areas of the United States with small Irish populations would not cover those events.

Once they have decided that something is hard news, news workers must decide how to present it. Journalists use the word **objectivity** to summarize the way in which news ought to be researched, organized, and presented. Most journalists

hard news a news story marked by timeliness, unusualness, conflict, and closeness

objectivity presenting a fair, balanced, and impartial representation of the events that took place by recounting a news event based on the facts and without interpretation, so that anyone else who witnessed the event would agree with the journalists' recounting of it; the way in which news ought to be researched, organized, and presented

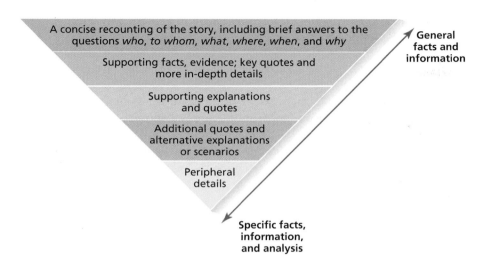

Figure 2.5

The Inverted Pyramid
The Inverted Pyramid approach to reporting the news begins with the most general statement of the story and grows increasingly more specific.

would agree that it is impossible to present a totally objective view of an event, if that means a view that is the absolute truth with no personal viewpoints inserted. The fact is that no two people will see the same thing in exactly the same way. Most journalists would say that what they mean by objective reports is reports that present a fair, balanced, and impartial representation of the events that took place.

Over the decades, journalists have agreed upon certain characteristics that an objective story will have. These characteristics give a reporter the tools to describe an incident efficiently in ways that his or her editor (or any other editor) will consider fair and impartial. Here are four major characteristics of an objective story, particularly with regard to print news:

- It should be written in a form that journalists call an *inverted pyramid*. That means that the reporter should place in the first paragraph (the *lead paragraph*) a concise recounting of the entire story. Typically that means "leading" with the six Ws—*who* did it, *what* they did, to *whom* (or with whom), *where* they did it, *when* they did it, and *why* (see Figure 2.5). That is the most general statement of the story—the base of the pyramid. In the paragraphs that follow, the reporter should give increasingly specific information about the material in the lead paragraph. (The ever more specific information supposedly corresponds to the increasingly narrow pyramid.)
- An objective story should be told in the *third person*. That means writing as if the journalist is a novelist telling the tale but is not involved in it. So, for example, an objective report of a riot can state, "The crowd ran wildly around the square breaking store windows." It would not be objective for the reporter to write, "I saw the crowd run wildly around the square breaking windows."
- An objective story should report at least *two sides* of a conflict. If a politician is accused of corruption, the objective report must also note the politician's denial of the charges.
- An objective story uses quotes from those involved or from experts on the topic to back up statements.

These characteristics can be used in creating objective news stories for any medium. If you watch television news programs carefully, however, you may note that reporters also convey the idea of objectivity in a visual way. Here are three camera rules for an objective story:

- There should be a title on the screen telling the viewer who the reporter is interviewing.
- The camera should film the reporter or a person being interviewed from the height of a normal person, not from the ground staring up at the person or from above the person staring down.
- The camera should give as much time to a person representing one side of the conflict as it does to a person representing the other side. Anything less would be considered biased.

In addition to being objective, hard news reports are also held to strict standards of accuracy. **Accuracy** means reporting factually correct information. Many news organizations expect their reporters to check "facts" with at least two sources before they use them in stories. Reputable news-oriented magazines often have fact checkers who review stories for accuracy before they are released to the public.

accuracy reporting factually correct information

Investigative Reports **Investigative reports** are in-depth explorations of some aspects of reality. This news subgenre shares the same standards of objectivity, accuracy, and fairness or balance with hard news. However, a major difference between hard news and investigative reports is the amount of time journalists can devote to the project. When it comes to hard news, journalists typically work on tight schedules; their time limit (**deadline**) for the completion of an assignment is often only a few hours after they begin it. In contrast, journalists who work on investigative reports have quite a bit more time to do their research, interview their sources, and write their script. Their deadlines can be days or weeks from the time they begin, or even longer.

investigative reports in-depth explorations of some aspects of reality

deadline the time limit for the completion of an assignment

Often, though not always, the investigative reporters seek to uncover corruption or other problems in government or business, and the tone of the report resembles that of a detective story. A few television news series, such as *60 Minutes*, *Dateline NBC*, and *20/20*, present this type of material.

Editorials Opinions regarding hard news are usually reserved for editorials. Unlike hard news and investigative reports, an **editorial** is a subgenre of news that expresses an individual's or organization's point of view. Some editorials are written in the name of (and express the point of view of) the person who wrote the piece, whereas others are written in the name of the entire news organization—for example, the newspaper that printed the piece or the television station that aired it.

editorial a subgenre of news that concentrates on an individual's or organization's point of view

News organizations may also allow their reporters and knowledgeable people who do not work for their firm to present editorial comments. **Columnists** are individuals who are paid to write editorials on a regular basis—usually weekly, monthly, or daily. Editorials by the most famous columnists, such as Dave Barry and Anna Quindlen, are carried by many news outlets across the United States and even around the world. On the Web, columnists may show up within journalistic websites (such as http://www.cnn.com or http://www.slate.com) or on opinion sites called **blogs**, in which writings are in the style of journal entries, often in reverse chronological order. A well-known example is The Huffington Post group of political-opinion blogs. They include regular columns by Arianna Huffington, humorist Harry Shearer, and Congressman John Conyers, as well as opinion pieces from invited celebrities such as actor John Cusack and political comedian Bill Maher.

columnist an individual who is paid to write editorials on a regular basis—usually daily, weekly, or monthly

blogs journalistic websites or opinion sites in which writings are in the style of journal entries, often in reverse chronological order

The clearest attempt to maintain the separation between hard news reporting and editorial commentary is made by newspapers, where "analysis" is a common label indicating editorializing, and special Opinion sections (often called "op-ed" sections, due to their customary placement opposite the Editorial section) are increasingly becoming regular features. Similarly, many broadcast stations clearly label as editorials any on-air comments made by management that take a position on particular policies, issues, and controversies.

Soft News   Although news workers generally consider hard news reporting a place for objective, accurate, and balanced reporting with little (if any) editorial commentary, they consider another news category, **soft news**, to be an area in which the reporter's opinions and biases can show through. As you may be able to tell by its name, this is the kind of story that news workers feel may not have the critical importance of hard news, but nevertheless would appeal to a substantial number of people in the audience. Cooking spots, articles on the best ways to shovel snow without injuring your back, video clips highlighting local students in community plays or recitals—these are topics that news workers consider soft rather than hard news. Another name for soft news is the human interest story.

www.huffingtonpost.com
The Huffington Post is a popular political-opinion blog.

Information

One way to understand the difference between news and information—a difficult distinction to draw, for some—is to say that **information** is the raw material that journalists use when they create news stories. On the most basic level, a piece of information is a fact, an item that reveals something about the world. Generally, we must bring together many pieces of information in order to draw conclusions about a person, place, thing, or incident.

All of us use pieces of information as tools in our personal and professional lives. Students gather information as part of paper-writing assignments. Accountants bring together the facts of a client's expenses and wages to fill out the client's tax return. Professors compile information to prepare (it is hoped interesting) lectures. Similarly, journalists often stitch together facts when they create a news story.

Sometimes searching for relevant facts means speaking to individuals (as reporters might), looking at old bills (as accountants might), or reading scholarly books (as professors might). Often, however, people find the information they want in special collections of facts called *databases*. Journalists search motor vehicle records, collections of trial transcripts, gatherings of old newspaper articles, and city real-estate files. Students, too, use databases: computerized and manual library catalogs are databases; so are dictionaries, LexisNexis, Factiva, and the *Reader's Guide to Periodical Literature*.

Even though it is not as heavily discussed as entertainment or news, information is a widely used and lucrative mass media commodity. Many companies bring together information and package it in a multitude of ways. A trip to any library's reference collection will reveal an extensive array of alphabetized and categorized facts on an enormous number of subjects that are waiting to be used for papers, dissertations, books, or just to settle arguments.

soft news   the kind of news story that news workers feel may not have the critical importance of hard news, but nevertheless would appeal to a substantial number of people in the audience

information   the raw material that journalists use when they create news stories

But although a major library's collection of print and computer databases may appear quite impressive, it is merely the tip of a huge iceberg of information that mass media firms collect and offer for sale. The information industry creates and distributes much of its product for companies, not individual consumers.

Information Gathering and Distributing   One major segment of the information industry aims to help businesses find, evaluate, and understand their current customers. Trans Union Credit Information Co. and Equifax Inc., for example, hold collections of information about the income and debts of hundreds of millions of people worldwide. These firms are in the business of selling selected segments of that information to banks, insurance companies, and other organizations that are interested in the creditworthiness of particular individuals.

These information activities affect you directly when you are approved (or turned down) for a loan or a credit card. This part of the information business also provides lists of names to the marketers who send you postal mail or email—or phone you (often in the middle of dinner) with "great" offers. Catalog companies, too, often rely on information companies to help them find new customers.

Information Research and Retrieval   Another major segment of the information industry focuses on providing quick retrieval of data for people whose work requires them to get facts quickly. Consider the services provided by LexisNexis, for example. The Nexis information service enables journalists, professors, students—in fact, researchers of all kinds—to search for and retrieve virtually any fact in more than 2.5 billion searchable documents. Lexis, a sister service, enables attorneys and paralegals to find, analyze, and validate information from countless legal documents by keywords via computer networks. For example, through Lexis' database, legal professionals can retrieve background information on public and private companies, find information about individuals, identify an organization's assets, and research judges, expert witnesses, and opposing counsel, among other things.

The subscription for services such as those offered by Equifax, LexisNexis, and other similar firms in the information business can be quite costly. Information industry executives tie their high prices to the expense of collecting the data, trying to ensure their accuracy, storing them and protecting them from hackers, preparing print or computer retrieval methods, and distributing the data to clients. But the high price of information is also based on the realization that certain types of information can be extremely valuable, allowing companies to make (or save) millions of dollars. Quick access to the right information helps businesses and governments go about their work efficiently.

Education

education   content that is purposefully crafted to teach people specific ideas about the world in specific ways

When it comes to genres of media, **education** means content that is purposefully crafted to teach people specific ideas about the world in specific ways. Education is a huge segment of the media marketplace. Spending for "instructional materials" by elementary and high schools reached $5.4 billion in 2005. Spending on college instructional materials hit $4.8 billion. Much of this money was spent on textbooks, the medium that most of us conjure up when we think of instructional materials for schools.

But the genre of education extends far beyond textbooks and other types of printed materials. Consider for a moment the wide variety of media that you've encountered in your long trek through school. Textbooks, workbooks, course-packs, wall maps, flash cards, software, and online services—these and more account for the almost $10 billion of spending in the educational media marketplace.

In addition, there is a vast amount of educational media material that is produced primarily for home use. When you were a child, your parents might have set you in front of the TV set to view *Sesame Street* or *Reading Rainbow*. Perhaps you watched *Bill Nye, the Science Guy*, or *Where in the World is Carmen San Diego?* when you got a bit older. Maybe your parents gave you the *Math Blaster*, *Fraction Fever*, *LeapFrog*, or *JumpStart* computer programs for a birthday present. These are just a few of the products that media companies have explicitly designed to teach basic skills.

Advertisements

An **advertisement** is a message that explicitly aims to direct favorable attention to certain goods and services. The message may have a commercial purpose or be aimed at advancing a non-commercial cause, such as the election of a political candidate or the promotion of a fundraising event.

As we will see in Chapter 15, advertising involves far more than explicit messages. People who work in the advertising industry help their clients with a range of activities from package design to coupon offers. A broad definition of advertising even includes **product placement**, which is the paid insertion of products into TV shows and movies in order to associate those products, often quietly, with certain desirable characters or activities.

No matter what the medium, advertising practitioners speak about three broad subgenres of advertisements:

- Informational ads
- Hard-sell ads
- Soft-sell ads

Informational Advertisements   **Informational ads** rely primarily on a recitation of facts about a product and the product's features to convince target consumers that it is the right product for them to purchase. An advertisement in *Stereo Review Magazine* that carefully details the specifications and capabilities of a set of Bose speakers would be informational in nature. Similarly, a television announcement aired during PBS's *This Old House* noting the program's support and use of Andersen Windows and Doors is another example of an informational ad.

Hard-sell Advertisements   **Hard-sell ads** are messages that combine information about the product with intense attempts to get the consumer to purchase it as soon as possible. For example, a TV commercial in which a car salesman speaks a-mile-a-minute about the glories of his dealership, shouts about a two-day-only sale this weekend, and then recites the address of the dealership four times before the spot ends is a hard-sell ad.

Soft-sell Advertisements   **Soft-sell ads** aim mostly to create good feelings about the product or service by associating it with music, personalities, or events that the creators of that product or service feel would appeal to the target audience. Television commercials for a wide variety of products, including soft drinks,

advertisement   a message that explicitly aims to direct favorable attention to certain goods and services

product placement   the process by which a manufacturer pays—often tens of thousands of dollars and sometimes far more—a production company for the opportunity to have its product displayed in a movie or TV show

informational ads   advertisements that rely primarily on the recitation of facts about a product and the product's features to convince target consumers that it is the right product for them to purchase

hard-sell ads   messages that combine information about the product with intense attempts to get the consumer to purchase it as soon as possible

soft-sell ads   advertisements that aim mostly to create good feelings about the product or service by associating it with desirable music, personalities, or events that the creators of that product or service feel would appeal to the target audience

Soft-sell ads like "Got Milk?" aim to create a "hip" feeling about a product that will lead consumers to want to be identified with it.

Take 9.
On the set they're screaming "action" all day.
And thanks to the 9 essential nutrients in milk, I've always got what it takes to nail it.

got milk?

beer, and athletic footwear, are soft-sell ads. Remember the "Got Milk?" ads for milk producers, the "Whassup" commercials for Budweiser, or the "Mac vs. PC" ads for Apple? These are classic examples of ads that aim to create a "hip" feeling about a product that will lead consumers to want to be identified with it.

It is important to note that these three types of ads—informational, hard-sell, and soft-sell—differ in degree, not kind. That is, they differ in the amount of stress they place on facts about the product, the intensity of the sales pitch, and the emotional connection between the consumer and the product. There are, however, circumstances in which much longer ads are created, and the advertisers can then combine informational, hard-sell, and soft-sell tactics. If you watch TV shopping channels such as HSN, you might see this mix. A hostess may provide a demonstration of a gold necklace that mixes specific information about the necklace ("beautiful 14-karat gold, thirty inches long, with a sturdy lock, as you can see…") and hard-sell encouragement ("these necklaces are going so fast that if you don't call us right now, we might run out of them") with soft-sell tactics that include joking around by people on the set and an attempt to build an entertaining environment for selling.

Mixing Genres

You have probably noticed that soft-sell advertising sometimes shows up as part of entertainment-oriented TV shows. When the CBS television show *Survivor* displayed the Target Stores emblem as part of the action, that was a clear case of mixing genres. Clearly, Target executives believed that audiences would get a favorable feeling for their stores if they saw it pop up within a popular entertainment program. For reasons that we will explore in Chapter 15, hybridity involving advertising and entertainment is becoming increasingly common. It is not, however, the only blending of advertising with other genres. Think of a political commercial that runs in a report on the evening news; an informational ad that becomes part of a database for consumers trying to find out about a product; and an elementary school math text that teaches students addition and subtraction by using the names of real products whose companies paid for the inclusion. (Some math textbooks *are* including real products in the name of realism, though to date no advertiser seems to have paid for inclusion.) A media literate who understands the mixing of genres and the reasons for it will be alert to the practice and know to ask whether it is happening and why.

Of course, advertising is not the only genre that mixes with other genres. Media practitioners who work in the fields of entertainment, information, and education explore the value of hybridity in order to attract and hold audiences. Media practitioners involved in education and advertisements often borrow comedic, dramatic, festival, and gaming elements to attract and hold audiences. Writers for *Sesame Street*, for example, often deliver their educational messages in segments that resemble situation comedies, game shows, and musical variety programs. Entertainment elements are difficult to find in the work of the producers of information, who wish to maintain an air of careful competence. Think, too, of programs such as *The Daily Show* and *The Colbert Report* on the Comedy Central cable channel, which use the setting and even the character types of news interview programs to create humorous imitations of the styles of those news shows—that is, to create **parodies**—that intend to entertain as well as make serious political points amid the laughter.

The primary genres of entertainment, news, information, advertising, and education are the fuel that drives the mass media business. Media practitioners take them and their subgenres quite seriously. If you talk to a person who writes family situation comedies, auto advertisements, or history textbooks, he or she is likely to be quite aware of the history of that form and to have strong notions of what was good and bad about past materials. As in the examples of horror movies given earlier, media practitioners often even adapt popular ideas from the past in the hope that these ideas can be converted into today's successes.

parody a work that imitates another work for laughs in a way that comments on the original work in one way or another; a subgenre of *entertainment*

The Business of Mass Media

Knowing how to use genres and their formulas to create materials that are popular with audiences is a highly valued skill in mass media industries. But there's a lot more to trying to get a work valued by audiences than just thinking it up. As we mentioned earlier, all kinds of media organizations must produce, distribute, exhibit, and finance their content in ways that maximize its chances of success with audiences.

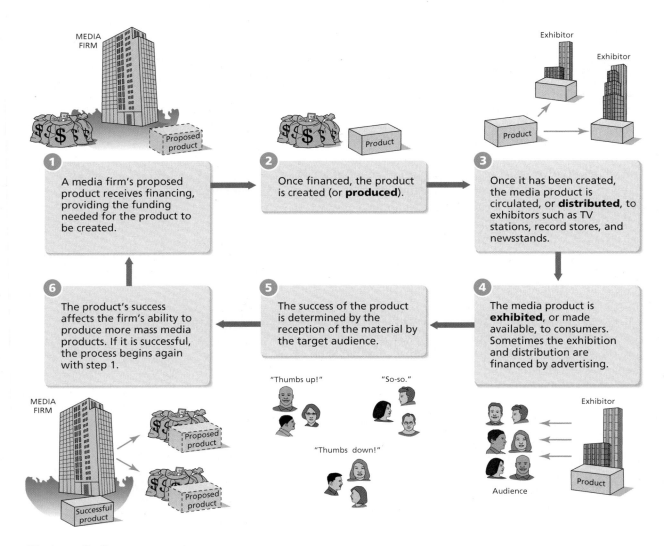

1. A media firm's proposed product receives financing, providing the funding needed for the product to be created.

2. Once financed, the product is created (or **produced**).

3. Once it has been created, the media product is circulated, or **distributed**, to exhibitors such as TV stations, record stores, and newsstands.

4. The media product is **exhibited**, or made available, to consumers. Sometimes the exhibition and distribution are financed by advertising.

5. The success of the product is determined by the reception of the material by the target audience.

6. The product's success affects the firm's ability to produce more mass media products. If it is successful, the process begins again with step 1.

Figure 2.6

The Business of Mass Media

Production, distribution, and exhibition, central to the functions of all media organizations, must first secure financing before they can proceed.

As Figure 2.6 shows, production involves creating the content. Distribution involves circulating the material to exhibitors (e.g. music stores, TV stations). The exhibitors, in turn, make it available to consumers. All of this activity requires money up front (financing) and involves government regulation of one sort or another. Let's examine these steps, which lie at the heart of what goes on in mass media industries, one at a time.

Production of Mass Media Content

production   the creation of mass media materials for distribution through one or more mass media vehicles

Production is the beginning of the chain of events that brings mass media content to audiences. **Production** for the mass media means the creation of materials for distribution through one or more mass media vehicles.

Silicon Freelancers

Tales of Hollywood agents busily wheeling and dealing with powerful movie studios for celebrity freelancers such as actors and directors are nothing new to anyone who has even a cursory knowledge of the entertainment industry. But did you know that such power brokers also exist in the computer software industry?

It's common knowledge in high-tech circles that a programmer with the talent to write concise, elegant code quickly and dependably is hard to find. With the proliferation of the Internet, software development cycles have quickened so drastically that talented programmers can make a lot more money moving among firms that desperately need their services than by staying in one place.

Many of the industry's most famous products such as Acrobat and the original Apple Macintosh operating system were designed by freelance programmers. They hire agents who act as high-tech power brokers, getting huge rewards for them while bringing the freelancers nearly triple their previous full-time salaries and supplying the companies with top temporary talent.

Software talent brokers act much like Hollywood talent agents for their freelance clients by building relationships over long periods of time with the production companies and code writers. Agents often fill a vital middle role in a fast-paced industry, where lean and mean firms want immediate results and software writers are famously shy of the nasty haggling that sometimes goes with bagging a six-figure salary.

Media Production Firms

A **mass media production firm** is a company that creates materials for distribution through one or more mass media vehicles. The Washington Post Company, which publishes the *Washington Post*, is a production company. So is Routledge, the publisher of this book, and its parent company, Informa. So are Time Inc. magazine company (a division of Time Warner), which creates *Time* magazine; General Electric's NBC Universal, which produces *NBC Nightly News*; and http://www.myspace.com (a division of News Corporation), a web platform for sharing all sorts of print, audio, and audiovisual materials.

Who Does the Work?   The making of all these media products requires both administrative personnel and creative personnel. **Administrative personnel** make sure the business side of the media organization is humming along. They must thoroughly understand the media business they are in, and their daily jobs—in, for example, accounting, law, marketing—have much to do with the success of the organizations for which they work.

Their work does not, however, relate directly to the creation of their firm's media materials. **Creative personnel** do that. They are the individuals who get initial ideas for the material or use their artistic talent to put the material together.

In all media industries, working on the creative side of a production firm can be done in two ways, on-staff or freelance. An **on-staff worker** is a worker who has secured a full-time position at a production firm. For example, most, though not all, art directors in advertising agencies are on-staff workers. They work for the same agency all the time; the projects they work on may change, but the company that issues their paycheck remains the same. **Freelancers**, on the other hand, are workers who make a living by accepting and completing assignments for a number of different companies—sometimes several at one time. Most movie actors

mass media production firm a company that creates materials for distribution through one or more mass media vehicles

administrative personnel workers who oversee the business side of the media organization

creative personnel individuals who get the initial ideas for the material or use their artistic talents to put the material together

on-staff workers workers who have secured a full-time position at a production firm

freelancers workers who make a living by accepting and completing creative assignments for a number of different companies—sometimes several at one time

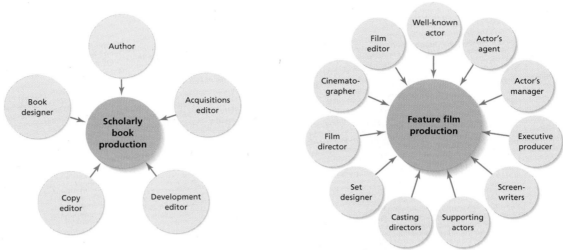

Figure 2.7

Individuals Involved in Two Types of Media Production

The mass media production process is almost exclusively a collaborative process.

work as freelancers, for example; when they finish one film, they look for work on another film, which may be made by a different company.

Although freelancing can be highly lucrative for some (we are familiar with the names of well-paid freelance creatives such as the novelist John Grisham or the film actor Tom Cruise), historically freelancing has been a difficult road for many creatives. Even when salaries are high (and they frequently are not), many freelance creatives do not work as often as they would like because of the heavy competition for desirable assignments. Historically, this competition has given tremendous power to the production companies that hire these freelance creatives. Freelancers, from actors, to book editors, to ghost writers, to cinematographers, have reported that production companies have used this power to "borrow" innovative ideas discussed in job interviews, force them to work unusually long hours, and withhold their due credits when the assignment is completed.

In order to establish a power of their own, many freelance creatives have banded together to create talent guilds. A **talent guild** is a union formed by people who work in a particular craft, such as the Writers Guild of America, Screen Actors Guild, and Directors Guild of America. These guilds negotiate rules with major production firms in their industries regarding the ways in which freelance creatives will be treated and paid.

The administrative and creative personnel of mass media production firms recognize that the previous successes of individual freelance creators—their positive track records—can help reduce the risk that a project will fail. In an effort to manage their risks, movie companies typically will not allow high-budget movies to be made unless a high-profile actor (such as Matt Damon or Will Ferrell) signs on.

Similarly, book-publishing firms have been known to pay popular writers hundreds of thousands of dollars for the rights to their next work. In 2006, various firms agreed to pay $7 million for books to Warren Buffett's ghostwriter, more than $8 million to former U.S. Federal Reserve head Alan Greenspan, over $10 million to evangelist Joel Osteen; and a measly (relative to the above) $2 million for two books from fiction writer and Pulitzer Prize-winner Jhumpa Lahiri.[7]

Magazine firms also have dangled grand salaries in front of editors who have boosted the visibility and sales of competitors' periodicals. These deals make news.

talent guild   a union formed by people who work in similar crafts to help negotiate rules with major production firms in their industries regarding the ways in which freelance creatives will be treated and paid

Increasing Pressures on Special Effects Shops

TECH & INFRASTRUCTURE

Titanic, *The Lord of the Rings: The Return of the King*, *Pirates of the Caribbean: Dead Man's Chest*, *Harry Potter and the Sorcerer's Stone*, and *Star Wars: Episode I—The Phantom Menace* are the five highest-grossing films of all time.* And as anyone familiar with these films is aware, they all feature mind-blowing visual and audio effects.

Today, special effects are seen as critical to the success of blockbuster films. As such, producers are willing to spend between 25 and 40 percent of their budgets on effects, according to Eric Hanson, a visual effects designer. Even non-effects based genres, such as romantic comedies and dramas, feature hundreds of effects shots.

While this may sound like good news to those in the visual effects industry, they are expected to complete their work in less and less time. Many attribute these timing demands to 2005's *War of the Worlds*, a film whose special effects were completed in an unprecedented three months. Soon thereafter, film producers began to request the "War of the Worlds schedule," which is nearly impossible under normal circumstances.

Variety editor David Cohen notes that not only are studios placing scheduling demands on effects houses, but they are also pressured to produce "more products at a higher quality." In fact, the number of special effects shots today is triple what it was only a decade ago.

Some effects specialists have grown so frustrated with the studios that they have left their careers, and more may be on the way. Addressing the difficulties workers had with the third *Pirates of the Caribbean* film, Cohen quipped, "If the visual effects industry had its way, the [film] might have been named, '*Pirates of the Caribbean: At Wit's End*'."

*From the Internet Movie Database's listing of the "All-Time Worldwide Box Office." http://www.imdb.com/

Sources: David Cohen, "Blockbusters Take Tool on F/X Shops," *Variety*, accessed 6/14/07, www.variety.com; Rachel Rosmarin, "Hollywood Goes High Tech," *Forbes*, accessed 6/17/07, www.forbes.com

When Elizabeth Tilberis, the influential editor of *Harper's Bazaar* magazine, died in 1999, it was reported that her salary had been $1 million a year.[8] When she was editor of *Talk* magazine in the 1990s, Tina Brown was rumored to make more than that, and to have hired an assistant at a yearly salary of about $500,000.[9]

How Does Production Take Place?   The personal vision of an actor, novelist, or scholar can sometimes make it to the screen or the page. Inserting such a personal vision into a work is called *authorship*. Generally, however, production in media industries is a **collaborative activity**, in which many people work together to initiate, create, and polish the end material. The collaborative nature of production holds true for every mass media product, from movies to scholarly books. Some types of production require more creative hands than others. When there are many creators, the "author" of the work may not be a person, but rather a group or company.

Compare the production of a scholarly book with that of a typical commercial movie starring a well-known actor (see Figure 2.7). In addition to the writer, a scholarly book requires an acquisitions editor, who finds the author and might help with the initial plan for the work; a few readers (usually other scholars) who suggest ways in which the writer can improve the book; a copy-editor, who helps with the manuscript's style; and design personnel, who craft the look of the book and perhaps its jacket.

collaborative activity   an activity in which many people work together to initiate, create, and polish the end material

Now consider the film. The well-known actor is chosen by an executive producer or studio head, with the assistance of the actor's business representatives. In addition, the film will need screenwriters to write and rewrite the script; other actors to work with the star; a casting director with assistants to choose the other actors; a set designer and assistants to plan the backdrops; a director and assistants to organize the filming; a cinematographer and assistants to photograph the scenes; an editor and assistants to put the scenes together into a finished movie; and many more. Although individual authorship of the scholarly book may be fairly clear, the same cannot be said of the movie. Because so many people are involved on the creative side, it is often very difficult to argue that the final version of a Hollywood film is one person's vision.

We commonly regard the results of production in terms of individual items—a particular movie, book, magazine, TV show. Actually, though, it is possible to find many cases in which what is produced is not an individual item, but rather a stitching together of already-existing products that, taken together, comprise a whole. Take ABC television as an example. ABC creates many, but not all, of the programs that it airs. It leases some programs from other production companies, which grant the network the right to sell time between parts of the shows to advertisers. ABC then sends these shows to TV stations in cities and towns via satellite, and they, in turn, broadcast the shows to the public.

But if you look at ABC's work another way, you will realize that the company could be considered to be heavily involved in TV production even if it didn't actually produce any of its shows. That conclusion comes from seeing production not in terms of individual programs but in terms of the **schedule**, or the pattern in which the programs are arranged. ABC employs programmers who create regular schedules for different parts of the day. The goal of these schedules is to attract viewers to ABC and to keep them watching ABC's shows and commercials for a number of hours. During the mid-2000s, for example, ABC fielded a successful Thursday evening schedule (*Ugly Betty*, *Grey's Anatomy*, *Men in Trees*) from 8 to 11 p.m. Clearly, the product that ABC programmers were creating was not an individual show but a flow of shows, put together with a particular audience-attracting goal in mind.

In mass media industries, **format** is the term commonly used to describe the rules that guide this flow. A format is the patterned choice and arrangement of elements that make up specific media material. The material may be a flow of programs, such as ABC's schedule, or it may be an arrangement of video, audio or text presentations that people upload to a website, such as on http://www.myspace.com, http://www.joost.com, and http://www.heavy.com. Most radio stations use formats that convey their personalities by combining certain types of songs, disc jockeys' sounds, and jingles that identify the station. The concept of format applies to magazines, too. *Time*'s creative personnel are involved not only in the production of individual articles that appear in the periodical, but also in choosing the topics of the articles to begin with and arranging the articles in a flow that is designed to convey an image and entice readers through the magazine.

schedule   the pattern in which media programs are arranged and presented to the audience

format   the rules that guide the flow of products that are put together with a particular audience-attracting goal in mind; a formula that describes a particular media product

Distribution of Mass Media Content

Most of us tend to think of production when we think of mass media industries. After all, it is the output of this production—the newspapers we read, the cable

TV shows we watch—that grabs our attention, that makes us happy or angry, interested or bored. Moreover, most public discussion about mass communication tends to center around production. The latest gossip about which actor will be in which film, the angry comments a mayor makes about the violence on local TV news, the newest CD by an up-and-coming music group—these are the kinds of topics that are most often the focus of our attention when we discuss media.

However, media executives and media literate citizens know that production is only one step in the arduous and risky process of getting a mass media idea to an audience, and that distribution is just as important as production. **Distribution** is the delivery of the produced material to the point where it will be shown to its intended audience; it is an activity which takes place out of public view.

distribution   the delivery of the produced material to the point where it will be shown to its intended audience

We have already mentioned that ABC acts as a distributor when it disseminates television programming to TV stations via satellite. When Philadelphia Media Holdings delivers its *Philadelphia Inquirer* to city newsstands, when Twentieth Century Fox moves its movies to the Regal Cinema Theaters, and when Sony Music sends its newest releases to http://www.apple.com to be sold over the iTunes website, they are each involved in distribution to exhibitors.

Note that these firms—Philadelphia Media Holdings, Twentieth Century Fox, and Sony Music—use their own distribution divisions rather than rely on other independent distribution firms to do the job. This background ought to underscore for you the importance of successful distribution in the world of media business. Some executives argue that while "content is king," distribution ought to share the crown. The reason is simple: without a distributor, a production firm's media product would literally go nowhere. It would stack up in the warehouse or a computer, eventually to be destroyed. To get a feel for the power in distribution, consider that you could "publish" a book quite easily. That is, you could take any work of art you've created—some doodles, a love poem, notes to this book—and get it photocopied and bound at the nearest photocopy store, like Kinko's. Say you splurge and print five hundred copies. For a bit more money than you'd spend in the copy shop, you could put a fancy binding on the product, so that it would look like a "real" book.

Of course, now that you have printed the book, the trick is to sell it. You might try to get the university bookstore to carry it, but chances are the store won't. Borders or Barnes & Noble Booksellers probably won't touch your book with a ten-foot pole. It's likely, in fact, that no legitimate bookstore will carry it. This is not necessarily because your writing is bad; your book might actually be a true work of art. The real reason that your chances of getting your book into a bookstore are so poor is that your book does not have a powerful book distributor behind it. If, however, you could persuade a major publishing company to allow its distribution sales force to pitch your book to bookstores, especially large chain bookstores, you might have a pretty good chance to get your book on to bookstore shelves.

Production, then, is useless without distribution. Without a powerful distributor, the material that a production firm's executives believe could be tremendously successful will have much less chance of achieving its potential. Some people believe that the Internet reduces the importance of distribution, because just about anyone can post—that is, distribute—just about anything online for very little cost. But putting something on a personal website or even on a backwater page of a popular exhibition site such as MySpace or YouTube does not ensure that anyone but your friends will go to it. Perhaps you will get lucky, and the clip you posted

The Disappearance of the Record Store

For decades, the Tower Records store on the corner of Broadway and 4th Street was a staple of New York's Greenwich Village district. Locals would scan their collection of indie albums and underground magazines; tourists would marvel at the store's massive inventory; and up-and-coming bands would get exposure while performing live in-store.

But in 2006, the flagship store, along with the rest of Tower's 89 chains nationwide, went out of business after filing for Chapter 11 bankruptcy protection. A representative from Tower remarked, "The brick-and-mortar specialty music retail industry has suffered substantial deterioration recently."

Indeed, CD sales had been declining since 2000, but the closing of Tower and more than 700 other U.S. music retailers made 2006 a particularly difficult year for the recorded music industry. By 2007, CD sales had slipped another 20 percent.

The plunge was no doubt a response to what *Wall Street Journal* reporter Ethan Smith described as "a seismic shift in the way consumers acquire music." Many people abandoned music stores in favor of online retailers such as Apple's iTunes, which offers low-cost downloads from its extensive digital library. Piracy remains another threat to the music industry, despite increasing efforts to eliminate illegal file-sharing.

The fact that retail behemoths like Wal-Mart and Best Buy sell CDs at a fraction of the price is another factor in the disappearance of specialty music retailers. According to one

CD sales have been declining since 2000, as many consumers have turned to downloading to get new music.

estimate, these chains represent about 65 percent of the retail music market.

Smith explained that these changes have rendered the recorded music industry "powerless." He continued, "Its struggles are hardly unique in the media world…Though consumers are exposed to more media in more ways than ever before, the challenge for media companies is finding a way to make money from all that exposure."

Sources: "Fans Mourn Tower Records Liquidation," MSNBC, accessed 6/15/07, http://www.msnbc.msn.com/id/15251144/; Ethan Smith, "Sales of Music, Long in Decline, Plunge Sharply," *Wall Street Journal*, March 21, 2007 page A1; "Tower Records Will Auction its Assets," *New York Times*, accessed 6/15/07, www.nytimes.com

to YouTube will become a popular "viral video" viewed by millions. In most cases, however, the key is to have the clout to place the content in a position where many people have a good chance of seeing it. That means getting the attention of a powerful distributor.

What makes a **powerful distributor**? Simply put, a distributor's power is measured in terms of the firm's ability to ensure that the media products it carries will end up in the best locations of the best exhibitors to the best audience. To understand what that means, we have to look at exhibition.

the power of a distributor the firm's ability to ensure that the media products it carries will end up in the best locations at the best exhibitors to the best audience

Exhibition of Mass Media Content

The exhibition of mass media material is closely linked to the distribution in the sense that both are steps in bringing the content to the audience. Sometimes the same company carries out both activities. Because exhibition is quite a different business from distribution, though, it often involves different firms.

Exhibition is the activity of presenting mass media materials to audiences for viewing or purchase. When media executives speak about the importance of exhibition, they often mention **shelf space**. Shelf space is the amount of area or time available for presenting products to consumers. Think of video stores with their long rows of shelves and racks. As large as typical chain stores are today, production firms want to rent and sell more types of DVDs than will fit in the racks of even the biggest stores. As a result, store executives must decide which categories of products, and which company's products within those categories, are carried and which get more room than others.

Consequently, video distributor firms that rely on stores to present their products to consumers must compete furiously for shelf space. The distributors that wield the most power are those with products that the stores need to have because consumers demand them. These distributors will have more ability to negotiate shelf space for new products than will distributors of goods that are not so important to the stores.

The same is true elsewhere in the media business. Magazine and book producers must compete for shelf space in bookstores, on newsstands, and in supermarket aisles. Moreover, some spots in stores and on newsstands are more valuable than others. The area toward the front of a bookstore is most valuable because all customers pass through it. Racks on a newsstand that are at eye level are more valuable than those at floor level because consumers are likely to look at the racks at eye level first.

For cable TV, movies, broadcast TV, radio, the Web, mobile phones and other media, the concept of shelf space has to be stretched just a bit, but it applies just the same. Executives think of the limited number of channels of a cable system as its shelves. Similarly, some broadcast television executives see the twenty-four hours in a day as their stations' shelves, because time limits what they can air. In cable, radio, and broadcast TV, certain time slots and channels (or stations) are more valuable than others. The same goes for high-traffic pages on websites such as http://www.auto.com and space on the starting areas (the "decks") of cellphones that provide a limited selection of links to areas of the Web. These are the more prominent positions in the electronic "store."

Now imagine a particular case: feel the tension that Marisol Durán, a salesperson for a newly formed independent book distribution firm, experiences as she waits to speak to a purchasing executive at a large bookstore chain such as Barnes & Noble. Marisol represents small publishing firms specializing in science fiction. Because of their small size, these firms don't have the money to hire their own salespeople. She knows that Barnes & Noble's shelves hold many books, but she also knows that the number of books published each year alone would take up far more space than those shelves can hold. She has been successful in placing many of the titles she carries in bookstores that specialize in the science fiction genre. She has ambitions beyond these small stores, however. A chance to catch the eyes of science fiction readers who shop at Barnes & Noble or at Borders would, she believes, surely result in a strong increase in sales.

exhibition   the activity of presenting mass media materials to audiences for viewing or purchase

shelf space   the amount of area or time available for presenting products to consumers

She knows, however, that she would get a better hearing at Barnes & Noble—and would place more books there—if she worked for the distribution arm of a publishing house such as Random House or Simon & Schuster, two giants of the book business. One reason is that such publishing giants can afford to advertise and promote their titles to the public better than her struggling publishers can, and such publicity can strongly affect sales.

The large publishers may also be better able than smaller ones to offer **trade incentives**—payments in cash, discounts, or publicity activities that provide a special reason for an exhibitor to highlight a product—that could influence large stores like Barnes & Noble to carry their books. To make sure that a bookstore chain exhibits key titles at the entrances to its stores, for example, a publisher might have to offer—through its distributor—to pay the bookstore chain a sum of money for taking up that space. Bringing the author in for special book readings and book signings and helping to pay for ads in newspapers (a practice called **cooperative advertising**) might also be part of the deal.

As this hypothetical experience suggests, linking up with a powerful distributor is of great benefit to producers in every mass media industry. Not surprisingly, the major production companies either own or are otherwise strategically linked to the major distribution organizations. In these cases, it is important to keep in mind that power over production and distribution is self-reinforcing: creative personnel with strong track records are attracted to the production firm in part because it has powerful distribution. In turn, the company has powerful distribution in part because its production arm attracts creative personnel with strong track records.

In some industries, major firms consolidate their strength by owning not only the distribution organizations, but the major exhibition firms as well. Television networks like NBC, CBS, and ABC, for example, have production divisions that create fiction, sports, and news programs. They also own broadcast TV networks that distribute their programs and broadcast stations in key cities that exhibit them. This control of the entire process from production through distribution to exhibition is called **vertical integration**, and it represents yet another way in which media companies try to reduce the risk that their target audiences won't even have an opportunity to choose the material competitors create (see Figure 2.8).

trade incentives payments in cash, discounts, or publicity activities that provide a special reason for an exhibitor to highlight a product

cooperative advertising advertising paid for in part by media production firms or their distributors in order to help the exhibitor promote the product

vertical integration an organization's control over a media product from production through distribution to exhibition

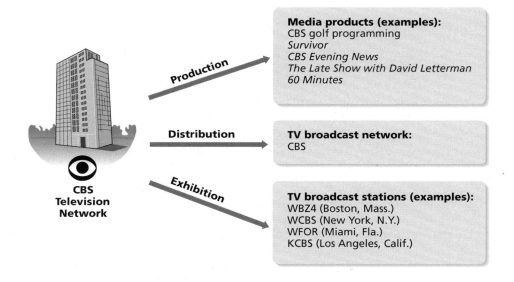

Figure 2.8
Vertical Integration
CBS—which owns production divisions, distribution channels, and exhibition venues—is a successful example of vertical integration.

Media products (examples):
CBS golf programming
Survivor
CBS Evening News
The Late Show with David Letterman
60 Minutes

TV broadcast network:
CBS

TV broadcast stations (examples):
WBZ4 (Boston, Mass.)
WCBS (New York, N.Y.)
WFOR (Miami, Fla.)
KCBS (Los Angeles, Calif.)

Production

Distribution

Exhibition

CBS Television Network

Financing Mass Media Content

As you read the previous pages on the production, distribution, and exhibition of mass media materials, it may have occurred to you that each activity must require a lot of money. Starting a publishing company, even a very small one, costs hundreds of thousands of dollars. Creating a one-hour television program costs more than a million dollars. Starting a new magazine can also cost even more. Want to buy a radio station? Despite the recent slowdown of growth in radio advertising, stations still go for tens, even hundreds, of millions of dollars.

The cash coming into a mass media firm can be divided into two categories:

- Money to fund new production
- Money to pay for already completed products

We'll explore each in detail.

Funding New Production

Executives in mass media enterprises may need to raise funds to expand into new areas, or they may want to build up areas in which they are already operating. A movie exhibition chain may want to expand by building new theaters in Europe. A publishing firm might want to start a new unit to create oversized coffee-table books. A company might want to buy an AM radio station. In such cases, executives may not want or be able to use the company's current revenues to cover the costs of the new venture.

A company generally has two ways to get money in anticipation of production: it can take out loans, and/or it can encourage investments in the company.

Taking Out Loans A **loan** is money that is borrowed from an organization, usually a bank, for a certain price (a percentage of the loan called an interest rate). To get a loan, executives must persuade the lending organization that their plans will realistically bring in the cash they expect so that the firm will be able to repay the amount of the loan (its principal) plus the interest in a timely way. The lender will also want to be sure that it has a claim on some of the current value (assets) of the firm—for example, the real estate of an exhibition chain or the current holdings of a radio station owner—in case the firm does not pay back the loan.

Investment banks are companies that arrange to lend millions, even tens and hundreds of millions, of dollars to companies, and also arrange stock offerings. Some investment banks specialize in particular industries, and the executives of these investment banks feel they understand quite well the risks involved. Large investment banks hire experts in particular industries to guide the banks' lending activities in their areas of expertise. These investment bankers assess the firms that want loans and put together the terms of agreement. When very large amounts of money are involved, the investment banker will organize a **syndicate**, a group of banks that agree to share the risks and rewards of the lending deal. Because it takes on more responsibility, the lead bank (the bank that organizes the syndicate) makes more money on the deal than the others.

Encouraging Investments While bankers worry that firms will not be able to pay back the money they have borrowed, executives of those firms worry about how much money the loans are costing them. That is, paying the interest on the

loan money borrowed from a company, usually a bank, for a certain price (a percentage of the loan called an interest rate)

investment banks companies that arrange to lend millions, even tens and hundreds of millions, of dollars to companies, and also arrange stock offerings

syndicate a group of banks that agree to share the risks and rewards of a lending deal, organized by investment banks when very large amounts of money are required

stock offering selling units of ownership in the company, or shares of stock, to organizations and individuals

loans requires cash that the company could use for other purposes. Consequently, executives may prefer to raise money through **stock offerings**. A share of stock is a unit of ownership in a company. All corporations, whether they are owned by only a few people or millions of people, issue stock. When a company engages in a stock offering, it sells these units of ownership to organizations and individuals.

For example, let's say that DigitalDynamics, a media organization that creates specialized sites on the Internet, wants to expand. One of its computer engineers has just created a device that executives believe will revolutionize the industry and make the firm a leader.

The three founders of the company still own all the stock; since there is no public market for the stock, the value of each of their holdings equals the assets of the firm divided by three. The founders (who also run the firm) are concerned that taking out loans in addition to the loans they already have would make the interest payments too high for the firm to afford, since they don't expect the new device to be profitable for at least a year. They decide to open up ownership of the company to people other than themselves.

Working with the company's accountants and with outside specialists, the company's founders determine the value of the company. That amount includes the worth of its equipment and also its goodwill—that is, the value of its reputation among its clients and potential clients in the online world. The founders decide that the company should issue six million shares; each of the founders will keep one million of those shares, and DigitalDynamics will offer the other three million at $2 each. Consequently, if the company is able to sell all of the nonpartners' shares, it will receive $6 million, which will be enough to expand the venture.

venture capitalists individuals or companies that invest in startup or nonpublic firms in the hope that the firms' value will increase over time

In view of its small size, DigitalDynamics will probably sell its stock to **venture capitalists**. Venture capitalists are individuals or companies that invest in startup or nonpublic firms in the hope that the firms' value will increase over time. These people and firms are in the business of assuming the high risks of investing in such firms in the hope of receiving high rewards. In the case of DigitalDynamics, they are assuming that the company's earnings will increase because its new device will bring in more business. That increase in earnings would make the company more valuable, and so each share will be worth more than the amount the venture capitalists paid for it. If the company were then sold, the venture capitalists would get substantially more money than they invested.

There are other ways in which DigitalDynamics can raise more money. Assume, for example, that after the sale of stock to the venture capitalists, DigitalDynamics' board of directors (which now includes some of the venture capitalists) decides upon an **initial public offering (IPO)** of the company's stock. The board needs to convince an investment banker that the company's future is so great that investment companies and individual investors would buy five million new shares of the company's stock at $10 a share. The investment bank agrees to manage (or underwrite) the offering for a fee. Because five million new shares will be created, the shares that already exist will represent a smaller percentage of the ownership than they did before the IPO. Still, the market value of the early stockholders' shares has gone from $2 to $10 a share. DigitalDynamics, meanwhile, has $50 million more to chew on.

initial public offering (IPO) the offering for sale to the general public of a predetermined number of shares of stock of a company that previously was owned by a limited number of individuals and the listing of the company's shares on a stock exchange

Funding When Production is Already Complete

profits the amount of money brought in by the completed products minus expenses

A primary indicator of the health of any company is its **profits**—the amount of money brought in by the completed products minus expenses. Even if a company is run efficiently and its expenses are low, it still needs to bring in ever-increasing amounts of revenue in order to increase its profits and satisfy its investors and lenders. In mass media firms, there are several ways to bring in revenues:

■ **Direct sales**

The purchaser pays the producer, distributor or exhibitor for the item and can use it in any way she or he sees fit—keep it forever, throw it away, give it to someone else, or even resell it. In college textbook publishing, for example, most of the money comes from sales to consumers (the students).

> **direct sales** a strategy to gain revenue in which the consumer pays the producer, distributor, or exhibitor for the item and can use it in any way she or he sees fit

■ **License fees**

A person or organization pays the producer for the use of a product, but the producer has ultimate control over the way it is used. For example, a toy company may pay Warner Brothers for the right to use the image of Bugs Bunny on toy banks for five years. Similarly, if you have Microsoft Word on your computer, what you have actually bought is a license to use it. (Remember the package telling you that if you unwrap the disk, you are accepting the "license agreement"? One consequence is that according to the agreement, you are prohibited from reselling the software to someone else.)

> **license fees** a strategy to gain revenue in which a person or organization pays the producer for the use of a product but the producer has ultimate control over the way it is used

■ **Rentals**

A producer, distributor, or exhibitor charges for the right to employ (read, view, or hear) a mass media product for a certain period of time, and then gets the product back. (For example, movie rentals—the store typically buys the video from the production firm and tries to make a profit by renting it to you and many others.)

> **rentals** a strategy to gain revenue in which a producer, distributor, or exhibitor charges for employing (reading, viewing, or hearing) a mass media product for a certain period of time, and then gets it back

■ **Usage fees**

The amount the producer, distributor or exhibitor charges for a mass media product is based on the number of times the product is employed. (For example, an Internet database of articles may charge you for the number of articles or "page views" you print.)

> **usage fees** a strategy to gain revenue in which the producer, distributor, or exhibitor charges for a mass media product based on the number of times it is employed

■ **Subscriptions**

The producer, distributor or exhibitor charges for regularly providing a media product or service. (Think of a magazine subscription, a subscription to a cable system, and a subscription to a company that provides you with Internet service.)

> **subscriptions** a strategy to gain revenue in which the producer, distributor, or exhibitor charges for continually providing a media product or service

■ **Advertising**

A company buys space or time on a mass medium (a page in a magazine, thirty seconds on a radio station) in which it is allowed to display a persuasive message (an advertisement) for a product or service. We will have a good deal to say about the workings of the advertising industry in Chapter 15. What is important to remember here is that the advertising industry is the dominant support system for the mass media. If advertising did not exist, the amount you pay for magazines, newspapers, Internet content, and cable television, not to mention broadcast television and radio, would skyrocket. Reliable estimates suggest, for example, that because of advertising, people on average pay half of what they would otherwise pay for magazines, and substantially less than half for newspapers.

> **advertising** a strategy to gain revenue in which a company buys space or time on a mass medium (a page in a magazine, thirty seconds on a radio station) in exchange for being allowed to display a persuasive message (an advertisement) for a product or service

The mention of magazines and newspapers brings up another important point about the sources of cash in mass media industries. Many companies in these industries benefit from what economists call a *dual revenue stream*. That is, they take in money from two sources: advertisers and consumers. Magazine and newspaper firms, for example, both sell ads and ask consumers to pay for each issue. Local TV broadcasters, on the other hand, live off only a single revenue stream, advertiser support; viewers do not have to pay them. This revenue stream happens to be quite an outpouring: in 2005, local TV stations took in $24.6 billion from advertisers. But as competition tightens in the television industry, as costs go up, and as advertisers have the option of placing ads in other media if the local stations raise their advertising rates, the single revenue stream does not look as lucrative as it once did.

By now, the complexity of trying to navigate the mass media environment should be quite clear. But wait—there's more! Not only do media practitioners have to worry about production, distribution, exhibition, and finance, they also have to concern themselves with **government regulation**. Government regulation involves a wide variety of activities and laws through which elected and appointed officials at local, state, and federal levels exercise influence over media firms. The different forms of regulation are so important to what media firms can and cannot do when it comes to production, distribution, exhibition, advertising, and finance, that we devote the entire next chapter—Chapter 3—to them.

government regulation
a wide variety of activities and laws through which elected and appointed officials at local, state, and federal levels exercise influence over media firms

Media Literacy and the Business of Media

At this point, you may be asking yourself two questions: how does knowing about the business of media help me to be a more aware consumer of mass media materials? And what difference might being an aware consumer make in my life? The questions speak, of course, to the important topic of media literacy, which we introduced in Chapter 1.

To begin to answer these questions, think back to the billboard scenario that began this chapter. Remember that the premise was that community leaders in the neighborhood where you live had begun to complain about billboard advertising featuring beer and sex, and you wanted to help these community leaders influence billboard executives to change their ad policies. At the beginning of this chapter, most of what you could do was list what you didn't know. Now (after reading the chapter), you ought to know enough to help your community deal with billboard (or "outdoor") firms.

■ For a starter, you know that billboard companies are the exhibition point of a chain of events that often also involves companies that create the ad ideas and other firms that actually make the posters and distribute them to the billboard owners. Your community group will try to persuade the exhibitors to change their policies, but if they refuse, you now know that there may well be two other levels of firms to which you can bring your demands. You might put pressure on the ad agencies that thought up the ads, or on the companies that manufactured them and delivered them to the billboard firm. The ad agencies may be more sensitive to organized pressure and anger than the billboard company.

■ You now bring to your talk with company executives a basic understanding of the advertising genre that will give you credibility with them and help you make your arguments. You know, for example, that sex and violence are often used in soft-sell advertising. The issue here is twofold: whether the practice is ethical when it is used for selling beer and whether it is ethical in areas where there are children who might consider the ads attractive and hip and so consider the combination (sex and beer) attractive and hip.

■ Our discussion of the way media firms think about audiences and the importance of segmentation and targeting to today's media should sensitize you to the issues that outdoor firms consider when they put their billboards up and that advertisers think about when they decide to place their ads on the billboards. By examining the locations of the most objectionable billboards, you might be able to show the billboard firms that you know that their supposed targets—adults—are not their only targets. You might, for example, find several of the objectionable billboards within a few blocks of high schools. That can get you into an interesting discussion about the ethics of targeting that audience and lead to leverage that you can apply to the firms.

There are many aspects of this business that we haven't yet given you the tools to address. We haven't yet discussed mass media conglomerates in any detail, so you may not feel comfortable talking about the cross-media strategies that liquor firms might be using with the help of media conglomerates. Nor have we talked about the possibility that you might be able to get help in your crusade from a government agency.

Even if there is still much to learn about this billboard issue as well as other aspects of media, the hope is that you have already begun to watch TV, read the newspaper, and use the Web with a new awareness of what is going on. Have you begun to dissect the formats of your favorite TV shows or magazines? When you open up "junk" mail, have you tried to figure out what target audiences you fit into and where the firms got your name? When you've gone into a music store, have you thought of the relationships among exhibition, distribution, and production? Have you watched and read the news with an eye to the subgenres that journalists use and, if it is hard news, the way they present the sense of an "objective" approach to the world through their use of the verbal and visual conventions we discussed?

If not, you ought to try; it will open up new ways to view reality and the forces that create it.

CHAPTER REVIEW

For an interactive chapter recap and study guide, visit the companion website for *Media Today* at www.routledge.com/textbooks/mediatoday

QUESTIONS FOR DISCUSSION AND CRITICAL THINKING

1   Investigate whether and how the three largest U.S. mass media companies operate in the three largest mass media industries.
2   In what ways are the local television hard news stories both different from and similar to the network TV hard news stories?
3   Can you see why companies in the information business might have to deal with ethical and legal issues of privacy? What privacy issues come to mind, and how do they affect you?
4   What does it mean to say that production in mass media firms is a collaborative process?
5   Why might media practitioners not want their products to appeal to certain audiences, even if those audiences are large?

INTERNET RESOURCES

Columbia Journalism Review (http//: www.cjr.com)
> *Columbia Journalism Review's* mission is to encourage and stimulate excellence in journalism in the service of a free society. It is both a watchdog and a friend of the press in all its forms, from newspapers to magazines to radio, television, and the Web.

Editor and Publisher (www.editorandpublisher.com)
> *Editor and Publisher* is a 116-year-old magazine covering the newspaper industry in North America. This site provides detailed economic and demographic profiles of and links to newspaper markets in the United States and Canada.

I Want Media (www.iwantmedia.com)
> This website focuses on diversified media news and resources. It provides quick access to media news and industry data, and is updated throughout the day.

Veronis, Suhler and Associates (http://www.veronissuhler.com)
> Veronis Suhler's Internet Research Library contains reliable data and valuable sources for the industry and financial information you need. Veronis Suhler's Internet Research Library delivers links to the websites that can answer your research questions.

KEY TERMS

You can find the definitions to these key terms in the marginal glossary out this chapter. Test your knowledge of these terms with interactive flash cards on the *Media Today* companion website.

accuracy

adequate revenue

administrative personnel

advertisement

advertising

analysis of existing data

audiences

blogs

collaborative activity

columnist

content

cooperative advertising

creative personnel

deadline

demographic indicators

demographics

direct sales

distribution

dramady

editorial

education

entertainment

exhibition

focus group

format

formula

freelancers

genres

government regulations

hard news

hard-sell ads

hybrid genres

hybridity

information

informational ads

initial public offering (IPO)

investigative reports

investment banks

journalist

license fees

lifestyle categories

line

loan

mass media production firm

media practitioners

objectivity

on-staff workers

parody

patterns of action

power of a distributor

product placement

production

profits

psychographics

rentals

research and development (R&D)

schedule

setting

shelf space

soft news

soft-sell ads

stock offering

subgenres

surveys

syndicate

talent guild

targeted

track record

trade incentives

typical characters

usage fees

venture capitalists

vertical integration

CONSTRUCTING MEDIA LITERACY

1   Claritas is a company that helps marketers divide the United States into lifestyle segments based on postal (ZIP) codes. Go to http://www.claritas.com on the Web to explore their products and services. Explain three ways in which Claritas is "constructing" America. If marketers use the constructions, how might it affect the ways people view U.S. society and even themselves?

2   Go to the ZIP code look-up page on http://www.claritas.com. It allows you to put in a neighborhood's ZIP code and find out what lifestyle stories Claritas connects to them. Put in two neighborhoods that you know are different from one another economically or culturally. Compare the ways Claritas constructs them.

3   To what extent do lists of popularity based on survey ratings or rankings affect the music you buy, the books you read or the movies you see? Do you find the lists helpful, or are you often disappointed when you base your media habits on the popularity rankings?

4   Think of a "subgenre" of entertainment that you particularly enjoy—horror movies, football films, workplace sitcoms, doctor shows, or some other one—and try to track examples of these on TV or in the movies over the past half century. (One resource to use is the Internet movie database, http://www. imdb.com, which covers theatrical films and television series.) Judging by descriptions of the programs and maybe by articles you can find about the shows, can you identify a formula for the subgenre? If so, how has the formula changed over time?

CASE STUDY   Teens as a Constructed Audience

The idea   One way to get a feel for the idea that audiences are constructed is to see how advertisers actually construct audiences. In this case study you will go through recent advertising trade magazines to see how marketing and media executives talk about an important audience—teens. You will also explore what their construction of teens means for the ways they try to reach them and persuade them to buy products.

The method   To conduct this study, you need to know how to use a periodical database in your school's library. The most popular databases are Factiva and LexisNexis. Knowing how to use these sorts of databases will help you learn a lot about the state of media today. It may also help you get a summer, or a permanent, job in a media firm.

1   Ask someone who knows how to use the database to show you how to do a full-text search of the weekly trade magazine *Advertising Age* for the past six months. Tell that person that you would like to investigate how *Advertising Age* used the term *teen* or *teenager* during that time.

2   You may find that *Advertising Age* used the term a lot during that period. Ask your professor what proportion of the articles you should read. If there are a hundred articles or more, the class might divide into groups of two or three people in each group. That way each group can share findings on all the articles and summarize them.

3 For each article, note the title and date and then answer the following questions on a sheet or paper:

    a   On what topic does it mention teenagers?

    b   How does it describe teenagers? To what extent, and how, does it divide teens by gender, class, spending power, physical characteristics, personalities, or other categories?

    c   Does the article make comparisons between teenagers and other groups in society? If so, how?

    d   What does the article say about teenagers' value to advertisers, uses of different media, and uses of different products?

    e   What, if anything, does the article say about how media firms create media to attract teens?

    f   What, if anything, does the article say about how media firms and advertisers are creating advertisements to attract teens? With what messages and images do they think they can persuade them?

4 Once you and your group have taken notes on all the articles, make an outline of a report that discusses what you learned about how teenagers are constructed by advertisers, why, and with what consequences for commercial messages and for media.

3

FORMAL AND INFORMAL CONTROLS ON MEDIA CONTENT: GOVERNMENT REGULATION, SELF-REGULATION, AND ETHICS

After studying this chapter, you will be able to:

1 Explain the reasons for and the theories underlying media regulation

2 Identify and describe the different types of media regulation

3 Analyze the struggle that exists between citizens and regulatory bodies in the search for information

4 Discuss the ways in which media organizations practice self-regulation, both internally and externally

5 Explain the meaning, importance, and difficulties of applying and following basic ethical principles within mass media organizations

6 Identify and evaluate some modern ethical dilemmas facing media practitioners today

7 Harness your media literacy skills in order to comprehend how media regulation affects you as a consumer

"The First Amendment is inconvenient. But that is beside the point. Inconvenience does not absolve the government of its obligation to tolerate speech."

–ANTHONY KENNEDY, SUPREME COURT JUSTICE

Media Today

"What progress we are making. In the Middle Ages they would have burned me. Now they are content with burning my books."
Sigmund Freud, 1933, Jewish-Austrian psychiatrist (1856–1939)

On May 10, 1933, the Nazi-led government of Germany organized several book burnings at universities around the country. One took place in Berlin at Wilhelm Humboldt University. Guided by top-level politicians, students from the University came together to select books to destroy from their university library. They chose to burn books by Jewish and Marxist authors and by other authors that the Nazi government found disreputable, including such world-famous thinkers as Heinrich Heine, Sigmund Freud, Thomas Mann, Erich Maria Remarque, Albert Einstein, Walter Benjamin, Karl Marx, Jack London, and Margaret Sanger.

The students transported the books to the Franz Joseph Platz, a large plaza next to the school. Denouncing the authors and their ideas, they tossed thousands of books into a bonfire. German newspapers, which were allied with the government, triumphantly reported that Germany was beginning to purge itself of the alien and decadent corrupters of the German spirit. Many newspapers and magazines outside Germany responded with surprise and shock; in the United States, journalists and authors expressed outrage. A study of American reaction to this and other book burnings that took place during the 1930s concluded that the American public generally was upset about these incidents, even though they took place so far away.[1] What was especially shocking to many Americans in 1933—and remains shocking even today—is the idea that a government could command so much direct, destructive power over mass media content. In addition to orchestrating book burnings throughout the rest of the 1930s, the Nazis controlled German newspaper reaction to those book burnings.

American schoolchildren are taught that such government control over "the press" is contrary to this nation's democratic ideals. Yet many Americans sometimes wish that the government would do something about what they consider media that are out of moral control. They complain about sex, violence, racism, sexism, and other aspects of media content. They cry out for some sort of government action to stop the objectionable images and words.

To what extent can U.S. government officials respond to their concerns? To what extent *should* they respond? What influence does the U.S. government exert over the mass media? What are the legal limits on government intervention? These are among the questions that we address in this chapter.

We noted in Chapter 2 that the vast majority of newspapers, magazines, books, radio shows, movies, and television shows that reach Americans are commercially produced. However, that doesn't mean that the government is out of the picture. Quite the contrary: government regulations have a tremendous impact on the kinds of businesses media firms can enter and the kinds of materials they are allowed to create and show to audiences.

Government officials often encourage media companies to regulate themselves in order to alleviate public concerns, leading media executives to fear that government actions to punish them will follow if they don't act the way the government wants them to. Amid all their business requirements, the executives have to decide what moral principles—what ethics—should guide the creation and circulation of mass media materials. In addition, outside advocacy organizations that want mass media firms to adopt the advocates' principles for creating media content put further pressure on media organizations to behave "ethically."

Government Regulation of the Media Marketplace

regulation with regard to mass media, laws and guidelines that influence the way media companies produce, distribute, or exhibit materials for audiences

When we talk about the **regulation** of mass media, we mean laws and guidelines that influence the way media companies produce, distribute or exhibit materials for audiences. Government regulation of mass media covers a wide range of territory. It can mean regulation by federal, state, county, or city government. Such regulation is carried out for different reasons, and in different ways, in different countries. Americans are often horrified by the extent of government control in other countries compared to that in their own country. Still, every government justifies its approach to regulation on the grounds that it is the best for that society. Sometimes many people in the society agree with the laws and guidelines, even though outsiders consider them unacceptable. Other times, people in the society believe that the laws are unfair and would like to see them change, but feel powerless.

Approaches to Media Regulation

Scholars who compare media systems around the world describe four different approaches to government regulation of the media. These approaches describe the amount of control government should have over the media, from high levels of control to low levels of control. (See Figure 3.1.) Those four approaches are:

- Authoritarian
- Communist
- Libertarian
- Social responsibility

Let's look at each of these ways of thinking about the government's role in media regulation individually.

authoritarian approaches approaches to media regulation that require the owners of mass media firms to be avid supporters of the authoritarian regime, with workers who are willing to create news and entertainment materials that adhere strictly to the party line; typically adopted by dictators who want to keep themselves and the elite class that supports them in direct control over all aspects of their society

Authoritarian Approaches **Authoritarian approaches** to media regulation are aimed at controlling what the population sees, reads, and hears through media outlets. These approaches are typically adopted by dictators who want to keep themselves and the elite class that supports them in direct control over society. Authoritarian rulers often claim that they are rescuing their people from evils that the society may have experienced in the past. They justify controlling the media and other aspects of life by saying that these activities are necessary in order to unify the public and educate it in the truth.

The authoritarian approach does not require that all the media outlets be owned by the government. It *does* require that the owners of mass media firms support the authoritarian regime, with workers who are willing to create news and entertainment materials that adhere to the party line. Those who dissent are stripped of their media holdings and prevented from speaking against the regime.

Figure 3.1

Approaches to Government Regulation of the Media

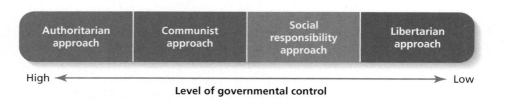

Level of governmental control

Such governments also make it illegal for people to read or listen to media materials from other countries that the government doesn't sanction.

Versions of the authoritarian approach were proudly practiced by the regimes of fascist Germany and Italy before and during the Second World War. The governments of Burma and Uzbekistan today can be described as among those operating under this philosophy of strict government control of the media. According to a 2007 Radio Free Europe/Radio Liberty report about Uzbekistan, "truly independent newspapers, radio, and television stations are almost nonexistent in Uzbekistan, [and] the government has turned its attention to the Internet, blocking news websites and creating pro-government sites that cover events from the government's viewpoint."[2]

Communist Approaches Like authoritarian approaches, **communist approaches** to government regulation believe that the government should determine what the population sees, reads, hears, and experiences through media outlets. They depart from authoritarian approaches, however, in the way they justify this control. They follow the writings of Vladimir Lenin, a leader of the Russian communist revolution. Lenin argued that the purpose of communist society was to help create a nation, and eventually a world, in which the common people would share everything. In this ideal society, there would be no rich or poor classes. People would be paid what they needed in order to live comfortably, no matter what kind of job they held.

Lenin believed firmly that the mass media were important vehicles for teaching people the values of communism. The media system of a communist society, he said, should be considered part of its educational system. Following Lenin, countries with communist governments—North Korea and Cuba, for example—teach their creators of news and entertainment that they must learn how to see the world through the eyes of communist beliefs. Armed with these understandings, their goal is to convey these beliefs in everything they produce for public consumption.

Libertarian Approaches On the other end of the spectrum from authoritarian and communist approaches to media control are **libertarian approaches.** It comes down to opposing views of human nature—people who endorse the authoritarian or communist approach to regulation of the media have little regard for the

communist approaches approaches to media regulation that hold that the government should determine what the population sees, reads, hears, and experiences through media outlets, in order to convey communist beliefs in everything the media produce for public consumption

libertarian approaches approaches to media regulation that hold that individuals are capable of making sound decisions for themselves and that government should intervene only in those rare circumstances where society cannot be served by people going about their own business; the mass media do not represent such an area, since individuals and companies will create mass media materials without prodding from the government

Book burnings were one of the means Nazis used to control media during the Second World War.

individual in society; libertarians, in contrast, operate under the belief that individuals are capable of making sound decisions for themselves.

Libertarians believe that any government restrictions placed on the dissemination and expression of ideas infringe upon the rights of the individual. In their view, government should intervene only in those rare circumstances in which society cannot be served by people going about their own business. For example, according to libertarians, government needs to intervene to provide a military because individuals would not be likely to coordinate such an activity by themselves. The mass media, however, are not an area in which government needs to intervene, since individuals and companies can readily create mass media materials without the government's help.

Moreover, say libertarians, in a free-flowing media system individuals will be able to make their own decisions about what is true and what is false. Libertarians get this notion from English writer and philosopher John Milton. In his 1644 pamphlet, *Areopagitica*, Milton called for a **marketplace of ideas** in which different opinions would compete for public approval. Milton felt that truth would always win out in such a contest.

"Where is this approach practiced?" you might ask. The answer is: nowhere. That is because in democratic societies, where it *might* be practiced, critics consider the libertarian approach to mass media to be unrealistic. They say that giving media companies total freedom to do as they like would lead to control of the media by a few

marketplace of ideas the belief, asserted by John Milton in *Areopagitica*, that in a free-flowing media system, individuals will be able to make their own decisions about what is true and what is false, because media competition will allow different opinions to emerge and struggle for public approval (as in a market), and in the end, the true opinion will win out

John Milton's *Areopagitica*, first published in 1644 as an appeal to Parliament to rescind the Licensing Order which was designed to bring publishing under government control by creating a number of official censors to whom authors would submit their work for approval prior to having it published.

huge corporations. There would not be any real struggle for "the truth" to come out because there would not be enough different viewpoints presented. As such, political democracies tend to choose the social responsibility approach to government regulation—to which we now turn—over the libertarian one.

Social Responsibility Approaches   **Social responsibility approaches** to government regulation are in agreement with the libertarian belief in the importance of the individual and the marketplace of ideas. Supporters of social responsibility approaches believe, however, that the *real* competition of ideas that libertarians seek will never happen without government action to encourage companies to be socially responsible by offering a diversity of voices and ideas. They also say that sometimes what individuals or companies want to publish— for example, child pornography—might be harmful to a large number of people in the society.

Sometimes a media conglomerate may exert power in an unfair way by destroying other media firms, which in turn might remove the voices of important media organizations in society. Still other times, the interests of media corporations might make it impossible for the opinions of individual citizens—or even citizens running for political office—to be heard by large numbers of people. Circumstances such as these require media regulation, say the supporters of social responsibility approaches. According to this view, government's role is to make sure that companies allow—and even encourage—social responsibility in the media system so that a diverse marketplace of voices and ideas can flourish.

Of course, definitions of social responsibility will vary among societies, and even within societies. The ideal in social responsibility approaches is to strike a balance among the needs and rights of the individual, of media organizations, and of the society as a whole. That balance may be struck by passing laws aimed at forcing private media companies to pay attention to their social responsibilities. This desire for a balance may also lead the government to provide public funding for nonprofit media organizations that aren't owned by the government; in the United States, the Corporation for Public Broadcasting, which distributes money to public broadcasters, is an example. In other circumstances, the government may feel that a state-owned media organization is the best way to accomplish goals that the private media system cannot or will not carry out. That is the philosophy that created the British Broadcasting Corporation, which is supported to a great extent by a tax on people who live in the United Kingdom.

The differences among the four approaches are shown in Figure 3.2. The categories may look quite distinctive in the illustration, but sometimes in real life things get ambiguous. Where, for example, should we put China? Its government is not run by a charismatic dictator or a military junta. Nor is China really a "communist" state anymore; despite the name of its ruling party, capitalism is making headway there. Of course, China is not a multiparty democracy (a traditional part of the social responsibility model) but other parts of the model may apply: the Chinese government does allow private print and broadcast media to exist, and it has loosened some of its restrictions on criticizing government activities, especially when it comes to corrupt activities of local administrators. In fact, it would not be surprising if a Chinese official were to argue that his country espouses the "social responsibility" model of media. The official might say that the Chinese government wants to have the best balance between government and private control over media in order to encourage the best balance between the individual and society and, as a result, both social harmony and national security.

social responsibility approaches approaches to media regulation that agree with the libertarian belief in the importance of the individual and the marketplace of ideas, but hold that the real competition over ideas will never happen without government action to encourage companies to be socially responsible by offering a diversity of voices and ideas, and also argue that sometimes things that individuals or companies want to publish—for example, child pornography—might be harmful to a large number of people in the society

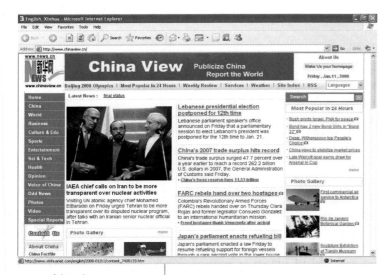

www.chinaview.cn,
the English language
website of China's official
government news agency

Critics of China would reply that the government's claim of regulation in the interest of social harmony and diversity is merely a cover to apply antidemocratic media regulations. While the government allows private Internet companies, in the name of social harmony and security it enforces many rules about what websites and people can discuss online about the central government. Under the umbrella of social responsibility, the government even blocks websites (such as those about the Chinese religious sect Falun Gong) that it says incite social unrest. In fact, the human rights group Amnesty International has claimed that the Chinese government approach to the online world has spawned a "Chinese model" that other countries have imitated: "an Internet that allows economic growth but not free speech or privacy—is growing in popularity, from a handful of countries five years ago to dozens of governments today who block sites and arrest bloggers."[3]

We might conclude, then, that the four regulatory approaches do not describe all situations. Societies may fall between these types, and it might be best to see authoritarian, communist, social responsibility and libertarian as starting points for analyzing the media structures of different societies rather than as absolute categories that can accommodate every situation. We should also not assume that claiming a social responsibility model automatically means accepting certain norms about freedom of the press. Clearly, definitions of social responsibility, and of the preferred balance between individual and society, will vary widely.

Figure 3.2

Differences Among the Regulatory Approaches
The four regulatory approaches typically reflect (1) different types of government, (2) different attitudes toward media ownership, and (3) different attitudes toward whether the media should care about society's or the individual's needs and interests.

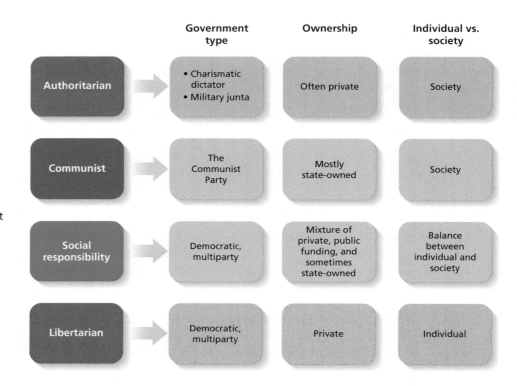

	Government type	Ownership	Individual vs. society
Authoritarian	• Charismatic dictator • Military junta	Often private	Society
Communist	The Communist Party	Mostly state-owned	Society
Social responsibility	Democratic, multiparty	Mixture of private, public funding, and sometimes state-owned	Balance between individual and society
Libertarian	Democratic, multiparty	Private	Individual

Political, Economic, and Cultural Influences on Government Regulation of the Media

It's important to note that even when countries have the same approach to government regulation of the media—whether the approach is authoritarian, communist, social responsibility or even libertarian—the actual laws that they pass may be quite different. Political, economic and/or cultural factors may help to explain the differences in the ways countries translate the same approach into actual regulation. Let's take a look at each.

Political Influences　**Political influences** refer to the types of power that officials can exert. The leaders of some countries have more power to impose their will over their nation's institutions than do the leaders of other countries. A dictator with a strong army to enforce his orders will typically be able to exert more direct control over his country's television stations and newspapers than a dictator who does not yet feel strong enough to pull every aspect of his society under his control.

political influences the types of power that government officials have to impose their will over the nation's institutions, including the media

Economic Influences　**Economic influences** revolve around the costs of carrying out certain types of regulation. For example, the governments of some countries may feel that putting media arrangements in place may be too expensive, while the governments of other countries may not be bothered by such costs. A country that adopts the social responsibility approach may use tax money to maintain an active educational TV broadcasting system, whereas another country may force privately owned TV stations to devote a certain number of hours a day to education. Similarly, some nations may pass laws mandating the use of government funds to help schools get connected to the Internet, whereas other countries can't afford such efforts.

economic influences the costs associated with carrying out certain types of government regulation

Cultural Influences　**Cultural influences** center on the historical circumstances that lead societies to accept certain media systems rather than others. The special history and customs of particular societies lead different governments to feel differently about the moral acceptability of certain regulations. Consider the post-World War II German government, which like the United States has adopted a social responsibility approach to media regulation. In an attempt to protect the nation from repeating its horrific Nazi past, German laws today make it illegal for any mass media outlet in the country to speak in favor of Nazi ideology or to deny Germany's intentional destruction of Europe's Jews during World War II. Such laws would undoubtedly be considered unconstitutional in the United States. As we will see, the United States has a very different tradition with respect to limits on the press.

cultural influences the historical and social circumstances that lead societies to accept certain media systems and government regulations

U.S. Media Regulation and the First Amendment

In the United States, the legal foundation for government's relation to the press is the First Amendment to the Constitution, which reads:

> Congress shall make no law respecting an establishment of religion, or prohibiting the free exercise thereof; or abridging the freedom of speech, or of the press, or of the right of the people peaceably to assemble, and to petition the Government for a redress of grievances.

The Bill of Rights, as this parchment copy is now known, is on permanent display in the Rotunda of the National Archives in Washington, D.C.

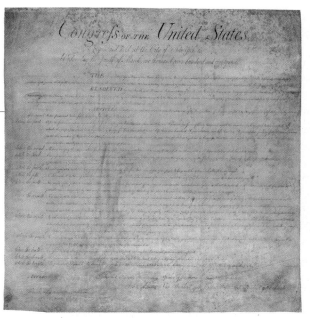

The First Amendment's statement that "Congress shall make no law ... abridging freedom of speech, or of the press," seems to rule out *any* type of government interference in journalistic organizations ("the press"), and maybe even in media that do not present only news. The country's Founders were determined that in the new nation, no one would need the government's permission to communicate ideas to a wide public.

The reality of lawmaking has been quite different, however. Over the decades, the federal government has been deeply involved in regulating all sorts of media firms in ways that lawmakers insist do not conflict with the First Amendment. Debate continues about the precise meaning of the First Amendment. The U.S. Supreme Court has involved itself numerous times in sorting out fights between government agencies interested in curtailing mass media content and companies interested in protecting and extending it.

What Does the First Amendment Mean by "No Law," and Where Does it Apply?

From the time the First Amendment was passed, lawmakers and lawyers have understood that its phrase "make no law" means that the federal branches of government could not make laws abridging press freedoms. They debated, however, whether the First Amendment applies to the states as well. The issue is an important one. Imagine you are the publisher of a newspaper that prints controversial views about politicians throughout the United States. You would like to be sure that the Constitution protects your work, no matter which politicians object to it. If the legislature of the state in which you work has the right to stop you from publishing your views, your newspaper would likely go out of business.

In 1925, this question was resolved by the Supreme Court, in the case of *Gitlow* vs. *New York*. Socialist agitator Benjamin Gitlow published a circular called *The Left Wing Manifesto*, calling for an uprising to overthrow the government. This upset local authorities, and Gitlow was convicted in the state of New York for the statutory crime of criminal anarchy. Gitlow then appealed his case to the U.S. Supreme Court. His lawyers argued that the Constitution (and therefore the First Amendment) should override any state law that contradicts it.

The U.S. Supreme Court agreed with Gitlow and his lawyers, ruling that the First Amendment's phrase "Congress shall make no law" should be interpreted as "government and its agencies shall make no law," regardless of the location or level of government. The Court reasoned that in the Fourteenth Amendment, Congress had ensured that fundamental personal rights and liberties could not be trampled by the states.

What Does the First Amendment Mean by "The Press"?

Here is another important question: when the Founders wrote that "Congress shall make no law…abridging the freedom of speech, or of the press," how did they define the term *press*? The Founders could not have possibly imagined the complex world of media messages and channels in which we currently live. So which segments of the media are included under the First Amendment's definition of "the press"?

You can probably imagine the difference the answer to this question makes. If only news companies fall under the protection of the First Amendment, then book publishers, magazine firms, websites, movie companies and advertising firms are open to government interference. That might place a chill on the creation of entertainment and fiction, as companies would fear getting in trouble with federal and state governments.

These issues have been of great importance to media firms and free-speech advocates. In recent decades, though, court decisions and political interpretations of what precisely the First Amendment means by "the press" have expanded the definition to include all types of mass media, not just the journalistic press.

Film   The Supreme Court established the First Amendment's protection of movies in 1952, in the case of *Burstyn* vs. *Wilson*. In its ruling, the Court declared:

> Expression by means of motion pictures is included within the free speech and free press guaranty of the First and Fourteenth Amendments. It cannot be doubted that motion pictures are a significant medium for the communication of ideas. Their importance as an organ of public opinion is not lessened by the fact that they are designed to entertain as well as to inform.
>
> (*Burstyn* vs. *Wilson*, 343 U.S. 495,
> The Supreme Court of the United States, 1952)

This ruling was significant in that it overturned the Court's long-standing 1919 decision in *Mutual Film Corp* vs. *Ohio Industrial Commission*, which had ruled that films were not a protected form of expression, because of their nature as novelty and entertainment pieces.

TV and Radio   TV and radio's protection under the First Amendment was established by the Supreme Court in 1973, in the case of *CBS* vs. *Democratic National Committee*. In preparing the Court's decision, Justice William Douglas wrote:

> TV and radio stand in the same protected position under the First Amendment as do newspapers and magazines. The philosophy of the First Amendment requires that result, for the fear that James Madison and Thomas Jefferson had of government intrusion is perhaps even more relevant to TV and radio than it is to newspapers and other like publications. That fear was founded not only on the specter of a lawless government but of government under the control of a faction that desired to foist its views of the common good on the people.
>
> (*CBS* vs. *Democratic National Committee*,
> 412 U.S. 94, Supreme Court of the United States, 1973)

Other Forms of Entertainment　The Supreme Court established the protected status of entertainment content in its 1967 ruling in the case of *Time Inc.* vs. *Hill.* The Court invalidated a New York Court of Appeals decision that the purpose of a *Life* magazine article was entertainment and marketing, and so the article wasn't covered by the First Amendment. In explaining the Court's reasoning, Justice William Brennan quoted two previous Supreme Court decisions, *Winters* vs. *New York* and *New York Times Co.* vs. *Sullivan.* He wrote a strong declaration that all sorts of materials, not just news, enjoy First Amendment protection:

■ "The guarantees for speech and press are not the preserve of political expression or comment upon public affairs, essential as those are to healthy government. One need only pick up any newspaper or magazine to comprehend the vast range of published matter which exposes persons to public view, both private citizens and public officials. ... The line between the informing and the entertaining is too elusive for the protection of ... [freedom of the press]." (*Winters* vs. *New York*, 333 U.S. 507, 510.)

■ Erroneous statement is no less inevitable in such a case than in the case of comment upon public affairs, and in both, if innocent or merely negligent, "it must be protected if the freedoms of expression are to have the 'breathing space' that they 'need ... to survive.'" (*New York Times Co.* vs. *Sullivan*, supra, at 271–272.)[4]

Advertising　In 1976, the Court ruled that even advertising and other forms of commercial speech are included in the First Amendment's definition of "the press" and therefore enjoy protection. In *Virginia State Board of Pharmacy et al.* vs. *Virginia Citizens Consumer Council*, a majority of the justices found that a state law making it illegal for pharmacists to advertise their prices was unconstitutional. Judge Harry Blackmun bluntly expressed the Court's position: "What is at issue is whether a State may completely suppress the dissemination of concededly truthful information about entirely lawful activity, fearful of that information's effect upon its disseminators and its recipients." He also answered bluntly: "Reserving other questions, we conclude that the answer to this one is in the negative."[5]

Based on such reasoning, in 2007 a Los Angeles federal judge refused to stop the hamburger chain Jack in the Box from running ads that poked fun at Carl's Jr.'s high-end sirloin hamburgers from Angus cows by implying that the meat comes from the cow's hind section. Carl's Jr.'s parent company had filed suit against Jack in the Box, claiming its ads were false and misleading. In one spot poking fun at Carl's, the Jack character uses a diagram to point out that sirloin comes from the cow's midsection. When asked to point to the "Angus section," Jack responds, "I'd rather not." Carl's parent company argued that the ad and others like it were confusing consumers into thinking its Angus burgers come from the "rear-end and/or anus of beef cattle." But the judge said there wasn't enough evidence that the ads were hurting the chain for him to stop the commercials from airing. He did say he would reconsider if Carl's presented persuasive evidence that the ads were deceiving people in the ways it claimed.[6]

What Does the First Amendment Mean by "Abridging"?

abridge to reduce in scope, to diminish

The term **abridge** means "to cut short, curtail." In fact, the Supreme Court has often approved government restrictions on speech or the press that place limits on the time, place, and manner of an expression. Such restrictions are legal as long as those limits:

- Are applicable to everyone
- Are without political bias
- Serve a significant governmental interest
- Leave ample alternative ways for the communication to take place

The issue has come up a lot in the area of outdoor advertising. Over the decades, communities upset about both the clutter that billboards bring and the content of some of them—sexual images and unwholesome products—have tried to create laws regulating them. Based on the points above, courts have ruled that any laws restricting outdoor advertising have to apply to all business and cannot reflect any prejudice toward any particular lawful business. That approach satisfies the four criteria above. Following this logic, federal courts have ruled that liquor ads could not be singled out for a ban on highways on the presumption that teen drivers would be influenced by them. The reasoning is that free speech should be protected as long as there are other ways to warn teenagers about the dangers of drinking and driving.

Anti-cigarette activists argue that outdoor cigarette advertising ought to be an exception to this approach. At this point, cigarette companies have stopped using large billboards as part of a "voluntary" agreement with the federal government to limit commercial messages for the product that, while it harms people, can still be bought legally. In 2007, however, U.S. Senator Ted Kennedy championed legislation that would let the Food and Drug Administration regulate tobacco and its advertising, including banning outdoor ads within 1,000 feet of schools or playgrounds, ending giveaways of promotional items, and limiting sponsorships of athletic, musical or social events. Pro-advertising interests contended that such restrictions would be unconstitutional, and the law did not pass.[7]

Whether or not courts would consider these broad prohibitions against cigarette advertising acceptable, the argument around Kennedy's proposal does highlight the point that when it comes to abridgment or regulation, as we will see, some types of media expressions are protected more than others (see Figure 3.3). Moreover, we must also recognize that regulation is not limited to the content level. Government decisions that affect the economic health of a company or industry can also be thought of as an abridgment of "the press" because such

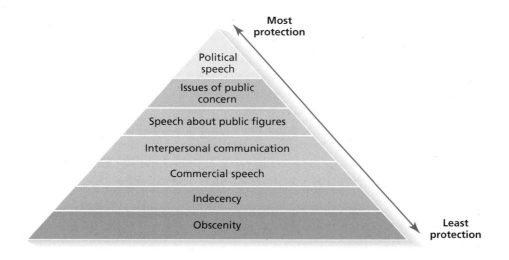

Figure 3.3

Levels of Protected Communication in the United States
The level of protection that the U.S. government provides depends upon the type of speech—from constitutionally valueless speech (no protection), to speech given intermediate protection (some protection), to fully protected speech (full protection).

91

decisions often affect the media products that the companies produce, distribute and exhibit.

Types of Media Regulation

Certain kinds of media regulation have been found constitutional numerous times by the Supreme Court. We can divide these types of governmental regulation into three categories:

- Regulation of content before it is distributed
- Regulation of content after it has been distributed
- Economic regulations

Let's look at each of these three types separately.

Regulating Content Before Distribution

prior restraint government restriction of speech before it is made

When the government restricts speech before it is made, it is engaging in **prior restraint**. Since the 1930s, the U.S. Supreme Court has consistently ruled that the practice of regulating or restricting speech before it is made violates both the spirit and the letter of the First Amendment. At the same time, however, the Court has held that in some specific circumstances—rare though they may be—such censorship before the fact is in the interest of the public good.

To understand the importance of the Supreme Court's approach, consider the landmark 1931 case of *Near* vs. *Minnesota*, in which the Court struck down a Minnesota law that allowed prior restraint. This law gave judges the authority to allow police to halt the distribution of "malicious, scandalous or defamatory publications." Such authority was granted against anti-Semitic newspaper publishers Jay Near and Howard Guilford who wrote in their *Saturday Press*, "every snake-faced gangster and embryonic yegg in the Twin Cities is a JEW," and accused the Minneapolis police chief of turning a blind eye to Jewish crime.

injunction a court order requiring a person or organization to perform or refrain from performing a particular act

The trial court declared the paper a nuisance and issued an **injunction**—a court order requiring a person or organization to perform or refrain from performing a particular act—that said if Near and Guilford printed such "defamatory" and "scandalous" comments again, they would automatically be punished for being in contempt of court. Near appealed against the injunction, and although the Minnesota Supreme Court upheld the trial court, the U.S. Supreme Court, in a five to four decision, reversed the state decision and allowed the *Saturday Press* to continue publication.

You might wonder why. After all, wouldn't squelching this sort of verbal garbage be a victory for decency? Writing for the majority, Chief Justice Charles Hughes stated that even though the articles were despicable, there was a more important principle at stake. He said that the main purpose of the First Amendment is to prevent prior restraint on publication. Hughes added that he agreed that charges of government scandal might very well cause a public scandal. But, he said, "a more serious public evil would be caused by authority to prevent publication."

In writing his decision in the *Near* case, Chief Justice Hughes cited instances in which prior restraint would be acceptable under certain circumstances. And, in fact, over the years, the Court has been strict about not allowing prior restraint when political ideas are involved. It *has* allowed the regulation of content before publication in some cases involving:

The Saturday Press

Vol. 1, No. 4   Minneapolis, Minn., Oct. 15, 1927   Price 5 Cents

A Direct Challenge to Police Chief Brunskill

The Chief, in Banning This Paper from News Stands, Definitely Aligns Himself With Gangland, Violates the Law He Is Sworn to Uphold, When He Tries to Suppress This Publication. The Only Paper in the City That Dares Expose the Gang's Deadly Grip on Minneapolis. A Plain Statement of Facts and a Warning of Legal Action.

Possibly there are moments news stands FOR WE HAD when "a soft answer turneth BEEN TOLD BY THE GAM-away wrath" but as against BLING SYNDICATE THAT

Respectfully Submitted

There seems to be an impression among gentlemen of peculiar bent that the suppression of our street sales has rendered abortive our attempt to cleanse this city of gang rule. These gents are intellectual single-trackers; twenty - two caliber saps rattling around in a four hundred thousand city. Lest they become too hilari-

testify before your body he would be more than glad to give you sufficient evidence upon which to base an indictment of the acknowledged gang-leader, Mose Barnett—the man who threatened Mr. Shapiro just a comparatively few days before the assault upon his person and property was made by four gunmen.

The Saturday Press stood at the center of the precedent-setting case of *Near* vs. *Minnesota* (1931).

- Obscenity
- National security
- Military operations
- Clear and present danger to public safety
- Copyright
- Courtroom proceedings
- Education
- Commercial speech

Let's take a brief look at each of these special cases in which prior restraint may be allowed.

Obscenity and Pornography   The Supreme Court has ruled that obscene materials are not protected by the First Amendment. The trick, however, has been to decide the exact meaning of the word *obscenity*.

The term *obscene* means "offensive to accepted standards of decency or modesty." One problem, of course, is that different people may have different standards of what constitutes obscenity; books such as D.H. Lawrence's *Lady Chatterley's Lover*, Walt Whitman's *Leaves of Grass*, and J.D. Salinger's *Catcher in the Rye* may not be acceptable to some in the society, but may be considered genuine works of art by others. Of course, the same holds with respect to images on websites. In 2007, the European Commission posted a montage of "sex scenes" from European films on a new video-sharing website in order to make an artistic point about cooperation ("Let's come together") and draw attention to its area of the site. Some, though, didn't see art there at all and decried the online video as "immoral."[8] Related to these disagreements about obscenity is the dilemma that the public's collective standards of what is obscene and what is not obscene change and shift almost constantly. Communities that deemed a book or film obscene in the 1970s might not agree with that assessment today.

In 1957, the U.S. Supreme Court made a significant advance in the freedom of expression with regard to sex. It held that:

obscene material material that deals with sex in a manner appealing to prurient interest

> Sex and obscenity are not synonymous. **Obscene material** is material which deals with sex in a manner appealing to prurient interest. The portrayal of sex in art, literature and scientific works, is not itself sufficient reason to deny material the constitutional protection of freedom of speech and press. Sex, a great and mysterious motive force in human life, has indisputably been a subject of absorbing interest to mankind through the ages; it is one of the vital problems of human interest and public concern.
> (*Roth* vs. *United States*, 354 U.S. 476, 1957)

Additionally, the Court ruled, "The standard for judging obscenity, adequate to withstand the charge of constitutional infirmity, is whether, to the average person, applying contemporary community standards, the dominant theme of the material, taken as a whole, appeals to prurient interest" (*Roth* vs. *United States*, 354 U.S. 476, 1957). In this way, the Court made it clear that a media product must be considered in its entirety, and not just in excerpt. It also made it clear that the standard to be used must be community-based; that is, what is deemed obscene in Bloomington, Indiana, may be seen as merely pornographic in Boston, Massachusetts, and may be judged as purely artistic in Los Angeles, California.

pornography the presentation of sexually explicit behavior, as in a photograph, intended to arouse sexual excitement

The word *obscenity* is often linked to the word **pornography**, which can be defined as "pictures, writing, or other material that is sexually explicit." Pornographic materials are not subject to prior restraint unless they are declared obscene. For more than a century, conservative and liberal groups have argued over the presence of obscenity in a gamut of materials accused of being pornographic—from books (*Are You There God? It's Me, Margaret*), to magazines (*Hustler*), to video games (hidden sexual content in *Grand Theft Auto: San Andreas*) to music (Crime Mob's *Rock Yo Hips*, for example[9]).

According to a three-part rule devised by the U.S. Supreme Court in the 1973 case of *Miller* vs. *California*, a mass media product—whether it is pornographic in nature or not—would be declared obscene if it meets all three of the following tests:

- First, an *average person*, applying current standards of the community, would have to find that the work as an entirety reflects an obsessive interest in sex.
- Second, the work has to portray in a *clearly offensive manner*—in pictures or writing—certain sexual conduct specifically described as unallowable by state law.
- Third, a *reasonable person* has to agree that the work lacks serious literary, artistic, scientific, or political usefulness.

It is important to note that even if pornographic materials do not meet these tests of obscenity, they can still be restricted under import regulations, postal

A Selection of Challenged or Banned Books in the 2000s

"Profanity"

I Know Why the Caged Bird Sings by Maya Angelou
Challenged as required reading for Hamilton, Montana, freshman English classes (2002). At issue are scenes in which the author explores her sexuality through intercourse as a teenager and the depiction of a rape and molestation of an eight-year-old girl; homosexuality is another theme explored in the book that has drawn criticism.

The Color Purple by Alice Walker
Challenged, along with seventeen other titles in the Fairfax County, Virginia, Elementary and Secondary libraries (2002).

Both books were challenged (2002), by a group called Parents Against Bad Books in Schools. The group contends the books "contain profanity and descriptions of drug abuse, sexually explicit conduct, and torture."

"Gay positive"

My Brother has AIDS by Deborah Davis
Challenged at the Montgomery County, Texas, Memorial Library System (2004) along with fifteen other young-adult books with gay-positive themes.

"Adult themes"

Brave New World by Aldous Huxley
Challenged, but retained in the South Texas Independent School District in Mercedes, Texas (2003). Parents objected to the adult themes—sexuality, drugs, and suicide—found in the novel. Huxley's book was part of the summer Science Academy curriculum.

"Degrading"

To Kill a Mockingbird by Harper Lee
Challenged at the Stanford Middle School in Durham, N.C. (2004), because the 1961 Pulitzer Prize-winning novel uses the word "nigger." Challenged, but retained in the Normal, Illinois, Community High School sophomore literature class (2004) despite concerns the novel is degrading to African Americans.

"Promotes witchcraft"

Bridge to Terabithia by Katherine Paterson
Challenged in the middle school curriculum in Cromwell, Connecticut (2002), due to concern that it promotes witchcraft and violence. The book is the recipient of the 1978 Newbery Medal for children's literature.

"Stupid"

Harry Potter and the Chamber of Secrets by J.K. Rowling
A federal judge overturned restricted access to the Harry Potter book after parents of a Cedarville, Arkansas (2002), fourth-grader filed a federal lawsuit challenging restrictions, which required students to present written permission from a parent to borrow the book. The novel was originally challenged because it characterized authority as "stupid" and portrays "good witches and good magic." Challenged, but retained in the New Haven, Connecticut, schools (2003) despite claims the series "makes witchcraft and wizardry alluring to children."

"Violence"

Of Mice and Men by John Steinbeck
Challenged in the Normal, Illinois, Community High School (2003) because the book contains "racial slurs, profanity, violence, and does not represent traditional values." An alternative book, Steinbeck's *The Pearl*, was offered but rejected by the family challenging the novel.

"Inappropriate"

The Joy Luck Club by Amy Tan
Challenged at the Arrowhead High School in Merton, Wisconsin (2004), as an elective reading list assignment by a parent because the book contains "sexually explicit and inappropriate material."

"Degrading"

The Adventures of Huckleberry Finn by Mark Twain
[Samuel L. Clemens].
Challenged in the Normal, Illinois, Community High School sophomore literature class (2004) as being degrading to African Americans. *The Chosen* was offered as an alternative to Twain's novel. Pulled from the reading lists at the three Renton, Washington high schools (2004) after an African-American student said the book degraded her and her culture.

Source: Adapted from Robert P. Doyle's "Books Challenged or Banned in 2002–2003," "Books Challenged or Banned in 2003–2004," and "Books Challenged or Banned in 2004–2005." Illinois Library Association. http://www.ila.org/advocacy/banned.htm, accessed 01/29/2007.

regulations, zoning ordinances, and other laws. For example, child-abuse laws have been used to bar materials that feature nude children. Similarly, concern about a large number of "porno" stores in certain areas of New York City led the city to prohibit merchants from selling specific hard-core sexual materials in all but a few locations in the five boroughs. Beginning in the fall of 1996, anyone wanting to make money from selling those kinds of videos and books exclusively or predominantly would have to set up shop in very specific and often inaccessible areas.

National Security   The U.S. Supreme Court has consistently ruled that the government has a right to censorship via prior restraint when the **national security** of the United States is at stake. For example, a newspaper can be stopped from disseminating the names of U.S. intelligence agents, or a television station from broadcasting the numbers and names of soldiers heading to the front, or of ships leaving a port when the nation is on a war footing.

In the last few decades, however, the Court has made it clear that the term *national security* should be defined narrowly. In 1971, the federal government tried to justify prior restraint by applying a very broad interpretation of national security. Daniel Ellsberg, a government researcher, investigated U.S. policy in Vietnam and subsequently prepared a detailed Pentagon study on the subject. Ellsberg, who strongly believed that the American public was entitled to an inside look at Pentagon decision-making, secretly copied the entire study (even though the document was stamped "top secret") and handed it over to Neil Sheehan, a reporter for the *New York Times*. Government officials were alarmed when the *New York Times* began publishing excerpts from the study, which became known as the *Pentagon Papers*.

Claiming harm to national security, the Nixon administration got a district court to order the *Times* to halt the series, but the newspaper did not do so, and instead turned to the U.S. Supreme Court. In its argument before the Court, the government claimed that publication of the *Pentagon Papers* had put national security at risk—but that claim proved to be weak and without merit. The Court sub-

national security   one of the circumstances that permits government censorship via prior restraint; an example is the right to restrain speech about military activities during times of war

The Supreme Court ruled that the government could not halt the publication of the *Pentagon Papers* despite the government's claim that publication had put national security at risk.

sequently ruled that the government could not stop publication of the *Pentagon Papers*. In the Court's decision, Justice Hugo Black wrote:

> Only a free and unrestrained press can effectively expose deception in government. And paramount among the responsibilities of a free press is the duty to prevent any part of the government from deceiving the people and sending them off to distant lands to die of foreign fevers and foreign shot and shell. In my view, far from deserving condemnation for their courageous reporting, the *New York Times*, the *Washington Post*, and other newspapers should be commended for serving the purpose that the Founding Fathers saw so clearly. In revealing the workings of government that led to the Vietnam War, the newspapers nobly did precisely that which the Founders hoped and trusted they would do ...
>
> (*New York Times* vs. *United States*,
> U.S. Supreme Court, 403 U.S. 713, 1971)

Despite the government's defeat in this case, the Court held that it could conceive of circumstances in which the national security of the United States could override First Amendment guarantees against prior restraint. The ruling thus upheld prior cases in which the Court had held that the government would be within its rights in restraining reports on troop movement and other military activities in wartime, if those reports constituted a "clear and present danger" to U.S. national security.

Military Operations   The regulation and control of media content during times of war has taken place since the Civil War. At times, media personnel have been required to submit their scripts and stories for governmental review before distribution.

During World War I, Congress passed the Espionage Act (1917) and the Sedition Act (1918), which together formalized wartime censorship of the press by preventing "disloyal" publications from being mailed via the U.S. Postal Service. During World War II, the Espionage Act was again put into effect—allowing the government to control broadcasting from 1941 until 1945. During this time, the Office of Censorship had the power to censor international communication at its "absolute discretion." With a staff of more than 10,000 censors, the office routinely examined mail, cables, newspapers, magazines, films, and radio broadcasts. Its operations constituted the most extensive government censorship of the media in U.S. history and one of the most vivid examples of the use of executive emergency powers.

In cases in which the United States is involved in a military operation but has not officially declared war, the government may seek to control access to information, rather than officially censoring that content. When U.S. troops were sent to the Caribbean island of Grenada in 1983, the Pentagon took control of all transportation to and from the island, and refused to transport reporters to the island to cover the conflict. Journalists protested this military news "blackout." In 1989, when U.S. troops were sent to Panama, the Pentagon instituted a system of **pool reporters**—selected members of the media who are present at a news event and share facts, stories, images, and firsthand knowledge of that event with others. Journalists were skeptical about the system, and as it turned out, their skepticism was well founded. Reporters in the press pool were held in a briefing room at a military post, and were given briefings that consisted of little more than history lessons on the relationship between the United States and Panama. As a conse-

pool reporters   selected members of the media who are present at a news event and share facts, stories, images, and firsthand knowledge of that event with others

More than 600 reporters and photographers traveled alongside coalition troops as "embedded journalists" to report on the U.S. invasion of Iraq in March 2003. Some critics worried that the journalists would lose their objectivity as they relied on the troops for their safety, but other observers welcomed increased public access to the battlefield.

embeds   reporters who receive permission from the military to travel with a military unit across the battlefield

unilaterals   reporters who receive permission from the military to travel across the battlefield without military escort

bad tendency   materials that may be restricted because they are distributed in a time of war, domestic unrest, or riot, even though they do not meet the level of clear and present danger

quence, journalists soured on the idea of a specially chosen pool of reporters, and the practice faded.

In the Iraq War that began in 2004, the military allowed **embeds**—reporters who received permission to travel with a military unit across the battlefield. The Defense Department required all embeds to agree not to break military information embargos, not to report on ongoing missions without clearance, and not to reveal deployment levels below large numbers such as troop corps and carrier battle groups. Nevertheless, some news outlets such as CNN and the UK's ITN with embeds pushed the limits of these requirements, and they were periodically threatened with losing the right to have embeds. Despite the restrictions, many of the embeds in Iraq were able to report the battlefield in great detail; one book calls the initial U.S. invasion of Iraq "the most covered war in history."[10] According to one reporter who studied the embed approach, journalists who were embedded in Iraq "experienced a freedom to do their jobs that journalists had not had since the Vietnam War."[11]

Critics have pointed out that a disadvantage of the embeds was the tendency for them to be highly sympathetic to the troops with whom they lived and on whom they depended for survival. These critics argue that self-censorship was sometimes the result. To meet these criticisms, the military allowed other journalists to work as **unilaterals**—to travel through the war zone by themselves.

Clear and Present Danger   The U.S. Supreme Court has long held that speech can be limited before it is distributed if the result of that speech is likely to pose a threat to society. But what determines whether that speech (or media content) poses a threat? The answer has varied over the decades, with more recent Supreme Court decisions making it difficult to restrain speech based on the clear and present danger test.

The earliest justification for imposing prior restraint because of social threats involved the **bad tendency** test. Under this rule, the government could restrain media material if it had any tendency to cause social evil. As you might imagine, this rule has the potential to cover a lot of territory; for example, a speech by a labor organizer that holds even a small chance of creating a disturbance could be open to prior restraint. The bad tendency test was eventually ruled unconstitutionally vague and hasn't been used since the early 1900s.

Taking its place is the **clear and present danger test** set forth by Supreme Court Justice Oliver Wendell Holmes. The difference between the clear and present danger test and the bad tendency test is that Holmes' approach suggests the importance of the social evil being *likely* to happen (not just that it might happen) and that it would happen imminently (that is, soon after the material is released).

The case that Holmes used to put forth his idea would probably not be considered a clear and present danger by today's standard. It centered on two socialists who distributed anti-draft pamphlets during World War I, and who were convicted of violating the Espionage Act of 1917. When the Supreme Court heard their appeal in a 1919 case called *Schenck* vs. *United States*, Holmes wrote for the majority of justices that the socialists could be convicted. Ordinarily, the pamphlets would be protected by the First Amendment, he said. But, Holmes continued, distributing the pamphlets during wartime was similar to the kind of danger created by "crying fire in a crowded theater." His point was that the government has a right to restrict the speech of anyone (or any organization) whose words might clearly cause social harm in particular circumstances. Holmes' comparison of circulating the leaflets to crying fire in a crowded theater was an odd one. He ignored that the prosecution in that case never produced evidence that anybody refused to be drafted directly because of the circulars. His willingness to give broad leeway to such fears, however, influenced courts for decades to come.

Then, in 1957, the Supreme Court in *Yates* vs. *United States* interpreted "clear and present danger" in a narrower, more literal way when it overturned a conspiracy conviction because the danger was too far removed (that is, not imminent and perhaps not even likely). Similarly, in a 1969 case, the Court ruled that even speech by the Ku Klux Klan is protected unless it is specifically directed toward producing imminent lawless action. These cases set a legal precedent: although the government can still impose prior restraint because a media product will likely cause imminent social harm, it's rare to find cases that fit these criteria.

Copyright   When we speak about **copyright**, we mean the legal protection of an author's right to a work. According to the U.S. Constitution, the purpose of copyright is "to promote the progress of science and the useful arts." The framers of the Constitution believed that only if people could profit from their work would they want to create materials that could ultimately benefit the nation as a whole. At the same time, the framers wanted lawmakers to strike a balance between the rights of authors to gain personally from their work, and the right of the society to draw on the information.

The hesitancy of government agencies to stop the press from circulating content does not apply to copyright violations, for two reasons. The first is that authors ought to be able to control how their work—their *intellectual property*—is used. The second is that authors should be *paid fairly* for the use of their work.

The **Copyright Act of 1976** lays out the basic rules as they exist in the United States today. The law, as later modified (in 1978 and again in 1998), recognizes the rights of an individual creator (in any medium) from the time he or she has created a work, and protects a creative work for the lifetime of its author plus seventy years.

As an example, let us say that Hector, an English student, writes a poem. From the moment Hector finishes the poem, he holds an automatic copyright on the poem for his lifetime plus seventy years. He may, if he decides, send the poem to the U.S. Copyright Office to register it for a small fee. Even if he does not do this,

clear and present danger test   as stated by Justice Oliver Wendell Holmes, "expression can be limited by the government when the words are used in such circumstances and are of such a nature as to create a clear and present danger that they will bring about the substantive evils that Congress has a right to prevent"

copyright   the legal protection of an author's right to a work

Copyright Act of 1976   a law that recognizes the rights of an individual creator (in any medium) from the time he or she has created a work, and protects a creative work for the lifetime of that author plus seventy years

however, he is protected as long as he can prove that he wrote the poem before anyone else did. (In order to prove when a work was created, some people mail a copy of the work to themselves and do not open it. The cancellation by the post office serves as proof of the date the material was sent. Let's say that Hector does that with his poem.)

Hector is proud of his poem, and he sends it to his friend Paloma, a former classmate in a summer poetry workshop. Now let's say that Paloma is envious of Hector's poem. She submits the poem to a literary journal as her own, and the journal accepts it, pays her a small honorarium, and publishes it under her name, not Hector's. At this point, Paloma has violated U.S. copyright law, and she can be prosecuted if Hector pursues the case, since she falsely passed herself off as the poem's true author.

But even if Paloma had not lied about the poem's authorship—let's say she was so proud of Hector and his poem that she submitted it to the journal under Hector's name to surprise him—Paloma (and the journal) probably would not be allowed to publish the poem—or even parts of it. Apart from not asking Hector's permission to publish the poem, Paloma has also violated the second proposition of copyright law—that authors must be paid fairly for the use of their works. Sometimes, even a line of a poem or a song may be considered crucial to the work's value. As you can see, Paloma and the editors of the literary journal would have to think hard before they printed all or part of Hector's poem without getting his permission.

The copyright rules for musical compositions are similar to those for poems. If a magazine or website wants to publish selected words or music from a tune by Paul McCartney, it needs the permission of his publisher. Copying parts of copyrighted musical material from someone else who had paid for it is also not legal. For decades, while businesses paid attention to this law, individuals ignored it. Friends would often lend records to their friends so that they could copy them onto tapes or CDs. If recording industry executives minded, they generally didn't make noise about it. One reason might be that the taped copies were not as good in sound quality as the originals. As we will see in Chapter 10, when we discuss the recording industry, their perspective has changed drastically. With the advent of perfect digital copies and the ability to share them over the Internet, recording industry officials are hauling into court people who share and record copyrighted music without the publisher's permission. We will review the pros and cons of this activity in Chapter 10, but here it is relevant to note what those officials have not emphasized: even copying part of a song without permission can make one a copyright violator.

Fair Use

Although Congress has generally supported the right of copyright holders over the desire of individuals to copy their material, one exception involves writers or academics who want to quote from copyrighted material in order to carry out critical analyses. A poet, artist, or novelist might charge an exorbitant rate for use of their works that would make it impossible for a scholar to share critical responses to it. To get around these problems, the law provides **fair use regulations.** Generally, they indicate that a person or company may use small portions of a copyrighted work without asking permission. Nonprofit, educational purposes have more leeway than for-profit ventures.

Another important consideration in fair use decisions is the commercial damage that copying may cause to the copyright material. A third criterion in favor of fair use is the transformative use of the copyrighted material. A use is **transformative** when it presents the work in a way that adds interpretations to it so that some

fair use regulations provisions under which a person or company may use small portions of a copyrighted work without asking permission

transformative when use of copyrighted material presents the work in a way that adds interpretation to it so that some people might see it in a new light

people might see it in a new light. So, for example, a magazine essay on John Updike's novels that quotes various passages from them to show how his views of suburbia have changed over time would likely be considered fair use. By these criteria, when scholarly critiques of popular culture quote from copyright materials to make their points, that is almost surely fair use.

Despite fair use regulations, college copy shops must contact publishers and get permission when they want to use entire articles in "bulk packs" for classes. And you may not know it, but photocopying a work for your own pleasure is normally not fair use. One curious exception to fair use guidelines relates to the videotape recorder. The Supreme Court ruled in 1984 that homeowners may record copyrighted TV shows for their personal, noncommercial use. A majority of the justices reasoned that taping was legal because people use the tapes for *time shifting*—that is, taping for later viewing what they would have watched anyway.

Today, time shifting is a way of life for many people who record TV shows and movies on digital video recorders (DVRs). Legal though the practice is, it has brought interesting headaches to media companies and their advertisers, as people view the programs they copied but not the commercials that support them. Even greater headaches have come with the rise of digital technologies that make it simple for people to copy all sorts of copyrighted materials (including music and movies) in circumstances that do not fall within the fair use rules. Some copyright owners call these behaviors "piracy" and demand that audiences stop doing it. The activities raise important legal and ethical issues that we will explore in chapters to come.

Parodies

A **parody** is a work that imitates another work for laughs in a way that comments *on the original work* in one way or another. It is perfectly legal to create parodies of copyrighted material. A number of major court cases have ruled that when artists add new perspective to a copyrighted material, in the process critiquing it and encouraging people to see it in different ways, that is fully legal. Supreme Court Justice David Souter even suggested that parodies have stronger rights than other kinds of fair use material in that the creator of a parody "may quite legitimately aim at destroying [the original] commercially as well as artistically."[12] The problem with parodies from a legal standpoint, though, is that the line between them and copyright violation is sometimes hard to figure out.

For one thing, not all comically altered versions of songs are fair use. That may explain why Weird Al Yankovic is so conservative when it comes to using his musical parodies. Weird Al is a performer who has based his professional career on writing and recording parodies of popular songs. Pieces such as *My Bologna* (a take on the Knack's *My Sharona*), *I Love Rocky Road*, *Another One Rides the Bus*, *Eat It*, *Like a Surgeon*, *I Think I'm a Clone Now*, and *Smells Like Nirvana*, have given him long-term popularity with a huge number of fans around the globe. Yet Weird Al is actually pretty conservative regarding his parodic creations. His lawyers may have pointed out to him that while his lyrics are funny, they don't really criticize the originals; nor does his musical take on the

parody a work that imitates another work for laughs in a way that comments on the original work in one way or another

Weird Al Yankovic has built a career on writing and recording parodies of popular songs.

101

originals vary much from them. Perhaps as a result, Weird Al notes he always seeks permission from the artists and writers of the songs before he puts his spin on them. "The parodies are all in good fun and good taste," he says, "and most of the artists normally take it that way. I prefer to have them on my team and I like to sleep well at night."[13]

Education   Prior restraint in education—especially with regard to primary and secondary education—involves newspapers created by students as part of their schoolwork. In 1988, in the case *of Hazelwood School District* vs. *Kuhlmeier*, the Supreme Court held that a principal's decision to remove two articles from a high school newspaper—one describing students' experiences with pregnancy, and another discussing the impact of divorce on students at the school—was perfectly legal. The newspaper was written and edited by a journalism class, as part of the school's curriculum.

Following school policy, the teacher in charge of the student newspaper submitted page proofs to the school's principal, who objected to the pregnancy story because the pregnant students, although not named, could easily have been identified from the text, and because he believed that the article's references to sexual activity and birth control were inappropriate for some of the younger students.

The Court held that, "A school need not tolerate student speech that is inconsistent with its basic educational mission, even though the government could not censor similar speech outside the school." The Court reasoned that because the school newspaper was part of the school's educational curriculum (it was open only to students taking journalism courses), it was not entitled to First Amendment protection. The wording seems to grant freedom of the press to school newspapers that are not part of the curriculum; college newspapers would seem to fit into this protected category.

commercial speech
messages that are designed to sell you products or services

Commercial Speech   Yet another area in which the courts have allowed prior restraint over mass media content is what the legal profession calls **commercial speech**. Advertisements make up a large part of this domain, but it also includes all kinds of messages that are designed to sell you products or services, from straightforward TV and magazine ads, to Internet pop-up ads, to phone calls that try to convince you to buy stocks. Over the decades, the U.S. Supreme Court has made clear its view that the Constitution allows the government a level of control over commercial speech that it does not tolerate when noncommercial content is involved.

Sometimes, government officials don't know of a false ad until it is released, but because of their prior-restraint powers they can immediately stop an ad that is false and deceptive. In a classic case, in the 1970s the Campbell Soup Company's ad agency put marbles in the bottom of a bowl of soup to emphasize the soup's chunkiness by making it look as if it contained many big pieces of meat and vegetables. Responding to complaints from competitors, the Federal Trade Commission (FTC), which oversees much of the commercial speech domain, forced the company to withdraw the ad. In the 2000s, the FTC has stopped what it considers to be false or unsubstantiated claims by more than sixty dietary-supplement and weight-loss advertisers across all kinds of media. By its own account, it has not caught all the offenders. The difficulty with enforcement, according to one Commissioner, is that there is so much of it that the agency cannot effectively police this area of advertising by itself. She urged the industry and media firms to help.[14]

Prior Restraint and Student Journalism on the Web

CRITICAL CONSUMER

Freedom of the press, issues of security and concerns about school image are bumping into one another as more and more high school journalism classes publish their papers online. School administrators that have allowed their students a lot of leeway when producing paper-bound news work are having second thoughts when the students turn to cyber-journalism.

Most of the restrictions have to do with publishing the last names of students, or their names next to their photos. Administrators worry that the wide reach of the Internet means that some stalkers may collect the names and photos with the intention to do harm. They also argue that the Federal Education Records Privacy Act, enacted in 1974, limits what Web newspapers may reveal about students online because of the Internet's reach far beyond the school.

Some champions of student journalism worry that school administrators will go beyond concerns about privacy to limit what Web newspapers can write about. Administrators are quite aware that Web editions make student views available to alumni and legislators who live away from the community. Worried about their image and the politics of funding, administrators may use their right to exercise prior restraint as a way to keep students' critical comments from being widely circulated.

Such was the case at California's La Serna High School, where in 2006, student journalists were banned from pub-

lishing the June issue of their newspaper *The Freelancer*. According to students, the ban was as a form of retribution for their May issue, which included a feature on students' attitudes toward sex. Some students considered pursuing legal action under a California law protecting student journalists, yet nothing has been filed to date. In a similar vein, during the spring of 2007, the student newspaper at St Francis High School in Minnesota was taken offline after it published a photo of a student destroying an American flag. Administrators said they feared the photo might be offensive to the veterans in the area. By the end of the summer, the administration still had not backed down.

Gene Policinski, vice president and executive director of the First Amendment Center, criticizes cases like these that overlook students' right to "exercise control rooted in good journalistic considerations." Instead, he argues, we should "consider the benefits of a healthy student press, staffed by young, educated journalists and advised by trained professional educators."

Sources: Dave Orrick, "Outcome of Minnesota Censorship Case Remains Unclear," National Scholastic Press Association, accessed 3/6/08, www.studentpress.org/nspa; Lisa Napoli, "Schools' Online Publications Face Curbs of their Own," *New York Times* Online, May 7, 1999, www.nytimes.com; Gene Policinski, "Why We Need a Strong Student Press," American Press Institute, February 12, 2007. Online. www.americanpressinstitute.org

As the Jack in the Box case described earlier suggested, whether or not an ad is deceptive will sometimes be a matter of strong argument. Children's advocacy groups have claimed that ads aimed at children under the ages of eight or twelve are by their very nature deceptive, since kids have a hard time understanding that they are being manipulated. Following that reasoning, in 2006 two advocacy organizations, the Center for Science in the Public Interest and the Campaign for a Commercial-Free Childhood, as well as two Massachusetts parents, announced plans to sue the Kellogg Company and Viacom, which owns Nickelodeon. They accused both companies of "unfair and deceptive" junk-food marketing to children under the age of eight, and they wanted the state government to stop them from releasing commercials with certain messages. Not surprisingly, the companies argued that they were doing nothing illegal.[15]

Regulating Information After Distribution

With respect to some areas of content, the courts have stated that authorities must wait until after distribution to press charges of illegal activity. Unlike regulating content before distribution, which usually involves a conflict between the government and the media, regulating content after it has already been distributed—through libel and privacy law, for example—often involves a conflict between an individual and the media.

defamation a highly disreputable or false statement about a living person or an organization that causes injury to the reputation that a substantial group of people hold for that person or entity

libel written communication that is considered harmful to a person's reputation

libel per se words and expressions that are always considered libelous

libel per quod words, expressions, and statements that, at face value, seem to be innocent and not injurious, but may be considered libelous in their actual contexts

slander spoken communication that is considered harmful to a person's reputation

Defamation, Libel, and Slander A **defamation** is a highly disreputable or false statement about a living person or an organization that causes injury to the reputation that a substantial group of people hold for that person or entity. *Libel* and *slander* are two types of defamation.

Libel is written communication that is considered harmful to a person's reputation. Some words and expressions are always considered libelous—false printed accusations that an individual is "incompetent," or that an organization is "disreputable," for example, are considered by courts as statements that, on their face, defame and are called **libel per se** (see Table 3.1 for a list of "red flag" words and expressions that courts have generally considered libelous per se).

Some words, expressions and statements that seem, on their face, to be innocent and not injurious may be considered **libel per quod** in their actual contexts. In other words, statements that aren't defamatory on their own may become libelous when one knows other facts. For example, saying that Bradley is married to Marisol doesn't sound libelous; but if you know that Bradley is married to Nadia, being married to Marisol would make him a bigamist. And that statement *is* libelous. Related to libel is **slander**, or spoken communication that is considered harmful to a person's reputation.

Although libel and slander are both forms of defamation, they are controlled by different laws. What is important to remember is that when either libel or slander (or both) occurs, a person's reputation and character are damaged in some way. An example everyone agrees is libel is a former entry in the web encyclopedia Wikipedia about the retired newspaper editor John Siegenthaler Sr. The elderly Siegenthaler is a hero to those who know his role in encouraging and writing about Civil Rights in the 1960s. Yet someone added horrible statements to his biography on the collectively created web encyclopedia Wikipedia. The passage claimed

Table 3.1 Libel per se

Listed below are some "red flag" words and expressions that courts have generally considered libelous per se:

ignoramus	rascal	amoral
bankrupt	slacker	unprofessional
thief	sneaky	incompetent
cheat	unethical	illegitimate
traitor	unprincipled	hypocritical
drunk	corrupt	cheating
blockhead		

that Siegenthaler was connected to the assassinations of both Robert Kennedy and President John F. Kennedy. When Siegenthaler protested the libelous entry, it was pulled from Wikipedia, as were echoes of the claims that had appeared on the websites http://www.reference.com and http://www.answers.com. Later, the author of the malicious entries came forward, apologized profusely and said he was playing a joke on what he thought was a prankster website. Clearly, by then, the reputation-damaging contentions had spread through the Web. Siegenthaler didn't sue the person for libel, though he certainly could have done so.

It is also important to recognize that there are two categories of libel plaintiffs: public figures and private persons. A **public figure** may be an elected or appointed official (a politician) or someone who has stepped (willingly or unwillingly) into a public controversy (for example, movie stars and TV stars, famous athletes, or other persons who draw attention to themselves). A **private person** may be well known in the community, but he or she has no authority or responsibility for the conduct of governmental affairs and has not thrust himself or herself into the middle of an important public controversy. Because the claim about Siegenthaler related to a time in his life when he did put himself in the midst of an important public controversy, he might well be considered a public figure with respect to the law.

In 1964, the case of *New York Times* vs. *Sullivan* profoundly altered libel law, and set legal precedent that is still in effect today. On March 29, 1960, a full-page advertisement titled "Heed Their Rising Voices," was placed in the *New York Times* by the Committee to Defend Martin Luther King, Jr. and the Struggle for Freedom in the South. The ad criticized police and public officials in several cities for tactics used to disrupt the civil rights movement and sought contributions to post bail for the Reverend Martin Luther King, Jr., and other movement leaders. The accusations made in the advertisement were true for the most part, but the copy contained several rather minor factual errors. L. B. Sullivan, police commissioner in Montgomery, Alabama, sued the *New York Times* for libel, claiming that the ad had defamed him indirectly. He won $500,000 for damages in the state courts of Alabama, but the U.S. Supreme Court overturned the damage award, reasoning that Alabama's libel laws violated the *New York Times'* First Amendment rights.

In issuing its opinion, the Supreme Court said that the U.S. Constitution (First and Fourteenth Amendments) protected false and defamatory statements made about public officials only *if* the false statements were not published with *actual malice*. The Court defined **actual malice** as reckless disregard for truth or knowledge of falsity. Note that actual malice considers a defendant's attitude toward truth, not the defendant's attitude toward the plaintiff. This differs from **simple malice**, which means hatred or ill will toward another person. By his own admission that he concocted the anti-Siegenthaler story, the blogger might be said to have written his piece with actual malice. Yet his claim that he thought the site was for pranksters (and therefore not believable) might make it difficult to have the "reckless" charge stick. If Siegenthaler had sued him for libel, the particulars would be up to a court to decide.

In general, because actual malice is difficult to prove, this ruling makes it difficult for a public official to win a libel suit. Additionally, the Supreme Court has broadened the actual malice protection to include public figures as well as public officials. The Court's reasoning is simple: the actual malice test sets a high bar, but it does so to protect the First Amendment rights of the media. At the same time, however, it allows media outlets to pursue legitimate news stories without the constant fear of being sued by the subjects of news stories. In the end, concern for the First Amendment takes precedence over libel laws as they relate to media.

public figure a person who is an elected or appointed official (a politician), or someone who has stepped (willingly or unwillingly) into a public controversy

private person an individual who may be well known in the community, but who has no authority or responsibility for the conduct of government affairs and has not thrust himself or herself into the middle of an important public controversy

actual malice reckless disregard for truth or knowledge of falsity

simple malice hatred or ill will toward another person

U.S. Libel Laws Meet the Internet

While countries around the world have enacted legislation to protect their citizens against libel, or defamatory written language, the United States is widely known for its press-friendly libel laws. Often, contentious language is protected under the free speech and press provisions of the First Amendment. As legal writer Steven Pressman notes, "It is almost impossible for a writer to be found guilty of libel if the writing deals with opinions rather than facts." What's more, the burden of proof in U.S. libel law requires that the person bringing the suit must prove that he or she has been libeled. This can be contrasted with libel laws of many other countries, where the defendant must show that what is written is truthful or justified.

Until recently, as legal expert Wendy Tannenbaum points out, U.S. libel laws enabled publishers to believe "that if they complied with U.S. laws, their liability would be low." Yet as media content is increasingly being published on the Web, the libel laws of the digital era are being questioned. In some cases, charges to U.S. journalists have been brought to foreign courts whose libel laws are much more stringent.

Commenting on the status of libel regulation in a new media environment, *CNET* reporters noted that, "In the United States, one of the most aggressive protectors of free speech in the world, Internet libel law is in flux."

Sources: Declan McCullagh and Evan Hansen, "Libel Without Frontiers Shakes the Net," *CNET*, December 11, 2002, accessed 3/6/08, http://news.com.com/Libel+without+frontiers+shakes+the+Net/2100-1023_3-976988.html; and Steven Pressman, "An Unfettered Press: Libel Law in the United States," International Information Programs, accessed 3/6/08, http://usinfo.state.gov/products/pubs/press/press08.htm; and Wendy Tannenbaum, "Questions of Internet jurisdiction spin web of confusion for online Publishers," *The News Media & the Law*, Winter 2003 (Vol. 27, No. 1), Page 33. Libel & Privacy.

Supreme Court decisions have also made it hard for a person who is neither a public figure nor an official to sue a media firm for libel. The Court has ruled that the First Amendment requires proof of **simple negligence**—lack of reasonable care—even when private persons sue the mass media for libel.

simple negligence lack of reasonable care

In order to win a libel suit, a plaintiff—whether a public figure or a private person—must prove that five activities occurred. The jury must be convinced that all of these five elements apply to the case in order for the First Amendment to be set aside in favor of an individual's right.

1   The defamatory statements were published.

publication in libel law, a process that occurs when one person—in addition to the plaintiff and the defendant—sees or hears the defamatory material in question

The term *publication* does not necessarily mean printing, as in a magazine or a newspaper. For the purposes of a court deciding a libel case, **publication** occurs when one person—in addition to the plaintiff and the defendant—sees or hears the defamatory material. You can "publish" something by making and circulating a video on the Internet, for example.

2   The defamatory statements identified the plaintiff (although not necessarily by name).

Some courts have ruled that it only takes one person to recognize and identify the plaintiff from a likeness, a description, or a story in context; the plaintiff does *not* have to be identified by name. Say, for example, that Joachim creates a DVD in which a character who looks and acts like his next-door neighbor is depicted as a person who regularly steals from Joachim's garage.

3   The defamatory statements harmed the plaintiff.

A plaintiff in a libel case can prove that he or she suffered **harm** by showing that the defamatory statements led to loss of income (actual financial loss) or physical and emotional discomfort. Continuing with our example, say that Joachim distributes a hundred DVD copies of the video throughout the neighborhood. He also posts the DVD on the "bulletin board" area of the local Neighborhood Club's website. His neighbor shows the court that people in the area have continually asked him if he is a thief. He argues that his local business has suffered because of the video. The man's lawyer brings forward the man's psychiatrist, who attests that the man's marriage and family life have suffered because of the stress Joachim's video has caused.

4   The defendant was at fault.

In order to win a libel suit, a plaintiff must prove **fault**, but how this is proven can vary from case to case. Depending upon the circumstances, fault may be established according to three factors: (1) who has brought the lawsuit, (2) the nature of the lawsuit (what it is about), and (3) the applicable state laws.

5   The defamatory statements were false.

Proving **falsity** in a libel case is a question of the burden of proof—who has to prove that the defamatory statements are false? If the plaintiff is a public figure, he or she must prove that the defamatory statements are not truthful or accurate. If the plaintiff is a private person, however, he or she must prove that defamatory statements are untrue only if those statements are regarding a matter of public concern. If the defamatory statements are of a private nature, then the burden of proof shifts to the defendant, who must prove that the defamatory statements are indeed true. In our example, then, it is Joachim who must prove that what his video depicts about his neighbor his true.

Defenses to libel come in three forms: truth, privilege, and fair comment and criticism.

1   Truth

Claiming and subsequently proving the **truth** of the defamatory statement in question is an absolute defense against a charge of libel. But how do you prove that the statement is true? The evidence presented in court must be both direct and explicit; that is, it must go to the heart of the libelous charge. Additionally, it must be substantial truth; the statement doesn't have to be entirely true, but the part that "stings" must be true. The real test is whether the proven truth leaves a different impression of the plaintiff in the minds of the jury than that left by the falsehood. Because truth can be so very hard to prove, this defense is rarely used.

2   Privilege

U.S. courts have held that the public's right to know takes precedence over a person's right to preserve his or her reputation. However, certain materials such as grand jury indictments, arrest warrants, and judicial proceedings are considered **privileged**. If a defendant claims, and subsequently proves, that the defamatory statement in question was privileged (and thus is not public), he or she has presented a valid defense against charges of libel. Only certain professions (doctors, lawyers, psychologists), or individuals (chiefly a spouse) can maintain that privilege; if any nonprivileged third party was part of the communication, the privilege is broken.

---

harm   in libel law, loss of income (actual financial loss) or physical and emotional discomfort

fault   in libel law, a condition that may be established according to who has brought the lawsuit, the nature of the lawsuit, and the applicable state laws

falsity   in libel law, untruth; one party or the other (either the defendant or the plaintiff) must prove that the defamatory statements are either true or untrue, and who must bear this burden of proof depends on whether the plaintiff is a public figure or a private person

truth   an absolute defense against charges of libel; to prove that a statement is true, and therefore not defamatory, the evidence presented in court must be both direct and explicit, and the statement must be substantial truth—it doesn't have to be entirely true, but the part that "stings" must be true

privilege   a defense to libel that holds that while the public's right to know takes precedence over a person's right to preserve his or her reputation, certain professions (doctors, lawyers, psychologists), or individuals (chiefly a spouse) can maintain privilege; if any nonprivileged third party was part of the communication, the privilege is broken

fair comment and criticism a defense against libel in which the defendant claims, and proves, that the defamatory statement in question was part of the defendant's fair comment and criticism of a public figure who has thrust himself or herself into the public eye or is at the center of public attention; this defense is good only when it applies to an opinion, not to an assertion of a fact

3   Fair comment and criticism

The third defense is claiming, and proving, that the defamatory statement in question was part of the defendant's **fair comment and criticism** of a public figure who has thrust himself or herself into the public eye or is at the center of public attention. This defense is good only when it applies to an opinion, not an assertion of a fact. There's a world of difference between saying "I think he's a crook," and saying, "He's a crook."

The FCC and Content Regulation   Despite its concern for a protected press, the Supreme Court has accepted the idea that the Federal Communications Commission can regulate broadcast content. In general, the basic principles of freedom of speech and of the press apply in electronic media just as they do in print media. From the early days of broadcasting, Congress has viewed broadcasting as different from print because the available wavelengths for radio and TV signals were limited (or scarce). According to Congress, this *wavelength scarcity* justified the creation of an agency such as the FCC to oversee the distribution of frequencies and to ensure competition of ideas over the airwaves.

Congress' notion of wavelength scarcity applies to broadcasting only—not to cable or satellite television. That has sometimes put Congress and the FCC in the strange position of announcing content regulations for broadcasters that do not apply to the hundreds of cable and satellite channels that a large proportion of U.S. homes receive. For example, in 1996 the FCC announced that each week broadcast TV stations must air three hours of educational television programs aimed at children aged sixteen and under that serve their "intellectual, cognitive, social, and emotional needs." Broadcasters complain that it is unfair that they alone, not cable or satellite networks—are required to spend the time and money on such programming. They also say that the requirement is outdated in an era of specialized children's channels such as Nickelodeon and the Disney Channel. Supporters of the rule argue that broadcasters should have greater obligations than other media firms because broadcasters are using valuable public airwaves that reach virtually everyone. The rule's supporters also claim that broadcasters do not always mount programs that match the spirit of the FCC rule. In the case of Univision, the country's largest Spanish-language broadcaster, the Commission agreed. In 2007 it forced Univision to pay a record $24 million fine for airing telenovelas (soap operas) with children during the time it claimed it was fulfilling the children's educational requirement from 2004 to 2006.[16]

equal time rule an order of Congress that requires broadcasters to provide equal amounts of time during comparable parts of the day to all legally qualified candidates for political office

Fairness doctrine a rule implemented by the FCC in the late 1940s that requires broadcasters to provide some degree of balance in the presentation of controversial issues

A much older requirement of broadcasters, one originating from Congress but enforced by the FCC, is the **equal time rule**. It requires broadcasters to provide equal amounts of time during comparable parts of the day to all legally qualified candidates for political office. Carrying this idea further, in the late 1940s the FCC stated the **Fairness doctrine**. This rule required broadcasters to provide some degree of balance in the presentation of a controversial issue. Say, for example, that a broadcaster aired an editorial supporting one side of a controversial issue—for example, the closing of an expensive "magnet" school in a city. The broadcaster would then have to make time (in a new story or by providing or selling the group advertising) for those who disagree.

As you might imagine, many broadcasters disliked the Fairness doctrine because it threatened to take away their control over "their" airwaves. By the mid-1980s, they argued to the FCC that new electronic media—for example, cable—were creating so many electronic choices that the requirement should be abolished. In the deregulatory climate of the day, the FCC suspended (though it didn't repeal) the Fairness doctrine. Even so, because the Fairness doctrine was not repealed, it

Self-regulation or Market Pressure: the Imus Case

IS IT ETHICAL?

You may recall the controversy that surrounded radio talk-show host Don Imus in 2007, after he made disparaging comments about the Rutgers University women's basketball team. A week after the incident, MSNBC announced that it would drop its telecast of his *Imus in the Morning* radio program. The following day, CBS made public its decision to fire Imus.

Civil rights activist Reverend Jesse Jackson declared CBS's dismissal of Imus as "a victory for public decency." He continued, "No one should use the public airwaves to transmit racial or sexual degradation." Jackson's sentiment reflected a sense of faith in the self-regulatory powers of the media.

Yet not everyone was convinced that this self-regulation stemmed from the broadcasters' ethical consciousness. Instead, some believed that the broadcasters' decision to cancel Imus's radio program was prompted by disapproval from marketers.

At least eight advertisers—among them corporate behemoths like General Motors, Sprint Nextel, GlaxoSmithKline, Procter & Gamble, and American Express—immediately pulled their sponsorship of the show. As a representative from Sprint explained, "We do not want our advertising associated with content which we, our customers and the public find offensive."

Radio talk-show host Don Imus (left) speaks with Rev. Al Sharpton (right) during Sharpton's radio show, in New York, where Imus apologized for insensitive remarks he made about the Rutgers women's basketball team.

Andrew Hampp, a columnist for trade magazine *Advertising Age*, argued that the loss of ad dollars was a driving force behind CBS and MSNBC's dismissal of Imus. In fact, MSNBC lost roughly $2.5 million in ad revenue. "If the whole Imus debacle tells us anything," Hampp noted, "it is that today the marketers are truly the reigning power in the fragmented media world."

While the upshot of the Imus controversy remains the same, this case raises important questions about who really controls media content—and for what reasons.

Sources: Andrew Hampp, "Imus Mess Makes Arbiters of Advertisers," *Advertising Age*, April 16, 2007, accessed 3/6/08, www.adage.com; "CBS Fires Don Imus Over Racial Slur," *CBS News*, April 12, 2007, accessed 3/6/08, http://www.cbsnews.com/stories/2007/04/12/national/main2675273.shtml

could someday be revived by a more activist commission, and the equal time rule still remains in effect.

Privacy **Privacy**—the right to be protected from unwanted intrusions or disclosures—is a broad area of the law when it comes to media industries. Almost every state recognizes some right of privacy, either by statute or under common law. Most state laws attempt to strike a balance between the individual's right to privacy and the public interest in freedom of the press. However, these rights often clash.

Invasion of privacy is considered a **personal tort,** or behavior that harms another individual. The law is aimed at protecting the individual's feelings. Courts often describe these feelings as "reasonable expectations of privacy." Only a person can claim a right of privacy; corporations, organizations, and other entities cannot.

Public figures have a limited claim to a right of privacy. Past and present government officials, political candidates, entertainers and sports figures are generally

privacy the right to be protected from unwanted intrusions or disclosures

personal tort behavior that harms another individual

considered to be public figures. They are said to have voluntarily exposed themselves to scrutiny and to have waived their right of privacy, at least regarding matters that might have an impact on their ability to perform their public duties.

Although private individuals can usually claim the right to be left alone, that right is not absolute. For example, if a person who is normally not considered a public figure is thrust into the spotlight because of her participation in a newsworthy event, her claims of a right of privacy may be limited.

As the law now stands, there are four areas of privacy:

- False light
- Appropriation
- Intrusion
- Public disclosure

Let's look at them one at a time.

False Light

false light   invading a person's privacy by implying something untrue about him or her

Publishing material that puts an individual in a **false light** has been considered an invasion of personal privacy by the courts. Suppose a TV station is creating a news report about the growing use of heroin by middle-class residents of your city. To illustrate the idea that "average" citizens are increasingly involved in the problem, the producer films footage of people walking down the streets of the city; you happen to be one of them. Turning on the local news one evening, you see a report that shows you quite clearly walking down the street just as the narrator notes that average residents are becoming hooked on heroin. You are angry that the station has placed you in a "false light" and invaded your privacy when you walked down the street. You consider suing the station on the grounds that the story made it appear that you were a heroin user.

distortion   a type of false light privacy invasion that involves the arrangement of materials or photographs to give a false impression

embellishment   a type of false light privacy invasion in which false material added to a story places someone in a false light

fictionalization   a type of false light privacy invasion in which reference is made to real people or to thinly disguised characters that clearly represent real people in supposedly untrue stories

False light can take place in a number of ways. The example above constitutes **distortion**, which is the arrangement of materials or photographs to give a false impression. Another type of false light is **embellishment**, in which false material added to a story places someone in a false light. Yet a third way is **fictionalization**, which involves making reference to real people or presenting thinly disguised characters that clearly represent real people in supposedly untrue stories.

The courts do not particularly favor false light cases because very often they conflict with freedom of speech. The most important case, *Time* vs. *Hill*, decided by the U.S. Supreme Court in 1967, set out the modern standard for false light privacy cases. According to the Supreme Court's decision in that case, a plaintiff is required to prove "by clear and convincing evidence" that the defendant knew of the statement's falsity or acted in reckless disregard of its truth or falsity. Using this standard, it would be difficult for a person who is deemed a public figure—an NBA basketball player who makes extra money by licensing his name on products—to win a case. The "public nature" of the athlete's activities gives writers and broadcasters considerable leeway to report on his or her affairs.

Appropriation

appropriation   an invasion of privacy that takes the form of the unauthorized use of a person's name or likeness in an advertisement, poster, public relations promotion, or other commercial context

Appropriation means the unauthorized use of a person's name or likeness in an advertisement, poster, public relations promotion, or other commercial context. It is illegal because of the harm it causes. The law protects individuals from being exploited by others for their exclusive benefit. As with libel, a person's entire name need not be used. If the person could reasonably be identified, the appropriation claim will most likely be valid.

Courts have continuously interpreted the law in a way that enables news organizations to use a person's name or likeness when publishing a newsworthy story.

They have even extended this privilege when the news organization is a private, for-profit organization that derives income from advertising. However, almost all courts have held that the use of the name and likeness must be newsworthy. The issue came up, for example, with regard to a famous photograph of a sailor kissing a nurse in Times Square. A U.S. district court held that the initial publication of the photograph in *Life* magazine was appropriate to illustrate a newsworthy event, but that *Time*'s subsequent sale of reprints to the public without permission from the man and woman pictured was not.

Courts have been quite clear that the exception allowing the use of such images is limited to newsworthy purposes. They have explicitly denied exceptions even for charitable or informational purposes. For example, courts have ruled that photographs of living cancer survivors could not be exhibited for public informational and educational purposes without the individuals' prior written consent.

Public Disclosure

The term **public disclosure** refers to truthful information concerning the private life of a person, that a media source reveals, that would both be highly offensive to a reasonable person, and is not of legitimate public concern. Courts have ruled that this is an invasion of privacy. For example, revealing private, sensational facts about a person's sexual activity, health or economic status can constitute an invasion of privacy under the law of public disclosure.

How the information was obtained and its *newsworthiness* often determine liability in cases of public disclosure. If a journalistic organization obtains information unlawfully—whether or not the information is truthful—the organization may be held liable for invasion of privacy under the rules of public disclosure. Additionally, courts may consider several factors in determining whether

public disclosure truthful information concerning the private life of a person, revealed by a media source, that would be highly offensive to a reasonable person and is not of legitimate public concern is considered to be an invasion of privacy

In Alfred Eisenstaedt's famous photograph, a sailor kisses a nurse in New York's Times Square on August 14, 1945, the day of victory over Japan, which marked the end of World War II.

information that is published is newsworthy, including the social value of the facts published, how deeply the article intruded into the person's private affairs, and the extent to which the person voluntarily assumed a position of public notoriety. For example, in a 1951 case, a woman who had been involved in a car accident sued a reporter who revealed that she was living with a man who was not her spouse. That fact was not pertinent to the story, which was otherwise newsworthy, and the reporter was held liable.

More recently, however, courts have made it difficult to win a public disclosure suit against journalists. Just as concerns for the First Amendment have given mass media firms a great deal of latitude when it comes to libel and appropriation, First Amendment considerations have tended to grant media businesses the right to reveal information about individuals. Consider a Florida rape victim's 1989 case against the *Florida Star,* a Jacksonville newspaper. A reporter-trainee for the paper had learned the full name of a rape victim whose initials were in a county sheriff's report. The *Star* published the name, even though a Florida law prohibited an "instrument of mass communication" from making public the identity of rape victims. The victim sued the paper for emotional distress and won. However, the U.S. Supreme Court reversed the decision. The justices said that the government is allowed to punish a paper for publishing lawfully obtained, truthful information only if the government can show that the punishment is "narrowly tailored to a state interest of the highest order."

Intrusion

intrusion an invasion of privacy that takes place when a person or organization intentionally invades a person's solitude, private area, or affairs

Intrusion, the fourth area of invasion of privacy, takes place when a person or organization intentionally invades a person's solitude, private area, or affairs. The invasion can be physical (for example, sneaking into a person's office) or nonphysical (such as putting an electronic listening device outside the office but in a position to hear what is going on inside). Intrusion claims against the media often center on some aspect of the news-gathering process. This tort may involve trespassing or the wrongful use of tape recorders, cameras or other intrusive equipment.

Defenses against allegations of privacy invasion are fairly straightforward. If a person *consents*, there can be no invasion of privacy. However, the reporter should be sure that the subject has not only consented to be interviewed, but also consented to having the interview or photographs published or aired. When minors or legally incompetent people are involved, the consent of a parent or guardian may be necessary. A written release is essential for the use of pictures or private information in advertising or other commercial contexts.

Truth can be a defense, but only in false light cases. A litigant claiming false light invasion of privacy who is involved in a matter of public interest must prove that the media intentionally or recklessly made erroneous statements about him or her. However, truth is not a defense to a claim based on publication of private facts.

If the public has a legitimate interest in the story as it was reported, *newsworthiness* can be a defense to the charge of invasion of privacy. But if a report that is of legitimate public interest includes irrelevant private information, publication of those private facts may warrant legal action.

Privacy in the Digital Age

Concern about media organizations and government agencies searching for personal details has grown with the enormous rise in the use of computers to collect and combine data about individuals from many sources. Responding to these fears, Congress has passed laws that limit the ability of companies and government agencies to use and share data without the knowledge of the individuals involved.

Web User Beware

Keeping control over important personal information can be tricky in today's digital world, and laws don't always help. Many people know that federal law prohibits their doctors and health firms from releasing information about them to marketers who want to send them advertisements. They may not know, however, that this law covers only a small segment of companies that can learn about their health information. And Madison Avenue really wants to know what is in your medicine cabinet. Drug companies spend as much as $18 billion annually on advertising and education, according to a 2005 report in the *Journal of the American Medical Association*. They'd just love to find more effective ways to target customers. What better way than to gain up-to-the-minute access to everyone's health records?

The idea of a central repository of health information that can help health professionals has great appeal. So does the idea of making it easier for us to see our medical records. The devil, however, is in the details. On sites such as WebMD and Revolution Health, setting up a personal health record is "free"—supported by advertising. This should raise alarm bells, because Madison Avenue has a long tradition of covertly trolling for consumers' personal information for marketing.

Every day, people unwittingly disclose personal health information when they use coupons for prescription drugs, subscribe to disease-based magazines, register at websites or complete surveys seeking personal information. Often, the real motive behind these activities is to compile profiles on individuals and households. Check the diabetes box, and your health condition appears permanently in the marketer's file. List sellers offer contact information on millions of individuals by disease profile. Companies that buy these names offer magazine subscriptions, raise funds and sell medical products and services.

Commercial repositories of personal health records increase the stakes for consumer privacy several-fold. Companies that charge consumers little or nothing for storing those records will profit by allowing marketers to use far more information about consumers than traditional lists could. Existing regulations do not cover personal health-record firms unless they also are healthcare providers or health plans. Once a consumer consents to the disclosure of medical records to a personal health records company, those records lose the protection of federal health privacy rules.

Companies may say that they will not share individually identifiable information with advertisers or others without consent. Unfortunately, it is too easy for a consumer to unknowingly give consent. A pre-checked box may be unobtrusively included on a Web page that a consumer must click through. Marketers expect that most consumers will not notice or bother to uncheck the box.

Companies may claim to respect your privacy. For example, a personal health records site may sell marketers the ability to advertise to diabetics, and you may be one of them. When you go to your personal record, you will see ads, discount coupons and articles targeted to diabetics. The marketers who pay for them will not know your name—or they won't until you make a common mistake. To obtain your identity, advertisers will try to entice you to click onto their websites. Once there, your personal information may end up anywhere. One click can result in an irretrievable revelation of your medical status to another company that profits by reselling personal data.

No administrative or legislative responses are on the horizon. Consumers must fend for themselves. Read the labels: Who is funding these services and who profits? And be careful in giving out information about yourself.

Sources: Joseph Turow, Robert Gellman and Judith Turow, "Why Marketers Want Inside Your Medical Cabinet," *San Francisco Chronicle*, March 5, 2007, p. D9; and Joseph Turow, Robert Gellman and Judith Turow, "Personalized Marketing of Health Products the 21st Century Way," AMA Virtual Mentor, 2007; 9: 206–209, accessed 3/6/07, http://virtualmentor.ama-assn.org/2007/03/pfor1-0703.html

Clearly, much of this concern with privacy is not tied specifically to the creation and circulation of mass media content. It does, however, affect activities within mass media industries because government actions to limit or broaden a company's ability to deal with information about individuals can affect how a mass media organization approaches its audiences and the profits it can make from them.

The Cable Telecommunications Act of 1984 provides an example. The lawmakers who wrote it were sensitive to concerns by various privacy-protection groups about new "interactive" cable technologies that deliver programs to homes without subscribers' knowledge in order to learn what they watch and how they live. That could happen if cable companies provided subscribers with keyboards and invited them to order products directly on screen, to participate in TV games that ask about their recreational activities, or to answer polls that require information about their voting behaviors and beliefs. This sort of information about every subscriber could then be requested by a government agency or sold to marketers or other media firms, who could merge the data with more information about the person from other places.

To satisfy some of the privacy-protection groups' concerns, the Cable Telecommunications Act requires cable companies to report to their subscribers what personal information is collected about them and how it is used. The Act further prohibits the cable operators from releasing to the government or other companies "personally identifiable information" without subscribers' consent. The Act does not prohibit the cable firm from using the information it gathers. It might, for example, send advertisements for upcoming romantic pay-per-view films to teenage girls in its system who have boyfriends, while targeting ads for financial news programs at politically conservative men who are over the age of fifty. The Act also does not prohibit a cable firm from selling its information to other firms as long as it does not tell the other parties the specific names involved. For example, a greeting card company might ask the cable firm to send ads about its Valentine's Day cards to the teenage girls who have boyfriends. As long as the cable firm does the actual mailing, it is not doing anything illegal.

As limited as it might be in protecting privacy, because of this feature of the 1984 Cable Act, cable firms are restricted far more than companies that create and distribute mass media materials via other media. The only other laws that specifically prohibit media firms from sharing information about their audiences are the **Video Privacy Protection Act (or VPPA) of 1988** and the **Children's Online Privacy Protection Act (or COPPA) of 1998**. The VPPA prevents disclosure of personally identifiable rental records of "prerecorded video cassette tapes or similar audio visual material."[17] Congress enacted the law out of anger at the disclosure of Supreme Court nominee Robert Bork's video rental records in a newspaper, presumably in an attempt to embarrass the Yale University professor.

COPPA states that if a website wants to get information from children under thirteen years old, it must receive parental permission. (The law requires the Federal Trade Commission (FTC) to create rules covering how permission can be granted, and the FTC has done that.) Moreover, the parent must be able to tell the website not to give the information to marketers and to ask the site to delete the data in the future.

But these rules are exceptions. The fact is that most firms that create and distribute mass media materials consequently have few direct constraints when it comes to protecting privacy. Companies both offline and online increasingly have the ability to silently and secretly gather information about people using their services. In Chapter 14, we will discuss how much of the Web's commercial activity is based on serving particular ads to individuals based on the demographic and psychographic information that sites have about the people; where they have been on the Web; and even their offline media activities. In other chapters we will see how traditional media are using data about their audiences, too. Magazine firms, for

Cable Telecommunications Act of 1984 a law that requires cable companies to report to their subscribers what personal information is collected about them and how it is used, and prohibits the cable operators from releasing to the government or other companies "personally identifiable information" without subscribers' consent

Video Privacy Protection Act (VPPA) of 1988 a law that prevents disclosure of personally identifiable rental records of "prerecorded video cassette tapes or similar audio visual material"

Children's Online Privacy Protection Act (COPPA) of 1998 a law that applies to the online collection of personal information from children under the age of thirteen; it spells out what a website operator must include in a privacy policy, when and how to seek verifiable consent from a parent, and what responsibilities an operator has to protect children's privacy and safety online

example, can buy information about you from other sources and use it to attract advertisers interested in reaching people like you. Or consider mass media firms that invite you to phone 800 numbers. Did you know that they can learn the telephone number (and usually the ZIP code and neighborhood) from which you are calling even if you have placed a block on your line to stop caller identification (Caller ID) technology? The law allows telephone companies to derail Caller ID blocking for calls to 800 numbers.

Economic Regulation

Economic regulations placed on media organizations greatly affect the ways in which those organizations finance, produce, exhibit, and distribute their products. Two types of media economic regulation are most common: antitrust laws and direct regulation by government agencies.

Antitrust Laws   Government regulators who want to expand the marketplace for ideas without directly making rules about content may seek to limit excessive market control by mass media corporations. **Excessive market control** is behavior by one company or a few companies that makes it nearly impossible for new companies to enter the marketplace and compete. For example, a production company might gain this kind of power by buying up competitors and making sure that exhibitors do not deal with any new competitors. Of course, distributors and exhibitors might do the same thing: a few bookstore chains might swallow up their retail competition to the point that all publishers must deal primarily with them. When it comes to mass media, the excessive control over the market might directly affect consumers or advertisers, or both.

Control of the market by one firm is called **monopoly**. Control by a select few firms is called **oligopoly**. Great concern over train and steel monopolies and oligopolies in the late 1800s led U.S. legislators to begin to take special actions with respect to these activities, in order to maintain competition. These laws came to be known broadly as **antitrust policies**, and in the following decades they were carried out in three ways:

- Through the passing of laws
- Through enforcement of the laws by the U.S. Department of Justice and by state attorneys general
- Through federal court decisions that determine how far the government ought to go in encouraging competition and forcing companies to break themselves up into a number of smaller companies

Over the years, regulators and the courts have ruled that certain activities by firms involved in mass communication represent excessive market control. Typically, they have involved the use of vertical integration by a few firms to control an industry. We will note the most important of these cases when we deal with particular industries in the chapters to come.

Direct Regulation by Government Agencies   The **Federal Trade Commission (FTC)** and the **Federal Communications Commission (FCC)** are the two most important federal agencies involved in regulating the mass media.

The first thing to remember when comparing the two agencies is that the FTC's coverage can include any of the mass media—print or electronic—as long as the

---

excessive market control behavior by one company or a few companies that makes it nearly impossible for new companies to enter the marketplace and compete

monopoly control of the market by a single firm

oligopoly control of the market by a select few firms

antitrust policies policies put in place to maintain competition in the U.S. economy, carried out through the passing of laws, through enforcement of the laws by the U.S. Department of Justice and by state attorneys general, and through federal court decisions that determine how far the government ought to go in encouraging competition and forcing companies to break themselves up into a number of smaller companies

Federal Trade Commission (FTC) a federal agency whose mission is to ensure that the nation's markets function competitively; its coverage can include any mass media—print or electronic—as long as the issue involved is related to the smooth functioning of the marketplace and consumer protection in that sphere

Federal Communications Commission (FTC) a federal agency specifically mandated by Congress to govern interstate and international communication by television, radio, wire, satellite, and cable

issue involved is related to the smooth functioning of the marketplace and consumer protection in that sphere. By contrast, the FCC is specifically mandated by Congress to govern interstate and international communications by television, radio, wire, satellite, and cable.

The **FTC** describes its overall mission in the following manner:

> The Federal Trade Commission enforces a variety of federal antitrust and consumer protection laws. The Commission seeks to ensure that the nation's markets function competitively, and are vigorous, efficient, and free of undue restrictions. The Commission also works to enhance the smooth operation of the marketplace by eliminating acts or practices that are unfair or deceptive.
>
> In general, the Commission's efforts are directed toward stopping actions that threaten consumers' opportunities to exercise informed choice. Finally, the Commission undertakes economic analysis to support its law enforcement efforts and to contribute to the policy deliberations of the Congress, the Executive Branch, other independent agencies, and state and local governments when requested.[18]

Implied in this mission statement are three responsibilities that very much relate to media today: creating technical order, consumer protection, and encouraging competition.

Creating Technical Order

Many of the FTC's most important activities are aimed at simply creating *technical order* in an electronic environment that could become chaotic without some kind of regulation. It is through the FCC that radio stations get licenses that allow them to broadcast on specific wavelengths (the numbers we associate with the stations). The FCC is also in charge of allocating the frequency spectrum among various other technologies, including satellites and cellular phones. Although some of these technical activities have nothing to do with mass media, many of them do. Most major news organizations use satellites and cellphones for their work. Many consumers pay to get TV programming via satellite. Increasingly, too, consumers are even getting news, information, and advertisements through their mobile phones. FCC decisions about how much and how to allocate spectrum space helps to define which and how many companies can afford to get into this business in different parts of the country. That, in turn, affects the number of companies consumers have to consider and how much they will pay.

Consumer Protection

In the area of *consumer protection*, the Federal Trade Commission is involved in issues ranging from combating deceptive advertising to protecting children's privacy on the Web. As we have noted, the FTC was placed in charge of implementing and administering the Children's Online Privacy Protection Act. To implement the Act, the FTC had to create rules that specified exactly what websites were covered by the Act, exactly what rules should apply to them, and when the rules would go into effect. To administer the Act, the FTC had to create a system for monitoring websites on a regular basis to make sure that they were adhering to COPPA.

Encouraging Competition

Encouraging competition means enforcing federal antitrust laws. As we have seen, these are laws designed to prevent one or a few companies from controlling such a large percentage of an industry that they can dictate high prices and so harm the consumer.

It was with this responsibility in mind that the FTC decided to review the announcement by Google in 2007 that it would like to purchase the firm DoubleClick. Google's competitors raised the antitrust issue within two days after Google's announcement came out. Microsoft executives pointed out that the $3.1 billion acquisition would combine the largest providers of online advertising and create a force that could control the marketplace. "By putting together a single company that will control virtually the entire market ... Google will control the economic fuel of the Internet," said Brad Smith, general counsel for Microsoft. Smith added that the deal would affect Americans' privacy because, he said, a Google–DoubleClick combination would have "an unprecedented degree" of personal information about a person's activity on the Internet.[19]

Two days after the Microsoft complaint, Google said that the FTC had in fact launched an antitrust review of its plan to buy DoubleClick. After its review, the FTC commissioners voted 4–1 not to block Google's proposed purchase of DoubleClick. The majority statement noted that "after carefully reviewing the evidence, we have concluded that Google's proposed acquisition of DoubleClick is unlikely to substantially lessen competition." The commissioners added that the FTC lacks the legal authority to stop the merger on the grounds that it would harm consumer privacy—even though, they emphasized, the Commission "takes consumer privacy very seriously." As you might imagine, many privacy advocates were not happy with that decision.[20]

The Struggle with Government over Information Gathering

Although opportunities for prior restraint on speech by governments are rather limited under the U.S. Constitution (as we have noted), government officials have tried to prevent journalists from gaining access to certain types of information in other ways. Over the decades, press organizations have worked to reduce these obstacles.

Gathering Information on Government Documents and Meetings

One way in which the government can limit speech—especially speech about the workings of the government—is to restrict access to government documents. In the past, media professionals were often prevented from gaining access to crucial materials and documents. Documents about the military or foreign policy are often kept from public scrutiny because they jeopardized important security matters. But sometimes the secrecy is aimed at covering government officials' mistakes. Sometimes, too, it was aimed at allowing government officials not to have to account to the public at large about decisions that they made. Consider, for example, the number of contractors and subcontractors of different nationalities working at U.S. and Iraqi military bases during the Iraq War. In response to demands from Congress, in 2006 the U.S. Central Command began a census of the number of civilian "contractors" working on U.S. and Iraqi bases to determine how much food, water and shelter was needed. But Congress didn't release that information publicly, perhaps partly because the large number—more than 180,000—exceeded the number of combat troops and might have encouraged new levels of debate on the resources the United States was spending on the war. As we will see below, it took special journalistic enterprise under a special law called the Freedom of Information Act for a reporter to learn that number.[21]

Gathering Information on News Events

During breaking and continuing news stories, journalists seek access to the people and locations that are central to the news event at hand. But instances of breaking news aren't the only times when journalists need access to people, places, and events that are newsworthy. Journalists also need access to government meetings—at the federal, state, and local levels—where important decisions about how to run government and how to spend taxpayer money (among other things) are made. Historically, however, many government organizations have maintained strict closed-meeting policies.

As much as politicians would like to work outside the light of the press, journalistic coverage of public meetings can be important to the democratic process. Imagine deliberations by a county government about whether and where to locate a new landfill—a controversial issue in any community. Reporters would undoubtedly report on the county's decision to think about creating the landfill. Coverage of the deliberations themselves would be important to citizens of the area who would worry about the location of the landfill, the nature of the material to be buried there, and the effect the landfill would have on their family's health and the value of their property. Having careful journalists at the proceedings might mean that people in the community can discuss what is going on based on straightforward reporting rather than on leaks and rumors that reflect the interests of different sides of the controversy, and might encourage local officials to guide the process more openly and honestly than they otherwise would.

Gathering Information from Confidential Sources

There are some important and powerful news stories that would never be written if the journalists who reported the information were forced to reveal their sources. Perhaps the source is too afraid to speak to anyone without the promise of anonymity; perhaps the source fears retaliation if his or her identity is made public. Perhaps the result of such a source remaining quiet is that valuable information goes unheard, and the public good is harmed. In such cases, the journalist may claim an **evidentiary privilege**, which is a journalist's right to withhold the identification of confidential sources. Just because a journalist claims evidentiary privilege, however, does not mean that he or she will be granted that privilege by the courts. The U.S. Supreme Court decided in 1972, for example, that the First Amendment offers reporters no protection from grand jury subpoenas.

The subject became a major issue among journalists when *New York Times* reporter Judith Miller was jailed by a federal prosecutor for failing to reveal the name of a source. Miller had acknowledged that a Bush administration official had told her the name of a CIA operative, Valerie Plame. The apparent reason for the disclosure was an effort to embarrass her and her husband, who had spoken out against the Bush administration's claims that the United States needed to invade Iraq because its president, Saddam Hussein, possessed weapons of mass destruction. Believing that the person she said was her source, "Scooter" Libby, didn't want her to testify, Miller spent 85 days in jail until Libby allowed her to identify him. (To make matters especially complex, Libby denied he had revealed

evidentiary privilege a journalist's right to withhold the identification of confidential sources

New York Times reporter Judith Miller (right) was jailed by a federal prosecutor for failing to reveal the name of a source who had told her the name of a CIA operative, Valerie Plame (left).

Plame's identity to Miller.) During that time, lawyers representing the *Times* tried to argue Miller's First Amendment rights, and her champions argued for the importance of shield laws. But three courts, including the Supreme Court, declined to back Ms Miller. Some observers, moreover, said that this case was not the one to stress the autonomy of reporters. The critics said the *Times* was protecting not a whistle-blower but an administration campaign intended to squelch dissent.[22]

In general, protecting sources has not been easy. Journalists argue that they should have an automatic right to conceal the identity of their sources (and related notes and videos) if they are questioned about those sources in a court-room. Many police and government investigators counter that journalists are no different from anyone else and shouldn't have the privilege of protecting people who may be lawbreakers. Journalists reply that people who might be afraid to speak to government authorities (possibly because they are speaking against those authorities or because they are criminals) may talk to reporters if they believe they will be protected from retaliation. Being able to talk to such people is crucial to covering the world, journalists argue. Forcing journalists to reveal the identity of their sources could deter people from talking to them and so harm the public interest.

Allowing Information Gathering

Parallel with reporters' struggles to keep their sources confidential have been their attempts to uncover information that government agencies have tried to keep secret. During the past few decades, the Federal Freedom of Information Act, along with local and state sunshine and shield laws, has helped journalists to learn information that is important for the public's understanding of social policies but might otherwise have remained out of view.

Freedom of Information Act (FOIA)   On the federal level, a major win for openness came in the form of the **Freedom of Information Act (FOIA)**, which

Freedom of Information Act (FOIA)   an act passed by Congress in 1967 that allows citizens to request government records and reports that have not yet been made public, so long as these records and reports do not relate to nine specific areas: national security, agency interpersonal activities, statutory exemptions, trade secrets, some intra-agency and inter-agency memos, issues involving personal privacy, police investigations, protection of government-regulated financial institutions, and information about oil and gas wells

Congress passed in 1967. The Act allows citizens to request government records and reports that have not yet been made public, so long as those reports and records do not involve nine specific areas:

- National security
- Agency interpersonal activities
- Statutory exemptions
- Trade secrets
- Some intra-agency and inter-agency memos
- Issues involving personal privacy
- Police investigations
- Protection of government-regulated financial institutions
- Information about oil and gas wells

Government agencies have sometimes tried to use these nine sensitive areas as barriers to prevent reporters and others from gaining access to other types of information. Bureaucrats and other government workers have enough leeway under FOIA to make it easier or harder (depending upon their priorities) for the press and the public to gain access to information. So, the struggle for access to government information continues. Still, the work of many journalists has benefited from the Freedom of Information Act.

Sunshine Laws Over the past forty years, the alliance between journalism and advocacy organizations has persuaded many states to pass **sunshine laws**—regulations that ensure that government meetings and reports are made available to the press and to members of the public. The extent of openness varies from state to state, but a journalist's ability to explore the workings of government is much improved compared to earlier in the century.

The federal **Government-in-the-Sunshine Act**, which took effect in 1977, requires more than fifty government agencies, departments, and other groups to open their meetings to the public and the press, except under specific conditions.

Shield Laws The U.S. Supreme Court has ruled that the First Amendment doesn't give journalists the right to protect their sources. Nevertheless, press organizations have managed to convince legislators in thirty states and the District of Columbia to pass **shield laws** that afford the media varying degrees of protection against being forced to disclose information about their sources.

These laws vary greatly from state to state. In many states without shield laws, state courts have recognized some form of qualified privilege. In others, the state constitution may include "free press" provisions, which are similar to the First Amendment and afford qualified protection. There are several states, however, such as Hawaii and Wyoming, where no privilege to protect unpublished sources of information has been recognized by the courts or the legislature.

Media Self-regulation

There are a number of media industry pressures—both external and internal—aimed at ensuring that media professionals operate in an ethical manner. Pressure from members of the public, advocacy groups, and advertisers are examples of forces from outside particular media industries that influence the creation of con-

sunshine laws regulations that ensure that government meetings and reports are made available to the press and to members of the public

Government-in-the-Sunshine Act a federal Act passed by Congress in 1977 that requires more than fifty governmental agencies, departments, and other groups to open their meetings to the public and the press (except under specific conditions)

shield laws laws passed in thirty states and the District of Columbia that afford the media varying degrees of protection against being forced to disclose information about their sources

tent. It is these outside pressures that often influence the self-regulation mechanisms that industries create. Let's start with external pressures and then move inside media industries.

External Pressures on Media Organizations to Self-regulate

Every public squabble over what media firms should or shouldn't do involves parties at interest, called **stakeholders**. These are parties outside of media industries who care particularly about an issue, and use their economic and political power to influence the outcome to their benefit. Such stakeholders include members of the public, public advocacy organizations, and perhaps most importantly, advertisers

Pressure from Members of the Public　　When individuals are disturbed about media content, they may contact the production firms involved to express their displeasure and demand alterations in the content. Pick any topic—from racism to religion, from politicians to business people—and you will probably find that some sector of society is concerned about the portrayal of that topic in the mass media. People who see the mass media as a series of windows on the world often want to see the people, behaviors, and values that they hold dear portrayed in the media products they use.

As we noted in Chapter 2, media executives understand that they must think of their audiences as consumers who buy their products or whom they sell to advertisers. The complaining individual might be successful in getting the content changed or even removed if he or she convinces the media executives that they might otherwise lose a substantial portion of their target market. But an individual's concern will garner little attention if it is clear that the person does not belong in the target audience. The editors from *Cosmopolitan* magazine, which aims at twenty-something single women, for example, are not likely to follow the advice of an elderly-sounding woman from rural Kansas who phones to protest what she feels are demeaning portrayals of women on covers of the magazine that she sees in the supermarket. Yet the magazine staff might well act favorably if a *Cosmo* subscriber writes with a suggestion for a new column that would attract more of the upscale single women they want as readers.

Pressures from Advocacy Organizations　　Individuals who are particularly outraged about certain media portrayals may try to find others who share their concerns. They might join or start **advocacy organizations**, or **pressure groups**, which work to change the nature of certain kinds of mass media materials.

Some advocacy organizations are specific to media—like the Center for Media Education, which concentrates on children and television; the Committee for Accuracy in Middle East Reporting in America (CAMERA), which is devoted to promoting its view of accurate coverage of Israel in the media; and the Center for the Study of Commercialism, a critic of advertising and marketing. Examples of organizations that pay strong attention to media as part of more general concerns are People for the American Way, which supports politically liberal approaches to social problems; Gay & Lesbian Alliance Against Defamation; and the conservative American Family Association, which monitors all aspects of society for attacks on its image of the family.

Representatives of these organizations may try to meet with the heads of media firms, start letter-writing campaigns, or attempt to embarrass media firms by attracting press coverage about an issue. If their target is an advertiser-supported

stakeholders parties outside media industries who care particularly about an issue and may try to use their economic and political power to influence the outcome to their benefit

advocacy organizations or pressure groups collections of people who work to change the nature of certain kinds of mass media materials

President of the Gay & Lesbian Alliance Against Defamation Neil Giuliano speaks at the 17th annual GLAAD Media Awards, which recognize and honor media for their fair, accurate and inclusive representations of the lesbian, gay, bisexual, and transgender community and the issues that affect their lives.

medium, they may threaten to boycott the products of sponsors. They may also appeal to government officials for help.

Pressure from Advertisers   Advertisers can be an incredibly powerful force in pressuring the media to make changes in their content. The reason is that many firms like to buy time and space for their commercial messages around media content that reflects well on their products. Companies such as Hallmark and Procter & Gamble, which spend enormous amounts of money on advertising, sometimes have the clout to persuade media firms to tone down certain kinds of portrayals that anger segments of the population.

Consider, for example, efforts by marketers to generate more "family-friendly" programming to sponsor during prime time on television networks. In 1998, such advertising giants as Johnson & Johnson, AT&T, Bristol-Myers Squibb, Coca-Cola, Ford Motor Company, General Motors, Gillette, IBM, Kellogg's, McDonald's,

Procter & Gamble, and Unilever United States became concerned that the increased level of sex and violence on TV was angering many of their customers. The standard TV programming was also making it difficult for them to reach both parents and children at the same time.

In response, the marketers created the **Family Friendly Programming Forum**. It seeks to stimulate the production of shows meant to appeal to broader, multigenerational audiences and suitable to run between 8 and 10 p.m. (Eastern and Pacific times). The initiative is indicative of the increasing attention being paid to such viewers, who remain crucial to the success of mass marketers even in an era in which programs and products are aimed at ever narrower segments of the general population. "We want to sit and watch TV with our families and not be embarrassed," explained Steve Johnston, vice president for advertising and brand management at Nationwide Mutual Enterprises in Columbus, Ohio.

Critics of this coalition fear that it wants to create programs that romanticize a kind of fictional nuclear family. The advertisers insist, however, that it is possible to be both contemporary and family-friendly. "We have to be realistic; families may not be gathered around one TV anymore, and they're not your traditional families," said Susan Frank, executive vice president and general manager of the Odyssey Network in Studio City, California, a cable channel owned by Hallmark Cards that focuses on family-oriented programming. "But there are times you can bring family members together with content that's thought-provoking, done in a good, quality way," she added. "You have to be relevant to the way people live today."

By 2007, the Association of National Advertisers was working with the Forum to publicize select primetime programs "for their contributions to outstanding family entertainment." In a news release, forum co-chairman Kaki Hinton said, "Working with our network partners, in eight short years we have achieved our goal of ensuring that there is always at least one show that families can watch during prime time every night of the week."[23] Although this project has itself created controversy, it does show how powerful advertisers can respond to concerns they perceive in their target audience and act to influence media.

One question critical media consumers should ask themselves is whether it is ethical to pressure mass media organizations to alter their activities. After all, we've all learned the importance of freedom of the press and the dangers of censorship. We might therefore consider any attempt to interfere with what media executives do to be an unethical infringement of that freedom—a kind of censorship.

Some mass media executives add that they are already responsible to the most important pressure consumers can place on them: the pressure of the marketplace. These executives argue that if their target audiences don't like certain products, they won't buy those products and the content will be discontinued. Pressures from outside this relationship, they continue, are unfair to the creators and the audience.

However, some individuals and groups feel that certain aspects of media content are so offensive that they have a right to change these aspects even if they don't represent a majority of the audience. This activity is not an infringement of the First Amendment, they argue, because the initiative comes from private groups, not from the government.

Internal Pressures on Media to Self-regulate

Media executives face difficult challenges when they worry about pressures from outside their organizations and industries. They worry about maintaining their credibility with the public at large (and especially their target audiences), but at the same time they do not want pressures from outside entities (especially the

Family Friendly Programming Forum a forum created by a coalition of marketers in order to stimulate the production of shows meant to appeal to broader, multigenerational audiences and suitable to run between 8 and 10 p.m. (Eastern and Pacific times)

123

government) continually interfering with their firms' activities. To achieve one or both of these goals, executives in media industries set up self-regulation policies and codes. This *internal self-regulation* can take a number of forms, including editorial standards and ombudspersons at the level of individual organizations, and professional codes of ethics, content ratings, press councils, and journalism reviews at the industry level.

editorial standards written statements of policy and conduct established by media organizations as a form of self-regulation

policy books guidelines for fairness, accuracy, and appropriateness of station content, etc., adopted by media organizations in the interest of self-regulation

operating policies policies, most often used by print media organizations, that spell out guidelines for everyday operations, such as conflicts of interest, acceptable advertising content, boundaries of deceptive information-gathering practices, paying sources for news stories, etc.

editorial policies policies, most often used by print media organizations, that identify company positions on specific issues, such as which presidential candidate the paper supports, and whether the paper is in support of certain governmental policies

ombudsperson an individual who is hired by a media organization to deal with readers, viewers, or listeners who have a complaint to report or an issue to discuss

Editorial Standards Most media organizations have established **editorial standards**—written statements of policy and conduct. In the case of the network television industry, these policies are maintained and enforced by a department known as *Standards and Practices*, which makes difficult decisions regarding the acceptability of language in scripts, themes in plot lines, and images used in visual portrayals. At the local television station level, policy and conduct are most often guided by **policy books**, which help to lay down guidelines for fairness, accuracy, and appropriateness of station content, among other things.

Newspapers and magazines are most often guided by two kinds of editorial standards. The first, **operating policies**, spell out guidelines for everyday operations, such as conflicts of interest, acceptable advertising content, boundaries of deceptive information-gathering practices, and paying sources for news stories, among other things. The second, **editorial policies**, identify company positions on specific issues, such as which presidential candidate the paper supports and whether the paper is in support of certain governmental policies.

Ombudspersons An **ombudsperson** is hired by a media organization to deal with readers, viewers, or listeners who have a complaint to report or an issue to discuss. Although an ombudsperson is employed directly by a media organization, his or her role is to act as an impartial intermediary between the organization and the public.

Professional Codes of Ethics When executives perceive a need for their industry as a whole to maintain a certain level of public credibility or to fend off public attacks, they often mobilize to enact one of the oldest approaches to self-regulation: the professional code of ethics. These codes are often administered by societies or associations that companies have established to represent their interests to the outside world and to deal with forces within their business that might lead to actions that members would consider unprofessional.

Examples of such organizations are the Society of Professional Journalists, the American Society of Newspaper Editors, the Radio-Television News Directors Association, the American Advertising Federation, and the Public Relations Society of America. Each has an established code of ethics—that is, a formal list of guidelines and standards that tell the members of the profession, in this case media practitioners, what they should and should not do. See Figure 3.4 for the Code of Ethics adopted by the Society of Professional Journalists in 1996.

Adherence to these codes of ethics is voluntary and cannot be enforced beyond removing a member from the society that administers the code. Most media professionals are wary and even fearful of the idea of a code of ethics that the government makes mandatory. They argue that such a code could unduly restrict the expression of free speech and encourage harmful lawsuits.

Content Ratings and Advisories Another way in which media organizations regulate themselves is through the adoption of *ratings systems*, like those of the film, television, and computer media industries. These ratings are often quite

Code of Ethics

Preamble

Members of the Society of Professional Journalists believe that public enlightenment is the forerunner of justice and the foundation of democracy. The duty of the journalist is to further those ends by seeking truth and providing a fair and comprehensive account of events and issues. Conscientious journalists from all media and specialties strive to serve the public with thoroughness and honesty. Professional integrity is the cornerstone of a journalist's credibility.

Members of the Society share a dedication to ethical behavior and adopt this code to declare the Society's principles and standards of practice.

Seek Truth and Report It

Journalists should be honest, fair and courageous in gathering, reporting and interpreting information.

Journalists should:

► Test the accuracy of information from all sources and exercise care to avoid inadvertent error. Deliberate distortion is never permissible.

► Diligently seek out subjects of news stories to give them the opportunity to respond to allegations of wrongdoing.

► Identify sources whenever feasible. The public is entitled to as much information as possible on sources' reliability.

► Always question sources' motives before promising anonymity. Clarify conditions attached to any promise made in exchange for information. Keep promises.

► Make certain that headlines, news teases and promotional material, photos, video, audio, graphics, sound bites and quotations do not misrepresent. They should not oversimplify or highlight incidents out of context.

► Never distort the content of news photos or video. Image enhancement for technical clarity is always permissible. Label montages and photo illustrations.

► Avoid misleading re-enactments or staged news events. If re-enactment is necessary to tell a story, label it.

► Avoid undercover or other surreptitious methods of gathering information except when traditional open methods will not yield information vital to the public. Use of such methods should be explained as part of the story.

► Never plagiarize.

► Tell the story of the diversity and magnitude of the human experience boldly, even when it is unpopular to do so.

► Examine their own cultural values and avoid imposing those values on others.

► Avoid stereotyping by race, gender, age, religion, ethnicity, geography, sexual orientation, disability, physical appearance or social status.

► Support the open exchange of views, even views they find repugnant.

► Give voice to the voiceless; official and unofficial sources of information can be equally valid.

► Distinguish between advocacy and news reporting. Analysis and commentary should be labeled and not misrepresent fact or context.

► Distinguish news from advertising and shun hybrids that blur the lines between the two.

► Recognize a special obligation to ensure that the public's business is conducted in the open and that government records are open to inspection.

Minimize Harm

Ethical journalists treat sources, subjects and colleagues as human beings deserving of respect.

Journalists should:

► Show compassion for those who may be affected adversely by news coverage. Use special sensitivity when dealing with children and inexperienced sources or subjects.

► Be sensitive when seeking or using interviews or photographs of those affected by tragedy or grief.

► Recognize that gathering and reporting information may cause harm or discomfort. Pursuit of the news is not a license for arrogance.

► Recognize that private people have a greater right to control information about themselves than do public officials and others who seek power, influence or attention. Only an overriding public need can justify intrusion into anyone's privacy.

► Show good taste. Avoid pandering to lurid curiosity.

► Be cautious about identifying juvenile suspects or victims of sex crimes.

► Be judicious about naming criminal suspects before the formal filing of charges.

► Balance a criminal suspect's fair trial rights with the public's right to be informed.

Act Independently

Journalists should be free of obligation to any interest other than the public's right to know.

Journalists should:

► Avoid conflicts of interest, real or perceived.

► Remain free of associations and activities that may compromise integrity or damage credibility.

► Refuse gifts, favors, fees, free travel and special treatment, and shun secondary employment, political involvement, public office and service in community organizations if they compromise journalistic integrity.

► Disclose unavoidable conflicts.

► Be vigilant and courageous about holding those with power accountable.

► Deny favored treatment to advertisers and special interests and resist their pressure to influence news coverage.

► Be wary of sources offering information for favors or money; avoid bidding for news.

Be Accountable

Journalists are accountable to their readers, listeners, viewers and each other.

Journalists should:

► Clarify and explain news coverage and invite dialogue with the public over journalistic conduct.

► Encourage the public to voice grievances against the news media.

► Admit mistakes and correct them promptly.

► Expose unethical practices of journalists and the news media.

► Abide by the same high standards to which they hold others.

Sigma Delta Chi's first Code of Ethics was borrowed from the American Society of Newspaper Editors in 1926. In 1973, Sigma Delta Chi wrote its own code, which was revised in 1984 and 1987. The present version of the Society of Professional Journalists' Code of Ethics was adopted in September 1996.

Figure 3.4

The Society of Professional Journalists' Code of Ethics

Source: Copyright © Society of Professional Journalists: www.spm.org. Reprinted with permission.

Video game Ratings Systems

In 2007, British censors banned the violent computer game *Manhunt 2*, making it illegal to supply the game anywhere in the U.K. The game, which immerses users in violent virtual experience as they try to escape from an insane asylum, was rejected by the British Board of Film Classification (BBFC) because of "its unrelenting focus on stalking and brutal slaying."

The classification came after a highly publicized case involving a teenager who murdered a 14-year-old boy after he was allegedly inspired by the original *Manhunt* game. According to a spokesman for *Manhunt* producer Rockstar Games, "We are disappointed with the recent decision to refuse classification of *Manhunt 2*. While we respect the authority of the classification board … we emphatically disagree with this particular decision."

The ban of *Manhunt 2* marks the U.K.'s first classification refusal in a decade and appeared to set a precedent in other countries. In Ireland, for example, the Irish Film Censor's Office also banned the game for its "gross, unrelenting and gratuitous violence." In the United States, a game can only be banned if it is decided by a court to be obscene, and no game has been banned to date. Instead, the U.S. self-regulatory agency, the Entertainment Software Rating Board, gave *Manhunt 2* an "Adults Only" classification, meaning that it was deemed unsuitable for persons under the age of 18. Yet reporter Tony Smith notes that various loopholes exist in the U.S. legal system. He explained, "Unlike the U.K.'s rating system, overseen by the BBFC, the U.S. scheme is not backed by legislation to prevent, say, a retailer selling an adult-oriented game to a minor."

As this book goes to press, there is talk that the publisher of *Manhunt 2* may appeal the "Adults Only" rating in the United States in favor of a "mature" classification, which would ensure its distribution at more retail platforms.

Sources: Charlotte Gill, "Family's Delight as Horror Video Game is Banned," *Daily Mail*, June 20, 2007, accessed 3/6/08, http://www.reghardware.co.uk/2007/06/21/manhunt_gets_us_rating; and Tony Smith, "Manhunt 2 Rated 18+ in U.S." *The Register Hardware*, June 21, 2007, accessed 3/6/08, www.reghardware.co.uk.

controversial. Some people believe that they are not informative enough; others believe that the ratings allow companies to place all the responsibility on the audience by creating whatever violent or sexually explicit materials they want and then simply slapping a rating on the material.

Film

A voluntary film rating system was adopted by the Motion Picture Association in 1968 and revised in 1990. The ratings place films into one of five categories:

G: *General audience—all ages admitted.* This is a film that contains nothing in theme, language, nudity and sex, violence, etc., that would be offensive to parents whose younger children view the film.

PG: *Parental guidance suggested—some material may not be suitable for children.* This is a film that clearly needs to be examined or inquired into by parents before they let their children attend.

PG-13: *Parents strongly cautioned—some material may be inappropriate for children under thirteen.* This is a film that leaps beyond the boundaries of the PG rating in theme, violence, nudity, sensuality, language, or other content, but does not quite fit within the restricted R category.

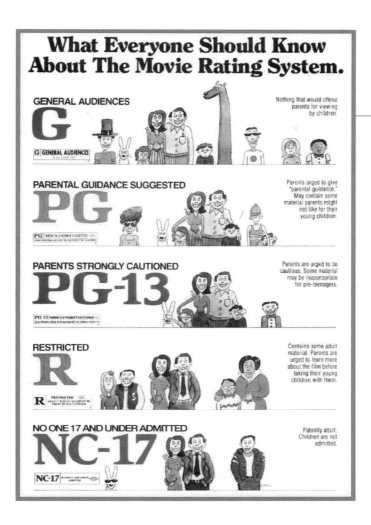

The MPAA produces promotional items like this poster to guide movie consumers on how to best use the film rating system.

R: *Restricted—under seventeen requires accompanying parent or adult guardian.* This is a film that definitely contains some adult material, possibly including hard language, tough violence, nudity within sensual scenes, drug abuse, or a combination of these and other elements.

NC-17: *No one under seventeen admitted.* This is a film that most parents will consider patently too adult for their youngsters under seventeen. No children will be admitted.

The basic mission of the rating system is a simple one: to give parents advance information about movies so that they can decide what movies they want their children to see and what movies they don't want their children to see.

Film ratings are determined by a full-time Ratings Board, located in Los Angeles, California. The board is made up of eight to thirteen people who are not specially qualified in any way, other than the fact that they all have "parenthood experience." When a film is submitted to the Rating Board, each member estimates what most parents would consider to be an appropriate rating for the film. The criteria the board considers are: theme, violence, language, nudity, sensuality, and drug abuse, among other elements. After a group discussion, the board votes on the film's rating, which is decided by a majority vote.

The Ratings Board stresses that there is no requirement that films be submitted to it. Any producer, filmmaker, or distributor who does not want to participate in the ratings process can send his or her film to the free market without any rating at all. This appears quite voluntary, doesn't it? But as a media literate consumer (or aspiring producer), can you see what's wrong with this picture? The answer is that if producers of a film refuse to submit it for rating, it will be extremely difficult (if not impossible) to persuade theater companies to show the picture. Some newspapers and websites may not even accept ads for the film. That is an invitation to lose money. So unless the film is pornography (and so moves through a very different production-to-distribution system), working with the Ratings Board is really a requirement.

Television

Up to two thousand hours of television are available in American homes each day. To help parents sort through this huge volume of material and choose programs they want their young children to see—or not to see—the television industry has developed TV parental guidelines. The parental guidelines are modeled after the familiar movie ratings, and consist of the following six categories:

TV-Y: *All children.* This program is designed to be appropriate for all children, including children ages two to six.

TV-Y7: *Directed to older children.* This program is designed for children age seven and above.

TV-G: *General audience.* Most parents would find this program suitable for all ages. It contains little or no violence, no strong language, and little or no sexual dialogue or situations.

TV-PG: *Parental guidance suggested.* This program contains material that parents may find unsuitable for younger children. The theme itself may call for parental guidance and/or the program contains one or more of the following: moderate violence (V), some sexual situations (S), infrequent coarse language (L), or some suggestive dialogue (D).

TV-14: *Parents strongly cautioned.* This program contains some material that many parents would find unsuitable for children under fourteen years of age. This program contains one or more of the following: intense violence (V), intense sexual situations (S), strong coarse language (L), or intensely suggestive dialogue (D).

TV-MA: *Mature audience only.* This program is specifically designed to be viewed by adults and therefore may be unsuitable for children under seventeen. This program contains one or more of the following: graphic violence (V), explicit sexual activity (S), or crude indecent language (L).

Because of the vast amount of daily TV programs, the networks and producers of each show determine the parental guidelines for that show. A monitoring board has been formed by the National Association of Broadcasters from a broad range of television industry experts. The board's mandate is to make sure that there is as much uniformity and consistency in applying the parental guidelines as is possible. The board examines programs whose guidelines may have been inappropriate and reviews publicly criticized programs to ensure the accuracy of the guidelines for those programs.

Electronic Software/Video Games

As a result of threatened federal intervention, in the early 1990s the gaming industry set about creating a rating system for games. The Entertainment Software Rating Board (ESRB)—an independent, self-regulatory entity that assigns ratings,

These Parental Guidelines icons represent the television industry's rating system.

enforces advertising guidelines, and helps ensure responsible online privacy practices for the interactive entertainment software industry—was established in 1994. Its ratings are designed to give consumers information about the content of an interactive video or computer entertainment title and the ages for which the title is appropriate. The ratings that suggest age-appropriateness are found on the front of the box and are not meant to tell consumers what to buy or to serve as the only basis for choosing a product. Content descriptions, found on the back of each game box, tell consumers whether the game contains elements that may be of interest or concern. ESRB ratings and their definitions are listed below:

EC: *Early childhood.* May be suitable for children ages three and older. Contains no material that parents would find inappropriate

E: *Everyone.* May be suitable for persons ages six and older. These titles will appeal to people of many ages and tastes. They may contain minimal cartoon, fantasy, or mild violence and/or infrequent use of mild language. This rating was formerly known as Kids to Adult (K–A).

E10+: *Everyone ten and older.* May be suitable for ages ten and older. Titles in this category may contain more cartoon, fantasy, or mild violence, mild language, and/or minimal suggestive themes.

T: *Teen.* May be suitable for ages thirteen and older. Titles in this category may contain violence, suggestive themes, crude humor, minimal blood, simulated gambling, and/or infrequent use of strong language.

M: *Mature.* May be suitable for persons ages seventeen and older. Titles in this category may contain intense violence, blood and gore, sexual content and/or strong language.

AO: *Adults only.* Should only be played by persons eighteen years or older. Titles in this category may include prolonged scenes of intense violence and/or graphic sexual content and nudity.

Content descriptors: Found on the back of the box. Indicate elements in a game that may have triggered a particular rating or may be of interest or concern.

Each ESRB rating is based on the consensus of at least three specially trained raters who view content based on numerous criteria. Raters must be adults and typically have experience with children through prior work experience, education, or by being caregivers themselves. To eliminate the risk of outside or industry influence, the identities of the raters are kept confidential, and they are not permitted to have any ties to or connections with any individuals or entities in the computer/video game industry. The raters review written submission materials and DVDs or videotapes, provided by the publisher, capturing all pertinent content in the game. This includes the most extreme instances across all relevant categories,

ESRB ratings, introduced in 1994, are designed to give consumers information about the content and age-appropriateness of computer and video games.

including but not limited to violence, language, sex, controlled substances, and gambling. After reviewing the DVD or video of all the pertinent content in the game, which may involve an ESRB staff member playing a beta or alpha version of the game, each rater recommends an appropriate rating category and content descriptor(s). The ratings are then compiled and a consensus is drawn from the three ratings. Finally, ESRB staff review the final rating recommendation and rating feedback, and then issue a certificate to the game's publisher with the official rating assignment. The publisher can either accept the game's rating as final or revise the game's content and resubmit the game, at which time the process starts anew. When the game is ready for release to the public, publishers must send final copies of the product to the ESRB where the packaging is reviewed for accuracy.

Ratings systems such as these are an increasingly common form of self-regulation. It's not clear how much use people make of different types of ratings systems and how helpful people find these systems. Nevertheless, media executives like these systems because they allow the industry to shift the burden of responsibility for content to parents and other members of the audience. Government officials also like them because it takes some of the public pressure off them to force companies to change their content.

Press Councils   A **press council** is an independent group of people who monitor complaints from media consumers, including complaints about unbalanced coverage, inadequate coverage, and erroneous coverage. Press councils differ from ombudspersons (discussed earlier in this chapter) in that they are made up of more than one person, and they are not directly employed by any one media organization.

One of the most active press councils in the United States is the Minnesota News Council, founded nearly thirty years ago. The council is made up of thirteen media professionals and thirteen members of the public. The Minnesota News Council aims to promote fairness in the news media by giving members of the public who feel that they have been damaged by a news story an opportunity to hold the news organization accountable. The council's role has been expanding in recent years to include reaching out to the media and the public to create awareness that will reduce the reasons for complaints.

The Minnesota News Council makes it clear, however, that it has no authority—and wants none—to order any news organization to do, or not to do, anything. It exists in order to help the public and the media create a moral force for fairness. People who come to the council with complaints are not interested in recovering money damages (if they were, they would sue); they are interested in vindication. To qualify for a hearing, one must waive the right to sue.

press council an independent group of people who monitor complaints from media consumers, including complaints about unbalanced coverage, inadequate coverage, and erroneous coverage

Journalism Reviews   **Journalism reviews**—publications that report on and analyze examples of ethical and unethical journalism—are yet another internal force that helps the media to self-regulate. These reviews include publications such as *Quill*, *Columbia Journalism Review*, and *American Journalism Review*. Take a look at the print copies of these journals or their counterparts on the Web. What you'll see are vehicles that are intent on talking about the realities of the news business as well as standing up for the values of their profession and for the rights of journalists around the world. The *Columbia Journalism Review*, for example, has run articles on the power of New York-based media; on what happens when reporters party with their sources—the uses and ethical dilemmas of this practice; and on the differences in news perspectives between the traditional media and new organs such as *Inside* magazine. The *CJR* website also has a link to the Committee to Protect Journalists, which reports on attempts to intimidate or injure reporters around the world.

journalism reviews publications that report on and analyze examples of ethical and unethical journalism

Ethics

The word *ethics* has appeared several times in this chapter in connection with arguments about the moral principles that ought to guide the creation and circulation of mass media materials. **Ethics** is a system of principles about what is right that guides a person's actions. Ethics has come to be recognized as the study of concepts such as *ought*, *should*, and *duty*. Let's look a bit more carefully at the topic of ethics and the way in which it relates to business requirements.

ethics a system of principles about what is right that guides a person's actions

Classical Ethics

Over the centuries, philosophers have developed various approaches to understanding what is ethical and what is not. By applying one or more of these classical approaches to ethics, we can better evaluate—from an ethics standpoint, at least—our behavior and the behavior of others. The five ethical approaches that follow—*the Golden Mean, the Golden Rule, the categorical imperative, the principle of utility,* and *the veil of ignorance*—have particular relevance to media professionals. Let's look at them one at a time.

The Golden Mean   The Greek philosopher Aristotle believed that an individual's acts are right and virtuous if they are means of two extremes. This idea led to the development of Aristotle's **Golden Mean**, which represents the average of the extreme actions for both the intellectual and moral virtues. While Aristotle was certainly not the first to develop the saying "moderation in all things," he was certainly one of its major proponents.

Aristotle reasoned that an individual could be happy if he or she chose the path between the two extremes that would lead him or her on the best course. Yet he also stated that each person should seek his or her own Golden Mean; each person is different, and what might be too much for one person could possibly be too little for another. To apply Aristotle's Golden Mean, begin by identifying ethical extremes and then seek a balance between the two. For those prone to one extreme, the balance comes from leaning toward the other extreme. The farther away you are from one extreme, the more you must lean toward the other.

Golden Mean Aristotle's belief that an individual who combines both intellectual and moral virtues while following reason can be happy, and that an individual's acts are right and virtuous if they are the mean of two extremes

Consider an example of a Golden Mean approach to ethical behavior: a TV network program director may try to get the producers of a particularly violent program to reduce the amount of mayhem on their show by telling them to cut out all violent car chases and fights. The program director realizes that the program's creators won't fully adhere to this extreme order. He believes in the Golden Mean: if he pushes them toward the other extreme, maybe they will end up in the appropriate middle when it comes to using violent action on the show.

Golden Rule or Judeo-Christian Ethic the admonition to "do unto others as you would have them do unto you"

The Golden Rule   The **Golden Rule**, also known as the Judeo-Christian Ethic, refers to the admonition to "do unto others as you would have them do unto you." This maxim has long been proposed as an ethical guideline. Kung Fu Tzu (Confucius) presented his version five hundred years before the birth of Christ as a proscription: "Do not do to others what you would not want done to you."

Continuing with our earlier example, following this rule might mean that producers of sex and violence on TV would recognize that they wouldn't want their children being bombarded with such materials, so they would stop bombarding other people's kids with them.

The Categorical Imperative   German philosopher Immanuel Kant developed the theory of the categorical imperative, which holds that individuals should follow ethical principles as if these principles could be applied in any situation. That way, Kant believed, we would be able to develop rules of order, or duties. The word *maxim*, in this sense, means the principle on which the action was based—the type of principle that people formulate in determining their conduct. So, if a person won't lie out of principle, he or she should be willing to apply that principle universally. Many have pointed out that this is simply a reformulation of the Golden Rule, and it's easy to see why.

Under the categorical imperative, an individual would act only in ways in which he or she would want everyone else to act, all the time. Thus, it would be permissible for us to lie only if we wished everyone to lie all the time. We could murder with impunity only if we would allow others to do so. Kant reasoned that rational beings wouldn't tolerate a state of existence in which everyone could lie or kill without compunction. And, of course, that's true. How could we live in a society in which we would expect a lie for every question we asked, or one in which murder were the rule rather than the exception?

A contemporary example relating to the categorical imperative involves invading other people's private information. If we, as individuals, would not want such a thing to happen to us, we should then act toward other people in the same way. Similarly, executives working for media firms that have the capability of secretly collecting information from people who visit their websites should ask whether they would want that done to them. If they followed the categorical imperative, they would use an "opt in" approach to information collection. That is, they would ask everyone for permission to collect and use the data, just as they might want to be asked.

the principle of utility John Stuart Mill's theory promoting an action based on its utility, or usefulness; often rephrased as "the greatest good for the greatest number," the basis of utilitarianism is the idea that the rightness or wrongness of any action can be judged entirely in terms of its consequences

The Principle of Utility   British philosopher John Stuart Mill believed in **the principle of utility**—so-called because it promoted an action based on its utility, or usefulness. The basis of utilitarianism is a single, guiding precept: the rightness or wrongness of any action can be judged in terms of its consequences. Motives are therefore irrelevant—completely the opposite of Kant's theory of the categorical imperative. Mill believed that good consequences give pleasure, whereas bad consequences result in pain. According to utilitarianism, the right course of action is the one that promotes the greatest pleasure or minimizes pain for those affected by the decision-making.

Under this principle, a person or company would have to evaluate the costs and benefits of harassing co-workers, televising violent programs, or secretly collecting information from friends or customers. If the individual or the company determines that more pain than benefit will result from doing these things, they should stop. For example, an online magazine might conclude that collecting and storing personal information from adults without their permission could lead to bad feelings if readers found out, and therefore could cause it to lose those subscriptions. The result might be that the magazine would set up a procedure to get permission from its customers after informing them what data it would collect and how it would use that data.

The Veil of Ignorance   Philosopher John Rawls' theory of the **veil of ignorance** holds that in any given situation, justice emerges only when all parties are treated without social differentiation. From this perspective, fairness is the fundamental idea in the concept of justice.

For example, a journalist would determine the just thing to do by determining the fairest option, and would make the ethical decision without considering his or her own personal interests. All people going behind this veil of ignorance would have to forget who they are and what their own values and ideologies are, and step into the shoes of the others involved in the ethical situation. Behind this veil of ignorance, journalists would be more objective in their reporting because their inherent biases would not come into play, as the person reporting the story would put aside his or her own values and ideas.

Journalists can use Rawls' idea of the veil of ignorance to write a truly fair story. Reporters who cover the same beat day after day can start to make assumptions about people and use those assumptions in the stories they write. But journalists who go behind the veil of ignorance should try to look at the story as if they are coming in contact with the people involved for the first time and should bury any preconceived notions about the people. This is a very idealistic look at journalism, but Rawls argues that journalists who use his suggestions will probably be better and fairer journalists.

veil of ignorance John Rawls' theory that holds that in any given situation, justice emerges only when all parties are treated without social differentiation; from this perspective, fairness is the fundamental idea in the concept of justice

Making Ethical Decisions

Every day you will find yourself in situations in which ethical decisions need to be made—whether those situations involve the mass media or not. How will you make these decisions? What sort of moral reasoning process should you follow—not only as a media consumer but, more importantly, as a good citizen?

Bob Steele, a senior faculty member at the Poynter Institute, outlines a model that media literates and professionals alike can use to evaluate and examine their decisions and to make good ethical decisions. Steele is concerned specifically with journalism, but the ethical-thinking process that he suggests can work for all sorts of media practitioners and consumers.

Steele says, ask yourself these ten questions:

1   What do I know? What do I need to know?
2   What are my ethical concerns?

3   What is my journalistic (or informational, entertainment, advertising, or educational) purpose?

4   What organizational policies and professional guidelines should I consider?

5   How can I include other people, with different perspectives and diverse ideas, in the decision-making process?

6   Who are the stakeholders—those affected by my decision? What are their motivations? Which are legitimate?

7   What if the roles were reversed? How would I feel if I were in the shoes of one of the stakeholders?

8   What are the possible consequences of my actions in the short term and in the long term?

9   What are my alternatives to maximize my truth-telling responsibility and minimize harm?

10 Can I clearly and fully justify my thinking and my decision to my colleagues, to the stakeholders, and to the public?

Answering these questions is difficult. It is a bit easier if you have thought through where you stand in relation to the ideas of classical ethics, the Golden Mean, the Golden Rule, the categorical imperative, and the principle of utility. Try it.

Ethical Duties to Various Constituencies

Combined with larger philosophies of ethics, Bob Steele's questions can help media practitioners think about their day-to-day responsibilities and prepare for events that raise grave ethical dilemmas. Ethical dilemmas often come about because we are torn in a number of directions over an issue. The perspective that media-ethics scholars Clifford Christians, Mark Fackler, and Kim Rotzoll[24] bring to this topic can help bring a sharper focus to the topics Steele raises when it comes to knotty ethical situations. In order to reach a responsible decision, these scholars write, an individual must clarify which parties will be influenced by a decision and which ones the person feels particularly obligated to support.

Consider yourself, for a moment, as a media practitioner trying to carry out an important assignment—writing a news story, directing a film, writing a TV movie, or any of a myriad of other activities. Fackler and his colleagues stress that as we carry out these activities, we have obligations to five parties, or constituencies. These five parties are *ourselves*, *the audience*, *the employer*, *the profession*, and *society*. To these five, we will add one more: the people to whom we've made promises, such as publics and sources.

Duty to Self
As a media practitioner, you clearly feel a duty to make sure your actions do not harm yourself. In fact, a key goal of your work is to make yourself look good—to shine in your job—and to act in ways that allow you to feel ethically correct.

Duty to Audience
As a media practitioner, you also have a duty to make sure that what you do takes the nature and expectations of the audience into consideration.

Duty to the Employer
The company that pays your salary is also an important consideration. At the very least, a practitioner owes the firm good work—a product that meets the expectations that caused the person to be hired in the first place.

Duty to the Profession

Most practitioners feel an allegiance to their profession. Movie scriptwriters feel an obligation to keep up the reputation and pay of the people who ply that craft. Similarly, reporters feel a responsibility to help other journalists who are in trouble and to make sure that their profession is taken seriously by editors and publishers.

Duty to Promiseholders

If you made promises to people during the course of covering a news story, putting a movie together, or making an ad, you may (and should) feel an obligation to those people when you move forward with your work. If a source requested anonymity, you can't divulge the name even if your editor thinks the article would be better if it were there. If you promised a young TV talk-show host the first interview about your new film, you are obligated to give that show the first interview, even though Jay Leno wants you first.

Duty to Society

Many practitioners also feel an obligation to society at large. You live in a real world, with neighbors, children, stores, churches, and governments. If you produce recordings, edit movies, write sitcoms, or illustrate children's books, you may feel that what you produce should have a positive social impact. At least, you may say, what you produce should not have a negative social impact.

Forming Ethical Standards for the Mass Media   If you think about the ethical systems we presented, about Bob Steele's ten questions and about the constituencies that Mark Fackler and his colleagues discuss, you will see that ethical standards for the mass media often involve at least three levels:

- The personal level
- The professional level
- The societal level

Most media practitioners find that they cannot exist on one level only. How their standards develop at each level has to do with their *values* and *ideals*. From these two sources come their *principles*—the basis for their ethical actions at every level.

Values are those things that reflect our presuppositions about social life and human nature. Values cover a broad range of possibilities, such as aesthetic values (something is harmonious or pleasing), professional values (innovation and promptness), logical values (consistency and competency), sociocultural values (thrift and hard work), and moral values (honesty and nonviolence).

Ideals are a notion of excellence, a goal that is thought to bring about greater harmony to ourselves and to others. For example, American culture respects ideals such as tolerance, compassion, loyalty, forgiveness, peace, justice, fairness, and respect for persons. In addition to these human ideals, there are institutional or organizational ideals, such as profit, efficiency, productivity, quality, and stability.

Principles are those guidelines we derive from values and ideals and are precursors to codified rules. They are usually stated in positive (prescriptive) or negative (proscriptive) terms. Consider, for example, the motto, "Never corrupt the integrity of media channels"—a principle derived from the professional value of truth-telling in public relations—or the statement "Always maximize profit"—a principle derived from belief in the efficacy of the free-enterprise system. The ideals, values, and principles of the media will differ according to the differing goals and loyalties of each.

values   those things that reflect our presuppositions about social life and human nature

ideals   a notion of excellence, a goal that is thought to bring greater harmony to ourselves and to others

principles   those guidelines we derive from values and ideals that are precursors to codified rules

Media Literacy, Regulation, and Ethics

Reading through the preceding paragraphs about ethics, it might have occurred to you that people who work in mass media organizations may sometimes feel strong conflicts among the various constituencies that we've mentioned. As we saw in Chapter 2, the creation, distribution, and exhibition of news, entertainment, educational, and informational materials take place in a highly competitive business environment. The high risks involved in that environment often create pressure on individuals to conform to organizational activities that, while legal, the individuals might consider ethically unsavory. An individual's duty to the media organization may conflict with his or her duty to society; an individual's personal values may conflict with the organization's values.

These considerations relate to a wide range of topics in different media. Consider the use of graphic violence in TV dramas, in local TV news programs, in ads, and in rap recordings; it also surfaces in other aspects of media content. Many of the distributors and exhibitors of the material, and even its creators, may personally abhor some elements of what they are doing. In their business lives, though, they may feel they have to use those elements. Why? Because they "work"—that is, they seem to sell the product to the right audience in a manner that supports the organization and brings paychecks to its members. A well-paid writer of TV movies once yelled at the author of this textbook for asking him questions that implied respect for his craft. "I write junk!" he shouted. He added that he knew he used violence and sex as props to advance his plots and that he wrote according to the most blatant pop-cultural formulas. "I do it because I have a family to support and a big mortgage to pay off for this house in Brentwood! I do it, but I know it's junk. Don't forget that!"

Actually, what this writer said can also illuminate the second problem of media ethics: its ambiguous nature. The writer may condemn his own scripts as contributing to the violent and mediocre nature of popular culture, but the producers of the programs that were based on these scripts might well argue that they were handsome creations that explore issues of good and evil in ways that are accessible to large audiences. You might think that it would be more difficult to defend the local news formula. One argument that its champions have advanced, though, is based on its popularity. Is it wrong, they ask, to create an accurate program about goings-on in a locality that many people want to watch?

There may also be ambiguity regarding how to apply the ethical principles. Ethical criteria may seem straightforward, but they are not always so. Take the principle of not misleading people—a notion that most people would agree is a basic ethical principle. Look at the Campbell Soup case, noted earlier, in light of this principle. When the company's ad agency used marbles in the soup to boost the soup's chunkiness, was that "misleading"? Campbell's argued that the company was trying to emphasize a genuine feature of its soup that the camera couldn't easily reflect without the marbles. The Federal Trade Commission disagreed, but that doesn't mean that Campbell's employees felt that they were acting unethically—do you?

Sometimes, though, executives do acknowledge that the business competition leads them to act unethically. One way to guard themselves and their competitors from improper behavior is by encouraging rules that prohibit it. From one point of view, then, media laws and regulations can be seen as a way to formally enforce agreed-upon norms of behavior by government officials with respect to media practitioners and by media practitioners with respect to the government and the society as a whole. The First Amendment, Freedom of Information Act, and Video

Privacy Protection Act are, for people who agree with them, rules that reflect ethical values regarding the government's relation to media, information, and the public. Similarly, antitrust laws, laws against deceptive advertising, and self-regulatory ratings voice norms about how media firms and media practitioners ought to behave.

Media Regulations and the Savvy Citizen

Even if you're not a media practitioner, thinking about the rules that guide the media is crucial. The more you know about how the media are regulated, how government and internal regulations protect you, and how those regulations sometimes intervene in ways you may not want them to, the more your awareness as a media consumer increases. So does your ability to act in support of your ethical concerns.

You can undoubtedly think of many examples of anger against the media. Activists who believe in women's right to choose abortions might be deeply offended by the portrayals of teen pregnancies in a TV movie shown by one of the networks. They might feel that to sit back and do nothing about these portrayals would invite further support of the anti-abortion position by the producers when they work on other shows. They might also believe that the portrayals will reinforce in the audience unfortunate images of, and actions toward, teen abortions in society. They might therefore mobilize to prevent the network from repeat showing of that film and to force the network to air a film or series that is more sympathetic toward teenagers who choose abortions.

But consider this complexity: at the same time that the activists are voicing their complaints, groups that find any portrayal of abortion to be reprehensible might make totally opposite demands to the network. They might argue that such portrayals encourage children and others to think that abortion is acceptable in society, and that that would erode family values—the very values that define American society. Consequently, they might demand that the network never portray any abortions.

Three points about these opposing groups and their demands deserve attention here. One point is the similarity in their approach: although they are far apart ideologically, their concern about the media comes not so much from a worry about how the members of their immediate groups will react to the movie as from concern about how members of society who are less informed on the subject—especially children—will relate to the material. This type of concern is common among media activists. Arguments with media firms are often based on fear about the media's effect on other segments of society.

A second point is that the two groups are poles apart on the question of what it is ethically correct for the media to do in this case. One side has notions of ethically proper images that involve certain positive portrayals of abortion. The other side considers any portrayals that depict abortion as playing a legitimate part in mainstream society to be unethical.

Finally, it should be clear that this is an ethical conflict that cannot be resolved by government regulation. As we have seen, the First Amendment protects the creators of media materials, including most forms of entertainment, from government interference. The First Amendment would apply in the abortion fight. In other circumstances, however, other laws might take precedence, and a concerned citizen would need to understand that it is appropriate to ask the government to intervene. We have seen, for example, that the libel of a non-public figure in a TV entertainment program would likely allow the person who was insulted to have her or his day in court.

Knowing the laws that relate to particular media in particular circumstances is critical to understanding the rights and responsibilities that apply to you, media firms, and government when it comes to materials you like or don't like. In many cases, you will find that no governmental law will help you to force certain media organizations to act in what you believe is an ethical manner. You will also find out that there are few easily agreed-upon media ethics in a nation as complex and varied as the United States. Of course, people who care about media ethics should not give up trying to persuade media organizations to alter their notions of proper behavior. However, persuading media organizations to do things involves much more than simply insisting on the ethical value of one person's or one group's suggestions; as we have seen, there may be others who insist on the ethical value of totally opposite actions. So it is also necessary to understand the following: controversial proposals will not likely be accepted by media organizations as a result of social debate, unless the party making the proposal is able to exercise economic and political power.

CHAPTER REVIEW

For an interactive chapter recap and study guide, visit the companion website for *Media Today* at www.routledge.com/textbooks/mediatoday

QUESTIONS FOR DISCUSSION AND CRITICAL THINKING

1   In what way do the authoritarian and libertarian philosophies of media systems represent opposing views of human nature?
2   How has the meaning of "the press" in the First Amendment changed over the course of U.S. history?
3   From a legal standpoint, what is the difference between obscenity and pornography?
4   What does it mean to say that using part of a copyright work is fair use because the use is *transformative*?
5   "Media laws and regulations can be seen as a way to formally enforce agreed-upon norms of behavior by government officials with respect to media practitioners and by media practitioners with respect to the government and the society as a whole." Explain this statement and bring two examples to support it.

INTERNET RESOURCES

University of Iowa's list of Internet resources on media law (http://bailiwick.lib.uiowa.edu/journalism/mediaLaw/)
    This is a useful annotated collection of materials about law, for experts and non-experts, available around the Web.

Court decisions regarding freedom of speech in the United States (http://www.bc.edu/bc_org/avp/cas/comm/free_speech/decisions.html)

    From Boston College Law School, this series of links is arranged in historical and thematic order.

Journal of Mass Media Ethics (http://jmme.byu.edu/)

    According to its website, "the *Journal of Mass Media Ethics* is devoted to explorations of ethics problems and issues in the various fields of mass communication. Emphasis is placed on materials dealing with principles and reasoning in ethics, rather than anecdotes, orthodoxy, dogma, and enforcement of codes."

The Reporters' Committee for Freedom of the Press (http://www.rcfp.org/)

    Based in Arlington, Virginia, RCFP is a nonprofit organization dedicated to providing free legal help to journalists and news organizations since 1970.

KEY TERMS

You can find the definitions to these key terms in the marginal glossary throughout this chapter. Test your knowledge of these terms with interactive flash cards on the *Media Today* companion website.

abridge	embeds
actual malice	embellishment
advocacy organizations	equal time rule
antitrust policies	ethics
appropriation	evidentiary privilege
authoritarian approaches	excessive market control
bad tendency	fair comment and criticism
Cable Telecommunications Act of 1984	fair use regulations
Children's Online Privacy Protection Act of 1998	Fairness doctrine
	false light
clear and present danger	falsity
commercial speech	Family Friendly Programming Forum
communist approaches	fault
copyright	Federal Communications Commission (FCC)
Copyright Act of 1976	Federal Trade Commission (FTC)
cultural influences	Freedom of Information Act (FOIA)
defamation	Golden Mean
distribution	Golden Rule
economic influences	Government-in-the Sunshine Act
editorial policies	harm
editorial standards	ideal

injunction

intrusion

journalism reviews

libel

libel per quod

libel per se

libertarian approaches

marketplace of ideas

monopoly

national security

obscene material

oligopoly

ombudsperson

operating policies

parody

personal tort

policy books

political influences

pool reporters

pornography

press council

pressure groups

press privilege

principle

principle of utility

prior restraint

privacy

private person

privileged warrants and judicial
    proceedings

public disclosure

public figure

publication

regulation

shield laws

simple malice

simple negligence

slander

social responsibility approaches

stakeholders

sunshine laws

transformative

truth

unilaterals

value

veil of ignorance

Video Privacy Protection Act of 1988

CONSTRUCTING MEDIA LITERACY

1   Why do you think many people get upset about the burning of books? Can
    you find modern counterparts to the Nazi book burnings?

2   If you were a judge in a murder trial, would you allow cameras into your court-
    room? Why or why not?

3   The Children's Online Privacy Protection Act (COPPA) requires websites to
    get parents' permission if they want to get identifiable personal information
    (for example, full name, email address, phone number) from children under
    age thirteen. When the bill was first introduced to Congress, many privacy
    advocates wanted to raise the age to seventeen or under, or at least older than
    thirteen. Do you agree that this should have happened? Why do you think it
    didn't?

4   If it were up to you, would you reinstate the Fairness doctrine? Why or why
    not?

CASE STUDY   Journalists and Ethical Dilemmas

The idea   Reading about the ethical dilemmas that media practitioners experience is not the same thing as experiencing them first hand. You might be able to understand these dilemmas and the ways media practitioners and their organizations deal with them better by talking directly to them about it.

The method   Interview a local journalist about an ethical dilemma that he or she confronted during his or her career. Come prepared with questions, and take notes during the interview, or ask the journalist for permission to record it. To get the journalist to be most honest, you may have to promise that when you write your essay about the talk, you will not reveal his or her name.

Ask what the dilemma was. With whom did the journalist share the dilemma inside and outside of his/her media organization? How did the journalist resolve the dilemma? Why? How did it affect the story that the journalist wanted to tell?

In writing an essay about the interview, ask yourself if the resolution the journalist found for the dilemma fits with one or more of the ethics models described in this chapter. Also consider whether you would have resolved the dilemma in the same way or a different way.

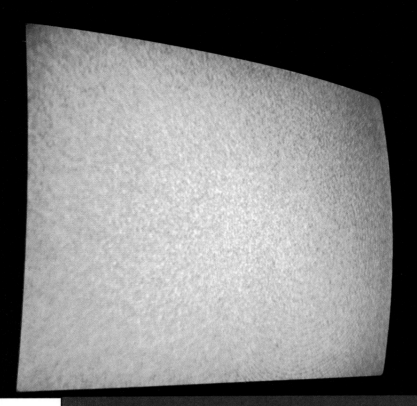

4 MAKING SENSE OF RESEARCH ON MEDIA EFFECTS AND MEDIA CULTURE

After studying this chapter, you will be able to:

1 Identify and explain what mass media research is as a practice, how it is conducted, and the ways in which it can be evaluated

2 Recognize and discuss the purpose, practices, and theories of the mainstream approaches to mass media research

3 Evaluate and distinguish among the three main goals of mainstream approaches to mass media research

4 Recognize the shift from mainstream approaches to mass media research to critical approaches

5 Recognize and discuss the purpose, practices, and theories of critical approaches to mass media research

6 Recognize and discuss the purpose, practices, and theories of cultural studies approaches to mass media research

7 Analyze how being media literate with regard to mass media research and media effects gives you access to tools for understanding and evaluating the media's presence and influence in your life

"There are in fact no masses; there are only ways of seeing people as masses."

RAYMOND WILLIAMS, CULTURAL PHILOSOPHER

Imagine a communication major, Jessica, who is a junior at a college near a large U.S. city. Jessica works on the Culture and Arts beat for the school's daily newspaper, which means that companies send her free tickets to plays, movies and concerts because they want her to write reviews about them for the paper. Jessica works late into the night at the newspaper office, trying to finish her reviews for the paper's website and its print edition. In the office, three flat screens bracketed to the wall are constantly tuned to the three major network stations in the area, and as she writes her reviews Jessica can't help but pay attention to what they are showing about the city: mostly stories of murder, robbery, and fires.

"Where is the coverage of all the great plays and concerts that I know are happening all around the city every day?" Jessica asks herself. She knows, too, that the level of violence in the city has receded substantially during the previous two years. Jessica is worried that viewers are getting the wrong impression, and that the local news is fostering a sense of fear. As the days go by, she decides that these sensational stories are problematic—both for what they show and for what they don't show. The news programs, she realizes, are ignoring the efforts of the mayor, the city commissioners, the school board, and the many other departments that keep the city working—or, sometimes, not working.

"It's hard to believe someone intelligent would watch this stuff," she tells her boyfriend Jim one day over lunch in the student center. "Well," Jim offers, "Loads of people around here pay attention to those shows. They may watch for the sports summary or the weather. The crime and violence just come along for the ride."

"But why?" Jessica presses him as she finishes her iced tea. "Why would stations put this junk on? And why would intelligent people not get angry and complain? Showing people an image of the city as filled with stories about violence and fires every day without giving them a sense of how the city works and the good things that are going on is dangerous. It can make people needlessly afraid, hopeless, and even wanting to leave. And anyway, why should sensational murder stories push out stories about concert series, art exhibits, and city government that can have much more impact on viewers' lives and on the future of the area?"

Jessica finds that a number of friends at the paper share her concerns about the local news. She becomes increasingly angry. One friend, a campus antipoverty activist and criminology major, confides that four months earlier he had met with the news directors of the three major television stations in the city. They listened politely to his complaints, he says, but in the end they did nothing. "The need to attract large numbers of viewers for advertisers obviously exceeds their desire to be publicly responsible," he suggests. Undeterred, Jessica is determined to go beyond what her friend has done. She decides to start a public advocacy group to try to put public pressure on the stations to change local news.

But how should she start? Jim suggests that she start with the basics: "You need to be more knowledgeable about the effects of TV and even on how local TV news operates. If you go out there and start complaining publicly with so little knowledge, even with a group behind you, you may come off looking foolish. And the people who run the stations will have had their way." Jim suggests that her first step might be to talk to her advisor. "Get his input into how this all works, what the effects of these sorts of images are, and the best ways to influence the companies that put them on the air," he says.

Jessica thinks that is a pretty good idea, so she lays out her concerns to her advisor, Communication professor Dave Berg. "It certainly is an interesting topic," Professor Berg says. "In fact, it's an issue I would love to pose to the graduate students in my 'media theory' class. Why don't you come to the class next week and I'll get the students to help you brainstorm about ways to understand local news from a variety of angles?" Jessica tells him that's a great idea. She secretly worries, though. "The grad students might just spout complicated 'ivory tower' phrases that have little to do with the real world and that just confuse me needlessly," she tells herself. Nevertheless, she shows up in the graduate class on that Thursday, finding seven enthusiastic grad students. It seems that she has hit on a hot-button topic with a substantial proportion of the seminar class. In fact, they are eager to express their viewpoints, and to link them to scholarly research.

The aim of this chapter is to bring you to the same realization as our fictional Jessica: that there is no ivory tower here. We will show that mass communication researchers have been grappling for decades with the most important social issues that have surrounded society's most important media, from newspapers to movies, from television to the Internet. We will look at the ways in which their research has contributed to, and even sparked, public debates about how we should think about media activities and media content. The aim is to help you become more aware than you otherwise might be of these developments, and of the impact that scholarly work on mass media continues to have on the ideas and activities of government, business, and the public at large.

The Nature of Mass Media Research

research the application of a systematic method to solve a problem or understand it better than in the past

mass media research the use of systematic methods to understand or solve problems regarding the mass media

Research is the application of a systematic method to solve a problem or understand it better than in the past. **Mass media research**, then, involves the use of systematic methods to understand or solve problems regarding the mass media.

The area is huge: mass media research is a large tree with many branches. One branch has to do with audiences. Media firms pay to find out who watches television, reads magazines, surfs the Web, or listens to the radio. Another branch relates to predicting the success of certain media materials. For example, a movie company might want to estimate how popular a film will be with its target audience if it is advertised in a certain way. A third branch centers on the relative success of advertising campaigns, such as whether a series of deodorant commercials using a famous sports personality leads to a greater increase in sales than a series of commercials for the same deodorant that featured "regular" people.

We will refer to these types of research in other chapters, but here our focus is very different. The research we are concerned with in this chapter tries to answer questions that relate to society's bottom line, not to a company's bottom line. This type of research asks about the role mass media play in improving or degrading the relationships, values, and ideals of society, and the people who make up that society, including questions such as:

- Does violence in news and entertainment encourage violence and/or cause people to be frightened when they leave their homes?
- Where do people get most of their information about candidates during political campaigns?
- Can we design advertising campaigns that will discourage teens from smoking cigarettes?
- What do the history and contemporary nature of advertising tell us about our society?
- What and who are the powers behind America's media arrangements, and how might they be affecting what Americans read and hear?
- What influence do advocacy groups have on the shaping of public policy regarding the media?

Addressing these sorts of topics is quite a complex task. It's hard to say that we have definite answers to each of these questions. After several decades of research, however, we certainly have a lot of evidence to consider.

Approaches to Mass Media Research

Broadly speaking, we can distinguish between research that is *empirical* and research that is *conceptual*, and also between research that is *quantitative* and research that is *qualitative*. The boundaries between these categories can be fuzzy, and academics can do more than one type of research at the same time. Still, each approach to research brings with it its own way of looking at the world and evaluating evidence.

conceptual research research that focuses on the perspectives or philosophies that we should use when we think about the media or media research

Conceptual and Empirical Work   **Conceptual research** focuses on the perspectives or philosophies that we should use when we think about the media or media research. Many scholars who study media ethics carry out conceptual work. Drawing on a long history of thought about moral behavior, their goal is to help

144

media practitioners, members of the public, and other scholars to think about how media firms ought to proceed in ethically challenging social and corporate environments. Scholars who comment on the history of mass communication research are carrying out important conceptual work. Their intent is to explore the concerns and beliefs about media effects that have guided professors over the decades, as well as the assumptions about individuals and society that are reflected in their conclusions.

In contrast, **empirical research** involves investigating and reporting on actual things in the world. In empirical research, it is important for the investigator to have well-elaborated ideas about the part of the world that he or she is studying. The best scholarly empirical research is *guided* by concepts.

The main difference between conceptual and empirical research, however, is that the former deals exclusively with concepts and their implications, whereas the latter uses concepts as jumping-off points for studying concrete parts of the world.

Consider one of the questions we asked earlier, "Can we design advertising campaigns that will discourage teens from smoking cigarettes?" You may think that answering this question does not involve a lot of concepts—that it simply involves setting up a series of anti-smoking ads and seeing if they persuade teens. It turns out, though, that a researcher who is investigating this question will systematically turn to large bodies of psychological and sociological knowledge about persuasion in order to get ideas regarding the best ways to set up such advertising campaigns and the best ways to think about, and measure, their effects. Those bodies of knowledge are themselves based on the findings of previous research. In empirical social research, the findings of studies lead to ideas about how things work that are used and tested in other studies.

Bodies of knowledge that contain tested explanations about how phenomena work are called **theories**. In the case of the ad campaign, the researcher might use the theory of reasoned action, developed by Martin Fishbein and Icek Ajzen in the late 1960s, to create the building blocks for the commercials. According to the **theory of reasoned action**, the most important determinant of a person's behavior is intent. The individual's *intention* to perform a behavior is a combination of his or her attitude toward performing the behavior and a subjective norm—that is, the individual's sense of how others whom he or she cares about evaluate the behavior. From these basic building blocks comes an entire body of writings and studies that have tested and expanded Fishbein and Ajzen's model.

A media consultant setting up an anti-smoking commercial based on the theory of reasoned action would use the theory to create parts of the commercial and generate *hypotheses* about how the target audience would react to these elements. **Hypotheses** are tentative predictions made in order to draw out and test the logical consequences of a theory or set of concepts. The aim of this empirical study would be to determine if the hypotheses about the elements' influence on the viewers of the commercial hold true. To do that, a researcher would probably carry out an **experiment**, a study in which groups of randomly chosen people are exposed

Media researchers examine the effects of a media product on its intended audience.

empirical research research that involves investigating and reporting on actual things in the world

theories bodies of knowledge that contain tested explanations of how phenomena work

theory of reasoned action a theory, developed by Martin Fishbein and Icek Ajzen, that posits that the most important determinant of a person's behavior is behavior intent, and that an individual's intention to perform a behavior is a combination of his or her attitude toward performing the behavior and a subjective norm

hypotheses tentative predictions made in order to draw out and test the logical consequences of a theory or set of concepts

experiment a study in which groups of randomly chosen people are exposed to one stimulus while other groups of randomly chosen people are given a similar presentation without that stimulus

control groups in an experiment, the groups that receive the presentation without the experimental elements

quantitative research research in which the researcher collects and reports data in numerical form

questionnaire a quantitative research tool consisting of a series of questions with answers that can be translated into numbers

survey a form of quantitative empirical research that involves systematically asking questions of a population of people and then presenting numerical tallies of the results

sample a subset of a population that is selected through systematic methods in such a way that the answers from the subset can be considered generalizable to the entire population of concern

content analysis a quantitative research tool that counts aspects of products as opposed to aspects of individuals; it allows a researcher to systematically choose a sample of mass media material, examine certain aspects of that material, and then present the results quantitatively

qualitative research making sense of an aspect of reality by showing how different parts of it fit together in particular ways

to a stimulus (in this case, the commercial with the elements that will test the hypotheses) while other groups of randomly chosen people are given a similar presentation without that stimulus (in this case, a commercial without those elements). The groups that receive the presentation without the experimental elements are called the **control groups**.

In our example, the researcher would ask the people in both the experimental and the control groups questions that would indicate whether or not they smoke and gauge their attitudes toward cigarettes. Then the groups would see the assigned commercials. Afterwards, the researcher would find ways to determine any changes in the attitudes and behaviors regarding smoking of those in the experimental group compared to those of the control group (which did not see the experimental elements) and whether these have supported the hypothesis. The results would lead the researcher to draw certain conclusions about the usefulness of the hypotheses (or of the elements in the commercial) for getting smokers to change their attitudes or behavior.

Quantitative and Qualitative Research The experiment is only one form of empirical research used by scholars attempting to explore the social implications of mass media. It can be classified as one of the *quantitative research methods*. The phrase **quantitative research** merely means that the researcher collects and reports data in numerical form. In an experiment of the sort mentioned above, investigators typically gauge the attitudes and behaviors of their subjects by asking them to fill out **questionnaires** or series of questions with answers that can be translated into numbers. (For example, 1 may stand for "doesn't smoke cigarettes," while 5 stands for "smokes four or more cigarettes per day.")

Another popular form of quantitative empirical research involving people is the **survey**. A quantitative survey is a research tool that involves systematically asking questions of a population of people and then presenting numerical tallies of the results (see Figure 4.1). A researcher could conduct a survey, for example, of parents whose households are connected to the Web. Since millions of families in the United States fit that description, survey researchers take a *sample* of the population. A **sample** is a subset of a population that is selected through systematic methods in such a way that the answers from the subset can be considered generalizable to the entire population of concern.

Not all quantitative empirical research relating to mass communication involves people. Researchers who study mass media content often use a method called **content analysis** that is quantitative but that counts aspects of media products rather than aspects of individuals. Content analysis is a technique that allows a researcher to systematically choose a sample of mass media material and examine certain aspects of that material. The results are presented quantitatively; for example: "Twenty percent of local news stories involved fires and 20 percent involved robberies, but only 15 percent involved city government."

Now let's turn things around a bit: not all empirical research is quantitative. Mass communication researchers conduct a lot of research that is empirical (that is, it systematically examines aspects in the world at large) but is *qualitative*. **Qualitative research** involves making sense of an aspect of reality by showing how different parts of it fit together in particular ways. One example is an historian who sifts through an enormous number of government documents to reach an understanding of the formation of the Federal Communications Commission. Another example is a person who watches every American movie since 1960 that

Joseph Turow/Annenberg Public Policy Center

The Internet and the Family 2000 Survey

PARENTS VERSION—Posted Unweighted Data[1]

Hello, my name is _____ from a national public opinion research company. We are conducting an important study for the University of Pennsylvania about families. Let me assure you that this is not a sales call, and the answers you provide are strictly confidential and will only be used together with those of other respondents

S1 We're interested in the kinds of things people use in their homes today. As I read to you a short list of things some households have, please tell me whether you have one in your home.

a. A microwave oven?

Yes	98%
No	2%

b. A VCR?

Yes	99%
No	1%

c. A PC or personal computer?

Yes	100%

S2 Does any one in your household use a personal computer at home to connect to the Internet for e-mail or any other purpose—that is, to go online?

Yes	98%

2. How many children between the ages of 8 and 17 years of age are living in your household?

One	48%
Two	36%
Three	12%
Four	3%
Five or more	2%

3. May I please speak to either the mother, father, or guardian of the children 8–17 currently living at home?

Yes	100%

4. Do you have a second phone line or cable connection in your home that you use primarily for connecting to the Internet?

Yes	46%
No	54%

5. Have you personally ever gone online, that is, used the Internet, the World Wide Web, or e-mail? IF YES: Is that for e-mail *only* or do you do other things on the Internet as well?

E-mail *only*	21%
Other Internet (with or without e-mail)	74%
Neither	6%

6. How would you characterize your abilities to go online or navigate the Internet? Would you say you are a beginner, an intermediate user, an advanced user, or an expert user?

A beginner	26%
An intermediate user	6%
An advanced user	21%
An expert user	7%
Don't know	*

7. In the past month, how many times did you go online from (READ EACH ITEM)—did you go online every day, every other day, every few days, a few times during the month, or one or two days? **Based on those who go online n = 945**

	Work	Home	Other places
Every day	30%	37%	3%
Every other day	6%	17%	2%
Every few days	7%	18%	3%
A few times	6%	11%	6%
One or two days	4%	6%	5%
Don't know (do not read)	1%	*	2%
None (vol.)	39%	4%	74%

[1]Unless otherwise noted, unweighted base = 1.001

Figure 4.1

Continued ...

8. How long has your family had an online connection at home?

Less than six months	14%
Between six months and a year	17%
More than a year, but less than two years	22%
More than two years	46%
Don't know (vol.)	1%

9. There are a number of *positive things* that people say about the Internet. Please tell me **whether** you strongly agree, somewhat agree, neither agree nor disagree, somewhat disagree, or strongly disagree when it comes to the following statements:

	Strongly Agree	Somewhat agree	Neither agree nor disagree	Somewhat disagree	Strongly disagree	DK (Vol.)
a. The Internet is a safe place for my children to spend time *50*	11%	39%	10%	23%	16%	1%
b. Access to the Internet at home helps my children with their school work *89*	63%	26%	3%	4%	4%	1%
c. The Internet can bring my children closer to community groups and churches *40*	14%	26%	15%	23%	20%	3%
d. Online, my children discover fascinating, useful things they never heard of before *85*	50%	35%	4%	7%	2%	1%
e. People worry too much that adults will take advantage of children on the Internet *59*	29%	30%	5%	16%	19%	1%
f. The Internet can help my children to learn about diversity and tolerance *66*	29%	37%	13%	11%	8%	2%
g. Children who do not have Internet access are at a disadvantage compared to their peers who do have Internet access *74*	42%	32%	4%	13%	9%	*

10. There are a number of *concerns* that people express regarding the Internet. Please tell me whether you strongly agree, somewhat agree, neither agree nor disagree, somewhat disagree, or strongly disagree when it comes to the following statements:

	Strongly Agree	Somewhat agree	Neither agree nor disagree	Somewhat disagree	Strongly disagree	DK (Vol.)
a. Children who spend too much time on the Internet develop anti-social behavior *42*	16%	26%	12%	22%	21%	4%
b. I often worry that I won't be able to explore the Web with my children as well as other parents do *25*	10%	15%	8%	25%	42%	1%
c. I am concerned that children give out personal information about themselves when visiting web sites or chat rooms *74*	44%	30%	4%	9%	11%	1%
d. Families who spend a lot of time online talk to each other less than they otherwise would *51*	25%	26%	8%	22%	19%	2%
e. I am concerned that my child/children might view sexually explicit images on theInternet *72*	48%	24%	4%	11%	13%	*
f. I am concerned that my child/children might view violent images on the Internet *61*	32%	29%	6%	18%	15%	*
g. Going online too often might lead children to become isolated from other people *59*	27%	32%	6%	18%	17%	1%
h. My children's exposure to the Internet might interfere with the values and beliefs I want to teach them *42*	18%	24%	7%	23%	27%	*

Figure 4.1 continued

This excerpted survey on the Internet and Family was conducted by Joseph Turow and the University of Pennsylvania's Annenberg Public Policy Center in January and February 2000. The survey was completed via telephone interviews that were conducted with a nationwide cross-section of 1,001 parents who have children aged 8 to 17 in homes with Internet connections, and 304 children aged 10 to 17 (half of which were selected from families in which the parents were also interviewed).

portrays homosexuality and writes a book that charts the treatment of this theme in U.S. films.

Like quantitative research, qualitative research often relies on sets of concepts (sometimes called **frameworks**) to guide understanding. The historian may be exploring whether ideas about the influence of business on government regulation make sense when looking at the formation of the FCC. The scholar studying homo-

frameworks sets of concepts that guide understanding

sexuality in U.S. films may draw on literature about minorities in American culture to help her make sense of and organize her material.

Tools for Evaluating Mass Media Research

You may be asking yourself how anyone knows whether these experiments or surveys or content analyses or historical studies really reflect reality; how can anyone be sure that the research they read or that they help people conduct is worth serious attention? The answer is not simple. Everyone who is concerned about the social implications of media—researchers, policymakers, media executives, and members of the public—has to think critically about research. Over the decades, researchers have developed a variety of ways for trying to think about the drawbacks of research findings.

Here are some topics to think about when you read about research:

- *The nature of the sample*. If the study has used a sample (of people or of content), how representative is it of the group about which the researcher is drawing conclusions? If the researcher studies teenagers and claims that his findings apply to the entire U.S. population, that's a problem. If a researcher studies situation comedies and claims that her findings apply to all of TV programming, that's a problem. These samples simply don't seem to be applicable to the larger group.

- *The size of the sample and the way it's collected*. Statisticians have determined how many people must be studied if a survey is to be reflective of a larger population. They have also devised methods for systematically determining which people are to be included in and excluded from samples. Similarly, researchers who conduct experiments have developed careful, systematic ways of choosing subjects. Does the research you are reading discuss these issues?

- *The design of the study*. What do you think about the way the study was set up? If it is a qualitative study, what do you think about the way the researcher posed the issues and went about gathering evidence for answers? If it is a quantitative study—a survey, an experiment, or a content analysis, for example— what do you think of the questions asked? One important point to consider is whether they were *leading questions*. **Leading questions** imply the answers the researcher wants in the way the questions are posed. For example, if I ask you, "Do you like to watch shows that are terribly violent?" you may feel that saying that you like violent shows will make you look bad to me. You might therefore say no even though you like violent shows. Research based on leading questions is not very persuasive because one can never know whether people answered the way they did in order to please the researcher or because they believed what they said.

  leading questions questions that imply the answers the researcher wants in the way the questions are posed

- *The reliability of the study*. Researchers consider reliability an important attribute of empirical studies. When a study is called **reliable**, that means that the results can be reproduced by repeating the conditions in the study. Another survey that asked the same questions and got a sample the same way would yield basically the same findings, even though the specific people participating in the sample would be different. If a study's methods are unclear, or if the answers to its questions depend greatly on the person asking the question, most people would consider the study too ambiguous to be a reliable reflection of real-world

  reliable the results can be reproduced by repeating the conditions in the study

conditions. It pays to emphasize that this concern about reliability applies mainly to empirical studies.

When it comes to conceptual research, we often place great value on the unique interpretive abilities of philosophers or ethicists. We expect them to show us how they arrived at their insights. We typically can judge whether or not we accept their conclusions by looking at the bodies of knowledge they brought together that stimulated their thinking, but we don't expect that just about anyone who had read the same materials could have come up with the same ideas. Creativity, intelligence, logic and persuasion often take the place of reliability when we judge conceptual research.

■ *The soundness of the analysis.* When reading the work of philosophers and ethicists, we typically decide whether or not we accept their conclusions by evaluating their analysis. We look at the bodies of knowledge they have brought together and we judge how logical their thinking is in relation to that material. The same approach applies to our evaluation of a researcher's analysis of his or her empirical data. We should ask whether the way the researcher is analyzing the data makes sense from the standpoint of basic logic—for example, whether a conclusion about a group's use of television is really justified by the numerical findings. We should also ask whether the researcher has analyzed the data well enough to understand truly what is going on. For example, after dividing certain TV viewing data between men and women, the researcher may conclude that gender is the great divider. A closer look at the data, however, might disclose that the real difference is not men and women in general but specifically between the Latino men and Latina women. Of course, as a reader you wouldn't have the ability to examine the researcher's data to find that out. But you should ask yourself what types of analysis the researcher should have done and be suspicious if they haven't been carried out.

■ *The validity of the study.* All types of studies ought to be judged in terms of their validity. **Validity** refers to the extent to which the study accurately describes the circumstances that exist in the real world. Determining this is often more difficult, and more controversial, than it may sound. Consider a researcher who wants to determine whether violent cartoons encourage children to commit violence. The researcher decides to set up an experimental situation in which children are exposed to cartoon characters hitting each other and are given the opportunity soon afterwards to hit dolls that look like those cartoon characters. Another group of children, a control group, is shown a nonviolent cartoon but is presented with the same dolls soon after seeing their video. Her findings show that the children in the experimental group are far more likely to hit the dolls and to hit each other while hitting the dolls than are the children in the control group.

Assume that the researcher conducts all her work impeccably. The nature of her sample, its size and the way it's collected, the design of the study—all these elements make for a study that's elegant, with results that are reliable. But, as a media literate consumer must still ask, are the results valid? That is, can we believe that what the researcher has found in her experimental situation has any relationship to what children would do in the real world?

Those who say that it is not valid would argue that it's unlikely that children will find themselves in situations where dolls representing violent cartoon characters show up near them right after they watch cartoons in which these characters star. The naysayers would argue that it was this

validity the extent to which the study accurately describes circumstances as they exist in the real world

unlikely scenario and the excitement it caused among the children that led to their hitting the cartoon-character dolls and hitting each other while hitting the dolls.

Those who say it *is* a valid study would argue that although the scene the children confronted after the cartoon isn't exactly what they see at home, many do have dolls representing cartoon characters at home and many do have opportunities to copy the violence that they see on the tube. Moreover, in their excitement in copying the violence and action they see in the cartoons, many may, in fact, end up hurting (purposefully or not) the children who are watching with them.

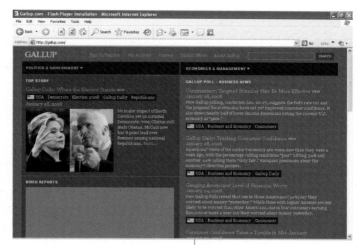

www.gallup.com, website of the Gallup organization, which is widely regarded as a conductor of reliable studies.

CASE STUDY   Evaluating a Scholarly Article

It takes some training to evaluate a scholarly article. The main thing to remember is that just because a study has been published in an academic journal doesn't mean that it is perfect. Sometimes, published articles have many flaws as well as good points. Hone your scholarly reading skills in the following manner:

1   Read an article about an empirical study that is published in a scholarly journal such as the *Journal of Communication*, *Journal of Broadcasting and Electronic Media*, *Critical Studies in Media Communication*, or *Journalism and Mass Communication Quarterly*.

2   Write a summary of the main points of the article in a page or less, focusing on the major questions, the theory the authors are working with to help understand or address those questions, the method used to carry out the study, the major findings, and the authors' conclusions about what the study means.

3   Then evaluate what you like and don't like about the study from the standpoint of the features discussed in this chapter: the nature of the sample, the size of the sample and the way it's collected, the design of the study, the reliability of the study, the soundness of the analysis, and the validity of the study.

4   In general, do you think the topics or questions that the author addressed are important? Why or why not? How convinced are you that the way the authors addressed those topics sheds an important light on the topics or questions?

The point here is not to scare you, but to alert you to what it means to be a literate consumer of mass media research. If you understand the basics of evaluating research and you get an overview of the kinds of concerns media researchers have had over the decades, you will be able to ask the right questions and critically evaluate the answers to those questions.

The Early Years of Mass Media Research in the United States

To find the first major academic consideration of mass communication in the United States, we must go back to the first two decades of the twentieth century—

nearly one hundred years ago. Two major issues relating to the media preoccupied the thinkers of the day. The first was the media's role in helping to keep a sense of American community alive. The second was the media's role in encouraging bad behavior among children—an issue that faded rather quickly, only to reappear many years later.

Searching for Community: Early Critical Studies Research

The early twentieth century was a time of enormous social change in American society. The industrial revolution was in full swing, and factories were turning out machine-made consumer products at low cost in numbers that had never been seen before. Many of these factories were located in cities, and they drew millions of workers who streamed out of farming communities in order to take advantage of the higher salaries and better opportunities of urban life.

Even more numerous than the workers who came to the cities from U.S. farms were the immigrants from central and eastern Europe who were teeming into American ports looking for a piece of the American dream. For many, the dream was a bit of a nightmare, at least at first. A large number of the newcomers, poor and not knowing the English language, led a difficult, even hand-to-mouth existence that contrasted dramatically with the lives of the wealthy urban industrialists of the day and the relatively modest, yet still quite comfortable, situation of most nonimmigrants.

Social observers in this period considered this a very serious situation. It wasn't just the poverty that concerned them. They also worried that this new urban, often non-English-speaking population who knew little of American values would endanger the small-town democratic community that they believed had characterized American society before the late nineteenth century. Could the traditional sense of community—that shared sense of responsibility that people felt toward their neighbors and their nation—be sustained in cities where so few people knew or cared about one another? Could the torrents of immigrants be brought into the mainstream of American society so that they considered its values their own?

Now, you may not agree that the questions these social observers asked were the correct ones. You may feel that these people were romanticizing small-town communities. Or you might argue that those who already lived in the United States did not have the right to impose their "American" values on the new immigrants. These are quite legitimate objections, but at the turn of the twentieth century, many people saw U.S. society's biggest problems as preserving a sense of small-town community and making sure immigrants "assimilated."

The pessimists among them concluded that there really was no hope; that urban society, and especially immigrant urban society, would destroy the connectedness that they associated with small-town America. Drawing upon late nineteenth-century European writings on the dangers of the "crowd" (or the "masses" as they were sometimes called), the prejudiced among them saw these urban crowds as having dangerously irrational tendencies. There was, they felt, a good reason to keep immigrants away from U.S. shores.

A Society of Shared Ideas   How are the mass media related to this issue? Well, a group of prominent sociologists at the University of Chicago argued publicly and in their scholarly writings that it was precisely because of the mass media that the situation in "mass society" was not nearly as bleak as some thought.

The influx of European immigrants in the early twentieth century caused many social observers to take a hard look at what constitutes a *community*.

Professors Robert Park, John Dewey, and Charles Cooley suggested that the widespread popularity of newspapers and magazines in the early twentieth century allowed for the creation of a new type of community (see Figure 4.2).

These researchers argued that the media brought together large numbers of geographically separated, diverse individuals who would otherwise be disconnected from one another and from a common notion of society, and allowed them to share ideas about the society without assembling in the same geographic area. They said that if media firms acted responsibly, Americans could learn ideas that were essential to their democracy from their messages. Robert Park conducted a study of the immigrant press in the United States, and concluded that, far from keeping the foreigners in their own little ethnic worlds, the immigrant newspapers were helping people (over time) to acclimate to American society. Immigrants, he said, were using their foreign-language media to learn how to be good citizens.

Cooley and Dewey were social philosophers. Their work tended to be conceptual rather than empirical. Park, a former newspaper reporter, was more empirically oriented. All three were the most prominent members of what became known as the Chicago School of sociology. Many of their ideas are fresh and interesting

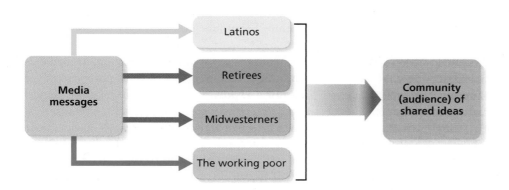

Figure 4.2

A New Type of Community
The media has the power to bring disparate individuals together by broadcasting the same notions of society to large numbers of people who might otherwise never interact—thereby creating a new type of community.

even today. Not everyone agreed with them then (and not everyone agrees with them now). Nevertheless, they were among the first U.S. academics to show how systematically presented ideas and research about the mass media could feed into important social issues.

Fearing Propaganda: Early Concerns About Persuasion

At about the same time that Cooley, Dewey and Park were writing about the possibility that mass media could help society maintain an informed democratic public, other researchers were expressing strong concerns about unethical rulers using the power of the mass media to reach huge numbers of people for undemocratic ends.

propaganda messages designed to change the attitudes and behavior of huge numbers of otherwise disconnected individuals on controversial social issues

Harold Lasswell, a political science professor at the University of Chicago, saw mass media organizations as powerful weapons of persuasion because they reached enormous numbers of geographically dispersed people in very short periods of time. Never before in history had this been possible, Lasswell and other researchers pointed out. They feared that powerful interest groups in a society would use mass media for propaganda purposes. These researchers defined **propaganda** as messages designed to change the attitudes and behavior of huge numbers of otherwise disconnected individuals on controversial social issues. Under the right conditions, they feared, such propaganda would enable people in power to spread lies about their opponents through the media and manipulate large numbers of people so that they would act together in support of the views of the people in power (see Figure 4.3). Those in the society who opposed these rulers would be at a substantial disadvantage.

One reason that such fears abounded in the United States had to do with the successful manipulation of newspaper reports and photographs by both the Allies and the German government during World War I. The head of the U.S. propaganda effort, George Creel, wrote a popular book, *How We Advertised America* (1920), in which he boasted that expertly crafted messages—on billboards, on records, and in movies—had moved huge numbers of people to work for the war effort. In addition, *The Brass Check* (1919), a book by the social critic Upton Sinclair, alleged that major advertisers were demanding favorable coverage in exchange for their purchase of ad space. Other reports detailed how public relations professions were supporting the aims of major corporations by secretly planting stories that echoed these corporations' viewpoints in U.S. newspapers. Newspapers themselves, critics contended, skewed their coverage of certain events to support particular political viewpoints.

Identifying and Analyzing Propaganda   Many liberal thinkers of the day saw these activities as fundamentally threatening to democracy, since citizens often had no idea of the intentions behind the messages they were seeing and hearing.

Some writers, such as the prominent journalist Walter Lippmann, argued that the most important culprits hindering U.S. newspapers' objective portrayal of the world were not propaganda forces such as advertisers or public relations practitioners.[1] Rather, said Lippmann, the culprits were U.S. journalists themselves. Because they were mere mortals with selective ways of seeing things, and because they worked in organizations with deadlines, restrictions on story length, and the need to grab readers' attentions, news journalists often portrayed predictably patterned (stereotyped), limited views of the world. Lippman believed that this was

Figure 4.3

Examples of Propaganda

When is propaganda *really* propaganda? The critical, media literate consumer must learn to recognize that even persuasive material circulated by those who seem to be "in the right" are pieces of propaganda all the same. These American (left) and German (right) propaganda posters from World War II show that both sides used persuasive, even manipulative, messages to garner support for their side and anger toward the opposition.

an important problem to examine and publicize because, he said, news sources play a critical role in society. In a book called *Public Opinion* (1922), he argued that the news media are a primary source of the "pictures in our heads" about the vast external world of public affairs that is "out of reach, out of sight, out of mind" (1922, p. 29). Lippman's notion that the media create "the ideas in our heads" about what is going on in the world is referred to as **agenda setting**. Many journalism professors in the 1920s and beyond picked up on Lippman's theory of agenda setting as a justification for examining the content of newspapers and the work that people in the news business perform.

Other academic thinkers of the era were more likely to emphasize the propagandistic aspect of the press. Academics of the 1920s and 1930s, such as Leonard Doob, Alfred McLung Lee, Ralph Casey, and George Seldes, saw the importance of systematically exploring the forces guiding media companies. They also saw great value in analyzing media content. Their aim was to lift what they felt was a veil of secrecy over what media firms did. They felt that by publicizing their findings, they could help citizens to protect themselves from the undue power of media organizations. They called the activity *propaganda analysis*.

Propaganda analysis involves the systematic examination of mass-media messages that seem to be designed to sway the attitudes of large populations on controversial issues. It is carried out through content analysis. Specially trained coders examine a population of messages (articles, movies, radio shows) for elements that the researchers believe are significant. Say, for example, the analysts in the late 1930s were concerned that U.S. newspapers were portraying the communist Soviet Union in unrelentingly negative ways that might harm chances for a United States–Soviet

agenda setting the notion that the media create "the ideas in our heads" about what is going on in the world

propaganda analysis the systematic examination of mass media messages that seem to be designed to sway the attitudes of large populations on controversial issues

collaboration against Hitler's Germany. To find out what influential newspapers were doing, the researchers might systematically examine two years of articles about the Soviet Union in major U.S. newspapers. The researchers would be trained (and tested on their ability) to note a variety of topics included in the coverage of that country, from music to crime to politics. They would also be trained to mark specific details about those topics. After analyzing the findings, the researchers would be able to come to quantitative conclusions about the messages about Russia that major press outlets were presenting to large numbers of Americans.

Some writers on the history of mass communication research have suggested that propaganda analysts took a **magic bullet or hypodermic needle approach** to mass communication (see Figure 4.4). By this, they mean that the propaganda analysts believed that messages delivered through the mass media persuaded all people powerfully and directly (as if they had been hit by a bullet or injected by a needle) without the people having any control over the way they reacted. For example, critics say that propaganda analysts believed that a well-made ad, an emotionally grabbing movie, or a vivid newspaper description would be able to sway millions of people toward the media producers' goals.

Actually, the terms *magic bullet* and *hypodermic needle* are too simplistic to describe the effects that propaganda analysts felt the media had on individuals. For one thing, the propaganda analysts certainly did not believe that all types of messages would be equally persuasive. (They stated, for example, that audiences would more likely accept messages that reinforced common values than messages that contradicted common values.) For another, they emphasized that propaganda is more likely to work under circumstances of media monopoly than when many competitive media voices argue over the ideas presented. They believed, too, that people could be taught to critically evaluate (and so not be so easily influenced by) propaganda.

Nevertheless, it is true that propaganda analysts of the 1920s and 1930s tended to focus on media producers and their output. They assumed that most members of the society shared similar understandings of that output. They emphasized the importance of this sharing of meaning and so didn't focus on the possibility that different members of the audience might interpret messages differently.

You may have realized that this emphasis on shared understanding also describes the hope of members of the Chicago school of sociology that the new media could help America overcome the problems of mass society. It was, however, an emphasis that not all academic researchers agreed upon. Another way of seeing media influence—one that suited very different social questions—was developing.

magic bullet or hypodermic needle approach the idea that messages delivered through the mass media persuade all people powerfully and directly (as if they were hit by a bullet or injected by a needle) without the people having any control over the way they react

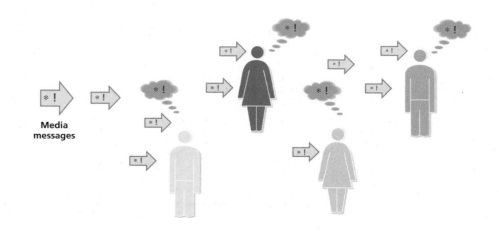

Figure 4.4
The Hypodermic Needle or Magic Bullet Approach has been used by researchers as a punching bag to illustrate what they believe is a simplistic view of media effects.

Media messages

Kids and Movies: Continuing Effects Research

By the mid-1920s, large numbers of parents, social workers and public welfare organizations were worried about whether specific films might be negatively affecting youngsters. Invented just a few decades earlier, the movies had become very much a part of Americans' leisure activities by the 1920s. As children and teenagers became accustomed to moviegoing, adults fretted that the violence, sexual suggestiveness, and misrepresentations of reality in many of the films they watched might bring about a slew of problems in their lives. Among the ills suggested were bad sleep patterns, improper notions of romance, and violent conduct.

These ideas may sound very modern to have been around as early as the 1920s. You may know (and we'll note later in the book) that in recent years television programs, comic books, video games, sports programs, the Internet, songs—as well as movies—have all been accused of encouraging these same problems among U.S. youth.

The Social and Psychological Effects of Films   These early controversies over movies marked the first time that social researchers carried out systematic research to determine whether these accusations had any basis in reality. The most important of these projects, formally titled *Motion Pictures and Youth*, is typically called the Payne Fund Studies because a foundation called the Payne Fund put forward the money for this wide-ranging exploration. The research effort was led by Professor W. W. Charters of Ohio State University and was conducted by the most prominent psychologists, sociologists, and educators of the day. The studies, published in 1933, look at the effects of particular films on sleep patterns, knowledge about foreign cultures, attitudes about violence, and delinquent behavior.

The researchers used a range of empirical techniques, including experiments, surveys and content analysis. One especially interesting survey was qualitative: a sociologist interviewed female college students about the extent to which and ways in which movies had affected their notions of romance. A noteworthy experiment was aimed at determining whether children who have seen violent films sleep more restlessly than those who have seen only nonviolent films. The children in the experiment were shown a movie featuring a lot of fighting, whereas those in the control condition saw a film with no combat at all. To determine the effects of the films on sleep, the researchers had the children sleep where they could observe them. Among other aspects of the children's sleep, the researchers measured their "restlessness" by attaching equipment to their beds that would note how often they moved and turned. They found that the children who had viewed the violent film tossed and turned more than the ones who had not.

Some popular commentators in the 1930s suggested that the results showed that individual movies could have major negative effects on all children—a kind of hypodermic needle effect. Most of the Payne Fund researchers themselves, though, went out of their way to point out that youngsters' reactions to movies were not at all uniform. Instead, these reactions very much depended on *specific social and psychological differences* among children. A sociologist in the group, for example, concluded that a particular film might move a youngster to want or not want to be a criminal. The specific reaction, the sociologist found, depended to a large extent on the social environment, attitudes, and interests of the child.

The psychologists in the group, for their part, pointed out that the way children reacted to films often depended on individual differences in mental or cognitive ability. So, for example, two researchers looked at children's emotional reactions to a film by hooking them up to instruments that measured their heartbeat and the amount of sweat on their skin. They found that children varied widely in

Contemporary parental concerns about violence and suggestiveness in video games and other media may date back to 1920s worries about the effects of the then relatively new technology of film on children.

social relations
interactions among people

emotional stimulation, and suggested that differences in response to specific scenes were caused by varied abilities to comprehend what they saw on the screen.

Social Relations and the Media

At Columbia University's sociology department, beginning in the early 1940s, a new contribution to this emphasis on people's different reactions to media materials emerged. It was the idea that **social relations**—interactions among people—influence the way individuals interpret media messages. The basic idea is straightforward: when people watch movies, read newspapers, listen to the radio or use any other medium, they often talk with other people about what they have seen or heard, and this can affect what they think about what they have just seen or heard. To understand how media content affects one person differently from another, then, we might want to know whom they spoke with about the material.

This sequence of images, which appeared in *Look* magazine in 1963, re-opened the floodgates of public concern over the effects of media-depicted violence. Media researcher Dr Albert Bandura shot this series of photos during what is often referred to as his "Bobo doll research," in which children in a laboratory setting were observed behaving violently with a blow-up Bobo doll after watching a film of people behaving violently.

Media Influence and Opinion Leaders   Curiously, until the early 1940s researchers didn't think of placing social relations alongside individual social and psychological differences as a major factor in helping determine the different under-standings that people draw from the media. The point was made loudly, however, by Paul Lazarsfeld and his colleagues at Columbia. The discovery started in a large-scale survey of the voting attitudes and activities of people in Erie County, Ohio, about the 1940 presidential election.

Lazarsfeld and his colleagues interviewed four similar samples of approxi-mately 600 people about their use of radio and newspapers as it related to the elec-tion. The researchers split the people up in this way because they were exploring a technique called a *panel survey*. In a **panel survey**, the same individuals are asked questions over a period of time. The purpose is to see whether and how the atti-tudes of these people change over time. In the early 1940s, panel surveys were an innovative design. Lazarsfeld wanted to find out whether asking people questions once a month during the election campaign (May to November) would lead to their answering questions differently from the way they would answer if the inves-tigators asked them questions a few times during the period, only once during the period, or only at the end of the period. After comparing the answers given by the four samples, Lazarsfeld concluded that surveying people every month did not affect their answers. The good thing about surveying them every month, however (despite its expense), was that the researchers could track the changes in the peo-ple's opinions regarding the candidates.

When the Columbia researchers concentrated on the roles that radio and news-papers played in individuals' decisions regarding the campaign, they found that news about the race seemed to change few people's voting intentions. However, when Lazarsfeld and his colleagues turned away from the issue of direct media influence to knowledge about the election, they got a surprise. The researchers were struck by the importance of voters' influence on one another. In short, vot-ers who participated in the survey reported that instead of being exposed to the election through news coverage, they learned what was going on through discus-sions with friends and acquaintances.

Building from their data in a somewhat shaky manner, Lazarsfeld and his col-leagues offered the **two-step flow model** (see Figure 4.5). This model states that media influence often works in two stages: (1) media content (opinions and facts) is picked up by people who use the media frequently, and (2) these people, in turn, act as opinion leaders when they discuss the media content with others. The oth-ers are therefore influenced by the media in a way that is one step removed from the actual content.

As an everyday example, think of a friend whose taste in movies is similar to yours and who is much more likely than you to keep up with the latest news about films. When the movie companies put out new releases, he not only reads news-paper and magazine reviews, but also checks the Web and reads the trade press. At least once a week, over lunch, you and that friend talk about the new releases and discuss the possibility of seeing "the best one" that weekend. Clearly, media discussions of the new movies are influencing you through your friend. The two-step flow is first from the various media to your friend and then to you.

Paul Lazarsfeld, his colleague Robert Merton, and other members of Columbia's sociology department went on to conduct several other studies on the relationship between opinion leaders, the two-step flow, and the mass media. In addition to these important works (which were influential because of their inno-vative methods as well as because of their findings), the Columbia program con-ducted research that looked at several aspects of the relationship between the media

panel survey   asking the same individuals questions over a period of time in order to find out whether and how the attitudes of these people change over time

two-step flow model   a model, developed by Paul Lazarsfeld and his colleagues, that states that media influence often works in two stages: (1) media content (opinions and facts) is picked up by people who use the media frequently, and (2) these people, in turn, act as opinion leaders when they discuss the media content with others, who are therefore influenced by the media in a way that is one step removed from the actual content

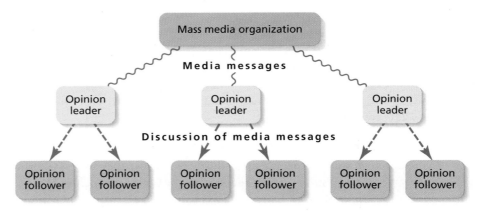

Figure 4.5

Model of the Two-step Flow of Media Influence

Through their social relations research, Lazarsfeld and his colleagues found that media messages often move in two distinct stages—from media organizations to opinion leaders, and then from opinion leaders to opinion followers, through discussion and interaction.

active audience the idea that people are not simply passive recipients of media messages; they respond to content based on their personal backgrounds, interests, and interpersonal relationships

uses and gratifications research research that studies how people use media products to meet their needs and interests; it asks (and answers) questions about why individuals use the mass media

and their audiences. Increasingly, the conclusions of these and other researchers emphasized the idea of the active audience. By **active audience**, they meant that people are not simply passive recipients of media messages. Rather, they respond to content based on their personal backgrounds, interests, and interpersonal relationships.

The best-known aspect of this research, which came to be known as **uses and gratifications research**, studies how people use media products to meet their needs and interests. The aim of this research was to ask (and answer) questions about why individuals use the mass media. Underlying these studies is the belief that it is just as important to know what people do with media as it is to know what media do to people. You may remember that in Chapter 1 we discussed why people use the media and raised such topics as enjoyment, companionship, surveillance, and interpretation—all are ideas that sprang from scholarly writings about the uses and gratifications people make of and get from the mass media.

Uses and gratifications research typically employs two research methods. One method involves interviewing people about why they use specific media and what kinds of satisfactions (gratifications) they get from these media. Often such research involves a small population so that the research can be conducted in depth. The second research method involves surveys that try to predict what kinds of people use what media, or what certain kinds of people do with particular media.

Consider a researcher who is interested in whether computers in nursing homes can enrich the lives of seniors. He might want to use both of these methods. One way to start such a project would be to go to nursing homes that provide Internet access and interview residents about the extent to which they use the Internet and what they get out of it. You might object that such a small-scale study is not clearly generalizable to other situations. You're right about that, but the researcher might sacrifice getting a representative sample of the population in return for the ability to really learn the habits and ideas of these people. He then might test what he learns in other circumstances or through large-scale surveys. In fact, the researcher might want to use the survey technique to canvass nursing homes with Web access around the country. One goal might be to find out whether certain characteristics

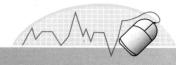

Could These Results Have Occurred by Chance?

MEDIA RESEARCH

Think about how many statistics you come across in a typical day. Your local newspaper reports that the democratic candidate for mayor is trailing behind in the public opinion polls. A nightly TV news special opens with the startling statistic that childhood obesity has quadrupled in the past forty years. An article on your favorite sports website reports that a link has been found between participation in athletic activities and career income.

With the ubiquity of survey research presented in the mass media today, it is important to develop a critical perspective toward research findings. One important question to ask relates to the fact that researchers do not poll everybody in the society. Apart from anything that might be wrong with the studies, we need to know whether the polls reflect the total population or just unrepresentative parts of the population. Put another way, we need to know the likelihood that the results could have occurred by chance.

To answer, you must look for the study's statistical significance level, which is the likelihood an association found in a sample really exists in the larger population. Significance levels are calculated through statistical analyses and are reported as the number of times in a hundred that if the poll were taken with the same number of questions and the same distribution of answers the finding would have been a mistake. The number is called the p-value and is reported between 0 (no likelihood that chance was involved) and 1 (total likelihood the results are accidental). Many researchers will recognize a study as statistically significant if the p-value is less than 0.05, meaning the proba-

bility that the results are due to chance is less than 5 in 100.

To understand the role of statistical significance in research better, let's return to the topic of childhood obesity. In 2006, researchers from the Dartmouth Medical School published findings that having a TV set in the bedroom puts children at a higher risk for obesity. Their study, which examined data from more than 2,300 high-school students, revealed that those with TV sets in their bedroom had a higher body-mass index and were significantly more likely to be overweight compared to those without a TV in their bedroom (27.3 percent vs. 17.7 percent). They reported a p-value of "less than or equal to 0.05," and thus characterized the finding as "statistically significant."

The significance level is just one factor to think about when you come across research in the media—and elsewhere. Researchers Elizabeth Blackmore and Wendi Rockert point out that adopting a critical stance to research findings can make you "a more informed consumer and ultimately more able to arrive at personal decisions which may incorporate what you learn from the media."

Sources: A. M. Adachi-Mejia, M. R. Longacre, J. J. Gibson, M. Beach, L. T. Titus-Ernstoff, and M. A. Dalton, "Children with a TV in their Bedroom at Higher Risk for Being Overweight," *International Journal of Obesity* (2006): 1–8; Elizabeth Blackmore and Wendi Rockert, "Becoming Critical Consumers: Research and the Media," National Eating Disorder Information Center, accessed 6/12/07, http://www.nedic.ca/knowthefacts/documents/Becomingcritical consumers.pdf; Bruce Thompson, "The Concept of Statistical Significance Testing," ERIC Clearinghouse on Assessment and Evaluation, Washington, DC, accessed 2/14/08, http://www.ericdigests.org/1995-1/testing.htm.

of seniors—their age, their health, or their attitudes about the future, for example—predict the kinds and extent of their Web use.

The Limits of Propaganda: Limited Effects Research

Amidst all this interest in how difficult it is for media to change people's attitudes and behaviors, even propaganda research was turned on its head. Remember how powerful the propaganda analysts of the 1920s and 1930s considered the mass media to be? Well, in the 1940s, social psychologists were pointing out that even

American servicemen answering questionnaires in Carl Hovland's *American Soldier* research.

media materials specifically designed to persuade people would succeed only under limited circumstances and with only certain types of people.

World War II and Cold War Research   The issue was by no means just a theoretical one. Propaganda became an important tool during World War II in the 1940s and during the height of the cold war with the Soviet Union in the 1950s and 1960s. During the Second World War, military officials became especially interested in the ability of movies, filmstrips, and other media to teach soldiers about the reasons for the war and to increase their motivation to serve. Research on the power of these media was carried on as part of a wide investigation called *The American Soldier*.

Because a soldier's duty is to do what he or she is told, a team of social psychologists under the leadership of Carl Hovland conducted careful naturalistic experiments with large numbers of people, a task that is typically difficult to accomplish. A **naturalistic experiment** is a study in which randomly selected people are manipulated in a relatively controlled environment (as in an experiment) without knowing that they are involved in an experiment. Some (who make up the experimental group) see the media message that is being evaluated, while others (the control group) do not. Researchers ask both groups the same questions at different points in time—usually before and after the experimental group sees the message, but in some designs only afterwards. The researchers take care to separate the questionnaire from the viewing so that the subjects don't suspect the relationship between the two. The before/after answers of the two groups are then compared. This approach is typically more like "real life" than a typical experiment, in which groups of randomly chosen subjects know that they are involved in an experiment and often participate in a laboratory setting.

Hovland and his colleagues used a variety of techniques with different subjects, but all were shown movies explaining America's reason for entering World War II. The 4,200 soldiers involved in the study were not told they were involved in an experiment. Instead, they were told they were being given a general opinion survey; the questionnaires they were given before seeing the film were different

naturalistic experiment   a study in which randomly selected people are manipulated in a relatively controlled environment (as in an experiment) without knowing that they are involved in an experiment

from those they received a week after seeing the film to disguise the real purpose of the questionnaire. Some of the experimental groups were also given questionnaires nine weeks after seeing the movie to study the long-term effects of the film. Control groups did not see the movies, but they were given questionnaires to fill out to see if changes happened without their having viewed the movies.

What Hovland's naturalistic experiments showed was how difficult it was to change an individual's opinions. As an example, consider the researchers' findings when they evaluated the effects of *The Battle of Britain* (a short film that explored in vivid detail how Britain fought bravely against the Nazis, why the United States went to war to help Britain, and why it was necessary to fight to win) on men enrolled in the military. The team found that the movie had strong effects on what men learned about the battle; how much they learned depended on their educational background. When it came to convincing the men in the study that the British and French were doing all they could to win, however, the film had much less effect; few soldiers who were suspicious of the French and British before they saw the film changed their opinion.

The film was also ineffective in strengthening the overall motivation and morale of the soldiers. Specifically, one item on the questionnaire given after the experimental group saw the film asked whether the soldiers preferred military service at home or joining the fighting overseas. Only 38 percent of the control group said they wanted to fight. For the film group—supposedly fired up by the film—the comparable figure was 41 percent, not a significant difference.

After World War II, Carl Hovland took a position at Yale University and continued his focus on propaganda. His aim was to understand what kinds of appeals could be more effective than others, *all other aspects of the communication environment being equal*. His Yale Program of Research on Communication and Attitude Change asked a wide variety of questions. Each of the program's different projects took a slightly different approach from one another, but the projects typically used Yale University students as subjects. The students were exposed to different experimental conditions and were asked to answer questions about the conditions by filling out a questionnaire. In this way, the researchers explored (for example) whether a spokesperson's credibility made a difference. They also looked at whether and when fear appeals were more persuasive than appeals that did not use fear, and even whether an audience that was active in discussing the message was more likely to be persuaded than one that just sat and listened.

The program yielded fascinating results that were undoubtedly used by cold war propagandists and TV advertisers. But the studies were laboratory experiments, conducted in an environment set up to encourage attitude or behavior change in a statistically significant percentage of subjects.

Even Hovland himself agreed that the findings did not contradict what by the 1950s was the mainstream verdict about media influence: under normal circumstances, where all aspects of the communication environment could not be equal, the mass media's ability to change people's attitudes and behavior on controversial issues was minimal.

Consolidating the Mainstream Approach

The seeds planted by the Columbia School, the Yale School, and to a lesser degree the Payne Fund Studies bore great fruit in the 1950s and beyond, as researchers in many universities and colleges built upon their findings. We can divide these later

© Mike Baldwin / Cornered

"TV's too violent. Better wear a helmet."

approaches into three very broad areas of study: *opinion and behavior change, what people learn from media,* and *why, when, and how people use the media.* Let's look at these one at a time.

Studying Opinion and Behavior Change

Many researchers have been interested in understanding the conditions under which the opinions or behaviors of certain types of individuals and not others could be influenced by certain types of content. Some of these researchers, using surveys or experiments, became involved in the most contentious issues involving media in the second half of the twentieth century—those centering on the effects of TV violence on children and the effects of sexually explicit materials (pornography) on adults.

A huge amount of literature on these topics appeared. In general, researchers seem to agree that the ways in which most adults and children react to such materials depends greatly upon family background, social setting, and personality. At the same time, they also agree that consistent viewing of violent television shows or movies may cause some children to become aggressive toward others regardless of family background. Researchers have come to similar conclusions about violent sexual materials, the kind in which men hurt women or vice versa. There is mounting evidence that for some viewers, irrespective of their background or initial attitudes, heavy exposure to such materials may desensitize them to the seriousness of rape and other forms of sexual violence. For example, in one study, viewers of sexual violence had less concern about the supposed victim of a violent rape than the control group viewers who hadn't seen such materials. Because most of these findings are based on lab experiments, though, there is a significant amount of debate about whether they apply to the real world.

Studying What People Learn from Media

A large number of researchers have been interested in who learns what from mass media material, and under what conditions. There are many facets to this study area, but two particularly important ones stand out. The first is whether media can encourage children's learning of educational skills. The second looks at who in society learns about current national and world affairs from the media.

Can Media Encourage Learning Skills in Children? When it comes to children's learning of educational skills, most people tend to think of *Sesame Street.* On television since 1969, the program has been the subject of much research into what children learn from it. Researchers have found that the program can teach boys and girls from different income levels their letters and numbers, and can be credited with improving the vocabulary of young children.

Professor Ellen Wartella, an expert on this topic, summarizes other findings on children's learning of education skills this way:

Since the success of *Sesame Street*, other planned educational programs, such as *Where in the World is Carmen Sandiego*, *Bill Nye the Science Guy*, *Square One Television*, *Reading Rainbow*, *Gullah Gullah's Island*, *Blues Clues* and *Magic School Bus*, have been found both to increase children's interest in the educational content of programs and to teach some of the planned curriculum. In addition, other children's shows, which focus less on teaching cognitive skills but more on such positive behaviors as helping others and sharing toys, can be successful. The most important evidence here comes from a study of preschool children's effective learning of such helping or pro-social behaviors from watching *Mister Rogers' Neighborhood*.[2]

Sadly, perhaps, an overview of available research in the area suggests that learning and acting out pro-social behavior from TV programming is more likely with kids aged three through seven than with older children. Perhaps the older children have already developed their individual personalities, so it becomes harder to change them.

Which Individuals Learn About National and World Affairs from the Mass Media?
Researchers who examine what individuals in society learn about national and world affairs from the mass media would probably argue that they, too, are looking at pro-social learning, but of a different kind. The basic belief that guides their work is that a democratic society needs informed citizens if public policies are to be guided by the greatest number of people. Some of their questions center on Walter Lippman's agenda-setting theory which we discussed earlier in this chapter.

Agenda-setting scholars agree with the mainstream position that differences among individuals make it unlikely that the mass media can tell you or me precisely what opinions we should have about particular topics. They point out, however, that by making some events and not others into major headlines, the mass media are quite successful at getting large numbers of people to agree on what topics to think about. That in itself is important, these researchers argue, because it shows that the press has the power to spark public dialogue on major topics facing the nation.

Professors Maxwell McCombs and Donald Shaw at the University of North Carolina, Chapel Hill, demonstrated this agenda-setting effect in research for the first time in a 1970 article. They surveyed Chapel Hill voters about the most important issues in the presidential campaign. They also conducted a content analysis of the attention that major media outlets in Chapel Hill paid to issues in the presidential campaign. McCombs and Shaw showed that the rankings of the importance that voters placed on certain issues in the presidential election campaign were related not to the voters' party affiliation or personal biases but to the priorities that the media outlets in Chapel Hill presented at the time.

That one study on the influence of the media agenda on the public

Just how much do children learn from what they see and hear in the media?

When Politics Meets Social Research

Government interest in research on social problems can sometimes lead to high profile arguments about who should conduct the research as well as about the significance of the findings. Questions of ethics surrounding them often swirl furiously. The Surgeon General's Report on Television and Social Behavior provides an example.

TV violence was a subject of much concern to parents and politicians alike during the early 1970s in the wake of rising crime as well as civil rights and anti-Vietnam War riots. Some people blamed the high quotient of violence in television programming for leading young people to see violence as a solution to problems in real life. At the request of the president, the U.S. Surgeon General decided to commission a series of studies to investigate the impact of violence on television to answer a basic question: could TV violence really cause individuals to commit violence?

The question had very real implications for the television industry. If violent TV shows were found to instigate more violence, the television networks would face harsh criticism and possibly be forced to take some of their most popular shows off the air. That would result in the loss of millions of dollars in advertising revenue.

ABC, CBS, and NBC executives expressed deep reservations about the project. They said they were concerned that researchers with a history of anti-TV sentiments would be chosen to guide the process of selecting and evaluating the investigations. Concerned about such criticism, the Surgeon General submitted his list of potential appointees for his "advisory board" to network executives for review before he selected them. ABC and NBC objected to several of the nominees, and they were taken off the list. ABC and NBC also proposed nominees, and eventually five network representatives were allowed to serve on a committee of twelve.

Critics of the process suggested that the Surgeon General had interfered unethically in the research process. They said that network interference prevented highly respected violence researchers, such as Professor Albert Bandura, from getting funding because of network objections. Moreover, the critics said, when the final report was completed, the summary that the advisory committee approved was a tentative one because of the industry influence. The summary said that violence on television had only limited effects on certain people under certain circumstances. Researchers who had reported to the committee argued that, in fact, they had concluded quite differently. They felt that their findings had demonstrated more negative effects of television violence than the advisory committee reported.

This was not the first time that high-profile research was influenced by a political tug-of-war, nor will it be the last. Do you think that the Surgeon General behaved unethically in allowing the TV networks to veto advisory board members? Or was he just being wisely practical in realizing that if the networks deemed the board "tainted" they would never accept any of its suggestions regarding TV violence?

Source: Willard Rowland, *The Politics of TV Violence* (Beverly Hills: Sage Publications, 1983).

agenda led to a torrent of others (more than two hundred!). The agenda-setting power of the press has generally been shown to operate in both election and non-election studies across a variety of geographic settings, time spans, news media, and public issues. Researchers have also described an effect called *priming* as a "close cousin of agenda-setting."[3]

priming the process by which the media affect the standard that individuals use to evaluate what they see and hear in the media

Priming means the process by which the media affect the standard that individuals use to evaluate what they see and hear in the media. The idea is that the more prominent a political issue is in the national media, the more that idea will prime people (that is, cue them in) that the handling of that issue should be used to evaluate how well political candidates or organizations are doing their jobs.

But the power of agenda setting and priming is by no means the entire story. Researchers have found that mass media agenda setting has the ability to affect people's sense of public affairs priorities, and that mass media coverage primes people with respect to the criteria they use to evaluate particular issues. Nevertheless, researchers emphasize that individual backgrounds and interests weaken these effects—that is, they bring about a lot of variation in what issues people pick up as important, how they prioritize these issues, and whether or not they use these issues as evaluation criteria. The weakening of these effects occurs primarily because people's differences lead them to pay attention to different things in the media. As with the Yale studies described earlier, the strongest agenda-setting effects have been found in experimental studies. That suggests that a major condition for obtaining these effects is attention, because in experiments subjects are essentially forced to pay attention, whereas under naturalistic conditions some people do and others don't, based on their interest in what is going on.

If it is sometimes difficult to get people to pay attention to current events via the headlines, imagine how difficult it is to get them to pay attention to less obvious aspects of our political culture. In fact, in the decades since World War II, researchers have found a wide variation in what individuals learn from the mass media. Education has consistently been a major factor that is positively associated with differences between those who pick up knowledge of public affairs and those who do not. It seems that people are more likely to remember the events and facts that media present if they have frameworks of knowledge from schooling that can help them make sense of the news events they see or hear.

In the late 1960s, Professors Phillip Tichenor, George Donahue and Clarice Olien of the University of Minnesota came upon a sobering survey finding that relates to the difference in the amount of current events information that different people learn from the media. They found that in the development of any social or political issue, the more highly educated segments of a population know more about the issue early on and, in fact, acquire information about that issue at a faster rate than the less-educated segments. That is, people who are information-rich to begin with get richer faster than people who are information-poor, and so the difference in the amount of knowledge between the two types of people will grow wider.

Professors Tichenor, Donahue and Olien concluded that this growing **knowledge gap** was dangerous for society in an age in which the ability to pick up information about the latest trends is increasingly crucial to success (see Figure 4.6). Because the information-rich in society were often the well-schooled and well-off financially, a growing knowledge gap might mean that the poorer segments of society could not participate meaningfully in discussions of social issues. It also might mean that they would not know about developments that would help them prepare for, and get, better jobs.

Studying Why, When and How People Use the Media

Some of the most basic questions that researchers ask about mass media in society center on who uses them, how, and why. As we noted earlier, it was a group of scholars at Columbia University who created the first notable research program that went beyond basic factual descriptions of the numbers of newspaper readers and radio listeners to ask what motivated people to use certain kinds of content.

They asked, for example, "Why do people like such programming as radio soap operas and quiz shows?" This question may have gotten sneers from some of their elitist colleagues. Nevertheless, over the decades, this uses and gratifications research has received a lot of attention. The focus is on when, how, and why people use various mass media or particular genres of mass media content.

knowledge gap a theory developed by Tichenor, Donahue, and Olien, that holds that in the development of any social or political issue, the more highly educated segments of a population know more about the issue early on and, in fact, acquire information about that issue at a faster rate than the less-educated ones, and so the difference between the two types of people grows wider

A World Class Idea

In 1970, an eleven-page article by three professors at the University of Minnesota appeared in the journal *Public Opinion Quarterly*. "Mass Media Flow and Differential Growth in Knowledge," by Phillip Tichenor, George Donahue, and Clarice Olien, presented the idea that a knowledge gap exists between socioeconomic classes. The idea was that those who are information-rich are able to gather new information faster than those who are information-poor. Both groups gain information, but there is a difference in the rate at which they gather it. Tichenor, Donahue, and Olien supported their contention that there is a growing knowledge gap through a study of people's understanding of newspaper and scholarly journal articles. Now, more than thirty years later, scholars have accepted that the notion of a knowledge gap holds for other media as well. Hundreds of articles have been written on knowledge gap issues with topics ranging from health communication to interactive media.

While the original study was done in Minneapolis, the knowledge gap theory has expanded to cover activities of people all over the world. Scholars have used the knowledge gap in dealing with such diverse topics as leprosy in India, democratic education in Argentina, vaccination knowledge in the Philippines, European information policy, AIDS education in Norway, mental health images in Canadian newspapers, migration in Thailand, earthquake predictions in Japan, and knowledge of voters in municipal elections in Sweden. The theory has captured the imagination of academics throughout the planet.

Tichenor, Donahue, and Olien emphasize that rather than having an equalizing effect by making information widely and inexpensively available, mass media may actually widen the gap between the information-rich and information-poor. This conclusion demands attention, as it causes us to pause and reflect on the dark side of information dissemination in our mediated society.

Source: Phillip Tichenor, George Donohue, and Clarice Olien, "Mass media flow and differential growth in knowledge," *Public Opinion Quarterly*, Summer 1970, 159–170.

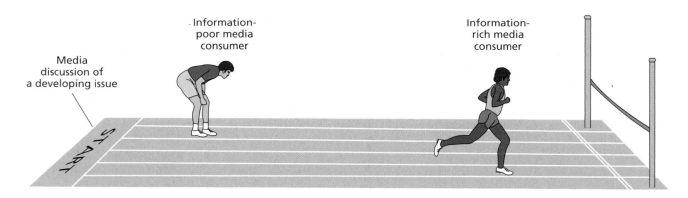

Figure 4.6

The Knowledge Gap

In the development of any social or political issue, people who are information-rich to begin with will become information-richer much more quickly than people who are information-poor to begin with. For this reason, the difference in the amount of information between the information-rich and the information-poor grows exponentially wider.

True to the spirit of the mainstream approach, uses and gratifications research has at its core a belief in the active audience. The term means that individuals are not just passive receivers of messages. Rather, they make conscious decisions about what they like, and they have different reasons for using particular media, depending on different social relationships as well as on individual social and psychological differences. Moreover, people are physically active when they use media. When it comes to TV, for example, studies have shown that people do not sit quietly, transfixed by the tube, as some cartoon stereotypes would have it. Rather, they move around, do other things, and talk to friends and family.

A huge amount of literature explores how people use a variety of media and why. Some very interesting work connects uses and gratifications research with effects research, linking how or why people use media content with the extent to which it changes their opinions, actions, or ideas about the world.

Much of this work is interesting and important in its own right. It is useful to know, for example, what percentage of poor families have been connecting to the Internet compared to the percentage of middle-class and wealthy families. The findings that there are sharp differences in income between families that are online at home and those that are not has sparked discussion of a **digital divide** in the United States—a separation between those who are connected to "the future" and those who are being left behind (see Figure 4.7). That, in turn, has led to efforts by governments and corporations to place Web-linked computers with instructors in libraries and community centers that are within easy reach of people who cannot afford the Internet at home.

Activists argue that there is a lot more to do in this area. Of particular concern are economically disadvantaged children in the United States and elsewhere in the world who are falling behind in their ability to be part of the modern world. More than a few of their advocates point out that while providing them with new technology is a beginning, it is not enough. Teaching them how to use the technology in ways that will benefit themselves and their societies is a critical part of bridging the digital divide.

digital divide the separation between those who have access to and knowledge about technology and those who (perhaps because of their level of education or income) do not

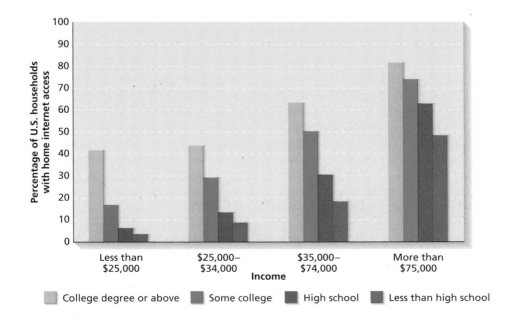

Figure 4.7
The Digital Divide
Now, more than ever, the gap between those people and communities who can make effective use of information technology and those who cannot is widening. While a consensus does not exist on the extent of this digital divide (and whether this digital divide is growing or narrowing), researchers are nearly unanimous in acknowledging that some sort of divide exists at this point in time, as this figure shows.

Bridging the Global Digital Divide

To most people, the fact that many of the two billion children in the world's developing countries are inadequately educated is a formidable problem. Yet, to researchers at the Media Lab of the Massachusetts Institute of Technology, this problem is not without a solution.

These scholars are working alongside professionals from the technology, education, and business industries in an effort to provide each one of these children with a laptop—and an education.

One Laptop Per Child (OLPC) is the brainchild of Nicholas Negroponte, a scholar-turned-philanthropist who developed the organization after seeing firsthand the remarkable effects of laptops on children in a remote Cambodian village. "The first English word of every child in that village was 'Google,'" Negroponte says.

Today the OLPC organization seeks to produce and distribute "a children's machine designed for 'learning learning.'" Their latest model is the XO, which costs about $100 to produce and is made to be both durable and power-efficient.

Children are not the only ones to benefit from OLPC's efforts. Negroponte explains that children take the laptop home from school and teach the whole family how to use it. For those families with no electricity, the laptop becomes a tremendous source of light. "Talk about a metaphor and a reality simultaneously," Negroponte continues, "It just illuminated that household."

Of course, this program is not without its critics. Members of the technology industry contend that a high-quality computer cannot be designed at such a low cost. Others, meanwhile, question the priority of this issue and wonder whether OLPC individuals should be devoting their

www.laptop.org, the website of One Laptop Per Child

time and energy to other issues, such as nutrition and healthcare.

Microsoft founder and philanthropist Bill Gates is among those who believe that we should devote our resources to more pressing issues confronting the developing world. Although Gates for years supported international education issues, he has now shifted his priorities to healthcare and the distribution of vaccines. In fact, he has been quoted as saying that poor families trying to live on $1 a day "are not going to, like, sit around and browse eBay or something. What they want is for their children to live."

Where do you stand on this controversy, and why?

Source: Sam Howe Verhovek, "Bill Gates Turns Skeptical on Digital Solution's Scope," *The New York Times*, November 3, 2000, on the Web; One Laptop Per Child website, accessed 6/18/07, http://laptop.org/en/vision/index.shtml; Leslie Stahl, "What If Every Child Had a Laptop?" *CBS News*, May 20, 2007, on the Web. www.cbsnews.com.

The Rise of Critical Approaches

mainstream approaches
the research models that developed out of the work of the Columbia School, the Yale School, and the Payne Fund Studies

As you can see, the **mainstream approaches**—the research models that developed out of the work of the Columbia School, the Yale School, and the Payne Fund Studies—have led to valuable work that helped many researchers contribute to society's most important debates. At the same time, however, other researchers insist that the questions asked by mainstream approaches are not really the most important ones when it comes to understanding the role of mass media in society.

Moving from Mainstream to Critical

According to critics of the mainstream approach, there are two major problems with even the best mainstream research. One problem is its stress on *change rather than continuity*. The other is its emphasis on the active role of *the individual*—the active audience member—in the media environment and not on the power of *larger social forces* that control that media environment.

Let's look at the first problem. By *a stress on change over continuity*, critics of mainstream research mean that much of this research focuses on whether a change will occur as a result of specific movies, articles or shows. Critics say that this approach ignores the possibility that the most important effects of the media have to do not with changing people but with encouraging them (or reinforcing them) to continue certain actions or perspectives on life.

Mainstream researchers might focus, for example, on whether a girl will hit her little brother after watching the violent antics of a *Three Stooges* film or whether a woman will learn about politics from a website or TV news program. Now, there's nothing wrong with such questions, the critics allow. But, they add, fascination with these questions of change often hides the importance of the media in encouraging the *reinforcement* of actions and beliefs among many in society.

Mainstream researchers emphasize that most people's opinions and behaviors don't change after they view television or listen to the radio. What the researchers don't emphasize, the critics point out, is that the flip side of change—reinforcement—may well be a powerful consequence. In fact, the critics argue, reinforcement is often the major consequence of mass media messages. Media may repeat for us values that we have come to love, ideas about the world that we have come to trust, social-class relationships that we have come to accept, and beliefs about the way people who are not like us look and act that we have come to accept. These are the ideas that hold a society together, the critics say, so it is a shame that the mainstream people have played them down.

But the critics often go further. They argue that mainstream research has placed so much emphasis on the individual's relationships to media—the second major problem we identified—that it has ignored social power. It has neglected to emphasize that there are powerful forces that exert control over what media industries do as part of their control over the society.

What really ought to be studied, say the critics, is the way these powerful groups come to influence the most widespread media images in ways that help them stay in power. From this perspective, agenda setting and the digital divide are not just phenomena that point to what people learn and how differently they learn. They are phenomena that help the powerful classes in the society retain their power.

Clearly, we have here a major difference of opinion about how to look at mass media, where their powers lie, and which of their aspects should be studied. Many critics of the mainstream approach prefer an avenue of research that recalls the most sophisticated of the propaganda analysts. Like the propaganda analysts, contemporary critical scholars emphasize the importance of systematically exploring the forces guiding media companies. They also place great value on analyzing media content to reveal the patterns of messages that are shared broadly by the population. Like the propaganda analysts, their aim is often to expose to public light the relationship of media firms to powerful forces in the society. They want to publicize their findings in order to encourage public understanding and, sometimes, to urge government regulations that would promote greater diversity among creators of media content and in the content itself.

The "critical" label describes a wide variety of projects relating to the mass media. Three prominent perspectives that guide critical researchers are the *critical theory of the Frankfurt School, political economy research,* and *cultivation studies.*

The Deep Political Influence of the Media: the Frankfurt School's Critical Theory

The Frankfurt School is a shorthand name for a group of scholars who were associated with a place called the School for Social Research during the 1930s and 1940s. This shorthand name comes from the original location of the institute in Frankfurt, Germany. The researchers who made significant contributions to this school of thought are Theodor Adorno (philosopher, sociologist, and musicologist), Walter Benjamin (essayist and literary critic), Herbert Marcuse (philosopher), and Max Horkheimer (philosopher, sociologist). Each of these philosophers shared the basic view of capitalism set forth by the nineteenth-century philosopher Karl Marx. According to Marx, **capitalism** is the ownership of the means of production by a ruling class in society. Marx insisted that in societies that accept this economic approach, capitalism greatly influences all beliefs. He further insisted that capitalism and the beliefs it generates create economic and cultural problems. They exploit the working class and celebrate that exploitation in literature and many other aspects of culture. Marx believed that the direction of history was toward labor's overthrow of the capitalist class and the reign of workers in a society in which everyone would receive what he or she needs.

The Frankfurt School focused on the cultural aspect of this issue, and its members were pessimistic about it. Marxist and Jewish, they were exiled from Germany to the United States because of the rise of Nazism during the 1920s and 1930s. In New York (where they established the New School for Social Research), the members of the Frankfurt School explored the relationship between culture and capitalism in an era in which economic depression, war and mass exterminations made it difficult to be optimistic about the liberating potential of culture. Their writings about the corrosive influence of capitalism on culture came to be known as **critical theory.**

Many media scholars today feel that the members of the Frankfurt School tended to overemphasize the ability of mass media to control individuals' beliefs. Nevertheless, over the decades, the philosophies collectively known as *critical theory* have influenced many writings on mass media. Writings by Adorno stress the power of "the culture industry" to move audience members toward ways of looking at the world. Writings by Marcuse suggest to researchers how messages about social power can be found in all aspects of media content, even if typical audience members don't recognize them. For example, **co-optation** is a well-known term that Marcuse coined to express the way capitalism takes potentially revolutionary ideas and tames them to express capitalist ideals. For an example of co-optation, consider how advertisers take expressions of youthful rebellion such as tattoos and colored hair and turn them into the next money-making fads. Marcuse would say that this sort of activity shows how difficult it is for oppositional movements to create symbols that keep their critical meanings.

Political Economy Research

The Frankfurt School writers typically assumed the economic structure's effects on culture and then analyzed the culture. **Political economy** theorists, by contrast, focus specifically on the relationship between the economic and the cultural. They look at when and how the economic structures of society and the media system reflect the political interests of society's

capitalism   as defined by Karl Marx, the ownership of the means of production by a ruling class in society

critical theory   the Frankfurt School's members' theories focusing on the corrosive influence of capitalism on culture

co-optation   a term coined by Marcuse to express the way in which capitalism takes potentially revolutionary ideas and tames them to express capitalist ideals

political economy   an area of study that focuses specifically on the relationship between the economic and the cultural, and looks at when and how the economic structures of society and the media system reflect the political interests of society's rich and powerful rich and powerful. In this vein, the professor and media activist Robert McChesney examined ownership patterns of media companies in the early 2000s. He concluded in his 2004 book *The Problem of the Media* that we have reached "the age of hyper-commercialism," where media worry far more about satisfying advertisers and shareholders than providing entertainment or news that encourages people to understand their society and become engaged in it.[4] McChesney blames government legislators and regulators for allowing the rise of huge media conglomerates that control large portions of the revenues of particular media industries for the purposes of selling advertising time and space. One alarming consequence, he contends, is a journalistic system that focuses more on attracting the attention of audiences than trying to build an informed society like that imagined by Jefferson and Madison. As alarming to McChesney is the notion that because U.S. media firms are so powerful internationally, this commercially driven perspective on journalism is spreading through the world. He and political economist Edward Herman put that idea succinctly in a 1997 book called *The Global Media*: "Such a [global] concentration of media power in organizations dependent on advertiser support and responsible primarily to shareholders is a clear and present danger to citizens' participation in public affairs, understanding of public issues, and thus to the effective workings of democracy."[5]

Another writer from a political economy perspective, Ben Bagdikian, points out in his book *The Media Monopoly* that huge media firms are often involved in many businesses outside of journalism. General Electric, parent of NBC News, makes nuclear power plants and train locomotives, for example. Disney owns theme parks around the world as well as ABC News. News workers who are employed by these firms may be afraid to cover controversies that involve those operations; in fact, corporate bigwigs may keep them from doing so (see Figure 4.8).

The problem is not just theoretical: when ABC News investigative reporter Brian Ross was putting together a report on child abuse issues in theme parks, he was ordered by executives of the Walt Disney Company, which owns ABC News, not to report on possible problems with childcare in Disneyland. ABC officials denied that the corporate linkage influenced their decision to pull an investigative report on allegations involving Disney. "Disney: The Mouse Betrayed," a 20/20 segment produced by Brian Ross, alleged, among other things, that Disney World

Author and media critic Ben Bagdikian is the winner of almost every top prize in American journalism, including the Pulitzer, and is one of the most respected media critics in the United States.

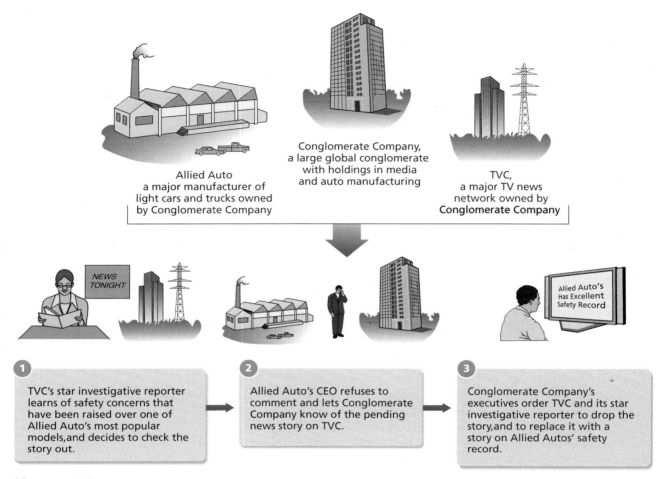

Figure 4.8

Afraid to Cover Conglomerate Controversies: A Hypothetical Example

A conflict of interest can arise when conglomerates with a direct stake in businesses outside of journalism own many of the media outlets through which the public is informed. In this hypothetical example, Conglomerate Company, which has holdings in TV news and in the auto industry, orders its news arm to "kill" a negative story about the safety ratings of the cars it produces. What are the ethical implications of Conglomerate Company's actions? What about harm to the public good? How often do you think this sort of situation takes place in the real world? To what extent is it possible to find out?

in Florida fails to perform security checks that would prevent the hiring of sex offenders and has problems with Peeping Toms. According to an ABC spokeswoman, news president David Westin's killing of the story had nothing to do with any network reluctance to criticize its parent company. "The fact that this particular story involved Disney was not the reason it did not make air," claimed ABC officials. Similarly, when Time Inc. merged with Warner Communications in the 1980s, some writers for *Time* magazine felt that their colleagues were intimidated from reporting honestly on the way the merger was proceeding and what it might mean for the media system.

The work by McChesney, Herman, and Bagdikian is only the tip of the iceberg of research that looks into the economic relationships within the media system and tries to figure out their consequences for issues of social power and equity. This work doesn't portray media executives as a bunch of cigar-smoking honchos who care nothing of the public. Rather, most critical political economy work is concerned with looking at how institutional and organizational relationships create requirements for media firms that lead the employees of those firms to create and circulate certain kinds of material and not others. These scholars might explore, for example, whether (and how) major advertisers' relationships with television networks affect programming. They would look at the extent to which advertisers' need to reach certain audiences for their products causes networks to signal program producers that shows that aim at those types of people will get preference.

The topics political economists choose vary greatly. Some, like Herbert Schiller, explore global issues. An example is the study of factors that encourage the spread of Western (often U.S.) news and entertainment throughout the world. These political scientists consider such activities to be *cultural colonialism*. **Colonialism** means control over a dependent area or people by a powerful entity (usually a nation) by force of arms. England and France practiced colonialism in places such as India and Vietnam for many years. **Cultural colonialism** involves the exercise of control over an area or people by a dominant power, not so much through force of arms as by surrounding the weaker countries with cultural materials that reflect values and beliefs supporting the interests of that dominant power. The political economists who explore cultural colonialism argue that by celebrating values such as commercialism and immediate gratification, the cultural colonizers encourage markets for goods that reflect those values and so help their own country's business interests.

colonialism   control over a dependent area or people by a powerful entity by force of arms

cultural colonialism   the exercise of control over an area or people by a dominant power, not so much through force of arms as by surrounding the weaker countries with cultural materials that reflect values and beliefs supporting the interests of that dominant power

Other political economists focus on the concerns of media in individual countries. They look, for example, at the extent to which ethnic or racial minorities can exert some control over mainstream media. Their fear is that social minorities often do not get to guide their own portrayals in their nation's main media. The result is underrepresentation and stereotyping of these groups by producers who are insensitive to their concerns. These political scientists urge changes so that minority producers and actors can have input regarding their groups' depictions.

Cultivation Studies   Cultivation researchers are also interested in depictions, but in a different way. Such studies are different from political economy studies in that they focus not on industry relationships but on the information about the world that people pick up from media portrayals. You might object that this sounds very much like what many mainstream effects researchers do. On the surface it does. Where cultivation researchers differ is in the perspective they bring to the work and how they interpret their findings. **Cultivation studies**, then, emphasize that when media systematically portray certain populations in unfavorable ways, the ideas about those people that mainstream audiences pick up help certain groups in society retain their power over the groups they denigrate. Stereotypes, they believe, reinforce and extend ("cultivate") power relationships.

cultivation studies   studies that emphasize that when media systematically portray certain populations in unfavorable ways, the ideas about those people that mainstream audiences pick up help certain groups in society retain their power over the groups they denigrate

Cultivation work is most associated with Professor George Gerbner and his colleagues at the University of Pennsylvania's Annenberg School for Communication from the 1960s through the 1980s. Gerbner began his work with the perspective that all mass media material—entertainment and news—gives people views of the world. Those views, he said, are mass-produced output of huge corporations. These corporations have a vested interest in perpetuating their power along with the power of established economic and cultural approaches in U.S. society. Their power is seen especially in the way violence is used in television entertainment, the most widely viewed entertainment medium in the United States.

Across all channels on the tube, argues Gerbner, TV violence is a kind of ritual ballet that acts out social power. Although TV violence may sometimes encourage aggression, most of the time it cultivates lessons about strength and weakness in society. For example, Gerbner contends that the "hidden curriculum" of TV violence tells us that women and blacks, who tend to be the objects of violence, are socially weak. White males, who tend to be perpetrators of violence (including legal violence by the police or military), are socially strong.

Moreover, Gerbner argues, the overall message of TV violence is that we live in a scary, mean world. He and his colleagues found support for this view through a two-pronged research design. First, they conducted content analyses of many hours of television entertainment programming, using a careful definition of violence and noting who is violent to whom and under what conditions. Next, they conducted a telephone survey of a random sample of the U.S. adult population and asked the people questions about how violent the world is and how fearful they are. They found that heavy viewers of television are more fearful of the world than light viewers. Over time, these viewers also engage in more self-protective behavior and show more mistrust of others than do light viewers.

Gerbner maintains that although this phenomenon affects the individual, it also has larger social implications. The message of fear helps those who are in power because it makes the heavy viewers (a substantial portion of the population) more likely to agree to support police and military forces that protect them from that scary world. Not incidentally, those police and military forces also protect those in power and help them maintain control over unruly or rebellious groups in society.

Gerbner's cultivation research and the critical approaches of political economists and the Frankfurt School helped to add another dimension to the way U.S. scholars looked at the mass media. In the past couple of decades, a third broad avenue of inquiry has added to the mix of ideas about media power and consequences. This avenue is widely known as *cultural studies*.

Cultural Studies

cultural studies studies that start with the idea that all sorts of mass media, from newspapers to movies, present their audiences with technologies and texts and that audiences find meaning in them; scholars then ask questions that center on how to think about what "making meaning" of technologies and texts means and what consequences it has for those audiences in society

Let's say that you accept the importance of emphasizing the connection between mass media and social power, but you're a bit uncomfortable with what you feel is the too-simplistic perspective of the political economy and cultivation theorists. "Media power isn't as controlling as they would have it," you say. "While I agree that media systems are created by dominant social groups to promote their own interests, I don't believe that everybody in the society necessarily buys into the images of power that these systems project. People have minds of their own, and they often live in communities that help them resist the aims of the powerful."

If that's your perspective, you would probably find one of the many approaches within cultural studies to be up your alley. Cultural studies was developed in Europe and had been used there for many years before it attracted a large following in the United States, which it did during the 1980s. Writings in this area often tie media studies to concepts in literature, linguistics, anthropology, and history. **Cultural studies** scholars often start with the idea that all sorts of mass media, from newspapers to movies, present their audiences with technologies and texts, and that audiences find meaning in them. Major questions for these scholars center on how to think about what "making meaning" of technologies and texts means and what consequences it has for those audiences in society. As you might imagine, there are many ways to answer these questions.

Historical Approaches to Cultural Studies

One way is to answer them from a historical perspective. Professor Lynn Spigel, for example, explores the expectations that men and women have had for audio-visual technologies in the home and how those expectations have tied into larger social issues. She points out, for example, a historical relationship between home TV use and social fear:

> Communications technologies have promised to bring the outside world into the home since the late 19th century. At the time of industrialization, when urban centers were linked to the first suburban towns, there were endless speculations about the joys and potential pitfalls of a new design for middle-class living which would allow people to be joined together in an electrical public space without ever going outside. Middle-class families could, in this way, enjoy social encounters while avoiding the elements of urban space—such as labor unrest or ethnic immigration—which made them feel most threatened.[6]

Anthropological Approaches to Cultural Studies

Another way to look at what technologies mean in the context of social class and social power is to take an anthropologist's approach and closely examine the way people use media. While such studies may sound like mainstream uses and gratifications research, they aren't. Cultural studies researchers are much more interested than mainstream researchers in putting a critical spin on their work that ties people's uses of the media to their class, racial or gender positions within the society. Here, for example, is Professor Ellen Seiter writing in 1997 on differences in the use of television and computers between men and women in the home:

> Television sets and computers introduce highly similar issues in terms of placement in domestic space, conflicts among family members over usage and control, value in the household budget, and we can expect these to be articulated with gender roles in the family. Some research on gendered conflicts over computers (Giacquinta; Murdock; Haddon) reproduces themes of family-based studies about control of the television set. Already researchers have noted a strong tendency for men and boys to have more access to computers in the home. Television studies such as Ann Gray's, David Morley's and my own work suggest that women in nuclear families have difficulty watching a favorite television show (because of competition for control of the set from other family members, and because of shouldering the majority of childcare, housework and cooking). If male family members gravitate towards the computer as hobbyists, the load of chores relegated to female family members will only increase, and make it more difficult for female members to get time on the home computer. Computers require hours of trial and error experimentation, a kind of extended play demanding excess leisure time. Fully exploring the Internet needs time for lengthy downloading, and patience with connections that are busy, so much so that some have dubbed the World Wide Web the World Wide Wait.[7]

Linguistic and Literary Approaches to Cultural Studies

You probably found the paragraphs by Ellen Seiter and Lynn Spigel quite straightforward and easy to understand. The same can't be said typically for the areas of cultural studies that apply linguistic and literary models to the meaning of media texts. They tend to use the complex phraseology of linguistics and the jargon of literary analysts to make their points. That is unfortunate, because some of the scholars involved in this area often proclaim that their goal is to encourage viewers and readers to "resist" the dominant models of society that are suggested in the text.

Moreover, these discussions are actually quite interesting and important, once you cut through the language. A major topic of discussion is just where the meaning of a text lies. Is it preset into the written or audiovisual material (the book, the TV show), is it in the way a person using the material understands it, or is it in some relationship between the two? That may sound like an odd question, but it is significant because it speaks to the power of the media to guide people's understanding of the world.

polysemous   open to multiple meanings

At one extreme are scholars who believe that a text is open to multiple meanings (they say that it is **polysemous**) because people have the ability to subject media content to endless interpretations based on their critical understanding of the world. So, for example, Professors Elihu Katz and Tamar Liebes interviewed people in Israel and Japan to find out how they understood the popular 1980s U.S. TV series *Dallas*. They found that Japanese viewers, Israeli viewers from Morocco, and Israeli viewers from Russia had quite different interpretations of the program and its relevance to their lives. According to such findings about multiple interpretations, people in this camp have a clear idea of where they should apply their public interest energies. They would say, for example, that trying to limit the power of media conglomerates is not nearly as important as teaching people how to interpret media critically, in ways that resist any support of the dominant system.

Against this notion of a program or book being open to multiple meanings is the opposite idea that the meaning is in the text itself. Scholars with this view argue that the shared culture of the society leads individuals to share the basic meaning of the text. To them, firms that create agendas in news and entertainment have enormous power that cannot be overcome simply by teaching criticism. Active work to limit the power of these conglomerates is also necessary.

Philosophically, most scholars take a position between these two extremes. They accept the notion of polysemy but they argue that most people's interpretations of media texts are very much shaped by the actual texts themselves and by the industrial and social environments in which these texts are created. They stress that texts are likely to "constrain" meaning in directions that benefit the powerful. That is, because of the way the text is created, viewers or readers notice the "preferred" meaning, the meaning that members of the establishment would likely find most compatible with their own thinking. Certainly, audience members can disagree with this take on the world. Even if they do, however, they may get the strong idea that most other people would not disagree with the text's approaches to racial, gender, ethnic, and religious stereotypes; tales of who is strong and who is weak; or portrayals of what the universe is like, how we (as Americans and humans) fit in, and how we should act toward it. Such scholars might be likely to enthusiastically support media criticism as well as public actions to limit the power of huge media conglomerates.

Using Media Research to Develop Media Literacy Skills

We now return to the story of Jessica. She has heard those grad students discuss everything that you've read in the past several pages, as they present ways of looking at the issues about local news that she has brought to them. Each student gives her a thumbnail summary of the history and nature of different aspects of mass communication research. Jessica's head is spinning from the variety of ways to look at the same media material, the hundreds of questions it is possible to ask.

You may feel the same way she does. But if you think about it a bit more, you'll see that understanding the history of mass media research provides tools with which to figure out three key ideas that a media literate person must know. One is where you stand with respect to the effects of media on society. A second is how to make sense of the discussions and arguments about media effects. A third is how to get involved in research that can be used to explore concerns you might have about mass media.

Where Do You Stand with Respect to Media Effects?

While reading this chapter, it's likely that you found yourself agreeing with some of the media approaches, and disagreeing with others. Maybe you dismissed political economy as a lot of baloney, but you felt that uses and gratifications research and some aspects of cultural studies really make sense. That's fine; part of becoming media literate involves taking an informed stand on why the media are important. Learning about the ways in which people have grappled with concerns about the mass media over the decades can help you sort out your concerns. You personally may be more convinced that the individual interpretations and uses of the media are what make a difference for people. You may not be convinced by those who emphasize social issues, such as political economists, cultivation researchers, and even people involved in studying agenda setting.

It's really important, though, that you do not close your mind to all of these possibilities. New ideas keep coming up; your ideas about life keep changing, as well. You can keep up with what media researchers are saying by reading press articles about them, or maybe even going to journals such as the *Journal of Communication*, *Journalism Quarterly*, or the *Journal of Broadcasting & Electronic Media*. What you have learned here and what you learn in the future may well affect how you relate to the media yourself, how you introduce your children to different media, and what you tell parents who ask your opinion on how to think about the media's consequences for their children.

How to Make Sense of Discussions and Arguments About Media Effects

When you *do* read about research in the popular press or in academic journals, think back to this chapter to help you place the work in perspective and critique it. Here are some questions you should ask yourself:

- *Are the questions the researcher is asking interesting and important?* Think of the issues you have learned about in this chapter. How important are the ones dealt with in the study you are considering? Do you wish the researchers had

Table 4.1 Comparing the Theories in This Chapter

Theory/Research Study	Approach	Participating Researchers	Aim	Example
Chicago School	Early philosophy and sociology of media	Dewey, Cooley, Park	Searching for community	The immigrant press
Propaganda Analysts	Early concerns about media persuasion	Lasswell, McClung, Casey	The activities of media producers and the resulting content	Content analyses of newspapers
Payne Fund Researchers	Early research on children and movies	Charters	Explorations of media effects via multiple methods	How violent movies affect children's sleep patterns
Columbia School	The media and social relations	Lazarsfeld, Katz, Merton	Research on how interpersonal relations intervene in media effects	The "two-step flow" influence of radio and newspapers during a presidential election campaign
American Soldier propaganda research	The limits of propaganda	Hovland	Movies, learning and persuasion	An evaluation of the effects of *The Battle of Britain*
Yale Program of Research on Communication and Attitude Change	The limits of propaganda	Hovland	Research on the conditions that encourage audience persuasion	Experiments to determine whether and when fear appeals were more persuasive than appeals not using fear
Various	Mainstream effects research		Studying behavior and opinion change	
Various	Mainstream effects research		Can television encourage learning skills in children?	Research on what youngsters learn from *Sesame Street*
Various	Mainstream effects research	McCombs and Shaw Tichenor, Donahue, and Olien	Which individuals learn about national and world affairs from mass media?	Research on agenda setting; research on the knowledge gap
Various	Mainstream effects research		Why, when, how people use the media	Investigations of the active audience; research on the digital divide
Frankfurt School	Critical approaches to mass media	Adorno, Marcuse, Horkheimer	The relationship between capitalism and culture	Critical theory about the culture industry
Various	Critical approaches to mass media	Ben Bagdikian, Herbert Schiller	Political economy research	Research on media monopolies
Annenberg School	Critical approaches to mass media	George Gerbner	Cultivation studies	Research on TV violence and perceptions of a mean world

Theory/Research Study	Approach	Participating Researchers	Aim	Example
Various	Cultural studies	Spigel	Historical approaches	Historical relationship between home TV use and social fear
Various	Cultural studies	Seiter, Murdock, Haddon	Anthropological approaches	Differences between men and women in use of TV and computers
Various	Cultural studies	Katz and Leibes	Literary and linguistic approaches	Research on polysemous meanings

    devoted their energies to other topics that you consider more relevant to your life or the life of the country?

■ *Into what research tradition does the study fall*? Is it a study of priming, an example of cultivation research, a study of message persuasion, or a representation of another one of the streams of work that we have discussed (see Table 4.1)?

■ *How good is the research design?* While journal articles lay out the method used in research quite carefully, press reports of research often don't give you a lot of information about how the work was carried out. Even in the popular press, however, you can often find some of the specific questions the investigators used and some details about the method. When you think about the research design, be skeptical. Think about the type and size of the sample. If the study was an experiment, how realistic was it?

■ *How convincing is the analysis?* If the researcher is claiming that the media caused something to happen, are there any other explanations for the findings? Does it appear that the researcher thought about reliability? How valid does the study seem in terms of the real world? These and other questions should roll around in your head as you decide whether or not to accept the conclusions of the researchers or others who are quoted.

■ *What do you wish the researchers would do next in their research?* Asking this question, involving whether or not you like the research, will encourage you to think more deeply than you otherwise might about the role of media in society. Talking with your friends about especially interesting or problematic research is another way to play out some of the meanings that the research holds for you and for others in society.

How to Explore Concerns You Might Have About Mass Media

What are the implications of the research for your personal life as well as for public policy? For example, a well-done study of attitudes toward the Web and uses of the Web by people over the age of seventy might have great meaning to you if you work in a senior center and want to get seniors engaged with the Internet. The study might inform members of Congress who are thinking of providing funding to connect senior centers to the Web. The study might also be relevant if you have a parent or grandparent in that age range and you have wondered whether and how to introduce email and other Web-related technologies to her or him.

A desire to learn the implications of research for her personal life and public policy, you'll remember, is what brought communication major and student journalist Jessica to Professor Berg's graduate seminar. She now understands that all the research perspectives that the students have presented, from mainstream effects and uses and gratifications research to cultivation research to political economy and cultural studies, can be relevant to understanding local news in her city.

"There are so many possible important approaches to this issue that I almost feel paralyzed just worrying which to choose," she says to the assembled group. "*Where* should I begin? *How* should I begin?"

As they continue discussing her concerns, though, Jessica realizes that she must choose the approach to mass media that best fits the concerns she personally has about the media and the specific questions that she is asking. She goes home convinced that what she has had all along is a critical studies take on the issue.

Jessica suggests to her friend, who is a criminology major and anti-poverty activist, that they get a group together to conduct a systematic content analysis of local news in the city with the help of one of the professors. Their goal is to find out exactly how much emphasis on violence and sex and how little attention to government issues and city arts activities there is in the city's morning and evening newscasts. After the content research is completed, the group will interview local TV reporters and executives to try to understand the economic and organizational considerations that lead the local news stations to cover the city in certain ways. Jessica also enlists a journalism graduate student to prepare a review of agenda-setting and cultivation literature, to make the point that the TV station's systematic presentations of a violent city and their ignoring of government can have a real impact on the way adults and children perceive their surroundings. When all that is done—Jessica estimates it will take five months—she and her group will present their material to the TV stations, and also to newspaper reporters and city leaders. Their hope is that the work will encourage citizens, city officials, and maybe even some local advertisers to place pressure on station heads to tone down the violence and play up the role of government in people's lives. "Maybe I'm quixotic," Jessica tells her group, "but I really do think it can be done."

Jessica's story is not an unusual one. Every day, all sorts of mass communication research, from all sorts of perspectives, is brought to bear on a multitude of public issues. Local, state, and federal governments draw on the results of mass communication research, and they often commission it. Of course, scholars don't always do research with specific public policy questions in mind. Nor, it should be emphasized, do they "cook" their results to conform to their particular political points of view. Nevertheless, as we have seen in this chapter, over the past century academics have asked questions not from the irrelevance of an ivory tower but as human beings concerned with the best ways to think about some of the most important topics of their day. As you read the rest of this book, consider that the topics and issues raised are all subject to systematic investigation from one or more of the perspectives sketched above. You might find carrying out such an inquiry fascinating and rewarding.

CHAPTER REVIEW

For an interactive chapter recap and study guide, visit the companion website for *Media Today* at www.routledge.com/textbooks/mediatoday

QUESTIONS FOR DISCUSSION AND CRITICAL THINKING

1 Explain what is meant by the statement, "the best scholarly empirical research is *guided* by concepts."

2 In what ways do the early concerns of communication researchers—the ability of the media to communicate cultural values to diverse audiences, or the use of propaganda through the media to rally support for the positions of those in power—play out in the contemporary media environment?

3 What kinds of educational effects might mass communication channels have on child and/or adult audiences?

4 What might a political economist like Robert McChesney or Ben Bagdikian say about the issue of television violence and children?

5 In what ways, if at all, do practices like priming and agenda setting on the part of the media limit our perspectives on issues and events in the world?

INTERNET RESOURCES

Association for Education in Journalism and Mass Communication (www.aejmc. org/)

> The AEJMC exists to promote the highest possible standards for education in journalism and mass communication, to encourage the widest possible range of communication research, to encourage the implementation of a multi-cultural society in the classroom and curriculum, and to defend and maintain freedom of expression in day-to-day living.

Center for Research on the Influences of Television on Children (www.utexas.edu/research/critc/)

> CRITC, the Center for Research on the Influences of Television on Children, studies the impact of various kinds of television viewing on children's behavior and development. It has conducted studies of how children decode the medium of television; how they understand its forms and formats, as well as its content.

Center for Media and Public Affairs (www.cmpa.com/)

> The Center for Media and Public Affairs (CMPA) is a nonpartisan and nonprofit research and educational organization which conducts scientific studies of news and entertainment media. CMPA has emerged as a unique institution that bridges the gap between academic research and the broader domains of media and public policy.

Critical Studies in Mass Communication (http://www.tandf.co.uk/journals/titles/ 07393180.asp)

Critical Studies in Media Communication provides a home for scholarship in media and mass communication from a cultural studies and critical perspective. It particularly welcomes cross-disciplinary works that enrich debates among various disciplines, critical traditions, methodological and analytical approaches, and theoretical standpoints.

Journal of Communication (http://www.blackwell-synergy.com/loi/jcom)

The *Journal of Communication* is the flagship journal of the International Communication Association and an essential publication for all communication specialists and policymakers. The *Journal of Communication* concentrates on communication research, practice, policy, and theory, bringing to its readers the latest, broadest, and most important findings in the field of communication studies.

Journal of Broadcasting and Electronic Media (http://www.tandf.co.uk/journals/ HBEM)

The *Journal of Broadcasting and Electronic Media* is the scholarly journal published quarterly by the Broadcast Education Association. Considered one of the leading publications in the communication field, the journal contains timely articles about new developments, trends and research in electronic media written by academics, researchers and other electronic media professionals.

Media Effects Research Lab at Pennsylvania State University (www.psu.edu/dept/ medialab/)

The Media Effects Research Laboratory at the College of Communications in the Pennsylvania State University is a facility dedicated to conducting empirical research on the psychological effects of media content, form, and technology. Several experimental studies involving hundreds of subjects have been conducted in the lab since its opening in 1997.

Newsweek Media Research Index (www.vmr.com/research/index.html)

The Newsweek Media Research Index is a directory of major studies and reports spanning four decades. This index is made available through the generosity of *Newsweek*. It represents an extraordinary bibliography of over 700 studies, journal articles, conference papers and books, including many international contributions.

KEY TERMS

You can find the definitions to these key terms in the marginal glossary through-out this chapter. Test your knowledge of these terms with interactive flash cards on the *Media Today* companion website.

active audience

agenda setting

capitalism

colonialism

conceptual research

content analysis

control groups

co-optation

critical theory

cultivation studies

cultural colonialism

cultural studies

digital divide

empirical research

experiment

frameworks

hypotheses

knowledge gap

leading questions

magic bullet or hypodermic needle
   approach

mainstream approaches

mass media research

naturalistic experiment

panel survey

political economy

polysemous

priming

propaganda

propaganda analysis

qualitative research

quantitative research

questionnaire

reliable

research

sample

social relations

survey

theories

theory of reasoned action

two-step flow model

uses and gratifications research

validity

CONSTRUCTING MEDIA LITERACY

1 Which of the perspectives on media effects do you find most interesting? Why?
2 To what extent have you seen polysemy work when you and a friend go to the movies? Give an example.
3 Scholars point out that the digital divide may show itself differently in rela-tively wealthy countries such as the United States and United Kingdom com-pared to poor countries such as Bangladesh or the Sudan. Using newspaper or magazine articles, bring some examples of such differences.
4 How do you think your ideas of romance have been shaped by movies and popular songs?
5 Have you ever gotten angry at media portrayals? What, if anything, did you do about it? Do you think that you would go so far as to do what Jessica did? Why or why not? What realistic steps could you/did you take?

chapters

5 A WORLD OF BLURRED MEDIA BOUNDARIES

6 UNDERSTANDING THE STRATEGIES OF MEDIA GIANTS

We live in an age of media giants—large companies with major businesses that influence several media areas. Firms such as Disney, News Corporation, Time Warner, Google, and Sony are setting a pattern for twenty-first century operations. That pattern is global and requires an ability to control content across media boundaries.

In this section, we examine the strategies of media giants and their impact on the media system. We also introduce concerns by media critics that a small number of media conglomerates have too much influence over the news, entertainment, information, and even education materials that surround us in our daily lives.

media giants and

two

part two

media giants and cross-media activities

cross-media activities

5

A WORLD OF BLURRED MEDIA BOUNDARIES

After studying this chapter, you will be able to:

1 Identify and discuss the six guiding trends shaping the world of mass media

2 Analyze and discuss media fragmentation's impact on media organizations and their consumers

3 Recognize and evaluate the audience segmentation strategies of media organizations

4 Identify and explain the benefits and challenges of distributing products across media boundaries

5 Analyze and discuss the impact of digital convergence on media organizations and their consumers

6 Recognize the trend toward globalization in the mass media and evaluate its consequences

7 Recognize the trend toward conglomeration in the mass media and evaluate its consequences

8 Harness your media literacy skills by taking a critical view of the six trends discussed in this chapter

"All these years … you've gone through the day without e-mail like this in your pocket. Or stock updates like this in your pocket. Or Internet like this in your pocket. And you survived. The question is, 'How?'"

–iPhone Advertisement

Media Today

If you flip through the pages of this book, you'll notice that in the chapters to come, we look at mass media industries individually. You'll see, for example, that there are separate chapters on the book, newspaper, film, and Internet industries—with good reason. Each industry has its own way of doing things, its own approaches to production, distribution, and exhibition.

Yet, if we want to understand how the mass media work today, there is also a good reason for thinking of the mass media industries as related rather than separate. Top media executives certainly think of them as related. Those executives point out that the boundaries of media industries are becoming increasingly blurred. That is, it is getting more and more difficult to know where the movie industry ends and the television industry begins; where the Internet industry ends and the newspaper industry begins; where the advertising industry ends and the public relations industry begins, and so on. Materials that are created for one mass media industry are increasingly showing up in others in one form or another. The *Harry Potter* series, for example, has moved from its original format as a book to the advertising poster, the movie screen, the website, the soundtrack, the action figure, the DVD, and the television, among other things.

"Wait!" you may hear yourself saying. "These kinds of cross-media connections have been going on for decades. Instead of My Little Pony and Wubbzy, my parents and grandparents had Howdy Doody and Bullwinkle stuff that crossed media: from TV to movies and toys and lunch boxes, comic books, and posters. Has anything really changed? Hasn't this always been a standard part of the mass media world?" Good question. A glance back in time does reveal that media industries have always interacted. Still, what is happening at the start of the twenty-first century represents a major change. Within the past fifteen years, the quick movement of all sorts of materials across a variety of mass media industries has become critical to the financial health of virtually all types of media firms.

The aim of this chapter and the one that follows is to help you critically examine these cross-media activities. How do they work? What effects might they have on society and on you as a consumer? It is useful to address these questions before you study individual mass media industries. Being sensitive to the cross-media picture will help you be better able to think about the way the individual industries we discuss operate in the larger media system.

Six Current Guiding Mass Media Trends

Six related trends describe the mass media world at the beginning of the twenty-first century:

- Media fragmentation
- Audience segmentation
- Distribution of products across media boundaries
- Globalization

- Conglomeration
- Digital convergence

Mass media executives see media fragmentation and audience segmentation as special challenges that force media producers to move materials across media outlets in search of profits. And they see digital convergence, conglomeration and globalization as potential solutions to the difficulties of cross-media distribution while also adding to their ways of maximizing profit. Media critics worry that these activities pose serious dangers to a democratic society. They are especially concerned about ill effects of globalization and conglomeration. To understand why, we must first understand what's going on in all these activities. Let's start with media fragmentation.

Media Fragmentation

media fragmentation the increase in the number of mass media and mass media outlets that has been taking place during the past two decades

As we discussed in Chapter 1, the term **media fragmentation** refers to the increase in the number of mass media and mass media outlets that has been taking place during the past two decades. (See Figure 1.1 on page 7.) During the past thirty years, we have seen skyrocketing growth in mass communication via cable TV, UHF TV, VCRs, the personal computer, telemarketing, DVDs, out-of-home media, and the Internet. Of course, along with the growth of these media, we also saw the growth of *mass media outlets*. That is, the number and variety of particular media sources in the United States have skyrocketed. They now include, for example, tens of cable networks, many independent television stations, and millions of personal computers with technology connecting them to the outside world.

The process isn't stopping. As you read this, companies are working to find even more ways to distribute and exhibit news, information, advertising, and entertainment in as many places as possible, with substantial consequences for the way executives think about media industries. For leaders of long-standing firms, the changing world poses major challenges.

Audience Erosion

audience erosion a decrease in the percentage of the population using a particular mass medium or a specific media outlet

The most far-reaching of these challenges is *audience erosion*. **Audience erosion** refers to a decrease in the percentage of the population using a particular mass medium (such as newspapers in general) or a specific media outlet (such as a specific newspaper). Strictly speaking, audience erosion may happen for many reasons. Readers of a magazine may not like the stories it features anymore, or they may stop buying it because the company decides to charge a higher price. Similarly, a TV network may lose a lot of viewers if those viewers find that the programming of a network's competitors is more interesting.

When most media executives talk about audience erosion, though, they mean erosion that is taking place because of media fragmentation. The dramatic increase in the number of media and media outlets has given people more choices for news, entertainment, information and education. That has led to declines in audiences in many media industries and for many media firms.

As we will see in forthcoming chapters, the most important erosion of magazine and radio audiences began before the 1980s, as a result of the commercial introduction of television in the 1940s and (for AM radio) FM in the 1960s. Movie producers have also noticed that the number of tickets sold at theaters in the United

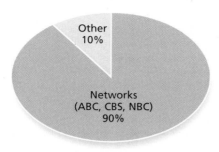

Primetime in the 1990s*

*According to Nielsen Media Research

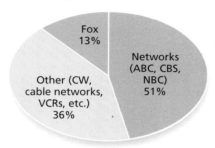

Primetime in the late 2000s*

Figure 5.1
Eroding Audiences
Audience erosion had most
notably affected the prime-
time ratings of the "Big
Three" networks—ABC,
CBS, and NBC—as this
figure shows.

States has been flat for many years, even though the population has grown substantially.

From the 1980s onward, though, media and advertising practitioners have had a sense that the audiences for all media are eroding at an increasing pace. Much of that sense undoubtedly has to do with the startling, dramatic splintering of audiences for broadcast television. From the late 1940s until the early 1980s, ABC, CBS, and NBC consistently received 90 percent of the evening ("primetime") audience, according to the Nielsen audience ratings company. To put it differently, fully 90 percent of all those watching television were tuned to one of the broadcast networks. By the mid-2000s, though, the three-networks' "share" had slid to about 51 percent—that's a 54 percent drop (see Figure 5.1). According to Nielsen, the missing population could be found at the relatively new Fox network (which had about 13 percent of the audience); at the smaller, newer broadcast networks (for example, the CW and Univision); and at cable networks, DVDs and video games.

Today, for many broadcast network executives, and certainly for many leaders of the radio, magazine, book, newspaper, and movie industries, the goal is not even to try to attract "everybody." It is to define and hold an audience niche—to earn the loyalty of specific portions of the population and hold onto them while other companies in the fragmenting media world try to attract other groups.

Media fragmentation and audience erosion have therefore mobilized media executives to think about their desired audiences more carefully. That has led them to engage in audience segmentation.

Audience Segmentation

The term **audience segmentation** means that producers and distributors try to reach different types of people with messages tailored specifically for them. No individual media materials can attract *all* of the approximately 300 million individuals in the United States. Instead, these materials reach segments, or parts, of society. These

audience segmentation
the process by which
production and distribution
are targeted to reach
different types of people
with messages tailored for
them

Media organizations often set their sights on a target audience and tailor their products according to the audience segment they are pursuing. The women's magazines shown here each go after specific types of women—for example, women aged eighteen to thirty-five.

targeting   the process by which a mass media organization sets its sights on having as its audience one or more of the social segments it has identified in the population

segments vary greatly in terms of the number of people involved and the time it takes for most of them to receive the material. *Grey's Anatomy* is an example of a television program that reaches tens of millions of viewers virtually instantaneously. The destruction of New York's World Trade Center by terrorists on September 11, 2001 provides an instance of how huge audiences can build over a period of time. Although many saw the horrors live on television, many more learned about them in news programs and newspapers that appeared after it happened.

Then there are cases in which the number of people reached by particular mass media materials is relatively small. We all know that this happens when a TV show, movie, or musical recording fails to attract the large audience its producers intended. Increasingly, though, the pursuit of relatively small audiences by firms involved in the production, distribution, and exhibition of messages is purposeful and profitable.

When a mass media organization sets its sights on having as its audience one or more of the social segments it has identified in the population, that behavior is called **targeting**. Consider, for example, a magazine company that, for decades, has put out a periodical aimed at women in general. "Women" is, of course, an audience segment—quite a large one. Greater audience segmentation on the part of the publisher might involve deciding to go after specific types of women—say, women aged eighteen to thirty-five who are mothers. Targeting would involve advertising to women who fit that profile in the hope that they will subscribe to the magazine.

Some **target segments** may be quite large—in the millions. Others might comprise only hundreds or tens of thousands of individuals. The targeted media typically portray the place of the members of these segments in the larger society—their problems, triumphs, and futures. A magazine for African-American women, for example, might explore the challenges that its readers face when they try to find mentors in their workplace. A magazine for golfers might rate the best restaurants near golf courses. A gardening magazine might assess the future of gardening societies in the United States.

Why would a media company want to reduce its audience by segmenting and targeting in that way? The answer is that segmentation and targeting are based on business considerations. Why and how executives engage in segmentation and targeting differs somewhat depending on whether or not their media outlet is supported primarily by advertising funds. Recall from Chapter 2 that some media companies rely mostly on advertising for their revenues. Other companies get support from a balanced combination of advertising and subscription. Still others get most of their support from individual purchases or subscriptions. (**Subscriptions** are purchases for a series of products that are paid for in advance.)

Let's take a look at how segmentation works both when outlets are not advertiser-supported and when they are.

Segmentation When Outlets are not Advertiser-Supported

Why would a media outlet not be supported by advertising? So much media in the United States *is* ad-supported that it may well seem odd to us when a particular medium isn't. Take books. Although you may have seen some ad inserts (for cigarettes, for example) in paperbacks, we're not used to thinking of books as featuring advertising, except maybe advertising for other books. The same is true for music albums. Instead of being supported by advertising, customers pay for them outright.

When a media outlet is not advertiser-supported, it must target segments of the population that are large enough or wealthy enough to cover the costs of the media product. Consider a low-budget horror movie that also has strong romantic elements. If the movie costs "only" $10 million or $15 million to make, a relatively small audience can support it. Nevertheless, because there is so much competition, studio executives will not give such a movie the green light unless they are convinced that a segment of the movie-going audience is likely to find the particular film interesting.

Producers make that determination by conducting or drawing on previous **market research**. Market research is different from the social research we discussed in Chapter 4, because its focus is on selling products. Certainly, some market research may be useful to social researchers, and some social research findings might help media producers. Moreover, market researchers often use the same techniques that social researchers use. They carry out surveys, for example, and may even conduct experiments. So, based on a national survey by a commercial research firm, the producers may be able to show that "teenagers who like horror films" and "women eighteen to thirty-five who like gothic romances" are two categories that are large yet specific enough to be expected audiences for such a film.

You might think that very expensive films, such as one of the *Spiderman* or *Harry Potter* films, would have to go after just about everybody in order to justify their more than $150 million budgets. Certainly, energizing huge numbers of potential movie viewers is good; mega-hits such as *Star Wars* make so much money

target segments the desired segments that a media organization is trying to reach

subscriptions purchases for a series of products that are paid for in advance

market research research that has, as its end goal, the gathering of information that will help an organization sell more products

Table 5.1   Targeting an Audience Segment: Two Ends of the Spectrum

Action film (R rating)	Children's film (G rating)
■ Show promotional trailers in theaters that exhibit other action films. Include some of the film's romance in the trailer so that women will not mind seeing the movie with men.	■ Show promotional trailers in theaters that exhibit other children's films. Include scenes that imply to adults that they will like the film too.
■ Commercials during wrestling, football, baseball.	■ Commercials on Saturday morning TV, Nickelodeon, Friday night TV.
■ Sweepstakes in connection with a beer company.	■ Give out movie-related toys at Burger King or (if it is a Disney film) McDonald's.
■ Radio commercials on hard rock stations.	■ Contests on cereal boxes.

that they warm the hearts and dreams of most movie executives. Still, the producers of even an expensive film have an audience segment in mind. The creators of *Terminator 2: Judgment* Day, with Arnold Schwarzenegger, seem to have decided that their main audience would be males, especially non-U.S. males who like Schwarzenegger and the action genre. Producers of *Harry Potter* films also seem to have had particular, or core, audience segments in mind: children and their parents who will see the film several times and buy the many toys and clothes related to it (see Table 5.1).

Some people object to the idea that media materials for children are created with the primary motivation of selling merchandising to kids. Media critics have complained for decades that many of the U.S. media operate on the ethically questionable premise that children are as much of a target market as adults. However, the critics do not have much clout in the new, interconnected media world, especially when media materials are not directly ad-supported. But even when they are, the name of the game is to spin off products for sale with or without ad-support in order to accumulate extra revenue from as many sources as possible.

Segmentation When Outlets are Advertiser-Supported

When a media outlet is advertiser-supported, production, distribution, and exhibition executives must identify population segments that sponsors will want to reach at prices that will pay for the media materials. Take a look at *Advertising Age* or similar magazines that discuss the advertising industry. You will see that media and advertising practitioners continually pay for market research that breaks society into an enormous number of segments. This sort of research is often not very different from the market research we discussed earlier. The idea is to observe or survey samples of the population and then draw conclusions about how certain parts of the sample are different from other parts.

The more marketers find a group attractive, the more they are prone to take that group apart to look for subgroups that have uniquely attractive features. For example, women of childbearing age interest marketers because they purchase most of the goods for their homes. But marketers often don't stop there. They distinguish among single, married, and divorced women; between women with children and those without; between women in upscale and downscale households; and between women who work outside the home and those who work at home. [1]

Recall from Chapter 2 the terms *psychographics* and *demographics*. These terms refer, respectively, to personality characteristics (optimist, ambitious) and social categories (teenager, Asian-American) that researchers use to distinguish among consumers. Marketers also separate people by their lifestyles—the kinds of activities they tend to engage in.

One of the firms that uses lifestyles and demographics in market research is Claritas. It creates descriptions of neighborhoods around the United States using segmentation techniques that start with the premise that "birds of a feather flock together." That is, it assumes

www.adage.com, the website of *Advertising Age* magazine

that neighborhoods can be defined in terms of clusters of similar demographic information and behaviors of the households in them. Companies that buy its research often use this information to decide where and on what media to place advertising money.

The Alltel telephone company, for example, found that middle-class clusters that Claritas labels "Mobility Blues," "Starter Families," and "Mid-City Mix," plus higher-income clusters labeled "Executive Suites" and "Winner's Circle," were good prospects for phone services that combined local, long distance, and cellular. These households spent more than $50 a month on local phone service plus $45 to $65 on cellular service. The company targeted its marketing efforts at communities that are home to lots of these clusters, and saw bundled wireline sales in one market (Jacksonville, FL) go from 0 to 5 percent in ten months.[2]

As an example of how firms use psychographic research, consider the following comments about *Fortune* magazine by the vice president of marketing at the BMW North America car company. *Fortune* is "superb at capturing our psychographic: a 30–40-year-old person who works hard, plays hard." In fact, the vice president went on to say, studies of *Fortune* also show that its readers actually read the ads that advertisers place there. Phil Sawyer, director of advertising research for market research firm Roper Starch, noted that "In our *Read Most* scores—which measure how many readers read half or more of the ad copy—*Fortune* readers score 16 percent vs. 13 percent for newsweeklies on two-page spreads, for example. *Fortune*," he concluded, "brings you a quality customer."[3]

Often media executives commission this sort of research to show *why* advertisers should pay to reach their audiences. Sometimes, if sponsors show little interest in those audiences, or if there is too much competition for a particular audience slice, the executives may rethink the segments they have chosen. Executives of new media outlets are often more practical. They will go out of their way to build content around audience segments that advertisers want to reach but that are underserved by media.

The *Fortune* case provides a good example of the rethinking of audiences in order to win more ad sponsorship. In the late 1990s, *Fortune*'s executives decided that the magazine should have more readers among America's rising number of wealthy young business people. These readers were of interest to luxury advertisers who did not think of *Fortune* as a place to find such people, and so were looking to other magazines. Consequently, executives mapped out a new editorial approach that mixed in each issue investigative, hard-news stories with the kind of gossipy stories that *Fortune*'s staffers knew attracted young adults to their sister publication, *People*. The combination attracted a young but very upscale audience that advertisers could not find in *People* or many other places.

Distribution of Products Across Media Boundaries

Traditionally, understanding mass media has meant seeing the newspaper, book, broadcast, radio, recording, and other mass media industries as separate worlds. A couple of decades ago, this approach was reasonably accurate. The difficulty with it today is that the boundaries between various mass media industries are blurring tremendously (see Figure 5.2).

Executives routinely create products for use in a number of mass media. Newspaper companies, for example, are increasingly moving their reporters' work—and even their reporters—to cable TV, broadcast TV, computer software, and the World Wide Web. People in "the film business" also know that it is becoming more and more difficult to determine where the film industry ends and where a host of other industries begin. Contemporary movie companies support their creations when they cross media boundaries with their materials by propelling them far beyond theaters through deals with the broadcast television, cable TV, home video, satellite TV, toy, book, and recording industries, among others.

Exactly what does the phrase *cross media boundaries with their materials* mean? It means creating content that can be used and appreciated in different media. As an example, consider the movie *Enchanted*. The Walt Disney Company, which provided most of the money for the film and distributed it, released it to U.S. movie theaters during the summer of 2007. But Disney had no intention of limit-

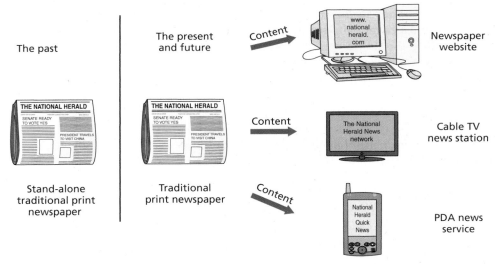

Figure 5.2

The Blurring of Media Boundaries

In the past, a newspaper was just that—a stand-alone newspaper, delivering content through printed images and words. Today, and likely even more so in years to come, a newspaper is so much more, with content moving across media boundaries—from the traditional print piece to the paper's website, to the paper's own cable news network, to a downloadable version of the paper's top stories on your PDA device ... and beyond!

ing the showing of the movie to theaters. Instead, Disney saw the theatrical release of the motion picture as the first step in a marketing effort to place the film in a variety of media. These included pay-per-view television (as in hotels), digital video disks (DVDs), videotapes, pay cable television (for example, HBO), and regular broadcast TV (on Disney-owned ABC, no doubt).

As this example shows, crossing media boundaries sometimes simply means transferring the exact same content to other media. Other times, though, it involves transforming the content so that it will fit the medium or the audience for that medium. An audio CD of *Enchanted*'s songs is an example. So is a book (actually, there were three age-appropriate versions), a video game and a website based on the movie.

The need to cross media boundaries is related to two major goals. The first is to cover the costs of production and extend the revenue possibilities. The second is to make a substantial proportion of the target audiences in a variety of media locations aware of the material's existence. Marketing executives call that achieving a good share of mind. Let's take a look at each goal separately.

CASE STUDY Cross-media Marketing of Movies

The idea To get a sense of the cross-media power of major movie companies and the conglomerates to which they belong, track the cross-media marketing activities that are being used and the windows in which the film will appear.

The method Pick a movie that a major studio—Warner Brothers, Columbia, Disney, Paramount, Twentieth Century Fox or Universal—has released as a major summer or Christmas film. The *Harry Potter*, *Pirates of the Caribbean*, and *Shrek* flicks are examples. Then use a newspaper-and-magazine database such as Factiva or NexisLexis to investigate the coverage the film received in the month before it was released. Check out (1) the various types of press articles about the movie; (2) toys and other licensed products (such as T-shirts and masks) that the studio may have licensed with the film's release; and (3) the publicity the movie has gotten through tie-ins with other product marketers, such as food companies, stores, and phone companies.

Write a report of what you learned, including who the target audience in the United States was for the movie and how the movie company tried to reach it. In view of what you have learned about cross-media activities, address the following questions: if you were a member of the target audience, would you have heard about the movie before its release? What notions about the film and its stars would you have heard (that is, what agenda about the movie did the publicity create)? And through what media would you have heard that?

Reasons for Crossing Media Boundaries: Covering Costs

There was a time not too long ago when media companies could cover all their costs of doing business by concentrating on one medium. Book companies that aim at the general public could put out the works of popular novelists and hope to make a worthwhile profit from the hardback version. Even major movie companies, which have always spent a lot of money on their productions, assumed that they would make back their costs during the theatrical release of their motion pictures in the United States. Money from anywhere else—outside the United States, television—was easy profit.

This expectation of making a profit by releasing content in one medium no longer holds for many mass media firms; their costs have simply gotten too high. In the book industry, for example, well-known authors often get advance payments in the millions of dollars by pitting book publishers against one another in bidding wars for their manuscripts. In the movie business, salaries of stars and directors that can soar far above $20 million and the enormous cost of marketing a film make it highly unlikely that the tickets that U.S. audiences buy will lead to a profit.

One popular solution to the problem of profitability has been to try to increase revenues by moving the content across media. Different media industries have tended to address this challenge in different ways. Let's take a look at two particular approaches—those of the TV and film industries, and those of the print media industries.

Covering Costs in TV and Film In the television and film businesses, where production costs are quite high, the challenge of covering costs has forced production organizations to design their output with an eye toward moving it across mass media boundaries.

Consider broadcast television, for example. The major networks—ABC, CBS, Fox, and NBC—commission the most-viewed programs, those in prime time. But network executives have found that the costs of producing programs are often far greater than the amount that advertisers (who are aware of audience erosion) are willing to pay for network time. In short, the executives can't cover the high cost of producing these shows with the revenues from advertisers alone.

To address this situation, the network executives will often refuse to pay the full cost of episodes of a new series or made-for-TV movie that they intend to air only a few times. By doing so, the network executives force the production firm that is producing the series or movie to make up the financial difference by finding cable, airline, hotel, video, or other outlets in the United States and abroad that want to air repeats of the programs after they show up on the networks. So, for example, reruns of *Law and Order* show up on the U.S. cable network. Spots from network news division shows such as *60 Minutes* and *Dateline NBC* show up between movies on airplanes.

As this last example suggests, network executives sometimes try to keep control over their costs and potential earnings through **vertical integration**, a term that we first discussed in Chapter 2. Recall that it means having control of all phases of a media product, from production through distribution to exhibition. In our cross-media case, it means that by getting one of its own production units to create the products it distributes, the network can control distribution and even exhibition in the cable, home video, airline and other industries—and all the revenues that come with it. So, for example, the ABC-TV network (whose parent is The Walt Disney Company) may pay Walt Disney Productions to create a TV movie that will be shown on ABC as part of its Sunday evening schedule. After two showings on ABC-TV, Disney might distribute the film to another exhibition outlet it owns—the Disney Channel or the Lifetime cable channel. Some months later, Disney Home Video may sell the film to department and video stores to get further revenues from it. By controlling the distribution and sometimes even the exhibition of its own product, Disney can make a lot of money from it—money that it would not see if the movie aired on ABC-TV alone.

Network-owned production firms do not create all the programs that appear on the networks. However, when network executives do accept programs

vertical integration an organization's control over a media product from production through distribution to exhibition

from unrelated production firms, they often require the production firm to bring the network in as a partner. Such *partnering* means giving the network a share in the ownership of the program. The production firm Atlantis Alliance, for example, shares ownership in the primetime drama *CSI* with CBS Productions; the program airs on CBS. That way, when the Atlantis Alliance makes money on the show in cable, syndication, or other places, CBS will receive part of those revenues.

Naturally, many production executives see partnering as a kind of extortion—the network demanding a piece of the action in return for a time slot. Network executives justify this demand by arguing that the network deserves a reward for helping to promote the program so that it can succeed after its network run. They add that when production firms have a network as a partner, they can use the first broadcast run as a launching pad for revenue-making runs in other places.

The traditional way to make money from programs with a long network run has been to rent them to local stations; this activity is called **syndication**. In recent years, syndication has taken on a much broader meaning. Some production firms license their programs first to local stations and then to cable networks. *Seinfeld* fits this description; so do virtually all the series on the TV Land cable network. Others go directly to cable with their shows. In a few cases, notably with *The X Files* and TV classics such as *M*A*S*H*, producers have even turned episodes into home video titles.

Executives use the term **windows** to describe the series of exhibition points for audiovisual products through which revenues are generated. The ABC-TV example that was just presented suggests how this can work in television. When companies make theatrical films, their series of windows is typically quite a bit more varied than that of TV producers. You can see that if you compare the number of windows mentioned in the ABC television case with the number mentioned in our earlier discussion of *Enchanted*.

The reason for this is that for many years movie producers have realized that the number of tickets sold at U.S. theaters has been flat, even though both the cost of movies and the American population have grown substantially. Instead of watching newly released movies in the theaters, many people now watch films as they move through the gamut of windows spread over a few years—from pay-per-view cable at home, to pay cable (for example, HBO or Starz!) to home videocassettes or DVDs, to digital satellite devices like DirecTV, to network TV, to syndication. And that's just the domestic (U.S.-based) set of windows. Add to that list of windows the similar international exhibition gamut from which producers and distributors pull in money.

Two other activities that film producers and even some TV producers often engage in to make money from their creations are *product placement* and the sale of *creative rights*. A **product placement** involves a manufacturer paying—often tens of thousands of dollars and sometimes far more—a production company for the opportunity to have its product displayed in a movie or TV show. Remember Reese's Pieces in *E.T.*? Kellogg's cereals on *Seinfeld*? Apple Computers in *Independence Day*? FedEx in *Cast Away*? Doritos, Mountain Dew, Reebok, and Target Stores on *Survivor*? All these are examples of product placements.

Sometimes products get into TV shows and movies because the producers need a product and ask the manufacturer if it wants to participate. That's how FedEx got into *Cast Away*. Increasingly, a production firm looking for extra money will make a deal with a product placement company that is looking to reach specific audiences for one or more of its clients. The contractual agreement that results often specifies the length of time the product will appear on screen.

syndication licensing or renting to local stations or cable networks the right to air programs with a long network run (generally at least one hundred episodes)

windows the series of exhibition points for audiovisual products through which revenues are generated

product placement the process by which a manufacturer pays—often tens of thousands of dollars and sometimes far more— a production company for the opportunity to have its product displayed in a movie or TV show

Figure 5.3

The Increased Value of Other Windows to the Hollywood Majors

The six major U.S. movie distributors (Paramount, Walt Disney, Sony Pictures, Twentieth Century Fox, Universal, and Warner Brothers) are making far more money now than in the past from circulating movies through different windows—to hotel and airline viewings, in-home pay-per-view, home video sales and rentals, various types of television outlets, and more.

Source: Hy Holinger, "MPA Study," Hollywood Reporter, June 15, 2007, accessed 3/7/08, http://www.hollywoodreporter.com/hr/content_display/news/e3ic5575a8c4f61aadd68a0d344f476d5da

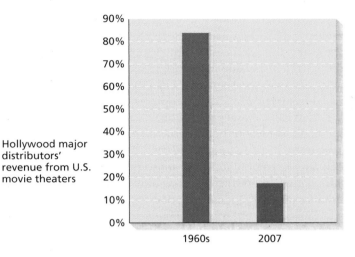

Hollywood major distributors' revenue from U.S. movie theaters

creative rights allowing companies that make or sell clothing, food, toys, or other goods the right to use characters or scenes from the film or TV show to attract customers

While product placement involves using a film or TV show to hype the products of other companies, the sale of **creative rights** involves encouraging other companies to hype the film or TV show through their products. When it sells creative rights, a producer allows companies that make or sell clothing, food, toys, or other goods the right to use characters or scenes from the film or TV show to attract customers. Some products based on creative rights can last for years (think of *Star Wars* or *The Simpsons* toys); some last only for a few months (think of *Power Puff Girls* cereal or *Rugrats* vitamins). But with certain event films or children's films, the sale of creative rights can bring the production company (and, depending on the deal, the distributor) a bonanza.

This cash flow from distributing products across media boundaries has proved particularly significant for revenues in the film industry. In the 1960s, the major film distributors raked in close to 90 percent of their revenues from domestic theatrical rentals (your basic U.S. movie theaters); in the late 1990s, domestic rentals accounted for only 13 percent of the incoming cash (see Figure 5.3). This low percentage should not be taken to mean that the release of films into U.S. theaters is unimportant. On the contrary, a strong domestic theatrical release is the platform upon which the profit from all the other windows stands. That's because most consumers who pay to see films in the nontheatrical windows take their cues from what succeeded at the box office. Consequently, a film that bombs at the U.S. box office will simply not be that attractive to executives who purchase films for other outlets. Table 5.2 summarizes the various tactics used by the electronic media.

Covering Costs in Print Media   The amount of money it takes for an established magazine or newspaper firm to publish a new issue is typically far less than the amount of money needed to produce a new movie or TV series. Nevertheless, the operating costs of print media firms can be substantial, and print media companies are increasingly looking for ways to use, reuse, and repurpose the content they have. Their logic is not that different from the logic of movie and TV executives: the more windows of opportunity to eke more revenues from this material, the better.

Consider the New York Times Company as an example. You may think of it as just the newspaper that bears its name, but the $3.5 billion company actually extends far beyond this: it owns seventeen newspapers, eight network-affiliated television stations, and two New York City radio stations. Because news creation is such an expensive, labor-intensive business, the Times Company works hard to take fruits of its journalistic labors for its own papers and sell them to other papers,

Table 5.2   **Covering Costs: A Recap of the Tactics Used in the TV and Movie Industries**

Strategy	Television example	Movie example
Distribution to a variety of windows	Beginning with network TV and moving to home cable, hotels, and airlines	Beginning with theaters and moving to hotels and airlines, then home video, pay-per-view cable at home
Vertical integration	ABC network buying movie from Walt Disney Productions	Viacom-owned Nickelodeon cable releasing movie through Viacom-owned Paramount Pictures
Partnering	Atlantis Alliance with CBS on the series *CSI*	Dreamworks and Universal on the movie *Gladiator*
Syndication	Wolf films sells TBS Cable the right to air *Law and Order* after its network runs	Warner Brothers sells local stations the right to air a group of WB theatrical films after their appearance in other windows
Product placement	Reebok products on *Survivor II*	FedEx name in *Cast Away*
Sale of creative rights	*Power Puff Girls* cereal	*Rugrats* vitamins

use them for its websites, and to repurpose them for databases. In addition to using the news in its own papers, the firm runs news and feature **syndicates.** These are firms that, for a subscription fee, continually provide hard and soft news, respectively, to newspapers around the world. The *New York Times* also uses its daily news stories on its Internet properties such as http://www.nytimes.com, http://www.boston.com, and http://www.newyorktoday.com. When the news stories, photos, and illustrations are not "new" anymore, the conglomerate approaches them differently (or *repurposes* them). It incorporates them into news, photo, and graphics archives that sell stories, photos, and charts to companies and individuals that need such material. The Times Company also leases all the articles in its papers to database firms such as LexisNexis, which pays it money when people use the databases to read Times-owned articles.

> **syndicates** firms that, for a subscription fee, continually provide hard and soft news to newspapers around the world

Magazine and book publishing firms similarly look for ways to distribute their products. Consider the deal that Golden Books Family Entertainment made with Sony Wonder, the video subsidiary of the Sony Corporation. Golden Books Family Entertainment calls itself the leading children's book publisher in North America. As a result of its book publishing operation, the company owns one of the world's largest libraries of family entertainment copyrights, including *The Lone Ranger*, *Lassie*, *Underdog*, and *Shari Lewis*. One way in which the company uses its copyrights beyond the printed page is through joint ventures that turn material from Golden Books and other sources into videos that are sold in book and department stores.

Reasons for Crossing Media Boundaries: Achieving a Good Share of Mind

A media product will be successful only if the product's target audience learns about it and thinks about it. Marketers refer to getting a substantial percentage of their target audience to think about their product as *achieving a good share of mind*. Think about what happens when a company moves a mass media product across media outlets: more people get to notice the product's existence—and get to notice it more often—than if it just stayed in one medium. That exposure can help business. The idea is a basic one: if you see that a film is playing in many the-

achieving a good share of mind making a substantial proportion of the target audiences in a variety of media locations aware of the material's existence

aters, even if you don't pay to see it in the theater, you might pay to see it when it hits another window—the home-video release, or the pay-perview showing.

But **achieving a good share of mind**—making a substantial proportion of the target audiences in a variety of media locations aware of the material's existence—requires a lot more than simply getting people to notice a product as it moves in its entirety through a number of windows. In the highly fragmented and competitive media environment, executives have concluded that they must chase target audience segments across as many exhibition outlets as possible in order to convince them to see a movie, watch a TV show, or read a book or magazine. That is why, for example, you see movie stars appearing on morning talk shows, evening celebrity shows, and late-night talk shows just before their latest films appear in theaters. These stars are also on the covers of magazines that cater to the films' target audiences. Pick just about any major movie that has just come out and you will see the pattern repeated.

When we look at the chapters on advertising (Chapter 15), and public relations (Chapter 16), we will see that moving people and ideas across different media outlets is basic to what executives in those industries do. During the past couple of decades, mass media executives have learned that they must use a wide variety of mass media for advertising and public relations activities to make their target audiences aware of their products. Some of this activity involves standard advertising and public relations activities—putting a commercial on TV, or trying to get your movie discussed on *Entertainment Tonight*. But many mass media production and distribution executives go further. They use the licensing of creative rights as a way to publicize their mass media products while making extra money on the product.

Examples include *Harry Potter* toys, *Star Wars* sweatshirts, and *Shrek* lunchboxes. Media executives view such paraphernalia as more than just a fun thing for people to buy. These items remind consumers of their interest in the movie and provide them with a continuing reason to pay for *Star Wars* movies, books, home videos, and cable showings. Media executives use the term *brand* to describe products such as *South Park, American Idol,* and *60 Minutes.* By **brand** they mean a clearly identifiable image that attracts target audiences over and over again. Executives believe that they can extend the life of a powerful brand over many years by achieving the right kind of publicity and combining new products with reissues of old ones. That strategy amplifies the ability of the product to contribute to the company's bottom line.

brand a name and image associated with a particular product

Media executives use the word *brand* to refer to media outlets as well as individual products. The owners of media outlets such as *Cosmopolitan*, MTV, and Paramount stress to advertisers and consumers that these names do not just stand for a magazine (in the case of *Cosmopolitan*), a cable channel (in the case of MTV), or a film company (in the case of Paramount). Instead, the owners of these outlets say, each of these names stands for a certain personality, a certain kind of content, and a certain type of audience, no matter where the name appears. So, *Cosmopolitan* will be recognized as the *Cosmopolitan* brand whether it appears on a magazine, on a book, or on cable TV, and MTV's image crosses media from cable to clothes to books to music. Executives believe that such cross-media branding is increasingly necessary to keep existing advertisers and audiences and to get new ones as sponsors and consumers scatter to different channels.

Globalization

In the face of media fragmentation, audience erosion, and the need to move materials to more outlets in order to increase revenues, U.S. production and distribu-

A vast range of products—from books to movies to toys to video games to clothing to backpacks and more—help promote the *Harry Potter* brand.

tion executives have been looking to markets beyond those in America—to the global marketplace—as a way to solve their revenue problems.

It's not as if U.S. mass media firms have been ignoring the rest of the world until now. On the contrary, the movie, recording, radio, television, book, and magazine industries have all—to some extent—been distributing their products internationally for a long time. However, during the first three-quarters of the twentieth century, "going global" meant taking materials that had already generated profits in the United States and adding to those profits by selling them elsewhere.

Today, a new mindset about the world outside American borders has emerged. Its logic is as follows: media fragmentation and audience erosion make it difficult for mass media distributors to reach the huge audiences they would like in the United States. Producers' use of audience segmentation to attract advertisers or cultivate consumer loyalty also inevitably lowers the number of American consumers that go to the producers' products. Global consumers are a way to make the audience larger.

Rather than simply being a place to pick up extra money from products that have already made their profits in the United States, then, countries around the world should be viewed as part of the initial marketplace for these mass media materials. The potential market thereby becomes huge, even in the face of audience erosion. Moreover, the world's population potentially provides producers and distributors with larger audiences than ever for targeted, niche materials.

For media critics, there are two questions about this approach that particularly stand out. First, who's to say that there are audience segments outside the United States that have tastes similar to those of Americans? Second, don't those parts of the world that have strong and growing consumer economies—Europe, Asia, and Latin America—have their own mass media firms that create materials aimed at their own consumers?

In order to answer these questions, we must first realize that much of the U.S. media business is already highly global at its core. The importance of the world market has become so strong that during the past quarter century many major mass media firms based in foreign countries have bought important U.S. media holdings. As illustrated in Figure 5.4, the Sony Corporation, headquartered in

Bertelsmann

(Germany)

Books: Selected U.S. Holdings
- Random House
- Doubleday
- Bantam Dell
- Ballantine
- Crown Publishing Group
- Fodor's
- Knopf

Magazines: Selected U.S. Holdings
- *American Homestyle*
- *Family Circle*
- *Fast Company*
- *Inc.*
- *McCall's*
- *Parents*
- *YM*

Music: Selected U.S. Holdings
- Arista Records
- RCA Records
- BMG Music
- Bad Boy Records
- LaFace Records
- Windham Hill Group

Multimedia: Selected U.S. Holdings
- Barnes&Noble.com
- Cdnow.com
- Lycos
- BMG Direct
- Tripod

SONY

(Japan)

TV and Film: Selected U.S. Holdings
- Sony Pictures Entertainment
- Sony Pictures Classics
- Columbia Pictures
- TriStar Pictures
- Columbia TriStar
- Columbia TriStar Home Entertainment
- The Game Show Network
- Jim Henson Productions
- Mandalay Entertainment

Music: Selected U.S. Holdings
- Columbia Records
- Epic Records Group
- Sony Classical
- Legacy
- Nashville
- Sony Wonder
- Sony Music Video (SMV)
- Word Entertainment
- Columbia House

Multimedia: Selected U.S. Holdings
- Sony Online
- Sony PlayStation
- The Station@sony.com
- Columbia TriStar Interactive

Figure 5.4

The Global Nature of U.S. Mass Media Ownership
Bertelsmann (of Germany) and Sony (of Japan) each have significant U.S. media holdings under their corporate umbrellas, as this figure shows. They have created a joint venture, Sony BMG, to manage their music holdings.

Japan, owns Columbia Pictures and Sony Music. Rockstar, a major video game company (the *Grand Theft Auto* series is one of their achievements), is based in the United Kingdom. The German firm Bertelsmann owns the Random House and Doubleday book publishing companies.

Worldwide Tastes in Media vs. American Media Tastes

Consider the first question, which raises the problem of finding audience segments that have tastes similar to those of Americans. Recording companies have decided that they can't, in fact, take it for granted that people throughout the world share

American tastes. Tastes in music are often vastly different within each country, let alone worldwide. But the costs of producing a CD or selling digital copies through iTunes are so relatively low that it is often quite profitable to pursue audience segments within a country. Consequently, even the biggest firms have split themselves into different subsidiaries that concentrate on different parts of the world and funnel the profits back to the home office. At the same time, executives in these subsidiaries are on the lookout for musicians or acts that have the potential to be worldwide successes.

Consider the example of the cable television programmer MTV, a subsidiary of Viacom. MTV boasts that it is "the leading multimedia brand for youth the world over," with a channel in 164 countries and territories. MTV has the divisions for the United States, as well as for Africa, Brazil, Canada, China, Europe, Germany, India, Italy, Japan, Korea, Latin America, Russia, Southeast Asia, Taiwan/Hong Kong, and U.K./Ireland. The company estimates that about 419 million television homes in the world now have access to one form of MTV or another (in taking its product to other countries, MTV says it strives to strike the right balance between sending the same product globally and paying attention to local tastes). The company notes that it "tailors its channels to local cultural tastes with a mixture of national, regional and international artists, along with locally produced and globally shared programming."[4] For example, the company says that its African subsidiary, called MTV base, "plays a minimum of 30 percent African music content, drawn from all over Africa, with a minimum of 4–6 African music videos played every hour. Music genres include Afro-Beat, Dancehall, Kwaito, Hip-Life, M'balax, Zouk and Coupe, Decale, alongside international genres like Reggae, Hip-Hop, R&B and NeoSoul."[5]

Traditionally, the U.S.-based movie industry has taken a very different approach. Rather than making different films for different parts of the world, the major producer–distributors (often just called "the majors") actively look for themes, plots, and actors that will play well around the world. Movie industry executives have concluded that this often means action films with huge special-effects budgets, internationally popular stars (like Arnold Schwarzenegger or Jackie Chan), and little important dialogue so that people don't have to know English, or even read subtitles, to understand the action. The advertising industry runs the gamut from global to regional to local planning of ads. In television, program producer–distributors typically try to sell U.S.-made shows to other countries. Often that makes up the difference between the money U.S. television networks pay them to air the shows and the money it costs to make individual episodes. In 2006, for example, a new U.S. series cost an average of $2.75 million an episode, and the U.S. networks paid the production firms about $1.5 million per episode; foreign returns helped fill in the rest.[6] Smaller production firms, especially those working in cable, have tried to get sufficient funding for their work by lining up cable, satellite, and broadcast outlets, some American and some not, that will pay at the start for the right to show it. For their part, U.S. cable network executives who want to extend their brands to other countries have been adjusting their programming (and its language) depending on the countries they want to reach.

Local Media Organizations vs. Global Media Organizations

At the same time that they are distributing their American products to countries around the world, major U.S. media organizations are acutely aware that their international presence angers local media production organizations in other coun-

Viacom's Joint Venture in India

The entertainment conglomerate Viacom has been most visible in India through a subsidiary called MTV Networks in India. It owns Indian versions of the youth-oriented music networks MTV and VH1 as well as the children's channel Nickelodeon. A Viacom press release called MTV Networks in India "the industry's most engaging multi-platform entertainment brands." Nevertheless, the conglomerate's executives clearly felt that they needed help in trying to reach wider segments of the world's second most populous nation with products from their movie and television businesses.

In 2007, Viacom therefore formed a joint venture with the Television Eighteen Group (TV18), a media company rooted in TV but with ambitions to spread far beyond it. In 2007, the two firms announced the creation of a 50/50 joint venture Indian operation, Viacom-18. What they said they were trying to accomplish makes a great case study of this chapter's discussion of cross-media activities, with the added international dimension. According to Viacom's president, Phillipe Dauman, "India is one of Viacom's priority markets for expansion internationally." He added that TV18 represents a guide into the Indian audience and media in a much deeper way than Viacom could do alone. The alliance will meld television, film, and online materials from both firms into a variety of television and Internet vehicles. Dauman said that the partnership "will transform and significantly enlarge our business … across platforms, and opportunities for advertisers to reach the full spectrum of demographics." Viacom and TV18 also intend to create a new motion picture partnership, The Indian Film Company, which will release Indian-made films as well as Viacom products. Viacom's stated reason fits right into this chapter's discussion: "The film operation of Viacom-18 will provide strong synergies with the TV and digital media business, as well as complement our Paramount and Dreamworks studios."

For TV18, an ambitious, growing, but relatively small Indian company, the joint venture with the American behemoth represents a great opportunity to leap forward in presence on the national scene. "We are confident," said the firm's managing director, "that Viacom-18 will entertain India's burgeoning film and television audiences. Viacom-18 will also propel the TV18 Group into the league of a truly diversified and broad-based media conglomerate."

Source: "Viacom and the TV18 Group Announce the Creation of New Joint Venture in India," *PR Newswire* (US), May 22, 2007, 7:51 GMT.

---

tries. These organizations worry that locally made films will be swept aside at the box office by the Hollywood behemoths.

For their part, executives from the U.S. media organizations worry that this anger will result in laws restricting U.S.-made films or prohibiting the majors from building multiplex theaters in other countries. But they also see a plus side to international politics. The tax laws of some countries allow movies to be produced much more cheaply than in the United States. U.S. firms can get some of those tax benefits if they take on production partners from those countries and make movies there.

Because of these concerns and opportunities, major U.S.-based movie production firms such as Warner Brothers and Columbia Pictures have begun to fund and produce some films specific to particular areas of the world—France and India, for example—that seem to have a good chance at making a profit in those countries but might have relatively little interest for Americans. In addition, the major U.S. film producers have been getting more involved than ever in international *coproductions*. A **coproduction** is a deal between two firms for the funding of media material. So, for example, Warner Brothers may collaborate with Roadshow Pictures of Australia in the financing of a movie. The two companies would split the costs and perhaps the distribution duties. They would also split the profits between them.

coproduction a deal between two firms for the funding of media material

In addition to coproductions, the major firms are also engaging in more international *pickups* than in the past. A **pickup** is a film that is not produced by a major firm but that a major firm agrees to distribute in the United States or other areas of the world. The increase in international pickups means that the major firms are agreeing to distribute more and more films made outside the United States with non-American casts.

To mass media executives, the goal of their global activities is to lower their risk of failure by making sure that they control as many distribution and exhibition routes as possible to the largest audiences. As we have seen, that is the goal of their activities within the United States, as well. But this goal creates a key issue for production firms: what happens if competitors who have control of distribution and exhibition routes in the United States or around the world refuse to pick up their products? Fear of this nasty predicament is what has led to the next trend, conglomeration.

pickup a film that is not produced by a major firm but that a major firm agrees to distribute in the United States or other areas of the world

Conglomeration

A **conglomerate** is a company that owns a number of different companies in different industries. A **mass media conglomerate** is a company that holds several mass media firms in different media industries under its corporate umbrella. (See Figure 5.5 for a diagram of one such conglomerate, Time Warner.) Mass media conglomerates are not new. What is relatively new is the approach to them that their corporate leaders are taking.

Until the 1980s, the executives who ran media conglomerates typically did not require the different parts of their firm to work with one another. To them, the value of owning magazines, TV stations, music labels, and the like lay in the ability of each business to generate profits separately for the parent firm. But even then there were exceptions to this rule. As early as the 1950s, Walt Disney used his theatrical movies in his TV and theme park subsidiaries. The animated film *Snow White and the Seven Dwarfs* appeared both in movie theaters and segments on TV's *Disneyland* series. The name of the series promoted the Disneyland amusement park, which, in turn, promoted the film *Snow White* and other Disney films and characters in many manifestations—dolls, posters, and other merchandise. But Disney's elaborate cross-subsidiary activities had few imitators for decades.

Things began to change in the 1980s for a number of reasons. One was simply that top media executives and financiers got caught up in the greedy merger-and-acquisition mania that swept through corporate America during that decade. An even more intense period of combinations took place during the mid-1990s. The multibillion-dollar linkages between such companies as Time and Warner and then between AOL and Time and Warner, Twentieth Century-Fox and News Corporation, Sony and Columbia, Disney and ABC, and CBS and Viacom raised serious questions even while they were taking place:

conglomerate a company that owns a number of different companies in different industries

mass media conglomerate a company that holds several mass media firms in different media industries under its corporate umbrella

- Were these deals worth the huge amounts of interest on the loans that helped them get off the ground?
- Were they worth the huge fees to lawyers and investment bankers?
- What would they bring to the corporation that justified the extraordinary cost and effort of forming the new companies?

In response to sometimes skeptical Wall Street investors, the chief executives of these and other companies contended that they saw the media world evolving

TIME WARNER

Warner Bros Entertainment

Warner Bros Pictures

Warner Bros Pictures International

Warner Independent Pictures

Warner Bros Television Group

- Warner Bros Television
- Warner Bros Domestic Television Distribution
- Warner Bros Domestic Cable Distribution
- Warner Bros International Television Distribution
- Warner Bros Animation
- Telepictures Productions

Warner Bros Home Entertainment Group

- Warner Home Video
- Warner Bros Online
- Warner Bros Digital Distribution
- Warner Bros Interactive Entertainment (Warner Bros Games)
- Warner Bros Technical Operations
- Warner Bros Anti Piracy Operations

Warner Bros Consumer Products

Warner Bros International Cinemas

Warner Bros Studio Facilities

Warner Bros Theatre Ventures

DC Comics

- *MAD Magazine*
- *Vertigo*
- *Wildstorm*

New Line Cinema

New Line Cinema

- New Line Distribution
- New Line Home Entertainment
- New Line International Releasing
- New Line Marketing
- New Line Merchandising/Licensing

New Line Records

New Line New Media

New Line Television

New Line Theatricals

Picturehouse

AOL

AOL

- ADTECH
- Advertising.com
- AIM
- CompuServe
- GameDaily.com
- ICQ
- Lightningcast
- MapQuest
- Moviefone
- Netscape
- Relegence
- Spinner.com
- TACODA
- Third Screen Media
- Truveo
- Userplane
- Weblogs, Inc.
- Winamp
- Xdrive

Time Warner Cable

Time Warner Cable

- Road Runner
- Digital Phone
- Time Warner Cable – Business Class
- Time Warner Cable – Media Sales
- Time Warner Cable Albany
- Time Warner Cable Austin (includes Waco)
- Time Warner Cable Buffalo
- Time Warner Cable Charlotte
- Time Warner Cable Eastern Carolina [Raleigh, Wilmington]
- Time Warner Cable Greensboro
- Time Warner Cable Kansas City
- Time Warner Cable Los Angeles
- Time Warner Cable Mid Ohio (Columbus)
- Time Warner Cable National (based in Denver, CO, nonclustered systems)
- Time Warner Cable New England (Portland, ME)
- Time Warner Cable New York & New Jersey
- Time Warner Cable North Texas (Dallas)
- Time Warner Cable Northeast Ohio (Akron & Cleveland)
- Oceanic Time Warner Cable (Hawaii)
- Time Warner Cable Rochester
- Time Warner Cable San Antonio
- Time Warner Cable San Diego
- Time Warner Cable South Carolina (Columbia)
- Time Warner Cable Southwest Ohio (Cincinnati, Dayton)
- Time Warner Cable Southwest (El Paso, Harlingen, Corpus Christi, et al)
- Time Warner Cable Syracuse
- Time Warner Cable Wisconsin (Milwaukee & Green Bay)
- Capital News 9 Albany, Albany, NY
- MetroSports, Kansas City, MO
- News 8 Austin, Austin, TX
- News 10 Now Syracuse, Syracuse, NY
- News 14, Carolina Charlotte, NC Raleigh and Greensboro, NC
- NY1 News, New York, NY
- NY1 Noticias, New York, NY
- R News, Rochester, NY
- SportsNet New York

HBO

HBO

- HBO On Demand
- Cinemax
- CinemaxOn Demand
- HBO Video
- HBO Mobile
- HBO Independent Productions
- HBO Domestic and International Program Distribution
- HBO On Demand International (Israel, United Kingdom)
- HBO Mobile International (United Kingdom, Ireland, Belgium, Netherlands, Germany, Austria, Switzerland, Italy, Spain, South Africa, South Korea)
- Picturehouse (joint venture with with New Line Cinema)

- HBO Adria
- HBO Asia
- HBO Brasil
- HBO Czech
- HBO Hungary
- HBO India
- HBO Ole
- HBO Poland
- HBO Romania
- HBO Serbia

Turner Broadcasting/Turner Entertainment Digital Network

Cartoon Network

- Adult Swim
- AdultSwim.com
- Boomerang
- Cartoon Network Asia Pacific
- Cartoon Network Europe
- Cartoon Network Latin America
- Cartoon Network Studios
- Cartoon Network.com
- Williams St. Studio

CNN

- CNN/U.S.
- CNN Airport Network
- CNN en Espanol
- CNN en Espanol Radio
- CNN Headline News
- CNN Headline News in Latin America
- CNN Headline News in Asia Pacific
- CNN International
- CNN Mobile
- CNNMoney.com
- CNN Newsource
- CNN Pipeline
- CNN.com
- CNNRadio
- CNNStudentNews.com
- CNN to Go

Court TV (now TruTV)

GameTap

NASCAR.com

PGA.com

Pogo

Superdeluxe.com

TheSmokingGun.com

TBS

Turner Classic Movies

- TCM
- TCM Asia Pacific
- TCM Canada
- TCM Europe
- TCM Classic Hollywood in Latin America
- TCM.com

TNT

- TNT
- TNT HD
- TNT Latin America

Toonami

VeryFunnyAds.com

Time, Inc.

Time Magazines
Southern Progress Corporation
Time Inc. South Pacific
Grupo Editorial Expansion
IPC Media
Time, Inc. Business Units

Time Warner Investments

Global Media Group

Figure 5.5

The Time Warner Conglomerate Time Warner's control over creation, promotion, and distribution makes it a highly vertically and horizontally integrated media conglomerate. Time Warner is organized into nine business units; they are shown at the head of the colored boxes. All but two of the businesses (Time Warner Investments and Global Media Group) have several divisions; they are in bold type. The divisions, in turn, often have business units within them. They are listed with bullets. For more specifics go to: http://www.timewarner.com/corp/businesses/index.html

in a way that required them to have holdings in several mass media industries if their companies were to remain major players in the next century. Their argument went something like this:

> Audience erosion is inevitable in established media as the fragmentation of old and new media channels takes hold. At the same time, the rising costs of producing content for these media require an ability to take the money back across a variety of sponsored and unsponsored windows in different media industries. Crossing a variety of media outlets is also necessary for getting the proper share of mind for the content and demands publicity that will lead the target audience to the theaters, videos, TV shows, books, magazines, websites, and theme parks that recycle the material in one way or another.
>
> The danger for a media firm is that its competitors will prevent it from accessing the distribution and exhibition outlets that it needs if it is to carry out its revenue-generating mission. True, we can make agreements with other firms that allow us to use outlets owned by them on the condition that they can use our outlets. Ultimately, though, a company's destiny in the new media world will be determined by its ability to own, alone or with others, the distribution and exhibition outlets that it needs in order to reach its audiences. Perhaps ten or fifteen companies from around the world will achieve this power. We want to be one of them.

As this imaginary speech suggests, top executives for mass media conglomerates argue that they have to take bold steps if they are to be major players in the next century. They have to move beyond encouraging the subsidiaries of their conglomerates to seek profits independently.

Recall that we have used the term *vertical integration* to describe an organization's control of a media product from the production of content through its distribution and exhibition. Vertical integration is now legal in the TV industry and, to a certain extent, in the theatrical motion picture industry. In circumstances where vertical integration hasn't been legalized (as was the case in the movie and broadcast TV industries until recently), companies have tried to grab control of two of the three stages—production and/or distribution and/or exhibition—to keep their industry clout.

What the leaders of media conglomerates urge today is *horizontal integration* in addition to as much vertical integration as possible. **Horizontal integration** has two aspects. First, it involves the ownership of production facilities, distribution channels, and/or exhibition outlets in different, even potentially competing, companies across a number of media industries. Second, it involves bringing those parts together (integrating them) so that each can profit from the expertise of the others.

Synergy

A term that is similar to horizontal integration and that and became a buzzword among media executives for a while is *synergy*. **Synergy** describes a situation in which the whole is greater than the sum of its parts. When Time Warner's DC Comics provides the characters for Time Warner's Warner Brothers movies, which in turn provide the inspiration for *Batman* clothing, and when all of these elements get publicity through Time Warner's AOL Internet services and its TNT and TBS cable networks, that is synergy at work.

horizontal integration the ownership of production facilities, distribution channels, and/or exhibition outlets in a number of media industries and the integration of those elements so that each can profit from the expertise of the others

synergy a situation in which the whole is greater than the sum of its parts; the ability of mass media organizations to channel content into a wide variety of mass media on a global scale through control over production, distribution, and exhibition in as many of those media as possible

209

The goal of synergy underscores that at the turn of the century executives of mass media conglomerates were defining market power in a sweeping way. They saw it as the ability to channel products into a wide variety of mass media on a global scale through control over production, distribution, and exhibition in as many of those media as possible. They considered the best content for these cross-media activities to be genres that are likely to cross geographical borders, reach audiences that are attractive to advertisers, and not raise the political hackles of certain governments. These executives believed that children's programs, sports, variety shows, action adventures, direct marketing, headline news, and certain kinds of music were the genres that travel best globally across media.

How can an American company get away with having that much clout across so many media, you may ask. Aren't there laws against the accumulation of this kind of capability, just as there are against vertical integration? The answer is no, since no one claims that any company that has such cross-media capabilities controls a large portion of the distribution channels and exhibition outlets in particular industries. Another reason for the U.S. government's laxity regarding horizontal integration by huge media firms is a concern about foreign media powers. Mass media products are this nation's second largest export, after airplanes. Government officials fear that if they restrict the capabilities of U.S.-based media firms, it will give their rivals in countries without such restrictions the power to surpass them. If there are to be media behemoths in this world, American politicians want the giants to be American.

In fact, according to a 2007 list of the "top 30 global media owners" prepared by the ad-buying company ZenithOptimedia, U.S. media companies do dominate the global media scene. Using 2007 data of the revenues companies make from activities supported by advertising, ZenithOptimedia found that seventeen of the top thirty are U.S.-based, four are Japanese, three each are from France and the U.K., two from Germany and one each from Spain and Italy. In its list, the biggest media firm is U.S.-based Time Warner, with $32.2 billion in revenues (see Table 5.3). A far number two is News Corporation, also based in the United States, though with roots in Australia. It brought in $20.6 billion in revenues. By ZenithOptimedia's counting, seventh-place Bertelsmann, a German company with $10.6 billion in revenues, is the largest media firm outside the United States.

But no tally of such companies can be definitive because there are many ways to define a "media company." Some lists of top media firms (such as ZenithOptimedia's) don't include Sony Corporation, for example, because the rankings are based primarily on revenues from activities that support advertising. Companies that receive cash principally from consumers through admission tickets or product sales aren't included. That probably explains why Sony Corporation didn't make ZenithOptimedia's list. But with Sony's worldwide activities in movies, television, video games and music, it would be foolish not to see it as a powerhouse mass media firm. Besides, those who created the list ignored the fact that the movies and video games distributed by Sony and other firms *are* increasingly presenting paid-for commercial messages in one form or another—whether directly in traditional advertising or through product mentions within the ongoing action.

Every list of powerful global media firms will have its critics, and Table 5.3 is no exception. Yet the aim of the table is not to create another set of rankings based on revenues but to place companies into rough groupings based on their movement of materials across media and across the world. Many companies on this list will be mentioned in this book, if they haven't been already. Those in tier 1 surely have the ability to create, distribute, and exhibit multiple product genres across a variety of media on a highly sustained, visible, and global basis through their own

Table 5.3 Top 30 Global Media Owners

	Media owner	Media revenue 2006 U.S.$ million	Media revenue 2005 U.S.$ million	Percentage change 2006/2005
1	Time Warner	32,217	29,834	8.0
2	News Corporation	20,574	17,816	15.5
3	General Electric	16,188	14,689	10.2
4	The DirecTV Group	14,755	12,958	13.9
5	Walt Disney Company	14,638	13,207	10.8
6	CBS Corporation	13,550	13,389	1.2
7	Bertelsmann	10,573	9,622	9.9
8	Google	10,493	6,065	73.0
9	Cox Enterprises	10,358	9,452	9.6
10	Advance Publications*	7,700	7,536	2.2
11	Gannett	7,532	7,162	5.2
12	BSkyB	7,337	6,871	6.8
13	Clear Channel Communications	6,464	6,078	6.4
14	Yahoo!	6,426	5,258	22.2
15	Tribune Company	5,260	5,339	-1.5
16	Vivendi	4,554	4,331	5.2
17	Mediaset	4,260	4,317	-1.3
18	Viacom	4,217	3,963	6.4
19	Yomiuri Shimbun Holdings*	3,846	3,970	-3.1
20	Hearst Corporation*	3,525	3,276	7.6
21	Fuji Television Group	3,261	3,338	-2.3
22	ITV plc	3,225	3,387	-4.8
23	Grupo Televisa	3,126	2,746	13.9
24	Asahi Shimbun Company*	3,093	3,401	-9.1
25	DMGT	3,086	3,078	0.3
26	Lagardère	3,059	3,090	-1.0
27	New York Times Company	3,044	3,152	-3.4
28	TF1	3,016	3,358	-10.2
29	Axel Springer	2,821	2,796	0.9
30	NTV	2,304	2,522	-8.6

*estimate

Source: ZenithOptimedia, which defines *media* as services and content supported by advertising. See the text for further explanation.

joint ventures alliances formed between a large media firm and one or more of the thousands of smaller firms that are eager to extend their niches in the global media environment; the companies either work together or share investments

holdings. These are the companies that stand astride the most powerful lines of worldwide mass communication. The firms in tier 2 also have a global or cross-media capability, but not the reach of the tier 1 firms. As for the companies in tier 3, they typically are powerful in one or two industries (typically broadcasting and cable) within a particular country and have few, if any, worldwide media brands. They need help from other firms in order to compete globally across media boundaries. To get that help, they can join up with larger firms or turn to one or more of the thousands of smaller firms that are eager to extend their niches in the global media environment. Called **joint ventures**, these alliances involve companies agreeing to work together or to share investments. The television network Animal Planet, for example, is a joint venture between Discovery Communications and the BBC in all parts of the world except the U.K. and Italy, where Discovery controls it.

7-Eleven Morphs into *The Simpsons* Version of Itself

CULTURE TODAY

When scholars talk about "material culture," they mean the buildings, the furniture and the landscape that surround us in our everyday life. In the mass media, material culture helps make things appear realistic. Movies and television programs take aspects of the physical around them and use them as background in the story. Sometimes, though, the material culture stands out. That's what happens with product placements—for example, the Coca-Cola glasses on the TV program *American Idol*. Other times, creators use material culture as key parts of the story. In the Spiderman movies, for example, the campus of Columbia University, monumental skyscrapers, and modest homes of Queens become important to giving a highly unrealistic story an air of authenticity.

Although it's common to see the material culture of American life brought into popular culture, it's rare to see the furniture and signs and architecture from movies and television transported to our everyday lives. That's what made 7-Eleven's transformation of its convenience stores in twelve North American cities and in Denmark so unusual. During part of July, 2007, several 7-Eleven stores in those places were transformed overnight into Kwik-E-Marts, the convenience stores familiar to viewers of the fabled Fox animated television show *The Simpsons*. Not only was the look of the stores changed to match the animated ones: they and most of the more than 6,400 stores in the United States, Canada, and Denmark brought to life several products that until then existed only on TV—Buzz Cola, a Radioactive Man Comic Book, Krusty O's cereal, and Sprinkilicious donuts.

The 7-Eleven in Burbank has been given a "Simpsons" makeover, turning it into a Kwik-E-Mart. A total of twelve stores in North America, including one location in Vancouver, Canada, were given the makeover in anticipation of the release of *The Simpsons Movie* in 2007.

Naturally, there was a marketing strategy behind this singular cross-media activity. 7-Eleven had determined that its primary customers and the audience for *The Simpsons* overlap, and it wanted to show them that the chain understands and cares about them. In a printed statement, 7-Eleven's senior director for national marketing put it this way: "Many brands have product placement in a movie, but we were intrigued with the idea of bringing fiction to life—'a reverse placement,' if you will. As the number-one show among men ages 18–34, teens, boys 12–17 and kids 6–11, *The Simpsons* reaches our core audience."

Source: Tanya Irwin, "Seven-Eleven Brings *The Simpsons*' Kwik-E-Mart to Life," *Marketing Daily* July 2, 2007 at http://publications.mediapost.com

Note, though, that joint ventures are not limited to third-tier or second-tier firms. Time Warner's 2006 annual report contains several examples of how the company is extending its reach internationally with the help of local "partners." These are firms that know the territories, the government officials, and the interests of audiences. As we noted in our discussion of trends in globalization, this knowledge of audience is becoming increasingly important. Media firms realize that they can most easily attract audiences in different countries by customizing their programming to fit these countries' different languages and cultures.

Time Warner's Turner cable networks, for example, are familiar to U.S. viewers and those around the world through such brands as CNN and the Cartoon Network. While Time Warner owns those services in some parts of the world, in a number of regions Turner has launched local-language versions of its channels through joint ventures with local partners. These include CNN+, a Spanish language 24-hour news' network distributed in Spain and Andorra; CNN Turk, a Turkish language 24-hour news' network available in Turkey and the Netherlands; Cartoon Network Japan and Cartoon Network Korea (launched in November 2006), both local-language 24-hour channels for kids; and BOING, an Italian language 24-hour kids' animation network. CNN is distributed through CNN-IBN, a co-branded, 24-hour, English-language general news and current affairs channel in India. Turner also has joint-venture interests in services in China.

The distribution of materials across media boundaries globally and nationally has become so much a part of what media firms do that we all take this activity for granted. You probably aren't surprised when you see a CNN weather report in a hotel elevator, on your friend's home computer, on an airport monitor, or maybe even on your mobile phone. It seems so natural to see content discussed or displayed in many different places, that we may believe that it was always that way. As we will see in the history chapters coming up, it wasn't. In today's world, the movement of much content across media is becoming more common at least partly because it is technologically easier. The reason for this involves the next trend we will discuss, digital convergence.

Digital Convergence

Convergence means coming together. **Digital convergence** refers to the use of computer technologies to allow different media to share the same or similar materials. Digital convergence is a remarkable development that is changing the way in which media firms do business and the way in which audiences use media. It is also encouraging and accelerating the blurring of media boundaries and the development of conglomerates that move materials across those boundaries. In the process, it is creating public controversies and forcing both government officials and companies to rethink their models of media in society.

A Remarkable Development

When people use the word *digital*, it is a quick way of referring to the use of computers. Computers use digits—1s and 0s—to carry out their functions. Of course, people who program computers have learned to manipulate these digits to produce an astonishing array of possibilities. Today, computers are central to much of what people in industrialized societies do every day. If you go to the bank, shop at the supermarket, or even drive in your car, you are coming into contact with computers in one way or another.

convergence coming together

digital convergence the coming together of computer technologies as the basis for production, distribution, and even exhibition in many media industries

During the past two decades, virtually every media industry has found it efficient to use computers in the production of its products. Book, magazine, and newspaper publishers regularly use computers for the creation of text, the creation of formats, and the printing of the final product. Computers are used quite commonly in movie and television production for such activities as title production, editing, and special effects. Although much of the photography for prime-time television and theatrical movies is still film-based, directors and cinematographers are steadily moving toward the use of digital movie cameras. Digital *still* photography has certainly become an important part of the outdoor advertising (i.e. billboard) industry, which uses computers to create those wall-size posters and bus-wraps that are showing up in many parts of the country.

Just as significantly, the use of computers is also showing up in the distribution and exhibition of traditional mass media products. The *New York Times* and the *Wall Street Journal* have for a long time sent digital copies of their papers to printing plants in different parts of the country so that the papers can be printed and circulated there. Public relations firms send emails and post videos on websites to communicate with members of the press and other media. Music companies release digital recordings of their latest artists to exhibition outlets such as iTunes, Rhapsody and Napster. The major movie distributors have experimented with the satellite delivery of computerized versions of movies that can then be projected on the screen through special digital projectors.

We will discuss each of these developments in more detail when we get to the chapters on the book, newspaper, magazine, recording, movie, advertising, and public relations industries. The point here is to demonstrate more broadly that the digitization of production, distribution, and exhibition is changing the media system as a whole. Because of digital convergence, media are converging like never before. The reason is quite basic: once mass media materials are converted to digits, they can be transformed into almost any form imaginable. Words that were intended for the printed page can also be used for a website, a database, or a CD-ROM; they can even be used in a voice recognition system that can read the words. Movies intended for the big screen can (given fast computers, enough *data compression*, and the proper memory chips) be shown over the Web or transferred easily to DVDs. Parts of films can also be used in the creation of digital video games. The music from digital movies can also be used in such games, and it can be moved from the soundtrack into CDs or onto the Web.

Encouraging Cross-media Distribution

Many of these activities are less than a decade old. They have, however, become so common that you probably consider them a natural part of everyday life. That is because companies have adopted them quickly as part of their attempts to increase their revenues through cross-media distribution. The digitization of content actually encourages cross-media distribution because it turns the material into **cross-platform data**. That means that the material has been converted to digits that can easily be used as resources for the creation of material in other media.

The clearest example of this activity is the use of content by newspaper for websites and databases. Hundreds of U.S. newspapers have websites, and many of them license their articles to database companies such as LexisNexis and Dow Jones Interactive. This **repurposing**—the industry term simply means the reuse of content for different aims—could never take place if computers were not in the creation of the papers in the first place. It would simply be too expensive to scan or retype all the articles and photos so that they could be accessed by computers.

cross-platform data digitized material that can easily be used as resources for the creation of material in other media

repurposing the reuse of content for different aims

The use of computers in printing is also making electronic books much more economical than they would otherwise be. As we will see when we discuss the book industry, books in electronic form are an emerging medium for members of the general public as well as in schools. The transformation of text into voice is currently a developing technology that nevertheless presents many cross-platform possibilities for book, magazine, and newspaper publishers. Presently, print-to-voice technologies still don't have the diction and inflection to make many people comfortable listening to them for long periods. Consequently, audio "books" are still created by having real people read the text. This is quite likely to change in the not too distant future. Once technologists create software that causes the computer to read text in ways that really sound human, yet another set of realistic cross-platform possibilities will open for publishers. People will not necessarily read the news on commuter trains and in cars. For not much more than the print versions, they might download their favorite papers in their favorite voices into tiny recorders and listen to them on the way to work or while jogging in the morning.

Exactly this sort of listening already takes place with music, of course. Although typical CDs that you purchase in stores are not in a digital format that allows you to move them automatically across digital devices, many people have software that enables them to "rip" these CDs into a digital format called MP3 that creates cross-platform digital versions. Using an MP3 player, they can listen to the songs on their computer or carry them anywhere in an MP3 player. Using their computers, they can also create their own disks, which they can then use on computers and other digital players.

As yet another example of the power of digital convergence, consider Moviefone. A subsidiary of Time Warner, it provides the public with information about where and when films are playing in many major cities. Moviefone started as a telephone service with a website, but now is exclusively web-based at http://www.moviefone.com. Funded by advertising from production firms and extra charges from the tickets it sells, Moviefone allows you to type in your ZIP code, and up will come a list of theaters in your area with the movies they are playing and their showtimes. For many of the theaters, you can purchase a ticket directly from the Moviefone site so that you won't have to stand in line at the box office. (Some theaters have signed up with a competing service, Fandango.) Just click the time you want, state the number of tickets, and pay the total by punching in your credit card number. (Moviefone assures you that its site is secure.) You print out the confirmation, and when you arrive at the theater, you insert your credit card into a special reader that is linked to Moviefone's Web computer. If you've done everything correctly (and we're sure you have), your tickets should be printed right then and there.

Note that this activity very much fits our definition of mass communication even though it takes place through a vehicle—a website—that has not traditionally been considered mass media. Moviefone is an example of the industrialized production and multiple distribution in mass communication. When we think of the work of media industries, too often we consider the creation of the products but leave out the work it takes to get them to the people the companies intend to reach. Yet distribution is at least as important to the success of a firm as production. Moviefone's success is not primarily based on its list of which theaters are playing which films and when; that information can be found in almost any daily newspaper. It was figuring out a way to distribute that list in an efficient, customer-friendly, and advertiser-friendly way that made the difference for the company.

Moviefone started as a telephone service, but it is now exclusively web-based at www.moviefone.com

peer-to-peer computing (P2P) a process in which people share the resources of their computers with computers owned by other people

Encouraging Controversy

One of the most important features of MP3 technology is that people can send copies of the MP3 files to their friends via email, and those friends can then listen to that music on *their* computers and portable devices. That sounds quite useful and a great deal of fun (as you may know). However, it is this aspect of digital convergence that has most shaken up media industries and caused broad social and legal controversy.

At the turn of the twenty-first century, Napster was the most visible manifestation of the issues surrounding digital convergence. It was the most popular early version of what came to be called **peer-to-peer computing**. That is a process in which people share the resources of their computers with computers owned by other people. Napster served as a facilitator, or go-between, in this process. It allowed a person who had signed up with its service to search for MP3 files—usually songs—that resided in the computers of other Napster members who were online at that time. Linking to Napster and typing in a request would cause Napster to search its members' computers for files with that name. Once such files were found, Napster would display a list of them. Clicking on the file you wanted would automatically lead Napster to begin copying it from the computer of the contributing Napster member. In that way, it was possible to find thousands of songs on the computers of Napster members around the world.

The ability to do this excited millions of people. They realized that they could build their own libraries of exactly the music "singles" they wanted without having to go to a store and buy albums made up mostly of songs that didn't interest them.

At its core, this development raises critical questions for all sorts of media firms. In an era where all of content is in digits, how can we keep control over it? Place yourself in the position of an executive of a media conglomerate who found out that all the latest hit songs in his music company's catalog were being traded on Napster. You would probably feel that this trading means that your firm is losing a great deal of money as people download singles rather than buy them or the albums connected to them. More important, you might see Napster as a sign of greater menaces to come.

"Who says it will stop with music?" you might say. "In the near future, our company's books, magazines and even movies may be swapped freely by people who have no right to do so. In fact, these products have already been traded. The movie *Pirates of the Caribbean* was available for download not long after it appeared in theaters. Napster and activities like it threaten our control over our copyrights. Control over our copyrights is the lifeblood of our company, the fuel that allows us to create products for a variety of media industries. If we can't keep control over our products, we can't make money, and we ultimately can't exist."

These apocalyptic concerns are what drove the then top five music companies—Universal, EMI, Warner Records, Sony Records, and Bertelsmann Music Group—which control over 90 percent of the world's recorded music, to sue

Napster for copyright infringement in the hope that it would be shut down. Supporters of Napster contended that Napster itself should not be blamed for the illegal behavior of individuals using it. They also noted that Napster's peer-to-peer model could be used to share legitimate, noncopyrighted material. Napster's opponents replied that the peer-to-peer service was primarily a tool for the illegal use of copyrighted material, and thus Napster ought to be made to pay for the violations of its members.

After listening to the legal wrangling, the judge agreed with Napster's foes that the service owed them money, but she didn't shut it down. Instead, she ordered Napster to remove from its system all the songs that copyright holders told the firm were there illegally. At the end of 2001, Napster had effectively shut down. Eventually, Bertelsmann bought it and transformed it into a pay service.

In the meantime, new peer-to-peer services were emerging that had no central, Napster-like organization at their core that could be sued. Instead, software with names such as Gnutella, BearShare, Limewire and BitTorrent that was distributed free on the Web simply helped people find songs, videos, and movies in other computers and copy them to their computers. To consumers who were angry at conglomerates that they felt were less than consumer-friendly or responsive, using these services meant punishing those conglomerates and getting what they themselves deserved. To executives who were worried about their firm's future in an era of digital convergence, such services promised a disastrous loss of profits if they were not controlled.

Forcing New Models

Media executives, copyright attorneys and technologists have been trying to figure out how to create profitable business models in an era in which digital convergence threatens to allow consumers to move material across media platforms without charge almost as easily as companies can do it. Because the music industry has been the hardest hit, it has been the most active in formulating responses. The Recording Industry Association of America and the five major music companies have taken a number of tacks beyond the Napster suit:

- They have hired companies to track down and sue people, including college and high school students, who are circulating a substantial number of copyrighted songs on the Web. The recording industry claims that a relatively small number of people are doing a huge percentage of the sharing of hit songs. Go after these people, say industry executives, and you'll stop much of the copyright infringement.
- They have hired consultants to create forms of music that cannot be circulated without corporate permission. These activities have included making it impossible for someone to move music from a CD to a computer and innovations that keep music that a corporate website sells from being circulated beyond the person who has bought it. Parallel to these developments is the creation of "watermark" technology that will allow a company to place an unerasable registry sign on every file it places on the Web. That will allow it to keep track of all files that it releases to the Web and to note if the people who have these files in their computer are the ones who paid for them.
- Companies have gotten together to start and license downloading services that will sell music to consumers using the secure technology just discussed. Two

Apple's iTunes Store has sold more than 3 billion songs since it launched in 2003, capturing roughly 70 percent of all digital music sales.

approaches are being used. One sells songs or albums one at a time and charges per transaction; Apple Corporation's iTunes is by far the most popular. The other streams songs off the Web on a subscription basis. That is, the consumer pays a fixed fee per month and gets to listen to songs or download them for an extra fee. Rhapsody and the new Napster are examples.

The recording industry, however, is far from alone in worrying about the effects of digital convergence. Movie and book executives are busy trying to figure out ways to circulate their products in various forms while at the same time making money off them and keeping control over them throughout the world.

Media Literacy: Taking a Critical View of Blurring Media Boundaries

We have seen that the continual flow of new digital technologies poses major opportunities and challenges for global, cross-media giants such as Viacom, News Corporation, and Time Warner. The enormous changes that we have sketched in this chapter also challenge us as citizens to ask what they mean for society.

Many people worry that a few huge media conglomerates are causing problems because of their substantial power within and across many important media industries. The often-used phrase *conglomerate power* reflects a fear by some in the United States and around the world that a few large media corporations are accumulating sufficient assets to allow them to dominate the major channels of mass communication. They argue that giant corporations with interests in a number of media industries use internal synergies and joint ventures to spread their content efficiently across as many media as possible. They point out that in addition to using well-recognized mass media such as broadcast TV, cable TV, home video, theatrical movies, comic books, newspapers, magazines, radio, and books, these firms are turning to the World Wide Web, theme parks, toys, clothes, and a huge variety of other outlets to spread the word about a firm's new creation.

Overall, investment experts who follow media companies agree that we are now rapidly moving toward a time when no more than ten to fifteen companies will control the most prominent channels of production, distribution, and exhibition of content in the world. This consolidation does not mean that the media giants will have exclusive access to the public; they will undoubtedly make deals with other companies to distribute and exhibit those companies' material as well. Moreover, it is likely that many individuals and small companies will have the ability to post textual and audiovisual materials on the Web for virtually anyone to notice. The giants will, however, become the major gatekeepers to the public across a wide swath of media. In order to reach either huge, mass-market audiences or relatively small, targeted audiences in the surest, most efficient ways possible, one will have to utilize the services of Time Warner, News Corporation, Viacom, CBS, Disney, or one of a few other huge firms.

We are not far from such a situation today. Some observers, such as journalism scholar Ben Bagdikian, argue that the number of firms dominating U.S. media has already dwindled to six. It's rare to see a theatrical movie do well if it isn't

Herbert Schiller

A common criticism of academics is that they inhabit an ivory tower high above the heads and problems of the world outside university walls. That's not true of many mass media researchers. It especially is not true of Herbert Schiller. For Herbert Schiller, motivation sprang from belief in the injustices created by giant media companies when they have too much power over the creation (and also destruction) of culture. Through a series of books, Schiller influenced communication scholars throughout the world and helped to focus communication studies to deal critically with the control of culture.

After working for the army in World War II and earning a degree from NYU, Schiller began studying communication at the University of Illinois, where he worked closely with the Institute for Communications Research. His first book, *Mass Communication and American Empire*, argued that American media had a detrimental impact on local cultures throughout the world. Highly influenced by Marxist political economy, the book created controversy in academic circles when it was published in 1969.

Schiller's contribution to the study of communication was to question how politics and economic policy affect media. The larger corporate and political structure and the desire to increase profits shape media, and media create and carry culture. Schiller offered some of the earliest critiques of the developing information society as he explored the power and influence of various media and information organizations, from *Reader's Digest* to the Gallup polling company.

Schiller next went to the University of California at San Diego where he was able to write several books on the impact of media, including *The Mind Managers* in 1973. In this work, Schiller argued that large media conglomerates had immense power over culture, not just over trade. In fact,

Herbert Schiller

Schiller viewed the consolidating of media companies as a threat to culture. At the time, the wired home—"the electronic cottage"—was the media's ideal of the future family life. Schiller begged to differ. "The prospect is so overwhelmingly gruesome—this electronic cottage, this utopian society," he wrote. "It's an inversion of what any kind of reasonably attractive society is all about." The theme of corporate greed and increasing private control over public spheres ran through all of Schiller's eight books.

Schiller remained a harsh and outspoken critic of the corporate media landscape until his death at age eighty in 2000. Without a doubt, he helped to shape media criticism for generations of communications scholars.

Sources: Vincent Mosco, *The Political Economy of Communication* (London: Sage Press, 1996); Myrna Oliver, "Author Studied Corporate Influence on Culture," *Los Angeles Times*, February 2, 2000, p. A26; Jack Williams, "Herbert Schiller, 80, Founder of UCSD Media Department," *San Diego Union-Tribune*, February 2, 2000, p. B5.

distributed by one of the majors or their subsidiaries (such as Disney's Miramax). Most bestsellers in the book industry come from a handful of publishers (such as Random House's publication of John Grisham or Danielle Steele novels). Just a few companies own the cable and broadcast channels that reach the vast majority of people. The same is true in the magazine, home video, and recorded music industries. Moreover, Time Warner, Disney, News Corporation, Viacom, Sony, and

Bertelsmann are each top firms in a number of these industries. Through alliances, General Electric (which owns NBC-Universal), Microsoft, CBS, and a few other conglomerates have also been able to command huge global audiences in several media domains.

Three Common Criticisms of the Growth of Conglomerates

What's the problem about this situation? Certainly, the companies' stockholders—thousands of people around the world who have invested in these companies—are happy when these firms bring in global profits. Why not let them count their money while we enjoy the latest news on Time Warner's CNN cable network, read the latest news from Time Warner's Time magazine, get lost in a bestseller from Warner Books, go to the movies to see the latest action film from Time Warner's Warner Brothers or New Line Entertainment, stop at Wal-Mart to buy a recent movie distributed by Warner Home Video, watch the Warner-made series *Smallville* on the partly Warner-owned CW TV network, and then play a video game from Warner Brothers and Electronic Arts based on the Warner Brothers movie *Dark Knight*? After all, it's all very enjoyable.

That's missing the point, say scholars and activists who are concerned about the growth of huge media conglomerates. Over the past several decades, these scholars and activists have written many books and articles outlining their concerns about the dangers of allowing corporations to acquire too much control within and across mass media industries. Here, briefly, are three of their major arguments.

- When a small number of firms exercise power over production, distribution, and exhibition, they narrow the mainstream agenda of society.
- When a small number of huge firms exercise power over production, distribution, and exhibition on a global basis, they accelerate the homogenization of world society in the interest of commercialism.
- When a small number of huge firms exercise power over production, distribution, and exhibition, the democratic political process is jeopardized.

Let's look at these criticisms one at a time.

Narrowing Society's Mainstream Agenda   When a small number of firms exercise power over production, distribution, and exhibition, they narrow the mainstream agenda of society. This criticism harks back to our discussion

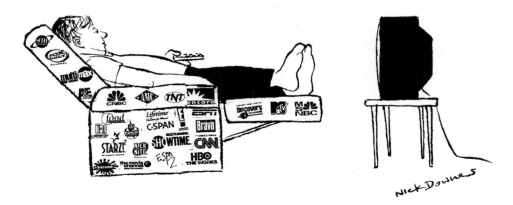

of agenda setting in Chapter 4. An **agenda,** in this context, is the list of items that people in a society talk about. The argument here is that when a handful of companies have so much control over the content that most people receive, the diversity of news and entertainment they can get is limited.

Critics of media consolidation such as Ben Bagdikian and Robert McChesney say that they are concerned about making sure a multiplicity of voices will be heard across media industries. One way to encourage diversity, they contend, is through ownership of mainstream media by diverse segments of the population. These critics point out, though, that the federal government's emphasis on deregulation has led to a sharp decline in the ownership of electronic media channels by members of historically disadvantaged groups such as women and ethnic and racial minorities. In 1995 and 1996, for example, the number of TV station owners who were members of minority groups declined by 10 percent, according to Commerce Department figures. There weren't many of these owners to begin with. The most recent U.S. government data on this topic dates back to 2000. The study found that members of minority groups and women owned less than 3 percent of broadcast properties in the United States.[7]

Media conglomerates, these critics point out, have grabbed so many of the powerful broadcast and cable outlets that minorities and the viewpoints that they might share with the rest of society are often locked out. The critics argue that having members of historically disadvantaged minority groups owning electronic media properties means that people with sensitivity to minority views have power to choose these properties' programming. That increases the chances, they contend, that more programming that reflects these groups' perspectives will make it to the air and thus to the public agenda.

Another aspect of conglomerates that narrows society's agenda, according to critics, is the cross-media mind set of their executives. As we noted earlier, capturing a large part of the audience's share of mind is critical to the leaders of major media firms. When they spend huge amounts of money to produce a new film, when they have a slate of new shows for the TV season, or when they have a new rock group on tour, they must have maximum publicity in front of the target audience if they hope to make a profit. In response to this need, conglomerates and their joint-venture partners turn their own media outlets and those of partners into formidable publicity machines.

Earlier in this chapter, we mentioned *Harry Potter* as an illustration of cross-media branding by Warner Brothers in search of good share of mind. Critics point out that although these tactics help the companies, they make it more difficult for voices not supported by the conglomerates to make it into the target audience's consciousness. It's hard to outshout Fox or Time Warner. That is the case, say the critics, even on the hugely popular **social media** sites MySpace, YouTube, and FaceBook. The term social media has come to mean sites that allow people to create networks of acquaintances and friends and to share their writings and audiovisual materials with them. The critics charge, though, that MySpace, YouTube, FaceBook, and similar sites are becoming major places for large media firms to spread their songs, movie trailers, television shows, and commercials. Often the sites receive payment for firms that want to "seed" the sites with these materials in the hope that people who like them will point them out to those on their networks. Marketers have learned they can gain attention by sponsoring contests that encourage people to create commercials for the marketers' products, with the winners having the commercials shown on TV. The use of social media sites for commercial cross-media aims shouldn't be surprising, say the critics. After all, they are money-making operations; in fact, the biggest ones, MySpace and YouTube, are

agenda the list of items that people in a society talk about

social media sites that allow people to create networks of acquaintances and friends and to share their writings and audiovisual materials with them

owned by two major mass-media conglomerates, News Corporation and Google, respectively.

Critics also raise broader concerns about the agenda-grabbing power of huge media conglomerates. What happens, the critics ask, when information is released by the Justice Department or some other organization that reflects critically upon part of the conglomerate? Will a news organization that is owned by the conglomerate rush to do an investigative story on the subject? Will it do a story at all?

Robert McChesney, Joseph Turow, and others have written that journalists seem to be losing their ability to address the role and nature of corporate power in the United States media because the organizations they work for are part of that powerful establishment. Although research on this issue is too scant to give a definitive answer, journalists are often wary about reporting on the activities of their own companies. This problem is serious enough when their companies are separate entities that are not attached to entertainment giants. When cross-media conglomerates are involved, though, the issue of reporting becomes even more problematic.

How will ABC News cover a corporate problem at Disney? Should we believe *Time* magazine's version of what is going on inside Time Warner? What are we to make of *TV Guide* articles about the Fox network, given that News Corporation owns all of Fox and part of *TV Guide*? The topic gets more complex still when we realize that most people probably don't know what firm owns *TV Guide*; nor do they have any idea when they read reviews of a *Harry Potter* film in *Entertainment Weekly* that Time Warner produces and distributes both. Do media outlets have an ethical responsibility to make people aware of ownership patterns?

People who work for conglomerates play down the importance of these questions. They argue that there are enough news firms to ensure that even if a company doesn't report on itself, another will report on it. Media critics aren't so sure that such coverage will be widespread, since the conglomerates that control mainstream distribution have an interest in not making waves about ownership patterns.

The Threat of Commercialism and Homogenization When a small number of huge firms exercise power over production, distribution, and exhibition on a global basis, they accelerate the homogenization of world society in the interest of commercialism.

Just about everywhere you go, critics point out, you can get MTV, CNN, NBC News, and Hollywood movies. Through these and other media channels, people all over the world are increasingly sharing the same media materials. Right now, the programs are shared only by the wealthiest people. Over time, though, that will change, and billions of people will tune to Sony, Time Warner, and News Corporation for entertainment and news.

Critics such as Dan Schiller and Vincent Mosco worry that the power of global media conglomerates to distribute materials worldwide will lead the local media industries of many countries to join the conglomerates in producing and distributing U.S.-style fare. As a result, the prominence of indigenous cultures will decline in the media of many countries.

A related concern that media critics such as Sut Jhally raise is that when companies around the world import or produce materials with U.S. partners, these companies are often communicating subtle and not-so-subtle messages that individual wealth and consumption of goods are what count in society. Although some populations around the world share this view, many do not. When these messages are heard over and over, though, they may persuade some impressionable people, especially younger ones, that commercialism is valuable. Western media materials therefore become the advance guard for Western companies that want to sell people in those countries the kinds of products that are shown in the movies, in magazines, and on TV.

Defenders of the large media firms vigorously disagree. First of all, they say, in most countries local media materials are still the most popular ones. The defenders add that when media firms go global, many of them increasingly adapt their programming to the societies that they serve. MTV, a case in point, is programmed differently in Germany, in Russia, in Latin America, in India, and elsewhere. Besides, say the defenders, even when people do see the same programs, they will interpret them differently because they come from different cultures. So, even if local cultures do change as a result of such media fare, they will not become part of a single global culture. Cultures will still remain different because of the way in which people understand the programming

While critics see the sameness created by cross-media materials, the defenders of these movements actually celebrate what they see as the creativity on the part of companies in creatively bringing material to consumers. In his book *Convergence Culture*, for example, Henry Jenkins argues that a new type of media consumer is developing, who revels in a "convergence culture" and who actually influences media firms in their creating. These consumers, he claims, have a strong influence on what we see in media "in part because advertisers and media producers are so eager to attract and hold their attention."[8]

Defenders of global media conglomerates are often not embarrassed to stand up for commercialism. With the fall of Soviet communism, they argue, the world is moving toward a capitalist, commercial model. The transformation of the television systems of many countries so that they accept advertising is evidence of this movement. The popularity of Western media materials, with their capitalist values, should not be a surprise. They simply reflect what people around the world want.

The critics of global media conglomerates respond that the popularity of Western media reflects not so much the values that people want as their attraction to stunningly produced images of sex, violence, and action. In the end, though, the values do get sold, especially to the young.

At heart, the argument is about whether global media firms reflect or create changes in world culture. Some critics agree that they do a bit of both. In any event, they say, the ultimate concern lies in the next argument.

Harm to the Democratic Process   When a small number of huge firms exercise power over production, distribution, and exhibition, the democratic political process is jeopardized.

Critics such as Edward Herman and Noam Chomsky argue that politicians are so worried about getting favorable treatment from the press during an election campaign that they play ball with large media firms, fearing that they will not get enough coverage during the election campaign if they don't. These critics also say that the news divisions of conglomerates may not report much on bills in which they collectively have a vested interest. This failure, critics argue, allows politicians to proceed with less attention to the public interest than they would if they had to worry about intense news coverage.

Defenders of media bigness insist that such lapses of journalistic responsibility do not happen, but critics insist that they do and will. In fact, the large media conglomerates' potential power over the political process may even be greater outside the United States, in countries where democracies are fragile. Such power, say the media critics, seriously threatens to undermine the rule of law.

Determining Your Point of View
as a Critical Consumer of Media

The issues regarding media conglomerates are clearly complex. So are those related to media fragmentation, audience segmentation, the distribution of products across media boundaries, digital convergence, and globalization. In the interest of media literacy, it's important that you see these developments as social phenomena that ought to be looked at critically. You might end up deciding that what is happening is fine, or you might decide that important changes should be made.

Table 5.4 outlines some views that people who are for or against the six developments might offer, and it suggests some questions that media-literate individuals might want to ask in order to extend their knowledge and decide which perspectives to support. At the heart of the debate that is reflected in the table is an idea we discussed in Chapter 1: how the mass media reflect portraits of society to society. The belief here is that mass media ought to help people in a society to understand their society and the various groups that make it up. Do the six developments help or hinder the achievement of this goal? The table offers differing views.

The "pro" views suggest that the movement toward media and audience splintering and corporate bigness is not necessarily a problem. In fact, the views suggest that fragmentation allows for the recognition of audience needs that hadn't before been recognized. They suggest that cross-media activities and digitization can encourage minority-oriented media, making it realistically possible to pay for their content by releasing it in several versions. And they argue that globalization and huge media conglomerates have a positive social role to play in introducing countries around the world to new technologies and new perspectives.

The "con" view sees these developments quite differently. It critiques media fragmentation as being contrary to the interests of having people of a society come together to share ideas and arguments with one other. It sees audience segmentation as a marketing tool that can needlessly emphasize people's differences rather than their similarities. A related problem is that the broad marketing approach that comes with this segmentation is used for the purpose of selling to people, not encouraging them toward civic commitments. That is also a difficulty with cross-media activities, especially when carried out by media conglomerates. In fact, according to this view, media globalization and conglomerates take the problems that media and audience fragmentation bring and spread them internationally. Media conglomeration also creates circumstances that make it difficult for journalists to cover the activities of these huge corporations, since the journalists often work for one or another of them.

These topics are as important as they are interesting. As these developments take hold, they will affect all our lives profoundly. Think about where you stand on these issues when you read the next chapter, where we go in detail into the corporate strategies of some of the largest media firms. Think about them, too, when you tackle individual industries in the rest of the book. Remember that today every mass media industry is part of the big, cross-media picture.

Table 5.4 **Contrasting Views on the Social Pros and Cons of Media Trends**

Trend/issue	The pros	The cons	Questions for media literates to ask
Media fragmentation	■ Provides more media channels and outlets for people to use ■ Provides more opportunity than before for a diversity of media voices	■ Makes it difficult for "society" to talk to itself because people are spread across so many different outlets ■ The media are not as diverse as one might think because the outlets reflect formulas of media conglomerates	■ What do you and others mean by words such as "diversity" and "society"? ■ How much "diversity" of media genres do the many media channels really present? ■ Is media fragmentation merely encouraging huge conglomerates to own many more outlets than before? ■ How important is it for different groups in society to share their ideas and argue in media used by many people who do not belong to their groups?
Audience segmentation	■ Shows that media firms recognize many segments of the population ■ Encourages a diversity of media content because media firms and marketers want to attract the various segments	■ Audience segmentation sometimes encourages social divisions by emphasizing differences between people, not their similarities ■ Audience segments are based on categories designed to sell to people and do not encourage them to be good citizens	■ Which segments in society may benefit from advertiser and media interest and which may not? ■ To what extent do individuals who belong to audience segments (say, "tweens") accept the views media personnel have about them? ■ How does audience segmentation shape the media content that you and others get? ■ How does that affect the way you personally look at the world?
Distribution of products across media boundaries	■ Allows businesses to make money back on products that otherwise wouldn't be worth producing ■ Increases the audience for media materials in an age of media segmentation and audience segmentation	■ Makes much of mass media into promotional vehicles for other mass media	■ Can reading trade media magazines alert you to understanding how particular cross-media activities are orchestrated by marketers? ■ Do cross-media activities increase a media product's "share" of your mind? ■ When talking with your friends, which products are you more likely to discuss: those that are distributed across media boundaries or those that stay in one medium?

(Continued on following page)

225

Table 5.4 Contrasting Views on the Social Pros and Cons of Media Trends (continued)

Trend/issue	The pros	The cons	Questions for media literates to ask
Digital convergence	▪ Once information is digitized, the cost of moving useful material from one medium to another is low ▪ Makes it easy to move information from one medium to another, which is useful to people in both work and recreation ▪ Allows ordinary people to use media images for their own purposes and exhibit them on MySpace and similar sites	▪ Digital convergence makes it possible to surround narrowly defined customer groups with tailored content across several media in ways that make it difficult for different segments to share each other's views	▪ To what extent is this creation of "electronic gates" of information, entertainment and advertising between groups taking place? ▪ To what extent is digital convergence encouraging people to create their own audiovisual materials that question the mainstream media? ▪ What areas of society benefit most from digital convergence, and what areas benefit least?
Globalization	▪ Gives people from different countries a shared mirror on certain parts of the world ▪ Encourages the use of media technology, which can help some countries' economic development	▪ Often perpetuates cultural colonialism ▪ Drowns out much nation-specific entertainment ▪ Perpetuates and extends a marketing view of the world	▪ Is there a diversity of countries from which media firms are getting the materials they send around the world? ▪ What is the nature of the debates about globalization in various countries?
Conglomeration	▪ Large media conglomerates can afford to take risks on content that smaller companies wouldn't take ▪ Large media conglomerates can spend money on technological innovations that smaller companies cannot afford	▪ Media conglomerates often drown out distinctive social voices ▪ Media conglomerates have the resources to exert enormous pressures on government to pass laws that benefit them and not smaller media firms ▪ Media conglomerates often include major journalism firms, and that makes it hard for journalists to report on the activities and implications of conglomeration	▪ What "risks" are conglomerates taking, and what kinds of distinctive social voices do they appear to be drowning out? ▪ How active are media conglomerates in lobbying government, on what subjects, and how successful have they been? ▪ To what extent and in what way do the news companies of media conglomerates cover their own firm?

CHAPTER REVIEW

For an interactive chapter recap and study guide, visit the companion website for *Media Today* at www.routledge.com/textbooks/mediatoday

QUESTIONS FOR DISCUSSION AND CRITICAL THINKING

1 How is media fragmentation related to audience segmentation?
2 Over the years, the major television networks have tried to stop audience erosion, without much success. What are some of the ways in which they have tried to do that?
3 "The more marketers find a group attractive, the more they are prone to take that group apart to look for subgroups that have special features that attract them." Explain this statement and give an example that is not mentioned in the chapter.
4 What does it mean for media companies to achieve "good share of mind"? Give an example, and explain why crossing media boundaries can help firms achieve good share of mind.
5 Using news as an example, explain the three criticisms of mass media conglomerates. Also, show how the criticisms are related to one another.

INTERNET RESOURCES

Center for Digital Democracy (http://www.democraticmedia.org/)
According to its mission statement, the Center for Digital Democracy is "committed to preserving the openness and diversity of the Internet in the broadband era, and to realizing the full potential of digital communications through the development and encouragement of noncommercial, public interest programming."

Websites of media conglomerates
To get a good idea of the cross-media and global activities of first-, second- and third-tier media conglomerates, check out their "corporate websites"—the websites they have set up for investors—and take a look at the companies they own and the media products they release. Getting to these websites is not at all intuitive. Some sites have obvious web addresses—for example, http://www.timewarner.com. http://www.newscorp.com is a bit of an unusual twist on News Corporation. But the New York Times Company's corporate site is quite unintuitive: http://www.nytco.com. The best way to find the corporate website of a media firm is to use a search engine such as Google, type the name of the company in quotation marks, and add the word *corporate*. So, for example, to get

to the Sony Corporation's corporate website, go to http://www.google.com or http://www.yahoo.com and type "*Sony Corporation*" into the search box.

FreePress.net (http://www.freepress.net/docs/talk_radio.pdf)

Free Press is a national, nonpartisan organization working to reform the media. Through education, organizing and advocacy, it promotes diverse and independent media ownership, strong public media, and universal access to communications.

Media Access Project (http://www.mediaaccess.org)

Founded in the early 1970s, the Media Access Project is a "public interest media and telecommunications law firm which promotes the public's First Amendment right to hear and be heard on the electronic media of today and tomorrow."

KEY TERMS

You can find the definitions to these key terms in the marginal glossary throughout this chapter. Test your knowledge of these terms with interactive flash cards on the *Media Today* companion website.

achieving a good share of mind	media fragmentation
agenda	peer-to-peer computing
audience erosion	pickup
audience segmentation	product placement
brand	repurposing
conglomerate	social media
convergence	subscriptions
coproduction	syndicates
creative rights	syndication
cross-platform data	synergy
digital convergence	target segments
horizontal integration	targeting
joint ventures	vertical integration
market research	windows
mass media conglomerate	

CONSTRUCTING MEDIA LITERACY

1 In your opinion, which of the six trends described in this chapter is having the most impact on media today?

2 Can you think of methods that the major television networks could have used in their attempts to stop audience erosion?

3   Some business observers doubt that synergy is as helpful to a mass media conglomerate as its supporters believe. Argue for or against this view, bringing evidence to support your argument.

4   How much of the news, information, and entertainment that you receive from mass media on a daily basis does not come from mass media conglomerates?

6 UNDERSTANDING THE STRATEGIES OF MEDIA GIANTS

After studying this chapter, you will be able to:

1 Evaluate the core businesses of two contemporary media conglomerates—The Walt Disney Company and News Corporation—as well as the core business of Google, a large web-based corporation that is on the way to becoming a cross-media conglomerate

2 Examine and evaluate other large media firms to better understand their scope and power

3 Recognize and understand the three main operating strategies of News Corporation

4 Recognize and understand the three main operating strategies of The Walt Disney Company

5 Recognize and understand the three main operating strategies of Google

6 Harness your media literacy skills in order to develop your own critical view of cross-media activities and their impact on society and on individuals

"The usual democratic expectation for the media—diversity of ownership and ideas—has disappeared as a daily experience of a generation of American readers and viewers."

—Ben Bagdikian, Media Critic

Media Today

Have you ever considered how often and how much you live in "Disney World"? You may be thinking that you've been to the place only once or twice, or even that you've never been there at all. But whether or not you have ever *gone* to the physical place we call Walt Disney World Resort is not really the point of the question. In fact, you can live in Disney World even if you've never been to a Disney-owned theme park. That is because so much of the media world is shaped by The Walt Disney Company that you may be immersed in its products for many hours of your week, whether or not you know it.

- Do you get your news from ABC television? ABC is owned by Disney. How about the TV shows you watch—are any of those on ABC?
- On cable TV, if you're an ESPN fan, a Lifetime fan, an A&E or SOAPnet fan, you're in Disney territory.
- What about your radio listening—is one of the sports stations you listen to part of ESPN Radio?
- What about going to the movies? Obviously, if you see a Disney film, you're in Disney World, but did you know that Touchstone Pictures, Pixar, and Miramax Films also fall under the Disney umbrella?
- Books, magazines, and toys, anyone? Hyperion is a Disney book company. *ESPN Magazine* is a Disney periodical. And if you or a toddler you know is into the *Little Einstein* series on the cable TV Disney Channel, you might know that there are toys and books based on it, too.

In fact, Disney's presence extends even further to include music recordings, home video, the Web, video games, and much more. If you knew how many of the media products you use come from The Walt Disney Company—alone or in combination with partners—you might be surprised at how much time you spend in its world each week. The same can be said about other huge media firms such as Time Warner, Viacom, NBC Universal (part of General Electric Company), News Corporation, Bertelsmann and Google. Together, these companies create mass media worlds that we visit more often (and for a longer time) than we often realize.

In Chapter 5, we discussed the most important activities of mass media firms at the beginning of the twenty-first century—media fragmentation, audience segmentation, distribution of products across media boundaries, digital convergence, globalization, and conglomeration. Whereas that chapter mapped the considerations that drive cross-media activities, this chapter explores the way in which two conglomerates—Walt Disney Company and News Corporation—are deeply involved in those activities in the real world. We'll also take a close look at Google, a large web-based corporation that is on the way to becoming a cross-media conglomerate.

Three Contemporary Media Giants

conglomerate a company that owns a number of companies in different industries

strategies overall, broad plans to accomplish set goals

Three definitions will be useful at the start of our journey. As we saw in Chapter 5, a **conglomerate** is a company that owns a number of companies in different industries. A mass media conglomerate, then, is a company that holds several mass media firms in different media industries under its corporate umbrella. Even when media executives think they have sound **strategies**—or overall, broad plans to accomplish their goals—to guide their firms, they regularly reexamine their approaches to make sure they are moving in the best possible direction. That kind of continual rethinking takes place in small and midsized mass media companies as well as at all levels of major conglomerates such as News Corporation and Disney. The reason for this has to do with the far-flung cross-media activities of these two firms. For its part, Google really doesn't yet fit our definition of a conglomerate. Its business is primarily located on the Web and involves serving advertisements to people based on what it knows about. As we will see, however, Google's strategies for expansion beyond the Web may soon place it among the ranks of key media conglomerates.

We will examine these three companies because their activities have such a large impact on the output of many media. Another reason to look at huge conglomerates like these is that they often affect what smaller firms can do—whether they can go it alone or must find merger partners or enter into joint ventures with the conglomerates, and even whether they can survive.

We could easily have chosen other firms to make these points. Disney, News Corporation, and Google are the specific subjects of our analysis here for three reasons:

- All three exert enormous influence on the media world.
- Each firm has different ways of facing up to the challenges of the new media environment. Each, for example, has different ways of approaching media fragmentation, audience segmentation, distribution of products across media boundaries, digital convergence, and globalization.
- All three engage in activities that you may recognize but may not have considered from the perspective of a critical consumer.

The Walt Disney Company

One look at the investor section of The Walt Disney Company's corporate website (http://corporate.disney.go.com/investors/index.html) and it's clear: Disney is quite aware and proud that it reaches people around the world in many ways. The company's mission statement emphasizes the global aim of its activities:

> The Walt Disney Company's objective is to be one of the world's leading producers and providers of entertainment and information, using its portfolio of brands to differentiate its content, services, and consumer products.

Let's unpack the corporate strategies reflected in this statement. To do this, we'll use a useful tool—the company's annual report. Even the images on the cover of a company's annual report can provide important clues about where the executives believe the firm's most important activities lie. You can find the annual report of just about every public media firm on the Web. The quickest way is to go to the company's website and click on the link to *investor relations*. There you will find the annual reports or a category called SEC (that is, Securities and Exchange Commission) filings. Another name for the annual report is Form 10-K.

Some annual reports, such as those of CBS and Google, look very bureaucratic, like a report to a government agency. Others, like Disney and News Corporation, are fancy affairs with pictures and executive statements that clearly aim to impress readers about certain aspects of the firms. Consider the cover of Disney's 2006 annual report which can be found online at http://corporate.disney.go.com/investors/annual_reports/2006. It shows Sheriff Woody, the leader of the toys in the hit movie series *Toy Story*, leaning against the post of a building in what looks like a western town in one of Disney's theme parks. To his left, and also leaning against a post, is a little boy, much shorter but wearing jeans similar to Woody's as well as a hat very much like his. The entire photo is black-and-white except for the boy, whose color image is highlighted by a bright yellow shirt and hat, and lit from the side by the sun. Glimmers from the sun show up as white stars at the top of the post and in front of Woody's head. Toward the bottom right of the photo is a phrase: *Where dreams come true*.

This image makes a number of points about the way Disney sees itself and its future. It evokes the company's ability to make a hit movie. It reflects pride in Disney's family- and child-oriented content. It suggests the company's ability to move its creations across media—in this case, to translate movie images into theme park attractions. Finally, it underscores the power of Disney as an influence on culture—its capacity to "make dreams come true." In the image, the boy's dreams about his hero Woody come true as they stand side by side. And who knows: maybe the people who put together the photo also meant to suggest impishly that Disney has the ability to make its characters' dreams come true. Like Disney's Pinocchio becoming a real boy, Woody has become a life-size figure outside the animated film, in the theme park.

The choice of a *Toy Story* character for the 2006 annual report's cover (as opposed, for example, to the company's *Pinocchio* or *Little Mermaid*) is quite purposeful. It is a reference to Disney's purchase of Pixar that year, as well as to Disney's relationship with Pixar from the creation of the first *Toy Story* film in 1995. Disney's role in Pixar's success beginning with *Toy Story* was primarily as the company's distributor. Not only was the role lucrative for Disney, it helped to keep the conglomerate's association with hit animation in the public mind at a time when Disney's own animated films were not performing terrifically at the box office. After *Toy Story*, Disney went on to produce six other animated films (for example, *Finding Nemo* and *Cars)* that were enormously successful at the box office and in home video. Unfortunately, by the early 2000s, Disney CEO Michael Eisner did not get along well with Pixar's executives, and the distribution contract was in danger of not being renewed. When Robert Iger took over as Disney's CEO in 2005, he moved to repair relationships and determined that it was in Disney's long-term interest to own Pixar outright, not just distribute Pixar-created movies. The annual report's cover, then, is a celebration of Pixar being fully folded into The Walt Disney Company, and into its strategies.

Disney CEO Iger makes this point triumphantly in his "Letter to Shareholders" included on the first page of the company's annual report. (You can find it online at the Disney corporate site.) Iger writes:

> Synonymous with the Disney name is creative strength, and this year we made a tremendous move to build upon that great tradition with the acquisition of another globally recognized powerhouse of creativity and technology, Pixar Animation Studios.

Compare this sentence with the mission statement quoted above, and you'll see important similarities. Both emphasize the strong audience awareness of the firm's content—its "portfolio of brands" and "recognized powerhouse of creativity." And both emphasize that this recognition is global. There *are* differences. The mission statement specifically goes beyond the mention of content to note the

Does Mickey Mouse Have a Personality?

CRITICAL CONSUMER

Psychologists have long grappled with the question of whether an individual's personality is formed during childhood or whether it continues to take shape over the course of one's life. Although you might argue that Mickey Mouse is not an individual *per se*, people in and out of the Disney empire have worried about his personality—in fact, about whether he really has one.

The story of Mickey Mouse's creation is perhaps as legendary as the cartoon himself. He was developed by Walt Disney in the late 1920s, a period that Disney later described as "when the business fortunes of my brother Roy and myself were at lowest ebb, and disaster seemed right around the corner." During a cross-country train-ride, Disney came up with the idea for a cartoon mouse named Mortimer; at his wife's suggestion, he changed the name to Mickey.

Mickey debuted in the 1928 cartoon *Steamboat Willie*, and by the end of the 1930s he had appeared in more than 100 films. Yet as Mickey was becoming the central figure behind The Walt Disney Company, his personality became what one writer described as "less edgy, duller, and less subversive." As Disney archives director David Smith explained, "You didn't want to do naughty things with your corporate logo. He suddenly became sacrosanct."

Mickey's personality was briefly revived during the 1950s with the broadcast of the *Mickey Mouse Club* program. But as the Disney Company produced more and more films, his personality became eclipsed by the more dynamic charac-

ters of Donald Duck, Goofy, and others. In fact, Mickey has appeared in only two cartoons since 1960.

By the time Mickey Mouse celebrated his seventy-fifth birthday in 2003, many claimed that his personality had all but disappeared. Describing him as boring, neglected, and irrelevant, among others, they blamed Mickey's lackluster persona on Disney's globalization efforts. "The years have dulled Mickey's personality," notes reporter Mike Schneider, "a result of him becoming the corporate face of a multibillion dollar entertainment empire." Some have even speculated that Disney is planning to remake the character.

While Mickey's personality in the twenty-first century remains yet to be seen, the early life of Mickey Mouse remains an important part of cartoon history. Animation artist David Johnson notes that the debut of Mickey Mouse brought something extraordinary to the world of animated characters. "[This] ungainly rodent with a falsetto voice squeaked his way not only into his own newly-created niche but soon had an entire world waiting to cheer on each new exploit. This unprecedented phenomenon, whose impact and popularity continues to this day, defies any simple solution."

Sources: Mike Schneider, "Disney Icon Mickey Mouse Turns 75," *Newsday*, November 18, 2003, online: http://www.newsday.com; David Johnson, "Personality of the Early Cartoon," *Animation Artist Magazine*, 2000, online: accessed 3/7/07, http://www.animation artist.com/InsideAnimation/DavidJohnson/Personality.html Jesse Green, "Building a Better Mouse," *New York Times*, April 18, 2004, online: Factiva Database

conglomerate's additional focus on "services and consumer products." Iger's sentence about Pixar adds the importance of technology to the company's activities.

Three Main Strategies

Disney's mission statement and the comment about Pixar's role in Iger's "Letter to Shareholders" both hint at where Disney sees its strengths in its competitive environment. Using these and other tools like the rest of the annual report in general, other recent Disney annual reports, and the approach that Disney has taken towards its holdings, we can see three major strategies that management believes will help Disney grow. They are:

- exploit as much synergy as possible among subsidiaries
- emphasize the global movement of content
- adopt new distribution technologies.

Let's consider what the strategies mean, how they relate to one another, and how they relate to the company's overall mission.

Exploit as Much Synergy as Possible Among Subsidiaries   As we discussed in Chapter 5, **synergy** describes a situation in which the whole is greater than the sum of its parts. To implement this strategy, Disney looks for ways for the company's subsidiaries to profit from the distribution of new and old material in a wide array of media industries. It turns movies into DVDs and uses their plots for books and video games, for example. Another part of the strategy is to get the subsidiaries to work with one another to find new ways to profit from the creation, distribution, and exhibition of materials. For example, the Disney theme parks and cruise line work with the Disney movie division to bring popular film characters and plot ideas into the parks and cruises. (For a list of the companies Disney owns, see Table 6.1 on page 240.)

Historically, Disney has used the content of many of its animated films—from *Snow White and the Seven Dwarfs* to *Beauty and the Beast*—for theme parks, books, stores, magazines, Broadway musicals and the licensing of creative rights. As we saw in Chapter 5, **licensing** involves a firm granting other companies (usually manufacturers) permission to profit from the use of the firm's trademarked or copyrighted material in return for payment. The aim of licensing is the same as the aim of all uses of the content: both to draw attention to the material (in this case the animated film) and to profit from it in as many ways as possible. In recent years, Disney has not only continued this synergy strategy, but has extended it quite regularly to live-action movies. Disney succeeded somewhat with a live-action *101 Dalmatians* based on the Disney animated film, and a *Country Bears* film based on an attraction at several Disney theme parks. The company hit a synergy-and-licensing home run with its *Pirates of the Caribbean* movies, which also took inspiration from a Disney theme-park amusement.

However, not all of Disney's live-action films fit this pattern. Disney has released many movies (such as *Scary Movie* and *The Queen*) under the Miramax banner that have little, if any, connection with the rest of Disney. Nevertheless, while these films sometimes bring the company strong revenues, there is a conviction at Disney that the company will usually derive greater profit over the long term from movies that carry the Disney name and are aimed at families, movies such as *The Lion King*, *Beauty and the Beast*, and *Pirates of the Caribbean*. Such Disney movies have become key "franchises" to be mined by the conglom-

synergy   a situation in which the whole is greater than the sum of its parts; the ability of mass media organizations to channel content into a wide variety of mass media on a global scale through control over production, distribution, and exhibition in as many of those media as possible

licensing   a firm granting other companies (usually manufacturers) permission to profit from the use of the firm's trademarked or copyrighted material in return for payment, with the aim of drawing attention to the material and profiting from it in as many ways as possible

franchise   a brand that is highly profitable across time as well as across media

erate. In show business, a **franchise** is a media property that has a life beyond its original appearance as a film, TV series, or book series; often that life extends across media.

Disney's executives are well aware that people associate the name Disney with desirable family entertainment. That makes it relatively easy to distribute productions based on Disney characters or plot lines in a mind-boggling variety of places—through subsidiaries owned by the company, through joint ventures with other firms, or through licenses to other companies. Disney CEO Iger describes the importance of these activities this way:

> [C]learly innovation and imagination continue to be essential components … as we seek to build our outstanding creative franchises across different businesses, platforms and markets, drawing in new and traditional audiences spanning multiple generations. One such example can be seen in the continued, runaway success of *Pirates of the Caribbean: Dead Man's Chest*, which was the number one movie of 2006 and the third-biggest release in motion picture history, surpassing the $1 billion mark at the worldwide box office. But we didn't stop there. *Pirates* books topped the best-seller lists, characters from the movie were added to the *Pirates* attractions at Disneyland and Walt Disney World, our Halloween costumes were the hit of the season and even adults got into the spirit with strong sales for our line of high-end *Pirates*-themed couture. And the *Pirates* DVD, released just before Christmas, broke records, selling five million units in its first day of release, while the iTunes downloadable version has also done remarkable business. We're confident that *Pirates* fever will continue into this year as we await the release of our third installment of the franchise, *Pirates of the Caribbean: At World's End*, which opens in May.[1]

In the case of *Pirates of the Caribbean*, the desire to promote and build off a theme park ride served as the jumping-off point for making the movie. The movie, in turn, became a platform that stimulated many other *Pirates* products, including new parts of the park attraction.

nodes   particular areas of a conglomerate

Disney executives are well aware that particular areas, or **nodes**, of their conglomerate are more likely than others to generate cross-media hits. The Disney Channel has taken on that reputation within the company when it comes to connecting with youngsters. Iger's "Letter to Shareholders" notes that "As an incubator or creator of creativity and talent, Disney Channel is second to none, generating the kind of popular new characters and stories that have made it a top television destination for kids from toddlers to tweens." During the past few years, the biggest cultural phenomenon out of the Disney Channel has been its *High School Musical* film series. Disney's 2006 annual report notes proudly that *High School Musical* "truly took the world by storm, setting records across multiple categories [that is, media platforms], including *Billboard's* best-selling record of the year, and a *New York Times* best seller, not to mention outstanding ratings on Disney Channel." But wait—there's more: "Our millions of *High School Musical* fans can look forward to even more fun in the coming year as we debut a sequel to the movie, a national concert tour, thousands of licensed musical performances in local schools and drama clubs across the country and a new line of merchandise."

Apart from *High School Musical*, Disney Channel has *Hannah Montana*, *Mickey Mouse Clubhouse*, and *Little Einstein*, in addition to classic Disney characters to attract kids and their parents. Clearly, one reason that Disney marketers try to get kids to like these figures is that they hope the kids will pester their parents to use products with these brands on them and not others. Is this strategy simply an honest understanding of the way families operate, or is it an exploitation of branding in the interest of synergy? If you spend time around young children, your answer may depend on how much they pester you on such topics.

When it comes to Disney, it's not very hard at all to see how children's attraction to these characters successfully drives corporate synergies across a variety of media. Kids and their parents grow up with Disney characters and story lines in activities that are cross-generational. Parents (and grandparents) remember Disney as a happy part of their childhood, and so they tend to pass on the "tradition." One can move from Mickey Mouse teething rings (a licensed product) to Disney plush toys for babies (also licensed) to early childhood toys (more licensed stuff) and videos from Baby Einstein (a Disney subsidiary). As toddlers grow into kindergarteners, videos based on Disney movies and cartoons become "age-appropriate," as do Disney broadcast TV programs and Disney (cable) Channel. Visiting a Disney theme park reinforces the purchase of a wide range of products, from sweatshirts to watches. So does taking a vacation on the Disney Cruise Line, which conveniently makes Walt Disney World Resort a prominent stop. If you really want to be part of the Disney world, you can purchase a home in Celebration, Florida, a Disney-built housing development not too far from the theme park that incorporates the company's philosophy of living into the architecture.[2]

Emphasize the Global Movement of Content   As we have seen in the mission statement, a critical part of Disney's strategic activities is to be a leader in producing and distributing its products, not just in the United States but around the globe. As recently as a decade ago, Disney executives acknowledged that they did not take global distribution seriously enough and that they did not make much of an attempt to achieve the global exploitation of the kinds of synergies that made Disney brands highly profitable in the United States. In the 1999 annual report, then-chairman Michael Eisner wrote, "Disney is in the ironic position of being one of the best-known brands on the planet, but with too little of its income being generated outside the United States. The United States contains only 5 percent of the world's population, but it accounts for 80 percent of our company's revenues."[3]

In 1999, Disney created a subsidiary company called Walt Disney International in order to boost revenues outside the United States. Since then, the company has moved aggressively to generate income in many countries. In tune with a desire to make sure that all its activities and distribution platforms are as interrelated as possible, in 2007 Disney announced the formation of an "integrated global television distribution division with responsibility for the international distribution and sales of the far-reaching portfolio of entertainment and news content produced by The Walt Disney Company." One of Disney's executives was assigned to oversee the distribution of Disney's audiovisual products, including "all feature films, television series, kids' programming, made-for-TV movies, miniseries, news documentaries, TV animation and direct-to video content—and their distribution to all platforms, including the burgeoning video-on-demand [that is, ability to watch a TV show when you want to] and broadband [i.e., high speed Internet] markets."

Highlighting all sorts of Disney content for people around the world also seems to be a major aim of three theme parks outside the United States—Disneyland Resort Paris, Tokyo Disney Resort and the part-owned Hong Kong Disneyland. Disney executives have acknowledged that the parks have not performed well financially, but they characterize them as crucial statements of the company's

Disney to China: "It's a Small World After All"

China's consumer market is expected to grow considerably in the next few years, so it is perhaps not surprising that The Walt Disney Company recently identified China as one of its top priorities.

In 2007, Disney released its first locally made motion picture in China, *The Magic Gourd*, which is based upon a classic children's novel by Zhang Tian Yi. Disney chief financial officer Thomas Staggs notes that unlike films exported from the United States, those produced in-market enable the brand to be more relevant to the regional marketplace. Local production also enables media companies to avoid China's import restrictions on foreign films.

Other efforts by Disney to tap into the Chinese market include China Central Television station's recent broadcast of the animated program *Lilo & Stitch* and talk of a new Disneyland theme park in Shanghai. Not only would the park generate revenue through ticket sales, but executives

believe that it would also leverage the Disney brand in external retail locations. In fact, they estimate that in 2008, 6000 retailers throughout China will carry Disney branded merchandise.

Not all of Disney's forays into China have been quite so successful. When Hong Kong Disneyland opened in 2005, for example, many condemned what they considered to be an unfair partnership between the Hong Kong government and Disney. Others believed that the theme park disregarded local customs and posed a threat to the environment.

Disney is, of course, not alone in confronting these issues. As U.S. reporter Craig Simons points out, "Disney's challenges highlight the difficulties international brands face as they try to tap into China's lucrative and growing market."

Sources: Katie Allen, "Film Industry: Magic Kingdom Woos China with Tale of an Enchanted Vegetable," *Guardian Financial*, June 11, 2007, p. 27; Craig Simons, "China Park's Rocky Debut Deflates Ambitious Disney," *The Atlanta Journal Constitution*, February 11, 2007, p. 1F.

commitment to engaging consumers far beyond North America. One Disney executive noted that the parks boost sales of Disney-branded products and movies. "There is," she said, "good synergy between other Disney products and our parks."[4]

But Disney also recognizes that the way to attract populations around the world is to provide content that resonates with their worlds. While it is placing its traditional parade of characters (often in translation) in different platforms around the world, the company is also increasingly creating materials for particular markets. In Latin America, for example, it created local versions of its U.S. television series such as *Desperate Housewives*. In 2007, it increased its non-U.S. activities by teaming up with an Indian studio to collaborate on movies there. In addition, Disney embarked on co-producing an animated Chinese-language film in China called *The Magic Gourd*. Thomas Staggs, Disney's chief finance officer, said that the release of *The Magic Gourd* marked the beginning of a clear commitment to TV shows and feature films not made in the United States in developed and developing countries. He stressed that the locally made productions will nevertheless have all the classic storytelling elements. That way, the Disney brand would come through and so help the sale of all Disney products, whether they are films, toys or theme parks. "That ability to drive our different businesses under a common umbrella sets us aside from our peers," he contended.[5]

Adopt New Distribution Technologies   In addition to Disney's newly energized global approach to its business, the company has been aggressive in using new forms of digital distribution to get its image and products out to its various target audiences. As early as 1999, CEO Michael Eisner suggested in Disney's annual report that the Internet would be another place for the exploitation of synergy between divisions to further the Disney mission. He declared that:

> There can be little question that the Internet is the next major development
> in the realm of information and entertainment. During the coming years,
> broadband transmission will make it possible for the Internet to become
> a true entertainment medium. This is where our library, news and sports
> assets will be put to good use. So will our expertise in creating filmed
> entertainment.[6]

In 2006, Robert Iger added to this commitment, noting that changing audience media-use patterns were forcing Disney to distribute its products via new digital technologies. People's desire to access media materials at times of their choosing along with a reluctance to pay a lot for content meant that Disney needs "to continue to anticipate and meet changing demands for our content by providing it on the platforms they use most on a well-priced, well-timed basis."

In the early years of digital technologies Disney was reluctant to dive into them, since it feared that perfect digital copies of its valuable programming would be pirated. Since then, however, it has changed its corporate mind. The company has sold TV shows and movies on Apple's iTunes web downloading site; it has experimented with a mobile phone service that delivered ESPN sports news and highlights; and it has even used the Disney name to brand a mobile-phone business called Disney Mobile that through use of Global Positioning System (GPS) technology allows parents to know where their kids are.

The central area for digital activities, from Disney's point of view, will be its corporate websites, especially http://www.disney.com, http://www.abc.com, and http://www.disneychannel.com. By 2007, http://www.abc.com was streaming popular advertiser-supported television series on demand and for free on its website. Executives came to the conclusion that the ability to view content through the Web wasn't stopping people from buying DVDs or watching the ABC, ESPN or Disney Channel networks. So, in 2007 they moved to implement what they considered the next required features for the http://www.disney.com website:

> Highly customizable, multi-faceted and rich in content, all based on the
> age and interests of the user. Guests will be able to watch videos, movies,
> television shows and shorts, as well as to listen to music, create their own
> play lists and enjoy a stunning array of games. The site will also offer
> direct vacation planning services and information, as well as enhanced
> online communities and shopping capabilities. In short, Disney.com will
> be the one-stop online destination for the world of Disney.

News Corporation

Take a look at News Corporation's 2006 annual report and you'll see both differences from as well as similarities to Disney's strategic vision. (You can view it online at http://www.newscorp.com/Report2006/AR2006.pdf.) The similarities are basic,

Table 6.1 The Walt Disney Company Holdings, 2006

Film
Walt Disney Pictures
Touchstone Pictures
Hollywood Pictures
Miramax Films
Buena Vista Home Entertainment
Pixar

Broadcast Television
ABC Network
Owned and Operated Television Stations
WLS Chicago
WJRT Flint
KFSN Fresno
KTRK Houston
KABC Los Angeles
WABC New York City
WPVI Philadelphia
WTVD Raleigh - Durham
KGO San Francisco
WTVG Toledo

Cable Television
ESPN
ABC Family
Disney Channel
Toon Disney
SOAPnet
Lifetime Network (partial)
A&E (partial)
E! (partial)

Radio
WKHX Atlanta
WYAY Atlanta
WDWD Atlanta
WMVP Chicago
WLS Chicago
WZZN Chicago
WRDZ Chicago
WBAP Dallas
KSCS Dallas
KMEO Dallas
KESN Dallas
KMKI Dallas
WDRQ Detroit
WJR Detroit
WDVD Detroit
KABC Los Angeles
KLOS Los Angeles

KDIS Los Angeles
KSPN Los Angeles
KQRS Minneapolis - St. Paul
KXXR Minneapolis - St. Paul
KDIZ Minneapolis - St. Paul
WGVX Minneapolis - St. Paul
WGVY Minneapolis - St. Paul
WGVZ Minneapolis - St. Paul
WABC New York City
WPLJ New York City
WQEW New York City
WEVD New York City
KGO San Francisco
KSFO San Francisco
KIID Sacramento
KMKY Oakland
WMAL Washington DC
WJZW Washington DC
WRQX Washington DC
KQAM Wichita
KKDZ Seattle
WSDZ St Louis
WWMK Cleveland
KMIX Phoenix
KADZ Denver
KDDZ Denver
WWMI Tampa
KMIC Houston
WMYM Miami
WWJZ Philadelphia
WMKI Boston
WDZK Hartford
WDDZ Providence
WDZY Richmond
WGFY Charlotte
WDYZ Orlando
WMNE West Palm Beach
WEAE Pittsburgh
WDRD Louisville
WPPY Albany, NY
KPHN Kansas City
WQUA Mobile
WBML Jacksonville
WFDF Flint
WFRO Fremont, OH
WDMV Damascus, MD
WHKT Norfolk Radio Disney
ESPN Radio (syndicated programming)

Music

Buena Vista Music Group

Walt Disney Records

Hollywood Records

Lyric Street Records

Publishing

Book Publishing Imprints

Hyperion

Miramax Books

ESPN Books

Theia

ABC Daytime Press

Hyperion Audiobooks

Hyperion East

Disney Publishing Worldwide

Cal Publishing Inc.

CrossGen

Hyperion Books for Children

Jump at the Sun

Volo

Michael di Caupa Books

Disney Global Children's Books

Disney Press

Global Retail

Global Continuity

Magazine

Automotive Industries

Biography (with GE and Hearst)

Discover

Disney Adventures

ECN News

ESPN Magazine (distributed by Hearst)

Family Fun

Institutional Investor

JCK

Kodin

Top Famille (French family magazine)

Video Business

Quality

Parks and Resorts

Disneyland Resort

Walt Disney World Resort

Tokyo Disney Resort

Disneyland Resort Paris

Hong Kong Disneyland

Other

Buena Vista Theatrical Productions

The Disney Store

Disney Cruise Line

ESPN Zone

Disney Toys

The Baby Einstein Company

Walt Disney Internet Group

Source: "Who Owns What," *Columbia Journalism Review.* Online. Updated June 27, 2006. http://www.cjr.org/resources/

since most media executives—including those at News Corporation and Disney—share common understandings of the changes riling their businesses. So it would be a sound prediction to guess that News Corporation CEO Rupert Murdoch, like his counterpart at Disney, would emphasize the need for synergies among subsidiaries, global activities, and new technologies in his Letter to Shareholders. And, in fact, News Corp's mission statement on its website is similar to Disney's: "Creating and distributing top-quality news, sports and entertainment around the world." But News Corporation is quite a different company from Disney, with a different background and a very different leadership. As a result, the company places different priorities on these needs, and it interprets them quite differently from Disney.

Take the issue of globalization. News Corporation executives would probably sniff (or sneer) at Disney CEO Iger's note about the importance of spreading globally—in their view, News Corporation has globalization in its genes. A globe of the world is the company's logo. Moreover, the firm's ties to the world at large are made prominently on the cover of every annual report since at least 1997. (Check out http://www.newscorp.com/investor/annual_reports.html to see past covers of the company's annual reports.) Sometimes versions of the globe or maps of the world make up the dominant image. Other times the cover is built around images of the company's holdings in different countries. In 2005, it featured a gate-fold containing a human eye, a globe, and text that reads "The eyes of the world are on us."

Of course, from a literal standpoint, this statement is more a hope than a reality. It might be more accurate to say that for decades, News Corporation has had its eyes on the world. The company's roots are international. News Corporation Ltd is an American company with origins in Australia. Its CEO and majority stockholder is Rupert Murdoch, a man well known for his tenacity in achieving his goals. One small example: during the late 1980s, when he was building the Fox television network in the United States, Murdoch purchased Metromedia's chain of television stations. In the process, he came up against a federal law prohibiting non-U.S. citizens from owning more than a small percentage of a U.S. broadcast station. The FCC had long interpreted this law as barring non-U.S. companies from indirectly owning or controlling more than 25 percent of a television station. Because he could not convince Congress to change the law, Murdoch took the next logical step: he abandoned his Australian citizenship and with great fanfare became an American citizen so that he could purchase U.S. television stations and build his TV empire.

Murdoch's rapid change in citizenship underscores both the importance of an American broadcast network to News Corporation and Murdoch's intense focus on building his company. His second wife, Anna, who filed for divorce in 1998, said she was shocked when Murdoch became an American citizen in 1985. "I never thought he'd do it. I realized then how strong his ambitious drive was."[7] And drive he did. Before the 1980s, News Corporation's financial strength came from its collection of powerful newspapers in Australia and the United Kingdom. By the mid-1990s, Murdoch had transformed the print-oriented Australian company into a multimedia firm with worldwide clout. Murdoch's major goal for the conglomerate, as stated in both the company's 2000 and 2006 annual reports, is "transformation"—to continue reshaping the firm so that it has a leadership position in the new global cross-media economy. News Corporation's activities respond directly to the trends toward media fragmentation and digital convergence that we discussed in Chapter 5. News Corporation also follows the trends regarding audience segmentation, globalization, conglomeration, and the distribution of products across media boundaries.

Murdoch is quite aware of the increased number of audiovisual channels that are competing to stand out in the marketplace, the fragmented audiences that result from giving people so many channel choices, and the increasingly global and computer-based nature of the media business. "We have always sought new markets and new avenues for distribution," he asserts in the Chief Executive's Review in the 2006 annual report. "Our company launched Australia's first national paper and America's first new television network in 40 years. We helped pioneer the TV DVD market. We upended a decade and a half of received wisdom about what works in the cable news market. Now we are bringing that same innovative, entrepreneurial spirit to the Internet."[8]

A list of some of the conglomerate's holdings suggests the extent and manner in which News Corporation is moving toward that global goal. According to the *Columbia Journalism Review*, News Corporation owns part or all of the subsidiaries listed in Table 6.2 (p. 248). In terms of media power, they range from the quite local (a television station in Philadelphia) to the national (the U.K.'s *Sunday Times*) to the international (Twentieth Century Fox).

Rupert Murdoch

Who would have guessed that a man in his mid-seventies would become the face behind one of the defining pop cultural phenomena of the twenty-first century? Although few anticipated it, that is exactly what happened in 2005, when media mogul Rupert Murdoch bought social networking site MySpace. As chairman of the megacorporation News Corp, Murdoch had been trying to make his mark on the world of digital media for some time. The purchase of MySpace seemed to do just that.

Of course, Murdoch boasts a long track record of successes in media ownership. He began in the newspaper business in the 1950s when his father gave him control over the Australian *Adelaide News.* After his successful run with that paper, notes one reporter, "it was one international acquisition after another en route to building a global media giant." By the end of the 1980s, he had acquired the *Mirror* in Sydney; the *News of the World, Sun, The Times,* and the *Sunday Times* in London; and a number of newspapers in the United States.

To further grow his power in the U.S. media market, Murdoch changed his citizenship from Australia to the United States so that he could purchase American television stations. His current holdings in the United States include the Fox TV Network, HarperCollins Books, and Twentieth Century Fox.

Today, News Corp is recognized as the world's third largest media conglomerate, owning products in the television, film, book, newspaper, magazine, and Internet industries. The scope of this media empire reaches into the United States, Australia, Continental Europe, the United Kingdom, Asia and the Pacific Basin.

News Corp is also known for being one of the few conglomerates led by a single individual, and as such, Murdoch has

Chairman and CEO of News Corporation, Rupert Murdoch

been compared to great media moguls like William Randolph Hearst and William Paley. One reporter has even called him "the single most powerful media magnate ever."

Yet with the acquisition of MySpace and a number of other digital enterprises, Murdoch added a new adjective to his repertoire: Internet visionary. It's hard to know if he is one or if his advisors persuaded him to get strongly into the Internet space. Murdoch, though, furthers the mystique. "I love being called that," he told *Time* reporter Eric Pooley, "but the truth is, I'm just lucky and nimble."

Source: Eric Pooley, "Exclusive: Rupert Murdoch Speaks," *Time International*, June 28, 2007, online: http://www.time.com; William Shawcross, "Rupert Murdoch," *Time International*, October 25, 1999, p. 116.

Three Main Strategies

News Corporation's holdings will undoubtedly have changed by the time you're reading this. Media conglomerates are continually adding to their holdings when companies that match their strategic plans come on the market, and selling firms that are not performing well or that no longer match the executives' vision for the company.

The point here is not to be absolutely precise about what the company owns. Rather, it is to identify the *key strategies* that News Corporation's management is using in its bid to establish media platforms through which to distribute its content globally. Three strategies, in particular, stand out:

- Expand rapidly into the Internet and other new digital realms
- Nurture diverse global channels of distribution
- Emphasize entertainment, news, and sports

Let's look at these strategies one at a time.

Expand Rapidly into the Internet and Other New Digital Realms

The centerpiece of Murdoch's message in News Corporation's 2006 annual report is what he calls "the transformation of our company from a traditional media company into a major digital player." In large part, that happened through News Corporation's purchase of http://www.myspace.com, the Internet's most popular social networking site. The company also bought other smaller Internet properties (for example, the IGN gaming site and the Rotten Tomatoes moviegoing site) and

Buying Space on MySpace

For advertisers, buying space on the popular social-networking site MySpace might seem like a no-brainer: it reaches more than 100 million users, many of whom are in the coveted 18–34-year-old demographic; user interests are displayed prominently on profiles, eliminating the need for psychographic research; and it reportedly costs only ten cents for 1,000 impressions.

Nevertheless, according to knowledgeable observers, News Corporation had some difficulty attracting advertisers to MySpace. Why? For one, many marketers expressed concern about the site's distasteful content, including what has been described as the "glorification of drinking, drug use, and sex." Among those who have refused to advertise on the site for this reason are marketing goliaths like Pepsi-Cola, McDonald's, and NBC Universal.

So in 2006, News Corp attempted to allay marketers' concerns by deleting an estimated 200,000 profiles that contained hate speech and other objectionable content. It also hired a safety czar to monitor the site content.

Yet perhaps the company's most innovative solution to this problem concerns the advertising itself. Rather than placing ads directly on users' profiles, advertisers can now create

their own brand profiles, allowing other MySpace users to become "friends" with certain companies and their products. For example, when Wendy's fast food chain created a profile for its animated hamburger character, nearly 100,000 people added the cartoon as a friend.

The brand profile idea was the brainchild of MySpace co-founder Chris DeWolfe and provides what one reporter called "a neutral home to advertisers that…don't want their ads associated with the risqué content of some members' profiles."

DeWolfe and others realize, however, that they must strike a balance between satisfying the needs of advertisers and the demands of its massive user base. If the site becomes too commercial, warns *New York Times* reporter Saul Hansell, it could end up scaring off its audience.

Sources: Saul Hansell, "For MySpace, Making Friends Was Easy. Big Profit Is Tougher." *New York Times*, April 23, 2006, online: http://www.nytimes.com; Jennifer LeClaire, "MySpace Removes Objectionable Content in Advertising Bid," *E-Commerce Times*, July 19, 2007, online: http://www.ecommercetimes.com; Pete Lerma, "Is MySpace an Advertiser Space?" *Clickz*, July 25, 2006, online: http://www.clickz.com

folded all of them into a new division called Fox Interactive Media (FIM). But with its "120 million-plus users worldwide," it was MySpace that catapulted News Corporation into the ranks of Google and Yahoo—what Murdoch calls "the Internet elite." In fact, it was the power of MySpace to attract so many people with different interests that made Google want to use the site to attract people to ads on its search engine: for the right to be the exclusive search engine for MySpace and to show text ads related to the searches, Google agreed to pay News Corporation $900 million over four years. That amount more than made up for the approximately $700 million News Corporation had reportedly paid for MySpace just a year earlier.

www.myspace.com

Naturally, News Corporation announced its intention to keep improving its sites and draw more advertisers to them. In addition, the company's 2006 annual report presents two other aims for its involvement in the digital realm. One is to extend News Corporation's operations beyond the Web to cellphones and other digital devices. As we noted in Chapter 5, the term *digital* extends far beyond the Internet. It refers to any media that carry messages in the language of bits that computers speak. When materials are transmitted digitally, or can be translated into digital format, they can be made compatible with the Web and with a range of other mobile and stationary technologies. Stationary technologies include electronic boards in stores, malls and on streets; think of electronic signs in places such as Times Square. Mobile examples include cellphones, personal digital assistants (PDAs), cellphones that include PDAs (these are often called smart phones), and handheld multimedia players such as the iPod. At this point, News Corporation is concentrating on entering the mobile market. The firm has entered into a deal with the Apple Company to make many of its broadcast and cable television shows (for example, *24* and *Nip/Tuck*) available for purchase and download into iPods as well as computers. It has started a joint venture with NBC Universal to create a major website that will bring together the content of both firms for people to download—and see ads alongside the material. News Corporation also assembled a group to create short segments ("mobisodes") based on Fox programs (such as *Prison Break*) that can be viewed on handheld devices. Mobile devices are also the target of special music, art, games, video clips and other content based on popular Fox content such as *Family Guy*, *American Dad*, *Napoleon Dynamite*, and *Ice Age*.

As News Corporation CEO Murdoch lays it out, News Corporation has special qualities to win in the digital world. "Some boast high traffic but little content. Others have plenty of content but little traffic. Only News Corporation combines high traffic with vast amounts of compelling content. Our situation is unique—and powerful."

Nurture Diverse Global Channels of Distribution   To Murdoch, power in the digital space places a new twist on the importance of distribution. Being able to attract large audiences on the Web and elsewhere in the digital environment will truly give News Corporation the possibility of the global audience's eyes that it has always sought. According to Murdoch:

News Corporation's core mission has always been to provide as many consumers as possible with the highest quality content through the most convenient distribution channels. That was the strategic imperative behind our entry into the satellite business, and that same imperative now propels us into the digital world. All the historic constraints inherent in distribution—prohibitive entry costs, hard-to-reach locations, sluggish technology—are being swept away by digital technology. For the first time in media history, complete access to a truly global audience is within our grasp.[9]

Apart from a highly optimistic vision of News Corp's future power because of digital technology, Murdoch's words reflect the primary ability that his company has always sought: clout over distribution. The central images on the front page of the firm's corporate website during summer 2007, for example, were logos of the company's global properties—Twentieth Century Fox movie studio, Sky TV satellite platform, *The Times* and the *Australian* newspapers and many more. The company is divided into divisions that reflect the focus on media vehicles throughout the world: filmed entertainment, television, cable, direct broadcast satellite television, magazines and advertising inserts, newspapers, books, and other assets (primarily Fox Interactive Media and the News Outdoor billboard company).

You may be thinking that in view of Murdoch's strongly held view that the Internet and other digital pathways will sweep away the need for clout in these areas, a question arises: Why would the company continue to emphasize traditional distribution mechanisms? Perhaps not surprisingly, Murdoch has thought of that question, too. "To the casual observer," he writes in the 2006 annual report, "News Corporation's entry into digital media may seem to be a departure from our past business models and practices. But in truth there is fundamental continuity to our approach." He goes on to say that keeping distribution clout in traditional media of various stages of growth is critical to building a future digital News Corporation. The reason is that the older distribution avenues, which have principally been paid for, are the revenue engines that allow the conglomerate to keep growing. He sees this as a three-stage strategy in which newly profitable, high growth businesses move the company ahead and please investors while mature parts of the company fund the growth areas of the future.

> We have always grown this company by intelligently managing a mix of business in various stages of growth and development. Established businesses produce modest growth yet sizable—and reliable—cash flows. Businesses in the middle stage are the primary growth drivers of the company, delivering strong profit growth. And our youngest efforts are being nurtured and developed by the cash generated by our mature businesses, to allow them to find their footing and realize their potential as the company's future growth drivers.[10]

At heart, however, Murdoch seems to appreciate and understand distribution more than content production. That's still the case to a large extent. Reminders of specific content did show up—Bruce Willis of the new *Die Hard* movie, Kiefer Sutherland from the *24* TV series, and the Silver Surfer from the new *Fantastic Four* film, for example—but the company logos and people using company media stood out. The same applies to Murdoch's "Letter" in the 2006 annual report. While he certainly mentions successful movies and series (and pictures of products are peppered throughout the report), it is the corporation's power to reach audiences for these materials that takes center stage. The perspective is quite different from the one we saw in Iger's letter about Disney, where attention to content outweighed attention to distribution. The different emphases reflect different historical and contemporary strengths of the two conglomerates.

Emphasize Entertainment, News and Sports   Murdoch is well aware that it is the content that material firms distribute that helps News Corporation remain competitive and grow. That explains the conglomerate's third strategy: identifying popular entertainment, news and sports content, and pumping them through those distribution channels.

Although Disney notes the same three types of content on its website and in Iger's letter, its main corporate focus is clearly on family entertainment. News Corporation doesn't emphasize one genre over the other. The website and annual report remind the reader that News Corporation does have some mighty popular brands of content in each area. Oddly, for the head of a company that emphasizes that global activities are at its heart, Murdoch's letter doesn't mention specific entertainment, sports or news content. The rest of the annual report does glance at the company's properties for India and China. But the discussion of content (as contrasted with the discussion of distribution) centers squarely on U.S.-made news, entertainment and sports.

In the entertainment area, Murdoch stresses his company's ability to choose movies (*Fantastic Four*, *Star Wars III*) that have legs in the theaters and on home video and to produce the mega-hit *American Idol* as well as fictional TV series (*The Simpsons*, *24*) that not only draw fans in their initial airing but that get repeat viewing in home video. As for sports, Murdoch assures shareholders that "in the coming seasons, Fox will remain the premier sports network on U.S. television." He notes that the firm renewed its contracts with Major League Baseball, NFL football and NASCAR "at attractive rates." Possibly in a nod to the firm's attempts to cultivate young viewers, he mentions that Fox Sports also inked a new deal to broadcast the college football Bowl Championship series. And to show that News Corporation executives are responding to changing audience capabilities, he notes that, "Sporting events are—along with live news—as close to DVR-proof as programming gets."

Despite his comment about DVR-proof live news, it is in discussing the company's activities in this area that Murdoch gets cautious. He writes that the Fox News cable channel "set another record for operating income and revenue growth." He notes that the company is bringing successful Fox News Channel techniques to its broadcast TV station. Yet he acknowledges that while circulation at most of News Corporation's newspaper properties "remains strong," it is declining throughout the industry. He continues that "survey after survey shows that newspapers are less integral to people's lives with each passing year." To Murdoch, the problem is not with the news genre. He argues that "Younger consumers prefer alternative means of getting the news, such as reading the online versions of newspapers for free." He continues that News Corporation's commitment to the Internet and other new channels of distribution will allow it to keep its news areas growing:

> The hunger for news and information…is not fading. It is intensifying. And
> as a content provider, we are well positioned to capitalize on that hunger,
> provided that we are smart about reaching younger consumers in the ways

Table 6.2 News Corporation Holdings, 2007

Television
Fox Broadcasting Company
Fox Television Stations
WNYW New York City
WWOR New York City
KTTV Los Angeles
KCOP Los Angeles
WFLD Chicago
WPWR Chicago
KMSP Minneapolis
WFTC Minneapolis
WTXF Philadelphia
WFXT Boston
WTTG Washington DC
WDCA Washington DC
KDFW Dallas
KDFI Dallas
WJBK Detroit
KUTP Phoenix
KSAZ Phoenix
WUTB Baltimore
WRBW Orlando
WOFL Orlando
WOGX Ocala
WAGA Atlanta
KRIV Houston
KTXH Houston
WJW Cleveland
WTVT Tampa
KDVR Denver
KTVI St Louis
WITI Milwaukee
WDAF Kansas City
KSTU Salt Lake City
WHBQ Memphis
WGHP Greensboro
WBRC Birmingham
KTBC Austin
DBS & Cable
FOXTEL
BSkyB
Star
DirecTV
Sky Italia
Fox News Channel
Fox Movie Channel

FX
FUEL
National Geographic
  Channel
SPEED Channel
Fox Sports Net
FSN New England
  (50%)
FSN Ohio
FSN Florida
National Advertising
  Partners
Fox College Sports
Fox Soccer Channel
Stats, Inc.

Film
Twentieth Century Fox
Fox Searchlight Pictures
Fox Television Studios
Blue Sky Studios

Newspapers
United States
  New York Post
United Kingdom
  News International
  News of the World
  The Sun
  The Sunday Times
  The Times
Australia
  Daily Telegraph
  Fiji Times
  Gold Coast Bulletin
  Herald Sun
  Newsphotos
  Newspix
  Newstext
  NT News
  Post-Courier
  Sunday Herald Sun
  Sunday Mail
  Sunday Tasmanian
  Sunday Territorian
  Sunday Times

The Advertiser
The Australian
The Courier-Mail
The Mercury
The Sunday Telegraph
Weekly Times

Magazines
InsideOut
donna hay
SmartSource
The Weekly Standard
TV Guide (partial)

Books
Access
Amistad
Caedmon
Avon
Ecco
Eos
General Books Group
Fourth Estate
HarperAudio
HarperBusiness
HarperCollins
Harper Design
  International
HarperEntertainment
HarperLargePrint
HarperMorrow
HarperResource
HarperSanFrancisco
HarperTorch
Perennial
PerfectBound
Quill
Rayo
ReganBooks
William Morrow
William Morrow
  Cookbooks

Children's Books Group
  Avon
  Greenwillow Books
  Joanna Cotler Books
  Eos
  Laura Geringer Books
  HarperAudio
  HarperCollins Children's
  Books
  HarperFestival
  HarperTempest
  Katherine Tegen Books
  Trophy
  Zondervan
HarperCollins UK
  HarperCollins Canada
  HarperCollins Australia

Other
Los Angeles Kings
  (NHL, 40% option)
Los Angeles Lakers
  (NBA, 9.8% option)
Staples Center (40%
  owned by Fox/Liberty)
News Interactive
Fox Sports Radio
  Network
Sky Radio Denmark
Sky Radio Germany
Broadsystem
Classic FM
Festival Records
Fox Interactive
IGN Entertainment
Mushroom Records
http://www.myspace.
  com
National Rugby League
NDS
News Outdoor
Nursery World
Scout Media

Source: "Who Owns What," *Columbia Journalism Review*. Online. Updated May 14, 2007. http://www.cjr.org/resources/

they prefer to be reached. Right now our print businesses have more total readers than they ever had, thanks to the Internet. All of this is to say that, while in a certain sense our digital and Internet efforts are specific and part of a defined segment of our company, in the broader sense our effort to redefine this company for the digital age is being and must be applied to every segment.[11]

Google

It's quite likely that Google's presence has greatly influenced News Corporation CEO Rupert Murdoch's statement that his company's "print businesses have more total readers than they ever had, thanks to the Internet." News Corporation has undoubtedly found what other large companies that own websites have seen: a substantial proportion of Internet users do not come to their websites by directly typing in the web address (for example, http://www.fox.com). Rather, they do it by going to a web search engine's site and typing in the topics they want to find. A **web search engine** is an information retrieval system designed to help find information on the World Wide Web. You undoubtedly use a web search engine every day. So how would you use it to find the names of the people in TV's animated *Simpsons* family on Fox television? One way is to go to a search engine and type *Simpsons Fox Television* into the search box. Do it on Google (at http://www.google.com), and several links will appear that send you to online places with the information. The first three links, it turns out, lead to News Corporation sites (http://www.thesimpsons.com, http://www.fox.com, and http://www.fox.com/schedule).

If you ask most people to conduct a web search, the chances are that they will use Google. Even though there are many other web search engines—Yahoo, AltaVista, Lycos, Dogpile are just a few—Google is by all accounts the dominant one. The Nielsen Company's web ranking subsidiary estimates that Google attracts 55 percent of all search requests in the United States; some estimates say the percentage is even higher and that Google is even stronger in other countries. Google doesn't charge users for searching. But because it brings so many people worldwide to the advertising it shows them, Google has been raking in money. Its revenue in 2006 was about $11 billion, and its stock market value (the number of shares multiplied by the shares' value) in mid-2007 was around $160 billion—14.5 times revenues.[12] Contrasted with firms at the very top of the media food chain, Google's take was substantial but not dominating. News Corp's 2006 revenues, for example were $25 billion. Yet News Corp's mid-2007 market value of about $70 billion was only 2.8 times its annual revenues. That Google's was so much higher indicates that Wall Street clearly felt that the company has much more growth in it than does News Corporation. And many marveled that a company founded in 1998 took just a few years to become, in the words of one writer, "a tech and media titan."[13]

web search engine an information retrieval system designed to help find information on the World Wide Web

www.google.com

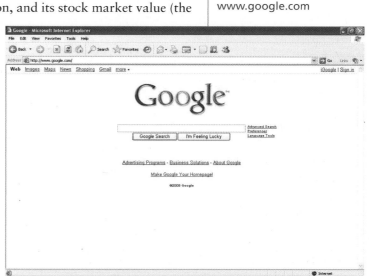

249

Google Founders Sergey Brin and Larry Page

MEDIA PROFILE

The rise of Internet search behemoth Google is in many ways a classic Cinderella story: it was developed in the college dormitory of Stanford students Sergey Brin and Larry Page and launched from their friend's basement. Within a few years, the brainchild of these middle-class suburbanites had grown to become the world's most popular search engine.

Page, the son of a computer science professor and a computer programming teacher, claims to have fallen in love with computers at the age of six. Not surprisingly, then, he earned his Bachelor's degree from the University of Michigan with a concentration on computer engineering. Brin also seems to have inherited his scientific skill-set; his father was a mathematician economist. As a child, he emigrated with his family from Moscow and went on to earn a Bachelor's degree in mathematics and computer science from the University of Maryland at College Park.

Page and Brin met in 1995 at Stanford University, where each was pursuing a computer science doctorate. Working from their dorm rooms, they developed a new type of search system that listed results based on popularity. In 1998, they ended up putting their doctorates on hold so that they could launch their system commercially. They decided to name it Google after the mathematical term "Googol," which describes a one followed by a hundred zeros.

Now, more than a decade later, Google has achieved unprecedented growth as a search provider and is a recognized leader in the software, technology, and advertising service industries. Its string of recent acquisitions includes online video streaming site YouTube and Internet ad service provider DoubleClick.

Google founders Sergey Brin (left) and Larry Page (right)

Google Inc. employs more than 10,000 people worldwide and has been ranked by *Fortune* magazine as the number one best company to work for. Particularly well-known is the company headquarters—known as the Googleplex—which features a gym, two swimming pools, several cafeterias, and a lobby decorated with a piano and lava lamps.

Both Page and Brin remain deeply involved with the company as president of products and president of technology, respectively. And despite their company's unabashed success, they like to show that their daily lives invoke Google's more humble beginnings. Until recently, Page and Brin each owned a Toyota Prius; and, in 2007, Brin admitted that he continues to shop at Costco.

Sources: Will Smale, "Profile: The Google Founders," *BBC News*, April 30, 2004, online: http://news.bbc.co.uk; Google Company Website, http://www.google.com

Three Main Strategies

But while Google is a household name in many places around the world, it is quite likely that many people don't really understand how the company makes its money and sees its strategies for growth. The aim of the next several paragraphs is to help you begin to understand that. The reason for the exploration is to help make you more literate about the important influence that Google is exerting on the direction of the media system, as well as on society. As with News Corp and Disney, you can get a sense of that influence by reading the company's annual reports and its website. The following three strategies are suggested by those sources as well as information from a wide-ranging tracking of Google and its activities over its short life.

■ Continue to improve the global attractiveness of the search engine
■ Expand Google's advertising activities to as many media as possible
■ Create non-search products that will keep users coming back despite competition

Let's take them one at a time.

Continue to Improve the Global Attractiveness of the Search Engine

Google's "Letter from the Founders" says it quite concisely: "Search remains the heart of Google." The desire for a better web search is what got Larry Page and Sergey Brin energized to start the company in 1998; today it is web users' preference for Google that allows the company to serve billions of ads to them and make billions of dollars. Brin and Page's central insight when they created Google involved the ranking of website results after the search. They reasoned that when it came to a search term, the best sites were those that used the term and were linked by other sites. According to this view, the best sites are ones nominated by other sites. The more link nominations a site with the term received, the more that site deserved to be ranked highly.

Now, this approach to ranking websites certainly has its shortcomings. For one thing, it privileges sites that have been around long enough to have developed a lot of link nominations. Fascinating but newer sites relevant to the search term would not show up as highly. Another drawback is that it implies that popularity means credibility and accuracy, which may or may not be the case. A third difficulty is that people can try to rig rankings by trying to make sure that their sites link to a particular site they want to see high up on ratings when a particular word is entered into the search engine. Despite these drawbacks and others that we'll discuss in the chapter on the Internet, Google works very well for most people. The company continues to hire additional computer programmers to improve its operation. Moreover, Google is trying to create particular search engines for people in specific professions or with particular interests. These are called vertical search engines, and Google and its competitors are racing to build the most popular ones. To quote the founders:

> Our search must also work well for different levels of expertise. Sometimes it is patients who seek medical information on Google, but other times it is doctors themselves. To go more deeply into technical fields, we have developed Google Scholar™, the most comprehensive search for scholarly work. And we also launched Google Patent Search as well as News archive search, which adds nearly 200 years of newspaper archives to Google News™. In addition, information providers and individuals can now help us improve search within their fields of expertise by creating Custom Search Engines on their own sites that provide more specific search results related to their interests.[14]

Apart from vertical search, the company is hard at work trying to maximize search results for people who want to know what's in videos (it owns the video site YouTube), for people who want to chart and learn about local geographies and businesses (through Google Earth, for example), and for mobile devices. As Brin and Page describe their work, it is crucial to millions of people—literally in a life-and-death sense. Interspersed among the paragraphs of their letter on the corporate area of Google's website are comments from Google users who testify to its importance for their health, their careers, and their personal relationships. "Sometimes," the Brin–Page letter states, "it is just a casual curiosity that sends them searching, but at other times, their need for information can be critical—and what they find can even save a life. That is why we work so hard to provide the best possible information for every query, on any topic, in any language, in any country."

For Google, that last phrase is crucial. Because of its potential worldwide reach via the Internet and a belief that everybody who uses the Web needs to have a way to search it, Google sees itself as a global firm. The Google website says, "We strive to provide our services to everyone in the world." And, in fact, the Google interface is available in 116 languages. Google News provides an automated collection of frequently updated news stories in 11 languages aimed at 34 different international audiences. The company also offers automatic translation of content between various languages and provides localized versions of Google in many developing countries. Employees outside the United States now make up nearly a third of the company, based in such cities as Beijing, Trondheim, Istanbul, Tel Aviv, Copenhagen, Vienna, Taipei, Warsaw, Haifa, Moscow, St Petersburg, Sydney, Mumbai, Cairo, and Delhi. Brin and Page note that "with international sources comprising 43 percent of Google's revenues in 2006, we continue to grow our global monetization efforts."

Expand Google's Advertising Activities to as Many Media as Possible What do Brin and Page mean when they write about "monetization efforts"? Primarily, they mean advertising, for about 98 percent of Google's

Globalizing Google

WORLD VIEW

Have you ever tried to access Google from outside the United States? If so, you probably noticed that you were automatically directed to one of the Internet search engine's country-specific domains such as http://www.google.com.mx (Mexico), http://www.google.co.uk (United Kingdom), or http://www.google.co.jp (Japan).

Google currently hosts more than a hundred domains internationally, each of which features local search results and appears in the regional language or languages. Google India, for example, is available in five different languages including Hindi and Bengali. Particularly popular is Google's advanced translation engine, which uses statistical extrapolations based on language patterns to translate entire websites.

Google's strong international presence is not surprising given the fact that more than half of its users live outside the United States. Yet some of its efforts to cater to local markets have received harsh criticism. Many have attacked Google executives for willfully censoring some of the content in China.

Others claim that Google infringes on users' privacy by using their IP addresses to track them geographically. This is, of course, how they are able to direct you to a regional Google search engine.

Google maintains that these initiatives enable them to "facilitate access to information for the entire world." What do you think?

Source: Bill Sofky, "How Google Translates Without Understanding," *The Register*, May 15, 2007, online: www.theregister.co.uk

revenues come from that. That is an enormous percentage—far higher than the proportion of money Disney and Fox make from ads compared to sources such as subscriptions and ticket purchases. The revenue source underscores what a lot of people do not understand about Google: the company is fundamentally in the business of serving advertisements to people based upon evidence it collects about who they are, what they care about, and what they might do. More specifically, Google's money-making activities center on serving ads to people. Its primary business involves serving those ads to people in two types of web locations.

The first location is its search engine. Businesses bid to have Google place their text ads next to Google's search findings on particular words. Say you sell binoculars, and you want to advertise it to Google users. You may bid a certain amount of money for a text ad linked to your binoculars website to appear (that is, to be served) when a person types the word *binoculars* into Google's search engine box. If Google accepts your bid, you must agree to pay each time a person clicks on your ad. Google calls this activity its AdWords program. Quite different is Google's AdSense advertising program. That involves thousands of websites not owned by Google who agree to allow Google to place ("serve") text advertisements on their sites' pages in return for sharing the revenues. As with AdWords, Google accepts bids on words from advertisers who want to advertise on sites that are relevant to those words. Google's computers scan the many pages on the thousands of websites and, based on special formulas, determine what pages on what sites are most relevant to those words. That is where the text ads for those words show up. As with AdWords, advertisers pay based on the number of clicks on Google's text ads.

This process may sound complex, and it is—by design. The reason: Google is constantly trying to perfect its understanding of the conditions under which people who enter particular search words or who go to particular sites are likely to click on text ads. That has led the company to record and analyze the activities of tens of millions of users without their knowing they are being tracked. Often, Google has personal information about them (for example, if they registered for Gmail) and sometimes it does not. These analytical procedures have two purposes. One is that they help Google to refine its search strategy. The company can learn, for example, how people with certain interests search compared to people with other interests. Just as important, Google's analyses of its users' activities can help the firm to refine its advertising serving model. Google is quite secretive about its activities in this area. It seems clear from various close observers of the company that its statisticians are continually trying to associate user activities and backgrounds to their clicking on ads and even completing transactions (such as buying things). Using special tracking files called cookies and other technologies, the company seems to be constructing enormous databases about its users. It has personal information about many of them through their registration with Google products such as Gmail and iGoogle, which gives users personalized search results in turn for allowing Google to store their web-surfing histories. But even those who are anonymous to Google still contribute enormously to its knowledge about how they act in searching and toward text ads on websites. Google's goal seems to be predicting whether a particular individual from a particular region with particular characteristics and search history would be more responsive to one type of ad for one type of product over another type of ad for another type of product.

The company's business, then, involves not just serving advertising. It involves serving advertising in ways that are guided by databases about the users. While Google has competitors in this database-driven ad-serving business—Yahoo and Microsoft are two—Google is by far the dominant player in the large and lucrative area of text advertising on the Web. But the company's executives don't want to stop there. As they see it, the company should be able to take the database-guided ad-serving approaches it uses with the Web and apply them to serve ads to other media. Certainly, mobile phones and digital television are obvious places, and Google is already sending ads to mobile phones and to the YouTube video website, which it owns. But Google is also turning its sights on traditional ad vehicles such as newspapers and radio. In 2005, the company purchased a company called dMarc Broadcasting that aims to help advertisers buy ads on radio stations in ways that are similar to the bidding system that Google uses for its advertising services. Google has also made deals with several newspaper companies to coordinate the selling of some of their newspaper space in this manner. Currently, these print and broadcast activities are undeveloped, partly because the non-digital nature of their products makes it impossible for Google to serve ads directly to them in the same ways it does via the Internet. Google executives clearly hope that when it becomes economically feasible to customize the ad space of newspapers and the commercials of local radio based on what is known about their audiences, Google will be the dominant player.

Google's collection of data about its users makes many privacy advocates nervous. One worry is that the personal data Google has collected about the interests of millions of people might be used to give some people more rewards (better discount coupons, free access to websites others pay for) than others get because of the way Google has interpreted its data about them. Another concern is that the information may get into the wrong hands and be interpreted in a way that could harm individuals. For example, leaked information about the diseases a particular person searches for or the websites about psychological problems that a person frequents might lead health advertisers or malicious spammers to bother the person. Certain leaked information about someone's click and search behavior may even make it difficult for the person to get health insurance coverage. The company argues that it abides by all laws about handling people's information wherever it operates, but that still hasn't stopped critics from worrying that its databases may cause individuals harm. We will deal with the issue of database privacy in some detail in Chapter 14's discussion of the Internet and related digital media.

Advertising and media firms also worry that Google's enormous financial resources and its aggressive interests in controlling the serving of advertising will do them harm. Page and Brin say in their 2006 "Letter from the Founders" that, "Our goal is to create a single and complete advertising system," and the company's activities online, in mobile phones and in the newspaper and radio businesses suggest they are serious. Advertising and media executives began to express alarm in 2007, when Google announced its intention to buy DoubleClick. DoubleClick is the king of display advertising on the Web—ads that include graphic information beyond text such as logos, photographs or other pictures, location maps, and similar items.[15] Google tried to enter that part of the business on its own, did not get much traction, and so determined that buying DoubleClick was the better way. That concerned Google competitors Microsoft and Yahoo, because they saw the new company as an instant powerhouse in both display and text that would make it even harder to compete with. But advertising agencies began to worry about the merger, too. They saw Google as being so powerful in knowledge of audience members' activities across so many media that it would become the controlling force for serving all sorts of ads in virtually all media. Much as it was serving ads to websites and splitting revenues with them, Google would serve text and display ads to radio, cable and broadcast networks and share the revenues with them. So much advertising money would be going through Google that the company could determine ad-serving policies and prices for the entire media system.

That sort of expansion, critics of the deal told the FCC and Congress, deserved to be stopped for antitrust reasons.

Create Products That Will Keep Users Coming Back Despite Competition   All the material about AdWords, AdSense, ad-serving and databases is not quite what Google executives want their users to hear. The public rhetoric of the company centers on the usefulness of its search engine and its related mission to "organize the world's information."[16] When Google does discuss its advertising business, it is as a secondary activity and in a way that makes it sound almost like a public service, explaining that its "relevant" advertising "makes the advertising useful to you as well as to the advertiser placing it."[17] Of course, a really big question must have occurred to Google's leadership: what would happen to Google's advertising if another company discovered a better way to search for information and the number of people using Google (or the number of times they came to Google) began to decrease? It's a critical question, because advertisers expect websites or web networks to deliver huge numbers of people so that even the narrow segments of the audience they want to reach (for example, pregnant women who live in London) will contain very many individuals. A progressive slide in audience may lead advertisers to move on to sites that have more "scale" (that is larger populations) and seem to be on the upswing in popularity.

One way that Google tries to avoid such a doomsday scenario (for a firm so heavily dependent on ads) is to pour enormous amounts of money to support talented people and cutting edge technologies that continually improve the chances that individuals get exactly the materials they would want to see and hear when they search. Eric Schmidt, Google's CEO, told the *Financial Times* in 2007 that the goal is to maximize the personal information it holds about its users so that they will feel comfortable asking the search engine "What should I do tomorrow?" and "What job should I take?"[18] Another way to keep the huge scale of its user population is to create technologies and services that may be hard for competitors to duplicate and that would encourage people to keep coming back even after they considered that a different search engine could give them better results. Google, for example, is reputed to be using its enormous revenue to build a network of computer servers that is bigger than that of any other company. Positioned around the world, their purpose is to make sure users always think of Google when they want lightning-fast results.

As for programs that keep people coming back, (and which allow Google to learn about people's habits), the standouts include Gmail email service, Google Docs and Spreadsheets (that allow someone to create, store and share documents on the Web) and Google Books. Google Books is perhaps the most ambitious and controversial of these. It involves literally scanning millions of books in a number of major university libraries. The idea is not to release digital versions of the entire book into the Web. Rather, Google intends to show users a few lines of the book that contain their search terms. In many cases, they would then get the book from the library or purchase it. Despite the small amount of the text that is revealed, some publisher and author groups believe that Google's act of scanning and storing the books infringes on their copyrights. Google rejects their argument and is continuing with the project. The company undoubtedly realizes that this enormous project that involves so many resources and risks a major lawsuit is an undertaking that will be unique in its scope. Consequently, it will be yet another facet of the firm that keeps people coming back even in the face of enormous competition.

Table 6.3   Google Inc. Acquisitions, 2001–2007

Company/Product	Business Area
Orion	Advanced search method
Applied Semantics	Advertising technology
Measure Map	Blog analysis
Pyra Labs	Blogger
Genius Labs	Blogging
Current Communications Group	Broadband Internet
Baidu (2.6% stake)	Chinese language search engine (all shares were sold in June, 2006)
Neven Vision	Computer vision
Neotonic Software	CRM technology
GreenBorder Technologies	Desktop enterprise security
Panoramio	Geospatial Photo-sharing Service
Deja's Usenet archive	Google Groups
Skia	Graphics software
AOL (5% stake)	Internet
Akwan Information Technologies	Latin American Internet operations
Keyhole, Inc.	Mapping software; used in Google
Where2	Mapping software; used in Google
Endoxon	Mapping solutions
Xunlei (partial acquisition)	Network, file-sharing
FeedBurner	Online RSS Feeds
Sprinks	Paid listings unit of Primedia
PeakStream	Parallel Processing
Picasa	Photo management software
Tonic Systems	Presentation software
Zenter	Presentations Software
dMarc Broadcasting	Radio advertising software and platform
Kaltix	Search engine technology
@Last Software	SketchUp, 3-D modeling
Dodgeball	Social networking
Trendalyzer	Software
Android	Software for handheld devices
Outride, Inc.	Spin-off from Xerox PARC
ZipDash	Used in Google Ride Finder
Marratech video conferencing software	Video conferencing
Adscape	Video game advertising
YouTube	Video sharing
GrandCentral	VOIP Phone Aggregation
Urchin Software Corporation	Web analysis.
Reqwireless	Web browser and Mobile email
2Web Technologies	Web-based spreadsheet
JotSpot	Website applications
Ignite Logic	Website creation technology
Phatbits	Widgets engine
Upstartle	Writely, online word processing

Source: *Wikipedia*, accessed 7/17/07. http://en.wikipedia.org/wiki/List_of_Google_acquisitions

Media Literacy and Corporate Strategies

At this point in its short life, Google is only beginning to be and act like a conglomerate. It has made many acquisitions (see Table 6.3), but it has integrated almost all of them into the core of the company to help it increase its abilities with respect to searching and advertising. Moreover, virtually all of its revenues come from the Web. Still, the company has begun to expand into other media through small subsidiaries that depart from the fixation on the Web. In not too many years, Google executives foresee their ability to serve ads across a variety of media. They may even help media firms decide what kinds of noncommercial content should be served to what people, based on those individuals' characteristics. These cross-media activities will likely be quite different from those of Disney and News Corporation, but Google's influence on the ads and even the content people see is nevertheless likely to be profound.

As we have seen in this chapter, media conglomerates are increasingly trying to find profits in the movement of products and ideas across media boundaries. More and more, executives are moving their targeted brands across media boundaries to pursue their customers in a highly competitive environment. The executives' mandate is to follow the consumers with their brand, expose the brand to new target consumers, and by doing so allow advertisers to reach certain types of consumers in as many places as possible. Even when media executives think they have good strategies for carrying out this and other mandates, they constantly re-examine their approaches to make sure they are moving in the best direction possible. That kind of continual rethinking takes place in small and midsized mass media companies, but it is especially common at all levels of major corporations such as News Corporation, Disney, and Google.

Cross-media strategies have become a major engine that drives the contemporary media system. Critics of media conglomerates argue that these activities are dangerous to society because they allow a small number of huge firms to dictate what society will see across its most important media channels. From a critical perspective, a blunt way to express what we have seen in this chapter is to say that many media channels today have become "retread" machines. Media firms see different mass media channels simply as new places to display their wares.

As an example relating to cross-media activities, consider the kind of database-guided personalization that we see particularly in Google, but—as we will see in forthcoming chapters—all companies and their advertisers are building audience databases and pursuing personalization technologies. We therefore ought to pay attention to these activities and try to think through how they might affect the media materials that we confront on a daily basis. It would seem that the more channels a company uses to send us news, information, and advertising, the more likely we are to notice that material. Similarly, the more materials we receive that reflect our individual interests, the more we are likely to pay attention. Critics further argue that the benefits of personalization across media channels are often outweighed by the problems of privacy that they bring.

How would you feel if you knew that the relevant material that you receive also means that you don't get offers and commercials and even programs that other people, with different data profiles, receive? As yet, this doesn't happen very often—though it *does* happen, as later chapters will show. In an era of so many cross-media activities and a fixation on a personalized-media future, try to imagine the benefits of the opposite: a world in which different media were seen as unique, fresh ways to look at the world that surprised people because they offered views so different from what they would expect. Of course, as we have seen, the structure of media costs and opportunities makes the disentangling of these channels highly unlikely. As a media literate person, however, you should consider alternatives and your opinion of them even if they do not presently seem realistic. You should realize, too, that you can't prove that media channels would be wildly different if cross-media activities ceased. Nevertheless, this sort of mind game does keep you asking the kinds of critical questions that can help you to understand better what does and doesn't exist in the mass media.

Cross-media activities and personalization activities are only two of the issues that we could tease out in thinking about media giants and their power. To keep your critical edge, it is important to consider what individuals and societies may not be receiving as a result of corporate power. Because we are so surrounded by the products of mass media industries, we may forget that very different alternatives can, and often do, exist. One goal of media literacy may be to think about alternatives, identify them, and then encourage media companies to pursue them. Trying to encourage change in the media is a tough challenge, but understanding the considerations that guide media firms in what they do is a crucial way to start.

CHAPTER REVIEW

For an interactive chapter recap and study guide, visit the companion website for *Media Today* at www.routledge.com/textbooks/mediatoday

QUESTIONS FOR DISCUSSION AND CRITICAL THINKING

1 In what ways are the News Corporation and Disney corporate strategies similar? In what ways are they different?
2 How is Google different from these media conglomerates?
3 Why are conglomerates increasingly concerned with moving their products globally as well as within their home countries?
4 Why are some social critics upset with media conglomerates?

INTERNET RESOURCES

The annual reports of media conglomerates online

> The best way to find the corporate website of a media firm is to use a search engine such as Google, type the name of the company in parentheses and add the word *corporate*. So, for example, to get to the Sony Corporation's corporate website, go to Google or Yahoo and type *Sony corporate* into the search box. Once on the corporate site and directed to investor services, look for annual reports. You may need to click on the term *SEC filings* to get to them.

FreePress.net (http://www.freepress.net/docs/talk_radio.pdf)

> The website states that "Free Press is a national, nonpartisan organization working to reform the media. Through education, organizing and advocacy, we promote diverse and independent media ownership, strong public media, and universal access to communications." Founded by professor and media activist Robert McChesney, it often presents strong critiques of the activities of media conglomerates.

KEY TERMS

You can find the definitions to these key terms in the marginal glossary throughout this chapter. Test your knowledge of these terms with interactive flash cards on the *Media Today* companion website.

conglomerate	strategies
franchise	synergy
licensing	web search engine
nodes	

CONSTRUCTING MEDIA LITERACY

1   How would you respond to the remark, "Google's business is search"?
2   How much of your media time in a typical day do you spend with material produced by Time Warner, Disney, Viacom, CBS, News Corporation, Sony, NBC-Universal and Comcast? Try to keep track of what media you use and what companies own them. It isn't easy keeping track, and you may find it difficult to figure out the ownership of certain media—cable networks, for example. But the extent to which you rely on them might surprise you.
3   The next time you go to the movies, keep track of the number of product placements you see. To what extent do you think the placements give you a clue about the producer's intended audience?
4   If you were a school-supplies advertiser, would you be concerned about using MySpace for reaching tweens and teens? Why or why not?

CASE STUDY   Analyzing the CEO's Statement in an Annual Report

The idea   The chief executive's (CEO's) statement in a media firm's annual report is often a useful way to present a vision of its strategies to investors and to justify the vision and the way it is being accomplished. Understanding that will help you understand many of the actions of the company that affect consumers.

The method   Choose a large media corporation and go to its most recent two annual reports online. Read the CEO's statement in each. Also, take a look at the covers of the annual reports and the other matter created for investors, such as photos of the company's products and stars. (Don't worry about the financial numbers in the back; one has to be quite specialized to understand these.) In addition, read five articles in trade magazines (through a database such as Nexis or Factiva) that discuss the company's activities in the past year. Using this chapter's analyses of Disney, News Corporation and Google as examples, write a report that answers the following questions: (1) What is the CEO's vision for the company—the idea of what the company's mission is and why? (2) How do the CEO and others in the company see the competitive environment that the firm is facing? (3) What strategies (broad ways to think of what to do) and what specific activities do they present for overcoming these and other obstacles? (4) How are these strategies and activities affecting the kinds of materials consumers receive from that company? In your report, also comment on what you think the media critics mentioned in this chapter would say about the company's activities.

chapters

7   **THE BOOK INDUSTRY**

8   **THE NEWSPAPER INDUSTRY**

9   **THE MAGAZINE INDUSTRY**

Traditionally, when we think of *print* media industries, we think of reading materials manufactured from ink and paper. The largest of these print media industries—the book, newspaper, and magazine industries—are the focus of this section.

In Chapters 7 through 9, you'll learn about the history of the industries and their work today. We'll explore social and ethical concerns regarding the ways the industries carry out their work. We'll also investigate a change that ties into what we discussed in Part 2: the transformation of newspapers, magazines, and books into forms that have nothing to do with paper and ink.

the

three

print media

7 THE BOOK INDUSTRY

After studying this chapter, you will be able to:

1 Consider today's books in terms of the development of books over the centuries

2 Differentiate among the different types of books within the book-publishing industry

3 Analyze ethical pitfalls that are present in the book-publishing industry

4 Explain the roles of production, distribution, and exhibition as they pertain to the book-publishing industry

5 Realize and evaluate the effects of new digital technologies on the book-publishing industry

"If I rely on just the bookstore sales, I won't make a living. Putting [my book] online does not put my livelihood at risk; you make a living finding new ways to do business."

– CORY DOCTOROW, SCIENCE FICTION WRITER AND BLOGGER

Media Today

Were you one of the millions of people who signed up with bookstores to reserve a copy of the seventh and final installment of the *Harry Potter* series, in 2007? Even if you weren't, the frenzy was hard to miss. The book was released just as the third *Harry Potter* movie opened in theatres. As publicists trickled out word that two major characters would die in the book, interest in the novel reached new heights. Further focusing attention on the release, author J. K. Rowling and her British publisher, Bloomsbury, made sure that bookstores would begin selling the novel at the same time around the world: 12:01 a.m. on Saturday July 21 in the eastern United States. Bookstores opened at odd hours so that their customers could get their copies at exactly the release time. In the United States, the online company http://www.amazon.com not only sold the book at about half the publisher's suggested price, it guaranteed delivery to the "lower 48" states by 7 p.m. Saturday if customers bought it from the Amazon website by 5 p.m. on July 19.

In the age of the Internet, total control over the novel's release was predictably impossible, despite the publishers' best efforts. Scanned copies of the U.S. edition appeared online a couple of days in advance of its release. Moreover, reviewers from the *New York Times* and *Washington Post* got their hands on the novel and wrote assessments before the book hit the shelves. Despite these breaches of secrecy (or maybe because of them), the book garnered record-breaking sales worldwide. According to Scholastic, *Harry Potter*'s publisher in the United States, *Harry Potter and the Deathly Hallows* became the fastest-selling book in U.S. history; an unprecedented 8.3 million copies were sold within the first 24 hours of the book's release. In the U.K., the market auditing company Nielsen BookScan reported that 2.6 million copies of *Deathly Hallows* were sold in the first 24 hours at bookstores, making it the fastest selling book in the country's history.

The sales were also brisk in non-English-speaking places. In Germany, for example, 398,271 copies of the novel were sold in the first 24 hours.[1]

Harry Potter is a fascinating example of the cross-media hype that is keeping certain segments of book publishing successful today. Yet many book-industry executives will tell you that relying on such hit-making is not typical. Titles such as the *Harry Potter* series that aim at the general public do gather billions of dollars—$21.3 billion in 2005. Yet they represent only a small slice of a huge business that includes books for elementary schools, high schools, colleges, graduate schools, professional training centers, and more.

The book you are reading now is a product of one area of the book industry, the college textbook segment. If you think of the "extra" materials that come with the book—the website and the terms you can download to your mobile device, for example—you will realize that book publishers in the new media environment are going beyond the printed page. Their biggest long-term concerns involve figuring out how to compete in a digital environment, where paper is only one way to deliver the information in books. The challenge, as they see it, is to keep the essential features of a book that have drawn readers over the centuries, while giving those features wondrous new digital spins that will keep the book healthy for centuries to come.

For one of the oldest communication media—books are older than newspapers—and for an industry that has typically been pretty set in its ways, that is a tall order. It's by no means an impossible one, though, as we will see. If you were involved in the task, probably the first thing you would have to do is ask two basic questions: what are the essential features of a book that have drawn readers over the centuries? And what are the essential elements of today's book industry that would encourage or discourage bold new movements into the digital age?

The Meaning of a Book

UNESCO, the United Nations Education, Scientific and Cultural Organization studies the availability of books around the world. They define a **book**, as a "non-periodical printed publication of at least 49 pages excluding covers." We can break this definition down into five important parts that come together to distinguish a book from other media:

1 A book is *printed*. It is created using one or more machines rather than written or painted by hand.
2 A book is a *publication*. It is printed in multiple copies for circulation to more than its creator.
3 A book comprises *at least 49 pages*. The UNESCO definers evidently meant to exclude short documents. We would call those pamphlets, not books.
4 A book has *covers*.
5 A book is *not a periodical*. That is, it is not updated under the same title on a regular basis, like magazines and newspapers.

The History of the Book

While the history of the book as we know it can be traced back only about 500 years, the idea of the book is much older. Scholars consider the papyrus roll in Egypt around 3,000 BC an early ancestor of the modern book. Papyrus was made from a reed-like plant in the Nile Valley, and it resembled paper. Scribes laid out sheets of papyrus, wrote on them, copied a text on one side of the sheets, and then rolled up the finished manuscript. The Greeks adopted the papyrus roll from the Egyptians. They stored their rolls in great libraries. In fact, the Greeks considered the book so important that they began to use it, rather than the memory of speeches (what is called the oral tradition), as the main way to make ideas "public"—or, available to large numbers of people. Greek writers of the era refer to a market in books and to prices paid for them. Large libraries maintained **scriptoria** where many books were copied by hand. Unfortunately, relatively little of this material has survived.

The Romans picked up the idea of papyrus rolls from the Greeks. Apart from libraries, a fairly large number of Romans, especially those of the upper class, owned manuscripts. The interest in these works led to a small-scale Roman industry of papyrus rolls. "Publishing" entrepreneurs used slave labor to create multiple copies at relatively low prices. One writer asserts that "In many ways these enterprises were prototypes for modern publishing houses. Roman publishers selected the manuscripts to be reproduced;

book according to UNESCO, a "non-periodical printed publication of at least 49 pages excluding covers"

scriptoria areas located in ancient Greek libraries where books were copied by hand

The *Harry Potter* series of books—and now toys, films, and other spin-offs—has become a business in itself.

advanced money to authors for rights to the manuscripts, thus assuming the risks of publication; chose the format, size, and price of each edition; and developed profitable markets for their merchandise."

But it was a long way from the slave-driving papyrus scroll businesses to Random House. Part of the difference had to do with the look of the book (its **format**) and the technology to make it. Manuscripts began to take on the look of a book around AD 100, when Christians invented the **codex**—a document in which papyrus pages faced one another and were bound together, instead of rolled up. This form made it easier to find a particular passage quickly—the reader didn't have to unravel a large roll—and it enabled writers to write on both sides of the pages. The codex was followed by innovations in the material used for the manuscripts—animal skins (vellum and parchment) and then, by the fifteenth century, paper.

If you were transported to Europe of that period, you would recognize books. They were pages bound together and collected under hard covers. They were different from today's books in one important way, however—they were written by hand. Like the Greek scriptoria workers, fifteenth-century monks patiently copied manuscripts that they considered holy or otherwise important. They sometimes also added beautiful drawings to illustrate what was written. As you might imagine, it took a long time to produce these books, so relatively few were produced. Scholars have estimated that in all of Europe of the early 1400s, the total number of books was in the thousands.

Gutenberg and the Advent of Movable Type

It was during this time that a revolution in printing took place so that only a hundred years later, the number of books in Europe was about nine million. The instigator of this revolution was the printing press, created by Johannes Gutenberg.

Gutenberg, who lived in what is today Germany, didn't create his new machine totally from scratch. The Chinese had independently developed the art of manuscript production around the time of the Christian era. Lampblack ink was introduced in China in AD 400 and printing from wooden blocks in the sixth century. Europeans became familiar with both these innovations before the 1400s.

What made Gutenberg's approach unique was his creation of **movable type**—individual letters of the alphabet made out of wood or metal that can be rearranged in any number of combinations to make different words. Unlike

format   the look of a book

codex   the first manuscripts that began to take on the look of a book: papyrus leaves faced one another and were bound together, instead of rolled up; this form made it easier to find a particular passage quickly

movable type   individual letters of the alphabet made out of wood or metal that can be rearranged in any number of combinations to make different words; invented by Johannes Gutenberg

This page of hand-illuminated manuscript is from one of Johannes Gutenberg's Bibles, produced during the fifteenth century.

Figure 7.1

Woodblocks vs. Movable Type

Once it became available on more than a limited basis, printing with "movable type" was immediately recognized as a truly extraordinary technological advance over woodblock printing.

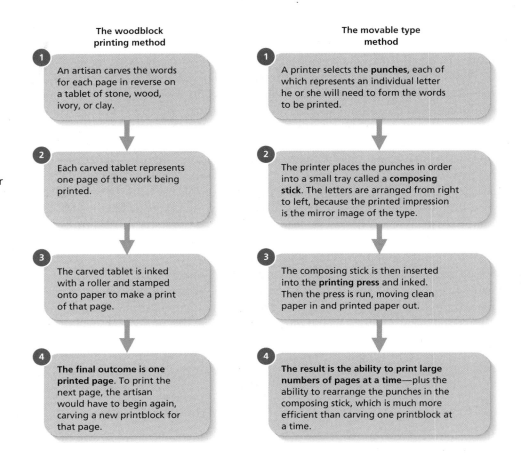

The woodblock printing method

1. An artisan carves the words for each page in reverse on a tablet of stone, wood, ivory, or clay.

2. Each carved tablet represents one page of the work being printed.

3. The carved tablet is inked with a roller and stamped onto paper to make a print of that page.

4. **The final outcome is one printed page.** To print the next page, the artisan would have to begin again, carving a new printblock for that page.

The movable type method

1. A printer selects the **punches**, each of which represents an individual letter he or she will need to form the words to be printed.

2. The printer places the punches in order into a small tray called a **composing stick**. The letters are arranged from right to left, because the printed impression is the mirror image of the type.

3. The composing stick is then inserted into the **printing press** and inked. Then the press is run, moving clean paper in and printed paper out.

4. **The result is the ability to print large numbers of pages at a time**—plus the ability to rearrange the punches in the composing stick, which is much more efficient than carving one printblock at a time.

a woodblock, which could only be used for one message, movable type could be used over and over because it could be constantly rearranged (see Figure 7.1). Gutenberg made a frame to hold the arranged type in place. He covered the type with ink, placed paper on top of the inked bed of type, and then applied pressure to the paper with a corkscrew device that was adapted from a wine press. The process enabled anyone who was strong enough to work the press to create multiple, identical copies of text that were as good-looking as those written by the most careful scribes of the day. Gutenberg's most famous creations, his forty-two-line Bibles, are quite beautiful even by today's printing standards. Once it became available on more than a limited basis, printing with movable type was immediately recognized as a truly extraordinary technological advance over woodblock printing. Gutenberg's idea caught on quickly. By 1500, printing presses had been established in 242 cities across various countries.

The Impact of the Book on Society

During the 1400s and early 1500s, most books were print versions of what monks had previously made by hand: works such as the Bible, books of hours (prayer books), and religious calendars. Beginning in the 1500s, book printers began to produce books that challenged the dominant (Catholic) church and that circulated nonreligious (secular) ideas. This growth of anti-Catholicism and secularism in books both reflected and influenced the rise of new ideas about the world. As more and more people learned to read, the books helped foster important changes in European understandings. In the sixteenth through eighteenth centuries, these changes helped encourage the Protestant Reformation, the Renaissance, the growth of science, and ideas about democracy.

Book printing, then, stood in the center of remarkable changes that helped make civilization the way it is today. The changes came slowly, and there were many fights in Europe and Britain among printers, booksellers, authors, publishers and rulers about what could be published and by whom. We'll concentrate on Britain, because its experience most influenced the development of printing in what would become the United States.

The Book in Britain

The history of the book in Britain was marked by strong governmental control that began to loosen at about the same time as Britons were settling the North American colonies in large numbers. For centuries after the first printing shop opened in 1487, British printers were controlled by the government. The British Crown feared dissent and worried that printing presses in the wrong hands could lead to uprisings. As a result, British kings and queens kept close control over all printers and printing. For example, in 1509 King Henry VIII put out a list of prohibited books and established a **licensing system,** under which only people with written authority from the Crown could use a printing press. Queen Mary Tudor, Henry's daughter, extended those controls through the establishment of the Stationers' Company—an organization that regularly searched printing houses to report on the nature of the work in progress and the identities of customers. As a result of such measures, the books printed in England from the late 1400s through the 1600s reflected the religious and political convictions of the ruling monarchy.

In 1637, licensing procedures became even more stringent, reducing the total number of printers to twenty-three, and assigning severe penalties for violators. It was this act that prompted John Milton to write and publish a pamphlet called *Areopagitica*, in which he pleaded for freedom of the press and argued passionately against censorship. Milton claimed that a free exchange of ideas would create a **marketplace of ideas** in which different opinions would compete for public approval. Milton felt that truth would always win out in such a contest. This notion became the rallying cry for those in Britain and America who wanted press freedom. It led to a British law passed in the 1680s that guaranteed free expression for members of Parliament. In Britain's American colonies, this belief encouraged some printers to argue that the press should be free to attack the government.

The demand for a free press marked only part of the changes that were taking place in British book publishing. In the sixteenth and seventeenth centuries, booksellers often acted as publishers, paying for the making of the book, so they could sell it. Printers were paid little for making the books, and the booksellers claimed total ownership over the material, meaning they could print it elsewhere at will. As a result, the author had no control over the work. By the eighteenth century, however, the figure of a publisher separate from the bookseller began to develop. This created a new three-way relationship—between the author (who wrote the work), the publisher (who supported the author in the creation of a book and paid for its printing with the belief it would be saleable to the public), and the bookseller (who sold the book to consumers).

licensing system in the history of print media, a system put in place by King Henry VIII in 1509 under which only people with written authority from the Crown could use a printing press

marketplace of ideas the belief, asserted by John Milton in *Areopagitica*, that in a free-flowing media system, individuals will be able to make their own decisions about what is true and what is false, because media competition will allow different opinions to emerge and struggle for public approval (as in a market), and in the end, the true opinion will win

The desire to encourage authors to create, and publishers to support them, led to the Copyright Act of 1709, the first of its kind in any country. It protected printed works for set periods of time, and also set forth penalties for those who stole other people's copyrights.

The Book in the British Colonies

The idea of copyright and of books that were free from government control migrated to the British colonies which later became the United States. The first press in the British colonies was brought to Cambridge, Massachusetts, in 1639, and focused on religious publications. Soon after, however, more printers came to Massachusetts and other colonies, turning out a wide variety of materials. Works of theology formed the leading category of books. Almanacs, primers, and law books were the staples of book production.

The process of printing these materials was labor-intensive, and not all that different from what it was in Gutenberg's time. The methods of getting the books to the reading public were also quite different from today. There were booksellers; often these were the printers themselves. Rich people might buy leather-bound books by subscription—giving the printer money in advance to turn out handsome volumes. And many who bought books, particularly unbound cheap paper books, got them from street vendors—hawkers—who walked through cities and towns calling out about their printed wares.

As late as 1810, books were typically published by small printing companies, often family-run businesses. The presses these companies used were still not much different from Gutenberg's. Printing took root in the biggest cities on the East Coast, but it also spread west with the general national expansion. By wagons, by barges, and by whatever other means came to hand, printers dragged their presses and type across the new nation. Once they had settled in a place, these printer-entrepreneurs turned out pamphlets, local laws, commercial announcements, bills, legal forms, newspapers and books.

U.S. Book Publishing Becomes an Industry

Then came a technological change that transformed the American book industry. The change was the invention of the steam-powered printing press. By the 1830s, developments in society and in technology came together to encourage a new approach to printing. On the cutting edge of technology was the steam-powered *cylinder press*. It was called a cylinder press because the paper was fed to the flatbed type by one, or sometimes two, cylinders. The machine had been invented by Frederick Koenig in Saxony (today a part of Germany), had been improved in England, and had reached new levels of efficiency with the work of R. Hoe and Company in the United States.

In 1830, a Hoe steam-powered cylinder press could produce 4,000 double impressions on paper in one hour. This was four times faster than earlier German and British versions, and an astonishing twenty times faster than the colonial flatbed press. The potential for turning out huge numbers of copies quickly encouraged the development of cheaper methods for making paper. The speed of the Hoe press and the new low cost of paper meant that for the first time it was technologically possible to create huge numbers of printed pages for about a penny a copy, a price low enough that even working people could afford them. Around the same time as the steam-powered cylinder press came developments such as low-cost paper, mechanical typesetting, new methods of reproducing illustrations and inexpensive cloth bindings.

To these technological developments add crucial cultural developments: the increase in literacy and the huge influx of immigrants into the United States. The growth of canals and railways during the nineteenth century meant that publishers could transport books to the inner parts of the American continent. These long trips also led people to buy books to read on the journeys.

Between 1825 and 1875, the book business developed into an industry. Large companies began to emerge, with departments specializing in different types of books aimed at different markets. The tremendous social changes during this period also affected book publishing and made the sale of large numbers of copies realistic. With transportation and communication becoming easier, a publisher could expect to sell copies over a wider territory than was previously possible. In addition, the market was growing because literacy continued to rise. According to one historian, education grew so rapidly that by the 1840s the United States had produced "the largest reading audience anyone had ever seen."

By 1855, the United States surpassed England in book sales. That in itself probably would not have bothered British publishers, who might have sold to the United States as well as the United Kingdom and the English-speaking parts of its empire. But the British publishers lost out because the American competitors published popular British novels in the United States without paying royalties to the authors or publishers. The problem from the British standpoint was that the federal government refused to recognize the legitimacy of copyrights taken out on books in foreign countries. Consequently, titles by highly popular British authors such as Walter Scott and Charles Dickens could be reproduced and sold by U.S. publishers with impunity. It was not until 1891, when foreigners began copying American works without paying, that the U.S. joined the International Copyright Convention at the insistence of U.S. publishers who were losing revenues because of it.

Despite the lure of cheap British titles for publishers in the nineteenth century, books by American authors also brought in a good deal of revenue. Dictionaries and books on law, medicine, and theology that were produced in the United States were selling well. By 1860, textbooks made up the largest part of U.S. book production, as they do today. There were successful U.S. fiction authors, too. Harriet Beecher Stowe's *Uncle Tom's Cabin*, published in 1852, had racked up 500,000 sales by 1857,

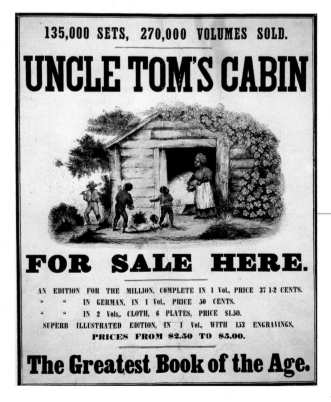

Uncle Tom's Cabin is arguably the most socially influential American novel ever published. As this advertising poster suggests, the book had a worldwide audience; it was translated into thirty-seven languages and has never gone out of print.

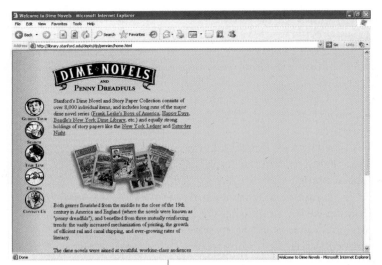

Stanford Dime Novel and Story Paper Collection, housed at http://www-sul.stanford.edu/depts/dp/pennies/home.html collects more than 8,000 examples of the genre.

dime novel a type of paperback book published in the early 1860s, so called because their price was ten cents per copy

domestic novel a type of paperback book published in the 1870s, mostly aimed at women

and continued to sell 1,000 copies per week. Around that same time, Washington Irving's works were posting 800,000 sales, a writer named T. S. Arthur was selling more than a million copies of his books, and James Fenimore Cooper's publisher was selling 40,000 copies of Cooper's books each year.

The Advent of Dime Novels and Domestic Novels

While works of fiction by individual authors continued to be popular, a new sort of fiction appeared in the early 1860s. Published in paperback, these books reflected the increasing industrialization of the publishing industry. Called **dime novels** because of their price of ten cents a copy, these books were less important for their content than for the factory-like system in which they were created and distributed. The emphasis was on inexpensive publishing of predictable successes. Authors were given fees, not royalties, and their payment depended on the length of the novel, the type of novel, and the writer's reputation. The writers were expected to work according to pre-established adventure, western, and detective formulas that were aimed mostly at men and boys. The books were marketed by mail subscription in a series and in a variety of retail outlets.

In the 1870s, more traditional publishers began to turn out their own versions of predictable sellers. These **domestic novels,** aimed at women, were tearjerker stories about heroines who sin in their personal lives, suffer the consequences, and then repent. They were the predecessors of TV's soap operas and the publishing industry's Harlequin romances. The book publishing industry as a whole also began to copy the marketing tactics of the dime-novel producers. By the end of the century, all publishers were trying to sell inexpensive books individually and in series—for example, a series of Shakespeare's plays or Dickens' books. And like the dime-novel producers, more traditional publishers were trying to broaden the distribution and exhibition of their products. High quality books increasingly could be bought—not just in bookstores and through the mail—but in department stores and discount outlets as well.

Conglomerates Enter the Book Industry

By the mid-twentieth century, book publishing in the United States was a highly segmented business. More than 22,000 publishing houses issued 49,000 new titles or editions every year, producing a total of nearly two billion books per year. Exceptions to this segmentation were the several large companies dominating the high-profile consumer fiction and nonfiction areas. The rest of book publishing began to follow in this direction during the 1960s. That was when large corporations began to see gold in the growing textbook market. In the ensuing decades, major corporations such as Time Warner, CBS, and Advance Publications bought up companies in the book business. In addition, European book companies bought American book-publishing companies beginning in the 1980s. For example,

The Advent of the Serial

The first highly popular paperback novels in the United States were not really books at all; nor were they written by primarily American writers. Instead, they were publications that looked very much like newspapers, and they contained mostly British novels in serial form, meaning that they appeared over several weeks.

The first such "story paper" was developed in 1839 by New York journalists Park Benjamin and Rufus Griswold. They named their weekly publication *Brother Jonathan*, which was an early national symbol for an American and was later replaced with Uncle Sam.

Benjamin and Griswold designed their publication to look like a newspaper to take advantage of the lower postage rates reserved for that medium. At that time, the federal government refused to recognize the legitimacy of copyrights taken out for books in foreign countries. Thus, by using British novels, Benjamin and Griswold could keep costs down by not paying royalties. As a result, they were able to maintain a successful publication while only charging twenty-five cents a copy, a low price for a book.

Although *Brother Jonathan* ceased publication in 1843, it spawned many imitators. Known as the "Mammoth Weeklies," this was a new generation of story paper. Firms would mail entire volumes in the now-familiar book format, but without covers, to those who paid for them, supposedly as "supplements" to the story papers.

More conventional U.S. book publishers tried to compete by drastically lowering their prices for books by British authors. In the end, the publishers managed to win their struggle with the paperback printers when the U.S. Postal Service declared that the supplements would no longer be carried at newspaper rates, but had to go at the higher book rates.

Although the ruling pushed the supplement publishers out of business, they left a legacy: They had shown that, after centuries of being available only to a comparatively small elite, books could reach large numbers of people. Cheap books, paperbound or not, were firmly established, never to disappear.

Sources: Michael Davitt Bell, "Beginnings of Professionalism," *Culture, Genre, and Literary Vocation: Selected Essays on American Literature* (Chicago: University of Chicago Press, 2001), pp. 67–133.

Bertelsmann of Germany added Doubleday, Bantam, Dell, and Random House to its worldwide publishing empire; the Holtzbrinck Group of Germany bought Holt, Rinehart & Winston (renaming it Henry Holt); and Britain's Penguin Publishing Company added New American Library and E. P. Dutton to its roster of firms.

The emergence of large, multinational conglomerates changed all facets of book publishing. Owning several firms that targeted different types of readers became a common strategy. Bertelsmann's Random House, for example, had several firms under its umbrella in 1998, and some of those firms had departments that specialized in particular kinds of books (foreign reprints, for example), particular types of subject matter (high-class novels, romances, quality nonfiction), and particular readers (children, members of ethnic groups). People who remembered consumer publishing before the 1960s also claimed that it had lost a genteel quality. Previously, they said, editors and publishers were in the business to generate truly good literature and great nonfiction. With the merging of book publishing into the big business of big media, they claimed, the politeness gave way to dog-eat-dog competition and mercenary calculation of a book's value that smacked more of Hollywood than the book business of old.

Let's take a look at the publishing world of today and then peer into its future.

Book Conglomerates

CRITICAL CONSUMER

How do you put a price tag on a mass media product whose value is immeasurable? Books have long been thought of as being not so much moneymakers as important and worthwhile products to be published for their own sake. Book companies could make money by relying on the revenues from the occasional bestseller. But Andre Schiffrin, a former editor at Pantheon, tells how media conglomerates are changing that model—and not for the better.

When Bertelsmann, a huge German media conglomerate, took over Random House (Pantheon's parent company) in the late 1990s, the idea was no longer to publish books that would serve the public interest by offering new ideas or challenging old perceptions. Bertelsmann wanted to work from a profit model, which meant that "Pantheon would no longer publish political works," as Random House's incoming chief editor told his staff.

Schiffrin, who earlier in his career had brought such political material as *Marx for Beginners* and the works of Noam Chomsky to print in the United States through Random

House, was outraged and quit his position. Schiffrin notes that highly influential authors like Kafka and Brecht had initial print runs of only a few hundred; under a profit-only model, these writers would never have been introduced. He sees the Bertelsmann takeover as part of a larger trend towards a diminishing number of independent bookstores and fewer and fewer huge corporate interests owning more and more presses.

Indeed, in the decade since this takeover, large retail chains and national bookstores have forced many independent booksellers to close up shop; meanwhile, the publishing world has become even more concentrated.

This raises the question of whether a certain book's chances of being published depend on the conglomerate's political and economic agenda, instead of what may be beneficial to society.

Sources: Anthony Amove, "Publish and Perish, "*In These Times* (Institute for Public Affairs), December 25, 2000; http://www.union writers.org/campaigns/media-democracy/docs/monkerud-media.php

The Book Industry Today

Book publishing is big business. Economists project that by 2010, expenditures on books and book-related materials in this country will reach about $47 billion. Book publishing is a growing and generally healthy industry. The people who work in it make a variety of distinctions among types of books. The most basic distinction is between professional and educational books, on the one hand, and consumer books, on the other. Let's take a look at each category.

Educational and Training Books

pedagogy the use of features such as learning objectives, chapter recaps, and questions for discussion; this is characteristic of educational books

Educational and professional books focus on training. Most professional and educational books are marked by their use of **pedagogy** (or learning materials), which includes features such as learning objectives, chapter recaps, questions for discussion, and the like. Although a good deal of what professional and educational publishers turn out looks like traditional books, the publishers are the first to acknowledge that a growing proportion of what flows from their firms doesn't look like the standard book. They point to math workbooks, corporate training manuals, college coursepacks, online versions of textbooks, and text-related videos. Because some of the materials are not standard books (or even books at all, as we understand the term), some writers on the topic have come to refer to this area

The Scarcity of Textbooks

Reading this textbook probably does not seem odd to you. After all, you have been reading textbooks your entire life, and college classes often require at least one expensive textbook, sometimes several. A textbook is as natural to you as a desk or a chalkboard. However, for many students in the world, a textbook is a precious and scarce item, or perhaps only a dream. For example, in rural areas of sub-Saharan Africa, there is one textbook for every thirty children. Many parents cannot afford the fees that schools with limited funding must charge.

Worldwide, more than 125 million children are not in school. Lack of schooling has led to the illiteracy of more than one billion members of the earth's population. Efforts to increase school funding and enrollment are underway, but poor countries are struggling under the weight of debt, and industrialized nations have not made good on promises to provide the funding necessary to support schooling.

Foreign-owned debt continues to devastate the budgets of Third World nations, leaving them strapped for funds that are desperately needed in other areas, such as textbooks.

Educational deficiencies mean that these nations are further hindered in their efforts to compete in the globalized economy, which they fear will widen the existing gross gap between rich and poor nations.

The problem has not gone unnoticed, as many have called for steps to debt relief so that poorer nations can use their funds in areas where they are badly needed. Humanitarian aid has also helped in some areas. For more than two decades the Sabre Foundation of Massachusetts has helped to "support the educational infrastructure vital to countries in either conflict, or in transition, or countries that are already on the road to development." Particularly successful has been its book donation program, which by the end of 2006 had sent 2.3 million new books and CD-ROMs to Africa.

Sources: Justin Forsyth, "Globalization: Education Makes Moral and Economic Sense," *The Independent*, December 12, 2000, Features, p. 11; Rumman Farugi, "A New Approach to Debt Relief," *International Herald Tribune*, Opinion, p. 4; The Sabre Foundation website "Book Donation Philosophy," online, accessed 8/5/07, http://www.sabre.org/about/Book_Donation_Philosophy.php

broadly as "educational and training media." Experts consider the area as part of book publishing, because the non-book products are often closely connected to traditional books in the learning environment. The business is large; it brought just over $21 billion in revenue during 2005. The basis for most of the categories in this industry, though, is the book. People who work in the industry recognize three types of educational and training books: el-hi, higher education, and corporate training manuals.

El-hi Books and Materials

El-hi books and materials are created for students in kindergarten through twelfth grade. Growth in the educational book market was spurred by an increase in the birth rate during the 1980s, as the large generation known as the baby boomers—people born between 1945 and 1961—had children. The increased number of students in the educational system resulted in increased orders for el-hi textbooks. Although those numbers have peaked, observers of the el-hi market predict the federal government's No Child Left Behind Act, and a general commitment to improving education at state levels of government, will lead school districts to be able to keep purchasing textbooks and materials that involve evaluation and testing of student knowledge based on the texts.

el-hi books and materials educational books published for use by elementary, middle, and high school students

Higher Education Materials

These are books that focus on teaching students in college and post-college learning. The textbook you are now reading falls

professional books books that are dedicated to postgraduate training primarily for people in the fields of business, law, medicine, technology and science, library science, and education

into this category. The "baby boomlet" of the 1980s mentioned in the previous paragraph has led to a spike in college enrollments, and the increased numbers of college students mean more textbook business in this area. The boomlet has led to a need for more **professional books** as students graduate from college. These titles provide postgraduate training, primarily for people in the fields of business, law, medicine, technology and science, library science, and education. These books are aimed at people whose professions require them to have a personal reference library. The higher education market involved sales of $6 billion in 2006.

Outsourced Corporate Training Materials   These involve books and related materials that help to keep people who are working up to date on their areas as well as help bring them to the next level of knowledge. "Outsourced" simply means that a company hires a firm to train its employees rather than doing it within the company. Many corporations sponsor these sorts of educational experiences, either in classroom settings or through programs taught over the Internet. One analyst points out that these programs are increasing as the baby boom generation begins to retire and corporations feel a need to train the next generation of top executive talent. Although publishing texts and other works for this market may not seem as exciting as turning out a Stephen King novel, think of the money involved. In 2005, companies spent about $11 billion on outsourced corporate training.

Consumer Books

consumer books books that are aimed at the general public

Unlike the publishers of professional and educational books, publishers of **consumer books** are aiming their products at the general public. They target readers in their private lives, outside their roles as students and highly trained workers. Informal teaching is certainly a significant part of consumer publishing, in areas as varied as religion (the Bible), science (*A Brief History of Time*), history (*Guns, Germs and Steel*), cooking (*Rachel Ray Express Lane Meals*), and ethics (*The Book of Virtues*). Noneducational genres are also a major part of consumer book publishing; these include everything from romance novels to joke books to travel books. Publishing personnel use these subject classifications and many more when they create titles.

When it comes to defining the major categories of the consumer book-publishing business, though, publishers identify them quite differently. Using terms originated by the Association of American Publishers (AAP), people involved in publishing talk about the following categories:

- Trade
- Mass market paperback
- Religious
- Book club
- Mail order
- University press
- Subscription reference

Rather than describing the subject matter of books, all the AAP categories (with the exception of religion) refer to the way in which books are distributed or produced. Let's explore each of these categories one at a time. Table 7.1 shows the number of books sold for each of these categories.

Table 7.1 Net Sales of Consumer Books, 2005

Type of book	Number of books (in millions)	Percentage of consumer books shipped
Adult trade	455.9	27.2
Juvenile trade	403.4	24.1
Mass market paperbacks	420.5	25.1
Religious	192	11.5
Book clubs	130.9	7.8
Mail order	44.6	2.7
University press	28.2	1.7
Total	1,675.5	100.1

Trade Books **Trade books**—general-interest titles, including both fiction and nonfiction books—are typically sold to consumers through retail bookstores (both traditional and Web-based) and to libraries.

Publishing personnel further distinguish between adult and juvenile trade books. In 2005, they shipped about 456 million of the former and 403 million of the latter to retailers. Employees also distinguish between trade books that are *hardcover* ($1.7 billion worth of juvenile and $5.1 billion worth of adult units shipped in 2005) and those that are *paperbound* (a combined total of $5.6 billion shipped).

When it comes to juvenile hardcover sales, sales of the past few years went up and down depending on whether a new *Harry Potter* book emerged. In 2005, for example, *Harry Potter and the Half-Blood Prince*, published by Scholastic in the United States, sold 13.5 million copies and in doing that accounted for 8 percent of all hardback juvenile books sold in the United States. But *Potter* has not been the only large driver of juvenile hardback sales. That same year, the newest title in the immensely popular *Lemony Snicket* series, *The Penultimate Peril*, sold more than 1.7 million copies. Moreover, earlier editions of the series continued to sell so well in 2005 that they claimed the sixth through tenth spots on the list of best-selling hardback juveniles for the year that the trade magazine *Publishers Weekly* (*PW*) compiled. As for children's paperbacks, the *Chronicles of Narnia* fantasy books have been successful due to the release that year of the *Chronicles of Narnia* movie based on them. In fact, in 2005, *Narnia* titles occupied the top nine spots on *PW*'s list of juvenile trade paperbacks.

Mass Market Paperbacks **Trade paperbacks** is a term used to refer to standard-size books that have flexible covers. Smaller, pocket-size paperback books are called **mass market paperbacks.** They are designed to be sold primarily in so-called **mass market outlets**—newsstands, drugstores, discount stores, and supermarkets. Many types of books come in this format, but romance novels and science fiction tales are among the most common.

In recent years, mass market paperbacks have lost some sales to trade paperbacks. Superstore booksellers such as Barnes & Noble prefer to carry the larger books rather than the smaller ones because they are more profitable. Traditional

trade books general-interest titles, including both fiction and nonfiction books, which are typically sold to consumers through retail bookstores and to libraries

trade paperbacks standard-sized books that have flexible covers

mass market paperbacks smaller, pocket-sized paperback books

mass market outlets venues where mass market paperbacks are generally sold, including newsstands, drugstores, discount stores, and supermarkets

275

Harry Potter Goes Green

I'm sure you can think of dozens of items that are made from recycled paper—from greeting cards and letterheads to paper towels and grocery bags. But did you know that books can be added to this list?

Publishers have been printing selected manuscripts on recycled paper since the late 1990s. Yet it was J. K. Rowling's *Harry Potter and the Deathly Hallows* that took eco-friendly publishing to a whole new level. When the book was released in 2007, it was printed on recycled paper in sixteen countries, including in Canada, where publisher Rainforest has been printing the *Harry Potter* series on "green" paper since 2003.

Scholastic, the series' U.S. publisher, agreed to print the first 12 million copies of *the Deathly Hallows* on paper made from at least 30 percent post-consumer waste fiber. In addition, the 100,000 deluxe editions were printed on 100 percent recycled paper. According to a report from the Canadian organization Markets Initiative, which works with book publishers to shift their titles onto eco-friendly papers, the

English-language editions of this book will save more than 197,000 trees, an area 2.5 times the size of Central Park.

The efforts of Rainforest, Scholastic, and other *Harry Potter* publishers around the world have set a precedent in the book industry. An estimated 300 publishers have since announced plans to increase the number of books they print on eco-friendly papers, while dozens of printers have begun to stock recycled paper.

Sarah Nelson, editor-in-chief of the trade magazine *Publishers Weekly*, reaffirmed the book's lasting legacy on the industry. "The world of publishing may never see the likes of *Harry Potter* again, but that doesn't discount its importance to readers, to the booksellers and to the way publishing has melded its needs with that of the environment."

Sources: Alana Herro, "Harry Potter Fights Evil, Saves Trees," Worldwatch Institute, online, accessed 7/30/07, www.worldwatch. org; Jessica Goldberg, "How Harry Potter's Saving Trees," *E-magazine*, online, accessed 7/30/07, http://www.emagazine.com/view/ ?3819

---

mass market locations have begun to carry the larger books as well. In response, publishers of mass market paperbacks have begun to release so-called premium paperbacks. They are a couple of dollars more expensive than regular mass market paperbacks, but they feature larger type than regular mass market paperbacks, and look classier. Early indications are that the new format may well be a success.

religious books trade books that contain specifically religious content

Religious Books   As noted earlier, of the categories of consumer books, "religious" is the only one that centers on the content of books. **Religious books** are essentially trade books that contain specifically religious content. They are sold in general bookstores as well as in special religious bookshops. The success of this category seems to vary with the level of interest in the topic. Judging by unit sales, interest seems to have dropped sharply during the 1980s, but rebounded equally as powerfully during the 1990s and 2000s. In 2005, revenue from the sale of religious books in the U.S. was $3 billion. That figure includes sales of the Bible, the bestselling book of all time. It also includes Joel Osteen's books *Your Best Life Now*, which was the bestselling religious book of that year.

book clubs organizations through which individuals who have joined can select books from the club's catalog and purchase them through the mail or via the club's website, often at a discounted price

Book Clubs   This industry category is used for books distributed through **book clubs,** organizations through which individuals who have joined can select books from the club's catalog and purchase them through the mail or via the club's website, often at a discounted price. There are general-interest clubs, such as Book-of-the-Month Club, and special-interest clubs that aim at people with specific enthusiasms—cooking, the outdoors, history, the military, and many other topics. When you join a club, you get a certain number of books for a small amount of money, and then the company sends you a catalog every month with new choices that you can purchase. Sometimes the initial membership agreement requires you to purchase a certain number of books during the course of the year. Traditionally, book clubs have worked on a **negative-option plan**: unless you specifically cancel your membership, you will continue to receive books on a monthly basis. In addition, the book club will send you its "main selection" every month unless you request some other action. In recent years, though, Bookspan, the company that owns the Book-of-the-Month Club, has allowed members to choose their books instead of sending the company's book choice to them.

Most book clubs do not originate books; instead they acquire the right to sell the publishers' books to club members. These rights are typically exclusive; that is, no other book club will be allowed to offer that particular book. Once it has these rights, the book club typically contracts with a printer to create a separate edition of the book for its members. In a nation with so many bookstores and the Internet to find books, though, the allure of book clubs is not huge. The entire sales of this publishing segment amounted to $1.3 billion, a small fraction of consumer trade book sales. One area where book clubs do seem to be getting some traction, and where Bookspan is placing a lot of its energies, is in creating niche book clubs that help readers find books of quite special interests and that encourage web-based book discussions among members.

Mail-order Books   You've undoubtedly seen TV ads or received promotional mailings for books on home repair, the Civil War, or gardening. You call an 800 number and give the operator your credit card number, and within several days the book shows up on your doorstep. That's **mail order.**

Both book clubs and mail order businesses ship titles directly to the consumer. The principal difference between the two is that the mail order publisher actually originates new titles—creates new, original books—whereas the book club sells existing titles. Mail order publishing has been taking a much smaller role in the book industry over the last fifteen years. In fact, the biggest force in the industry, Time Warner, sold its famous Time-Life Books mail order business in 2005. Although mail order sales made up 10.5 percent of the U.S. consumer book industry in 1982, the number had dropped to 2.7 percent in 2005. Of course, people still buy many books through the mail—for example, after ordering online from http://www.amazon.com—but this book-selling business does not fit the definition of mail order.

University Press Books   The nature of the publisher, not the distribution method, is what defines this AAP category. In truth, **university press books** could fit several of the categories previously named, since they are essentially trade books that end up in libraries and bookstores. Some of their titles are sold primarily through the mail to scholars who are interested in particular topics.

Why, then, the separate label? Presumably, this is because people in the book publishing industry believe that university presses are a different kind of publisher. Typically, they are not-for-profit divisions of universities, colleges, museums, or research institutions, and they publish mostly scholarly materials—that is, books that are read by professors and graduate students. Even when they publish titles that have broad popular interest and end up in bookstores, the AAP and industry convention is not to lump those titles into the "trade" categories, but still to consider them university press books.

negative-option plan   a membership agreement under which a consumer continues to receive a product until the agreement is fulfilled or the subscription is cancelled

mail order books   books that are advertised on TV or in promotional mailings that can be ordered directly from the publisher and are shipped to the consumer's home

university press books scholarly titles published by not-for-profit divisions of universities, colleges, museums, or research institutions

subscription reference books titles such as "great books" series, dictionaries, atlases, and sets of encyclopedias that are marketed by their publishers to consumers on a door-to-door or direct-mail basis; the distribution typically involves one large package deal—several volumes at a time—with a deferred payment schedule

Subscription Reference Books   The term **subscription reference books** refers to "great books" series, dictionaries, atlases, and sets of encyclopedias that are marketed by their publishers to consumers on a door-to-door or direct-mail basis. It is a separate category from mail order because the distribution typically involves one large package deal—several volumes at a time—with a deferred payment schedule.

Consumers receive the encyclopedia or set of "great books" right away, but they pay for the material by subscription, over a number of months. Perhaps your parents bought the *World Book Encyclopedia* or *Encyclopedia Britannica* in this way; millions of people have done so. During the past two decades, this category has been affected negatively by the rise of Internet references; the *Britannica* and *World Book* are themselves available online. Their sales have remained a tiny 0.1 percent (that's one-tenth of one percent) of book industry sales.

Variety and Specialization in Book Publishing

No matter how obscure a subject is, there is probably a book about it. In fact, there may even be a publisher specializing in the topic. Take a virtual stroll through many of these titles via your nearest university library's catalog or through the "subject" section in *Books in Print*, a reference volume that you can find in print or online in any library or bookstore. Even though you've been dealing with books all your life, a close examination of the breadth of titles available is likely to surprise you.

Are you interested in maritime issues? *Literary Marketplace*, a standard reference volume on book publishing, lists sixty-one imprints in the United States that deal with the subject. Among the other specialties noted, fifty-two firms mention Hindu religion, forty-seven note real estate, thirty-seven list wine and spirits, and twenty-two claim veterinary science. Many of the publishers involved are quite small. Names such as Cornell Maritime Press, International Marina Institute, Lloyds of London Press, and Naval Institute Press are not exactly household names. *Literary Marketplace* devotes more than ten pages to listing "small presses," which it considers to be firms that publish fewer than three books per year. Among those included in the 2005 edition were Anti-Aging Press of Coral Gables, Florida; Moonstone Press of Potomac, Maryland; and Quillpen Publishing of Trenton, Michigan.

Financing Book Publishing

These examples only begin to suggest the immensity of the book-publishing business in the U.S. Approximately 83,000 publishing houses issue about 291,000 new titles or editions every year, producing a total of more than two billion copies of books each year.[2]

Part of the reason for this huge number is that publishing a basic book really doesn't cost that much, although some titles (such as this textbook) can be very expensive to put together. For a few thousand dollars, a person can put out a handsome product. The low entry costs allow zealous entrepreneurs or people who are committed to disseminating certain ideas to get in on the activity.

Typically, these companies can stay afloat if they find a highly specialized niche. Belnice Books, for example, concentrates on puppet and drama books for children, parents, and teachers; it has published one or two titles a year since 1981. Falcon Company, founded in 1941 and based in San Diego, California, centers its output on studio ceramics and crafts. Examples are *Ceramic Woodchimes* and *Advanced Ceramic Manual*. Bess Press, founded in 1976, is a Honolulu, Hawaii-based publisher that issues various books on Hawaiian and Pacific history and culture.

Although many small publishers are founded every year, a handful of companies still dominate the most lucrative areas of the book-publishing business. Here are a few examples:

- Three titles—*Merriam Webster*, *Random House*, and *American Heritage*—regularly dominate the field of English-language dictionaries, with a combined 90 percent or greater share.
- Under various imprints, only five publishers accounted for 88 percent of hardcover consumer trade books on the U.S. bestseller lists in 2006. In order of their shares of books on the list, these publishers were:
  —Random House
  —Penguin
  —Simon & Schuster
  —Hachette Book Group, USA
  —Holtzbrinck
  —Hyperion
- Moreover, five of those same companies made the list of seven firms that accounted for 90 percent of all consumer books on the paperback bestseller lists. The top seven were:
  —Random House
  —Penguin
  —Simon & Schuster
  —Hachette
  —HarperCollins
  —Holtzbrinck
  —Houghton Mifflin[3]

These figures raise a logical question: if producing a book is often so relatively inexpensive, how is it that only a few companies dominate parts of the industry? The answer is that some parts of book publishing can be extremely expensive, and the greatest expenses are typically related to aspects other than the physical creation of the book.

The overwhelming majority of publishers do not own the basic machinery of bookmaking—a printing press and a machine that places bindings on finished pages. Typically, publishers contract out these services to firms that specialize in these activities. Publishers also contract out **composition** services, the work involved in inserting into a manuscript the codes and conventions that tell the page-making program or the printing press how the material should look on the page.

If color photographs and special layouts are involved, this kind of work can be quite expensive. To sell the book at a reasonable price, the publisher has to sell many thousands of copies simply to make back the manufacturing costs. Still, the ability to contract out such services at reasonable costs is what makes the mere entry into book publishing so easy.

At its heart, though, book publishing is not really about writing, editing, or printing. It is about finding, preparing, marketing, distributing, and exhibiting titles in ways that will get particular audiences to notice them and buy them. This process takes place in different ways in different sectors of the industry. Much more money is required in some sectors than in others to compete at the top level. As a result,

composition the work involved in inserting into a manuscript the codes and conventions that tell the pagemaking program or the printing press how the material should look on the page

in these sectors, the wealthiest companies can take the lead and keep it. To give you a sense of what book publishing means, we'll focus on comparing adult hardcover trade publishing and university press publishing from the standpoint of production, distribution, and exhibition.

Production in the Book Publishing Industry

As we've noted, the production of books involves finding them and preparing them for the marketplace. The same basic activities take place at every kind of book publisher.

Production in Trade Publishing

acquisitions editor a person who recruits and signs new authors and titles for the company's list of books

royalties shares of a book's sales income which are paid to an author, usually based upon the number of copies sold

An **acquisitions editor** recruits and signs new authors and titles for the company's list of books. In major firms, because of the cost of running the company, acquisitions editors must find and produce a certain number of new titles that have a certain sales potential. The titles can come as completed manuscripts or as proposals for manuscripts. A contract is drawn up that promises payments to the author. Sometimes the payments are in the form of a flat fee for producing the work. Often the payments are in the form of **royalties**—shares of the sales income, usually based on the number of copies sold. After the acquisitions editor receives a completed manuscript, permission to go ahead with publication must typically be granted by an executive committee (sometimes called a publication board) of the firm. Once the go ahead is received, the manuscript goes to a developmental editor. That person reads and edits the work carefully in order to make sure that it is clear and internally consistent. After the author addresses the developmental editor's suggestions, the manuscript is transmitted from the developmental editor to a production editor in the production department. The production editor then arranges all of the technical aspects of the book—from design, to pagination, to copyediting—until the book is in final page-proof form (see Figure 7.2).

This process sounds straightforward, but it can be quite complex. Probably the hardest step is the first, and it belongs to the acquisitions editor—identifying the "right" manuscript. You might not think that finding manuscripts would be a big deal; we all know people who are eager to get their ideas into print. Yet acquisitions editors will tell you that they have to deal with two major considerations when they sift through proposals: they have to find topics that match the personality of their imprint, and they have to find authors who can write ably about those topics and whose books can make profits for the firm. Getting the topic and the author together is the really hard part, the editors will tell you. Not surprisingly, acquisitions editors have developed strategies to overcome this challenge and reduce their risk of failure. These strategies require the editor to be familiar with the sales goals of the firm, with the intended audience, and with the way in which books are marketed to that audience.

literary agent a person who, on behalf of a client, markets the client's manuscripts to editors, publishers, and other buyers, based upon knowledge of the target market and the specific content of the manuscript

Adult hardcover trade acquisitions editors rarely read unsolicited manuscripts or proposals for manuscripts unless these are brought to them by known literary agents. **Literary agents** are people who, on behalf of a client, market the client's manuscripts to editors, publishers, and other buyers, based upon knowledge of the target market and the specific content of the manuscript. These agents work for companies called *literary agencies* and act as the initial eyes and ears of trade editors. Agents understand the personalities of different imprints, and they make their

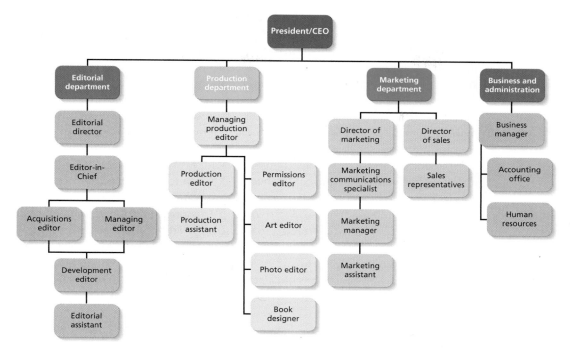

Figure 7.2
The Organizational Structure of a Typical Book Publishing House

pitches to the ones best suited to particular authors. This system saves editors enormous amounts of work, although some authors undoubtedly fall through the cracks because of it. If an agent succeeds in placing a work, the agent receives a commission, typically 10 percent of all income related to the book that is received by the author.

Trade presses usually sell their titles through bookstores. Consumers find out about them by browsing through the shelves, reading reviews in newspapers and magazines, or noting discussions with the author in print or on TV.

In hardcover trade publishing, achieving success with a book means selling at least 50,000 copies. Achieving **bestseller** status means selling more than 75,000 hardcover copies or 100,000 paperback copies. And beyond the bestseller looms the realm of the **blockbuster,** which is a book that sells well over 100,000 hardcover copies—constituting an immense success. Major trade presses spend enormous amounts of money on marketing and publicity departments that have the expertise and resources to take books with the potential to be bestsellers or blockbusters and help them to sell the requisite number of copies. The acquisitions editor's job is to find books with that potential.

bestseller   a title that has sold more than 75,000 hardcover copies or more than 100,000 paperback copies

blockbuster   a title that has sold well over 100,000 hardcover copies

Production at a University Press

Publishing at a university press is very different from adult hardcover trade publishing in this respect: in university press publishing, a "hit" realistically means selling several thousand copies. A title reaches hit status if it commands respect from professors, who then tell their students and university libraries to buy it.

The different pressures on scholarly and trade publishers lead to quite different approaches to recruiting and acquiring authors whose books may or may not be hits. To reduce the risk that academics will not like their books, editors at scholarly presses will try to get manuscripts by well-known professors from well-known universities. Because acquiring only books from these professors would not yield enough titles for their lists, the editors go after the next best thing: young professors on their way up the academic ladder. To find them, the editors turn to consultants: well-known academics with a reputation for being able to spot innovative new work in their field that their colleagues are likely to appreciate. Sometimes these academics get paid for their services. In addition to the help of consultants, many academic editors will read unsolicited manuscripts sent to them by professors from around the country in the hope of finding something good.

In contrast to the way trade books are sold, university presses usually publicize their books at academic conferences and by mail. Academic associations rent space at their conventions to booksellers. Salespeople set out titles that they think the professors and graduate students who are attending the convention might like and discuss the books with interested passersby. In addition, the marketing departments of these publishing companies send brochures specifically to academics that specialize in a book's topic; the brochures contain descriptions of the author and the topic along with blurbs by other professors who like the work.

Books on Demand

TECH & INFRASTRUCTURE

Publishers are well aware that not every book will top the bestseller list. In fact, most books sell no more than a few thousand copies, leading wary publishers to weed through submitted manuscripts carefully, looking for appealing titles. As a result, many manuscripts that are on specialized topics or that are written by unknown authors fail to get published because of business constraints, even if they are well written. These manuscripts may find life in a new method of book publishing: books on demand.

Instead of printing a batch of several thousand books, books are printed individually as they are demanded. Gopher PLC, a Scotland-based publishing house, operates in this way. An author may submit a manuscript, just as he or she would to any publishing house. If a work is approved, an editor prepares the manuscript while an artist perfects the cover and the layout. Gopher supports the work just like any other publisher; the only difference is that each book is printed only when needed. Books are stored electronically, which allows for easy editing, storage, sending, and printing of a manuscript. When a client selects a specific title via the Internet, the order is sent to Gopher's digital printing press, where a 300-page book can be printed and bound in three minutes. The book is then packaged and sent to the customer.

One such digital press is the InstaBook Maker, which takes up less than a square meter of space and can print seventy-two book pages a minute. After the last page is printed, it takes only seventeen seconds for the book to be completed. The size and speed of new digital printers allow for cheaper and quicker printing, making on-demand publishing possible and potentially quite profitable. Books can be stored electronically and accessed through the Internet, allowing a manuscript to be sent from anywhere to the printer.

Not only is InstaBook Maker being used at publishing houses like Gopher and the U.S.-based Denlinger's Publishers, but it is also being made available to the public. In 2004, the independent bookstore Bookends in Ridgewood, New Jersey, became home to America's first in-store print-on-demand publishing system. As Victor Celorio, president of InstaBook Corp, said, "We believe that Bookends, with its long tradition as a home for people who write books and people who read books, is the perfect place to show what the InstaBook Maker can add to the literary community."

Sources: Susan Mansfield, "Books to the Future," *Aberdeen Press and Journal*, June 17, 2000, features, p. 15, "First Digital Bookstore and Self Publishing Center Launches in the United States," May 12, 2004. Press Release. Online.

Book Production and the Electronic Age

During the past few years, the biggest book publishers have been active in creating books for the electronic market—placing titles for sale online at the same or a lower price than hard-copy versions. Some observers have wondered what the rush is about, since there is actually rather little money being made from the sale of electronic books. Portable, high-resolution viewers for downloading and reading e-books are quite expensive and rather clunky, they point out. Moreover, they ask, why would people want to read consumer books from a screen when they can crawl into bed or lounge in an airport reading a portable paperback version? Daniel O'Brien, an analyst who studies electronic books for Forrester Research, calls electronic books a solution in search of a problem. "Our research with consumers indicates very little interest in reading on a screen," he told the *New York Times*. "Maybe someday, but not in a five-year time frame. Books are pretty elegant."

Still, many in the industry are more optimistic. Jack Romanos, president of Simon & Schuster, one of the first traditional publishers to begin selling electronic books, argues that "the logic of electronic books is pretty hard to refute—we see it as an incremental increase in sales as a new form of books for adults and especially for the next generation of readers."

Some saw the gold rush accelerating after best-selling horror author Stephen King posted his thriller, *The Plant*, on the Web in 2000. Readers could go to his site (http://www.stephenking.com), read a sample of the book, and—if they liked what they read—could make an online payment and download the entire book. King declared on his site that he and readers could become publishing's worst nightmare. However, few people continued to pay for installments, and within months King wrote on his site that he would not continue the story for the foreseeable future. Despite the failure, King and others insisted that cyberspace was a place where an author could sell books without a publisher. Publishing executives realized, however, that even online authors need the marketing and accounting expertise that publishers provide. They rushed to be the first to conquer cyberspace for fiction and nonfiction writers.

The result is that in the early years of the twenty-first century, major book publishers, technology companies, online booksellers, and new electronic book middlemen are experimenting with digital books. The atmosphere is rich with innovation, although it's still not clear how big the market is. In 2007, Amazon injected excitement into the e-book business by coming out with the Kindle, a $399 wireless portable reading device with which customers could download books from Amazon as well as subscribe to a variety of newspapers and magazines. Amazon boasted that it sold out its initial inventory in five hours. Nevertheless, skeptics insist that there is no large interest among consumers for such gizmos and that Amazon's costs selling books through the device would likely exceed its returns.[4] Supporters of digital readers argue that in the years to come increased portability, clarity—and the saving of trees—will win over huge proportions of readers. Clearly, the jury is still out.

One area that clearly seems to have had some success is the sale of textbooks in digital form. A number of school districts around the United States have experimented with giving their students laptops loaded with their textbooks instead of giving hard copies of the books. By doing that the districts can get updates of the books every year more cheaply; the kids can use the laptops for their work at school and at home; and the children's backs aren't strained terribly by the weight of heavy textbooks that they must lug home every day.

Another area that has drawn the interest of academic publishers is the release of books online and offline at the same time. Yochai Benkler's 2006 book *The Wealth of Networks*, about the social and economic implications of the Internet, is an example. Yale University Press allowed Benkler to post it on the Web at the same time that the company sold it through traditional channels. The logic was that most of the people who got a taste of the nearly 500-page book online would be enticed to purchase the physical book. But Yale, MIT Press, the University of Michigan Press and other academic presses are trying to push beyond the boundaries of traditional publishing in their online activities. Sometimes authors invite comments about the book online in order to encourage serious discussion of the topic. In some cases, the author uses the discussion to create an updated, corrected, or extended edition of the book, which may eventually be published in traditional as well as digital form. Will all of this pay for itself? Is there truly a reasonable business model here? The leaders of major university presses aren't sure, but they believe it is in their interest and in the interest of scholarship to find out.

In the long run, it may well be that electronic book publishing is, to quote the editor in chief of *Publishers Weekly*, "the next major thing after Gutenberg." Still, don't hold your breath waiting for the disappearance of the book. Even the just-quoted editor was adamant that books won't go away. What seems certain is that book industry executives will respond to competitive pressures from electronic and other currents around them.

Ethical Pitfalls in Book Production

The process of finding and developing ideas and authors for books is filled with ethical pitfalls for authors, agents, and publishers. One of the biggest issues is that of stealing ideas. **Plagiarism**—using parts of another person's work without citing or otherwise crediting the original author—unfortunately seems to be much more common than many in publishing would like to believe. Sometimes such an act is clearly illegal, as when an author lifts sentences or paragraphs from copyrighted material. Plagiarism is not illegal when the author uses material that has not been protected by copyright; however, it remains a serious breach of ethics.

plagiarism using parts of another person's work without citing or otherwise crediting the original author

Kaavya Viswanathan's 2006 debut novel *How Opal Mehta Got Kissed, Got Wild, and Got a Life* was recalled by its publisher after accusations of plagiarism.

Ethical Issues for Authors Literary scholars and critics have concluded that many writers have been guilty of plagiarism, although the issue rarely makes the front pages. You might remember the recent case of Harvard student, Kaavya Viswanathan. In 2006, Little Brown publishing company released her first novel, *How Opal Mehta Got Kissed, Got Wild, and Got a Life*. Soon afterwards, her publisher asked bookstores to remove the book from their shelves after it confirmed accusations that she used paragraphs from two other novels without citing them. One of the most prominent authors to be accused of plagiarism in recent years was Alex Haley, the author of *Roots*,

Plagiarism in the Twenty-first Century

CRITICAL CONSUMER

During the last decade, a slew of plagiarism scandals have plagued the publishing industry. Among the most noteworthy was the allegation that legendary singer Bob Dylan stole lyrics from nineteenth-century poet Henry Timrod. Another recent case involved a Harvard student whose debut publication had to be reworked after it was found to be strikingly similar to several other novels.

One plausible explanation for the recent surge in plagiarism accusations is the rise of the Internet, which makes it easier for artists and audiences alike to find similarities between works of different authors. Furthermore, as the *San Francisco Chronicle*'s Steven Winn notes of the digital age, "From the Napster wars to hypertext publishing to the Supreme Court's decision to extend copyright protection by 20 years, the fundamental concepts of public domain, authorial primacy and shared cultural legacy are up for grabs."

Yet Charles Isherwood, a columnist for the *New York Times*, suggests that there is a more subtle reason for the explosion of plagiarism cases in the early years of the twenty-first century. According to Isherwood, we have witnessed "a shift in cultural attitudes toward the meaning and uses of personal experience." He continues, "We are living in an age marked by heightened sensitivity to the idea of one's own life, and one's own words, as a commodity with prospective commercial value."

Isherwood conjectures that as artists become increasingly fearful of plagiarism, they may stop drawing inspiration from the past. "Shakespeare drew on Plutarch's lives; Henry James's notebooks were filled with what he called données, bits of dinner party gossip that occasionally bloomed into fictional flower; innumerable historical novels have drawn on biographies and memoirs," he gives as examples of great literature which have been based on others' work.

As we enter into a new era of technology—and of cultural expression, it will no doubt become increasingly important to determine where to draw the line between inspiration and plagiarism.

Sources: Charles Isherwood, "Her Life, His Art, Your Call," *New York Times*, December 3, 2006, online: http://www.nytimes.com; Steven Winn, "The Lines, They Were A-Changin' But Not Enough To Save Dylan From Plagiarism Accusations," *San Francisco Chronicle*, July 17, 2003, online: http://www.sfgate.com

the bestselling book that became one of the most-viewed television miniseries of all time. In 1978, Harold Courlander sued Haley for extensively lifting material for *Roots* from Courlander's book *The African*. That book itself did quite well when it appeared in 1967: it sold 300,000 and was translated into several languages.

Haley eventually agreed to settle. Courlander received $650,000 just before the judge issued a ruling. Yet until Haley's death, he continued to claim that the numerous similarities between the books were unintentional and minor, even though a lot of evidence introduced in court indicated that he had used *The African* substantially in writing *Roots*. Courlander himself felt that the basic issue of copying never really made it onto the public agenda. He noted that although he had felt vindicated at the time of the court settlement, public interest in the incident quickly disappeared. Haley, he added, "was a very persuasive public speaker" who dismissed questions about the settlement. "Nobody really raised the issue of literary ethics, and he continued to receive honorary degrees—it didn't slow him up. This troubled me. No one seemed interested in the basic issues," Courlander said.

Ethical Issues for Editors and Literary Agents Editors and literary agents, as well as authors, also confront major ethical issues. Let's say you're an editor and you get a manuscript chapter out of the blue from an unknown author.

She proposes a nonfiction book about how mothers who travel frequently on business balance home and work. You don't know the writer and you don't intend to use her. You do, however, like the topic, and you can think of at least two authors who have written for you who would do a great job with such a book. What do you do? Should you go ahead with it? Is it ethical to take one person's ideas for a book and pay someone else to write it?

Or, let's say you are a literary agent just starting out on your own. You already represent a few authors, but you need to bring in more money. You know that among literary agents, the rule is that you charge a percentage of an author's earnings, but you do not demand a fee for simply representing an author. The reason is that agents who accept fees have been known to represent authors simply to get their money, not because the agents really thought the authors would succeed in finding a publisher. You also know, however, that there are many aspiring writers out there who would love to have your input, even for a fee. You tell yourself you can be honest with them. Should you do it?

Reducing the Risks of Failure During the Production Process

These sorts of questions come up all the time as authors, agents, and editors struggle to make books, and in turn, to see those books make money. Book publishers use a number of strategies to reduce the risk of failure. Among them are:

- Conducting prepublication research
- Making use of authors with positive track records
- Offering authors advances on royalties

Let's look at each of these strategies individually.

prepublication research research conducted in order to gauge a title's chances of success with its likely audience

Conducting Prepublication Research   You might wonder whether companies involved in publishing university press and trade books conduct **prepublication research** to gauge a title's chances of success with their likely audiences. In fact, they do, but they do it in a rather informal way. Editors may meet with people who are representative of their audience and ask them questions about the book being developed. In scholarly publishing, editors often pay a few professors to read the manuscript and comment on its prospects for success. Going a lot further in research—testing each title with large numbers of likely consumers to gauge their reactions—might raise the expense of publishing the book so much that if it was to make a profit, it would have to be priced at an unrealistically high level. The only systematic research that publishing executives carry out regularly is seeing how previous books on a topic sold. That information gives them an indication of whether going ahead with the book is worth the company's money.

track record the previous successes or failures of a product, person, or organization

Making Use of Track Records   Of course, some authors have already proved their worth: they have **track records,** or histories of successes, in the book marketplace. Editors naturally like to sign these authors because doing so lowers the risk of failure. The authors' names are so well known in their area of publishing that their new titles almost sell themselves.

In academic publishing, prestige tends to be the best tool for successfully snagging an author with a substantial track record. Typically, the acquisitions editor who wants to snag such authors must work for one of the most prestigious scholarly presses—Harvard, Yale, Cambridge, Oxford, MIT, Chicago and a few others.

Targeting in the Book Industry

CRITICAL CONSUMER

We live in a highly segmented media world where TV programs, radio stations, magazine titles, and websites are targeted to specific groups of people in a society. It is perhaps not surprising, then, that the book industry is becoming increasingly segmented.

One noteworthy change in the industry has been the explosive growth of niche imprints tailored to reach such groups as women, Christians, and conservatives. Many publishing houses have also launched imprints to cater to racial minorities including Random House's One World Books, which emphasizes African authors, and Rayo, HarperCollins' Latino imprint.

Another site of increased segmentation in the book industry is on the exhibition front. Many bookstores segment literature by race, including Borders, which has for decades featured a separate African-American authors section.

To some, the rise of minority imprints and separate bookstore sections makes it easy for people to find books that they can relate to. This, in turn, helps certain groups to maintain a distinct cultural identity.

Yet others wonder whether organizing books by categories such as race makes it difficult for authors to secure a mainstream audience. On a larger level, these practices may reify group divisions. Commenting on bookstores' segregation of African-American authors, longtime publisher Bennett J. Johnson says it "reinforces the notion that the United States remains a nation of 'two separate societies'."

Wall Street Journal reporter Jeffrey A. Trachtenberg describes these two arguments as a "debate between assimilation and maintaining a distinct identity." Which side of the debate do you fall on and why?

Sources: "Emerging Majorities Influence Publishers, Retailers to Develop Targeted Imprints and Books," *Marketing to the Emerging Majorities*, July 1, 2007, Volume 19, Issue 7, Factiva database; Jeffrey A. Trachtenberg, "Why Book Industry Sees the World Split Still by Race," *Wall Street Journal*, December 6, 2006: p. A1.

Of course, the most prestigious presses continue to collect the most prestigious academic authors, and thus to dominate the scholarly sector.

In adult trade publishing, almost anything goes with regard to authors with positive track records or authors who for other reasons are expected to have high sales. The authors who garner large advances and are successful in sales are often those who are:

- Previously hugely successful (John Grisham, Stephen King, Patricia Cornwell)
- Controversial (Senator and Presidential candidate Hillary Clinton, former *New York Times* reporter Jayson Blair, cultural critic Michael Eric Dyson)
- Well known outside of book publishing (Madonna, Larry King)

Offering Advances on Royalties   Offering authors an **advance on royalties**—a payment before the book is published of money that the publisher anticipates the author earning through royalties on the book—to sign a contract is not as common in academic as in trade publishing, possibly because academic titles do not sell that many copies and possibly because the firms can lure academic writers without advances, as they are called. The amount of money that trade publishers offer in order to lure star authors can be impressive. For example, Simon & Schuster offered Houston televangelist Joel Osteen $10 million in 2006 for the right to publish his 2007 book, *Become a Better You*. The reason? His book *Your Best Life Now: 7 Steps to Living at Your Potential*, published by small publisher

advance on royalties   a payment before the book is published of money that the publisher anticipates the author earning through royalties on the book

Preacher Joel Osteen, whose internationally televised services at Lakewood Church in Texas reach millions of viewers each week, reportedly received a more than $10 million advance from Simon & Schuster to publish his 2007 book, *Become a Better You*. The advance was based on the success of his 2004 book *Your Best Life Now*, which sold millions of copies for its publisher, FaithWords.

Faithwords, had sold millions of copies since its release in 2004. Probably at least as important was that its audience bought audiobooks, calendars, and other spinoffs that seemed to suggest the pastor's writing career has legs. He also has television and radio gigs that continually keep him in the eye of the people who would buy his books.

When such large deals are signed, observers inevitably ask if they are worth the money. Sometimes they loudly conclude they aren't. Consider the case of *Thirteen Moons*, the second novel by Charles Frazier. Frazier's previous (and first) novel was *Cold Mountain*, which the relatively small Atlantic Monthly Press published. As a result of the huge success of that book, Random House grabbed him from Atlantic Monthly by offering Frazier an $8 million advance for *Thirteen Moons*.

Publishers Weekly called it the highest amount ever paid for a single novel and questioned the logic of the publisher's action. The magazine's reasoning went this way: "Random ordered a 500,000-copy first printing. As of January 22, Nielsen BookScan reported 225,000 copies sold, though Random House says total sales are closer to 300,000 copies. For most books, that would be impressive. But *PW* calculates that, based on standard publishing formulas, Random needs to sell about a million hardcovers and two million paperbacks to earn out its advance."[5] That, *PW* suggested, was unlikely.

Those who are involved with the deals clearly believe that they are worth it. In addition to considering whether the book will sell enough in hardcover to justify the advance, the publishing firm considers the title's future attraction to paperback and foreign publishers. The reason is that in return for the advance, the hardback publisher typically gets the opportunity to sell the paperback and foreign rights to other publishers. In the case of an attractive title, the hardback publisher might make back a substantial portion of the advance through the sale of these rights. As the advance to Osteen suggests, the largest advances typically go to authors whose involvement in other media can help them sell copies. A title based on a popular movie or one that is written by a popular sports figure will similarly have the instant recognition among certain audiences that will help it move off the shelves.

Of course, not all titles succeed, no matter what strategies the publishers might have taken to reduce the risk of failure. *Publishers Weekly* lists standard reasons that books with hopes for great sales ended in disappointment: "one too many sequels, a book where a magazine article would do, a celebrity whose day has come and gone." When a string of similar books sells strongly at the outset but ends with disappointing sales, acquisitions editors generalize about what people appear not to want to buy anymore, at least for a while. It also works the other way. When one or two books on a topic take off, editors begin to think a trend is at work and they look for books that relate to the same or similar topics. The large number of Sudoku puzzle books pouring into stores is one example. Another, perhaps stranger and more tentative example, is a seeming mini-trend of books that try to promote atheism. *Publishers Weekly* pointed out in 2007 that at the same time that religious books were selling well, three titles against religion had also been garnering large numbers of readers: Christopher Hitchens' *God Is Not Great: How Religion Poisons Everything* (published by Twelve), Richard Dawkins' *The God Delusion* (Houghton Mifflin) and Sam Harris' *Letter to a Christian Nation* (Knopf). A *PW* reporter noted that "These brainy, skeptical takes on God and religion have quickly ascended to the top of national bestseller lists" and in interviewing editors found they saw the topic as a reaction to fundamentalism among substantial segments of U.S. society. To them, that meant room for more, and a chance for substantial sales. As a Houghton Mifflin editor said, "If another great book came along tomorrow that I felt really advanced the issue, I'd snap it up."6

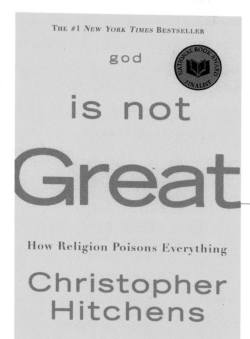

THE #1 NEW YORK TIMES BESTSELLER

god

is not

Great

How Religion Poisons Everything

Christopher Hitchens

When books on a particular topic begin to sell well, publishers take notice of the trend and look to publish similar books to capitalize on demand. Christopher Hitchens' *God Is Not Great* was one of three skeptical books on religion to top bestseller lists in 2007.

Distribution in the Book Industry

Ideas that are not well conceived or well executed and trends that have passed their peak can explain the failure of titles in every sector of book publishing, from juvenile hardback to mail order. Similarly, acquisitions editors and other executives in all areas of the industry realize that distribution can play an important part in making or breaking a title. In mail order and book club publishing, effective distribution means making sure that the right customers get the right book catalogs and that their orders get filled on time. In the other publishing sectors, effective distribution means getting the right number of copies of a title to the stores, schools, and libraries that order them.

The Role of Wholesalers in the Distribution Process

The biggest trade publishers—Random House, Simon & Schuster, HarperCollins—distribute books to the largest bookstore chains (Barnes & Noble, Borders, and Books-A-Million) and a few others, such as the online bookseller, http://www.amazon.com. Otherwise, these publishers and others rely on three huge wholesalers—Baker & Taylor, Ingram, and Brodart—to distribute their books to bookstores and libraries. These wholesalers stock huge numbers of titles from a great number of publishers in massive warehouses. This system allows librarians and book dealers to obtain a variety of books more quickly than if they had to order from individual presses.

The process works this way: a wholesaler purchases copies of a book from a publisher at a discount and then resells them to a retailer (the exhibitor) at a somewhat lower discount. Both the wholesaler and the publisher share the risks in their relationship. When a wholesaler purchases a certain number of copies of a title, it

Figure 7.3

The Role of the Wholesaler
The wholesaler plays a crucial role in the book publishing process.

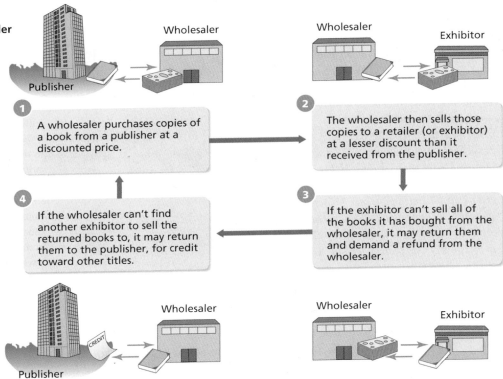

1. A wholesaler purchases copies of a book from a publisher at a discounted price.

2. The wholesaler then sells those copies to a retailer (or exhibitor) at a lesser discount than it received from the publisher.

4. If the wholesaler can't find another exhibitor to sell the returned books to, it may return them to the publisher, for credit toward other titles.

3. If the exhibitor can't sell all of the books it has bought from the wholesaler, it may return them and demand a refund from the wholesaler.

is committing itself to devoting valuable warehouse space to that title and to fulfilling orders for the book. The publisher, though, is not off the hook when the wholesaler receives the title. In the book industry, copies of the book that don't sell can ordinarily be returned to the publisher for credit toward other titles (see Figure 7.3). As a result of this returns policy, publishing executives must be realistic regarding the **print run**, or the number of copies that are printed.

print run   the number of copies that are printed

Assessing a Title's Popularity

Throughout the distribution process, wholesalers keep a careful eye on indicators that help them to gauge how popular a book will be.

Popularity Indicator 1: the Size of the Print Run   The size of the print run signals to wholesalers how popular a publisher expects a book to be. That indication helps the wholesalers decide how many copies of the title to stock. Looking at the publishing imprint also helps. Wholesalers associate certain imprints with certain levels of marketing power as well as with certain types of books. Imprints, therefore, telegraph expected sales. A distributor is more likely to stock up on a title with the Random House imprint than to take a large quantity of a title from Pantheon or Schocken, even though Random House owns those imprints.

Popularity Indicator 2: the Content of Reviews   Review media are also vehicles for estimating the popularity of a forthcoming title. Review media are periodicals such as *Kirkus* and *Choice* that receive early versions of books from their publishers. Review magazine staff members read the books and predict their popularity among different audiences.

Popularity Indicator 3: the Scope of the Marketing Plan   Finally, the publisher's marketing plan serves as a hint to wholesalers about a title's future.

The marketing plan describes the specific ways in which the publisher will get the word out about the title to its target audience. Although the marketing plan of a small university press will probably be limited to a few mailings to appropriate libraries and academics, a trade publisher with high expectations for a title will typically do much more. The firm's publicity department might inform distributors that it will advertise the title in magazines and newspapers that deliver an audience similar to the book's.

In addition, publicists may promise to send the author on a *book tour* that will draw a lot of attention to the title. A **book tour** is a series of appearances that an author makes in various cities in order to promote a title and stimulate sales. The publicist tries to make sure that in each city the author will discuss the book with TV personalities, radio talk show hosts, and newspaper columnists. In addition, publicists might arrange for the author to appear in bookstores to talk about the book and sign copies for customers. The belief in book publishing is that a vigorous and well-put-together book tour can spike the sales of a title substantially.

book tour a series of appearances that an author makes in various cities in order to promote a title and stimulate sales

Exhibition in Book Publishing

The concern that trade publishers and distributors feel about printing and circulating the appropriate number of copies is shared by the stores that exhibit and sell the books to the public. However, this sort of tension is not the norm in publishing for the simple reason that a large percentage of the titles that publishers produce every year do not end up in bookstores. Juvenile books and Bibles are sold in stores, but most university press products end up in libraries. The mail order, subscription, and book club sectors of the industry distribute titles from their warehouses directly to customers. Publishers in those businesses advertise for new customers through television and magazine ads and by phoning prospects whose names they have gotten from companies that rent lists of likely consumers to marketers. In addition to drawing new purchasers, mail order, subscription, and book club publishers face the challenge of maintaining an inventory that piques the buying interests of their customers and keeps them coming back.

Exhibition in Textbook Publishing

Textbooks are yet a different story. The "exhibition" area for el-hi texts is not primarily the schools, it is special evaluation boards that inspect various titles to determine their appropriateness for children in their area. In many states, this evaluation takes place at the state level. California and Texas are the largest states with centralized selection, and board decisions can influence whether a textbook publisher has a chance of selling thousands upon thousands of copies. As you might imagine, textbook company executives pay a lot of attention to the likes and dislikes of members of the selection boards in these states. The executives often instruct their authors to make sure they write in ways that will appeal to the selection boards of California and Texas.

This activity, in turn, has bred resentment among teachers and parents in states that buy fewer books. They have expressed anger that the attitudes of a few people should have so much influence over what American children learn. You may not have known it when you were in grades K through 12, but el-hi textbooks are controversial commodities.

At the college level, the instructors choose the titles they want to use and ask students to buy them. (Sound familiar?) Presumably, if the students don't like the

Huge chain bookstores, like this one owned by Barnes & Noble Booksellers, are the most popular place for buying books in the United States.

text, their feedback will encourage their teachers to look for a replacement. College textbook publishers regularly send professors free copies of new textbooks in the hope that they will like what they see better than they like whatever they are currently using and will order the book for their classes. Acquisitions editors must be alert for new trends in teaching that would suggest new text ideas, even while they encourage authors of current books to update their titles with new editions.

New editions of texts have two purposes. Most obviously, a new edition includes new facts or ideas that have come to light or have been incorporated into the course as it is usually taught since the earlier edition went to press. But there is also a strong marketing motive for new editions. Textbook publishers know that many students sell their texts after they use them and that the books then go on sale in the used-book market. The result is that publishing revenues from an edition plummet after the first year because students purchase used copies. The production of a new edition every three years or so is an attempt to derail this process, since students cannot get the updated version from used-book vendors. Revised versions of popular titles keep textbook publishers in business.

College students have for many years complained about the high price of textbooks. During the last several years, a number of advocacy groups and politicians have taken up their cause, asserting that they are indeed paying too much and that publishers are encouraging professors to order too many extra materials—workbooks and online materials, for example—with the texts. Publishers reply that their costs are high, that the used book market means that many students who sell their books to it pay far less than the original price, and that the extra (or "bundled") materials are useful to instructors and students. Nevertheless, during the past several years a number of states have taken action. Connecticut in 2006 passed a law requiring publishers to disclose textbook prices to college faculty, presumably so they would consider that in their decisions. Virginia in 2005 passed a law discouraging faculty from asking students to buy new editions that are just minimally different from older ones that can be bought on the used-book market. And that year Washington State passed legislation that gives students the option of buying texts without buying CD-ROMS or other bundled materials. In the end, even in these states, the teachers of these college courses do make the final choices.

Exhibition Via Bookstores

Most of us purchase the individual books that we read from bookstores like Barnes & Noble or Borders. Think about where you went the last time you bought a hardback title for yourself or a friend. Did you purchase it from http://www. amazon.com or another online bookseller? (For a discussion of online media, see Chapter 14.) If, like most people, you purchased the title in a place with real doors and shelves, do you remember if it was a chain bookstore or an independent bookseller? An independent bookseller is a company that is based in a particular area and has at most a few locations (often only one). A chain bookstore is part of a large company that has outlets around the United States. Borders, Barnes & Noble, and Books-A-Million are the largest bookstore chains.

Traditionally, the independent bookstore was the place where Americans went to buy hardback trade books. During the past few decades, though, the chains have come on strong. They first appeared in the malls that began to spring up throughout America during the 1960s and 1970s. During the 1990s, they began to emerge as huge, freestanding superstores with more than 60,000 square feet of space; more than 100,000 titles; better prices than the independents; and coffee, croissants, and music to boot. Using sophisticated computer programs, the chains can route different sorts of books to different locations, depending on the population in the area they serve. They also attract customers by bringing touring authors to sign their books.

The independents, which are often family businesses started primarily out of a love for books and whose owners may not have great business skills, have been hard pressed to compete. Not only have their customers been flocking to the chains, but because the word in the industry has been that independent booksellers won't last much longer, wholesalers have shortened the time they give the independents to pay them for books, making it even more difficult for the independents to survive. At the same time, major publishing houses have been extending longer credit terms and more promotional money to the chains. The situation angered the American Booksellers Association (ABA), the organization representing the smaller

Founded in 1953 by poet Lawrence Ferlinghetti and Peter D. Martin, San Francisco's City Lights Bookstore is one of the few truly great independent bookstores still running in the United States.

293

booksellers. In 1994, it filed suit against six publishing companies, charging that they were extending more favorable business terms to chains than to independents.

Five of the six houses settled the cases out of court (Random House didn't), but the ABA noted that independent bookstores were still operating at a competitive disadvantage. By the mid-1990s, it was clear that sales by independents were declining, while those by the chains were growing. In 1995, the chains sold more books than the independents for the first time. Independent booksellers were saying that the arrival of chain stores in an area created instant trouble for them.

Exhibition Via the Web

The rapid spread of home computers and the Internet has already brought about a wealth of changes in the book industry. We've already mentioned online bookstores such as http://www.amazon.com and http://www.barnesandnoble.com. These now regularly sell billions of dollars' worth of books. In the first three months of 2007, for example, Amazon sold $2.8 billion dollars' worth of books.[7] Few book publishing executives believe that Web bookstores will eliminate their material-world ("brick-and-mortar") counterparts, simply because many people like to walk around and look at books to decide what they want. Nevertheless, virtual exhibitors are changing the business, expanding consumers' choices of books and causing more problems for independent retailers.

Amazon is considered the thousand-pound gorilla of book exhibition online. To get a gauge on the current position of Amazon, consider its role in selling the *Harry Potter* book with which we started this chapter. According to Nielsen Bookscan, which claims to cover 65–70% of all exhibition sales, Barnes & Noble beat Amazon as the leading *Hallows* seller in the United States during the first day of its release in July 2007, although Amazon likely sold more copies of the book worldwide than any other company. Borders took third place among the major U.S. outlets. But the big stores were not the only places Americans went to find the title. Many non-chain book outlets also reported strong sales of the title: 2,100 at Anderson's in Naperville, IL; 1,187 at New York City's Strand, while Books of Wonder in New York sold over 1,500; and Skylight Books in Los Angeles sold 400 copies. The owner of Books of Wonder said that his store's midnight party for the *Harry Potter* book was "the best event we've ever had. What was really nice was that because it moved so smoothly, people actually bought other books. It was really one of the highlights of my career as a bookseller."[8] So while the big chains and the online exhibitors are certainly shaping the book business, the smaller book outlets, while sometimes embattled, are not down for the count—at least for now.

Media Literacy and the Book Industry

The adaptation of the book industry to the new media environment underscores two major themes of this text: the convergence of media into digital forms and the blurring of media boundaries. We have seen digital convergence in developments such as the Amazon Reader and the emergence of publishing on the Web. These activities also reflect the blurring of media boundaries, of course. We have also noted other types of boundary blurring, especially when it comes to trade books. Publishers promote trade book titles across a variety of media, from television shows, to magazines, to newspapers, to the Web.

As Chapters 1 and 5 noted, mass media executives today increasingly believe that to reach their target audiences, they must pursue these audiences across media

"We have a calendar based on the book, stationery based on the book, an audiotape of the book, and a videotape of the movie based on the book, but we don't have the book."

boundaries. We should therefore expect not only more multimedia promotion of books, but more books that are *presold*. A **presold title** is one that publishers expect will sell well to specific audiences because it ties into material that is popular with those audiences across other media. So, for example, a book by Oprah Winfrey, highlighted on her show, is presold to fans of her TV show and magazine.

Can you see why some book lovers might be anxious about this fixation on presold books and books that can be easily publicized across media boundaries? They worry that the books with the highest profile in bookstores and in the media are those that are reflections of popular characters or plot lines from other media—television, radio, magazines, the movies, or the Web. In an age in which the most powerful media conglomerates own the largest book companies, these cross-media relationships are not likely to change. In fact, for reasons we suggested in Chapters 5 and 6, cross-media activities may accelerate in the name of synergy. As a media literate person, you might want to ask the following questions as you move through the book world:

- To what extent are the books that are getting most of the media attention today generated as a result of an author or character's popularity in another medium?
- Are we seeing an increase in cooperative activities between movie companies and book publishers owned by the same conglomerate? That is, are movie companies mostly using the publishers to sell books that publicize the movies, and are book companies trying to come up with titles that can become films?

An optimist would answer "surely not." She or he would point out that there are many publishers who publish trade books that have no connection to TV or movies and who have no interest in making a TV show or movie of these books. A pessimist would concede this point but would emphasize that increasingly the titles that get the most publicity both in and out of the bookstore are those that fit the cross-media, conglomerate profile. As this chapter has shown, the history of the book is a long and complex one. Books have changed through the ages, with the currents of culture and interests of those who have the power to produce them. This long view is useful to take when you think about the future of the book.

presold title a book that publishers expect will sell well to specific audiences because it ties into material that is popular with those audiences across other media

CHAPTER REVIEW

For an interactive chapter recap and study guide, visit the companion website for *Media Today* at www.routledge.com/textbooks/mediatoday

QUESTIONS FOR DISCUSSION AND CRITICAL THINKING

1   What were the initial reasons for a copyright law in England?
2   How do nonfiction consumer books differ from college texts?
3   What are some of the strategies that publishers use to try to reduce the risk of failure?
4   What are the major differences between large bookstore chains and the independents?

INTERNET RESOURCES

Literary Marketplace (http://www.LiteraryMarketplace.com)
This site is a useful place to search if you want to learn about large or small publishers on particular topics. You can identify publishers by state, by size, by more than 170 subject terms or create a customized term through the keyword search. Although the site charges for use of certain areas, much of it is free with registration.

Publishers Weekly (http://www.PublishersWeekly.com)
This is the website of the major trade magazine of the book publishing industry. You need not pay a subscription to use much of it, and it is a good way to learn about fads and fashions in the business of books.

The Institute for the Future of the Book (http://www.futureofthebook.org)
According to its mission statement "The printed page is giving way to the networked screen. The Institute for the Future of the Book seeks to chronicle this shift, and impact its development in a positive direction." The website describes an innovative approach that the Brooklyn-based Institute is taking toward digital publishing, carries essays by its leaders and fellows, and has commentary threads by those interested in the Institute and its work.

Book History Online (http://www.kb.nl/bho/)
A project of the National Library of the Netherlands, this is a database in English on the history of the printed book and libraries. It contains titles of books and articles on the history of the printed book worldwide. You can search for materials about the history of books in any country and any century through a simple though powerful search engine.

KEY TERMS

You can find the definitions to these key terms in the marginal glossary throughout this chapter. Test your knowledge of these terms with interactive flash cards on the *Media Today* companion website.

acquisitions editor
bestseller
blockbuster
book clubs
book tour
codex
dime novels
domestic novels
el-hi
format of a book

higher education
    materials
mail order
mass market outlets
mass market
    paperbacks
movable type
negative-option plan
pedagogy
plagiarism

prepublication research
presold title
print run
professional books
royalties
subscription reference
    books
track record
trade paperbacks
university press books

CONSTRUCTING MEDIA LITERACY

1   What are the threats to variety and diversity in the book industry? Do you think people who worry about such threats exaggerate the problem? Why or why not?
2   What segments of the book industry will gain, and which ones will lose, if a large number of people start using digital book readers? (Hint: consider the suppliers of paper.)
3   What ethical issues relating to book publishing concern you the most? Why?
4   In what ways is the book publishing industry contributing to the digital media environment?
5   If you were working in book publishing, what career would you choose? Why?

CASE STUDY   Independent vs. Chain Bookstores

The idea   The number of independent bookstores has diminished over the past few decades as big chains and online bookselling have made it difficult for them to compete. Many independents have folded, and others have adapted so they compete successfully. How are independents faring in your community?

The method   Using electronic databases such as Nexis or Factiva, find statistics and discussions about the national trends regarding independent bookstores. What is happening and why? Is the decline of independents accelerating, decelerating or remaining the same? Why?

Then identify independent bookstores in your community. If they don't exist now, when did they cease business, and what took their place? If they do exist, what do they seem to be doing to compete with the chains in your area? Interview the owners or managers of the bookstores to get their perspectives. Write a report of your findings in which you lay out what you have found and suggest whether or not you believe the balance of independents and chains in your community is a good one.

8 THE NEWSPAPER INDUSTRY

After studying this chapter, you will be able to:

1 Describe key developments in U.S. newspaper history

2 Explain the production, distribution, and exhibition processes of various types of newspapers

3 Recognize and discuss the challenges faced by the newspaper industry today and some approaches to dealing with them

4 Describe the ways that newspapers have begun to reach out to audiences through digital technologies, on the Internet and elsewhere

5 Apply your media literacy skills to evaluate the newspaper industry and its impact on your everyday life

"Half of the American people have never read a newspaper. Half never voted for President. One hopes it is the same half."

–GORE VIDAL, WRITER

Media Today

About sixty years ago, a communication researcher named Bernard Berelson decided that a newspaper strike that had shut down eight major papers in New York City offered a great opportunity to find out what missing a daily paper meant to people. Interviews with many regular readers convinced Berelson that what people really cared about was not so much the front-page headlines—they could get those from other media sources. Rather, people missed reading the parts of the paper that had direct connections with their personal interests—the comics, crossword puzzles, advice columns, sports sections, even the classified advertisements.

Professor Berelson's study underscores two important points about newspapers. One is that they are filled with much more than what people in mass media industries describe as *news*. In fact, the content of newspapers runs the gamut of the media genres described in Chapter 1. They carry entertainment (the puzzles, some of the columns), information (stock listings, for example), education (historical discussions, some columns for children), and, of course, advertisements.

The second point emphasized by the study is that—in the minds of readers—newspapers do not compete only with other newspapers. When Professor Berelson conducted his study, he and others saw radio and magazines as the only substantial competitors to the daily newspaper (television was only a very new technology at that time). Today, many companies are taking slivers of what newspapers have been presenting for a century—the puzzles, classified ads, the stock listings, the national and international news—and finding ways to profit from them in other media. Broadcast television, cable and satellite-delivered television, magazines, the Internet, and more, are drawing revenues from activities that used to be confined to newspapers. In particular, newspaper executives see the Internet as the place that most of their readers go to find out what is happening, and they are trying mightily to remake themselves on the Web and elsewhere so as to remain relevant and profitable. How is this reinvention taking place? What considerations are shaping it? In the face of these changes, what are the prospects for the newspaper? For people who work in the newspaper industry, or who want to work in it, these are critical questions.

We will tackle these questions before this chapter is over. First, though, it is important to put these challenges in perspective by sketching the story of newspapers' development in the United States. A look back shows that newspapers have always been adapting to challenges. In fact, the very idea of what a newspaper should look like has transformed over the past couple of centuries. As the next few pages will show, one reason has to do with new technologies—faster presses, new ways of reproducing pictures, new trucks—that companies have used to design, print and distribute papers. Another reason has to do with political and social circumstances. The people who have led newspapers have responded to governments, advertisers, and audiences in ways that have altered their product in important ways.

The Development of the Newspaper

newspapers   printed products created on a regular (weekly or daily) basis and released in multiple copies

People who study **newspapers** agree that they are printed products created on a regular (weekly or daily) basis and released in multiple copies. By this definition, newspapers did not exist before Johannes Gutenberg invented the printing press in the mid-1400s (see Chapter 7). And while Gutenberg's printing press made it possible for newspapers to be produced, having the technical means to do so did not immediately result in an explosion of newspaper publishing.

In England, regular newspapers weren't even produced during most of the 1600s. One reason was that England's ruling monarchs feared newspapers and greatly restricted their production. These rulers felt that if newspapers were to report on happenings in the land, it might provoke political discussions that could lead to overthrow. Additionally, England was politically and socially detached from the rest of the world for much of this period. Newspapers published in Europe tended to mix political news with business news. Merchants were the main audience because they needed to know what was going on politically and economically throughout Europe and in the "New World" that was being colonized by European nations. Only in the late 1600s, when England's ruling monarchs were forced to yield power to a feisty Parliament and the nation began to flex its naval and trading muscles, did newspapers become a regular feature in the country.

The Rise of the Adversarial Press

The idea of a press that would be free of government control developed slowly through the 1700s, and newspapers were at the center of the debate. In the early years of the British colonies, newspaper publishers tended to be either postmasters appointed by the local governor, or printers who had succeeded in winning government printing contracts. As a result, they were unlikely to circulate ideas that were politically suspect. Over time, though, renegades challenged the authorities. One such independent soul was James Franklin, printer and publisher of the *New England Courant*. The brother of the more famous Ben Franklin, James wrote that "to anathemize [that is, ostracize] a printer for publishing the different opinions of men is as injudicious as it is wicked."

Others voiced similar opinions, like Andrew Hamilton, a Philadelphia lawyer representing John Peter Zenger, a New York printer, in 1735. Zenger was charged with "seditious libel" for printing facts in his newspaper that reflected badly on the royal governor. Even though a guilty verdict was the proper outcome under British law, Hamilton persuaded the jury that his client was innocent. The reason, he stated, was that "Nature and the Laws of our country have given us a Right—the Liberty—both of exposing and opposing arbitrary Power… by speaking and writing Truth."

adversarial press   a press that has the ability to argue with government

This belief in an **adversarial press**—a press that had the ability to argue with government—was taking hold among the intellectuals in the British-American colonies. It was strengthened when Britain attempted to impose taxes on paper to pay for its expensive war with France during the 1760s and 1770s. Lawyers and printers were hurt most by the rules. They banded together to publish strong denunciations of the British colonial policy of taxation without representation. The anger rose to a pitch that culminated in the American Revolutionary War.

The Birth of the First Amendment

Even after the Revolutionary War, printers and intellectuals continued to advocate for the ability to argue publicly with the government. By 1787, the constitutions of nine of the original thirteen states had sections protecting the press from government interference. Still, there was a lot of debate when George Mason of Virginia suggested, at the convention to ratify a new constitution in 1787, that "I wish [the Constitution] had been prefaced with a bill of rights." The debate was between two political groups that had evolved by that time—the Federalists, who supported a strong federal government and commercial interests, and the Antifederalists, who felt that the states should be stronger than the federal government.

The tide turned in favor of a bill of rights when James Madison, a Federalist, helped push through the Constitution's first ten amendments. Ratified in 1791, the First Amendment said in part that "Congress shall make no law… abridging the freedom of speech, or of the press." The point of the First Amendment, in other words, was to make sure that the adversarial relationship between the press and the authorities would continue. Congress remained free to enact laws that restrained the press, but that didn't impede the adversarial relationship—for example, laws pertaining to copyright, slander, libel, and indecent language.

Newspapers in Post-revolutionary America

Newspapers were deeply involved in the political debates of the post-revolutionary period. As late as 1815, they were typically published by small printing companies, often family-run businesses. Nevertheless, newspapers achieved a dominant social and political position relative to books and magazines by the beginning of the 1800s. In 1820, the United States was home to 512 newspapers; 24 of them were published daily, 66 two or three times a week, and 422 once a week. The dailies tended to be in the cities with the largest populations. (*Largest* has to be understood in terms of the era. Philadelphia, the city with the most people in 1800, was quite small by today's reckoning: it had seventy thousand residents. Today its population is well over 1.5 million.)

Many of the newspapers were allied with political parties, and much of the news that appeared took the form of fierce political argument against an opposing viewpoint. Some newspapers were even supported by party officials, who helped arrange valuable government printing contracts for the editors. Readers knew that the *Minerva*, edited by Noah Webster, was a Federalist newspaper, and they understood that the *National Intelligencer* supported Thomas Jefferson and his Antifederalist philosophy.

Even though newspapers were widely available, the great majority of Americans did not read them. Part of the reason for this was illiteracy, but even for those who could read, the cost of purchasing a newspaper was often too high to afford. The printing process was a totally handicraft operation. The presses these companies used were not terribly different from Gutenberg's. Paper was either handmade from rag by the printer, or shipped from England. The labor-intensive nature of the process meant that in the early 1800s, publishers had to charge from six to ten dollars a year, in advance, for a newspaper subscription. That was more than most skilled workers earned in a week. Because of the cost, **circulation**—the number of newspapers people paid for or received free in one publishing cycle—was rather small, even relative to the population size. A circulation of 1,500 was common in all but the largest cities.

circulation the number of newspapers people paid for or received free in one publishing cycle

Newspapers Become Mass Media

By the 1830s, developments in society and in technology came together to encourage a new approach to the newspaper. Together, the steam-powered cylinder press created by Hoe and Company and the development of low-cost paper (see Chapter 7) made it possible to create huge numbers of newspapers for about a penny a copy, a price low enough that even working people could afford.

But could the common working people read? Would they read? Hoe introduced the steam-powered press at just the time when entrepreneurs were willing to take risks to find out the answer. If they had any chance to overturn the established press order, this was the time to do it. The 1820s and 1830s were a period in which American leaders began to emphasize the power of the "common man."

Andrew Jackson's election to the presidency in 1829 on a platform that celebrated the rough-hewn side of America, reinforced the idea that the working class had assumed much greater political importance than in the past. Literacy among the working class continued to increase, and large numbers of workers began to take an interest in reading affordable newspapers. The brief popularity of union-supported newspapers during the 1820s was evidence of this interest. When the unions declined after that decade, their papers declined as well. A number of entrepreneurs took note, however, that there might be an untapped audience for daily newspapers. A few tried to create a paper that sold for a low price—some for only a penny a copy—but they failed.

Then, in 1833, a struggling printer named Benjamin Day started the *New York Sun* and sold it for a penny on a per issue basis. The slogan on the *Sun*'s masthead was "It Shines for All." This slogan was not just a pun on the newspaper's name; it reflected Day's desire to entice great numbers of people, not just those with money, to read its material. Day got his wish. Within six months, the paper's circulation reached about eight thousand, almost twice that of its nearest rival. Within the next few years, successful imitators of the *Sun* appeared in New York, Philadelphia, and Baltimore. The idea became so popular, in fact, that there were often a number of **penny papers** competing for readers in the same area.

penny papers newspapers produced in the early 1830s that were sold on the street at a penny per copy

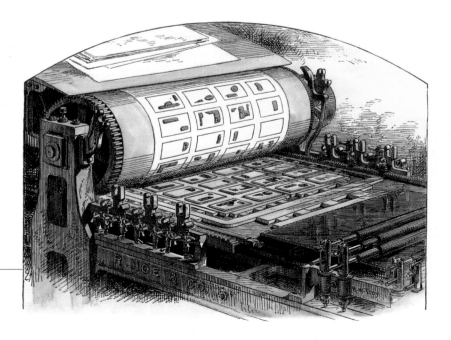

This engraving from 1865 shows an advanced Hoe rotary press.

THE SUN.

NUMBER 1.]   NEW YORK, TUESDAY, SEPTEMBER 3, 1833.   [PRICE ONE PENNY.

PUBLISHED DAILY,

AT 222 WILLIAM ST............BENJ. H. DAY, PRINTER.

The object of this paper is to lay before the public, at a price within the means of every one, ALL THE NEWS OF THE DAY, and at the same time afford an advantageous medium for advertising. The sheet will be enlarged as soon as the increase of advertisements requires it—the price remaining the same.

Yearly advertisers, (without the paper.) Thirty Dollars per annum—Casual advertising, at the usual prices charged by the city papers.

☞ Subscriptions will be received, if paid in advance, at the rate of three dollars per annum.

FOR ALBANY—PASSAGE ONLY $1.

The large and commodious steamboat COMMERCE, Capt. R. H. Fitch, will leave the foot of Courtlandt street on Friday, at five o'clock, P. M. for Albany, stopping at the usual landing places to land and receive passengers Passage $1. For particulars apply to the Captain on board. REGULAR DAYS.

From New York, Mondays, Wednesdays, Fridays. From Albany, Tuesdays, Thursdays, Saturdays.   a29

AN IRISH CAPTAIN.

"These are as sweet a pair of pistols as any in the three kingdoms;" said an officer, showing a pair to a young student of his acquaintance, "and have done execution before now; at the slightest touch, off they go, as sweet as honey, without either recoiling or dipping. I never travel without them."

"I never heard of highwaymen in this part of the country."

"Nor I." replied the officer, "and if I had I should not trouble myself to carry the pistols on their account—Highwaymen are a species of sharks who are not fond of attacking us lobsters; they know we are a little too hard to crack. No, my dear sir, highwaymen know that soldiers have not much money, and what they have they fight for."

"Since that is the case, how come you to travel always with pistols?"

"Because," answered the officer, "I find them very useful in accommodating any little difference I may accidentally have with a friend, or which one friend may chance to have with another."

"Provided you had a good cause;" replied the young student.

"I should not be squeamish respecting the cause, provided I had a good battle: that, my dear, is what is the most essential to a conscientious officer, who wishes to improve himself in his profession. I have much reason, therefore, to wish for a war; and at the present juncture, it would be much to the advantage of the nation in general, as it is dwindling into a country of ploughmen, manufacturers, and merchants. And you must know, too, that I am pretty fortunate, having already stood thirteen shots, and I never was hit but once."

"Thirteen! what, have you fought thirteen duels?"

"No, no!" replied the captain, "the last shot fired at me completed only my sixth duel."

Wonders of Littleness.—Pliny and Elian relate that Myrmecides wrought out of ivory a chariot, with four wheels and four horses, and a ship with all her tackling, both in so small a compass, that a bee could hide either with its wings. Nor should we doubt this, when we find it recorded in English history, on less questionable autho-

"It Shines for All"—The banner of Benjamin Day's *New York Sun*, the first of the penny papers.

Newspaper circulation figures skyrocketed into the tens of thousands within a decade, and newspaper publishers found that even the best steam-powered flatbed presses, which produced a few thousand pages an hour, were inadequate for the job. That was when Hoe's rotary (or "type revolving") press entered the picture on a widespread basis. Instead of placing the type on the flatbed, Hoe put it on a cylinder, with different parts of the cylinder holding type for different pages of the paper. By 1855, Hoe's ingenious machine could print twenty thousand sheets per hour. With this sort of power, newspaper executives were confident that they could turn out huge numbers of copies for an ever-growing readership.

Changing Approaches to News

To the typical newspaper reader of the early 1800s, the *Sun* and its imitators must have appeared shockingly different from their predecessors. Unlike the other papers of the day, these papers didn't print partisan political commentaries; instead, they were filled with stories of crime and love, humor and human interest. In the earliest years, they frequently included exaggerations and hoaxes, such as descriptions of life on the moon. Over the next few decades, though, the *Sun* and other penny papers developed the basic approaches to financing the paper, defining news, and organizing the news process that we still see in U.S. journalism today.

In the mid-1800s, it was common to see and hear newsboys like this one hawking papers on the street corners of most large American cities.

hawkers young boys who sold newspapers on the streets, and who made about thirty-seven cents for every hundred copies they sold

Financing the Paper

From the start, Benjamin Day's slogan, "It Shines for All," reflected his philosophy regarding the way to make money from the paper as well as reflecting his approach to its content. He believed that a publication that was affordable by the working class could make its profits one issue at a time. The paper was sold on the streets by ambitious **hawkers**—often young boys—who made about thirty-seven cents for every hundred copies they sold. This form of distribution encouraged publishers to search for presses that could print drawings across the front page to lure readers' attention as competing hawkers screamed through the streets. When special events—a murder trial, a natural disaster—took place after a paper was printed, publishers hyped circulation by releasing special issues that covered the incident. These "extra" editions were possible because new presses offered faster, larger, and cheaper print runs than their predecessors had. As a result, increased circulation meant increased profits for the publisher.

Profits also grew due to an increase in the amount of newspaper space sold to advertisers. As circulation figures grew into the thousands and tens of thousands, companies that hadn't advertised in newspapers before began to see the penny press as a way to reach large numbers of people. Publishers quickly realized that the most ad money went to the papers that had the most readers. Because having the latest news seemed to be what drew readers to a particular newspaper when penny papers competed, publishers began to put revenues into improving news coverage. The hope was to raise both circulation and ad revenues at the same time.

Defining News

In this competition over news, publishers developed a new consensus about how to think of news; one that moved ever closer to the *news* genre that we discussed in Chapter 2. The development spanned several decades—from the 1840s through the Civil War in the 1860s. Compared to the papers of the early 1800s, the change was drastic. Those dailies tended to relay information that came from somewhere else. They printed such things as discussions of trends that had appeared in other newspapers, letters from readers expressing political opinions, government reports, speeches by political leaders that the editors admired, and shipping reports. The penny papers, in contrast, defined their primary role not as relayers of information but as aggressive searchers for events and developments that their readers would find compelling. That vision meant hiring people—reporters—to actually "gather" stories.

As the penny press developed, its publishers tried to attract more and more readers by adding new sections that reported on a variety of possible interests, including those of the wealthier classes of society. James Gordon Bennett's *New York Herald* was especially innovative in appealing to different segments of the population within the same issue. By the late 1840s, Bennett's paper had a sports section, a critical review column, society news, and a strong financial section.

With special sections as well as general news coverage, a large part of the competition among papers involved the claim that the paper's reporter was first with a story. As a result, reporting events quickly became a hallmark of the news process. Reporters tried just about every quick mode of transportation they could think of to speed their words along, from the carrier pigeon, to the pony express, to the railroad. The invention of the telegraph in 1844 was particularly important to what became known as **news gathering**.

Elements of today's news jargon began to develop around this time. The **byline** (which tells who wrote the story) emerged, as did the **dateline** (which tells where and when the reporter wrote it). So did different sizes of **headlines**, which informed readers of the content and the relative importance of a particular story.

During the Civil War, a new element was added. Because reporters on both sides of the war feared that the telegraph wires would be cut, they began to summarize their major facts quickly at the beginning of their dispatches. Only after this summary did they elaborate on the incident or battle they were describing. This style of factual reporting is called the *inverted pyramid* style (see Figure 2.5 on page 55). It is the style used for most hard news stories today.

Organizing the News Process

One consequence of the new financial and news considerations was that newspapers became complex organizations. The newspaper of the early 1800s tended to be created by a single printer-publisher-editor-reporter, with apprentices who were sometimes family members. That was possible when the work involved simply relaying information. It would not do, however, when creating a newspaper meant quickly finding and preparing material that would entice huge numbers of readers on a daily basis. Newspaper companies soon became large organizations, with different departments to take care of financing, creating, printing, distributing, and marketing their product.

In addition to becoming more complex internally, newspaper companies began to interact with other organizations that helped them to get news to their readers quickly and efficiently. The Western Union telegraph company was one such organization; it helped reporters relay news quickly. Another was the Associated Press. It was established in 1849 by seven New York City newspapers as a cooperative news-gathering organization. Newspapers in other cities were invited to join the service, which charged a membership fee in return for sending its stories to the paper over the telegraph wires.

Clearly, the newspaper business was evolving into an industry. Publishers were using ever-faster printing presses and other communication technologies to pursue larger and larger audiences. The era of mass communication had begun. Still, it would be wrong to get the idea that the major urban newspapers of 1850 or 1860 could be mistaken for those of today. One major difference was the absence of photographs in the press of the mid-1800s; the technology for printing photographs in newspapers hadn't been invented yet. A bigger difference was the tone used by that era's major dailies compared to ours.

The notion of *objectivity* as it is used by today's journalists in hard news had not yet been developed. Today, once news workers have decided that something is hard news, they must decide how to present it. They use the word **objectivity** to

---

news gathering the process by which reporters and editors gather and organize the news they include in their publication

byline a statement identifying who wrote the story

dateline a statement identifying where and when the reporter wrote the story

headline an identifying tag appearing at the top of a news story, cueing readers in on the content and relative importance of the story

objectivity presenting a fair, balanced, and impartial representation of the events that took place by recording a news event based on the facts and without interpretation, so that anyone else who witnessed the news would agree with the journalists' recounting of it; the way in which news ought to be researched, organized, and presented

summarize the way in which news ought to be researched, organized, and presented. It is possible, they believe, to recount a news event based on the facts and without interpretation, so that anyone else who witnessed the news event would agree with the journalists' recounting of it. The goal of a hard-news reporter, then, is to summarize an event in an *objective* manner—that is, to present a fair and impartial representation of what happened (see Chapter 2 for a more detailed discussion of objectivity).

But this approach didn't yet exist in the mid-1800s. Publishers such as James Gordon Bennett (of the *New York Herald*) and Horace Greeley (of the *New York Tribune*) had no qualms about lacing their editions with long articles that included spirited attacks on political or philosophical rivals that would appear strange in daily newspapers today. Greeley, in particular, used his paper as a forum for wide-ranging discussions of new schemes to improve society. In the 1850s, for example, the *Tribune* devoted many pages to explaining socialism, and Greeley himself plunged into long debates with famous opponents of socialism on the desirability of a socialist society.

A Revolution in Newspaper Publishing

The technological and organizational developments in newspaper publishing from the 1830s through the 1860s paved the way for a big leap forward. The era of mass circulation in the 1880s, when newspapers with truly huge audiences emerged, had arrived. Two profound changes took place in the ways in which newspaper owners thought of their products. The first had to do with readership—the newspaper's new goal to attract hundreds of thousands, even millions, of customers. The second had to do with the financial support of the product. In earlier decades, readers' subscriptions had covered a large percentage of the publisher's costs, but advertisements soon began to provide most of the revenues.

A Readership Revolution

In the years following the Civil War, the United States went through an unprecedented period of industrialization. Factories, located in cities, were turning out an enormous number of products. They were hiring huge numbers of foreign workers as well as American-born farmers who were attracted to a new way of life. As the nation got wealthier, educational services increased. More children than ever before went to public schools and literacy was on the rise. These changes meant that there were far more potential readers for newspapers than ever before. The growth of U.S. cities meant that large numbers of people were living in densely populated areas. Large-scale newspaper distribution was suddenly much easier than it had been in previous decades. What made the potential for newspapers particularly great was the existence of merchants and other business that became interested in using newspapers to reach huge audiences.

An Advertising Revolution

That meant advertising. The key to attracting customers, the manufacturers reasoned, was to take advantage of the crowded city. Signs throughout neighborhoods, on walls and on streetcars and trucks, were a popular way to trumpet the virtues of branded products and the stores that sold them. But manufacturers saw a high-circulation daily newspaper as a particularly valuable way to advertise consumer goods. Publishers new and old were eager to oblige. They aimed their content at the large, diverse populations that major manufacturers and department stores eagerly sought. The number of English-language, general-circulation dailies increased from 489 in 1870 to 1,967 in 1900. Foreign-language newspapers also grew steeply in number and readership.

Inventors and newspaper owners worked together to make the newspaper attractive to huge audiences. They developed efficient techniques for printing wide headlines and advertisements. Speed became ever more important—not just in gathering news, but also in turning it out. By the early 1890s, the finest Hoe press could turn out 48,000 twelve-page newspapers in an hour. Owners of large papers were installing several presses to keep up with their quickly rising circulation. Full-color presses, first used in Paris, were adapted in the United States and used especially for Sunday comics. In 1897, high-quality reproductions of photographs made their first appearance, in the *New York Tribune*.

Newspaper firms kept the price of their dailies at around a nickel even as the cost of printing technology and paper rose. A new business philosophy was developing. Newspapers were relying mostly on advertising instead of circulation revenues for their profits. The percentage of newspaper revenue coming from advertising rose from 50 percent in 1880 to 64 percent in 1910.

Print Journalism in the Early Twentieth Century

In this competitive environment, the daily newspaper changed dramatically, taking on a form close to that of the kind of paper we are used to today. With color comics, syndicated columnists, hefty sports sections, photograph-filled Sunday magazines, and more, the newspaper became a mosaic of features designed to attract as many different types of people as possible. The complex product gave rise to a complex corporate structure, with advertising and circulation departments that were often as large and as important as the news departments themselves.

Major cities in every region of the nation had one or more newspapers that used the new approach. The *Atlanta Constitution* and the *Louisville Courier-Journal* were stars of the South. In the Midwest, the *Cleveland Press* and the *Detroit News* emerged as powerful evening papers. The West saw the *Los Angeles Times* and, in San Francisco, the *Examiner* and the *Chronicle*. Publishing entrepreneurs such as E. W. Scripps, William Randolph Hearst, and William Patterson built fortunes through their ability to sell ads by building circulation through well-liked features, fast-breaking news stories, coverage of sensational events, human interest tales, and civic campaigns that brought community goodwill.

The Era of Yellow Journalism

These developments reached their height in New York City, where Joseph Pulitzer and William Randolph Hearst competed for circulation and advertising leadership. The highly publicized fight between Pulitzer and Hearst over a Sunday comic character called "The Yellow Kid" seemed to symbolize the ferocity of the competition among papers in many cities. To this day, the newspapers of the 1890s are said to be part of **yellow journalism**. The term is used for a newspaper characterized by irresponsible, unethical, and sensational news gathering and exhibition. The publishers of these papers used sensational stories of sex and murder, and huge publicity gimmicks to lure each other's readers. Hearst brazenly used any story that would

yellow journalism a term used to refer to the newspaper products of the 1890s, which were characterized by irresponsible, unethical, and sensational news gathering and exhibition

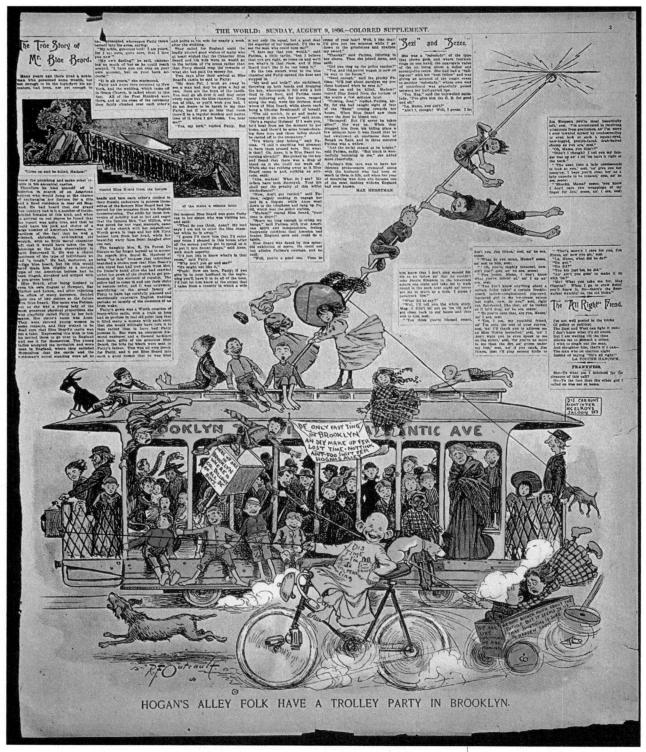

In addition to standing for a certain type of newspaper competition, *The Yellow Kid* represented a technical advance in color printing. Richard F. Outcault's drawing of an urchin, wearing a yellow nightshirt through New York's slums, was selected to test the use of color in Joseph Pulitzer's *New York World* on February 16, 1896.

boost circulation. When the U.S. battleship *Maine* blew up in Havana harbor, Hearst offered a fifty-thousand-dollar reward to the person who could prove who did it. And when the United States went to war with Spain over the incident, both the *World* and the *Journal* covered the conflict in jingoistic, highly emotional tones.

At the turn of the century, the excesses of yellow journalism began to alarm people both inside and outside the newspaper business. Self-regulation became a by-word, and universities established schools and departments of journalism, often with the help of wealthy newspaper publishers; their goal was to turn journalism into a respected craft, with its own clear set of procedures and norms. The first university journalism school was at the University of Missouri; Pulitzer's estate funded the graduate school of journalism at Columbia University.

The Newspaper Industry Consolidates

Between 1910 and 1930, the number of U.S. dailies fell from 2,200 to 1,942. More significantly, the number of cities with competing daily papers fell from 689 to 288 during this same period. Part of the reason was competition: the high cost of equipment combined with circulation wars killed many papers. Another part of the reason, though, was the desire of the largest newspaper owners to reduce competition in the various cities in which they operated. These owners tried to ensure that they would attract most of the daily circulation, and therefore most of the advertising money, by buying and killing off other newspapers in places where they owned papers. The result was the creation of powerful **newspaper chains**, companies that owned a number of papers around the nation. By 1933, the six most powerful chains—Hearst, Scripps-Howard, Patterson-McCormick, Block, Ridder, and Gannett—controlled about one-quarter of all daily circulation in the United States. Hearst alone controlled almost 14 percent of daily and 24 percent of Sunday circulation in 1935.

newspaper chains companies that own a number of newspapers around the nation

The Rise of the Tabloids

The 1920s saw the rise of papers that were printed in a **tabloid form**—that is, on a page that was about half the size of a traditional newspaper page. They became popular because they included a number of photographs, they were easy to handle on public transportation, and they featured sensational coverage of crimes and movie stars. The most popular of this sort of newspaper was the *New York Daily News*, which dubbed itself "New York's Picture Newspaper." Like its imitators, in its earliest years the *Daily News* seemed to reflect the idea of a newspaper that had been stripped of the real news that the new journalism schools were trying to promote. What the reader got instead was large doses of the entertainment part of the traditional paper: gossip, comic strips, horoscopes, advice columns, sports, and news about movie stars. Though there are still some echoes of this "jazz journalism" in today's *Daily News,* this particularly sensationalist style doesn't characterize it anymore. You can see more of this type of journalism in such weekly entertainment papers as the *National Enquirer* and perhaps even in headline-mongering dailies such as the *New York Post.*

tabloid form a printing format that uses pages that are about half the size of a traditional newspaper page

Newspaper Industry Woes

The high-flying years that newspaper firms saw in the early 1900s ended with the Great Depression of the 1930s. During that decade, unemployment, low wages, and a more restrained society led consumers to buy one traditional paper instead of a traditional paper and a tabloid. Some people who had once purchased several papers on a daily basis found that they could not afford even one.

Between 1937 and 1939, the situation was so bad that one-third of salaried employees in the newspaper industry lost their jobs. The dominant reason for newspaper failures was a drastic decrease in spending by advertisers. Although loss of business was one factor that discouraged advertisers from buying space in papers, another was that they were shifting a substantial portion of their advertising funds to radio, which was just beginning to grow as an advertising medium.

Declining Dailies Radio was the newspaper industry's first substantial daily competitor for advertising. In the late 1940s, television arrived, adding to newspaper executives' worries. Still, in the years immediately following World War II their circulation figures rose and profits were strong. Yet by the year 2007, the number of dailies had decreased, ownership concentration had increased, and the number of cities with competing dailies was reduced to a handful (see Table 8.1).

Katharine Graham

MEDIA PROFILE

By the 1980s, Katharine Meyer Graham was regarded as one of the most powerful women not just in the newspaper business, but in the country as well. This was not necessarily a position she sought or wanted. Born in 1917 to Eugene and Agnes Meyer, an influential couple in the worlds of finance and politics, Katharine was introduced to the newspaper industry when her father rescued the *Washington Post* from extinction at a bankruptcy auction.

Katharine worked as a reporter in San Francisco and for her father's paper, but she never had any intention of staying in the business. Her plans abruptly changed in 1939 when she met Philip Graham, whom she wed within six months. A lawyer by training, Philip was persuaded to join the *Washington Post* as associate publisher in 1946. Within two years, Eugene Meyer transferred ownership to Philip and Katharine, although her role did not extend beyond that of the publisher's wife. A brilliant newspaperman, Philip suffered from intense self-doubt and manic depression. In 1963, he committed suicide, and a distraught Katharine decided to assume the presidency of the *Post*.

She questioned her ability to lead the paper at first, and her predominantly male board and staff also felt she did not deserve the position and gave her little support or respect. However, Katharine set out to learn every aspect of the business, and she appointed powerful reporter Ben Bradlee to be the *Post*'s managing editor.

She developed a vast knowledge of the industry and an effective management style so quickly that she soon shed her Washington housewife image and became a tough-minded yet principled executive.

Katharine steered the paper through the biggest editorial controversies in history—the publication of the Pentagon Papers and the bringing to light of the Watergate scandal, which toppled President Nixon's administration.

Moreover, under her stewardship, the Washington Post Corporation went beyond publishing a solid regional paper to become the fifth largest U.S. publishing company and a Fortune 500 multimedia empire. Graham's son Donald succeeded her as CEO and chairman of the board in 1991 and reigned supreme as a political and social force in Washington. Katherine Graham passed away in July of 2001, but her legacy as the first woman to head a Fortune 500 company, as a Pulitzer Prize winner, and as a leading figure in political, media, business, and social circles will live on.

Source: Nancy Signorelli (editor), *Women in Communication: a Biographical Sourcebook*, 1996 Greenwood Press. Reproduced with permission of Greenwood Publishing Group, Inc., Westport, CT.

Table 8.1 The Decline of U.S. Daily Newspapers

Year	Total Papers	Total Circulation
1940	1,878	41,132
1945	1,749	48,384
1946	1,763	50,928
1947	1,769	51,673
1948	1,781	52,285
1949	1,780	52,846
1950	1,772	53,829
1960	1,763	58,882
1970	1,748	62,108
1980	1,745	62,202
1985	1,676	62,766
1990	1,611	62,328
1991	1,586	60,687
1992	1,570	60,164
1993	1,556	59,812
1994	1,548	59,305
1995	1,533	58,193
1996	1,520	56,983
1997	1,509	56,728
1998	1,489	56,182
1999	1,483	55,979
2000	1,480	55,773
2001	1,468	55,578
2002	1,457	55,186
2003	1,456	55,185
2004	1,457	54,626
2005	1,452	53,345
2006	1,437	52,329

Source: *Editor and Publisher International Yearbook 2007.*

What can account for changes in the newspaper industry? Among several factors were a strong and steady increase in the price of newsprint, rising wages and salaries, and the loss of advertising to television as well as to radio. Labor strikes in several cities also hurt. Many of these strikes were sparked by craft-union anger over executives' desire to replace the typesetting machine operators with computers. Together with the other difficulties that weakened the papers, the disputes resulted in suspensions or mergers, especially in large metropolitan areas. In 1947, 181 of the nation's cities had competing papers, whereas only 38 cities had them in 2006.

Declining Readership   Exacerbating all these changes was the fact that the percentage of the U.S. population reading daily papers declined between the 1930s and the 1990s. About 40 million copies were sold each day in 1930, when the population was 122 million; in 2000, when the population was about 250 million, only 60 million copies were sold. But the number of newspapers for each household decreased from 1.32 in 1930 to 0.68 in 1990 and to 0.43 in 1994.

Competition from the Web   At the end of the 1900s, newspaper companies generally remained quite profitable, as local advertisers still used them to reach large numbers of people. But as the industry moved into the twenty-first century, many newspapers began to suffer not just larger annual losses in readership than in earlier years, they began to see signs that their growth in advertising money was also decreasing. As you might guess, a primary concern for those in the industry is competition from the Web. In order to fully grasp the ways in which the Web is changing newspapers' production, distribution, and exhibition activities, it is important to understand the types of papers that exist, the companies that run them, and the support they receive from advertisers. This will also make it clear that the newspaper industry today is quite varied, and it is important to get a sense of that variety before making generalizations about "the newspaper's" future.

An Overview of the Modern Newspaper Industry

dailies   newspapers that are published at least five times a week

weeklies   newspapers that are published once a week

Perhaps the broadest way to think about newspapers in the United States is to divide them into **dailies** (those that are published at least five times a week) and **weeklies** (those that are published fewer than four times a week). According to the newspaper trade magazine *Editor & Publisher*, in 2006 there were 1,437 dailies and 7,319 weeklies. Of the dailies, morning papers outnumbered evening papers for the first time: 833 to 614. Of the newspapers mentioned, 907 had Sunday editions. That was a substantial rise from 1970, when there were only 586 Sunday editions (see Table 8.2).[1]

Daily Newspapers

Daily newspaper circulation has moved downward over the past quarter century, even though the nation's adult population has grown by more than a third. In 2006, it hovered at about 52 million, about three million fewer than in 2000 (see Table 8.3). During the past few years, the three newspapers that distributed their dailies across the country—the *New York Times*, the *Wall Street Journal*, and *USA Today*—managed to hold their own in circulation, or to have only slight drops.

Year	Morning	Evening	Total M&E[1]	Sunday
1950	322	1,450	1,772	549
1955	316	1,454	1,760	541
1960	312	1,459	1,763	563
1965	320	1,444	1,751	562
1970	334	1,429	1,748	586
1975	339	1,436	1,756	639
1980	387	1,388	1,745	735
1985	482	1,220	1,676	798
1990	559	1,084	1,611	863
1991	571	1,042	1,586	874
1992	596	995	1,570	891
1993	623	954	1,556	884
1994	635	935	1,548	886
1995	656	891	1,533	888
1996	686	846	1,520	890
1997	705	816	1,509	903
1998	721	781	1,489	897
1999	736	760	1,483	905
2000	766	727	1,480	917
2001	776	704	1,468	913
2002	777	692	1,457	913
2003	787	680	1,456	917
2004	814	653	1,457	915
2005	817	645	1,452	914
2006	833	614	1,437	907

Table 8.2 — Number of U.S. Daily Newspapers

[1] "All-day" newspapers publish several editions throughout the day.
They are listed in both morning and evening columns but only once in the total.
Source: Newspaper Association of America, accessed 2/19/07, http://naa.org/thesource/14.asp#number

Circulations in small cities such as Brockton, Massachusetts or in rural areas, such as Pike County, Kentucky were also stable or even increased. Large city newspapers, though, saw relatively large drops. For example, in 2005 dailies in the top 50 markets lost an average 4.1 percent in circulation, while the average across the country was a loss of 3.1 percent. Some big-city drops were startling. In web-savvy

Table 8.3 U.S. Daily Newspaper Circulation, 2000–2006

Year	Morning	Evening	Total M&E	Sunday
2000	46,772,497	9,000,350	55,772,847	59,420,999
2001	46,821,480	8,756,566	55,578,046	59,090,364
2002	46,617,163	8,568,994	55,186,157	58,780,299
2003	46,930,215	8,255,136	55,185,351	58,494,695
2004	46,887,490	7,738,648	54,626,138	57,753,013
2005	46,122,614	7,222,429	53,345,043	55,270,381
2006	45,441,446	6,887,784	52,329,230	53,175,299

Source: Newspaper Association of America, accessed 2/19/07, http://naa.org/thesource/14.asp#number

San Francisco, for example, the *San Francisco Chronicle* lost 17 percent of its circulation in 2005. Less drastic, but still troubling to management, was the *Miami Herald*'s decline of 4.3 percent. Table 8.4 lists the top twenty U.S. daily newspapers by 2006 circulation.

As we have discussed, circulation declines are nothing new, and declines in big-city papers have been going on for a while. The *New York Daily News* provides the most dramatic example. Between 1950 and 1990, the *Daily News* fell from being the most popular daily newspaper to being seventh in daily circulation.

Table 8.4 Top Twenty U.S. Daily Newspapers by Circulation[1]

USA Today	2,269,509	Dallas Morning News	404,653
Wall Street Journal	2,043,235	Phoenix Republic	397,294
New York Times	1,086,798	Boston Globe	386,415
Los Angeles Times	745,766	Chicago Sun-Times	382,796
New York Post	704,011	Newark Star-Ledger	378,100
New York Daily News	693,382	San Francisco Chronicle	373,805
Washington Post	656,297	Minneapolis Star Tribune	358,887
Chicago Tribune	576,132	Atlanta Journal-Constitution	350,157
Houston Chronicle	508,097	Detroit Free Press	345,861
Long Island Newsday	410,579	Cleveland Plain Dealer	336,939

[1] As of September 30, 2006.

Source: Editor & Publisher International Yearbook, 2007.

The *Daily News* lost almost three million Sunday readers and just over one million daily readers at a time when the population of its area was increasing. A cause of the circulation drop of a few big-city papers are free newspapers, in particular a daily called *Metro*. Owned by a Swedish publisher, *Metro* now publishes in 100 cities in 20 countries in Europe, Asia, and North and South America. It claims a reach of 22.8 million readers daily.[2] In Philadelphia, Boston and New York, the free daily is a joint venture with another paper (for example, the *Boston Globe*). The target is commuters to and from work. The *Washington Post* has its own free publication called *Express* that is aimed at riders. Although the free paper may erode some of the other daily's circulation, the parent company may consider the gains in ad revenue from the freebie worth it.

Another, more important, culprit affecting daily newspaper circulation is the Internet, particularly the strong growth of high-speed ("broadband") Internet connections in U.S. households. One analyst suggests that this trend has affected big-city papers more than dailies in mid-sized or smaller markets because there are many highly regarded online news sites (as well as cable TV channels) that cover national and international news. Because the major metropolitan dailies have tended to focus on these types of stories, their readers find that the Web can provide them with great alternatives. Newspapers in smaller markets, though, tend to place more emphasis on local news, and that is harder to find on the Web. Consequently, their hard-copy circulation isn't as negatively affected.[3]

Daily Newspaper Chains   It's important to note that with the exception of the free papers that they often own alone or with the *Metro*, daily newspapers tend not to have competition from other dailies. Moreover, most of the dailies in the United States are controlled by a few large firms. In 2000, for example, newspaper chains (or groups) controlled about 1,083 dailies; only about 400 were independent. More recent data are not available, but observations of mergers and acquisitions in the industry suggest that the number of independent dailies has certainly not grown. The logic of chain ownership has traditionally been quite strong. A daily newspaper that was the only one in its area could pretty well dictate prices to local advertisers—car dealers, department stores, movie theaters—that wanted to reach high percentages of the population on a regular basis. Consequently, daily newspapers' margins of profit have been quite high, far higher than most other industries.

In recent years, newspaper executives and their investors have begun to worry that this logic no longer holds. Losses in readership, and increased competition for local advertising by the Internet, free newspapers, and other local media have led investors to downgrade the monetary value of some of the biggest newspaper companies.

It isn't as if newspaper chains are actually losing money. As the *Financial Times* newspaper put it in 2007, "most newspaper chains are still wildly profitable by conventional measures—generating pre-tax margins of 20 percent or more."[4] Yet their executives are finding it difficult to maintain those levels and deliver the earnings growth that Wall Street demands. With revenues stagnant, most have resorted to cost-cutting to appease shareholders. Moreover, declining margins of profit and concerns for the long-term future of the business have led some of those firms to sell out to others. In the past few years, major news chains such as the Tribune Corporation, Knight Ridder, and Dow Jones have bitten the dust; they have been taken over by firms that have kept the most attractive properties and sold the others to the highest bidders. Critics worry that many of the remaining chains will try to pay for their acquisitions—and keep up profit margins—by reducing their reporting and editorial staff and cutting back on news coverage.

Weekly Newspapers

circulation the number of units of a magazine or newspaper sold or distributed free to individuals in one publishing cycle

alternative weeklies a paper written for a young, urban audience with an eye on political and cultural commentary

shoppers free, nondaily newspapers, typically aimed at people in particular neighborhoods, that are designed primarily to deliver advertisements, but which may also carry some news and feature content

Weekly newspapers have been somewhat less buffeted by the enormous challenges that daily newspapers have been experiencing (see Table 8.5). In 2006, the total **circulation** of weeklies—that is, the number of papers people paid for or received free in one publishing cycle—hit about 50 million. Of those, about 21 million go to people who pay for them. About 28 million are distributed free. Although the circulation of paid weeklies is falling somewhat, free weeklies are growing in circulation, particularly in medium-sized and small cities and suburban areas. Newspaper-industry analysts predict that the circulation of free papers will grow in the next several years, while circulation of paid weeklies will decline, as readers increasingly use the Web and free publications.[5]

Many weeklies have succeeded in carving out topic or audience areas that (so far) daily newspapers have not been able to cover easily. Four coverage topics stand out. Three are geographic—coverage of neighborhoods within cities, of suburbs, and of rural areas. The fourth area of coverage focuses on certain types of people—particular ethnic, racial, occupational, or interest communities. Often those communities cannot support a daily paper, and so a weekly takes hold. A hot type of city paper has been the **alternative weekly**. It is a paper written for a young, urban audience with an eye on political and cultural commentary. **Shoppers** are another popular form of weekly newspaper that bears noting. These are typically aimed at people in particular neighborhoods who might shop at local merchants, are designed primarily to deliver coupons and advertisements but may also carry some news or feature content.

Table 8.5 **Total U.S. Weekly Newspapers**

Year	Total Weekly Newspapers	Average Circulation	Total Circulation
1996	6,580	6,977	45,911,510
1997	6,581	7,194	47,340,474
1998	6,642	7,338	48,742,278
1999	6,646	7,399	49,170,488
2000	6,579	7,295	47,990,892
2001	6,476	7,339	47,527,348
2002	6,699	7,467	50,023,378
2003	6,704	7,490	50,212,925
2004	6,692	7,444	49,814,806
2005	6,659	7,319	49,541,617

Source: Newspaper Association of America, accessed 2/19/07, http://naa.org/thesource/16.asp

Newspaper Niches

As the newspaper categories just mentioned suggest, the variety that exists among daily and weekly papers is fascinating. When was the last time you read the *Eielson Air Force Base Goldpanner*, a weekly North Pole paper that claims a circulation of about four thousand? Are you a lawyer in Philadelphia? If so, you might know that the five-times-a-week *Legal Intelligencer* in Philadelphia counts five thousand subscribers. If you're a resident of New Orleans, perhaps you will be interested in the *Gambit Weekly* of New Orleans, a self-described locally-owned "alternative weekly" that distributes forty thousand copies to over

El Diario/La Presna is the oldest Spanish-language newspaper in the United States. Its Sunday edition has a full week-in-review of Latin American news, an arts and culture calendar, and highlights of Latino sports leagues.

375 locations throughout the area. Did you say you're a college student? You're probably aware that virtually every campus has a newspaper, most of which are free to students and supported by advertising. The largest college papers are the University of Minnesota's *Minnesota Daily* and Michigan State's *State News*, both with circulation figures of about thirty-five thousand copies daily.

The African-American press includes about 280 newspapers. Two of these, the *Blytheville (Ark.) Times* and the *Chicago Daily Defender*, are daily; almost all the others appear weekly. Among foreign-language newspapers, Spanish is the most common. Latino papers range from the seven-days-a-week *El Diario* of New York City (circulation 50,000) to the weekly La Jara, Colorado, *Conejos County Citizen* (circulation 657) to the twice-monthly *El Veterano* (published in Vineland, New Jersey, and claiming a circulation of 480,000). Spanish, though, is only the tip of an iceberg of foreign-language newspapers in the United States. Daily or non-daily newspapers target speakers of Mandarin, Vietnamese, Russian, Yiddish, and Ukrainian, among many other languages.

Financing the Newspaper Business

No matter what their size, topic, or language, newspapers need to make money. They can generate revenues in two ways: from *advertising* or from *circulation*. Advertising is by far the most dominant source of money. On average, daily newspapers receive about 80 percent of their revenues, and weekly newspapers receive about 90 percent of their revenues, in this way. Individual papers may have higher or lower percentages. Larger newspapers and weeklies that charge for their copies receive a higher share of their revenues from circulation than do smaller papers and free weeklies. Either way, it adds up to a lot of money.

Advertising

In 2005, physical daily and weekly newspapers together brought in about $53 billion in advertising.[6] But the term *advertising* as it applies to newspapers really refers to four different areas: retail advertising from companies with local outlets, classified ads, national ads, and inserts.

Ethnic Newspapers

Today, while many newspapers across the nation are struggling with declining circulations, ethnic papers have over the past decade increased in both size and readership. In fact, a poll conducted in 2005 by New California Media (now New American Media) found that 29 million ethnic adults, or 13 percent of the U.S. adult population, consider themselves "primary consumers" of ethnic media.

As such, ethnic papers have become a mainstay in regions with large immigrant populations, including in California, Texas, New York, and Washington, DC. The DC metropolitan area alone distributes about a dozen Spanish-language papers and three Korean-language dailies, among many others, reports the *Washington Post*. Elected State Representative Ana Sol Gutierrez says that minority-language newspapers act as "a lifeline to the community." She continues, "The main media simply [do] not address the issues or provide the information that various ethnic groups need to have."

One such ethnic group is the growing population of Vietnamese Americans. As Vietnamese immigration to the United States only began in the wake of the Vietnam War, most are first- or second-generation Americans. As such, many Vietnamese Americans rely on the ethnic press to remain connected to their country of origin while also keeping informed about issues in their community. Today, Vietnamese immigrants have dozens of dailies and weeklies to choose from, and roughly 80 percent read ethnic papers regularly. The publishers of many of these papers are committed to fulfilling their social responsibility role by getting readers the type of information they are not likely to come across in the mainstream media or in their daily lives.

For example, *Mach Song*, a Vietnamese monthly which publishes in 20 cities across the United States, printed an article encouraging battered women to get help. The article prompted several domestically abused women to contact a social service agency. Other Vietnamese newspapers have also done stories on such sensitive issues as gambling, addiction and abortion. According to Nguyen Dinh Thang, publisher of *Mach Song*, "We would like to break the silence on critical issues on the community... If you choose to ignore it, they don't go away. We have to transmit the information."

Sources: "Ethnic Media in America: The Giant Hidden in Plain Sight," report from California New Media, June 7, 2005, accessed 2/18/07, http://www.ncmonline.com/polls/full_em_poll.pdf; Phuong Ly, "Ethnic Papers Seeking to Make Voices Heard; Publications Eye Larger Role," *Washington Post*, January 2, 2003, online: Factiva database.

classified ad a short announcement for a product or service that is typically grouped with announcements for other products or services of the same kind

national ads advertisements placed by large national and multinational firms that have branch stores and other operations that do business within the newspaper's geographic area

Retail Advertising Retail advertising is carried out by establishments located in the same geographic area as the newspaper in which the ad is placed. Think of ads from computer electronics stores, department stores, hospitals, car dealerships, restaurants, realtors, and movie theaters. Some of these advertisers may be parts of national chains, but the purpose of the ads is to persuade people to shop in the local outlets. Retail advertising is the most important of the four main areas of newspaper advertising. It makes up about 50 percent of the total in daily papers and an even higher percentage in weeklies.

Classified Advertising The second most lucrative type of newspaper advertisement is the classified ad, which makes up near 40 percent of the revenue pie. A **classified ad** is a short announcement for a product or service that is typically grouped with announcements for other products or services of the same kind. Newspapers typically sell classified ad space by the line to people who want to offer everything from houses to beds to bikes.

National Advertising **National ads** are advertisements placed by large national and multinational firms that do business in a newspaper's geographic area.

Airline and cruise line ads are often national purchases. Political advertisements and movie ads also often fit the "national" tag. The distinction between retail and national ads may not always be clear. Sometimes what appear to be retail ads are actually national ads. The reason is that national marketers often provide **co-op advertising** money to retailers that carry their products. In co-op advertising, manufacturers or distributors of products provide money to exhibitors in order to help the exhibitor with the cost of promoting a particular product. A soup manufacturer, for example, might provide a local supermarket chain with an allowance to purchase ads that highlight the manufacturer's soups. The money may be used to buy time on local radio and TV, as well as in local newspapers.

Freestanding Inserts   Inserts, often called **freestanding inserts (FSIs)**, are preprinted sheets that advertise particular products, services, or retailers. FSIs are not printed as part of the paper itself, but are inserted into the paper after the printing process has been completed. Typically, an FSI is sent to the newspaper firm, which charges the advertiser for placing it in the newspaper and distributing it. FSIs are most numerous in Sunday papers and can be devoted to one or multiple advertisers. Both types often carry discount coupons, which provide incentives for people to buy a product by giving them a certain amount off the retail price. Supermarkets, hardware chains, and other large retailers often create their own FSIs. Some FSIs are entire booklets that describe products and announce sales.

The FSIs that carry products of more than one advertiser typically are created by an FSI company. News America Marketing, a subsidiary of News Corporation, is a major firm involved in this work. This insert company makes deals with advertisers to carry their messages in FSIs in specific areas around the country at specific times. The advertisers pay the FSI firm; that firm generates the sheets, pays the newspapers to carry the sheets, and pockets the profits.

Although national ads and FSIs together provide only about 17 percent of revenues, newspaper executives nevertheless consider them important. FSIs are a relatively inexpensive way for newspapers to gain revenue, since all the newspaper

co-op advertising
advertising in which the manufacturers or distributors of products provide money to exhibitors in order to help the exhibitor with the cost of promoting a particular product

freestanding insert (FSI)
preprinted sheets that advertise particular products, services, or retailers, most often accompanying the Sunday edition of a newspaper; FSIs are not printed as a part of the paper itself, but are inserted into the paper after the printing process has been completed

Free-standing inserts (or FSIs) like the ones shown here are used to get maximum impact at a minimal cost, pinpoint a target market, and target customers in their home.

has to do is fold them into the issue. As for money from national advertisers, daily newspaper executives, especially, see that as a potential growth area, since the current amount is so relatively small.

When advertisers buy space in newspapers, a major way they evaluate it is by looking at the **cost per thousand readers** (often abbreviated **CPM**, for **cost per mil**). This is the basic measurement of advertising efficiency in all media; it is used by advertisers to evaluate how much space they will buy in a given newspaper or other medium and what price they will pay. If a full-page ad in a particular newspaper that reaches one thousand people costs ten thousand dollars, the CPM is ten dollars. Because advertisers often compare media in terms of CPM, even firms that have the only daily newspapers in their cities worry about coming up with ad prices that can compete with radio, TV, or even local ads inserted into national magazines.

cost per thousand readers or cost per mil (CPM)
the basic measurement of advertising efficiency in all media; it is used by advertisers to evaluate how much space they will buy in a given newspaper or other medium, and what price they will pay

Advertising Challenges Facing Newspapers

During the past few decades, a major goal of newspapers was to attract national advertising. Newspaper executives realized that because newspapers around the country had different advertising formats and different procedures for placing them, major national advertisers found the process of placing ads cumbersome and inefficient. That changed in the early 1990s, as the Newspaper Association of America and other groups drew on advanced technology and cooperation among newspaper firms to make it easy for advertisers to send the same ad to many papers around the country quickly and efficiently. Among the most effective has been the National Newspaper Network (NNN). The NNN can place national advertising in every newspaper in the United States, no matter what its circulation or ownership.

The activities did increase the amount of national newspaper advertising. Certain periods have been better than others, though, because the health of the economy has a lot to do with national firms' decisions to buy newspaper space. The same is true for retail advertising. For example, buyouts and bankruptcies of major department store chains often mean the loss of a portion of the dollars spent by those retailers on newspaper ads. As for classified advertising, a good economy leads more employers to advertise for jobs than does a poor economy.

During the past few years, however, the Internet has confronted newspaper executives with a new source of competition. They are beginning to see that some retail, national, local, and classified advertisers are following their target audiences to the Internet, taking money that traditionally has gone to newspapers and using it for online advertising. The lucrative classified area is a particular concern. Online help-wanted sites, real estate sites, auto sites and general classified sites such as http://www.craigslist.com are drawing lots of traffic. They provide users with continually updated information, interactivity, and immediate responsiveness that papers cannot possibly match. Although optimistic executives believe that classified advertising in traditional papers will continue, an increasing number believe that the industry's advertising climate is changing fundamentally and that they cannot take their past ad successes for granted.

In response, most newspapers have established websites with which they try to capture the retail, national and classified funds that have gone online. Sometimes it means making a deal with classified advertisers to place both print and online ads for a package price. That is something the *Atlanta Journal-Constitution* has tried, for example. Sometimes it means setting up a continuous local auction on the website where the paper gets a portion of the money made from the sales. The

Augusta Chronicle in Georgia has tried that. Sometimes it simply means offering readers the ability to place free classified ads online in order to lure them to the site so they will see paid retail or national ads.

Another approach that newspaper firms have used to capture advertising that goes to the Web is to create non-newspaper sites that copy their competitors. Examples are http://www.cars.com, a car buying and selling site; http://www.apartments.com, where people can find places to rent in specific cities; and http://www.careerbuilder.com, a help-wanted site. These new businesses often involve joint ventures on the part of several firms. For example, six newspaper companies came together to

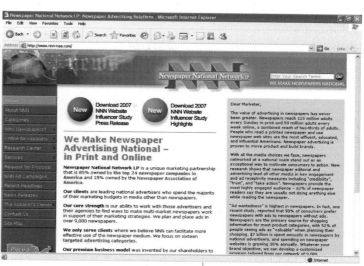

www.nnn-naa.com, website of the National Newspaper Network

start a firm called Classified Ventures, which owns various classified sites, including http://www.apartments.com. Clearly, executives believe that the cooperation they had shown in starting the National Newspaper Network will have to be extended to more areas in the new competitive environment. In 2007, the CEO of the Newspaper Association of America said that during this time of "transition" in the business, newspaper companies "have to continue to work together closely and productively and with a shared sense of commitment."[7]

It is important to note that the advertising money they collect from activities online, though growing strongly, represents a small percentage of the ad revenues they bring in. In 2005, for example, daily newspaper companies made about $2 billion from online advertisers. That sounds like a lot until you recognize that they draw $47 billion worth of ads to their printed pages.[8]

Circulation Challenges Facing Newspapers

Another major revenue challenge for newspapers has been circulation. We have already noted that the circulation for weeklies (especially free weeklies) has been steady, whereas a downturn in readership of the dailies has caused alarm among newspaper executives. Although newspaper income from circulation is far less than that from advertising, it is still critical because advertisers typically buy space in newspapers because of their circulation.

Historically, one factor encouraging the decline of readership has simply been the death of papers through bankruptcy or consolidation. Veronis Suhler (VS), a company that provides investment banking services to communication firms, has pointed out that the long-term decline in circulation has followed the long-term reduction in the number of newspapers. When papers consolidate or go out of business, the surviving papers do not capture all the lost circulation. In other words, the number of newspaper readers in an area shrinks when the number of papers decreases.

During the 1990s and into the twenty-first century, the rate at which daily newspapers died moderated. The circulation issue that now concerns many daily newspaper executives is whether young people will stop reading papers because they are so heavily involved in electronic media. Research in 2005 revealed that 66 percent of people 55 years and older read daily newspapers on weekdays and Saturday; 72 percent read the Sunday paper. When it came to 18–24-year-olds,

Figure 8.1

Who Reads Newspapers?
This graph, based on research conducted in 2005, shows that Americans over 55 read the daily newspaper in much greater numbers than Americans age 18 to 24. Newspaper executives are trying to secure younger adult readership by using both print and digital strategies.

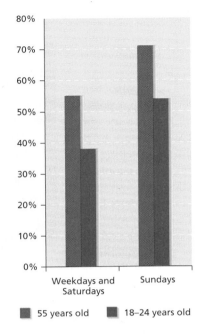

though, only 38 percent were weekday readers, and only 46 percent read the Sunday paper. A look at reading by these age groups over time shows that while still high percentages of older Americans (and especially those past 60) have continued to read the newspaper, the percentage of younger people reading it continues to decline.

One interpretation of these numbers is that, "The aging of America is a positive trend for newspaper companies." This interpretation may be too rosy, however. Even if more people pick up the newspaper when they pass the age of 55, that still leaves a large part of the rest of the population not doing it. And it suggests that newspaper circulation will not grow at anywhere near the pace of the entire population. Moreover, say pessimists, while 55-year-olds today may be more comfortable with print than with online news, in ten or fifteen years that may not be the case. The result might be that the increasing losses of young-adult readers that newspapers are seeing now may show up even among older readers.

Newspaper executives are trying to deal with these concerns using both print and digital strategies. Print strategies involve trying to create products that are both attractive to readers and profitable. Digital strategies involve trying to rethink the presentation and delivery of news. Both strategies affect the agendas of news that newspaper firms are offering their audiences. Let's look at both through our familiar categories of production, distribution, and exhibition.

Production and the Newspaper Industry

In discussing the production of newspapers, we will focus on two general areas. One involves the creation of the content that goes into the papers, and the other involves the actual technical process of putting together a newspaper.

Creating Newspaper Content

The creation of a newspaper's content differs between dailies and weeklies, and between newspapers with large circulations and those with small ones. We can, however, generalize about the basic approach to creating content (see Figure 8.2). The newspaper's **publisher** is in charge of the entire company's operation, which includes financial issues (getting advertising, increasing circulation), production issues, and editorial issues. **Editorial** in this case has two meanings. In a narrow sense, it means the creation of opinion pieces by the firm's editorial writers. More broadly, it means all non-advertising matter in the paper.

publisher   the individual in charge of all of a newspaper's operations, including financial issues, production issues, and editorial issues

editorial   a term used to describe both all nonadvertising matter included in the newspaper and opinion pieces created by a newspaper's editorial writers

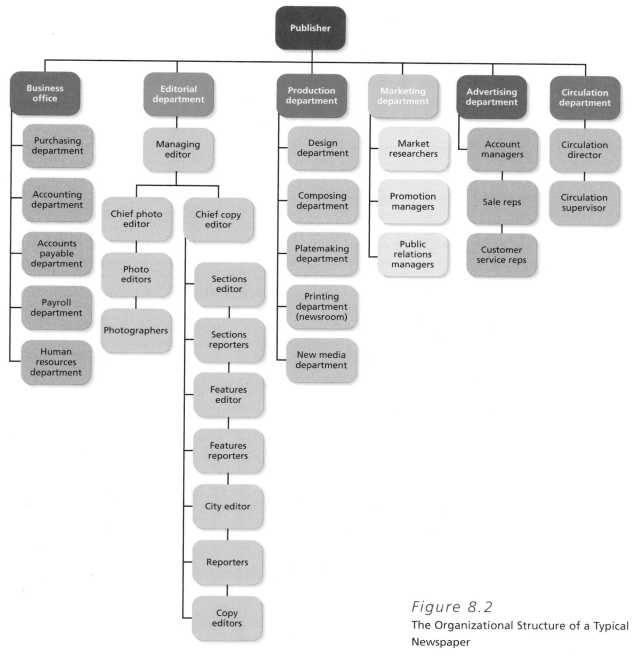

Figure 8.2

The Organizational Structure of a Typical Newspaper

advertising-editorial ratio
set by the publisher, this ratio determines the balance between the amount of space available for advertisements and the amount of space available for editorial matter in one issue of a newspaper

news hole   the number of pages left over and available for editorial matter, based upon the number of pages needed to run advertisements

editor   the executive in charge of all the operations required to fill the news hole

managing editor
individual who coordinates the work of the sections or departments within the newspaper

general assignment reporters   newspaper reporters who cover a variety of topics within their department

beat   a specific, long-term assignment that covers a single topic area

freelancer   a worker who makes a living by accepting and completing creative assignments from a number of different newspapers— sometimes several at one time

wire service   an organization that, for a fee, supplies newspapers with a continual stream of hard news and feature stories about international, national, and even state topics via high-speed telephone and/or cable connections

syndicate   a company that sells soft news editorial matter, cartoons, and photographs to newspapers for use

The publisher sets an **advertising-editorial ratio,** which determines the balance between the amount of space available for advertisements and the amount of space available for editorial matter in one issue of a newspaper. A typical daily newspaper carries 60 percent advertising and 40 percent editorial content. Weeklies have a higher percentage of advertising; some are virtually all advertising. For any particular issue of the paper, the number of pages left over and available for editorial matter (based on the number of pages needed for advertisements) is called the **news hole.** The executive in charge of all the operations required to fill the news hole is called the **editor.** He or she is aided by a **managing editor,** who coordinates the work of the sections (or departments) of the paper if there are any.

In a daily urban newspaper, typical departments might be sports, lifestyles, entertainment/leisure, business, TV, city news, a "neighborhoods" section, and real estate. Each department has one or more reporters assigned to it, and the editor may tell them what topics to cover, when, and where. Reporters who cover a variety of topics within their department are called **general assignment reporters.**

If the newspaper's editor and publisher consider a department especially important, they may give the editor the money and personnel to assign reporters to particular places or topics—for example, city hall and crime in the city news department, college athletics in the sports department, or movie reviewing in the entertainment/leisure department. Such specific long-term assignments are called **beats.**

However, a fair amount of a paper's editorial matter will not be written by members of the newspaper's staff. Sometimes an editor may hire individuals who accept creative assignments from a number of different newspapers to write such things as music or book reviews; these people are called **freelancers.** If the paper is owned by a group—Gannett or Knight Ridder, for example—that group may have its own news service that provides stories created by other papers in the chain. A substantial number of stories also will come from **wire services** such as the *Associated Press* and *Reuters.* These services, for a fee, supply via high-speed telephone and/or cable connections, a continual stream of hard news and feature stories about international, national, and even state topics for which the newspaper may have no reporters. Special wire editors and others continually check the stream of stories that "come over the wires" for likely material.

Syndicates also provide important materials for newspapers. A **syndicate** is a company that sells soft news editorial matter, cartoons, and photographs to newspapers for use. There are hundreds of syndicates that supply a variety of content for different departments and different audiences, including:

- The Washington Post Writers Group, the syndication arm of the *Washington Post,* circulates the work of columnists such as Ellen Goodman, George Will, and David Broder
- Copley News Service sells editorial cartoons
- Universal Press Syndicate offers a wide range of choices, from "Dear Abby" and Jeane Dixon's "Your Horoscope" to Marshall Leob's "Your Money" column to the "Doonesbury" comic strip

As you might imagine, syndicates supply some of the most popular parts of a paper.

For every issue, editors from all departments draw on all these sources to make up the paper. Under the watchful eye of editors, reporters on beats and those assigned to particular stories carry out their assignments. When it comes to the print version, everyone knows the paper's **deadline**—the time when the final version of their work has to be in. The news staff enters the stories into computers,

Project Censored

Are you tired of the routine coverage and lack of real diversity presented by the standard daily news media? You could turn to Project Censored, a nonprofit alternative media watchdog organization that tracks major stories that have not been given the full coverage they deserve by the mainstream media.

Every year, Project Censored researchers compile what they consider to be the twenty-five most important news stories that were not reported on by the major newspapers. For example, in 2007, the project reported that in the Congo region of Africa, more than six million people have died in the past decade as a result of invasions over the region's natural resources. Allegedly, many of these attacks have been sponsored by Western corporations vying for control over the region's diamonds, gold, and minerals used for electronics.

For a host of reasons, this important story was left out of any mainstream news coverage; it is just the kind of story that Project Censored seeks to uncover. Government and corporate censorship, Project Censorship's leaders say, can cause vital news to be excluded from the realm of possible stories. The organization utilizes the help of student interns and prominent media scholars to research and publicize its findings.

Based at Sonoma State University in California, Project Censored has been working the investigative alternative journalism beat for more than thirty years. It publishes its findings in annual compilations called the Censored Yearbook, and it works with other alternative media organizations like Fairness and Accuracy in Reporting (FAIR) to get its message out. Too many important stories are left uncovered, the project says, with serious consequences for democracy and action. After all, an informed citizenry is one of the key concepts of a democratic society, and if people aren't fully informed, some of society's worst ills may never be addressed. Project Censored feels a responsibility to pick up where traditional journalism leaves off and, according to its website, to "inform the public, advocate for independent journalism, and strive to spark debate on current issues involving media monopoly."

Source: http://www.projectcensored.org

---

which are linked to the managing editor and copyeditors, as well as to others on the paper. **Copyeditors** read the stories the reporters write and edit them for length, accuracy, style, and grammar. Headlines are written, and photographs and design work to accompany the stories are selected. Computer-ready syndicated material is chosen and added to the mix. The newspaper is ready to be printed.

Until around 2005, that was it: the work cycle of a newspaper centered on the time at which one or more editions had to be printed. When newspaper organizations began putting their material online, they followed this approach. To a large extent what readers saw on the Web was a reproduction of the printed product. Updates rarely happened, and editors were hesitant to put a story online that would reveal happenings that would override or contradict the printed product. That reluctance changed rather quickly, as newspaper executives realized that they were now competing with local and national television sites, including all-news channels—that were continually updating stories and presenting new ones. Newspaper executives decided they had to do that, as well, and so many sites have become round-the-clock—or **24/7**—operations. Today, stories are just as likely to premiere online as in the printed edition.

Moreover, the difference between the online and offline reportorial staffs is blurring. For certain topics not covered in the printed version—say, technology or certain local neighborhoods—the website might hire special staff. In general, though, the expectation today is that reporters will create for both the print and

deadline the time when the final version of an assignment has to be in

copyeditors the individuals who edit stories written by reporters; they edit for length, accuracy, style, and grammar, and write headlines to accompany the stories

24/7 around-the-clock news operations that continually update stories and present new ones

online products. That often means that they have to learn new skills that go beyond straightforward reportage. "Creating" for the online "paper" often means preparing a photographic or videographic version of the written material. In many cases, it also means writing a web log, or **blog.** That is a sort of diary or journal that may describe the events surrounding the coverage and that invites reader responses.

As you might imagine, this is a lot of work, and reporters have complained that the need to produce ever more materials for analog and digital forms does more than get them tired. Piling on the new reportorial tasks, they say, makes them focus so much on getting out the product in different ways that they have little time to conduct time-consuming legwork and thinking that will help them get below the surface of stories. Publishers and editors, though perhaps sympathetic, state that an expectation of intense cross-media activity is the direction in which the news world is moving.

If you've been to an online newspaper, you have probably noticed that the contents do not stop with the staff's takes on the day's news. Increasingly, newspaper websites aim to encourage their audiences—called **users** on the Web—to engage with the site in numerous ways. On many sites, for example, you can email a reporter whose story you have read; join a "community" of readers to discuss particular news topics; create a blog around any topic you like; search the week's news by using key words of your choosing; browse an archive of newspaper issues that may go back decades and beyond; watch video reviews, product demonstrations or news stories from the paper's staff or one of the wire services; click on an article so that the computer will read it to you; and (of course, and importantly for the sites) click on ads.

The Technology of Publishing the Paper

Despite this seeming cornucopia of material in the digital version of the daily or weekly newspaper, many people do read the printed version or both. Creating a website for them to read on a 24/7 schedule is a challenging and expensive activity. It requires information-technology professionals who tie the journalists into a world involving the creation of sites with many layers and the storage of huge amounts of material. Interestingly, much of the printed product starts out digital, too. Computers and related digital technologies are the mainstays of contemporary newspapers. Reporters now can go anywhere with portable computers and, if there is a telephone connection, send stories to the home department in a form that can be immediately read and printed. Even when local phone service isn't available, some reporters have telephones that beam messages to satellites so that they can "phone in" their stories. Similar portable transmitters allow photographers to beam images to the newspaper from the place of action. Digital cameras, which translate the world directly into computer code, allow images to be entered into the computers instantly.

Key to the activity is a process called **pagination**—the ability to compose and display completed pages, with pictures and graphics, on screen. In large daily and weekly newspapers, the technology enables the editors to transmit these images to the plates of the company's printing presses. See Figure 8.3 to see how *USA Today* uses electronic pagination in its production process.

Smaller papers use similar, though much less expensive, approaches. With personal computers, editors can use desktop publishing software to create the paper's layout. They can then take the results to a local printing shop, where the material can be printed relatively inexpensively. The costs of the operation are low enough that classified notices and ads from local merchants can support these small papers.

blog   a sort of diary or journal that may describe the events surrounding the coverage and that invites reader responses

users   the audience of newspaper websites

pagination   the process by which newspaper pages are composed and displayed as completed pages, with pictures and graphics

Printing: to Outsource or Not to Outsource?

TECH & INFRASTRUCTURE

For many media companies, outsourcing is a way to control costs and to remain focused on key areas of expertise. In the newspaper industry, publishers have traditionally outsourced everything from ad production and cartoon creation to Web operations and subscription delivery. Yet most newspaper companies have been unwilling to hand over the reins to their printing operations.

This is particularly startling given the high cost of maintaining a press as well as the fact that several national dailies have outsourced with great success. However, most newspaper executives cite concerns over commercial printers' reliability and proximity.

A more likely explanation, notes media economist Robert Picard, is a psychological one. According to Picard, the identity of a newspaper is so firmly linked to the notion of "the press" that the two have become virtually synonymous. Recently, though, the high costs of in-house printing have begun to outweigh benefits. A number of smaller papers across the United States and in Europe have already made the switch to commercial printers. And in 2006, the *San Francisco Chronicle* became the largest metropolitan paper to outsource its printing when it made public its 15-year contract with a Canadian printer.

In announcing the *Chronicle*'s decision, president and publisher Frank Vega said that this would ensure that the paper could "concentrate on what we do best, which is to gather news and information and advertising." Vega went on to say that he expects that many other major newspapers will adopt this type of model in the years ahead. Others agree that as newspaper profits continue to dwindle, companies will no longer be able to afford in-house printing operations. *Editor & Publisher* writer Jim Rosenberg says that, faced with declining circulation, publishers will have to make a choice to "either become printers with customers, or become printers' customers."

Sources: George Raine, "Chronicle Hires Firm to Print Newspaper," *San Francisco Chronicle*, November 18, 2006, online: http://www.sfgate.com; Jim Rosenberg, "Ironing Out a Problem?" *Editor and Publisher*, March 1, 2006, Lexis-Nexis.

The result has been the rise of free weekly papers that focus on sports, shows, politics, or neighborhood events in sections of large urban areas. Typically, the staff is quite small and the advertising-editorial ratio is quite high. Nevertheless, some observers see these smaller local newspapers as providing a wider range of information to their audiences than the dailies provided when they had monopolies.

Distribution and the Newspaper Industry

Newspaper distribution means bringing the finished issue to the point of exhibition. For a newspaper, that might be a person's house, a newsstand, a supermarket, or a vending machine—or to a computer or mobile device. Distributing a website on a 24/7 schedule is at least as challenging as creating it. The company's information-technology professionals must coordinate the serving of stories to users whose computers or mobile devices (typically "smart" cellphones) come to the sites, the serving of ads to those users (often with the help of separate ad-serving companies), and attempts to learn about users (in part to help sell ads) by getting them to register and by tracking their activities on the sites. Because these activities make the newspaper firms part of the larger Internet industry (along with

newspaper distribution
bringing the finished newspaper issue to the point of exhibition

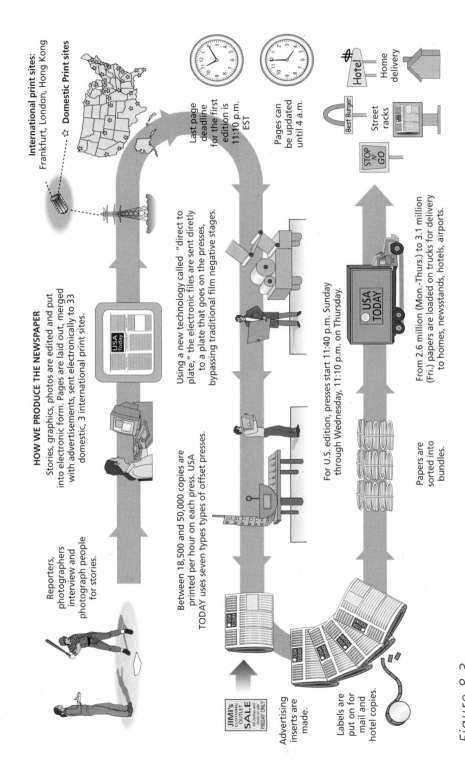

HOW WE PRODUCE THE NEWSPAPER

Stories, graphics, photos are edited and put into electronic form. Pages are laid out, merged with advertisements, sent electronically to 33 domestic, 3 international print sites.

International print sites:
Frankfurt, London, Hong Kong

☆ **Domestic Print sites**

Reporters, photographers interview and photograph people for stories.

Between 18,500 and 50,000 copies are printed per hour on each press. USA TODAY uses seven types of offset presses.

Using a new technology called "direct to plate," the electronic files are sent diretly to a plate that goes on the presses, bypassing traditional film negative stages.

Last page deadline for the first edition is 11:10 p.m. EST

Pages can be updated until 4 a.m.

Home delivery

Street racks

For U.S. edition, presses start 11:40 p.m. Sunday through Wednesday, 11:10 p.m. on Thursday.

From 2.6 million (Mon.–Thurs.) to 3.1 million (Fri.) papers are loaded on trucks for delivery to homes, newsstands, hotels, airports.

Papers are sorted into bundles.

Advertising inserts are made.

Labels are put on for mail and hotel copies.

Figure 8.3

How *USA Today* is Produced

USA Today is the United States' only national, daily, general-interest newspaper. It is printed each Monday through Friday at 33 locations across the country and is available nationwide.

Source: Copyright © 2000, USA Today. Reprinted with permission.

news sites that have no relation to newspapers), we will discuss these topics in Chapter 14.

Distributing physical newspapers is enormously challenging as well. Newspaper firms, especially dailies, typically distribute their own products. The task is carried out by the circulation department's personnel, under the authority of the business manager and publisher.

Determining Where to Market the Newspaper

The most basic question the circulation department must confront has to do with the geographic area in which it will market the paper. Many considerations go into making the decision. Among them are:

- The location of consumers that major advertisers would like to reach
- The location of present and future printing plants
- Competing papers
- The loyalty to the paper, if any, that people in different areas seem to have

Any or all of these considerations can change, of course. New major advertisers may be found, new printing plants can be built in certain places and not others, and marketing can try to encourage loyalty to the paper and beat the competition. The newspaper's business people, however, must examine the costs and benefits of every decision. The solutions they arrive at must necessarily vary with the newspaper's circumstances.

Executives at the *New York Times*, for example, have decided that their audience is an upper-income, educated class of readers that reaches far beyond the borders of New York City. As a result, they distribute a digital version of the paper by satellite to printing plants throughout the United States every day. The *Times* contracts with local companies to distribute the paper in those areas.

Most daily newspapers do not have such lofty circulation goals, but their executives do have to decide on the limits of their marketing territory. In deciding on those limits, they may be losing out on some ads from chain stores that have branches in the outlying areas that they have excluded. On the other hand, the paper won't incur the substantial costs of marketing and delivering papers beyond its primary territory.

Alternative Distribution and Marketing Tactics   In recent years, some newspaper groups have been having their cake and eating it, too, when it comes to winning chain store ads and not incurring the high costs of "fringe" circulation. Their tactic has been to buy dailies that serve adjacent communities. The groups then offer advertisers, particularly national and regional retailers, a single buy for the larger geographical area. The newspaper groups also save substantial amounts of money by combining their existing production facilities and staff. At the same time, each individual paper keeps its traditional coverage area and the loyalty of the readers in that area.

One example of a group using this tactic is Media General Newspapers, a group that owns, among other media holdings, three daily papers along U.S. Highway 29, an important business and residential corridor from Danville, Virginia, to the outskirts of Washington, DC. A shopper company that takes this approach is Newport Media, which owns weekly *pennysavers* across New York City, Long Island, and New Jersey. The firm boasts that it can offer advertisers "near 100 percent saturation advertising."

Newsprint and Recycling

More than 69 percent of old newspapers in the United States were recovered and recycled in 2005, representing more than 9.7 million tons of old newspapers out of a total supply of nearly 14 million. A growing proportion of the printed paper is made from recycled paper fiber. According to the Newspaper Association of America, in 1989, the average amount of recycled fiber in newsprint was 10 percent; by 2005 it was more than 32 percent. Newspapers are also recycled to make other products, from cereal boxes to insulation materials. Here is a breakdown for 2005:

Use of Recycled Newspapers

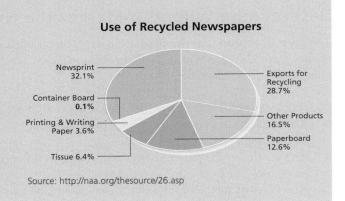

Newsprint 32.1%
Container Board 0.1%
Printing & Writing Paper 3.6%
Tissue 6.4%
Exports for Recycling 28.7%
Other Products 16.5%
Paperboard 12.6%

Source: http://naa.org/thesource/26.asp

A Critical View of Marketing and Distribution Tactics in the Newspaper Industry

Whereas newspaper firms see distribution policies as a marketing issue, media critics have pointed out that decisions to emphasize certain areas and not others can affect the makeup of the newspapers themselves, as publishers encourage editors to develop features and pursue news that will be of interest to the target audience. A particularly distressing development, say the critics, is that major daily newspapers have been concentrating their circulation efforts on the suburbs as opposed to the core cities that used to be their audience base. The reason is that during the past several decades, many of the upper- and upper-middle-class families that advertisers covet have moved to the suburbs, although they may work in the city.

The critics point out that along with marketing efforts to build up suburban circulation have come editorial policies that emphasize the interests of the upscale suburban groups over those of lower-middle-class urban dwellers. An increase in articles about suburban business, education, and lifestyles, for example, along with a de-emphasis on stories that are relevant to lower-middle-class urban dwellers, clearly signals what is the most desired audience. In addition, opinions on the editorial page might reflect the publisher's desire to appeal to certain income levels rather than others.

In the Philadelphia area, Philadelphia Media Holdings has used its ownership of two newspapers—the *Philadelphia Inquirer* and the *Philadelphia Daily News*—to channel the most desirable audiences to one of the papers and to guide the rest of the population to the other daily, where advertisers who want to reach them can do so. In its marketing, the *Philadelphia Inquirer* reaches out to business people who live in the suburbs and certain upscale parts of the city. The *Philadelphia Daily News*, in contrast, markets itself as a blue-collar daily for people who live in Philadelphia's many middle- and lower-middle-class neighborhoods.

Mirroring the different marketing philosophies are very different editorial policies. The *Inquirer* stresses international and national news, has a strong business section, and is decidedly upscale in its discussions of the arts and leisure activities. Compared to the *Inquirer*, the *News* is much more dedicated to city news and puts more emphasis on syndicated entertainment features. People argue as to which paper has the better sports section. A look at the ads and the classifieds also clearly indicates that these are papers for very different populations.

Exhibition in the Newspaper Industry

The digital *Inquirer* and *Daily News* do share areas on one distribution site, http://www.philly.com. Like other online news outlets, it is distributed through exhibitors—typically cable and telephone companies—to computers, smart phones and other devices wherever users can and want to pick it up. In the physical world, the exhibition point of a newspaper is more specific and depends upon its type. Free weeklies are often placed in special boxes in stores or on streets, with placards inviting people to take a copy. Weeklies and dailies that cost money can, of course, also be found in stores and in coin-operated boxes on streets as well as on newsstands.

However, circulation executives for paid weeklies and dailies prefer the exhibition point for their papers to be their readers' homes or places of work, as opposed to a newsstand. The reason is that delivery to a home or office implies a subscription to the paper, a paid-in-advance commitment to receive the product. Such commitments help the paper's business people sell advertising in the paper by enabling them to guarantee that advertisers can reach a fixed number of consumers in particular locations.

Achieving Total Market Coverage

Historically, paid-subscription daily or weekly newspapers could guarantee to advertisers that their ads would reach virtually every home in the newspaper's coverage area. However, because of the nationwide decrease in the percentage of homes receiving newspapers, the major dailies or weeklies in a region can no longer automatically provide advertisers with what people in the industry call **total market coverage (TMC)**. This problem, though, means opportunities for others. One direct competitor is the "shopper" firm, like Newport Media, which was mentioned earlier. Its marketing literature boasts that its free papers can offer, "customized home distribution programs" that will result in "near 100 percent saturation" of the audiences that advertisers desire.

Other competitors offering TMC to advertisers are **direct mail firms,** which mail ads directly to homes. Companies that specialize in delivering circulars that might otherwise be newspaper inserts are called **marriage mail outfits;** they produce sheets and brochures from several advertisers that are bundled together (hence the term *marriage*) and sent via the post office to every address in a particular area. With this approach, names are not nearly as important as reaching every house or apartment. In fact, the required postal cards accompanying the ads are often addressed simply to "current resident." There is little, if any, nonadvertising matter in the package. Some would say that what we have here is quintessential junk mail.

total market coverage (TMC) reaching nearly all households in its market area

direct mail firms advertising firms that mail advertisements directly to consumers' homes

marriage mail outlets advertising firms that specialize in delivering circular advertisements that might otherwise be inserted as FSIs in newspapers; these firms produce preprinted sheets and brochures from a number of advertisers, bundle them together, and send them directly to consumers' homes

New Exhibition Strategies for Newspapers

Retailers have found that marriage mail and shoppers are efficient ways to get their FSIs out to entire neighborhoods when local newspapers cannot offer that kind of service or when they are more expensive. As you can imagine, marriage mail firms and shoppers have siphoned away newspapers' coveted supermarket advertising and FSIs. But the newspapers are fighting back. One way is to compete directly. Some newspapers have started their own shoppers and marriage mail operations or have bought their competitors. Other papers have supplemented their regular paid circulation to certain key areas with a weekly TMC circulation. They accomplish that goal by delivering a special version of the newspaper (usually a compilation of stories or a sports section) to every nonsubscribing home in an area. Ads and FSIs are included with the package.

In addition to competing head on to keep TMC dollars, business executives at many paid-circulation newspapers try to persuade advertisers that they lose credibility when they use marriage mail and shoppers instead of "real" local newspapers. The Gannett Company went so far as to conduct research in the mid-1990s to support its claim that newspapers were more useful to advertisers than ads mailed directly to consumers. The firm reported that consumers are nearly three times more likely to read and use newspaper inserts than to read and use advertisements they get in the mail. The reason, said Gannett, is that people see the newspaper with its ads as useful while people see the bundle ads as junk. Unlike their reaction to mailed advertisements, "people welcome newspapers into their homes. They read ads instead of pitching them." So, concluded Gannett, "when advertisers pay for direct mail, they pay for distribution [only]. When they pay for newspaper advertising, they pay for impact."

A Key Industry Issue: Building Readership

Despite such boastful statements and the belief of some investors that young adults who are not reading newspapers now will begin to read them as they get older, publishers and editors are extremely concerned with the recent downturn in newspaper readership trends. They know that physical newspapers charge more per thousand readers for advertising than their websites do and bring in far more advertising revenue than their Web versions. In the foreseeable future, their organizations could not survive without a healthy print edition. They therefore believe they need to find ways to get people to read physical newspapers at a time when news and entertainment are available from so many electronic sources. At the same time, many newspaper executives believe that they must adapt their organizations to new digital media. A 2006 study by the Newspaper Association of America (the NAA) found that compared to 2005 there were strong gains in online reading of newspapers among people in the age brackets that newspapers and their advertisers covet most: adults 18 to 24 (up 9 percent) and adults 18 to 34 (up 14 percent).[9] These are clearly audiences that the newspaper companies want not only to keep, but to increase.

As a result, then, many newspapers are pursuing two types of approaches to building readership. One group of approaches might be called analog strategies, which involve the physical paper. The other might be termed digital strategies, which involve the website and other Internet-related ways that the paper can intersect with the lives of its readers. We will look at each group separately.

Building Print Readership

One question is basic, "What does a physical newspaper have to look like to attract more people, now and in the future?" Newspaper executives have been working hard to develop answers. Here are a number of approaches that they have tried, together and separately.

More Attractive and Colorful Layouts   The movement in this direction started with the launching of *USA Today* by the Gannett Company in 1982. The paper was designed to attract the interest of travelers around the United States, particularly at airports, train stations, and bus stations. Right from the start, consumers seemed impressed with the paper's look. It had color photos at a time when that was quite rare in newspapers. It had eye-catching graphics and charts filled with interesting facts. Critics complained that the attraction was just skin deep, that the trivial topics, short articles, and beautiful graphics did not truly give readers an understanding of what was going on. They said it lacked substance. In a reference to the food produced by McDonald's, which some believe is a bland, institutional, insubstantial meal, critics called *USA Today* McPaper.

USA Today has come a long way since 1982, and many of its critics admit that it is a far more serious paper today than it was back then. What many publishers and editors thought they had learned from the paper's quick popularity, though, was that a carnival of color and short articles was a necessity in an era in which people do not seem to want to read long articles and often read the newspaper while watching television.

Many papers (including the *New York Times*) have now switched to color presses and embarked on major redesigns aimed at stopping readers in their tracks and getting them to want to read every issue. Other features designed to be reader-friendly include fewer stories on the front page, more liberal use of white space, quick news summaries and notes about "what's inside," and more use of charts and pictures to convey information. Individual stories, too, have gotten shorter. The aim is to create a quick and not too taxing read.

USA Today is known for its bold color and visuals. The newspaper combines words and graphics that tell what happened in the last 24 hours and what to expect in the next 24 hours. This approach to layout, color, and story length has influenced many American newspapers.

Sections Designed to Attract Crucial Audiences   Newspapers aim to create a collection of articles that is relevant to the audiences that newspaper companies care about. For many papers, that means the people aged twenty-something to forty-something (and hopefully relatively well off) that most major national and local advertisers covet. To find out what those target audiences want, publishers employ research firms to conduct surveys and focus groups. The idea is to concentrate on news that people can "use"—that is, news that is clearly relevant to their lives.

Large chains such as Gannett and McClatchy have been testing this approach to newspaper publishing in at least some of their dailies. Their executives argue that it is only good business to find out what kinds of things people want to read about and to give them what they want. And, in many cases, readership has increased. Moreover, some papers have made themselves more audience-friendly, while retaining or improving their reputation for solid coverage of news and information. During the 1980s and 1990s, for example, the *New York Times* aggressively beefed up its daily business section and created sections on science, food, and the home that appeared on different weekdays. Editors designed the new sections to gain favor with key audiences and advertisers interested in them. In addition to achieving that goal, the *Times* also won raves from critics for its solid coverage of often underreported topics.

Emphasizing Localism   Many newspaper executives have come to the conclusion that it is reporting on the communities in which their readers live that gives them a leg up on competition from other media firms, especially online news sources. Newspaper consultant George Hayes put it bluntly: "One should never underestimate the importance of being local! Newspapers own that."[10] Being local can mean many things. It may mean publishing news about local school events, photos of county fair winners, and letters to the editor that discuss community affairs. It may mean polling readers through surveys or focus groups to find out what they think are the most important issues in local, state or national election campaigns. It may mean covering problems in the area and editorializing with vigor about ways to solve them. Newspapers are using these and other techniques to encourage people in their areas to see them as related to their lives on a regular basis.

Even papers in the biggest U.S. cities, which have tended to emphasize national and international coverage more than the goings on in neighborhoods, have begun to increase their attention to local news. In some places, it means increasing the attention that city and regional stories get on the front page. That has been happening at the *Philadelphia Inquirer*. In many papers it means expanding or adding sections that relate to the goings on in neighborhoods. Those sections are typically distributed once a week to the places that they cover. That specificity allows advertisers to target segments of the newspaper's market without buying the entire distribution of the paper. As newspapers increase their stress on localism, the number of sections is likely to grow, as is their frequency. The *Washington Post* may be a pacesetter in this regard. In 2007, it experimented with creating a twice-a-week section for a particularly wealthy DC suburb that its advertisers wanted to reach.

Related to this desire to reach out to various segments of readership are some major newspaper publishers' investments in, or outright purchase of, weekly and smaller daily papers in the markets that surround them. Some of these papers are useful to have because they represent direct competition for advertising. Other properties executives consider useful include free commuter dailies, ethnic publications and alternative weeklies. These fill a different but still important niche: with lower rates they attract smaller advertisers who would not advertise in the larger daily.

Building Digital Newspapers

It was only a few years ago that newspaper publishers viewed the Web as necessary but unprofitable. That has changed. As the CEO of the McClatchy chain said in 2007, "It used to be online audiences were worthless to newspapers; now we are making money."[11] The bulk of this money comes from advertising, for almost all newspapers allow readers to browse their sites without charge. Sometimes, the papers' websites do require visitors to fill out registration forms that ask for basic demographic information and sometimes inquire about their interests. That information is used to help the paper attract advertisers by claiming to be able to serve ads to different types of people—men, for example, or women, or under 50 years old. And, in fact, the growth of advertising on newspaper websites has been substantial, though in the past year or so has leveled off from the enormous gains of 2005 and 2006.

The need for building digital newspapers is two-fold. First, it is to keep the sites interesting so that readers keep coming back and new readers visit. Second, it is to generate enough revenues from these readers that the growth of the digital area can make up for slow or negative circulation and advertising growth on the print side. These challenges are, of course, related, and they are daunting. The main reason is that there are so many places on the Internet users can get news that newspapers risk losing readers and advertisers to those many alternatives.

To make and keep their sites attractive to readers, newspapers have been continually updating the print and audiovisual materials mentioned earlier. Many offer users the ability to download audio stories automatically to their MP3 players; this activity is called **podcasting**. Another offering is the **RSS feed**. That is a flow of stories on topics the reader has chosen that the newspaper sends to the individual's personal website (at http://www.myspace.com or http://www.myyahoo.com, for example) so that the user does not have to go to the paper's website to see it. Still another service is the **mobile feed**—stories specifically formatted for the user's cellular phone, "smart" device or personal digital assistant. The overall aim of the podcasts, RSS feeds, and mobile feeds is to encourage users to pull toward them parts of the newspaper that they like. Although the newspapers don't charge for these services—digital users have shown that they won't pay for general news content—each of the feeds comes with advertising. And newspapers have been busy trying to figure out how to serve ads efficiently to people based on both their registration material and their activities online (for example, their interest in the automotive section or the style section) so that advertisers looking for people with those interests and backgrounds will pay a premium to reach them.

The interest in targeting users for advertisers parallels a belief by newspaper publishers that a key way for them to distinguish themselves from other news sites their users can visit is to emphasize the local. This is the digital version of the "own the local" strategy that newspapers are pursuing with their print versions. Because the digital world allows for so much more content than in a physical paper, some publishers have begun to say they are following a "hyper-local" strategy online. That is, they want to reach out to many more geographic and demographic segments of the newspaper's area than the physical paper ever could—and garner advertisers who want to reach those very local segments. For a big-city paper, being hyper-local means covering school meetings across many neighborhoods, contin-

podcasting audio recordings that can be downloaded to MP3 players

RSS feed a flow of stories on topics the reader has chosen that the newspaper sends to the individual's personal website (at MySpace or MyYahoo, for example) so that the user does not have to go to the paper's website to see it

mobile feed stories specifically formatted for the user's cellular phone, "smart" device or personal digital assistant

Four major newspapers online:
www.washingtonpost.com, www.nytimes.com,
www.latimes.com, www.usatoday.com

ually listing restaurants and entertainment activities in different parts of the city, reporting on many school and amateur sporting events, hosting the discussions of neighborhood clubs—in short, trying to become the go-to place for information about what is going on in the area. Carrying out this goal can be costly, and newspaper executives must balance their level of localism with the advertising that it brings in. In many cases, they can rely on volunteers to populate some of the local pages; in others, they hire special web reporters whose job it is to work out of their cars, sending digital reports to the paper as they move from community event to community event.

In search of digital advertising, some large newspaper companies have been buying media properties that enlarge their audiences. The *New York Times* owns the encyclopedia-like site http://www.about.com, for example, and the *Washington Post* owns the opinion/feature articles site http://www.slate.com. By selling these visitors as well as the newspaper-site users, the firms can attract more advertisers than their individual papers would. This approach certainly applies to the *Wall Street Journal*, owned by News Corporation. News Corp can package the sale of ads in the online *Journal* with ads for its other online sites based on what it knows about the demographics of the readers and their digital activities.

Media Literacy and the Newspaper Industry

A few large corporations with strong holdings in the newspaper industry, such as the *New York Times*, have gone beyond websites to experiment with electronic newspapers. In one version, a flexible sheet or monitor would replace the paper. Subscribers would be able to tell the newspaper firm what kinds of hard and soft news they would most like to read, and the paper would be customized to individual interests. In another version, every evening a subscriber would plug the sheet into a computer connection at home. During the night, stories, features, comics, and ads that were customized for the subscriber would be transmitted from the newspaper firm and stored in the monitor. In the morning, the subscriber would unplug the sheet and take it around the house or on the subway or to the office. Rather than turning the page, the reader would tap the story on the screen, and more of it would appear on the monitor, along with colorful ads. In the evening, the process would start over again.

Such futuristic scenarios may indeed come to pass, but for the next several years (at least) the newspaper will still most probably appear on newsprint, on your computer, and on small handheld devices. No matter what the delivery system, though, editors must still attract readers, and their activities need to make money. That ability to make money is at the heart of the concerns that knowledgeable observers have about the newspaper's future. Some of them believe that the print version is doomed to disappear and that the digital versions of most will not be able to make enough advertising money to support the staff that is required to put out an acceptable product. One controversial writer, the media consultant Henry Blodget, wrote bluntly on his blog in 2007 that "Newspapers are Screwed." More sober, but still pessimistic, was the 2007 assessment by the famously savvy investor Warren Buffett. Buffett, who owns a portion of the *Washington Post* and has a long connection with the business, wrote that "fundamentals are definitely eroding in the newspaper industry, [and] the skid will almost certainly continue." He went on to state that, "The economic potential of a newspaper Internet site—given the many alternative sources of information and entertainment that are free and only a click away, is at best a small fraction of that existing in the past for a print newspaper facing no competition."[12]

Many in the newspaper industry don't agree with him, of course. Some are sure that physical papers will always exist alongside digital versions and that the two will bring in enough money to make newspaper publishing a viable business. As an *Editor and Publisher* writer notes, "Others have looked at history and concluded that as print has survived the advent of radio, movies, and television, newspapers will survive the rapid development of cyberspace technology and find their place in the future."[13] Tony Barbieri, a University of Maryland journalism professor and former managing editor of the *Baltimore Sun*, doesn't automatically buy that rosy view. He argues that Buffett's analysis will prove correct only if the industry does not change, but he thinks executives will eventually find a good business plan. "I think even newspaper executives are smart enough to see that we need a new revenue model in our industry," Barbieri told the trade magazine *PR Week*.[14]

These cross-currents of concern are obviously crucial to consider if you have an interest in pursuing a career in the newspaper industry. But they are also important to understand as a citizen concerned about the flow of news through our society. Most observers, including Buffett, invoke the civic importance of the newspaper industry when talking about it and worrying about its demise. By saying that, they imply that newspapers are providing knowledge that other sources of news—online, on TV, and in print—do not present. The point deserves critical examination. From the standpoint of local, regional, national, and/or international news, what unique roles do newspapers play in presenting the world to readers? Apart from many jobs (not an inconsiderable concern in itself), what would be lost to society if the future of newspapers is, in the words of one writer, "fundamental doom"?

There are indeed important roles that newspapers—especially local newspapers—can play in the life of society that are not easily duplicated by other existing sources. To ensure the future of the newspaper, though, it is necessary to make these roles clear, to pursue them, and to find ways to support them. This is the profound challenge that the newspaper industry and people outside the industry who care about newspapers will have to confront for years to come.

CHAPTER REVIEW

For an interactive chapter recap and study guide, visit the companion website for *Media Today* at www.routledge.com/textbooks/mediatoday

QUESTIONS FOR DISCUSSION AND CRITICAL THINKING

1 Why is the penny press important to the development of the contemporary U.S. newspaper?
2 What are some similarities and differences between daily and weekly newspapers?
3 What effects can advertising have on the production, distribution, and exhibition of a newspaper?
4 When might a newspaper want total market coverage, and when might it want to carry out segmentation?
5 What are the arguments of people who believe that printed papers are doomed to disappear, and those who disagree with them?

INTERNET RESOURCES

Chronicling America: Historic American Newspapers (http://www.loc.gov/chroniclingamerica)

Chronicling America, a project of the Library of Congress and National Endowment for the Humanities, represents, says the site, a "long-term effort to develop an Internet-based, searchable database of U.S. newspapers with descriptive information and select digitization of historic pages." The site allows you to find out which libraries hold which newspapers and in what form—original or microfilm. You can also see digitized versions of front pages of newspapers—for example, the *New York Sun*—going back more than one hundred years.

Newspaper Association of America (http://www.naa.org)

On its website, the NAA calls itself "a nonprofit organization representing the $55 billion newspaper industry… NAA members account for nearly 90 percent of the daily circulation in the United States and a wide range of nondaily U.S. newspapers." This site, then, is a good portal into the mainstream U.S. newspaper business. Various areas cover advertising, circulation, electronic publishing, diversity, and other aspects of the newspaper business.

Association of Alternative Newsweeklies (http://aan.org)

The Association of Alternative Newsweeklies (AAN) calls itself "a diverse group of 130 alt-weekly news organizations that cover every major metropolitan area in North America." This website reflects the breadth of its membership through a directory of its member publications, an ability to receive email newsletters on various topics of the business, an archive of articles about alternative weeklies, and more.

International Newspaper Marketing Association (http://www.inma.org)

This organization focuses on the marketing aspects of the newspaper business, with perspectives reflecting its diverse membership representing 70 countries. Its website contains useful papers and conference reports reflecting changes in the ways newspapers are trying to increase circulation and advertising.

KEY TERMS

You can find the definitions to these key terms in the marginal glossary throughout this chapter. Test your knowledge of these terms with interactive flash cards on the *Media Today* companion website.

adversarial press	marriage mail outfits
advertising-editorial ratio	mobile feed
alternative weekly	national ads
beats	news hole
blog	newspaper chains
byline	newspaper distribution
circulation	objectivity
classified ad	pagination
co-op advertising	podcasting
copyeditors	publisher
cost per thousand readers (CPMs)	retail advertising
dailies	RSS feed
dateline	shoppers
direct mail firms	syndicate deadline
editorial	tabloid forms
freelancers	total market coverage (TMC)
freestanding inserts (FSIs)	users
general assignment reporters	weeklies
headline	wire services
managing editor	yellow journalism

CONSTRUCTING MEDIA LITERACY

1   What relevance does the history of newspapers have to understanding the current situation of the newspaper?
2   From what you have read and see around you, how pessimistic or optimistic are you about the newspaper's future? Why?
3   If you or some friends do not read a newspaper or visit a newspaper site, what would it take to encourage you (or them) to do that? Are the steps the industry is taking persuasive?
4   Do you agree with those who argue that localism—even hyper-localism—is the way for newspapers to remain relevant and profitable in an age of so many information sources? Why or why not?

CASE STUDY   Analyzing a Newspaper's Attempt to Engage Its Audience

The idea: As the chapter notes, many newspaper websites today are attempting to attract audiences by creating a variety of ways to receive the sites' content as well as encouraging them to interact around, and even contribute to, the websites' content. Examples are blogs, conversation areas, RSS feeds, and mobile capabilities. The purpose of this assignment is to encourage you to explore the techniques that your local paper is using and to carry out a hands-on examination of them.

The method: Examine your local newspaper's website for ways that it is trying to interact with audiences and to encourage audiences to interact with each other around its content. Spend a week using these tools yourself. Then write a report of about four pages about your experience. In your paper, answer the following questions: to what extent did it allow you to get closer to news you want? To what extent did it extend your understanding of various sorts of news? Did the blogs or chat areas make you want to come back to the site more than you would if you hadn't connected with them? In general, how successful were these techniques in creating bonds between you and the newspaper?

9 THE MAGAZINE INDUSTRY

After studying this chapter, you will be able to:

1 Sketch a history of magazines and the importance of knowing it

2 Describe the physical and digital production, distribution, and exhibition of different types of magazines

3 Explain the view that magazines are brands that need to follow their readers

4 List the risks and barriers involved in launching a new magazine

5 Analyze critics' concerns regarding the influence of industry ownership and advertising

"Most women's magazines simply try to mold women into bigger and better consumers."

– GLORIA STEINEM, WRITER

Media Today

Attendees at a breakfast arranged by the Magazine Publishers of America must have been surprised when Ann S. Moore, the top executive at Time, Inc., the largest magazine publisher in the United States, talked about the anxiety her job had brought her. It was May 2007, and Moore had gone through months of layoffs, and the sale or shut-down of several magazines under the Time umbrella. With her staff, she had also been immersed in trying to remake her magazine division of Time Warner into a powerful force that could attract large and desirable audiences and advertisers—not just in print but on the Web and other areas of the digital environment. According to the trade magazine *Advertising Age*, Moore said that the goal—transforming her company from a firm focused on paper into a multimedia player—had been wrenching, professionally and personally.

"Steering an organization through change is hard," she said, knowing that many of the magazine-publishing executives in her audience were feeling the same pressures. But she also pointed to successes that had come out of her work—for example, growing revenue at *Sports Illustrated* and *People Magazine*, partly because of their popular websites. Her advice to her peers: "You know, everybody stay calm," she suggested. "This is a great business we're in."[1]

As Ann Moore suggests, the industry is changing dramatically in order to fit into the new media world. Magazine companies are killing magazines, rethinking magazines, trying out new magazines, and going online in their bid to succeed in the face of the changing demands of their marketplace. Critics say that not all of these changes have served readers well. They charge that the huge conglomerates that own the most popular magazines have been turning them into cross-media brands that are in danger of losing their editorial independence from advertisers.

How are we to understand and evaluate this concern? What forces are shaping the future of magazines, and what might that mean for the news and fashions that circulate through our society? To begin answering these questions, we first have to get a grasp on the industry itself. This chapter introduces the enormous cauldron of activity that is the magazine business through the by now familiar categories of history, production, distribution, and exhibition. We start with history as a way to show how we got to where we are now. A sketch of the past also demonstrates that our era is not the first in which the magazine industry has had to grapple with major change.

The Development of Magazines

The word *magazine* comes from French; it means storehouse. **Magazines** were, and still are, collections of materials (stories, ads, poems, and other items) that their editors believe will interest their audience.

By the 1700s, magazines were being published regularly in England, as the growing power of Parliament allowed for more public arguments about governing than in the past. Political magazines and literary magazines made their debuts. Some, such as the famous *Tatler* and *Spectator* served up both politics and litera-

magazine a collection of materials (stories, ads, poems, and other items) that editors believe will interest audiences

ture by famous writers of the day. Of course, these magazines were aimed at, and were read by, England's wealthy elite. Not only were most people of the time illiterate, they couldn't afford to buy the magazines.

The same was true in the American colonies of England. Similar to newspapers, magazines aimed at relatively wealthy people, often merchants or plantation owners with literary and/or political inclinations. The first magazines appeared in 1741 in Philadelphia; Benjamin Franklin was one of the printers who tried his hand at publishing a periodical. Printers in Boston and New York soon followed, and the colonies saw many attempts at periodically released magazines. One estimate has it that around one hundred magazines appeared and disappeared by the time of the Revolutionary War.

After the establishment of the United States, the rapid turnover of magazines continued. However, magazines seemed to fail as fast as they were introduced. One reason (aside from illiteracy and the expensive production technique) was the cost of transportation. Magazines were heavy, and the increased load led some postal workers to refuse to carry them.[2] In 1825, fewer than one hundred magazines were published. Still expensive collections of commentary and literature for the well-educated, magazines were often more hobbies or extensions of book company activities than serious money-making enterprises. In fact, most editors and writers for American magazines during the first quarter of the nineteenth century received very little compensation for their work, or didn't get paid at all. Magazines were a labor of love that reached a small community of readers. They were also dull-looking, with few pictures—and the ones that appeared tended to be crude block prints.

The Transformation of Magazines into Mass Media

You might recognize the early newspaper and even the early book in this description. In fact, just as entrepreneurs took advantage of the rise in education, the new steam-powered presses, and postal loopholes to expand the market for newspapers and books after 1830, there were those who used the new technological and social environment to advance the business of magazines.

Between 1825 and 1850, the number, the nature, and the business of magazines changed dramatically. In 1850, about 600 magazines were published in the United States. As high as that figure is compared to the fewer than 100 magazines that existed in 1825, it only suggests the ferment that was taking place: in the period from 1825 to 1850, between four thousand and five thousand new magazines were introduced in the United States. Most of them died quickly, but the fact that new periodicals continued to be launched meant that business people were beginning to see that there was a large market emerging for magazines. The magazines that survived were still more expensive than newspapers, and they assumed a higher intellectual level. But even so, as a group they began to exert increasing influence on the nation's cultural life.

Magazines dedicated to diverse subjects began to draw audiences that numbered in the tens and hundreds of thousands. Two outstanding periodicals launched around that time that are still in circulation today are *Harper's Monthly* (founded in 1850) and *Scientific American* (founded in 1845).

The Rise of Women's Magazines

An especially important development of the magazine age was the rise of magazines aimed at women. The most important one was *Godey's Lady's Book*,

NUMB. 1

The SPECTATOR.

Non fumum ex fulgore, fed ex fumo dare lucem Cogitat; ut fpeciofa dehinc miracula promat. Hor.

To be Continued every Day.

Thurfday, March 1. 1711.

I Have obferved, that a Reader feldom perufes a Book with Pleafure 'till he knows whether the Writer of it be a black or a fair Man, of a mild or cholerick Difpofition, Married or a Batchelor, with other Particulars of the like nature, that conduce very much to the right Underftanding of an Author. To gratify this Curiofity, which is fo natural to a Reader, I defign this Paper, and my next, as Prefatory Difcourfes to my following Writings, and fhall give fome Account in them of the feveral Perfons that are engaged in this Work. As the chief Trouble of Compiling, Digefting and Correcting will fall to my Share, I muft do my felf the Juftice to open the Work with my own Hiftory.

I was born to a fmall Hereditary Eftate, which I find, by the Writings of the Family, was bounded by the fame Hedges and Ditches in *William* the Conqueror's Time that it is at prefent, and has been delivered down from Father to Son whole and entire, without the Lofs or Acquifition of a fingle Field or Meadow, during the Space of fix hundred Years. There goes a Story in the Family, that when my Mother was gone with Child of me about three Months, fhe dreamt that fhe was brought to Bed of a Judge: Whether this might proceed from a Law-Suit which was then depending in the Family, or my Father's being a Juftice of the Peace, I cannot determine; for I am not fo vain as to think it prefaged any Dignity that I fhould arrive at in my future Life, though that was the Interpretation which the Neighbourhood put upon it. The Gravity of my Behaviour at my very firft Appearance in the World, and all the Time that I fucked, feemed to favour my Mother's Dream: For, as fhe has often told me, I threw away my Rattle before I was two Months old, and would not make ufe of my Coral 'till they had taken away the Bells from it.

As for the reft of my Infancy, there being nothing in it remarkable, I fhall pafs it over in Silence. I find, that, during my Nonage, I had the Reputation of a very fullen Youth, but was always a Favourite of my School-Mafter, who ufed to fay, *that my Parts were folid and would wear well.* I had not been long at the Univerfity, before I diftinguifhed my felf by a moft profound Silence: For, during the Space of eight Years, excepting in the publick Exercifes of the College, I fcarce uttered the Quantity of an hundred Words; and indeed do not remember that I ever fpoke three Sentences together in my whole Life. Whilft I was in this Learned Body I applied my felf with fo much Diligence to my Studies, that there are very few celebrated Books, either in the Learned or the Modern Tongues, which I am not acquainted with.

Upon the Death of my Father I was refolved to travel into Foreign Countries, and therefore left the Univerfity, with the Character of an odd unaccountable Fellow, that had a great deal of Learning, if I would but fhow it. An infatiable Thirft after Knowledge carried me into all the Countries of *Europe*, where there was any thing new or ftrange to be feen; nay, to fuch a Degree was my Curiofity raifed, that having read the Controverfies of fome great Men concerning the Antiquities of *Egypt*, I made a Voyage to *Grand Cairo*, on purpofe to take the Meafure of a Pyramid; and as foon as I had fet my felf right in that Particular, returned to my Native Country with great Satisfaction.

I have paffed my latter Years in this City, where I am frequently feen in moft publick Places, tho' there are not above half a dozen of my felect Friends that know me; of whom my next Paper fhall give a more particular Account. There is no Place of publick Refort, wherein I do not often make my Appearance; fometimes I am feen thrufting my Head into a Round of Politicians at *Will's*, and liftning with great Attention to the Narratives that are made in thofe little Circular Audiences. Sometimes I fmoak a Pipe at *Child's*; and whilft I feem attentive to nothing but the *Poft-Man*, over-hear the Converfation of every Table in the Room. I appear on *Sunday* Nights at St. *James's* Coffee-Houfe, and fometimes join the little Committee of Politicks in the Inner-Room, as one who comes there to hear and improve. My Face is likewife very well known at the *Grecian*, the *Cocoa-Tree*, and in the Theaters both of *Drury-Lane*, and the *Hay-Market*. I have been taken for a Merchant upon

The Spectator, an extremely influential early British magazine founded by Joseph Addison and Richard Steele in 1711, aimed to prepare its readers for intelligent conversation in polite society. It was the first daily periodical to cover literary and cultural matters from philosophy to etiquette, rather than focusing strictly on news.

Godey's Lady's Book, launched by Louis A. Godey in 1830, led the wave of new periodicals aimed at women. It had the highest circulation of any magazine in the mid-nineteenth century in the United States.

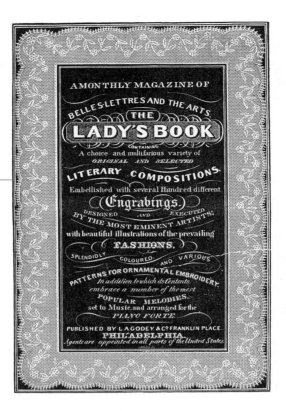

a monthly launched in 1830. By 1850, it had the highest circulation of any magazine in the United States, reaching more than 150,000 readers; it included hand-colored engravings of fashions, along with articles and fiction stories. Louis A. Godey was the first in a string of famous male editors of periodicals for females. He was helped tremendously in his work by his female assistant editor, Sarah Josepha Hale, who joined him in 1837. Hale was a determined champion of education for women at a time when many didn't see the point of it. (She also gained a type of immortality by writing "Mary Had a Little Lamb" and persuading President Lincoln to declare Thanksgiving a national holiday.)

In the same way that the rise of the penny press spawned a new structure for creating the newspaper, the expansion in magazines beginning in the 1830s changed the structure of the business. The notion of the freelance magazine writer evolved. As today, they made their living by selling their works to different periodicals. Notable examples—some known today and some not—were Lydia Sygourney, Edgar Allan Poe, Margaret Fuller, and Henry Wadsworth Longfellow. The magazine editor, who was now paid a decent wage, also took on a new role. Although not quite the administrator and strategist of today, the editor began working with writers rather than doing the writing himself or herself.

Fundamental Changes in Magazine Publishing

Chapter 8 notes that the transformation of newspapers in the first half of the 1800s set them up for even greater changes in the second half of the century. Magazine publishers were responding to the same forces: faster printing technologies, new ways to reproduce pictures and even photographs, huge population growth, an increase in literacy. One difference between the way newspapers and magazines reacted to these developments was that newspapers focused on reaching people in the local areas in which they were published, while more and more magazines aimed to attract national audiences of sizes that no U.S. media had previously reached. The huge expansion of the railroad in the second half of the nineteenth century helped them do that. Trains permitted the efficient transportation of all sorts of mail, including magazines. The expansion of the postal service to rural areas (through rural free delivery routes) meant that most of the nation could receive periodicals easily. Moreover, the Postal Act of 1879 substantially lowered the cost of mailing magazines.

Adding to the technological possibility of reaching millions of readers was publishers' realization that advertisers were suddenly interested in using magazines to reach huge national audiences. Many of these manufacturers were using factory methods to create products that had been made by hand, often by the user's family, only a few years before. Other plants were turning out products—toothpaste, corn flakes, safety razors—that no one had made previously. The large number of items being produced encouraged competition between manufacturers of similar goods. One result was the creation of **brands**—products with distinctive names and identities that make them stand out from their competitors. But in order to make money on a particular brand of soap or any other mass-produced item, a manufacturer had to make sure that hordes of people recognized the brand and bought it.

brand a name and image associated with a particular product

Frank Munsey was a magazine owner who showed how advertising could pay most of the costs of producing the magazine. His low subscription prices for *Munsey's* magazine lured many readers. He used those large numbers to attract advertisers who wanted to reach those readers, and he charged the advertisers for reaching them. He proved quite successful, and the approach caught on. For the first time, the specific goal was to attract hundreds of thousands, even millions, of customers in order to deliver them to advertisers. In earlier decades, readers' subscriptions had covered a large percentage of the publisher's costs; now advertisements provided most of the revenues. On the strength of this approach, in 1901 the *Ladies' Home Journal* became the first magazine to pass one million in circulation. Two years later the readership of the *Saturday Evening Post* was an unprecedented two million. The *Post* brought in advertising revenues of $25 million that year.

New Roles for Mass-circulation Magazines

The most popular magazines at the turn of the twentieth century provided their readers with an exciting mixture of sensational news about problems in their society with entertaining stories and helpful advice.

Sensational News: the Work of the Muckrakers

From 1900 to 1912, the *Ladies' Home Journal*, *Collier's*, *Everybody's*, *McClure's*, *Munsey's*, the *Saturday Evening Post*, and other magazines joined with great enthusiasm in crusades against big business, against corruption, and for social justice. A group of American journalists, novelists, and critics known as **muckrakers** attempted to expose the abuses of business and the corruption in politics.

muckrakers American journalists, novelists, and critics who, in the early 1900s, attempted to expose the abuses of business and the corruption in politics

The term *muckraker* was coined by President Theodore Roosevelt in a speech in 1906, in which he agreed with many of the muckrakers' charges, but asserted that some of their methods were sensational and irresponsible. He compared them to a character in John Bunyan's book *Pilgrim's Progress* who had a muckrake in his hands; he could look no way but downward and was interested only in raking

The term "muckraker" was coined by President Theodore Roosevelt, depicted in this 1906 editorial cartoon cleaning up corruption in the meat packing industry.

A NAUSEATING JOB, BUT IT MUST BE DONE

the filth. Since the 1870s, there had been recurrent efforts at reform in government, politics, and business, but it was not until the advent of the national mass-circulation magazines that the muckrakers had sufficient funds for their investigations and a large enough audience to arouse nationwide concern. The writers were mostly newspaper reporters who liked both the extra money and the national exposure that such magazines offered. Their work sometimes had enormous impact.

All aspects of American life interested the muckrakers, the most famous of whom are Lincoln Steffens, Ida Tarbell, David Graham Phillips, Ray Stannard Baker, Samuel Hopkins Adams, and Upton Sinclair. In the early 1900s, magazine articles that attacked trusts—including those of Charles E. Russell on the beef trust, Thomas Lawson on Amalgamated Copper, and Burton J. Hendrick on life insurance companies—did much to create public demand for regulation of these great corporations. Probably the most far-reaching of these stories were those in *McClure's* and the *Ladies' Home Journal* about the dangers of food and medicine. These articles helped encourage the passage in 1906 of the first Pure Food and Drugs Act.

The muckraking movement lost support around 1912. However, historians agree that had it not been for the revelations of the muckrakers, the Progressive movement would not have received the popular support needed for effective reform.

Entertainment Roles: the *Ladies' Home Journal* and the *Saturday Evening Post*

Overall, though, the focus of magazines in the first two decades of the twentieth century was more on entertainment—storytelling, humor, and information—than on sensational news. Colorful covers were combined with stories by famous writers and articles about famous people, often from the new media of sound recordings and cinema. The advertisements were also standouts: some were full page, in color, and designed to be a pleasure both to behold and to read. Because of their ads, mass-circulation magazines were often quite hefty. The *Ladies' Home Journal* stood out in this respect. It sometimes carried more than $1 million of ads in a single issue, and an issue often ran to more than two hundred pages.

The *Ladies' Home Journal* and the *Saturday Evening Post*, both published in Philadelphia by the Curtis Publishing Company, were undoubtedly the most important periodicals of their era. Cyrus Curtis, the publisher of these magazines, was an advertising, marketing, and distribution wizard who helped shape the close relationship between advertisers and magazines. The *Saturday Evening Post's* editor, George Horace Lorimer, aimed to appeal to all the adults in the United States. Under Lorimer's direction, the *Saturday Evening Post* attained its greatest success, partly because of his astute judgment of popular U.S. tastes in literature. Lorimer published works by some of the best U.S. writers of the time: Stephen Crane, Frank Norris, Theodore Dreiser, Jack London, Willa Cather, Ring Lardner, F. Scott Fitzgerald, and Sinclair Lewis. In addition, he brought such European authors as Joseph Conrad and John Galsworthy to U.S. readers. Lorimer held conservative views, and this was reflected in the articles he published in the magazine. Upton Sinclair wrote that the material in the *Saturday Evening Post* was as "standardized as soda crackers; originality is taboo, new ideas are treason, social sympathy a crime, and the one virtue of man is to produce larger and larger quantities of material things." However, Lorimer did employ the radical David Graham Phillips, who wrote more than fifty articles criticizing the rich and powerful. By December 1908, Lorimer was able to announce in the *Saturday Evening Post* that for the first time the journal was selling more than a million copies a week. Circulation continued to increase under Lorimer's stewardship, and by the end of 1913 it had reached two million.

Edward Bok, editor of the *Ladies' Home Journal*, edited his periodical as if he were writing for all the nation's women. Bok, a Dutch immigrant, was one of the most powerful magazine editors, if not the most powerful, in U.S. history. By 1900, the *Ladies' Home Journal* was the best-selling magazine in the United States. In addition to using his magazine to promote ideas on interior decorating and the appearance of cities, Bok showed great courage on social issues. During his tenure at the *Ladies' Home Journal*, he used the magazine to campaign for women's suffrage, pacifism, conservation of the environment, improved local government, and sex education—regardless of the effect on subscriptions. In campaigning for sex education, for example, Bok lost thousands of subscribers by running an article about syphilis. The topic shocked readers; it was, in fact, the first time that even the word "syphilis" had been used in a popular magazine. He also instituted the Curtis advertising code, a type of self-regulation, which specifically banned financial, tobacco, playing card, and liquor advertising in the firm's magazines.

The *Ladies' Home Journal*, the *Saturday Evening Post*, and many other mass-circulation magazines thrived during the first four decades of the century. During the 1920s, more specialized magazines made successful debuts. One type focused on the idea of distilling information for busy people. *Reader's Digest*, a compendium of "must read" articles, and *Time*, a weekly news summary, first appeared in 1922 and 1923, respectively. Both had predecessors in magazine history, and both had their imitators. The second type of magazine reflected an elite, knowing cynicism and humor that seemed to be the mark of the so-called Jazz Age, the 1920s. The *New Yorker* was the most successful of these magazines.

Magazines Later in the Twentieth Century

During the 1960s and 1970s, the magazine industry again found itself in an environment that demanded fundamental change, thanks to the new medium of television. By the late 1950s, most U.S. homes (86 percent) had at least one television set; that number had jumped to 93 percent by 1965. The huge popularity

From 1899 to 1969, millions of Americans saw themselves each Tuesday in the cover art of the *Saturday Evening Post,* the most popular magazine in the country.

of the television began to hurt mass-circulation magazines such as the *Saturday Evening Post.* Large advertisers abandoned magazines for TV because it could help them reach even larger portions of the U.S. population than mass-circulation magazines at a comparable cost. Not only that, but television allowed for dynamic ads with moving pictures and sound, features that print media couldn't offer.

Advertisers' shift to television marked the beginning of the end of America's mass-circulation magazines, despite their large readerships. For example, *Coronet* ceased publication in 1963, even though it had a circulation of 3.1 million. Around that time the *Saturday Evening Post* and several other magazines like it also died.

It took the magazine industry a few years to adjust to these stunning reversals, but by the early 1970s, executives had developed a new approach to their business. Instead of trying to reach "everybody" and compete with TV, magazine executives decided to develop periodicals that were designed to attract narrow slices of the population that certain types of advertisers wanted to reach. Certainly, there were already magazines that were tailored to particular ethnic, religious, occupational, and hobby groups, but the new magazines tried to go beyond those categories and tap into the newer, narrower interests and lifestyles of the relatively affluent in U.S. society—target audiences that advertisers especially wanted. Small, targeted audiences became especially profitable for magazines as technology developed in the 1970s and 1980s. New computer-driven printing technologies allowed companies to make substantial profits with magazines that reached hundreds of thousands, or even tens of thousands, of people instead of millions.

The potential for great profits drew big companies. Giant firms dominated the magazine industry as the industry moved into the twenty-first century. Time Warner's Time Inc. magazine company is the advertising and circulation leader. Other leading consumer magazine groups are Hearst Magazines, Advance Publications, and Meredith Publishing Company. But if the 1990s were a time of strong revenues and confidence, the 2000s are, as noted earlier, a time of worry and sober concern with the future. Let's look at the current profile of the industry.

An Overview of the Modern Magazine Industry

Earlier, we described magazines as collections of materials (stories, ads, poems, and other items) that their editors believe will interest their audience. While this notion of what a magazine is makes sense on the surface, it still leaves lots of ambiguity. But frankly, even people who work in the magazine industry don't seem to have a consistent definition of a magazine. Some, for example, put comic books under the magazine tent, while others don't. What's more, one could argue that the difference between a weekly magazine and a weekly newspaper is sometimes in the eye of the creator or beholder, not in any particular features to which anyone can point.

The Magazine Association of America, which doesn't define the term in its annual handbook, reports that 19,419 different magazine titles were published during 2006 in North America.[3] Most magazines are monthly (issued once a month), although semimonthly magazines (issued twice monthly), bimonthly magazines (issued once every two months), and magazines issued ten times each year are also common.

American newsstands regularly display about 2,600 magazine titles. Many others can be seen in the periodicals section of large university or city libraries. Magazines differ widely in both circulation and topic. As a mind-boggling example, consider that the 19,000 magazines that the Magazine Publishers of America refers to include *AARP: The Magazine* (circulation 23 million), *Inc.* (circulation 682,000), *American Woodworker* (circulation 270,000), and *Gun Dog* (circulation 31,000)—all in the same list!

Five Major Types of Magazines

People who work in the magazine industry categorize magazines in several ways, but there seems to be general agreement that if a periodical fits into one of the following five categories, it is to be considered a *magazine*:

- Business or trade magazines
- Consumer magazines
- Literary reviews and academic journals
- Newsletters
- Comic books

Let's see what each of these categories includes.

Business-to-business Magazines/Trade Magazines

A **business-to-business (B-to-B) magazine**, also called a **trade magazine**, focuses on topics related to a particular occupation, profession, or industry. Published by a private firm or by a business association, it is written to reach people who are involved with that occupation, profession, or industry.

Standard Rate and Data Service (SRDS), a firm that collects information about magazine audiences and ad rates and sells it to advertisers and ad agencies, devotes an entire reference directory to business magazines. The directory divides business specializations into over 200 categories. Examples are: advertising and marketing, automotive, banking, building, ceramics, computers, engineering and construction, healthcare, and hotels, motels, clubs, and resorts.

The titles within SRDS's categories are as varied as the subjects they cover. Notable business publications include *Geriatrics*, *Architectural Record*, *Emergency Medicine*, *Institutions* (covering the food service industry), *Professional Builder*, and *Medical Economics*.

Are you interested in what funeral directors read? You'll find nine magazines, among them *American Funeral Director*, *The Director*, and *Morticians of the Southwest*. *The Director* is the official publication of the National Funeral Directors Association. *Morticians of the Southwest* is a regional publication (that

business-to-business or trade magazine a magazine that focuses on topics related to a particular occupation, profession, or industry

editorial profile   a summary of a magazine publisher's publication philosophy, designed to inform potential advertisers of the kinds of articles that will surround their ads

is, its circulation is limited to one part of the country), whereas the other two reach readers nationally.

Like the other magazines in the SRDS business directory, each funeral magazine presents its **editorial profile**—a summary of its publication philosophy that is designed to inform potential advertisers of the kinds of articles that will surround their ads. A careful reading of the editorial profile also provides a sense of the comparative position, or niche, that a publisher is trying to establish for a magazine. *American Funeral Director*'s profile, for example, centers on the practicalities of a mortician's business—"cremation, pre-need, funeral business topics, professional vehicles, computers and software, insurance, lifestyle and travel planning, profitable business operation tips/tools, and other content of specific interest to those working in the profession."

Consumer Magazines

consumer magazines   magazines aimed at the general public

Consumer magazines are aimed at people in their private, nonbusiness lives. They are sold both by subscription and on newsstands and magazine racks in stores. They are called **consumer magazines** because their readers buy and consume products and services that are sold through retail outlets and that may be advertised in those magazines. Think of a magazine that you or your friends read for fun—for example, *Men's Health*, *Time*, *People*, *Essence*, *Woman's Day*, *Vanity Fair*, *Details*, *Spin*, *Wired*, or *Maxim*. It's likely to be considered a consumer magazine.

The SRDS consumer magazine directory lists 75 categories, from Adventure and Outdoor Recreation to Youth. Two major categories are Women's Magazines and Men's Magazines. The magazines listed under these labels aren't the only ones targeted to women or men in the United States. Instead, they're merely tags that magazine publishers want SRDS to use in presenting them to would-be advertisers—"beauty" magazines (for women) or "sports" magazines (for men) might be other listings. Still, the "women's" and "men's" categories provide an idea of the number of magazines specifically aimed at gender categories.

The Women's Magazines category alone contains 137 magazines, including titles such as *Allure*, *American Woman*, *Cosmopolitan*, *Harper's Bazaar*, *Harper's Bazaar en Español*, *Woman's World*, *Playgirl*, *Woman's Health Monitor*, and *YM*.

The category also contains the periodicals that have long been the giants of the women's magazine business: *Family Circle, Good Housekeeping, Ladies' Home Journal, Woman's Day, Redbook,* and *Better Homes and Gardens.* These and many other periodicals for women are called **service magazines.** That is, they provide advice for women across a wide spectrum of life issues—how to dress, how to cook, how to discipline kids, how to catch a man, how to make love.

If it's hard for you to think of men's magazines that fill this "service" role, that's because there are many fewer such magazines for men than there are for women. One sign is that the Men's Magazines category has far fewer titles than the Women's Magazines category—39 compared to 137. Another is the list of titles in the category. Among the better known are *Details, Esquire, Field and Stream, GQ, Men's Fitness, Men's Health, Men's Journal, Outdoor Life, Playboy, Cigar Aficionado, Maxim,* and *Wired.* As you can see, only a few of these magazines—*Esquire, Men's Health, Men's Journal,* and maybe *Maxim*—could legitimately claim the broad service label. Magazine industry executives have puzzled for decades over the reasons for the relatively small number of service magazines for men. Some observers have suggested that the traditionally "macho" role for males in U.S. society has made it less acceptable for them to share intimate parts of their lives with one another, in person or in print. In fact, although magazines for men about men may not be plentiful, periodicals on traditionally male subjects certainly are. SRDS links several magazine subject areas to men—for example, Automotive, Fishing and Hunting, Fitness, and Sports—and each of these areas has many titles. Take a look at the periodicals listed under any one of these topic categories, and you'll see how specialized many magazines are. There aren't just one or two or ten magazines about automobiles—there are more than a hundred.

Literary Reviews and Academic Journals

This category includes hundreds of publications with small circulation figures. **Literary reviews** (periodicals about literature and related topics) and **academic journals** (periodicals about scholarly topics, with articles typically edited and written by professors and/or other university-affiliated researchers) are generally nonprofit; funded by scholarly associations, universities, or foundations, and sold by subscription through the mail. Examples are the *Journal of Communication* (a scholarly journal from the International Communication Association), *The Gettysburg Review* (a literary review of short fiction, poetry, essays, and art), *Foreign Affairs* (a journal of opinion from the Council on Foreign Relations), and *Harvard Lampoon* (the oldest humor magazine in America).

Because their readers are often quite highly placed in academia, politics, or business, these periodicals often have clout that far exceeds their small circulation. Moreover, journalists often look to some of these publications for fresh ideas that they can discuss in broader-reach newspapers and magazines. Some of the most influential ideas in history have come from scholarly journals and reviews—for example, the first mapping of DNA in the journal *Science;* key theories about humans' apelike ancestors in the journal *Nature;* weighty discussions at the start of the cold war about how the United States should deal with the Soviet Union in *Foreign Affairs.*

In recent years, controversy has swirled around what you might imagine is the rather scholarly arena of academic journals. Seeing captive markets (because every field has just a few key journals) and low labor costs (because most academic editors volunteer their time), big companies have moved into the business. They have raised subscription prices enormously, to the point that college

service magazine a type of consumer magazine, aimed at women, which provides advice for women across a wide spectrum of life issues

literary reviews small-circulation periodicals about literature and related topics; usually funded by scholarly associations, universities, or foundations

academic journals small-circulation periodicals that cover scholarly topics, with articles typically edited and written by professors and/or other university-affiliated researchers

Academic Journals and Open Access

Chances are, your university library houses a collection of academic journals that is eclectic, impressive—and expensive. A subscription to the brain sciences journal *Brain Research* costs more than $20,000; many others are upwards of $10,000. In fact, subscription rates for academic journals have risen on average 226 percent from 1986 to 2000.

Despite the high price, university librarians feel under tremendous pressure to continue their subscriptions. "Librarians have long felt voiceless in negotiations with publishers," explains *Chronicle of Higher Education*'s Lila Guterman. "Since every journal's contents are unique, university libraries feel compelled to subscribe to journals that their faculty members need, almost regardless of cost."

A potential solution to this issue is the notion of "open access." Spearheaded by former head of the National Institutes of Health Harold E. Varmus, the open access model makes journals available to scholars at no cost. Instead, authors pay a small fee to get their work published. Not only does this reduce the direct costs to universities,

but it also helps authors get cited since their work is more freely available.

While the open access movement is not without its skeptics, a number of publishers have already adopted this model. In 2007, Marquette Books announced that it would make eight of its communication journals available free of charge, making it the first private publisher to provide open access. According to Marquette's publisher, "At a time when most for-profit publishers are increasing the costs of their journals, we decided to go the opposite route and offer all of our journals free of charge." He added, "We want the scholarship in our journals to be read by as many people as possible."

As a student and researcher, where do you fall on the issue of open access?

Sources: Lila Guterman, "The Promise and Peril of 'Open Access,'" *The Chronicle for Higher Education*, January 30, 2004, online: http://www.chronicle.com; "Marquette Books Goes 'Open Access' With Communication Journals," Press Release, August 21, 2007, www.marquettejournals.org

and university libraries have been painfully squeezed as journal costs rose far faster than inflation.

Newsletters

newsletter a small-circulation periodical, typically four to eight pages long, that is composed and printed in a simple style

A **newsletter** is a small-circulation periodical, typically four to eight pages long, that is composed and printed in a simple style, unlike the large, sometimes glossy-page periodicals we have discussed until now. Part of the reason is cost. Newsletters typically go to small numbers of people at a frequency that would make a more production-heavy publication too expensive. The rather plain look of a newsletter often matches its editorial purpose: to convey needed information in a straightforward way. People receive these publications by mail, by fax machine, or, increasingly, online.

When we hear the term *newsletter*, many of us may think of the information bulletin of a church or school. We are less likely to know about the large number of newsletters that are used in business. They often center on specific areas of an industry, and they are published frequently; most come out weekly or biweekly, but a few are daily. They address decision-makers in those areas and provide statistical trends and gossip about that area of the business. The aim is to help these decision-makers do their jobs better. Executives pay a lot of money for those newsletters, from a couple of hundred to a few thousand dollars per subscription.

Comic Books

As you may well know, many comic books are neither comical nor books. The term **comic book** for a periodical that tells a story through pictures as well as words developed in the 1930s as publishers of cheap ("pulp") magazines that presented detective, romance, action, and supernatural-science stories tried to take advantage of the popularity of newspaper comic strips to boost sagging sales. They put their material into comic-strip form and sold it in a complete story unit as a comic book.

Archie and his friends Jughead, Betty, and Veronica have remained teenagers at Riverdale High since the comic book debuted in 1942.

comic book   a periodical that tells a story through pictures as well as words

Today, comic books run a wide gamut of topics. The label covers *Alvin and the Chipmunks* as well as *Green Lantern*, *Blade*, and *Conan*. Although historically most comic books were aimed almost exclusively at preteens, nowadays many tilt toward far older readers. Archie Comics is traditional, aiming at girls and boys aged six to eleven with *Archie*, *Betty and Veronica*, *Sabrina the Teenage Witch*, and the like. IDW Publishing is among the new breed. In its monthly comic books, it targets teens and young adults with heroic adventure and science fiction tales such as *The Transformers*, *30 Days of Night*, and *Fallen Angel*. Other companies produce products that are clearly aimed at adults. The Kitchen Sink Press publishes *Gay Comics*, an anthology of the American homosexual experience, and *Twisted Sisters*, another anthology that includes comic tales depicting the romance problems of both heterosexual and homosexual women.

By far the largest firms in terms of overall circulation are Marvel Comics Group and DC Comics. Marvel alone turns out more than fifty different comic book titles, limited series, quarterlies, and special editions that feature more than 3,500 characters and together reach about 5.7 million people a month. Marvel also has different targets for its superhero books. Some, such as *Marvel Adventures Fantastic Four*, aim at youngsters, whereas others, such as *Astonishing X-Men* and *Amazing Spider Man*, go after teens and adults.

Some executives in the magazine industry don't consider comic books part of their industry; the American Magazine Association doesn't report on them. The reasons for this attitude vary. Some people cite the comic books' mostly pictorial emphasis and note that "real" magazines are more text-oriented. Some note that comic books are distributed in special stores, not in the places where magazines can usually be found. Others mention the much cheaper paper that many comic books use. These criticisms don't really hold water. For one thing, many children's periodicals and "nudie" publications emphasize pictures, and magazine executives consider them to be in the fold. For another, comic books were sold on newsstands for most of their existence; it is only in the last couple of decades that producers have built up new distribution and exhibition routes. As for paper, the quality of paper varies across the vast world of magazines.

It is true that comic books today use a broad spectrum of formats. Some, the more traditional, look like small magazines with inexpensive newsprint and stapled bindings. Others have wider, heavier, glossier pages; glued bindings; and sometimes even rigid nonmagazine-like covers. Comic book publishers are increasingly turning to the Internet. In November 2007, Marvel Comics launched Marvel Digital Comics Unlimited, posting thousands of past and present comics online, while DC and Dark Horse comics began posting sample issues on MySpace. We must conclude that history and custom lead magazine and comic book people to view one another differently.

Financing Magazine Publishing

One feature that comic books clearly share with other magazines is the presence of advertising. Of all forms of magazines, only newsletters and academic journals have not made ads an important source of cash. The amount of money we're talking about is substantial. In 2005, advertisers spent $8.7 billion on space in business magazines and $12.7 billion on space in consumer magazines. For individual business (trade) and consumer periodicals, advertising typically provides the largest percentage of revenues. Consumer magazines receive between 50 and 60 percent of their money from ads, whereas business magazines rely on advertisers for an even higher proportion of their funds—between 70 and 80 percent). Table 9.1 lists the periodicals that draw the most ad money, and Table 9.2 lists the advertisers who spend the most money on magazine advertisements. According to the Magazine Publishers Association, the top fifty advertisers in magazine spending—about $8.5 billion—equaled 35 percent of all the revenue that magazines brought in.

Controlled-circulation Magazines

Most of the other money the magazines bring in comes from readers. From the numbers presented in the previous section, you can see that readers collectively

Table 9.1 **Top Ten Magazines by Advertising Revenues, 2006**

Rank	Magazine	Total gross ad revenue, 2006 (in millions of dollars)
1	*People*	850
2	*Better Homes and Gardens*	800
3	*Time*	631
4	*Parade*	626
5	*Sports Illustrated*	623
6	*Good Housekeeping*	477
7	*Newsweek*	472
8	*USA Weekend*	431
9	*InStyle*	391
10	*Parade*	275

Source: R. Craig Endicott, "Magazine 300," *Advertising Age.*

Table 9.2 **Top Ten Magazine Advertisers by Total Ad Dollars Spent**

Rank	Company	Total ad dollars spent, 2006 (in millions)
1	Procter & Gamble Co.	838.5
2	Altria	418.3
3	General Motors	390.4
4	GlaxoSmithKline	331.7
5	Ford Motor Company	326.1
6	L'Oreal SA	318.1
7	Johnson & Johnson	304.7
8	Time Warner	258.6
9	Toyota Motor Corp	252
10	Pfizer Inc.	251.3

Source: Magazine Publishers of America, Top 50 Magazine Advertisers.

pay more for consumer magazines than they do for business magazines. It turns out that although some trade magazines are quite a bit more expensive than consumer periodicals, nearly two-thirds of their readers actually pay nothing for the trade periodicals they receive in the mail. Business-press publishers have learned that so many advertisers want to reach personnel in certain industries that it is possible to support the production of a periodical and the mailing of it to readers without charging the readers. This type of magazine is called a **controlled-circulation magazine**. Consider, for example, *Medical Economics*, a magazine for doctors about the business of medicine. Its circulation is "controlled" in the sense that the publisher, rather than the reader, decides who gets it. *Medical Economics* creates a list of doctors whom advertisers would likely consider useful targets and mails issues to those people only. Postal rules require that once every year publishers ask those readers if they want to continue receiving the material.

One type of consumer magazine that often has controlled circulation is the **custom magazine**. It is typically created for a company with the goal of reaching out to the company's customers or other people (such as government officials) that it wants to impress. One major custom publisher, Hachette Filipacchi, puts the goal this way: "Through a precise understanding of our client's strategic marketing and communication objectives, coupled with our proven ability to motivate consumers through meaningful and relevant content, we create one-to-one communications that foster a long-term relationship with a client and its customers."[4]

Advertisers have bought the idea. According to the Custom Publishing Council, custom publishers distribute about 34 billion copies a year. *American Way*, given out on American Airlines flights, is one example of a custom magazine. *WebMD the Magazine*, sent to 85 percent of physicians' waiting rooms in the United States, is another. The custom field is populated by firms that specialize in this area, but some of the largest consumer magazine publishing firms, such as Hachette

controlled-circulation magazine a magazine whose production and mailing is supported not by charging readers, but (typically) through advertising revenues; the publisher, rather than the reader, decides who gets the magazine

custom magazine a controlled-circulation magazine that is typically created for a company with the goal of reaching out to a specific audience that the company wants to impress

357

Filipacchi and Time Inc., have custom divisions. Many custom magazines carry advertising only for the company, whereas others (such as *American Way*) solicit ads from many different sponsors that don't compete with American Airlines. You'll never see a United Airlines ad in an issue of *American Way*.

Paid-circulation Magazines

paid-circulation magazine a magazine that supports its production and mailing by charging readers money, either for a subscription or for a single copy

The opposite of controlled circulation is **paid circulation**—in which the readers of a magazine pay for that magazine by purchasing either a subscription or a single copy. The overwhelming majority of consumer magazines work on this model. The reason is that because of the enormous competition for advertising among consumer periodicals, they cannot raise their ad rates enough to cover all their costs. As a result, they must rely on a dual revenue stream, with readers picking up some of the tab. In the consumer area, advertisers like to see readers pay. They worry that if you had the opportunity to get *Money* magazine free or dirt cheap, you might not bother to read it, and so you would not see the ads. That concern doesn't seem to be as strong among business-magazine advertisers. Maybe it should be.

circulation the number of units of a magazine/ newspaper sold or distributed free to individuals in one publishing cycle

Advertisers who are considering buying space in business or consumer magazines try to find out as much as they can about the readers of those magazines before they put down their money. The most basic information is **circulation**—the number of units of the magazine sold or distributed free to individuals in one publishing cycle. Publishers can hire one of a number of organizations to inspect ("audit") their shipments on a regular basis and certify that the number of copies the publishers claim to circulate is, in fact, the number they do circulate. The Audit Bureau of Circulation (ABC) is the best known of these organizations; the Business Publications Audit of Circulation (BPA) is another. Small publications that don't want to pay for audits, or that can't afford them, often come up with a "sworn circulation" number from the publisher that they hope potential advertisers will take seriously. The circulation of *Medical Economics* (about 169,000) is audited by BPA, whereas the circulation of *Pharmaceutical Representative* magazine (about 72,000) is sworn.

For consumer magazines and the larger business magazines, information about readership begins rather than ends with audits. The enormous number of magazines that are competing for ad dollars means that in order to survive, a magazine firm must present research findings that prove to potential advertisers that its readers are of the kind and in the quantity that the advertisers want. Often, that means paying research companies to obtain information about readers that might lure sponsors. Publishers invest money in their own databases about readers as well as in custom and syndicated research.

media kit a database compiled by a magazine that tells potential advertisers attractive key facts about its readers

Look at ads in any trade magazine aimed at the advertising industry, and at the **media kits** that magazines circulate to entice advertisers. You'll quickly notice how periodicals try to outdo one another in boasting about why their readers are better buys than other magazines' readers. In 2007, for example, *Seventeen*'s online media kit used data from the MRI research firm to make the claims that *Seventeen* reaches not only "America's teens" (5.9 million of them), but that it grabs "the older, more sophisticated teen" (more 16–19 year olds than *Teen People*, *CosmoGirl* or *Teen Vogue*) and also "dominates the young women's market" (reaching 6.8 million 18 years and older). The kit also boasts that *Seventeen* influences readers' understanding of fashion, beauty and music trends in ways that will boost advertisers. In May, September and December of 2006, for example, it ran a *17 Deals* program: "an exciting in-book and online program that highlights the coolest products that our readers must check out."[5]

Market Segmentation

One note in *Seventeen*'s media kit is that the magazine will be able to target ads by certain regions of the country. In fact, many consumer and business magazines today offer advertisers the possibility of paying for certain portions, or **segments,** of the readership. During the printing process, certain ads, and even special articles, are bound into copies that go to certain people, and other ads and articles are printed in copies that go to other people. As you might imagine, printing different ads in a magazine based on characteristics of the audience can be expensive, and small-circulation titles may not be able to offer it. In fact, publishers of small titles would consider this sort of segmentation unnecessary because they are niche-oriented already. But large-circulation magazines have a particular incentive to break their readership into segments, to allow advertisers to zero in on readers by geography or demographic type.

> **segments** portions of a magazine's readership that an advertiser wants to reach

Consider *Reader's Digest*, which has an audited circulation of ten million. Apart from a national run-of-book ad, the magazine sells advertisers the ability to appear in one or more of ten "regional editions," which themselves have substantial readership. The *New England* edition, for example, reaches 435,000; the *Great Lakes*, 1.5 million; and the *Pacific* edition, 1 million. Also available are four special editions with particular demographic qualities that might be of interest to certain advertisers: *Family* (5.5 million adults 18–54 and/or children in household); *Boomer* (4.5 million adults 55+); *Elite* (1.5 million adults 18–54 with household incomes $50,000 or more); and *Elite Gold* (1 million adults 18–54 with household incomes $75,000+). For advertisers who find these segments useful, the savings can be substantial. While *Reader's Digest* lists a four-color full-page in its national edition at $269,000, a full page in *Elite Gold* is $114,500, and one reaching *New England* is $31,265. Of course, the number of people reached is substantially smaller with these editions, but for geographically or demographically focused advertisers who want to be associated with *Reader's Digest* in the minds of readers, it might be a good deal.

The very large circulation of *Reader's Digest* allows it to offer segments large enough to make the cost of printing ads for particular groups efficient. It was this desire to offer large segments that led Time Magazines to start a subsidiary called MNI, which allows advertisers to purchase segments that cross several magazines, some owned by Time and others owned by other firms. So, for example, advertisers who buy the Executive segment have their ads sent to "business leaders" who are among the subscribers to *Business Week*, *Fast Company*, *Forbes*, *Inc.*, *Fortune*, *Fortune Small Business*, and *Money*. They can also choose to target those business leaders in those magazines based on particular states. Other segments available through MNI are Health and Beauty, Family, Men, Style, Luxury, Home, News, and Hispanic.

Despite the diversity and the large numbers of magazines, there is one generalization that is safe to make at the start of the twenty-first century: magazines increasingly need to be specialized with a clear sense of the audience they want to reach, the topics they want to cover, and the personality (that is, attitude and viewpoints) they want to present if they are to remain competitive in their industry. Publishers are quite aware of the need for this approach. Let's look at how they go about it.

WORLD VIEW

Magazines in China Come of Age

"Welcome to the World's Most Exciting Magazine Market," headlined a recent article in *Magazine World* that discussed China's booming publishing industry. Indeed, the number of magazines in China has grown from roughly 1,000 in 1975 to more than 9,400 today.

Not only has the number of publications grown, but the quality of these periodicals has also improved. Zhang Bohai, Chairman of China Periodicals Association, notes that, "Creative ideas, touching stories, colorful pictures and printing quality of a world class standard are becoming more and more available in the market." Bohai says that this, coupled with publishers' savvy marketing tactics, has led to a steady rise in circulation since the mid-1980s.

In China, where 90 percent of magazine revenue comes from newsstand sales, a higher circulation corresponds directly to a greater profit. Yet publishers are already beginning to rethink their revenue model as magazine advertising in China continues to increase.

The shift to an advertising-sales approach is also being driven by the large number of global publishers eager to tap into China's lucrative consumer market. Annie Yuan, an advertising research director, explains that, "With the fast development of the Chinese economy and the emergence of a sizable group of middle-incomers with high disposable income, major international publications have been setting up in China."

Sources: Zhang Bohai, "Welcome to the World's Most Exciting Magazine Market," *Magazine World*, issue 52, April 2007, 16–17; Lu Xiang, "China, The Story So Far," International Federation of the Periodical Press, February 28, 2006, http://www.fipp.com; Annie Yuan, "China Magazines—Attractive Propositions," *Media and Marketing Europe*, November 30, 2006, Factiva.

Production and the Magazine Industry

magazine publisher the chief executive of a magazine, who is in charge of its financial health

In the magazine industry, the term *publisher* refers not to the company making the magazine, but to a person who works there. A **magazine publisher** is the chief executive of a magazine and is in charge of its financial health. Under the publisher are the business departments (in charge of advertising and circulation), the technical production department, and the editorial department. The magazine's editor-in-chief works for the publisher; several editors may, in turn, work for the editor-in-chief (see Figure 9.1).

Magazine publishers today typically work with their editors to build their magazines around distinct topics that they hope will attract distinct slices of the American population. In turn, the publishers hope (or expect) that their magazines will pull in advertisers who need to reach those population slices with the best medium possible.

Magazine Production Goals

What makes a magazine the best medium possible? To advertisers and publishers, the answer is a magazine that:

- Draws an attractive audience
- Draws an audience that is loyal to the content and personality of the magazine—its "brand"
- Provides an environment conducive to the sale of the advertisers' products
- Provides this audience and environment at an efficient price

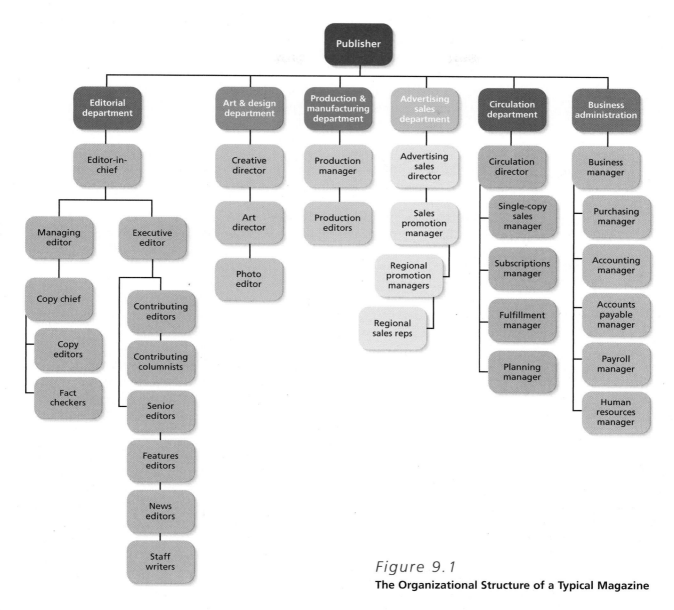

Figure 9.1

The Organizational Structure of a Typical Magazine

- Provides a way for advertisers to associate with the magazine's brand and audience beyond the magazine's pages

Let's look at these features one at a time.

Drawing an Attractive Audience　Typically, magazine publishers want to reach what they call **upscale readers.** These are upper-middle or upper-class people with substantial disposable income—that is, money beyond the amount needed for basic expenses that they can spend on special or expensive items. Because so many periodicals reach these sorts of people, a magazine has to be distinctive enough to draw particular upscale readers whose social characteristics and lifestyles fit a profile that interests enough advertisers to support the magazine.

To make the case that they have a distinctly attractive audience, magazine firms turn to the syndicated and custom research described earlier. *Smart Money*, for example, uses MRI data to argue that its readers are financially well off, home-owning folks—"every marketer's dream."[6] Similarly, seeking to position itself as

upscale readers upper-middle or upper-class people with substantial disposable income (money beyond the amount needed for basic expenses)

the place for expensive car announcements, *AutoWeek* draws on information from its own databases and the JD Power research company to boast to potential advertisers that its readers are "twice as likely as average U.S. vehicle buyers to purchase a vehicle costing $30,000 or more...and more than three times as likely to purchase a vehicle costing $50,000 or more!" Furthermore, according to the magazine's interpretation of the JD Power data, advertisers need to reach *AutoWeek* readers because they are opinion leaders who will share with others what they read: "Their auto expert behavior shines through as advice-givers to others."[7]

Drawing a Loyal Audience   In today's competitive media environment, it is not enough for a magazine to have a distinctly attractive audience on its rolls. Several other magazines, or radio stations or cable stations, may make similarly alluring claims. A magazine's business executives therefore must convince advertisers that the magazine is edited so effectively that the people who receive it read it consistently and thoroughly—presumably so thoroughly that they pay attention to the ads. On this theme, an ad for *Men's Vogue* in *Advertising Age* depicts actor Hugh Jackman reading it and asserts, "Once they get it, they never let it go."[8] In another ad to the trade, *Forbes* magazine calls itself a "capitalist tool" and tells potential advertisers, "There's a movement 20 million people strong. Moving Global Markets. Shaking Up Boardrooms. Embracing the Free Flow of Capital. It's called *Forbes*. And Here's Why You Should Join: Bigger Wins."[9] Making a case for all of its consumer magazines (including *Wired*, *Architectural Digest*, and *Vanity Fair*) the publisher Condé Nast argues that people develop a passion for

In 2005, Condé Nast introduced *Men's Vogue*, a men's magazine aimed at over-35 professional males, and *Domino*, a shopping magazine for home products modeled after their successful fashion-oriented shopping magazine, *Lucky*.

them. That emotion, says Condé Nast, translates into a tight connection with everything associated with the title: "A more engaged reader. A connection that drives culture. And a most effective media choice" for advertisers, presumably because the attention and aura carries to the ads.[10]

Creating a Conducive Environment

As the Condé Nast and *Forbes* statements suggest, publishers understand that from an advertiser's standpoint a magazine is above all a platform for persuasive messages. Advertisers particularly like magazines with articles and photos that fit with the tone and spirit of their products or services.

It is no accident that in *Ladies' Home Journal* and other women's service magazines, you're likely to find ads for foods in the recipe section. In fact, publishers and editors often develop new magazine sections with an eye toward specific types of advertisers that would find these sections good places to parade their goods. As far back as 2000, *National Geographic* was pretty explicit about the favorable environment it presents for advertisers. The magazine said in a trade magazine ad that it "brings unique portraits to readers who have an insatiable curiosity of the world we live in with a truth that compels them to embrace our brand and your advertising message."[11]

Setting an Efficient Price

Publishers know that they must present advertisers with a competitively low **cost per thousand** readers if they want to get or keep business. Of course, a cost per thousand is truly low only if the consumers the magazine reaches are the consumers that the advertiser is targeting.

Say, for example, that you represent an advertiser that wants to use *Time* to reach upper-class executives who are interested in world affairs. If you advertise in the general edition of *Time* magazine, you might get a relatively low cost per thousand (say fifteen dollars) when all the readers are taken into account. When you consider only upper-class executives who read the magazine, however, your cost per thousand may actually be much higher, because you are paying to reach so many people that you do not want. It is more efficient, you may have realized, to use one of the special *Time* editions that target highly paid executives. In fact, *Time*'s printing technology is set up so that your ad can target people based on their executive status and their geography—executives living in the Northeast, for example. The CPM may be higher than the CPM for *Time*'s general audience, but you will get the specific audience you want.

"Wait!" you might object. "Why shouldn't another magazine publishing firm come out with a magazine that is specifically designed for upper-level executives interested in world affairs? If it were done well, it could be as efficient a buy as *Time*'s special edition, and its special content could also create a pleasing environment for advertisers aiming at this group. Telling the target audience that the content was made just for them could, in addition, engender a particularly strong loyalty to the magazine that would be a magnet to advertisers."

That's good thinking—and it's an idea that would make *Time*'s publisher shudder. One way that relatively large-circulation magazines such as *Time* are trying to blunt the increased competition from more targeted (or niche) magazines is by using new technology to customize magazine content for particularly attractive audiences. The process involves using computer-guided printing presses to selectively channel particular articles and ads into magazines that will be mailed to individuals with certain characteristics. We've already noted that one way that Time carries out this ad-targeting activity is through its MNI subsidiary. Like our *Reader's Digest* example, that involves changing only ads. When it comes to

cost per thousand or cost per mil (CPM) the basic measurement of advertising efficiency; used to evaluate how much space an advertiser will buy in a given newspaper, and what price they will pay

reaching really valuable readers for advertisers, though, *Time* customizes not just the ads but the editorial matter as well. Here is how it works:

Time offers to marketers three "targeted demographic editions." These are ways to reach only the wealthiest segments of *Time*'s audience with particular interests and purchasing profiles. The *Time Global Business* edition is sent to 1.5 million readers "with a business job title or in a business household." The *Time Affluential* edition regularly reaches 800,000 "of our highest income subscribers." And the *Time Style and Design* edition goes quarterly to "*Time*'s more affluent and style-savvy readers …based on their income levels and interest in fashion, style and design." Other weeks, these special targets receive the regular national edition, or maybe MNI's targeted ad editions.

Sports Illustrated, owned by *Time*'s parent company, Time Warner, has been sending 400,000 readers who say they like a particular football team special coverage of that team. *Farm Journal,* one of the earliest magazines to customize its articles as well as its ads, holds the record for different versions of a magazine. Every month the company puts together customized contents to match the special farming needs of its 430,000 readers; these needs are listed in a database that is updated through telephone surveys. Each issue comes out in as many as 12,000 different versions. Advertisers have the option to match their ads to different types of readers. So, makers of hog-farm equipment and supplies can talk only to hog farmers without the waste in circulation.

Producing the Magazine as Brand

An increasingly important way that a major magazine company tries to keep advertisers and get new ones is to position every title not just as paper-bound reading material but as a personality—a brand—with which readers want to engage in many areas of their lives. Doing this, magazines have become central actors in the movement of materials across media boundaries that we discussed in Chapter 2. One major way in which they interact with their audience is through digital media. Another is by expanding into other media and staging events. In both, the magazines invite strong advertising participation.

Digital Magazines   Until around 2001, magazine companies hardly used the Internet or any other digital platform. Publishers didn't think it was cost-effective to create material just for the Web, and they were afraid that if they posted their magazine content online, it would discourage readership of the hard copy magazine issues. In the next few years, though, their attitude changed drastically. They realized that their audiences were increasingly using the Internet, sometimes to the detriment of reading magazines. Advertisers noted that too, and magazine executives began to worry that they might lose readers and money to the Web.

The result was that many magazine firms are moving strongly to use the Web to extend relationships with their readers beyond the printed page. That is the case with trade (business-to-business) magazines, as well as consumer magazines. Even though the Web still contributes only a very small portion of revenues (around 5 percent with consumer magazines, 8 percent with business-to-business), executives see it as key to their future. Most observers believe that consumer magazines have not been as aggressive as trade magazines in reaching out to their audiences online and drawing advertisers. That may change, however. In 2006, Hearst Magazines announced the creation of a digital unit, Hearst Digital Media, expressly to develop the firm's online properties. The same year, Condé Nast hired specific "web editors"

Pushing Time Ahead

You may remember from your history textbooks the *Chicago Daily Tribune*'s infamous election headline gaffe of 1948, "Dewey Defeats Truman." (By morning it was clear that Truman beat Dewey.) But even today, in an era of 24/7 news and real-time communication, media producers struggle to provide audiences with the most current content. This is particularly true for those in the monthly magazine industry, where there is a two-month lag between an issue's closing and on-sale date.

For example, *Shape*'s October 2005 issue included a travel spread encouraging people to tour New Orleans, a city which had been devastated by Hurricane Katrina several weeks earlier. That same year, *Glamour* published a short news piece commemorating the fiftieth anniversary of Rosa Park's landmark act of civil disobedience. Yet while the article referred to Parks as "now 92 and living in Detroit," she had passed away two months before the issue's December cover date.

While such errors can be attributed to bad fortune, the schedule on which the magazine industry operates is also partially to blame. Publishers plan editorial features up to a year in advance, and magazines typically go on sale weeks or more before their cover date. As they try to anticipate and influence the future, producers seemingly "push time ahead."

According to Brooke Duffy, who authored a study on the timing routines of women's magazines, this forward-looking timing schedule is based upon producers' considerations of readers, advertisers, and other key constituents. In order to prevent the sort of timing accidents described above, producers have admitted to filling their pages with evergreen content, covering topics that are not dependent on time, and eschewing features that are likely to be outdated, such as those involving research findings.

Only very recently have producers begun to rethink the benefits of pushing time ahead, in part because twenty-first-century advertisers and readers have new expectations about the timeliness of media. Some magazines have taken advantage of the Web to correct outdated content that appears in the print version; others supplement their monthly content with web-based features that are updated weekly or even daily.

Looking ahead, as magazine websites become increasingly important platforms to reach readers and advertisers, the issue of timing will play a critical role in the dynamics between the print and online periodicals. This may ultimately have an impact on what information you receive from magazines—and when.

Source: Excerpted from Brooke Erin Duffy, "Pushing Time Ahead: The Digital Challenges Facing Women's Magazines," unpublished Manuscript, Annenberg School for Communication, University of Pennsylvania, 2007.

for all 29 of its consumer magazines. *Time* announced that its new managing editor would have oversight of both the magazine and its online site. If you go to the websites of magazines by these and other big firms, you can see how they have begun to create sites that involve their users with podcasts, music, videos, blogs, and opportunities to interact with one another as part of the magazine's community.

The Web has become a big selling point with advertisers. Recall that *Seventeen* magazine's media kit noted that *17 Deals* was "an exciting in-book and online program." Just about every publisher nowadays emphasizes advertisers' ability to buy space both in print and online in order to engage the reader deeply. Increasingly, too, they are trying to engage readers on their mobile phones. That means encouraging them to download ring tones and photos, to enter contests from the phone, to read articles and in general to interact with the magazine while they are on the move. The men's magazine *Maxim*, for example, sells a daily sports prediction game that mobile users can play. Here, as with other activities, the idea is to reach

Oprah Winfrey, Cross-media Phenomenon

MEDIA PROFILE

In addition to being one of America's most beloved talk show personalities, Oprah Winfrey is a cross-media marvel whose arms of influence reach across television, film, print, and more. She personally represents the kind of cross-media branding that so many companies are trying to accomplish with their magazines.

O, The Oprah Magazine, which was launched in 2000 as "the women's personal growth guide for the new century," is among her most successful ventures. The magazine instantly became a newsstand favorite, and it continues to receive accolades from readers and the publishing industry alike. Its featured columns include "A Million Ways to Save the World," "Books that Make a Difference," and "Phenomenal Women," the latter of which profiles women who have overcome personal adversity to reach their goals. These unique features invoke the senses of inspiration, empowerment, and self-discovery that are the core of Oprah's persona—and her brand.

In fact, Lorraine York, a professor of English who has developed a course on Winfrey's influence on various cultural industries, credits *O, The Oprah Magazine* with elevating Oprah to brand status. By appearing on the cover of every single issue, York explains, she "embodies the information and advice that appear inside."

The Oprah brand has also made its way to her enterprises in television (*The Oprah Winfrey Show*), cable (the Oxygen net-

Oprah Winfrey

work), film (*Their Eyes Were Watching God*), Internet (http://www.oprah.com), and radio (Oprah & Friends on XM Satellite Radio), as well as her Book-of-the-Month club. "What's really brilliant," says York, of Winfrey's media empire, "is that each branch, in effect, advertises the others."

Sources: Denise Davy, "Deconstructing the Oprah Effect," *The Hamilton Spectator*, July 7, 2007, Factiva, accessed 2/19/08, http://hearstcorp.com/magazines/property/mag_prop_o_2000.html; http://www.omediakit.com

out to magazine readers with the magazine's personality (and its ads)—and encourage them to reach out to the magazine—wherever they are.

Of course, one concern publishers have is that if they let people read their magazines online for free, they may not pay for offline subscriptions. All publishers provide web users with an encouragement to subscribe to the print issues, which they can do online. Beyond this common approach, they have different responses. Some magazines, such as *Time*, place virtually all of the material in their hard-copy editions online in the belief that people will still purchase the hard copies. Others, such as *Maxim*, provide lots of material online but make it clear that to get the articles in the latest issue of the magazine, you have to get the magazine. Still others, such as *Variety*, allow visitors into small parts of their sites for free but charge for admission to other areas.

Expanding into other Media and Events   Remember the *Forbes* advertisement that "There's a movement 20 million people strong"? Toward the end, the ad insists that the magazine is a personality that exists for its readers and advertisers beyond the magazine's covers: "In print, online, and in person," it states, "*Forbes* offers global platforms for bigger impact." What *Forbes* means by "in person" is that the magazine stages conferences where readers can meet the kind of influential business people that the magazine wants to associate with its brand. The company charges thousands of dollars for many of these events—with titles such as "The Forbes Family Business Forum," "Leadership Networks Forum," and "The New Director: Inside the Fishbowl." Some are by invitation only, and marketers have an opportunity to buy an association with them. Even if readers can't go, their existence and reporting about them provides a special aura for the magazine. Many trade magazines stage executive-level events, as well, targeted to the particular businesses that their publications cover.

Magazine events are by no means confined to this elite level. Look at any magazine's media kit, and you'll see how executives try to help their advertisers reach their readers beyond the page and website. One of *Seventeen*'s offerings, for example, is for marketers to associate themselves with mall events that it stages in different parts of the country. "Rock the Runway," it says "spotlights the hottest fashion, beauty and music trends during one of the biggest shopping seasons of the year: Spring/Prom! These high-energy events in five major markets feature a major Center Court event including a 'Get Discovered' photo shoot, fashion presentations, live concert, and interactive sponsor activities. Hosted by *Seventeen*'s renowned style pros, these events will attract young shoppers in record numbers."[12]

In addition to mounting events, magazines are moving their brands into other media. You may be familiar with the Martha Stewart Collection of upscale merchandise at Macy's and Bloomingdale's. This venture is in addition to the image of pleasing domesticity that celebrity Martha Stewart projects not just in her magazine but through satellite radio and various forms of TV, as well. More tilted to a partying life are the activities instigated by *Maxim*. Its Sirius satellite radio channel projects the tone of all its projects when it boasts on the Web, "Girls, comedy, sports, music: Maxim Radio is the best thing to happen to men ...since women!" The description adds that "Maxim Radio takes *Maxim* magazine's amazing ability to speak to guys and pours it into a national, live radio station."[13] Also sporting the Maxim name through licensing deals are home furniture, a fabric collection in Macy's department store, and a chain of lounges. If you visit Cancun, Mexico, you can stay at Maxim Beach, a nightclub and beach club that a restaurant chain has opened in partnership with the magazine. All these products aim to benefit from, and reinforce, the image of masculine excitement that *Maxim* wants to project.

Distribution and the Magazine Industry

Magazine distribution refers to the channel through which the magazine reaches its exhibition point, the place where the reader sees it. When it comes to websites and other digital activities, distribution means sending content through website providers (cable or phone companies, for example) and through mobile providers (for example, AT&T, Verizon or Sprint), which act as exhibitors. In the case of mobiles, getting to people's phones sometimes means making deals with the providers to share revenue from products such as ringtones and games. When it

magazine distribution   the channel through which a magazine reaches its exhibition point

Figure 9.2

Sources of Magazine Revenue, 2007

As this figure shows, magazines typically earn more revenue from advertising than from subscription and single-issue sales combined. Source: Data from Magazine Publishers of America, The Magazine Handbook, 2007/08, p. 18: http://www.magazine.org/content/Files/magHandbook07_08.pdf

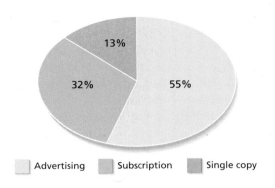

Advertising   Subscription   Single copy

subscription   a long-term order, paid in advance, for the receipt of a magazine for a predetermined period of time or number of issues

single-copy sales   the number of copies of a magazine sold not by subscription, but one issue at a time

comes to print, business magazines and newsletters to subscribers typically take place through the mail. The exhibition point is either the subscriber's workplace or the subscriber's home. Comic book companies distribute their products by themselves or through wholesalers to special stores that stock them.

In consumer magazine publishing, print distribution takes place in two ways. One is through the mail by **subscription,** a long-term order, paid for in advance, for the receipt of a magazine for a predetermined period of time or number of issues. The other is through companies that distribute magazines from many companies to retail outlets where **single-copy sales,** or the sale of copies one issue at a time, take place (see Figure 9.2). Each avenue has its benefits and obstacles. From the standpoint of a small publisher, the mail is a useful distribution channel because the U.S. Postal Service (USPS) must accept all comers; therefore, a magazine from a major firm will not have precedence over a magazine from a minor firm. But small publishers are also angered by USPS' charges. In a bid to encourage magazine firms to help it deliver issues efficiently, USPS has raised rates less for magazines that prepare large numbers of copies in bundles by ZIP codes than for firms that send out relatively few copies. The approach privileges big mailers over small ones and, say small publishers, makes it difficult for magazine publishers with small circulations (and who worry about raising subscription charges) to stay afloat.

Small magazine firms may have to rely on rented lists for their solicitations. They may also turn to direct-mail subscription firms such as Publishers Clearinghouse, which advertise many magazines by mail or online. However, these subscription firms charge a lot for their services—about 90 percent of the price the subscriber pays. That means that the magazine firm benefits from the reader only as a target for its advertisers. Moreover, during the past few years these firms have generated many fewer subscriptions than before. That is because in the past, these firms used the chance of winning a sweepstakes as a lure. The Federal Trade Commission has forced them to redesign their mailings to make it clear that the recipient has not actually won the sweepstakes already and to tell people that they don't have to buy periodicals to have a chance of winning.

Large magazine companies, although they sometimes take the sweepstakes route, can do much more. With their own expensively produced databases of potential readers, they can mail highly targeted ads that entice desirable readers to subscribe; that way they get to keep the subscription money themselves. Large magazine firms are also able to put a lot of money and effort into one of the most difficult aspects of their business—getting readers to renew their subscriptions for another year. It sometimes takes several mailings and a lot of money to do that.

Much to publishers' chagrin, it is becoming ever-more difficult to recruit new subscribers to magazines. One traditional route to seducing new subscribers, direct mailing of ads about the magazines, has declined sharply. As recently as 2002, direct mail through sweepstakes and other means brought in about 35 percent of all new subscribers. By 2007, that number was down to 25 percent. The rise in postal costs along with the lower success rates makes this method discouragingly expensive. Cards blown into the magazines that people see in stores or other places represent another method of reaching out to people. They still work, though not as well as in the past.[14]

While creating, building, and maintaining a magazine's circulation by mail is difficult, doing it through magazine distributors is even harder. Magazine firms usually use one of a handful of national distribution firms to reach a couple of hundred regional wholesalers, who, in turn, service well over 100,000 local retailers—typically supermarkets, drugstores, convenience stores, and newsstands. At retail, the field is complex and highly competitive, with the largest magazine racks carrying only about two hundred titles. In addition, people's chances of seeing magazines in supermarkets, traditionally a major place for buying single copies, have diminished. That is because average visits to supermarkets by household members dropped drastically between 1999 and 2005, from 83 to 64.[15] For these and other reasons, only a small number of magazines (notably *Woman's World*, *First For Women*, and *US Weekly*) use single-copy sales as their main way to readers. At the same time, single-copy sales can bring in more per-copy revenues than subscriptions, which are often sold at substantial discounts off the cover price. Display on the newsstand and in the supermarket is an important way to introduce the magazine to new readers, who might use cards inside the periodical to become subscribers.

The distributor, the wholesaler, and the retailer (the dealer) are able to make money because they pay a discount off the cover price. The total discount that a publisher typically gives up is about 50 percent; that is, if an issue's cover price is one dollar, the distributor, wholesaler, and retailer together make fifty cents on each issue. But, as in the book-publishing industry, the publisher typically takes responsibility for unsold copies. If a wholesaler gets too many copies and returns proof of the unsold ones, the publisher refunds the money to the national distributor (which credits the wholesaler and retailer) and absorbs the loss.

Exhibition and the Magazine Industry

The challenge from the magazine publisher's standpoint is not just providing the wholesaler with only a few more copies than the retailers will sell. It is also to make sure that the wholesaler is placing the title in the retail outlets in which it will sell best, and in places in those outlets where it will best be seen. Walk over to a magazine stand or a supermarket checkout area, and you will see the great number of magazines vying for your attention. In view of the large number of magazines that wholesalers have to stock, they may not pay much attention to new magazines from small companies unless the magazines are heavily advertised. In fact, it may be difficult for small companies to get retailers to accept their periodicals, and when they do get picked up, they may not get prominent positions on the rack.

The largest magazine firms have an additional advantage at the newsstand. Companies such as Time Inc., Condé Nast, and Hearst own their own national distribution firms. They therefore have more influence with wholesalers concerning where and how their magazines should be placed with retailers. The large

Securing display position for magazines in retail spaces such as the Barnes & Noble store seen here can be highly competitive. Therefore, few magazines use single-copy newsstand sales as their primary means to reach readers.

companies also have the cash to pay retailers slotting fees, or payments that ensure that their products will be placed prominently at the front of magazine racks or at the checkout counters of supermarkets. Smaller firms can't get this kind of treatment. In fact, during the past several years, major distributors have been buying up small firms because they couldn't compete.

Cover Lines

TECH & INFRASTRUCTURE

The next time you visit a supermarket, look at the magazine racks near the checkout counter. It might help you to realize that magazine publishers have quite a challenge. They must convince consumers to buy their magazine.

That environment is why publishers consider magazine cover lines so important. Cover lines are come-on phrases that call out to potential readers, signaling to them that the magazine is one that they might like to read (and buy).

Consider *Woman's Day*, a periodical that aims at women aged eighteen to fifty-four with families and that relies mostly on newsstand and supermarket sales. Its editors have developed these cover line principles:

- On the newsstand, the top 50 percent of the cover is the most visible. Consequently, it is important to place at least four to five cover lines there. The most important cover line can go on a banner above the logo.

- Most of the other cover lines should begin on the left side of the cover, because people read from left to right.
- Cover lines should be placed in descending order of the readers' priority.
- Numbers attract readers. The cover should emphasize lines such as "100 Ways to Cut 100 Calories," or "46 Meals in Under 4 Hours." The numbers should be printed within an inch or so of the left binding, because on store racks, the right sides of magazines are often covered by other periodicals.
- Cover lines on stories that are likely to be popular with a segment of the target audience can be added on the cover's right side. They also tell the consumer that she will be getting a lot for her money.

Source: Joseph Turow, *Breaking Up America: Advertisers and the New Media World* (Chicago: University of Chicago Press, 1997), pp. 93–98.

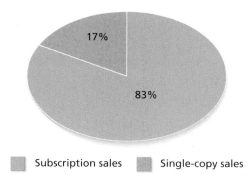

17%

83%

Subscription sales   Single-copy sales

Figure 9.3

Single Copy or Subscription?

In 2005, 83 percent of total circulation in the consumer magazine industry was from subscriptions, while single-copy sales made up only 17 percent.

Source: Veronis Suhler Stevenson, Communications Industry Forecast 2006–2010.

In general, single-copy sales are not moving in a direction consumer magazine publishers like. From 2000 to 2006, the share of single copy circulation declined from 15.9 percent of all consumer magazine copies distributed to 13.3 percent of the copies distributed (see Figure 9.3).[16] That is a particular problem for magazines that rely on single copies to recruit new subscriptions. They have to find new ways to get potential readers to see the value of a long-term relationship with their magazines.

Media Literacy and the Magazine Industry

Now that we've begun to have a good grasp of the way the magazine business works, it will be useful for us to step back as citizens and understand some of the complaints that social critics have lodged against the industry. Two of the major objections that critics have noted are *conglomeration* and *the influence of advertisers*. Let's take a look at each.

Conglomeration

Car and Driver and *InStyle* are very different magazines with different target audiences. Despite their differences in content, the periodicals share one crucial element: a powerful corporation backing them. *InStyle* is owned by the magazine powerhouse Time Magazines, which is itself owned by Time Warner. Hachette Filipacchi, the major magazine firm that owns *Car and Driver*, is owned by the major French media conglomerate LeGardere. Making it big in the consumer magazine industry today requires more than just a good idea and a cross-media perspective. It requires the muscle of a big firm. In fact, as we've already noted in the past few pages, the current magazine environment benefits big, rich firms. Publishers need to have huge amounts of cash and clout if they are to be noticed at the production, distribution, and exhibition levels.

Critics complain that this is the kind of influence that only the largest conglomerates can exert. People outside the mainstream may have fascinating ways of looking at society that the executives of corporate juggernauts such as Time, Hachette Filipacchi, Hearst, Condé Nast and Meredith would consider odd, or even ideologically offensive. No matter how interesting their ideas, though, individuals and small firms have a far smaller chance of launching successful consumer periodicals than do major corporations. The unequal competition is not just connected to the print edition. Rich websites that have become the norm of media properties are expensive to create and keep up. In general, small firms find it nearly impossible to put together the kind of cross-media packages that today's advertisers demand. That makes their chances of staying in business over the long haul even dimmer than in earlier years, when putting out a magazine meant just working on a hard-copy periodical.

Advertiser Influence on Content

As the preceding paragraph suggests, many of the changes in today's magazine industry reflect the enormous competition for advertiser support. You probably realize that a great deal of what we have said about the U.S. magazine industry throughout this chapter comes down to attempts to attract advertisers. This fact raises another concern of media critics: the influence of advertisers on magazine content.

They note that as the executives of consumer and business magazines feel increasing competition from other media as well as from other periodicals, the possibility of direct and routine advertiser influence on editorial matter looms larger and larger. Some publishers and editors may not consider this a problem. After all, they will point out, advertisers have always had a profound influence on the magazine industry because they pay most of the costs. As a result, the very basic decisions about target readers—whom to attract and whom to ignore—are typically made with commercial sponsors in mind. Similarly, as we have noted, decisions about what types of sections to place in a new periodical, or to add to a mature one, are made with an eye toward potential advertisers. Recipe columns draw food ads. Travel columns draw travel ads. The list can go on.

Magazine publishers and editors have consistently recognized that this kind of sponsor influence is the unavoidable price of doing business in a commercial world. On the other end of the spectrum, one long-standing principle of magazine editing is that ads must be clearly separated and differentiated from other content—by using a different layout and a different font, for example. U.S. postal regulations require that ads that don't clearly look different from editorial matter be labeled "Advertisement."

Situations in which advertisers are mentioned or shown as part of the editorial content of the magazine are more difficult. Some companies, such as Time Magazines, have had explicit policies separating the business and advertising activities of the magazine from its editorial activities. The separation is supposed to ensure that editors do not worry about offending advertisers, since they do not deal at all with people from the ad department. Nevertheless, for obvious reasons, most magazine editors do not go out of their way to antagonize regular sponsors, and this can sometimes lead to ethical problems. Should, for example, a women's magazine run articles about the dangers of smoking if its major advertisers are cigarette firms?

Research on the relationship between smoking ads and the lack of articles about smoking in women's magazines suggest that cigarettes have quietly "bought" protection from bad publicity by paying for ad space. Publishers counter that, because cigarettes are legal, they have a right to carry these ads. Besides, publishers say, cigarette companies often purchase expensive space, such as the back cover, that is difficult to sell on a regular basis.

Publishers and their editors often face other difficult decisions relating to advertisers. Say you are running a controlled-circulation magazine and a potentially large advertiser agrees to purchase space on condition that the advertiser's activi-

Jean Kilbourne and Magazines

CRITICAL CONSUMER

Jean Kilbourne is a widely hailed expert on addictions, gender issues, and the media. Her major focus, magazine advertising's impact on teenage girls and eating disorders, has sparked much critical debate on the issues of body image and self-esteem. Winning the "Lecturer of the Year" award twice from the National Association of Campus Activities, Kilbourne's commitment to spotlighting these issues for college students is fierce. She has spoken at length at one-half of all the colleges and universities in the United States.

Kilbourne uses slides and other visual aids in her lectures to highlight magazine advertising messages that influence the way men and women perceive relationships and each other, from marriage and dating to love and friendship. She is well known for her wit and warmth, as well as her ability to present provocative topics in a way that unites rather than divides, encourages dialogue, and moves

and empowers people to take action in their own and in society's interest. Kilbourne asserts that through their advertising and their focus on consumption, magazines teach people values that serve to create dissatisfaction and needs that can be satisfied only by the purchase of products.

Increasingly, she says, media are blurring the line between advertising and content. She argues that this is especially noticeable in magazines aimed at teenage girls. There readers are encouraged by both content and ads to focus on makeup, dieting, and wearing the right outfit. The same goes for men's magazines. In this sense, magazines and their advertising help shape the way people think about what is important in their lives.

See also http://www.jeankilbourne.com

ties are also regularly mentioned in the editorial matter of the periodical. What do you do? If your magazine needs (or covets) the money, would you say to yourself that the advertiser would probably be mentioned in the magazine anyway, so it would be fine to agree? The American Business Press code of ethics states that such activities are prohibited. Trading ads for editorial coverage certainly occurs in the business press, but because this practice is rarely admitted, no one really knows how often it takes place.

What about consumer magazines? How vulnerable are they to mixing advertising and editorial matter and to making themselves merely the instruments of the highest bidders? Magazine specialists J. William Click and Russell Baird quote a former editor of *Good Housekeeping* as contending that although "to set out deliberately to antagonize advertisers would be senseless …when there was reason to investigate and expose, there was no hesitation." But Click and Baird also note that "editorial integrity is much easier to maintain if the [magazine] is in solid financial condition and does not desperately need to woo advertisers." The problem is that as magazines compete for narrower audiences than ever before and as publishers worry about losing advertisers to a bad economy and other media, worries about their financial stability increase.

An article about breaking into the magazine industry quoted the advertising production manager of *Entrepreneur* as encouraging editorial people to cooperate with the advertising staff. Speaking to aspiring publishers, he said, "You'll want to work hard to develop a strong relationship between your advertising and editorial production departments. One of the reasons we're so successful is that we've always worked well with our editorial team to develop the give and take that's necessary to make both sides of the business happy and successful."[17]

Many people in the magazine industry would cringe at these sorts of relationships. But with even the largest magazines struggling, signs are emerging that the lines between the business and editorial departments are beginning to blur in some magazines, that the publishers of some magazines are actively encouraging "partnerships" with advertisers that they feel reflect their audiences' lifestyles. The practice of seeing magazines as brands that set up events and Internet sites sometimes encourages dimmed lines between the editorial department and advertisers. An example is when a fashion magazine mounts a show of the latest dresses and the bulk of the clothes going down the runway are by the companies that are sponsoring the event.

Or consider Hachette's *Car and Driver* website's decision to develop "virtual test drives" based on car reviews from the magazine. The videos are sponsored by car companies as part of advertising packages that include the print magazine, the website and perhaps other associations with the *Car and Driver* brand. Although the magazine's writers have no hesitation in giving a negative review to a car they evaluate, Hachette's marketing director of men's titles acknowledged that the videos about the car would likely eliminate the negative aspects of the review to make sponsors (likely the car company) comfortable. "If the editorial staff has said that the vehicle is overweight, we'll never say it's light," he said. Instead, "We'll focus on other aspects of the vehicle on behalf of the consumer."[18]

The extent of widespread editorial sensitivity and collaboration will become one of the most basic questions that we can ask about the changing magazine industry. In the interest of your media literacy, it will be useful to follow this trend through industry trade magazines such as *Advertising Age* and *Folio*. In the long run, the integrity of the U.S. media system is at stake in the outcome.

The magazine industry is an enormously varied business that runs the gamut from widely read consumer periodicals to narrowly read newsletters. There are huge differences in types of readership and sources of financial support. Perhaps the one major similarity among magazine practitioners is that all are being buffeted by the changes taking place in the broad media environment. New electronic media present both challenges and opportunities. Competition for readers, always intense, is becoming more intense. In decades past, such challenges have led to profound changes in several parts of the industry. There are signs that advertisers are having a growing influence on content in some areas of consumer magazines. It will be interesting to see how the magazine industry adapts to the twenty-first-century media world—and how that affects what we get from magazines and how we get it.

CHAPTER REVIEW

For an interactive chapter recap and study guide, visit the companion website for *Media Today* at www.routledge.com/textbooks/mediatoday

QUESTIONS FOR DISCUSSION AND CRITICAL THINKING

1 Why did President Theodore Roosevelt use the term muckrakers to describe the investigative magazine writers of his day? By using the term, did he mean to compliment or disparage them?
2 Why did magazines such as *Coronet* and *The Saturday Evening Post* stop publishing in the 1950s and 1960s despite high circulation numbers?
3 Describe benefits and drawbacks of controlled-circulation and paid-circulation magazines.
4 "Magazines increasingly need to be specialized with a clear sense of audience they want to reach, the topics they want to cover, and the personality (that is, attitude and viewpoints) they want to present if they are to remain competitive in their industry." Why?
5 What does it mean to say that publishers believe they need to treat their magazines as brands?
6 Why is conflict between "church" and "state" more pronounced in major magazine companies today than in the past?

INTERNET RESOURCES

Folio Magazine (http://www.foliomag.com/)
   Folio is the major trade magazine of the magazine publishing industry. On the website you can read articles from the magazine and a newsletter, learn about industry events, and browse through a directory of companies, from list brokers to publishing technology firms, that supply the industry with the wherewithal to carry out its tasks.

Magazine Publishers of America (http://www.magazine.org)
   Established in 1919, the Magazine Publishers of America (MPA) calls itself the industry association for consumer magazines. It is a strong advocate for magazines to advertisers and the government. The website reflects these roles in addition to having sections about magazine careers, magazine retailing, and other aspects of the industry. The site also hosts the American Association of Magazine Editors.

International Regional Magazine Association (http://www.regionalmagazines.org)
   This is a group of companies that produce magazines aimed at particular geographic areas—for example, *Vermont Life* and *Oklahoma Magazine*. The site includes a reference area with links to useful sites that are relevant to all sorts of magazines.

Custom Publishing Council (http://www.custompublishingcouncil.com)

The Council "is focused on promoting the growth and vitality of this dynamic marketing discipline." Its website includes an explanation of custom publishing, profiles of custom publishers, and research, case studies and how-to-articles that explain and promote this type of magazine publishing.

KEY TERMS

You can find the definitions to these key terms in the marginal glossary throughout this chapter. Test your knowledge of these terms with interactive flash cards on the *Media Today* companion website.

academic journals	magazine distribution
brands	media kits
business-to-business (B-to-B) magazine	muckrakers
	newsletter
circulation	paid-circulation magazine
comic book	publisher
consumer magazines	readership segments
controlled-circulation magazine	service magazines
cost per thousand	single-copy sales
custom magazine	subscription
editorial profile	trade magazines
literary reviews	upscale readers

CONSTRUCTING MEDIA LITERACY

1 Make a case for the argument that comic books are not magazines.
2 Based upon your own use of print magazines and Internet resources, in what ways does the Internet present a significant threat to the print magazine industry at this time? How might you see this changing in the future?
3 You are the editor of a women's magazine, which is having a hard time selling ads. Cigarette companies are offering to buy full page ROB sponsorships. Should you accept the ads? Should you run articles about the dangers of smoking if you know your major sponsors might leave? What would you do? Why?

CASE STUDY   Exploring Magazine Media Kits Online

The idea   Many magazines post their media kits online for prospective advertisers to consider. The kits can provide interesting insight into the different ways that magazines try to position themselves among the competition and promote their ability to reach certain audience segments.

The method   Choose two magazines that you believe aim at similar audiences—for example, two women's magazines or two consumer automotive magazines. In Google, type the name of the magazine in quotation marks and the words "media kit" in quotation marks. For example, type "car and driver" "media kit."

Explore each media kit along the following lines: the magazine's description of its goals or mission; the way it talks about its editorial material; the ways it describes its circulation; the ways it talks about its audience and audience segments; the various ad formats and offers for reaching its audience and audience segments; and the media activities in which it engages beyond the magazine pages. Then write a five-page report that explains similarities and differences among the ways the magazines argue their place and advantage within their industry.

chapters

10 THE RECORDING INDUSTRY

11 THE RADIO INDUSTRY

12 THE MOTION PICTURE INDUSTRY

13 THE TELEVISION INDUSTRY

14 THE INTERNET AND VIDEO GAME INDUSTRIES

The industries engaged in electronic media are a part of a broad landscape that's changing rapidly, in which the boundaries among businesses are blurring. Will radio, recordings, movies, television, and electronic games merge into one vast electronic network we call the Web? If the answer is no, what forces are stopping this from taking place? If the answer is yes, who will control the Web and with what consequences?

This section will help you to answer these questions. Chapters 10 through 14 examine the recording, radio, movie, television, and Internet and video game industries. We'll investigate social controversies related to each of the industries and focus a critical eye on the impact and influence of the most powerful firms.

four

the electronic media

electronic media

10 THE RECORDING INDUSTRY

After studying this chapter, you will be able to:

1 Sketch the history of the recording industry from the standpoint of its relation to technological and social change

2 Explain how a recording is developed—from the time an artist creates a song to the time the recording ends up in your CD collection

3 Explain the ways in which artists and labels turn profits

4 Recognize the promotional techniques used by record labels to push sales

5 Decide where you stand on the major controversies facing the recording industry today

"For so long, the record industry had control. But now that monopoly has ended, they don't know what to do."

–RICK RUBIN, MUSIC EXECUTIVE

"Piracy is an insidious act performed in an almost offhanded way by people who would never consider stealing anything else."

– GLEN BALLARD, SONGWRITER AND MUSIC PRODUCER

Media Today

How many people do you know (including yourself) who have downloaded music from Internet sites without paying for it? If you answered "everyone" or "too many to count," you're like many people who are taking advantage of digital technologies to share perfect copies of songs without reimbursing the copyright holders. Though illegal, the activity is widespread. The Recording Industry Association of America (RIAA), the major association that represents the recording industry, doesn't put a particular number on digital piracy, but states on its website that "the pirate marketplace currently far dwarfs the legal marketplace." The RIAA goes on to state that "the piracy habits of college students remain especially and disproportionately problematic" and it goes on to justify one of the major tools it has used in attempts to combat piracy: suing college students who do it. As you might imagine (or might have experienced), that has led to anger and angst in dormitories across the United States.

It has not, however, stopped illegal digital copying. In fact, unlawful downloading has grown along-side a smaller but still-substantial rise in legitimate digital purchases. Together, these activities represent the most profound change in a century regarding all aspects of the recording industry, from production to distribution to exhibition. Not everyone is suffering because of the transformation. Some companies and artists have learned to adapt quite well to the new realities, and others are working hard to figure out how to adapt.

Who is winning, who is losing, and why? How are their actions affecting the kind of recorded music that is circulated in the United States and the rest of the world? The aim of this chapter is to help you address these questions and think about how they affect you. To understand where the industry is now and why it is responding to digital challenges so nervously, it is useful to take a quick look at where it came from. As you'll see, over the past hundred years or so, a handful of recording companies developed the power to control much of the music that Americans heard. In the early twenty-first century, they fear they are losing that control, and they are fighting it.

The Rise of Records

As late as 1880 or 1890, a person growing up in a middle-class U.S. household had no recorded music in the home in the sense that we understand it today. That's not to say that homes didn't have music. For one thing, family members often played musical instruments. Pianos were especially popular in middle-class homes. Many family members learned to play, and there was a vigorous and growing industry that published sheet music and sold it in music stores around the country.

How did parents and their children know which of the latest sheet-music compositions to buy? Sometimes the salesperson at the store would play the piece for the customer, to give the customer an idea of what it sounded like. People also often heard the songs they wanted to buy from musicians and singers who came through town: symphony orchestras, marching bands, and touring vocalists. If

Before the rise of recorded sound in the late nineteenth-century, most American families entertained themselves at home by singing and playing musical instruments. Pianos were especially popular in middle-class homes.

minstrel show a touring show popular in the mid-nineteenth century, in which performers dressed up in special "blackface" makeup, made jokes, and sang songs that, though supposedly drawn from "black songfests," actually had little to do with the African-American lifestyles and rhythms they claimed to mimic

vaudeville shows a touring show comprised of several types of acts that were popular in the United States from the late nineteenth century through the 1920s

Tin Pan Alley term describing the popular-music publishing industry of the early twentieth century

For more than 150 years, vaudeville was America's most popular form of entertainment. People who sit glued to their TV sets today would have been flocking to their local auditorium to see programs like the one advertised here.

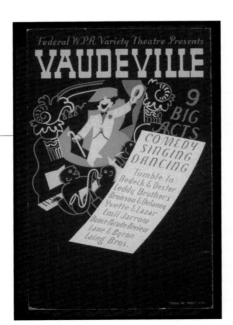

audience members at these concerts liked a particular piece, they would purchase a copy from the sheet-music proprietor.

Two particularly important touring sources for popular new songs were the *minstrel show*, which was popular around the mid-nineteenth century, and the *vaudeville show*, which was popular from the late nineteenth century through the 1920s.

Minstrel Shows

The **minstrel show** purported to be derived from a black songfest. Performers (usually white, but sometimes black) dressed up in special "blackface" makeup and made jokes and sang songs that actually had little to do with the African-American lifestyles and rhythms that they claimed to present.

Minstrel shows first appeared in the early 1840s and were very popular until they were eclipsed by vaudeville in the 1890s. At the height of their popularity, dozens of minstrel show companies toured the United States; some even played theaters in England. By 1910, the genre was nearly obsolete, as can be seen from advertisements appealing to nostalgia for an age of minstrelsy that was already past. Though the minstrel show had all but vanished, some variety performers and motion picture actors, notably Al Jolson, adopted the minstrel's blackface makeup in the 1920s and 1930s.

Vaudeville Shows

Vaudeville shows had some things in common with minstrel shows (including some blackface singers) but drew from a broader range of social experiences. Within one show, vaudeville presented comedy acts, acrobats, animal acts, and even famous people simply talking to the audience about their lives. Much of vaudeville, however, involved music. And an entire popular music-publishing industry, based on one street in Manhattan and nicknamed **Tin Pan Alley**, grew up to serve the needs of vaudeville; in turn, it used vaudeville to publicize its music.

The competition among song publishers to promote their songs around the country was strong. It was common knowledge in vaudeville that "song pluggers" often paid popular vaudeville performers a lot of money to sing a particular publisher's tunes on stage. Sometimes the performer's face appeared on the sheet music as a way to hype the song.

Listening to Music at Home

People who couldn't play sheet music could enjoy other forms of music in their homes, even before the advent of records. Wind-up music boxes were a popular way of providing in-home music. Inside these music boxes were metal rolls with specially arranged pegs on them. As the rolls turned, the pegs struck steel combs. When the combs were struck, they played notes, and so the music box played a song. By around 1890, people were buying much larger music boxes that used interchangeable disks to hit the metal bars, so that one music box could play many songs.

Another popular "music machine" was the player piano, which used a perforated roll of paper and a pneumatic mechanism to get the keys to hit the strings. Some player pianos reproduced not only the notes recorded on the paper roll, but also other characteristics of the original performance, such as the pressure applied to individual keys and the loudness of notes.

The Advent of the Record Player

Despite the popularity of such mechanical players, there were systematic attempts in the nineteenth century to reproduce the actual sound vibrations of a performance. The first device that could record and play back sound was invented by Thomas Alva Edison in 1877. What Edison called a **phonograph** recorded sound on tin foil with spiral grooves on it that was wrapped around a metal cylinder (see Figure 10.1). To record, a person would use a crank to turn the cylinder while speaking into a tube with a vibrating diaphragm. Air pressure from the diaphragm

phonograph   invented by Thomas Alva Edison in 1877, this device recorded and played back sound on tin foil wrapped around a metal cylinder with spiral grooves on it

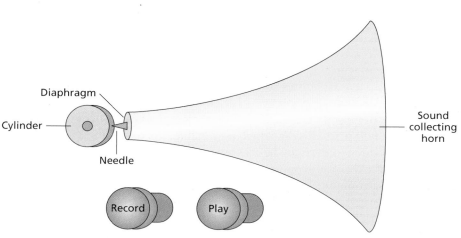

Figure 10.1

Edison's Phonograph

In Edison's original phonograph, a diaphragm directly controlled a needle, and the needle scratched an analog signal onto a tinfoil cylinder. You spoke into Edison's device while rotating the cylinder, and as the diaphragm vibrated, so did the needle. Those vibrations impressed themselves onto the cylinder, thus making a recording. To play the sound back, the needle moved over the groove scratched during recording, causing the needle and the diaphragm to vibrate and play the recorded sounds.

Figure 10.2

Berliner's Gramophone

The gramophone's major improvement over Edison's phonograph was the use of flat, wax records with a spiral groove (instead of a tinfoil cylinder), making mass production of records easy.

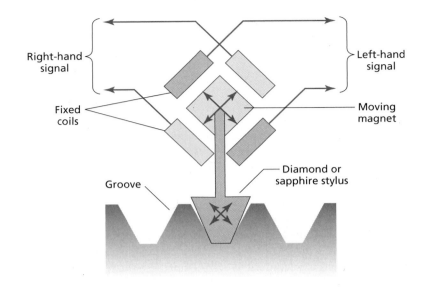

caused a needle "stylus" to vibrate against the foil so that grooves of different depths and lengths were created. To play back the recording, the person would connect the stylus to a hollow horn, place the stylus on the cylinder, and turn the crank.

Edison's first recorded statement was the poem "Mary Had a Little Lamb," by magazine editor Sarah Josepha Hale (see Chapter 9). His company's publicity department extolled the invention highly and sold it as a business recording device, but the foil was hard to use properly; by 1880, a disappointed Edison described his invention as "a mere toy, which has no commercial value." The machine's fortunes changed in 1885, however, when Chichester Bell and Charles Tainter introduced wax rather than foil as the recording medium; they called the device a **graphophone.**

In 1887, Emile Berliner modified the invention still more by abandoning Edison's cylinder model and using zinc disks for recording. To record, Berliner covered the surface of the disk with a wax substance that could be recorded upon. After the sound waves had been recorded on the wax coating, the disk was immersed in acid, which ate through the grooves in the wax and cut into the zinc (see Figure 10.2). He called the device a **gramophone.**

Although the Berliner system was very loud, the quality of playback was not as good as that of Edison's cylinder. The real weak point was the playback machine. This machine had a small crank that was connected to a belt that moved the turntable. You needed to hold the machine while you were cranking and at the same time lower the needle onto the record, which was turning (you hoped) at 70 revolutions per minute (rpm). You also had to continue cranking for as long as you wanted to listen. Hardly anyone could keep the turntable moving at the right speed, and even if they could, someone else had to hold the machine so that the cranking wouldn't jolt the needle and disrupt playback. Despite these problems, Berliner had made an important discovery: He could use the zinc disks to make molds that would press out copies of the records on hard rubber. The molds could be used to make copies in almost unlimited numbers.

Unfortunately for Berliner, there was little demand for his records as a result of the manual machine that had to be used to play them. (Some people compared operating the machine to using an eggbeater.) The reason for the success that he did have was his price. Since the Berliner Gramophone had no spring motor or battery, it was cheap. At a time when the average worker was earning only $6 a

graphophone Chichester Bell and Charles Tainter's 1885 modification of Edison's phonograph, which featured a wax cylinder rather than a tin foil cylinder for recording and playback

gramophone Emile Berliner's 1887 modification of both the phonograph and the graphophone, which featured wax disks for recording and playback, rather than a cylinder

week, Edison's North American Phonograph Company was selling its machines for $150, targeted at businesses. Berliner's activities awakened Edison to the money-making possibilities of his invention. His company tried to maintain control over the device by claiming that it retained the patent rights to all cylinder versions of the machine.

In the end, however, it was Emile Berliner's machine that won out, at least in part because of shrewd marketing. He and a partner had established the Victor Talking Machine Company. Its trademark was a dog named Nipper looking into the speaker of the gramophone (hearing "His Master's Voice"). In 1906 the firm marketed the *Victrola*, the first talking machine that was also a piece of furniture. Consumers preferred the flat disks over cylinders because they sounded better and were easier to store without breaking. In 1912, even Edison's company realized that Victor had won and began producing disks.

By that time, Americans' interest in recorded music had grown tremendously. The annual production of phonographs (both cylinder and disk players) grew from 150,000 in 1899 to 500,000 in 1914. In 1910, at least 20 million records were sold. By 1921, the number of records sold reached 140 million. The popularity of recordings encouraged AT&T to perfect the "electrical recording" in 1924, amplifying the voices of musicians and singers for the first time. All-electric record players, which allowed much better reproduction of sound, also became available. Records had become part of American life.

The Effect of Records and the Record Player on the Early Music Industry   Records had also begun to change the music industry. One effect was to make the sheet-music business much less important. Think about it: the phonograph made music available to everyone. If you had no piano (or if you couldn't play it), for a small amount of money you could still listen to recorded versions of the latest music, expertly performed. To get people to buy sheet music, publishers had to lower their prices for songs drastically—from forty cents per copy in 1902 to ten cents in 1916. Music publishers found themselves making more money from the sale of recordings of their music (royalties) than from the sale of sheet music.

The effect of records on popular songs was even more extraordinary. Before the phonograph, Tin Pan Alley's songwriters had created tunes that could be played and sung by amateurs at home. Now they could write more complicated works, since people could buy them on disks and did not have to play them. Musical arrangements could be more intricate, with harmonies and ranges suited to better-trained musicians. For example, compare the 1892 song "A Bicycle Built for Two"—with its simple melody and easily managed lyrics—with "Stardust" (1920), a hard-to-play melody that didn't even have lyrics initially. (This book can't sing, but maybe you can find recordings elsewhere.)

One more point about the effects of records: because their playing time was set by the manufacturers at about three minutes, songwriters and arrangers had to work with about two choruses of songs. This lyric format became the standard unit for decades until the arrival of long-playing records, and it had enormous consequence for the nature of the popular song. The sixteen-bar narrative song, which had been popular for nineteenth-century sing-alongs, did not fit this format and fell by the wayside. Lyrics had to be short and direct.

Records and the Rise of Radio

The 1920s marked a decade in which the recording industry confronted another industry that would be critical to its existence over the next eighty years:

Record companies worried that radio might discourage the purchase of recorded music, but sales remained brisk for types of music that radio stations wouldn't play, such as jazz and blues. Records of "torch" singer Bessie Smith are said to have helped keep Columbia afloat.

commercial radio. A large part of the development of commercial radio in the 1920s involved playing music over the airwaves. Initially, that created problems for the record industry. Record companies worried that radio might discourage the purchase of recorded music. In fact, the presence of popular music on the airwaves—often "live" rather than recorded—created severe problems for the phonograph industry during the mid-1920s, as people listened to radio instead of buying disks. The Victor Talking Machine Company, worried about the future of its business, merged with RCA. The Columbia Phonograph Company, also fearful that its business was trickling away, tried to profit from broadcasting by financing a radio network to be called the Columbia Broadcasting System. The project lost money, Columbia pulled out, and what became known as CBS proceeded on its own. (Years later, in 1938, CBS purchased Columbia Records.)

There were, however, some types of music that radio stations wouldn't play: jazz, blues, hillbilly music, ethnic songs, and other compositions that executives did not consider refined enough to broadcast. That created opportunities for record producers. African Americans were particularly avid record buyers; records of the black "torch" singer Bessie Smith are said to have kept Columbia afloat. Soon Victor and Columbia expanded their "race" catalog and even issued jazz under their more general-market labels. In addition, many small record companies appeared (for example, Brunswick, Vocalion, Okeh, Cameo) that recorded materials a person wasn't likely to hear on the radio. As one media historian notes, "radio, putting pressure on records, was edging them firmly into a new world."[1]

Radio remained a double-edged sword for the record industry. The variety of music available on radio expanded in the 1930s. That sounds good, but partly because people could get music without paying for it, the economic depression of the early 1930s hit the recording industry harder than many others. Record sales fell to one-tenth of 1929 levels, and some companies went bankrupt. By 1935 only Victor (now part of RCA) and Columbia-Brunswick remained significant. Just as things were looking terribly bleak for the industry, though, sales increased again. Singing stars from radio and movies, such as Bing Crosby, along with newly popular "swing bands," such as those of Benny Goodman and Artie Shaw, encouraged millions of youngsters and young adults to buy records. Two new companies emerged as important in American and international music: Decca (a U.S.-British firm) and EMI (a British firm).

Music publishers and composers were beginning to think of radio as a new source of stable income. They also saw it as a better platform for publicizing songs and encouraging record sales than the now-dying vaudeville. They began to get substantial royalties from radio through the American Society of Composers, Authors and Publishers (ASCAP), which charged stations and the networks an annual license fee for broadcasting music. By using the lists of music played on some stations and paying people to audit the songs of other stations, ASCAP decided how much of the money each of its individual members should receive. Broadcasters, angry at what they contended were ASCAP's excessive fees, started their own licensing organization, Broadcast Music Incorporated (BMI). The competition lowered music costs for broadcasters and showed how important radio had become to the musical recording world.

Rethinking Radio and Recordings, 1950–1980

Major changes that occurred in American society after World War II ended in 1945 deeply affected the radio, and as a result, the record industry. Two of the most important developments were the rise of television and the emergence of the baby boom generation.

The Development of Formats

Television, a new medium during the late 1940s, rapidly began to draw audiences and advertisers away from radio. The national radio networks found that they could not afford to mount the expensive programs and support live orchestras that had made up so much of their broadcasts throughout the previous two decades. They gave back a lot of their time to local stations, which found it more profitable to play records rather than bring in performers for live shows. In order to draw advertisers, radio executives decided to do what TV wasn't doing: go after specific local audience segments by devoting most of their stations' time to broadcasting music that those segments would tune in to hear. Playing records was inexpensive compared to creating drama or comedy or adventure series; often record companies would send records to the radio stations for free, in the hope that the stations would play them and their listeners would buy them. As a result, stations around the country developed different formats. A **radio format** is the personality of a station organized around the kind of music it plays (country, rock, hip-hop) and the radio personalities (called disk jockeys or DJs) who are hired to introduce the recordings and advertisements

That's how baby boomers entered radio's universe. In the mid-1950s, the creators of radio formats realized that the generation of youngsters born in the early and mid-1940s was becoming the richest generation in history. These people had money to spend and time to spend it, and they wanted to listen to their own music. A few enterprising disk jockeys (Alan Freed and Murray "the K" Kaufman were two) developed quick-moving "rock 'n' roll" formats that included new music that borrowed heavily from African-American rhythm and blues.

Radio station owners worried, though, that the sensual, even sexual, language of some of the songs—not to mention the race of their singers at a time when overt bigotry was still strong—might cause controversy. DJs consequently tended to play "cover" records by white singers that made the lyrics more acceptable to parents and regulators. (For the same reason, the DJs transformed the phrase *rock 'n' roll*, a sexual metaphor if there ever was one, into a type of dance.) On the air, the DJs introduced songs with lingo and sounds that they felt teenagers could identify with. The idea caught on throughout local radio and it reshaped record executives' ideas about what music to record.

From the standpoint of the record industry, the increasingly specific formats of radio stations enabled record promoters to target their intended audiences much

radio format the personality of a station organized around the kind of music it plays, and the radio personalities who are hired to introduce the recordings and advertisements

Berry Gordy

Berry Gordy intrepidly turned $800 into $61 million and made a makeshift recording company, Motown Records, into the largest African-American-owned business in the world. He does admit to one fear regarding music: he can't sing. As the songwriter-producer-agent-publisher from Detroit says, "I've always been insecure about singing to people because they would cut me off, or they had to leave in a hurry to go someplace."

Luckily for Gordy, there have been a myriad of artists throughout the course of his career willing—in fact, vying—to perform for him. From its founding in 1959 until its sale in 1988, Motown produced more than 30,000 songs like "To Be Loved" (1957) and "Shop Around" (1959), in addition to launching the careers of stars such as the Supremes, Marvin Gaye, Stevie Wonder, and the Jackson 5.

Gordy was born in 1929 to a family that was, in his own words, "blessed with a work ethic going back generations." As an adult, he struggled to make a living as a lightweight amateur boxer, a record store owner, and an assembly line worker at the Ford Motor Company. In his heart, though, burned the entrepreneurial spirit. As one of Gordy's artists, Jackie Wilson, later said, Gordy was "a little man with a big dream."

Securing an $800 loan from his family in 1958, Gordy turned an apartment in central Detroit into a makeshift recording studio and began writing what would later become some of the greatest hits of the 1960s, 1970s, and 1980s. He also began seeking out talent to sing the songs. Through William "Smokey" Robinson, the Marvelettes, the Temptations, and other groups, he created the "Motown sound," which was popular with both white and black teenagers. By exposing a new generation of white teenagers to black music, Gordy and his stars are credited with helping to bridge the gap between blacks and whites in the 1960s. This racial unity helped further the civil rights movement that was being led by Gordy's friend, Dr Martin Luther King, Jr.

The ability of Berry Gordy and his other Motown songwriters to mold groups and turn out hit songs became legendary. As Michael Jackson said at the 1997 induction of the Jackson 5 into the Rock and Roll Hall of Fame, "Berry prom-

Motown legend, Berry Gordy

ised us four consecutive number one records …and delivered them all. I'll never forget it." In 1998, Gordy himself was honored by the Songwriters Hall of Fame with the Sammy Cahn Award for lifetime achievement.

He sold Motown to MCA and Boston Ventures for $61 million in 1988; they sold it to Polygram in 1993 for $300 million. But Gordy retained his real jewel—Jobete Music, the publishing firm that holds the copyrights on the songs that he and other Motown songwriters created over the decades. In 1997, he sold a 50 percent stake in that to the huge British music firm EMI for $132 million. EMI's song-marketing ability will ensure that Gordy's most amazing legacy, Motown catalog's 15,000 songs, including "My Girl," "I'll Be There," "Heard It Through the Grapevine," and "Ain't No Mountain High Enough," will be heard for a long time to come.

In 2001, Gordy established a relief fund for former Motown musicians and writers who are down on their luck. The Gwendolyn B. Gordy Fund, to which Gordy donated $750,000 in the name of his late sister, assists artists from the 1960s and 1970s.

more carefully than before. College radio stations, for example, became useful vehicles for introducing "alternative" music, which most commercial stations would not touch until it had sold well in stores. Recording executives hated the fact that they had to rely on the interests of radio programmers to get their music out to potential customers. The pressure to get "airplay" encouraged bribes with money, drugs and other gifts, and produced a number of scandals.

New Developments in Technology

The explosion of music formats in radio was a great benefit to the recording industry. It came at a time when the technology of recording and playback was changing. First, Columbia and RCA introduced records that played at slower speeds ($33^1/_3$ and 45 rpm instead of the previous 78), which permitted longer recordings. Second, the sound quality of records was enhanced by the introduction of high fidelity and stereophonic record players. Third, almost unbreakable vinyl replaced highly breakable shellac as the material for making records. All these developments encouraged consumers to purchase recorded music. Recording executives noted that radio, and especially teen-oriented rock 'n' roll radio, was driving a high percentage of the purchases. When a song was played over and over again on the air, it stood a good chance of selling a lot of copies.

Aiding this growth were the long-playing record, FM radio, the transistor radio, and the tape player. Long-playing records allowed rock musicians to try out ideas that were much longer and more conceptual than the traditional three-minute song that had been standard since the start of records. "Sgt. Pepper's Lonely Hearts Club Band" by the British rock group the Beatles in 1967 was a milestone of this development. Although the entire album would not typically be played on standard rock 'n' roll radio, portions ("cuts") of it were.

Listening to albums outside the home became much easier with the developments of the transistor radio and the tape player. The transistor, invented at Bell Laboratories in the 1940s, quickly became a replacement for the vacuum tube in radio devices. Transistors were much lighter, less fragile, less bulky and more energy-efficient than tubes. That allowed for lightweight radios with small batteries that could be carried virtually anywhere. And while transistor radio allowed people to access stations on the go, the tape recorder did that and more. The idea of recording and playing sound on tape originated in Germany right before World War II; German tape recorders were discovered by Allied soldiers towards the end of the war. By the 1960s, tape recording was allowing musicians more freedom in the way they created and edited their works, changing the way in which records (and music) were created. By the same token, tape players powered by transistors and light batteries were changing the way audiences, especially teens and young adults, listened to music. Now the albums of their choice were portable, so people could take them to the park or the beach and play them in their cars.

Toward a New Digital World: the 1980s and 1990s

The spread of cable television in the 1980s provided an opportunity for recording companies to reach out to target audiences beyond radio. At the forefront of cable music were MTV and VH1, two cable networks owned by the same firm (Viacom) that played nonstop music videos supplied by music companies. MTV pioneered the twenty-four-hour music-video approach in the early 1980s. Other music-video programs, on broadcast television as well as on cable networks such as Black Entertainment Television (BET), also seemed to influence music purchases.

The CD was the record industry's newest attempt to entice people to recordings. It was brought to the market in 1983 by a number of Japanese firms. CD technology abandoned Thomas Edison's analog method of reproducing sound in favor of a digital approach. That is, instead of creating grooves that held sound analogous to the original sound, the recording process laid down digital codes that could tell a computer chip how to reproduce the sound. In playback, a laser beam read the codes and sent them to the chip, which, in turn, sent them through the amplifier to the speakers. The recording industry promoted the CD as an alternative to the standard vinyl record; it argued that CDs had superior sound, were more durable, and would never wear out. Although there were skeptics (and there still are), recorded music sales surged as people rebuilt their collections of records and tapes with CDs. By the late 1990s, though, this rebuilding had run its course, and the growth rate of recorded music sales slowed a bit. The digital nature of the CD, however, made it straightforward to create copies of albums in the home computers that spread through the United States and the rest of the world during the 1990s. Although people had long been making copies of records through their tape recorders, that analog method degraded the sound quality. CD copying worried executives because the digital reproductions are identical to the original.

As CD piracy became rampant in the United States and around the world, the recording industry was hit by another stream of copying. The spread of the Internet in the late 1990s marked the start of uploaded music (often from CDs) for all to share. So, while recording firms still saw radio as the major promotional medium for their business, they worried that the new technologies would reduce the sales that might result from their promotional work because people could get the music off pirated CDs and the Web and pay little or nothing at all. The concern raised enormously important issues for the industry: What would the rise of these and other Web technologies do to the music industry? To what extent, and how, would it transform the production, distribution, and exhibition of music in the twenty-first century? Would the traditional role of radio for the recording industry change as a result of all this?

Answers to these questions—and to the related ones we asked at the start of this chapter—are beginning to emerge. Let's look at how the recording industry is arranged today, including the ways it is changing in response to the digital challenges that face it.

An Overview of the Modern Recording Industry

A broad look at the recording industry in the United States makes three things about the industry very clear:

- Its ownership is international
- Its production is fragmented
- Its distribution is highly concentrated

Let's look at each of these statements individually.

International Ownership

To get an idea of the international nature of the recording business, consider that only one of the four largest recording companies—Universal, Sony BMG, Warner, and EMI—is even partly based in the United States. EMI is a British firm. Sony BMG Music Entertainment is a global joint venture equally owned by German Bertelsmann AG and the U.S. subsidiary of Sony of Japan. Universal is owned by Vivendi, a French conglomerate. Warner is owned by a Canadian group led by Canadian Edgar Bronfman. The country of origin of each of these firms, however, does not typically dictate the kind of music it tries to circulate in the United States.

"Think globally; act locally" is a phrase that is very apt for executives in the recording industry. Fifteen or twenty years ago, however, their perspective was quite different. Then the major firms concentrated on taking American and British hits and making them into worldwide megahits. Now, while many top American and, to a lesser extent, British artists still sell well globally, the real action and money seems to be in finding top local and regional talent.

Fragmented Production

This realization leads us to the second statement about the recording industry: that it is fragmented at the production end. In this context, *fragmentation* means that there are literally thousands of companies turning out recordings that they would like to sell. These recording firms are called *independents* because they are not owned by the major companies mentioned above, which are also the major distributors in the industry. Although the United States has always had many small firms producing recordings, the number of independents has soared in the past decade. In fact, independent record distributors as a group have become the third largest distributor of recorded music in the United States, after Sony.

One reason for the rise of independent firms is that newly affordable powerful personal digital recording technology has enabled small companies to produce compact disks. The availability of this technology has led to a flood of independent recordings. Many small production firms circulate their products to stores or sell them directly on the Web or at concerts instead of hooking up with the major distributors. Some independents are actually quite large operations. An example is Rounder Records, which specializes in bluegrass and other "American roots" music.

Concentration of Distribution

Still, the four major recording companies are the distributors of choice because of the immense power they bring to the marketplace (see Figure 10.3). Because they represent many popular artists, they have access to stores and radio stations for the promotion of new acts that small distributors might not have. Being large organizations, they are able to spend a lot of money to push artists that their executives believe have promise. In fact, these distributors insist that their size and their strong international presence give them a stature and credibility that make them the distributors of choice. The Universal Music Group's website proudly stated in 2007 that "UMG leads the music industry in global sales with an estimated worldwide market share in 2005 of 25.6 percent. Its global operations encompass the development, marketing, sales and distribution of recorded music through a

www.universalmusic.com, website of Universal Music Group, the largest group of music labels in the recording business.

Figure 10.3

**Music Distributors by
Percentage of Total Albums
Sold, 2007**

Source: Nielsen Soundscan Press
Release, January 3, 2008.

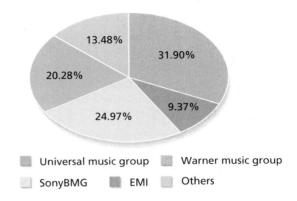

Universal music group   Warner music group
SonyBMG   EMI   Others

network of subsidiaries, joint ventures and licensees in 77 countries, representing approximately 98 percent of the music market."[2]

Unique Features of the Recording Industry

U.S. Sales and Audiences

Within the worldwide recording industry, the United States accounted for about 33 percent of all recording sales. In 2006, the industry sold just over one billion recordings in the United States and had revenues of $11.5 billion. Who buys all this music? From a gender standpoint, the split has long been around 50 percent male, 50 percent female. When it comes to age, the record industry targets its marketing to young people because traditionally they have bought more recordings than people in other age groups. According to the Recording Industry Association of America (RIAA), people 15–24 years old accounted for 22.6 percent of the spending on recordings in the United States in 2006—more than their percentage of the population. People aged 45 and older accounted for 26.1 percent of the spending—less than their presence in the population (see Table 10.1).

album a collection of a dozen or more individual musical recordings

single a product that contains only one or two individual musical recordings

Singles vs. Albums

The recording industry releases its product in two lengths: *singles* and *albums*. An **album** is a collection of a dozen or more individual songs, whereas a **single** con-

Table 10.1	How Does Age Relate to Music Purchases?		
Age group	**Percentage of music purchases**	**Age group**	**Percentage of music purchases**
10–14 Years	7.6	30–34	10.2
15–19	12.8	35–39	10.6
20–24	9.8	40–44	9.0
25–29	12.7	45+	26.1

Source: Recording Industry Association of America, *2006 Consumer Profile.*

Table 10.2 **Top Selling Recording Artists**

Artist	Certified units in millions	Artist	Certified units in millions
The Beatles	170	Madonna	63
Elvis Presley	118.5	Bruce Springsteen	62.5
Garth Brooks	116	Mariah Carey	61.5
Led Zeppelin	109.5	Michael Jackson	60.5
The Eagles	91	Metallica	57
Billy Joel	79.5	Van Halen	56.5
Pink Floyd	73.5	Whitney Houston	54
Barbra Streisand	71	U2	50.5
Elton John	69.5	Kenny Rogers	50.5
AC/DC	68	Celine Dion	49
The Rolling Stones	66	Fleetwood Mac	48.5
George Strait	65.5	Kenny G	48
Aerosmith	65.5	Neil Diamond	48

Source: http://riaa.com/goldandplatinumdata.php?table=tblTopArt, accessed 8/31/07.

tains only one or two songs. Singles are the building blocks of radio formats, and the airplay of these singles is often how the public first learns about an artist. However, artists and labels make their money from album sales, and the recording companies often do not price physical singles so they are worthwhile purchases relative to the albums. As a result, in 2005 sales of physical singles were negligible compared to albums: $10.5 billion versus $13 million. By contrast, though, web sales of singles through iTunes and other sites are often far less expensive than albums—99 or even 79 cents compared to several dollars. In that space, buyers go after their favorite songs. In 2005, they paid for 366.9 million singles and only 13.6 million albums.[3]

Diverse Recording Media Formats

Whether the recording is a single or an album, commercially sold music can be placed on a number of media. Those that are best known today are:

- Compact disks (CDs)
- Cassettes
- Videos
- Vinyl records
- Audio DVDs
- Super audio CDs
- Digital platforms

Table 10.3   Top Ten All-Time Best-Selling Albums

The following albums have been certified by the RIAA as the best-selling albums of all time, based upon RIAA statistics.

1	*Eagles: Their Greatest Hits* The Eagles/Elektra, 1976	6	*Back in Black* AC/DC/Elektra, 1980
2	*Thriller* Michael Jackson/Epic, 1982	7	*The Beatles* (The White Album) The Beatles/Capitol, 1968
3	*The Wall* Pink Floyd/Columbia, 1979	8	*Come On Over* Shania Twain/Mercury Nashville, 1997
4	*Led Zeppelin IV* Led Zeppelin/Swan Song, 1971	9	*Rumours* Fleetwood Mac/Reprise, 1977
5	*Billy Joel: Greatest Hits Volumes I & II* Billy Joel/Columbia, 1985	10	*The Beatles* The Beatles/Apple, 1968

Source: Recording Industry Association of America Top 100 Albums, http://www.riaa.org/Gold-Best-5.cfm, accessed 8/31/07.

download   to transfer data or programs from a server or host computer to one's own computer or digital device

digital rights management (DRM)   technologies that try to prevent consumers from copying digital material (including music) or from converting it to other formats; in the recording industry, DRM takes the form of codes included on digital music files that set certain limits on how many times or on what specific device a person can play the music

ringtones   bits of songs (or even new musical compositions) that people download to their mobile phones so that they play when someone calls them

The first six media are physical; that is, a person can hold them in his or her hand. Among the physical media, about 94 percent of the units that recording companies ship are compact disks. CDs are, in fact, durable and have excellent sound quality. Audio DVDs and super audio CDs are engineered to have even better sound, but they are new, expensive technologies which so far haven't caught on; each shipped only about half a million units in 2005. Cassettes, which constitute less than 1 percent of recorded music shipments, have declined markedly because of the tremendous success of CDs in the 1990s and 2000s. As recently as 1995, cassettes made up a quarter of all shipments; in 1990, they constituted half of them. Portability and convenience made them popular despite their lower fidelity and fragile nature. The declining cost of portable CD equipment for pedestrian and car use has eroded cassette use, however.

The term *digital platforms* stands for the several ways that people can purchase music without holding a medium in their hands. All typically involve a form of **downloading,** which means that the company sends the song as a digital file to the buyer's computer or computer-like device (for example, a mobile phone). In order to stop sharing of the songs, the file the person buys will sometimes come with a **digital rights management** (DRM) code for the device that plays it. That code sets certain limits on how many times or on what specific device a person can play the music. It also gets many buyers angry; we'll look at that in more detail, later. In addition, some companies that sell digital music download the files in forms that can be played only on particular devices with the right hardware or software. Apple's iTunes site uses the AAC format that works only on iPods. That doesn't seem to bother many consumers, because iPods are so popular. Apple is by far the leading purveyor of music; it has sold over a billion downloads (audio songs and music videos) from its site.

Although people's payment for owning songs is the most common way recording companies make money from digital platforms, they do have two other major opportunities. One involves streaming and the other involves ringtones. **Ringtones** are bits of songs (or even new musical compositions) that people download to their

Table 10.4 **Physical and Digital Music Unit Sales and Dollar Values**

	2003	2004	2005	2006
Physical Units	798.4	814.1	748.7	642.6
$ Value	11,854.4	12,154.7	11,195.0	9651.4
Digital Units		143.9	383.1	625.3
$ Value		183.4	503.6	878.0

Numbers are in millions, net after returns.

Source: Recording Industry Association of America, *2006 Consumer Profile.*

mobile phones so that they play when someone calls them. **Streaming** takes place when a website sends an audio file to a computer-like device so that it can be heard while it is coming into the device and then disappears. Some sites such as Yahoo Music and Rhapsody sell subscriptions for streaming. You pay $75 a year and you can stream as many songs as you want, but you cannot keep them. (The sites do give you the opportunity to buy the song or an album, though.) Yahoo and many other sites also give users the opportunity to listen to pre-chosen music streams based around certain genres—for example, jazz or classical—for free if they listen to commercials. Because it is much like a radio station, the activity has come to be known as **Internet radio.**

The money made from physical recordings dwarfs the sale of digital recordings, for now. According to the Recording Industry Association of America (RIAA), in 2006, physical music sales totaled around $9.6 billion while digital sales totaled $878 million[4] (see Table 10.4). Certainly, $878 million is not chicken feed, and the growth of digital payments is very strong; it was 74 percent over 2005, according to RIAA. Nevertheless, the recording industry is concerned about a number of developments. First, physical sales of music (CDs, videos, and vinyl LPs) have been dropping since 2000. Sales in 2006 plummeted about 14 percent compared to 2005. Second, the sales of individual digital songs, while growing strongly, cannot make up for the drop in albums, which normally bring in much more money. In 2006, for example, the industry sold 643 million physical units of music (albums and singles of all kinds), yielding $9.6 billion in revenues. Online unit sales that year were quite similar—625 million—but because the units tended to be singles rather than albums, the cash that came in was far less ($878 million). Third, and as a result of the industry's economic woes, executives are determined to lose as little as possible of their business to piracy, as we will see.

streaming an audio file delivered to a computer-like device from a website so that it can be heard while it is coming into the device but cannot be saved or stored

Internet radio pre-chosen music streams based around certain genres—for example, jazz or classical—free of charge to listeners, paid for by commercial advertisements, much like a radio station

Diverse Music Genres

The recording industry releases music in many genres, targeted to different slices of the music-buying public. According to the RIAA, in 2006, rock music remained the most popular genre of physical product; it accounted for one of every three recordings sold in the United States. As Table 10.5 shows, country held the second spot, with rap/hip-hop and R&B/urban music closely behind, followed by pop. You may (or may not) be surprised that classical music made up only 1.9 percent

Table 10.5 Genres of Music Sold as Physical Recordings

Genre	Percentage	Genre	Percentage
Rock	33	Religious	5.5
Country	13	Children's	2.9
Rap/hip-hop	11	Jazz	2
R&B/urban	11	Classical	1.9
Pop	7	Other	7.3

Source: Recording Industry Association of America, *2006 Consumer Profile*.

of the recordings, while "religious" (which includes gospel, inspirational and spiritual recordings) made up a higher 5.5 percent.

So we know what kind of musical recordings have moved more quickly than others. But how do those products get to their audiences in the first place? What happens between the time someone gets an idea for a song and the moment the recording of that song is sold? To answer this basic, but difficult, question, we turn to issues of production, distribution, and exhibition.

Production and the Recording Industry

Chances are, you know someone who is in a band. Maybe the band plays at local college bars, and the members practice when they are not working at day jobs to pay the bills. Perhaps the band's members have even recorded a demonstration (or "demo") song at a local studio and given you a copy. They are working hard while they wait for their big break: a contract with a record label, which they know will bring them fortune and fame in Hollywood. Will they still take your phone calls when they become big stars?

Across the country, many aspiring recording artists are waiting for their big break. Most of these artists never record a professional album and eventually move on to other, more lucrative lines of work. The age-old advice to struggling artists—Don't quit your day job—is especially true in the record business.

Artists Looking for Labels; Labels Looking for Artists

label a division of a recording firm that releases a certain type of music and reflects a certain personality

Many struggling bands dream about recording for a label of one of the major record production and distribution companies—the likes of Warner, Universal, and RCA. A **label** is a division of a recording firm that releases a certain type of music and reflects a certain personality. It is very much like an imprint in the book industry. For example, among Universal's many labels are Island Def Jam (for rap and hip-hop), Verve (for jazz and blues), MCA Nashville (for country), and Mercury Records (for classical). Realistically, artists know that they are much more likely to start their recording careers with small independent firms that are willing to

Latin Music

Until the early part of 2007, Latin music had been the most consistent genre in the record industry. Sales of Latin music records—those with at least 51 percent Spanish-language content—had increased since 2001, even posting all-time high marks in 2006, a monumentally difficult year for the rest of the record industry. In early 2007, however, sales of Latin music albums dropped considerably. This trend has been described as a delayed response to changes in digital music technology. Since Latin markets lag mainstream trends by a few months or years, music downloads, both legal and illegal, could be eating away at recent album sales.

There are other theories for the seemingly sudden dip in Latin music sales. Some blame high gas prices. It has also been argued that the sharp decline was the result of circumstances specific to the Hispanic population, namely increased pressure on local authorities to deal with illegal immigration. Latin industry insiders have noted that immigrants are reluctant to shop at bodegas selling Latin music or attend concerts by Mexican artists for fear of being deported.

Additionally, some see the problem as a consequence of the fact that most Latin albums are purchased not from independent retailers but mass-merchants such as Wal-Mart. Since large stores generally carry only established artists, the diminished relevance of indie record stores can have a direct effect on the development of up-and-coming musicians, thus hamstringing the genre's potential growth.

On the whole, Latin music seems susceptible both to the problems facing the mainstream music industry, as well as issues specific to the Hispanic population in the United States. That said, many new types of Latin music have created stable niches in the Latin market—reggaetón and bachata, for example—although none has been able to curb the decline seen in Latin record sales of late.

Sources: Leila Cobo, "Latin Notas: The Immigration X-Factor; Crackdowns On Citizenship May Be Hurting Latin Music Biz," *Billboard*, August 11, 2007, Leila Cobo "The Latin lag," *Billboard*; Leila Cobo, "Sales slow for Latin music; Distributors say sales have been dropping for three years," *Billboard*, July 8, 2007.

take a chance on them. They hope to sign with one of the majors once they have proved themselves.

The point person in a recording company for signing new artists is the label's **A&R** person. A&R stands for **artist and repertoire**, a term that dates back to the time when record executives saw themselves as shaping artists by choosing the collection of songs (the repertoire) that an artist played or sang. Today, the function of the A&R person is to screen new acts for a firm and determine whether or not to sign those acts. Like baseball scouts looking for the next Cy Young Award winner, A&R people are constantly searching for new acts for their label (see Figure 10.4).

Suppose your friends, after years of paying their dues in nightclubs throughout the state, are approached by the A&R person for Universal's Interscope record label. Somehow, the record company executive learned about the band, perhaps through hearing a demo record or attending a performance at a local bar, and wants to sign it to a record deal. At this point, certain relationships come into play. Negotiating the terms and conditions of these relationships is very important. Many struggling artists, unfamiliar with the business side of the artistic process and desperate to make it in the record industry, have entered into bad, one-sided agreements. Billy Joel, *NSYNC, Janet Jackson, and Tupac Shakur are only a few of the well-known musical acts who have fallen into this trap.

Many artists on their way up realize the necessity of hiring a competent manager to coordinate the development of the artist's career; help to arrange business opportunities for the artist; and handle the receipt, disbursement, and accounting

artist and repertoire or A&R describes the function of screening new musical acts for a recording company and determining whether or not to sign these acts; the record executives consider it their duty to shape artists by choosing the collection of songs (their repertoire) to be played or sung by the artist

397

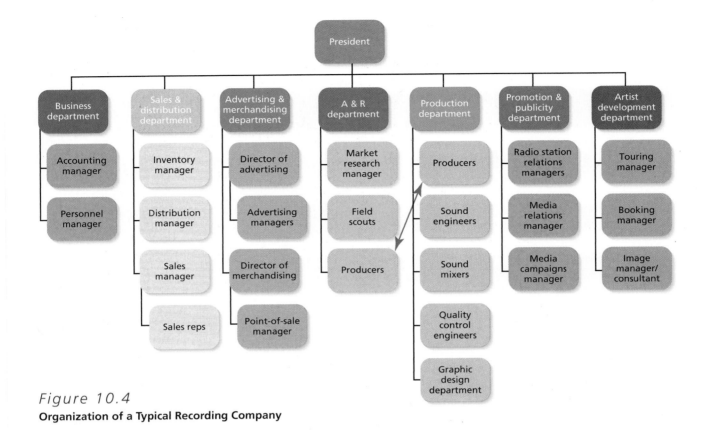

Figure 10.4
Organization of a Typical Recording Company

of the artist's revenues. In return for these services, the manager earns a percentage, typically 10 to 25 percent, of all the revenue the artist earns. Of course, artists try to hire a manager who will further their career, preferably one who knows the intricacies of the music business and most of the important people in the business. Despite artists' understandable wish for a manager who will act exclusively on their behalf, good managers often handle several artists at once.

Other business relationships for the band quickly follow. Most acts hire an attorney and an accountant to assist their manager in handling their often complex business affairs. Artists may also join a union such as the American Federation of Musicians (AFM) or the American Federation of Television and Radio Artists (AFTRA), which provides access to television and motion picture work, represents the artist's interests with various media industries, and offers benefits such as group health insurance. Joining a royalty-collecting association, such as ASCAP or BMI, is also important. But of all these contractual relationships, the most important one is the one the artist develops with a record label. Simply put, the music industry today revolves around the issuance of recorded music and the joint effort of the artist and the company to sell as many records as possible. The most difficult negotiation an artist carries out is with his or her record label.

Finding Music to Record

Artists, of course, need music to perform. Many popular artists today perform music that they have written themselves. Yet at some point in their careers, virtually all artists record music that someone else wrote. There are several ways for an artist or group to find music. Music-publishing companies maintain catalogs of songs, and many record stores sell printed copies of music, usually intended to be played on a guitar or piano. When an artist uses any song in these libraries commercially, songwriters and their publishing companies expect to be paid a share of the money the production firm receives; this payment is called a **royalty**.

Royalties

There are important legal steps that songwriters must take, such as filing their songs with the U.S. copyright authorities, in order to ensure that they make money from a song they have written even if they do not sing it themselves. But it is difficult for the owner of a song to keep track of where and how the song is performed. For example, songwriters are entitled to compensation whenever a radio station plays their songs, a band performs their work at a nightclub, or a record company releases their songs.

Agencies like ASCAP, BMI, and Harry Fox exist to make sure that publishers and songwriters are compensated for the use of their work. These agencies take over the daunting task of verifying compliance with the law on behalf of the rights holder. ASCAP, or the American Society of Composers, Authors and Publishers, is the largest of the performing-rights organizations and represents more than 120,000 songwriters and publishers. Though the airing of one covered song on a radio station may result in a royalty payment to ASCAP or its agents of only a fraction of a penny, these small amounts add up. According to its annual report, in 2006, ASCAP received more than $785 million on behalf of its member songwriters and publishers. After operating expenses, the organization distributed $680 million of that money. ASCAP uses formulas derived from surveys that rank the popularity of each songwriter's songs during the year to determine each member's share of the revenue after expenses and distributes that share to each member.

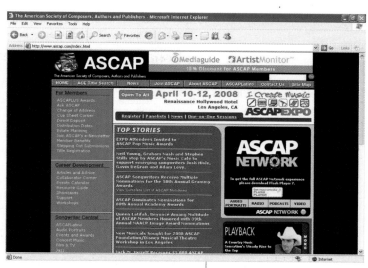

www.ascap.com, website of the American Society of Composers, Authors and Publishers, which licenses performance rights and distributes royalties for hundreds of thousands of music creators worldwide.

royalty the share of money paid to a songwriter or music composer out of the money that the production firm receives from the sale or exhibition of a work

Compensating Artists

Artists are compensated for their performance on recorded music in one of two ways. Artists who help to make an album, but are not central to it, are paid an hourly fee. In accordance with the rules of their union, these studio musicians or singers are paid at least the industry scale. The central artists on the recording, in contrast, typically are not paid by the hour. They receive royalties for their work. Many artists believe that they can hit the jackpot if their recordings sell well and so prefer royalties over flat fees. A typical recording industry contract will give an artist or group 10 to 15 percent of the retail price of an album. At the same time, many studio musicians and singers are quite comfortable with their more predictable payments. Artists who are in great demand as backup talent for albums receive far more than scale and can make a very good living.

Producing a Record

The firm that has signed a contract to record an artist's album will often line up a producer to oversee the recording of the album and its final sound. The producer, like the artist, is generally compensated on a royalty basis. A typical royalty percentage for a good producer is 2 to 4 percent of the total retail sales of the album.

The producer is responsible for obtaining copyright clearances, lining up session musicians if needed, staying on budget, and delivering a high-quality master tape to the record company. An important first task for a producer is to line up a good place to record. Studios with good equipment and good engineers can be found all over the world, and producers carefully select a studio where the artist will be comfortable and productive. It may come as no surprise to you that many major albums are produced in quiet, out-of-the way places where the artists are unlikely to be disturbed.

A producer also works to keep the project on budget. Each extra day in the studio can cost thousands of dollars. Record companies can financially penalize the recording artist for cost overruns by taking the money out of the artist's royalties. After the recording sessions have been completed, the producer and artist finish mixing the songs on the album. They pay special attention to making the songs fit the specific technical requirements of the label, such as the length of each song, and also to identifying any potential singles on the album.

First-time artists, however, often find themselves in a very weak position with their prospective label. They quickly learn that signing a recording contract does not mean becoming an instant millionaire. Most labels pay for manufacturing, distribution, and promotion, but they deduct recording costs from the artists' royalties. In major recording studios these costs typically run to as much as fifty thousand dollars for putting down the sound "tracks," mixing them, and preparing a master for reproduction. Moreover, for every twenty-dollar sale, the record label may pocket ten dollars on an initial contract. Therefore, an artist who spends fifty thousand dollars on a recording must sell 500,000 units—or go "gold"—just to break even!

Independent labels generally have even more restrictive artistic contracts than the majors do. Contracts with independent labels are for a longer period than those with the majors, provide lower royalty rates than those of the majors, require the artists to share the copyright on songs with the labels, and may even demand a share of the artist's merchandising monies. Independent-label executives respond that they incur sizable financial risks when they subsidize new artists. Recording companies can spend hundreds of thousands of dollars breaking a new artist, and many new artists, despite the best efforts of both sides, never contribute to the overall profitability of the record company. In addition, the executives argue, independent firms have to pay a percentage of their income to the firms that distribute their product.

The hope of making it truly big is always there for the artists, however. If they become superstars, their power relationship with the record label equalizes. For artists with proven market demand, their agents and lawyers can negotiate generous deals. At his height of popularity, Michael Jackson records reportedly received a royalty rate of 20 percent from a unit of Sony.

Self-producing CDs for Sale

For the many struggling singers and musicians who don't have contracts with any recording firm, there is another route. In view of the difficulty of getting noticed even by independent companies, artists may decide to produce their own CDs for sale and sell them at performances, and maybe even in some stores. The good news is that affordable, professional-quality equipment has recently become available in recording studios. In many cases, studio rates have been halved in the past few

Analog vs. Digital

Once compact disks had rendered record albums and cassettes nearly obsolete, it appeared that audio DVD or Super Audio CD (SACD) would emerge as the next must-have music technology. Both represent advances in sound recording and have heightened audio quality and storage capacity compared to CDs. However, even with an increasing number of titles available in both formats and the availability of hybrid forms that will work in regular CD players (though without the added quality), the progress of these newer formats on the market has been slow. Reasons for this include the popularity of Internet downloading of music (even though those formats are inferior to regular CDs) and the fact that the new formats are incompatible with each other. Historically, such competition between music formats has led to either the death of one or both. At this point it is hard to tell whether audio DVD or Super Audio CDs will take off. Here, though, is how they differ from the older record formats:

Vinyl albums use analog technology. This term comes from the word *analogous*, meaning that the recorded sound waveform is a copy of the original. Phonograph recording mechanically engraves sound waves directly on to a vinyl disk. Electrical signals are relayed from a microphone to a cutting tool that, following the sound waves, moves within a magnetic field to make grooves in the soft surface of the plastic record. The grooves are, in essence, a replica of the original recorded waveforms. Sound is generated when a special needle navigates the record's grooves at a regulated speed and sends electrical signals to speakers.

Compact Disks (CDs) utilize digital recording, which converts sound waves to a series of 0s and 1s known as bits (short for binary digits). A CD is encoded with small pits that represent the binary code for the recorded sounds. A laser beam decodes the sequence of bits off the reflective surface of the disk, which a computer within the CD player then reads and creates an electronic signal that corresponds to the value of each binary number. When the signals are played in order, the original sound is reproduced.

Audio DVD and SACD take digital one step further. They pick up higher sound frequencies than a CD, providing richer, more subtle acoustics. Audio DVD and SACD store about seven and four times the amount of data respectively, allowing for longer recordings on one disk. Both formats allow for 6-channel surround sound instead of 2-channel stereo sound that CDs are limited to. Also, audio DVD, when connected to a TV or computer, permits the display of video clips, liner notes, or text from the artist, for example.

Source: "Sound Recording and Reproduction," in *Encarta online Encyclopedia*, http://encarta.msn.com; Jack Schofield, "Technology: No Taste for High Quality Audio", *The Guardian*, August 2, 2007, p. GTP1; Panasonic DVD-Audio Q&A site.

years. Some artists don't even bother with studios. It is possible to make a perfectly acceptable recording in someone's basement, and people often do. Moreover, because of intense competition in the CD manufacturing business, the cost of making CDs has plummeted, too.

And who says you need a CD at the start? Many musicians load their work onto sites such as MySpace and Revver with the hope they'll get noticed. MySpace claimed in 2007 that it had more than eight million bands using the site. A press release stated that "MySpace music has allowed bands to share music and videos, announce tour dates and communicate with fans and others in the MySpace community, seamlessly integrating the Web into shared online and offline experiences."[5] And, in fact, go through MySpace music's various genres, and you'll find bands with a wide spectrum of public renown. In late 2007, you could come across Justin Timberlake (attached to Sony BMG's Zomba label), Sparta (signed with Disney-owned Hollywood Records), Smile Empty Soul (which lists its independent label

Singer Ingrid Michaelson rose to popularity without a record-label contract by distributing her music through her MySpace site seen here. Her songs were used on television shows like *Grey's Anatomy* and *One Tree Hill* and the exposure sent one of her songs to number 13 on the iTunes pop music chart.

as Bieler Bros Records/MRAfia Records), and The Morning Light, which says it has no record label. Some artists who started on MySpace went on to get contracts with recording companies and substantial radio airplay. Examples are Colby Caillat ("Bubbly") and Sara Bareilles ("Love Song").

Distribution in the Recording Industry

MySpace is, of course, a distribution venue, but you don't have to pay anything to get on it. You can sell your music from it, and while the site may take a cut of the sale, the amount is far less than a label takes. If The Morning Light can produce its music in a basement and release its songs on MySpace just a click away from Justin Timberlake, why would any group choose to sign with a recording firm, whether an independent or a major?

It's a good question, particularly if you pay attention to stories such as Ingrid Michaelson's. Her experience makes the MySpace model of distribution seem extremely attractive. An aspiring singer/songwriter/pianist and part-time teacher of theater to kids, Michaelson was 24 when in 2005 she set up a page on MySpace with the aim of networking with musicians and potential fans. Within a year, her soft vocals and romantic piano attracted a management company that specializes in finding little-known acts for TV shows, advertisers, movie companies and video games. The firm placed three of her songs on ABC's popular "Grey's Anatomy," and the exposure sent one of her songs, "The Way I Am," to number 13 on the iTunes pop music chart.

She had to pay 15–20 percent of her music royalties to the management company. But not having a label allowed her to keep most of what was left. As the *Wall Street Journal* pointed out, "Because Ms Michaelson doesn't have a record-label contract, she stands to make substantially more from online sales of her music. For each 99-cent sale on iTunes, Ms Michaelson grosses 63 cents, compared with perhaps 10 or 15 cents that typical major-label artists receives via their label."[6] By mid-2007, she had sold about 60,000 copies of her songs on iTunes and other digital stores. She used some of that money to press (and sell) her own CDs, arrange distribution for them, make T-shirts for concerts, and hire a marketing company to produce promotional podcasts.

What, then, *does* a label bring to an artist's career? The short answer is sustained cross-media exposure. Getting the ears of powerful concert promoters, radio program executives, and cable gatekeepers who select music for large, though targeted audiences is a task that requires a strong organization with much experience. Don't ignore that even Michaelson didn't get her TV exposure on her own; a management company led the way. Record labels have the ability to push her further. Because she had no record label or distributor, her two CDs, "Slow the Rain" and "Girls and Boys," which she put out herself in 2004 and 2006, weren't carried by many traditional music stores even in 2007.

The manager for several bands, including Death Cab for Cutie, adds that an unsigned artist risks losing momentum. "There's a lot more components to an artist's career than being featured prominently on a show, just as there's more to it than having one hit on the radio," he stated. Michaelson agreed. She told the *Wall Street Journal* in 2007 that she hopes to sign with a label eventually. But knowing the pitfalls of the business, she is playing it smart. First, she says, she wants to build up her reputation and fan base. "I want to make my presence known before that happens, so I can have some clout," she said.[7]

All these comments emphasize the point that distribution holds the key to potential success in the recording industry. As in other mass media industries, having good distribution avenues does not ensure that a recording will be a hit. Without strong ability to place recordings in stores and other exhibition areas, however, the chances that a recording will be a hit diminish considerably. And having a hit with a major label builds on itself so that the label can make a deal for the kind of visibility on MySpace and other music sites that a band without a marketing power behind it would not have.

Distribution does not simply mean being able to send recordings to a store. Although major firms such as RCA send recordings to their biggest retail clients directly, many of their albums, singles, and videos end up in stores through huge wholesalers. The wholesalers work with all the majors as well as with independent distribution firms that handle some of the recordings produced by independent companies. The real distribution power of RCA, Sony Music, Warner, and the other major producer-distributors lies in their ability to generate a buzz among an artist's potential fans that will induce retailers to carry his or her records and display them properly.

The task is an imposing one. The statistics must be frightening to anyone who is hoping to hit it big without the Big Four—Universal Music Group, Sony BMG, EMI, and Warner Music—who together control 75 percent of global music sales. Powerful distributors have the benefit of big promotional teams, liaisons with radio stations, and money for co-operative advertising. Let's take a look at these areas.

The Importance of Promotion

More than anything else, distributors contribute marketing expertise to building a recording artist's career. **Promotion** involves scheduling publicity for a recording artist, such as an appearance on the cover of *Spin* magazine and performing charity work that will make news. This includes liaisons with radio stations, or setting up cooperative activities with radio stations in different cities that reach the people who are likely to buy an artist's albums. The deal may entail generating excitement on the air about a concert tour by the artist that will come through the station's area. In return for the on-air promotion of a group and its rock concert, for example, a radio station might receive free tickets to give away and exclusive radio interview rights when the artist hits town. Promotion may also include cooperative advertising, which means that the recording firm provides a retailer with a portion of the money the retailer needs in order to buy space in local newspapers or time on local radio and TV stations. All this may sound easy, but in the competitive media environment, it is extremely difficult. Recording firms have particular difficulty motivating people to buy the albums of new groups because people need to hear music before they buy it. Attractive cover art is nice, but it is hard to visually "window shop" for a new album. You really have to hear the music.

The recording industry is therefore dependent on other media to inform its audiences about new products. Some retailers are trying to alleviate this problem by encouraging customers to sample new music before they buy it. A few stores allow you to try out any album, but most highlight a limited number of albums,

promotion the process of scheduling publicity appearances for a recording artist, with the goal of generating excitement about the artist, and thereby sales of his or her album

chosen because recording firms have paid to promote them. Moreover, despite the incorporation of listening posts into music stores, research has consistently shown that most customers credit radio airplay for getting them interested in buying particular music.

The Recording Industry and the Radio Industry   Historically, as we have seen, music distributors have directed a lot of marketing attention to the radio industry. That is still the case. Recording-industry promotion executives focus particularly on radio program directors, because they are the ones who choose the particular pieces from albums (the cuts) that get airplay on the station. The relationship between the two groups is quite symbiotic; that is, each lives off the other. Both are in the business of targeting a large but fairly narrow audience with a particular genre of music. A hit recording keeps listeners tuned in to a radio station and helps the station in its battle to win ratings; and airplay on the radio station converts listeners to buyers, fulfilling the goals of the record company and its artists.

Still, the needs of recording-company promoters sometimes conflict with those of the programmers. Many radio stations are conservative about adding new music. Program directors give preference to existing artists because those artists have a track record of success and because listeners are familiar with their sound. New artists are very much an uncertainty, and gambling on new material from unknowns might hurt the station's ratings. Music promoters also face the problem of competition. In any given week, a station may add only one new song to its playlist, whereas the various record labels may have a dozen new songs that they believe fit the station's format.

Radio station programmers, faced with the daunting task of deciding which of the many new songs that come out each week to add to their playlists, supplement their own impressions of the quality of music with outside data. Several firms, such as Broadcast Data Services, now electronically monitor radio stations across the country, verify the identity of every song played on those stations, and report these data to subscribers. A second system, known as SoundScan, automatically records the sales of music at participating retail stores. Each week the SoundScan findings are used to compile lists of record sales across the country. Based on such data, various trade publications compile weekly lists of the top-selling or most-played songs.

Radio programming executives often look at these lists to help them make decisions about airplay. Station program directors also monitor their own station's request line to see whether typical listeners want to hear more of a new song. Some conduct phone surveys of

The promotion of recording artists takes many forms, depending upon the artist and the audience. Publicists for singer Beyoncé Knowles likely believed that her appearance as the cover model of the 2007 *Sports Illustrated* Swimsuit issue would appeal to an important component of its audience.

listeners in which they play bits of songs and ask whether they would want to hear them on the station.

Music Promotion Techniques   Knowing that radio stations use various pieces of data to make decisions on airplay, record executives have to work hard to get the airplay in certain markets and on particular stations that will convince program directors on the largest stations to insert a song into a playlist rotation. There are many ethical ways of doing that. Over the decades, the enormous pressure to succeed in radio has also led to unethical tacks. There are reports, for example, that record company representatives have organized campaigns to flood stations with requests for a particular song. An even more unsavory activity aimed at placing songs on radio stations is **payola**—the payment of money by a promotion executive to a station program director to ensure that the program director includes certain music on the playlist. In the late 1950s, the federal government made payola illegal. In view of the millions of dollars at stake in the recording industry, though, you shouldn't be surprised that prosecutions for this kind of improper influence continue. Stories consistently circulate that newer versions of payola, in the form of drugs or other noncash favors, are given to radio executives or consultants in return for adding new songs to their stations' playlists.

payola an activity in which promotion personnel pay money to radio personnel in order to ensure that they will devote airtime to artists that their recording companies represent

Video, Internet, and Movie Promotions

Despite the importance of radio, music distributors do try to excite potential buyers about their music in other ways. TV is a critical medium for promoting many genres. During the past two decades, music videos have played an important role in driving rock, pop, and rap sales. Recording companies often help artists produce these videos because of the proven ability of a sizzling video to lead consumers to stores. The MTV network has been the major focus of television's rise as a video outlet. Other sources of video exhibition include Country Music Television, the Nashville Network, VH1, and Black Entertainment Television (BET). BET plays a crucial role in presenting music to African-American viewers.

As Ingrid Michaelson's experience shows, television series have also become important venues for new music, particularly by new performers. For TV producers who want to reach young adults, introducing indie artists is less expensive than paying huge amounts for stars, and it may signal to the audience that the program is in tune with the newest sounds. Although these sorts of programs may not be a place for major labels to place hit acts, the shows may be good for relative newbies. Moreover, the indie acts that make it to the TV series are getting the kind of promotion that may well make the major labels take a look at them and decide that the publicity makes them ready to move to higher levels of popularity.

As we have seen, the Web is similarly a place where hugely popular artists and unknown ones are out there waiting for fans. Most record labels have websites where you can read about your favorite artists, download photos, hear snippets of new songs, and sometimes even listen to these songs in their entirety. More controversially, record executives have been known to pay teens to spread buzz in chat rooms and through emails about an artist the company is trying to promote.

Increasingly, companies allow consumers on a variety of sites to download several songs from a new album in the hope that they will ultimately buy the CD anyway. Going further, recording firms have collaborated with those Web powers to highlight and sell album releases from artists such as Gnarls Barkley, Panic! At the Disco, Lily Allen, Fall Out Boy, Timbaland, Modest Mouse, and The Used. The publicity seems to pay off. In 2007, exclusive album releases on MySpace by

T-Pain, The Used, Timbaland, Modest Mouse, and The Shins coincided with those albums showing up that week in the number one or two position on *Billboard* magazine's popularity chart.

Concert Tours

Presenting concerts across the country is a time-honored way to promote an album. Performing is second nature for most groups; after all, many groups start out by playing local gigs in their hometown. A good manager tries to book a new group as the opening act in a tour by an established superstar, thus quickly introducing the new group to the established superstar's large audience. One often overlooked fact is that while tours have the potential to generate lots of money, the expenses are often quite high. Experienced help has to be hired, and trucks and buses must be rented. Schedules have to be reasonable so as not to wear out the artist. Millions of dollars can be lost if a major artist comes down with pneumonia and has to cancel performances. One technique for reducing the financial uncertainty of a major tour is to find a national sponsor, such as a beverage company.

At each stop along the tour, the artist seeks to build support for his or her records. The artist may visit local radio stations in an attempt to influence their decisions on airplay and help generate a large crowd at the arena. T-shirts, sweatshirts, and other memorabilia are given away free by promoters and sold at the concerts; so are albums. The total take from concert paraphernalia can be surprisingly high. Independent recording artists often make a substantial percentage of their income from such sales.

A local promoter may help make some of the arrangements and also share in the risks and potential rewards of putting on a concert. Involving a local promoter ensures that the arena chosen is the right size and configuration for the nature of the act. The promoter carefully prices concert tickets so that the house will be 60 percent full at the very least. After all, it costs virtually the same amount to perform for a small audience as to perform for a large audience, but empty seats generate no revenue.

Exhibition in the Recording Industry

After all the work of making the record and all the work of distributing it is completed, recordings are laid out for members of the public to choose. Recordings make it into the hands of the public through six major paths. They are:

- Digital downloads
- Traditional record stores
- Other retail stores
- Internet stores
- Record clubs
- Direct sales

Digital Downloads

It's useful to start with this exhibition mode because we've already described it during the discussion of various vehicles for recorded music. According to the RIAA,

Corporate Sponsorship of Music Stars

What do the burger wars have to do with the battle of the boy bands? Quite a bit, apparently. In 2000, McDonald's Summer Music Event offered McDonald's customers three original CDs featuring Jive recording artists *NSYNC, Britney Spears, and Sisqo, among others. Not to be outdone, Burger King let Backstreet Boys fans "have it their way" by launching three exclusive CDs featuring the band and sponsoring their "Black and Blue" world tour.

Corporate promotions featuring popular recording artists have long been a staple of marketing strategies. Is linking a brand name with a performer or group truly an effective way of converting the performer's fan base to the company's customer base? Companies like Microsoft believe it is. Microsoft hopes its investment in sponsoring tours by chart toppers like The Chemical Brothers, VHS or BETA, Suzanne Vega, and Smashing Pumpkins will pay off in increased sales of its Zune digital music player among hip teens, Gen-Xers, and others.

In some cases, however, the motives of corporate sponsors in the music world are not wholly profit-driven. The Live Earth 2007 global concert series powered by and highlighting artists like Alicia Keys, Dave Matthews Band, Madonna and the Red Hot Chili Peppers, was sponsored by corporations ranging from Pepsi to Stonyfield Farm Organic. Their efforts were linked to the tour's pledge to "to trigger a global movement to solve the climate crisis." In keeping with Live Earth's spirit, corporate supporters stated their commitment to help work to solve the climate crisis by raising awareness and leading a movement toward more sustainable practices.

Do altruism and social responsibility play a role, then, for corporations that tie their public relations and marketing efforts to popular music artists? Or are even the most socially responsible campaigns of this sort geared only to improving the bottom line?

of music purchased over the six paths, it represented the smallest of the revenues brought into the recording industry in 2006, 6.8 percent. Others who look at the digital environment see the revenues differently, though. Veronis Suhler Stevenson, a media investment consultancy, concluded, using Nielsen SoundScan data, that digital downloads made up 11.8 percent of spending on recorded music and it added the separate category of mobile phones (not mentioned in the RIAA table) and gave it a 6.6 percent share. By that calculation, payments through digital downloads already exceeded record clubs' contribution to sales in 2006, which the RIAA put at 10.6 percent. Undoubtedly, each party would have its legitimate explanation of the data. Both agree, however, that the paid downloading of individual songs, albums and music videos; the subscription-based or advertising sponsored streaming of music audio and video feeds; and the purchasing of ringtones represent a rapidly growing revenue source for the industry. At the end of 2007, Nielsen SoundScan concluded that digital music had accounted for 23 percent of music purchases that year. Clearly, the world of music distribution is changing quickly.[8]

Traditional Record Stores

For decades, the record store on the shopping street or in the mall was probably the best-known place to buy music. There were hundreds of music stores across the country. Prominent chains were Sam Goody and Tower Records. But both chains went out of business, and the stores that exist are struggling. Change came rapidly, for as recently as 1998, record stores accounted for 50.8 percent of the sales of recordings in the United States. By 2006, the percentage of sales linked to record stores had slid to 35.4 percent, and the trajectory over the years was pretty consistently southward. It seems that the decline can be blamed on two types of stores, other physical retail stores and Internet stores.

Other Retail Stores

The phrase "other retail stores" refers to any legitimate emporium that sells records along with other items. Department stores do that, as do electronics, clothing, and truck stops. In 2006, this category represented 32.7 percent of all recorded-music sales. Chains such as Trans World Entertainment, Best Buy, Barnes & Noble, Newbury Comics and Gray Whale sell lots of CDs, with a fairly wide range of titles. At other retailers the range of recordings sold is very thin, customized to the

| **Gold, Platinum, and Diamonds** | CULTURE TODAY |

Do you think you know your music? Who's certified as being the top-selling group of the twentieth century? The Beatles are the most successful recording act, with sales of more than 106 million albums—and that's just in the United States.

What about the top solo artist? No, it's not Elvis. Garth Brooks has sold 89 million albums, and his sales are climbing. Elton John is second, then Billy Joel, then Barbra Streisand, and then Elvis.

Here are some other award trivia:

- The first Gold single? Perry Como's "Catch a Falling Star" (RCA Records) in 1958, the year the awards were launched.
- The first Gold album? The cast album to *Oklahoma*, sung by Gordon Macrae and cast (Capitol Records).
- Johnny Taylor's "Disco Lady" was the first Platinum single.
- The first Platinum album certified by the RIAA was The Eagles' *Their Greatest Hits 1971–1975*. And now that album has sold over 26 million copies, becoming the best-selling album of the twentieth century.
- Michael Jackson's *Thriller*, which was one of the first Multi-Platinum albums ever certified, held the top album slot from 1984 until his record was tied and then eventually broken in 1999.

On March 16, 1999, the RIAA launched the Diamond Awards, honoring albums or singles with sales of ten million copies or more. Of all the artists in attendance, Sir Elton John best described the significance of the award when he said, "I think this is the biggest accolade you can be given because it means your fans have gone out and bought your records. And that's why we make records—for our public."

The list of Diamond titles represents some of the best and most influential recordings in history. From the Beatles to the Backstreet Boys, it is truly an audio timeline of the last fifty years. Representing all genres of music, these fifty-eight artists and seventy-eight titles have had total U.S. sales of more than 900 million copies.

In commenting on the RIAA's artists of the century, Hilary Rosen, president and CEO of the RIAA, stated, "These artists represent the very best of popular music and deserve the highest accolades the industry has to offer. All have been major trendsetters, as well as record-breakers. Their exceptional talent has opened doors for other artists to follow."

Source: Printed by permission of the Recording Industry Association of America, Inc. (RIAA®), Gold®, Platinum® and Diamond® and RIAA® are registered marks of the Recording Industry Association of America, Inc., accessed 2/20/08 at http://www.riaa.org/Gold-Intro.cfm

store's image. You may have noticed, for example, that the Starbucks coffee chain sells CDs that reflect a cool, sophisticated take on life. But the biggest business of CD selling is taking place at very large retailers such as Wal-Mart, Target and K-Mart. Wal-Mart, in fact, has become the largest single purveyor of musical records in the United States.

Many retail shops do not actually run their own record department. Instead, they farm out the section to an intermediary known in the business as a **rack jobber**. A rack jobber is actually a separate company that maintains a small retail space for recorded music within a store, following rules set by the retailer. Partnering with a rack jobber means that the merchant doesn't have to worry about keeping up with what is hot in the music industry, constantly ordering new products, and periodically adjusting the store's record displays. Typically, the revenue generated from sales of these products is split between the rack jobber and the owner of the retail store.

rack jobber a company contracted by a department store to maintain its rack of records, tapes, CDs, and/or DVDs

Internet Stores

Internet stores are online sites that sell CDs and mail them to the buyer; think of http://www.amazon.com (the clear leader), http://www.lala.com, http://www.ebay.com, and many more. With their efficiency, low costs, and wide selection, these virtual places seem to be taking away business from physical retailers. Whereas in 2003 they comprised 5 percent of record sales, according to the RIAA, in 2006 the number had nearly doubled to 9.1 percent. By comparison, "other retail stores" made up 50.7 percent of the pie in 2003 and only 32.7 in 2006. It seems that the long-term direction is in favor of these sorts of merchants and the ones that sell digital downloads.

Record Clubs

Another major way to distribute recordings is through clubs such as Columbia House. RIAA data indicate that these clubs have increased their percentage of industry sales in recent years, from 4.1 percent in 2003 to 10.5 percent in 2006. Individuals are enticed into joining these clubs by newspaper or magazine ads offering low-cost introductory specials, such as seven CDs for one cent. Members also sometimes agree to buy a certain number of albums later at the regular price. Often artists receive a lower royalty on sales of recordings through these clubs.

Direct Sales

Direct sales accounts for just 2.4 percent of all revenues. Products sold through the "direct" channel frequently are compilations of old songs on such themes as Christmas hymns or the greatest disco hits. They are sold directly to individuals through television ads. These ads may feature short selections of a song or its accompanying music video. The ads repeatedly urge you to call a toll-free number and use your credit card to place an order now.

Two Major Public Controversies

With all the changes riling the recording industry, you would think that the last thing record executives need is a public controversy that strikes directly at the core of their activities. It turns out that they have not one such controversy to worry about; they have two. One has to do with the lyrics in certain genres of popular music. The other has to do with the ways people are allowed to have access to songs on the Internet. Both raise serious social questions that have no easy answers.

Concerns Over Lyrics

A large number of music consumers are also parents. In this role, many have been less concerned about the ethics of music downloads than about the lyrics of the songs their kids get off the Web and buy from the stores. This is not a new concern. For decades, recording companies, artists, and stores have been pelted with complaints from parents and teachers around the country that their children are purchasing music with lyrics unsuitable for the children's—and maybe some parents'—ears.

Many of their concerns came to a head during the 1980s, when Tipper Gore, the wife of U.S. Senator Al Gore, joined with other wives of influential Washington politicians and businessmen to form the Parents Music Resource Center (PMRC). The PMRC had a number of goals. It aimed to lobby the music industry to print lyrics on album covers. It wanted explicit album covers kept under the counter. It demanded a records ratings system similar to that used for films, and also a ratings system for concerts. The group also suggested that the companies reassess the contracts of those performers who engage in violence and explicit sexual behavior on stage; and it proposed a media watch by citizens and record companies that would pressure broadcasters not to air songs that the group considered problematic.

The anger succeeded in leading major recording companies to put parental advisory labels on albums that warned parents about objectionable lyrics. The nation's leading retailer, Wal-Mart, has in fact refused to stock albums with controversial lyrics. As a result, some recording firms resorted to distributing two versions of an album: one with safer, censored lyrics and the original one that the musician intended to distribute.

The rise of gangsta rap in the late 1980s raised more concerns about violent or sexually explicit lyrics in censored and uncensored albums. Others objected to the depiction of women in many rap songs as well as in other musical genres. In the mid-1990s civil rights activist C. Delores Tucker launched a highly visible campaign to clean up rap music. She focused on Time Warner, whose subsidiary Interscope was home to hard-core rappers Snoop Dogg and Tupac Shakur. In 1995, Tucker and her allies succeeded in forcing Time Warner to get rid of Interscope. But Time Warner simply sold Interscope to Polygram (now Universal Music Group), and the label continued to turn out songs that Tucker and others reviled, through immensely popular artists such as 50 Cent and Eminem. A dozen years later, the battle reached another crescendo, with Al Sharpton and other public figures objecting particularly to racial epithets (particularly the N word) and sexual profanities (the omnipresent B word) in the music.

Some people have lauded these calls for reining in rappers and other songwriters with what they considered immoral lyrics. They have argued that popular music speaks to an enormous number of impressionable young people and teaches them about romance and love and relationships. Bleeping out a word here and there on the radio or a censored album doesn't erase many of the objectionable words and ideas in the songs, they have argued. Many of rap's defenders have responded that outsiders should not impose their values on an important field of artistic endeavor. Rappers, they have said, reflect views that many angry African Americans feel toward their surroundings; such hard-edge views need to be heard and understood, they argue. During the past few years, though, even rap's defenders have acknowledged that sometimes the lyric writers aim for the obscene, the violent and derogatory simply to stand out. In 2007, the filmmaker Byron Hurt released *Beyond Beats and Rhymes*, a documentary critical of rap that, in the words of a *Time* magazine writer, was notable "not just for its hard critique but for the fact that most of the people doing the criticizing were not dowdy church ladies but members of the hip-hop generation who deplore rap's recent fixation on the sensational."[9] Many rap artists disagreed strongly, and the arguments continued.

Concern About Access to Music

Of course, many of the songs that some people find so objectionable can be downloaded from the Web. Some parents worry that their children have access to this material too easily, and so a small industry of advice-givers and software creators has arisen to help people control the access that their young people have to certain music. Record executives, for their part, have been embroiled in broader struggles with a variety of groups about access to their company's music. The struggles can be broadly described under two terms, *piracy* and *digital rights management*.

Piracy   **Piracy** is the unauthorized duplication of copyrighted music. People concerned about this activity add two special types, counterfeiting and bootlegging. **Counterfeiting** also involves unauthorized duplication, but it is more serious because the copy is packaged to look like an authentic copy so that it can be sold as authentic. **Bootlegging** is the unauthorized recording of a musical performance and the subsequent distribution of that performance. For example, if you go to a concert, secretly record the program, and then sell your recording to your friends, you are bootlegging.

The counterfeiting of CDs and the bootlegging of concerts take place on a huge scale around the world. Most experts consider China the center of counterfeiting, but the sale of illegally created CDs takes place everywhere. In the United States, many people seem to have no problem buying what they know are counterfeited products, including music CDs. A 2007 Gallup poll of Los Angeles residents found that one in four residents bought pirated goods.[10]

While the counterfeiting of physical albums and the creation of bootlegged concert CDs remain a big problem, it is the illegal downloading of music around the world that has record executives particularly challenged. The plain fact is that when a person grabs a song off the Web without permission of the recording firm or copyright holder, it is against the law. It's not hard to do. Individuals continually make songs available online in a compressed file form called MP3. These files can be circulated quickly to anyone who wants them via special **peer-to-peer** (or **P2P**) downloading software. This type of software relies on the cooperation of many computers to exchange files over the Internet. Aside from being fast, P2P software such as BitTorrent makes it difficult for copyright owners to blame a website or company for the downloading. The MP3 recordings can be played on computers or on players, including iPods, that can be taken anywhere.

Paying for online music is rare in some countries. In 2007, almost 100 percent of music downloaded from the Net was illegal, according to Leong May See, Asia director for the International Federation of the Phonographic Industry, an umbrella group that includes Sony BMG Music, Universal Music, and Warner Music.[11] Most experts agree that in the United States illegal downloading is also rampant. While the amount of legal downloading via iTunes, Yahoo Music and other such services is growing substantially in the United States, it doesn't come close to the

piracy   the unauthorized duplication of copyrighted material for profit

counterfeiting   the unauthorized duplication of copyrighted music and packaging, with the goal of making the copy appear authentic for sale

bootlegging   the unauthorized recording of a music performance, and the subsequent distribution of that recording

peer-to-peer computing (P2P)   a process in which people share the resources of their computers with computers owned by other people

411

amount of illegal downloading that is taking place. Executives and government officials who worry about this situation point out that much of the U.S. economy is based on intellectual property. When people in the United States and the rest of the world take songs without paying for them, that takes billions of dollars away from the economy and subtracts jobs that would otherwise exist. Exactly how much money and how many jobs this costs the U.S. economy is a matter of argument. Some people who argue that numbers relating to piracy may be inflated point out that a lot of songs may be downloaded without fee by people who would not otherwise have bought that music.

Still, most people agree that the record industry is losing lots of money on all sorts of piracy. The industry is moving against this problem on a number of fronts, including raids and legal actions against people suspected of pirating CDs. The industry has also enlisted the help of the U.S. government to influence governments around the world to clamp down on the pirating of American albums offline and online. Inside the United States, the RIAA has embarked on a highly controversial activity. It has initiated lawsuits against people that it determines through analysis of web files have uploaded lots of music for others to share. In fact, from September 2003 through September 2007 it initiated more than 21,000 lawsuits. Many of these have been against college students, who have been involved in P2P activities using their schools' high-speed networks. Users who download music illegally face fines for each song, which can quickly add up to thousands of dollars.

The Electronic Freedom Foundation, which has railed against this approach, notes that overwhelmingly the people targeted are "children, grandparents, single mothers," rather than commercial copyright pirates. "The industry shows no signs of slowing its lawsuit campaign … filing hundreds of new lawsuits each month including, most recently, 400 per month targeted against college students," the report said. "Today downloading from P2P networks is more popular than ever… The lawsuit campaign has enriched only lawyers, rather than compensating artists for file sharing."[12]

The RIAA obviously has another view. Its website justifies its lawsuits against individuals this way:

> Just as we must hold accountable the businesses that encourage theft online, individuals who engage in illegal downloading must also know there are consequences to their actions. If you violate the law and steal from record companies, musicians, songwriters and everyone else involved in making music, you can be held accountable. With so many great legal music options available, there is really no excuse for music theft. Fans have a choice: pay a little now or a lot more later.[13]

digital rights management (DRM) technologies that try to prevent consumers from copying digital material (including music) or from converting it to other formats. In the recording industry, DRM takes the form of codes included on digital music files that set certain limits on how many times or on what specific device a person can play the music

Digital Rights Management   Some people complain that a major factor that stops people from paying for downloading music is not the price but all the restrictions that go along with it. They argue that in its desire to protect copyright, the industry has been too stingy about giving the people who purchase the music the right to use it as they please. At the center of this argument is **digital rights management (DRM)**—technologies that try to prevent consumers from copying digital material (including music) or from converting it to other formats. Recall from earlier in this chapter that in order to stop sharing of the songs, the file the person buys will sometimes come with a digital rights management code for the device that plays it. That code sets certain limits on what specific device a person can use to play the music. Moreover, subscription services will sometimes allow a person to keep songs on his or her computer on the condition that the person keeps paying the subscriptions. If the person cancels the subscription, the service will disable the songs.

For people not trained in the complexities of copyright law, this doesn't seem fair. The rules may be particularly confusing because there are many places online where music publishers encourage people to download songs free and without these restrictions for publicity reasons. By 2007, Amazon and Wal-Mart had come to believe that they could sell loads of songs off the Web if the music did not come with the onerous DRM restrictions. Their goal was to sell the DRM-free songs in the MP3 format that is open to all manufacturers of music players rather than in proprietary formats, like Apple's. By early 2008, Universal, EMI, and Warner had agreed to go along. Sony had announced it would sell tracks and albums in MP3 format on a new music site it was setting up. And while Apple's iTunes was still selling most major label tracks with DRM protections, it had also begun selling EMI and independent labels in MP3 format. Moreover, Apple chief Steve Jobs had written an open letter calling for the music industry to let iTunes sell songs without DRM. Although many called the letter self-serving—Apple was then under pressure from many European governments to alter or drop its proprietary DRM system—it pushed forward the debate in the music business about whether DRM was helping or hurting music distributors. The anti-DRM forces were gaining strength. By the time you read this, use of DRM in the sale of popular music may be more of an exception than a rule. It will likely not eliminate piracy, though it may encourage more people to go legal. And it certainly will have gone a long way to defining the new form of music distribution and exhibition in the United States and the world.

Media Literacy and the Recording Industry

For those executives who worry that getting rid of DRM in music sold online will encourage piracy, David Card, a New York-based senior analyst with Jupiter Research, said bluntly, "The thing is, nothing can stop piracy." His larger point was that while the record industry must be cautious about how it circulates its music, the best approach may be to give people what they consider the best music with the best price in the easiest way possible. Some people in the industry worry that it may not be enough. It's hard to compete with "free," they say, and too many people will download songs and other materials for free if they have the chance and know they won't get caught. The industry cannot afford to give away music, they say.

Putting aside for a moment the illegality of downloading music without permission, it is useful to think about many of this chapter's points about the recording industry from the standpoint of several parties involved. We already know the position of the RIAA and the established record companies about giving away music. They want to control when it happens totally, and they want to stop most of it. They say that their businesses are at stake. Let's look at other constituencies, struggling artists, artists with label contracts, and consumers.

Struggling recording artists and those who are still trying to find a label and make a name for themselves might well have a different viewpoint from established ones about some of these issues. For one thing, these players and singers are likely to resent the power that just a few large firms have over the music, and the musicians, that are heard in the United States and much of the rest of the world.

They realize that while music may be fragmented at the production end, it is highly concentrated at the distribution end, and it is likely to remain that way. Unlike the established artists, they may see the big recording companies not as allies but as enemies who are keeping them out of the distribution pipeline. To many aspiring artists, control of the music industry by Warner, Sony BMG, Universal, and EMI is preventing them from achieving the success they deserve. And they may be gleeful at the prospect of the Web weakening these companies' power.

Moreover, artists who are just starting out may not be upset by the trading of their music on the Web. In fact, they may welcome it. Aspiring musicians can place their material on websites much more easily than they could place it on radio. For basement bands and garage bands, the Web has become a great vehicle for getting their sound out and hoping that people will hear it.

Some artists on their way up—even those with label contracts—see the Web in the same way. They realize that the structure of their contracts with the recording companies mean that making lots of money through their albums is a long shot. They make most of their living through the concerts they give, and they may see the pirating of their albums as great publicity that will translate into the kind of popularity that will lead people to pay to hear them at concerts. So, in effect, they may be grateful that fans care enough about their music to steal it.

Many consumers care little about the problems that the recording companies and their stars have with piracy. In fact, millions of people act as if sharing copyrighted music with millions of other people on the Web is not a legal or ethical issue. The fact that a federal court has ruled that sharing music in this way is legally wrong hasn't stopped music lovers—especially teens and young adults—from scouring the Web for MP3 cuts of their favorite new and old works.

Is it just selfishness that leads to these wholesale copyright violations? Some commentators argue that consumers are ignoring the interests of the recording industry because for a long time the industry—and especially a handful of firms that are intent on controlling music across as many media as possible—has ignored their interests. The top record companies, they say, have continually taken advantage of the switch to new recording forms (such as tapes, minidisks, and CDs) to charge consumers far more than necessary for singles and albums. Moreover, they say, many consumers feel that albums are often rip-offs, that to buy two or three of a group's songs, they must purchase an album that also includes eight or nine other songs that are not terribly good. Consumers therefore have developed no loyalty to or concern for the firms and have no qualms about picking the songs that they really want off the Web without paying for them. Industry critics argue that rather than suing individual consumers for illegal downloading, the industry ought to try to understand what consumers want and respond to their interests. Industry officials reply that this has begun to happen.

In the end, of course, it is up to you to decide where you stand in relation to these issues. Arguments about piracy, and about the morality of certain songs, underscore the fact that recordings play a huge role in people's lives. Our trip through the recording industry in this chapter sketched the ways in which this industry produces, distributes, and exhibits products in the United States. That is changing in momentous ways. New technologies promise new opportunities, as well as challenges to traditional distribution, exhibition, and promotion routes. It will be interesting to see how the recording industry responds, and how that response affects not only the recordings we can buy but also how we can buy them in years to come.

CHAPTER REVIEW

For an interactive chapter recap and study guide, visit the companion website for *Media Today* at www.routledge.com/textbooks/mediatoday

QUESTIONS FOR DISCUSSION AND CRITICAL THINKING

1   How does the phrase "think globally; act locally" apply to the recording industry? To what extent does it apply to other media industries you have studied so far?

2   Who in the recording industry needs to know the personalities of particular labels? As a consumer, do you feel that it is important to look at the labels of recordings you buy? Why or why not?

3   Consider the following statement: "For a singer trying to establish herself, being signed by a major label is both a blessing and a curse." Explain why someone might make this claim.

4   Why is the U.S. government interested in helping the recording industry fight piracy outside the United States?

INTERNET RESOURCES

Recording Industry Association of America (http://www.riaa.org/)
> As its website says, "the RIAA works to protect intellectual property rights worldwide and the First Amendment rights of artists; conducts consumer, industry and technical research; and monitors and reviews state and federal laws, regulations and policies. The RIAA also certifies Gold, Platinum, Multi-Platinum, and Diamond sales awards, as well as Los Premios De Oro y Platino, an award celebrating Latin music sales." The website reflects these activities as well as presenting statistics about record industry revenues.

SonyBMG Music (http://www.sonybmg.com)
> An interesting site of one of the big four recording firms. It has information about its labels, artists, executives, its approach to copy protection and royalties, as well as a "parental guide."

Rounder Records (http://www.rounder.com/)
> Rounder is now one of the biggest independent record labels in the United States, with several specialized subsidiary labels. It was founded in 1970 by three university students. The website is a showcase for its activities, which center on American roots music, such as bluegrass.

Bemuso (http://www.bemuso.com)
> This site is aimed at DIY (do it yourself) music artists and independent labels. It is a primer about the recording business, with acerbic comments about the big record companies.

KEY TERMS

You can find the definitions to these key terms in the marginal glossary through-out this chapter. Test your knowledge of these terms with interactive flash cards on the *Media Today* companion website.

A&R (artist and repertoire)	payola
album	peer to peer
bootlegging	phonograph
counterfeiting	piracy
digital rights management (DRM)	rack jobber
downloading	ringtones
format	royalty
gramophone	single
graphophone	streaming
Internet radio	Tin Pan Alley
label	vaudeville shows

CONSTRUCTING MEDIA LITERACY

1 Where do you stand about the ethics of downloading copyrighted music off the Web without getting permission from the copyright holders? Explain your viewpoint.

2 Based on your experience and the experience of your friends, do you think that music CDs have a future? Why or why not?

3 If you were a member of an aspiring rock band, what vehicles might you use to get your band known? Would you want to work with a label? Why or why not?

4 Do you think the RIAA is ethically correct in suing individuals—not compa-nies—who share lots of music illegally online? Explain your viewpoint.

CASE STUDY   MySpace versus Amazon as Exhibitors

The idea   Owned by conglomerate News Corporation, the social website MySpace has worked hard to become an important platform for aspiring and established artists. In return, the recording industry has been using MySpace (along with other sites) as a platform for promoting its products. Amazon.com has also become an important place for noting and listening to music. There are many differences between the two sites, not least of which is that you cannot buy music directly from MySpace while you can from Amazon. But it is not hard to imagine that MySpace will sell music, too. From that standpoint, it is interesting to consider which makes the best exhibitor of music.

The method   Spend time exploring the MySpace Music site over a week. Study the main page and its links. Then focus on a music genre and the way its artists and their sites are laid out. Do the same regarding Amazon.com. Imagine that MySpace sells music on its site just as Amazon does. Write a report laying out your view on how the sites compare from the standpoint of (1) promoting aspiring and established artists; and (2) displaying songs and albums. Try to find out why MySpace does not sell music as yet, and about possible plans for doing so.

11 THE RADIO INDUSTRY

After studying this chapter, you will be able to:

1 Analyze through history why the radio industry is arranged the way it is

2 Explain the relationship between advertising and programming

3 Detail the role of market research in the radio industry

4 Critically examine the issues surrounding the consolidation of radio station ownership

5 Discuss ways in which new digital technologies are challenging traditional radio

Media Today

Consider the enormous challenges that face the radio industry. The home—the place where radio was once the dominant medium—has now been invaded by many channels that bring both sight and sound. Broadcast television, cable and satellite TV, CDs and computer-based jukebox programs, VCRs and DVD players, computer game systems, digital music players, and Internet music sites all compete with radio for people's attention. In the face of this invasion, one might expect traditional radio audiences to plummet. How well can the radio industry possibly compete for audiences and advertisers?

The answer is unclear. The radio business started the twenty-first century generally quite healthy, but its growth in audience and in advertising (its main method of support) has stagnated recently in the face of its competition. At the same time, optimists in the industry would tell you that the radio industry is changing—that radio stations are working to become important parts of the digital media revolution. This transformation will be substantial, because media powers have built the U.S. radio system to be powerful and to last. In fact, exploring radio today, you'd be hard-pressed to realize that it was once the central, most important medium in Americans' lives. Let's take a look.

The Rise of Radio

Our discussion of the record industry's rise in Chapter 10 shows how a new medium (in this case records) can have enormous consequences for a media industry that already exists (in this case sheet music and Tin Pan Alley songwriting). But things don't stand still in the world of mass media. Just as records were developing, a potential competitor was emerging. Its inventors called it *radio broadcasting*.

The Early Days of Radio

The origins of radio go back to the nineteenth century, and its initial purpose was not for entertainment. After Samuel Morse developed the telegraph in 1842, scientists began to look for ways to free messages from the telegraph wire and send them over the air using electric waves or frequencies. Guglielmo Marconi of Italy brought these ideas together and in 1895 succeeded in sending messages over long distances using the code of dots and dashes that Morse had developed.

Because the Italian government showed no interest in Marconi's find, he took it to England, where people quickly saw its value to the far-flung British Empire. The Marconi Company was formed, and during the next several years, it made money by equipping the commercial and military ships of England, the United States, and other countries with wireless telegraphy for communicating with one

The first radio transmitter was invented by Guglielmo Marconi in 1894, at the age of 20. Initially, he could only transmit signals over short distances, but a year later he finally succeeded in sending signals over longer distances.

radiotelephony or radio
the broadcast of speech and music through wireless transmission

broadcasting term referring to radio transmissions that can be widely received; originally an agricultural term meaning to scatter seed over a broad area rather than in particular places

another and with shore points around the world.

Other inventors added to the value of the wireless radio. On Christmas Eve 1906, Reginald Fessenden gave wireless operators on ships in various parts of the Atlantic Ocean a scare by broadcasting from Massachusetts not just dots and dashes, but a speech and music, played on a phonograph. This new twist on Marconi's device, suggesting as it did both radiation (dissemination) through the air and the telephone, got the name **radiotelephony—radio**, for short (see Figure 11.1).

U.S. inventor Lee De Forest took the invention even further. At first, radio transmissions could be heard only through earphones. DeForest's Audion vacuum tube, patented in 1907, made radio transmissions much clearer and made it possible for people to listen to the communication in groups through speakers. He envisioned stations sending out continuous music, news, and other material to anyone who was interested. The idea came to be known as **broadcasting**, from an agricultural term meaning to scatter seed over a broad area rather than in particular places.

Figure 11.1

Radio Waves

Radio waves are broadcast in several wave bands, often called long wave, medium wave, VHF (very high frequency) and short wave bands. Each band contains a range of radio wavelengths, and each station has its own particular wavelength within a band.

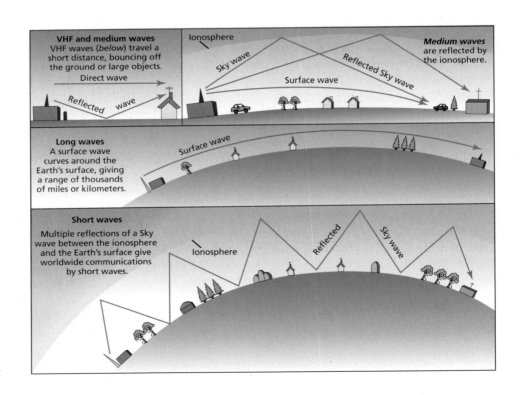

How the Radio Spectrum Works

All your life you have heard about "AM radio" and "FM radio," "VHF" and "UHF" television, "citizens band radio," "short-wave radio," and so on. Have you ever wondered what all of those different names really mean?

A *radio wave* is an electromagnetic wave that is propagated by an antenna. Radio waves have different frequencies, and by tuning a radio receiver to a specific frequency you can pick up a specific signal. In the United States, the FCC (Federal Communications Commission) decides who is allowed to use what frequencies for what purposes, and it issues licenses to stations for specific frequencies.

When you listen to a radio station and the announcer says, "You are listening to 91.5 FM WRKX The Rock!" what the announcer means is that you are listening to a radio station with the FCC-assigned call letters WRKX that is broadcasting an FM (frequency-modulated) radio signal at a frequency of 91.5 megahertz (MHz). *Megahertz* means "millions of cycles per second," so saying that the frequency is 91.5 MHz means that the transmitter at the radio station is oscillating at a frequency of 91,500,000 cycles per second. Your FM radio can tune in to that specific frequency and give you clear reception of that station. All FM radio stations transmit in a band of frequencies between 88 and 108 MHz. This band of the radio spectrum is used for no other purpose but FM radio broadcasts.

In the same way, AM radio is confined to a band from 535 to 1,700 kilohertz (kHz) (kilo means "thousands," so this means 535,000 to 1,700,000 cycles per second). So an AM radio station that says, "This is AM 680 WPTF!" means that the radio station has the FCC-assigned call letters WPTF and is broadcasting an AM (amplitude-modulated) radio signal at 680 kHz.

Common frequency bands include the following:

- AM radio: 535 kHz to 1.7 MHz
- Short-wave radio: bands from 5.9 to 26.1 MHz
- Citizens band (CB) radio: 26.96 to 27.41 MHz
- Television stations: 54 to 88 MHz for channels 2 to 6
- FM radio: 88 to 108 MHz
- Television stations: 174 to 220 MHz for channels 7 to 13

Why is AM radio in a band from 550 to 1,700 kilohertz while FM radio is in a band from 88 to 108 megahertz? It is all completely arbitrary, and a lot of it has to do with history. For example, AM radio has been around a lot longer than FM radio. The first radio broadcasts occurred in 1906 or so, and frequency allocation for AM radio took place during the 1920s. (The predecessor to the FCC was established by Congress in 1927.)

In the 1920s, radio and electronic capabilities were fairly limited; hence the relatively low frequencies for AM radio. Television stations were pretty much nonexistent until 1946 or so, when the FCC allocated commercial broadcast bands for TV. By 1949, a million people owned TV sets, and by 1951 there were 10 million TVs in America. FM radio was invented by a man named Edwin Armstrong in order to make high-fidelity (and static-free) broadcast of music possible. He built the first station in 1939, but FM did not become really popular until the 1960s.

Source: Adapted with permission from http://www.howstuffworks.com/radio-spectrum.htm, accessed, 2/20/07.

Determining the Use of Radio

De Forest's vision of how radio should be used is the one that eventually came to pass in the United States. However, the development of a radio system that centered on the broadcasting of music, news, and other types of programming took more than two decades. One reason had to do with fights between various inventors over the rights to various patents. Drawn out and expensive, the patent battles derailed the business plans of Fessenden and others.

Another reason centered around World War I. When the United States entered the war in 1917, the U.S. Navy took control of radio in the United States, got the government to declare a moratorium on patent suits, and developed radio in ways that would most benefit the military. After the war, the navy sought congressional permission to retain control over radio for reasons of national security. Its argument was that if enemies of the United States somehow got control of radio stations, they could disseminate propaganda and secret messages that could be damaging to the interests of the country.

However, business and government leaders believed that the best way to develop radio's great potential was to move it from the public to the private sector. In addition, members of Congress were aware of the American tradition that mass media were not under direct government control. A broadcast station could spread words further than an individual newspaper or magazine. Allowing the U.S. Navy to dictate its use would mean that a government agency would potentially be controlling the ideas presented to large segments of the population—a controversial proposition.

The Creation of the RCA

As a result of this debate, in 1919 Congress decreed that broadcasting was to be a privately sponsored enterprise, available to any citizen who paid for a license. But radio's split from government had a catch: to ensure that dominant control of radio would remain in friendly hands, the government forced the British-Italian Marconi Company to sell its interests to General Electric. The U.S. Navy then encouraged a number of American firms that owned major broadcast patents (notably, American Telephone and Telegraph (AT&T), General Electric (GE) and Westinghouse) to form a patent trust—that is, a company that would rule U.S. radio through patents.

RCA Radio Corporation of America

They called this trust the **Radio Corporation of America (RCA)**. Its purpose was to force anyone who was interested in setting up a broadcasting operation to pay RCA for the use of RCA's radio patents. RCA, in turn, would impose certain agreed-upon conditions for the use of the airwaves. RCA would thus be the most powerful force in developing the airwaves, ensuring that an organization close to the navy would remain in the driver's seat.

U.S. courts broke up this radio monopoly within a decade, separating RCA from GE, AT&T, and Westinghouse, but not before it had shaped the new medium in ways that are still with us. The two most important consequences of this decision were:

- The development of advertising to support radio
- The creation of networks to spread advertiser-sponsored programming around the country

These activities, in turn, led RCA and other firms that were involved in radio actually to beg the government to exert more control over broadcasting! Why? Read on.

Radio and Advertising   Today we're used to the idea of advertisements on radio; it seems natural. In 1919, though, this idea was not at all taken for granted. U.S. Secretary of Commerce Herbert Hoover even voiced the hope that the babble of advertising would never pollute the airwaves. How, then, could privately owned radio stations cover their costs?

In the 1920s, the answer came from the suppliers, manufacturers, and sellers of radio equipment. Equipment suppliers wanted to encourage the growth of radio in general. Manufacturers of radio equipment set up stations with regularly scheduled programs in the more specific hope that people would want to tune in and, thinking well of the manufacturers' activities, buy their sets.

Westinghouse was first; in 1920 it founded KDKA in Pittsburgh with the purpose of selling sets. RCA, General Electric, and AT&T also started stations during the next few years. Stores also got in on the action, using in-store stations as publicity for the radios they sold; other organizations also began radio stations as signs of goodwill. Some of the stations' call letters were self-congratulatory. Sears, Roebuck in Chicago started WLS (it stands for "world's largest store"), the Chicago Tribune Company started WGN (for "world's greatest newspaper"), and WSM in Nashville was begun by the National Life Insurance Company ("we shelter millions").

Even while these promotional stations were developing, some business people feared that they didn't make sense in the long run. The cost of running a serious station with popular programming was climbing into the tens, or even hundreds, of thousands of dollars. It seemed improbable that listeners would send stations money (although at least one station did ask for it).

This dilemma led to the sale of advertising, which started in a strange way. AT&T executives in New York became convinced that the way to make money through radio was to use a telephone model. That is, they reasoned that people would pay to speak over the radio, just as they paid to speak over the phone. When it didn't look as if individuals were really prepared to ante up for a chance at the microphone, the company agreed in 1922 to allow a company—the Queensboro Realty Company—to pay three thousand dollars for five "talks" extolling properties it had for sale. The rest, as they say, is history. Other stations picked up AT&T's idea and rushed to sell time on their airwaves. To draw listeners, the advertisers often mixed entertainment with their commercial pitches.

The Creation of Radio Networks The creation of radio networks was a logical extension of stations' desire to attract advertisers. A **radio network** is a group of interconnected stations. In the mid-1920s, as radio advertising took off, executives at RCA realized that they could encourage large advertisers to buy time on the company's several stations by linking them (**O&O stations,** or those that the network owned and operated) and other stations (**network affiliates,** or stations that transmit network signals but are not owned by the network) around the country through AT&T's telephone lines. The advertisers' programs could therefore be heard by many more people, and the cash received by RCA could be shared by the linked stations.

RCA's idea came together in 1926 in the establishment of the National Broadcasting Company (NBC). By that time, AT&T had sold its broadcast stations to RCA, so the company owned two stations in New York. It therefore started two NBC networks, the Red and the Blue, which carried different programs. That same year, another network, United Independent Broadcasters, was also formed. After stumbling badly, it was reorganized under new ownership in 1927 as the Columbia Broadcasting System (CBS). Though it struggled during its early months, CBS eventually stabilized and became a formidable competitor to NBC.

Government Regulation of Radio

The growth of advertising and the birth of NBC made it clear that radio was becoming a big business. For business-minded radio executives in the mid-1920s,

radio network a group of interconnected radio stations

O&O stations local radio stations which are commonly owned and operated by a network that often provides a regular schedule of programming materials for broadcast

network affiliates local radio stations that transmit network signals, but that are not owned by the network; in exchange for the transmission of their signals, the network agrees to compensate the affiliate with a portion of the revenues received from network advisers

though, radio's popularity had a major downside. A large number of small broadcasters, many of them amateurs, were creating havoc on the airwaves, interfering with commercial stations' ability to get their signals into homes reliably.

The Radio Act of 1912   In response to this problem, Congress passed the **Radio Act of 1912.** It gave the secretary of commerce the right to issue licenses to people who wanted to broadcast, and to decide what frequencies should be used for what kinds of services (for example, maritime use, military use, police use, and public broadcast). Once the available public frequencies had been established, the Commerce Department allowed individuals and companies to pay a small fee for a license to start up their broadcast operations. The broadcasters could use any frequency they wanted, as long as the frequency they used was within the designated range of public frequencies,

From the standpoint of broadcasters wanting to turn radio into a big business, the result was chaos. In the 1920s, a large number of stations came on the air across the United States, many on the same frequencies. Because they interfered with one another, it was difficult for audiences to hear any of them consistently. Some stations made informal agreements not to interfere with one another, and in some communities local stations went off the air so that residents could receive stations from faraway cities that they wanted to hear. More and more radio executives complained, however, that the airwaves had to be put in order if advertisers were to get their money's worth and radio was to grow as an industry.

They appealed to the federal government to stop giving out licenses. However, in 1926, the U.S. attorney general ruled, and the courts concurred, that the 1912 law did not allow the secretary of commerce to refuse a license, assign broadcast hours, or assign specific frequencies. The radio executives then demanded a rewrite of the Radio Act of 1912 in a way that recognized the right of stations to have exclusive frequencies. They wanted predictable places on the consumer's radio dial.

The Radio Act of 1927 and the Advent of the Federal Radio Commission   They got that rewrite. The Radio Act of 1927 created a **Federal Radio Commission (FRC)** whose mandate was to issue radio licenses and bring order to the airwaves. The FRC kicked some stations off the air and told the remaining ones the maximum power at which they could broadcast. The stations that were already the most powerful and that had the best technology got the best frequencies with the maximum power allowances. These stations were generally commercial broadcasters, and often they were network affiliates. Educational and religious stations were consigned to inferior positions on the dial, if they stayed on the air at all.

Congress did exact a price for creating a stable business environment for commercial broadcasters. The price was that a station that received a dial position would not own that position. Rather, the new Radio Act noted quite clearly that the airwaves belonged to the public and that the station was receiving its dial position through a license that would be renewed as long as it acted "in the public interest, convenience and necessity." Just what that phrase meant, no one was exactly sure; even today lawmakers are not quite sure. The 1920s was a time, however, when many people around the nation were nervous about the potential of new, highly visible mass media such as radio and movies to carry sexual or violent content that might harm the morals of youngsters and cheapen the American culture. The phrase was clearly inserted into the law to give the new commission enough power to induce broadcasters to keep their programming in line with general standards of good taste.

Radio Act of 1912   passed by Congress in 1912, this act gave the secretary of commerce the right to issue licenses to parties interested in radio broadcasting, and to decide which radio frequencies should be used for which types of services (i.e., public broadcast, military use, police use, etc.)

Federal Radio Commission (FRC) . created by the Radio Act of 1927, this commission's purpose was to issue radio licenses to those who applied for them, and to bring order to the nation's radio airwaves

The Federal Communications Act of 1934   This twin message was repeated in the **Federal Communications Act of 1934,** which turned the Federal Radio Commission into a larger Federal Communications Commission with responsibilities for regulating the telephone and telegraph industries as well as the radio broadcasting industry. It was a message that would become the pillar of the government's approach to broadcast television and, later, cable TV: the federal government would protect the ability of business interests to develop the public airwaves for commercial purposes, but, the other side of the message went, the government would be less likely to protect them if their programming or other activities created public controversies.

Federal Communications Act of 1934   the Congressional act that turned the Federal Radio Commission into a larger Federal Communications Commission, with responsibilities for regulating the telephone and telegraph industry as well as the radio broadcasting industry

Radio in the 1920s, 1930s, and 1940s

Network radio executives and their sponsors indicated that they had gotten the message. At the beginning of 1927, as the new law was being considered, a number of high-minded series were already in place on NBC's two networks. Network executives noted that the networks distributed many unsponsored hours of farm programs, religious programs, talks, and music-appreciation concerts for schools. The money for these "public service" activities came from sponsored programs

The Shadow was an enormously popular radio mystery program of the 1930s and 1940s. The narrator's introduction remains a familiar part of American popular culture: "Who knows what evil lurks in the hearts of men? The Shadow knows!"

425

Jack Benny began his career as a vaudeville performer, but came to national attention as host of *The Jack Benny Program,* which was one of the most highly rated radio shows from 1932 to 1955.

such as *The Maxwell House Hour, The Palmolive Hour, The General Motors Family Party, The Wrigley Review,* and *The Eveready Hour,* among others.

As their names suggest, each of these programs was entirely supported by an individual advertiser. When they sold time to advertisers, NBC and CBS simply gave a period of airtime to the advertisers and allowed them and their advertising agencies to create material. On radio, the ad agency typically produced the programs as well as the commercials. To find out how well a program was doing, the advertisers paid ratings companies to phone people at different times or to give families diaries to find out what station they were listening to at home. The networks, for their part, collected the advertisers' fees and distributed them to stations across the United States. People listened at home, often on radios powered by car batteries. By the 1930s they also listened in cars, because automobile manufacturers had begun selling radios.

Network Programming

In the 1920s, the programs that listeners could hear on NBC and CBS throughout the United States were mostly musical. Many were classical concerts, although popular dance music was on the rise. The presence of popular music on the airwaves—often "live" rather than recorded—created severe problems for the phonograph industry during the mid-1920s, as people listened to radio instead of buying disks. The Victor Talking Machine Company, worried about the future of its business, merged with RCA. The Columbia Phonograph Company, also fearful that its business was trickling away, tried to profit from broadcasting by financing a radio network to be called the Columbia Broadcasting System. The project lost money, Columbia pulled out, and what became known as CBS proceeded on its own. In 1938, however, CBS purchased Columbia Records.

But radio was much more than music. In the 1930s and 1940s, the medium's content was more like that of television today than like that of radio today. National networks dominated radio—the NBC Red and Blue; CBS; and, beginning in 1934, the Mutual Broadcasting Company. There were also a few smaller networks of stations in some parts of the country, such as the West Coast-based Don Lee Network and the New England-based Colonial Network. The FCC, concerned that NBC's ownership of two networks gave it excessive power over radio, ordered it to sell one of them, and the Supreme Court agreed. In 1943 the network let go of the weaker Blue, which became the American Broadcasting Company (ABC).

Radio listeners heard talk-and-variety programs (*The Breakfast Club, Arthur Godfrey*) in the morning, continuing dramas (*The Romance of Helen Trent, One Man's Family*) in the late morning and early afternoon, children's adventure programs (*The Shadow, Dick Tracy*) after school, and sports broadcasts during weekends. In the evening, in addition to musical-variety programs, listeners could hear the same genres of shows that TV viewers see today: situation comedies (*The Charlie McCarthy Show, Burns and Allen, The Jack Benny Program, Allen's Alley, Blondie*), general drama (*The Lux Radio Theater, The Mercury Theater of the Air*), quiz and game shows (*Take It or Leave It, The $64,000 Question, Truth or Consequences*), police shows (*The FBI in Peace and War*), detective programs (*Philo Vance*), doctor shows (*Doctor Christian*), mysteries (*The Black Castle, The Shadow*), and more.

News also developed into an important part of radio, but slowly in the beginning. In the 1920s, newspaper executives saw radio as a major competitor for advertising dollars. They consequently pressed the wire services (AP and UPI) to severely restrict their services to broadcasters. This press–radio war lasted for only a short while, though, as the wire services saw that there was money to be made from radio, and the newspapers realized that they could actually increase their sales by printing what was on the air. The major networks created their own news divisions and beefed them up during the Spanish Civil War and the outbreak of World War II in Europe. President Franklin Roosevelt recognized the importance of radio for informing the nation and embarked on a series of radio talks to promote his administration's policies. These popular broadcasts became known as fireside chats.

Rethinking Radio, 1950 to 1970

Major changes that occurred in American society after World War II ended in 1945 deeply affected the radio and recording industries. Two of the most important developments were:

- The rise of television
- The baby boom

President Franklin Delano Roosevelt used the radio to speak directly to the nation about his administration's policies through a series of broadcasts that came to be known as "fireside chats."

Radio and the Rise of Television

Television entered the picture near the start of the baby boom—around 1948. In that year, executives from NBC, CBS, and ABC began to shift much of the profits of their radio networks into building television networks. They saw TV as the wave of the future because it combined the sound of radio with the pictures of movies. In fact, some of radio's biggest stars—Jack Benny, George Burns, Ed Wynne—moved their programs to TV, and a number of other entertainers—Milton Berle, Sid Caesar—became major celebrities as a result of the home tube. Advertisers followed them.

By 1960, more than 90 percent of homes had one. Instead of listening to network radio, people tended to watch network television. With network audiences declining, nervous radio station owners began to drop their affiliations and look for other, non-network ways to make money. Whereas 97 percent of all radio stations were affiliated with a network in 1947, only 50 percent were network affiliates in 1955. Looking back, it seems clear that radio was undergoing a revolution.

The direction of that revolution was toward stations that played particular types of music. Radio executives decided that, in order to draw advertisers, they would do what TV wasn't doing: go after specific local audience segments by devoting most of their stations' time to broadcasting music that those segments would tune in to hear. Playing records was inexpensive compared to creating drama or comedy or adventure series; often record companies would send records to the radio stations for free, in the hope that the stations would play them and their listeners would buy them. As a result, stations around the country developed different music formats based on the kind of music they played (country, rhythm and blues, big band) and the radio personalities (called disc jockeys or DJs) who were hired to introduce the recordings.

The Baby Boom, Radio, and Recordings

You might remember from Chapter 10 that these new developments coincided with the **baby boom**. Because advertisers in the 1950s were interested in reaching them, many radio stations played music called rock 'n' roll with disc jockeys that specifically called out to them. Other stations targeted different age groups with different styles of music and DJs. This new sort of station that focused on particular music preferences caught on because radio was now more portable than ever. The development in 1948 of the **transistor,** a much smaller replacement for the Audion vacuum tube, led to the miniaturization of radio receivers. Now radio became something that people could literally take with them throughout the day—to the park, to the beach, or wherever. All of a sudden, the medium had a new life, and companies rushed to get new licenses. The number of stations jumped dramatically, from about one thousand in 1946 to nearly 3,500 in the mid-1950s. The largest proportion of these played specific types of music.

Ethics and Payola

The new station formats made local radio more important to music marketers than ever before. The things that DJs around the country decided to play grabbed listeners' attention, and that translated into record sales. Recording firms pressured their promotion personnel to persuade DJs to give "airplay" to the singers their

the baby boom the huge spike in the population that was created during the late 1940s through the 1950s as soldiers who returned from World War II married and started families

transistor device for amplifying, controlling, and generating radio signals; a smaller replacement for the Audion vacuum tube, leading to the miniaturization of radio receivers

Early rock and roll artists like Elvis Presley fueled an explosion of teen-oriented rock 'n' roll radio programming in the 1950s.

company was pushing. The pressure was so great, and the influence of certain DJs on audiences was apparently so strong, that many promotion people started paying DJs to highlight their firm's output. As we saw in Chapter 10, this process was known as **payola.** The amounts of money delivered to one DJ could run into the tens of thousands of dollars.

Were these transactions ethical? When newspapers disclosed the activities, many people thought not, since the disc jockeys were being paid by their stations to choose songs that they genuinely thought their audience would like, not songs that companies bribed them to play. The DJs who were caught accepting bribes could argue that they took money only for songs that they would have played anyway; the cash was just a perk of their job. Song salespeople, in turn, noted that paying to publicize songs was nothing new. Recall that back in the days of vaudeville, song pluggers greased the palms of performers to sing their publishing firm's songs.

When the radio version of this activity became public, political leaders, some genuinely indignant and some grandstanding for their own ends, argued angrily that this payola should not be allowed. DJs were fired, Congress held hearings on the subject, and the lawmakers amended the Federal Communications Act to make the practice illegal. Many radio stations took song selection away from individual disc jockeys and centralized the activity in the hands of the program director. Radio was so important to the promotion of records, however, that the practice continued in one way or another—often with the program director as the focus of the

payola an activity in which promotion personnel pay money to radio personnel in order to ensure that they will devote airtime to artists that their recording companies represent

activity. Expensive gifts, including sex and drugs, often took the place of money. Payola remains an ethical issue even today.

FM Radio and the Fragmentation of Rock Music

Despite public controversies over payola and over the airing of rock 'n' roll music, the growth of radio formats continued, based on the targeting of certain age groups and musical tastes. One factor that encouraged the changing of radio to include longer songs and the expansion of the number of station choices was the development of **FM**— which stands for **frequency modulation**— an invention of Columbia University engineer Edwin Armstrong during the 1930s. From the start, leading radio executives realized that the static-free sound of FM was far superior to the sound produced by the **AM** (**amplitude modulation**) technology upon which existing radio transmitters and sets were based. The problem, for the executives, was that for technical reasons the FM technology could not simply be used to improve AM radio. FM would have to either replace AM or coexist with it. Broadcasters worried that their huge investment in AM would be threatened if they undertook to develop FM as a substitute. They also worried that the development of a whole new set of FM stations would divide audiences, and therefore advertising monies, in ways that would substantially reduce their profits. These executives therefore used as much influence as they could with the FCC to derail attempts to develop FM radio. However, they also tried to protect themselves in case FM did catch on by getting FM licenses and simply duplicating on FM stations what they were airing on AM.

Edwin Armstrong, depressed over what he saw as the radio industry's attempts to derail his invention, committed suicide. Eventually, FM radio did emerge, though years later than its supporters wanted. By the 1960s, the FCC was not handing out new AM licenses, and the amount of money needed to buy an existing AM station was soaring. New business interests, seeing FM as an opportunity, pressured the FCC to encourage the growth of FM by passing a nonduplication rule, which the FCC did in 1965. This rule stated that an owner of both an AM and an FM station could not play the same material on both stations more than 50 percent of the time. The rule had the effect the supporters of FM wanted. FM stations, looking for things to play and not having many commercials, developed formats that played long cuts or even entire albums, an approach that AM stations resisted. Many listeners migrated to FM, liking the music and the static-free sound. FM radio began an astounding rise in popularity. In 1972, FM had 28 percent of the radio audience in the top 40 radio markets, with AM taking 72 percent. By 1990, these figures were reversed.

Challenges of Fragmentation and Digitalization, 1970 to the Present

Just as radio executives in the 1940s had feared, the popularity of the many new FM stations scattered audiences across more channels and made it harder for individual stations to draw advertisers. From the 1970s onward, and especially during the 1980s and 1990s, radio station executives found that they had to position their stations toward very particular types of people with very particular lifestyles and listening tastes if they were to attract sponsors. Industry consultants helped station executives relate particular social categories (age, race, gender, ethnicity)

frequency modulation (FM) a means of radio broadcasting, utilizing the band between 88 and 108 megahertz; FM signals are marked by high levels of clarity, but rarely travel more than eighty miles from the site of their transmission

amplitude modulation (AM) a means of radio broadcasting, utilizing the band between 540 and 1,700 megahertz; AM signals are prone to frequent static interference, but their high powered signals allow them to travel great distances, especially at night

to particular formats (album-oriented rock, Top 40, middle of the road, country, and multiple variations of these) to signal to people scanning the airwaves whether or not a station was for them.

AM stations struggled to find niches for themselves in the new radio world. Many had a hard time staying afloat, and some even went out of business. The ones that remained tended to focus on nonmusic (all talk, all news, all business/financial, all sports), religious, and ethnic (often Spanish-language) formats. In the 1990s, talk stations hit a sort of a jackpot. The popularity of such on-air characters as Rush Limbaugh, G. Gordon Liddy, Laura Schlessinger, and Oliver North drew millions to those stations and boosted their advertising.

Radio executives also redefined the idea of a network. The traditional notion of a network as a distributor of all sorts of programming to affiliates had faded with the rise of television. In its place emerged organizations that delivered material that was tailored to the new demands of segmented, targeted radio. The ABC radio network set the pattern for this approach in 1968, when it reorganized into four services—contemporary, informational, entertainment, and FM. Principally, it offered hourly news reports styled to mirror different formats. As the delivery of programming by satellite became possible in the 1970s, more and more networklike services arose to provide stations with everything from around-the-clock music formats to special music concerts that matched their formats. Cable television firms even began to offer their customers audio music services that could not be received over the air. More than twenty radio networks plied their trade in the late 1990s.

Executives in the traditional radio industry began to refer to their business as **terrestrial radio**. Terrestrial radio involves signals that are broadcast from transmission towers on the ground and picked up by radio sets. That is different from cable radio, where cable firms send music to customers through their wires, from satellite radio, which involves transmitting signals to satellites that retransmit them to radio sets, and from Internet radio, where audio is distributed to digital devices that access the Web location. Apart from encouraging new networks, the fragmentation of terrestrial radio encouraged consolidation—the purchase of several radio stations in an area by one company. Before the late 1990s, the FCC did not allow broadcasters to own more than one FM and one AM station in a given area. However, the Telecommunications Act of 1996 did away with such restrictions. The huge number of stations in certain areas, some of them in financial trouble, encouraged the commission to allow broadcast companies to snatch up several AM and FM properties in the same market. That sparked the creation of large radio conglomerates, most notably Clear Channel Communications, which controlled large proportions of radio advertising in markets across the country.

The rise of the radio conglomerates has sparked much criticism that in its current state much of terrestrial radio is repetitive, not innovative, and clogged with commercials. This criticism is happening at a time when digital media such as satellite radio, Internet-linked computers, iPods, MP3 players, mobile phones and related technologies are opening up new ways for people to get audio materials that radio has long provided to them. As we have seen, this is not the first time that radio executives stand between an old and new world. They have a lot invested in—and still make a lot of money from—traditional broadcast radio. So they are trying to understand how to adapt to, and compete with, the new technologies. Let's take a look at the established and emerging worlds of radio. We start with today's terrestrial radio world, then examine digital competition to the radio industry and the industry's response to it. As we will see, there certainly is a lot of music streaming out there.

terrestrial radio
traditional broadcast radio, which involves signals that are broadcast from transmission towers on the ground and picked up by radio sets

431

An Overview of the Terrestrial Radio Industry

It's certainly a world with a lot of stations. In 2007, there were more than twelve thousand radio stations in the country. At the same time, the ownership of the stations has become quite concentrated. As noted earlier, in recent years the federal government greatly relaxed its limitations on the number of stations one party can own. The Telecommunications Act of 1996 allows the owners of station groups to hold up to eight stations in large markets and up to five in smaller markets, with no limit on the total number they can have. Big firms bought up many stations, and the ownership of radio stations became more concentrated than ever. As a result, most large market stations are now part of station groups that are owned by major corporations such as Clear Channel, Cumulus, Citadel and Viacom.

When and Where People Listen to the Radio

Arbitron, the company that makes money supplying radio ratings to the industry and its advertisers, says in one of its brochures that radio has a "remarkable ability to attract listeners in every demographic group." It adds that "an overwhelming percentage (93 percent) of all people 12 or older listen to the radio each week." But what Arbitron means by "listen" is tuning in at least once for a short period during a week. A tougher gauge of attention to radio is time spent with it. The company acknowledges that between 1997 and 2006 the amount of time spent listening during the week has gone down. Men 18–24 have seen a decline of 17 percent, and teenage women have reduced their listening by 23 percent. The listening time for older men and women has gone down, too, but less. Arbitron points to the "numerous media alternatives available" as being the cause of the decline.[1]

We noted earlier that since the 1950s a large part of the explanation for radio's strength in the face of competition from other media has to do with its *portability*. Lightweight receivers have allowed people to use radio outside the home, where they have had less access to the medium's audiovisual competition. According to Arbitron, listening at home has been on a long-term decline. Whereas in 1986 53 percent of all radio listening (as measured in quarter hours) took place at home, by 2006 that percentage had dropped to 40 percent. In contrast, listening in cars increased during the same period, from 22 percent of all quarter-hour listening in 1986 to 34 percent in 2006. Listening elsewhere—at work, on the beach, in the park—remained pretty steady between those years, at 26 percent. Overall, fully 60 percent of all radio listening took place outside the home in 2006.

AM vs. FM Technology

As we have discussed, terrestrial radio stations broadcast using one of two technologies, AM or FM. The two technologies operate on different ranges of frequencies (called *bands*) and utilize two different means of broadcasting their signal. (See Figure 11.2.)

There are about 4,700 AM stations and 9,200 FM stations in the United States. Since the 1970s, listeners clearly have preferred FM. In 1981, AM stations attracted 41 percent of the listeners; in 2005, they managed to grab only 18.5 percent. To put it another way, AM's share of radio listeners fell by 55 percent between 1981 and 2000. At the same time, FM's share of listeners increased by 38 percent.

AM Signal

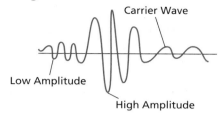

Carrier Wave

Low Amplitude

High Amplitude

FM Signal

Carrier Wave

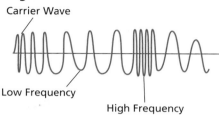

Low Frequency

High Frequency

Figure 11.2

AM and FM Signals

Both AM and FM radio stations transmit a carrier wave that is somehow changed or "modulated" to carry audio signals such as music or voice. With AM (amplitude modulation) radio, the amplitude or strength of the carrier wave's vibration fluctuates with the sound. With FM (frequency modulation) radio, the strength of the carrier wave remains constant, and instead it is the frequency or number of vibrations within the wave that changes based on the sound.

Commercial Radio Stations vs. Noncommercial Radio Stations

In addition to distinguishing radio stations by their positions in the AM or FM bands, we can also characterize them by the way they get the money they need in order to survive. In terms of funding, there are two types of radio stations:

- Commercial stations
- Noncommercial stations

The vast majority of stations—about 11,000—are **commercial stations**. As the name implies, these stations support themselves financially by selling time on their airwaves to advertisers. In 2006, advertisers spent a bit more than $20 billion on radio.[2]

Noncommercial stations do not receive financial support from advertisers in the traditional sense of airing commercials. Most noncommercial stations are located at the very left of the FM band (between 88 and 92 MHz) because these frequencies have been reserved by the government exclusively for noncommercial use. If your college or university owns a station, it may very well broadcast here. Because the FCC does not permit these stations to sell products directly, the stations support themselves through donations from listeners and private foundations, and from corporations, the latter in return for mentioning the firm or its products in announcements at the beginning and end of programs airing on the station. These announcements, called **billboards**, often sound suspiciously like the commercials these stations aren't allowed by law to run.

Radio Market Size

Radio stations can also be grouped according to the size of the market they serve (see Table 11.1). Listeners in small cities like Laramie, Wyoming, or Kenai, Alaska, may have only a handful of stations available to them. In fact, despite the availability of frequencies, many rural towns cannot attract the advertising or noncommercial support to field even a single radio station. Contrast that situation with

commercial station a radio station that supports itself financially by selling time on its airwaves to advertisers

noncommercial station a radio station that does not receive financial support from advertisers, but rather from donations from private foundations and listeners, or from commercial firms in return for mentioning the firm or its products at the start or end of programs airing on the station; most of these stations are located at the very left of the FM band (88 to 92 MhZ), because these frequencies have been reserved by the government exclusively for noncommercial use

billboards the mention of a sponsor's name or products at the start or end of an aired program in return for money

433

Table 11.1 Top Fifteen Radio Markets by Population, 2007

2007 rank	Market location	2007 population*
1	New York, NY	15,344,600
2	Los Angeles, CA	10,902,400
3	Chicago, IL	7,784,400
4	San Francisco, CA	5,969,400
5	Dallas-Fort Worth, TX	4,973,000
6	Houston-Galveston, TX	4,639,000
7	Philadelphia, PA	4,350,000
8	Atlanta, GA	4,267,500
9	Washington, DC	4,210,000
10	Boston, MA	3,874,600
11	Detroit, MI	3,866,500
12	Miami-Ft. Lauderdale-Hollywood, FL	3,538,400
13	Puerto Rico	3,328,500
14	Seattle-Tacoma, WA	2,328,100
15	Phoenix, AZ	3,173,200

*Metropolitan area, 12-year-olds and older

Source: Arbitron Radio Market Ratings, Fall 2007.

the one that exists in major markets like New York City or Los Angeles, where more than sixty stations compete for residents' ears. Moreover, despite the large number of stations fighting for listeners, a frequency in a large city can be worth hundreds of millions of dollars.

How can so many stations survive in a major urban environment? The answer lies in the second major reason radio has been able to compete in the new media world: segmentation, specifically, *format segmentation* and *audience segmentation*. To understand what these activities mean and how they guide the radio industry, let's turn to the categories of production, distribution, and exhibition.

Production in the Radio Industry

Research suggests that despite the large number of signals they may be able to receive, people tend to be loyal to no more than two or three stations. Think about the radio stations that you listen to at different times during the day. Most likely you listen to a station that plays music. Perhaps you listen to a "talk station," where listeners can phone in and speak their mind, or to an all-news station or an all-sports station.

Let's focus on the music station for the moment. What does that station create or "produce"? Unless the station is broadcasting a special concert, it almost certainly does not produce the music. Today, virtually all radio stations rely on recordings for their musical repertoire. Those recordings were created elsewhere; typically they are CDs made by recording companies.

Radio Formats

If you think about it, you'll realize that what music-oriented radio stations produce is an overall sound: a flow of songs punctuated by the comments of the DJs, the commercials, the station identification, the news, the weather, and sports. Radio industry practitioners call this flow of on-air sounds a **format**. A format is the personality of a radio station. As such, it attracts certain kinds of listeners and not others. That's just fine with the station's management because radio practitioners have found that, in their highly competitive media environment, the way to prosper is not to be all things to all people.

A radio station's music format is governed by four factors:

- Music style
- Music time period
- Music activity level
- Music sophistication

Music style refers strictly to the type of music a radio station plays, regardless of how the music is packaged for airplay. **Music time period** refers to the time of the music's release. "Current" music generally refers to music released within the last year, "Contemporary" music generally refers to music released within the past ten or fifteen years, "Oldies" generally refers to music released between the mid-1950s and the mid-1970s, and "Nostalgia" generally refers to music released prior to the mid-1950s.

Music activity level is a measure of the music's dynamic impact, ranging from soft and mellow to loud and hard-driving. The names of some music styles include built-in descriptions of the music's activity level: "hard rock," "smooth jazz." **Music sophistication** is a reflection of the simplicity or complexity of the musical structure and lyrical content of the music played. Although difficult to quantify, this factor often determines the composition of a station's audience. It is also reflected in the presentation of the station's on-air staff.

In both commercial and noncommercial radio, profits come from breaking the audience into different groups (segments) and then attracting a lucrative segment. For commercial broadcasters, a lucrative segment is one that many advertisers want to reach. For noncommercial broadcasters, a lucrative segment is a population group that has the money to help support the station or that corporate donors want to impress.

The fragmentation of the radio dial spurred the creation of many different radio formats, as radio executives struggled for ways to reduce their risk of failure amid enormous competition. They hoped that the formats they created would help them home in on audiences that would be large and desirable enough for local and national advertisers (or donors) to support. As Table 11.2 shows, the popular format with the largest number of stations is Country music. It is carried on almost 2,049 stations, representing about 15 percent of all stations. According to Arbitron, though, the News/Talk format garners the highest share of audience listening per average quarter hour between 6 a.m. and midnight. It grabs 17 percent of the audience, while Country lassos only 9 percent. In fact, adult contemporary, contemporary hit radio, Spanish, and Urban formats beat Country in shares of the national audience.

format the personality of a station organized around the kind of music it plays, and the radio personalities who are hired to introduce the recordings and advertisements

music style the aspect of a radio station's format that refers to the type of music the station plays

music time period the aspect of a radio station's format that refers to the release date of the music the station plays (i.e., "Contemporary," "Oldies," etc.)

music activity level the aspect of a radio station's format that refers to the measure of the played music's dynamic impact (i.e. "soft rock," "smooth jazz," etc.)

music sophistication the aspect of a radio station's format that refers to the simplicity or complexity of the musical structure and lyrical content of the music played

Table 11.2 **Radio Station Formats in the United States, December 2007**

	Total counts	Total AM	Total FM
Adult Contemporary	670	88	581
Adult Standards	379	323	49
Alternative Rock	384	12	357
Black Gospel	269	209	58
Classic Hits	505	35	467
Classic Rock	459	9	447
Classical	176	2	171
Contemporary Christian	920	52	827
Country	2049	537	1508
Easy Listening	27	3	22
Ethnic	132	94	32
Gospel	42	25	16
Hot AC	386	7	378
Jazz	151	8	137
Modern AC	20	0	19
Modern Rock	177	4	173
News/Talk	2025	1281	703
Oldies	738	295	430
Pre-teen	57	54	3
R&B	160	10	140
R&B Adult/Oldies	39	15	20
Religion (Teaching, Variety)	1231	364	513
Rhythmic AC	27	2	25
Rock	302	2	298
Soft Adult Contemporary	244	43	201
Southern Gospel	314	166	136
Spanish	917	478	414
Sports	574	517	57
Top 40	496	2	492
Urban AC	165	32	132
Variety	672	43	367
Format Not Available	9	4	5
Construction Permits	816	134	621
Stations off the air	140		

Source: Inside Radio, "Format counts," http://ftp.media.radcity.net/ZMST/insideradio/DEC07TOTALFormats.htm, accessed 02/22/2008.

Types of Formats   Table 11.3 presents a guide to radio formats, giving the format's target demographic, and a brief description of the people in the format's target audience. This list of formats, although long, is not exhaustive. By some counts there are more than 40 different formats, including "Hawaiian" and "Farm," with every format having variations. Moreover, new formats are born each year.

Selecting the Right Format   Because the format is the basis for attracting a target audience, radio station executives spend a lot of time deciding on a format. Often they hire **format consultants,** who help to analyze the competition and choose a format that will attract the most lucrative audience niche possible. Most of the formats are based on music, but to radio consultants, the bottom-line issue is a station's ability to gather a distinct audience for sponsors, not the aesthetics or diversity of its sound. People in the industry often use the term **narrowcasting** to describe the activity of going after specific slices of the radio audience that are especially attractive to advertisers. One well-known radio consultant explained that a radio station's need for distinct listeners was the reason behind narrowcasting. "As the [audience] pie gets thinner and thinner [because of the large number of competing stations], it's not so much whether you have ten thousand listeners at any given time …[but] what's the difference between [stations] A, B, C, and D."[3]

Radio industry executives suggest that the following five propositions about listening patterns help them divide, or segment, audiences into smaller and smaller pieces.

- Individuals tend to listen to only three radio stations at any particular period in their lives, with the most "preferred" of those stations taking up 65 to 70 percent of their listening time
- In the United States, there tends to be a large and widening divide between the music preferences of blacks, whites, and Hispanics
- Men and women often have separate musical interests
- People who are ten years apart in age tend to belong to different "music generations" with different tastes
- These music preferences can be useful tools for identifying people with distinct styles of living and buying

Determining Listening Patterns

Radio practitioners argue, for example, that they can construct formats that will divide the African-American audience by age and lifestyle. New formats often combine older formats to better target potential listeners. For example, several cities have urban/adult contemporary stations that combine the features of both adult contemporary and urban contemporary stations. They try to reach an older African-American audience by playing the "soft" tunes that were popular in these listeners' youth. In a similar vein, the news/talk format can be further divided into distinct subformats such as all news, sports talk, motivational talk, and political talk.

Consultants tend to describe formats by mentioning radio stations or particular artists that exemplify the sounds. The trick in radio, still another consultant contended, is to let a person know within two records what personality the musical menu exudes. It is the combination of a radio station's cues—the kind of music or talk, the presence of announcers and their speech patterns, the presence or absence of jingles and other identifiers (**interstitials**)—crafted in

format consultant an individual hired by a radio station to analyze the competition and select a format that will attract the most lucrative audience niche possible

narrowcasting going after specific slices of the radio audience that are especially attractive to advertisers

interstitials station or network identifiers and related signals that are interspersed between programs and commercials aired on the radio

Table 11.3 A Guide to Radio Station Formats in the United States, 2007

Symbol	Format Name	Description	Demographics
AC	Adult Contemporary	An adult-oriented pop/rock station with no hard rock, often a greater emphasis on non-current music	Women 25–54
AH	Hot AC or "Adult CHR"	A more up-tempo, contemporary hits format, with no hard rock and no rap	Adults 25–34
AP	Adult Alternative	Eclectic rock, often with wide variations in musical style	Adults 25–44
AR	Album Rock	Mainstream rock 'n' roll, can include guitar-oriented "heavy metal"	Men 25–44
AS	Adult Standards	Standards and older, non-rock popular music from the 1940s to the 1980s, often includes softer current popular music	Adults 35+
BG	Black Gospel	Current gospel songs and sermons	Adults 35+
CH	Contemporary Hit Radio (Top-40)	Current popular music, often encompassing a variety of rock styles, CH-R-B is dance CHR, CH-AR is rock-based CHR and CH-NR is new rock or modern rock-based CHR	Teens & adults 20–24
CR	Classic Rock	Rock-oriented oldies, often mixed with hit oldies of the 1960s, 1970s and 1980s	Men 25–44
CW	Country	Country music, including contemporary and traditional styles—CW-OL is country oldies	Adults 25+
CZ	Classic Hits	A rock-based oldies format, focusing on the 1970s	Adults 25–44
EZ	Easy Listening	Primarily instrumental cover versions of popular songs with more uptempo varieties of this format including soft rock originals, may be mixed with "smooth jazz" or adult standards	Adults 35+
ET	Ethnic	Programs primarily in languages other than English	Variety of ages
FA	Fine Arts—Classical	Fine arts "classical" music often includes opera, theater and/or culture-oriented news and talk	Adults 35+
FX	Farm News and Talk	Farm news, weather and information	Men 25+
JZ	Jazz	Mostly instrumental, often mixed with Soft AC, includes both traditional jazz and "smooth jazz" or "new AC"	Adults 25+
MA	Modern AC	An adult-oriented modern rock format with less heavy, guitar-oriented music than the younger new rock	Mostly women 25–44
MT	Financial Talk	All financial or "money-talk"	Adults 25+

Symbol	Format Name	Description	Demographics
NR	New Rock—Modern Rock	Current rock, mainstream "alternative" and heavier guitar oriented hits	Teens & adults 20–35
NX	News	All-news, either local or network in origin, stations may also have this description if a significant block of time is devoted to news	Adults 35+
OL	Oldies	Popular music, usually rock, with 80 percent or greater non-current music, CW-OL indicates country oldies and RB-OL indicates R&B oldies	Adults 25–55
PT	Pre-teen	Music, drama or readings intended primarily for a pre-teen audience	Children 12 & under
RB	R&B—Urban	Covers a wide range of musical styles, can also be called "urban contemporary"	Teens & adult 20–24
RC	Religious—Contemporary	Modern and rock-based religious music	All ages
RG	Religious—Gospel	Traditional religious music, BG indicates black-oriented and SG indicates country-oriented "southern gospel"	Adults 25+
RL	Religion	Local or syndicated religious programming, sometimes mixed with music	Adults 20+
SA	Soft Adult Contemporary	A cross between adult contemporary and easy listening, primarily non-current, soft rock originals	Mostly women 25+
SB	Soft Urban Contemporary	Soft R&B sometimes mixed with smooth jazz, often heavy in oldies	Adults 35+
SG	Southern Gospel	Country flavored gospel music, also includes the "Christian country" or "positive country" format	Adults 25+
SS	Spanish	Spanish-language programming, often paired with another type of programming, equivalents of English formats include: SS-EZ (easily listening); SS-CH (contemporary hits); SS-AC ("modern" music); SS-NX-TK (news-talk); SS-RA (ranchero music); SS-TP (salsa, tropical); SS-TJ (tejano); SS-MX (regional Mexican); or SS-VA (variety)	All ages
SX	Sports	Listed only if all or a substantial block of a broadcast day is devoted to play-by-play, sports news, interviews, or telephone talk	Men 25+
TK	Talk	Talk, either local or network in origin, can be telephone talk, interviews, information, or a mix	Adults 25+
VA	Variety	Incorporating four or more distinct formats, either block-programmed or airing simultaneously	All

Source: http://www.newsgeneration.com/radio_resources/formats.htm, accessed 9/22/07. Copyright, News Generation, Inc., 2001.

particular ways, that keep listeners of particular genders, ages, races, and ethnicities coming back.

Working with Formats

Once station management chooses a target audience and a format for a local station with the help of consultants, the station's personnel are typically responsible for working with the format—producing it and making it attractive to the target audience on a daily basis (see Figure 11.3).

The *general manager* is in charge of the entire station operation. He or she represents the owners of the station and is responsible for its activities. When it comes to the sound of the station, these include the work of the chief engineer, the news director, and the program director. The *chief engineer* makes sure that the station's sound goes over the air reliably and, with the help of the *compliance manager*, that the station's equipment complies with the technical rules of the Federal Communications Commission. The *news director* supervises news that is read over the air, perhaps assisted by one or two reporters. In preparation for delivering the news over the air, these workers scan the news wires for relevant stories and conduct brief interviews with local officials, such as police officers and city council members, to supplement their stories.

With the obvious exception of news-intensive stations, the overall amount of news on the radio has decreased over the last two decades, largely because the FCC has not required a local news operation as a condition of license renewal.

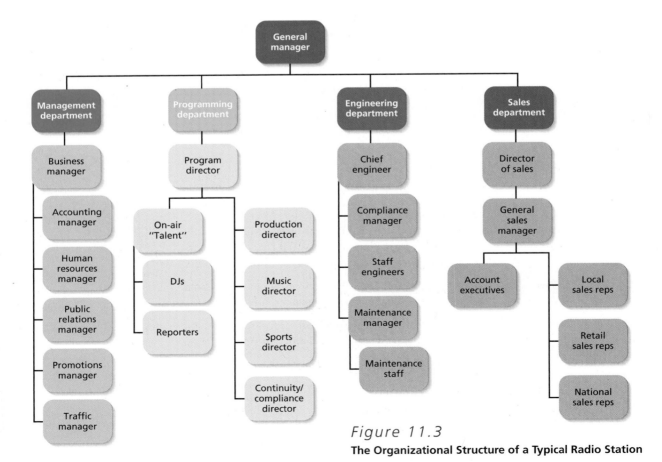

Figure 11.3

The Organizational Structure of a Typical Radio Station

Today, most radio newscasts run for only a few minutes, appear only in the morning, and cover only a handful of stories. Indeed, at some stations the news department has been dismantled, and any news that is broadcast is supervised by the program director.

The station's sound is under the command of the *program director*. He or she must make sure that the station's programming is consistent with the format and popular with the target audience. The program director controls the on-air functions of a station. Almost everything a listener hears over the air is the responsibility of the program director. The air personalities, or DJs, work for the program director. The program director is often assisted by a *music director* and a *promotions manager*. In many cases, these individuals also handle a shift on the air.

The average on-air personality (also known as **on-air talent**) works a four- or five-hour shift. Although this may sound like cushy work, it isn't. Running a format requires being able to handle many different, time-sensitive tasks simultaneously. During his or her hours on the air, a personality may play up to seventy-five

on-air talent term referring to radio workers whose voices and personalities are broadcast over the radio's airwaves

Payola Radio

Programming personnel at most radio stations are required to sign affidavits acknowledging that it is illegal to accept outside payments for playing records. However, an attorney representing one radio executive who was convicted of accepting bribes called it "business as usual." He claimed that the executive was also approached by other labels to trade payments for airplay of their artists.

Salvador Homero Campos, vice-president for programming at Sacramento-based Z-Spanish Radio Network, pleaded guilty to accepting as much as $15,000 a month in payola from Fonovisa Records, the biggest independent label in the Spanish music business. In the Fonovisa case, IRS and Justice Department agents combed through records and payroll data from broadcasters across the United States to see whether the bank accounts, assets, and lifestyles of radio station employees corresponded to their salaries.

Lawmakers noted the complicated structure of the payola scams such as "quarterbacking." Here, industry insiders describe that over a period of several months, labels pay tens of thousands of dollars to an independent contractor who, in turn, targets a portion of these moneys to radio programmers in exchange for adding songs to playlists. This effectively distances labels from direct transactions.

After an investigation, the FCC announced in April 2007 that the four big radio station owners—Clear Channel

Communications Inc., CBS Radio, Entercom Communications Corp and Citadel Broadcasting Corp—had agreed to a consent decree. The decree included a $12.5M settlement and the adoption of voluntary "rules of engagement" which were to ensure fair interaction between broadcasters and record labels and artists. This was to ensure that more local and independent acts had greater access to airplay.

However, several months after the announcement, some government officials were already questioning the effectiveness of the voluntary "rules of engagement" citing that some stations were requiring independent musicians to sign over any right to royalties and license to the music upon submission. Hence, the effectiveness of these measures in ensuring fair access is still under considerable question.

In addition to ruining the careers of those involved, the tarnished image of the companies named in such scandals may have long lasting effects, according to some analysts. Investigations such as those in the Latin and urban music markets may convince investors that music corporations are "throwing their shareholders' money away."

Sources: Chuck Philips, "Latin Radio Figure to Plead Guilty in Payola-Related Case," *Los Angeles Times,* February 13, 2001, p. A1; Chuck Philips, "U.S. Widens Probe into Bribery in Latin Radio," *Los Angeles Times,* November 3, 1999, p. A1; "Feingold Questions Big Radio's Commitment to Ending Payola," *Capitol Hill Press Releases,* July 11, 2007.

records and an equal number of commercials. In addition, the personality will answer the phone, perhaps give away a few tickets to lucky listeners, and update the weather forecast or sports scores. Keeping all these format elements in order while sounding friendly and happy on the air requires a fair amount of technical skill. Station employees carefully ensure that when a song ends, a new one smoothly begins. Otherwise, the station will transmit **dead air**—that is, nothing. Silence is a big taboo in radio because the mandate is to keep the target audience interested. Figuring out how to fill time attractively is a big challenge for a DJ. After their shift in the on-air studio, many disc jockeys move to a production studio, where they create items like commercials or comedy bits for later airing.

dead air the silence on the airwaves that is produced when a radio station fails to transmit sound

Producing the Playlist

Let's assume you have been named the program director of a new Top 40 station. What do you play to attract your target audience of young people in their teens and twenties? Your DJs need a *playlist* to guide them. The **playlist** is the roster of songs the DJs can put on the air (see Figure 11.4). The first step in creating a playlist

playlist the roster or line-up of songs that a radio can play on the air during a given period of time

KIIS FM playlist for 1.2.2008 to 1.27.2008		
Rank	Title	Artist
1	Hate That I Love You	Rihanna/Ne-yo
2	Low	Flo Rida
3	Clumsy	Fergie
4	No One	Alicia Keys
5	Kiss Kiss	Chris Brown/T-pain
6	Scream	Timbaland/Keri Hilson/Nicole Scherzinger
7	Flashing Lights	Kanye West
8	Hypnotized	Plies/Akon
9	Apologize	Timbaland/One Republic
10	Shawty Is A 10	The-dream/Fabolous
11	Take You There	Sean Kingston
12	Girlfriend	Bow Wow/Omarion
13	With You	Chris Brown
14	Love Like This	Natasha Bedingfield/Sean Kingston
15	Baby Don't Go	Fabolous/Jermaine Dupri
16	Good Life	Kanye West/T-Pain
17	The Anthem	Pitbull/Lil' Jon
18	Piece Of Me	Britney Spears
19	Tattoo	Jordin Sparks
20	Sensual Seduction	Snoop Dogg

Figure 11.4

A Sample Playlist

This excerpted playlist from KIIS 102.7—Los Angeles, California's number 1 Hit Radio Station—represents some of the songs that KIIS can play for a certain period of time—in this case, between January 2, 2008 and January 27, 2008.

is to listen to new music. Sometimes an artist is so well known that his or her songs will be played automatically, or a new song just sounds so good that it is immediately added to the playlist. But more often than not, adding a song requires careful thought. After all, listeners are fickle and will tune out of a station if it plays a song they don't want to hear. When in doubt, programmers use research.

Conducting Research to Compile the Playlist

Research can take many forms. Local stores may be polled to see what records are selling well. Stations in other cities that use the same format may be surveyed to see what they are playing. Executives check trade periodicals such as *Billboard* and *Radio and Records*. They go on the Internet to see what people are talking about and downloading, and they may even subscribe to a company that audits what songs people are downloading illegally. Also, stations may periodically survey representative listeners, either in person in a public place or via telephone, and ask them about their preferences. In these interviews, called **call-outs**, a station representative plays a snippet of a song and asks a listener to rate the song. Only songs that test well with the audience will receive substantial airplay.

Research has other uses as well. For example, **focus group** research can shape the overall direction of a station. To use this technique, the station or a research firm it hires gathers and interviews a small group of area residents (usually eight to ten) that fit the profile of the station's target audience. Only rarely are these individuals told beforehand the complete purpose of the session and the identity of the station. First, the individuals may be asked for their thoughts on various local radio stations. Then, as the interview progresses, they might be asked what they like and dislike about a certain station personality. The sessions are designed to get the spontaneous reactions of the participants. Radio industry executives believe that focus group research gives them a feel for what their target audience really thinks about the station.

call-outs periodic survey of representative listeners in which a station representative plays a snippet of a song and asks a listener to rate the song

focus group an assemblage of eight to ten carefully chosen people who are asked to discuss their habits and opinions about one or more topics

Maintaining the Format and Retaining the Target Audience

No matter what their format, programmers must perform the delicate balancing act of trying to please the largest possible segment of the station's target audience. A programmer's choice of records reflects the difficulty of the balancing act. To hold the interest of those who fall within the target audience but rarely listen to a particular station—that is, fringe listeners—the programmer wants to play only the best songs. Otherwise, when these occasional listeners tune in, they will quickly tune out again because the station is playing something they do not know or like. But other listeners who spend a lot of time listening to a radio station quickly tire of hearing the same songs over and over. This core audience for a station craves a wider variety of music. A programmer faces the dilemma of balancing the desires of loyal and occasional listeners.

With this balancing act in mind, most radio stations create an hourly **format clock** (also called a **format wheel**). This is a circular chart that divides one hour of the station's format into different, timed program elements (see Figure 11.5). The function of the clock is to maintain stability while making sure that key service elements show up at specific times. For example, a radio station may schedule its news at the top of the hour, followed by a hit song. To help listeners remember which station they are hearing, the clock instructs DJs to broadcast the station's call letters and frequency often. Stations may also use jingles to improve their

format clock or format wheel a circular chart that divides one hour of a radio station's format into different, timed program elements

443

Figure 11.5

Format Clock

Radio programmers and disc jockeys use a format clock like this one to program what will be played in one hour's time on their station—from local and national advertisements, to news, to songs, to station jingles and promotions—all to keep the listener tuned in.

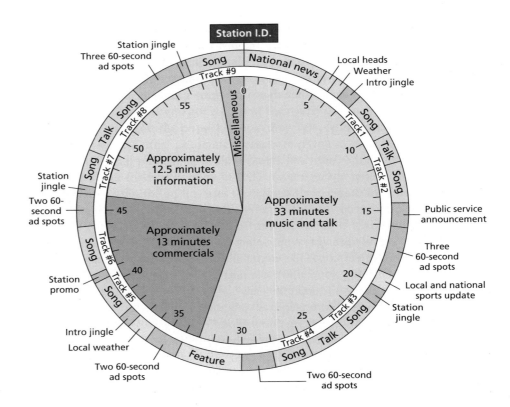

drive time early weekday mornings and late afternoons, when people are driving to and from work; this is the time during which radio stations expect to capture their largest audiences

listeners' retention of the station's identity. Perhaps most important from the station owner's viewpoint, the clock also dictates when air personalities play those vital commercials.

The clock also provides the framework for the scheduling and placement of music. Many stations use complex music-scheduling programs to make sure that individual songs are properly spaced and balanced. The clock guarantees that the most popular records are repeated more often while less popular records air less often.

The approach may vary somewhat during different times of the day. In radio, **drive time,** or the period when people are driving to and from work, is "prime time." That is, most radio stations expect to capture their largest audience during early weekday mornings and late afternoons. Given the large audience, advertising rates are also at their highest during these time slots. The morning shift is especially important for the station, and finding the right person or team to handle a station's early morning shift is often a great challenge. Funny morning personalities can command huge salaries. An axiom in the radio business is that a good morning personality will keep listeners tuned in to the station for the rest of the day.

Because so much listenership (and ad money) rides on it, drive time is the period during which program directors can afford the least amount of risk in terms of what is aired. Late at night or on weekends, when there are fewer listeners, program directors can be a bit more adventurous in format. Some stations also use these hours of lower listenership to introduce new music. Through its request lines, a station can hear from members of its audience about whether they like the new song or not. That might affect whether the program director will slot it in drive time.

It is interesting to note that most air personalities have little input into what music they play. Program directors and their general managers believe that the stakes are too high and the risk too great to allow a single DJ to decide what music to play based on his or her mood. In contemporary radio, a carefully crafted format must be consistent throughout the broadcast day.

Distribution in the Broadcast Radio Industry

The sound that the program director and air personalities produce every day sometimes goes from them directly to the station's airwaves. Station executives may also believe, however, that producing all of the station's programming locally is not the most competitive tactic. They may feel, for example, that broadcasting concerts by famous rock acts or programs with famous talk show hosts (depending on the format) might be the best way to attract the right kind of listeners to their station. Yet, paying for these programs is often far beyond the means of an individual radio station.

The Role of Networks and Syndicators

Most stations depend on *networks* or *syndicators* to supplement their local programming. Although some syndicators call themselves networks, people in the business of analyzing radio distinguish between the two.

A **network** provides a regular schedule of programming materials to its affiliate stations for broadcast, whereas a **syndicator** typically makes a deal for one show (or one series of shows) at a time. To illustrate the difference, when a talk station signs on to Salem Radio's Talk network, it gets a package of nine live, daily and weekend talk shows—for example, *Bill Bennett's Morning in America* and *The Dennis Prager Show*. By contrast, when the station makes a deal with Premiere Radio Networks (a subsidiary of Clear Channel) for the nationally syndicated conservative talk program *The Rush Limbaugh Show*, the deal can be for that program alone.

Networks and syndicators typically circulate their material to stations via satellite. Stations typically do not pay for the programming from a network. In fact, the network may pay the station for the privilege of using its airwaves; the amount is highly negotiable. Syndicators often do charge for their programs, although their fees are also negotiable. If a particular station reaches exactly the target audience a syndicator wants, the syndicator may charge that station very little for the show or even give it away.

Both networks and syndicators make most of their money by selling time on their programs to advertisers that want to reach the listeners of certain types of radio stations around the country. The network or syndicator may also give the local

network a company that distributes programs simultaneously to radio stations that agree to carry a substantial amount of its material on an ongoing basis; typically, a network will provide a regular schedule of programming material to its affiliate stations for broadcast

syndicator a company that licenses programming to radio stations on a market-by-market basis

Through Rush Limbaugh's three-hour daily political call-in show, he reaches approximately 20 million weekly listeners on nearly 600 stations across the United States.

445

station some of the advertising time that is available during the programming. In Philadelphia, for example, the station that airs *The Dennis Prager Show* will make money during the first six minutes of the hour by running its own commercials during the news. During the 54 minutes of the Prager's show, the show will break for 16 minutes of commercials. The Salem network will make money running commercials across its networks during five of those minutes. The remaining 11 minutes make up commercial time that the station can peddle to local or national advertisers.

Even noncommercial stations use networks. The largest, National Public Radio (NPR), distributes cultural and informational programming to its member stations across the country. It is probably best known for its news programs like *All Things Considered* and *Talk of the Nation*. The second-largest noncommercial network is Public Radio International (PRI), which distributes such well-known programs as *Marketplace* and *Prairie Home Companion*. Because noncommercial networks are largely prohibited from soliciting advertisements, these networks help defray their costs by getting foundations or companies to support the show in return for being mentioned on the air, as well as by charging a fee to their affiliated station. (The stations get their money from contributions from listeners, as well as from foundations and firms that pay to have their names mentioned locally.) Foundations and companies are attracted by the chance to parade their names in front of the typically well-educated, often prosperous, and influential audience that NPR and PRI deliver.

Format Networks vs. Traditional Networks

In general, radio networks reflect the dedication of the radio industry to targeting audiences through formats. The ultimate in long-form programming is the growing phenomenon of round-the-clock **format networks.** ABC Radio Networks (now a subsidiary of Citadel Broadcasting) provides ten round-the-clock formats, including Jackfm (broadly targeting 25–54-year-olds), Classic Rock (targeting the "lucrative 25–49-year-old demographic with the music they crave") and Today's Best Country (which "attracts a broad demographic of 18–54-year-old listeners").[4] These format networks provide a subscribing station with all the programming it needs. All the station owner has to do is insert local commercials. Automatic equipment keeps the station on the air, or the station can break into the programming with local news and weather. A station that is affiliated with one of these networks no longer needs to have a fully staffed programming department, which means a saving of perhaps hundreds of thousands of dollars annually. Of course, having no local programming staff also means having little or no local content.

Most radio executives believe, though, that giving a format a "home town" basis will draw more listeners than broadcasting only on-air talent from another part of the country. These stations use the traditional radio networks, which send only part of a day's programming, to fill specific needs, such as news and live concerts. Meshing a local format with the right network format (and so targeting a particular audience) is part of the business. The two news feeds provided by ABC Radio Networks can provide an example. The ABC News Radio format is intended to gel with news and talk stations, whereas ABC FM is designed to fit into certain types of music formats.

Syndicators also work to make their programming mesh with certain formats. Think of the weekly countdowns of hit songs carried by many music stations and hosted by personalities such as Ryan Seacrest ("American Top Forty") or Lon Helton ("Country Countdown, USA"). With different songs and different chatter,

format network
programming firm that provides a subscribing radio station with all the programming it needs to fill its airwaves 24 hours a day, 7 days a week; often the stations needs only to insert local commercial spots into the programming

these shows reflect the formats of the radio stations that carry them.

The growth of format networks notwithstanding, the number of radio stations associated with radio networks has recently declined. In part this seems to be related to the increase in the number of outlets that stations have been allowed to own within markets and across markets. Executives of these station groups believe that they own enough stations to make their own deals with national advertisers and so they do not have to share the money with networks. As for a high-profile program or concert that will especially excite listeners, their feeling seems to be that an occasional syndicated show can fill that bill.

Ryan Seacrest counts down the hits on radio as host of "American Top 40," which can be heard on more than 400 radio stations worldwide.

Exhibition in the Broadcast Radio Industry

At the end of the day, filling the bill comes down to paying the bills. From the standpoint of the radio station's owner, after all, the purpose of producing a format and/or buying one from a distributor (a network) is to make money at the exhibition point. That is the moment at which the format is actually broadcast from the station.

Advertising's Role in Radio Exhibition

For the general manager and the program director, the success or failure of their product depends on whether the station's sales force, led by the sales manager, can sell enough advertising to bring the station adequate profits. Radio ad people talk about two kinds of advertising coming into a station:

- Local spots
- National spots

In **national spot advertising,** airtime is purchased from a local station by major national advertisers, such as Nabisco, Paramount Pictures, and Maybelline, or their representatives. The word *spot* in the term *national spot advertising* distinguishes this kind of sponsorship from **network advertising,** in which sponsors (perhaps also Nabisco, Paramount, and Maybelline) purchase airtime not from the station, but from a network that serves the station. National advertisers use spot purchases to target certain cities with particular ads. Buying network ads is often more efficient when the aim is to reach a particular radio audience across the country.

Of the approximately $17 billion of advertising going into radio in 1999, about $16.3 billion went to radio stations as a result of national and spot commercial buys; the rest (about $700 million) went to networks. Of the money that went to

national spot advertising form of radio advertising in which airtime is purchased from a local radio station by national advertisers or their representatives

network advertising form of radio advertising in which national advertisers or their representatives purchase airtime not from local radio stations, but from the network that serves the radio station

447

radio stations, local advertising (as opposed to national spot advertising) accounted for about 75 percent of the total. Clearly, a radio station's sales manager knows that the most important market for the firm is the local one. Practically speaking, this market represents the advertising dollars the station can collect from businesses in the area. The station's sales staff must convince local companies—for example, area restaurants and hospitals—to advertise on the station.

Placing and Scheduling Commercials

In order to avoid alienating listeners, management sets an upper limit on the number of minutes per hour that can be sold for advertising. The prices of commercials are based on their length (typical lengths are thirty and sixty seconds) and when they air. A commercial that airs during drive time, the time with the highest listenership, will cost more than one that airs in the middle of the night. The goal of the sales department is to sell as many of the available minutes as possible for the highest price.

The sales manager works with the *traffic manager* to coordinate the placement of commercials. Despite the title, the traffic manager's responsibilities do not include reporting on accidents on the highway. Rather, the traffic manager ensures that advertisements are scheduled and broadcast correctly. For example, it is considered bad practice to schedule commercials from directly competing companies, say Pepsi and Coca-Cola, right after each other.

Learning Who Listens

Advertisers naturally need to be convinced that they will benefit from paying for time on a radio station. The most basic question they ask is, how many people are listening? Answering that question with certainty is nearly impossible. Newspaper and magazine companies can actually count the individual copies of the paper or

"Starting Monday, this radio station will switch from classical music to hard-core rap."

magazine that are sold to people. In the electronic media, however, the product being delivered is by definition untouchable; it is sent out free over the air. As a result, the people who choose to pick up the product—to listen to it—must be counted. Because it is nearly impossible to ask all the people in a community what radio station they listened to this morning, radio stations pay research firms to ask this question of a sample of the population that is designed to represent the entire community.

Conducting Market Research to Determine Station Ratings

The largest firm that conducts radio audience measurement is Arbitron. The area in which Arbitron surveys people about a station is called the station's market. Des Moines, Iowa; Los Angeles, California; and Madison, Wisconsin are radio markets of different sizes. On a regular basis, Arbitron selects a sample of listeners in each radio market to participate in its survey. Arbitron then repeatedly tries to contact its selected sample. Say Arbitron reaches you at your home and asks you to participate. Given your interest in the mass media, you agree. The Arbitron representative asks you to fill out a diary listing all your radio listening for a week and then to return the diary electronically, via the Internet. The company pays you a token fee—usually a dollar or two—for your cooperation.

The diary contains space for a week's worth of responses. You dutifully fill it out every time you listen to the radio. You promptly submit it through the company's website at the end of the week. The firm now has an accurate survey, right? Not so fast. This technique of audience measurement has some drawbacks. First, the research firm may have had difficulty getting a random sample of everyone in the area to participate. For example, some people, like college students or seasonal workers, move frequently or are hard to find, so they are often underrepresented in the survey sample. In addition, evidence suggests that people with busy lifestyles are less likely to participate than those who have more time on their hands. Therefore, the assumption that the sample is representative of the community is often invalid.

In addition, many of the people who do make it into the survey drop out or fail to fill out the diary completely. Though Arbitron designs the diary to be taken along throughout the day, many participants do not do so and then, at the end of a day or week, have to try to remember their station choices and to re-create their listening activity before they write it down in the diary. Even listeners who try to participate conscientiously may accidentally record incorrect information. If you are like many people, you sometimes jump between stations while you are in your car. Would you be able to record which ones you heard?

Recognizing these problems, Arbitron has rolled out a device called a **portable people meter (PPM)** for tracking radio listening, both at home and on the street. Arbitron's PPM service will replace Arbitron's current diary-based ratings. Current plans call for the PPM to be deployed in the top 50 radio markets by 2010. At the same time, Arbitron is exploring—and will be testing in the field—different approaches

portable people meter (PPM) Auditron's electronic device for tracking radio listening, both at home and on the street

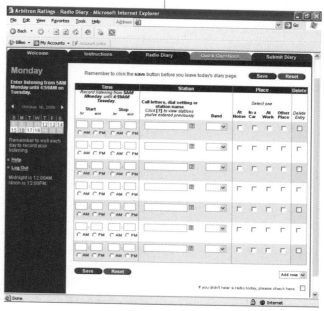

An Arbitron Radio Diary
Source: http://www.arbitron.com/downloads/ediary2.jpg

to using electronic measurement in markets ranked 51+. The PPM is a mobile-phone-sized device that consumers wear throughout the day. It works by detecting identification codes that can be embedded in the audio portion of any transmission. The PPM can determine what consumers listen to on the radio; what they watch on broadcast, cable and satellite TV; what media they stream on the Internet; and what they hear in stores and entertainment venues.

You've probably already noticed a flaw in this system: just because a person passes by a radio station's sound doesn't mean that he or she is really listening. It's certainly a problem, but executives believe the PPM is still superior to the diary method. By 2007, the service had rolled out in the Philadelphia and Houston markets. There were glitches with constructing the sample of PPM-carriers that was representative of radio listeners. The new approach was very much considered a work in progress.

Most local stations and advertisers use the diary-based Arbitron rating results because they are the best data available. When ratings are reported to subscribing stations, employees await the news with trepidation. Ratings are to station employees what report cards are to students: rows of raw numbers summarize many months of effort. One rating point equals one percent of the population in a market. Because typically there are dozens of stations broadcasting in major markets, the ratings for individual stations are often quite small. Stations are considered successful if they manage to garner only four or five rating points. Yet the raw number is often not the only thing of interest to a radio advertiser. The extent to which the advertiser's target audience—in demographic and lifestyle terms—is being reached with an efficient cost per thousand listeners is often more important. For example, a concert promoter may want to know which station in town attracts the lion's share of the young adult audience so that she can effectively buy advertising to attract a rock band's core audience.

Arbitron results give radio executives and advertisers information on such basic categories as listener gender, race, and age. These characteristics form the basis for discussions between a radio station's sales force and potential advertisers about the appropriateness of the station's target audience compared to those of other stations. To marshal evidence about other characteristics that might also attract advertisers, many radio stations subscribe to Scarborough Research surveys. Scarborough conducts telephone surveys of a market's population and asks people questions about various aspects of their lives, from purchasing habits to hobbies to radio listening preferences. Radio stations' sales forces often link these data with Arbitron data. They then use the findings to try to convince certain local advertisers that their station can deliver the most appropriate audience.

This doesn't always work, because Scarborough studies and others like them have their own drawbacks. Sometimes advertisers purchase time on a radio station primarily because they believe that the format is suitable for their product or message and because the sales staff has arranged to tie them to a promotion (a contest, an event in which prizes are given out) that will both highlight the advertiser and result in concrete responses from listeners toward the advertiser. Almost everyone knows of a radio station that has given away cash prizes, trips, or concert tickets. The prizes are geared to the demographic and lifestyle categories of the listening population that the station's management wants to attract.

A station whose ratings are up will often try to raise its advertising rates to reflect its increased popularity. Some station employees may directly benefit from the ratings report because their salaries are tied to ratings. But the celebration cannot last too long because a new ratings report card is always being prepared. Most large radio markets, like Chicago, are surveyed year-round by Arbitron.

When Stations Fare Poorly in the Ratings

When stations have fared poorly in the ratings process, managers may institute immediate changes. Sometimes managers blame simple internal factors like a poor choice of recorded music. They may also blame factors outside the station's control. For example, many music-intensive stations have poorer ratings during severe winters because listeners flock to competing news/talk stations for updates on school closings and icy roadways. In that case, a program director of a Top 40 station, for example, will recognize that the ratings fluctuation was due to unusual circumstances and may decide to make no changes in the hope that listeners will return to their normal habits with the approach of milder spring weather.

Often, however, poor ratings lead to personnel changes. A careful analysis of Arbitron data may indicate that a particular time slot is not performing as well as the program director and station manager expect it to. In this case, the on-air personality during that period is likely to be replaced. When stations have a history of poor ratings and revenue performance, station owners will frequently decide to try a new station format in an effort to grab a larger target audience and more advertisers. Overnight, a station that is known for playing classical music may start playing country tunes. With these wholesale makeovers, it is not unusual for all employees associated with the station's old format to lose their jobs.

Although management may consider it deadly to stick with an unprofitable format, instituting a new format on a radio station also has risks. Listeners to the old format are likely to feel abandoned and angry, and it may be tough to get the new target audience to find the station. Attempts to attract new listeners through publicity stunts and advertisements on billboards, on TV, and in newspapers can be quite expensive. And if the new format doesn't work, management may be in a worse situation than it was in before the change. Nevertheless, the formats of certain stations do change fairly frequently; their managers believe that the benefits of responding to the shifting interests of audiences and advertisers outweigh the costs and risks of change.

Broadcast Radio and Social Controversy

Radio industry executives point to their industry with a great deal of pride. They argue that the many formats and format variations that exist throughout the country indicate that the industry is diverse and in touch with its listeners. There are, however, important groups within U.S. society who argue that Americans should find some of the activities at the core of the radio industry troubling. In the interest of better understanding the environment of sound that surrounds us, let's note two related issues, radio consolidation and the radio industry's political clout.

Radio Consolidation

Media watchdog groups such as the Media Access Project and consumer groups such as Consumers Union argue that the purchase of hundreds of stations by large companies is reducing the amount of diversity in American radio (see Table 11.4). They and many other media critics say that the actual range of music broadcast, even in large markets, is not nearly as wide as one might think from merely looking at the number of stations. A major reason for this, they say, is that when the big radio firms buy up stations, they put in place cookie-cutter approaches to

Table 11.4 Number of Stations Owned by Top Broadcasting Companies in 2006

Rank	Owner	Number of stations
1	Clear Channel Communications	1,190
2	Cumulus Broadcasting Inc.	303
3	Citadel Broadcasting Corp.	225
4	Infinity Broadcasting	178
5	Educational Media Foundation	143
6	American Family Association Inc.	120
7	Salem Communications Corporation	104
8	Entercom	103
9	Saga Communications Inc.	86
10	Cox Broadcasting	78

Source: http://www.journalism.org/node/847, accessed 2/28/08.

formats that have proved efficient in other markets. The upshot of this standardization is that cities and towns around the country increasingly have the same lineup of formats with the same lineup of sounds—sometimes even played by 24-hour format computers in places far away. As a result of consolidation, they argue, radio doesn't reflect different regional or local tastes; nor does it encourage live performances by local artists. They add that the growth of round-the-clock format networks that has resulted from consolidation has further homogenized radio despite the large number of stations.

The Radio Industry's Increasing Influence over the Political Process

Watchdog and consumer groups have also joined with community groups to protest the influence over the political process that the radio industry's consolidation has brought. They point out that politicians need the coverage of radio stations in their home areas when they run for reelection. When just a few companies own stations that attract a large percentage of voters in a particular area, those companies may have a lot of leverage over the area's politicians. The politicians may fear that they will not get news coverage—or may get negative coverage—from those stations if they don't go along with the broadcasters' needs.

A case in point, say the advocates, is the political furor that arose when the chairman of the Federal Communications Commission under President Bill Clinton, William Kennard, came up with a plan to increase community involvement in radio. The growing consolidation in the radio industry along with a significant drop in minority ownership of stations led Kennard to support the creation of a new form of radio for the United States: low-power FM (LPFM) stations with transmissions reaching an area of 2 to 18 miles. In 1999, he announced that the goals of the LPFM program would be to provide new opportunities for community-oriented radio broadcasting, foster opportunities for new radio broadcast ownership, and promote additional diversity in radio voices and program services. He added that the new stations could provide a low-cost means of serving urban communities and neighborhoods as well as people living in smaller towns and communities. Kennard also stated that such stations could be added to the radio dial without causing interference with existing stations or with other organizations (such as airlines and emergency services) that use the radio spectrum.

Established radio broadcasters were quite upset when they heard of the plan. The National Association of Broadcasters (NAB), the industry's main lobbying group, claimed that the new stations *would* cause interference with existing signals. Clearly, though, what concerned radio broadcasters most about low-power FM stations was the increased competition for audiences (and thus lower advertising rates) that the existence of many more commercial stations would bring. They simply didn't want the competition.

Swinging into action, the NAB got Congress to pass a bill, called the Radio Broadcasting Preservation Act of 2000, that imposed such stringent engineering requirements on low-power stations that only a small number of the thousands Kennard had hoped to encourage could actually go on the air. The new, more conservative FCC chairman under President George W. Bush, Michael Powell, had no intention of fighting that battle. The NAB had won, something it was accustomed to doing. As a Salon.com article noted, "the ad-hoc LPFM coalition of educators, church leaders, grass-roots entrepreneurs, school administrators and minorities have discovered firsthand why their primary foe, the National Association of Broadcasters, is regarded as one of Washington's most powerful players."

Radio executives reply that these two concerns are overblown. They point out that in most markets, even when some consolidation takes place, many stations remain. They also argue that while the National Association of Broadcasters certainly has influence over lawmakers, it is certainly not all-powerful and wins battles when it shows politicians that its positions reflect the public interest. Advocates strongly disagree with both these contentions, and the arguments continue. One area that radio activists and industry executives likely do agree on, though, is that the availability of new digital music production, distribution and exhibition systems threaten to drain away much of radio's audience in the years to come. The activists point to what they consider radio's overloaded commercialism, lack of musical diversity and innovation as a reason people will flee broadcast radio. The executives simply note that new technology is allowing people to stream music in ways that force radio broadcasters to change the way they do business—and they are trying hard to do that.

Radio and the New Digital World

What are the new digital technologies that compete with broadcast radio? The major ones are satellite radio and Internet radio. Satellite radio has so far proven to be only a minor annoyance to the industry, but some observers have great hopes for it. Most observers agree that Internet radio threatens to cause the radio industry great damage in the long term if it doesn't adapt. Let's look at each.

Satellite Radio

Satellite radio is a technology through which a consumer can receive streaming channels of music and/or talk to a special receiver. It has little to do with the

satellite radio radio broadcast by transmitting signals to satellites that retransmit them to radio sets

453

technology of broadcasting as it developed over the past century. That this activity has come to be known as Internet radio shows the powerful hold that the medium has on people's understandings. It also suggests that this activity is likely to be seen as direct competitor to AM and FM radio.

At this writing there are two satellite radio firms, XM Radio and Sirius Radio. Each makes money through subscription (about $20 a month) as well as through advertising on some of the hundreds of channels it offers, with a wide variety of formats. The companies produce the programs, sometimes in joint ventures with other firms (Oprah's Harpo Productions, for example, for the XM channel, *Oprah and Friends*). The channels are uploaded to satellites and can be picked up in most places around the country by receivers that stores such as Radio Shack and Best Buy sell. In addition, Sirius and XM have each made deals with major car companies to offer their receivers as original equipment. Some of the equipment is portable, so that it is possible to listen at home and while outdoors, not just while in the car.

In 2007, about 14 million people subscribed to satellite radio. While that's a lot of people, it doesn't come close to the number of people (almost everyone) who

To Space and Back

1. Sirius and XM both produce live and taped programming, ranging broadly from Alanis Morissette, right, to sports and news.

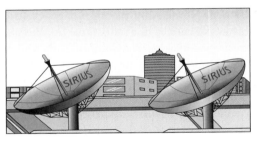

2. The programming is beamed to satellites from dishes operated by each company.

3. The satellites broadcast the signal back to Earth, where it's picked up directly by receiver units. The signal is also received and rebroadcast by repeater stations in metropolitan areas. XM uses two geostationary satellites (right) that remain constantly above the United States. Sirius uses three satellites, two of which are always over the country.

4. A receiver buffers the broadcast for a few seconds, so if it loses the satellite signal it can use one from a repeater station, helping insure a continuous broadcast. Overpasses and tall building are particular problems.

Figure 11.6

How Satellite Radio Works

http://www.space.com/businesstechnology/technology/satcom_radio_operations_031112.html

454

listen to radio during the week. Moreover, while broadcast radio brought in about $21 billion in revenues during 2005, satellite radio saw a much smaller amount—$752 million. In fact, the huge costs of setting up the system, paying enormous amounts to talents such as Howard Stern and promoting it through discounted subscriptions brought Sirius and XM to ask the Federal Communications Commission if they could merge, even though their initial licenses explicitly denied that. As you might guess, broadcasters did not want the FCC to waive the rule, and a fight ensued. In the meantime, satellite-radio boosters point out, the number of subscribers grew impressively. Some analysts projected that in just a few years satellite radio could grow to several tens of millions and begin to draw national advertisers away from broadcast stations and networks.

One selling point that satellite radio has used to draw adherents is that some of its music channels have no commercials, and that the channels that do are quite sparing in the commercial time they use. It is a point that is not lost on nervous broadcast radio executives, especially when they combine concern about satellite competition with worries about Internet radio.

Internet Radio

Like satellite radio, Internet radio is a metaphor. It could more appropriately be called **audio streaming**, for what it involves is the flow of music or other audio signals from their originator to a computer via the packet switching technologies that are at the core of the Internet. In its most basic form, the streaming of music from a website is different from the downloading of typical songs in that it is designed not to be saved by the computer through which it is playing, unless a special recording device captures it and translates it into a savable format (MP3, for example). On the Web are hundreds of sites that stream music. Sometimes the sites make money through the advertising placed on their sites. Sometimes, the sites require subscription fees. A tack of the biggest sites, such as Yahoo Music and Rhapsody, is to offer some music channels without charge but with commercials dispersed through the music. If a person pays the subscription fee, he or she can get more channels with no commercial interruptions.

Even the commercial interruptions that occur when you don't subscribe to a channel are nowhere near as long or frequent as radio station commercial breaks. At least as attractive as few or no commercial interruptions is the diversity of streams. Go to Yahoo Music or Rhapsody and you'll note possibilities that sound like radio station formats: including, Rock, Today's Big Hits, Classic Country, Oldies, Contemporary Christian and the like. But you'll also find niche channels that would never make it on traditional AM or FM stations—Celtic, India, Klezmer, Naughty Comedy, Modern Broadway, Forgotten Hits of the Nineties, and more. In addition, both Yahoo Music and Rhapsody encourage subscribers to "create your own station" by identifying artists across genres that will be streamed especially to them. The music site Pandora goes further. Its software identifies patterns in the musical compositions a person chooses to stream and then offers music that fits those genres or combinations of genres.

audio streaming an audio file delivered to a computer-like device from a website so that it can be heard while it is coming into the device but cannot be saved or stored

Music.yahoo.com, website of Yahoo! Music

www.rhapsody.com, website of Rhapsody Music

But these activities are only the start of the way people can shape music streaming to their own interests. Rhapsody trumpets the ability of its subscribers to share the lists of streams they have created. Say, for example, you are interested in movie scores in Warner Brothers films. Clicking through Rhapsody, you could create a set of list links to music that as a group would represent your understanding of Warner Brothers movie scores; it might be three hours long. You can then "publish" that on Rhapsody so that by clicking on a link, any subscriber could hear all the pieces you had strung together.

Traditional Radio's Responses to Digital Music

Radio executives view the rise of satellite radio and Internet radio with not a little bit of concern. The new music distribution networks perform many of the key functions that contemporary AM and FM stations do. They are available when people want them. And they help to guide listeners through the thicket of songs that they feel they should know about, or might want to learn about. In fact, Internet radio sites often present a lot of information about the music they are playing, including biographies of the artists and discographies (lists of the records they have put out).

The one advantage that broadcast radio has retained is its presence in virtually all automobiles. Americans report that fully one-quarter of their music listening takes place in the car, and much of that is still captured by traditional radio stations. While 96 percent of Americans in 2006 said they used an AM/FM radio in a car, only 1 percent said they used a satellite receiver, and only 3 percent said they used an MP3 player in a car.[5] Even the lack of auto competition may represent short-term relief, however. With the spread of satellite radio and the increasing ability to connect to the Internet outside the home via mobile phone handsets and other devices (see Chapter 14), it will not be long before many people will have the choice to stream sounds from the Internet or satellite virtually anywhere.

The radio industry has responded to the challenges posed by satellite radio and the Internet by addressing three major areas: commercial time, HD radio, and their own Internet participation.

Commercial Time

Executives for major station groups admit that the amount of time that they have traditionally devoted to commercials and promotions—as many as twenty minutes per hour—has driven some listeners away. Some stations have tried to soften the blow by bunching commercials together into long strings; listeners are guaranteed twenty minutes or more of music before they hear an ad, for example. Although this approach may assuage some in the audience, it may get advertisers upset if they are stuck in the middle of the commercial break, worried that many listeners have long since changed the station, if only temporarily.

In late 2004, Clear Channel, the nation's largest broadcast radio station owner, tried to set a new example with an approach it called "Less is More." Clear Channel committed itself to reducing its available ad time to no more than 15 minutes of ads per hour and no more than 6 ads in a row. Analysis of the loads of commercials of radio stations across the nation indicates that the number of commercials (particularly the number of long, 60-second commercials) did go down if one compares the first 3 months of 2005 and the first 3 months of 2006. Some observers explained the decline as related to advertisers' interest in buying radio commercials, not just to a desire by station owners to reduce commercial time. It remains to be seen whether many firms will follow Clear Channel's example over the long haul.

HD Radio

HD radio is a system in which digital signals of AM and FM stations are sent along with the traditional analog station sounds on the same frequencies allocated to the analog stations. The technology was developed by the company iBiquity Digital in 1991 and approved for use by the FCC in 2002. HD, by the way, does not stand for high definition (as in high definition television) but for hybrid digital/analog. As iBiquity's website (http://www.ibiquity.com) states:

> Your favorite station remains in the same place on the radio dial, but when you have a new digital HD radio receiver, your AM sounds like FM and FM sounds like CDs. In addition, the wireless data feature enables text information—titles, artists, weather or traffic alerts—to be broadcast directly to your receiver's display screen. And, FM HD radio stations are starting to "multicast," offering more than one stream. Simultaneously, one station can offer several audio channels as well as on-screen data. A station can run one channel of music and one of news, or two different music formats. Or run three completely different music formats in three different languages. And much, much, more.[6]

Radio executives see HD radio as a way to compete directly with satellite radio. You do have to purchase a new radio, but after that the stream of music or talk is free. Moreover, unlike satellite radio, HD can be local radio, not just a national feed. Right now, many FM stations across the United States offer two extra program streams on HD, often related to the FM station's genre. So, for example, a station playing a broad Spanish music format might have one digital channel playing Latin jazz and another specializing in Tejano. HD radio is in its infancy. Relatively few people have receivers and critics complain that the signal is typically so weak that stations sometimes fade in and out. Nevertheless, the radio industry has high hopes for HD as another way to reach listeners who want more stations but don't want to pay for satellite radio.

Internet Participation

Broadcast radio is moving rapidly to work with Internet radio. Just about every radio station management realizes that it has to have an Internet site. The site streams what the radio station is playing but it goes beyond that to deepen and engage the user with the personality that the station aims to project. Consider the site of Power99FM, the website for one of five Clear Channel radio stations in Philadelphia. This station focuses on "Bangin hip hop and R&B," to quote the

www.power99.com, website of Power99 FM

site. The site is filled with music and music videos that reflect the radio station's theme. Not only can a user stream individual songs or even albums, much of the material is available for free download. In September 2007, Kanye West's album *Graduation* was streaming on the site a few weeks before its release as part of the site's "sneak peek" music. An area of the site called "Stripped" goes beyond packaged albums to provide videos of artists in concert-like venues. In addition, Power99FM offers a free podcast which will send songs that conform to the specific interests that the user has indicated to their personal website. Much like MySpace, the site has a place where you can listen to music by unknown performers. In this case, aspiring artists must upload music to the site along with a request that the music be considered for inclusion.

Surrounding all this music is a large promotional and advertising environment. Listeners can go to the site to find out about contests and promotions that take place on the radio. It also conducts its own contests to involve visitors. You can sign up for a VIP club to "enter exclusive online contests for concert tickets, hot prizes, movie passes, sporting event tickets, cash, trips, cars, you name it." All of this comes with advertising for local and national companies. The streamed music did not include commercials in 2007, but it did include a short verbal publicity for the activity (for example, "Sneak peek: hear it here first"). It is a small step from that to a short commercial message.

All these activities leverage the power of the Clear Channel organization to create deals with recording companies and artists for the right to post material across Clear Channel's many websites. Like other Internet music sites, visitors can purchase the albums online from the site, for which the company gets a transaction commission. In fact, with the idea of guiding consumers to the purchase of music online and through broadcast, Clear Channel reinforced the company's sense of itself as very much a part of the new digital environment. In 2007, it was among the radio groups cheerleading a new development in HD radio technology: users who "tag" a song on a special HD receiver have the option to purchase it or find more information about it when their iPod is synced with iTunes software.

On its corporate website, Clear Channel notes that its "content can be heard on AM/FM stations, HD digital radio channels, on the Internet, via iPods, through Motorola's iRadio cellphone service, and via mobile-navigation devices from Cobra, Garmin, Kenwood and others." While Clear Channel may be the most aggressive about its move to digital, the other major groups are also involved. The websites of CBS Radio stations have many of the same features as the Clear Channel sites. Citadel Broadcasting, somewhat less involved in digital, nevertheless promotes the idea of "Right Now Radio." It involves streams of its radio station programming from their website or from a central site, with specially inserted commercials. These activities reflect a changing radio industry that senses it must define itself to its audiences and its advertisers as far broader than AM and FM radio.

Media Literacy and the Radio Industry

If you had to create an industry that streams music and talk formats to Americans, would the radio industry as it is now organized be what you would choose?

As this chapter has shown, the U.S. radio industry developed over decades in response to a variety of forces relating to industry, technology and society. Powerful organizations work hard to protect the industry's turf so that challenges to the ways radio firms approach the airwaves are difficult to mount. Yet challenges are taking place, mainly from companies and individuals with new digital technologies that ignore the traditional airwaves. To make sense of all these changes, their problems and possibilities, it may be useful not to think only of the radio industry as it currently exists. Rather, think of streaming audio, the industries that are involved in providing that, and the consequences they seem to be having on the variety and diversity of sounds and ideas that Americans can access.

Next time you take a long car trip, try to listen to as many radio stations as you can along the way. Pay attention to their formats and try to determine how much variety there is in the sounds you can hear in different parts of the country. Think, too, of this chapter's discussion of the way these formats are chosen, produced, and evaluated. Then consider what streaming audio in a car, or on a walk, or at work, or in the home might be like in a decade. Winds of change are certainly blowing from various directions. Relaxed federal ownership rules allow companies to own far more stations in a given market than ever before. Yet heightened competition from other media for audiences and advertising revenues poses new threats to traditional radio. How will these and other trends affect the landscape of streaming audio? Will the developments really introduce people to a greater variety of the music enjoyed by many communities in American society, or will they primarily allow individuals to fall into areas of comfortable sounds that are narrower than those found on contemporary radio? Are there ways to encourage a balance of both approaches? How would you like to see streaming audio develop? Why? Keep listening, and thinking.

CHAPTER REVIEW

For an interactive chapter recap and study guide, visit the companion website for *Media Today* at www.routledge.com/textbooks/mediatoday

QUESTIONS FOR DISCUSSION AND CRITICAL THINKING

1 What methods do stations use to signal their formats to listeners?
2 How do radio stations know who their listeners are?
3 What are ways in which radio stations deal with poor ratings?
4 What impact does consolidation have, according to media critics?
5 Why hasn't Internet radio taken more of traditional radio's audience?
6 What changes in technologies suggest that this situation might change?

INTERNET RESOURCES

National Association of Broadcasters (http://www.nab.org)
The National Association of Broadcasters (NAB) is the trade association that represents radio and television stations and networks before government bodies.

United States Early Radio History (http://www.earlyradiohistory.us/)
This site explores the history of radio technology and stations (but not programming) from the mid-nineteenth century to the early 1950s. Aside from essays on various historical periods, it has links to many websites with documents that expand on its writings.

Radio Days (http://www.otr.com/index.shtml)
This website contains essays about and examples of network radio from the 1930s and 1940s. There are mystery programs, private eye shows, comedy programs, and science fiction series.

Opry.com (http://www.opry.com/MeetTheOpry/History.aspx)
The Grand Ole Opry in Nashville was a staple for country music fans on radio from the time WSM started carrying it in 1925. This website reviews the past and present of the Opry, including its radio history.

Radio & Records (http://www.radioandrecords.com/RRWebSite/)
Radio & Records is a trade magazine of the radio and record industries. Its website offers useful information on station formats, ratings, and industry conventions.

KEY TERMS

You can find the definitions to these key terms in the marginal glossary throughout this chapter. Test your knowledge of these terms with interactive flash cards on the *Media Today* companion website.

AM	format clock
audio streaming	format consultants
billboards on non-commercial radio	format networks
broadcasting	format wheel
call-outs	interstitials
commercial stations	music activity level
dead air	music sophistication
drive time	music style
Federal Communications Act of 1934	music time period
Federal Radio Commission (FRC)	narrowcasting
FM	national spot advertising
focus group	network
format	network advertising

network affiliates

O&O stations

on-air talent

payola

playlist

Radio Act of 1912

radio network

radiotelephony

syndicator

terrestrial

transistor

CONSTRUCTING MEDIA LITERACY

1   In what ways do you think new technologies will affect traditional radio?
2   If you had the power to recreate the formats of radio stations in your area, how would you do it?
3   How important do you think "localism" should be in radio? How would you describe what it should mean?
4   Let's say more and more Americans started taking mass transit to and from work. How would that affect terrestrial radio, and what (if anything) could radio stations do about it?

CASE STUDY   Radio's People Meter Ratings

The idea When Arbitron instituted portable people meter (PPM) ratings in Philadelphia and Houston in 2007, it changed the way advertisers and radio station owners thought of their audience. In Philadelphia, the first sets of ratings showed dramatic differences from the old diary method of keeping track of people's listening habits. Some stations even changed their formats because of the findings. The PPM is an example of how an audience measurement technology can change the nature of reality for a media industry about its audience. It deserves to be examined in more detail.

The method Using a periodical database, follow the discussions that radio and advertising executives have had over the past several years about problems with Arbitron's diary method and with the benefits and problems that the PPM technology would bring. If everyone understood the problems with the diary method, why were station owners loath to move over to the portable people meter? What were problems that Arbitron found when it tried to implement the new technology? How hard was it to roll out the technology in Philadelphia, in Houston, and beyond? Is it right to assume that the PPM gives the radio stations and their advertisers the correct read on what stations are most popular and when? Do you think it represents the last word on radio ratings?

Write a report of your findings that addresses these questions and this more sociological one: in what ways does the PPM experience show how an audience measurement technology can change the nature of reality for a media industry about its audience?

12 THE MOTION PICTURE INDUSTRY

After studying this chapter, you will be able to:

1 Explain the history of movies in the United States and how it affects the industry today

2 Analyze the production, distribution, and exhibition processes for theatrical motion pictures in the United States and recognize the major players in each realm

3 Describe how movies are financed, and how they make money through various exhibition arrangements

4 Analyze the relationship between movie distributors and theaters

5 Explain the impact of new technologies and globalization on the movie industry

6 Determine where you stand on issues involving the impact of the American movie industry on world culture

"The words 'Kiss Kiss Bang Bang' which I saw on an Italian movie poster, are perhaps the briefest statement imaginable of the basic appeal of movies."

– PAULINE KAEL, MOVIE CRITIC

Media Today

You get to the theater a bit late with your date on a Saturday night, hoping the movie you want to see isn't sold out. Just your luck—it is. You agree on one of the other movies that the theater is showing. Next question: will you share buttered popcorn? Your date says no (too greasy); how about some Raisinettes? Where do you want to sit? This seemed like a good place, but the person in front is too tall. It might pay to move. Next issue: where will you go when the movie ends? Ice cream? No, too fattening. Coffee?

Movies and dating seem linked, don't they? But while people on the dating circuit go to the movies more often than other people in the United States, movie theaters draw more than just the romantic crowd. Check out the Saturday and Sunday afternoon theater hordes around malls, and you'll see a lot of children and their parents. Married baby boomers with older kids attend movie theaters fairly often, and senior citizens frequent early evening ("twilight") shows.

As for the movies themselves, even if you don't actually see many of them, you're likely to learn about the most expensive ones that are coming out. The advertising and publicity surrounding such movies is so intensive that you can't fail to learn what the basic plot is and who the stars are. Along the way, you may learn about the enormous salaries certain stars are getting for making a single film. You may also hear stars explain why they chose to act in particular films and how much their screen characters relate to their real personalities. You also don't have to look hard to learn how much money top films are taking in at theater box offices around the United States.

This chapter goes beyond the glitz of movies to sketch what these reports rarely explain: how the motion picture industry actually works. What companies are involved in production, distribution, and exhibition? Where does the money come from to support these activities? To what extent are new media technologies changing the way motion picture executives do their jobs?

The answers to these questions form the overall theme of this chapter: that the motion picture industry is at the center of much popular culture production in the United States and throughout the world. Films that are made for the "big screen" often influence a variety of other businesses—from home video to television, from toys to clothing. Moreover, the ways in which the movie industry is changing in response to new technologies and the needs of media conglomerates raise important questions about the control of popular culture in the twenty-first century.

How and why did a handful of companies associated with a place called Hollywood become so influential in the creation of America's popular culture? To answer these questions, we have to go back in time to a period when moving pictures were associated with magic shows.

The Rise of Motion Pictures

Magicians were the master showmen of Europe and the United States in the 1800s. What most people in their audiences didn't know was how important projected images were in their acts. As early as the 1790s, magic performances used slides to project mystical pictures onto smoke rising from canisters in their darkened theaters. This "magic lantern" effect grew more sophisticated through the 1800s. It makes sense, then, that magicians were particularly interested in the experiments in creating, and even projecting, moving pictures that inventors in the latter part of the century were conducting.

In one way or another, these experiments took advantage of the phenomenon known as **persistence of vision**, in which the human eye continues to see an image for a fraction of a moment after the object is removed from sight. In the early 1800s, inventors created devices that took advantage of this phenomenon to fool the brain. All of these devices involved preparing a series of drawings of objects in which each drawing was slightly different from the one before it. When the drawings were made to move quickly (say, if they were pasted next to one another on the side of a revolving drum), it appeared to the viewer that the objects were moving. Try it yourself by making a flip-book with an object (a dot, a face) in a slightly different position on each page; the image really seems to move!

Using Photographic Images to Simulate Motion

While some inventors were trying to make still drawings appear to move, others were developing the same idea using photographic images to simulate motion. One particularly important figure in this blending was Edward Muybridge, who emigrated to the United States from England. In 1878, Leland Stanford, a wealthy sportsman, recruited Muybridge to settle a $25,000 bet that he had made; he had bet that all four feet of a galloping horse were sometimes off the ground at the same time. Muybridge set up twenty-four cameras close to one another at a racetrack to take photos as a horse ran by. Stanford got his money (the photographs showed all four feet off the ground), and Muybridge's work got inventors to think that motion picture photography might be possible. The trick was to be able to take twenty-four photographs with one camera rather than with twenty-four different cameras.

It was Thomas Edison and his assistant, William Dickson, who figured out how to solve this problem in 1889. Dickson discovered that the key was to use the flexible photographic film that had recently been invented by George Eastman (the founder of the Kodak film and camera company). The photographer would turn a crank, moving the flexible film in front of the lens at a constant speed. The result would be several photographs, each slightly different from the previous one. When the strip of film was developed and passed quickly in front of the eye, it gave the illusion of a moving object.

Just as he had misunderstood the potential of his recording machine, however (see Chapter 10), Edison misjudged the value of his moving-picture device, which he called a **kinetoscope**. He insisted that the only way to make money from it was to place it in a box into which individuals would have to drop coins in order to watch movies.

Two Frenchmen, Louis and Auguste Lumière, proved Edison wrong in 1894, demonstrating that popular interest could be whipped up and money could be made by projecting movies to large groups.

persistence of vision natural phenomenon in which the human eye continues to see an image for a fraction of a moment after the object is removed from sight

kinetoscope a moving-picture device, invented by Thomas Edison and his associates in 1892, that allowed one person at a time to watch a motion picture by looking through the viewer

Shown here are the photographs Edward Muybridge took to help Leland Stanford win his bet that a galloping horse sometimes has all four feet in the air at the same time. Can you see why a talented inventor like Thomas Edison would see the seeds of motion pictures in photos like these?

Edison Vitascope a projector that made the showing of film on a large screen possible; invented by Thomas Armat and C. Francis Jenkins, and premiered in 1896

The Lumières refused to sell their cameras or projectors. Instead, they trained people around the world to *show* their movies using their equipment. They focused on documenting "real life"—street scenes, parades, royalty. In contrast, Robert Paul, a competitor in England, sold moving-picture cameras and projectors to anyone who wanted them. Magicians were some of the first to recognize the power of this new technology and put it to use. They put it in their act as part of the whole business of illusion making.

When film projecting caught on in the United States and elsewhere, Edison rethought his movies-in-a-box approach. His agents quickly arranged to buy the rights to a projector invented by Thomas Armat and C. Francis Jenkins. Calling it the **Edison Vitascope**, the inventors arranged for its public debut on April 23, 1896, at Koster and Bial's Music Hall, a vaudeville site in New York City. (It's where Macy's 34th street department store now stands.) When the Vitascope premiered, the sensation of the evening was a film entitled *Rough Sea at Dover*, made by Robert Paul. The view of waves crashing on Dover beach was so realistic that people in the front rows actually shrank back in their seats, fearful of getting wet.

Edison's choice of location for the unveiling of his Vitascope film was significant. Unlike the Lumière brothers, who were interested in documenting real life, the films from Edison's company were typically silent "entertainment" performances. (An especially famous one, *The Kiss*, depicts a man's attempt to kiss a woman as they sit on a park bench.) In linking his moviemaking to entertainment, Edison was following the tradition of the many magicians who had used photographs, including moving ones. Although films documenting life were certainly to become an important area of filmmaking, the major thrust of commercial moviemaking focused on entertainment.

Films Become Mass Entertainment Media

Until 1903, a film typically was less than a minute long, consisted of a single shot, and was generally shown during breaks between vaudeville acts in places such as

The Edison Vitascope, as advertised in 1896, was a modified "Phantascope," jointly designed by C. Francis Jenkins and Thomas Armat. Armat sold his rights to Edison, who then claimed the modified projector (which he dubbed the Vitascope) as his own invention. In later years, however, Edison acknowledged that the device was the work of Armat.

Koster and Bial's Music Hall. Two filmmakers who helped to change that approach were Frenchman George Méliès and American Edwin S. Porter. Méliès, a magician and graphic artist, made fantasy films with elaborately painted scenery and skillful camera effects; his film *A Trip to the Moon* is particularly well known for introducing animation and science fiction narrative to the movie business. Porter, who was experimenting with more realistic genres (he made *The Life of an American Fireman* and *The Great Train Robbery*, among other films), showed that moviemakers could go beyond simply filming stage plays and create a new art form through the use of imaginative editing and camera work. Along with close-ups and other innovations, *The Great Train Robbery* has a startling ending: a cowboy points his gun directly at the audience and shoots.

With the development of the film narrative came larger and larger audiences. Theaters called **nickelodeons** (so named because they charged an admission price of a nickel per person) sprouted up throughout the United States. The immigrants who were streaming into the United States from eastern and southern Europe in the early 1900s were especially attracted to nickelodeons—not only because of their low cost, but because the medium was silent. Stories were told through mime, with title cards inserted into the films at special moments to tell viewers exactly

nickelodeon an early movie theater that charged an admission price of five cents per person

what was going on. Because a filmmaker could change the language of the titles fairly simply to suit a particular audience, and because most viewers could usually follow the action even without the titles, the movies were popular with people who had just moved to the United States and didn't speak English.

The MPPC and the Fight Over Patents   By 1910, the demand for movies had become so great that small movie-production firms, many owned by immigrants, were churning out many films. The biggest film companies—Edison, Biograph, and Vitagraph—all based in the New York City area, were alarmed at the competition and at the fact that the small filmmaking firms generally were not paying royalties on the patents on camera and projection equipment that the big companies owned. In 1908, the ten largest companies banded together to form a trust called the **Motion Picture Patents Company** (**MPPC**), also known as the Movie Trust, the Edison Trust, or simply the Trust. Through this coalition, which lasted from 1908 to 1912, these producers and distributors attempted to gain complete control of the motion-picture industry in the United States, primarily through control of patents. The coalition's intention was to sue any company making or projecting movies without getting permission from the trust.

The MPPC entered into a contract with Eastman Kodak Company, the largest manufacturer of raw film stock, under which film would be supplied only to licensed members of the coalition. It even went so far as to dictate the form of the movies produced by its members and licensees. It decreed that movies should not be longer than ten minutes, because audiences would not tolerate longer films. The trust also refused to allow the names of actors to be listed on the screen, fearing that if actors became well known, they would ask for raises.

The MPPC, however, failed to stop its upstart competitors, many of whom were Eastern European Jewish immigrants who were intent on making their fortunes in a trade that, unlike railroading, auto building, and other entrepreneurial businesses, had few start-up costs. They broke the MPPC's filmmaking rules—by making longer films and revealing stars' names—and they succeeded. To escape from the demands of the MPPC, and to find whether that would enable them to film year-round, many of them moved their studios from New York to a suburb of Los Angeles, California, called Hollywood. The MPPC, for its part, was investigated by the federal government for antitrust violations and was dissolved by court order in 1917. (See Chapter 3 for a discussion of antitrust laws.) By 1920, the MPPC had disappeared altogether, along with the filmmaking companies that had once belonged to it.

The new immigrant-run studios, on the other hand, prospered—some eventually became the major film studios we know today—Columbia Pictures, Paramount, Warner Brothers, Universal, Twentieth Century Fox, and Metro-Goldwyn-Mayer (MGM). Not only were large audiences in the United States eager to see the movies these studios were making, but markets in Europe and elsewhere were wide open to them as well. Part of the reason was that the young European film industry had been destroyed during World War I. The American companies saw an opportunity for worldwide distribution of their products. By 1918, U.S. movie firms controlled about 80 percent of the world market.

Vertical Integration and the Advent of the Studio System

Keeping control of that business was a high priority. The immigrant studio chiefs were quite aware that they had defeated the previous movie regime, and they didn't want the same thing to happen to them. To protect and extend their

Motion Picture Patents Company (MPPC)   also known as the Movie Trust, Edison Trust, or the Trust, this coalition, which lasted from 1908 to 1912, was organized by the ten largest movie companies, whose producers and distributors attempted to gain complete control of the motion-picture industry in the United States primarily through control of patents

vertical integration an organization's control over a media product from production through distribution to exhibition

studio system the approach used by American film companies to turn out their products from the early 1920s to the 1950s

star system an operation designed to find and cultivate actors under long-term contracts, with the intention of developing those actors into famous "stars" who would enhance the profitability of the studio's films

A and B movie units an element of the studio system in which films were divided into two categories of production

A films expensively made productions featuring glamorous, high paid movie stars

B films lower-budget films that were made quickly

series pictures movies that feature the same characters, storylines, and sets across a number of films

block booking a tactic under the studio system in which distribution executives ensured that theaters showed both their A films and their B films; if theater owners refused to carry a certain number of a studio's B films, they would not be allowed access to certain A films produced by that studio

companies' power, they engaged in one or both of two key strategies: vertical integration and the studio system.

Vertical Integration Recall from Chapter 2 that in the mass media industries, **vertical integration** is control of all steps in the process from creator to audiences—production, distribution, and exhibition. Vertical integration dictated that a major film company should possess moviemaking facilities (the studio), a division that distributed its films to theaters (its distribution arm), and many theaters in the most important areas. If a firm had all these activities under its control, competitors could not stop its movies from being shown to the public.

The Studio System From the early 1920s to the 1950s, the **studio system** was the approach the movie companies used to turn out their products efficiently. One element of this process was the **star system**. This operation was designed to find and cultivate actors under long-term contracts, with the intention of developing those actors into famous "stars" who would enhance the profitability of the studio's films. Another element was the division of the studio into **A and B movie units**. **A films** were expensively made productions featuring glamorous, highly paid stars. **B films** were made more quickly, with much smaller budgets.

Sometimes the studios produced **series pictures**—movies that featured the same characters (and actors and sets) across a number of films, thus lowering the costs and increasing profits. The A films were the prestige films; they were designed to get audiences excited about them so that the audiences would think well of the companies that made them. The movie companies also used A films to force independent theaters (those that the film companies didn't own) to carry their films. Distribution executives simply said that if theater owners didn't carry a certain number of B films, they would not get the A pictures. They called this practice **block booking**.

Alone or together, vertical integration and the studio system kept the seven immigrant-built firms—sometimes known as **the majors**—at the top of the movie industry during the 1920s, 1930s, and 1940s. Small companies emerged to create niche pictures (children's films, comedy shorts, documentaries, and the occasional big drama), but the majors ran the industry.

This is not to say that times were always healthy for all of these companies. During the 1920s, and especially during the Great Depression years of the 1930s, many firms had a hard time staying afloat. In fact, it was during the late 1920s that a struggling Warner Brothers decided to gamble on a technique for adding talking and singing to movies. After experimenting with short **talkies**, or films that featured sound as well as images, the company released *The Jazz Singer* in 1927 starring the vaudeville singing sensation Al Jolson. The film was a hit, and it sparked a worldwide conversion of movie theaters to handle sound. A new era had begun. By the early 1930s, the majors were only turning out movies with sound.

Self-regulation and the Film Industry

Although special circumstances such as the desperate financial situation at Warner Brothers sometimes led a major film company to take risks, generally these firms tried to lower their risks by controlling their environment through strategies like the studio system and the star system. Another way that the majors controlled their environment was by adopting self-regulation in response to public controversies involving the movies they created. The problem was this: many people around the country believed that the violence and sex in the movies Hollywood

Star of stage, screen, radio, and vaudeville, Al Jolson has the monumental credit of being the first person to speak in a feature film (in *The Jazz Singer* as shown in this photo). Jolson often performed in what is known as "blackface"—where white men blackened their faces and performed songs and dances in the style of African Americans—a controversial part of the earlier era of show business. Ironically, *The Jazz Singer* and the advent of sound led to the demise of blackface's popularity. With sound came a greater emphasis on realism, and it soon became impossible for the motion picture industry to maintain that white actors in blackface could realistically portray African-American characters.

was turning out were poisoning youngsters' minds and debasing American culture. Film titles such as *Traffic in Souls* (about prostitution) and drug, sex, and murder scandals in the movie community linked Hollywood with sin as well as with glamour.

Complicating the situation for the studio heads was a 1919 Supreme Court ruling that movies were entertainment, and were therefore not protected by the First Amendment's free-speech guarantees (see Chapter 3). As states and towns passed censorship laws, the studios feared that they would have to make different versions of movies for different areas of the country. Instead, in 1922 they formed a self-regulatory body called the **Motion Picture Producers and Distributors of America**. Headed by Will Hays, it created a code that defined movie morality and had the power to enforce it. The plan worked: with the advent of the Hays Office (as it was sometimes called) the majors managed to stave off government regulation and keep the studios in control of their product. It also set a precedent for self-regulation in other media industries, including radio, television, and even comic books.

New Challenges for the Film Industry

By the late 1940s, the major U.S. movie companies were riding high. The difficult Depression years of the 1930s were behind them: people were going to neighborhood movie theaters an average of twice a week or more, and the studio system was working like a well-oiled machine. Just then, though, things began to fall apart. Two developments took place that led to major changes.

Anti-trust Woes   One was the 1948 settlement of an antitrust suit by the U.S. Justice Department against Paramount, Warner, MGM, and Fox—the majors that

the majors   the immigrant-built motion picture studios at the top of the movie industry during the 1920s, 1930s, and 1940s—Columbia Pictures, Paramount, Warner Brothers, Universal, Twentieth Century Fox, and Metro-Goldwyn-Mayer (MGM). The majors in the early twenty-first century are Disney, Warner Brothers, Twentieth Century Fox, Universal, Paramount, and Sony (Columbia)

talkies   films that featured sound (such as singing, talking, sound effects, etc.) as well as images

Motion Picture Producers and Distributors of America also known as the Hays Office, this self-regulatory body of the film industry created and enforced a code that defined movie morality, setting a precedent for self-regulation in other media industries

Hattie McDaniel

MEDIA PROFILE

Back in the days when Hollywood allotted very few major roles to African-Americans, Hattie McDaniel appeared in more than three hundred films. In 1940, she won the best supporting actress award for her role as Mammy in the film *Gone with the Wind*. This achievement made her the first African American to win an Academy Award and helped her to earn the reputation as the most successful black movie actress of her time.

Unfortunately, most of McDaniel's accomplishments were criticized by progressives in the black community. In almost every film she appeared in, McDaniel played the role of a maid or cook, a fact that did not go unnoticed. It was in 1935 that McDaniel first drew criticism for her work in *The Little Colonel*. Many members of the black community felt that her role as the happy black servant reinforced stereotypes that blacks had been content with slavery. Five years later the NAACP criticized McDaniel for her role as Mammy, even though many journalists in the black press viewed her work in *Gone with the Wind* positively.

In the late 1940s, Walter White, the executive secretary of the NAACP, began an intense crusade to diversify the roles played by blacks in Hollywood movies. He openly attacked any role that "smacked of Uncle Tomism, or Mammyism" and singled out McDaniel in particular. She stood up to her opponents and responded, "Hell, I'd rather play a maid than be one," a quote that became forever linked to the actress.

McDaniel firmly believed that actors ought to be allowed to choose any role they wanted. Born to a family of entertainers in 1895, she dropped out of high school to become a minstrel performer. Before making her film debut in 1931, the actress also dabbled in radio, worked in a club, and took a variety of menial jobs to support herself during the Depres-

Hattie McDaniel in *Song of the South*

sion. Having lived through tough times, McDaniel had no intention of throwing it all away.

Toward the end of her life, Hattie McDaniel won the starring role in *The Beulah Show*. At the height of its success in 1950, this program attracted a multiracial audience of 20 million Americans each night. Although she was once again playing the role of a maid, McDaniel generally received approval from the NAACP and the Urban League for her comedic work as Beulah. Playing this character allowed McDaniel to prove that blacks could perform comedic roles without degradation. McDaniel was so committed to this show that she continued to work on it following a heart attack she suffered in 1951. Sadly, she succumbed to breast cancer one year later, leaving behind a rich legacy in Hollywood.

Sources: *Contemporary Black Biography* (Detroit: Gale Research Inc., 1993); and Al Young, "I'd Rather Play a Maid than Be One," *New York Times*, October 15, 1989, Sec. 7, p. 13.

owned theaters. The suit had claimed that these companies' vertical integration was preventing producers who were not affiliated with them from getting their movies exhibited. The settlement forced the firms to split off their production and distribution divisions from the theaters where the films were exhibited. Government officials hoped that these actions would weaken the studios and encourage competition.

The Advent of Television   The second development of the late 1940s that led to major changes in the movie industry was the commercial introduction of television. Though it may have seemed fairly trivial to studio executives at the time, it turned out to be profoundly important. Chapters 9 and 11 note the major consequences that the flood of TV viewing had on the magazine and radio industries. The effect of television on the movie industry was also great. Curiously, those now-aging movie entrepreneurs who had fought the MPPC and created companies known the world over were unable to see the threat that radio-with-pictures posed for their business. Although they had ample opportunity to acquire TV stations and networks in a major way, they declined to do so. As attendance at movie theaters dropped, studio executives argued that the drop was temporary—it was a by-product of the postwar baby boom, which was keeping parents with babies at home. At any rate, they refused to help the new industry by allowing stations to telecast their movies. Yet by the mid-1950s, the movie studios realized that television was not going away. After Warner Brothers and the Walt Disney Company (one of the smaller movie firms) made deals to produce programs for the ABC TV network, the gates opened wide and all the studios rushed in. Hollywood was now in the TV business.

From the beginning of their participation in the new medium, movie executives realized that television was a place where their B pictures—the inexpensive products that had been their bread and butter through the 1920s, 1930s, and 1940s—could be shown. The challenge now became what to do with their traditional exhibition arena, the theaters. During the 1950s, movie studio executives believed that they could entice people back to "the big screen" by emphasizing its bigness. They made movies with ultra-wide projection technologies such as Todd-AO, Cinemascope, and Cinerama (think of today's *IMAX*). They even tried 3-D pictures, for which members of the audience had to wear special glasses. Although individual films such as *The Ten Commandments* drew huge crowds, the executives began to realize that neither ultra-wide screens nor 3-D gimmicks were going to bring the U.S. population back to the twice-a-week moviegoing habit that had been common during the 1940s.

Increasingly, studio executives no longer saw theatrical movies as part of Americans' weekly habits (now that they had TV); rather, they saw movies as individual events that had to lure people into theaters. The lack of audience predictability meant that the well-entrenched star system had at last become too costly. So the studios got rid of it, preferring instead to let talent agents find and cultivate actors and actresses.

Under this new way of seeing theatrical films as special events, movie executives began to release their most expensive films at times when most people were at leisure (for example, during summer vacation and around Thanksgiving and Christmas) and had the time to go to a movie. Executives also believed that people wanted to see stories in the movies that they could not see on television. TV executives, wary of the FCC's ability to withdraw licenses, had picked up a code of good practices that was modeled after the one used by network radio and the Hays Office. Now movie people began to question whether their code was too rigid.

Happily for movie executives, in 1952 the U.S. Supreme Court had overturned its 1919 ruling and stated that movies were entitled to First Amendment protection. The upshot was that as the 1950s gave way to the 1960s, producers and directors increasingly ignored the Hays Code and turned out pictures with scenes of violence, sex, addiction, and other subjects that would never have appeared a decade earlier. To replace the code, the industry began a very different self-regulatory activity: a **film ratings** system in which an independent panel of

film ratings system   the system by which a motion picture rating is assigned to a film by the Motion Picture Association of America (MPAA), with regard to the amount and degree of profanity, violence and sex found in the film

471

Increasing the "Gross" at the Box Office

IS IT ETHICAL?

Is it ethical for films to keep inching into formerly taboo territory in order to get laughs and make extra money at the box office? *Wedding Crashers* and *40-year-old Virgin* both presented comic situations that would have been unthinkable for a mainstream picture ten years earlier, yet each film played to packed theaters and grossed well over $200 million and $100 million respectively at the box office.

Michael DeLuca, head of production at New Line Cinema, points out that each generation becomes more tolerant than the previous one: "We are now dealing with a generation where the cat's out of the bag with every single subject…Society as a whole has moved into a taboo-free zone." Many producers justify their movies as giving the public what it wants, noting that anything too risqué will drive away audiences. Proponents of this view see the movies themselves as self-regulating—what meets the broadest tastes of audiences will make the most money.

"You have to measure your starting point where the last guy left off," said comedian and filmmaker Keenan Ivory Wayans. Other defenders point out that Charlie Chaplin, who is now considered innocent, was once looked upon as rude and dirty.

Critics claim that we are seeing a spiraling of lewd films that attempt to appeal to the lowest common denominator. Studios target frequent movie-goers in their teens and twenties, hoping that crudeness will enable them to sell tickets to these people. Many critics charge that adolescents copy the behavior they see in movies, leading to increased obscenity and the lessening of morals throughout society. During the 2000 presidential election, both candidates expressed concern about the movies coming from Hollywood. "I don't support censorship but I do believe that we ought to talk plainly to the Hollywood moguls and people that produce this stuff and explain the consequences," candidate George W. Bush said during the third debate.

What do you think?

Sources: "Exchanges Between Candidates in the Third Presidential Debate," *New York Times*, October 18, 2000, p. A26; Robert Welkos, "Movies Test the Limits of Bad Taste," *Los Angeles Times*, June 22, 2000, p. A1; "Top 20 Grosses of 2005", Exhibitor Relations Co., accessed on 02/25/2008 at http://www.ercboxoffice.com/erc/premium/index.php?d=39; Scott Bowles, "Hollywood Considers Ad Campaign to Boost Attendance," *USA Today*, March 16, 2006, p. 3D; Stephen Silvis, "Idiot's Delight," *Prague Post*, January 11. 2006; Sharon Waxman, "Hollywood Losing Biggest fans to Digital World," *New York Times*, October 10, 2005, p 14.

viewers assigned labels to movies that indicated their appropriateness for audiences of different ages (as discussed in Chapter 3). This meant that the film industry itself would no longer approve or disapprove a film's content; instead, it would provide film consumers with advance warnings so that they could make their own decisions about which films to see and which films to avoid. (The percent of films with each rating classification is given in Figure 12.1.)

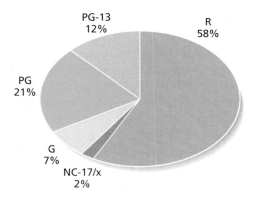

Figure 12.1

Percent of Films by Rating, 1986–2006

Changes in Technology

Between the 1960s and the 1990s came an unending stream of inventions that were reshaping the distribution and exhibition of movies in the twenty-first century. The development of the home videocassette recorder, initially opposed by Hollywood, quickly became a benefit as the studios developed a market in films to the home that eventually exceeded the revenues they were bringing in from theaters. The VCR gave way to the digital video disc (DVD) that continued to be a crucial element in the profits moviemakers earned. Also critical to the movie studios were cable and satellite technologies in ways that spawned hundreds of viewing options. Many of those licensed movies for viewing, and so became still more places for movie firms to make money from films. The rise of the broadband Internet in the mid-2000s provided yet another place where movies could be shown. A downside of these technologies for movie executives is that they made it easy to create counterfeit versions of Hollywood films. The movie industry fought bitterly against this activity in the United States and around the world.

An Overview of the Modern Motion Picture Industry

The most appropriate name for the enterprise that we're dealing with in this chapter is the theatrical motion picture industry. That is because the business is set up in such a way that much of its output (movies) initially goes to theaters. It is true that virtually all **theatrical films** (sometimes called **feature films**) now made commercially in the United States appear in nontheatrical locations after they have completed their runs in movie theaters in the United States and abroad. These movies are typically turned into videos for rental or sale; shown in hotels, airplanes, and homes on pay-per-view systems; shown on cable, satellite, and broadcast TV, and more. Still, "the movie industry" continues to mean the industry that produces films that will first be exhibited ("featured") in theaters.

At the beginning of the twenty-first century, Americans are purchasing about 1.5 billion tickets a year to see theatrical films, spending over $9 billion (the box office receipts, or the sum of money taken in for admission) at an average price of a bit over $6.50 per ticket (see Tables 12.1 and 12.2). That $6.50 may seem low

theatrical film or feature film a film created to be shown first in traditional movie theaters; once these films have had their run at movie theaters, often they are redistributed as home videos and DVDs for rental or for sale, as pay-per-view films in hotels and in homes, as in-flight movies on airlines, and as featured films on cable, satellite, and broadcast television channels

Table 12.1 **Domestic Gross Box Office Receipts, 1991–2006**	
Year	**Box office gross (USD millions)**
2006	9,487.8
2005	8,991.2
2004	9,539.2
2003	9,488.5
2002	9,519.6
2001	8,412.5
2000	7,660.7

(Continued on following page)

Table 12.1 (continued)

Year	Box office gross (USD millions)
1999	7,448.0
1998	6,949.0
1997	6,365.9
1996	5,911.5
1995	5,493.5
1994	5,396.2
1993	5,154.2
1992	4,871.0
1991	4,803.2
1990	5,021.8
1989	5,033.4
1988	4,458.4
1987	4,252.9
1986	3,778.0

Source: Motion Picture Association of America.

Table 12.2 Average Annual Admission Price at U.S. Movie Theatres, 1996–2006

Year	Avg. annual admission price (USD)
2006	$6.55
2005	$6.41
2004	$6.21
2003	$6.03
2002	$5.81
2001	$5.66
2000	$5.39
1999	$5.08
1998	$4.69
1997	$4.59
1996	$4.42

Source: Motion Picture Association of America.

Table 12.3   **Admissions by Age Group, 2006**

Age	Percentage of U.S. Admissions	Percentage of U.S. Population
12–24	36	22
25–29	10	8
30–39	18	17
40–49	16	19
50–59	9	15
60 +	9	20

The total admissions in 2006 were 1.3 billion.
Source: Motion Picture Association of America.

in view of what you pay to see a film, but keep in mind that this price includes discounts for senior citizens and children. Moreover, prices in some parts of the country are a good deal lower than those in other areas. In New York City, for example, moviegoers in Manhattan typically pay $11 per person or more to see a new movie. Across the river in some parts of Brooklyn, the price might be a couple of dollars lower.

Going to the movies continues to be an activity that is most common among young people. Around 36 percent of all tickets for movies in the United States are purchased by people aged 12–24, even though these people make up only 22 percent of the nation's population. People 25–29 years old represent 10 percent of the ticket holders, which is very close to their percentage in the population, whereas Americans 60 years of age and older, who make up about 20 percent of the population, account for 9 percent of the admissions (see Table 12.3).

During the past decade, between 450 and 600 movies a year made it to around 35,000 U.S. movie screens. Industry executives tend to pay most attention to the movies that bring in more than $200 million at the U.S. box office; they call such films **blockbusters** (see Table 12.4). There aren't very many blockbusters each year, but the ones that are tend to bring in a high percentage of the money that theatrical films as a whole make at the box office. In 2006, one film (*Pirates of the Caribbean: Dead Man's Chest*) exceeded $300 million at the box office; it made $423 million. Five movies made more than $200 million, and twelve brought in over $100 million. Together, the top 10 movies of 2006 brought in $2.2 billion, which comprised 23 percent of total domestic box office spending.

Movie executives pay attention to more than just U.S. theaters, however. What movie executives call the "international" (that is, non-U.S.) marketplace has been expanding rapidly. Around the world, moviegoing has been encouraged by the building of modern, air-conditioned **multiplexes**, or theaters with eight to fifteen screens, and **megaplexes**, or theaters with more than sixteen screens. As a result, box office receipts in the international sector grew substantially faster than U.S. box office revenues. In fact, from 2001 to 2006, the percentage of international receipts from outside the United States moved consistently upward, from 50 percent in 2001 to 54 percent in 2003 to 64 percent in 2006.

Radiating out from Hollywood are decisions and activities that influence the films that a huge number of people around the world see in their neighborhood theaters and, later, on their DVD and TV sets. Consequently, a large part of the

blockbuster   a film that brings in more than $200 million at the box office

multiplex   a modern, air-conditioned building that houses between eight and fifteen screens and has the capacity to exhibit a number of different films at the same time

megaplex   a modern, air-conditioned building that houses sixteen or more screens and has the capacity to exhibit a number of different films at the same time

Movie studios produce relatively few blockbuster films each year. However, the small number of very successful films like *Pirates of the Caribbean: Dead Man's Chest*, starring Johnny Depp, which earned $423 million in 2006, can generate a high percentage of the money that theatrical films as a whole make at the box office.

business focuses on getting films and people together in theaters. What does the "Hollywood" way of doing business look like? Let's start with production.

Production in the Motion Picture Industry

People tend to think that when they see the symbols for Twentieth Century Fox, Universal Pictures, Warner Brothers, and other famous Hollywood firms at the start of films, this means that those companies produced the movies. In most cases, however, they didn't.

Table 12.4 **All Time Top Ten Grossing Domestic Films**

Rank	Title	U.S. distributor and release date	Gross
1	*Titanic*	Paramount, 1997	$600,788,188
2	*Star Wars: Episode IV—A New Hope*	Fox, 1977 (re-released in 1997)	$460,998,007
3	*Shrek 2*	Dreamworks, 2004	$437,212,000
4	*E.T.—The Extra Terrestrial*	Universal, 1982	$434,974,579
5	*Star Wars: Episode I—The Phantom Menace*	Fox, 1999	$431,088,301
6	*Pirates of the Caribbean: Dead Man's Chest*	Buena Vista, 2006	$423,416,000
7	*Spider Man*	Sony, 2002	$407,681,000
8	*Star Wars: Episode III—Revenge of the Sith*	Fox, 2005	$380,270,577
9	*Lord of the Rings: Return of the King*	New Line, 2003	$377,019,252
10	*Spider Man 2*	Sony, 2004	$373,377,893

Source: All Time Top 1000 Grossing Films (U.S. Domestic Ranks in Millions) http://www.movieweb.com/movies/boxoffice/alltime.php, accessed 2/28/08.

The Role of the Majors

The companies that people most associate with Hollywood are called the **majors**. They are the most powerful companies in the movie business. The majors in the early twenty-first century are Disney, Warner Brothers, Twentieth Century Fox, Universal, Paramount, and Sony (Columbia).

Despite their prominence and power, these firms create only a small fraction (often one-third or less) of the movies to which their names are attached. The reason that their names are on the screen is that they are the distributors of the films. The films are often produced by other companies.

Distinguishing Between Production and Distribution

The distinction between production and distribution in the movie industry is a critical one to understand. Film production firms are involved in coming up with story ideas, finding scriptwriters, hiring the personnel needed to make the movie, and making sure the work is carried out on time and on budget. Film distribution firms, in contrast, are responsible for finding theaters in which to show the movies around the world and for promoting the films to the public. Distribution firms often contribute money toward the production firms' costs of making the film.

The one generalization we can make is that when you see the phrase "a Universal release," for example, you should be aware that it does not necessarily mean that the company's studio arm has fully financed and produced the movie. While Universal's studio does fully produce movies that its distribution division circulates to theaters, most of the films that Universal deals with as a distributor come from production firms such as Beacon. Universal typically kicks in a portion of the money, but the production firm takes on a lot of the risk itself.

The Role of Independent Producers

The example given here used Universal, but the same situation applies to all the major distributors. Why don't the majors produce all the movies that they distribute? The reason is straightforward: for a distribution firm to maintain a strong relationship with theaters, it has to provide a strong roster of films to help them fill their seats. If a distributor offers theaters fewer than fifteen or twenty movies a year, theaters will not take the distributor seriously and it will not be an influential force in the movie industry. Yet movies are both very expensive and very risky to make. They typically cost tens of millions of dollars each, and many of them lose money. A firm such as Universal cannot afford to risk the amount of cash that would be required to fully fund many films. Consequently, Universal's own studio generates five to ten films itself, and the company picks up the rest of its distribution roster from independent producers—that is, from production firms that are not owned by distributors.

Consider the 2007 movie *3:10 to Yuma*, which was released by the **independent distributor** Lionsgate. *Variety* learned that it was mostly financed by its executive producer Ryan Kavanaugh and his company Relativity Media, with Lionsgate acting as a minority investor of $42.5 million on the $87.5 million-plus project.[1]

independent distributor
a company other than the major studios that distributes movies

The Process of Making a Movie

If you speak to executives of a production company, they will tell you that the process by which a movie goes from an idea in someone's head to a film that the

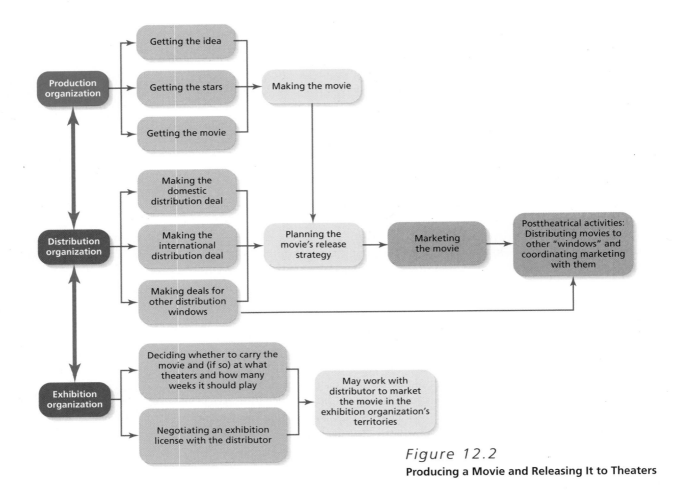

Figure 12.2

Producing a Movie and Releasing It to Theaters

distributor can ship to theaters is typically time-consuming and torturous as well as expensive (see Figure 12.2). They will also say that overseeing the filming and editing of their movies is only a small part of what their company does. Other important steps involve getting the idea, getting the stars, and getting the money. Only after these steps have been performed can the activities involved in actually making the movie take place. Let's look briefly at each stage in this process.

Getting the Idea An idea for a movie can come from virtually anywhere. Producers have gotten ideas for movies from places as diverse as television shows, comic books, short stories, and newspaper articles. Scriptwriters and books have traditionally been the most common sources, however.

Plot ideas from scriptwriters often come to production firms from the writers' **talent agents**, individuals who represent various creative personnel (such as actors, directors, authors, and screenwriters) and aim to link them with production firms in exchange for a percentage of the creator's revenues from the finished product. An agent's job is to gain a reputation around Hollywood for having good creative and business ideas so that when he or she knocks on a producer's door with a suggestion, the producer will listen. Agents know what has been popular. They also know what kinds of films certain producers like to make.

An idea for a film from an established writer will sometimes be only a few lines that go to the heart of the plot. ("Stallone in a busy tunnel under Manhattan's East River that's going to get crushed.") If the producer likes the idea, the writer

talent agent an individual who represents creative personnel (such as actors, directors, authors, and screenwriters) and aims to link them with production firms in exchange for a percentage of the creator's revenues from the finished product

might be paid to write a detailed outline, which is called a **treatment**. If the producer likes the treatment, the next step might be payment for a full script. Less-established writers may write an entire script without getting paid. That is called writing a script **on spec**. The writer's agent will pass around a spec script to various production firms in the hope that they will bid for it. Attractive scripts can fetch hundreds of thousands of dollars or more.

The second traditional source for film ideas—books—became especially popular in the late 1990s. Producers had long looked for successful books with stories that fit the types and budgets of films that they expected to make; now they were furiously trying to beat one another to new books, or even books that had not yet been published, with stories that seemed to suggest a cinematic gold mine. *The Horse Whisperer* was an early example of the stampede. In 1994, while the book was still in manuscript, the writer's agent orchestrated an auction of film rights that netted the author $3 million. The amounts involved can go much higher than that. According to the trade magazine *Variety*, producer Dino de Laurentiis plunked down $10 million in 1999 for film rights to Thomas Harris's sequel to the successful book and movie *Silence of the Lambs* before the sequel hit the bookstores. It was a shrewd move. The movie that resulted from that investment, *Hannibal*, was a major hit of 2001.

In movie-industry jargon, when top production executives approve the making of a movie, they give it the **green light**. Wherever the idea for a movie comes from, and however good it sounds to producers, it will have the chance of being given a green light only if it fits a movie production firm's ideas about what will succeed in the marketplace. Production company heads have ideas about segments of the market that are useful to target with particular types of films. Teens and young adults, for example, are thought to like horror films (*Halloween*). Women are thought to like romantic comedies such as *What Women Want*, while men are typed as adventure-movie (*The Bourne Ultimatum*) or gross-out film (*Superbad*) oriented. People over 45 are the targets of British-made small films that have a subtle comedic or deeply dramatic sensibility, or are just a bit unusual. Think of *The Queen* or *Atonement*. Of course, many women and men attend the movies together, so executives often try to leaven movies targeted to one type of audience with some material that another type would like. An adventure film will often have a strong romantic component, for example.

The rising importance of the non-U.S. market to Hollywood has meant that when executives green light a film they think about its potential around the world. Moreover, filmmakers in a number of countries, particularly in the European Union, have been voicing concerns that U.S.-based firms have been exporting films around the world but not giving anything back to other filmmaking communities. The potentially large audience for U.S. producers and distributors in China is hard to reach because the Chinese government limits the numbers of films that can be brought into the country.

These two developments have led major and independent production and distribution firms in a number of directions. Most prominently, the desire to attract international audiences has led them to make action movies that emphasize violence and hair-raising stunts and that require little knowledge of English to understand. Some of these films have been made in the United States; think of the Fast and the Furious films and those in the James Bond series. Others have been coproductions that blend the investment and production talents of a U.S.-based firm and a firm of another country. That has been taking place in France and India, for example.

The concern with the international market affects U.S.-made films as well. Historically, most U.S.-made comedies do not "travel" well, so a budget for a

treatment a detailed outline of an initial pitch to executives of a production or distribution firm; if the executives approve of the treatment, they will probably order a script to be written

on spec writing a script for a film without a contract to do so, with the hope that when the script is passed along to various production firms by the scriptwriter's agent, it will be bid for and purchased

green light a term used to describe production and distribution executives' approval of the making of a particular film

comedy will typically have to be low enough to be profitable from U.S. revenues alone. Adventures do travel well, and some action stars—Jackie Chan and Sylvester Stallone are examples—do better outside than inside the United States. Increasingly, U.S. firms are making movies for other parts of the world, with the notion that they may make money even if they don't do well in the United States. Universal Pictures was deeply involved in funding and distributing the latest installment of the British Mr Bean comedy in 2007 (*Mr Bean's Holiday*); the films traditionally do terrifically in the U.K. and very well in parts of Europe, but are weak in the United States.

Getting the Stars   When a production firm purchases a script or book, its executives typically have certain actors and directors in mind. Sometimes a major actor may get control of a property with the idea of starring in a film based on it. The actor's agent may even go further in dealing with production firms that are interested in the project: the agent may take a number of people from his or her roster of clients—actors, a well-known director, a highly regarded cinematographer—and tell production firms that the deal comes in a package. To many observers of the film industry, the fact that a number of talent agencies have the power to organize such major film deals with production firms is evidence that talent agencies are among Hollywood's most powerful players.

The money to pay actors and other creative personnel must, of course, come from the overall budget. The stratospheric salary requirements of the most popular stars (some make more than $20 million a picture) mean that only the major

Hollywood Meets Bollywood

Bollywood, India's Mumbai-based film industry, is the largest producer of films in the world. Churning out two hundred pictures a year in sixteen different South Indian languages, Bollywood is responsible for more tickets than any film industry in the world. Seeing dollar signs where there have previously been rupees, American film studios and production companies are looking to get in on the action.

Saawariya, the title of a Hindi film meaning 'beloved,' is a traditional Bollywood flick made by an Indian director and cast, complete with bright colors, melodrama and song-and-dance routines. However, unlike all previous Hindi-language Bollywood films, *Saawariya* was produced by Hollywood. Sony Pictures, pioneering what will undoubtedly be an increasing move of American studios into Indian markets, is hoping that *Saawariya*, and films like it, can break into the Indian market and supplement American audiences. This might be a difficult proposition, however, as the American studio is attempting to break into a marketplace dominated by domestic films.

In 2006, homegrown films in India and the United States accounted for around 95 percent of each country's box office sales, a percentage that dwarfs what is seen throughout Europe and Asia. In India, this translated to about 1,000 films and $2.1 billion. But the market is expected to expand to $4.4 billion in 2011, and Sony, like the other American companies that have Bollywood projects in the works, is hoping that its films will be able to fill a gap in the Indian film market that isn't satisfied by traditional American exports alone.

Walt Disney is also getting in on the action, partnering with Indian studio Yash Raj Films to make animated movies for Indians. On a larger scale, Warner Brothers is planning to produce three to six Bollywood films a year, all made with Indian talent. As of now, the rule seems to be replication rather than reinvention. In a nation where movies are the primary form of entertainment, Bollywood is still king.

Source: Anand Giridharadas, *Business Times Singapore*, August 9, 2007, via Nexis.com

studies and a few other production companies that expect to make extremely expensive movies can afford to hire these stars. Sometimes a production firm will make a deal with a famous actor or director in which the actor or director takes a lower salary but gets a percentage of the money that the production firm receives from the distributor. This is called a **back-end deal** or **percentage of the gross** in movie jargon. After his hit film *Borat*, Sacha Baron Cohen made a deal with Universal Pictures that included a payment of about $20 million for the rights to his next film *Bruno*, plus a "back-end" deal that guaranteed 15 percent of box office takings.[2]

Often back-end deals take effect before the production firm breaks even. Only the stars involved in the films have an opportunity to negotiate such deals, however. Some in the industry, in fact, have suggested that the high salaries stars are demanding are leading producers to hold off on hiring established, experienced actors in secondary roles in favor of more-affordable relative newcomers. Rules about actors' minimum pay and working conditions have been established through deals between the Screen Actors Guild and the major production firms. Similar arrangements for screenwriters have been made by the Writer's Guild of America. These **guilds** are unions established by writers, directors, and/or actors to protect their mutual interests and maintain standards. "Hot" writers and directors, like star actors, can demand far more than the minimum for their work, including back-end deals.

The guilds provide the less highly paid workers with a collective voice. Sometimes that results in a strike, as in 2007 and 2008, when writers expressed their frustration when the major studios and the Writers Guild of America could not come to terms with the Alliance of Motion Picture and Television Producers about how much pay the writers should receive from the major studios for work that appears on the Internet. The strike of over 10,000 Writers Guild members crippled Hollywood. It ended production on TV dramas and comedies, caused the Golden Globe Awards to be canceled, and delayed a number of movie productions.

Getting the Money Getting a well-known actor to agree to play the lead in a movie can help a production firm get the cash it needs in order to make the film. Getting the money is what makes generating a motion picture so painful. One reflection of the stomach-tightening nature of movie development is the

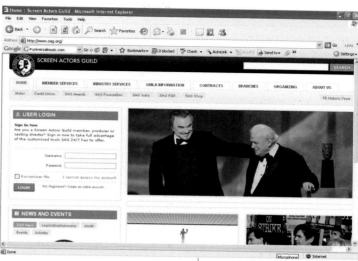

www.sag.org, website of the Screen Actors Guild

back-end deal or percentage of the gross a deal in which a production firm convinces a major actor or director to take a lower salary in return for a percentage of the money that the production firm will later receive from the distributor

guild a union established by writers, directors, and/or actors to protect their mutual interests and maintain standards

The Writers Guild of America, representing more than 10,000 film and television writers, went on strike on November 5, 2007 over a variety of issues in their negotiations with the Alliance of Motion Picture & Television Producers, including DVD residuals and guild coverage, and residuals for original content produced for the Internet.

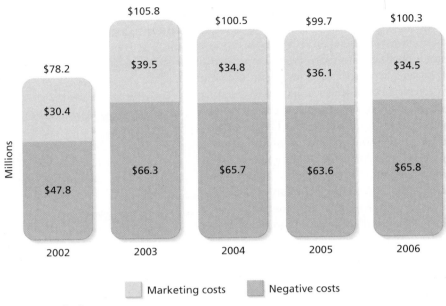

Figure 12.3

MPAA Member Companies Average Theatrical Production Costs, 2002–2006

The MPAA member companies are the major movie producers and distributors: Paramount, Disney, Sony, Twentieth Century Fox, Universal, and Warner Brothers. The negative cost is the amount of money it takes to complete the first copy of a movie. The marketing costs, often called P&A costs, represent the price of making a movie's prints that are projected in theaters and trying to persuade audiences to see it.

Source: Motion Picture Association of America.

fact that movies distributed by the major studios cost an average of nearly $60 million (see Figure 12.3). That number is a bit deceptive because it includes several movies made every year that cost near or above the $200 million mark. It also doesn't include movies put out by small distributors; they often cost far less than $50 million.

The fact is that the amount it costs to make a movie varies over a wide range, from way over $100 million dollars (*Spider Man*, *Pirates of the Caribbean*) to between $50 and $100 million (*The Simpsons Movie* reportedly cost about $75 million) to less than $50 million (*Knocked Up* cost $40 million to produce). The word in Hollywood is that it is the most expensive movies that tend to become megahits. Still, a moderately expensive film can also reap great benefits for its production firm. *Once*, a 2007 musical romance from Ireland, cost about $150,000 to make. In the United States alone it brought $7 million in box office returns.[3]

How much money a producer sets as the budget for a film doesn't necessarily depend on the producer's initial calculation of what is necessary to tell the story. In a logic that is peculiarly Hollywood's, the reverse is often true: a story is often chosen and developed to fit the budget that executives of a production firm can manage. Consequently, a production firm's heads decide what kinds of monetary risks they want to take (or can take). They then go about choosing a story, or tailoring it, to fit the budget they have.

Take as an example Dimension Films, the company that produced the hit movie *Scream* in 1996. Dimension Films was founded in 1992 as a division of Miramax Films (which is owned by The Walt Disney Company) to make

genre films. Genre films are movies that fit classic storytelling formulas (science fiction, horror, action) and are typically relatively inexpensive to make. Movie industry executives believe that successful genre films can be made with relatively low budgets. If a movie soars beyond its niche, as *Scream* and *Scream 2* did, its success makes up for films that brought the production firm little return.

Dimension Films is different from most other companies involved in the making of genre movies because in many ways its situation is more like that of a major studio. In Dimension's case, Miramax supplies the money and the distribution clout. Miramax's half owner, the Walt Disney Company, has a separate distribution firm, Buena Vista Releasing, for its divisions that make more broad-based movies, Walt Disney Productions and Touchstone Films. The reason for Miramax's existence as a distributor is that movie executives believe that niche pictures have to be released to theaters in a different way from broad-based movies. The difference is so great, they believe, that it pays to develop an organization with special expertise in this form of distribution.

When millions and millions of dollars are hanging in the balance, giving a film the green light is not easy. Not only must executives believe in the script, the director, and the stars, but they must have the money to make the film and a company to distribute it. If the production firm is part of a major studio, the chief executive officer of the studio typically discusses the proposed film with the production and distribution chiefs. Once the film and its budget are approved, the studio as a whole (encompassing both the production and distribution divisions) provides the money. It is the distribution division, however, that works to make the money back, and more, through a percentage of the **box office receipts**.

Independent firms have a harder time getting the money to make a film. If the independent firm has had previous successes, it may be fortunate enough to have a multi-picture distribution deal with a major that includes some financing. However, the independent may still have to use its own funds, or funds borrowed from banks, to make up the rest of the film's budget. The banks, of course, are hoping that the movie will make back its costs for the production firm so that they can retrieve their money with interest.

The most consistently successful independent production outfits are so tightly linked to particular distributors that they are virtually extensions of the distribution firm's own studio output. When it was independent, the Pixar animation firm had a distribution deal with Disney. Pixar films became so important to Disney's slate that eventually Disney decided to buy the company. On a lower level of financing, the independent production firm the Weinstein Company in the late 2000s had a long-term U.S. distribution deal with MGM. Many production companies do not have such long-term deals, though, and have to run the entire approval gauntlet time and time again.

Production companies that don't have long-term deals with distributors have to work a lot harder to find cash and a distributor. Sometimes wealthy investors will put up the money in the hope that they will get lucky and the film will be a hit. (Often these rich people also want to be close to the glamour of Hollywood.) Sometimes an independent production firm with a record of successes (a **track record**) will be able to convince a major bank to provide a revolving credit agreement for several pictures. When a production firm is seeking a loan for part of a film's budget, the loan will be easier to get if the production firm can show that an established star has been signed for the film and that an established distribution firm has agreed to take it on and to advance it money.

A popular way for independent producers to get the money for film projects is to sell the rights to distribute a particular movie to companies in different parts

genre film a movie that fits a classic storytelling formula (science fiction, horror, action) and is typically made relatively inexpensively

box office receipts the sum of money taken in for admission at movie theatres around the country

track record the previous successes or failures of a product, person, or organization

of the world (different territories). For example, a production firm's executives might get $2 million from an Asian firm that wants the rights to distribute the film to theaters (and perhaps home video rights) in Southeast Asia. Another distributor may bid $2 million for distribution rights in Australia and New Zealand. A third distributor might buy North American theatrical and home video rights. By accumulating these territory deals, often before the film is fully made, the production firm can show banks that a substantial portion of the film's budget is already in hand.

It's a difficult puzzle to put together. For example, for its 2007 movie slate (including Denzel Washington's *The Great Debaters*, Wayne Kramer's *Crossing Over*, and Anthony Minghella's *The No. 1 Ladies Detective Agency*), TWC brokered **distribution deals** (sometimes called **output deals**) with TF1 in France, Motion Picture Distribution in Canada, RAI Cinema for theatrical, home video and free TV in Italy, Paramount in the U.K., Australia/New Zealand's Village Roadshow, and German free TV.[4]

When a production firm with a solid record sells territorial rights, the firm may be able to negotiate receiving some of the box office revenues as well as up-

distribution deals or output deals arrangements in which production firms contract with particular distribution firms to market their films to exhibitors in particular parts of the world

Asian Film Trend

WORLD VIEW

When Rudyard Kipling suggested, "Oh, East is East and West is West, and never the twain shall meet" he probably couldn't have anticipated that *The Ring*, the American remake of a Japanese horror film, would have been one of 2002's biggest box office hits. Grossing a surprising $229.1 million worldwide, *The Ring* generated more than American horror classics *Friday the 13th* and *Nightmare on Elm Street*. This success ushered in a new trend in American filmmaking—the remaking of Asian hits.

The architect of this movement is Roy Lee, a Brooklyn-born Korean film producer who is known in Hollywood as the "King of Asian Film Remakes." While Lee is responsible for dozens of American remakes, he is most famous for the role he played in turning *Ringu*, the 1998 Japanese box office smash, into its 2002 American counterpart. Through a series of strange events, Lee was able to orchestrate the acquisition of *Ringu*, with Dreamworks picking up the $1 million tab for the remake rights.

After the success of the first movie, Dreamworks produced a sequel, this time asking Hideo Nakata, the director of *Ringu*, to helm the project. *The Ring Two* grossed $161.9 million, with Lee credited as an executive producer.

The Asian-remake trend hasn't been limited to horror films. *The Departed*, which banked Martin Scorsese his first

Academy Award for directing, was a remake of the 2002 Hong Kong crime thriller *Infernal Affairs*. The American version, staring Leonardo DiCaprio, Matt Damon and Jack Nicholson, was one of the most well received movies of the year, winning four of the five Oscar awards for which it was nominated, including Best Picture and Best Adapted Screenplay. The award for screenplay was especially notable, as the American version remained loyal to its Hong Kong predecessor.

The impact of Asian films is also seen in movies that are created and developed exclusively in the United States. At the 2007 Sundance Film Festival Geoffrey Gilmore, the festival's long-time director, remarked that Asia was the part of the world responsible for the best filmmaking of the last decade. He argues that Asian moviemakers' "reinvention of genres" influenced American films in plot, character development and visual effects, such as the notes *Spider Man 3* seems to have taken from the aerial fighting scenes in *Crouching Tiger, Hidden Dragon*.

Sources: Tony Ryanto, "Lee, King of Remakes, Translates East into West," *The Jakarta Post* June 23, 2007, via Nexis; Seo Dong-shi, "Sundance Man Has Passion for Asian Cinema," *Korea Times*, August 27, 2007, via Nexis.

front cash from the distributors. If the production firm really needs the money and has little influence in the deal, however, it may have to sign a contract that allows it to get only a little (if any) of the money that distributors receive from exhibitors around the world. Therefore, even if the movie does very well, the producer will see few of the benefits.

Getting to the Actual Making of the Movie As you can see, a lot of work has to be done on a movie project before the actual moviemaking even begins. The moviemaking process involves a large number of people. To get an idea of how many, watch all the credits at the end of the next movie you attend. (Tell the people with you that it's a class assignment.) Alternately, look up any movie on a site like the Internet Movie Database (http://www.imdb.com) or Hollywood.com (http://www.hollywood.com) and look at the cast and crew listings. Pay particular attention to the different jobs that are involved. Experienced personnel scout locations for certain scenes in the movie and try to minimize problems that might occur while filming there: casting directors help the director choose many of the actors; set designers, costume designers, makeup experts, and computer graphics personnel help create the physical shape of the space in which the actors work; stand-ins and stunt people help actors with boring or dangerous parts of the work; the cinematographer and the film crew create the look of the film as it will appear on screen; recording engineers make sure the sounds of the movie are appropriate (much of the dialogue will have to be re-recorded in a studio for clarity); a wide variety of personnel handle the equipment, the sound stage work, the salaries, the food, and all the other duties connected with a large project; and the editor decides (usually with the director) which versions ("shots") of different scenes should end up in the final version of the film.

Because of the large number of resources involved, every extra day of filming can be an enormous drain on the production firm's budget. Keeping the production on schedule is the role of the director, who controls the pace of filming, along with a **line producer**, who makes sure the equipment and personnel are there when they are needed. Some lenders, worried about spiraling costs, require production firms to hire **completion bond companies**. These are insurance companies that, for a large fee, will pay any costs of a film that exceed an agreed-upon amount. When a completion bond company signs on to a movie, especially one that is in danger of going over budget, it often sends its own executives to the sites where filming is taking place. By contract, those executives have the right to take control of some of the film's activities in order to keep it on budget.

line producer the individual responsible for making sure that the equipment and personnel necessary for a film's production are available when they are needed

completion bond company an insurance company that, for a large fee, will cover the costs of film production that exceed an agreed-upon amount

Theatrical Distribution in the Motion Picture Industry

When you're putting tens of millions of dollars into a movie, you want it to have a chance to reach the intended audience so your firm can make its money back (and hopefully turn a profit). As we've seen, helping a movie get that chance is the job of the distribution company. The most powerful companies in the movie business have distribution arms that have the reputation of being able to place films in theaters in the United States and around the world. Their power to move films is enormous. The major distribution firms have offices around the world, and the mandate for their personnel is twofold: to get the films they distribute into theaters, and to market these films effectively to target audiences.

Finding Movies to Distribute

The first order of business for a distributor is to get movies to distribute. You might suspect that the major distributors would have it easy, since they are linked to studios that create their own films. Certainly, they have a simpler time of it than the independent distributors. Executives in those firms have to scour the world for the rights to films that they feel will attract the audiences they know how to reach. But even the majors cannot afford to circulate only films that their studios make. They distribute several films from their own studio and get the rest from other places.

In recent years, the majors themselves have collaborated on the cost and distribution of particularly expensive films. The reason is that the executives of these firms want to lower the risk that they will lose enormous amounts of money if individual movies fail. So, for example, Paramount distributed *Titanic* in the United States while Fox distributed it internationally. Of course, sharing the costs also means sharing the profits. If Fox had distributed *Titanic* itself (as its executives originally intended), the company would have received all the profits of the movie, which took in more than $1 billion in theaters alone. At the time the movie was being made, however, its success was not at all guaranteed.

Releasing Movies

Once a distributor has set its slate of motion pictures and these pictures are completed (or nearing completion), the challenge is to choose a release date and a release pattern. The **release date** is the day on which the film will open in theaters. In setting a film's release date, executives take into consideration the kind of film it is, how popular its actors are, its target audience, and the other films in their slate. They also try to figure out when their competitors' movies will be released.

Typically, executives schedule the release of potential blockbusters in the United States during the summer or between Thanksgiving and Christmas. These are periods when students are off from school and when many adults spend extra time with their families. Because different societies may have different moviegoing habits, the release time of a film may be different around the world. In recent years, though, movie distributors have tended to release blockbuster films at the same time in many different countries—a practice known as a **day-and-date release**. The reasons have to do with concerns with piracy along with the technological ability to promote a movie efficiently across the world at the same time.

Release Patterns   In addition to the release date, distribution executives must agree on the release pattern in which the movie will be released to theaters around the country. Three release patterns are common in the United States: wide release, platform release, and exclusive release:

- A **wide release**, the most common pattern, typically involves opening a film in more than 2,000 theaters simultaneously. (At the higher end, wide releases are sometimes called **saturation releases**.) Putting a film in thousands of theaters beginning the same weekend is increasingly common as distributors rev up their marketing machines to hype potential blockbusters around the country (and the world) at the same time. In 2007, *Spider Man 3*, *Pirates of the Caribbean: Dead Man's Chest*, and *Shrek 3* all opened with far more than 3,000 engagements.

- A **platform release** involves the initial release of the movie in far fewer theaters in a relatively small number of areas. Executives are likely to choose this

release date   the day on which the film will open in theaters

day-and-date release   a simultaneous release date for a movie in different countries

wide release   opening a film in more than two thousand theatres simultaneously, usually accompanied by a large publicity campaign to incite people to see the film; the most common release pattern in the United States

saturation release   the initial release of a film in more than 2,000 theatres simultaneously

platform release   the initial release of a film in a small number of theatres in a relatively small number of areas; executives use this approach when they believe a film has the potential for wide appeal but needs time for newspaper reviews and other media discussions of the film to emerge and encourage the film's target audience to go see it

approach for films that they feel have potentially wide appeal but that need time for media reviews and other discussions of the film to emerge and ignite interest among the target audience. They hope to increase the number of theaters as the movie's popularity builds and thus encourage the snowballing of attendance.

- **Exclusive releases**, on the other hand, are not set up with the intention of "going wide." These films go to only a handful of carefully selected theaters around the country. Films with this distribution pattern are typically specialty films, often foreign, that their distributors believe will do well with very specific audiences in particular places around the country.

Of course, the number of movie theaters available to show a film is also an important consideration in distribution executives' decisions regarding release dates and release patterns. Theater-chain executives have their own ideas about what pictures they want in what locations, and they negotiate with the distributors regarding what pictures they will take and for how long. By law, movie distributors are not allowed to force exhibitors to book blocks of their films. Paramount, for example, is prohibited from telling the Regal theater chain that it can have a particular film only if it takes three other motion pictures. Over the decades, though, the major distributors and the major theater chains have developed ways to accommodate each other's needs.

Marketing Movies

One reason that theater chains like dealing with the major distributors is that the majors have very sophisticated marketing operations. To help reduce the risk of failure, distributors often conduct two types of research before a film is released. **Title testing** involves conducting interviews with filmgoers in shopping malls and other public places in order to determine the most alluring name for an upcoming picture. **Previewing** is a type of concept testing that takes place after a film is

exclusive releases the release of a film to only a handful of carefully selected theaters and target audiences throughout the country

title testing conducting interviews with filmgoers in order to determine which of a number of titles (or names) for an upcoming film will draw people in the target audience to the theater to see the film

previewing a type of concept testing to evaluate newly completed films, in order to determine what members of the film's target audience like and/or dislike about the film

Fueled by an aggressive marketing campaign and strong word-of-mouth, *Spider-Man 3* earned $336 million at the U.S. box office, making it the highest-grossing film of 2007 in the United States. Released in 16 territories, the film also set a worldwide record for its opening weekend earnings of $382 million.

487

rough cut a preliminary version of a film, shown before its final editing process and formal release

completed but before it is formally released. Theatergoers see a preliminary (**rough cut**) version of a movie and answer survey questions about what they like or don't like about it. The reactions may be used to re-edit parts of the film. The original sad ending of *Fatal Attraction*, for example, was changed to make it happier after it received negative audience reactions during previews.

Prints and Advertising (or P&A) The research and the activities that go along with it cost a lot of money. The expenses that distributors incur in getting their films to theaters and marketing them to the public are summed up by the industry acronym **P&A**, which stands for **prints and advertising**. The prints part means the cost of reproducing the original film negatives to circulate to theaters around the country and around the world. The advertising part means the money the distributor spends to publicize and advertise the film.

P&A or prints and advertising the expenses that distributors incur in making prints of their films for theaters and marketing the films to the public

publicity the process of creating and maintaining a favorable "buzz" about the film among its target audience

You're undoubtedly very familiar with both of these activities. Examples of **publicity** for a movie are setting up lavish parties for a film's cast on the day of the movie's premiere with the press in attendance; arranging interviews with the film's actors on television programs such as *The Tonight Show with Jay Leno* and *Entertainment Tonight*; putting previews of the film on YouTube and MySpace; and giving out free preview tickets to college students before a film formally opens. The aim of publicity is to get a favorable "buzz" going about the movie among its target audiences. The aim of advertising is to turn that buzz into actual moviegoing by telling people that the movie is playing near them and urging them to see it.

You may have noticed that the flurry of publicity and advertising for a film is intense and short (a few weeks at most), and that it takes place before and around the time the movie is released to the theaters. The reason is that distribution executives believe that although marketing can prepare moviegoers for a movie, after the first weekend of its release, word of mouth—the discussions that people who see the movie have with their friends—will determine whether more people will go to see it. The life of a film in theaters is no more than six months. The greatest proportion of the money received from a film comes in during the first few weeks; in fact, executives believe that they can predict the total amount of money a movie will make by looking at how it does during that short period of time.

tracking studies research on the public's awareness of and interest in a film, beginning two weeks before the film's release and continuing through the film's first month of release

Tracking In order to better understand how things are going, distribution executives support **tracking studies**, or research on the public's awareness of and interest in a film, beginning two weeks before the film's release and continuing through the film's first month of release. Three times during each of those weeks, a company called National Research Group surveys a random sample of Americans by phone. National's operators read a list of current or soon-to-be-released films to people who say they have recently seen theatrical movies. For every film on the list, the people are asked if they are aware of it and if they want to see it. These findings come too late to lead to any changes in the movie or its release pattern. Nevertheless, the film's marketers may use the results to determine whether revisions in their publicity and advertising plans are needed.

All this activity requires a lot of money. On major domestic releases in the early twenty-first century, P&A costs amounted to around half of the negative cost. The negative cost is the expense of making and editing the movie. According to the trade magazine *Variety*, the negative cost of *3:10 to Yuma* came to roughly $60 million, to which distributor Lionsgate added $27.5 million for prints and advertising.[5]

In rare instances, marketing a film costs even more than putting it together. *Scream*, the Miramax release mentioned earlier, reportedly had a negative cost of

Who's the Critic?

Lines like, "Another Winner!" and "This year's hottest new star!" were used on posters for 2001 films *The Animal* and *A Knight's Tale*, but as it turns out, the critic who supposedly wrote those lines—David Manning of the *Ridgefield Press*—was made up by a Sony marketing executive in order to put a positive spin on the hit-starved studio's films. Manning's name also appeared in exclamatory ads for Sony films *Hollow Man* and *Vertical Limit*. The *Ridgefield Press* is a real newspaper covering a small town in Connecticut, but it does not have a reviewer named David Manning, and it was not aware that its name was being used in film advertisements. Tom Nash, publisher for the *Ridgefield Press*, said he initially thought it was only a mix-up with a review service his paper uses.

"We thought it was a database error that mixed up a reviewer with our paper," Nash said. "We thought [Manning] was a Long Island News Day guy."

Sony wishes that were so: in truth, an unidentified Sony employee fabricated the Manning persona in July of 2001, using the name of a friend. After a brief international investigation, Sony admitted to creating the fake movie critic for advertising purposes, and suspended two of its advertising executives for 30 days without pay. Additionally, Sony immediately removed the manufactured blurbs from future print ads and launched its own investigation into the incident. "It was a case of incredibly bad judgment," said Sony spokeswoman Susan Tick. "We're taking all the steps necessary to determine who's been responsible and will act appropriately."

As a result of the Manning incident, the Connecticut attorney general has launched an investigation into the studio marketing practices, and two moviegoers in Los Angeles filed a suit claiming that Sony intentionally deceived consumers and violated professional business codes of conduct in using fabricated glowing reviews on four films. Sony agreed to an out-of-court settlement that would pay $1.5 million. Moviegoers around the country were eligible for a $5 refund as a result of the fake review, with any left over money from the payment to go to charity.

It is difficult to see why Sony executives braved the risk involved in making up such quotes, especially given the ease with which film companies can get favorable review quotes for just about any movie without resorting to "inventing" reviewers. Even movies with mostly negative reviews attract what the industry calls "quote whores"—reviewers who talk up nearly every film in hopes of having their name used in an advertisement.

But even in Hollywood, where studios go to great lengths to generate the ever-elusive buzz (often quoting virtually unknown critics or dubious publications), the Manning deception received a thumbs-down review from its own kind.

Where do you stand on this issue? In what ways do Sony's actions violate the public trust in what many people might consider "testimonial evidence" of an impartial movie critic? How critical should consumers be of film critics' quotes supporting certain films?

Sources: Josh Grossberg, *Sony Fakes A Film Critic*, E! Online News, http://www.eonline.com/News/Items/0,1,8370,00.html, download date 7/15/01; Whitney Mathieson, *Dave Manning, The Year's Hottest New Star*, USAToday.com, http://www.usatoday.com/life/columns/candy/2001-06-06-candy.htm, download date 1/16/02; BBCNews, *Sony Admits Using Fake Reviewer*, BBCNewsOnline, http://news.bbc.co.uk/hi/english/entertainment/film/newsid_1368000/1368666.stm, download date 1/16/02; BBCNews, *Sony Pays $1.5m over fake critic*, BBCNewsOnline, http://news.bbc.co.uk/2/hi/entertainment/4741259.stm, download date 08/03/05.

about $15 million and more than $20 million of marketing expenses to send it into wide release. In this case, though, the expenditure seemed to pay off. Three weeks after its debut, the trade magazine *Variety* was predicting that the movie would bring in $70 to $80 million in box office receipts.

But not all the money made at the box office comes back to the distributor. Let's look at the exhibitor's side of the story.

Theatrical Exhibition in the Motion Picture Industry

Just as about ten major distributors control over 90 percent of U.S. theatrical activity, so the largest 3 percent of movie chains control 60 percent of the screens on which the films are shown.

Recall that in 1948, the federal government and the major studios signed a settlement that prohibited the major film distributors (several of which are still majors today) from owning theaters. As a result, from the 1950s onward, large chains developed that were outside the ownership orbits of Hollywood moviemakers. The chains with the largest numbers of screens are Regal, AMC, Cinemark, Carmike, Cineplex Entertainment and National Amusements. The United Artists, Edwards, and Regal chains are owned by financier Philip Anschutz, who bought them when they were in severe financial straits.

The early years of the 2000s were disastrous for the largest theater chains. All lost enormous amounts of money, and most have either declared bankruptcy (and gone into court-supervised reorganization) or come close to it. The primary reason was a very expensive building spree. At the turn of the century, all the theater chains embarked on huge construction programs that involved borrowing huge amounts of money to create modern theaters with fancy food concessions and comfortable "stadium seating" (where the rows go up in steps, making it easier for people at the back to see the screen). Their aim was to create settings that would draw people to their theaters in an age when DVDs and large-screen TVs might keep them home.

Although the chains set up new screens, they didn't shut down their older theaters quickly enough, often because they couldn't get out of leases for the space. The result was that the companies were burdened by too many old screens as customers streamed to the new ones. The exhibitors found it difficult—sometimes impossible—to pay back their huge debts.

The Relationship Between Distributors and Theater Chains

The theatrical economy has strengthened since then, and the number of screens in the United States has remained much higher than in the mid-1990s. While there were 29,731 indoor and outdoor movie screens in 1996, the number rose to 38,415 in 2006, according to the National Association of Theater Owners. To distributors, the increase in the number of screens meant that exhibitors would be accepting more movies and keeping them longer. Exhibitors' need for films to show might also mean that distributors could demand more money per movie from exhibitors than they had in the past.

Tensions involving what movies to choose and how much to pay have long been part of the relationship between exhibitors and distributors. Just as distributors have to set up a slate of films to show to the public, exhibitors must have pictures that will fill the seats of their theaters. Executives who book movies want popular films to come out on a schedule that allows the chains to maximize the use of their theaters on a year-round basis. This desire has created tensions with the major distributors, who have traditionally tried to release most of their films during the summer and during the Thanksgiving and Christmas vacation periods. Nevertheless, because distributors and exhibitors need each other, distributors try to adjust some of their release strategies to accommodate theaters' needs, and theaters try to help distributors get screens for hoped-for blockbusters during times of the year when every studio, it seems, wants to have a place in theaters.

The relationship typically works this way: a theater chain often has booking divisions in different areas of the United States, depending on where it concentrates its screens. AMC, for example, has three booking divisions—one handling the Northeast, one the South, and one the West. Each division has a number of bookers. Say you work as a booker for a chain of movie theaters in a particular region of the United States. Movie distributors inform you months in advance of what films they intend to release, and when. That information allows you to begin thinking about the kinds of movies you might have in your theaters at different times of the year. As a particular film's release date gets closer, the distributor sends you publicity material about the film, and you also have the opportunity to see uncompleted versions. These uncompleted versions of films (often without music) are called rough cuts. Based upon this information and what you know about the other movies that are coming out around the same time, you make an estimate of how well you believe the film will do at the box office compared to the others.

The distributor of the movie, for its part, has an interest in getting the movie into theaters that fit its sense of audience interest in the film. If the film will have a limited or exclusive release, the distributor will want to place it in locations where the target audience for the film lives. Executives may try to place a movie aimed at African-American moviegoers, for example, in areas where many African Americans live. If distribution executives anticipate that a film will be a blockbuster, they will insist that an exhibitor that wants to carry the film place it in the largest theaters within its multiplexes. In areas where a couple of exhibition chains have competing theaters, the distributor may try to satisfy them all in order to keep its long-term business relationships solid. The distributor may offer the film exclusively to one chain in one area and to another in another part of the neighborhood. Or it may offer one potential hit to one company and another potential hit to the other company.

Financial Agreements Between Distributors and Theater Chains
Negotiations on the issues that are important to distributors and exhibitors may continue until just a few weeks before a movie's opening. Eventually, distribution and exhibition executives negotiate an **exhibition license** for each theater. The license specifies the date the distributor will make the picture available to the theater, the number of weeks the theater agrees to play the picture, and when and where competing theaters can show the same film. The exhibition license also sets the financial arrangements between the distributor and the theater chain. These arrangements take into consideration the distributor's huge expenditure on the film, on the one hand, and, on the other, the exhibitor's need to cover its costs and make a profit.

One common approach is for the distributor to take a certain percentage of the ticket revenues from the film, with the exhibitor keeping the rest. Another approach is the **percentage-above-the-nut** approach. It works this way: the executives of the theater chain and the distribution firm come together to agree on what it costs to operate each theater (the electricity, salaries, rent, maintenance, and the like). That break-even point is called the **nut**. For each picture, the theater chain negotiates what percentage of the amount "above the nut" it will pay to the distributor. Typically, an exhibitor will return around 90 percent of ticket revenues above the nut to the distributor. That percentage may get lower several weeks into the run of a film. "Discount" theaters, which may show movies a few months after

exhibition license an agreement between a distributor and an exhibition firm that specifies the date on which the distributor will make the film available to the exhibition firm's theaters, the number of weeks the theaters agree to run the film, and when and where competing theaters can show the same film; it also sets the financial arrangements between the distributor and the exhibition firm

percentage-above-the-nut an agreement drawn between a distributor and an exhibition firm in which the executives of the exhibition firm and the distribution firm agree on the costs of operating each theater (the electricity, salaries, rent, maintenance, and the like), a break-even point called the *nut*; then, film by film, the distributor and the exhibition firm negotiate what percentage of revenues "above the nut" the exhibition firm will pay to the distribution firm

they were first released, typically pay a substantially lower percentage above the nut to the distributor.

In the end, distributors typically get back about half the box office receipts. As a general rule, the 50 percent that exhibitors get covers their costs, plus about 10 percent. Although a 10 percent return isn't bad, theaters typically make a lot more money than their cut of the admission take through their concessions—popcorn, soft drinks, candy, and other food. Big theater chains, such as AMC, fully control their concession operations and do not have to share the profits of these operations with other firms. Selling food can be quite a lucrative proposition, particularly in view of the high prices the chains charge. (Remember the last time you bought a soft drink at a movie?) An increasing number of theaters now sell pizza and other noncandy foods.

Digital Theaters

Every year distributors spend huge amounts on a task that many in the industry believe should be eliminated. That task is sending films to theaters. This may sound like a very basic activity: placing reels of movie film in a box and shipping them to the theaters that will use them. But although the activity is basic, it is a monetary and logistical nightmare. For every film that goes out in wide release, distributors must make more than two thousand separate film prints. Every film must be shipped to a theater and then shipped back to the distributor. Many of the prints can be used again overseas, but the distributor must still pay shipping costs. Moreover, international releases of many films have increasingly been taking place at around the same time as North American releases, in part to take advantage of global marketing activities. That practice means even greater expense for creating prints.

One way to get around this problem, industry executives have suggested, is to deliver films to theaters via satellite and then to project them onto a screen. Much of the production of movies is already done digitally. An increasing number of directors are using digital cameras that use no film and are lighter than traditional gear. Even if film is used during shooting of the movie, the pictures are often transferred to computers for special effects and editing. It's a no-brainer to think that an all-digital process could be much easier and more efficient.

Companies already make projectors that they claim have both the clarity and resolution to match those of traditional motion picture technology. In fact, almost 150 theaters in the United States are already equipped to show digital movies. Distribution executives see a time in the not-too-distant future when much of the toil involved in circulating films will be eliminated. Instead of making prints and paying delivery services, distributors may connect to a satellite delivery service that allows them to circulate one master copy of their product to theaters around the world at virtually the same time. To foil piracy attempts, they envision sending the digital copy in a code that could be deciphered only by particular theaters.

The reason digital projection hasn't spread beyond a few theaters has less to do with the technology than with the expense. Each digital projector costs about $100,000. Multiply that times the 36,000 screens in the United States alone and you can see that the cost of moving to digital exhibition will be enormous. The major movie distributors would like the theater chains to help pay for digital projectors. Despite the arguments, observers within the industry suggest that the parties will eventually compromise and that we will see digital movie distribution as the standard within a decade or two.

Digital Film

After completing his first film, *El Mariachi*, in 1992 for only $7,000, director Robert Rodriguez was hooked on film making made cheap. Ever since, as technology has developed and Rodriguez's star rose in Hollywood, he has taken up a new role as digital movie making evangelist. Rodriguez insists on total control over his movies, from directing, to shooting, to editing, to composing music for his films. To maintain such tight control over the creative process while keeping the price down, Rodriguez relies on a stockpile of digital tools at his Troublemaker Studios. Using Sony HD Cameras, a Discreet visual effects software, Avid digital editing machines, and XSI 3D animation software, Rodriguez teamed with Frank Miller to produce *Sin City*, one of the more visually innovative movies in recent years. Then, Rodriguez led off the credits to *Spy Kids 3-D: Game Over* with the phrase: "A Robert Rodriguez Digital Film." The medium, as with the director, had officially arrived in Hollywood.

In general, digital technologies have made the production of films easier and cheaper, and many filmmakers are increasingly recognizing the advantages of digital cinema devices and starting to use them in filmmaking. The new tools are especially welcomed by indie (independent) and art-film auteurs, who have had trouble raising money to make their films. For instance, the indie film director Rene Besson produced her mini-film *Boxes* in 2000 for only $285. She said that with digital cinema tools, "movies can be made based on passion without having to beg, plead and compromise (to the sponsors) for every aesthetic choice."

Not only have digital cameras changed movie-making, but the editing system has also harnessed digital technology, with remarkable results. Computer software like Final Cut Pro puts the tools for editing mini-DV productions into the hands of the filmmaker. With software installed on a computer, the editing can take place in the filmmaker's home.

After digital films are edited on a personal computer, they can be sent to places such as San Francisco's the Orphanage. Its proprietary software transforms the video into a film product that can be projected on a contemporary movie theater's screen.

Inspired by the creative potential of the mini-DV format films, many Hollywood producers have begun to use a wide range of digital cinema tools. A number of well-known filmmakers have used digital film making to present their movies on a grander scale at IMAX theaters (e.g., Zack Snyder's *300* and Sam Raimi's *Spider Man 3*). Films like *Sin City* use digital features in their postproduction work as well, shooting almost the entire movie in front of a green screen, adding action and environmental effects later in the studio.

One major problem with digital production is the high cost of storing the materials. Unlike films, which can last for a hundred years in the proper vault, digital creations take up lots of room in computers and must be checked often for deterioration. A 2007 study by the Academy of Motion Picture Arts and Sciences titled "The Digital Dilemma" concluded that simply to store a digital master record of a movie costs about $12,514 a year compared to the $1,059 it costs to keep a conventional film master. Moreover, when a movie is made digitally from scratch, producers want to keep all the data connected with it; then the cost of preservation soars to $208,569 [6].

Clearly, the problem of digital storage is one that the industry needs to address. Nevertheless, most observers agree that the future is in digital production, distribution, and exhibition.

Sources: Brian Ashcraft, *The Man Who Shot Sin City*, WIRED Magazine On-Line, http://www.wired.com/wired/archive/13.04/sincity.html?pg=1&topic=sincity&topic_set=, download date April 2005; Michael Cieply, "The Afterlife is Expensive for Digital Movies," *The New York Times*, December 23, 2007, Sec. 3, p. 6.

Non-theatrical Distribution and Exhibition

Theatrical distribution is the pad that launches a film toward many other exhibition locations. As we have noted in earlier chapters, different types of exhibition points are called **windows** in industry jargon. The importance of theaters as a

windows the series of exhibition points for audiovisual products through which revenues are generated

movie's first window explains why distributors pay a lot of attention to marketing movies when they are first released to theaters. It is also the reason why distribution executives must maintain good relationships with their counterparts in the theater business despite the tensions we have noted. When it comes to making money off the movies, though, a number of other windows are terribly important. They include video stores and television exhibition of different sorts.

Traditional and Online Video Stores

During the course of a single year, the money that movie distributors receive from the sale of home videocassettes and DVDs of their movies exceeds the revenues they receive from theatrical showings. Generally, the movies that have done well in theaters are also the ones that do well in video. There are important exceptions, though. Children's videos and some types of horror films may have lackluster theatrical distribution but bring in enough money in video to justify the production. Revenues from home video come from two sources: sell-through outlets and rental outlets.

sell-through outlets stores in which consumers buy the videos rather than just renting them

rental outlets companies that purchase releases from film distributors and then rent them on a pay-per-day basis to individual customers

Sell-through outlets are stores in which consumers buy the videos rather than just renting them. Some stores such as Blockbuster, Target, and Wal-Mart sell videos in physical locations as well as online. Amazon (http://www.amazon.com) is an example of an online only video store.

Rental outlets are companies that purchase releases from movie distributors and then rent them to individual customers on a pay-per-day basis. The traditional way to carry this out is to go to a physical ("bricks and mortar") store such as one in the Blockbuster chain and pay to take out the video for a number of days; bringing it back late means paying for the extra days. In recent years, the rental business has seen the growth of subscription services, in which a person pays to be a member and then gets to take out a certain number of DVDs for any length of time. There are no late fees, but subscribers can only take out more videos if they return the ones they've currently checked out. In the model popularized by Netflix, a person signs up online and both receives and returns the DVDs by mail, with Netflix paying the postage. Seeing a competitive threat, Blockbuster went a step further. It allows subscription customers to return the videos either by mail or to its stores.

Blockbuster Video faced the competition of online DVD rental services like Netflix by integrating rental-by-mail services into its own business model, and went a step further by also allowing their own online customers to rent and return videos in Blockbuster's brick-and-mortar stores.

The growth of broadband Internet in Americans' homes led some online firms to offer downloadable movies for rent. They do it with the permission of the distributors and with digital rights management (DRM) software to prevent wholesale copying. Sites that allow one form or another of downloading include

CinemaNow, Vongo, ifilm, Movielink, Movieflix, AtomFilms, and iTunes Video. Using an example from Netflix, a medium-cost Netflix plan allows the subscriber to rent as many DVDs as he/she wants (three DVDs at a time) and watch without extra charge 17 hours of movies instantly on one PC. Higher cost plans allow more DVDs at a time and more hours on the PC. Amazon.com allows movie downloads for a variety of prices with the proviso that "Your rental video can be stored on your PC or TiVo DVR for 30 days. Once you press play, you have 24 hours to watch the video before it expires."[7]

www.netflix.com, website of online DVD rental service Netflix, which offers more than 90,000 titles to more than 6.7 million subscribers.

In 2005, subscription video sales represented about 19 percent of the video rental market and that number was climbing. Overall, DVD rentals that year came to $6.5 billion. DVD sales were much higher, $16.7 billion. Videocassette sales and rentals plummeted through the 2000s, as DVD players found a presence in nearly 80 percent of U.S. homes. In 2000, videocassette rentals and sales brought in $14.7 billion; by 2005 that number was $2.3 billion and sinking rapidly.[8] It should be noted that while most of these numbers represent theatrical movies, they also reflect the growth of DVDs of television programs that also represent largely Hollywood product, as we'll see in Chapter 13: The Television Industry.

Exhibition of Movies on Television

Television is an extremely important exhibition arena for theatrical movies. Actually, the word "television" stands for many exhibition points. Once a movie leaves the theater, and often even before it lands in home video, it begins a gauntlet of windows that typically start a couple of months after the theatrical release with pay-per-view cable and satellite outlets in hotels. The movie might then be released on DVD and also show up on home cable or satellite pay-per-view and "on demand" systems, as well as transatlantic or transcontinental airline flights. Later, it might appear on a subscription cable channel such as Showtime or HBO. Still later, the movie may run a number of times on a major broadcast or cable network. Eventually, a local television station might pick it up as part of a package of films it licenses for late-night or weekend airing. All this amounts to a lot of money. In fact, the post-theatrical windows can turn a hit film into a bonanza for the production and distribution firms. It can also turn a disappointment at the box office into a break-even or even mildly profitable film.

The Problem of Piracy

Profits in the motion picture industry are continually threatened in the United States and around the world because of film **piracy**—the unauthorized duplication of copyrighted films for profit. The activity is illegal under international copyright laws, but it is rampant around the world. You can see it pretty openly in many U.S. cities: vendors selling videos of films that are still in theaters. Sometimes pirated

piracy the unauthorized duplication of copyrighted material for profit copies are produced by having someone take a video camera into a theater and shoot the movie. In more sophisticated cases, pirates smuggle a movie out of the theater, copy it as a video master, and then return the original. These illegal practices made it possible to purchase cheaply many major films on the streets of major cities on the days that the films debut theatrically. Stripping the copy-protection codes off DVDs and uploading movies to the Internet means that many people can illegally download hit films for free.

Consider the ethical responsibility of the buyers of these DVDs as well as the behavior of the pirates. The U.S. movie industry estimates that such theft is costing the industry billions of dollars a year—money that it would have received if its companies had sold those DVDs. Within the United States, federal and local law enforcement groups have been trying to combat piracy. On a global level, the U.S. government, aware of the importance of the film industry to U.S. exports, has been pressuring the governments of countries in which enforcement of copyright regulations is particularly problematic. In addition, the Motion Pictures Producers Association of America (MPAA), the group that represents the major production and distribution companies, has hired detectives who roam the world trying to identify the pirates. As for Internet piracy, which the MPAA on its website calls "a global avalanche," the organization states that it has a multi-pronged approach," including educating people about the consequences of piracy, taking legal action against Internet thieves, working with law enforcement detecting piracy operations, and helping to advance technologies that will "allow the legal distribution of movies over the Internet." Like the recording industry's RIAA (see Chapter 10), the MPAA has sued Americans for copyright infringement in the smallest of towns and the biggest of cities. Damages for copyright infringement range from $30,000 to $150,000 per work and, if there is criminal prosecution, could include up to five years in jail."[9] Unfortunately for the industry, all sorts of piracy continue.

Under pressure from the United States, the Chinese government took action against rampant media piracy. As a part of that action, millions of pirated CDs and DVDs were destroyed by steamrollers.

Media Literacy and the Motion Picture Industry

Despite its expensive and risky nature, moviemaking in many ways lies at the center of American popular culture. As we have seen, U.S. theaters are merely the first stop in a gamut of exhibition windows through which American movies run. The films then travel to theaters around the world, to airplanes and hotel pay-per-view systems, to cable and satellite pay services, and to home videos. They go to pay cable channels such as HBO and Showtime, to regular cable channels such as TNT, to broadcast TV networks such as ABC, and eventually, perhaps, to late-night runs on local stations.

Not only are movies shown, they are discussed. Especially when movie companies first release films, huge waves of publicity blanket the mass media. It often becomes impossible to avoid hearing about certain movies. You'd almost have to be on another planet not to know something about the Spider Man and Harry Potter flicks. Moreover, movie stars and songs that come from movies are themselves major topics on television, in magazines, in newspapers, around the water cooler, and in the lunchroom.

It may be startling to realize how many of these performances and discussions across so many media in so many parts of the world are sparked by just a handful of corporations, the major movie distributors. Moreover, all the majors are tied to huge mass media conglomerates—Time Warner, Disney, Viacom (which owns Paramount), News Corporation (which owns Fox), and General Electric (which owns Universal). These conglomerates use their Hollywood assets as content for their holdings in different media industries around the world. Materials get packaged, sold, and hyped many times. In that way, even extremely expensive movies have a decent chance of making their money back, and blockbuster hits have a chance of making stratospheric sums.

Cultural Diversity and Cultural Colonialism

Some observers of popular culture look at these activities with dismay. They express two types of concern. One relates to the narrowing of cultural diversity. A second involves what they call cultural colonialism. Let's look at each of these.

The Narrowing of Cultural Diversity   Critics of the mainstream movie industry argue that movie executives are sending a rather narrow range of stories into American theaters and homes. Many contemporary Hollywood movies, they argue, are made according to simplistic formulas that use sex and violence in ways designed to ignite the interest of the central moviegoing audience easily: 14–24-year-olds. Expensive films that can become blockbusters are the name of the game in Hollywood because they have the potential to travel across so many different media and make so much more for the majors than small films ever will. But the major studios will not take artistic risks on such films because the stakes are so high. As a result, films that push the envelope and challenge the audience to see the world differently are few and far between.

Exhibitors also work against cultural diversity, say the critics. Overwhelmingly, they book movies that fit the Hollywood profile. Few theaters in the United States show "art films"—movies created on small budgets that often do not fit into Hollywood stereotypes and standard genres. Even fewer theaters show foreign-language films, even dubbed or with subtitles. The theater chains justify their choices by saying that Americans simply won't go to see these movies in numbers that justify booking them. The critics respond that the movie industry worked for

With its universal theme of love and determination, as well as its star Will Smith's status as one of the highest grossing actors in the world, *The Pursuit of Happyness* is an easy "pick up" for translation into foreign languages—in this case, Japanese.

decades to keep such films out of the mainstream in order to protect the standard Hollywood product. It will take time, they say, for Americans to develop the habit of watching non-Hollywood-style films.

The critics add that by not encouraging Americans to see movies made in other countries, the U.S. movie industry is keeping Americans isolated from important aspects of world culture. We live in a time, they say, when business is global, and Americans—especially young people—need to be able to understand the viewpoints of other people. Watching other people's movies can help that understanding enormously. The U.S. movie industry's activities are counterproductive in this regard, they say.

Cultural Colonialism   Another strong criticism lodged against the movie industry is that it represents a leading edge of American cultural colonialism. As we noted in Chapter 4, cultural colonialism is the process by which the media content of a dominating society (in this case, the United States) surrounds people of another society with values and beliefs that are not those of their own societies. Rather, the content's values and beliefs reflect and support the interests of the dominating society.

As you can see, this criticism is in some ways a mirror image of the first criticism. The concern over the lack of cultural diversity in movies argues that American society is being harmed. The concern about cultural colonialism, in contrast, argues that American-based companies are harming other countries. They are doing this, the argument goes, by drowning out the presentation of local cultural experiences in the media with Hollywood-based formulas.

The critics point out that this cultural colonialism helps American business by creating markets for consumer goods. Moviemaking in the United States is big business. (In fact, filmed entertainment of all sorts, for television and home video as well as the theaters, is one of America's top exports.) At the same time, critics say, it erodes local cultures because they can't compete with U.S. marketing glitz. It also encourages a "throwaway" view of the world that leads to a degraded global environment.

One result of the U.S. movie industry's focus on the international market in recent years has been the search by the majors for smaller, more literary movies—

so-called **art films**—that might connect with relatively cultivated audiences around the world. The conglomerates have set up divisions such as Miramax, Fox Searchlight, Sony Classics, and United Artists (MGM) to handle these films. You might think that critics and producers in other countries would be happy about this development. The problem is that so far all but a few of the movies that these divisions and others have picked up have been English-language pictures, from either the United States, England, Australia, or New Zealand. Distribution executives point out in frustration that American audiences, still the largest moviegoing audiences, don't like to watch movies that have been dubbed or that have subtitles. As a result, even European film companies have been moving toward making films in English and then subtitling them for non-English-speaking lands. The Americans are colonizing even the art-film world, critics say.

The critics point to the majors' worldwide success as evidence that cultural colonialism is taking place. The international power of the majors, they say, has made U.S. films dominant in the box offices of many countries around the world. True, several of the conglomerates that own the studios are not American. The filmmaking activity, however, is very much based in the United States and presents the U.S. view of the world. Furthermore, they add, the popularity of U.S. movies is merely the tip of a huge iceberg. Under the guidance of powerful multimedia conglomerates, U.S. theatrical product blankets all sorts of print and electronic media. U.S. stars are favorites the world over. And the U.S. way of life that is shown in the movies—with its strong commercialism, lack of environmental sensitivity, and urge toward immediate gratification—becomes an attraction for young people throughout the world.

Not surprisingly, Hollywood's supporters reject this view of their role in global culture. They point out that Hollywood employs many Americans as a result of the movie industry's global reach. They add that many countries support local filmmakers and encourage them to make movies that reflect their own societies. It is not the U.S. movie industry's fault that people like Hollywood films more than those types of movies.

Hollywood's defenders also argue that people around the world like U.S. movies because they are good stories filmed in a high-quality way. They also say that it is patronizing to believe that people in other countries see the movies in the same way that American audiences see them. Rather, they accept or reject what they see in movies from the vantage point of their own cultures. They may even understand the stories differently because they are coming at them with different cultural "eyes."

This is not an argument that will go away. It may, in fact, become louder as media conglomerates increase their use of Hollywood moviemaking in their bids to create global content for the many channels they need to fill. Where do you stand on these issues, and why?

art films small literary movies

CHAPTER REVIEW

For an interactive chapter recap and study guide, visit the companion website for *Media Today* at www.routledge.com/textbooks/mediatoday

QUESTIONS FOR DISCUSSION AND CRITICAL THINKING

1 Compare the ways that the earliest movie firms and the ones started by immigrants tried to keep control over the movie business.
2 Why can it be said that the B movie part of Hollywood migrated to television?
3 In what ways are movie theaters at risk of losing audiences as a result of the growth of video and DVD rentals and sales, pay-per-view and cable showings, video on demand, and other venues?
4 If the major U.S. movie companies make more money distributing their product outside theaters than in them, why is theatrical distribution so important?

INTERNET RESOURCES

Motion Picture Association of America (http://mpaa.org/)
According to its website, the MPAA "and its international counterpart, the Motion Picture Association (MPA) serve as the voice and advocate of the American motion picture, home video and television industries, domestically through the MPAA and internationally through the MPA." The site contains much interesting data about performance of the industry in the United States and abroad. It also presents the association's positions on piracy, film ratings, and U.S. movies internationally.

Internet Movie Database (http://imdb.com/)
Owned (but seemingly not biased) by Time Warner, it is truly (in its own words) "the biggest, best, most award-winning movie and TV site on the planet."

The Greatest Films (http://www.filmsite.org/filmh.html)
Tim Dirks has put together a fascinating and useful website that moves across film history by decade. The site also includes "quotes," "genre," and "reference" sections.

Writers Guild of America, West (http://www.wga.org/), **Directors Guild of America** (http://www.dga.org), **and Screen Actors Guild** (http://www.sag.org) are the key labor unions for theatrical movies made in the United States. The websites present news about and for their members and insight into critical aspects of the movie business.

Variety (http://www.variety.com/)
This legendary show business magazine provides deep coverage of the movie industry, including film reviews. Many aspects of the site are open to subscribers only, but visitors can get a flavor of the topics they cover.

KEY TERMS

You can find the definitions to these key terms in the marginal glossary throughout this chapter. Test your knowledge of these terms with interactive flash cards on the *Media Today* companion website.

A and B movie units

A films

B films

back-end

block booking

blockbusters

box office receipts

completion bond companies

day-and-date release

digital theaters

Edison Vitascope

exclusive releases

exhibition license

feature films

film distribution firms

film production firms

film ratings

genre film

green light

guilds

independent distributor

kinetoscope

line producer

majors

marketing cost

megaplexes

Motion Picture Patents Company

Motion Picture Producers and
    Distributors of America

multiplexes

negative cost

nickelodeons

on spec

P&A

percentage of the gross

percentage-above-the-nut

persistence of vision

piracy

platform release

previewing

publicity

release date

rental outlets

rough cut

saturation release

sell-through outlets

series pictures

star system

studio system

talent agents

talkies

territories

theatrical films

title testing

track record

tracking studies

treatment

vertical integration

wide release

windows

word of mouth

CONSTRUCTING MEDIA LITERACY

1 How big an impact do you think the movie industry has on American pop culture?

2 Do you agree that the export of Hollywood movies crowds out or taints foreign cultures? Why or why not?

3 Support or refute the following statement: Hollywood movie companies should take risks in producing a more stylistically diverse set of films, instead of producing films that simply use the formulas audiences want.

4 To what extent do you agree or disagree with the argument that Hollywood is a major instrument of American cultural colonialism?

CASE STUDY   The Exhibition of Independent and Non-English Language Films

The idea: Critics of movie exhibition in the United States argue that most Americans have no chance to be familiar with films that are off the beaten track. They specifically point to movies distributed by firms not affiliated with the major studios—Fox, Disney, Sony, Universal, Paramount, and Warner Brothers. How true is this criticism in the area in which you live or attend school?

The method: Chart the movie theaters within twenty miles of your house. If you can find historical data, track the movies that were exhibited in them over the past three months. If you cannot find such data, track the movies that are exhibited in each theater over the next month. For each film, note the name of the production studio, the distributor, country of origin, language, and (if you can find it) the countries in which the film's story takes place. Write a four-page report describing what you have found.

13 THE TELEVISION INDUSTRY

After studying this chapter, you will be able to:

1 Compare and contrast broadcast, cable, and satellite television

2 Explain the role of advertisers in these three forms of television

3 Name and describe the different types of cable and satellite services

4 Identify the ways in which broadcasters, cable companies, and satellite companies produce, distribute, and exhibit programming

5 Describe the issues facing the TV industry and society in a rapidly changing TV world

"TV will be transformed. People will look at it as historically quaint that you had to watch something that others chose for you."

– MITCH KAPOR, SOFTWARE ENTREPRENEUR

Media Today

You probably have your favorite television shows. Indeed, there may be a night or two a week when you build your plans around viewing a favorite program. For most of us, television is a relaxing form of cheap, familiar entertainment. You may even feel that there is a comforting predictability about the medium. The box is always there, and your favorite shows always seem to be there, whether in new episodes or in reruns.

Yet the business behind the box is anything but predictable these days. The whole idea of what television means is up for grabs as the traditional ways of creating, sponsoring, distributing, and exhibiting programming clash with new approaches and new technologies. This chapter explores the U.S. television industry at a time of enormous change. It presents the basic building blocks for understanding how things are done now, why they may be changing in the decades ahead, and how they relate to the trends toward conglomeration and globalization that we have mentioned in previous chapters.

The Rise of Television

To really understand the TV enterprise and the tensions involved in its current transformation, you have to understand how it started. You have to know, for example, that American regulators and industry executives saw the medium as related closely to radio. Back in the first half of the twentieth century, both radio and TV were centered on broadcasting—the use of public airwaves to send audio (for radio) and audiovisual (for television) signals to sets that Americans bought for their homes. Moreover, the companies that gained control of television and shaped its commercial development were by and large the same firms that had become giants in radio.

Television in its Earliest Forms

The commercial introduction of television in the United States took place in 1946, right after World War II. Yet the idea of television had been around for some time before that. The word *television* was used as early as 1907 in the magazine *Scientific American*. Even earlier, in 1879, the British humor magazine *Punch* published a picture of a couple watching a remote tennis match via a screen above their fireplace. Three years later, a French artist drew a family of the future watching a war on a home screen. Pretty prophetic, huh?

Although the idea of television was in the air, the actuality of **television broadcasting**—scanning a visual image and transmitting it electrically, generally with accompanying sound, in the form of electromagnetic waves that when received could be reconverted into visual images—was harder to accomplish. Laboratory

television broadcasting the transmission of visual images, generally with accompanying sound, in the form of electromagnetic waves that when received can be reconverted into visual images

work started in Germany during the 1880s and continued in the United States, Scotland, Russia, and other countries throughout the next several decades. The first telecast of a drama took place in 1928 from General Electric's experimental studio in Schenectady, New York.

Between 1935 and 1938, the Nazi government in Germany operated the world's first regular television service, sending propaganda broadcasts to specially equipped theaters. Engineers did not consider the technology used for these performances very acceptable, however. The whirring mechanical disk that was used to scan the broadcast images had too many drawbacks. During the 1930s, an RCA team brought together inventions that allowed electronic rather than mechanical scanning. This technology seemed to be the way to go. RCA introduced the system at the 1939 World's Fair in New York; in introducing the new medium during formal ceremonies, President Franklin D. Roosevelt became the first U.S. president to appear on the tube. Regular broadcasts began and TV sets went on sale, but television did not take off. World War II intervened, and resources were diverted to defense production.

It was after the end of World War II—in 1946—that commercial television came into being in the United States. From the start, commercial television was tied to the companies that controlled radio—including NBC (owned by RCA), CBS, and ABC. Recognizing a direct threat to the radio business, executives from those firms poured their profits into developing television stations and networks. But between 1948 and 1952, the Federal Communications Commission declared a freeze on new station licenses and new television manufacturing in order to review its standards for television. It decided to use the desirable **very high frequency** (VHF) band of frequencies—those between 30 and 300 MHz—for channels 2 through 13, and an **ultra high frequency** (UHF) band of frequencies—those between 300 and 3,000 MHz—for channels 14 through 83. All the best channels and network affiliates were on the VHF band; in fact, most televisions didn't even have a UHF dial during the first two decades of television.

Television Gains Widespread Acceptance in the 1950s

When the freeze on new licenses ended, it was as if a national dam had broken. People poured into stores to buy televisions. People who couldn't afford them, or who wanted to wait until the televisions improved stood outside TV stores during the day watching the screens and went to bars in the evening to do the same thing. By 1955, almost two-thirds of all U.S. households—64.5 percent—owned TVs. By 1961, that number had grown to 88.8 percent. Today, 99 percent of all U.S. households—a total of 111 million households—report owning at least one TV set.

Recall from our discussion in Chapter 12 that the rise of television hurt movie theaters, as Americans stayed home to watch the tube. As TV clearly gained a permanent hold on the population's interest in the early 1950s, movie studio executives refused to deal with broadcasting executives. As a result, most network television in its first commercial decade was broadcast from New York, not Hollywood, and it was **broadcast live**—that is, it was broadcast as it was actually being performed, rather than being taped, filmed, or recorded. Variety shows with vaudeville and radio stars, as well as dramas from aspiring theatrical ("Broadway") writers and actors, gave television an accessible, real-world feel that was missing from many Hollywood films. The 1950s, which historians have nicknamed the **golden age of television** included powerful, original dramas such as *Marty*, *Judgment at Nuremberg*, and *Requiem for a Heavyweight*, and the standard-setting comedy

very high frequency (VHF) a band of radio frequencies falling between 30 and 300 MHz; VHF signals are widely employed for television and radio transmissions. In the United States and Canada, television stations that broadcast on channels 2 through 13 use VHF frequencies, as do FM radio stations. Many amateur radio operators also transmit on frequencies within the VHF band

ultra high frequency (UHF) a band of radio frequencies from 300 to 3,000 MHz; UHF signals are used extensively in television broadcasting, typically carrying television signals on channels 14 through 83

broadcast live broadcast while actually being performed; not taped, filmed or recorded

golden age of television the period of time from approximately 1949 to 1960, marked by the proliferation of original and classic dramas produced for live television

During the early 1950s, people who could not afford a television of their own often watched the TVs displayed in store windows.

performers that appeared, including Milton Berle, Sid Caesar, Imogene Coca, and Ernie Kovacs.

It was an age that ended quickly. The grittiness of TV's live dramas made some major advertisers nervous. Hollywood's version, a world that was more upscale and that was populated with beautiful people, seemed to fit better with the advertisers' commercials for automobiles and other symbols of the good life. And Hollywood was finally getting interested. Even in the early 1950s, West Coast film producers and actors outside Hollywood's studio system had begun to sell new-filmed series to television. The most important of these were Desi Arnaz and Lucille Ball, whose *I Love Lucy* was an enormous hit with audiences on CBS television. Movie and network executives were quick to recognize the advantages of having a hit on film—as opposed to broadcast live. Unlike the live performances of Berle or Caesar, an *I Love Lucy* episode could be aired over and over again, or **syndicated**. These "repeats" could even be leased to local television stations on a market-by-market basis, to be aired when the network was not operating.

Recognizing the huge potential of such activities, the studios began to deal with television on a regular basis. Warner Brothers was the first major studio to do so, with a production deal in 1954 to supply ABC with three westerns— *Cheyenne*, *Sugarfoot*, and *Maverick*. The floodgates were open, and within a few years live television was rare. The medium had gone Hollywood.

syndication the licensing of mass media material to outlets on a market-by-market basis

Television in the 1960s

Meanwhile, the broadcast television industry was rapidly moving ahead. Advertisers were rushing toward the new medium as it became clear that TV was the most efficient way in history to reach a high percentage of the U.S. population. By the early 1960s, the approach to selling advertising time on TV had changed. Instead of

I Love Lucy was first broadcast in 1951 on CBS, and soon became a show so beloved (thanks to syndication) it actually runs more frequently today than it ran in the 1950s! *I Love Lucy* ran for six years of original episodes (180 in all), and stopped production in 1957, despite the fact that it was still the number 1 show on American television. But good planning kept *I Love Lucy* fresh for decades after the show's original run, as from the start, Lucille Ball and Desi Arnaz insisted on filming the shows in front of a live studio audience. Three separate cameras were used, allowing the show to be edited into its final form. Not only did this become the later standard for all sitcoms, it also ensured that high-quality prints of *I Love Lucy* would be preserved for syndication for years to come.

television program ratings
audits of people's viewing behaviors that gauge which shows households are viewing and how many are viewing them; they help network executives decide which shows should stay, which should be dropped from the lineup, and how much advertisers should pay to hawk their products during breaks in the program

advertisers buying the time and mounting the show (as they had done in network radio and early television), network executives began to plan the schedule and order the shows. This allowed advertisers to buy time on various programs, thereby reaching people at different times and on different networks. The AC Nielsen company supplied **television program ratings,** or audits of people's viewing behavior. Nielsen's ratings gauged which shows households were viewing and how many households were viewing them. TV network executives could use the ratings to decide which shows should stay, which should be dropped from the lineup, and how much advertisers should pay to sell their products during breaks in the programs.

Television executives soon found themselves in the midst of political and social problems raised by their new medium. In the early 1960s, public anger over rigged quiz shows, over the large amount of violence on the home tube, and over what many influential individuals in society considered idiotic entertainment ("a vast wasteland," the FCC's head called it) led to congressional hearings. After the urban riots of the mid- and late 1960s, many politicians, educators, and others blamed television for the nation's violence. TV executives, taking a cue from their movie-industry predecessors, made the appropriate apologies, toned down the violence for a few years and somewhat adjusted their self-regulatory mechanisms. Generally, though, they continued to air Hollywood-produced programs (and made-for-TV movies, a new form of entertainment in the 1960s) that they believed would appeal to the largest number of people in order to grab the highest ratings.

The Advent of Fin-Syn and Prime-Time Access Rules   In fact, during the 1960s, the commercial success of the three television networks and their affiliates was so great that production firms in the industry began to complain that the networks had too much power. Some producers argued that because of the financial success of reruns, the networks were forcing producers to hand over a share in the ownership of a show in exchange for the network agreeing to air it. Other producers noted that the networks took up such a large part of evening programming that it was virtually impossible to sell new syndicated material to stations for airing. The consequence, critics argued, was that television was totally controlled by three companies (ABC, CBS, and NBC) that had an economic stranglehold on the industry and limited the diversity of voices that could be heard.

The Justice Department and the FCC agreed. In 1970, the FCC passed the **primetime access rule (PTAR)**, forcing the networks to stop supplying programming to local stations for a half hour of evening programming during **primetime** (the period chosen turned out to be 7:30 to 8:00 EST) six days a week. This regulation was supposed to help new TV companies come up with new ideas for syndicated programming. In practice, however, the ruling helped large Hollywood firms get stations to buy their cheap quiz shows, game shows, and gossip programs. PTAR's results were far-reaching; in fact, they can be seen quite readily every day on the home tube. For its part, in 1970, the Justice Department established **financial interest and syndication rules, or fin-syn rules.** These rules prohibited ABC, NBC, and CBS from owning most of the entertainment programming they aired, and it also limited their involvement in producing shows for syndication.

Despite these drawbacks, ABC, NBC, and CBS were flying high in the 1970s. Government rulings were limiting their revenues only slightly, and the few UHF stations that existed hardly affected the earnings of the networks' own stations or their affiliates. But in a situation eerily similar to what had happened with movies in 1948, an emerging technology would soon begin to erode the dominance of broadcast TV. The technology was **coaxial cable,** a type of copper cable in which one physical channel that carries the signal is surrounded by another concentric physical channel. Coaxial cable is able to carry information for a great distance.

The Rise of Cable Television

Coaxial cable was not really a new technology in the 1970s. It was invented in 1929 and was first used commercially in 1941 by AT&T, which had established its first cross-continental coaxial transmission system in 1940. By the 1940s, coaxial cable was recognized as a way to carry telephone, radio, and television signals across long distances. In the late 1940s, entrepreneurs realized that coaxial cable could be used to supply broadcast TV signals to communities that had no stations and couldn't use regular rooftop antennas to pick up signals from faraway cities.

Imagine living in a Pennsylvania town somewhere between Pittsburgh and Philadelphia. You are surrounded by hills, so you cannot receive signals from either city. Then some people come along with a bright idea: they place a huge antenna on the tallest hill, string cable from there to people's homes, and charge them for the service. All of a sudden you can get both Philadelphia and Pittsburgh stations for a small subscription fee—it's a great deal.

That's the way **cable television** started, as a **community antenna television (CATV) service** for small towns and suburbs that needed better reception. In fact, this was the way most cable-industry executives saw their business until the late 1970s. In the 1950s and 1960s, broadcasters were quite happy to have cable companies relay their signals to out-of-the-way areas. Broadcasters recognized early, though, that if cable companies started laying wires in and around cities, they could dilute the value of the broadcasters' stations. Residents of a Chicago suburb could, for example, enjoy the sports programming of Cincinnati, New York, or Atlanta channels. These could be relayed to the cable operator by microwave transmission facilities and distributed to the operator's customers via the coaxial cable.

primetime access rule or PTAR a 1970 FCC rule that forced the networks to stop supplying programming to local stations for a half hour during prime time —8 to 11 p.m. (7 to 10 p.m. in the central and mountain time zones) six days a week

financial interest and syndication rules, or fin-syn rules rules established by the U.S. Justice Department prohibiting ABC, NBC, and CBS from owning most of the entertainment programming they aired, and limiting their involvement in producing shows for syndication

coaxial cable a type of copper cable used by cable TV companies between the community antenna and user homes and businesses; it is made up of one physical channel that carries the signal surrounded by another concentric physical channel and is able to carry information for a great distance

cable television the process of sending TV signals to subscribers through a wire (usually a coaxial cable, but increasingly via fiber optic lines)

community antenna television (CATV) service an early name for cable television

Government Regulation of the Cable Television Industry in the 1960s and 1970s

During the 1960s, the FCC agreed with broadcasters' arguments that the government had to protect "free" broadcasting in metropolitan areas from cable operators who demanded payment for their signals. As a result, the agency formulated the Cable Television Rules that made it nearly impossible for cable firms to expand their operations to the center and the suburbs of major cities.

By the mid-1970s, the forces supporting cable television began to gain more political clout. Realizing that encouraging cable would expand the number of television options available to Americans, the FCC changed its rules to allow cable firms to expand into metropolitan areas (and to compete directly with traditional broadcasters).

Another federal policy that opened the TV world to competition between technologies was the **free skies** entrepreneurial approach to satellite use in the 1970s, which for the first time allowed satellites to be used freely for a wide variety of business purposes. This approach permitted two developments that pointed to cable TV's future impact on national advertising—the advent of HBO and Ted Turner's Superstation.

free skies a policy instituted by the U.S. government that for the first time allowed satellites to be used freely for a wide variety of business purposes

Home Box Office and Ted Turner's Superstation

In 1976, Home Box Office (HBO), a subsidiary of Time Inc., began to deliver fairly recent films to cable systems around the United States via the Satcom 1 satellite. Cable systems that purchased a satellite dish could carry HBO, charge subscribers an additional fee, and share the proceeds with HBO. Instantly, HBO gave cable a national brand and a unique service: programming that home viewers could not get from over-the-air stations.

Close on HBO's heels was Atlanta broadcaster and sports financier Ted Turner. Early in 1976, he announced that he was going to make the programming of his Atlanta UHF-TV station available to cable systems via the same Satcom 1 satellite used by HBO. Coining the term **superstation** to describe his concept, Turner reasoned that cable system owners and viewers would appreciate the mix of old movies, Atlanta Braves baseball, and Atlanta Hawks basketball that his station provided. Turner would benefit financially in several ways—from the transmission fee charged to cable firms for picking up the signal, from the broad attention his teams would receive, and from the extended audience his advertisers would get. By the end of 1976, Turner's station was being carried by twenty cable systems in different parts of the country.

superstation term coined by Ted Turner to describe his cable station concept, which aired old movies, Atlanta Braves baseball, and Atlanta Hawks basketball that his station provided. Turner benefited financially in several ways—from the transmission fee charged to cable firms for picking up the signal, from the broad attention his teams would receive, and from the extended audience his advertisers would get

The rise of HBO and Turner's Superstation received a lot of attention and ignited talk in the press that a new TV world was just around the corner. Naysayers could argue correctly, though, that not much had really changed. HBO didn't even carry ads. As for the broadcast channels that cable systems retransmitted to their subscribers' homes, they simply expanded the audience for standard commercials a little. The number of channels delivered to people's homes was larger than before, but not astoundingly so. In the mid-1970s, most systems (75 percent of them) still carried fewer than twelve channels, including the three or more local channels that homeowners had received before they paid for cable. To top it off, a great portion of America still didn't have cable: even as late as 1978, only about 17 percent of American homes received cable television.

Nevertheless, the movement to a new television world had begun. The early 1980s saw the launching of a raft of new satellite-delivered television channels—most prominently the Cable News Network (CNN), Nickelodeon, and Music

Television (MTV)—that further enticed upscale viewers to subscribe to cable even if they could easily receive the broadcast networks. The **cable networks,** or program channels offered by a cable system beyond what is broadcast over the airwaves in their area, benefited from a dual revenue stream. Their most important source of support was the exhibitors—the cable television systems that carried their programs. Recognizing that original networks generated new subscribers, the cable companies paid a monthly fee (about fifteen cents per subscriber) to the new networks. The second source of support was national advertisers. They saw these program services as helping them to reach selected audiences in the same way that magazines did. Because homes with cable TV in the 1980s tended to be wealthier than those without it, advertising on MTV or CNN enabled a sponsor to reach upscale people with particular interests—an opportunity the broadcast networks rarely offered.

cable networks program channels offered by a cable television system to its customers in addition to what is broadcast over the airwaves in their geographic area (now more appropriately called *cable/satellite networks*, since they can be delivered to the consumer through cable television systems or via satellite)

A Fragmented Television Era

As the number of cable networks grew, cable system operators added channels and the number of choices available to cable subscribers grew. Many observers noted, however, that the sheer number of channels—150 in some areas in the early twenty-first century—should not be equated with diversity. A large proportion of cable programming was made up of reruns from broadcast TV. Nevertheless, the activities of the cable industry multiplied the number of viewing possibilities at any one time.

So did the growth of broadcast television channels beginning in the late 1970s. At that time, the FCC, aiming to inject competition into the over-the-air business, started assigning a large number of new, mostly UHF, broadcast TV licenses. As a result, the number of independent TV broadcasters (those not affiliated with ABC, NBC, or CBS) soared, from fewer than 100 in 1979 to 339 in 1989. Airing mostly old TV shows, movies, and sports, these stations managed to garner high enough Nielsen ratings and find enough advertisers to sustain themselves.

videocassette recorder (VCR) an electronic device for recording and playing back video images and sound on a videocassette tape

New Networks Emerge

By 1986, the number of independent TV broadcasters around the United States was great enough to convince media mogul Rupert Murdoch that he could accomplish a feat no one had been able to do since the 1950s: start a fourth network that could compete seriously with the Big Three. His Fox network started out shakily, but in the ensuing years, on the strength of a popular Saturday morning children's lineup and quirky, youth-oriented evening programs such as *The Simpsons*, *Married...with Children*, and *The X-Files*, it managed to draw advertisers and become a permanent TV fixture. Trying to imitate that success, in the mid-1990s Time Warner launched the WB network, and a strong broadcast-station firm called Chris Craft, together with Viacom, launched UPN. By 2006, the WB and UPN merged into one network, called the CW. Two Spanish-language networks, Univision and its less popular rival, Telemundo, became mainstays of the quickly growing U.S. Hispanic population.

digital versatile disk (DVD) an optical disk technology with two layers on each of its two sides, holding up to 17 gigabytes of video, audio, or other information; *DVD-Video* is the usual name for the DVD format designed for full-length movies and played through a box that will work with your television set

New Technologies Mean New Opportunities and New Challenges

TV options were further enlarged by the spread of the **videocassette recorder** (the **VCR**), the **digital versatile** (or digital video) **disk** (the **DVD**), and **direct-to-home**

direct-to-home satellite service a digital technology that delivers up to 150 channels to a plate-sized receiver on a subscriber's house; these services include the DBS format in the United States and the DVB format in much of the rest of the world

satellite services. The last of these digital technologies, new in the 1990s, beamed up to 150 channels to a plate-sized receiver on a subscriber's house. Carrying mostly recent movies and cable networks, direct-to-home satellite viewing initially served as a substitute for cable television in rural areas where cable wasn't available, or in communities where subscribers didn't like their local cable operator.

The merger of computer and television technologies led to the beginnings of digital television, for which over-the air standards were set in 1996. Observers debated whether the new DVD—a device that could store music, data, and video—would replace or complement the VCR. (By 2007, it pretty well replaced it.) Audiovisual choices were exploding. Regulators tried to keep up. The **Telecommunications Act of 1996** allowed anyone to enter any communications business and let any communications business compete in any market against any other business, and so allowed telephone and cable companies to compete with each other for the first time.

The result was that more than ever, people were going to different places for their TV viewing. In one sense, family members were spending a lot of their viewing time separated from one another. Survey companies found that by 1995, more than 66 percent of U.S. homes had multiple television sets—10 percent more than a decade earlier. About 28 percent had three or more sets. By 2007, 84 percent owned a DVD player, and 86 percent received cable, satellite transmission, or phone transmission of TV signals. Moreover, almost one out of five households had a digital video recorder (DVR), which allowed people to record shows and view them later. It also allowed viewers to race through the commercials. The increasing number of choices encouraged parents to watch separately from their children—and encouraged different children in the family to watch separately as well. TV executives worried that the growing DVR use meant fewer people were attending to commercials.

In another sense, people were also watching programs from new sources. Not only were they viewing cable and broadcast TV, they were going online to view videos from amateur and professional sources. They were moving through audiovisual video game adventures online, on computers, or via game players. And in growing numbers they were even viewing videos on their mobile phones and other handheld digital devices like iPods.

Consolidating Ownership

With technological changes such as these came changes in the ownership of the television business. Despite the fragmentation of television and the competition between channels, a few conglomerates had a substantial amount of power over this new audiovisual environment. Those conglomerates stood at the center of the Hollywood industry that fifty years earlier had pretended that TV would go away. Now Disney, News Corporation, Time Warner, Viacom, Sony, and General Electric (through NBC Universal) took command not just of theatrical moviemaking but also of distribution in the home video (VCR and DVD) business, controlling a huge share of the market. In addition, the Telecommunications Act of 1996 eliminated the fin-syn rules, making it possible for the first time since the 1960s for a major movie studio to own a broadcast network. Disney, News Corp, Time Warner and GE did just that. By the end of the twenty-first century's first decade, all of these conglomerates also owned lucrative cable networks that further extended their audiovisual distribution capabilities.

Increasingly, then, competition meant a battle among titans in television, as in other media. Small producers, distributors, and exhibitors had a difficult time sur-

Telecommunications Act of 1996 a law that allowed anyone to enter any communications business and let any communications business compete in any market against any other business

TV Ratings and Kids

TECH & INFRASTRUCTURE

The Telecommunications Act of 1996 enabled parents to exercise greater control over the television content to which their children were exposed. In addition to requiring TV manufacturers to produce sets with a V-Chip that allows parents to block objectionable programming, a rating system was enacted to alert viewers to the nature of program content. The ratings strategy was highly controversial because its categories were based on the age of the viewer, like those of the motion picture industry, and not on the program's content (e.g., violence, adult language, sex).

Joanne Cantor of the University of Wisconsin-Madison conducted several studies that showed that the age-based ratings system did not help parents make informed television content decisions for their families. Cantor and other researchers analyzed national surveys that showed parents' overwhelming preference for a content-based ratings system over one based on age-appropriateness.

In addition, these researchers found that a TV ratings system akin to the movie industry's ratings was fairly uninformative and unpredictable. They coded more than 1,400 PG-rated movies to determine what elements contributed to the rating: adult language, violence, and/or sexual content. Of these movies, 26 percent were rated PG on the basis of language only and another quarter contained both violence and coarse language, but 18 percent had no sex, violence, or coarse language. Based on these findings, the odds were that an age-based TV rating system would not give parents the information they needed in order to assess whether a program's content might be harmful to kids.

Cantor also examined whether ratings and advisories produced a "forbidden fruit" effect, leading some children to want to watch programs that the system implied might be inappropriate. Blander ratings like "viewer discretion advised" did not affect the attitudes toward viewing programs of kids in any age or gender group. However, ratings that could be seen as more restrictive, such as "parental discretion advised" or film ratings of PG-13 or R, did heighten the appeal of the programs for older kids, especially older boys.

Professor Cantor's research raises provocative questions about whom the ratings really benefit—the parents or the broadcasters.

viving; they often could do so only by creating an alliance with one of the major firms. At the same time, a couple of new twenty-first century titans also emerged to add new meaning to competition in "television." These were Google and Yahoo, Internet firms that were posting videos online. So were smaller websites such as Joost and Revver. These developments raised the question of what exactly television meant in the twenty-first century, and they led the longstanding TV powers to begin to rethink what they were doing in the television industry. As a result, today's TV industry involves activities that are both traditional and experimental. Let's look at both.

An Overview of the Modern Television Industry

We'll start with the traditional, mainstay activities of the business, where most of the action and money remain. It's useful to think of today's television world as divided into three domains:

- TV broadcasting
- Cable services
- Satellite services

Table 13.1 Household Penetration Rates of Television Services in the United States, 2006

Television service	% of households (total HH = 113.4)
Overall television households	98.2
Basic cable households	64.0
Pay cable households	32.0
Satellite households	25.0
Video On Demand	26.3
RBOC television	1.0

Source: Motion Picture Association of America and Veronis Suhler Stevenson

Of the two subscription technologies, cable is by far the most popular. In 2006, it reached about 64 percent of American homes, while satellite reached about 25 percent. A variation of cable TV, through phone companies called RBOCs, reached about 1 percent with their subscription television service (see Table 13.1). We'll discuss them in a bit.

Let's take a look at the three domains.

Television Broadcasting

Television broadcasting, or the broad, over-the-air transmission of audiovisual signals, has historically been the most popular of the three. Its signals are transmitted from towers owned by local stations on frequencies allocated to them by the Federal Communications Commission (FCC). People can receive the signals without charge by simply turning on a television set. More than 99 percent of American households can do that.

About 1,400 television stations existed in 2007. Each station is licensed by the Federal Communications Commission to send out signals in a particular area of the country. As we have seen, the FCC gives out licenses to operate on frequencies in one of two bands of the electromagnetic spectrum: the VHF band and the UHF band. Because VHF can deliver clear pictures to more people than UHF can, VHF stations have been considered more valuable. The FCC has ruled that as of April 2009, however, all stations will move to a new part of the spectrum and broadcast using digital rather than analog technology. That part of the spectrum will be auctioned by the government for use by other companies and public service organizations. By then, according to FCC rules, new TV sets will have to be able to receive the new digital signals.

Most of the 1,400 stations are what people in the TV industry call *commercial*; the rest are *noncommercial*. **Commercial stations** make their money by selling time on their airwaves to advertisers. **Noncommercial stations** receive support in other ways, such as viewer donations and donations from private foundations and commercial firms in return for billboards. **Billboards** are mentions of a sponsor's name or products at the start or end of programs airing on the station.

commercial television station a broadcast television station that supports itself financially by selling time on its airwaves to advertisers

noncommercial television station a broadcast television station that does not receive financial support from advertisers, but rather supports itself through donations from listeners and private foundations, and from commercial firms in return for mentioning the firm or its products in announcements at the beginning and end of programs airing on the station

billboard the mention of a sponsor's name or products at the start or end of an aired program in return for money

Digital TV Conversion

As the long-planned Digital Television Transition nears, the Federal Communications Commission is taking steps to ensure that consumers will not be adversely affected. Initially conceived as a way to free up space on the broadcast spectrum by harnessing new technology, the move will also allow the FCC to utilize the airwaves for public and safety services as well as for advanced wireless services. Televisions currently run on analog at 700 MHz and public and safety services use frequencies that are congested, jeopardizing efficacy. Additionally, using 700 MHz for wireless broadband could go farther and in a straighter line than the frequencies currently used, improving speed. The changeover is set to take place on February 17, 2009. In anticipation, the FCC required all new televisions manufactured after March 1, 2007 to include a digital tuner.

Additionally, the FCC has adopted rules to ensure that all cable customers—even those with analog televisions—receive local stations via their cable company. The FCC's ruling gives cable providers two choices for compliance: "(1) carry the digital signal in analog format, or (2) carry the signal only in digital format, provided that all subscribers have the necessary equipment to view the broadcast content." The Commission voted to extend this window until 2012, so that companies and technologies, as well as users, have ample time to adapt to new technologies. In the meantime, the FCC is spreading the word through its website dedicated to the transition, found at http://www.dtv.gov

Since advertising is so important for the support of broadcast stations, you should not be surprised to learn that people who work in the television industry divide the United States into 210 markets. New York City is the largest, followed by Los Angeles and then Chicago. The New York City market boasts about seven million homes. Glendive, Montana, the smallest market, has 4,000 (see Table 13.2).

Table 13.2 **The Top Ten Broadcast Television Markets in the United States, 2007**

Rank	Designated market area (DMA)	TV households	Percentage of U.S.
1	New York, NY	7,391,940	6.553
2	Los Angeles, CA	5,647,440	5.007
3	Chicago, IL	3,469,110	3.076
4	Philadelphia, PA	2,939,950	2.606
5	Dallas-Ft. Worth, TX	2,435,600	2.159
6	San Francisco-Oakland-San Jose, CA	2,419,440	2.145
7	Boston, MA (Manchester, NH)	2,393,960	2.122
8	Atlanta, GA	2,310,490	2.048
9	Washington, DC (Hagerstown, MD)	2,308,290	2.046
10	Houston, TX	2,050,550	1.818

From "U.S. TV Household Estimates Designated Market Area (DMA)–Ranked by Households" from Television Bureau of Advertising Online. Source: Nielsen Media Research, Inc.

www.pbs.org

television network an organization that distributes television programs, typically by satellite and microwave relay, to all its affiliated stations, or stations that agree to carry a substantial amount of the network's material on an ongoing basis, so that programs can be broadcast by all the stations at the same time

Big Four the four largest television networks: ABC, CBS, Fox, and NBC

vertical integration an organization's control over a media product from production through distribution to exhibition

owned and operated or O&O broadcast television stations that are owned and operated by a network that often provides a regular schedule of programming materials for broadcast

More than 80 percent of local TV stations have linked up or affiliated with a *television network* for at least part of their broadcast day. A **television network** is an organization that distributes television programs, typically by satellite and microwave relay, to all its affiliated stations, or stations that agree to carry a substantial amount of the network's material on an ongoing basis, so that the programs can be broadcast by all the stations at the same time. ABC, CBS, Fox, and NBC are the broadcast networks that regularly reach the largest number of people. They are advertiser-supported, as are three smaller networks: the CW, MyNetworkTV and ION. Two commercial Spanish-speaking networks also exist. They are Univision and Telemundo, owned by NBC. The Public Broadcasting Service (PBS) is the network for noncommercial stations.

The **Big Four** commercial networks—ABC, CBS, Fox, and NBC—are the giants of the broadcast television business, primarily because of their role in coordinating the distribution of shows to hundreds of local stations, which then transmit the shows to homes. But ABC, CBS, Fox, and NBC are more than just distributors. They are **vertically integrated** operations. Each company has divisions that produce news, sports, situation comedies, dramas, and other types of programs for use on the network. Each company also owns stations (sometimes called broadcast outlets) in the biggest cities; these outlets serve as exhibition anchors for their respective networks. In the TV industry, these local stations are called **O&O**—short for **owned and operated.**

Local stations that are not owned by broadcast networks and yet transmit their signals and programs are called **network affiliates.** A network affiliate transmits the network's **program feed** (that is, the succession of shows) on a daily basis. In return, the network promises to compensate the affiliate with a portion of the revenues received from advertisers that have bought time on the network.

Many affiliates are part of **station groups,** or collections of broadcast television stations owned by a single company. In the wealthiest station groups, such as Allbritton Communications, each station is an affiliate of one of the major networks. Stations in other groups hook up mainly with WB or UPN.

According to the Federal Communications Commission, no group may own more than two television stations in any market. That dictum is based on the desire to limit the power of broadcast groups in any one area. The FCC has also ruled, however, that a company can own two networks as long as both are not among the Big Four networks. Observers saw the ruling as a way to help Viacom after the conglomerate's merger with CBS. The company was in the uncomfortable legal position of owning both the CBS TV network and the struggling UPN. Some FCC members feared that UPN, which ran series tilted toward African-American audiences, would be in danger of failing if Viacom wasn't allowed to keep it.

A broadcast station that is not affiliated with one of the Big Four networks is called an **independent.** (Industry executives often consider CW, MyNetworkTV and ION affiliates to be independents because they air relatively few hours of network programming per week.) Practically speaking, independents must find all (or almost all) of their programming themselves. Actually, even network affiliates and

O&Os must look to sources other than ABC, CBS, Fox, and NBC for some of their programming. The reason is that the Big Four do not distribute twenty-four hours' worth of shows. As we will see later in this chapter, the broadcast industry has no shortage of companies trying to interest independents, affiliates, and O&Os in programming.

We have already suggested another set of key industry players: advertisers. With the help of companies called advertising agencies (which Chapters 15 and 16 discuss in some detail), advertisers pay for time between programs and segments of programs. In return, broadcasters allow advertisers to use this time to air **commercials**—short audiovisual pieces

www.ionline.tv, website of the Ion Television network

that call attention to their products or services. A lot of money changes hands in this activity. In 2005, advertisers spent about $45 billion on television broadcast advertising. Viewers of broadcast TV do not have to pay to receive the programming. Consequently, almost all the money that broadcast stations and networks receive has come from a single revenue stream—commercials. That is still the case, though the networks and local stations are beginning to take advantage of digital media to develop sources of revenue other than broadcast commercials.

Cable and Satellite Services

One way in which cable and satellite services differ from broadcasting is their reliance on two major revenue streams:

- Advertisers pay to have their commercials shown during programming
- Consumers pay to get the service in the first place

Both revenue streams are substantial, although the money received from subscriptions is far greater than advertisers' contributions. In 2005, American consumers paid around $59 billion to receive cable or satellite services. Advertisers paid $22 billion to advertise on these services.[1]

In the case of the cable and satellite television industries, we can see quite clearly that more kinds of key players are involved in them than in broadcast television. Consider cable television with its cast of organizations. Then there is the satellite area, with its *direct broadcast satellite* operations.

The Cable Television Business Cable television refers to businesses that provide programming to subscribers via a wire (historically a coaxial cable, but increasingly a fiber optic line). The cable television business is by far the most developed in the cable and satellite area. Stripped to its basics, a **cable** is a type of flexible tube or pipe through which programs are exhibited in the home. The retailer that physically installs the cable and markets the program service to consumers in a particular geographic area is called a **cable television system** (see Table 13.3). A cable television firm that owns two or more cable systems is a **multiple system owner (MSO)** (see Table 13.4). Much like a store, every cable system has a certain amount of shelf space, which in this case is the channels it carries through its pipes. Each system offers consumers in its community an array of channels that includes

network affiliates local broadcast television stations that are not owned by broadcast networks and yet transmit network signals and programs on a daily basis; in return, the network promises to compensate the affiliate with a portion of the revenues received from advertisers that have bought time on the network

program feed the succession of shows sent from a network to its network affiliates

station group a collection of broadcast television stations owned by a single company

independent broadcast station a broadcast television station that is not affiliated with one of the Big Four networks

commercials short audiovisual advertisements that call attention to certain products or services

Table 13.3   Top Ten Cable Systems, 2007

Rank	System	Basic subscribers
1	Cablevision Greater New York	3,009,064
2	Comcast Greater Chicago Region	1,800,000
3	Comcast San Francisco Bay Area Region	1,700,000
4	Comcast New Jersey	1,400,000
5	Time Warner of New York & New Jersey	1,400,000
6	Comcast Michigan Region	1,320,000
7	Comcast Philadelphia Metro	1,100,000
8	Comcast Washington State	1,095,000
9	Bright House Networks, Tampa Bay Division	1,030,000
10	Comcast Mid-South Region	1,024,307

Source: Multichannel News online, accessed 1/21/08.

cable   a type of flexible tube or pipe through which programs are exhibited in the home

cable television system the cable television retailer that physically installs the cable and markets the program service to consumers in a particular geographic area

multiple system owner (MSO)   a cable television firm that owns two or more cable television systems

subscription networks nonbroadcast program channels for which people pay a monthly subscription fee to receive them via cable or satellite

special networks as well as independent local broadcast stations and network affiliates. Called cable networks because they first appeared on cable, the nonbroadcast channels are more appropriately called **subscription networks** because people pay a monthly fee (a subscription) to receive them via cable or satellite.

Table 13.4   Top Ten MSOs, June 2007

Rank	MSO	Subscribers
1	Comcast Cable Communications	24,141,000
2	Time Warner Cable	13,391,000
3	Cox Communications	5,424,000
4	Charter Communications	5,376,800
5	Cablevision Systems	3,139,000
6	Bright House Networks LLC	2,327,100
7	Suddenlink Communications	1,416,800
8	Mediacom Communications Corp.	1,344,000
9	Insight Communications	1,341,000
10	CableOne	696,700

Source: National Cable Television Association.

Recently, traditional telephone service providers, notably AT&T and Verizon, have also begun to offer a multichannel television service in many parts of the country, competing with the cable TV firms. Although they wouldn't be called cable companies by people in the business, Verizon and AT&T do use wire technologies (as opposed to the unwired satellite approach) to reach people's homes. Some people in the business call them **RBOCs**, which stands for Regional Bell Operating Companies—a reference to the old Bell Telephone system from which those firms sprang. Verizon and AT&T have different technical philosophies, but they share the idea of using advanced communication lines called fiber optics to send cable programming to TV sets. Down the line, the RBOCs, and especially Verizon, will pose a formidable threat to providers of television services. At this point in time, though, the threat posed by RBOCs to traditional cable firms and to the satellite business is small because they are just beginning to roll out their services.

The Satellite Business   **Satellite television** means programming that comes directly to the home from a satellite orbiting the earth. In 2007, 59 percent of U.S. households with a TV were hooked up to a cable service, and about 25 percent subscribed to a satellite operation. You may have seen old-style satellite dishes, large structures that typically sat behind people's homes. The backyard satellite dish business was built in the 1980s on the proposition that a homeowner could cut out the cable system by installing a dish-shaped instrument in the backyard and getting programs directly from the satellite that sends them to the cable system. Unfortunately for the homeowners, though, most networks now encode their programs so that a person with a dish cannot view them free of charge. Although 200,000 people still have backyard dishes, most have been replaced by **direct broadcast satellite (DBS)** technology. Introduced in 1994, it allows a household to receive hundreds of channels. The signals are delivered digitally to a small dish installed on the side of a house or apartment building; a set-top box converts the digital signals to analog signals that are accepted by the TV. The DBS satellites operate from orbits directly above the earth's equator and just over 22,000 miles up. DirecTV and EchoStar (the Dish) are currently the largest DBS companies in the United States.

For the foreseeable future, it seems clear that competition over television will be among broadcast, cable, and satellite providers. TV executives fear that audiences will continue to flee to the new channels and away from the Big Four. You might also have gathered that cable and satellite systems are themselves engaged in sometimes ferocious fights for consumers. To get an idea of how these providers are jockeying for viewers' eyeballs, we have to understand the basic elements of the evolving television industry. To do that, we turn to our familiar categories of production, distribution, and exhibition. Production takes up the lion's share of this discussion, simply because there are so many different ways to look at it.

RBOCs or Regional Bell Operating Companies   a term used to describe Verizon and AT&T who have determined to compete with traditional cable MSOs. Although they wouldn't be called cable companies by people in the business, Verizon and AT&T do use wire technologies (as opposed to the unwired satellite approach) to reach people's homes

satellite television programming that comes directly to the home from a satellite orbiting the earth

direct broadcast satellite (DBS)   technology that allows a household to receive hundreds of channels which are delivered digitally to a small dish installed on the side of a house or apartment building; a set-top box converts the digital signals to analog signals that are accepted by the TV. The DBS satellites operate from orbits directly above the earth's equator and just over 22,000 miles up

Production in the Television Industry

Production is a tricky word when it comes to the television business. In the broadest sense, at least three forms of production are going on at different levels of the industry. To get a sense of what this means, think of your local cable television system. Chances are, your local cable system produces very few of its own programs. (Maybe it aids in the production of an access channel, where local officials and citizens can state their problems and parade their interests.) But making shows is not

lineup the menu of channels that a cable television system offers potential subscribers

format the collection of elements that constitutes a channel's recognizable personality, created through a set of rules that guide the way the elements are stitched together with a particular audience-attracting goal in mind

the only way a cable TV system can be involved in production. Your local system is very much involved in producing the number and nature of network channels that it offers potential subscribers; this menu of channels is called a **lineup**.

Each network, in turn, is engaged in a second sort of production. Take the MTV network as an example. Its personnel create the **format**—the flow of series, news and videos that defines MTV's overall personality and helps it stand apart from other networks in cable system lineups. Of course, MTV personnel select the programs that are crucial building blocks of their network. However, these are often created by other firms that have very little input into decisions about the formats or lineups in which they appear.

Trying to understand production in the television world, then, means getting a grip on the considerations that affect the lineup of channels, the formats of individual channels, and the elements of individual programs. Let's look at each of these categories as it relates to the cable/satellite/RBOC and broadcast TV businesses.

Producing Channel Lineups

Creating a channel lineup is a high-priority job for cable and satellite exhibitors. Executives from these companies believe that the number and kinds of programming networks that they offer potential customers are major features that attract people to pay for their service. MTV, Nickelodeon, VH1, E!, CNN, C-Span, TBS, AMC, ESPN, ESPN2, the Cartoon Network, HBO: for which of these or other networks would you consider subscribing to another service if your cable or satellite system didn't carry it?

With so much riding on customer satisfaction, you would think that cable and satellite executives would simply poll their customers and put on everything they want to see. The firms do, in fact, conduct surveys of consumers, and executives do look at ratings reports that indicate how many people watch different networks. Nevertheless, the choice of networks is based as much on three other considerations as on consumer feedback. These considerations are:

- The technological limitations of the system
- The amount of money a network demands from exhibitors
- Whether or not the exhibitor owns a piece of the network

digital compression technology a development that allows both cable and satellite delivery firms to pack anywhere from four to twelve digital video signals into the same 6-MHz slot currently occupied by a standard (analog) channel

Technological Limitations Technological limitations restrict the number of channels that a cable or satellite service can deliver. **Digital compression technology** allows a cable company or satellite delivery firm to pack anywhere from four to twelve digital video signals into the same 6-MHz slot currently occupied by a standard (analog) channel. Satellite firms send all their programming digitally, and cable firms are encouraging their customers to move from analog to digital service using a converter box. How many more signals cable systems can carry depends on the nature of their existing pipelines and the amount of money they are willing to spend. Even when new devices emerge that can expand the number of channels, firms that offer subscription video have to weigh the often-huge cost of adding these new devices against the revenue the additional channels may bring in.

High definition TV signals use substantially more bandwidth than standard TV signals, a factor that has affected the number of HDTV channels cable and satellite firms have offered. As a telecommunications analyst said in 2007, "HDTV takes an enormous amount of (transmission) capacity. They're going to be sticking 10 pounds of potatoes into a 5-pound bag. Something will have to give."[2]

A *USA Today* columnist added that cable and satellite companies may have to "throw some weaklings overboard to make room for a coming onslaught of high definition channels."[3]

Covering Costs   In addition to technological limitations and the costs of upgrades, the lineups set by cable and satellite exhibitors depend on the amounts of money that particular networks charge exhibitors for carrying their networks. These costs are called **license fees.** The notion that a subscription video network should charge exhibitors for carrying it goes back to the early 1980s, when advertising support for cable networks such as CNN and A&E was meager and cable systems agreed to chip in to help the networks survive.

Cable and satellite systems typically pay between fifteen and twenty-five cents for each subscriber for many of the networks they carry. With millions of subscribers out there, this can add up to real money, money that the delivery service could use for technology upgrades. Consequently, when cable and satellite systems make decisions about their lineups, the mix of channels that they choose is influenced by the amount they will have to pay to those channels. A channel that charges more than another with the same level of audience popularity will have less chance of getting on a system than one that demands lower license fees.

Of course, one way in which a cable or satellite system can provide relatively expensive channels and continue to make technological improvements is to charge subscribers more money. That was what many cable operators did during the 1990s, despite federal laws aimed at keeping prices down. Still, the possibility of competition and a desire for consumer goodwill led firms to keep their most basic rates relatively low and to charge more for extra packages of programs. This strategy of charging different amounts for different levels of programming is called **tiering.** The number and variety of tiers has gone up dramatically in recent years, especially among cable firms. The most common types are described below.

Basic Cable
In many cable systems, this entry-level service offers the customer all the broadcast channels available in the area, channels with local government and other "access" programming, and a small number of subscription channels, such as TBS and TNT. In some areas, these starter tiers cost less than $10 per month. Relatively few viewers choose this tier, though, and satellite firms don't have an equivalent limited offering (Echostar's DISH packages start with fifty channels).

Expanded (or "Enhanced") Basic
This tier really gets the subscriber into the menu of cable programming. Comcast's version of this tier in 2007 provided 70 channels at around $51 per month. A few of the expanded basic networks, such as the two C-SPAN services that air programming from Congress, rely on the cable exhibitors to foot all of their bills. Most of these networks are advertiser-supported as well as cable-supported, however. Apart from TBS and TNT (which tend to appear in basic lineups), common networks in the enhanced lineup are CNN (news), ESPN (sports), USA (general programming), Discovery (science and nature), Nickelodeon (programming aimed at children), the Cartoon Network, the Nashville Network (country music), Fox News, Lifetime (programming aimed at women), MTV (music), A&E (historical and cultural documentaries), Black Entertainment Television, and the Weather Channel. Below them, a large number of advertiser-supported networks clamor to get on cable systems. Country Music Television, Animal Planet, Food Network, HGTV (Home & Garden Television), and the Travel Channel are among the dozens of candidates trying to make it into the video pipelines. Some of them are

license fees   the costs that particular networks charge exhibitors for carrying the networks' lineups in the exhibitors' cable or satellite systems

tiering   the strategy by which different levels of television programming are priced differently

521

so eager, and so confident of advertiser support, that they are not demanding any subscriber payments from cable or satellite systems.

Digital Cable

In an attempt to compete with the larger number of channels that DirecTV and Echostar offer, some cable companies have been using digital compression technology to deliver over one hundred channels to their customers. Many of these channels offer pay-per-view movies or music audio services. The cable systems charge extra for this digital tier. In 2000, about ten million homes subscribed to digital cable.

The fast growth in DBS and the rise of digital cable has led cable/satellite networks to fear that they might lose their audiences to new competitors. As a result, they have created additional channels that they hope will attract audiences and lock out potential competitors from satellite services and digital cable services. Showtime Networks, for example, offers sixteen separate channels, including Showtime, ShoToo, ShoCASE, ShoExtreme, ShoFamily, Flix, and Sundance. All sixteen carry separate programming streams (feeds) for the East and West Coasts of the United States. Some critics wonder whether this splintering of channels will simply divide a network's audience into tiny pieces rather than attract many new customers to the services. That might be inefficient for both the networks and the cable or satellite firms.

Premium Channels

This term refers to HBO, Encore, Showtime, Cinemax, Encore, and other networks that charge individual monthly fees for receiving their programming, although discounted "packages" are available. Premium sports channels are also part of the pay cable menu in many areas. Cable and satellite systems share the fees with the pay networks.

The penetration of premium services is higher in DBS households than in cable homes—88 percent of DBS households compared to about 79 percent of cable households. One explanation is that DBS households tend to be more financially secure than cable subscribers. Another is that their very choice of DBS suggests that they are more likely to value having many channels and to be willing to pay for them.

Pay-per-view (PPV)

In this type of programming, the cable or satellite company charges the customer for viewing an individual program, such as a boxing event, a live broadcast of a concert, or a newly released motion picture. The customer must wait for the specific time that the program airs to view it, or the customer can use a digital video recorder (DVR) to capture the program at that time. Depending on the sophistication of the system, the customer phones the firm or simply enters a choice into a set-top box. The charge appears on the customer's bill.

Video on Demand (VOD)

This is a more interactive technology than PPV. With video on demand, a customer simply uses the remote control to navigate to a menu of programs and then to click on the program he or she wants to watch. Unlike PPV, where the customer has to wait for the show to appear at a certain time, the program immediately appears for viewing.

As this description suggests, VOD requires the customer to be able to communicate directly with the computer providing the programming. That is possible in most cable television systems, because the wire connected to the television carries a signal two ways—from the system's regional delivery location (called the head end) to the home set and back. Satellite companies, however, don't typically provide the ability of a home television remote to communicate instantly with the computers delivering the programming. Consequently, they cannot offer true video on demand. They try to make up for it by providing their customers with digital video recorders that download selections viewers might want to try, but the selections are more limited than the ones that cable firms provide. Seeing a competitive advantage, cable firms have been trumpeting their VOD offerings, many of which are free and some of which are in high definition. Cable executives are disappointed, though, that customers spend relatively little of their VOD time with movies or other programs for which they must pay. In 1996, Comcast found that almost 95 percent of all VOD viewing involved free programming.

The Exhibitors' Ownership Role in the Network A third important consideration that influences the lineup of a cable system is whether the MSO or its parent company owns the network. It stands to reason that if a company has a financial interest in the success of a channel, it would include it. So, for example, if you live in an area served by Comcast, you'll probably find that it carries SportsNet, E!, Style, The Golf Channel, and G4—all owned wholly or partly by Comcast. Time Warner Cable similarly carries networks that it owns. That doesn't mean that cable systems that do not own these channels will not carry them. It does mean, however, that if a major cable MSO decides to create a channel, it will put it on enough systems in favorable channel locations to give it a good chance of success. That kind of boost would not be so easily available to independent companies with interesting channel ideas.

Producing Broadcast Channel Lineups

You may be wondering if anything resembling what we have discussed regarding lineups in the subscription video industry exists in broadcast. The answer is: it doesn't exist now, but it will soon. To understand what this means, you have to realize that broadcast television is currently going through an enormous transformation that has given every local broadcaster as many as four channels to program. The change may well make every local TV station a kind of mini-cable system that will have to deal with questions of channel lineups similar to those faced by cable systems. At the core of this change in how broadcasters do business is the industry's shift from the traditional analog to the new digital transmission of programming. Chapter 2 explains the technical difference between **analog** and **digital** materials. Recall that **analog** electronic transmission is accomplished by adding signals of varying frequency or amplitude to carrier waves of a given frequency of alternating electromagnetic current. By contrast, **digital** electronic technology generates, stores, and processes data in the form of strings of 0s and 1s. Each of these digits is referred to as a *bit* (and a string of 8 bits that a computer can address as a group is a *byte*). For our purposes, the movement to digital transmission of TV signals has two consequences:

- It allows those signals to be accepted by, and manipulated in, computers.
- It permits what technicians consider the best form of **high definition television (HDTV)**, which provides five channels of CD-quality digital surround sound and about five times more picture information (picture elements, or pixels) than conventional television. If you've ever seen a show on HDTV, you know that the picture is of movie-theater quality.

head end a cable system's regional delivery location

analog electronic transmission accomplished by adding signals of varying frequency or amplitude to carrier waves of a given frequency of alternating electromagnetic current. Broadcast and phone transmission have conventionally used analog technology

digital electronic technology that generates, stores, and processes data in the form of strings of 0s and 1s. Each of these digits is referred to as a *bit* (and a string of 8 bits that a computer can address as a group is a *byte*)

high definition television channels (HDTV) a television display technology that provides picture quality similar to that of 35 millimeter movies with sound quality similar to that of today's compact disk. Some television stations have begun transmitting HDTV broadcasts to users on a limited number of channels, generally using digital rather than analog signal transmission

Widening Bandwidths   Standard TV sets cannot pick up HDTV signals—or any digital signals, for that matter. Moreover, to transmit an HDTV signal, a broadcaster requires a lot of frequency space. Excited by the possibility of bringing HDTV to U.S. homes (and encouraging U.S. leadership in the technology), Congress came up with a controversial solution: it instructed the FCC to give every broadcast TV station a new, wider bandwidth so that it could begin a transition to digital HDTV broadcasting. The plan was to allow the broadcasters to continue to send out their shows on their analog channels and at the same time transmit the same programming in digital HDTV on their new channels. Lawmakers were convinced that over the course of a decade or so, Americans would buy new sets or converter boxes that would allow them to receive the digital programming. TV stations would then give the spectrum space used for the analog transmission back to the government.

Congress has set the switch to digital TV beginning March 2009. Critics have denounced the free allocation of multichannel spectrum to broadcasters as a scandalous giveaway. But the switchover is moving forward. The FCC has required that all new TV sets with a diagonal screen size of 24 inches and smaller sold after March 2007 will have tuners that receive the digital signals. The larger flatscreen HDTV or HDTV-ready sets that increasing numbers of Americans are buying also have digital reception capabilities.

By 2009, broadcasters will have to send all their programs in the digital format—but that's not necessarily the high-definition flavor of digital TV. Many broadcasters figure that they may send out HDTV signals during the evening, when the large number of viewers available will justify beaming shows in expensive, spectrum-hogging HDTV. At other times, they reason, they can make more advertising money by doing what is called channel **multiplexing or multichannel broadcasting**. That involves splitting their new digital signals into two, three, or even four separately programmed channels and sending them in the form of a complex signal that is separated at the receiving end instead of broadcasting one channel of HDTV. So, rather than just Channel 6, a network could broadcast on Channels 6a, 6b, 6c, and 6d.

That's where questions related to program lineups enter the picture. Should each channel aim as broadly as possible, or should it focus on a particular topic (food or sports, for example), as many cable systems do? Should the stations target people at home, in school, in hospitals, in nursing homes, at work? Should the channels be related to one another thematically—all of them programming news but programming different types of news, for example? How different should the channels be from the offerings of other stations? How involved should the network with which the local station is affiliated be in creating programming for the channels? What will advertisers think about all this?

These are among the questions TV broadcasters have begun to ask about their new digital world. They also face the challenge of trying to persuade—or get the government to require—local cable systems to carry their digital and HDTV signals. Although federal law requires cable systems to carry local stations, the cable firms are reluctant to carry the multiplexed channels of these stations. They argue that these channels would take up so much space on their systems that they would interfere with the systems' ability to carry the popular national networks that cable outlets typically exhibit.

The issues and requirements show the power of Congress and the Federal Communications Commission to affect the number of TV stations in an area. Historically, that number has been pretty stable. Substantial struggles have surrounded FCC decisions to allocate more broadcast television channels to an area.

multiplexing or multichannel broadcasting sending multiple signals or streams of information on a carrier at the same time in the form of a single complex signal, then recovering the separate signals at the receiving end

Existing broadcasters haven't liked the idea, because it means that more over-the-air stations will be competing with them for advertising dollars. For these reasons, as well as because of technical limitations, the number of broadcast stations in an area doesn't change very often. Moreover, the commission is not allowed by law to mandate a mix of programming styles among the channels in an area. Unlike the situation in cable and satellite services, then, the notion of production in broadcast television mainly applies to two areas: the arrangement of a schedule on individual channels and the creation of individual programs.

Producing Individual Channels: Cable, Satellite, and Broadcast

The task of producing a channel is huge, whether it is carried out for a cable/satellite network such as CNN or for a broadcast station. Imagine yourself with twenty-four hours of airtime to fill every day of the year. How would you do that in a way that would make money for the channel's owners? That is the challenge that confronts programmers, the people in charge of operations as different as the Weather Channel and MTV on subscription video and WWOR (Channel 9) in New York and KNBC (Channel 4) in Los Angeles on broadcast TV.

WWOR and KNBC are stations, not networks, and they are mentioned in order to bring up an important difference between broadcast and cable or satellite TV. As noted earlier, the FCC allocates channel licenses to particular parts of the country, which means that broadcast channels serve particular areas. A firm that holds a channel license can then choose to affiliate with a network that sends programming to it and to other broadcast stations around the country. In contrast, cable/satellite channels are not allocated by any government agency and are not rooted in specific locations. They are like the broadcast networks in the sense that they distribute their materials at the same time to a variety of exhibitors around the United States and sometimes around the world.

Determining the Channel's Intended Audience   The most basic issue that confronts a local or network programmer relates to the intended audience: *Whom should the programmer try to attract as viewers?* This critical question is typically thrashed out by a number of top executives in the organization. The answer generally depends on four considerations:

- The competition
- The available pool of viewers
- The interests of sponsors
- The costs of relevant programming

These considerations are interrelated. Competition means the programming alternatives that already exist. If a channel that emphasizes history is already succeeding, starting a similar channel may not be useful unless you are sure that you have a clearly more attractive way of doing it or that there are enough people who are interested in history to accommodate two somewhat different approaches to the subject. But even if there are enough history buffs around, executives who are thinking of starting a second history channel must ask whether there are enough *advertisers* that want to sponsor programs on such a channel. If the channel is in the cable/satellite domain (as it probably would be), the executives have to ask whether they could successfully place a second history channel on enough systems to interest advertisers. They also have to ask whether the costs of history programs

www.hgtv.com, website of Home and Garden Television, a cable network

ratings   the audits of people's viewing behavior that help to determine where much of the money for programming and advertising should go

people meter   a small box installed by Nielsen on television sets in about 5,000 homes that it has chosen as a representative sample of the U.S. population. The meter holds a preassigned code for every individual in the home, including visitors. Nielsen asks each viewer to enter his or her code at the start and end of a TV viewing session. Information from each viewing session is transmitted to Nielsen's computers through television lines and is the basis for the firm's conclusions about national viewing habits

are appropriate in view of the projected revenues that would be received from advertisers that wanted to reach the projected audience. If the programs are so expensive that the costs can't be recovered from advertisers and cable subscriptions, the channel won't succeed, regardless of how interesting it is.

Programmers for cable/satellite channels often focus on rather specific topics to guide their choices of materials. They aim to reach people with particular lifestyle habits or interests. Think of HGTV (Home and Garden Television) or the Golf Channel. In contrast, broadcast stations, because they reach virtually everyone in their area, do not differentiate themselves so narrowly. When they go after new audiences, they choose broad segments of the population that advertisers want to reach. In some large cities, for example, where the FCC added several UHF stations and increased competition for audiences, a few stations have decided to pursue Spanish-speaking viewers, or non-English-speaking viewers generally, to maximize their profits.

Whether they are working for a network or a local station and whether they are programming in English or in another language, programmers want to keep audiences tuned to their channel. For commercial stations, the reason is simply that the more of the target audience that is watching, the more the channel can charge for its commercials and the more money it can bring in. Even noncommercial stations want to reach large numbers of their target audiences, however, because this tells supporters that the stations are accomplishing their aim. It also means that more people might contribute money to the stations.

Ratings   In the television industry, the audits of people's television viewing behavior that help to determine where much of the money for programming and advertising should go are called **ratings**. One firm, Nielsen Media Research, dominates this business. The stations, networks, and major advertisers foot most of the bill for the firm's reports. Nielsen uses meters and diaries to determine what people are watching and when.

For a snapshot of what America is watching, Nielsen uses an instrument called a **people meter**. The company installs this small box on all the television sets in over 12,000 homes that it has chosen as a representative sample of the U.S. population. (Actually, the number of homes is rising. Nielsen has announced that it wants to reach a sample of 37,000 homes by 2011.) The meter holds a preassigned code for every individual in the home, including visitors. The research firm asks each viewer to enter his or her code at the start and end of a TV viewing session. Information from each viewing session is transmitted to Nielsen's computers through television lines and is the basis for the firm's conclusions about national viewing habits.[4]

However, meters in 12,000 homes scattered around the country can't tell stations in individual markets how many people are watching them and who these people are. To get these data, Nielsen uses two approaches. For nonstop research on the largest 39 markets, Nielsen installs what it calls an audimeter on every television in the home of several hundred people in each market. This meter measures whether a TV set is being viewed and notes the channel (a specific over-the-air

Hispanic Television

Many of the nation's 40 million Hispanics tune in to Spanish-language television on a regular basis. It shouldn't surprise you to learn that Spanish-language television is set up a lot like English-language TV. Instead of CBS or ABC, Hispanics have two broadcast networks, Univision and Telemundo. Like their English-language counterparts, these networks utilize dozens of local affiliates across the country.

Univision claims the lion's share of the Spanish-language audience (75 percent). It is closely associated with Mexico's Televisa network, and its schedule mostly consists of imported shows from Mexico and other Latin American countries. Telenovelas (which are basically soap operas) are a key component of its prime-time schedule. Sports programming, such as soccer and boxing, is a common weekend feature. The network has also become well known for its nightly U.S. programs. Jorge Ramos, one of Univision's anchors, is basically the Tom Brokaw of the Spanish-speaking community. Boosted by the popularity of its news programming, Univision's affiliates regularly earn higher ratings than the affiliates of some English-language networks in cities such as Miami and Los Angeles.

Telemundo, purchased by Sony in 1998 and then NBC in 2001 has always been a far second to Univision, controlling only 25 percent of the Spanish-language audience. Its first season under Sony proved disastrous, resulting in free advertisements that cost the network more than $1 million in potential revenue. Telemundo turned to several strategies to recover including a partnership with TV Azteca and attempts to provide original programming that reflects the experiences of Latinos in the United States.

More recently, trends in television viewing among Hispanics have been changing due to the increasing number of second- and third-generation Latinos. Of the Hispanics born within the United States, 75 percent watch English-language television; and only 26 percent of this group watch any Spanish-language programming. This has resulted in a rise in demand for English-based Hispanic-oriented programming; what some call the "Latinization of America." Subsequently, there has been an increase in courtroom shows featuring English-speaking judges of South American decent and English-language adaptations of popular telenovelas. Some analysts claim that it is this area where the greatest possibilities of growth lie for networks such as Telemundo.

Sources: Jeff Zbar, "Law and Disorder are Hot," *Advertising Age*, March 27, 2006; Jay Sherman, "Experts Say Net Missed Chances; Ratings Are Up, but Telemundo Still No Match for Univision," *Television Week*, April 10, 2006; "Know Cristina," accessed 2/28/08, http://www.cristinaonline.com/english/know_cristina/index.asp.

number, a specific cable number, the VCR, or a video game). Unlike the people meter, the audimeter notes only whether someone is watching, not who is watching. Its results therefore allow the company to generalize about TV use for the household, not for specific individuals.

Nielsen finds a way to generalize about the habits of individual viewers in these markets by comparing the data collected from the people meters with entries in **diaries** that are distributed six times a year to another sample of viewers in the same markets. These diaries are also used to determine viewing habits during four months of the year—February, May, August, and November—in all 210 television markets. Broadcast industry workers call these months the **sweeps** because the ratings measurements during these periods are comparable to giant sweepstakes in which winners and losers are determined. The diaries are sent to representative samples of households in each market. Nielsen asks the family members to fill in the viewing experiences during the month for each member of the household.

Nielsen's results are arrayed as *ratings* and *shares*. Ratings and shares, in turn, can be discussed in *household* and *people* terms. **Household ratings** represent the

Nielsen diaries a method used by A.C. Nielsen Company to determine television ratings information, which requires selected individuals to keep a written record or "diary" of their television use during a given time period

sweeps the survey of TV viewing habits in markets across the United States, as performed by A.C. Nielsen four times per year—during the months of February, May, August, and November; competition among TV programmers is especially keen during these periods

www.nielsenmedia.com, website of Nielsen Media Research, the leading provider of television information services in the United States and Canada.

household ratings
ratings that represent the percentage of households in which the channel was turned on, compared to the number of households in the channel's universe (the local area, or the number of people who receive the cable network)

people ratings particular demographic categories of individuals within each household—for example, those eighteen to forty-nine years old or those who are female

household shares the percentage of households in which a particular channel was turned on, compared to the number of TV-owning households in the area where the channel can be viewed

percentage of households in which the channel was turned on, compared to the number of households in the channel's universe (the local area, or the number of people who receive the cable network). **People ratings** refer to particular demographic categories of individuals within each household—for example, those 18–49 years old or those who are female. For a particular channel during a particular time, a **household share** represents the percentage of households in which the channel was turned on compared to the number of TV-owning households in the area where the channel can be viewed.

Because of their wide **reach,** or the percentage of the entire target audience to which they circulate, broadcast networks often answer to advertisers in terms of their **national rating points.** In 2007, every national household rating point represented 1.1 million homes (about 1 percent of U.S. homes with a TV). National people ratings are expressed in terms of the number of individuals in the United States who fit into a particular category. Each rating point in the 18–49-year-old category, for example, represented 1.24 million viewers (1 percent of the U.S. total for people in that age range in 2007).

If *The Tonight Show*, for example, distributed nationally on NBC, receives a 5.4 household rating and a 16 household share, what does that mean? The rating means that of the 111.16 million households in the United States that own a TV set, 5.4 percent (6 million households) had at least one TV tuned to Leno. That may look like a very small percentage, but the program airs at 11:30 p.m. Eastern and Pacific times, when many people are asleep. The 16 household share means that of the households in which people are viewing at that time of night, about one in six (about 16 percent) has a set tuned to Leno. Of course, households often have people viewing different TV sets. Increasingly, then, networks and their advertisers prefer ratings and shares to be expressed not in terms of households but in terms of categories of individuals who are viewing. So, for example, you might read in the trade press that *The Tonight Show* received a 19 share among the 18–49-year-olds in its audience.

Nielsen reports each program's rating and share for a particular night to its clients (typically advertising executives). But it reports more than that. In the 2000s, advertisers began to pressure Nielsen to report ratings and shares not just for the average viewing of programs but—and even primarily—in terms of the viewing of commercials within and around the shows. After all, for advertisers the shows are there mainly to get the right people to watch the commercials. Nielsen determines ratings and household viewings during commercials and reports them in terms of the **average commercial minute**. That way, advertisers have measurements not just for each program taken as a whole but of the commercials that run during the programs. In addition, Nielsen determines the ratings for that program and its average commercial minutes not just by whether a person viewed it the evening it ran on broadcast or cable. The company includes in the ratings people who recorded it on DVRs and viewed them within a three day period. This approach—measuring the average commercial minute of a program within a three-day window—is called the **C3 standard** that is used for today's ratings reports.

Preparing a Schedule   The size of a program's audience helps determine the amount of money a station or network can charge an advertiser for time during that program. Consequently, ratings are always on the minds of the programmers who produce schedules for their stations or networks. Many programmers break down their work into creating discrete **schedules,** or patterns in which programs are arranged, for different **day parts,** or segments of the day as defined by programmers and marketers.

The most prominent of these day parts is the period from 8 to 11 p.m. (7 to 10 p.m. in the central and mountain time zones), when the largest number of people are viewing. Called **primetime,** these are the hours in which the Big Four broadcast networks put on their most expensive programs and charge advertisers the most money for thirty seconds of commercial time. Primetime is the most prestigious day part, although not necessarily the most profitable. The CBS network, for example, makes more profits from its afternoon soap opera schedule (for which it pays relatively little) than from its pricier evening fare.

In primetime, as in all day parts, the different goals of different channels lead to different schedules. As noted earlier, household ratings are usually not as important as individual ratings to advertisers and programmers. Age, gender, and sometimes ethnicity are particular selling points. The Fox network, for example, wants to reach children on Saturday morning, whereas NBC is interested in "selling" adults to advertisers during much of Saturday morning. It's a no-brainer, then, that an animated comedy about kids is a more appropriate choice for Fox than for NBC.

When adults are the targets, most programmers start with the assumption that they must attract mostly people between 18 and 49 years old, because this is the market segment that most television advertisers want to reach. Although people older than 50 actually have more money than those who are younger, advertisers believe that once people pass the age of 49, they are pretty well set in their ways and are not as susceptible as younger adults to new product ideas. Advertisers are also aware that people who are 50 and older are less likely than younger adults to be taking care of children at home. More people in a household means more repeat purchases of goods such as soap, cereal, and frozen foods.

The building block of a television schedule is the *series*. A **series** is a set of programs that revolve around the same ideas or characters. Series can be as varied as *Grey's Anatomy*, a weekly dramady about physicians in a Seattle hospital; *Nightline*, a daily late-night news-interview program; or *Are You Smarter than a 5th Grader*, a quiz show that pits an adult's knowledge against knowledge held by kids. The reason series are useful to programmers is that they lend predictability to a schedule. Programmers can schedule a series in a particular time slot with the hope that it will solve the problem of attracting viewers to that slot on a regular basis.

Programmers generally try to bring viewers to more than just one show on their station or network. Their goal is to attract certain types of people to an entire day part so that the ratings of that day part, and therefore its ad fees, will be high. Keeping people tuned to more than one series also means keeping them around for the commercials between the series. In TV-industry lingo, the challenge is to maximize the audience flow across programs in the day part.

That's a tall order when so many viewers clutch that ultimate ratings spoiler, the remote control, securely in their hands for the duration of their viewing sessions. The idea of audience flow is particularly precarious when a substantial portion of households (20 percent in 2007) have digital video recorders that can

reach   the percentage of the entire target audience to which a media outlet will circulate

national rating points   a measure of the percentage of TV sets in the United States that are tuned to a specific show. In 2001, each national rating point represented just over one million U.S. TV homes

average commercial minute   Nielsen's reporting standard for determining ratings and household viewings during commercials. This information gives advertisers measurements not just for each program taken as a whole, but for the commercials that run during the programs

C3 standard   Nielsen technique of measuring the average commercial minute of a program by including in the ratings people who recorded commercials on DVRs and viewed them within a three day period

schedules   the pattern in which television programs are arranged

day part   a segment of the day as defined by programmers and marketers (examples: prime time, daytime, late night, etc.)

primetime   the hours in which the Big Four broadcast networks put on their most expensive programs and charge advertisers the most money for commercial time

series   a set of programs that revolve around the same idea or characters

The Broadcast Networks and African Americans

In the summer of 2007, just as network programmers were preparing to publicize the fall schedules that they had worked hard to craft, the National Association for the Advancement of Colored People (NAACP), along with some Latino and Asian advocacy groups, called the latest network lineups the least diverse in recent years. This echoes the criticisms launched by the NAACP almost ten years ago when they accused the major networks of "whitewashing" their prime-time lineups and creating schedules from which minorities were woefully absent.

In 1999, the absence of minorities was particularly evident in the new series announced then. TV executives had attributed this to factors such as the rise of cable, especially Black Entertainment Television, and the then new networks such as WB and UPN, who have since merged into CW. They stated that these networks were pursuing black audiences with programs with all-black casts, making it harder for the major networks to attract African Americans with casts that were mixed. In addition, the need to attract the highest-paying advertisers led the Big Four to target upscale whites. This resulted in a sharp division between the shows that black and white audiences watched. Black leaders countered by stating that black audiences left the Big Four because the Big Four had abandoned blacks. Subsequently, they threatened boycotts and lawsuits (contending that network stations were neglecting their responsibility to serve the broad public) if network programmers didn't revise their actions substantially. The jawboning seemed to have some effect and the Big Four began to play catch-up and sought to increase multicultural content.

For the fall 2007 schedule, minorities were featured in most of the 29 new major network series. TV executives point to series such as CBS' *Cane*, which features a predominantly minority cast to show the Big Four's continued commitment to diversity. However, most of the regular minority characters were support roles for white leading characters. The small number of people of color in lead roles has troubled group leaders who had been encouraged by recent initiatives and programs by the Big Four to increase multiculturalism.

Currently, the CW remains the main avenue for multicultural programming. Along with scheduling three new series, the CW has renewed many of its African-American comedies (such as *Everybody Hates Chris* and *Girlfriends*). It is these types of series, containing lead roles for minorities, which groups such as the NAACP claim the major networks continue to lack.

Sources: Gary Levin, "TV in Black and White," *USA Today*, July 7, 1999; Lisa de Moraes, "Holy Catch-Up," *Washington Post*, July 30, 1999, p. C1; Greg Braxton, "White Still Primary Color," *Los Angeles Times*, June 6, 2007.

---

lead-in a program that comes before, and therefore leads into, another program

sampling trying out a new series by watching it for the first time

lead-out the program that follows the program after the lead-in

capture one network's program while they watch a different channel. Still, Nielsen ratings do suggest that certain scheduling techniques can improve audience flow. One is the use of a strong lead-in to programs that follow. A **lead-in** is simply a program that comes before, and therefore leads into, another program. Ratings suggest that a strong lead-in tends to bring its audience to sample the program that comes after it. The chance for **sampling,** or trying a new series for the first time, is increased if the **lead-out**—the program that follows the new series—is popular. Many people who are interested in seeing the first and third programs will stick through the second if they consider it at all good.

Say you're a programmer, and you have a new series that you want to give the maximum chance to succeed. By the logic of lead-ins and lead-outs, you should place the new series between two well-established shows that appeal to the same audience. This position, called a **hammock** by TV people, will give the right viewers a huge opportunity to sample the show.

Television programmers use other scheduling tricks as well, but the ideas of audience flow, lead-ins, lead-outs, and hammocking are the basis for much of the arrangement of programs on television. Producing a schedule is similar to putting together a huge jigsaw puzzle—although producing a TV schedule is often harder than solving a jigsaw puzzle, because while the puzzle solver needs to look at only one picture, the programmer must examine not only his or her channel but also many competing channels.

Sometimes what seems like a good program for a particular position in the schedule, or **time slot**, may be judged unacceptable because it is aimed at the same kinds of people (in terms of age, gender, ethnicity, or interests) who are flocking to a popular program on another channel at the same time. When programmers don't want to compete directly with a popular series, they turn to **counterprogramming**. That means placing a program that aims to attract a target audience different from that of other shows in a particular time slot. So, for example, in 2007 some local stations began to place game shows in the late afternoon (4–6pm) time slot as counterprogramming to talk shows that their competitors were running at that time.[5]

Producing Individual Programs

The heads of firms that produce television shows must be aware of all the complexities that their clients—the programmers—face. To program producers, being successful doesn't just mean coming up with an idea that programmers like (as difficult as that may be). It also means coming up with an idea that programmers for local stations, broadcast networks, or cable/satellite networks need at a cost they can afford.

Daily news programs tend to be the focus at the local broadcast level. Local programmers believe that morning, evening, and late-night news shows give viewers a sense of their station's commitment to the area. Early- and late-evening newscasts that draw good ratings also bring the station loads of revenue. Apart from news, local broadcasters tend to produce little of their own material.

For many production companies, the biggest prize is for one of the broadcast networks to order a prime-time series. That can be tough because often network-owned production companies sometimes seem to have an inside track. Even apart from the competition with the networks' production divisions, however, the chances of getting such an order are not high. Network programming executives meet with many producers to hear brief summaries of program ideas. Creators may present several of these summaries, called **pitches**, at one sitting. Most of the time, the network people say that they are not interested. Sometimes they tell the creators that they will pay for a **treatment**, a multipage elaboration of the idea. The treatment describes the proposed show's setup and how it relates to prior popular series. It also discusses the collection of elements that will propel the series and give it a recognizable personality—the setting; the characters; typical plots; and the general layout, tone, and approach. This collection of elements, which often are created using a set of rules that guide the way the elements are stitched together with a particular audience-attracting goal in mind, is called the format of a show. (We have already seen how networks such as MTV can have formats.)

If network officials like the format and believe that it fits their programming strategy, they may commission research to try out this idea and the ideas of other producers with audiences. This activity is called **concept testing**. It involves reading one-paragraph descriptions of series formats to people who fit the profile of likely viewers. Sometimes these people are contacted by phone, and sometimes they are questioned in preview theaters where they have been invited to evaluate new shows. Researchers ask these viewers if they would watch the series based on the

hammocking the strategic placement of a program between two other programs; positioning a new series between two well-established shows that appeal to the same target audience often gives the right viewers an opportunity to sample the new series

time slot a particular position in the schedule

counterprogramming placing a program that aims to attract a target audience different from that of other shows in the same time slot; often done in order to avoid competing directly with a popular series

pitches brief summaries of program ideas

treatment a multipage elaboration of a television series producer's initial pitch to network programming executives; the document describes the proposed show's setup and the way in which it relates to prior popular series

concept testing research commissioned by network executives in order to determine whether the format of a proposed series appeals to members of the series' target audience; this often involves reading a one-paragraph description of series formats to people who fit the profile of likely viewers

pilot a single episode that is used to test the viability of a series

preview theater a venue to which members of a target audience are invited to engage in concept testing or to evaluate newly completed series pilots

license the contract between a production company and network executives that grants the network permission to air each episode a certain number of times; usually thirteen episodes of a series are ordered

descriptions. If a producer's concept receives high marks from the appropriate audience, the interested network may contract for a sample script and a test program, called a **pilot.**

When the pilot is completed, the network tests it, too. Often the process involves showing the pilot to a group of target viewers, either on specially rented cable TV channels or in **preview theaters.** When cable TV is used, the individuals chosen are asked to view a movie or series pilot on the channel at a certain time. After the program, the viewers are asked questions over the telephone about what they saw. Viewers in preview theaters sometimes sit in chairs equipped with dials that they can use to indicate how much they like what they see on the screen. These responses, along with their written comments, help network executives decide whether or not to commission the series.

Let's assume that everything works out fine with a series' concept testing and pilot. The network executives then give the production company a contract for several episodes—typically thirteen. The contract is for permission—called a **license**—to air each episode a certain number of times. You might think that with such a deal in hand, production firm executives would be wildly ecstatic, sure that the show will enrich their firm. Not so fast. For one thing, the network may reduce the firm's potential profits by asking for co-ownership of the show as a way of paying for the risk the network is taking to fund and air it. Moreover, even with network backing, the show may not last long. Many prime-time series receive bad ratings and are yanked by the networks even before their first thirteen episodes have aired.

Another item that makes production executives nervous is that network licensing agreements typically do not cover the full costs of each episode even for shows from companies they own. If an hour drama is slated to cost the production firm $2.5 million per episode, the network may pay $1.5 million. The producers have to come up with $1 million per episode themselves. Over thirteen episodes, that will put them $13 million in the red.

Why would any company do that? The answer is that production firms see network broadcast as only the first of a number of TV domains in which they can make money from their series. They can make money from local stations, from cable networks, from stores, from the Internet and from broadcasters outside the United States. And if a show succeeds on TV, these extra windows can become goldmines. To learn more about how the money comes in, we need to shift the discussion from production to distribution.

Distribution in the Television Industry

As noted earlier, a broadcast television network is involved in the distribution of material. When a network licenses programs from its own production divisions or from outside producers, it sends them to its affiliates, and they broadcast them (usually simultaneously) to homes. Not all TV programs are distributed in this way, however. One reason is that not all broadcast TV stations are affiliated with networks, and the independents need to get their programming from somewhere. Another reason is that even network stations do not broadcast the network feed all the time. Certain hours in the morning, in the afternoon, in the early evening, and after 1 a.m. belong to the stations. Therefore, they can take for themselves all the ad revenue they bring in during these periods. But first they must find programs that attract an audience at a reasonable price.

Syndication

Many nonnetwork distributors are very willing to help local stations find attractive shows. Their business is called **syndication**. It involves licensing programs to individual outlets on a market-by-market basis (see Tables 13.5 and 13.6). One way to attract audiences "off network" is with programs that are newly created for syndication. Examples are *The Oprah Winfrey Show* talk show, the celebrity news program *Entertainment Tonight*, the cooking show *Rachael Ray*, and the game show *Wheel of Fortune* are made to be shown every weekday, and that is typical of new syndicated programming. This five-day-a-week placement is called **stripping** a show. Local programmers believe that in certain day parts, putting the same show in the same time slot each weekday lends predictability to the schedule that their target audiences appreciate.

Stripping is also a popular tactic with the other major method through which stations get programming: off-network syndication. In **off-network syndication**, a distributor takes a program that has already been shown on network television and rents episodes of that program to TV stations for local airing. Consider *Law & Order: Criminal Intent*, a police and law drama produced by Wolf Films and NBC Universal, and showed on a first-run basis on NBC television and USA cable network. In 2007, NBC Universal Domestic Television Distribution syndicated it to local stations on a stripped basis. The distributor made deals with stations covering 95 percent of the country.[6]

Not all network programs make it into off-network syndication, though. The popularity of stripping means that a lot of episodes are required, and so shows with fewer than 100 episodes are unlikely candidates for syndication. Programs that the networks take off the air quickly because of bad ratings don't have a chance to go into reruns. Also, situation comedies are more likely than dramatic programs to be desired by local stations. The sitcoms get better ratings in reruns and tend to attract the audience profiles (young mothers and children) that local stations need after school and before the five and six o'clock news, which is typically the time during which network affiliates schedule reruns.

syndication the licensing of mass media material to outlets on a market-by-market basis

stripping five-day-a-week placement of a television show; programmers believe that in certain day parts, placing the same show in the same time slot each weekday lends a predictability to the schedule that their target audiences appreciate

off-network syndication a situation in which a distributor takes a program that has already been shown on network television and rents (licenses) episodes of that program to TV stations for local airing

30 Minute Meals with Rachael Ray airs every weekday evening on the Food Network. Local programmers believe that airing the same show in the same time slot each weekday lends a predictability to the schedule that their target audiences appreciate.

533

Table 13.5 **Top Syndicated Programs by Households, 2007**

Rank	Program	LIVE+SD HH AA
1	*Wheel of Fortune*	7.5
2	*Jeopardy*	6.1
3	*Oprah Winfrey Show*	5.5
4	*Judge Judy*	4.9
5	*Entertainment Tonight*	4.8
6	*Dr Phil Show*	4.5
7	*Everybody Loves Raymond*	4.1
8	*CSI Miami*-Syn	4.0
9	*Family Guy*-Syn	3.9
10	*Two and a Half Men*-Syn	3.9

"Live+SD HH AA" means the average audience household rating for the week in terms of people who viewed the program at the time it aired or on a digital video recorder the same day it aired.
Source: Nielsen Media Research Syndication Service via TVBonline.

Table 13.6 **Top Syndicated Programs Audiences Aged 25–54, 2007**

Rank	Program	LIVE+SD AA A25–54
1	*Oprah Winfrey Show*	2.4
1	*Two and a Half Men*-Syn	2.4
1	*Wheel of Fortune*	2.4
4	*CSI Miami*-Syn	2.3
4	*Entertainment Tonight*	2.3
4	*Everybody Loves Raymond*	2.3
7	*Family Guy*-Syn	2.2
7	*Seinfeld*	2.2
9	*Seinfeld*-Wknd	2.0
10	*Jeopardy*	1.9
10	*Judge Judy*	1.9

"Live+SD AA A25–54" means the average rating for the week in terms of people aged 25–54 who viewed the program at the time it aired or on a digital video recorder the same day it aired.
Source: Nielsen Media Research Syndication Service via TVBonline.

Subscription, Out-of-Home, and International Distribution   If producers fail to place their reruns on local stations, there are other avenues that they can use. Cable and satellite networks have become voracious consumers of off-network programming, in part because these programs are less expensive than new shows and in part because they reliably attract certain categories of viewers. *Nick at Night* and *TVLand* are two subscription video networks that air television programs that people in their thirties and forties viewed when they were young. The *Lifetime* channel goes after programs that in their broadcast network lives were popular with women, and the *Family Channel* looks for material that few moms and dads would find objectionable.

Another venue for making extra money from television programs is what marketers call **out-of-home** locations; sometimes they are called **captive audience** locations. These include places such as airline waiting areas and store check out lines where people congregate and would likely pay attention to TV clips and commercials. CNN distributes its news programming as the Airport Channel. NBC sends parts of its programs to a supermarket checkout TV network. CBS provides some of the news and entertainment programs it owns to airlines; it also owns a network that sends some of its programs (with commercials) to healthcare offices. ABC News provides material for a company that puts video screens on gas station pumps.

out-of-home locations or captive audiences   places such as airline waiting areas and store check out lines where people congregate and would likely pay attention to TV clips and commercials

Foreign countries have also been a useful market for certain types of reruns. Broadcasters around the world purchase U.S.-made series as components of their schedules. The popularity of programs from the U.S. rises and falls, and in many cases home-grown programming gets better ratings than the U.S. material. Generally speaking, action dramas do better than sitcoms in this market, since American humor doesn't cross borders as easily as sex appeal (*Baywatch* was popular around the world) and violence (so was *Walker, Texas Ranger*). The mid-2000s was a hot period for U.S. series. *CSI*, *Lost*, *Desperate Housewives*, *House*, and *Ugly Betty* drew lots of attention and record prices in the U.K. In Europe, the series *24* and *Without a Trace* attracted large audiences. The reason, according to the show business magazine *Variety*: "The writing on U.S. dramas is more compelling, the storylines more complex and the production values more cinematic. And serendipitously, a number of younger-skewing foreign stations—Rupert Murdoch's Sky Italia, Cuatro in Spain and Flextech in Britain—have realized that Yank shows can add cachet to their skeds [that is, schedules]." The article continued with an idea relevant to our discussion of foreign coin as a way to help pay for the production deficits that firms incur when they license their programs to the U.S. networks: "The popularity of U.S. series abroad could not come at a better time, as studios struggle with rising production costs. The season's crop of newcomers cost an average of $2.75 million an episode, and the foreign returns help fill a gap of $1–1.2 million in the license fees studios collect from networks."[7]

Challenges to Traditional TV Production and Distribution

Ten years ago, maybe even five, the description just presented of television production and distribution would have been adequate. The growth of digital media, however, has presented many new challenges to the TV industry that are encouraging important new avenues for production and distribution. You might already guess some of these challenges from earlier discussions. The Internet has become a competitor to the traditional TV set for viewers' time; so have video games and the DVD player. TV ratings are slipping as a result and advertising rates are not rising as high as license fees in many cases. Producers and network executives are trying to find ways to profit from the programs that they make and circulate.

New Avenues for Network Distribution

The television networks have been especially active in pursuing ways to get viewers engaged with their programming in as many media as possible. The aim is not to replace the viewing of their programming on traditional channels. It is, however, to allow for ways for viewers to connect with shows they enjoy but didn't have time to view, or want to view again soon after it aired. Both these possibilities allow the networks to sell time to advertisers that want to reach those audiences. At this point, broadcast and subscription networks use four ways to make extra money from their programming: insisting on DVR ratings, allowing cable firms to offer programs through video on demand, encouraging people to view programs with commercials on the Internet, and offering shortened or promotional versions of the programs for use on mobile handsets. Let's elaborate a bit on each.

Insisting on DVR Ratings   The main cable and broadcast networks have convinced advertisers that they should determine the ratings of a program not just by its viewing on a particular night and time. Rather, they argue, audiences increasingly use digital video recorders to postpone their viewing, and when they view those programs they should be counted. After lots of discussion, major advertisers and Nielsen agreed that the viewers of programs on DVRs up to three days after their airing would be added to the programs' ratings. That agreement became part of the C3 approach to ratings described earlier.

Offering Programs Through Video on Demand   **Video on demand (VOD)** is a great way to allow people who want to see an episode to view it at their leisure. The programs can be shown with commercials or without them, depending on the deal the network makes with the initial advertisers. At this point, Nielsen doesn't count VOD viewing in the ratings, but that could change.

Encouraging Viewers to Download Programs with Commercials on the Internet   During the past few years, an increasing number of homes have been paying for fast broadband connections to the Internet. They allow users to view audiovisual presentations with acceptable clarity, and many are doing it. As a result, just about every television network is posting some of its programming on the Web for people to view. The shows stream—that is, they start playing when you click on their links, and they are not designed to be saved on the user's computer. The program streams come with commercials that are much shorter in number and time than the ones people see on traditional TV. The catch, however, is that online a viewer cannot speed through ads.

Different networks have different philosophies about how much programming to put online and where. The biggest networks, though, have decided that putting shows only on their own sites is not enough. CBS, for example, has been making deals with many places on the Web, including the Joost video site (in which it has invested), to display links to its shows. Sites that bring viewers to CBS programs share in ad revenues. NBC and Fox have collaborated on a website for their programs and others that they call Hulu. Similar to CBS, though, both networks also will encourage other places on the Internet to post their programming.

video on demand (VOD) a television viewing technology whereby a customer uses the remote control to navigate to a menu of programs and then to click on the program he or she wants to watch. Unlike pay per view, where the customer has to wait for the show to appear at a certain time, the program immediately appears for viewing

Offering Programming for Use on Mobile Devices   Many media and advertising executives see the mobile phone as the next great place for programming. A growing number of Americans have phones that can play videos. Mobile phone companies offer such programming and have made deals with firms such as Mobilo to sell such services to their customers. Television and cable networks have been trying to figure out ways to create sponsored mobile offerings that people would want to watch on the go. Fox tried a mobile version of its cult hit, *24*. The other networks have been experimenting with promotional videos for programs in the belief that some viewers would find them interesting on the go.

New Avenues for Production Firms

The television networks have been more aggressive about taking advantage of the new media environment than have TV production firms. The producers have, however, recognized the value of DVDs and have been selling boxed sets of popular TV series such as *The West Wing*, *24*, and *Grey's Anatomy*. One direction that producers have only begun to take is to make material specifically for the Web. With so many amateur videos showing up on places such as YouTube and MySpace, the notion of distributing a professional TV series on the Web might sound intriguing. The producers would need, however, to find places to show the material that would get attention and justify the large amounts of money such a series might cost.

High-profile Hollywood talent has been involved in working on web-initiated programming. When the Budweiser beer company started Bud.TV in 2006, it turned for material to Kevin Spacey's Triggersteet Productions, Matt Damon's LivePlanet Productions and the Warner Bros Television Group's Studio 2.0—an outfit created for less expensive web-based projects. Consider, too, the path of Emmy award-winning writer/producer team Marshall Herskovitz and Edward Zwick (*My So-Called Life*, *Thirty-Something*, *Glory*). In 2007, they decided to take the pilot of an ad-sponsored program called *Quarterlife* that did not make it to traditional network television and to recreate it in smaller bits as an Internet series. They enlisted the enormously popular site MySpace (owned by News Corporation) to distribute the series' 36 episodes, and did not count out showing it elsewhere on the Web as well. At the moment, it's not clear how successful they were, but their move did point to a distribution platform for new professionally created television programming outside of the traditional channels. It's a new world for video professionals, and it stretches the term television far beyond what people would have thought a decade ago.

Exhibition in the Broadcast Industry

Local stations, cable systems, satellite delivery systems, wired phone and wireless phone companies take on the role of exhibitor when they deliver material directly to viewers. Like theaters in the movie business and stores in the book-publishing industry, the broadcast exhibitors are retailers. Their business is to attract the number and the kind of viewers who can help them make a profit for their shareholders.

The early twenty-first century finds the television exhibition system in the midst of a major upheaval. Local broadcasters, the bedrock of the medium since its commercial introduction in the late 1940s, are facing ever-escalating competition from the cable, satellite, Internet and even mobile phone businesses. Moreover, those other businesses have the potential for making money from both subscription fees and advertising, whereas local broadcasters make money only from advertising. To make matters even more difficult for local broadcasters, the increased number of channels that cable and satellite services bring into people's homes has meant that ratings for the network and local programming that broadcast stations deliver have been declining rather steadily. Local television stations still make money—in the biggest metropolitan areas, they make huge amounts of money—but observers wonder whether this will still be true later in this century as hundreds of channels race into American homes.

Network affiliates are particularly worried about the declining ability of ABC, CBS, and NBC to grab the lion's share of the U.S. television audience. Local TV executives are also concerned about the networks' strong and increasing participation in the subscription video world. Disney-owned ABC controls cable/satellite networks ESPN, ESPN2, the Disney Channel, and Disney Family, among others. NBC-Universal controls MSNBC, CNBC, USA, SciFi, and Bravo. All the broadcast networks are placing hit programs on the Web, with the consequence that viewers don't have to watch local channels (and their commercials) to see prime time TV. Network executives reply that since their O&O properties are extremely important to them (as a group they often make more profits than the networks), they would not do anything that would fundamentally harm local service. They are also helping the local stations to beef up their websites, where they make money from advertising. These are among the places viewers can find network shows. Nevertheless, the tension between the two parties continues.

Another tension in exhibition involves the conversion to digital television that is currently taking place. This conversion essentially will give every network and broadcast station the capability of sending out either one high-definition television signal or a number of regular-definition channels. What will the stations broadcast on the extra channels if they choose to go the regular-definition route? Will some of the channels require a decoder to allow the local station to tap into subscription as well as advertising revenue? What will be the relationship between local and network broadcasters in this environment? Answers to these questions will emerge over the next few years.

Tensions are also running high in the cable exhibition business. For decades cable systems were the only major exhibitors competing with local TV stations. Now cable operators worry that their power will be eroded substantially by DBS firms such as DirecTV and Echostar's DISH, as well as by broadband services from Verizon and AT&T that will duplicate cable services.

Television and Media Literacy

Through its many exhibition modes, television stands at the center of much of American culture. As we have seen, Americans spend enormous amounts of time with it, companies spend billions of dollars feeding programming endlessly to the tube, and governments (particularly the federal government) spend many hours deciding how to regulate it. From the standpoint of media literacy, it will be useful to apply our knowledge of the industry from this chapter to concerns about three interrelated areas: audience, content, and control.

Audience Issues

This chapter makes it clear that audiences are critically important to the people who run the various parts of the television industry. Go to any meeting of industry executives or turn to any trade magazine on the industry and you're likely to note intense discussions of the size of the audience and its nature. The term **tonnage** shows up frequently; the word describes a hefty number of viewers and indicates that, at least in network television, reaching large numbers of people for advertisers is still a key goal. Also showing up a lot, though, are phrases such as "eighteen to forty-nine-year-olds," "eighteen to thirty-four-year-olds," "bilingual Hispanics," "the African-American audience," and "high-spending teens." They indicate a strong and growing concern with targeting that parallels what we have seen in other media industries.

When you hear or read these terms, step back and think about what they really mean. You might remember our discussion in Chapter 2 about how mass media executives consider people primarily as consumers of media materials and other products. The audience research that media firms conduct and the ways in which they interpret that research are aimed at figuring out two things: what people who are attractive to certain types of advertisers are like, and how to get these people to be loyal consumers of certain media products and certain advertised products.

These considerations of the audience take place in all media industries. A chapter on television is an interesting place to emphasize them because so many of us are so often part of TV's audience or audiences. But as we think about being part of that audience, we also ought to think of another point made in Chapter 2: mass media executives do not think about audience members in the same way that audience members think about themselves. A TV network may be interested in whether you are in the 18–49 age bracket, but you may consider age relatively unimportant in your life. Churchgoing or friendships, lifestyle categories that may have little significance to the media firms, may well be key to the way you see the world.

When you come across the audience labels that television companies and their advertisers promote, think about how they are created for commercial purposes. Realize that what the executives leave out in considering the audiences for their programming may be just as important as what they put in. Also, consider what it means to define so much of U.S. society through lenses created for commercial purposes. For many broadcast network TV executives, the optimal viewer is an eighteen to twenty-four-year-old female or male who has the money to buy things. As we have seen, these executives' dedication to reaching people in this demographic segment shapes much of the way programs are selected and schedules are crafted. From *Friends* to *Survivor* to *American Idol*, TV executives' way of looking at the world shapes the way we as viewers see it.

Critics of the medium, and of all advertiser-sponsored media, have a term for this approach to audiences. They call it the **commodification of audiences.** By commodification they mean that everything in life, both private and public, is being shaped by the values of business and commercialism. In this logic, such categories as age, gender, and ethnicity and such ideas as friendship and knowledge are understood only in terms of their monetary value. People within certain age brackets are more important than people in other brackets because they bring in more money. Women and men are described by characteristics that relate to what, and when, they buy things.

Because of the TV industry's commodification of audiences, the critics say, people themselves are treated as products to be compared and sold to advertisers based on their value to those advertisers. By extension, the television programs that are

tonnage describes a hefty number of viewers and indicates that, at least in network television, reaching large numbers of people for advertisers is still a key goal

commodification of audiences the idea, held by critics of the advertiser-supported media's approach to audiences, that everything in life, both private and public, is being shaped by the values of business and commercialism

created to attract audiences typically are not aimed at making people better citizens, smarter individuals, or more friendly neighbors. Rather, they are designed to get their attention so that they will watch the commercials. The critics further argue that a TV industry built around programming that demands attention for the purpose of commercial persuasion is not an industry that can hope to better society.

Content Issues

Many critics of the U.S. television industry believe that it is the industry's commercial motives, and the resulting commodification of its audience, that has led to what they consider programming that emphasizes violence, sex, and sensationalism at the expense of quality. Sure, the critics say, there *are* some good programs on TV—programs that compellingly challenge audiences to think about themselves or the world around them. But much programming, they insist, exists simply to get people's attention in the most basic ways possible so that they will watch the commercials. TV producers have learned that human beings are drawn instinctively and quickly to images of sex, violence, and other types of fast-paced "action." They therefore exploit these images in the most efficient manner possible in order to gather the audiences they need.

There are many advocacy groups that don't emphasize the commodification argument but that nevertheless have problems with sex, violence, and sensationalism on TV. Parent, teacher, religious, and other groups have expressed grave concerns about what they consider to be too much sexuality, violence, and stereotyping on television, as well as a scarcity of programs that seriously try to educate as well as entertain children. Table 13.7 sketches some of their major concerns and the typical replies of industry executives.

Most of the time, the industry replies have not persuaded the advocacy groups. Individuals and organizations have advocated a wide variety of solutions, ranging from boycotting the offending networks to boycotting their advertisers to passing laws that would require certain kinds of programming. Every so often, their ideas strike a responsive chord with society at large, possibly because of particularly offensive programs. Government regulators sometimes step in and put pressure on offending producers and networks. Nervous advertisers may also use their clout to tone down the obnoxious programming. Critics contend that these steps work for only a short while; the sex, violence, and stereotyping come back with a roar when public concern turns to other things.

Industry officials naturally say that they prefer self-regulation to government regulation. They especially prefer "rating" systems that alert parents and others to potentially objectionable aspects of shows while not taking away producers' ability to create such shows. This approach has been in effect in the movie industry since the 1960s, as we noted in Chapter 14. In the late 1990s, a rise in public concern about television's portrayal of sex and violence and its use of vulgar language led industry critics, members of Congress, and industry executives to agree on a similar system for broadcast TV. They added an interesting technological addition, however: beginning in 2000, all television sets sold in the United States must come with a so-called V-Chip.

Invented in Canada, the **V-chip** is a small computer device that allows parents to block programs automatically from a television set if the programs are transmitted with a code that will activate the chip. The codes are content ratings that reflect concerns about violence, sex, and "strong" language. (The V in V-chip stands for violence.) Table 13.8 gives the ratings categories that most networks have agreed to present at the beginning of their programs and in codes that can be

V-chip a small computer device that allows parents to block programs automatically from a television set if the programs are transmitted with a code that will activate the chip; the codes are content ratings that reflect concerns about violence, sex, and "strong" language (the V in the V-chip stands for violence)

540

Table 13.7 Concerns and Replies Regarding Current TV Issues

Issue	Some Concerns	Some Industry Replies
Violence on television	TV violence is encouraging children and even adults to see physical force as the solution to problems, to see the world around them as more mean and dangerous than it really is, and to be less sensitive than they might otherwise be to real-world violence.	Violence is a part of life, and television reflects life. Some of the greatest literature includes violence. Much of the violence on TV is unrealistic, and most viewers can distinguish between TV violence and the reality.
Sex on television	Television portrays sex and sexuality in a casual manner, not linked to love. Nudity (on cable) or seminudity (on broadcast) is seen too often. Sex is often not linked to issues of birth control or safe sex.	Sex is part of life, and television reflects life. If programs with this sort of content were not popular, producers would not offer them.
Stereotyping on television	On television, people who belong to certain groups, especially women, people who have physical handicaps, and members of minority ethnic groups, are portrayed in patterned ways that sometimes demean them. Fat people are often the object of humor, for example, and highly intelligent black men are few and far between. Such images extend and reinforce patterns of prejudice in the society at large.	Stereotyping is part of life, and television certainly reflects that part, as well. Yet while it does still exist on TV, stereotyping is much less a part of programming today than it was years ago. As the United States becomes more and more a multiethnic society, television is increasingly reflecting that diversity.

read by the chip. Advocacy groups, members of Congress, and the FCC chairman in the late 1990s saw the V-chip as a way to give harried parents power over what their children were watching even when they were not in the TV room with their children. Researchers found that most parents didn't understand how the chip works and didn't use it. Critics suggested that all it really did was let the TV industry off the hook for the programming it created.

Industry Control Issues

More generally, critics have complained that the major companies in the television industry have become so powerful that it is difficult, if not impossible, for public groups to influence their activities. For one thing, the critics say, the federal government's move to deregulate the industry to encourage competition and the growth of new services has meant that executives feel increasingly confident that business can effectively sidestep government and public concerns when it comes to shaping television's future. For another, they add, although on some levels competition between the satellite, cable, broadcast, and telephone industries may be fierce, the number of major companies involved in the competition is getting smaller all the time. Moreover, these companies are the media conglomerates that we've discussed in previous chapters.

The names should be familiar by now—Time Warner, News Corporation, Disney, CBS, and General Electric. These and a few other firms have their hands across cable, satellite, and broadcast TV and the Web. In these media, they are

Table 13.8 TV Rating Categories

Rating	Meaning	Description
Children's categories		
TVY	All children	Animated or live action; shows' themes and elements are specifically designed for a very young audience, including children from ages two to six. Program not expected to frighten younger children.
TVY7	Directed at older children	Program designed for children ages seven and up. May be more appropriate for children who have acquired the developmental skills needed to distinguish between make-believe and reality. Themes and elements in this program may include mild physical or comedic violence and may frighten children under the age of seven.
General categories		
TVG	General audience	Although this rating does not signify a program designed specifically for children, many parents may allow younger children to watch this program unattended. It contains little or no violence, no strong language, and little or no sexual dialogue or situations.
TVPG	Parental guidance suggested	May contain some material that some parents would find unsuitable for younger children. The program may contain infrequent coarse language, limited violence, and some suggestive sexual dialogue and situations.
TV14	Parents strongly cautioned	Program may contain some material that many parents would find unsuitable for children under fourteen years of age. May contain sophisticated themes, sexual content, strong language, and more intense violence.
TVM	Mature audience only	Specifically designed to be viewed by adults and therefore may be unsuitable for children under seventeen. May contain mature themes, profane language, graphic violence, and explicit sexual content.

involved in production, distribution, and/or exhibition. Clearly, they play major roles in other media as well, from airlines to supermarkets to healthcare sites. Critics say that their influence throughout the TV industry cements the control that a small number of firms has over the dominant channels leading to Americans' minds. More optimistic observers point to the millions of video clips on the Internet as evidence that the creation of television programming is not locked up by just a few firms. Those who disagree reply that while these clips certainly exist on places such as Revver, MySpace and YouTube, they have nowhere near the impact on the population that the major TV distributors have.

In addition to raising important points about social power, these arguments also highlight an interesting development that we have only implied until now: the changing meaning of *television*. It used to be that when you said you were watching TV, it meant that you were watching a stationary, noninteractive box in your home. Now, as this chapter has shown, television can mean so much more than that, in home and out of home. Where does television end and video begin? If you view an audiovisual clip on your mobile device, are you watching television? Does it matter, and to whom? These are just a few extra questions that this chapter has raised about television today.

CHAPTER REVIEW

For an interactive chapter recap and study guide, visit the companion website for *Media Today* at www.routledge.com/textbooks/mediatoday

QUESTIONS FOR DISCUSSION AND CRITICAL THINKING

1 What is meant by "the golden age" of television?
2 Think about ideas you might have for a new television series. What steps would you need to follow to get your series on the air?
3 How many types of television distribution now exist?
4 Describe the C3 TV ratings system.

INTERNET RESOURCES

Internet Movie Database (http://imdb.com)
A useful catalog of television programs that have appeared over the decades.

Variety (http://www.variety.com/)
This show business magazine specializes in coverage of television programming. The website requires subscription, but your college may have a password for students.

Broadcasting & Cable (http://www.broadcastingcable.com/)
It says it covers "the business of television," and that includes local and national broadcast and cable developments. The website also includes information about industry events and conferences.

KEY TERMS

You can find the definitions to these key terms in the marginal glossary throughout this chapter. Test your knowledge of these terms with interactive flash cards on the *Media Today* companion website.

analog	cable networks
average commercial minute	Cable Technical Advisory Committee
basic cable	cable television
Big Four commercial networks	cable television system
billboards on TV	captive audience
broadcast live	coaxial cable
C3 standard	commercial stations
cable	commercials

commodification of audiences
community antenna television
   (CATV) service
concept testing
counterprogramming
day parts
diaries
digital
digital cable
digital compression technology
digital versatile disk (DVD)
direct-to-home satellite services
expanded (enhanced) basic
financial interest and syndication
   (fin-syn) rules
format
free skies
golden age of television
hammock
head end
high-definition television (HDTV)
household ratings
household share
independent station
lead-in
lead-out
license
license fees
lineup
multichannel broadcasting
multiple system owner (MSO)
multiplexing
national rating points
network affiliates
noncommercial stations

off-network syndication
out of home
owned and operated (O&O) stations
pay per view (PPV)
people ratings
pilot
pitches
premium channels
preview theaters
prime time
prime-time access rule (PTAR)
program feed
RBOCs
reach
sampling
satellite television
schedules
series
station groups
stripping
subscription networks
sweeps
syndication
Telecommunications Act of 1996
television broadcasting
television network
television program ratings
tiering
time slot
treatment
ultrahigh frequency (UHF)
vertically integrated
very high frequency (VHF)
videocassette recorder (VCR)

CONSTRUCTING MEDIA LITERACY

1   What program scheduling strategies can you note on yesterday evening's broadcast network television schedule?

2   "Audiences are not real things. They are constructed by media firms." What do you think this statement means? Do you agree with it? Why or why not?

3   Where do you stand with regard to critics of TV who say that violence, sex, and stereotypes are problems on the small screen?

CASE STUDY   Out of Home Television

The idea   As noted in the chapter, television can now be seen in many places outside the home, and the major providers of broadcast and cable programming (CBS, NBC-U, ABC) are providing some of that material. How common is out of home television where you live, and who is providing it?

The method   Use your postal ZIP code as the geographical territory and try to uncover the use of out of home television sets in stores, healthcare offices, travel depots, and other waiting and shopping areas. What is the programming like, and what is the format? Is the material repurposed—that is, taken from general broadcast or cable TV—or is it new material? Try to determine who the program producers and distributors are in each case. Write a report of your findings.

14 THE INTERNET AND VIDEO GAME INDUSTRIES

After studying this chapter, you will be able to:

1 Sketch the development of the computer, the Internet, the Web and video games

2 Explain the workings of the Internet industry

3 Discuss business models in the online world

4 Describe video game genres

5 Sketch the production, distribution and exhibition of video games

6 Chart major social controversies surrounding the Internet and video games

"The Internet is the first thing that humanity has built that humanity doesn't understand, the largest experiment in anarchy that we have ever had."

– ERIC SCHMIDT, GOOGLE CEO

Media Today

As recently as fifteen years ago, college students were unlikely to have heard of the Internet. Those who recognized the term were probably computer-engineering majors who were working on special projects with their professors. Now, a large majority of undergraduates use the Internet regularly—from various sites on campus and from home. In fact, a large majority of American homes are connected to the Internet, most with high-speed connections. And increasing numbers of people are accessing the Web through computer devices known as smart phones. Not all of these developments are the work of mass media industries (that is, industries that focus on the industrialized production and multiple distribution of messages through technological devices). As we saw in Chapter 1, when you send a computer message (electronic mail, or email) to a friend, that action is mediated interpersonal communication, much like a telephone conversation. When an organization works methodically with other organizations to reach members of the public, however, that activity is mass communication.

A great deal of mass communication activities take place on the Internet. Millions of people go to websites to watch television shows, read newspapers, download music, and do so many things that have traditionally been associated with separate non-computer media industries. Yet the Internet itself has an industrial aspect to it, with production, distribution, exhibition, and finance activities that are both different from and similar to traditional media industries. One aim of this chapter is to understand how the commercial Web is organized.

A second aim is to survey another business rooted in the digital technology: the video game industry. People play video games both on and off the Web—on their computers or on separate consoles connected to monitors. In fact, the total revenue of the U.S. video game industry exceeds $10 billion. The cash flow is not all that different from what the movies bring in at the theatrical box office in the United States. Moreover, while theatrical attendance is rather stable, the number of people playing and buying video games is growing quite strongly.

This chapter, then, examines two relatively new mass media industries that center on advances in computer technology: the *commercial aspects* of online services and the video game industry. You probably deal with these industries every day without thinking very much about how they work or how they relate to other media. Here's your chance to find out, and to think about the implications of these media for yourself, people close to you, and the society at large.

An Industry Background

The first point to make about computer-centered mass media is that the crucial difference between them and other media technologies is that they are **digital** rather than **analog**. A simple way to understand the distinction between digital and analog is to think about what distinguishes an old-fashioned vinyl record from a CD. If you look at a record, you will see grooves. When the phonograph needle moves through the grooves, it picks up vibrations that were made by the sound coming from the singer's vocal cords. When the record was made, a machine cut grooves

digital electronic technology that generates, stores, processes, and transmits data in the form of strings of 0s and 1s; each of these digits is referred to as a *bit* (and a string of bits that a computer can address individually as a group is a *byte*)

analog electronic transmission accomplished by adding signals of varying frequency or amplitude to carrier waves of a given frequency of alternating electromagnetic current. Broadcast and phone transmission have conventionally used analog technology

that reproduced these vibrations into the vinyl. The record grooves, then, hold a literal physical reproduction—an **analog**—of the singer's sound that can be reproduced with the right equipment.

The CD, by contrast, does not contain a physical reproduction of the sound. Instead, during the recording process, computers transform the singer's voice patterns into a string of binary digits, or *bits* (0s and 1s). Each sequence, or string, of 0s and 1s represents a different sound. The strings serve as a code—a symbolic representation of the sound. This digital code is placed on the CD in an order that conforms to the sequence of sounds made by the singer. When you turn on your CD player, a laser beam reads the code and sends it to a computer chip in the player. The computer chip is programmed to recognize the code and to understand which strings of numbers represent which sounds. At the speed of light, the chip transforms the code into electrical impulses that, when sent through an amplifier and sound system, end up reproducing the singer's voice.

The basic idea applies, too, to digital music files that reside in your computer, digital music player, or mobile phone. In that case, you don't even have a piece of plastic that carries the tune into the device. Rather, you download a digital file in one of a number of formats (MP3, WAV, AAC, or others), and if your device has the ability to recognize and decode the file, it transforms it into sounds that reproduce the original. If the file you are using is not copy-protected (and MP3 and WAV files are not) you can copy the music from your phone to one of your other players. Being able to move digital files (music or not) from one device to another is an example of the **convergence** of media technologies—the ability of different media to interact with one another easily in parallel digital formats. Convergence also means that different media can end up carrying out similar functions because they all accept digital information. So, for example, a computer can take on the functions of a DVD player, a CD player, and a cable television set.

Just as important, the application of computer codes to mass media materials allows audience members to manipulate the materials to suit their interests. Audience members who are connected to the producers of an audio or audiovisual program via a cable or telephone line can respond to those producers via the com-

convergence the ability of different media to interact with each other easily because they all deal with information in the same digital form

An iPhone or a laptop that can take on the functions of multiple devices—a telephone, DVD player, a CD player, and more—are just two examples of media convergence. Think about the digital devices that you use everyday. Do they combine technologies that were traditionally separate?

One of the earliest computers weighed nearly 30 tons, but today's computer technology can be found in countless lightweight, handheld devices.

puter. The producers, in turn, can send out a new message that takes the response into consideration. This sort of manipulation and response, which is much easier in digital than in analog technology, is what people mean when they speak of **interactivity.** We are leaving the analog age, they point out, and entering the age of digital interactive media.

interactivity the ability to track and respond to any actions triggered by the end user, in order to cultivate a rapport

The Rise of Computers and the Internet

The roots of digital interactive media can be traced at least as far back as a primitive computing machine that French mathematician Blaise Pascal built in the 1600s. Around the same time, German mathematician Gottfried Leibnitz set out important theoretical principles for the use of **binary digits,** the zero-to-one system that is at the core of digital technology. Morse Code—the dot-dash system devised by American inventor Samuel Morse when he created the telegraph in the

binary digits the zero-to-one system that is at the core of digital technology

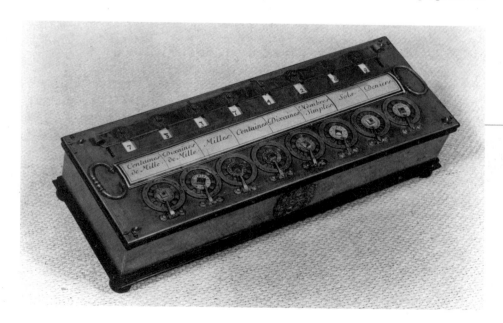

This mechanical adding machine, built by French philosopher and mathematician Blaise Pascal in 1642, was the first digital calculator. His design may not have been commercially successful, but it did lay the groundwork for today's computer engineering.

The Electronic Numerical Integrator and Computer (ENIAC) was so big that it took up an entire room. The two women in this 1946 photograph are programming the computer by adjusting its wiring. These women and four others—Kay McNulty, Betty Jennings, Betty Snyder, Marlyn Wescoff, Fran Bilas, and Ruth Lichterman—hired to run ENIAC were the first computer programmers in history.

ENIAC or Electric Numerical Integrator and Computer the world's first operational electronic digital computer

transistor a device that amplifies current and regulates its flow, acting as a switch or gate for electronic signals

microprocessor a miniaturized version of the central processing unit (the "brains") of a computer processor on a single microchip (sometimes called a *logic chip*); designed to perform arithmetic and logic operations that make use of small number-holding areas called *registers*. Typical microprocessor operations include adding, subtracting, comparing two numbers, and fetching numbers from one area to another

1840s was an important example of the use of a binary code to represent letters in the English alphabet. It wasn't until a hundred years later, though, that scientists figured out how to build a machine that could use binary digits to perform much more complex manipulations of mathematical data.

In 1940, at Harvard University, mathematician Howard Aikin constructed a computer that used the binary system to calculate; it used open and closed mechanical gates to represent binary digits. The machine was huge and noisy. A profound advance came in the mid-1940s when electrical engineers at the University of Pennsylvania replaced the mechanical gates with electronic "gates" in the form of vacuum tubes. These engineers constructed **ENIAC** (Electric Numerical Integrator and Computer), as this machine was called, to help the U.S. military figure out the trajectory of missiles in flight. Like the Harvard machine, ENIAC was very big. It took up a large room, weighed thirty tons, and used about eighteen thousand tubes.

What was brilliant about ENIAC, though, was its use of electronic rather than mechanical components as the basis of its operation. The usefulness of this thinking was confirmed in the 1950s, when scientists at Bell Labs invented the **transistor**, which featured the same capabilities as the vacuum tube in a smaller package. Private firms began to turn out computers, and over the next couple of decades, these computers got smaller and simultaneously faster and more powerful. By the 1970s, inventors had created the **microprocessor**, a miniaturized version of the central processing unit (the "brains") of a computer on a single chip. The microprocessor made it possible to build complex calculators and video games. As early as 1975, the Midway arcade company sold a Japanese home-arcade game cartridge called Gunfight that relied on a computer microprocessor for displaying its images.

The Advent of the Personal Computer

The invention of the microprocessor also led to the creation of the personal computer (PC), a computer that could fit on a desk. The first people to use PCs were hobbyists who built PCs from kits. By the early 1980s, Apple Computer, Commodore Corporation, Tandy Corporation, Osborne, and IBM were building fully assembled PCs for home as well as business use. An entire industry developed

Personal computers like the Apple II GS seen here began to find their way into homes and businesses in record numbers in the 1980s. *Time* magazine named the personal computer its "Person of the Year" for 1982. In 2006 *Time* would return to computers again for its "Person of the Year", this time honoring "You," the anonymous online contributors to blogs and sites like Wikipedia and YouTube.

rather quickly to create programs that could get personal computers to do useful things for people. Software companies marketed word processing programs that made the computer function like a super typewriter. Spreadsheet programs helped companies calculate projected expenditures and earnings. Educational programs helped kids do schoolwork. Computer games helped people have fun and persuaded them to buy computers in the first place. Just as surely as network television programs did, these computer programs involved mass communication. Over the next decade, in fact, executives in the television industry began to worry that the computer software industry was luring audiences away from their traditional TV sets.

Online Capability

The typical 1980s-vintage personal computer that sat in a home office consisted of a video display, a keyboard, a microprocessing unit, and a storage device (a replaceable, or "floppy," disk drive and often a permanent, or "hard," drive). What the earliest home-based computers generally didn't have was a way to send messages to computers elsewhere in the world. Before too long, however, computers did come equipped with the ability to go online—to receive digital information from anywhere by telephone. The hardware that made online activity possible is the **modem,** a device attached to the computer that performs a digital-to-analog conversion of data and then transmits the data to another modem. That modem reverses the process, performing an analog-to-digital conversion that permits the computer to which it is attached to use the data (see Figure 14.1).

An entire industry developed around the use of the modem. Commercial online networks, such as Prodigy and America Online, aggressively offered consumers the ability to play games with people across the nation, get help with homework through online encyclopedias, and chat with people about common interests. By the mid-1990s these firms came into competition with an enormous online network that threatened to push them aside: the **Internet.**

The Internet was developed by the National Science Foundation (NSF) from a project started by the U.S. Department of Defense. ARPANet, as it was first known,

modem a device attached to the computer that performs a digital-to-analog conversion of data and then transmits the data to another modem, which reverses the process

Internet a worldwide system of computer networks; a network of networks in which users at any one computer can, if they have permission, get information from any other computer (and sometimes talk directly to users at other computers)

Figure 14.1

How a Modem Works

A voiceband modem—short for modulator-demodulator—allows computers to "talk" to one another over great distances by modulating, or converting, the digital computer signals into sounds that can be transmitted over telephone lines. A modem on the other end then demodulates the signal—that is, it converts the analog sounds back into digital information that can be understood by another computer. Today, cable and DSL modems are more commonly used as faster connections between computers, and unlike voiceband modems, they do not need to modulate or demodulate the digital signals that they transmit.

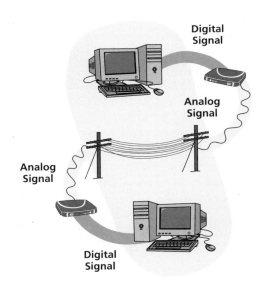

hyperlinks highlighted words or pictures on the Internet that, when clicked, will connect the user to a particular file, even to a specific relevant part of a document

The earliest form of the Internet was developed in 1969 by Advanced Research Projects Agency (ARPA) of the Department of Defense and it was first known as the ARPANet. As this map from 1973 shows, the network allowed users of research computers at distant locations to communicate with one another.

was conceived by the Advanced Research Projects Agency (ARPA) of the Department of Defense in 1969 to create a network that would allow users of a research computer at one university to "talk to" research computers at other universities. A side benefit of ARPANet's design was that, because messages could be routed or rerouted in more than one direction, the network could continue to function even if parts of it were destroyed in the event of a military attack or other disaster. At its core were three parts: a computer code (software) that allowed messages to be addressed and sent to particular individuals, a series of interconnecting computer networks that could coordinate the transmission of these messages around the nation and even around the world, and modem hardware that made it possible to use regular analog telephone lines to send digital computer messages.

Although the network was initially meant for scientific use, non-scientists within universities and executives from companies outside universities saw linking their computers to this network as a new and speedy way to communicate with others around the world. Universities and private firms spent huge sums of money to purchase computers and make sure that they could handle the rush of Internet traffic. The research, education, and business benefits that accrued through the Internet, though, would have cost much more if the work had been done in other ways—through travel or regular phone calls, for example.

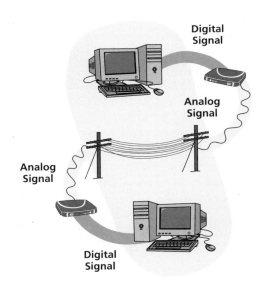

ARPA Network, Geographic Map
September 1973

The Hyperlink and the World Wide Web

But some computer scientists had even more ambitious ideas. They did not want the Internet to be a vehicle for simply transferring messages or documents between individuals. Instead they wanted to create a way for large groups of people to access and work on the same files. And they wanted to be able to send people to those documents through **hyperlinks**—highlighted words or pictures that, when clicked, will connect the user to a particular file, even to a specific relevant part of a document. Researchers at CERN, a nuclear research center in Geneva, Switzerland made this possible in 1989. Tim Berners-Lee and Sam Walker from the United Kingdom and Robert Cailliau from Belgium created **HTML** (HyperText Markup Language)—a computer language system that allowed people to access a system of interlinked documents that could be accessed through the Internet. HTML is used to define the structure, content and layout of a web page by using what are called *tags* that have attributes. As the viewer of a web page you don't see the HTML; it is hidden from your view. However, you do see the results. A key aspect of this system—what they called the World Wide Web—was that users could go to the materials by typing in a specific World Wide Web address or a clicking on a link in a document that contained the address which would automatically "link" them to that place.

Internet messages had to be transmitted in text form. Sending graphical images was possible, but the images had to be decoded by the receiver before viewing. That situation changed in 1993, when computer scientists at the University of Illinois created the **browser**, a graphical way to access the World Wide Web. Using software like Netscape Navigator or Microsoft Internet Explorer, a computer user can easily view complex drawings or photographs. As computer experts devised increasingly sophisticated and easy-to-use browsers for finding information, students and their professors began to "surf" the Web. The idea that millions of well-educated people around the world could access pictures, sound, and even video intrigued marketers and media firms. They started websites and tried to entice potential customers to visit them.

By the mid-1990s, the Internet had moved far beyond its original military and academic purpose to become a vast communication system. Much of the activity in **cyberspace** (that is, in the online world of computer networks) still involved mediated interpersonal communication—individuals interacting one-on-one with other individuals through written words, voice, and video. But a large and growing portion of the online world involved commercial attempts to reach out to various audiences. Companies sprang up to create sites on the Web or the commercial online networks, to determine who was coming to these sites, and to encourage advertising on them. The digital world of the Internet, in short, had become a new mass medium.

HTML (HyperText Markup Language) a computer language system that allowed people to access a system of interlinked documents that could be accessed through the Internet. HTML is used to define the structure, content and layout of a web page by using what are called *tags* that have attributes

browser software that interprets Hypertext Markup Language (HTML) and displays it on a computer screen

cyberspace the online world of computer networks

The Rise of Video Games

The period from the 1940s through the 1990s is also roughly the period in which the video games developed to become a mainstay in many American homes.[1] The birth of video games can be traced back to two separate streams of developments that initially were unrelated to the computer. The first stream involved the **pinball machine**, a coin operated game in which a player scores points by causing metal balls to move in certain directions (often with flippers) inside a glass covered case. These games were made popular by David Gottlieb beginning in the early 1930s at **entertainment arcades**—commercial locations featuring coin-operated machines such as pinball machines, fortune tellers, and shooter games.

While the mechanical pinball game was a fixture of arcades, scientists working on video electronics and computers were amusing themselves with games that could be played on TV-like displays. In 1958, for example, scientists at the Brookhaven National Laboratory set up a video tennis game on an oscilloscope for play during its annual visitors' day. Similarly, computer students at MIT, Stanford

pinball machine a coin operated game in which a player scores points by causing metal balls to move in certain directions (often with flippers) inside a glass covered case

entertainment arcade a commercial location for coin-operated machines such as pinball machines, fortune tellers, and shooter games

and other schools began to use their universities' computer systems to create games such as Spacewar! that tied to their love of science fiction. Activities such as this at the University of Utah influenced Nolan Bushnell and Ted Dabney, in 1972, to start Atari. It became the first successful U.S. company to create video arcade games.

During the late 1970s and the early 1980s arcade video games became very popular with entertainment genre such as shoot 'em ups (*Defender*), racing games, maze games (*Pac-Man*) and platform games that challenged players to navigate a series of levels through ladder-like structures while dodging obstacles (*Donkey Kong*). This arcade fever encouraged toy companies such as Mattel and electronics companies such as Magnavox to try to make video games for the home. Mattel released a hand-held game machine with a screen, but most of the games were placed on computer chips that were placed into cartridges that in turn were inserted into electronic boxes ("consoles") that were attached to TV sets. There were several failures among the console games, and for a time in the 1980s, gaming attention shifted from consoles to a new invention, the personal computer. Companies sold disks that could be played on specific computers—for example, the Commodore 64, the Apple II, and the IBM PC. Strategy video games and simulation video games, genres that had already been used for some consoles, generated a lot of interest during this time as particularly appropriate for computer play; *Dune* (strategy) and *SimCity* (simulation) were particularly popular.

When the Internet began to be used by more and more academics in the 1980s, it too became a location for playing games. People even figured out how to use Internet **bulletin boards**, in which many users could send text messages to one another, as a place where many people could share a game. Multi-player computer games that combined elements of chat rooms and fantasy role-playing games, such as *Dungeons & Dragons* emerged as extremely popular in these environments and the games became known as multi-used dungeons—MUDs for short. They were the predecessors of today's massively popular multi-player online role-playing games (MMORPGs) like *World of Warcraft*, with millions of players worldwide.

bulletin boards   software that allows users to exchange messages with other users, read news, publish articles and perform other activities such as play games

MUDS or multi-user dungeons   fantasy role-playing games such as Dungeons and Dragons, they were the predecessors of today's online games, with hundreds of thousands of players

The best-selling arcade game of all time, *Pac-Man* is widely considered one of the definitive classic video games of the 1980s. The remarkable popularity of the game upon its release in 1980 was dubbed "Pac-Man Fever," and the phenomenon launched countless toys and merchandise, an animated *Pac-Man* TV series on ABC, and even a pop music single that sold 2.5 million copies.

By the time the early 1990s came around, then, the basic types of video game vehicles had been established. Although some had almost vanished during the previous years, the next decade would reveal that many different types of video game platforms—consoles, computers, handheld, and Internet—could co-exist. At the end of the first decade of the twenty-first century, video games and the commercial Internet are very much intertwined as places to distribute, play, and buy the many types of gaming products. It will be useful, then, to first take a look at the commercial Internet industry and then focus on the video game business. Our primary lenses for both explorations will be the by-now familiar categories of production, distribution, and exhibition.

An Overview of the Modern Internet Industry

Reaching out from home or from work through the computer has become common for many people in the United States. In 2005, more than 73 million households had Internet access. That number represented about 64 percent of all U.S. households and 95 percent of computer households. As Table 14.1 shows, the percentage of American men and women who say they use the Internet (at home or out of home) is around the same. Internet use is more likely with younger than older adults, with higher education, with greater income, and with parents with children under age 18. Black men tend to say they use the Internet less than white men; this difference may be related to income and education.[2]

The Pew Internet and American Life Project continually surveys the U.S. population regarding its Internet uses, knowledge and habits. Figure 14.2 reflects answers a representative national sample gave Pew regarding the commercial uses that people make of the Web. The table distinguishes between people who access the Web through dialup telephone connections to a service provider such as Earthlink and people who access the Web through providers of high-speed—**broadband**—connections. As you can see, reading news, going to online stores (e-commerce), playing games, reading blogs, and downloading music are quite popular. So is creating spaces on social or community sites such as MySpace, Facebook and Linked In. Viewing network TV videos is growing, as well. Most of these activities—the news, music, games, network TV—are related to media industries with offline as well as online products.

In the chapters about these individual industries we have explored their online activities and strategies. The overall theme has been that today it is impossible for a media firm to remain separate from the Internet. Our purpose here is not to repeat these points, but to examine features of the online world that affect all companies, to explore some businesses that are unique to an Internet environment, outline ways that companies make money online, and to consider some of the social issues that are relevant to these activities.

broadband technologies
equipment that allows for the quick reception and transmission of a wide array of signals to come into the computer at the same time

Production and Distribution in the Internet Industry

When it comes to the commercial Internet, it is useful to discuss production and distribution together. That is because these two activities are often very much intertwined. When a company (say the New York Times) produces a website (or works with a specialized firm to create the site) and posts it online, it is engaging in production and distribution of the site. Now, it is the case that companies and

Table 14.1 U.S. Internet Use, 2006

Social category	Men (percent)	Women (percent)
Overall	68	66
Age		
18–29	80	86
30–49	76	79
50–64	63	66
65+	34	21
Race		
White	70	67
Black	50	67
Income		
<$30,000	49	48
$30,000 to $50,000	66	76
$50,000 to $75,000	84	87
>$75,000	90	95
Educational status		
No high school diploma	32	27
High school	58	56
Some college	79	79
College grad/grad degree	89	89
Parental status		
Parent of child under 18	81	80
Not parent of child under 18	61	57

Source: Veronis Suhler Stevenson, Communications Industry Forecast, 2006–2010, p. 438.

individuals often create content for sites that they don't control. Consider the example of a video production firm that creates a travel video for the Times website. Or the videos, songs and photos that individuals post on MySpace, Heavy, Facebook or other social media sites. Creative products by the people who visit the sites are often called **user generated content**. Still, even in these situations, the commercial firm that is distributing these works also acts as a production firm because it creates the elements on the sites that organize where these materials go.

Funding Internet Content It stands to reason that companies produce and distribute websites in order to make money. How they try to make money varies

user generated content creative products, such as videos and music, generated by the people who visit websites such as MySpace, Heavy, and Facebook

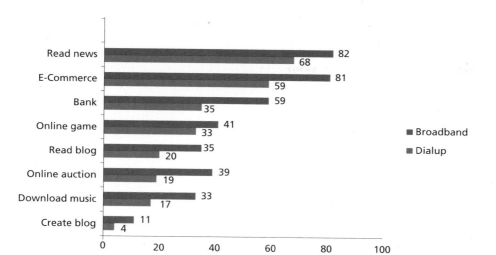

Figure 14.2
U.S. Internet Use by Access

Read news — 82 / 68
E-Commerce — 81 / 59
Bank — 59 / 35
Online game — 41 / 33
Read blog — 35 / 20
Online auction — 39 / 19
Download music — 33 / 17
Create blog — 11 / 4

■ Broadband
■ Dialup

widely. Some companies see their sites as primarily carrying out image-making activities. Others see their sites as directly selling products. Still others display content aimed at making money by attracting audiences through subscriptions or through advertising. Sometimes, firms approach sites with more than one of these goals. Let's take a look at each.

Sites Involved in Image-making

The idea behind using a site for image-making activities is typically to encourage fans of a product or service to purchase the product or service offline. Kraft Food's Jell-O website (http://www.kraftfoods.com/jello/), for example, is a site that provides recipes based on various forms of the product. The site also allows people to see commercials for the product and to download the commercial song as performed by Pat Benatar. The site also urges people to use various forms of the product with other Kraft items (Cool Whip, for example). In addition, Kraft used its site for a recipe exchange and message boards ("share ideas with others about dinner, entertaining"), a suggested food calendar, contests, and the videos of its "cooking school." None of these activities directly make any money for Kraft. Instead, they cultivate a friendly, healthful, family-oriented image for Kraft food that they hope will yield purchases in supermarkets and other physical stores.

Sites Selling Products or Services

If you have ever bought anything online (and a large majority of Internet-enabled individuals have) you know a website that sells products or services. This selling method has much in common with an old-fashioned catalog, except that online you sometimes have an opportunity to see a video of the products in operation. It should come as no surprise that the most popular bricks-and-mortar stores are among the most popular online stores; Wal-Mart, JC Penney, and Home Depot draw millions to their websites. People in the industry refer to firms with both an online and an

www.kraftfoods.com/jello/, the website for Jell-O®, promotes a fun, friendly, image for the product by posting music, video, and other interactive features, as well as recipes.

557

click-and-mortar companies firms with both an online and an offline sales presence

offline sales presence as **click-and-mortar companies.** Financial analysts sometimes prefer the click-and-mortar firms over pure web companies because the former have their warehouses and transportation services and they have the deep pockets needed to absorb the years of losses that are likely to result from their web operations. Analysts also suspect that consumers are more likely to be comfortable buying from the Web if they are buying brands they already know. Moreover, if something goes wrong with the products they buy online, they can take these products back to the bricks-and-mortar version of the store to receive face-to-face customer service.

Content Sites Selling Subscriptions

content site sites that attempt to build revenues by attracting audiences to content provided on the site

publisher the company running a website

A website that primarily shows printed or audiovisual material is called a **content site**; the company running it is called a **publisher.** Think, for example, of http://www.cnn.com or http://www.carfax.com. The idea of a publisher charging people to see the content of a site may sound great, but it is one that hasn't worked very well on the web. People who are spending hundreds, even thousands, of dollars for hardware and monthly payments to receive the Internet seem to have come over the decades to expect that media content will be free or very low cost. Exceptions tend to be in the business area. Industry trade magazines such as *Variety* sometimes charge for people to get into their websites, or into substantial parts of those sites. (They may show ads, as well.) In addition, specialized information sites, such as http://www.lexis.com, charge for entry. But over the past decade consumer newspapers and magazines that have tried subscriptions have abandoned them for all but archives of their periodicals. Instead, they have turned to advertising as the way to support their online ventures.

Content Sites Selling Advertisements

The bookstore, newspaper, radio, music, movie, and television sites that we have discussed throughout this text post advertisements on their websites. Sometimes the ads are for their own products. Very often, they are for other companies' goods or services, and the companies make money for posting the ads that reach the people who visit the sites. Then there are sites such as Monster, CareerBuilder and HotJobs that make money off the posting of classified ads.

search engine websites that allow users to find sites relevant to topics of interest to them

web crawlers or web spiders programs used by search engines that search the Internet to retrieve and catalog the content of websites

algorithm a complex set of rules that search engines use to come up with sites that relate to your search terms

Search Engines Although the kind of content production that these firms carry out is similar to analog material—whether music or classifieds—there is one type of content creation that is unique to the digital world: the search engine. The Wikipedia online encyclopedia defines a **search engine** as "an *information retrieval system* designed to help find information stored on a *computer system*." The search engine developed out of a need by people using the Web to be able to find sites relevant to topics of interest to them. You undoubtedly have gone to Google, Yahoo, MSN, Ask, Dogpile, or another search program to find out about a person, location or fact for a professional or personal reason. Search engines work by using **web crawlers** (also known as **web spiders**). These are programs which automatically browse the World Wide Web to create copies of all the visited pages. The search engine software will then catalog or "index" the downloaded pages so that a person searching for a word in them will find it quickly. Depending on the search engine, the spiders index more or less of the Web, but they never catalog the entire Web. Not only would it take too much time (and the crawlers have to keep doing their jobs over and over again to update their findings), there are some parts of the Web that they cannot enter because they are protected by passwords. When you type in search terms, you activate a complex set of mathematically-based rules, called an **algorithm,** that come up with sites that relate to your search terms.

Algorithms are the "secret sauce" of search engines. It is quite well known, though, that Google's approach to search involves a particular definition of popularity: the number of websites that are linked to a site that uses the search term. So, for example, if you type "Nikon" into a Google search box, the top links that appear will be for sites with the word "Nikon" to which many other sites link. The main list of sites that you get in response to writing Nikon in the Google search box is called Google's **natural search results**. That means that the sites came up based on Google's algorithm without any influence from Nikon or any other advertiser. Yahoo and other major search engines also set their ads apart from the natural search results. This point is important because the way these search companies survive is by sending advertising to their users. If natural results were intermingled with ads, users might have a tough time knowing whether a link was placed higher because it was really relevant or because a company paid for its placement there.

natural search results
websites that come up based on a search engine's algorithm without any influence from any advertisers

Distributing Advertisements on the Web　Advertising of all types brought in $17.5 billion to websites in 2005; the growth rate was in the double digits. According to the Internet Advertising Bureau, in 2005 72 percent of web advertising flowed to the ten most popular sites on the Web. In fact, the top 50 sites grabbed 95 percent of the revenues. The remaining 5 percent is still a very large number—half a billion dollars—an amount over which many sites would want to compete. Nevertheless, those who believed that the Web would allow a

Google in China

WORLD VIEW

In light of Google's decision to censor search results in China, some are questioning just how closely the company adheres to its motto: Don't Be Evil. Faced with what amounted to a choice between omitting objectionable material and pulling out of the Chinese search engine race entirely, the Mountain View, a California-based company, made what Google officials described as an excruciating decision to stay online at the expense of providing free access to content.

Initially, searches on Google.cn, the official Google China site, were slowed or blocked because the company didn't provide adequate barriers to information the Communist government deemed inappropriate. Consequently, in an attempt to tap into the market of several hundred million Chinese web users, Google agreed to restrict access to such subjects as Taiwan's independence and the 1989 Tiananmen Square massacre. As a result, when a user attempts to access blocked subject matter, he is alerted that the information he is seeking has been removed. The search engine hopes that, in spite of these restrictions, Google.cn will become the most popular search engine in the world's largest country.

Many outside observers, however, are extremely concerned by the precedent, "This is a real shame," said Julien Pain,

head of Reporters Without Borders' Internet desk. "When a search engine collaborates with the government like this, it makes it much easier for the Chinese government to control what is being said on the Internet." Google wasn't the only Internet company Reporters Without Borders took issue with, as the media watchdog contended that similarly problematic decisions were made by Yahoo and MSN.com when they entered the Chinese market.

Even so, China isn't the only country that mandates some restrictions to Internet access. In France and Germany, for example, Google agreed to censor references to Nazi paraphernalia, as is required by French and German law. In both those countries, however, Internet users have access to Google mail. That service is not provided to Google users in China, out of concern that the Chinese government would order the search engine to turn over personal information. This fear is warranted; in 2005, Yahoo turned over the private email account information of a Chinese journalist to the Communist government, a decision that was widely criticized as it ultimately led to the journalist being jailed.

Source: Associated Press, "Google Spells Censorship in China," *Wired*, January 24, 2006.

great spread of ad money across a broad range of large and small sites must be disappointed by these findings.

Broadly speaking we can distinguish between two types of ads on the Web, text ads and display ads. **Text ads** typically comprise a few lines of writing about the offered product or service that link to the advertiser's website. **Display ads** add graphics and sometimes video to text and usually take up more space on a web page. Let's look at the two types in a bit more detail.

Text Ads

The most widespread text ads on the Web are those placed by email advertising companies, advertising networks and search engines. An email advertising company is a firm that sends commercial messages to people's email addresses. Sometimes, as in the case of Google's Gmail, text ads lie at the bottom of an otherwise normal email between two or more people. Sometimes the entire email message is an advertisement. The norm (and in some states the law) regarding email advertising is that the recipient has to agree to receive such ads or have a relationship with the firm that is sending them. That consent is called an **opt-in** rule for sending the advertising. Legitimate companies that send email ads also provide the opportunity for recipients to **opt-out**—to not continue to receive the ads. Ads that people do not want to receive are known as **spam**. The amount of spam from all over the world into people's mailboxes is so great that an industry has grown up to sell programs that attempt to filter the ads so they will not appear with legitimate mail. Many Internet service providers such as Comcast and Earthlink also filter the email people receive to stop spam.

An **ad network** is a collection of many websites that a company knits together in order to sell ads on them. The ad-serving company shares its revenues with the sites on which it places the ads. The terms by which search engines and ad networks get paid for advertising differ by company, but let's use Google as a specific example. Google has both a search engine advertising program, which it calls AdWords, and an ad network, which it calls AdSense. To make money from advertisers for its search page, it puts out bids for search words. Say, for example, that you are a camera manufacturer. You might bid on the term "digital camera"—that is, state how much you are willing to pay Google if your ad shows up and someone clicks on it. If Google accepts your bid your text ad will come up next to Google's search results when a person types "digital camera" into the search box. Google will charge you, however, only if the person clicks on the link of your text ad, thus indicating a serious interest.

When an Internet user clicks on an ad that shows up on Google's search page, Google alone makes the money. The situation is different with Google's AdSense network. Google computers scan the pages of the sites in the network and choose ads for products that seem to resonate with the topics on the page. So, for example, if the page discusses cameras, Google might serve up an ad for a camera to that page. This activity of scanning a publisher's web page and serving ads that match the topic of the page is called **contextual advertising**. As with the AdWords, the advertiser pays only if the user clicks on the ad.

Display Ads

Display ads are messages that combine text and graphics. If you go to an ad-supported site, chances are you will see the two basic forms of display ads, banners and pop-ups. **Banners** are square or rectangular commercial messages that sit on a page of the website. Many of them are **rich media** ads. That is, they contain animated or video presentations that activate automatically or can be activated by clicking on the ad.

---

text ads typically comprise a few lines of writing about the offered product or service that link to the advertiser's website

display ads add graphics and sometimes video to text and usually take up more space on a web page

opt-in a rule for sending email advertising that states the recipient has to agree to receive such ads or have a relationship with the firm that is sending them

opt-out a rule for sending email advertising that provides the opportunity for recipients to not continue to receive the ads

spam ads that people do not want to receive

ad network a collection of many websites that a company knits together in order to sell ads on them

contextual advertising the activity of scanning a publisher's web page and serving ads that match the topics of the page

banners square or rectangular commercial messages that sit on the page of a website

rich media ads that contain animated or video presentations that activate automatically or can be activated by clicking on the ad

One type of ad that many people dislike is the **pop-up ad**. Pop-ups are commercial messages that jump out at you (typically in square and rectangular form) when you go to a web page or click on a picture or word. Creators often build animated images and sell them in order to grab the attention of web users in an environment filled with ads. In addition, increased competition for viewer attention has led advertisers to be quite creative (and sometimes annoying) with their placement of banners and, especially, pop-ups. The latest web browsers have software that prevent pop-ups from showing up if the user chooses to eliminate them. One kind of forced viewing that remains is the **interstitial**. It jumps out at you, often as an entire page, as the publisher's site is loading or between the site's page loadings.

As more and more people have access to broadband technology in their homes and offices, display ads are adding video components. Even search and advertising network ads, that have traditionally been text based, have been moving toward the presentation of boxed videos instead of the text links. Moreover, as publishers such as CNN and CBS put professional videos online, they incorporate commercials into the videos. These commercials are typically only 15 seconds long, but the audience cannot move quickly past them. This forced viewing annoys many viewers, and Google has tried to find other forms of advertising for the videos it places on its YouTube site.

Web Ads, Targeting, and Data mining

The pitch that content sites make to advertisers is that they attract the best potential customers for their products. Because the online world is so diverse, they argue, advertisers can find sites that reach people with very specific interests. But the executives of content sites go further than that. They provide advertisers with technology that, they claim, can actually ensure that certain ads will be seen by some people on their sites and other ads will be seen by different people.

Web marketers argue that this ability to target individuals makes online advertising more "customizable" than any other mass medium in history. They call this advertising activity **mass customization**—-the use of sophisticated technology to send large numbers of people messages tailored to their individual interests. So, for example, http://www.iVillage.com can send different ads to a woman who says that she is in her twenties and to one who claims to be over forty, even if they are reading the same article.

Because tailoring messages in this way requires information about particular members of the audience, website owners engage in online data gathering to find out as much as they can about the individuals who visit their domains. Creating a description of someone based on collected data is called **profiling**. One straightforward method a firm can use to get data for profiling is to ask people to register to get access to a site. When you try to get into http://www.nytimes.com for the first time, for example, you will have to answer a number of questions about your work, your income, and your address before you are able to enter the site.

That information is probably not terribly reliable because you could make up everything except your email address. (The *Times* computer checks to see that that is correct.) A second profiling method (which yields different sorts of data) is to ask people what topics they want to learn about through the site. *Wall Street Journal Interactive*, for example, asks you to choose news and entertainment categories as guides to the material it sends you. A third method of profiling yields still other kinds of data: having the computer silently track your choices as you move through a particular website or across websites. These choices are stored on your computer in a tiny hidden text file called a **cookie**. Every time you visit the site, the cookie is activated and records your movements, or **clickstream**, through

pop-ups commercial messages that jump out at you (typically in square and rectangular form) when you go to a web page or click on a picture or word

interstitial pop-up ads pop-up ads that jump out at you between page loadings

mass customization the use of sophisticated technology to send large numbers of people messages tailored to their individual interests

profiling creating a description of someone based on collected data

cookie information that a website puts on your computer's hard disk so that it can remember something about you at a later time; more technically, it is information for future use that is stored by the server on the client side of a client/server communication

clickstream computer jargon used to describe movement through websites

the site. Over time, the company that created the cookie develops a profile of your interests that it can bring together with other profiles to offer to advertisers. The company can also track your behavior within its site, and some advertising networks track your behavior across sites.

For websites, the ideal is having all three types of data about their visitors to sell to advertisers. And even sites that don't rely on ads—such as the image-making and direct selling sites we discussed earlier—want to know these sorts of things. They believe that very specific audience data can help them better customize their content and more persuasively encourage people to buy their products or services.

data mining the process of gathering and storing information about many individuals—often millions—to be used in audience profiling and interactive marketing

The process of gathering and storing information about many individuals—often millions—to be used in audience profiling and interactive marketing is called **data mining.** In addition to the three forms of online data just mentioned, miners try to find offline information on individuals—for example, drivers' license records, mortgage information, and credit ratings—that they can link by computer to other data in the website's collection. Because of the wide interest in data gathering on the Web, an entire data-mining industry has grown up around this activity. Its goal is to help web companies sort through the many pieces of information they have on the individuals who come to their site so that the producers of the sites can profitably use mass customization in editorial and advertising content. Figure 14.3 illustrates this data-mining process in action.

As you can see, the Web's content is not only constantly changing, but the particular content distributed by a website may well vary with the individual. One person may see different things based on what the site knows about him or her. Sites that use cookies and sophisticated data-mining techniques to create profiles of their visitors can literally create very different sites for different personalities. Moreover, what is "produced" for any one person can change instantly, depending upon the way the person responded to material distributed to him or her an instant earlier.

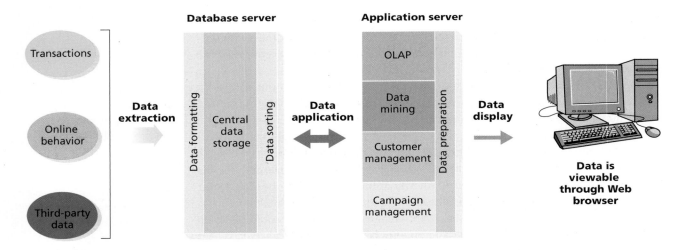

Figure 14.3

The Data-Mining Process in Action

This figure illustrates how information on individuals is "extracted" from various sources and analyzed. The database server stores the information for the application server, which takes the information and sorts it to make profiles (data mining), to create lists of types of profiles (data management), and to create web ad campaigns and other online targeting activities. OLAP stands for online analytical processing, an activity that analyzes new and old data about an individual in real time.

Offerings such as "my Yahoo" and the options that Amazon.com encourages people to use to make its site more specific to them are examples of this sort of personalization. The truth is, though, that the great majority of sites do not have the sophisticated technology that would enable them to truly tailor content based on the profiles and real-time activities of their visitors. Most of the time, **personalization of content** does not mean writing a different story based on the known characteristics of the individual clicking on the material. Instead, it means sending one story rather than another, or sending the business section rather than the sports section.

Web executives assert that this sort of personalization is coming soon. They point out, too, that a large amount of personalization is already taking place in web advertising. The distribution of ads to visitors is especially critical to content sites because they depend so heavily on the revenues that advertising brings. Their claim to advertisers is that because of their interactivity and profiling, they can reach individuals who fit the profile the advertisers are seeking more effectively than any other medium. If you are getting the feeling that these activities have the potential to violate the privacy of web users, you are not alone. As we will note in more detail at the end of the chapter, they have led to a national dialogue on privacy in the Internet age.

personalization of content a strategy for providing tailored content, based upon profiles and real-time activities of a website's visitors

Exhibition in the Internet Industry

A media firm's executives may be very proud of their company's website and the banners that they can sell to advertisers. Ultimately, though, a commercial website is successful when the kinds of people the company wants as visitors log on in sufficient numbers and take actions that justify the hundreds of thousands of dollars it often costs to create and maintain the site. "How does this relate to exhibition?" you may ask. The answer is that the exhibitor is the company that provides the technology through which the person can go to the site. This may seem like a basic activity, a little like picking up a wireline telephone and making a call. While to an extent it's like that, the potential role of exhibition firms in making decisions about the kind of sites people can visit has led to much controversy.

Before we get to the controversy, let's start with basic questions about "going" to a site: how do people "get" online? When they do get online? How do they find out about particular sites? And, equally important for media firms, how can advertisers who buy banners be persuaded that the kinds of people they are paying to meet at particular sites actually get those ads distributed to them? Let's examine these topics one at a time.

Getting Online   If you're a college student, there's a fair chance that much of your contact with the online world is through your school. In that case, the school typically picks up the tab for your email and your connections to the college's online resources (such as the library catalog) as well as to the World Wide Web. Providing this kind of access to students can cost an academic institution loads of money. It is, however, considered part of the cost of educating students today.

People outside colleges are not so fortunate. They must find an Internet service provider (**ISP**) individually, and they often have to pay for them. Broadly speaking, they have four choices for an Internet service provider, a cable company such as Time Warner or Comcast, a phone company such as Verizon or Sprint, a packager of Internet service such as Earthlink, and a mobile phone company. ISPs typically provide their customers with a browsers and the ability to receive email.

If you've been online in your college or university, you've undoubtedly heard the word **WiFi**—short for **wireless fidelity**. It's a radio technology (called IEEE

Internet service provider (ISP) a company that sells access to the Internet

wireless fidelity or WiFi a radio technology (called IEEE 802.11) designed to provide secure, reliable, fast wireless connectivity

The Pew Internet and American Life Project

The rise of the Internet has led to a host of questions regarding its impact on society. While it is agreed that the Internet affects the way people live and interact, it is an ongoing process to understand the nature(s) of this influence. The Pew Internet and American Life Project (http://www.pew Internet.org) produces reports that examine the impact of the Internet on a variety of aspects of American life. The project covers the following 11 areas: demographics; E-Gov and E-Policy; education; family, friends and community; health; Internet evolution; major news events; online activities and pursuits; public policy; technology and media use; work. According to its mission statement, "The Project aims to be an authoritative source on the evolution of the Internet through collection of data and analysis of real-world developments as they affect the virtual world."

Utilizing nationwide random telephone surveys and online surveys, the project collects both quantitative and qualitative data to aid research initiatives throughout the country and the world. Both individual and group use is tracked through the surveys, painting detailed portraits of the Internet in its many forms and functions. The Internet and American Life is a project of the Pew Research Center, a

www.pewinternet.org

nonpartisan "fact tank" that provides information on the issues, attitudes and trends shaping America and the world." (http://www.pewresearch.org). Funding is provided by the Pew Charitable Trust, an independent nonprofit organization dedicated to improving public policy, informing the public, and stimulating civic life.

Source: http://www.pewtrusts.org

802.11) that engineers designed in the late 1990s (after earlier work in Holland using a different technology) to provide secure, reliable, fast wireless connectivity. Many consumer devices use WiFi. Amongst others, personal computers can network to each other and connect to the Internet, mobile computers can connect to the Internet from any WiFi hotspot, and digital cameras can transfer images wirelessly. There are four types of WiFi—a, b, g, and n—and each provides faster connection to the web router (see Figure 14.4). Because WiFi frequencies don't travel more than a few hundred yards, it can't be used for purposes that cover many miles. That is the purpose of WiMAX. It is based on a different radio technology (IEEE 802.16) and can in fact cover many miles. The U.S. cellular company Sprint Nextel announced in mid-2006 that it would invest about $5 billion in building a WiMAX technology over a few years in order to sell mobile Internet users high-speed access to data[3] (see Figure 14.5).

Addressing the Web You probably know that you reach sites on the World Wide Web by typing a string of letters, called a web address, into a browser. The structure of web addresses is generally administered by the Internet Corporation for Assigned Names and Numbers (ICANN). ICANN is a private, nonprofit organization that the U.S. government helped set up in 1998. More international than

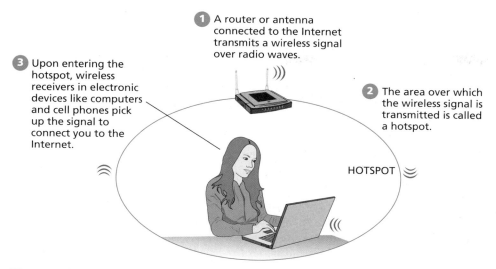

1 A router or antenna connected to the Internet transmits a wireless signal over radio waves.

3 Upon entering the hotspot, wireless receivers in electronic devices like computers and cell phones pick up the signal to connect you to the Internet.

2 The area over which the wireless signal is transmitted is called a hotspot.

HOTSPOT

Figure 14.4

How WiFi works

WiFi, or "wireless fidelity," technology allows an Internet connection to be broadcast and received using radio waves. Technology in computers, video game consoles, cellphones, MP3 players, PDAs, and other wireless-enabled devices can pick up the signals to connect to the Internet when they are within the range of a wireless network. The area in which one can connect to a wireless network is known as a hotspot. Depending upon the network provider, access to the hotspot may be available for free or restricted to subscribers and pay-as-you-go users.

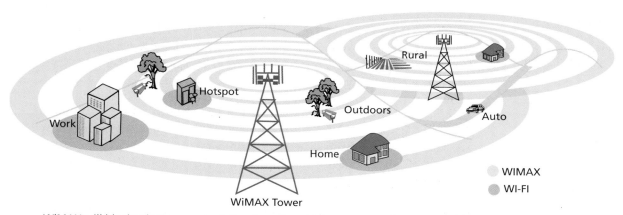

Rural

Hotspot

Outdoors

Auto

Work

Home

WIMAX

WI-FI

WiMAX Tower

WiMAX will blanket large areas to deliver broadband Internet access that moves with you beyond Wi-Fi hotspots.

Figure 14.5

WiFi versus WiMax

WiFi frequencies typically have a limited range of about 500 feet, but newer WiMax (Worldwide Interoperability for Microwave Access) technology aims to provide wireless network connections over much longer distances. WiMax uses towers similar to cellphone towers to broadcast a signal up to 30 miles. That's nearly 300 times as far! A WiMax receiver similar to the WiFi receiver found in most computers today receives the signal that connects you to the Internet. Like WiFi, WiMax is a global standards-based technology that is being adopted in many countries around the world. Sprint Nextel launched some of the first commercial WiMax networks in the United States in Chicago, Baltimore, and Washington, DC in early 2008.

the previous organization that performed these tasks, it is a technical coordination body for the Internet.

Web addresses are often called **URLs,** or **uniform resource locators;** they help to locate unique resources (i.e., sites) on the Web. Every web address must be unique so that the computers that connect computers on the Web can locate it. A URL has two parts, the domain name of the individual or organization, and the **top-level domain (TLD).**

Domain Names

The **domain name** is a word or connected phrase with which the person or organization wants to be identified on the Web. Routledge (this book's publisher) decided to use Routledge; it could also have used Routpub or some other identifier. As you might imagine, there are many fights over the use of domain names. Generally speaking, courts have ruled that trademark owners get to keep their names online. Only Coca-Cola can use coca_cola, for example. The issue gets more problematic if two companies in different industries have the same name. When that happens, first come, first served is typically the rule. Alternatively, one party may pay the other to bow out.

Using a domain name means registering with one of the ICANN-approved registry companies that help people establish their URLs on the Web. Each registrar sets the price it charges for registering names, and prices vary significantly among different registrars. In addition, some registrars offer discounted or free registration services to those who pay for other services, such as *web hosting.* **Web hosting** means providing space on a computer for the actual website with the domain name.

Top-level Domains

In a site's address (its URL), the domain name is connected to its top-level domain, the most general part of the domain name in an Internet address. The TLD is actually the first step in telling the Web computers that connect other computers on the network where to go in a search for the computer that hosts the site. Until 2001, there were only five main TLDs. They indicated whether the organization was a web-related organization (.net), a U.S. government agency (.gov), an educational institution (.edu), a nonprofit organization (.org), or a commercial firm (.com). The U.S. military also has a suffix (.mil). With .mil, .gov, and even .edu restricted to specific types of sites, individuals and companies from all over the world began to complain that the domain names they wanted to use had already been taken in the dot-com and/or dot-net TLD. The resulting discussions led ICANN to approve seven new top-level domains (see Table 14.2). So, for example, if a company finds that http://www.tires.com is taken, it might try to register http://www.tires.info or http://www.tires.biz.

Many web addresses include top-level country names (ccTLDs)—for example .uk for the United Kingdom, .jp for Japan, and .il for Israel. The rules and policies for registering domain names with these country codes vary significantly, and some are reserved for use by citizens of the corresponding country. Anyone from anywhere can apply for the three-letter TLDs, however.

For an individual trying to get to a website, all these behind-the-scenes activities result in the website URL that must be typed into the browser. Each URL starts with http://. That opener, **HTTP** (which stands for *hypertext transfer protocol*) is often followed by www. (for World Wide Web) and then by specifics about the site—its domain name and its TLD. When you know these basics, getting to some sites is often pretty intuitive. To get to ESPN's site, type http://www.espn.com. For the general Disney location, type http://www.disney.com. The White House is at

---

uniform resource locator (URL) Internet location of a website

top-level domain (TLD) most general part of the domain name in an Internet address. A TLD is either a generic top-level domain (gTLD), such as "com" for "commercial," "edu" for "educational," and so forth, or a country code top-level domain (ccTLD), such as "fr" for France or "is" for Iceland

domain name one word or a connected phrase with which the person or organization wants to be identified on the Web

web hosting providing space on a computer for the actual website with the domain name

HTTP or hypertext transfer protocol the set of rules for exchanging files on the World Wide Web

Table 14.2   **The New Domain Names**

TLD	Purpose	Registry Applicant
.aero	Air-transport industry	Société Internationale de Telecommunications Aeronautiques SC (SITA)
.biz	Businesses	JVTeam, LLC (now known as NeuLevel)
.coop	Cooperatives	National Cooperative Business Association (NCBA)
.info	Unrestricted use	Afilias, LLC
.museum	Museums	Museum Domain Management Association (MDMA)
.name	Individuals	Global Name Registry, LTD
.pro	Accountants, lawyers, and physicians	RegistryPro, LTD

At its meeting on November 16, 2000, the ICANN board selected seven new top-level domains (TLDs). The new TLDs and their intended purposes are listed above.

http://www.whitehouse.gov. The University of Pennsylvania web address is http://www.upenn.edu.

Of course, not all addresses are this straightforward, though, and so people may well need to use search engines to find them.

The Net Neutrality Controversy   Note that in mentioning the ESPN, White House and Penn websites we assumed that everyone could go to them no matter what ISP they use. It's possible that some companies restrict their workers' ability to use the firms' computers to visit sites the companies feel will waste workers' time (game sites, for example) or embarrass other employees (for example, pornography sites). But computer users connected to the Internet can typically go to any website that is open to the public. (Parents, if they want, can then filter certain sites so that their children can't go to them.) Imagine, though, if the Internet service provider for your home computer began to make decisions that it would allow only certain websites to reach its clients but not others. They might do that in order to get websites to pay them to "exhibit" the sites in people's homes. Or they may tell websites that they might slow them down (thus encouraging users to go to other sites) unless they pay fees to get the fastest speeds.

As a consumer, you may think this is a terrible idea because it might make it difficult or impossible to reach certain sites. But some ISP executives argue that they should have the right to charge some sites for "exhibition" because the sites use up enormous amounts of bandwidth (by providing videos, for example) that they have to provide to their customers and for which they do not get compensated. Website executives and consumer advocates respond that the ISPs do get back that money by charging their customers for access. Moreover, they argue that the Internet has become so important to society that to restrict or diminish the use of it could have unfortunate consequences for what people know and what they can share with one another.

This argument is called the **net neutrality** controversy. The term refers to the desire by websites and advocates to make sure that ISPs do not charge sites for transmission. At this point in time, no ISPs seem to violate the idea of net

net neutrality   the desire by websites and advocates to make sure that ISPs do not charge sites for transmission

neutrality. As mentioned, some companies may restrict employees' web access even though the ISPs deliver them. Also, some mobile phone devices that can access the Internet won't deliver certain parts of it (for example, videos and music streaming sites) because of drawbacks in the software or hardware. There have been reports that some mobile phone providers purposely place these deficiencies on the phones so that customers will have to use (and pay for) similar services on special sites that the phone companies set up.

An Overview of the Modern Video Game Industry

The term *video game* obscures a complex industry with several different types of products and different production, distribution and exhibition processes. They make up a big business. In the U.S., video game companies of all sorts—the ones that sell consoles and accessories and the ones that sell games—brought in almost $13.5 billion in revenue in 2006—an 18 percent increase over the previous year.[4] The goal here is to help you develop a framework with which to explore these activities further. We start with a definition: **video games** are entertainment products powered by computer chips and displayed on monitors that require users to experience and interact with challenges in a series of tasks. As you can infer from this definition (and from what you may know about video games), any discussion of the business has to take into consideration two key features: the hardware and the software.

Video Game Hardware

Hardware refers to the devices on which the video games are played. As you might have gathered from the brief outline of video game history presented earlier, a number of hardwares coexist.

Games are sold for the gaming console, the stand-alone desktop or laptop computer, the Internet-linked computer, the interactive television connection, the handheld game device, and the mobile phone. Let's dig a bit into each of these.

The Gaming Console   With computers in so many homes, a person might wonder why people would find a need for a gaming console. After all, a gaming console is a computer on which you play games. But that's the point. Gaming consoles are built—optimized—for the speed and graphics that many games require. You could get many of those features on a desktop or laptop computer, but you'd likely have to know a lot about ordering special components, and you'd undoubtedly pay a lot more money than if you bought a standard computer.

Three companies—Sony, Microsoft, and Nintendo—make the consoles that people associate with contemporary gaming. Before Microsoft entered the fray in 2001 the competition was between three companies—Sony, Nintendo and Sega. Sony's PlayStation became so popular that Sega dropped out of making consoles and Nintendo was far behind. Moreover, it took a while for Microsoft to be a serious competitor. To give you an idea of the popularity of the Sony PlayStation, consider that in 2005, Playstation 2 accounted for eight of the top ten console titles sold during that year. Over time, the Xbox and its successor, the Microsoft's Xbox 360 (released in 2005) cut into Sony's lead.

In 2007, however, Nintendo came roaring back into competition with Sony and Microsoft consoles via its Wii. The Wii represented a kind of counterprogramming to the gaming approaches of Sony and Microsoft. Their consoles aimed at

video games
entertainment products powered by computer chips and displayed on monitors that require users to experience and interact with challenges in a series of tasks

hardware   the device or console on which video games are played

hardcore gamers—typically (75 percent) male and young (46 percent are under 18 years old) who enjoy playing complex adventures that require dexterity with hard-to-learn controls. The Wii, by contrast, is a gaming platform that Nintendo purposely built for people who may be intimidated by Playstation and Xbox controllers. Its graphics do not have as high a resolution as the other two machines, but its controller is extremely easy to use. Instead of pushing a series of buttons, the user can carry out the actions needed in the game by moving the entire device up, down or to the side, as if the user were in the actual game. The console is particularly suited to video versions of such physical games as ping pong and racket ball. The Wii seems to have hit a nerve among so-called **casual gamers**—women and men who are older than the hardcore types and like to play less intense (though not necessarily less difficult) games than the hardcore types. By mid-2007, the Wii was the best-selling console in the United States, ahead of the Xbox 360 and even further ahead of Sony's PS3.

The Standalone Computer Like hardcore console players, the players associated with games played on computers are male and young. Their population does, however, include a somewhat higher percentage of females (39 percent vs. 35 percent) and a somewhat higher percentage of "older" players (36 percent rather than 46 percent are under 18). Computer game players also seem to prefer strategy games over the adventure games that console players tend to buy. Although games purchased to play on the computer were extremely popular in the 1990s, such sales have declined as consoles became attractive to hardcore gamers and as broadband connections to Internet gaming increased. Sales of new entertainment software for the PC have declined every year since 2000; in that year it reached $1.9 billion dollars, but by 2005 that number had been cut in half. Even more startling is the drop in educational software from a $1 billion industry in the 1990s to less than $100 million in 2006.[5] One summary of the educational software market noted that disk-based games to teach kids reading and math "virtually disappeared from the shelves" as the Web brought new ways to access them.[6]

hardcore gamers typically (75 percent) male and young (46 percent are under 18 years old) who enjoy playing complex adventures that require dexterity with hard-to-learn controls

casual gamers women and men who are older than the hardcore types and like to play less intense (though not necessarily less difficult) games than the hardcore types

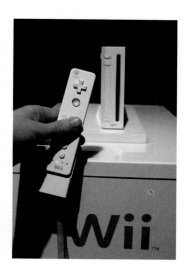

Video game consoles include the Sony PlayStation 3 (left), the Microsoft Xbox (center), and the Nintendo Wii (right).

PlayStation Nation: Ireland?

Japan has long been seen as a culture addicted to anything high-tech. Also, much of the most popular video game consoles have originated from there (e.g., Nintendo and Sony). Hence, it is not surprising that Japan has the highest PlayStation sales per capita. However, the country next on that list may come as a surprise: Ireland.

Between March and September 2007, Sony sold 40,000 PlayStation3s in Ireland and 700,000 PS2s in the seven years prior. Now, one in four homes in Ireland has a PS2. In addition, many Irish gamers are thought to have several different consoles in their homes. The high sales have led the Managing Director of Sony Computer Entertainment Ireland, Niall O'Hanrahan to exclaim that video games had "captured the hearts of the Irish public." However, this position for Ireland is not new. Ireland reached the number two position of PlayStation ownership almost a decade ago.

In 1998, when sales of PlayStation first made huge leaps in Ireland it was thought that it was due to the poor summer weather Ireland was experiencing at the time. This can no longer be a serious consideration as the popularity of the PS consoles has lasted too long to be attributed simply to weather. Even girls as young as six have been purchasing PlayStations. While this may be surprising, some gaming-enthusiasts in Ireland state that the Irish have always been into games and that the PlayStation trend is simply an extension of this. Whatever the cause, Ireland is continuing to be an increasing market for video games.

Sources: Eva Marie Gibney, "PlayStation Nation; Only the Japanese Own more PS2s than the Irish," *Daily Mail*, September 27, 2007; Karl Brophy, "Cool Summer Means Hot Business for Video Games," *Daily Mirror*, August 4, 1998.

The Internet-linked Computer While game-playing on stand-alone computers is falling, playing online is rising strongly. Actual gambling online is illegal in the United States, though Americans do access sites elsewhere in the world to participate. Aside from gambling sites, however, you can go to many websites that offer games to play. Most fall under the casual gaming category; it is supposedly a category preferred by women. It includes puzzle, card, board and word games, sometimes with fictional characters, and it is very popular. In fact, the Casual Games Association (http://www.casualgamesassociation.org), an industry trade group, estimates more than 200 million people worldwide play such games on the Internet.[7] Pogo (http://www.pogo.com) is a website that specializes in these sorts of games, with titles such as "Mahjong Garden Deluxe" and "World Class Solitaire." Pogo (and Yahoo Games and many other sites) also has arcade-like games and sports games. If you want to play games free, you will see a lot of ads; some even interrupt game play. Pogo allows you to get rid of the ads by paying a fee to play, and you can join Club Pogo to play a panoply of games without ad interruptions. One of the benefits of online connections is that people who care about games can chat about the topic or just about anything else in chat rooms set up on the various sites.

People interested in the more intense, complex and often violent adventure platforms aimed at hardcore gamers can also find them, and chat rooms to discuss them, online. On http://www.gametap.com, for example, you can find games such as Battlestations Midway, Shock Troopers, and Tomb Raider. Some of them are free (for viewing ads) while others charge to play. Increasingly popular with hardcore gamers are sites for **massively multiplayer online role-playing games** (**MMORPG**). These are video games in which a large number of players—as many

massively multiplayer online role-playing games (MMORPG) video games in which a large number of players interact with one another in a virtual world

as hundreds of thousands—interact with one another in a virtual world. In an MMORPG, a player uses a client to connect to a server, usually run by the publisher of the game, which hosts the virtual world and memorizes information about the player. The user controls a character represented by an **avatar**—a character which represents the user and which can be directed to fight monsters, interact with other characters, acquire items, and so on.

avatar a character which represents the user, and which can be directed to fight monsters, interact with other characters, acquire items, and so on

MMORPGs have become extremely popular since the wider debut of broadband Internet connections, now with millions of subscribers from hundreds of different countries. Some MMORPGs have as many as a million subscribers. MMORPGs have their roots in online, text-based adventures, which existed as early as the 1970s. Games were played on a pay-by-month basis, as are most contemporary MMORPGs. The genre surged into popularity throughout the late nineties, finding especially welcoming markets in Taiwan, South Korea, and America. In 1999, Sony Online Entertainment released *EverQuest*, a popular game to this day.

The newest consoles from Microsoft, Sony, and Nintendo are designed to allow large numbers of people to play their console games with others at the same time online. Microsoft and Sony, especially, see their newest consoles as potential entertainment hubs that allow connections between Internet and television for movies as well as games.

Handheld Devices, Mobile Devices and Interactive Television

Handheld game devices are portable machines that are primarily for game playing. Nintendo's Game Boy series has long been the leader in this area. The Game Boy Advance comes in two forms, a squarish palm size device and the micro, which is more rectangular and is designed not only to fit in your hands but (according to its website) in "the pocket of your tightest jeans." Its primary competitor is Sony's Playstation Portable (PSP), which can play music and movies as well as games. Somewhat bigger than these handhelds is the Nintendo DS, which allows players to chat with one another via a Nintendo WiFi-enabled Internet site. The DS is so popular that during several months in 2007 it was outselling every console in the United States.[8]

handheld game devices portable machines that are primarily for game playing

Also handheld, but a different sort of portable gaming platform, are **mobile phones**. The capability to use these devices for more than the most basic games with primitive graphics has grown as more Americans have been buying high-speed (3G) mobile devices with better graphics and memory capability than the phones of just a few years ago. The big video game software company Electronic Arts, for example, has a special website (eamobile.com) that sells a wide variety of games. The site sells people games customized to their phone carrier and specific handset. To use the game properly without corrupting the phone, you must download it directly to the phone. Prices tend to be less than $10. It's an activity that is rapidly gaining in popularity. According to the Veronis Suhler Stevenson consultancy, mobile gaming grew 162 percent in 2005 over the year before, earning $189 million.

mobile phones used as handheld portable gaming platforms

If you think that kind of growth is astonishing, take a look at the growth of gaming on cable, satellite, and RBOC TV systems between 2004 and 2005: 1,288 percent! One reason for this huge growth is that 2004 was the first year that this so-called interactive television (iTV) gaming has been available[9]; it has, however, clearly grown. Much of the iTV gaming is done via the set-top box so that even satellite companies (whose technologies do not allow for two-way interactions with customers) can get in on gaming. In 2007, for example, EchoStar's Dish Network was one company offering a game subscription service. Its customers could get DishGames, a collection of 16 games including asteroids and centipede, priced at $4.99 per month. Comcast cable has been more aggressive. In some areas it offers a wide variety of action games that require the high-speed broadband connections of its high-end (eight megabits per second) Internet service. The RBOC Verizon sees this area of high-speed gaming as a competitive advantage of its new high-speed FiOS service, which because of the quick response of its servers (what is called their "latency") would go beyond cable systems' capabilities to allow multiplayer gaming. According to one Verizon executive, the goal in the not-too-distant future is to run shoot-em-up titles such as *Doom* or *Quake* from servers in the network. "We definitely see multiplayer gaming as an opportunity, because we have low latency in the network."[10]

Video Game Software

You've undoubtedly gotten the idea throughout this section of the chapter—if you didn't know it before—that there is a huge number of video games to fit a wide variety of tastes. The major hardware makers also produce games specific to their systems; the intention is to persuade people to buy their systems because of the games exclusively associated with them. So, for example, Nintendo turns out the *Super Mario* and *Pokémon* titles, among others. Sony turns out the *Gran Turismo* racing game. Microsoft has an exclusive deal with Bungie Studios, which it used to own fully and in which it still has an equity stake, to produce the *Halo* series.

The launch of *Halo 3* illustrates the utility of this sort of exclusivity from the console-maker's standpoint. The game's global sales reached $170 million on its first day, making it the biggest launch in video game history to that point. By the end of the first week, it had reached sales of $300 million globally.[11] Not incidentally, from Microsoft's standpoint, the game has spiked sales of Xbox 360, the only console on which anyone could play the game. According to initial reports from retailers worldwide, Xbox 360 console sales nearly tripled compared with the weekly average before the launch of the new game.[12]

Although video games made by console and handheld manufacturers exclusively for their devices get a lot of marketing and press attention, by far the largest number of games are made by what the trade calls **third party publishers**. These are companies that are unaffiliated with hardware companies. Because of their unaffiliated status, third party publishers typically create games that work on a variety of systems. The NDP Group, a market information provider, organized the top-selling game titles during 2006 in two categories. It called "video games" those titles that are played on portable and console machines. NDP separately considered "PC game titles," those titles that are sold to be played on computers. The top company in each category was a third party publisher, Electronic Arts (EA), with games such as *Madden NFL 07*, *NCAA Football 07* (in consoles and portables) and *The Sims 2* (for computers). In fact, EA grabbed four of the top ten slots in the console and portable list, and it took five of the top ten in the list of computer game titles. Other third party publishers on the list are THQ (*Cars*), Activision (*Call of Duty 3*), Vivendi (*World of Warcraft*), Eidos (*Lego Star Wars*), and Take II Interactive (*Elder Scrolls IV: Oblivion*). A feature that undoubtedly helped sales is that all of these publishers' titles could be bought for a number of (though not all) Sony, Microsoft and Nintendo console systems.

Software Genres   It's likely that you noticed that the game titles just mentioned do not include the same types of games. As we saw in Chapter 2, creators in every mass media industry think of content in terms of categories, or **genres**. This approach helps them understand how to create in that genre; it often helps distributors and exhibitors in sending and choosing titles for certain outlets; and

third party publishers companies that are unaffiliated with hardware companies that typically create games that work on a variety of systems

genres major categories of media content

it sometimes helps consumers who are thinking about what materials they want to watch, play with, or hear. Most of the people who create video games for consoles, portables and computers broadly categorize what they do as entertainment, meaning that the games are intended primarily for enjoyment. In fact, the variety of video games is so great that aficionados (many of whom have shared their views on the Wikipedia online encyclopedia) have developed several subgenres of entertainment to describe them, and even subtypes—subgenres of those subgenres. Below, adapted from writings about video games posted on Wikipedia, are short explanations of the ten most important entertainment subgenres.

Action Games

These are challenges that emphasize combat or attempts to escape being captured or killed. Action games as a category probably has the largest number of sub-types among video games. Three popular ones are shooter, competitive fighting, and platform games.

- *Shooter games* involve a character going through a dangerous environment hunting for bad guys. First person shooter video games show the environment from the perspective of the character with the weapon; that character (whose full body you don't see) is controlled by the player. In third person shooter games, by contrast, the player does see the character moving through the environment as the player uses the controls.
- *Competitive fighting games* emphasize one-on-one combat between two characters, one of whom may be controlled by the computer. Examples are *Virtua Fighter* and *Soul Calibur II*.
- *Platform games* involve traveling by running and then jumping between levels and over obstacles in order to avoid being eliminated and to reach a goal. *Super Mario Bros*, the bestselling video game of all time that was first released in 1985, is a well-known example. More recent entries are *Banjo Kazooie* and *Psychonauts*.

Adventure Games

Unlike action games, adventure games are characterized by investigation that focuses on exploration and a story rather than challenges that require the quick use of reflexes. One Wikipedia writer states that, "Because they put little pressure on the player in the form of action-based challenges or time constraints, adventure games have had the unique ability to appeal to people who do not normally play video games. The genre peaked in popularity with the 1993 release of *Myst*."[13] Another Wikipedia writer notes that "games that fuse adventure elements with action gameplay elements are sometimes referred to as adventure games (a popular example is Nintendo's *Legend of Zelda* series)." The writer continues that "Adventure game purists regard this as incorrect and call such hybrids action-adventures."[14]

Casual Games

These are challenges with fairly straightforward rules that make them easy to learn and play. The word casual probably comes from the idea that a person can get into the game quickly and doesn't have to devote a major commitment of time to the idea of being a "gamer." Such commitment is often required for people who want to play adventure games and the other genres listed. Note that just because a game is deemed "casual" it doesn't mean that it is easy.

Simulation Games

Sometimes called sim games, these involve players in the creation and cultivation of certain worlds that are designed to be realistic. The idea is to see whether you can excel at accomplishing a task. The task might be sprawling—for example, building urban environments (*SimCity*). They might be narrower in focus, related to particular industries (*Stock Exchange, Roller Coaster Tycoon 3*). They might be even narrower still, focusing, for example, on raising pets (*Neopets*) or flying jets (*MS Flight Simulator*).

Strategy Games

Think of chess. What is needed in these games is a careful assessment of a situation and wise actions in order to win a competition or war. The difference between strategy and action games is that action games center almost entirely on actual combat while strategy games expect the player to focus on political diplomacy, the historical context, the procurement of resources, and the larger placement of troops. Examples are *Diplomacy, Command and Conquer,* and *Dune II*.

Sports Games

One could argue that some sports games really belong to the category of action game and that others are a combination of action and strategy games. But producers, distributors, exhibitors and consumers of video games consider sports-related competitions as a category unto itself. Some games focus on playing the sport (the *Madden NFL* series is an example). Others focus on the strategy behind the sport, such as *Football Manager*.

Of course, not all video games fall under the entertainment genre. A much smaller, though socially important, segment falls under the education genre. To quote a Wikipedia article on the topic, educational video games "are specifically designed to teach people about a certain subject, expand concepts, reinforce development, understand an historical event or culture, or assist them in learning a skill as they play."[15] You may be familiar with *Reader Rabbit, Zoombinis, Mavis Beacon Teaches Typing,* or *The Big Brain Academy: Wii Degree.* Actually, instead of education, some in the video game industry use the term **edutainment** to describe such teaching-oriented games. The reason is that they are designed to be a lot of fun as well as have educational outcomes for specific groups of learners.

Advertising Content and Video Games

It stands to reason that advertisers would become fascinated with a medium growing so rapidly in the past couple of decades as video games. Advertisers have been particularly interested in reaching a group that seems to gravitate to video games more than to other mass media, such as television and magazines: young men. Over the years, they have tried a variety of techniques to use games to reach this population segment and others with messages that would lead the target audiences to feel favorably toward the products and buy them. People in the ad industry call the activity **advergaming**, and in 2006 they spent $692 million on the activity.[16] The two most prominent ways in which they go about it are by creating custom games and by embedding ads in games.

Creating Custom Games   In this common activity, an advertiser links up with a game company to create a game that is exclusive to that marketer. One way to do it is to lead people to an advertiser's website to play games. The Jack Links meat-snacks company turned a TV commercial many of its customers found funny into three web-video games around a mythical Big Foot character who shows his

edutainment teaching-oriented video games that have educational outcomes for specific groups of learners

advergaming using games to reach specific segments of the population with messages that would lead the target audiences to feel favorably toward the products and buy them

574

Girl Games

While the stereotype of a video game enthusiast hasn't changed much lately, thanks to new gaming systems, the actual demographic of gamers has become significantly more diverse. Part of this evolution is tied to two Nintendo products, the handheld DS and the console Wii, which support games that both appeal to girls and have titles that specifically target female players. As a result, according to Nintendo, 33 percent of Wii's sold are purchased by women. Additionally, the proportion of male-to-female gamers is starting to narrow. As of 2007, 41 percent of gamers in the United States were female.

In the past, girls tended to lose interest in gaming between the ages of eight and twelve. However, a recent study indicates that the difference in gaming experience between men and women is quite close, with females having played for an average eight years, compared to ten years for males. There are indications that these trends will continue, as popular game makers are producing more games designed to appeal to female players. Some of these games, like Disney's *High School Musical*, *Hannah Montana* and *Princess* brands, are

marketed specifically to girls, while others, like EA Playground, *MySims*, and *EA Smartypants Trivia*, are designed with both male and female players in mind.

That said, it seems game makers are operating under the assumption that girls are inherently disinterested in hardcore, action oriented games. Electronic Arts, a major player in the video game market, created two new divisions—EA Casual and EA Sims—to make games that don't fall into the traditional gaming model. These games, which are more like *Tetris* and *SimCity* than *Halo* or *Grand Theft Auto*, are more likely to be targeted to a mixed-gender audience than their traditional counterparts. However, if the increasing number of women playing in gaming tournaments featuring traditional games such as *Dead or Alive 4* or *Counterstrike: Source* is any indication, the perceived difference in gaming interest between men and women may be more stereotype than reality.

Dean Takahashi, "New Video Games Target Girls," *San Jose Mercury News*, Sunday, October 7, 2007.

angry side with allegedly comic effect—for example, by swinging a big stick at animals. The company offered the potential of instant prizes for those playing the game, with a chance to enter a $50,000 grand-prize drawing. During the first four months of the game during the summer of 2007, over 300,000 people played the Jack Links games online.[17]

The classic way to do this is to distribute the game on a cartridge or disc. The Burger King fast food company did that during fall 2006. It teamed up with Microsoft in a campaign aimed at both making families feel good about the fast food chain as well as promoting the Xbox 360 console, which Microsoft wanted to push beyond hardcore gamers to a more mainstream audience. The gaming firm developed two racing games and one in which users play the King and sneak up on people, as the character does in the ads. They were designed so players with Xbox 360s could compete online. Burger King outlets in the United States sold the game for $3.99 with the purchase of a Value Meal.

Burger King officials judged the effort a great success. They said that outlets sold 3.2 million games, and contended that the promotion had directly contributed to a 40 percent quarterly increase in profits. "Creating your own game allows you to control every aspect of it, from the genre and characters to the tone in which the game is delivered," says Burger King's senior director, marketing impact, Martha Thomas Flynn. "For example, we used our own advertising characters, instead of the borrowed equity of another game's characters. We were also able to include a few surprises—something our consumers have grown to expect from us."[18]

America's Army is a military simulation game that was developed as a promotional tool for the U.S. Army. According to the game's website, www.americasarmy.com, more than 8 million players have downloaded the free PC versions of the game, which is also available in a variety of console and cellphone game versions. The game is rated "T" for teens, the target audience for military recruitment.

Not all games promote commercial products and services. Some organizations create and distribute games to encourage players to adopt commercial or political beliefs through the playing of games. The U.S. Army, for example, has released multiple versions of its game America's Army in free CD/DVD form and for online play. In addition, the Army collaborated with the Red Storm Entertainment video game company to develop and distribute America's Army: True Soldiers. Released in 2007, it was created specifically for the Xbox 360 and given an industry rating as acceptable for teens, the target audience for military recruitment. Clearly, the Army meant for its ideology to be built into the game. Prior to its appearance, the game's website noted that:

> Red Storm and the Army are working together to make sure that America's Army True Soldiers game play experience is an authentic Army experience. [The game] accurately portrays the values that guide Soldiers in the U.S. Army, by specifically incorporating gameplay based on mission accomplishment, teamwork, leadership, rules of engagement, and respect for life and property. Just like in real combat, honor and respect must be earned, and in the game the Play-Lead-Recruit feature allows players to earn respect as they move up through the ranks and become a true leader.[19]

Embedded Ads Some companies or organizations don't want to go through the trouble of paying for and distributing games, but they do want to reach certain target audiences. To accommodate them, game publishers increasingly place ads or products in the action so that players will see the commercial messages or use the products in the course of their play. The game publishers realize that ad insertion adds to their profits without adding much to development costs. As the trade magazine *Advertising Age* noted, "in a low-margin business with only $3 to $5 in profit on a $50 video game, even one extra dollar per box is significant."[20]

Digital Resistance? Digital Terror?

Hezbollah, the Lebanese organization of Islamic Shiite groups, has gotten into the video game business. More specifically, the first-person shooter genre home to some of the most successful games of today. Halo, Medal of Honor, Resident Evil all present certain versions of battle—sometimes historic, sometimes fantasy based. But Hezbollah's offering, Special Force 2, puts another spin on the first-person shooter, this time within a very different context. Real war, real death, and the real future of Lebanese and Israeli citizens is the premise for this game.

According to the United States, Hezbollah is an international terrorist organization; Israel classifies the group the same. Of course, Hezbollah sees itself differently: as a liberation vehicle for the Palestinian people against Israel. In 2006, Israel fought Hezbollah in a 34-day war after terrorists kidnapped Israeli soldiers. By the end more than one thousand people had died, most of whom were Lebanese citizens. Terror and violence were further sown into everyday life in Lebanon, as Israeli citizens were left to fear retaliation.

But with the brutality of war fresh in the collective memory, Hezbollah got to work on *Special Force 2*. The reason?

Recruitment. In order to lure more young resistance fighters, or Mujahedeen, to the organization Hezbollah brought the fight to the children—digitally. The goal of Special Force 2 is simple: kill or capture as many Israeli soldiers as possible; destroy their tanks; confiscate their weapons. The more soldiers killed and tanks blown up, the more points the player accumulates. Cross-border raids can succeed in kidnapping soldiers, and rockets find their target in Israeli villages. While the rubble is yet to be rebuilt in Lebanon, the resources were assembled to produce *Special Force 2*.

What does it mean to have a video game represent conflict that is still so fresh in the public memory? What does it mean to highlight ethnic conflict, or encourage the killing of civilians as justified by the concept of resistance? Finally, what does it mean to use video games as training or recruitment, a practice that the U.S. Army also engages in? In a fractured world of political and ethnic strife, what power does virtual gaming serve?

Source: Reuters, "Hezbollah Video Game Recreates Israeli War," *PC Magazine*, August 16, 2007.

In racing games, for example, cars pass realistic billboards with the names of products whose companies have paid for their presence. In fact, even the car that the player is driving may be offered because its manufacturer paid the gaming company for its presence. As this activity becomes routine, some companies are adding to it by giving people free add-ons that provide characters or more levels to the games. As an example, in summer 2007 Nissan USA, for example, sponsored add-ons for the *Forza Motorsport 2* Xbox game. It made free downloads available of a Nissan Sentra SE-R vehicle that players of the game could race in a high-performance competition that was to take place that season.[21]

But marketers and game publishers see these activities as only the beginning of a highly sophisticated process of targeting players with ads and add-ons that are specific to what the companies know about them. They realize that with increasing numbers of gamers playing online, it will be possible to send them these features on-the-fly, while they are playing, and to change the ads and offer different sponsored downloads depending on their game setting and level. This activity is called **dynamic in-game advertising**, and it is drawing a lot of attention from marketers, game firms and technology companies. In fact, Microsoft owns a video game advertising company called Massive that is one of the leaders placing ads in games. In 2007 it publicized a study it commissioned from Nielsen Entertainment

dynamic in-game advertising the process of sending ads into video games while individuals are playing, and of changing the ads and offering different sponsored downloads depending on their game setting and level

on the marketing benefits of ad units placed within video games that are played while connected to the Internet. According to Nielsen, many of the study's respondents reported that hot games such as *Need for Speed* created a halo effect for the ads, increasing their "cool quotient." Clearly, Massive hoped that such findings would further excite advertisers about the utility of dynamic in-game advertising.[22]

Distribution and Exhibition of Video Games

There are many ways to get games to the player. As noted earlier, some cable systems and RBOCs stream games to computers by subscription; the games do not remain on the computer. In the case of mobile games, the software does get downloaded and it must come directly to the phone; some of the payment is shared by the creator with the mobile phone company. Video games for consoles, PCs, and handhelds are typically distributed on disks or cartridges to stores by their manufacturers, sometimes through wholesalers, and sold through a variety of outlets. In the bricks-and-mortar world, you can find collections of the top games (and consoles) in huge retailers such as Wal-Mart, toy outlets such as KBToys as well as in consumer electronics stores such as Best Buy and Circuit City. There are also specialized video game retailers such as Gamestop that sell a wider variety of titles. In addition, you can purchase video games online, at Amazon.com or many other retailers. Used games show up on many sites, including Ebay. Some games (particularly casual games) are downloadable from the Internet, but many high-end games are not, either because the manufacturer wants to keep the software from being pirated or because they are too data-rich for most people to download in a reasonable amount of time.

While all this is pretty straightforward, selling video games isn't without controversy. That is because many games have levels of violence and sex that cause consternation among parents and civic leaders. You may remember from Chapter 3 that the industry has established the Entertainment Software Ratings Board (ESRB) as a self-regulatory mechanism to quell such concerns. Modeled after the motion picture ratings system, the ESRB ratings are used along with content descriptors in a way that is (according to its website) "designed to provide concise and impartial information about the content in computer and video games so consumers, especially parents, can make an informed purchase decision."[23] The six ratings (apart from "rating pending") are EC (early childhood), E (Everyone), E 10+ (Everyone 10+), T (Teen), M (Mature—17 and older), and AO (Adults Only). Content descriptors ran a wide gamut from "alcohol reference" to "intense violence" to "use of tobacco."

Despite this ratings system, some games have raised consternation among critics. In 2005, *Grand Theft Auto: San Andreas* was skewered by angry parents and advocacy groups as morally bankrupt. They argued that it teaches people how to engage in a crime spree with gusto. *Grand Theft Auto: San Andreas* was given an M by the ratings agency. Critics claimed that the rating and the accompanying descriptors were problematic because they didn't inform parents regarding the true level of violence and sex in the game. The controversy got hotter when players discovered that use of a certain code would unlock an explicit sex scene in the game. Even though Rockstar insisted that the sex scene and code were the work of a hacker, politicians such as Hillary Clinton and advocacy groups leaped on the company as misleading the ESRB, retailers, and parents. Rockstar pulled the game from the shelves at great cost, deleted the scene, and put it back on the market. Nevertheless, the incident served as an opportunity for groups to rail at retailers for allegedly selling games to kids as young as nine.

Rockstar Games' *Grand Theft Auto* is one of the best-selling video game franchises of all time, and its violent content has attracted considerable controversy since the first game debuted in 1998.

Take 2 sparked a game-selling controversy again in 2007, with a game called Manhunt 2. Its central character is an inmate who escapes a mental asylum and in the course of doing that horribly murders guards and prisoners. The game was banned in the U.K., Ireland, and Italy, and it was given an AO rating by the ESRB. Take 2's chairman defended the game on artistic grounds, stating that "The Rockstar team has come up with a game that fits squarely within the horror genre and was intended to do so," Zelnick said in a statement. "It brings a unique, formerly unheard of cinematic quality to interactive entertainment, and is also a fine piece of art," he added.[24] Take 2's financial situation was precarious, however, and Zelnick knew that major retailers such as Wal-Mart would not carry a title with an AO rating. Moreover, Sony and Nintendo do not allow AO rated games on their systems. So Rockstar toned down the sadism, and the ESRB gave it an M.

To some critics, the change was beside the point. They argued that even M ratings in stores were getting into the wrong hands, that game retailers too often sell M-rated video games to kids as young as nine years of age. They cited research at the Harvard School of Public Health that 81 percent of M-rated games were mislabeled and had missing content descriptors, thus potentially misleading parents.[25] The ESRB replied that the researchers had exaggerated problems they found and that a long list of content descriptors on packages would be impractical. Clearly, though, the arguments surrounding video game producers, retailing and ratings were not over.

Media Literacy and the Internet and Video Game Industries

The developments regarding computers and the online world that we've just discussed are merely the surface of a huge transformation in the way mass communication is taking place. With the aim of continuing media literacy, how can we organize our understanding of the social issues that these activities raise? One way is to look at how key activities that we have described in this chapter reflect major themes that we have noted for the media in general. Another way is to look at the social controversies that the activities we have discussed are igniting. Here we'll do a bit of both. The major themes we will look at are the blurring of media boundaries and the power of conglomerates. The social controversies that we'll look at briefly relate to privacy and the filtering of content for children.

Blurring of Media Boundaries

One theme that we have seen throughout this book is that increasingly the boundaries between media industries are blurring. Certainly, that theme applies to the Internet worlds. The activities that we have described in this chapter are recent, and they are affecting every mass medium. The rise of the dictionaries and other reference books on CDs, DVDs and online, for example, led publishers of reference books to rethink the way they present materials. Encyclopedias that used to be sold as books are now sold as pieces of plastic or online connections.

You may have noticed, in fact, that each of the chapters about other mass media industries in this book refers to the ways in which the industry is changing because of computers and the Web. Even media that aren't given entire chapters are changing dramatically. Consider greeting cards. With the growth of email, the greeting card industry has developed a major segment that allows people to send digital versions of cards—some of them even talking or singing—instantly across the country and around the world. It's not hard to imagine that in not too many years the online method may become the preferred way of sending cards. The greeting card industry, like the book industry, also relates to the Internet industry.

The digital convergence not only raises questions about where one media industry begins and another ends. It even raises questions about the traditional names we give to media. When a "magazine" online and a "newspaper" online are continually updating, what is the difference between a newspaper and a magazine? When CNN, *Time Magazine*, the *Washington Post* and ABC News are posting video and audio programs, is it useful to say online that one is a cable channel, the other a magazine, the third a newspaper and the fourth a broadcast network? Even though technologically the streaming of music online is far different from radio broadcasting, should we now talk of all streamed music as "radio"? What happens when the dominant way people access these media is through digital means (computers or heldheld devices, for example)? Will these media terms still be useful? Certainly it is possible to give satisfactory answers to these questions that distinguish among media, but there is no question that the digital world messes up distinctions we long took for granted.

The Power of Conglomerates

Another theme that has followed us throughout this book has been the rise of conglomerates as the central powers in mass media industries. Every person who wants to increase his or her understanding of the mass media system and its position in society must confront the nature and meaning of conglomerate clout. As we have seen in previous chapters, media critics worry that Time Warner, Viacom, News Corporation, Sony, Bertelsmann, and just a few other firms control or strongly influence the vast majority of the production, distribution, and exhibition avenues by which news, entertainment, and information are delivered to Americans and others around the world. The critics say that executives in these huge firms are unlikely to take artistic risks by bringing innovative works to the public. Rather, they are likely to choose and market mostly what they feel will be hugely popular.

Moreover, say the critics, the overwhelming presence of these firms in the marketplace makes it very difficult for smaller firms that are willing to take risks to compete. The big firms use their power to influence laws in order to keep themselves in power, and they don't discuss these activities in their media. The critics also argue that the conglomerates rarely advertise the patterns of their media ownership to the public at large. As a result, most people who use media owned by the biggest firms probably don't know it.

"Wait a minute!" you may be thinking while you read this.

I understand how the biggies can keep this kind of control in traditional mass media such as television and the movies. I can also see how a few companies, such as Microsoft, can take over a huge chunk of the computer software business. I noticed how three companies control the video-game console market, and how those same firms, Electronic Arts, and maybe a couple of other firms pretty well have a lock on the most popular game software. But the Web is different! Anyone can start a website—even I have one—so no one company can come in and stop people from going to the millions of sites out there. It would seem that the conglomerates would have an almost impossible time controlling cyberspace.

One might indeed think that, and at first glance it does seem that people are going to an enormous number of virtual spaces that have been created on the Web. Look a little closer, though, and we see that, to quote a *Newsweek* article, "Media consolidation has come to the Internet." *Newsweek* was commenting in the summer of 2001 about a study by market researcher Jupiter Media Metrix that just four companies—AOL Time Warner, Microsoft, Yahoo!, and Napster—control roughly half of the time Internet users spend online. That's down from eleven companies two years ago. Moreover, 60 percent of online time is controlled by only fourteen companies, a breathtaking plunge from 110 companies in 1999. That's "an incontrovertible trend toward online media consolidation," the authors of the report wrote.

Well, times have changed. AOL Time Warner is now just Time Warner, and may be preparing to sell AOL. Napster no longer exists. But some would say that the consolidation that *Newsweek* identified back in 2001 has actually intensified in the commercial part of the Web. As we noted earlier, in 2005 72 percent of web advertising flowed to the ten most popular sites on the Web. That advertising flow reflects traffic patterns. Google, Yahoo, and AOL (through its Advertising.com subsidiary) control most of that advertising flow, and their decisions about what ads (and for Google and Yahoo, what content should come up in search and news) has major consequences for the ways people see the world. Moreover, the major media powers have been moving to control the biggest sites. News Corporation owns MySpace (and since it bought it has made it more far more commercial than it was at its start), Google owns YouTube, and most people assume it is just a matter of time before a media biggie (say, Microsoft) picks up Facebook. CBS, Disney, Viacom and Time Warner are implementing Internet strategies that aim to keep the huge numbers of people who made up their audiences offline coming to them online and through mobiles. Their strategies differ, but they involve marketing muscle. They are able to drive traffic to their sites by cross-promoting these sites on cable and broadcast networks and in print through their own holdings or through joint ventures with other firms. Every time *Desperate Housewives* appears on TV, for example, the ABC network notes that the program can also be viewed online. And the sites the media conglomerates control are not necessarily few in number or with their name on it. CBS has a significant monetary interest in Joost, for example, and NBC and News Corp have set up Hulu as a site to attract certain target audiences to their programming. The idea is to use high-visibility programming from network television and movies to drive people to sites that fit their specific interests but are controlled by them.

Mark Mooradian, a Jupiter vice president and senior analyst back in 2001, noted that access to the Web itself is open to everyone. But not everyone has the muscle and experience of the leading mass media firms when it comes to using the Web to grab attention. His comment is as relevant today as it was then: "Does everyone have a microphone? Yes. But are some microphones louder than others? Absolutely."

The Filtering of Content

We've seen how video-game violence and sex have sparked concerns in the United States and around the world. We've also looked at the tussles around the self-regulatory system that the video game industry has established. These arguments recall the struggles around content in the movies and on TV—though in the United States neither medium has shown such graphic violent and sexual images as video games. Chapter 13 discussed the V-chip filter as a legal response to parental concerns about sex and violence in certain television programs. The concept of filtering web content that various groups consider offensive has been much more controversial.

Consider the circumstances that led to the arguments: the Web, as you probably know, is filled with images of explicit nudity and/or extreme violence that can be accessed by anyone with a web browser. People who object to these images realize that the First Amendment prohibits the government from making such sites illegal. In fact, a federal court in Philadelphia declared unconstitutional two congressional attempts to require that such sites determine the age of visitors before letting visitors access the material. Looking for another way to keep this material away from children, many parents and advocacy groups have turned to web filtering technology.

web filters computer programs that block objectionable sites from coming into a computer; sites are blocked either because they have been specifically censored or because a search engine used by the filter program has detected words that indicate that there is prose (and possibly pictures) on the site that the filter's creators want excluded

Web filters are computer programs that block objectionable sites from coming into a computer. Sites are blocked either because they have been specifically censored or because a search engine used by the filter program has detected words that indicate that there is prose (and possibly pictures) on the site that the filter's creators want excluded. Consider the situation at the Fort Worth Public Library in 2007. Debate on filters heated up there when it asked city council to give the go-ahead to install them for users younger than 17 years old. A policy against viewing adult websites and other inappropriate material was already in place. The staff was monitoring what patrons viewed, and anyone caught breaking the rules could lose his or her computer privileges. Some in the library did advocate filters, however, and the push for that on youngsters' computers started after a parent complained that her three sons had seen inappropriate images on a computer near the children's section.

The request caused a stir that brought out the arguments on both sides. Supporters of web filters say that they solve an important social problem and that they can be customized to the moral, religious, or political viewpoint of the person or organization installing them; liberals can use different filters from conservatives. They argue that filters should be placed on computers that children use in schools, libraries, and other public places. Many also insist that even in adult public areas, such as libraries, filters should be installed on web computers so that other patrons don't have to see nudity and librarians don't have the embarrassing task of asking a patron to get off an offensive website.

Opponents argue that filters are not really a very good solution for web computers in public places. For one thing, they say, filters are still fairly primitive. Some may block articles about breast cancer because the word *breast* was programmed in order to weed out sexually objectionable sites. Filtering technology is getting better, they concede, but it will never be 100 percent possible to ensure that filters are not systematically blocking important material. Another problem, the opponents contend, is that companies that sell filters do not as a rule reveal the sites that they block or the filtering rules that they use. They are secretive for competitive business reasons, but the result is that a person, group, or organization that uses a filter often does not really know how lenient or how strict it will be. Third, say some of the opponents to filtering, the idea that a public library or public organization would stop people from going to certain places on the Web smacks of censorship, and they are opposed to it. Parents can use filters in the privacy of their homes, and companies have a right to use them on their computer networks, but public computers should be free of filters.

Interestingly, many local librarians as well as many conservative groups support filters. Many schools have adopted filters, and a federal law ties U.S. government funding for school technology to the school's use of some philosophy or technology of filtering. But as the Fort Worth example showed, a lot of heat still exists around the subject. The controversy is likely to be around for a long time.

Privacy

So is the issue of digital privacy. Critics' concerns about the Web aren't limited to what companies deliver to people's computers via their websites and email. The concerns also extend to what the companies often try to take from people as they use their computers. At issue is the information that web firms want about the individuals and organizations with whom they interact.

Companies aren't the only targets of these worries. Activists fear that governments—federal or state—might encourage laws that give them powers to tap into people's computers or Internet activities. Officials from police agencies such as the Federal Bureau of Investigation (FBI) have already tried to prevent Internet software from helping potential criminals make their email totally uncrackable by law-enforcement authorities. In the wake of the 2001 attacks on the World Trade Center and Pentagon, Congress passed laws aimed at allowing the FBI and other agencies to follow digital trails more easily than in earlier years.

In general, concerned individuals and organizations argue that we are moving into a new era when it comes to information. It is an era, they say, in which governments will be able to find out far more about citizens than the citizens want them to know. And it is an era where companies will be able to find out far more about their customers than those customers realize. In the new digital age, the critics say, privacy must be a major social concern.

The topic has become a media issue only rather recently. As we noted in Chapter 3, in earlier decades of the century, privacy was often defined as "the right to be let alone," to use the phrase of Samuel Warren and Louis Brandeis in a famous 1890 *Harvard Law Review* article. In the twentieth century, privacy came to be a subject that people debated when they worried about governments, employers, or credit companies snooping into their personal lives.

In the past twenty years or so, concern about privacy has erupted noisily into the media realm. Most of the noise has related to corporate rather than government activities, because of a belief that laws are less strict with regard to business snooping. The first stirrings of concern began in the 1970s, when companies began to use computers to combine enormous amounts of information from public and private records about virtually everyone in the nation and sell this information to marketers. Among the largest of these companies are Experian, Equifax, Acxiom, and Choicepoint. Many marketers use these firms' universal databases (called that because they hold information on almost everyone) to find people whose profiles make them potential customers.

Acxiom, for example, maintains a storehouse of consumer information covering more than 200 million individuals and 124 million households in the U.S. Drawing on its continually-refreshed databases, Acxiom offers clients addresses, telephone numbers, demographics (for example, age, gender, race, occupation, number of children, marital status), and past purchasing behaviors of likely direct-marketing prospects. In a fact sheet on its website (www.acxiom.com) titled "The Power of Data," the company states that its information will help marketers "better understand your best customers—and find more like them." Acxiom also sells its ability to analyze the data. That involves creating predictive models of consumer behavior for identifying individuals and households that are relevant to particular marketers and those who are not.

In addition to these funds of knowledge, marketers themselves have been taking advantage of the constantly decreasing costs of computer power to create their own databases from information they learn about their customers, by asking them and by keeping records of their purchases. These storehouses of information are called **transactional databases.** A marketer that wants to learn more about the customers in its transactional database can turn to Acxiom. The company will match the names and addresses of the marketer's customers against its data on more than 124 million households. The resulting merged file could supply the marketer with a wealth of new information about each customer's purchasing behavior, estimated income, credit extended by mail-order firms, investments, credit cards, and more.

You may already be getting nervous that your favorite department store or catalog company knows more about you than you would like. But wait!—as they say on those hard-sell TV commercials—there's more!

The circulation of these data began to be a mass media issue as direct marketers increasingly used them for targeting. Members of the public got angry when advertisers used personal information to guide direct-mail advertisements and tele-marketing pitches to people's homes. Until then, many Americans didn't realize that advertisers knew so much about them.

But privacy really took off as a media issue with the rise of marketing on the World Wide Web in the mid-1990s. Recall our discussion of interactive marketing and cookie technology earlier in this chapter. Interactive media firms see the ability to track the clickstreams as a great way to find out what users want and how best to serve them. Moreover, the managers of websites see the ability to target content and ads to individuals based on the computer's knowledge of these individuals' interests and past behavior as crucial to their competitive advantage over magazines and cable television when it comes to attracting advertisers. Privacy advocates point out that tracking personal behavior, on or off the Web, is often done without the knowledge or permission of the consumer.

Rarely will media executives argue publicly that people should have no right to stop firms from collecting information about them. Under government pressures, many often concede that members of the public should have the right to know that material about them is being collected. Media executives emphasize,

transactional database a database that stores and sorts large quantities of data that reflects transactions—such as logs of phone calls, emails, mailings, or purchases

however, that in today's competitive media world, being able to show advertisers that a medium can deliver specific, desirable types of people is crucial for their survival. Supporters of data collection also use an ingenious argument that the invasion of privacy has its positive side. They argue that the more marketers know about people, the more they will be able send individuals materials that these individuals will find relevant to their lives. The result, they say, is that people will be unlikely to complain that they receive junk mail.

Nowadays, most web marketers say that they understand people's desire to keep certain information private. They also insist, however, that many individuals are willing to give up information about themselves if in return they get something that they consider valuable. Many privacy advocates agree that people should have the right to decide whether they want to give up private information as part of a transaction. They disagree with the web marketers on the way in which consumers should be informed about the data that will be collected about them, often without their knowledge.

Privacy advocates want members of the public to have to opt-in when it comes to giving out information. That is, marketers should not be permitted to collect information about a person unless that person explicitly indicates it is OK for them to do so (say, by checking a box online). Marketers contend that getting opt-in permission is too difficult because people either are too lazy to give it or are concerned about their privacy when the question is put to them in that way. The marketers prefer an opt-out approach. That means that they will be permitted to collect personal information from consumers as long as they inform people of what they are doing and give them the opportunity to check a "no" box or otherwise refuse to allow it.

Chapter 3 discusses the Children's Online Privacy Protection Act (COPPA). That law requires websites to get parents' opt-in permission. Some aspects of medical privacy regulations passed by the federal government also require an opt-in approach. The government is more lax with financial organizations (banks, credit card companies). It requires them to present consumers with an opt-out choice. In some situations involving financial organizations, such as the transfer of information among affiliates within a firm, federal law gives the consumer no choice at all over the sharing of personal information. Moreover, these exceptions aside, the federal government in the early twenty-first century stayed away from imposing rules on the use of personal information by websites. The reason: to encourage web commerce.

Yet consumer advocates, academic researchers and lawmakers have noted increasing public concern about privacy in the digital realm. Industry representatives have kept insisting that interactive sites and marketers could regulate themselves through an opt-out norm approach, although some sites still tell their visitors nothing about the information they collect about them. Compounding all these arguments is the international nature of the issue. The European Union (EU) uses an *opt-in* approach, for example, and U.S. companies have to promise to accept the stricter EU rules when they deal with European, though not necessarily with U.S., consumers. This distinction riles consumer advocates, who see the European approach as the fairest one.

Note, too, that these privacy issues are not related only to the Web. What people do on mobile devices is already of interest to many advertisers; some government agencies might want to see these data, as well. The same is the case with who plays video games, what they play, and how they play them. In fact, as home-based television viewing becomes a two-way activity, getting data about what individuals do with the medium will also interest marketers and, possibly, certain branches of government. As these types of surveillance take place, various advocacy groups will argue against them and ask for legal safeguards against the misuse and abuse of people's data. Clearly, the fight over U.S. consumer privacy in the digital age will continue.

CHAPTER REVIEW

For an interactive chapter recap and study guide, visit the companion website for *Media Today* at www.routledge.com/textbooks/mediatoday

QUESTIONS FOR DISCUSSION AND CRITICAL THINKING

1   Some people say that hyperlinks lie at the center of activities of the World Wide Web. What do they mean?
2   What is the ESRB ratings system? Explain why some critics argue that it isn't working.
3   To what extent do the major video-game genres relate to genres that also exist on other media?
4   Explain the ways advertisers have become involved in the Internet and in video games.

INTERNET RESOURCES

Association of Internet Researchers (http://aoir.org/)
> The Association of Internet Researchers (AoIR) is an international academic organization dedicated to interdisciplinary studies of the Internet. In addition to the annual AoIR conference, their mailing list provides a venue for its more than 2,000 subscribers to discuss the latest trends and issues in Internet research. The AoIR Guide to Ethical Online Research is available online at http://www.aoir.org/reports/ethics.pdf

Digital Games Research Association (www.digra.org)
> The website of the Digital Games Research Association (DiGRA) publishes original research on games for academics and professionals. The organization hosts a bi-annual conference for the international digital games research community.

The Electronic Frontier Foundation (http://www.eff.org/)
> Founded in 1990, the Electronic Frontier Foundation is an international non-profit advocacy group with the stated aim of championing "the public interest in every critical battle affecting digital rights."

The Entertainment Software Association (http://theesa.com/)

The Entertainment Software Association (ESA), the trade association for the computer and video game industry in the United States, regularly posts press releases, research, statistics, and industry sales reports on its website.

Gamasutra (http://www.gamasutra.com/)

Gamasutra is a website aimed at game developers that posts regularly updated news, features, and job postings for the computer and video game industry. Owned by CMP Media, it is the companion website publication to the magazine *Game Developer*.

KEY TERMS

You can find the definitions to these key terms in the marginal glossary throughout this chapter. Test your knowledge of these terms with interactive flash cards on the *Media Today* companion website.

advergaming	interstitial
algorithm	mass customization
analog	microprocessor
banners	MMORPG
behavioral targeting	mobile phones
binary digits	modem
broadband	MUD
browser	natural search results
casual gamers	opt-in
click-and-mortar companies	opt-out
clickstream	personalization of content
content site	pinball machine
search engine	pop-up
contextual advertising	RBOC
cookie	rich media
cyberspace	spam
data mining	text ads
digital	third party publisher
display ads	top-level domain (TLD)
domain name	transistor
edutainment	uniform resource locator (URL)
ENIAC	user generated content
entertainment arcade	video games
handheld game devices	web crawler
hardcore gamers	web hosting
HTTP	web spider
hyperlink	website or game publisher
Internet	WiFi
Internet resources	WIMAX

CONSTRUCTING MEDIA LITERACY

1 To what extent is media convergence already part of your everyday life?
2 Some observers have commented that parents in some families feel like immigrants to the United States when the family brings computers into the home for the first time. That is because, as in immigrant families, the children often "speak the language" better than the parents do. Did your experience with home computers fit this description? Do you have any friends whose experiences fit the description? Why or why not?
3 Where do you stand on the issue of net neutrality? Why?
4 If you were a parent of a ten-year-old, would you filter that child's web content? What if you were a parent of a fifteen-year-old?

CASE STUDY Developing a Website

The idea It may seem easy to develop a website that can make money. In fact, it is a highly creative act that requires a lot of business sense. Apart from getting a good idea, you have to figure out how to make money

The method Develop an idea for a profit-oriented website. Describe its target audience, its features, and its business model (that is, the way it aims to make money). To get a reality check, find a website that has a similar business model. Using a periodicals database such as Nexis or Factiva and drawing from a variety of periodicals, discuss how well it is doing and how it got to that point.

chapters

15 THE ADVERTISING INDUSTRY

16 THE PUBLIC RELATIONS INDUSTRY

The advertising and public relations (PR) industries play crucial and controversial roles in the media system. Advertising provides billions of dollars in support of print and electronic media. PR provides ideas, people, and sometimes technology to help mass media create content that reaches huge audiences. In exchange for these services, though, the PR and advertising industries exercise enormous influence over the media and their products.

Chapters 15 and 16 discuss these roles. In the process, they show that the largest advertising and public relations firms are controlled by a few agency holding companies with the power of guiding the flow of resources to many media. Moreover, the boundaries of advertising, PR and related forms of marketing communication are blurring, making it even more difficult to know when producers of mass media materials are secretly being paid to present products and ideas in particular ways.

advertising and

five

part five

advertising and public relations

public relations

15 THE ADVERTISING INDUSTRY

After studying this chapter, you will be able to:

1 Sketch the history of advertising in the United States

2 Describe various types of advertising agencies and how they differ

3 Analyze the process of producing and creating ads

4 Discuss branding and positioning and explain their importance to advertisers

5 Explain the debate between advertising's critics and defenders about the industry's role in spreading commercialism and the decline of democratic participation

"The trouble with us in America isn't that the poetry of life has turned to prose, but that it has turned to advertising copy."

– LOUIS KRONENBERGER "AUTHOR AND CRITIC"

If you're like most people, you are probably aware that advertisers buy space or time in various media in order to send you messages ("advertisements") about their products or services. You might know (perhaps because you've read previous chapters of this book) that where advertisers decide to place their money can make the difference between life and death for media firms. But even if you don't know these things, it's likely that you've talked with friends about ads. Maybe you've commented about how funny or how horrible they are, or how good-looking the men or women in them are.

We can define **advertising** as the activity of explicitly paying for media space or time in order to direct favorable attention to certain goods or services. Three points about this definition deserve emphasis. First, advertisers pay for the space or time that they receive. Second, advertising clearly states its presence. When you see an ad, you know what it is for, and you often know quite easily who is sponsoring it. Third, advertising involves persuasion—the ability or power to induce an individual or group of individuals to undertake a course of action or embrace a point of view by means of argument, reasoning, or emotional plea.

The aim of this chapter is to help you critically explore the quick-changing business that is behind the ads and the support of such a large part of the media. The next chapter will tackle public relations and marketing communication and examine the important links both have to advertising. Let's start by getting a sense of how the ad industry came into existence.

The Rise of the Advertising Industry

Advertising is as old as *selling* itself. During the time of the ancient Roman Empire, criers were paid to scream out messages about products for sale. There were "print" ads, too: archeologists have found a three-thousand-year-old ad for a runaway slave that was written in Thebes on papyrus. In medieval England, shopkeepers often posted a boy or man at the entrance to their shop to shout at the top of his lungs about the goods in the store. Signs posted over shops also beckoned consumers. Centuries later, after the printing press came into use in England, businesses added handbills and newspapers to their advertising mix. This routine presence of advertising was transferred to the British colonies in the New World. By the time Benjamin Franklin was born in Boston in 1706, advertisements were an expected and accepted part of almost all the day's periodicals.

Franklin was one of the most successful sellers and writers of advertisements in the thirteen American colonies. His advertisements were certainly different from those of today. Because the colonial printing press could accommodate only the simplest drawings, ads looked more like today's stodgy classified ads than like any of the more trendy advertisements in contemporary media. Still, like our modern-day ads, the ads of Franklin's era shouted messages for goods, for houses for sale,

advertising the activity of explicitly paying for media space or time in order to direct favorable attention to certain goods or services

for articles lost or stolen, plays showing in local theaters, and patented medicines. Then, as now, some advertisements stirred anger and controversy. (An ad in one of Franklin's papers, for example, was accused of inciting anti-Catholic feelings.) And then, as now, intellectuals worried about the power of shrewdly worded messages to stir people to purchase too much and believe outrageous things.

From the earliest days of advertising—through Ben Franklin's time and until around the 1840s—the act of advertising typically involved direct negotiations between someone who wanted to advertise a product and the owner of a newspaper or magazine. Say you were the owner of a dry-goods store and you wanted to announce a new shipment of fabric. You would write the announcement yourself, or maybe your spouse would help. Then you would walk over to the local newspaper office and pay for the space to make an announcement of your goods.

That system worked fine when only one or two newspapers were available and merchants wanted to sell goods in a relatively small area. But imagine the difficulty of buying announcements in a much greater number of papers. Say you are the producer of a horse buggy in 1840. You have heard about all the new penny-press papers that have attracted large audiences from Boston, Massachusetts, to Richmond, Virginia. Advertising your buggy in these papers would seem to be a good idea, but how can you negotiate efficiently with all of them? Sure, you could write letters, but such one-on-one correspondence with every paper would be terribly time-consuming.

The Birth of the Advertising Agency

advertising agency a company that specializes in the creation of ads for placement in media that accept payment for exhibiting those ads

These sorts of problems led to the development of the **advertising agency** in the 1840s, a company that specializes in the creation of ads for placement in media that accept payment for exhibiting those ads. Volney Palmer is credited with starting the first advertising agency. Palmer was essentially a space salesman. He made money by soliciting notices from merchants or manufacturers who wanted to sell to a wide territory. He would place these notices in a group of newspapers, to which he often had exclusive space-selling rights. Though merchants were expected to write the ads, they saved time and energy by having the ad agency reach far-flung audiences. The advertising agent typically received compensation from various newspapers in the form of 15 to 25 percent of the payment as commission.

The ad agency's function changed dramatically in the decades after the Civil War, when the United States experienced the rapid growth of manufacturing as a result of the Industrial Revolution. More and more, factory activity was based on the principle of continuous-process or "flow" production. Conveyor systems, rollers, and gravity slides sent materials through the production process in an automatic, continuous stream. As a result, companies could transform massive amounts of raw materials into finished goods.

These new approaches changed American business. The manufacturing capacity of the United States increased seven-fold between 1865 and 1900. Cities suddenly bulged with people as workers streamed in from farms and from other countries to work in factories. Many factories created products that had been made by hand only a few years before. Other plants turned out items—toothpaste, corn flakes, safety razors, cameras—that nobody had made previously.

But the trick to making lots of money was not just in the manufacturing of these products; it was in getting stores to carry them and consumers to buy them. The large number of items available for sale encouraged competition between manufacturers of similar goods. One result was the creation of *brands*. A **brand** is a name and image associated with a particular product. With brands, a company

brand a name and image associated with a particular product

did not make just soap, it made *Ivory soap* or *Pears' soap*. To make money on a particular brand of soap or any other mass-produced item, a manufacturer had to make sure that hordes of people knew about the product and asked their local retailers—grocery and department stores—for it.

In this new environment, the advertising agency's function changed. The manufacturers and stores now needed firms to help them create ads that would stand out from the competition. Around 1910, advertising agencies started copy and art departments to create both words and images for advertisements. Along with the agency's creation of the ad came its work on the **ad campaign**, which is a carefully considered approach to creating and circulating messages about a product over a specific period with particular goals in mind. That work included early forms of research on the marketplace and on consumers, as well as on the media that claimed to reach those consumers. Entrepreneurs started research companies to meet those needs. As part of their growing research operation, in 1914 advertising agencies helped to establish an independent organization, the **Audit Bureau of Circulation**, to verify the size of a periodical's audience. Among the major agencies involved in those developments was one that still exists: J. Walter Thompson, which is today called JWT and is part of the WPP Group.

Ad agencies created jingles, artwork, and trade characters that became part of American culture. Within the industry, two broad differences in the approach to creating ads emerged, approaches that are still used today. Some practitioners used **reason-why ads**—those that listed the benefits of a product in ways that would move the consumer to purchase it. Others swore by the effectiveness of **image ads**—those that tied the product to a set of positive feelings. Advertising practitioners eventually agreed that some types of products were better sold through reason-why pitches, whereas others could use the push of image ads.

Consumers, for their part, sometimes became annoyed with both types of ads, but that response wasn't new. People have complained about ads for as long as ads have been around. During the early twentieth century, however, anger about false or manipulative advertising threatened to lead to government regulation of the ad industry. To calm the population's concerns and reduce the chances of government regulation, leaders of the ad industry started organizations such as the Association of National Advertisers and the American Association of Advertising Agencies. Their purpose was to establish norms of proper ad-business behavior and to plead their industry's case with government regulators.

PEARS' SOAP

·a·Specialty·for·Children·

The Best for the Complexion. "A Balm for the Skin." Economical; It Wears to Thinness of a Wafer.
June, '87.

In this 1887 advertisement, Pears' Soap associates its product with family and children.

ad campaign a carefully considered approach to creating and circulating messages about a product over a specific period with particular goals in mind

Audit Bureau of Circulation an independent organization established in 1914 by advertising agencies to verify the size of a periodical's audience

reason-why ads advertisements that list the benefits of a product in ways that would move the consumer to purchase it

image ads advertisements that tie the product to a set of positive feelings

The Advent of Radio Advertising

Until the 1920s, virtually all of the advertising agencies' work appeared in print media—newspapers, magazines, signs, and flyers. Beginning in the 1920s, however, many ad people added radio to the media they used. Radio imposed responsibilities on ad people that they hadn't previously known. One basic new requirement was to learn about the growing number of stations around the country that were eager to get money for broadcasting commercial messages to their audiences. To help ad practitioners purchase local radio time most efficiently, **representation firms**—companies that sold time on many radio stations—came into existence. In connection with these sales, ad practitioners insisted that radio executives provide proof of their statements about the size of their audiences. A number of companies rushed in to conduct surveys of listeners in order to get this information, and the broadcast audience research (or rating) business was born.

representation firms in radio, companies that sell time to advertisers on many radio stations

Another imposition that radio made on the advertising industry resulted from its very nature. Radio required ad people to learn how to sell through sound rather than through text. Through the 1920s and into the 1930s, advertisers adapted tried-and-true print techniques—slogans, dramatizations, brand personalities—to the new medium. In addition, ad agencies that had large consumer-goods firms as clients often coordinated the creation of weekly network radio programs. Some agencies were responsible for coming up with an appropriate idea for the program, negotiating its time period and its cost with a network, and then producing the show from start to finish every week.

As we saw in Chapter 11, the radio industry grew rapidly during the Great Depression. Even though major advertisers put a lot of money into radio during that time, the overall ad support for media—especially for newspapers—dropped significantly throughout the 1930s. The amount of money moving through the advertising industry was far less than it had been in the 1920s. Although the economy rebounded during World War II, the advertising of consumer goods did not pick up dramatically because many major products, such as cars, were not made during the war years.

Advertising, the Postwar Era, and Television

The dam of pent-up consumer demand broke when World War II ended in 1945. As millions of soldiers came home, got jobs, and started families, production of consumer goods took off. Manufacturers and stores turned to advertising agencies to help them stir up demand for products, and by the mid-1950s the ad industry was healthier than ever.

The commercial introduction of television in the late 1940s brought a challenge to advertising practitioners that was similar to the one they had faced with radio. They adapted quickly to the new audiovisual environment, though. In fact, as we noted in Chapter 9: The Magazine Industry and Chapter 11: The Radio Industry, the large-scale movement of ad money into TV forced magazine and radio executives to make profound changes in the audiences they pursued and the content they chose. Increasingly, radio and magazines sold themselves as media that targeted particular groups that certain advertisers were chasing (young adults, for example), whereas television reached "everybody." The period clearly showed the power of the advertising industry as a whole to shape the direction of the media system.

In TV's early years, ad messages were live; as in radio, they often appeared as part of the program. Advertisers bought hour or half-hour blocks of time from the TV networks and sponsored entire shows; again as in radio, ad agencies produced these shows for their clients. But this approach changed after a decade. By the early 1960s, advertiser interest in fully sponsoring a show diminished.

Part of the reason was that TV network executives had concluded that it was more profitable for them to shape their schedules, and sometimes own their shows, than for them to allow advertisers to do so. Advertisers had their reasons for agreeing with this approach. They wanted to reach as many people as possible with the quickly growing medium. Tying up a large amount of money in one time period every week was not the best way to achieve this goal.

As a result, advertisers scattered their time purchases across the TV schedule. With tens of millions of Americans viewing the same show at the same time, network charges for advertising on these shows skyrocketed. With the increase in charges, the length of television commercials decreased. In the 1960s, one-minute commercials were common. By the 1970s, the most common duration had dropped to thirty seconds. By the 1990s, fifteen-second TV commercials were common.

Trends in the Second Half of the Twentieth Century

The growth of television brought millions of dollars into the advertising industry for the production of audiovisual commercials, as well as the purchase of the time for showing them. An entire research industry grew up around the agencies' need to show their clients that the work they were doing was reaching large audiences and getting people to buy the products.

Proving the effects of advertising on purchasing has never been easy, and it is sometimes impossible. Nevertheless, ad practitioners increasingly turned to a wide variety of consultants who claimed to be engaging in **motivation research,** or using social science techniques to learn what motivates Americans to buy certain goods. Some also studied whether **subliminal persuasion,** or quickly flashing messages, such as "buy popcorn," that reach the mind at a level below the conscious mind, in fact worked. However, whether or not these consultants' ideas about motivation research and subliminal persuasion actually did work, in the 1950s they became the subject of a number of books—notably Vance Packard's best-selling *The Hidden Persuaders*—that aroused public anger against advertising for messing with people's heads without their knowledge.

Still, the U.S. ad industry grew strongly, and two trends are most notable. The first was a shift toward a **global presence.** As American businesses expanded their operations around the world after World War II, they wanted their ad agencies to work with them on creating ads and buying media abroad. Until that time, only a few of the very biggest agencies, such as J. Walter Thompson, had had a global presence, but with the increased demand, many of the large agencies set up offices in several countries. By the 1990s, owning an "international network" was crucial to being a major player in the ad industry.

The second notable trend was the formation of advertising conglomerates—known as **agency holding companies.** These are umbrella firms that own two or more ad agencies, in addition to owning research firms, public relations consultancies, or other organizations that contribute to the business of selling products, services, or ideas in one way or another. One idea behind the formation of these holding companies was to be able to offer clients a range of services beyond advertising. The reason for placing more than one agency under a conglomerate's umbrella was to be able to serve firms that compete with one another. Traditionally, companies would not think of giving business to an agency that has such **client conflicts** for fear that confidential information might be shared among employees and get to competitors. If a totally different agency network is involved, though, most

motivation research the systematic investigation of the reasons people purchase products

subliminal persuasion persuasion that works by influencing the unconscious mind

global presence having strategic offices and representatives around the world

agency holding company a firm that owns full-service advertising agencies, specialty agencies, direct-marketing firms, research companies, and even public relations agencies

client conflicts serving companies that compete with one another

Table 15.1 The "Big Eight" Marketing Agency Holding Companies

Holding company	Headquarters	Worldwide revenue ($)	U.S. revenue ($)	U.S. percentage of total revenue
Omnicom Group	New York	11,376.9	5,743.9	50
WPP Group	London	10,819.6	4,195.9	39
Interpublic Group of Cos.	New York	6,190.8	3,441.2	56
Publicis Group	Paris	5,871.3	2,676.6	46
Dentsu	Tokyo	2,950.7	46.5	2
Havas	Suresnes, France	1,841.0	687.4	37
Aegis Group	London	1,825.8	489.4	27
Hakuhodo DY Holdings	Tokyo	1,337.0	0.0	0

Ranked by worldwide revenue in 2006 in millions of dollars.

Source: *Advertising Age*, accessed 3/7/07, http://adage.com/datacenter/datapopup.php?article_id=116383

advertisers don't mind—even if both agencies are controlled by one firm. They accept the claim that those parts of the two businesses are kept quite separate.

Interpublic Group of Companies—recognized as the first agency holding company—was started in the late 1950s by Marion Harper. At the time, many people laughed at him for buying firms but not merging them into his existing firm. By the late 1980s, however, the agency conglomerate model, often including two global agency networks and support companies for both, had become the norm. The biggest of these holding companies is Omnicom, based in New York. Others are Interpublic (also in New York), WPP (London), Dentsu (Tokyo) and Havas (Paris). As Table 15.1 shows, the top eight holding companies (which are by far the biggest) have substantial business outside the United States. In fact, in 2006 only one, Interpublic, made more than half of its revenue in the United States.

Another set of developments in the 1980s and beyond had far-reaching effects on the advertising industry. It was the multiplication of media channels as a result of cable television, satellite TV, video games and (beginning the mid-1990s) the World Wide Web. As we have discussed throughout this book, the enormous number of media outlets that were present in many homes (along with the presence of multiple TV sets) led audiences to scatter across them. That made it more challenging than ever for advertisers to reach the people they wanted as customers. The advertisers turned to their advertising agencies for help.

How did the ad agencies respond? What, in general, do ad agencies do? To answer, let's start with a broad overview of the industry and then turn to our categories of production, distribution, and exhibition.

An Overview of the Modern Advertising Industry

Advertising is a large and widespread operation. If Wall Street estimates are anywhere near accurate, the amount of money advertisers shell out is impressive (see

Table 15.2 **Advertising Spending by Media Industry, 2005***

Industry	$ (Billion)	Percentage of total
Broadcast television	42.7	21.7%
Cable and satellite television	22.3	11.3%
Newspapers	55.5	28.1%
Radio	20.1	10.2%
Yellow Pages	15.4	7.8%
Consumer magazines	12.9	6.5%
Pure-Play Internet **	11.1	5.6%
Business-to-business magazines	10.3	5.2%
Out-of-home***	5.8	3.2%
Other entertainment based advertising****	0.7	0.4%
Total ($ millions)	197	

*Numbers for traditional media industries include online advertising activities of firms within these industries

** Includes online revenues for firms (e.g. Salon.com) with no traditional media counterpart

***Includes billboards, kiosks, mall boards, transit ads and other outdoor advertising vehicles

****Includes cinema advertising, in-game video game advertising and advertising on film, music, video games and consumer book websites

Source: Veronis Suhler Stevenson, *Communications Industry Forecast, 2006–2010*, pp. 110–113.

Table 15.2). According to the media consultancy firm Veronis Suhler Stevenson, in 2005 advertisers in the United States spent around $65 billion in support of television programming and about $20 billion to fund radio broadcasting. In addition, the ad industry spent $55 billion on advertisements in newspapers (including their online versions), compared to the $11 billion that consumers shelled out to buy the papers. Advertisers funded consumer magazines (including their online versions) to the tune of about $10.5 billion, and consumers dropped a smaller $8.5 billion into the periodicals' coffers. When it came to supporting websites that are unattached to traditional media brands—industry people call them pure-play Internet sites—advertisers put out about $11 billion to support them.

That's certainly a lot of money, but ad support doesn't end there. These numbers don't include anywhere near everything that advertising spends on the mass media. They don't, for example, reflect the monies that advertisers spent to send ads to people's homes ("direct mail"), pay for Yellow Pages telephone book ads, and sponsor billboards or other outdoor ads. Nor do they reflect the amounts spent by sponsors who chose new miscellaneous approaches to placing ads—for example, on supermarket-based radio stations, on outdoor ads, and at informational kiosks at stores and shopping centers. The total amount is huge. As Table 15.2 indicates, Veronis Suhler Stevenson estimated that in 2005 about $197 billion was spent in the United States on all types of advertising.

Advertising Agencies

The number of companies involved in advertising is also huge. Just about every business advertises somewhere. Sometimes the executives of the business write the

New York City's Times Square is home to the highest density of illuminated outdoor advertising in the United States. Known as "spectaculars," the first electric sign was installed on Broadway in 1904.

business-to-business agencies advertising agencies that do work for companies that are interested in persuading personnel in other companies to buy from them instead of from their competitors

consumer agencies advertising agencies that do work for advertisers that are intent on persuading people in their nonwork roles to buy products

general ad agency an advertising agency that invites business from all types of advertisers

specialty agency an advertising agency that tackles only certain types of clients (or accounts)

Internet agency an advertising company that promotes its expertise in understanding the technology for reaching people online, for creating the ads and websites that will lead to customer responses, and for measuring those responses

direct-to-consumer (DTC) used most effectively by the pharmaceutical industry, this type of advertising presents a prescription drug as a medical solution and encourages viewers to ask their physician to order the medicine if appropriate

ads themselves and then place them in newspapers and magazines. Other times—and this is particularly true of larger firms—the executives turn to companies that specialize in the creation of ads and their placement in media that accept payment for exhibiting those ads. As we said earlier, these companies are called advertising agencies. The companies that hire them and pay for their work are called advertisers. In the ad industry, when an agency takes on an advertiser's business, it is said to take on an account.

There are about five thousand advertising agencies in the United States, and they are scattered throughout the country. The largest tend to be located in the largest cities, especially New York, Chicago, and Los Angeles. Ad agencies range from one-site operations with just a few people, to organizations with several offices and thousands of employees. The kinds of things ad agencies do also vary. We can describe them along four dimensions:

- Business-to-business agencies vs. consumer agencies
- General agencies vs. specialty agencies
- Traditional agencies vs. direct-marketing agencies
- Agency networks vs. stand-alone firms

Business-to-Business Agencies vs. Consumer Agencies **Business-to-business agencies** work for companies that are interested in persuading personnel in other companies to buy from them instead of from their competitors. A zipper manufacturer, for example, might want to inform a pants manufacturer about its great new development in the fly business. **Consumer agencies,** by contrast, work for advertisers that want to persuade people in their nonwork roles to buy products. An agency that touts a client's cereal to children and their parents is one example. Individual agencies typically do not do both.

General Agencies vs. Specialty Agencies A **general ad agency** invites business from all types of advertisers, whereas a **specialty agency** tackles only certain types of clients. One type of specialty agency that works in both the consumer and business-to-business areas is the **Internet agency.** This is a company that promotes its expertise in understanding the technology for reaching people online, for creating the ads and websites that will lead to customer responses, and for measuring those responses. A different type of specialty agency deals with healthcare advertising. A big source of clients is the pharmaceutical industry, as firms in this industry are constantly competing to persuade physicians that their prescription products are best. In recent years, pharmaceutical firms' desire to get consumers to nudge their doctors to order new prescription drugs for them has led to a specialty called **direct-to-consumer** (DTC) pharmaceutical advertising, and ad firms focusing on that business have developed. Advertising to ethnic and racial groups is also a big specialty in the consumer area. You can find agencies that claim to have particular knowledge of how to persuade African Americans; others that tout their abilities to move Latinos to buy; others that go after Irish Americans; still others that specialize in Asian or Russian immigrants—and the list can go on.

Traditional Agencies vs. Direct-marketing Agencies A traditional advertising agency creates and distributes persuasive messages with the aim of creating a favorable impression of the product in the minds of target consumers that will lead them to buy it in stores. **Direct-marketing agencies** have a different mandate. Their job is not just to create a favorable image that will eventually result in purchases. Instead, they have to shape consumer mailings, telephone marketing contacts, TV commercials, and other appeals to target audiences so as to elicit purchases right then and there. Traditional advertising practitioners generally consider direct-marketing approaches more gruff, fast-talking, and even obnoxious than the traditional rhetorical tools. For their part, direct-marketing people believe that they are the only ones who really show that advertising can sell things, since the results are immediate: people either buy the product or they don't.

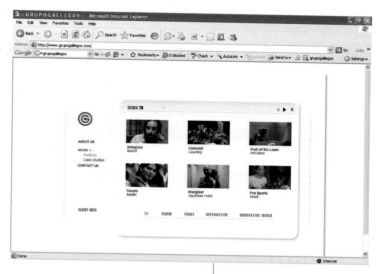

www.grupogallegos, the website of Grupo Gallegos, an advertising agency specializing in the Hispanic market.

www.the-dma.org, website of the Direct Marketing Association, a global trade association that promotes direct marketing with more than 3,600 member companies worldwide.

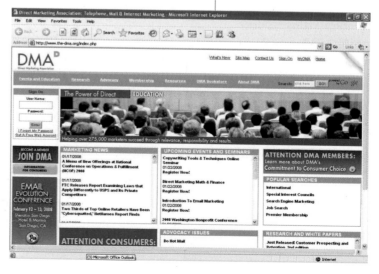

Tom Burrell

An aptitude test can give more insight into one's future than you think. At least, such a test turned out to be quite insightful for sixteen-year-old Tom Burrell from Chicago. Tom Burrell, now the Chairman Emeritus of Burrell Communications, took the test on the advice of a teacher at Parker High School, and the results were telling. Burrell scored highly in both his persuasive and artistic abilities—qualities that would serve him very well as a pioneering African-American executive in advertising.

Burrell continued to hone these skills while attending Roosevelt University, where he graduated in 1961 with a BA in English. While an undergraduate, Burrell took jobs in advertising that eventually earned him work as a copywriter at Wade Advertising during his senior year. He was assigned to well-known products such as Alka-Seltzer. Burrell's intelligence, work ethic and emerging marketing savvy earned him success not only as a copywriter, but also as a businessman. As he continued to advance, Burrell moved from Wade to Leo Burnett and then to Needham, Harper & Steers—all top Chicago agencies.

By 1971, Burrell had established himself as a productive and persuasive copywriter as well as a forward thinking organizational leader. In order to gain some room to grow in a leadership role, Burrell joined with Emmett McBain (of Vince Cullers Advertising) to start a new ad agency on Michigan Avenue in Chicago. McBain dropped out after a while, but the firm continued as Burrell Communications and thrived. In the late 1990s it reported over $128 million in annual billings. The agency is especially known for its ability to advertise to African Americans. Huge companies such as McDonald's, Sears, Coca-Cola and Procter & Gamble come to Burrell for advice and work advertising to African-American audiences. The firm has been so successful that it was one of the few African-American ad agencies to retain its independence and succeed through all of the buyouts in the 1990s. While the advertising and PR conglomerate Publicis now owns a 49 percent stake in the organization, the company retains its name Burrell Communications. The firm was also the first African-American agency to win *Advertising Age*'s Multicultural Agency of the Year award for its understanding of the urban consumer. To Burrell, the recipe for ad success returns to the elements of art and persuasion that stood out in high school. "Creative (work) is the most important element that ad agencies do," he told *Advertising Age*. "Everything else is in support of it."

Sources: "Burrell's Quarter Century," *Advertising Age*, June 3, 1996, p. C2; A. W. Fawcett, "Perseverance Pays Dividend at $128 Million Burrell Shop," *Advertising Age*, June 3, 1996, p. C2; "Interview with Burrell," *Advertising Age*, June 3, 1996, p. C10; "New CEOs Boost Burrell Strengths," *Advertising Age*, January 9, 2006, p. 5.

direct-marketing agencies
agencies that focus on consumer mailings, telephone marketing contacts, TV commercials, and other appeals to target audiences so as to elicit purchases right then and there

agency network
advertising agencies with branch offices in a number of different cities worldwide

Agency Networks vs. Stand-alone Firms   The biggest advertising agencies tend to be traditional, consumer-oriented companies (see Table 15.3). They often have offices in a number of cities in the United States as well as in foreign countries; the trade press calls firms such as these **agency networks.** These types of agencies are different from firms that have only one location. The agency networks typically work for large national advertisers such as Procter & Gamble, Phillip Morris, General Motors, Sears, Ford, and McDonald's. Because national advertisers tend to sell many products, they will often appoint a number of ad agencies to work for them, each working on a different product or a different set of products. In the late 1990s, for example, Kimberly-Clark Corporation used the Ogilvy & Mather agency to tout its Huggies baby diapers, the Campbell Mithun Esty agency to advertise its Depend diapers for adults, and the J. Walter Thompson agency to help with its Scott tissue products.

Specialty racial and ethnic firms sometimes enter the mix. For example, in addition to relying on Foote Cone & Belding for general advertising of its jeans

Table 15.3 **Top Ten Agency Networks, Ranked By 2006 Worldwide Network Revenue**

Rank	Agency network	Headquarters	Worldwide revenue
1	Dentsu	Tokyo, Japan	$2,487,000,000
2	McCann Erickson Worldwide	New York	$2,127,400,000
3	BBDO Worldwide	New York	$2,099,800,000
4	DDB Worldwide Communications Group	New York	$2,077,800,000
5	Ogilvy & Mather Worldwide	New York	$1,714,100,000
6	Young & Rubicam Brands	New York	$1,588,300,000
7	TBWA Worldwide	New York	$1,523,100,000
8	JWT	New York	$1,496,700,000
9	Publicis Worldwide	Paris, France	$1,243,800,000
10	Leo Burnett Worldwide	Chicago	$1,185,000,000

Source: AdAge Agency Report 2007 Index, accessed at, http://adage.com/article?article_id=116344 on 1/2/08.

and Dockers slacks, Levi Strauss used the full-service specialty agency Mendoza, Dillon & Associados for its advertising to Hispanic consumers. Similarly, Kellogg called on two general full-service ad agencies, Leo Burnett USA and J. Walter Thompson, to handle its cereals. But it also called on Vince Cullers Advertising, a full-service specialty agency, to sell the company's products to the African-American community.

Popular books, movies, magazine articles, and television shows encourage most people to think of a large and powerful "full service" ad agency such as JWT or Young and Rubicam when they think about the advertising industry. In today's complex marketing world, though, even large agencies such as JWT work with other organizations in the industry to carry out the three basic functions of ad work: **creative persuasion, market research,** and **media planning and buying.** We can explain how these three functions are carried out by exploring how they fit into our three familiar activities: production, distribution, and exhibition.

Production in the Advertising Industry

It is through their work with their clients that the biggest advertising agencies channel hundreds of millions, even billions, of dollars into various media; money which is a major source of support for American media industries. But the advertising industry does not really spend its money to support media. It spends money to persuade people to buy products, services, or ideas. How does it go about doing that?

The production of persuasive advertising messages goes on with the approval, and often the direct involvement, of executives from the client/advertiser. Because of the importance of keeping the account, the ad agency wants to ensure that its clients continually understand what the agency is doing for their products.

creative persuasion the set of imaginative activities involved in producing and creating advertisements

market research research which has, as its end goal, gathering information that will help an organization sell more products or services

media planning and buying a function of advertising involving purchasing media space and/or time on strategically selected outlets which are deemed best-suited to carry a client's ad message

Lionel Sosa

Hispanic Americans represent the fastest growing segment of the U.S. population. During the past several years, many major advertisers have begun to target the Hispanic audience. Since the 1980s, advertising agencies specializing in the Hispanic market have become an important and respected part of the media scene. Lionel Sosa is a pioneer in Hispanic advertising and among those responsible for the clout that today's Hispanic-American ad community enjoys.

Sosa was born in San Antonio in 1939 and from an early age was instilled with the idea that he could overcome pervasive discrimination to accomplish anything. His first career ambition was to work as an illustrator for the Walt Disney Company. After time spent in the Marines, he applied to be an animator at the studio but was turned down for the position. However, he soon found other outlets for his artistic abilities. He began designing neon and plastic signs and eventually opened his own graphic design firm, branding it Sosart. In the mid-1970s, Sosa decided to expand his business into an ad agency. The company later merged with another San Antonio firm to form Ed Yardang & Associates.

Sosa's big break came in 1978, when U.S. Senator John Tower, a Republican, hired Yardang & Associates to boost his popularity within the solidly Democratic Hispanic community. Tower won 37 percent of the Hispanic vote, edged out a victory in the race, and attributed much of the success to Yardang's work. Word spread among politicians and businesses that the agency knew the Hispanic market well. As the Hispanic population began to soar in the United States, corporations and politicians increasingly paid attention to its needs and desires. Sosa had the credibility and knowledge of the Hispanic markets that many did not. "It was a time when Hispanic advertising was in its infancy," he recalls, "people were just getting their feet wet."

Setting out on his own again in 1980, he founded Sosa and Associates, which later became Sosa, Bromley, Aguilar, Noble and Associates, and is now Bromley Communications. The firm attracted major clients, including Coca-Cola, Westinghouse, and former president George H. W. Bush. It developed a reputation for solid, high-quality work that rivaled the top national firms.

By 2000, Hispanic advertising had become so mainstream that general ad agencies had begun to purchase Hispanic-

Lionel Sosa

targeted agencies. Capitalizing on that trend, Sosa and his partners sold 49 percent of the company to the huge DMB&B Americas, a division of the firm that oversees the networking and operations of twenty ad agencies in Latin America and the United States.

Beyond getting more business, Sosa used his position as chairman to encourage companies to hire more Hispanic Americans in management roles. He insisted that executives would never really understand advertising to Hispanics unless they had members of this group in their ranks. "Until the corporations have more minorities in top and middle management," he argued, "they'll never have the sensitivity needed to make the most of the opportunity." Sosa served as chairman of the DMB&B Americas until 1995, when he partially retired at age 55. But he has not stopped working in advertising completely. He is now CEO of KJS Marketing, a firm started by his wife. Heading up a smaller firm allows him to spend more time with his family, and to pursue the public service projects he values so highly. One such is the web portal MATT.org, or Mexicans and Americans Thinking Together. Sosa has also written two books on how Latinos can achieve success, and has been the Hispanic Media Consultant for six Republican presidential campaigns, including that of George W. Bush in 2000 and 2004. Capping it all off, Lionel was named "One of the 25 Most Influential Hispanics in America" by *Time Magazine* in 2005, and has been inducted into the Texas Business Hall of Fame.

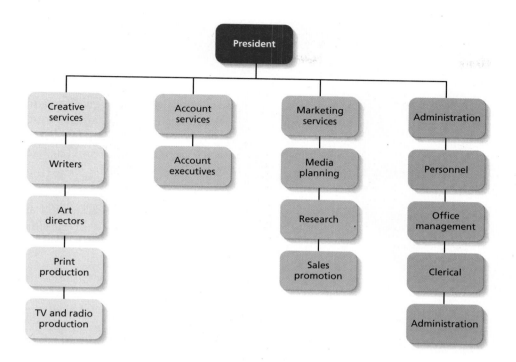

Figure 15.1
**Structure of a Typical
Advertising Agency**

Consequently, agency heads appoint an account executive for every account. The job of the account executive is to move information between the advertiser and the agency as well as to make sure that all production, distribution, and exhibition activities take place as planned.

Production activities most prominently involve the individuals whose work relates directly to the creation of their firm's media materials; people in the ad industry call such individuals **creatives** or **creative personnel.** They include copywriters (who write the words for the ads), art directors (who guide the creation of artwork), print production personnel (who supervise the final production of magazine and newspaper ads), and TV-radio production personnel (who supervise the final production of TV and radio commercials) (see Figure 15.1).

But the work of the creatives does not take place in a vacuum. Copywriters and art directors generally do not concoct a print ad or TV commercial out of just any ideas that come to them. On the contrary, they work hard to determine which ideas will lead target consumers to purchase the product. Typically, a client does not expect that an ad will be directed toward the entire population. For example, a cosmetics company would generally expect its lipstick ads to be directed to women (not men). However, for reasons having to do with the nature of the lipstick or the company's marketing strategy, company executives may want to advertise a particular lipstick to a few specific groups of women—say, women 18–34 years old, or executive women 18–34 years old. Dividing society into different categories of consumers is an activity called **market segmentation.** Agency creatives must understand the segments they are aiming at before they produce their ads.

In fact, both when ad agency executives are competing for new business and when they are working on products for current clients, they place a high priority on learning a lot about both the product they are seeking to represent and the audience they are trying to reach. What are the product's strengths? What do consumers think about it? What kinds of people buy it? Who are the best potential customers? Why do they—or don't they—buy the product?

creatives or creative personnel people whose work relates directly to the creation of their firm's media materials

market segmentation dividing society into different categories of consumers

we're cosmopolitan

COSMOPOLITAN
FUN FEARLESS FEMALE

Advertisers seek to position themselves in relation to a group of consumers and their particular interests and lifestyles. Who is the target audience for this advertisement for Cosmopolitan magazine? How is the ad attempting to appeal to its potential audience?

Answering these questions often requires drawing on the market research function of the ad agency. Such research might involve compiling the results of previous investigations on the product or its competitors. It might involve commissioning original surveys or experiments with potential customers to check the persuasiveness of a new ad or the success of one that already has been introduced to the marketplace. It might involve joining other firms in ongoing "syndicated" studies that inquire about social trends, general product use, media habits, or other characteristics of the American population.

Through these and other approaches, researchers construct detailed portraits of the intended audience and its position within the society at large. Then creatives mix those portraits with their own sensibilities and apply the results to their work.

Creating Portraits

Portraits of society are constructed through this meeting of research facts and artistry. Whether they are developing a magazine ad that details the joys of a Ford Mustang, a TV commercial that extols Pond's cold cream, or a video game that includes the McDonald's Hamburgler in its cast, the creator's goal is to suggest the product's usefulness for the audience. Of course, to do that, the ad people must have thoughts about the audience, particularly as it relates to the product they are selling. The goal is to imagine the product in a social environment that is appropriate for the intended audience and its values. Armed with these imaginings, a creative team can concoct a **sales pitch.** Inevitably, the sales pitch portrays the world of the intended audience, a problem in that world, and actions that show how the product can solve that problem.

sales pitch a presentation to a client, portraying the world of the client's intended audience and actions, in order to show how the client's product is valuable in that world

The next activity is to produce an ad, or a collection of ads, that illustrates the sales pitch in stories and settings that the creatives believe the target audience will accept. Often an agency develops different campaigns for distinct audiences. Editing and casting decisions take into consideration research findings about how different audiences look at the product and the world. This approach enables agencies to create an image of the product that matches what they believe will lead various audiences to feel good about the product and to purchase it.

Creating a specific image of a product that makes it stand out in the marketplace is called **branding** it. Ad practitioners consider the creation and nurturing of these product images—these brands—to be among their most important activities. The reason is their belief that people will pay more for a well-regarded brand than for a product they do not know or about which they have a bad feeling. Think about it: which would you rather buy from your supermarket for a party—Pepsi or Coke (whichever you prefer), or something called Pop-Soda Cola? Even if your supermarket guarantees the quality of Pop-Soda Cola and says it tastes "like the big guys," and even if it's a dime less expensive, you might feel funny serving it to your guests. Chances are you would choose Pepsi or Coke. These are brands you trust; perhaps, after years of seeing commercials, you may even think that these products belong at parties.

Advertising practitioners try to make a particular target group of consumers feel that a brand relates to their particular interests and lifestyles. Doing that is

branding creating a specific image of a product that makes it stand out in the marketplace

Dove's Contrary Approach to Beauty Ads

CULTURE TODAY

In a surprising move for a company trying to sell soap, the cosmetics brand Dove launched a video marketing campaign that focuses on what is wrong with advertisements for beauty products. The company's first Internet video, Evolution, shows an already attractive woman being fawned over by a team of hair and make-up stylists. When they are finished she is photographed, and the resulting image is digitally altered to raise her eyebrows and elongate her neck, amongst other changes. In the video's final shot, the completed picture is shown as a billboard, and the caption at the end reads, "No wonder our perception of beauty is distorted."

The second Dove Internet video, Onslaught, opens with a close-up of a young girl's face, and then jumps into a stream of clips and images from advertisements for beauty products, including some designed to make women "younger, smaller, lighter, fuller, tighter, thinner, softer." The video, which also shows a girl expanding and shrinking as she stands on a scale and women going under the knife for plastic surgery, tallied 70,000 YouTube hits on its first day.

The ads were created by the ad agency Ogilvy & Mather, and were designed "to skew the messaging toward mothers," said Tim Piper, who directed the spots. He continued, "Maybe this generation needs to talk to the next generation about the messaging they're getting from a very early time."

Some observers feel that this position is made somewhat problematic, however, by the fact that Ogilvy is the American agency for the Barbie doll. The critics say that the hypocrisy doesn't end there. The Onslaught spot ends with phrase "Talk to your daughter before the beauty industry does," a somewhat difficult proposition given that Dove itself is a part of the beauty industry. The company, while marketing a Campaign for Real Beauty, is owned by Unilever, a multinational corporation that counts Axe body spray and Slim Fast as two of its brands.

What do you think?

Sources: Jennifer Wells, "Ad Delves into the Ugly Side of Beauty," *Toronto Star*, October 3, 2007, B1; Bob Garfield, "'Onslaught' Is a Triumph—if You Don't Count the Hypocrisy," *Advertising Age*, October 8, 2007, p. 50.

positioning making a particular target group of consumers feel that a brand relates to their particular interests and lifestyles

called **positioning**. To position a product, agencies call on the research and creative activities that we have already discussed. Sometimes they will settle on a broad positioning for the product and then change it somewhat when advertising to particular target markets.

As a brief example, consider the position of Geico Direct, the fourth largest car insurance company in the United States. An insurance industry study described its brand image in the following way: "Geico occupies unique terrain in the auto-insurance space as a relatively inexpensive carrier that is fun. State Farm and Allstate, on the other hand, occupy more traditional territory (expensive and serious)."[1] It's not hard to understand why. You've probably seen the two long-running types of television commercials created by Martin Agency that present its pitch. One series stars an earnest British gecko and another centers on self-right-eous cavemen. Geico has created different versions of the commercials and also ads, many of which seem aimed at younger members of the driving public.[2] The caveman series of ads has become so popular, in fact, that they spawned a series of interactive websites called the Caveman's Crib. In October 2007, a spin-off series called *Caveman* debuted on ABC television.

Once the ads have been created—and sometimes while they are being created—they are tested. A variety of methods might be used, from focus groups to actually running the ads in certain areas and evaluating the results. One trial method for comparing the persuasiveness of two TV commercials is called the split-cable test. With this method, the advertiser arranges with a cable company to send one commercial to one particular neighborhood's TV sets and another commercial to a separate though similar neighborhood's TV sets during the same programs. Before the trial begins, the researchers monitor the sales of their products in stores in the two neighborhoods. After the split-cable showing of the commercials, the researchers recheck the stores to determine which commercial led to a greater increase in purchases.

Distribution in the Advertising Industry

Creating a series of ads and spending money to test them would be totally useless if the ad agency had no idea how and where to distribute them. Deciding how to distribute ads has been affected by improvements in technology. Because of cooperation between ad agencies and media firms, ad practitioners can now actually send finished print and television ads directly to media outlets by satellite. In some cases, print ads can be sent in digital form directly to the computers of the magazines or newspapers in which they will appear. From that standpoint, distribution of ads is constantly getting easier.

Because media fragmentation has dramatically increased the number of ad vehicles, however, deciding *where* to place advertisements is not getting easier; instead, it is becoming more and more challenging. Making these decisions is the work of an agency's media planners. To get an idea of the challenges they face, think of where you would place Geico's TV commercials, and also web ads that aim to convey the same message about the company to young adults.

The short answer is that planners would choose media that attract the young adult audience that Geico wants to reach with the commercials. But does this mean that any channel or website magazine that reaches a lot of twenty-one to thirty-four-year-old males is acceptable? What general criteria do ad planners use when they decide on media? The answers are important, since purchasing media can be

Apple's distinctive iPod advertising campaign uses a consistent silhouette style to promote the brand in television, print, and outdoor ads.

expensive. If an ad agency uses its media-buying budget to advertise in places that do not reach the target audience, or in places that reach that audience along with many other people who are not relevant to the ads, the advertiser will be wasting a lot of money. If Martin's planners and Geico's media-planner and buyer, Horizon Media, did that and Geico executives found out about it (as they undoubtedly would), both firms would lose an important client.

To avoid such disasters, media planners use computers that give them data about the number and kinds of people that various media outlets (specific magazines, radio stations, or TV networks) reach. Much of this information about individual media outlets is collected in syndicated studies by audience research firms such as Nielsen (for television and cable) and Comscore and Nielsen NetRatings (for the Internet); the Traffic Audit Bureau and Nielsen Outdoor (for billboard advertising); Arbitron and RADAR (for local and network radio); Audit Bureau of Circulation (for newspapers and magazines); and Simmons and MRI (for magazines). Sometimes the planners pay attention to custom research findings presented to them by individual media firms that want to impress them with further details. The custom research may add to the information about demographic characteristics that syndicated research provides; for example, it might explore the religious affiliations or occupations of an audience. The research might present **psychographic data,** information that links demographic categories to personality characteristics of an audience—for instance, whether they are "materialistic" or "confident" or people who want to lead rather than follow.

The research might also provide details about the lifestyles of the audience that could impress potential advertisers: how many vacations they took last year, what cars they drive, whether they play golf regularly. *Seventeen* magazine executives, for example, might commission research about how many of their teen readers have begun to use cosmetics or go to the movies each week or own cars. They would present these data to potential cosmetic, movie, and car advertisers in the hope of convincing them to include *Seventeen* in their media plan—that is, in the list of media outlets in which they advertise their products.

Outdoor and in-store media are of increasing importance for some marketers, and an insurance company such as Geico may be one. Outdoor media encompass

psychographic data
information that links demographic categories to personality characteristics of an audience

in-store media the print and audiovisual ads that people see when they walk into retail spaces

a great variety of stationary billboards and signs as well as moving media such as buses and trains. The term **in-store media** refers to a raft of print and audiovisual ads that people see when they walk into retail spaces. In a growing number of supermarkets, a company called MediaCarts sells ads on grocery carriages. Supermarkets show videos and ads at checkout too. In stores like Wal-Mart and Best Buy, PRN Corporation, owned by Thomson, sells ad space on checkout screens. Captivate, a company owned by Gannett, sets up office-building elevators with screens that run ads along with entertainment, weather or news. AccentHealth, a company owned by Discovery Holdings, has TV screens with CNN clips and targeted ads in more than 10,000 doctors' offices across the country.[3] And supermarket firms fill their stores with the audio announcements of sales, shelf signs, floor mats with ads, and video screens showing ads at checkout. The locations for ads seem to be boundless. In order to hype its shows during 2007, CBS even had a company stamp 35 million supermarket eggs with its trademark "eye" logo, as well as the names and logos of the programs in its fall television lineup.[4]

In evaluating a media outlet, media planners examine syndicated and custom demographic, psychographic, and lifestyle research to decide whether the audience segment they are aiming at can be found at that outlet. If it can, the planners then ask the following questions:

- What is the outlet's reach with respect to (ad planners use the term *against*) the target audience? That is, what percentage of the entire target audience (say, teenage girls) will the outlet reach?
- Considering the costs of running an ad there, how efficient is the outlet in reaching that audience compared to other outlets?

cost-per-thousand (CPM) the basic measurement of advertising efficiency in all media; it is used by advertisers to evaluate how much space they will buy in a given medium, and what price they will pay

In studying *Seventeen* for a makeup client, ad planners may find that it reaches 13 million readers, the overwhelming percentage of whom are teenage girls. Moreover, *Seventeen* provides lifestyle research that contends that many of these readers are trying makeup for the first time. Just as important, the planners learn that although the cost of buying space for a four-color, full-page ad in *Seventeen* is similar to the cost of buying such an ad in women's magazines with larger circulations, the **cost per thousand (CPM)** of teenage girls is quite a bit lower. That is because of the selectivity of the magazine: magazines such as *Glamour* reach lots of teenage girls, but an advertiser would not be able to target an edition directly to them, and so much of the ad money would be wasted. Because *Seventeen* reaches virtually only teenage girls, the CPM of the target audience is lower.

This factor makes *Seventeen* an efficient buy when compared to women's magazines, but how does *Seventeen* compare to other teen periodicals—*CosmoGIRL* and *Teen*, for example? Ad planners have to study their own research, their syndicated research, and the research presented to them by the magazine companies to make a decision. They might decide to see whether one or another of the teen magazines would give them a discount for the bulk of the makeup ad money. Or they might discuss the pros and cons of splitting their ad purchases equally among the major teen periodicals.

Considerations such as these constantly occupy media planners. They also worry about the placement of print ads and TV commercials. Placement concerns involve the *environment* of the ad as well as its visibility. **Environment** refers to the media material surrounding the ad. If you're advertising lipstick, you might want your ad placed in the vicinity of articles or TV programming that portrays good-looking people who might well be wearing makeup. You don't want it placed in the vicinity of articles celebrating a grunge look that avoids cosmetics. **Visibility**

environment the media material surrounding the ad

visibility putting the ad in a place where it is most likely to be seen simply means putting the ad in a place where it is most likely to be seen. In a group (or **pod**) of TV commercials, the first commercial is likely to be the one that is most noticed. Similarly, the back cover of a magazine is a good place to be; a foldout from the back or front cover (called a **gatefold**) may draw even more attention.

pod a group of television advertisements in succession

gatefold a foldout from the back or front cover of a magazine or book

Exhibition in the Advertising Industry

The goal of the production and distribution of an ad is to exhibit it across a variety of media to a target audience. Recall that advertisers call the entire set of advertisements using a particular theme to promote a certain product for a certain period of time an advertising campaign. Once the media plan for the campaign has been created, it is up to the advertisers' media buyers to carry it out. The buyers often work for separate media buying companies. (Recall, for example, that while Martin Agency creates and produces Geico's ads, it works with Horizon Media to plan ad-placement strategy; Horizon does the actual buying.) Every mass media firm publishes its rates for space or time. It also makes a pitch for different target audiences that advertisers crave. For example, MTV's online division has organized its sales staff to sell to advertisers "against" three psychographic groups: kids/family, men/gamer enthusiasts, and youth music. The division's digital sales

Advertising to Hispanics Outdoors

CULTURE TODAY

As demographic measurements become more and more precise, advertisers increasingly are looking toward outdoor advertising as a way to reach the burgeoning Hispanic market in the United States. Until recently, advertisers who wanted to connect with the Hispanic population would locate outdoor ads in areas with a high percentage of foreign-born residents, since those areas statistically predicted large Hispanic populations. Over time, however, the Hispanic population has become more geographically diverse, rendering these techniques less effective.

Nielsen Outdoor, the outdoor advertising arm of the Nielsen media research firm, uses the Global Positional System (GPS) to generate the same kind of viewership ratings they produce regarding television programs. Nielsen tracks their subjects, ordinary people who have been outfitted with small GPS devices, using 24 satellites maintained by the U.S. government. The GPS system provides Nielsen with 13,000 "fixes," or locations, per day for each subject. The fixes are then mapped according to a database of outdoor advertisements, like billboards or bus shelters, to determine what ads are most likely to be seen by what demographic. Additionally, Nielsen is working with the Traffic Audit Board,

the outdoor industry's non-profit circulation auditor, to develop an out-of-home ratings system to track traffic exposure more precisely.

The upshot of this, of course, is ad spending: advertisers will spend more than the $76 million dollars that went toward Hispanic-targeted outdoor advertising in 2004—a fact that will ring most true for Clear Channel Outdoor and CBS Outdoor's Latino Division, the two biggest players in the Hispanic outdoor market. They carry ads for banks, cellular, healthcare and insurance companies. For Arthur Rockwell, VP-sales for CBS Outdoor's Latino Division, the biggest draw of outdoor advertising is sazón, or the spice. "By incorporating out-of-home in the recipe, by adding the sazón, it not only fills in the reach gaps but makes everything else work that much better," Mr Rockwell says. "It reinforces other media."

Sources: Abbey Klaassen, "Outdoor Builds on GPS Data; Better Measurement Capability Helps Buyers Fill in Gaps in Ad Reach," *Advertising Age*, January 30, 2006, p. S8; Erik Sass, "Nielsen Claims Outdoor Ratings Breakthrough, Launches System As Industry Eyes Others," *Media Daily News*, December 7, 2005 7 a.m. ET, online at http://www.mediapost.com

director noted in 2006 that the company was reaching over thirty million unique visitors per month and so could deliver the large numbers—the "online scale"—that advertisers want.[5]

For media buyers representing large advertisers, however, these charges are just the starting point. They dangle the large amounts of cash that they control as they attempt to negotiate discounts from the basic rates. Some media companies want the business of big advertisers so much that they offer inducements beyond discounts to get them to sign up. These inducements, called **value-added offers,** cover a wide gamut of activities. A newspaper firm might help the advertiser create booklets about its product and distribute them to its readers. A TV network might give the advertiser "free" space on its Internet site. A magazine company might give the advertiser access to the media firm's large database of subscribers.

Cross-platform Deals

The rise of huge cross-media conglomerates such as Time Warner and News Corporation has added another wrinkle to dealmaking. The conglomerates have created divisions that aim to make **cross-platform deals.** These deals can take two forms. In the first type of cross-platform deal, known as a cross-conglomerate deal, the conglomerate may try to get an advertiser to buy ad space or time in as many of the conglomerates' holdings as possible. This approach can be difficult to put together, because it means that executives in several divisions of the conglomerate must be involved and must feel that their part of the company stands to make a profit from the deal. The second type of cross-platform deal involves an agreement with one part of the conglomerate, but across the many media brands that that division has established. For example, in 2007, NBC Universal made a deal with DirectTV to sponsor all its episodes *of Battlestar Galactica.* Apart from the standard sponsorships around the episodes, DirectTV was included in the show's SMS mobile alerts, DVDs, sweepstakes, and online sponsorships; and promotions on the Battlestar iTunes page, blogs, podcasts, and webisodes.[6]

Eventually, with the right technology, the goal is to help advertisers track individuals across many media, so as to reach them when they are most ready to receive ads. One hint of the way that might happen relates to mobile phone companies' ability to track their customers' locations. If the customers agree, the companies can send them ads, including discount coupons, based on their geographic location. This sort of advertising, which is sure to grow, is called **location-based advertising.** Such outdoor advertising might also develop cross-platform features—for example, if your phone company works with your supermarket to give you different coupons at checkout in the supermarket. The Microsoft Corporation is already carrying out a kind of location-based advertising activity in relation to gaming. Part of Microsoft's "Live Anywhere" strategy, the activity is called **cross-platform gaming** or **pervasive gaming.** It allows users to play the same game and same competitors in a variety of places. It also allows players to use one identity across platforms, as well as all-in-one scorekeeping, chat and friend lists. All this allows Microsoft to sell ads aimed at the same people with particular demographics across all three of Microsoft's gaming areas: the XBox, its online gaming sites, and its mobile gaming platform.[7]

Of course, advertising agencies expect their work to be exhibited on the media outlets with which they have made deals. Several companies exist to help ad buyers determine whether their work did indeed get printed or aired in the appropriate way and at the appropriate time. In addition, agencies and their clients are interested in what their competition is doing. Competitive Media Reports (CMR)

value-added offer a special service promised by a media firm to its most desired advertisers as an inducement to get their business

cross-platform deal a deal between a cross-media conglomerate and advertiser, which seeks to exploit as many of the conglomerate's holdings as possible

location-based advertising the process of sending commercial messages to people based on their geographic position

cross-platform gaming or pervasive gaming location-based advertising activity in relation to gaming that allows users to play the same game and same competitors in a variety of places. It also allows players to use one identity across platforms, as well as all-in-one scorekeeping, chat and friend lists. All this allows ad agencies to sell ads aimed at the same people with particular demographics across all gaming areas

is one firm that provides advertisers with information about where their competitors are advertising and how much they are spending.

Determining an Advertisement's Success

After an ad campaign is exhibited, the ad agency's research division will probably be involved with the advertiser in evaluating the campaign's success. In the case of a direct-marketing campaign, this evaluation is easy. If the campaign led to the purchase of a certain number of products (or a certain dollar amount), it may be judged a success. In the case of a web ad, evaluation depends on the nature of the response and the expectations of the marketers. If the ad is of the **click-through** sort, where the reader can use the mouse to get to a product site and purchase the product directly, the ad's success can also be evaluated through direct purchases. Yet, one can argue that the ad may be successful even if the people reading it do not click on it or, if they do click on it, they do not buy the product. They may buy it later, in a bricks-and-mortar store or online, and that could be difficult to track.

> **click-through ad** a web-based advertisement that, when clicked on, takes the user to the advertiser's website

In traditional advertising, immediate results are impossible to observe. It can be tough to determine how many teens bought lipstick as a result of the ad in *Seventeen*. Nonetheless, researchers try to find out. One way of noting the visibility of the campaign is to survey the target audience to see how many people recall the ads. Comparing the recall of those ads to the recall of other ads gives one measure of the ad campaign's ability to enter the consciousness of its targets. More directly related to the ad campaign's ability to move a product are comparisons of sales before and after the campaign. Of course, many factors, not all of them related to the campaign, can influence this comparison. But the researchers do the best they can to tease out these considerations and draw conclusions about the ads themselves.

Because the effectiveness of an advertising campaign is so difficult to measure definitively, advertisers constantly worry about whether the enormous amounts of money they are spending are worth it. Still, the revenues mass media firms collect from advertising continue to rise. A famous saying, sometimes attributed to the nineteenth-century merchant, John Wanamaker, helps explain the cash devoted to the activity. "I know that half of my advertising funds are wasted," he said. "The trouble is, I don't know which half."

Threats to Traditional Advertising

The concern that companies have had about measuring the value of their ads is as old as the advertising industry. Part of that worry comes from the awareness that people may not pay attention to ads, even if they are staring right at them. As radio and television began to air commercials, advertisers also worried that many members of the audience wouldn't sit still to watch their spots. Ad practitioners imagined large segments of listeners and viewers going to the bathroom or kitchen during commercial "breaks." The challenge then becomes to make the ads interesting, funny, disgusting or cute enough for target audiences to actually want to sit to hear, watch or read them. This has become an important goal of creativity in advertising.

During the past decade or so, though, advertisers have become increasingly concerned that consumers are using new technologies to help them avoid commercial messages so they don't even have to decide whether they want to attend to them. Marketers know that Americans are using digital video recorders (DVRs) to rush through broadcast, cable and satellite television shows. Online, they are using email filters and pop-up killers to get rid of unwanted ads. Advertisers fear that these technologies are only the beginning of a raft of approaches that allow audiences to enjoy ad-sponsored materials with hardly any confronting of the ads.

Sometimes the ways they express their concerns verge on the hilarious. Consider the worries that Jamie Kellner, CEO of Turner Broadcasting, expressed in 2002 about DVRs. He told the magazine *Cable World* that DVR users were "stealing" television by skipping the commercials. "Your contract with the network when you get the show is you're going to watch the spots. Otherwise you couldn't get show on an ad-supported basis. Any time you skip a commercial ... you're actually stealing the programming." When his interviewer asked him, "What if you have to go to the bathroom or get up to get a Coke," Kellner responded: "I guess there's a certain amount of tolerance for going to the bathroom. But if you formalize it and you create a device that skips certain second increments, you've got that only for one reason, unless you go to the bathroom for 30 seconds. They've done that just to make it easy for someone to skip a commercial."[8]

Over the next few years, it became clear that DVR makers were trying to make their devices ad-friendly—for example, by providing special places for advertisements on their devices and encouraging visits to advertisers' websites. Nevertheless, advertisers remained concerned. Their worries were bolstered by a 2005 survey by the Yankelovich Partners market research company that found 69 percent of American consumers "said they were interested in ways to block, skip or opt out of being exposed to advertising."[9] Fear continued that rapidly spreading technologies could make mulch of their traditional approaches to buying advertising.

What to do about it? Well, one approach was to make advertisements more relevant to specifically targeted audiences with the hope that they would know that and not skip them. Another tack was to make deleting or skipping the ads impossible; that's the case with in-game ads and the ads in online videos. Still another set of solutions that marketers are using involves bypassing traditional advertising altogether. To understand this last set of solutions, recall that at the start of this chapter we defined advertising as the activity of explicitly paying for media space or time in order to direct favorable attention to certain goods or services. The key word to notice here is *explicitly*. From the standpoint of a marketer, the advantage of being explicit about what you are selling is that you have a lot of control over when, where and in front of what audience your product will appear. You also have control over the message; the ad or commercial runs exactly as you intended it. The disadvantage of being explicit, though, is that the audience knows that you're trying to persuade it, and it may well try to get out of the way.

The alternative, many marketers understand, is trying to get in front of audiences through ways that don't announce their presence as persuasion. There are many ways to do that, and you've probably come into contact with all of them. You've already seen a definition for public relations, which involves the unannounced insertion of products or ideas into media materials. You've probably heard of product placement, when a brand is inserted into a TV show or movie as a result of a marketing deal. You may not have heard of viral marketing, buzz marketing, or environmental marketing. These businesses are growing tremendously—faster than the advertising business—as marketers look for a way to reach consumers in ways that will virtually force them to pay attention to their messages. We can group them under the label *public relations and other marketing communications*. These are important activities, critical to understanding the direction of many media today. We'll tackle them in Chapter 16: The Public Relations Industry.

Media Literacy and the Advertising Industry

Of course, the activity of advertising is here to stay, even as other forms of marketing communication come alongside it. As we have seen, companies spend $200 million a year on advertising. Advertising executives care about the money they allocate to the creation of ads and the purchase of ad space because this activity consumes lots of cash that could be used for other purposes. Media executives care about the money they *receive* from ads because it helps keep them alive. It's natural for them to be concerned, and it's natural for millions of other people to be concerned along with them because they work for companies that either spend or collect advertising money.

But what about people who are members of the larger society? What should citizens who want to live in a democratic, peaceful, thriving world think about the relationship between advertising and media? This is an important question, if only because advertising is all around us. Moreover, our everyday approach to ads is typically quite conflicted. We condemn the stupidity of some of them even while we hum commercial tunes and repeat commercial phrases (remember Budweiser's *Whassup?* ad campaign?). We hate it when ads intrude on our viewing, but we are

Is it Ethical to Advertise?

IS IT ETHICAL?

The question of ethics in advertising focuses on the morality of particular ads, particular types of ads and on the basic underlying tenets of the entire business of persuasion. In regard to the latter, the Catholic Church attempted to answer that question in a 35-page report titled "Ethics in Advertising." Published in 1997 by the Pontifical Council for Social Responsibility, the Church accuses advertisers of making "deliberate appeals to such motives as envy, status-seeking and lust" and urges them to avoid "manipulative, titillating and shocking ads."

Many advertising executives did not respond amiably, claiming that they should not be blamed for problems that they inherited rather than caused. One British executive responded: "[O]f course we resort to irrational motives and appeal to people's sense of status or lust or envy. That's what we are about." A decade after the Church's report, there is some evidence that the advertising industry has begun to change its stance on the applicability of ethics in marketing. The World Federation of Advertisers met in Canada in May 2007 under the banner "the ethical imperative: beyond compliance." However, critics say that this may be an attempt simply to avoid regulation and give advertisers a chance to mold ethics rather than allow ethical standards to mold them.

One of the most pertinent issues in recent years regarding ethics in advertising is that of advertising to children. Children are increasingly the target of advertising because of the growing amount of money spent on them and the influence they have over their parents—sometimes called "pester power." This is troublesome for advocates due to the vulnerable and impressionable nature of children that makes them more susceptible to messages. These messages can have negative impacts on their diet and lead to more materialistic behavior. As marketers are switching to more subtle means of advertising some governments have taken action. Both Norway and Sweden have banned advertising that targets children under twelve. Both Britain and Greece have strict restrictions on the types of advertisements allowed during children's programming. More subtle tactics by advertisers and the need for governments to regulate show that such self-regulatory "ethical" initiatives commenced by groups such as the World Federation of Advertisers may indeed be all "smoke and mirrors".

Sources: Belinda Archer, "The Eighth Deadly Sin," *Africa News,* April 11, 1997; "The Vatican's Ad Ethics Report Now On-line," *Advertising Age,* April 14, 1997, p.18; Vikki Leone, "Advertising: The Route of All Evil?," *The Age,* March 15, 2007; Simon Canning, "Ad Men Weigh into Ethical Guidelines," *The Australian,* May 3, 2007.

sometimes glad when commercials appear on TV so that we can go to the kitchen or bathroom. We sometimes buy what we see in ads even while insisting that they don't affect us. In general, we accept ads as a given in our society and don't think deeply about them.

Many scholars suggest that we really ought to think deeply about them. A few writers even suggest that the future of world civilization depends on redefining society's relationship to advertising. That may sound like an extravagant claim about an industry that sells cars and candy bars. But is it really that far-fetched? See what you think as we review three issues that center on advertising, the mass media, and society. One issue—the power of advertising conglomerates in the face of blurring media boundaries—carries forward two themes that we've seen throughout this text. The others—advertising and democracy and advertising and commercialism—focus on the ad industry but also relate to the media system as a whole. As we will see, all three issues are quite interrelated.

Advertising and Commercialism

commercialism a situation in which the buying and selling of goods and services is a highly promoted value

We start with commercialism because it is the term most associated with advertising and its impact on American life. **Commercialism** refers to a situation in which the buying and selling of goods and services is a highly promoted value. Many people say that the United States is a nation in which commercialism runs rampant. Everywhere we turn, we see a sales pitch.

Defenders of commercialism insist that Americans would never have the high standard of living that they now have, nor the products that they take for granted, were it not for the industrial competition that commercialism has encouraged. Detractors of commercialism question this notion of progress. They insist that many difficulties come along with making commercialism a central tenet of American society. The most common problem, they say, is leading people to purchase things that they don't really need.

hidden curriculum a program of study that people don't realize they are taking

From the time Americans are very young, the critics say, they are presented with a daily barrage of ads. These ads are important not primarily because they aim to sell individual products or services; sometimes they succeed at that, and sometimes they don't. Rather, the importance of the advertising barrage is that it is part of what some observers call a **hidden curriculum**. A hidden curriculum is a program of study that people don't realize they are taking. Advertising critics argue that what advertising teaches, and what Americans accept as a basic lesson from the ad "course" they receive, is that society is merely a huge marketplace, and that buying products and defining oneself through them is an essential aspect of life.

Supporters of advertising say that even if this hidden curriculum exists in as powerful a manner as its critics suggest, it is not harmful. People need to feel good about themselves, and advertising provides a vehicle—products—for doing that. Critics respond, however, that commercialism has dire side effects. Two that they especially highlight are the exploitation of children and the destruction of the global environment.

The Exploitation of Children Media critics contend that advertising to children is ethically unacceptable. They point out that children aged two through twelve are often treated just like any other consumers. Ad people know that children influence their parents' spending and, as they get older, also have their own purchasing power from gifts and allowances. The critics cite scholarly research showing that the youngest children (those under age four or five) often don't have the skills to be critical of advertisers' claims. As for the older kids, the critics con-

Ubiquitous Advertising

Is that wall moving? Why is the floor lit up underneath your feet? If you live in a city, those are probably advertisements you are seeing. Gone are the days when television, radio, and billboards were the primary conduits for advertising. In today's world of ubiquitous technology, the next big thing is ubiquitous advertising. It's a cliché at this point, but advertisers still talk a lot about thinking outside the box. Today, however, that box increasingly refers to both your television and your home. As advances in technology have driven down the prices of LCD and LED displays, it is becoming increasingly cost-effective to introduce video screens into scores of different situations. The most popular is known as **point-of-purchase** (POP) advertising. POP ads are based on the following concept: you are more likely to purchase a product when you are in shopping mode, whether that is walking around the city on your lunch hour or standing in a checkout line.

But the ads don't end there. More and more companies are buying into the idea that competition among brands and swelling marketing budgets mean that quantity (volume) is just as important as quality. It might not even be a traditional advertisement, but instead simply the name of the company or product. This process, known as branding, has allowed

companies to remind consumers to buy their product in even the smallest of spaces. Advertisers increasingly turn to this type of environmental conditioning to seed their product's message in the mind of the consumer. From static branding, usually featuring stickers or printed labels on generic products or places, to video billboards that serve up different moving images depending on the time of day, advertising is gaining more of a foothold in everyday life, and in some places even dominating the visual environment.

However, not everyone is sold on the tradeoffs of ubiquitous advertising that often provides free services or goods in exchange for ad space. Many municipalities have fought to keep ads off their buildings and streets, and billboards from their roads. Many people turn away from products that plaster their ads in more insidious places. But despite these many local protests throughout the country, it is clear that with big budgets and emerging technologies at their disposal, advertisers and the companies they represent are winning the battle for the nation's attention.

Sources: "Anywhere the Eye Can See, It's Likely to See an Ad," Louise Story, New York Times Online, January 15, 2007; "Advertising Away From Home, TV Ads Are Inescapable," Louise Story, New York Times Online, March 2, 2007.

---

tend that by getting children hyped for toys, foods, and other products that their parents must approve, the advertisers may be encouraging family arguments. In fact, marketers and media firms that invite children into a separate channel to advertise to them are quietly setting themselves up in opposition to the children's parents—a situation that, the critics argue, is morally highly questionable.

Destruction of the Global Environment Critics who argue that advertisers share the blame with polluters for the destruction of the global environment take the issue of teaching commercialism to kids to what they feel is its logical conclusion. When so many people are taught that the continual purchase of new products is the key to the good life, their resulting activities place an enormous burden on the earth's resources. The energy used to create the products they buy, the energy (and pollution) created by the use of the products, the garbage problems that are created when people throw away things that they could still use but that aren't fashionable—all these activities make the earth a more and more difficult place to inhabit. Supporters of advertisers counter that these problems are not really so bad, that people are living better now than ever before in history. The critics reply that the ecological disasters caused by commercialism are just beginning. As the

point-of-purchase (POP) advertising commercial messages displayed at the areas that people are likely to buy the products or services

billions of people in developing countries such as China buy into the commercialist philosophy of countries such as the United States, the pressure on the earth's environment will mount to unacceptable levels. Advertising critics such as Sut Jhally have argued that this predicament will literally lead to the end of the earth's ability to sustain human beings.

Advertising and Democracy

Writers such as Jhally extend their critique of advertising and commercialism into a critique of advertising and democracy. In doing so, they are trying to reverse a longstanding perception that advertising and democracy go hand in hand. Supporters of advertising have emphasized for decades that it is far better to have a media system that relies on advertisers for money than one that relies on the government. They point out that heads of states often try to control media in ways that preserve their power and take away the ability of citizens to understand other ways of looking at their worlds. Although outstanding examples of government-run media that encourage democratic thinking do exist (look at the British Broadcasting Corporation), many societies with government-owned media are not politically free. Because people cannot afford to foot the entire bill for their media menu, advertisers are a good alternative to government interference.

Advertising critics don't necessarily dispute the contention that government-controlled media often abuse democratic ideals. They insist, however, that advertisers also often guide ad-supported media in ways that hinder democracy. They do this by controlling content for marketing purposes in ways that are counter to encouraging citizen participation.

Consider the situation in the United States. The First Amendment does not protect media practitioners from advertiser control, critics note. In fact, because of their importance in funding the media, advertisers actually have a lot more power over the content of media in the United States than government agencies do. What advertisers get from that power, say the critics, are media vehicles that create a friendly environment for them among the audiences they target. This relationship between advertisers and media firms hinders democracy, the critics say, because their audiences get a selective view (or no view) of certain parts of the world that they don't know from personal experience. In effect, the advertising industry's power over media screens people from learning the perspectives of certain groups in society and discourages public discussions on certain important issues.

Some critics go even further with their complaints about the effect advertisers have on the public's knowledge about, and involvement with, parts of the world that they do not experience firsthand.

Sut Jhally, a leading expert on advertising and media studies, is the founder and executive director of the Media Education Foundation. In his frequent lectures and articles, Jhally asserts that advertising constantly pushes us toward consumer goods to satisfy our needs for love, friendship, and autonomy.

618

They say that the advertiser-media relationship has led to a situation in which much material is created primarily to get people interested so that they will see or hear commercial messages. The result, they add, is a media environment that attracts people with attention-grabbing stimuli such as sex and violence, yet puts them in a good mood when they watch, hear, or read the ads.

At its worst, say the critics, a media system driven by this mentality fosters a society of audiences, not of citizens. That is, it encourages people to pay attention to the media, but not to become actively involved in tackling the problems of the larger society, partly because the media focus so much on keeping them tuned in and entertained. Culture critic Neil Postman insisted, in fact, that because of the advertiser-media relationship, we in society are "amusing ourselves to death." Postman's argument is that the stress on unchallenging, feel-good pap in so much of the U.S. media (including the news) is leading American society down the path toward a situation in which society will be too involved in entertainment to cope with serious problems, and so these problems will destroy it. Sut Jhally, with his focus squarely on advertising's role in the deterioration of the global environment, would agree.

The Power of Conglomerates

During the past decade, the advertising industry has seen the same movement toward consolidation and rise of conglomerates that we have seen throughout the rest of the media systems. Some of the biggest agencies in the industry were acquired mainly by the four biggest ad organizations—Omnicom Group, WPP Group, Publicis and Interpublic Group. According to *Advertising Age*, these giants together accounted for about 54 percent of all the revenues that the top 500 U.S. advertising agencies earned during 2006.[10]

Ad industry critics such as Matthew McAllister have pointed to the rise of ad agency conglomerates in an era of blurring media boundaries as signaling a deepening of the problems of commercialism and democracy. Their reasoning has three steps. First, they emphasize the power that advertisers have always had over U.S. media. Next, they note the increasing movement of all material, including advertising, across media boundaries. Third, they suggest that as multimedia holding companies, the agency conglomerates are working with mass media conglomerates to turn as much media space as possible into ad-friendly space, deepening commercialism and threatening democratic dialogue even more than in the past.

The first point is one that we have seen already, in this chapter and throughout this book. Advertisers are extremely important to the survival of many U.S. media. Media executives must take the needs of potential advertisers into account when they make decisions about whom to reach and with what sorts of materials. Are women aged 25–54 a viable audience for a fashion magazine, or would advertisers be happier with younger demographics? If the latter, what kinds of columns and covers would best attract younger readers? If you multiply these sorts of questions and their answers thousands of times, you will understand that when people read a magazine, watch a TV show, get on many websites, or use any other ad-sponsored medium, they are entering a world that was created as a result of close cooperation between advertisers and media firms.

That cooperation, the critics note in their next step, increasingly involves the movement of all material, including advertising, across media boundaries. We've seen this, too, throughout our discussions of media industries. (You'll recall that Chapter 5 explains how and why this cross-media requirement developed.) The idea is to follow target audiences to as many places that they go as possible.

Ad-sponsored vehicles such as ESPN and *Sports Illustrated*, for example, are no longer tied to their original media (cable and magazines, respectively). The competitors for sports audiences now follow their audiences into one another's turf and even further, appearing in print, in video, on broadcast TV, on cable, on mobile devices, on airplanes—wherever the potential fan goes.

With all this advertising surrounding people, ad practitioners find it more and more difficult to get people's attention. Executives commonly use the term **ad clutter** to refer to the competing messages facing Americans virtually everywhere they turn, virtually every moment of the day. Their typical solution to cut through the clutter is more ads in more and more unusual places, from supermarket floors to bathroom stalls. This, of course, merely creates more clutter and encourages ad practitioners to buy more ads, and more creatively placed ads. The ensuing clutter keeps the process spiraling, with the result, say critics, that we are all being inundated with ads.

The critics go on to suggest the third point that centers on the relation between advertising holding companies and mass media conglomerates. As giant firms that own ad agencies, media-buying organizations, and more, the holding companies control billions of dollars worth of their clients' advertising budgets. Decisions by the top advertising conglomerates about where to spend that money can mean the difference between success and failure for some media outlets.

That's where the media conglomerates come in. Critics of advertising point out (as we have in this chapter) that companies such as News Corporation, Time Warner, and Viacom have set up divisions whose mission is to get as much ad money as possible for the company's media outlets through cross-platform deals. The agency holding companies, in turn, have set up divisions that work with the conglomerates to create cross-platform deals for their clients that achieve the clients' objectives and save them money compared to buying media vehicles one at a time. The result, say the critics, is acceleration of media clutter and, by extension, of the commercialism that deepens America's hidden ad curriculum and encourages content that is designed to keep people as audiences rather than citizens.

But the advertising industry is not alone in carrying out this process, some critics continue. The public relations industry is at least as much at fault. In addition, while advertising is at least visible, PR is often invisible. What is public relations, how does it work, and why should we care? To get answers, turn to Chapter 16.

ad clutter term used to refer to the competing messages facing Americans virtually everywhere they turn, virtually every moment of the day

CHAPTER REVIEW

For an interactive chapter recap and study guide, visit the companion website for *Media Today* at www.routledge.com/textbooks/mediatoday

QUESTIONS FOR DISCUSSION AND CRITICAL THINKING

1 Why would a company hire more than one ad agency to promote the same product?
2 Explain positioning and its relation to segmentation.
3 Why do some advertising critics dislike cross-platform deals by media conglomerates?
4 What does it mean to say that advertisers create portraits of America?

INTERNET RESOURCES

The Hartman Center for Sales, Advertising & Marketing History (http://library. duke.edu/specialcollections/hartman/index.html)
A Duke University site that displays thousands of old ads from the nineteenth and twentieth centuries.

Advertising Age (http://adage.com/index.php)
A major trade magazine of the advertising industry with a site that includes news, blogs, and industry data.

Mediapost.com (http://www.mediapost.com/)
This website offers to email to you, without charge, several daily bulletins about various aspects of advertising and media as well as classified job ads.

KEY TERMS

You can find the definitions to these key terms in the marginal glossary throughout this chapter. Test your knowledge of these terms with interactive flash cards on the *Media Today* companion website.

ad campaign	branding
ad clutter	business-to-business agencies
advertising	click-through
advertising agency	client conflicts
advertising campaign	commercialism
agency holding companies	consumer agencies
agency networks	cost per thousand (CPM)
brand	creative

creative personnel

creative persuasion

cross-conglomerate deal

cross-platform deals

cross-platform gaming

direct-marketing agencies

direct-to-consumer (DTC) advertising

environment

gatefold

general ad agency

global presence

hidden curriculum

image ads

Internet agency

location-based advertising

market research

market segmentation

media planning and buying

motivation research

persuasion

pervasive gaming

pod

point of purchase

positioning

psychographic data

public relations

publicity

reason-why ads

sales pitch

specialty agency

subliminal persuasion

traditional advertising agency

value-added offers

visibility

CONSTRUCTING MEDIA LITERACY

1   Do you agree with the notion that advertising provides a "hidden curriculum"? Why or why not?

2   How would you have responded to Jamie Kellner of Turner Broadcasting when he said that audiences have a responsibility to view ads?

3   To what extent is it possible for parents to shield their children from commercialism? Do you agree that shielding them is a good idea?

4   To what extend can you see market segmentation in the media that you use?

CASE STUDY   Exploring Ads All Around

The issue   We often don't pay attention to the many commercial messages that we see because of the clutter of advertising all around us. Knowing about this lack of attention, advertisers often send more ads our way with the aim of catching our attention, thereby increasing the clutter. The result is an everyday environment filled with ads. To see just how filled, it might be interesting to track the number of ads you see in just one part of your day.

The method   Count the number of ads you see from the time you get up until the time you get to work or to class. Take care to follow your normal routines and paths. Start with the sounds you hear or see from the radio and TV; the ads on the cereal box; the commercial messages on the clothes you wear; the ones on the signs you see on your way. Keep a record of what you saw and when—and in what amount of time. Write a report of your findings, and share it with your classmates to find out how similar or different you are from one another.

16 THE PUBLIC RELATIONS INDUSTRY

After studying this chapter, you will be able to:

1 Sketch the development of the public relations industry

2 Analyze the nine areas of the public relations industry

3 Explain how public relations, advertising, and other persuasion activities are coming together to produce *integrated marketing communication*

4 Discuss concerns that media critics have about the persuasion industries

"Some are born great, some achieve greatness, and some hire public relations officers."

– Daniel J. Boorstin, Historian

In our discussion of the advertising industry in Chapter 15, we defined *advertising* as the activity of explicitly paying for media space or time in order to direct favorable attention to certain goods or services. The first two elements of advertising—paying for space and explicitly advertising—are important to underscore because another major persuasion industry, public relations (PR), has been built on the premise that the best way to influence people through media is not to pay for space and not to announce your presence. Moreover, the past couple of decades have seen the fast growth of a third persuasion business, marketing communication, that mixes some aspects of advertising and some of public relations through activities such as placement of certain products in movies and the sponsorship of sporting events. All three activities involve the spending of billions of dollars and have major effects on the mass media content that so many people share. The aim of this chapter is to explain how and why that is so and to point to the growing number of circumstances in which elements of advertising and PR are mixed.

Distinguishing Between Public Relations and Advertising

You are probably much less familiar with PR than with advertising. In fact, it wouldn't be surprising if you've never talked with anyone about a public relations campaign. Most people don't have a clue as to which media materials they read, hear, or watch are parts of a PR campaign.

That's OK with public relations practitioners. They try very hard to avoid getting public recognition for stories that appear in the press. They believe that for their work to be most effective, viewers and readers should not know when TV programs and newspaper articles are influenced by the PR industry. The fact is, though, that a good deal of what we see and hear in both news and entertainment material is initiated by, or filtered through, public relations specialists.

What is Public Relations?

Perhaps the first thing to know about PR is that it is a very broad business. People sometimes talk about PR narrowly, equating it with **publicity**. Publicity is the practice of getting people or products mentioned in the news and entertainment media in order to get members of the public interested in them. Although public relations sometimes involves publicity work, it extends beyond it.

The following three examples may suggest the wide territory of the PR world:

■ You're the CEO of a large chemical firm, and you're worried that state legislators will pass environmental laws that will harm your company. At the same

publicity the process of getting people or products mentioned in the news and entertainment media in order to get members of the public interested in them

time, you don't want the legislators or the people of the state to believe that you want to pollute the environment. You hire a PR firm to help you devise a strategy for dealing with this dilemma.

- You're the head of investor relations for a large technology firm. You are sure that the firm's stock is undervalued, but key analysts at major brokerage firms don't seem to agree. You hire a PR firm to help you change that perception.

- As CEO of a pharmaceutical firm, you learn in a late-night phone call that one of your company's over-the-counter products has allegedly poisoned five people in the Midwestern United States. Although your firm has a crisis management team for emergencies of this type, you turn to a PR firm for further suggestions about how to handle the victims and their families, the press, politicians, and federal regulators.

public relations (PR)
information, activities, and policies by which corporations and other organizations seek to create attitudes favorable to themselves and their work, and to counter adverse attitudes

What do these different scenarios have in common? One expert has put it this way: **public relations** involves "information, activities, and policies by which corporations and other organizations seek to create attitudes favorable to themselves and their work, and to counter adverse attitudes."[1] That's a neat way of tying the examples together, and it also brings up another important issue: the relationship between public relations and mass media. If you think about the description and the three scenarios for a few moments, you'll see that they all suggest that public relations activities need not involve the technologies of mass communication. Much of the PR firm's plans for the state legislators, for example, may involve one-on-one lobbying, which is a straightforward form of interpersonal communication.

Still, in many aspects of their work, public relations practitioners do turn to the mass media. Those media activities are far more complex than merely getting good publicity for a client. For one thing, they often involve trying to counter negative media impressions of the client that were created by others. For another, media strategies typically fit into a larger PR communication strategy regarding the organization. PR work for the chemical firm, for example, may have an important mass media component, such as reaching out to reporters in the state capital with stories about the positive role the company is playing in the local economy and the care its leaders are taking with the environment. The public relations people might also believe that presenting the company in a good light to the viewing public might, in turn, encourage state politicians to believe that their constituents would applaud new laws that do not harm the firm.

At this point in the discussion, it may be useful to note two major ways in which advertising differs from PR in the mass media. First, advertisers pay for the space or time that they receive, whereas public relations practitioners typically do not. Second, advertising clearly states its presence. When you see an ad, you know what it is for, and you often know quite easily who is sponsoring it. A public relations activity, by contrast, typically hides its presence and its sponsor.

What advertising and PR have in common is that they deal in billions of dollars and play profound roles in American mass media. In fact, they are deeply involved in three important trends we have noted in media today: the movement of material across media boundaries, the rise of conglomerates, and the increase in audience segmentation and targeting. Not only do the ad and PR industries themselves reflect these trends, they encourage them in other mass media as well.

The multiplication of media and the growth of the Internet and other digital outlets have led to two major developments in the advertising and public relations industries themselves. One change is that more than ever marketers of all types are using advertising and public relations in concert to reach audiences with persuasive messages. A second development is that this concert is being orchestrated by large companies that own not just ad agencies and PR firms, but "branding" consultancies, polling firms, and other entities that add ingredients to a symphony that goes beyond advertising alone or PR alone in a mixture of the two for what broadly might be called marketing communication.

At this point you may be asking, "Where did public relations come from and how did it develop separately from advertising?" Not surprisingly, that's the topic of the next section.

The Rise of Public Relations

Public relations goes back a long way. In military reports that Roman generals such as Julius Caesar sent to the Roman Senate, historians have noted a kind of self-aggrandizing "spin" on events that we would today associate with a masterful public relations counsel. By the time of the American Revolution, the forms of public relations clearly had a modern feel. Anti-British colonists staged the Boston Tea Party and other events to gain public attention. They used popular symbols that colonists were likely to recognize easily—for example, the liberty tree and the minutemen—with the aim of mobilizing support for their cause. In addition, writers like Sam Adams, Tom Paine, Abigail Adams, and Ben Franklin developed messages that swayed public opinion against England. Think of the phrase *Boston Massacre*. As communication professor Joseph Dominick notes, what actually happened was that an angry mob got into a fight with British soldiers and a few people were killed. By calling this event a "massacre," leaders who wanted to eject the British were using inflammatory language to gain support for their position.

Early Pioneers in Advertising and Public Relations: Benjamin Franklin and P. T. Barnum

In Chapter 15, we discussed Benjamin Franklin's knack for writing advertisements in the 1700s. It turns out that he was a natural at selling himself and his various

The Boston Tea Party took place on the night of December 16, 1773, when a group of indignant colonists, led by Samuel Adams, Paul Revere, and others, disguised themselves as native Americans, boarded three East India Company ships, and threw their entire cargoes of tea into Boston Harbor. This early "publicity stunt" helped sway public opinion against the British government and helped stir the beginnings of the American Revolution.

ventures through advertising as well as through publicity and other forms of PR. One historian notes that "advertising and public relations, especially self-advertising and publicity, were as natural to Franklin as his restless intelligence and curiosity. Franklin, in all his roles and on behalf of all his varied activities, was always the untiring promoter." In fact, he was so successful a lobbyist and propagandist that in the 1760s he managed to persuade the British not to tax advertisements in the American colonies—even though ads were taxed in England.

Ben's characteristics point to the idea that until the middle of the 1800s, people who practiced these activities often didn't see them as especially separate. Many imaginative entrepreneurs touted their goods or services in a multitude of ways, some of which we would call advertising and some of which we would call PR. They simply didn't make these distinctions back then. If entrepreneurs thought of an activity that might lead customers to buy a product or an idea, they used it.

Phineas Taylor (P. T.) Barnum is another person famous for using both advertising and public relations seamlessly before the two industries developed in separate directions. You may know his name through the famous Ringling Brothers, Barnum and Bailey Circus. The circus certainly is a descendant of one of Barnum's pursuits, but he had many more. In the 1800s, he gained fame as a result of a broad spectrum of activities that mixed advertising, public relations, and showmanship in ways that made him both scorned and respected—and extremely wealthy. One of his first successes, for example, was generating an enormous amount of attention in the press when he exhibited an African-American woman who, he claimed, was the 161-year-old nurse of George Washington. Barnum also garnered great publicity for such oddities and hoaxes as a "mermaid" (in reality a dummy tied to a large fish tail) and the "marriage" of two short-statured people (which took place over and over again wherever his show stopped).

In 1842, circus pioneer P.T. Barnum (left) hired Charles Stratton, who became world-famous as "General Tom Thumb." Tom Thumb stood only 25 inches tall and weighted only 15 pounds, and was thus billed as The Smallest Man on Earth. Barnum and Thumb became close friends. During their dealings together, they traveled around the world and met various leaders and royalty, including President Abraham Lincoln and Britain's Queen Victoria and Prince Albert.

All of this made Barnum very wealthy. He didn't apologize for his tactics. He argued that his audiences liked to be fooled, and he even revealed to newspaper reporters some of the tactics he had used for previous hoaxes. Everything about his work was brash; his bold, highly pictorial advertisements and his brazen promotional activities deeply influenced other showmen such as "Buffalo Bill" Cody. Barnum's expertise at getting press coverage also served as a model for railroad publicists whose job was to lure people to settle near the tracks as railroads expanded west.

The late 1800s was a time of great change in the nation and its press, as you might remember from Chapter 7. Growing literacy, new technologies, new organizational arrangements associated with the penny press, changes in the economy after the Civil War, and other broad social changes gave Barnum and his cohorts a much larger readership than Ben Franklin had had one hundred years before. These changes also encouraged ventures that led directly to the creation of industries devoted to public relations and advertising.

The Public Relations Industry Comes of Age

Although ad agency conglomerates in the twenty-first century do tend to own public relations firms, including many of the largest, people in the advertising industry still consider the public relations industry a very different world from their own. During the 1900s, the two industries mostly grew apart. This trend, of course, was at odds with the ideas of Barnum and the other brash showmen of the 1800s, who clearly mixed advertising with public relations. However, their publicity/press agency model of the trade was not the one that was adopted by the PR practitioners who would set the tone for the emerging industry. Instead, these practitioners chose to emphasize a more elite role that was emerging for their profession: that of a PR "counselor" who could help guide the public images of large corporations in ways that satisfied management.

The social forces that made this sort of work lucrative—the growth of colossal companies aiming at large audiences in a national market economy—were the same ones that influenced the direction of the ad business. But whereas ad people had great opportunity in helping firms solve the problem of getting consumers to buy things in that economy, public relations practitioners gravitated to a very different corporate problem. This was an era in which the heads of large companies feared that the masses of consumers and workers might rise up against them in anger over negative articles about them that appeared in the press. Business leaders saw a major need to convince consumers and government officials not to interfere with their companies. The (often fabulously wealthy) chief executives wanted to make the case that their actions and the actions of their firms were in the best interest of the entire nation.

The job required people who could combine a Barnum-like feel for public image making with an understanding of politics that recalled that of Julius Caesar. In the late 1800s and early 1900s, railroad firms and utility companies such as AT&T and Consolidated Edison hired PR firms to get newspapers to portray them as concerned corporate citizens as well as to coordinate lobbying activities aimed at convincing federal, state, and local government officials to preserve their monopoly positions.

Of particular note during this time was an organization called the Publicity Bureau, which was the predecessor of the modern PR agency. Its first major account, in 1906, was aimed at defeating President Theodore Roosevelt's legislation to curb abuses of power by the railroads. The bureau's tacticians wrote essays favorable to the railroads and crafted them to look like news articles written by journalists. The bureau then paid to have those articles published in newspapers around the United States. The idea was to whip up public sympathy for the railroads and against the president's bill.

You might notice an ethical issue here. In fact, many of the early PR "counselors" would do whatever it took, even if that were shady or illegal, to take care of a client's needs. Their actions ranged from bribing lawmakers to vote in ways that helped the company to paying freelance journalists to write articles favorable to the firm. After a number of years, though, such routine ethical lapses started backfiring. Indignant journalists began exposing these practices, and then companies had to dig themselves out of even deeper public relations holes.

Ivy Lee and Modern Public Relations   One of the first individuals to help build the dignity of the corporate public relations business in the face of such embarrassments was a minister's son and former reporter named Ivy Lee. Lee went out of his way to cultivate a reputation of honesty among corporate leaders, government officials, and the press. In 1906, he convinced the heads of the Pennsylvania Railroad to "come clean" to journalists about their company's mistakes that had led to a rail accident. Lee argued that this sort of openness—which was unusual for its day—would lead reporters and consumers to trust the railroad for its straightforwardness.

Lee codified this view in a "statement of principles" that same year. "Our plan," he wrote, "is, frankly and openly, on behalf of business concerns and public institutions, to supply the press and public of the United States prompt and accurate information concerning subjects which it is of value and interest to know about." As distinct from the press-agency approach to PR, Lee's view of the business saw the PR counselor as a kind of in-house journalist with the main purpose of disseminating factual information in order to influence public opinion. Many members of the press appreciated this perspective and turned to Lee for inside information about his clients that they could not find elsewhere.

Lee's work for John D. Rockefeller's Standard Oil Company during problems at one of the firm's plants in Ludlow, Colorado, provides an example of how Lee used his press contacts. Fifty-three workers, wives, and children died during violent clashes that took place when representatives of the United Mine Workers tried to organize laborers at the company. Countering statements by the union that Standard Oil had hired goons to kill striking workers, Lee put out the company's version of events, which was that the victims had died in an accident that they themselves had caused. He tried to build credibility for this version by having John D. Rockefeller Jr., who actually ran his father's company, pose in overalls with union leaders and families of the workers.

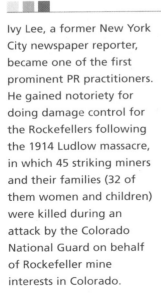

Ivy Lee, a former New York City newspaper reporter, became one of the first prominent PR practitioners. He gained notoriety for doing damage control for the Rockefellers following the 1914 Ludlow massacre, in which 45 striking miners and their families (32 of them women and children) were killed during an attack by the Colorado National Guard on behalf of Rockefeller mine interests in Colorado.

There were people both within and outside of the press who were sure that this account was false and that Lee had used his clout with journalists, and his reputation for openness, to circulate a deceitful version of the event deliberately. This criticism—that the purpose of public relations is to saturate the public with falsehoods that fit the needs of wealthy clients—is one that has dogged the business through the decades.

Public concern and awe about the alleged power of PR particularly developed when PR practitioner George Creel published his memoirs after World War I. Creel wrote of his wide-ranging campaign on behalf of the U.S. government to persuade the American people to rally around their country's entry into World War I. The Committee on Public Information, which he led, perfected many techniques that are common today—for example, the wide distribution of press releases to newspapers, the use of motion pictures to evoke emotional support for a cause, and the recruitment of local "opinion leaders" to convince people in their circles of friends of the correctness of the cause. His revelations caused a lot of people to become frightened of the power of PR "propaganda." Looked at differently, the idea that PR could successfully carry out such a major campaign using so many different techniques was great publicity for the young PR industry in search of corporate clients.

Edward Bernays and the "Science" of PR   Public relations professor James Grunig describes the approach to PR that both Ivy Lee and George Creel used as a "public information" model. Grunig notes that it is a **one-way model of public relations.** That is, this version of PR concentrates on sending persuasive facts that benefit the client to the press, without any attempts at systematically learning about the populations whom the client wants to persuade.

The first **two-way model of public relations** was championed by a practitioner named Edward Bernays beginning in the 1920s. A nephew of famed psychoanalyst Sigmund Freud, Bernays believed that it was essential to draw upon the social sciences to carefully shape the responses of audiences to the client's views of the world. Bernays is generally considered to be the first PR practitioner to offer all these ideas, together with a theory of how and why they would be successful. This "scientific persuader" business model is one reason PR historians call Bernays, rather than Ivy Lee, "the father of public relations." Other reasons are that Bernays wrote the first textbook on the subject and taught the first college course in public relations, at New York University in 1923.

Borrowing from philosophers of his day, Bernays justified public relations as a profession by emphasizing that no individual or group had a monopoly on the true understanding of the world; "truth" is relative, he said, and depends upon one's perspective. In his view, the role of the professional PR counselor was to lead general or particular audiences to see the truth from the client's perspective. He angered many people both inside and outside the PR business by his blunt assertions that PR practitioners could "engineer" the "consent" of audiences for their clients by learning to push the right psychological buttons. Nevertheless, throughout his long life (he died at 103), he championed the importance of PR for organizations and cultivated a reputation for doing work that was based on a careful, social-scientific study of the "nature and dynamics of public opinion," as he put it.

An example of this approach to PR is Bernays' decision to take into consideration children's attitudes toward soap and bathing when the Procter & Gamble company asked him to increase American families' use of Ivory Soap. His conclusion: change kids' attitudes toward bathing by promoting soap sculpture contests in schools. The idea was to get them to see Ivory Soap as a fun, friendly product that made washing and bathing inviting.

one-way model of public relations a model of PR that concentrates on sending persuasive facts that benefit the client to the press, without any attempts at systematically learning about the populations whom the client wants to persuade

two-way model of public relations first championed by a practitioner named Edward Bernays in the 1920s, this model of PR draws upon the social sciences to carefully shape the responses of audiences to the client's views of the world

Growth and Change in the PR Industry

The work and the writings of Ivy Lee, George Creel, and Edward Bernays inspired many people to get into the public relations business and many companies to hire them. During the Great Depression of the 1930s, large corporations turned to public relations counselors to help restore them to favor in the eyes of a population that was disillusioned with and angry at big business. Companies such as Carl Byoir & Associates and Hill & Knowlton came into existence and grew in this environment. World War II gave yet another boost to public relations as a needed activity in society. During this time of national crisis, the U.S. government called upon PR practitioners to use as many techniques as necessary—interpersonal and mass media, news and entertainment—to explain the war and encourage citizens to do their part to help win it.

The number of public relations practitioners continued to grow after the war, as companies and governments increasingly realized the importance of getting and keeping the public on their side. Two types of public relations practitioners emerged. The first worked in PR companies that acted as long- or short-term counselors to a variety of organizations. The second type, far more numerous than the first, worked full time doing PR for government agencies and private organizations. The titles of these practitioners—press officer, PR specialist, communications manager—depended on their activities and where they worked.

During the 1960s, public relations practitioners felt forced to rethink their approach to their audiences. The "scientific" model that they used, although two-way, saw target audiences as groups that were to be studied so that they could be manipulated. There was little room in public relations for suggestions that the government and corporate leaders for whom the industry worked would actually change their strategies or activities in response to research on what people wanted.

It was in the 1960s that that attitude began to change. It was a time of resistance, fueled by the Civil Rights Movement, the war in Vietnam, and a fiery consumerism movement. The latter had been sparked by *Unsafe at Any Speed*, a book written by Ralph Nader that revealed major safety problems in the rear-engine Chevrolet Corvair. The press—and public—outcry that accompanied these revelations became a PR nightmare for Chevrolet's parent, General Motors.

Ralph Nader began to earn his reputation as a crusader taking on major corporations 40 years ago, when he was catapulted into the national spotlight as a young Harvard law graduate whose stinging book *Unsafe at Any Speed* challenged the safety of the Chevrolet Corvair and American cars in general.

In the years that followed, many corporations, afraid that consumer anger would lead to lost sales, beefed up their customer relations programs. Some began an even more basic re-evaluation of their public relations strategies. Talk in the PR industry was of a more "symmetrical" two-way relationship with the public. In this approach to public relations, research would be used not only to shape messages aimed at audiences but also to figure out how the organization could position itself to most please its target audiences. The new role of public relations practitioners, in this view, would be to serve as go-betweens, as mediators between clients and the public.

Sometimes PR practitioners found that they did have the ears of top management and could, therefore, follow this business model. Much of the time, however, one of the other three models—that of press agent, public information distributor, and social-scientific persuader—held sway. Moreover, all of the models raise ethical issues that people in the industry and media-literate people outside it must confront. We explore this topic soon, as well. First, though, it will be useful to investigate the basic workings of the industry.

An Overview of the Modern Public Relations Industry

The number of individuals involved in public relations has risen sharply over the past few decades—from about nineteen thousand in 1950 to hundreds of thousands today. The Veronis Suhler Stevenson media consultancy estimates that in 2005 companies spent about $3.4 billion on public relations. Public relations in the twenty-first century is an activity in which most midsize and large companies are involved. Companies' involvement takes place in two ways, through direct involvement in corporate communication and through hiring a PR agency.

Corporate Communication Departments

Many large U.S. companies have public relations units, often called **corporate communication departments**. These departments typically have three functions: external relations, internal relations, and media relations. Let's take a look at each.

External Relations   External relations involve expressing the company's perspective to a variety of entities outside the organization. They include community groups, government officials, officials of various countries, and various citizen advocacy groups. Public relations employees also act as lobbyists for their company. That is, they try to convince state and federal legislators to pass certain laws that will benefit the company or to eliminate rules that may hinder the firm's progress.

Internal Relations   Internal relations involve being the voice of the company to employees, union groups, and shareholders. To that end, the external relations people may relate corporate newspapers, email notes, and (in really big companies) even television news shows about the company.

Media Relations   Journalists call many companies on a daily basis looking for information or wanting to speak to a particular executive. Media relations employees handle these calls, provide the answers, and coordinate the interviews

corporate communication departments public relations units that typically have three functions: external relations activities involve expressing the company's perspective to a variety of entities outside the organization; internal relations involve being the voice of the company to employees, union groups and shareholders; and media relations handle calls with journalists, provide the answers, and coordinate the interviews with executives

www.fleishmanhillard.com

agency holding companies firms that own large ad agency networks, public relations firms, and a multitude of branding, market research, and marketing communication firms

the Big Three the largest agency holding companies, including WPP, Omnicom, and Interpublic

with executives. They may also teach executives the best ways to act on camera or with a journalist.

Public Relations Agencies

While large companies may carry out day-to-day public relations agencies through in-house departments, they are also likely to hire "outside" PR companies for a variety of projects ranging from special lobbying to getting or controlling media exposure. According to the Public Relations Society of America, there are more than nine thousand PR firms currently plying their trade in the United States. Often these companies charge fees based on the number of hours that their employees work for a client. Sometimes clients make "retainer" deals with an agency, under which the company agrees to carry out a PR program at an agreed-upon rate per month.

Not all public relations companies do the same things. Large firms such as Fleishman Hillard help their clients with virtually any area of communication, including teaching their top executives how to speak on TV and in front of large groups. Many smaller public relations firms, however, specialize in a particular part of their industry's work. Examples of medium-size independent agencies that specialize include Healthstar (a healthcare agency); Cerrell Associates, a public affairs and environmental agency; and Integrated Corporate Relations, a company that helps firms speak to stock analysts, institutional investors, financial media "and other key corporate audiences."[2]

The biggest public relations firms are widely considered to be Fleishman Hillard, Weber Shandwick, Hill & Knowlton (which absorbed Carl Byoir in 1986), Burson-Marsteller, Incepta, Edelman Worldwide, BSMG Worldwide, Ogilvy PR, Porter Novelli, and Ketchum. All these companies with the exception of Edelman and Incepta are owned by one of the **agency holding companies** known as **the Big Three**: WPP, Omnicom, and Interpublic (see Table 16.1). As we saw in Chapter 15, agency holding companies are firms that own large ad agency networks, public relations firms, and a multitude of branding, market research, and marketing

Table 16.1	Major PR Firms Owned by the Largest Agency Holding Companies	
WPP	**Omnicom Group**	**Interpublic**
Burson-Marsteller	Fleishman-Hillard	Weber Shandwick
Hill and Knowlton	Ketchum	Golin Harris
Cohen and Wolfe	Porter Novelli	Rogers & Cowan
Ogilvy PR	Brodeur Worldwide	PMKHBH
Carl Byoir	Clark and Weinstock	Carmichael Lynch Spong
Dai Inchi	Cone	
Dewey Square		

Sources: Holding company websites.

communication firms. In fact, from the 1960s through the 1990s, the agency holding companies bought up 21 of the 25 largest PR firms.[3] The holding companies refuse to release data about the earnings, number of employees, or clients of the PR firms that they own. Their policy is based on the promise of total confidentiality for their clients, but it also means that it is difficult for outsiders to know what is going on within the industry's largest and most powerful firms.[4]

This gobbling up of the largest firms should not be surprising. Consistent with what we've learned about other media industries, the PR business in the 1980s and 1990s went through a period of rapid conglomeration and globalization. Big public relations firms merged with other big ones; big firms bought smaller ones, especially specialty firms; and public relations firms were bought by ad agency holding companies to create cross-industry communication firms. The number of such mergers has slowed in recent years, but the consolidation remains.

Globalization is a key to the activities of the biggest firms. Hill & Knowlton, part of the WPP holding company, reports on its website that it has 29 offices and 20 affiliated PR agencies across Europe, the Middle East and Africa.[5] It adds that it has a "vast presence" throughout South America, Central America, the Caribbean, and Mexico. As for the Asia Pacific, it says that, "For more than 40 years, through a network of wholly-owned offices and associates stretching from Beijing to Sydney and from Delhi to Tokyo, Hill & Knowlton has provided insights to guide clients through the opportunities and challenges of the world's fastest growing economic region." In these regions, as well as in the United States and Canada, it works for local firms as well as multinational conglomerates with the need for projecting influence with consumers and governments around the world.

Major Public Relations Activities

What are the demands on any public relations campaign? Why would companies (or, in some cases, individuals such as actors or authors) pay lots of money for representation by a public relations firm? The answer is that these clients need help in explaining their actions to government regulators, companies, and members of the public in ways that will help them complete a business deal, ensure them long-term favorable treatment, or get them out of trouble. A company that can help can be worth its high cost.

At the most basic level, PR practitioners help their clients:

- Understand the challenges that face them
- Formulate objectives that they would like to reach in meeting those challenges
- Develop broad approaches—**strategies**—for meeting the objectives
- Carry out particular activities—**tactics**—that put these strategies into action

strategies broad plans or approaches for meeting objectives

tactics the particular activities that put strategies into action

The uses for such expertise are wide. Here is how the Hill & Knowlton website describes to potential clients what the firm can do for them:

What does success look like to you? That's the first question we ask. We build up a clear picture of what you want to achieve. Then put in place whatever is needed to get that result.

There has been a huge increase in complexity, contradiction and uncertainty in all our lives and these magnify arguments in society. Brands, companies, governments and organizations face a new tougher set of challenges and the need for powerful, compelling communications has never been greater.

But effective communication is harder to achieve because of the increasing fragility of reputation, media fragmentation, audience proliferation and information overload. Now, more than ever, achieving measurable results—real brand and commercial results—demands that communicators meet a higher standard.

So how does Hill & Knowlton do superior quality work, even on the toughest tasks?

We start at an advantage: we have the desire to do so. We are unafraid of taking these tasks on, however difficult. We have a proven track record of doing so and delivering real brand and business outcomes.

We are also able to do so. As a firm, we are deliberately structured to meet even the most complex demands by connecting practice skills, sector expertise and geographic reach.

We put in place whatever is needed to help get the end result—your success.[6]

These statements about public relations are actually quite abstract comments about the importance of a company's ability to manage its environment. The way Hill & Knowlton and other PR firms put these environment-management goals into practice is through several categories of business activities.

The most prominent public relations activities are in these areas:

- corporate communications
- financial communications
- consumer and retail
- advanced technology and healthcare
- public affairs
- crisis management
- media relations

The labels indicate the broad landscape of activities in which public relations firms are involved and suggest the broad range of clients they serve. The biggest firms tackle many of these categories, though not always all of them. Moreover, some companies may combine someone or another category in organizing their expertise and personnel. As we sketch these activities below, notice that mass media are used consistently in every domain.

Corporate Communications

corporate communications the creation and presentation of a company's overall image to its employees and to the public at large

Corporate communications involves the creation and presentation of a company's overall image to its employees and to the public at large. Employers believe that if their workers share an understanding of company goals and activities, they will be both more satisfied with their jobs and more productive. Executives also want members of the public to believe that the company is a good corporate citizen, since that image might encourage purchases and help the firm get favorable treatment from local, state, and federal governments.

In many companies, a PR firm works in conjunction with human resources departments to carry out employee-relations tasks. These companies provide their employees with company handbooks, newsletters, and magazines. Experts in this area emphasize that all forms of interaction between a firm's leadership and its rank and file—even email—are vehicles for maintaining good morale and a sense of purpose. Some organizations with widely dispersed divisions even produce news programs just for employees that are sent via satellite to offices around the world.

The other side of corporate communications involves management's concern with the images of the company that are held by consumers. Even the largest companies often hire an outside public relations firm to help with their public image. Let's say that an automobile manufacturer wants to spread the notion that it is a technologically advanced, yet socially responsible company. PR counselors might suggest a number of activities that taken together would create that image in people's heads.

The PR company might create a booklet about the auto manufacturer's recent technological achievements that dealers can distribute. PR counselors might help the firm sponsor a solar-car race on college campuses. They might send the company's engineers to speak to reporters from around the country about the firm's cutting-edge work. PR specialists in digital communication may track the discussion of the firm on the Web and try to present responses on blogs, or videos on places such as YouTube, that position the firm in a positive light. Given a high enough budget, the company might even create a movie that explains scientific innovations relating to the car for science museums. Although such a film must be carefully positioned as a science film and not an ad, it can nevertheless associate the PR agency's client with innovations by showing its name a few times during the film as well as in the sponsorship credits.

Financial Communications

Financial communications involves helping a client's interactions with lenders, shareholders, and stock market regulators proceed smoothly. Sometimes the activities center around a particular client initiative. In 1995, for example, IBM turned to the financial PR firm Sard Verbinnen to support its attempt to buy Lotus Development Company. Lotus officials initially rebuffed the offer and characterized it as an unfriendly takeover attempt. IBM's public relations goal was to get out to government regulators, investors, and Lotus employees its position that folding Lotus into IBM would help both companies. They succeeded.

Financial communications work that is more typical than such one-shot initiatives revolves around top executives' need to keep investors' interest in their company's stock high. A low share price can make it tougher for the company to raise capital or make acquisitions, since sometimes payment is made in stock. Also, lenders and new investors judge a company at least in part by the performance of its stock.

The goal of a PR firm's financial communications specialists is to design a program that helps the firm communicate its value to its target audience. The nature of this communication program will depend on the specialists' analysis of the firm's image among investors. The specialists look at such factors as the company's size, its history, its financial record, industry identification, national or international scope, stock distribution, past communication efforts, and stock market recognition.

The idea is to shape a message about the company that is enthusiastic, yet falls within Securities and Exchange Commission guidelines that forbid misleading statements. Here are some of the types of work that a PR firm carries out to maximize a client's attractiveness to investors:

financial communications helping a client's interactions with lenders, shareholders, and stock market regulators proceed smoothly

- It prepares corporate and financial documents (such as annual reports) and financial fact books. Well-done photo layouts and well-turned phrases can make investors proud of their firm.
- It prepares company news releases and arranges interviews with financial journalists. When journalists, especially financial journalists, write seriously and positively about the firm, investors pay favorable attention to it.
- It coordinates shareholder meetings. A poorly run shareholder meeting can reflect badly on the ability of management to get a job done.
- It plans and arranges seminars, tours, and meetings with security analysts, portfolio managers, brokers, and professional investors. These events can help increase the visibility of the firm among the opinion leaders of the Wall Street community.

Consumer and Business-to-business Communication

On its website, H&K boasts that it helped its Brazilian beverage client Cerveceria Rio expand into Guatemala. It did it "using an intense media relations and opinion leaders campaign" to position the company "as socially responsible, focussing on the environment and benefits like job creation, market opening and international quality brands in a market dominated by a local monopoly beer producer and distributor."[7]

The PR firm also writes about its successful "central role" in convincing the International Olympics Committee to choose the city of London for the 2012 summer Olympics. H&K's website notes that the win for client London—"beating Paris, Madrid and Moscow—was one of the great sporting upsets of the past decade." How did it happen? "Through a carefully constructed international PR and lobbying campaign, H&K London, with the help of 27 global H&K offices, achieved twice as much overseas media coverage than the other 2012 bids combined." That media environment, says H&K, helped persuade the IOC.[8]

The first of these activities falls into the category of **consumer marketing**, whereas the second involves **business-to-business marketing**. Both activities center on using public relations, as opposed to advertising, tactics to project favorable images of the client and its products to businesspeople (the IOC) or general consumers, with the aim of getting them to buy. Advertising tactics typically involve purchasing media space or time in which to present short messages. PR practitioners, in contrast, use a wide variety of approaches to convince a client's target audience to see the client in a positive light. These approaches might range from sponsoring charities, to throwing glitzy parties for business clients, to giving away free promotional items, to instigating environmental action campaigns and providing scholarships for needy youngsters. PR staff members also work to get free media coverage of these activities. The aim is to build and maintain positive attitudes toward their client within its target audience and ultimately to pave the way for future sales.

This PR work usually supplements rather than substitutes for advertising. However, PR practitioners naturally argue that their work is at least as important as paid-for commercial messages. They see the goodwill generated by such events, and the news coverage of the events, as far more credible to target consumers than traditional advertising.

Advanced Technology and Healthcare Advanced technology and healthcare are two particularly high-profile industries for which both consumer and business-to-business PR take place. Advanced technology involves the prod-

consumer marketing the process of stimulating sales from people who are in their everyday, non-employee roles

business-to-business marketing the process of stimulating sales from people in their roles as company employees

ucts of computer manufacturers, silicon chip makers, and defense contractors, among others. The healthcare area includes hospitals, health-maintenance organizations, pharmaceutical firms, and provider organizations such as the American Medical Association and the American Nursing Association. Both industries have concerns related to government regulations; international sales; tensions with organizations that purchase their goods and services; and confused, angry, and even frightened members of the public. Companies in these industries hire PR firms to help them deal with these problems.

Take pharmaceutical companies as an example. They view public relations as invaluable for promoting both their products and their value to the nation. When it comes to their products, they start with the fact that prescription drugs reach the public through physicians. PR practitioners within the firm therefore work hard to establish relationships between physicians and the firm. Company representatives take physicians to lunch or dinner to explain the advantages of their products. They give doctors free samples. They send them articles from medical journals that mention the firm favorably. They may even give them medical instruments as gifts in the hope that such gestures will encourage their patronage.

Increasingly, pharmaceutical firms are also reaching out to the potential consumers of their products, hoping that they will urge their doctors to write prescriptions for these products. Some of this work is traditional advertising, carried out by ad agencies. A lot of PR work aimed at consumers goes on as well. Much of it is aimed at getting prescription drugs mentioned in newspapers and magazines and on TV programs.

Pharmaceutical companies need government approval of their drugs, and public relations employees play an important role in helping to sway government in a company's favor. Several years ago, Merck (a prominent pharmaceutical company) created a website called Merck Action Network to help its employees lobby Congress. Pharmaceutical firms also hire PR agencies for this work. One of the biggest public relations firms, Burson-Marsteller, argues that what it can offer companies is an ability to shape the opinions of people who count in the healthcare debates. "Burson-Marsteller's global Healthcare Practice is uniquely positioned to help clients navigate this complex medical, political, social and economic landscape, and in the process create and manage perceptions that deliver positive business results."[9] To carry out this persuasion process on many levels, it offers help for companies in the following areas:

- Pre-marketing of innovative drugs
- Public health-education campaigns
- Direct-to-consumer education and marketing
- Product lifecycle management
- Issues management
- Regulatory and policy issues
- Public education
- Grassroots communications
- Support and counsel on payer issues
- Medical education
- Obesity

Public Affairs

As you can see by the list above, in large PR firms, health units often join with public affairs specialists to achieve their government-oriented health goals.

public affairs PR public relations that focuses on government issues

Public affairs PR centers on government issues. Companies that depend on government contracts or that worry about lawmakers imposing regulations that will have a negative effect on them rely on public affairs experts to look out for their interests. Large firms may have their own public affairs departments within their corporate communication divisions; they may also hire outside firms to help them with this activity. Smaller companies may rely only on outside help. In both cases, the practitioners may apply their efforts in a number of directions.

communications PR sending out written materials to explain the firm's positions on various regulations

political action PR doling out money to individuals and groups that have been, or can be, politically helpful

government relations PR making sure that interactions between the firm and government officials are friendly

community involvement/corporate responsibility PR applying corporate funds to good works with the intention of gaining favor among elected officials as well as members of the public

international relations PR ascertaining the company's strategic interests relative to governments outside the United States and soliciting the help of the U.S. government in areas of difficulty. PR agencies also help foreign companies and governments establish good relations with American officials

- **Communications:** sending out written materials to explain the firm's positions on various regulations
- **Political action:** doling out money to individuals and groups that have been, or can be, politically helpful
- **Government relations:** making sure that interactions between the firm and government officials are friendly
- **Community involvement/corporate responsibility PR:** applying corporate funds to good works with the intention of gaining favor among elected officials as well as members of the public
- **International relations:** ascertaining the company's strategic interests relative to governments outside the United States and soliciting the help of the U.S. government in areas of difficulty; PR agencies also help foreign companies and governments establish good relations with American officials

Because these activities are so important to so many companies, an enormous number of PR practitioners have gotten involved in them. In the mid-1990s, one expert estimated that there were at the time some fifty thousand individual lobbyists and several hundred public relations agencies plying their trade in Washington, DC, alone.[10] There is no reason to think that the numbers are smaller today. These people exert much of their influence in the major corridors of power—the White House, the halls of Congress, and the myriad government agencies. As the Hill & Knowlton website puts it, "Commercial interests are intimately connected with and dependent on the decisions of governments and regulators… Competition for such influence is now more intense than ever and no organization can afford to be silent while others dominate the debate."

Public relations firms are sometimes paid to coordinate political lobbying campaigns that span nations. Take Hill & Knowlton's successful effort to help Botswana's diamond exports. With the rise of public concerns about "blood diamonds"—jewels that various armed groups in Africa used to finance their fighting—the Botswana government hired H&K to make sure that its diamonds would not be refused entry into key countries. H&K embarked on a major "information campaign" in Europe, the United States, the U.K. and Japan. It "generated support among Members of Congress, U.K. Parliamentarians, Members of the Japanese Diet and Members of the European Parliament as well as numerous media outlets. A number of political delegations from all four regions visited Botswana to meet with President Mogae and other Government Ministers at the highest level." The result, says H&K, is "significant political support for Botswana and its diamond industry and President Bush signed into law legislation favorable to Botswana in the form of the Clean Diamond Trade Act."[11]

Crisis Management

Public relations practitioners typically assume a reasonably stable client when they submit plans for public affairs, corporate communications, media relations, or financial relations in connection with advanced technology, healthcare, or other areas of business. It doesn't always work out that way, though, because the political or economic environment surrounding a client can sometimes change drastically. At other times, unforeseen events within the client's organization can spiral out of control and create a major problem. These changes are crisis situations, and a key area of the PR industry is set up to help companies manage crises.

Crisis management refers to the range of activities that helps a company respond to its business partners, the general public, or the government in the event of an unforeseen disaster affecting its image or its products. A classic example of crisis marketing in the healthcare area was Burson-Marsteller's handling of a 1982 crisis involving Tylenol for the manufacturer, Johnson & Johnson. Health officials named Tylenol as the product that had been used to kill seven people around Chicago. While law-enforcement and health officials were searching for the person or persons responsible (a culprit was never found), Burson-Marsteller's mandate was to make clear to the public that its client had America's best interest in mind and would take steps to ensure that Tylenol would be absolutely safe.

Large PR firms such as Burson-Marsteller not only specialize in helping companies when a disaster arises but also teach executives how to prepare for a crisis that might happen. These PR experts perform risk analyses and set up seminars to go over various scenarios with employees. In addition, they write instruction manuals, often in different languages, to help the staff of far-flung companies come together efficiently in times of emergency to try to keep the company's image from being tarnished.

Public relations campaigns that emerge from such thinking generally involve mass media. Although advertisements are one way to reach various constituencies, PR strategists believe that influencing the news about the client that these constituencies receive is more effective. The reason is that an advertisement so obviously represents the client's position that it may not be effective in convincing skeptics. In contrast, a properly influenced reporter will often present the client's interests as one legitimate side of a debate. Receiving this sort of legitimacy in the press can help rebuild a company's battered image with stockholders, with its employees, or with government regulators.

crisis management the range of activities that helps a company respond to its business partners, the general public, or the government in the event of an unforeseen disaster affecting its image or its products

Burson-Marsteller's handling of the 1982 Tylenol scare is considered a classic episode in crisis management.

Media Relations

media relations   all
dealings with reporters and
other members of media
organizations who might
tell a story about a client

You've undoubtedly noticed that many of the PR tactics that we've discussed involve the mass media. For PR practitioners, these activities fall under the heading of **media relations.** This term covers all dealings with reporters and other members of media organizations who might tell a story about a client. In some of these dealings, journalists take the initiative—for example, when reporters want to know what is going on during a company crisis. Other dealings with the media take place at the initiative of PR practitioners who want to spread the word about their clients' activities. Your university probably uses a PR staff to spread good news about research that is being carried out and about the success of its sports teams. The goal is to make both alumni and current students so proud of the institution that they will want to make financial contributions.

How do PR practitioners spread the news? Well, one of the most effective ways is by building good relationships with relevant journalists and editors. That way, the public relations staff will have the best chance at getting its organization's desired point of view across in a media story. Getting a desired viewpoint across usually means more than just answering incoming calls and sending out information. Most media relations work is proactive. So, in addition to providing interested parties with relevant facts and information for their stories, PR staff members have to go the extra mile by doing much of the journalists' job for them—for example, thinking up, selling, and sometimes even writing sample stories.

Of course, journalists have the final word on which stories they'll choose to rewrite and finally run. Although journalists do use stories initiated by PR firms quite often, they are often suspicious of their PR contacts. In addition, journalists have a large number of choices among PR-initiated stories, since so many companies are involved in media relations activities. These two circumstances create a lot of pressure on the PR practitioner. The next sections examine the public relations industry's production, distribution, and exhibition of material for the mass media in more detail.

Production in the Public Relations Industry

press release   a short essay
that is written in the form
of an objective news story

In general, the most basic product of a public relations firm's attempt to influence the media is the **press release.** A press release is a short essay that is written in the form of an objective news story. Because the goal is to get a reporter or editor to write about a particular aspect of the client's activities, a successful press release finds a hook in the client's tale that the reporter can use. PR practitioners know that reporters will dismiss as propaganda stories that simply tout the views of the firm's executives or present the firm's accomplishments. The trick, then, is to write a story with an angle that the journalist will see as interesting her or his audience and that can also include other firms and other points of view. A press release that is too obviously self-serving will rarely get picked up.

Because of the importance of knowing what attracts journalists to particular stories, PR firms and PR departments of organizations often hire former journalists as their press contacts. The Hill & Knowlton website proudly notes that "our staff includes seasoned former journalists from network radio and television, newspapers, news and business magazines. These specialists know and work with key editors, reporters, and writers and are up-to-date on the newest entrants into the media world, for example, interactive media developments." Hill & Knowlton underscores its ability to help clients systematically get into news stories that meet their business needs:

> We are skilled at message development in a rapidly changing news environment so our clients won't miss an opportunity to be part of a story. By being in touch with media on a daily basis, we find opportunities for clients to transform their messages into interviews and articles. And we know how to "shoot the angles" and find the best approach to any news organization for a story: through business pages, a feature section, an op-ed page, or an editorial calendar.

As these quotes suggest, writing press releases is just part of a PR firm's media duties. The company must also hire practitioners who can field questions from members of the press who come to them for stories. PR practitioners are also increasingly involved in coordinating the production of audiovisual materials that present their company's points of view to various constituencies. A mobile phone company, for example, might send a video to high schools to describe for students the new technologies it is using to keep rates down while providing the best service. A university might prepare a home page on the Internet that gives prospective students tours of the campus.

Companies involved in consumer public relations often decide to turn out their own TV "news" stories. For example, a computer chip manufacturer might create a short video for use on local news programs that shows how cutting-edge computer chips allow typical home users to perform an enormous number of tasks faster and make these tasks more fun. The trick to getting such a spot on the air is to make it seem like a "soft news" story created by the TV station. (See Chapter 2 for a discussion of soft news.) PR practitioners know that they should mention their client, the chip manufacturer, only in passing and show its logo only a couple of times. Subtlety is important. Overtly pushing the company and its products would be the kiss of death for a spot; a news show would never use it.

Distribution in the Public Relations Industry

Once materials for the media part of a public relations campaign have been prepared, the PR firm must distribute them to the proper publicity outlets. A **publicity outlet** is a media vehicle (for instance, a particular magazine, a specific TV interview program, a particular radio talk show) that has in the past been open to input from public relations practitioners. "Proper" in this case has two meanings: it refers to both outlets that reach the kinds of people the firm is targeting and outlets that are appropriate for the particular ideas, products, or services that the firm is trying to push.

Public relations practitioners keep lists of the publicity outlets in different areas that are appropriate for different types of products and for reaching different groups of people. When they are working on a particular campaign, they use these lists to determine which outlets to concentrate on and whom to contact. Sometimes only a press release will be sent. At other times, PR practitioners will be so familiar with the individuals involved that they will phone them directly. In fact, having good connections among media people, especially the press corps, is a crucial asset in the PR business.

publicity outlet a media vehicle (for instance, a particular magazine, a specific TV interview program, a particular radio talk show) that has in the past been open to input from public relations practitioners

Buzz Marketing

It's common knowledge that people you meet on the Internet might not be who they say they are. But not many people realize that Internet acquaintances might actually be paid salespeople who are trying to persuade you to buy something. This practice, called *buzz marketing*, is hailed by industry players as the next major step in online marketing. For companies that believe that word-of-mouth promotions are more successful than traditional advertising, the Internet offers a new solution. By paying people to visit chat rooms and message boards in order to hype a new product—usually a movie or musical act—marketers are able to create their own buzz without the general public knowing where it's coming from. In an effort to get the attention of teen consumers who are increasingly difficult to reach through traditional marketing avenues, Procter & Gamble created Tremor, an experimental teen marketing unit. The group identified 200,000 influential teens that have friends in different social circles and are more inclined to talk about products they use. The Tremor teens are given a sample of a product or service, sometimes before it has officially been released to the public, and they offer feedback about the product design or logo. Additionally, the panelists talk about the products with other teens, thus acting as word-of-mouth marketers of the P&G products. According to P&G, the teens are flattered to be part of the group and aren't asked to promote the prod-

ucts, which have included Cover Girl cosmetics, Old Spice deodorant, Valvoline and the DreamWorks SKG film *Win a Date With Tad Hamilton!*

Tremor's practices have raised a number of ethical issues, and the consumer advocacy group Consumer Alert filed a complaint with the Federal Trade Commission that alleges that Tremor targets teens with deceptive advertising. According to Gary Ruskin, executive director of Commercial Alert, P&G "are perpetrating large-scale deception upon consumers" because the teens they recruit aren't upfront about their connection with P&G when they talk about the products they've been given by the company. Tremor officials say this isn't the case because the teens aren't paid employees, but instead are given free samples of products and access to "cool" information. Commercial Alert, however, considers the teens paid marketers, and filed the suit with the FCC to determine whether the teens are upfront about their position as P&G employees when engaged in word-of-mouth marketing.

Sources: Zachary Rodgers, "Marketers Pay Their Way to the Youth Audience," The ClickZ Network, May 28, 2004, http://www.clickz.com/showPage.html?page=3360711, accessed 10/29/07; Bruce Horovitz, "P&G 'Buzz Marketing' Unit Hit With Complaint," *USA Today*, October 18, 2005, p. 1B.

Advanced distribution technologies have also become crucial to the PR industry during the past few years. PR practitioners use fax machines and email to send press releases. They track the discussions—the buzz—about their clients on chat rooms and blogs and they respond by paying people to go online and insert comments that reflect the positive spin that fits the aim of the PR campaign. They use satellite linkups to set up interviews with TV reporters from around the country and the world for their clients. They also use satellites to send video press releases to appropriate publicity outlets. These are packages of photographs, video clips, and interviews from which a reporter can choose to create a story. A video press release for a new adventure film, for example, might contain short clips from the movie, a background piece on the special effects used to make the movie, and separate as well as combined interviews with the male and female stars. Each piece would be designed to be used as a feature story on a local television newscast. The interviews will be shot in a way that allows news people in local stations to create the impression that the discussion was created exclusively for their broadcasts.

Exhibition in the Public Relations Industry

"But," you may ask, "why do TV and print journalists use this material? Haven't we learned that journalists pride themselves on their objectivity and independence?" Good question. The answer lies in the costs of news reporting in the print and electronic worlds. *Costs* here relates both to monetary expense and the amount of time involved. Reporting stories totally from scratch can cost a lot of money. It can also cost reporters an enormous amount of time, time that they often do not have because of deadlines.

Imagine how many reporters the *Washington Post* would have to assign to the Departments of State, Agriculture, Treasury, and the other cabinet-level divisions of the U.S. government if there were no systematic way to find out about meetings, speeches, reports, and other materials emanating from each. The paper could not afford to ferret out all that information, but it doesn't have to do so because each department's public relations division provides it with the basic schedule. Moreover, in key parts of the government, such as the State Department, public relations representatives summarize key issues for reporters and answer their questions.

In addition to allowing news organizations to allocate fewer journalists to government agencies, these press briefings help the journalists budget their time efficiently. The briefings allow the journalists to gather the basic information they need in order to write their daily stories. They can then spend the rest of their time following up issues raised by the briefing so that their story will stand out from those of other journalists who were also at the meeting.

It's clear, then, that an important reason that public relations so successfully permeates the mass media is that PR practitioners help the media get their work done. Communication professor Oscar Gandy calls this sort of help to media organizations and their personnel, **information subsidies.** The term means that PR people's help with information is akin to advancing money and time. Faced with a beautifully done clip that is part of a video press release, a TV station's news director may genuinely believe that some of the material in that clip is interesting enough to warrant a story. She or he also knows that the low cost of putting that spot on the air will offset the extra expenses of a locally produced story.

information subsidies
the time and money that PR people provide media practitioners that helps them get their work done

White House Press Secretary, Dana Perino, serves as the official liaison between the White House and members of the press, acting as a spokesperson and PR representative for the president and delivering the daily White House briefing.

Protecting Stars from Journalists

Influencing media coverage of the stars has become an industry in itself. Virtually all well-known actors and actresses hire publicity agents to shape their image through favorable press coverage. Pat Kingsley stands at the top of this industry. The founder of PMK, the most powerful public relations company serving the entertainment industry, she has a special ability to influence the press. An important reason is that she represents many of the stars who are most sought after by the press. In 2007, at the age of 75, Kingsley stepped down as CEO of PMK but continues to work creatively with clients through the company. She currently represents stars such as Michael Mann, Jodie Foster and Sally Field to name a few. To get to them, a reporter has to go through her. She has also represented Tom Cruise, Courtney Love, Arnold Schwarzenegger, Nicole Kidman, and Al Pacino in the past.

Kingsley is known to use her position to manipulate magazine and TV executives to cover her clients the way she wants. She often demands that in exchange for an interview, the executives use interviewers and photographers that *she* chooses. Invariably these will be most sympathetic to her clients. Sometimes strong-willed companies refuse her demands. NBC's *Today* program, for example, cancelled an appearance by actress Calista Flockhart when Kingsley informed the producers that the actress, her client, wouldn't discuss why she is so thin.

Actor Will Smith (right) and Publicist Pat Kingsley arrive for the premiere of *Hustle & Flow* in Hollywood.

Often, though, Kingsley's tactics prevail because the bounty she offers—exclusive cover pictures and magazine-show interviews of actors—can bring media firms lots of money. Journalism critics are troubled by her clout. What do you think?

Sources: Bernard Weinraub, "Gatekeeper to the Stars," *New York Times*, May 3, 1999, p. E1; Borys Kit, "Kingsley Does it Her Way in New PMK Role," *Hollywood Reporter*, September 27, 2007.

The danger of information subsidies from a client's standpoint is that they may not be used. News organizations receive many more offerings from PR firms than they have room for, and journalists can often be quite selective. The most successful, and most expensive, public relations practitioners work hard to establish strong relationships with members of the press to help grease the path to coverage. In the mid-1990s, the *New York Times* reported that Sard Verbinnen, the head of the PR agency with that name, would get pieces in the news by currying favor with journalists: giving an "exclusive" about a deal or an interview with a chief executive to one newspaper and then offering a behind-the-scenes look at a transaction to a reporter of another paper that did not get the original exclusive. By doing that, he would be able to call on both sources to help him with coverage when he needed it.

For Verbinnen or anyone else, though, coverage doesn't always work out the way the PR practitioner wants it to. Good journalists do their own independent investigations of material suggested by a press release or some other PR initiative.

Consequently, what begins as an attempt to present a favorable image of a firm or a person may backfire if the reporter finds material that contradicts the original report.

The Rise of Integrated Marketing Communication

Public relations, then, is potentially very useful but also unpredictable when it comes to getting a company, person, or product specific and favorable mass media coverage aimed at a particular audience. In contrast, advertising can provide quite predictable media coverage (since the advertiser pays for time or space), but it can be quite a bit more expensive than public relations work and may not be as persuasive as PR stories that appear as news.

During the past several years, the awareness that advertising and PR can complement each other has led executives to attempt to coordinate the two types of activities to get the best of both worlds. Some have dubbed this approach **integrated marketing communications (IMC)**, or sometimes simply **marketing communications**. The goal is to blend (integrate) historically different ways to communicate to an organization's various audiences and markets. Under the best of circumstances, integration means creating a campaign that sends different, yet consistent, messages around particular themes to present and potential consumers of a firm's products as well as to its employees, to the companies that sell to it and buy from it, and to government regulators.

In addition to traditional advertising and public relations, IMC often brings three related activities into its mix: branded entertainment, database marketing, and relationship marketing. Let's take a look at each.

Branded Entertainment

Branded entertainment involves associating a company or product with media activities in ways that are not as obviously intrusive as advertisements. The word "branded" refers to linking the firm or product's name (and personality) with an activity that the target audience enjoys. The three most common forms of branded entertainment are event marketing, event sponsorship, and product placement.

Event Marketing **Event marketing** involves creating compelling circumstances that command attention in ways that are relevant to the product or firm. These activities typically take place at sports and entertainment venues, via mobile trailers or road shows that publicize products, and in malls (see Figure 16.1). If you've gone to Florida or Texas for Spring Break, you may have seen companies such as Hawaiian Tropics set up bikini pageants. Often, these activities get more elaborate. In 2005, for example, the Bank of America wanted to promote its new "Keep the Change" savings program: when a customer makes a purchase with the BOA credit card, the amount is automatically rounded up to the nearest whole number and the difference is transferred to the customer's saving account. To emphasize the savings the company placed a 20 foot red sofa in high-traffic areas of several cities. Company representatives urged visitors to sit on the sofa and search in it for tokens redeemable for prizes. The idea was to reinforce the Keep-the-Change message that small change can yield big rewards.[12]

integrated marketing communications (IMC) a type of PR, the goal of which is to blend (integrate) historically different ways to communicate to an organization's various audiences and markets

branded entertainment associating a company or product with media activities in ways that are not as obviously intrusive as advertisements. The word "branded" refers to linking the firm or product's name (and personality) with an activity that the target audience enjoys. The three most common forms of branded entertainment are event marketing, event sponsorship, and product placement

event marketing creating compelling circumstances that command attention in ways that are relevant to the product or firm. These activities typically take place at sports and entertainment venues, via mobile trailers or road shows that publicize products, and in malls

event sponsorship situation in which companies pay money to be associated with particular activities that their target audiences enjoy or value. Examples include concerts, tours, charities, and sport

Figure 16.1
Shares of Spending on Consumer Event Marketing, 2005

PQ Media, a research firm, estimates that spending on event marketing in 2005 reached $27.94 billion. This table presents PQ's estimate of where that money was spent.

Source: PQ Media, cited in Veronis Suhler Stevenson, Communication Industry Forecast, 2006–2010, p. 172.

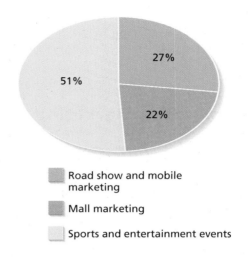

Road show and mobile marketing

Mall marketing

Sports and entertainment events

product placement agreement in which a firm inserts its brand in a positive way into fiction or nonfiction content

barter products used in movies and TV shows are provided by the manufacturer to the producers for free in exchange for the publicity

product integration the act of building plot lines or discussions for talk shows and reality TV around specific brands

Event Sponsorship In event marketing, the product is the focus of the activity. By contrast, **event sponsorship** occurs when companies pay money to be associated with particular activities that their target audiences enjoy or value. Examples include concerts, tours, charities, and sport. In the United States, Anheuser-Bush, PepsiCo, General Motors, Coca-Cola and Nike were the top sponsors in 2005.[13] Sport has long been the largest entertainment-sponsorship category, with NASCAR and the NFL particular draws for companies.

Product Placement **Product placement** takes place when a firm manages to insert its brand in a positive way into fiction or nonfiction content. Think of AT&T and Coca-Cola on the TV series *American Idol*, or the appearances of particular car models in movies, TV shows, and video games that you've seen. Traditionally, products used in movies and TV shows were provided by the manufacturer to the producers for free in exchange for the publicity. That is called **barter**, and it still represents the largest percentage. In recent years, paid product placement has been increasing, though observers say it still takes place less often than barter (see Figure 16.2). Some marketers have paid producers of so-called reality shows and talk shows to build plot lines or discussions around their brands. The activity is called **product integration**, and it is increasing, particularly online. In 2007, for example, Stouffer's Lean Cuisine sponsored an online comedy series with episodes three to five minutes long that consistently involved the company's products in the action.[14]

Figure 16.2
Shares of Paid vs. Barter Product Placement, 2005

PQ Media estimates that overall product placements on television were valued at $5.98 billion. The "barter" amount is an estimate of the value of the product given to the show and/or what the company's publicity on the show would cost if it were charged for advertising minutes.

Source: PQ Media, cited in Veronis Suhler Stevenson, Communication Industry Forecast, 2006–2010, p. 172.

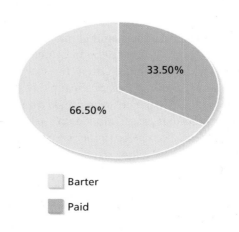

Barter

Paid

Database Marketing

Database marketing involves the construction of lists of customers and potential customers that can be used to determine what those people might purchase in the future. The marketer then contacts the people on these lists with advertising or PR messages. Although the use of lists in marketing dates back to at least the 1800s, the past few decades have seen a huge growth in the use of computers to store information about people and their habits. This growth in marketers' ability to cross-link and retrieve huge amounts of information about people took place at the same time that the introduction of toll-free numbers, more efficient mailing techniques, and fast delivery firms made shopping from home easier than ever. These changes led to a huge increase in targeted persuasion through direct marketing.

database marketing practice involving the construction of lists of customers and potential customers that can be used to determine what those people might purchase in the future. The marketer then contacts the people on these lists with advertising or PR messages

Relationship Marketing

Relationship marketing involves a determination by the firm to maintain long-term contact with its customers. This can be done by regular mailings of custom magazines, brochures, or letters or through frequent user programs that encourage repeat purchases and keep the person connected to the firm.

relationship marketing involves a determination by the firm to maintain long-term contact with its customers through regular mailings of custom magazines, brochures, or letters or through frequent user programs that encourage repeat purchases and keep the person connected to the firm

Agency Holding Companies

Every one of these activities has a growing presence in media. Moreover, marketers are linking them to one another and to advertising and public relations activities in their attempts to reach target audiences in as many ways as possible. While independent firms are certainly involved in these businesses, as we have noted both here and in Chapter 15, many of the major companies in each area are owned by one of the five **agency holding companies** that have emerged in the past twenty years to control the major advertising, public relations and marketing communication firms around the globe. These firms are deeply involved in advertising, PR and other media activities in the United States—WPP owns the JWT agency network, for example. They are also involved in helping their multinational clients with all sorts of communication services—from media research to branding—in a multitude of countries.

agency holding company a firm with global reach that owns full-service advertising agencies, specialty agencies, direct-marketing firms, research companies, and even public relations agencies

WPP provides an example of the scope of these firms. It has 100,000 employees, 2,000 offices in 106 countries, billings of $55.6 billion, and profits of $10.9 billion. Its website states that:

Within WPP, clients have access to all the necessary marketing and communications skills. [WPP] is structured as follows:

Advertising

Global, national and specialist advertising services from a range of top international and specialist agencies, amongst them Grey Worldwide, JWT, Ogilvy & Mather, The Voluntarily United Group and Y&R

Media investment management

Above- and below-the-line media planning and buying and specialist sponsorship and branded entertainment services from Mediacom, Mediaedge:cia, MindShare and others

Information, insight and consultancy

WPP's Kantar companies, including Research International, Millward Brown and many other specialists in brand, consumer, media and marketplace insight, work with clients to generate and apply great insights

Public relations and public affairs

Corporate, consumer, financial and brand-building services from PR and lobbying firms Burson-Marsteller, Cohn & Wolfe, GCI, Hill & Knowlton, Ogilvy Public Relations Worldwide and others

Branding and identity

Consumer, corporate and employee branding and design services, covering identity, packaging, literature, events, training and architecture from Addison, Enterprise IG, Fitch, Lambie-Nairn, Landor, The Partners, and others

Direct, promotion and relationship marketing

The full range of general and specialist customer, channel, direct, field, retail, promotional and point-of-sale services from 141 Worldwide, A. Eicoff, Grey Direct, OgilvyOne, RTC Relationship Marketing, rmg:connect, VML, Wunderman

Healthcare communications

CommonHealth, Grey Healthcare Group, Ogilvy Healthworld, Sudler & Hennessy and others provide integrated healthcare marketing solutions from advertising to medical education and online marketing

Specialist communications

A comprehensive range of specialist services, from custom media and multicultural marketing to event, sports, youth and entertainment marketing; corporate and business-to-business; media, technology and production services

The company states that they "encourage and enable our companies of different disciplines to work together, for the benefit of clients and the satisfaction of our people." In most cases, it seems, clients use only one or two of WPP's companies. However, the firm also notes that, "A recent development, and for a minority of clients, WPP itself can function as the 21st century equivalent of the full-service agency, acting as a portal to provide a single point of contact and accountability."[15] In the case of a few, the holding company's largest clients—Ford and IBM are examples—the entire holding company works to achieve the best possible marketing communication results across the gamut of new and old media.

Media Literacy and the Persuasion Industries

Using integrated communications, new media, and target marketing efficiently has for several years been a cutting-edge concern of executives and creative personnel in the persuasion industries. If we step back from their day-to-day challenges and turn our attention to what their activities mean for the larger society, we confront very different concerns regarding these aspects of mass media today. Here we will highlight three worries about the role that the persuasion industries in general, and public relations in particular, are playing in the contemporary world. Two of the issues—one on conglomerates and the other on target marketing—carry forward two themes that we've seen throughout this text. The other—on truth and the hiding of influence—centers on the persuasion industry but also relates to the media system as a whole. As you might imagine from everything you've learned in this book (we hope!), all three issues are interrelated.

Truth and Hidden Influence in the Persuasion Industries

We start with the issue of truth and hidden influence. We will review the issues together to make the point that when a company deliberately hides the sponsor or power behind a media message, its action very much represents a problem of truth. Leading an audience to get the wrong impression of a story by encouraging it to believe that the story had one author rather than another is very close to promoting a lie.

Critics of the persuasion industries argue that their practitioners can never really be truthful because their business is to portray people, products, and organizations purposefully in ways that do not reveal problems. Advertising and PR practitioners respond that there is nothing wrong with emphasizing the positive aspects of something, as long as what is emphasized is not demonstrably wrong. Their critics reply that it is possible to create an ad or public relations campaign that deceives even when the text in the ad is legally truthful. Think about all the ads you see in which men are attracted to women—or women are attracted to men—who use certain products. Technically, these ads are truthful because they never contend that using these products will automatically make you alluring. Still, the critics argue, there is a fundamental deception in photographs that imply over and over that material goods will make you sexually attractive.

A leading professor of public relations, Scott Cutlip, worries about the industry's problem with the truth. He admonishes that, "reality says ... that the public relations counselor should be seen as the advocate ... not as a dedicated purveyor of truth to serve the public interest. Many counselors serve as advocates of institutions and causes in the same way that lawyers serve clients, to put the best possible face on the facts they can, regardless of merit or truth." He adds that because of this, "as many PR practitioners shade the truth and deal in obfuscation as purvey accurate, useful information to the public via the news media."

Executives in the persuasion industries usually shrug off such complaints. They argue that not being able to suggest that a product will bring psychological benefits or that a company has a warm personality would seriously hamper their ability to create successful advertising and public relations campaigns. When it comes to ethics, they focus, instead, on circumstances that can hurt them legally or economically. Can the government hold them legally liable for deception in an ad or PR campaign? Are competitors making incorrect statements about their products that are likely to hurt sales? Will unscrupulous practices by competitors lessen the credibility of their industry and prompt government investigations?

To make the rules clear and to deter government regulators from intruding on their business, industry leaders have turned to self-regulation. Most notably, they have created professional associations that develop norms for the industry and write them into codes of good practice. The American Association of Advertising Agencies and the American Advertising Federation, for example, both circulate similar standards that their members promise to follow. Among their many prohibitions are misleading price claims and misleading rumors about competitors. In a similar vein, the Direct Marketing Association (DMA) compiles lists of "deceptive and misleading practices" that its members should avoid. The Public Relations Society of America also has a code of "professional standards" that includes such topics as safeguarding "the confidences of present and former clients," not engaging "in any practice which tends to corrupt the integrity of channels of communication or the processes of government," and "not intentionally" communicating "false and misleading information."

Some critics contend that public relations and advertising firms violate these rules every day. Moreover, no society can force a nonmember to even pay lip service to its rules. Attempts at enforcing complaints by one member against another do exist. If, for example, one advertiser believes that another advertiser is harming its products by broadcasting misleading or inaccurate commercials, the advertiser can complain to the National Advertising Division (NAD) of the Council of Better Business Bureaus. The NAD will investigate. If it finds the advertiser's work misleading, the charge is reviewed by the National Advertising Review Board (NARB), which consists of industry practitioners. That industry body will act as a referee and make a report on its conclusion available to the public. It will also suggest how the commercial might be changed. For the sake of self-regulation, advertisers typically agree to follow these suggestions.

Although critics of advertising point out that industry disputes over accuracy are only the tip of the iceberg of problems with the truthfulness of information, they acknowledge that at least an ad is out in the open for its audience to see. A person who sees an advertisement almost always knows that it is an ad and so can be sensitive to claims and images that may be exaggerated or are unsupportable. Public relations, in contrast, is by its very nature an activity that hides its creators from public view. That, say its critics, makes it almost impossible to examine its products for accuracy as one might examine an ad. In fact, as we noted previously, this is one of the persuasive advantages over advertising that PR practitioners cite. People naturally suspect an ad, they say, whereas in the case of PR they don't even know it is taking place.

The negative social effects of public relations' hidden nature can be considerable. As we have seen, many media activities today are influenced by the information subsidies that various types of public relations agencies supply. These subsidies can be as seemingly harmless as products placed by companies into entertainment or as clearly outrageous as orchestrating fake atrocity stories to sway the news media, the public, and Congress to support a war. In all cases, though, public relations practitioners are manipulating mass media content to their clients' commercial and political benefit without letting the public know about it.

People who don't consider the impact of public relations on news and entertainment may believe what they see because they trust the news or entertainment organization that they think is the source. They may act against their best interests because they don't realize that the real source of the story is quite different from the one that they believe instigated and interpreted it. At the same time, people who *are* aware of the power of PR over the mass media typically will still not be able to figure out whether or not a PR organization is behind a particular story, or how or why. The result of this inability to know may be a cynical view that everything in the media is tainted by PR and therefore is not what it seems. In either case, the hidden nature of public relations may have an unfortunate, even corrosive, effect on the way people understand those parts of society that are outside their immediate reach.

Targeting and the Persuasion Industries

The past two decades have seen tremendous growth in the ways in which advertisers and public relations practitioners create, combine, and use lists to reach target audiences. Americans have told pollsters in growing numbers that they worry that too much information about their lives and personal preferences is being exchanged without their knowledge. It also seems clear to direct marketers that people believe that they are receiving too much junk mail and too many telemarketing calls. Moreover, both pollsters and academics predict that the growth of online services will increase worries about privacy as more ways of collecting personal information (such as cookies) are created. (See Chapter 15 for a discussion of privacy.)

Another possible consequence of targeting that deserves mention involves marketing and media firms surrounding people with content that speaks so much to their own particular interests that those people learn little, and care little, about parts of society that do not relate directly to those interests.

Critics such as Joseph Turow (yes, this book's author) point out that the ultimate aim of twenty-first century marketing is to reach consumers with specific messages about how products and services tie in to their personal lifestyles. Target-minded media help advertisers and public relations practitioners do this by building what we might call "primary media communities." These are not real-life communities where people live. Rather, they are *ideas of connection* with certain types of people that are formed when viewers or readers feel that a magazine, radio station, or other medium harmonizes with their personal beliefs and helps them to understand their position in the larger world.

Some media are going a step beyond trying to attract certain types of people. They make an active effort to exclude people who do not fit the desired profile. This makes the community more "pure" and thereby more efficient for advertisers. Media executives accomplish this objective simply by purposefully placing material in their medium that they know will turn off certain types of people while not turning off others (and maybe even attracting them). The message of target radio stations, cable networks, and magazines is often that "this is not for everyone."

Jackass, a coarsely funny reality program, filled this role for MTV during the early 2000s when the network was working to position itself as a young adult-oriented channel. *Tell Me that You Love Me*, a graphically sexual show on HBO, did the same for that network. These programs had so much "attitude" that they sparked controversy among people who were clearly far removed from their "in" crowds. Executives involved with scheduling the shows hoped that the controversies surrounding them would crystallize the channels' images and guarantee that the channels would be sampled by the people they wanted to attract. The executives acknowledged that they also expected these "signature shows" to turn off viewers whom they didn't want in their audience.

An even more effective form of targeting goes beyond chasing undesirables away. It simply excludes them in the first place. **Tailoring** is the capacity to aim media content and ads at particular individuals. *Mass customization*, *clickstreams*, *web cookies*, and *interactive TV navigators* are terms we have learned that reflect an awareness that the long-term trajectory of media and marketing is toward customizing the delivery of content as much as possible. With just a little effort (habit, actually), people can listen to radio stations, read magazines, watch cable programs, surf the Web, and participate in loyalty programs that parade their self-images and clusters of concerns. With seemingly no effort at all, they receive offers from marketers that complement their lifestyles. And with just a bit of cash, they can pay for technologies that can further tailor information to their interests—through highly personalized news delivery, for example.

Customized media are still pretty expensive, so PR and advertising practitioners mostly reserve them for upscale audiences. The high cost of introducing

tailoring the capacity to aim media content and ads at particular individuals

interactive television that can customize programming for large populations has caused the process to take longer than some media firms would like. But the competition to develop interactive technologies has not faded. The momentum toward creating targeted spaces for increasingly narrow niches of consumers is both national and global.

All signs point to a twenty-first century in which media firms can efficiently attract all sorts of marketers by offering three things. One is **selectability**—the ability to reach an individual with entertainment, news, information, and advertising based on knowledge of the individual's background, interests, and habits. The second is **accountability to advertisers**—the ability to trace an individual's response to a particular ad. The third is **interactivity**—the ability to cultivate a rapport with, and the loyalty of, individual consumers.

Some companies, to be sure, will want to get their brands out to the broad population as quickly as possible and will find mass market media useful. They will support the presence of billboards, supermarket signs, and the few TV shows that still draw mass audiences, such as the Super Bowl, the World Series, and the Miss America Pageant. This kind of programming helps create immediate national awareness for a new car model, athletic shoe, or computer.

But even mass media will be targeted in the future. For example, Warner Brothers Television might try to reach as many people as possible to offset the high production costs of a TV movie about a nuclear disaster. Yet it might achieve this by public relations activities aimed at targeting people's personal TV navigators with tailored plot synopses—one for people who are interested in science, and a different one for people who like the lead actor. At present, it is cheaper to customize news and information programs than to customize top-of-the-line entertainment. For instance, NBC might tailor its election coverage to viewers with different interests. Consumers who care about foreign affairs, agricultural topics, or environmental issues might be able to choose the network feed that features detailed coverage of election results in their special-interest area.

Over and over, some media critics predict, different versions of news will present different social distinctions to different people. And even when the content is the same (as in the nuclear-disaster movie), producers will aim different PR and ad campaigns to different types of people or different media communities, thus encouraging the perception that the viewing experience in America is an enormously splintered one. The net result will be to push separation over collectivity.

These critics argue that it will take time, possibly decades, for the full effects of the emerging media world to take shape. Even when the new media environment does crystallize, consumers will still seek media that are not specifically aimed at them. Increasingly, though, the easiest path will be to go with the customized flow of media and marketing paraphernalia. For you and me—individual readers and viewers—this segmentation and targeting portends terrific things. If we can afford to pay, or if we're important to PR or advertising sponsors who will pick up the tab, we will be able to receive all the news, information, and entertainment we like. Who would not welcome media and sponsors that offer to surround us with exactly what we want when we want it?

A critical view of the situation would argue that while this may benefit us as individuals, it could potentially have a harmful effect on society. Customized media driven by target-oriented advertising and PR allow, even encourage, individuals to live in their own personally constructed worlds, separate from people and issues that they don't care about and don't want to be bothered with. This kind of segmentation of the population diminishes the chance that individuals who identify with certain groups will even have an opportunity to learn about others. In a soci-

selectability the ability to reach an individual with entertainment, news, information, and advertising based on knowledge of the individual's background, interests, and habits

accountability to advertisers the ability to trace an individual's response to a particular ad

interactivity the ability to cultivate a rapport with, and the loyalty of, individual consumers

ety in which immigration is increasing ethnic variation and tensions, the goal should not be to use the media to connect people. Rather, the media should encourage people to do the hard work necessary to become aware of other cultures' interests, to enjoy various backgrounds collectively, and to seek out media interactions to celebrate, argue, and learn with a wide spectrum of groups in the society.

The problem, say media critics, is that the advertising and public relations industries are working with media firms to go in the opposite direction. Their goal is to ease people into media environments that comfortably mirror their own interests so that they can be persuaded more easily. Media practitioners see nothing wrong with this approach. Media analyst Sut Jhally is among those who disagree. He argues that the tendency of the persuasion industries to play to people's self-interests rather than the larger society's interests is quite predictable. "The market," he says, "appeals to the worst in us ... and discourages what is best in us."[16]

Conglomerates and the Persuasion Industries

The growth of mass media and advertising/public relations conglomerates is an additional development that disturbs critics of the persuasion industries who worry about what they consider antisocial uses of hidden persuasion and target marketing. They worry that these huge companies will find it productive to work together to make integrated marketing communications an even greater part of the creation of media content than it is now.

What do they mean? We saw earlier that advertising agency holding companies own several public relations agencies as well as ad agencies and research firms. The biggest of the holding companies, such as Omnicom and WPP, own hundreds of companies with offices around the world. If you go to WPP's website or the website of the other Big Five agency holding companies, you will confront a bewildering array of firms. (To get an idea, take a look at the jumble of names in Figure 16.3, which reproduces the WPP holdings search page.) As we noted earlier in this chapter, they control the great percentage of top international PR firms.

As we discussed in Chapter 15, agency holding firms control about 65 percent of all the revenues brought in by the top 500 advertising agencies. Numbers such as these suggest that WPP, Omnicom, Publicis, Havas and Interpublic—with their huge media buying operations and their impressive direct marketing and branding firms—have enormous impact on the mass media. Unfortunately, however, it is very difficult to gauge their impact. They are secretive when it comes to discussing their integrated cross-media activities. The advertising, PR, and media trade press, which writes a lot about the individual advertising and PR firms that they own, rarely writes about the strategies and cross-discipline activities of the holding companies. Consequently, an area of the media business that is quite powerful is difficult to examine critically.

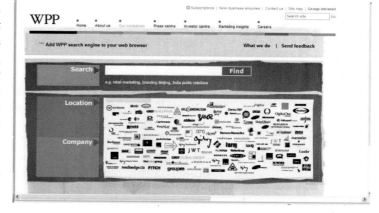

Figure 16.3
WPP's Holdings Search Page
Source: http://www.wpp.com/WPP/Companies#, accessed October 29, 2007

Realistically, it would be impossible for all the companies to work together. Nevertheless, the leaders of communications services firms emphasize that their clients will see a benefit from using a company that has general advertising, specialty advertising, general public relations, specialty public relations, media planning, media buying, and research services under one corporate umbrella. WPP puts the idea this way: "We encourage and enable our companies of different disciplines to work together, for the benefit of clients and the satisfaction of our people."

The development of huge persuasion-industry conglomerates is too recent for media scholars to have published a lot on the topic. Still, we might imagine that the trend would worry critics who condemn the hidden nature of public relations and excessive target marketing. "What is going on," they would probably say, "is that the most visible media outlets, which are owned by a few companies, are increasingly working in the interests of wealthy commercial clients with PR and ad agencies that themselves are owned by just a few companies. The mutual goal of these conglomerates is to shape media environments so that they will persuade individuals wherever they go to buy products and ideas, whether they know it or not."

It should be taken as a warning to media literate citizens to be aware of the situation when huge conglomerates have the capacity to present consumers with targeted content through media everywhere they go without the consumers knowing that they are being specifically targeted, by whom, and why. Some of the hidden persuasions may be useful—for example, if a cosmetic story on a news channel customized to you is pitched to your skin color, you may like the idea and not care who is behind it. Some hidden persuasion, however, may be disturbing to your sense of honesty and your ability to navigate the world critically. Consider, for example, a magazine story or news spot about a new electronic device you are thinking of buying. The piece pretends to be open-minded but really serves the interests of a particular manufacturer. Consider, too, an editorial on a newspaper site that appears to have been sent to everyone as the voice of the paper but was really written to harmonize with the political beliefs of people like you so that you will feel good about the paper and continue to subscribe.

The example of the editorial is based on a rumor and is certainly rare, if it exists yet at all. Nevertheless, it is a development that could take place. Some publishers might argue that there is really nothing wrong with personalized editorials and that they would be great for business. Ethical concerns about not telling people directly that the editorials are customized may not be considered an impediment to this activity at all because, after all, the editorial was written by an employee of the paper, not someone from outside the organization. Others may respond that presenting readers with editorial opinions without informing them that other readers received different editorials (or an editorial on the same topic but with a different view-point!) is contrary to the editorial tradition of laying an opinion out for all to read or hear.

The electronic-device example, in contrast, is extremely common. Much product evaluation in the mass media is deeply influenced by, if not the creation of, public relations activities. So is much writing about culture and politics, from news spots about fashion and travel to magazine profiles of corporate and political leaders. We may feel chagrined that we don't understand the hidden intentions of these stories even as we use them in our daily lives to make sense of how we think about other worlds and where we stand in ours.

CHAPTER REVIEW

For an interactive chapter recap and study guide, visit the companion website for *Media Today* at www.routledge.com/textbooks/mediatoday

QUESTIONS FOR DISCUSSION AND CRITICAL THINKING

1 Why would contemporary public-relations practitioners be more likely to invoke Edward Bernays than P. T. Barnum as a respected figure for their industry?

2 Explain how the consumer marketing and media relations categories of public relations activities will often overlap.

3 Why and how might a company use event marketing with respect to video games? Can you discover a situation in which that took place?

4 If reporters have as negative a view of PR as they typically say they do, why is the use of public relations output so widespread?

INTERNET RESOURCES

Public Relations Society of America (http://www.prsa.org/)

Based in New York City, the PRSA calls itself the world's largest organization for public relations professionals. This website presents an overview of the association's activities, with areas dedicated to jobs, networking, professional development, and publications.

The Museum of Public Relations (http://www.prmuseum.com/bernays/bernays_1929a.html)

This is an online overview of important figures and events in the history of public relations. It includes a video of Edward Bernays reflecting on his career and on the public relations profession.

Omnicom Group (http://www.omnicomgroup.com/)

One of the Big Five agency holding companies, Omnicom has a website that illustrates the astonishing breadth of advertising, public relations, and other marketing communications firms that such conglomerates own. The site includes case studies and a map of the firm's offices around the world.

KEY TERMS

You can find the definitions to these key terms in the marginal glossary throughout this chapter. Test your knowledge of these terms with interactive flash cards on the *Media Today* companion website.

accountability to advertisers	marketing communications
advertising tactics	media relations
agency holding companies	one-way model of public relations
barter	press release
branded entertainment	product integration
corporate communication	product placement
corporate communication departments	public affairs
	public relations
crisis management	publicity
database marketing	publicity outlet
event marketing	relationship marketing
event sponsorship	selectability
information subsidies	strategies
integrated marketing communications (IMC)	tactics
	tailoring
interactivity	

CONSTRUCTING MEDIA LITERACY

1   "Product placement is a harmless way to pay for a TV program, a movie, or some other form of media content." Do you agree with this statement? Why or why not?

2   Do you agree with the argument that placing persuasive messages into entertainment, information, or news programs without telling the audience is akin to lying? Why or why not?

3   "As media increasingly become digital and interactive, advertising, PR and marketing communications of various kinds will be used to follow individuals wherever they go and send them tailored messages." Do you agree that this can happen? Is it something to worry about? Why or why not?

4   If public relations activities are likely to be more believable to an audience than advertising, why do so many companies use advertising?

CASE STUDY Exploring Marketing Communication

The issue As this chapter and Chapter 15 note, traditional forms of public relations and advertising are two of the several approaches that marketers are using to reach target audiences. As we saw, *marketing communication* is the broad term that media and marketing personnel give to approaches that represent a wide gamut from product placement to event sponsorship and from buzz marketing to viral marketing. This case study will give you the opportunity to examine forms of marketing communication and their relation to mass media.

The method A convenient way to investigate marketing communication is to visit the website of the Big Five agency holding companies: Omnicom, WPP, Interpublic, Publicis, and Havas. Go to the website of one of these firms and explore the companies that they own that do not fall under the labels *advertising* or *public relations*. These companies are sometimes listed as "marketing services" firms. The websites typically describe these firms and give examples of their work.

Choose two of these subsidiaries that seem to deal with a form of outreach to consumers. An example might be a company that is involved in helping marketers develop "brand" images of products. Another might be interested in using the Internet to track consumer's discussions of products and decide how to react to those discussions. Still another might be involved in deciding how to use mobile media to reach customers.

For each of the two marketing-communication firms describe: (1) the work the company carries out, (2) why the company says it is important, (3) in what mass media the company's activities (or the result of the company's activities) take place, and (4) in what areas of the world the firm operates. Then bring an example of each firm's activities from the website and/or from another periodical. In view of what you've learned about each firm, comment on how you think firms that carry out the two forms of marketing communication they represent are influencing the media materials audiences receive.

Epilogue

The Need For Transparency

Let us not look back in anger, nor forward in fear,
but around in awareness.

JAMES THURBER

It is easy to sit up and take notice.
What is difficult is getting up and taking action.

AL BATTISTA

As the examples we've explored throughout this text suggest, a central concern in the developing world of media today relates to people's lack of knowledge about what powers and what agendas lie behind the news, information, and entertainment that confront them across so many channels. People find it difficult to keep straight the maze of ownerships, alliances, and entanglements that affect so much of what we see and hear today. Corporate relationships within Sony affect the circulation of music and characters from video games to recordings to movies and back. Internal organizational rearrangements within Time Warner affect everything from the lineup of your local cable system to the kinds of news you get from *Time, Sports Illustrated, Entertainment Weekly,* and CNN—and how the news travels across these sources.

The easy (and understandable) reaction is to simply throw up your hands and say "It's impossible to follow these issues. All of the media world is manipulated in ways we can't understand, so I'll just distrust it all." This is the path of cynicism. It's an approach that will make you suspect everything you come across in almost every medium, even when that response isn't warranted. You'll shut yourself off from good stuff, and you won't learn to be an educated critic of what is going on in the media or the world at large.

The other, better reaction is to apply the media literacy skills that you've learned through this book in two ways. The first way is to try to keep track of the connections among the media that produce, distribute, and exhibit the materials that you use on a regular basis. What companies create these materials? Are they part of conglomerates, joint ventures, or alliances of other types? Do any of these relationships explain the kinds of content you are getting in the ways you are getting them? If so, can you figure out whether any corporate strategies might explain why these materials and not others are being released—and why one perspective and not another is being used?

The second way to apply your media literacy skills is to take action. Work with individuals or groups to convince mass media organizations to be more open about the corporate connections that go into creating their content. Demand that entertainment and news organizations routinely disclose when press releases or public relations organizations are involved in instigating or contributing to a story. Insist that media firms prominently divulge all product placements. Write to executives of public relations and "communication services" firms to demand that they work with media companies to inform the public when the products of their activities make it into print, on the air, on film, or on the Web.

It's unlikely that media executives will take kindly to such requests. It's also unlikely that the government can force these sorts of corporate disclosures, because that is probably unconstitutional. Yet consistent, insistent pressure by various public groups for openness about the ways in which marketers and PR practitioners influence twenty-first century mass media might, over time, lead corporations to provide substantially more background about the commercial and political influences behind the mass media than the public now receives. Working toward more transparency in media today might well pay off big for what we all know about media tomorrow.

Notes

Part I

Chapter 1

1 The data in this paragraph come from Paul Verna, "Recorded Music: Digital Falls Short," *Emarketer Report*, February 2007.

2 See Elihu Katz, Jay Blumler, and Michael Gurvitch, *Uses of Mass Communication by the Individual* (Beverly Hills: Sage Publications, 1974).

3 John Harlow, "Brad and Jennifer Marry Among Friends at Sunset," *Sunday Times* (London), July 30, 2000, via LexisNexis.

4 For a summary of this work, see Lawrence Grossberg, Ellen Wartella, and D. Charles Whitney (eds), *MediaMaking* (Thousand Oaks, CA: Sage Publications, 2005), pp. 277–297.

5 See Elihu Katz, Jay Blumler, and Michael Gurvitch, *Uses of Mass Communication by the Individual* (Beverly Hills: Sage Publications, 1974).

6 Quoted in UCLA Graduate School of Education & Information Studies, "Literacies at the End of the Twentieth Century" (2000), page 5.

7 Sources consulted for these ideas include the following: Rene Hobbes, "The Seven Great Debates in the Media Literacy Movement," which can be found at http://interact.uoregon.edu/MediaLit/FA/mlhobbs/hbindex.html; Robert Kubey (ed.) *Media Literacy in an Information Age* (New Brunswick, NJ: Transaction Publishers, 1997); Ladislau Semali, *Literacy in Multimedia America* (New York: Falmer Press, 2000); Len Masterman, *Teaching the Media* (London: Comedia, 1985); Chris M. Worsnop, "20 Important Reasons to Study the Media," which can be found at http://interact.uoregon.edu/MediaLit/FA/articles/worsnop/cwindex.html; and Patricia Aufterheide, "Media Literacy: A Report of the National Leadership Conference on Media Literacy" (Washington, DC: Aspen Institute, 1992).

Chapter 2

1 Veronis Suhler Stevenson, *Communications Industry Forecast 2006–2010* (New York: Veronis Suhler Stevenson, 2006), p. 33.

2 *American Heritage Dictionary of the English Language*, fourth edition (Boston: Houghton Mifflin, 2006).

3 John Cawelti, *Six Gun Mystique* (Bowling Green, Ohio: Popular Culture Press, 1975).

4 Joseph Turow, *Playing Doctor* (New York: Oxford University Press, 1989).

5 See the "Bride and Prejudice" entry in the IMDB.com database: http://imdb.com/title/tt0361411/, accessed 3/6/08.

6 Interview with James Gandolfini on TV Guide website, http://www.hbo.com/sopranos/, accessed 3/6/08.

7 Sara Nelson, "The Price Isn't Right," *Publishers Weekly*, March 27, 2006, p. 5.

8 Peter Jensen, "'She Was Really Brave,'" *Baltimore Sun*, April 23, 1999, p. E1.

9 Dennis Loy Johnson, "Ex-staffer Bluntly Delivers Buzz About 'New Yorker,'" *Arizona Republic*, January 30, 2000, p. J5.

Chapter 3

1 Guy Stern, "The Burning of the Books in Nazi Germany, 1933: The American Response," Simon Wiesenthal Museum of Tolerance website accessed 3/6/08, http://motlc.wiesenthal.com/resources/books/annual2/chap05.html#4

2 Radio Free Europe/Radio Liberty, "Uzbekistan: Government Increases its Blocking of News Websites," *BBC Monitoring World Media*, April 26, 2007.

3 "'Online Freedoms Under Threat,' says Amnesty," *Guardian Unlimited*, June 6, 2007.

4 *Time Inc.* vs. *Hill*, 385 U.S. 374, Supreme Court of the United States, 1967.

5 *Virginia State Board of Pharmacy et al.* vs. *Virginia Citizens Consumer Council, Inc. et al.*, 425 U.S. 748 (1976).

6 Jennifer Davies, "Judge Won't Halt Jack's Ads Poking Fun at Rival," *San Diego Union-Tribune*, July 3, 2007.

7 Ira Teinowitz, "Ad Groups Fume in Tobacco War," *Advertising Age*, February 19, 2007.

8 Caitlin Roman, "European Commission Posts Video to New Online Channel with Sex Scenes from Popular Movies," *The Associated Press*, July 3, 2007.

9 Margaret Bernstein, "A Call to Clean Up," *Cleveland Plain Dealer*, May 10, 2007, p. E1.

10 Bill Katovsky and Timothy Carlson, *Embedded: The Media at War in Iraq* (Guilford, CT: The Lyons Press, 2004).

11 Paul Weidman, "Rules of Embeddedness," *The Sante Fe New Mexican*, September 10, 2004, p. 32. See also Kevin Smith, "The Media at the Tip of the Spear," *Michigan Law Review* 102, 6 (May 2004), p. 1329.

12 Julie Bisceglia, "Parody and Fair Use," *Entertainment Law Reporter*, May, 1994.

13 "Weird Al Yankovic Still Weird and White and Nerdy," *The New Zealand Herald*, March 2, 2007, via Nexis.com.

14 Sheila Anthony, "Let's Clean Up the Diet-ad Mess," *Advertising Age*, February 3, 2003, p. 18.

15 Editorial, "Selling Junk Food to Toddlers," *New York Times*, February 23, 2006, p. 26

16 Jim Puzzanhera, "FCC to Fine Univision $24 million," *Los Angeles Times*, February 25, 2007, p. A20; and Bloomberg News, "FCC Approves $12 Billion Sale of Univision Communications," *New York Times*, March 28, 2007, p. C6.

17 Law quoted from "The Video Privacy Protection Act," Electronic Privacy Information Center, website accessed 1/31/07, http://www.epic.org/privacy/vppa/

18 http://www.ftc.gov/os/ar961/overview.shtm

19 "Microsoft Hits Rival's Deal for DoubleClick," *Los Angeles Times*, April 16, 2007, p. C3.

20 Federal Trade Commission, "Federal Trade Commission Closes Google/DoubleClick Investigation," FTC website, December 20, 2007, accessed 6/3/08, http://www.ftc.gov/opa/2007/12/googledc.shtm

21 T. Christian Miller, "Contractors Outnumber Troops in Iraq," *Los Angeles Times*, July 4, 2007. p. A1.

22 See, for example, Don Van Natta, Jr., Adam Liptak, and Clifford J. Levy, "The Miller Case," *New York Times*, October 16, 2005, p. 1.

23 No author, "*Dancing with the Stars* triumphs at Family Television Awards in the U.S.," Indiantelevision.com, December 5, 2006, accessed 3/3/08, http://www.indiantelevision.com/headlines/y2k6/dec/dec39.htm

24 Clifford Christians, Kim Rotzoll, and Mark Fackler. *Media Ethics*, fourth edition (White Plains, New York, Longman: 1995).

Chapter 4

1 Walter Lippmann, *Public Opinion* (New York: Harcourt Brace & Company, 1922), p. 29.

2 Lawrence Grossberg, Ellen Wartella, and D. Charles Whitney, *MediaMaking: Mass Media in Popular Culture*, (Thousand Oaks, CA: Sage Publications, 1998), p. 307.

3 Lawrence Grossberg, Ellen Wartella, and D. Charles Whitney, *MediaMaking: Mass Media in Popular Culture* (Thousand Oaks, CA: Sage Publications, 1998), p. 349.

4 Robert W. McChesney, *The Problem of the Media: U.S. Communication Politics in the 21st Century*. (New York: Monthly Review Press), 2004.

5 Edward S. Herman and Robert W. McChesney, *The Global Media* (Washington, DC: Cassell, 1997), p. 1.

6 Lynn Spigel, "TV and Domestic Space Travels." Speech at Cornel University School of Architecture.

7 Ellen Seiter, "Television and the Internet." In J. Turow and A. Kavanaugh, *The Wired Homestead: An MIT Press Source book on the Internet and the Family* (Cambridge, MA: MIT Press, 1997), page 102.

Part II

Chapter 5

1 Cited in Joseph Turow, *Breaking Up America* (Chicago: University of Chicago Press, 1997), p. 64.

2 Simon Barker-Benfield, "Clustering Consumers not an Exact Science, but 'Generalizations Work' in Marketplace," *Florida Times-Union*, p. F1–12. http://www.jacksonville.com, accessed 8/21/2000, http://www.jacksonville.com/tu-online/stories/082100/bus_3737001.html.

3 Charles Pappa, "Fun Times on Business Front; Led by the Editor Who 'Gets It,' 'Fortune' Soars with Cheeky Copy," *Advertising Age*, March 12, 2001, p. S-10.

4 MTV Base, "About MTV Base," at http://www.mtvbase.com/mtvbaseafrica.com/terms/about.jhtml

5 MTV Base, "About MTV Base," at http://www.mtvbase.com/mtvbaseafrica.com/terms/about.jhtml

6 Elizabeth Guider, "Stars and Gripes Forever," *Variety*, November 13–19, 2006, p. 1.

7 See the transcript, "Media Diversity: Minority Media Owners Conquering New Frontiers: NTIA Minority Ownership Roundtable," *National Telecommunication and Information Administration*, July 18, 2000: http://www.ntia.doc.gov/ntiahome/minoritymediaroundtable/transcript.txt; accessed 3/7/08, also data at http://www.ntia.doc.gov/opadhome/minown98/toc.htm, accessed 3/7/08; and http://www.ntia.doc.gov/reports/97minority/overview.htm, accessed 3/7/08.

8 Henry Jenkins, *Convergence Culture* (New York: New York University Press, 2006), p. 23.

Chapter 6

1 Robert Iger, "Letter to Shareholders," *2006 Disney Annual Report*, p. 5.

2 Douglas Frantz and Catherine Collins, *Celebration, U.S.A.: Living in Disney's Brave New Town* (New York: Henry Holt, 1999).

3 The Walt Disney Company 1999 *Annual Report*, p. 3.

4 Craig Simons, "China Park's Rocky Debut Deflates Ambitious Disney," *Atlanta Journal-Constitution*, February 11, 2007, p. 1F.

5 Katie Allen, "Financial: Film Industry," *Guardian*, June 11, 2007, p. 27.

6 *The Walt Disney Company 1999 Annual Report*, p. 8.

7 Daniel Morrissey, "From One Paper Did a Media Empire Grow," *Toronto Star*, March 11, 2001, p. 1.

8 *News Corporation 2006 Annual Report*, p. 6.

9 *News Corporation 2006 Annual Report*, p. 5.

10 *News Corporation 2006 Annual Report*, p. 6.

11 *News Corporation 2006 Annual Report*, p. 9.

12 Clement James, "Google to Face AdWords Jury Trial," May 14, 2007, VNUNet.com, via Nexis.com; and Simon Avery, "How Google is Shaking Up the Ad World," *Globe and Mail*, June 8, 2007, accessed 3/7/08, http://www.reportonbusiness.com/servlet/story/RTGAM.20070608.wrgoogle08/BNStory/Business/home

13 Simon Avery, "How Google is Shaking Up the Ad World," *Globe and Mail*, June 8, 2007, accessed 3/7/08, http://www.reportonbusiness.com/servlet/story/RTGAM.20070608.wrgoogle08/BNStory/Business/home

14 "Letter from the Founders," http://www.google.com/corporate/

15 "Display Advertising" "Company Overview," http://www.google.com/corporate/ entry in Wikipedia, accessed on 7/18/07.

16 Caroline Daniel and Maija Palmer, "Google's Goal is to Organize Your Daily Life," *Financial Times*, May 23, 2007, p. 1.

17 http://www.google.com/corporate/

18 Caroline Daniel and Maija Palmer, "Google's Goal is to Organize Your Daily Life," *Financial Times*, May 23, 2007, p. 1.

Part III

Chapter 7

1 Martha Worboy, "Potter Finale Deathly Hallows Breaks Record for Book Sales in Canada," *Edmonton Journal*, July 24, 2007, p. D3.

2 R.R. Bowker, "Bowker Reports U.S. Book Production Rebounded Slightly in 2006," Press Release, May 31, 2007.

3 Daisy Maryless, "Bestsellers 06," *Publishers Weekly*, January 8, 2007, p. 24.

4 Kenneth Musante, "Wading into Amazon's Murky Water," CNNMoney.com, December 19, 2007; via Nexis.com

5 Lynn Andriani and Rachel Deahl, "At These Prices It's Hit or Miss," *Publishers Weekly*, January 29, 2007, p. 36.

6 Lynn Andriani, "Believe It or Not," *Publishers Weekly*, June 4, 2007, p. 22.

7 James Forsyth, "Technology File," *The Business*, August 4, 2007, via Nexis.

8 Jim Milliot, "Harry's in a League of His Own," *Publishers Weekly*, June 30, 2007, p. 4.

Chapter 8

1 National Association of Newspapers, "Number of U.S. Daily Newspapers," http://naa.org/thesource/14.asp#number, accessed 8/15/07.

2 E&P staff, "CEO of Global Free Paper Publisher Metro International Stepping Down," *Editor & Publisher*, February 13, 2007, via Nexis.

3 Veronis Suhler Stevenson, *Communications Industry Forecast 2006–2010* (New York: Veronis Suhler Stevenson, 2006), p. 493.

4 Joshua Chaffin, "Press Ahead," *Financial Times*, August 11, 2007, p. 16.

5 See, for example, Veronis Suhler Stevenson, *Communications Industry Forecast 2006–2010* (New York: Veronis Suhler Stevenson, 2006), p. 507.

6 Veronis Suhler Stevenson, *Communications Industry Forecast 2006–2010* (New York: Veronis Suhler Stevenson, 2006), pp. 501, 504.

7 Nat Ives, "Industry's Survival Plan: Unite," *Advertising Age*, May 14, 2007, p. 22.

8 Veronis Suhler Stevenson, *Communications Industry Forecast 2006–2010* (New York: Veronis Suhler Stevenson, 2006), p. 500, 502.

9 Veronis Suhler Stevenson, *Communications Industry Forecast 2006–2010* (New York: Veronis Suhler Stevenson, 2006), p. 484.

10 Quoted in Leslie Taylor, "Yeah, We're Going Digital—but with Dailies in Tow," *Advertising Age*, June 5, 2006, p. 4.

11 Jennifer Saba, "Counting on the Web," *Editor & Publisher*, May 1, 2007, via Nexis.

12 Quoted in Hamilton Nolan, "Analysis—Web Model Not Necessarily Papers' Savior," *PR Week*, March 12, 2007, p. 10.

13 Hiley Ward, "The Future of the Newspaper Industry," *Editor and Publisher*, May 3, 1997, p. 49.

14 Quoted in Hamilton Nolan, "Analysis—Web Model Not Necessarily Papers' Savior," *PR Week*, March 12, 2007, p. 10.

Chapter 9

1 Nat Ives, "Moore Admits It's Not Easy, but Wants You to 'Stay Calm,'" *Advertising Age*, May 28, 2007, p. 16.

2 Richard Campbell, Christopher Martin, and Bettina Fabos, *Media and Culture* (Bedford: St Martin's, 2008), p. 315.

3 Magazine Publishers of America, *Magazine Handbook 2007–2008*, p. 5, accessed 2/19/07, http://www.magazine.org/content/Files/magHandbook07_08.pdf

4 "Custom Publishing," Hachette Fillipachi website: http://www.hfmus.com/hfmus/our_platforms/custom_publishing

5 "*Seventeen* 2006 First-Half Marketing Opportunities," *Seventeen* website accessed 8/23/07, http://www.seventeenmediakit.com/r5/showkiosk.asp?listing_id=477078&category_code=mark&category_id=31774

6 http://www.smartmoney.com/mag/mediakit/pdf/R2.pdf, accessed 8/28/07.

7 http://www.autoweek.com/files/awmk_06/whatisaw.html, accessed 8/28/07.

8 *Advertising Age*, advertisement insert for Condé Nast magazines (including *Men's Vogue*), July 16, 2007, after p. 20.

9 *Advertising Age*, May 28, 2007, p. 5.

10 *Advertising Age*, advertisement insert for Condé Nast magazines, July 16, 2007, after p. 20.

11 *National Geographic*, "Uniform of the Day," *Advertising Age*, September 25, 2000, p. S6.

12 "*Seventeen* 2006 First-Half Marketing Opportunities," *Seventeen* website accessed 8/23/07, http://www.seventeenmediakit.com/r5/showkiosk.asp?listing_id=477078&category_code=mark&category_id=31774

13 "Maxim Radio," Sirius.com, accessed on 8/20/07.

14 Veronis Suhler Stevenson, *Communications Industry Forecast, 2006–2010* (New York: Veronis Suhler Stevenson, 2006), p. 578.

15 American Publishers Association, "Retail Update," November 2006. http://www.magazine.org/content/Files/retail%20update.pdf accessed 8/26/07.

16 Veronis Suhler Stevenson, *Communications Industry Forecast, 2006–2010* (New York: Veronis Suhler Stevenson, 2006), p. 578.

17 Steve Cooper, "Start Your Own Magazine," *Entrepreneur Magazine*, June 2006, and online: http://www.entrepreneur.com/article/printthis/160238.html

18 Robert Ames, quoted in "How Auto Mags are Turning Reviews into Digital Ad Revenue," *Advertising Age*, January 8, 2007, p. 4.

Part IV

Chapter 10

1 Erik Barnouw, *A Tower in Babel* (New York: Oxford University Press, 1966), p. 129.

2 "Universal Music Group: Overview," http://new.umusic. com/overview.aspx, accessed 8/31/07.

3 Veronis Suhler Stevenson, *Communications Industry Forecast 2006–2010* (New York: Veronis Suhler Stevenson, 2007), p. 408.

4 Recording Industry Association of America, "2006 Year-End Shipment Statistics," accessed 3/10/08,http://76.74.24.142/ 6BC7251F-5E09-5359-8EBD-948C37FB6AE8.pdf

5 "MySpace Announces First Nationwide Concert Tour," August 29, 2007. Accessed via Nexis.com

6 John Jurgensen, "Singers Bypass Labels for Prime-Time Exposure," *Wall Street Journal*, May 17, 2007, p. B1.

7 John Jurgensen, "Singers Bypass Labels for Prime-Time Exposure," *Wall Street Journal*, May 17, 2007, p. B1.

8 Nielsen SoundScan, "2007 U.S. Music Purchases Exceed 1.4 Billion," *Business Wire*, January 3, 2008, via Yahoo Finance.

9 Ta-Nehisi Coates, "Hip-Hop's Down Beat," Time.com, August 17, 2007, accessed 9/3/07.

10 Voice of America News (VOA English Service), "U.S. Business, Political Leaders Target Product Piracy," August 27, 2007, via Nexis.

11 Bruce Einhorn and Xiang Ji, "Deaf to Music Piracy; Chinese Search Engines Make it Easy to Steal Net Tunes," BusinessWeek Online, August 31, 2007, via Nexis.

12 Ryan Underwood, "UT Student Bases Internet Piracy Lawsuit on Privacy Grounds," *The Tennessean*, August 31, 2007, via Nexis.

13 http://riaa.com/faq.php

Chapter 11

1 Arbitron Company, "Radio Today: 2007 Edition," p. 91; http://arbitron.com/downloads/radiotoday07.pdf, accessed September 7, 2007.

2 Veronis Suhler Stevenson, *Communications Industry Forecast, 2006–2010* (New York: Veronis Suhler Stevenson, 2006), p. 332–333.

3 Jon Coleman, in Joseph Turow, *Breaking Up America: Advertisers and the New Media World* (Chicago: University of Chicago Press, 1997), p. 100.

4 "ABC Music Radio: 24-Hour Formats," http://www. abcradionetworks.com/Article.asp?id=341457, accessed September 8, 2007.

5 Veronis Suhler Stevenson, *Communications Industry Forecast, 2006–2010* (New York: Veronis Suhler Stevenson, 2006), p. 343.

6 Ibiquity, "What is HD Broadcasting?" http://www. ibiquity.com/hd_radio, accessed September 10, 2007.

Chapter 12

1 Dade Hayes, "Powering Up the Last Indie," *Variety*, August 27–September 2, 2007, p, 1.

2 Richard Simpson, "Borat's Pounds £24m payday," *Daily Mail*, November 21, 2006, p. 19, via Nexis.

3 Pamela McLintock, "Summer's Bottom Line," *Variety* August 20–26, 2007, p. 42.

4 Anne Thompson, "An Unfair Target," *Variety*, May 28–June 3, 2007, p. 5.

5 Dade Hayes, "Powering Up the Last Indie," *Variety*, August 27–September 2, 2007, p. 1.

6 Michael Cieply, "The Afterlife is Expensive for Digital Movies," *The New York Times*, December 23, 2007, Section 3, p. 6.

7 Amazon.com movie download section, accessed September 15, 2007.

8 Veronis Suhler Stevenson, *Communications Industry Forecast, 2006–2010* (New York: Veronis Suhler Stevenson, 2006), p. 382.

9 MPAA, "Internet Piracy," http://mpaa.org/piracy_internet.asp, accessed on 9/15/07.

Chapter 13

1 Veronis Suhler Stevenson, *Communications Industry Forecast 2006–2010* (New York: Veronis Suhler Stevenson, 2007), p. 270.

2 Stan Schatt of ABI Research, quoted in David Lieberman, "Cable Channels Undergo TV Makeovers," *USA Today*, September 11, 2007, p. 1B.

3 David Lieberman, "Cable Channels Undergo TV Makeovers," *USA Today*, September 11, 2007, p. 1B.

4 David Bauder, "Nielsen to Triple TV Sample," *Associated Press*, September 26, 2007, via Nexis.

5 John Dempsey, "Stations Game for Something New," *Variety*, June 25–July 8, 2007, p. 17.

6 Daisy Whitney, "Could Steve Whitfield be This Year's Rachael Ray?" *Advertising Age*, May 4, 2007, p. S12.

7 Elizabeth Guider, "Stars and Gripes Forever," *Variety*, November 13–19, 2006, p. 1.

Chapter 14

1 This brief historical sketch is based on a wide variety of articles in Wikipedia as well as on Steven Kent, *The Ultimate History of Video Games* (New York: Three Rivers Press, 2001).

2 Veronis Suhler Stevenson, *Communications Industry Forecast, 2006–2010* (New York: Veronis Suhler Stevenson, 2006), p. 438.

3 Sprint Nextel News Release, "Sprint Nextel Announces 4G Wireless Broadband Initiative," August 8, 2006, http://www 2.sprint.com/mr/news_dtl.do?id=12960, accessed 10/16/07.

4 NDP Group, "2006 US Video Game and PC Game Retail Sales," Press Release, January 19, 2007, http://www.npd. com/press/releases/press_070119.html accessed on 10/14/07.

5 Veronis Suhler Stevenson, *Communications Industry Forecast, 2006–2010* (New York: Veronis Suhler Stevenson, 2006), p. 415.

6 Veronis Suhler Stevenson, *Communications Industry Forecast, 2006–2010* (New York: Veronis Suhler Stevenson, 2006), p. 415.

7 Todd Spangler, "Verizon to Put Game Face on FiOS TV," *Multichannel News*, October 3, 2007, http://www.multi channel.com/article/ca6486821.html, accessed on 10/13/07.

8 See, for example (no author), "Sony Shrinks the Price of Its Portable Device," *St Petersburg Times*, April 4, 2007, p. 3D, via Nexis.

9 Veronis Suhler Stevenson, *Communications Industry Forecast, 2006–2010* (New York: Veronis Suhler Stevenson, 2006), p. 414.

10 Todd Spangler, "Verizon to Put Game Face on FiOS TV," *Multichannel News*, October 3, 2007, http://www.multichannel.com/article/ca6486821.html, accessed on 10/13/07.

11 Michael Sansbury, "X-Box Outplays Rivals and Movies," *The Australian*, October 11, 2007, p. 36.

12 Langston Werz, Jr., "Video Games," *Charlotte Observer*, October 8, 2007, p. 3D.

13 "Video Game Genres," Wikipedia, http://en.wikipedia.org/wiki/Video_game_genres, accessed 10/14/07.

14 "Adventure Game," Wikipedia. http://en.wikipedia.org/wiki/Adventure_game, accessed 10/14/07.

15 "Educational Game," Wikipedia: http://en.wikipedia.org/wiki/Educational_game, accessed 10/11/07.

16 Laurie Sullivan, "Beyond In-game Ads," *Advertising Age*, June 18, 2007, p. 1.

17 (No author) "Advergaming," *Brandweek.com*, July 23, 2007, via Nexis.

18 Robert Gray, "Play the Brand," *Marketing*, July 25, 2007, p. 33.

19 http://www.americasarmy.com/, accessed 10/15/07.

20 Beth Snyder Bulik, "In-game Ads Win Cachet Through a Deal with EA," *Advertising Age*, July 30, 2007, p. 8.

21 Laurie Sullivan, "Beyond In-game Ads," *Advertising Age*, June 18, 2007, p. 1.

22 Mike Shields, "Massive/Nielsen: In-Game Ads Heighten Brand Familiarity," *Brandweek.com*, August 8, 2007, via Nexis.

23 ESRB, "Game Ratings & Descriptor Guide," http://www.esrb.org/ratings/ratings_guide.jsp, accessed 10/14/07.

24 Reuters, "Banned Video Game Called 'Fine Piece of Art,'" *PC Magazine*, June 21, 2007, accessed 10/14/07.

25 Jonathan Silverstein, "Game Ratings Don't Always Tell the Whole Story," ABC News, April 5, 2006, http://abcnews.go.com/Technology/story?id=1808712&page=1, accessed 10/14/07.

Part V

Chapter 15

1 Myra Frazier, "Geico's $500 Million Outlay Pays Off," *Advertising Age*, July 7, 2007, p. 8.

2 Andrew Hampp, "10 Tunes in TV Spots," *Advertising Age*, December 18, 2006, p. 33.

3 Louise Story, "Away from Home, Ads Are Inescapable," *New York Times*, March 2, 2007.

4 Louise Story, "Anywhere the Eye Can See, It's Likely to See an Ad," *New York Times*, January 15, 2007.

5 Abbey Klaassen, "MTV Lures to Its Website Those Who Don't Buy TV," *Advertising Age*, 2006, p. 8.

6 Beth Snyder Bulik, "Why Sci-Fi Grabs More Than Geeks," *Advertising Age*, April 23, 2007.

7 Beth Snyder Bulik, "Microsoft Gaming Play Lets Advertisers Buy by Dem, not Platform," *Advertising Age*, July 23, 2007, p. 20.

8 Quoted in Joseph Turow, *Niche Envy: Marketing Discrimination in the Digital Age* (Cambridge, MA: MIT Press, 2006), p. 43.

9 Quoted in Joseph Turow, *Niche Envy: Marketing Discrimination in the Digital Age* (Cambridge, MA: MIT Press, 2006), p. 44.

10 No author, "Advertising & Media Market Share," AdAge.com, http://adage.com/images/random/agencysharepie2007.pdf, accessed 10/24/07.

Chapter 16

1 Robert Oskar Carlson, "Public Relations," in *The Encyclopedia of Communication* (New York: Oxford University Press, 1989), p. 391.

2 No author, "Many Independents Grow 20 percent +," *Jack O'Dwyer's Newsletter*, March 7, 2007, via Nexis.

3 Jack O'Dwyer, "PR Goes Marketing & Electronic," *O'Dwyer's PR Report*, August 2007, p. 3.

4 Jack O'Dwyer, "PR Goes Marketing & Electronic," *O'Dwyer's PR Report*, August 2007, p. 3.

5 http://www.hillandknowlton.com/index/regions/, accessed on 10/28/07.

6 http://www.hillandknowlton.com/, http://www.hillandknowlton.com/index/about_us, accessed on 10/27/07.

7 http://www.hillandknowlton.com/index/regions/latin_america, accessed on 10/28/07.

8 http://www.hillandknowlton.com/index/practices/marcom, accessed 10/28/07.

9 http://www.burson-marsteller.com/Practices_And_Specialties/Health-care/Pages/default.aspx, accessed 10/28/07.

10 Scott Cutlip, *The Unseen Power* (Hillsdale, NJ: Lawrence Erlbaum Associates, 1996), p. 768.

11 http://www.hillandknowlton.com/index/practices/public_affairs, accessed 10/28/07.

12 Veronis Suhler Stevenson, *Communications Industry Forecast, 2006–2010* (New York: Veronis Suhler Stevenson, 2006), p. 171.

13 Veronis Suhler Stevenson, *Communications Industry Forecast, 2006–2010* (New York: Veronis Suhler Stevenson, 2006), p. 171.

14 Claude Brodesser-Akner, "Here's a Marketer's Guide to Surviving a Writer's Strike," *Advertising Age*, October 22, 2007, p. 3.

15 http://www.wpp.com/WPP/About/WhoWeAre/Mission.htm, accessed 10/27/07.

16 Sut Jhally, "Advertising at the Edge of the Apocalypse." In Robin Anderen and Lance Strate, *Critical Studies in Media Commercialism* (Oxford, England: Oxford University Press, 2000), p. 33.

Photo Credits

Part I

Opener, © Shutterstock

Chapter 1

Opener © Shutterstock; page 5, © 2007 Gene Blevins/Corbis; page 6, photo by J. R. Eyerman © Time & Life Pictures/Getty Images; page 9, © iofoto/Shutterstock; page 13, © 2008 Jupiterimages Corporation; page 14, © 2006 Mario Anzuoni/Reuters/Corbis; page 20, © The New Yorker Collection 2000 David Sipress from cartoonbank.com, all rights reserved; page 22, © Steve Granitz/WireImage/Getty Images; page 24, © DreamWorks/Everett Collection; page 27, © Laura Stone/Shutterstock; page 31, © Anita Patterson Peppers/Shutterstock.

Chapter 2

Opener, © Ivan Cholakov/Shutterstock; page 44, © ABC, Inc./Everett Collection; page 47, www.InfoUSA.com; page 48, Warner Brothers/courtesy of Photofest; page 49, © NBC Universal, Inc/Everett Collection; page 50, © CBS Broadcasting Inc./courtesy of Photofest; page 53, © Home Box Office, Inc./courtesy of Photofest; page 57, www.huffington-post.com; page 60, www.bodybymilk.com; page 68, © Perov Stanislav/Shutterstock.

Chapter 3

Opener, © Gary Blakeley/Shutterstock; page 83, © Austrian Archives/Corbis; page 84, Special Collections and University Archives, Wichita State University Libraries; page 86, www.chinaview.cn; page 88, National Archives and Records Administration; page 93, Minnesota Historical Society; page 96, © Bettmann/Corbis; page 98, © Peter Turnley/Corbis; page 101, © Aaron D. Settipane/Shutterstock; page 109, © Chip East/Reuters/Corbis; page 111, © Alfred Eisenstaedt/Time & Life Pictures/Getty Images; page 119 (left), © Stefan Zaklin/epa/Corbis; page 119 (right), © Micha Walters/Reuters/Corbis; page 122, © Getty Images; page 127, © The Motion Picture Association of America; page 130, reprinted with permission of ESRB and ESA. Please be advised that the ESRB rating icons are copyrighted works and registered trademarks owned by the Electronic Software Association and the Entertainment Software Rating Board and may only be used with their permission and authority. Under no circumstances may the rating icons be self-applied to any product that has not been rated by the ESRB. For information regarding whether a product has been rated by the ESRB, or licensing questions, please call the ESRB at 917.522.3231.

Chapter 4

Opener, © Spauln/Shutterstock; page 145, © Cora Reed/Shutterstock; page 151, www.gallup.com; page 153, © North Wind Picture Archives; page 155 (left), © The Granger Collection; page 155 (right), © The Granger Collection; page 158 (top), © Waltraud Grubitzsch/dpa/Corbis; page 158 (bottom), © Albert Bandura; page 162, Do You Graphics, 410-442-1060, http://www.do-you.com, doyou @ix.netcom.com; page 164, © Mike Baldwin/Cornered/courtesy of CartoonStock.com; page165, © Ivan Josifovic/Shutterstock; page 170, www.laptop.org; page 173, photo by Ted Streshinsky.

Part II

Opener, © Mario Savoia/Shutterstock

Chapter 5

Opener, © Roca/Shutterstock; page 192, © PhotoEdit, Inc.; page 195, www.adage.com; page 203, © PhotoEdit, Inc.; page 212, © Paul Mounce/Corbis; page 216, www.moviefone.com; page 218, © PhotoEdit, Inc.; page 219, SIO Archives, University of CA; page 220, © The New Yorker Collection, 1999 Nick Downes from cartoonbank.com.

Chapter 6

Opener, © Emin Kuliyev/Shutterstock; page 243, © AFP/Getty Images; page 245, www.myspace.com; page 249, www.google.com; page 250, © Getty Images.

Part III

Opener, © Villedieu Christophe/Shutterstock

Chapter 7

Opener, © Arunas Gabalis/Shutterstock; page 264, © PhotoEdit, Inc.; page 265, © North Wind Picture Archives; page 269, © Bettmann/Corbis; page 270, http://www-sul.stanford.edu/depts/dp/pennies/home.html; page 284, © Hachette Book Group USA, reprinted with permission; page 288, reprinted by permission of Faithwords/Hachette Book Group; page 289, reprinted by permission of Hachette Book Group, USA; page 292, © Lee Snider/The Image Works; page 293, © Mark Ludak/The Image Works; page 295, © The New Yorker Collection 1998 Michael Maslin from cartoonbank.com, all rights reserved.

Chapter 8

Opener, © Vasily Smirnov/Shutterstock; page 302, © North Wind Picture Archives; page 303, The Granger Collection; page 304, The Granger Collection; page 308, The Granger Collection; page 317, http://www.eldiariony.com; page 319, © PhotoEdit, Inc.; page 321, www.nnn-naa.com; page 333, © PhotoEdit, Inc.; page 336, www.washingtonpost.com; page 336, www.nytimes.com; page 336, www.latimes.com; page 336, www.usatoday.com.

Chapter 9

Opener, © Dino O/Shutterstock; page 345, The Granger Collection; page 346, The Granger Collection; page 348, © North Wind Picture Archives; page 350, The Granger Collection; page 352, © The New Yorker Collection 1998 Michael Maslin from cartoonbank.com, all rights reserved; page 355, AP/Wide World Photos; page 362, Norman Jean Roy/*Men's Vogue*, © Condé Nast Publications Inc.; page 362, Max Kim-Bee/*Domino*, © Condé Nast Publications Inc; page 366, © Getty Images; page 370, © Lee Snider/The Image Works.

Part IV

Opener, © Velefante/Shutterstock

Chapter 10

Opener, © Agb/Shutterstock; page 382, The Granger Collection; page 382, LC-USZC2-5315 DLC Repository Library of Congress Prints and Photographs Division; page 386, The Granger Collection; page 388, © Getty Images; page 391, www.universalmusic.com; page 399, www.ascap.com; page 402, www.myspace.com/ingridmichaelson; page 404, © Corbis.

Chapter 11

Opener, © Andi Hazelwood/Shutterstock; page 420, The Granger Collection; page 425, The Granger Collection; page 426, The Granger Collection; page 427, The Granger Collection; page 429, © Bettmann/Corbis; page 445, © Mark Peterson/Corbis; page 447, © Lisa O'Connor/ZUMA/Corbis; page 448, © The New Yorker Collection 2002 Robb Armstrong from cartoonbank.com, all rights reserved; page 449, reprinted by permission of the Arbitron Company; page 455, www.music.yahoo.com; page 456, www.rhapsody.com; page 458, www.power99.com.

Chapter 12

Opener, © Ivan Cholakov/Shutterstock; page 465, The Granger Collection; page 466, The Granger Collection; page 469, © Bettmann/Corbis; page 470, The Granger Collection; page 476, © Bureau L.A. Collection/Corbis; page 481, www.sag.org; page 481, © Michael-John Wolfe/Shutterstock; page 487, © Corbis; page 494, © PhotoEdit, Inc.; page 495, www.netflix.com; page 496, © AP/Wide World Photo; page 498, © AP/Wide World Photos.

Chapter 13

Opener, © DeshaCAM/Shutterstock; page 507, © Bettmann/Corbis; page 508, © Getty Images; page 516, www.pbs.org; page 517, www.ionline.tv; page 526, www.hgtv.com; page 528, www.nielsenmedia.com; page 533, © Getty Images.

Chapter 14

Opener, © Rockstar Games, reprinted by permission; page 548, © Kimberly White/Corbis; page 549 (top), © Artiga Photo/Corbis; page 549 (bottom), The Granger Collection; page 550, The Granger Collection; page 551, © Bettmann/Corbis; page 552, image courtesy of the Computer History Museum; page 554, © Dennis Hallinan/Getty Images; page 557, www.kraftfoods.com/jello; page 564, www.pewinternet.org; page 569 (left), © Corbis; page 569 (middle), © 2007 Microsoft Corporation, reprinted by permission; page 569 (right), © Getty Images; page 576, www.americasarmy.com; page 579, © Rockstar Games, reprinted by permission.

Part V

Opener, © Timur Djafarov/ Shutterstock

Chapter 15

Opener, © Emin Kuliyev/Shutterstock; page 595, The Granger Collection; page 600, © gary718/Shutterstock; page 601, www.grupogallegos.com; page 601, www.the-dma.org; page 604, © Lionel Sosa, reprinted by permission; page 606, © Getty Images; page 609, © Justin Sullivan/Getty Images; page 618, © Sut Jhally, reprinted by permission.

Chapter 16

Opener, © PhotoCreate/Shutterstock; © page 627, North Wind Picture Archives; page 628, © Bettmann/Corbis; page 630, © Bettmann/Corbis; page 632, © Bettmann/Corbis; page 634, www.Fleishmanhillard.com; page 641, © Bettmann/Corbis; page 645, © AFP/Getty Images; page 646, © Corbis.

Index

A films 468
A movie units 468
ABC: News 52, 535; radio 426, 431, 446; TV 42, 66, 191, 509, 516, 538
abridgement 90–2
academic conferences 282
academic journals 353–4
AccentHealth 610
access to music 411–13
account executives 605
accuracy 56
acquisitions editor 280
action games 573
active audience 160, 169
activities 40
actual malice 105
ad campaigns 595
ad clutter 620
ad networks 560
addresses, web 564–7
adequate revenue 42
administrative personnel 63
Adorno, Theodor 172
AdSense 253, 560
advanced technology 638–9
advances on royalties 287–9
adventure games 573
advergaming 574–8
adversarial press 300
advertising/advertisements 42, 202, 592–622; accountability to advertisers 654; advertisers' influence on content of magazines 372–4; advertisers' pressure for media self-regulation 122–3; audience segmentation when outlets are advertiser-supported 194–6; challenges facing newspapers 320–1; commercial speech and regulation 102–3; content sites selling 558; distinguishing from PR 625–7; distribution 608–11; evaluation 613; exhibition 611–13; First Amendment and 90; genre 59–60; Google's strategy 252–5; on the Internet 520–1, 558, 559–63, 584–5; in magazines 347, 356–8, 363; media literacy and 615–20, 650–6; modern advertising industry 598–603; on MySpace 244; in newspapers 304, 306–7, 317–21, 332; postwar era 596–7; production 603–8; on radio 422–3, 445–6, 447–9, 596; rise of the advertising industry 593–8; source of revenue 73, 74; spending on 598–9; on TV 507–8, 517, 596–7; threats to traditional advertising 613–14; trends in second half of twentieth century 597–8; video games and 574–8, 612
Advertising Age 194, 195
advertising agencies 599–603; birth of 594–5; conglomerates 619–20
advertising campaigns 611
advertising-editorial ratio 324
advertising tactics 638

advocacy organizations 121–2, 540
AdWords 253, 560
African Americans 46, 530
age, and cinema-going 475
agency holding companies 597–8, 634–5, 649–50, 655–6
agency networks 602–3
agenda, society's 220–2
agenda setting 155, 165–7
albums 389, 392–3; best-selling 394, 408
algorithms 558–9
Alliance of Motion Picture and Television Producers 481
Alltel 195
alternative weeklies 316
AM radio 421, 430, 432, 433
Amazon 283, 294, 413
American Advertising Federation 651
American Association of Advertising Agencies 595, 651
American Booksellers Association (ABA) 293–4
American Broadcasting Company *see* ABC
American Business Press code of ethics 373
American Family Association 121
American Federation of Musicians (AFM) 398
American Federation of Television and Radio Artists (AFTRA) 398
American Revolutionary War 300
American Society of Composers, Authors and Publishers (ASCAP) 386–7, 398, 399
American Soldier research 162–3, 180
American Way 357, 358
America's Army 576
Amnesty International 86
amplitude modulation (AM) 421, 430, 432, 433
analog technology 401, 523, 547–8
analysis of existing data 46
Angelou, Maya, 95
Animal Planet 212
Annenberg Public Policy Center 147–8
Annenberg School 175–6, 180
annual reports 232–3
anthropological cultural studies 177
Antifederalists 301
antitrust laws 115, 117, 470
antitrust policies 115
AOL 581
Apple iTunes 218, 413
appropriation 110–11
Arbitron 449–50
Archie Comics 355
Aristotle 131
Armstrong, Edwin 430
ARPANet 551–2
Arthur, T.S. 270
artist and repertoire (A&R) person 397
Asian films 484
Associated Press 305

Association of National Advertisers 123, 595
AT&T 385, 423, 509, 519
Atari 554
atheism, books on 289
Atlantis Alliance 199
audience 40; active 160, 169; duty to 134; issues and television 539–40; magazine production and 361–2; movies 475; radio 432, 448–51; recording industry 392; role of 40–7
audience erosion 190–1
audience fragmentation 6, 7
audience research 40, 40–7, 609, 610
audience segmentation 41–5, 191–6, 224, 225; *see also* segmentation, targeting
audimeter 526–7
audio DVD 401
audio streaming 394–5, 455–6
Audit Bureau of Circulation 595
audits of circulation 358
authoritarian approaches to regulation 82–3, 85–6
authors 284–5
authorship 65
Auto Week 361–2
avatars 571
average commercial minute 528, 529

B films 468, 471
B movie units 468
baby boom 427, 428
baby boomers 387
back-end deals 481
bad tendency test 98–9
Bagdikian, Ben 173
Baird, Russell 373
Bandura, Albert 158
bandwidth, widening 524–5
Bank of America 647
banned books 95
banners 560
Barbieri, Tony 337
Barnes & Noble 292, 293, 294, 363
Barnum, P.T. (Phineas Taylor) 628–9
Baron Cohen, Sacha 481
barter 648
basic cable tier 521
Battle of Britain, The 163
Battlestar Galactica 612
beats 324
beauty product advertising 607
behavior change studies 164
behavioral codes 26
behavioral targeting 561–2
Belnice Books 278
Benjamin, Park 271
Benjamin, Walter 172
Benkler, Yochai, *The Wealth of Networks* 284
Benny, Jack 427
Berelson, Bernard 299
Berliner, Emile 384–5

Bernays, Edward 631
Bertelsmann 204, 210, 211, 580; book
    industry 270–1, 272; Napster 217
Bess Press 279
bestsellers 281
Beyond Beats and Rhymes 411
Big Four commercial networks 516
Big Three 634
Bill of Rights, The 88
billboard advertising 39, 74–5, 91
billboards 433, 514
binary digits 549–50
Black Entertainment Television (BET) 46,
    389, 405, 530
'blackface' 382, 469
block booking 468
blockbuster books 281
blockbuster films 475, 476
Blockbuster Video 494
blogs 56, 326
blurred media boundaries 188–228;
    audience segmentation 191–6, 224, 225;
    conglomeration 207–13, 218–23, 224,
    226; digital convergence 213–18, 224,
    226; distribution of products 196–203,
    214–15, 224, 225; globalization 203–7,
    224, 226; Internet and 580; media
    fragmentation 190–1, 224, 225; media
    literacy and 218–26
Bobo doll research 158
Bok, Edward 349
Bollywood 52, 480
book clubs 276–7
book tours 291
books 262–97; burning of 81, 83;
    challenged or banned 95; distribution
    289–91; exhibition 291–4; history
    264–6; impact on society 266–8; media
    literacy and the book industry 294–5;
    production 64, 65–6, 280–9; U.S. book
    publishing industry 268–71; source of
    ideas for films 479; types of books
    272–8; variety and specialization 278–80
Books-A-Million 292
Books of Wonder, New York 294
books on demand 282
bookstores 292–4
bootlegging 411
Borders 292, 294
Boston Massacre 627
Boston Tea Party 627
Botswana diamond exports 640
box office receipts 473–4, 475, 483
branded entertainment 647–8
branding 607; cross-media branding 202–3
brands 347, 594–5; producing magazines
    as brands 364–8
Bride and Prejudice 52
Brin, Sergey 250, 251–2, 254
Britain: colonies 267, 268; historic use of
    PR against 627; history of book
    publishing 267–8, 269
British Broadcasting Corporation (BBC) 85
broadband technologies 555
Broadcast Data Services 404
broadcast live 506
Broadcast Music Incorporated (BMI) 387,
    398, 399
broadcasting 420; radio *see* radio; TV *see*
    television broadcasting

Brother Jonathan 271
Brown, Tina 65
browsers 553
Bud.TV 537
Buffett, Warren 337
bulletin boards 554
Burger King 575
Burrell, Tom 602
Burson-Marsteller 639, 641
Burstyn vs. *Wilson* 89
business of mass media 38–79; audience
    research 40, 40–7; distribution 40, 61–2,
    66–8; economy of mass media 40, 41;
    exhibition 40, 61–2, 69–70; finance 40,
    61–2, 71–4; genres 40, 47–61; media
    literacy and 74–5; production 40, 61–2,
    62–6
business models 217–18
business-to-business agencies 600–1
business-to-business communication 638–9
business-to-business (B-to-B) magazines
    351–2
business-to-business marketing 638
buzz marketing 644
bylines 305

C3 standard 528, 529
cable 517, 518
cable networks 510–11, 518
Cable News Network (CNN) 213, 510–11,
    535
Cable Telecommunications Act (1984) 114
cable television 389, 513, 514, 517–19,
    538; production 520–3, 525–31; rise of
    509–11
Cable Television Rules 510
cable television systems 517, 518
call-outs 443
Campaign for a Commercial-Free
    Childhood 103
Campbell Soup Company 102, 136
Cantor, Joanne 513
capitalism 172
Captivate 610
captive audiences 535
Car and Driver 371, 374
Carl Jr. 90
Carol Wright database 584
Cartoon Network 213
CAS Marketing Solutions 47
casual gamers 569
casual games 573
catch phrases 22
categorical imperative 132
CBS 386, 610; Internet 581, 582; radio
    423, 425; TV 70, 191, 509, 516, 535,
    538
CBS vs. *Democratic National Committee*
    89
Center for Media Education 121
Center for Science in the Public Interest
    103
Center for the Study of Commercialism
    121
chain bookstores 292–4
chance 161
change, stress on in research 171
channel lineups 520; producing 520–5
channels: of communication 10, 15;
    television channels 525–31

Chevrolet Corvair 632
Chicago School of sociology 152–4, 180
children: advertising to 103, 615, 616–17;
    film ratings system 126–7; media and
    learning skills 164–5; research into
    effects of films on 157–8; television
    ratings system 128, 129, 513; video
    game ratings system 126, 129, 578–9
Children's Online Privacy Protection Act
    (1998) (COPPA) 114, 116, 140, 585
China 238, 360, 479; Google 559;
    government regulation 85–6
Chomsky, Noam 223
Christians, Clifford 134
Chronicles of Narnia books 275
cigarette advertising 91
circulation 301, 312–17, 331–2, 358;
    controlled-circulation magazines 356–8;
    declines in newspaper circulation
    310–12, 312–15; revenue challenges
    facing newspapers 317, 321–2
Citadel Broadcasting 458
City Lights Bookstore, San Francisco 293
Civil War 305
Claritas 195
classical ethics 131–3
classified advertisements 318, 320–1
Classified Ventures 321
Clear Channel Communications 431,
    457–8
clear and present danger 98–9
Click, J. William 373
click-and-mortar companies 557–8
click-through ads 613
clickstream 561–2
client conflicts 597–8
closeness of news 54
CNN 213, 510–11, 535
coaxial cable 509
codes of acceptable behavior 26
codes of ethics 124, 125, 651–2
codex 265
Cold War 162–3
collaborative activity 65
college newspapers 317
colonialism 175
Columbia Broadcasting System *see* CBS
Columbia Journalism Review 131
Columbia Phonograph Company 386,
    425
Columbia School of research 158–61, 180
columnists 56
Comcast 41, 571–2
comedy 48–9
comic books 355–6
commercial environment 30
commercial forces 32
commercial radio stations 433
commercial speech 102–3
commercial television stations 514
commercial time 456–7
commercialism 220, 222–3; advertising
    and 616–18
commercials 448, 517; *see also*
    advertising/advertisements
Committee for Accuracy in Middle East
    Reporting in America (CAMERA) 121
Committee on Public Information 631
commodification of audiences 539–40
commodities 18

communication 6–20; defining 7; elements of 9–11; mass *see* mass communication
communications PR 640
communist approaches to regulation 82, 83, 85–6
community 152–4
community antenna television (CATV) service 509
community involvement PR 640
compact disks (CDs) 390, 394, 548; self-produced 400–2
companionship 21, 23
competition: encouraging 117; Google's strategy 255
competitive fighting games 573
Competitive Media Reports (CMR) 612–13
completion bond companies 485
composition 279
computer server network 255
computers 549–53; video game playing 569–71; *see also* Internet, video games
concept testing 531–2
conceptual research 144–6
concert tours 406
confidential sources 118–19
conflict 54
conglomerates/conglomeration 232; advertising industry and 619–20; agency holding companies 597–8, 634–5, 649–50, 655–6; blurred media boundaries 207–13, 218–23, 224, 226; book industry 270–1, 272; common criticisms of growth of 220–3; corporate strategies *see* corporate strategies; cross-platform deals 612–13; Internet 580–2; magazines 371–2; News Corporation *see* News Corporation; and the persuasion industries 655–6; radio 431, 451–2; recording industry 390–1; reporting and 173–4, 222; synergy 209–13, 235–7; television 512–13, 541–2; Walt Disney Company *see* Disney Company
connectivity 27–8
consent 112
consolidation: newspaper industry 309; radio 451–2; TV 512–13
constructions, media materials as 30
consumer agencies 600–1
consumer books 274–8
consumer communications 638–9
consumer magazines 352–3
consumer marketing 638
consumer protection 116
consumerism 632–3
consumers: recording industry and 414; spending on media industries 40
content: advertiser influence on 372–4; creating to attract target audience 45–6; creating newspaper content 323–6; issues and television 540–1; measuring success of 46–7; ratings systems *see* ratings systems; regulation before distribution 92–103
content analysis 32, 146
content sites 558
contextual advertising 560
continuing effects research 157–8
control groups 146
controlled-circulation magazines 356–8

controversy: net neutrality 567–8; radio 451–3; recording industry 409–13
convergence 5, 213, 548; digital 213–18, 224, 226
convergence culture 223
cookies 561–2
Cooley, Charles 152–4
Cooper, James Fenimore 270
co-operative (co-op) advertising 70, 319
co-optation 172
coproduction 206
copyeditors 325
copyright 99–102; Napster and 216–17
Copyright Act (1709) (Britain) 268
Copyright Act (1976) 99–100
corporate communication departments 633–4
corporate communications 636–7
corporate responsibility PR 640
corporate sponsorship 407
corporate strategies 230–59; Disney 232–9; Google 249–56; media literacy and 257–8; News Corporation 239–49
Corporation for Public Broadcasting 85
cost per thousand (cost per mil or CPM) 320, 363, 610
costs: covering 197–201, 521–3; film production 482
Council of Better Business Bureaus 652
counterfeiting 411
counterprogramming 531
Courlander, Harold 285
cover lines 370
creative personnel (creatives) 63, 605
creative persuasion 603
creative rights 200, 201
Creel, George 154, 631
crisis management 640–1
critical studies research 152–4, 170–6, 180
critical theory 172
cross-conglomerate deals 612
cross-media activities: advertising 619–20; branding 202–3; distribution 196–203, 214–15, 224, 225; magazines 367–8; promotion of books 294–5; *see also* blurred media boundaries
cross-media strategies 257–8
cross-platform data 214
cross-platform deals 612–13
cross-platform gaming 612
crudeness 472
cultivation studies 175–6
cultural colonialism 175, 498–9
cultural diversity 497–8
cultural studies 176–8, 181
culture: global media companies and 222–3; influences on regulation 87; mass communication and 25–8; mass media, society and 23–8
current affairs 165–7
Curtis, Cyrus 349
custom games 574–6
custom magazines 357–8
customization 364, 561–2, 653–4
Cutlip, Sean 651
CW network 511, 516, 530
cyberspace 553
cylinder press 268–9, 302, 303

daily newspapers (dailies) 310–12, 312–16

Daily Show, The 12–13, 13–14, 14–15
data analysis 46, 150, 181
data mining 561–3
database marketing 649
databases 57, 584; database-guided advertising 253–4
datelines 305
Davis, Deborah, 95
Dawkins, Richard, *The God Delusion* 289
Day, Benjamin 302, 303, 304
day-and-date release 486
day parts 529
DC Comics 355, 356
dead air 442
deadlines 56, 324–5
Decca 386
decision making, ethical 133–4
decoding 10, 15
defamation 104–8
DeForest, Lee 420
democracy 618–19
democratic process 220, 223, 454–5
demographic indicators 44
demographics 43–4, 45, 195
developing countries 170, 273
developmental editor 280
Dewey, John 152–4
diamonds 640
diaries, Nielsen 527
Dickson, William 464
digital cable 522
digital compression technology 520
digital convergence 213–18, 224, 226
digital divide 169, 170
digital downloads *see* downloading
digital platforms 394–5
digital rights management (DRM) 394, 412–13
digital technologies 523, 547–9; book production and 283–4; Disney and distribution 238–9; Internet *see* Internet; movies 492–3; News Corporation's rapid expansion strategy 244–5; newspaper production 326–7; privacy in the digital age 112–15; radio and 430–1, 453–6; recording industry 389–90, 401; rise of computers 549–53; traditional radio's response to digital music 456–8; video games *see* video games
digital television 512, 515, 523, 524, 538
digital theaters 492
digital versatile (or video) disk (DVD) 473, 511–12; distribution of movies 494–5
digital video recorders (DVRs) 512, 612; DVR ratings 536
dime novels 270
Dimension Films 482–3
direct broadcast satellite (DBS) 519
direct mail 331, 369
direct-marketing agencies 601, 603
Direct Marketing Association (DMA) 601, 651
direct regulation by government agencies 115–17
direct sales 73, 409
direct-to-consumer (DTC) advertising 601, 602
direct-to-home satellite 511–12
Directors Guild of America 64
DirecTV 612

disk jockeys (DJs) 387; payola 428–30
Disney Channel 236
Disney Company 41, 207, 231, 232–9, 247, 483, 512, 581; holdings 240–1; main strategies 235–9; reporting on child abuse in theme parks stifled 173–4
Disneyland theme parks 173–4, 237–8
display ads 560, 560–1
distortion 112
distribution 40, 61–2, 66–8; across media boundaries 196–203, 214–15, 224, 225; in the advertising industry 608–11; books 289–91; Disney 237–8, 238–9; Internet 555–63; magazines 368–9; movies 477, 485–9, 493–5; News Corporation's global strategy 245–7; newspapers 327–31; PR industry 643–4; radio 445–7; recording industry 391–2, 402–6; regulation of content after 104–15; relationship between film distributors and theater chains 490–2; television 532–7; video games 578–9
distribution deals (output deals) 483–5
dMarc Broadcasting 254
doctor shows 50, 51
domain names 566
domestic novels 270
Donahue, George 167, 168
Donnelley Conquest/Direct database 584
DoubleClick 117, 254–5
Dove 607
downloading: films 494–5; illegal 216–17, 381, 411–12, 413–14; music 216–17, 381, 394, 406–7, 411–12, 413–14; TV programs 536
drama 48–9
dramady 52, 53
drive time 444
DS game console 571, 575
dual revenue stream 74
dynamic in-Ngame advertising 577–8

Eastman Kodak Company 467
EchoStar Dish Network 571
economic influences on regulation 87
economic regulation 115–17
economy of mass media 40, 41
Edison, Thomas 383–4, 385, 464, 465
Edison Vitascope 465, 466
editorial policies 124
editorial profile 352
editorial standards 124
editorials 56–7, 323, 372–3; personalized 656
editors: books 280, 285–6; newspapers 324
education: genre 58–9; government regulation and 102; research on children's learning from the media 164–5; video games for 574
educational books 272–4
educational TV programs 108
edutainment 574
Eisenstaedt, Alfred 111
Eisner, Michael 233, 237, 239
Electric Numerical Integrator and Computer (ENIAC) 550
Electronic Arts 571, 572
electronic books 215, 283–4
Electronic Freedom Foundation 412

electronic games see video games
electronic newspapers 337
el-hi textbooks 273, 291
Ellsberg, Daniel 96
embedded ads 576–8
embeds (embedded journalists) 98
embellishment 112
EMI 386, 391, 392, 413
empirical research 144–6
employee relations 636–7
employer, duty to 134
Enchanted 196–7
encoding 9, 15
Encyclopedia Britannica 278
enjoyment 21, 23
entertainment: Disney and family entertainment 236–7; First Amendment and 90; formulas 50–2; genre 48–52; magazines 348–9; News Corporation's strategy 247–9
entertainment arcades 553–4
Entertainment Software Rating Board (ESRB) 128–30, 578, 579
environment: of advertisements 610; commercial 30; conducive for advertisers 363; political 30
environmental destruction 617–18
equal time rule 108–9
Equifax Inc. 58
Espionage Act (1917) 97
ethics 32, 81, 131–5; advertising 615; book production 284–6; classical 131–3; decision making 133–4; duties to constituencies 134–5; media literacy, regulation and 136–8; payola 428–30; professional codes of 124, 125, 651–2; and research 166
ethnic newspapers 317, 318
European Union (EU) 585
event marketing 647–8
event sponsorship 647, 648
events 367
evidentiary privilege 118–19
excessive market control 115
exclusive releases 487
exhibition 40, 61–2, 69–70; advertising 611–13; book publishing 291–4; Internet 563–8; magazines 369–71; movies 490–2, 493–5; newspapers 331–2; PR industry 645–7; radio 447–51; recording industry 406–9; television 537–8; video games 578–9
exhibition license 491
expanded (enhanced) basic cable 521–2
experiments 145–6
external relations 633

FaceBook 221, 581
Fackler, Mark 134
fair comment and criticism 108
fair pay 99–100
fair use regulations 100–1
Fairness doctrine 108–9
fake reviews 489
Falcon Company 278–9
false light 110
falsity 107
family entertainment 236–7
Family Friendly Programming Forum 123
Farm Journal 364

fault 107
feature films 64, 65–6, 473–5; see also movies/films
Federal Bureau of Investigation (FBI) 583
Federal Communications Act (1934) 425
Federal Communications Commission (FCC) 108–9, 115–16, 506, 514, 515, 524
Federal Education Records Privacy Act (1974) 103
Federal Radio Commission (FRC) 424
Federal Trade Commission (FTC) 102, 114, 115–17
Federalists 301
feedback 10, 14–15, 16–17
Fessenden, Reginald 420
festivals 48–9
fictionalization 112
film distribution firms 477
film production firms 477
film ratings system 126–8, 471–2
films see movies/films
filtering, web 582–3
finance 40, 61–2, 71–4; book publishing 278–80; funding new production 71–2; funding when production is complete 72–4; Internet content 556–8; magazines 356–9; movies 481–5; newspapers 304, 317–22
financial communications 637–8
financial interest and syndication rules (fin-syn rules) 508–9, 512
First Amendment 87–92, 105, 137, 301, 618
Florida Star 112
FM radio 421, 430, 432, 433
focus groups 46, 443
Forbes 362, 367
foreign-language newspapers 317, 318
foreign TV stations 535
format clock (format wheel) 443–4
format consultants 437
format networks 446–7
formats 66; books 265; newspapers 333; radio see radio formats; recording industry 393–5; television 520; television programs 531
formulas 50–2
Fort Worth Public Library 582
Fortune 195–6
Fox network 191, 511, 516
fragmentation: audience 6, 7; media 190–1, 224, 225; production in recording industry 391; radio and 430–1; television 511–13
frameworks 148–9
franchises 235–6
Frankfurt School 172, 180
Franklin, Benjamin 344, 593–4, 627–8
Franklin, James 300
Frazier, Charles, Thirteen Moons 288
free newspapers 315, 316
free skies policy 510
Freedom of Information Act (1967) (FOIA) 119–20
freelancers 63–4, 324, 346
freestanding inserts (FSIs) 319–20
frequency, radio 421
frequency modulation (FM) 421, 430, 432, 433

Gallup 151
Game Boy 571
gaming 48–9
gaming consoles 568–9; *see also* video
　games
Gandolfini, James 52
gangsta rap 32, 410–11
Gannett Company 332, 333, 334
gatefolds 611
Gates, Bill 170
Gay & Lesbian Alliance Against
　Defamation 121, 122
Geico Direct 608
general ad agencies 600, 601
general assignment reporters 324
General Electric (GE) 512
genre films 482–3
genres 31, 40, 47–61; advertisements
　59–60; education 58–9; entertainment
　48–52; information 57–8; mixing 52, 61;
　music 395–6; news 52–7; video games
　572–4
geographic marketing area 329
Gerbner, George 175–6
Germany 81, 83, 506
Gibson, Charles 52
girls, and video gaming 575
Gitlow vs. *New York* 88
Giuliano, Neil 122
global media organizations 210–13;
　local media organizations and
　205–7, 222–3
global presence 597
globalization 203–7, 224, 226; Disney
　237–8; film production 479–80; Google
　252; News Corporation 241–2, 245–7;
　PR agencies 635; recording industry
　392–3; tastes and 204–5
Gmail 255, 560
Godey's Lady's Book 346
golden age of television 506–7
Golden Books Family Entertainment 201
Golden Mean 131–2
Golden Rule 132
Google 232, 249–56, 257, 513, 581;
　acquisitions 256; algorithm 559; in
　China 559; main strategies 250–5;
　MySpace 245; purchase of DoubleClick
　117, 254–5; text ads 560
Google Books 255
Google Docs and Spreadsheets 255
Gopher Publishing 282
Gordy, Berry 388
government documents 117–18
Government-in-the-Sunshine Act (1977)
　120
government meetings 117–18
government regulation 40, 74, 81, 82–120;
　approaches to 82–6; cable TV 510–11;
　direct regulation by government agencies
　115–17; economic regulation 115–17;
　First Amendment and 87–92; influences
　on 87; information gathering 117–20;
　media literacy, ethics and 136–8; radio
　89, 423–5; regulation of content after
　distribution 104–15; regulation of
　content before distribution 92–103; TV
　508–9, 510–11; types of 92–117
government relations PR 640
Graham, Katharine Meyer 310

Grammy Awards 24
gramophone 384–5
Grand Theft Auto 578, 579
graphophone 384
Great Depression 309–10
Greeley, Horace 306
green light 479
Greenspan, Alan 64
Grenada 97
Griswold, Rufus 271
Grupo Gallegos 601
guilds 64, 481
Gutenberg, Johannes 265–6, 300

Hale, Sarah Josepha 346
Haley, Alex, *Roots* 284–5
Halo 3 game 572
Hamilton, Andrew 300
hammocking 530–1
handheld game devices 571
hard news 54–6
hard-sell ads 60
hardcore gamers 569
hardware, gaming 568–72
harm 107
Harper, Marion 598
Harper's Monthly 346
Harris, Sam, *Letter to a Christian
　Nation* 289
Harry Potter: books 95, 263, 275, 276,
　294; brand 189, 202, 203, 264; films
　194
hawkers 304
Hays, Will 469
Hazelwood School District vs. *Kuhlmeier*
　102
HD radio 457
head end 522–3
headlines 305
healthcare 638–9
Hearst, William Randolph 307–9
Herman, Edward 173, 223
Herskovitz, Marshall 537
Hezbollah 577
hidden curriculum 616
hidden influences 597, 651–2, 656
high-definition TV (HDTV) 520–1,
　523, 524
High School Musical 236
higher education textbooks 273–4,
　291–2
Hill & Knowlton 632, 635, 635–6, 638,
　640, 642–3
Hispanic Americans 604, 611; television
　audience 527
historical cultural studies 177
Hitchens, Christopher, *God Is Not Great*
　289
Hoe steam press 268–9, 302, 303
Hollywood 467
Holmes, Oliver Wendell 99
Holtzbrinck Group 271, 279
Home Box Office (HBO) 510
homogenization 220, 222–3
horizontal integration 209
Horkheimer, Max 172
horror films 51
household ratings 527–8
household shares 528
Hovland, Carl 162–3

HTML (HyperText Markup Language)
　553
HTTP (hypertext transfer protocol) 566–7
Huffington Post political blog group 56,
　57
Huxley, Aldous 95
hybrid genres 52
hybridity 52, 61
hyperlinks 552–3
hypodermic needle approach 156
hypotheses 145

I Love Lucy 507, 508
IBM 637
ideals 135
ideas: for movies 478–80; marketplace of
　84, 267
identification, in libel law 106
IDW Publishing 355
Iger, Robert 233, 234–5, 236
ignorance, veil of 132
illegal downloading 216–17, 381, 411–12,
　413–14
image ads 595
image-making sites 557
immigration 152–3
Imus, Don 109
in-store media 609–10
independent bookstores 292–4
independent broadcast stations 516, 517
independent distributors 477
independent labels 391, 400
independent producers 477, 483–4
India 206
individuals 86, 121; active recipients of
　media messages 31; mass media in
　personal lives 20–3; research and
　emphasis on 171; use of mass media
　21–3
industrialization 306
industry 17; industrial nature of mass
　communication 6–7; media literacy
　and 29
information; gathering and distributing 58;
　genre 57–8; personal 47, 113, 114–15,
　583–6; research and retrieval 58;
　struggle with government over
　information gathering 117–20
information subsidies 645–7
informational ads 60
infoUSA 47
initial public offering (IPO) 72
injunctions 92
innovation 18–20
InstaBook Maker 282
InStyle 371
integrated marketing communications
　(IMC) 647–50
intellectual property 99–100
interactive TV (iTV) 571–2
interactivity 548–9, 654
internal relations 633
internal self-regulation 123–31
International Copyright Convention 269
international relations PR 640
Internet 29, 547; advertising on 320–1,
　558, 559–63, 584–5; competition for
　newspapers 312, 315, 320–1; digital
　divide 169, 170; Disney and 239;
　downloading *see* downloading;

Internet (*Continued*)
exhibition 563–8; exhibition in the book industry 294; game playing online 554, 570–1; getting online 563–4; and libel laws 106; media literacy and 579–86; music promotions 405–6; News Corporation's strategy 244–5; online capability 551–2; online magazines 364–7; online newspapers 325–6, 335–6; online video stores 494–5; and privacy 113, 583–6; production and distribution 555–63; radio stations and Internet participation 457–8; and recording industry 390, 411–13, 413–14; rise of 549–53; student newspapers published on 103; TV on 536, 537; use 555, 556, 557
Internet ad agencies 600, 601
Internet Corporation for Assigned Names and Numbers (ICANN) 564–6
Internet radio 395, 455–6
Internet service providers (ISPs) 563
Internet stores 409
interpersonal communication 7–8, 15; and mass communication 15–17, 18; mediated *see* mediated interpersonal communication; model of 11
interpretation 22–3
Interpublic 598, 619, 634
interstitial pop-up ads 561
interstitials 437
intrapersonal communication 8
intrusion 112
inverted pyramid 55, 305
investigative reports 56
investment banks 71
investments, encouraging 71–2
ION 516, 517
Iraq War 98, 117–18
Ireland 570
Irving, Washington 270
Isherwood, Charles 285
iTunes 218, 413
Ivory Soap 631

Jack in the Box 90
Jack Links games 576–7
Jackass 653
Jackson, Andrew 302
Jenkins, Henry 223
Jhally, Sut 618, 655
Jobs, Steve 413
Johnson & Johnson 641
joint ventures 206, 212–13
Jolson, Al 468, 469
journalism 307–9; *see also* newspapers
journalism reviews 131
journalists 53, 324, 326; embedded 98; evidentiary privilege 118–19
Judeo-Christian ethic 132
JWT (originally J. Walter Thompson) 595, 597

Kant, Immanuel 132
Kellner, Jamie 614
Kellogg Company 103
Kennard, William 452–3
Kennedy, Ted 91
Kilbourne, Jean 373
kinetoscope 464

King, Martin Luther, Jr. 105
King, Stephen, *The Plant* 283
Kingsley, Pat 646
Kitchen Sink Press 355
knowledge gap 167, 168
Knowles, Beyonce 404
Kraft Foods' Jell-O 557

labels, record 396–8, 402–3
Ladies' Home Journal 347, 348–9
Lahiri, Jhumpa 64
language 252; foreign-language newspapers 317, 318; strong language 540–1
Lasswell, Harold 154
Latimer, George Horace 349
Latin music 397
Law & Order: Criminal Intent 533
Lazarsfeld, Paul 159–60
lead-in programs 530
lead-out programs 530
leaders 26
leading questions 149
learning from media 164–7
Lee, Harper 95
Lee, Ivy 630–1
Lee, Roy 484
Lemony Snicket books 275
Lenin, Vladimir 83
Lexis/Nexis 58
Libby, 'Scooter' 118–19
libel 104–8
libel per quod 104
libel per se 104
libertarian approaches to regulation 82, 83–5, 85–6
license fees 73, 521
licenses 532
licensing 235
licensing system 267
lifestyle categories 45, 195, 609
Limbaugh, Rush 445
limited effects research 161–3
line producer 485
lines (products) 43
lineups 520; producing 520–5
linguistic cultural studies 178
Lippmann, Walter 154–5
listeners, counting 448–50
listening patterns 423, 437
literacy 29; media literacy *see* media literacy
literary agents 280–1, 285–6
literary cultural studies 178
Literary Marketplace 278
literary reviews 353–4
live broadcasting 506
loans 71
local newspapers 326–7
local spot advertising 447–8
local television stations 537–8
localism: global and local media firms 205–7, 222–3; newspapers and 334–5, 335–6
location-based advertising 612
Lorimer, George Horace 349
Lotus Development Company 637
low-power FM (LPFM) 452–3
Loyal Stationer's Company 267
loyalty 362

Ludlow massacre (1914) 630–1
Lumière brothers 464–5
lyrics, controversies over 410–11

Madison, James 301
magazine distribution 368–9
magazine publisher 368, 369
magazines 342–77; development of the industry 344–7; distribution 368–9; exhibition 369–71; finance 356–9; media literacy and 371–4; modern magazine industry 350–6; new roles for mass-circulation magazines 347–50; production 360–8; transformation into mass media 344–6; types of 351–6
magic bullet approach 156
Magic Gourd, The 238
mail order books 277
Maine battleship 309
mainstream agendas, narrowing of 220–2
mainstream approaches to research 158–71, 180
majors, the 468–9, 477
managing editor 324
Manhunt 2 game 126, 579
'Manning, David' 489
manuscripts 264–5
Marconi, Guglielmo 419–20
Marcuse, Herbert 172
market power 210
market pressure 109
market research 193, 194–6, 603, 608; compiling playlist 443; movies 487–8; radio station ratings 449–50; TV programs 531–2
market segmentation 605; *see also* segmentation
market size 433–4
marketing: movies 487–9; newspapers 329–31; *see also* distribution
marketing communications 647–50
marketing costs 482
marketing plans 290–1
marketplace of ideas 84, 267
marriage mail outfits 331, 332
Marvel Comics Group 355, 356
Marx, Karl 172
mass communication 11–18; and culture 25–8; defining 17–18; model of 19
mass customization 364, 561–2, 653–4
mass market outlets 275
mass market paperbacks 275–6
mass media 5, 17, 18; culture, society and 23–8; economy of 40, 41; in our personal lives 20–3; uses of 21–3
mass media conglomerates 207–13; *see also* conglomerates/conglomeration
mass media industries 17, 19; consumer spending on 40
mass media outlets 17–18, 190
mass media production firms 63–6
mass media research 32, 142–85; approaches to 144–9; cultural studies 176–8, 181; developing media literacy skills 179–82; early 151–63; mainstream approaches 158–71, 180; nature of 144–51; rise of critical approaches 170–6; tools for evaluating 149–51

mass production process 6
Massive 577–8
massively multiplier online role-playing games (MMORPGs) 570–1
Mattel 554
Maxim 366–7, 367–8
McChesney, Robert 173
McCombs, Maxwell 165
McDaniel, Hattie 470
McDonald's 407
meaning 178
media boundary blurring *see* blurred media boundaries
media fragmentation 190–1, 224, 225
Media General Newspapers 329
media influence 159–61
media kits 358–9
media literacy 28–34; and the advertising industry 615–20, 650–6; attributes 30, 33; and blurred media boundaries 218–26; and books 294–5; and the business of media 74–5; and corporate strategies 257–8; foundations of 29–32; Internet and video games 579–86; and magazines 371–4; mass media research and developing media literacy skills 179–82; and movies 497–9; and newspapers 337–8; and the persuasion industries 650–6; questioning media trends 33–4; and radio 459; and the recording industry 413–14; regulation, ethics and 136–8; skills 30, 32–3; and television 538–42
media planning and buying 603, 605, 608–11
media practitioners 40–1
media production firms 63–6
media relations 633–4, 642
media self-regulation *see* self-regulation
mediated interpersonal communication 8, 15; and mass communication 15–17, 18; model of 12
medium of communication 9–10, 11–12
megaplexes 475
Méliès, George 466
men's magazines 353
Merck Action Network 639
messages 7, 9–11, 15
Metro 315
Michaelson, Ingrid 402, 403
Mickey Mouse 234
microprocessor 550
Microsoft 117, 407, 581, 612: Xbox consoles 568, 569, 572, 575
military operations 97–8
Mill, John Stuart 132–3
Miller, Judith 118–19
Miller vs. *California* 94
Milton, John, *Areopagitica* 84, 267
Minnesota News Council 130
minstrel shows 382
Miramax Films 482, 483
mission statements 232, 234–5, 241
MNI 359
mobile feed 335
mobile phones 239, 245, 537; video games 571
modems 551, 552
monopoly 115
Moore, Ann S. 343

motion, simulation of 464–5
Motion Picture Association 126–7
Motion Picture Patents Company (MPPC) 467
Motion Picture Producers and Distribution Associates 469
Motion Pictures Producers Association of America (MPAA) 496
motivation research 597
Motown Records 388
movable type 265–6
Moviefone 215
movies/films 462–502; audience segmentation 192–3; covering costs 198–200, 201; First Amendment 89; local vs global media organizations 205–7; as mass entertainment media 465–7; media literacy and motion picture industry 497–9; moviemaking process 477–85; non-theatrical distribution and exhibition 493–5; overview of modern industry 473–6; piracy 495–6; production 64, 65–6, 476–85; ratings system 126–8, 471–2; research into effects on children 157–8; rise of the industry 464–73; and TV 471–2, 495, 507; theatrical distribution 485–9; theatrical exhibition 490–2; top grossing movies 476; worldwide tastes vs. American tastes 205
MP3 technology 215, 216
MTV 205, 206, 389, 405, 510–11, 611–12
muckrakers 347–8
multiple system owners (MSOs) 517; ownership role in the network 523
multiplexes 475
multiplexing (multichannel broadcasting) 524
multi-user dungeons (MUDs) 554
Munsey, Frank 347
Murdoch, Rupert 241, 242, 243, 245–7, 511
music 100, 215; concern about access to 411–13; concern over lyrics 410–11; digital convergence 215, 216–18; digital files 394–5, 548; diverse genres 395–6; downloads 216–17, 381, 394, 406–7, 411–12, 413–14; finding music to record 398–9; illegal downloading 216–17, 381, 411–12, 413–14; radio's responses to digital music 456–8; record player 383–5; sheet music 381–3, 385; tastes 204–5; *see also* recording industry
music boxes 383
music sophistication 435
music style 435
Music Television (MTV) 205, 206, 389, 405, 510–11, 611–12
music time period 435
Mutual Film Corp vs. *Ohio Industrial Commission* 89
Muybridge, Edward 464, 465
MyNetworkTV 516
MySpace 63, 221–2, 243, 244–5, 401–2, 581

Nader, Ralph 632
Napster 216–17, 218, 581
narrowcasting 437
national ads 318–19, 320

National Advertising Division (NAD) of the Council of Better Business Bureaus 652
National Advertising Review Board (NARB) 652
National Association for the Advancement of Colored People (NAACP) 530
National Association of Broadcasters (NAB) 128, 453
National Broadcasting Company (NBC) 423, 425–6; *see also* NBC-Universal
National Geographic 363
National Newspaper Network (NNN) 320
National Public Radio (NPR) 446
national rating points 528, 529
National Research Group 488
national security 96–7
national spot advertising 447
natural search results 559
naturalistic experiments 162–3
NBC-Universal 41, 63, 582; radio 423, 425–6; TV 191, 509, 516, 535, 538
NDP Group 572
Near vs. *Minnesota* 92
negative cost 482
negative-option plan 277
Negroponte, Nicholas 170
net neutrality controversy 567–8
network advertising 447
network affiliates 423, 516–17
network licensing agreements 532
network programming 425–7
networks: format networks vs traditional networks 446–7; radio networks 423, 445–7; TV networks 508–9, 510–11, 516, 536–7
new editions of textbooks 292
New York City 96
New York Daily News 309, 314–15
New York Herald 305
New York Sun 302, 303
New York Times 312, 329, 336
New York Times Company 201
New York Times vs. *Sullivan* 90, 105
New York Times vs. *United States* 96–7
New York Tribune 306, 307
New Yorker 349
Newport Media 329, 331
news: changing approaches to 303–6; costs of news reporting 645; defining 304–5; events 118; gathering 305; government regulation of information gathering 118; genre 52–7; News Corporation's strategy 247–9; PR and 'news' stories 643; radio and 426–7, 440
News America Marketing 319
News Corporation 41, 210, 211, 232, 239–49, 512, 580, 582, 620; holdings 248; main strategies 243–9; MySpace 222, 243, 244–5, 581; O. J. Simpson memoir 26
news hole 324
newsletters 354
newspaper chains 309, 315–16
newspaper distribution 327–31
newspapers 298–340; building readership 332–6; decline 309–12; development of the newspaper industry 300–12; distribution 327–31; exhibition 331–2; finance 304, 317–22; as mass media

newspapers (*Continued*)
302–3; media literacy and 337–8; modern newspaper industry 312–17; niche newspapers 317, 318; production 322–7, 328; revolution in newspaper publishing 306–7
newsworthiness 111–12, 112
Nickelodeon 510–11
nickelodeons 466–7
Nielsen diaries 527
Nielsen Media Research 526–8
Nielsen Outdoor 611
Nintendo 568, 572; DS 571, 575; Game Boy 571; Wii 568–9, 575
nodes 236
noise 10, 11, 15
noncommercial radio stations 433
noncommercial TV stations 514
nut 491

objectivity 54–6, 305–6
obscenity 93–6, 472
off-network syndication 533
Office of Censorship 97
Ogilvy & Mather 607
Olien, Clarice 167, 168
oligopoly 115
ombudspersons 124
Omnicom 598, 619, 634
on-air talent 441–2
on spec writing 479
on-staff workers 63
One Laptop Per Child (OLPC) 170
one-way model of public relations 631
online capability 551–2; *see also* Internet
online magazines 364–7
online newspapers 325–6, 335–6
online video stores 494–5
open access 354
operating policies 124
opinion leaders 159–61
opinion studies 164
opt-in: collecting personal information 585; email advertising 560
opt-out: collecting personal information 585; email advertising 560
organizational communication 8–9
Osteen, Joel 287–8
out-of-home locations 535
outdoor advertising 39, 74–5, 91, 600, 609–10, 611
output deals (distribution deals) 483–5
outsourcing 327; corporate training materials 274
owned and operated (O&O) stations 423, 516
ownership 86, 221; consolidation and TV 512–13; recording industry 390–1; role of TV exhibitors 523; *see also* conglomerates/conglomeration

p-value 161
Pac-Man 554
Packard, Vance 597
Page, Larry 250, 251–2, 254
pagination 326
paid-circulation magazines 358–9
Panama 97–8
Pandora 455

panel surveys 159
papyrus rolls 264–5
parasocial interaction 21
Parents Music Resource Center (PMRC) 410
Park, Robert 152–4
parodies 61, 101–2
partnering 199, 201
patents 467
Paterson, Katherine 95
patterns of action 50, 51
pay-per-view (PPV) 522
Payne Fund studies 157–8, 180
payola 405, 428–30, 441
pedagogy 272
peer-to-peer computing (P2P) 216–17, 411
Penguin Publishing 271, 279
Pennsylvania Railroad 630
penny papers 302–4
Pentagon Papers 96–7
People for the American Way 121
people meter 526
people ratings 528
percentage-above-the-nut 491–2
percentage of the gross 481
Perino, Dana 645
persistence of vision 464
personal computers (PCs) 550–1
personal information 47, 113, 114–15, 583–6
personal torts 109
personalization of content 257–8, 563, 656
persuasion 154–6; subliminal 597
persuasion industries 625; conglomerates and 655–6; media literacy and 650–6; targeting and 652–5; truth and hidden influence 651–2; *see also* advertising, public relations
pervasive gaming 612
Pew Internet and American Life Project 555, 556, 564
pharmaceutical companies 639
Philadelphia Daily News 330–1
Philadelphia Inquirer 330–1, 334
Philadelphia Media Holdings 67, 330
phonograph 383–5
photography 464–5
pickups 207
pilot programs 532
pinball machines 553–4
piracy: movies 495–6; music 411–12, 413–14
Pirates of the Caribbean films 65, 235, 236, 475, 476
pitches 531
Pitt, Brad 21
Pixar 233, 483
placement of ads 448, 610–11
plagiarism 284–5
Plame, Valerie 118–19
platform games 573
platform release 486–7
player pianos 383
playlist 404, 442–3
Playstation 568, 569, 570
Playstation Portable (PSP) 571
podcasting 335
pods 611
Pogo 570
point-of-purchase (POP) advertising 617

policy books 124
political action PR 640
political economy research 172–5
political environment 30
political ideologies 28
political influences 32, 87
political parties 301
political process 220, 223, 452–3
Polmer, Volney 594
polysemy 178
pool reporters 97–8
pop-ups (pop-up ads) 561
popularity indicators (books) 290–1
pornography 93–6
portable people meter (PPM) 449–50
Porter, Edwin S. 466
portraits 606–8
positioning 607–8
Postal Act (1879) 347
Postman, Neil 619
post-revolutionary period 301
power of a distributor 68, 69, 70
Power99FM 457–8
premium channels 522
premium paperbacks 276
prepublication research 286
presidential news conferences 24
presold titles 295
press: First Amendment and defining 89–90; *see also* newspapers
press briefings 24, 645
press councils 130
press releases 642–3
pressure groups 121–2, 540
prestige 286–7
preview theaters 532
previewing 487–8
primary media communities 653
prime time 191, 509, 529
prime-time access rule (PTAR) 508–9, 529
priming 166–7
principle of utility 132–3
principles 135
print media: covering costs 200–1; *see also* books, magazines, newspapers
print run 290
printing press 265–6; steam-powered 268–9, 302, 303
prints and advertising (P&A) 488
prior restraint 92–103
privacy 254; in the digital age 112–15; government regulation 109–15; Internet and 113, 583–6
private persons, libel and 105
privilege 107
PRN Corporation 610
Procter & Gamble 631, 644
producers, record 399–400
product integration 648
product placement 60, 199–200, 201, 614, 648; in reverse 212
production 40, 61–2, 62–6; in advertising industry 603–8; books 64, 65–6, 280–9; funding new production 71–2; funding when production is complete 72–4; Internet 555–63; magazines 360–8; movies 64, 65–6, 476–85; newspapers 322–7, 328; PR industry 642–3; radio 434–45; recording industry 391, 396–402; television 519–32, 537

production editor 281
profession, duty to 135
professional books 274
professional codes of ethics 124, 125, 651–2
profiling 561–2
profits 72
program director 441
program feed 516, 517
programs, producing for television 531–2
Project Censored 325
promiseholders, duty to 135
promotion 403–6
propaganda 154–6; limits of 161–3
propaganda analysis 155–6, 180
protected communication, levels of 91
psychographic indicators 45
psychographics 44–5, 195–6, 609
psychological effects 157–8
public, the: influence on production and distribution 33; pressures for media self-regulation from 121
public affairs PR 639–40
Public Broadcasting Service (PBS) 516
public communication 9
public disclosure 111–12
public figures 105, 109–10
public meetings 118
Public Radio International (PRI) 446
public relations (PR) 202, 614, 624–59; distinguishing from advertising 625–7; distribution 643–4; exhibition 645–7; growth and change in the industry 632–3; integrated marketing communications 647–50; major activities 635–42; media literacy and the persuasion industries 650–6; modern PR industry 633–5; practitioners 632, 633; production 642–3; rise of PR industry 627–31
public relations agencies 634–5
Public Relations Society of America 651–2
public service broadcasting 425
publication 106
Publicis 619
publicity 488, 625
Publicity Bureau 629
publicity outlets 643
publishers: content sites 558; magazines 368, 369; newspapers 323
Pulitzer, Joseph 307
Pure Food and Drugs Act (1906) 348
Pursuit of Happiness, The 498

qualitative research 146–9
quantitative research 146–9
Quarterlife 537
questionnaires 146

rack jobbers 409
radio 418–61; advertising on 422–3, 445–6, 447–9, 596; and digital technology 430–1, 453–6; distribution 445–7; exhibition 447–51; fragmentation and digitalization 430–1; government regulation 89, 423–5; in the 1920s, 1930s and 1940s 425–7; Internet radio 395, 455–6; media literacy and 459; overview of the terrestrial industry 432–4; postwar 387–9, 427–30;

production 434–45; recording industry and 385–9, 404–5, 428–30; records and the rise of 385–7; response of traditional radio to digital music 456–8; rise of 419–25; and social controversy 451–3
Radio Act (1912) 424
Radio Act (1927) 424
Radio Broadcasting Preservation Act (2000) 453
Radio Corporation of America (RCA) 386, 422–3, 425, 506
radio formats 387–9, 435–7, 451; maintaining and retaining the target audience 443–5; selection 437; types of 437, 438–9; working with 440–2
radio networks 423, 445–7
radio station ratings 449–51
radio waves 420, 421
radiotelephony 420
railroads 629
Random House 271, 272, 279
rap music 32, 410–11
Ratings Board 127–8
ratings: DVR ratings 536; radio stations 449–51; TV programs 508, 526–8, 536
ratings systems 124–30; movies 126–8, 471–2; TV 128, 129, 513, 540–1; video games 126, 128–30, 578–9
Rawls, John 133
reach 528–9, 610
Reader's Digest 349, 359
readership 321–2; building 332–6; declining 312; revolution in 306
readership segments 359
reason-why ads 595
receiver 10, 15; people as active recipients of media messages 31
record clubs 409
record labels 396–8, 402–3
record player 383–5
record stores 68, 407–8
recording artists: best selling 393, 408; compensating 399; and labels 396–8; and piracy 413–14
recording industry 380–417; CDs 390; distribution 391–2, 402–6; diverse recording media formats 393–4; effect of digital convergence 216–18; exhibition 406–9; media literacy and 413–14; modern industry 390–2; postwar 387–9; production 391, 396–402; public controversies 409–13; radio and 385–9, 404–5, 428–30; rise of the industry 381–7; unique features 392–6
Recording Industry Association of America (RIAA) 217, 381, 395, 412
records 547–8; effect on music industry 385; rise of 381–7; and the rise of radio 385–7; technological developments 389
recycling 276, 330
Red Storm Entertainment 576
Regan Books 26
regional bell operating companies (RBOCs) 519
regulation 74, 81, 82–131; government regulation see government regulation; issues and TV 541–2; media literacy, ethics and 136–8; self-regulation see self-regulation

reinforcement 171
relationship marketing 649
release date 486
release patterns 486–7
reliability 149–50
religious books 276
rental outlets 494
rentals 73
representation firms 596
repurposing 214
research 144; audience research 40, 40–7, 609, 610; market research see market research; mass media research see mass media research
research design 149, 181
research and development (R&D) 18–20, 46
retail advertising 318, 320
retail stores 408–9; bookstores 292–4; magazine distribution 369, 370; record stores 68, 407–8; video stores 494–5; with online presence 557–8
reviews, book 290
Rhapsody 395, 455, 456
rich media ads 560
ringtones 394
Rockefeller family 630–1
Rockstar Games 578, 579
Roosevelt, Franklin D. 427, 506
Roosevelt, Theodore 347, 348, 629
Ross, Brian 173–4
Roth vs. United States 94
Rotzoll, Kim 134
rough cut 488
Routledge 63
Rowling, J.K. 95, 263; see also Harry Potter
royalties 280, 399; advances on 287–9
RSS feed 335

sailor's kiss photograph 111
salaries 64–5
sales/selling: recording industry sales 392, 395; sites selling products or services 557–8
sales pitch 606
sample 146; nature of 149; size 149
sampling 530
satellite radio 453–5
satellite television 513, 514, 517, 519; production 520–3, 525–31
saturation release 486
Saturday Evening Post 347, 348–9, 350
Scarborough Research 450
schedules 66, 529–31
Schenck vs. United States 99
Schiffrin, Andre 272
Schiller, Herbert 175, 219
school newspapers 102, 103
Scientific American 346
Scream 482, 483, 488–9
Screen Actors Guild 64, 481
scriptoria 264
Seacrest, Ryan 446, 447
search engines 249, 251–2, 558–9; see also Google
Sedition Act (1918) 97
Sega 568

segmentation: audience 41–5, 191–6, 224, 225; book industry 287; magazines 359; market 605; when outlets are advertiser-supported 194–6; when outlets are not advertiser-supported 193–4
segments, target 193, 359
Seiter, Ellen 177
selectability 654
self, duty to 134
self-production of CDs 400–2
self-regulation 81, 109, 120–31, 651–2; external pressures 121–3; internal pressures 123–31; movie industry 468–9
sell-through outlets 494
serial form novels 271
series 529
series pictures 468
service magazines 353
Sesame Street 61, 164
setting 50, 51
7–11 convenience stores 212
Seventeen 358–9, 366, 367, 610
sex 540–1, 542, 578, 582
Shadow, The 426
share of mind 197, 202–3
shares 527–8
Shaw, Donald 165
sheet music industry 381–3, 385
shelf space 69
shield laws 120
shooter games 573
shoppers 316, 331, 332
Shrek films 24
Siegenthaler, John, Sr. 104–5
significance level 161
silent films 466–7
simple malice 105
simple negligence 106
Simpson, O.J. 26
Simpsons, The 212
simulation (sim) games 574
Sinclair, Upton 154, 348, 349
single-copy sales 368, 369, 371
singles 392–3
Sirius Radio 454, 455
slander 104–8
small-group communication 8
Smart Money 361
social currency 21, 22
social effects 157–8
social media sites 221–2
social relations 158–61
social responsibility approaches to regulation 82, 85–6
society: duty to 135; impact of books 266–8; mainstream agenda of 220–2; mass media, culture and 23–8; media literacy and representations of 31–2
Society of Professional Journalists 124, 125
soft news 57
soft-sell ads 60
software, gaming 572–4
software talent brokers 63
Sony BMG 390–1, 392
Sony Corporation 204, 210, 512, 572, 580; fake critic 489; Playstation 568, 569, 570; Playstation Portable (PSP) 571

Sony Music 67, 413
Sopranos, The 52, 53
Sosa, Lionel 604
SoundScan 404
source of communication 9, 12–13, 15
spam 560
special effects 65
Special Force 2 game 577
specialization 278–80
specialty agencies 600, 601
Spectator, The 344, 345
Spider-Man 3 487
Spigel, Lynn 177
split-cable test 608
sponsorship 407; event sponsorship 647, 648
sports 247–9
sports games 576
Sports Illustrated 364
stakeholders: ethical duties to 134–5; and media self-regulation 121–3
standalone computers 569
Standard Oil 630–1
Standard Rate and Data Service (SRDS) 351
standards, ethical 135
star system 468, 471
stars: PR and 646; securing for making films 480–1
station groups 516, 517
statistical significance level 161
steam-powered printing press 268–9, 302, 303
Steele, Bob 133–4
Steinbeck, John 95
stereotypes 28; stereotyping on TV 542
Stewart, Jon 12–13, 13–14
Stewart, Martha 367
stock offerings 72
Stowe, Harriet Beecher 269–70
strategies 232, 635; corporate *see* corporate strategies
strategy games 574
Stratton, Charles ('General Tom Thumb') 628
streaming 394–5, 455–6
stripping 533
student newspapers 102, 103, 317
studio system 467–8
subcultures 25
subgenres 48; entertainment 48–50; news 54–7
subliminal persuasion 597
subscription firms 368–9
subscription networks 518
subscription reference books 278
subscriptions 73, 193; content sites selling 558; magazine distribution 368–9; TV distribution 535
suburbs 330
sunshine laws 120
super audio CD (SACD) 401
superstation 510
Supreme Court: First Amendment 88–91; regulation of content after distribution 104–15; regulation of content before distribution 92–103
Surgeon General's Report on Television and Social Behavior 166

surveillance: individuals' use of mass media 21–2, 23; privacy and digital media 583–6
surveys 46, 146, 147–8
Survivor 50, 51, 61
sweeps 527
syndicates 71, 201, 324
syndication 199, 201, 507, 533–5
syndicators 445–6
synergy 209–13, 235–7

T-Pain 52
tabloid form 309
tactics 635
tailoring 653–4
Take 2 579
talent agents 478, 480
talent guilds 64, 481
talkies 468, 469
Tan, Amy 95
tape recording 389
target audiences 41–7; creating content to attract 45–6; defining 41–5; measuring success of content with 46–7
target segments 193, 359
Target Stores 61
targeting 43, 192–3; advertising 605–8; books 287; magazines 350, 363–4; movie audiences 479; newspapers 334; and the persuasion industries 652–5; radio formats *see* radio formats; TV channels 525–6; web ads 561–3
tastes 204–5
Tatler, The 344
technical order 116
technological change: effect on movies 472–3; TV 511–12
telecom TV 519; production 520–3
Telecommunications Act (1996) 431, 432, 512, 513
telegraph 305, 419
Telemundo 511, 516, 527
television 29, 387, 504–45; advertising on 507–8, 517, 596–7; cable *see* cable television; challenges to traditional TV production and distribution 535–7; covering costs 198–200, 201; distribution 532–7; educational programs 108; exhibition 537–8; First Amendment and 89; fragmentation 511–13; in the 1960s 507–9; interactive TV and game-playing 571–2; media literacy and 538–42; modern TV industry 513–19; and movies 471–2, 495, 507; music promotions 405; production 519–32, 537; radio and the rise of 428; ratings system 128, 129, 513, 540–1; research on the effects of violence in 175–6; rise of 505–9; satellite *see* satellite television; shares of prime-time audience 191; widespread acceptance in the 1950s 506–7; worldwide tastes vs. American tastes 205
television broadcasting 505–6, 513, 514–17; exhibition 537–8; producing channel lineup 523–5; producing individual channels 525–31
Television Eighteen Group (TV18) 206

television networks 508–9, 510–11, 516, 536–7
television program ratings 508, 526–8, 536
Tell Me that You Love Me 653
Terminator 2: Judgment Day 194
terrestrial radio 431, 432–4
territorial rights 483–5
text ads 560
text-to-voice technology 215
textbooks 272–4, 283; exhibition 291–2
theater chains 490; relationship to distributors 490–2
theatrical distribution 485–9
theatrical exhibition 490–3
theatrical films (feature films) 64, 65–7, 473–5; *see also* movies/films
theories 145
theory of reasoned action 145
third party publishers 572
'Thumb, General Tom' (Charles Stratton) 628
Tichenor, Phillip 167, 168
tiering 521–3
Tilberis, Elizabeth 65
Time Inc. 63, 174, 343, 350
Time Inc. vs. *Hill* 90, 112
Time magazine 349, 363, 364
time shifting 101
time slot 531
Time Warner 41, 207, 208, 210, 211, 512, 580, 581, 620; AOL 581; local partners 213
timeliness 54, 365
Tin Pan Alley 382, 385
Titanic 486
title testing 487
tonnage 539
top-level domains (TLDs) 566–7
total market coverage (TMC) 331
Tower Records 68, 408
Toy Story 233
track record 46, 64, 286–7, 483
tracking studies 488
trade books 275; production 280–1
trade incentives 70
trade magazines 351–2
trade paperbacks 275
traditional advertising agencies 601, 602–3
training books 272–4
Trans Union Credit Information Co. 58
transactional databases 584
transformative use 100–1
transistor radios 389, 428
transistors 389, 428, 550
transmission 9–10, 13–14
treatment 479, 531
Tremor 644
truth: legal suits 107, 112; and the persuasion industries 651–2
Tucker, C. Delores 410
Turner, Ted 510
Turner cable networks 213
Twain, Mark 95
Twentieth Century Fox 67
24/7 news operations 325
two-step flow model 159–60
two-way model of public relations 631, 632, 633
Tylenol 641

typical characters 50, 51

ubiquitous advertising 617
unilaterals 98
ultra high frequency (UHF) 506, 514
uniform resource locators (URLs) 566–7
United Independent Broadcasters 423
United Mine Workers 630
United States Postal Service (USPS) 368
universal databases 584
Universal Music Group 390–1, 391–2, 413
university press books 277; production 64, 65–6, 281–2
Univision 108, 511, 516, 527
unusualness 54
UPN 511, 516
upscale readers 361
USA Today 312, 326, 328, 333
usage fees 73
use of mass media 21–3; researching 160–1, 167–9
user generated content 556
users 326
uses and gratifications research 160–1, 167–9
utilitarianism 132–3
Uzbekistan 83

V-chip 540–1, 542
validity 150–1
value-added offers 612
values 135
variety 278–80
vaudeville shows 382–3
veil of ignorance 133
venture capitalists 72
Verbinnen, Sard 637, 646
Verizon 5, 519, 572
vertical integration 70, 198–9, 201, 209; movie industry 467–8; TV networks 516
vertical search engines 251
very high frequency (VHF) 506, 514
VH1 389
Viacom 103, 204, 206, 512, 516, 580, 581, 620
Victor Talking Machine Company 385, 386, 425
Victrola 385
video games 547; advertising and 574–8, 612; distribution and exhibition 578–9; hardware 568–72; media literacy and 579–86; ratings system 126, 128–30, 578–9; rise of 553–5; software 572–4
video on demand (VOD) 522–3, 536
Video Privacy Protection Act (1998) (VPPA) 114
video stores 494–5
videocassette recorder (VCR) 101, 472–3, 511–12
videos, music 405
Vietnamese Americans 318
violence: in films 157, 158; on TV 166, 175–6, 508, 540–1, 542; in video games 578–9, 582
Virginia State Board of Pharmacy et al. vs. *Virginia Citizens Consumer Council* 90
visibility 610–11
Viswanathan, Kaavya 284

Vitascope 465, 466

Wal-Mart 409, 410, 413
Walker, Alice 95
Wall Street Journal 312, 336
Walt Disney *see* Disney Company
Walt Disney International 237
war 97–8; Iraq War 98, 117–18; World War I 154, 424, 631; World War II 162–3, 632
War of the Worlds 65
Warner Brothers 507
Warner Communications 174
Warner music group 390–1, 392, 413
Wartella, Ellen 164–5
Washington, Denzel 26
Washington Post 334, 336
Washington Post Company 63
wavelength scarcity 108
WB network 511
web addresses 564–7
web crawlers (web spiders) 558
web filters 582–3
web hosting 566
web search engines 249, 251–2, 558–9; *see also* Google
WebMD the Magazine 357
website publishers 558
weekly newspapers (weeklies) 312, 316
Western Union 305
wholesalers 289–90, 369, 369–70
wide release 486
Wii game console 568–9, 575
WiMAX 564, 565
windows 199, 200, 201, 493–4
Winfrey, Oprah 366
Winters vs. *New York* 90
wire services 324
wireless fidelity (WiFi) 563–4, 565
Woman's Day 370
women's magazines 346, 352–3
woodblock printing 265, 266
word of mouth 488
World Book Encyclopedia 278
World War I 154, 422, 631
World War II 162–3, 632
World Wide Web 552–3; *see also* Internet
WPP 595, 598, 619, 634, 649–50, 655, 656
writers, film 478–9
Writers Guild of America 64, 481

Xbox game consoles 568, 569, 572, 575
XM Radio 454, 455

Yahoo 513, 559, 581
Yahoo Music 395, 455
Yale Program of Research on Communication and Attitude Change 163, 180
Yankovic, Weird Al 101–2
Yates vs. *United States* 99
yellow journalism 307–9
Yellow Kid, The 307, 308
YouTube 221–2, 581

Zwenger, John Peter 300
Zwick, Edward 537

Related titles from Routledge

Key Readings in Media Today

Brooke Erin Duffy and Joseph Turow, Editors

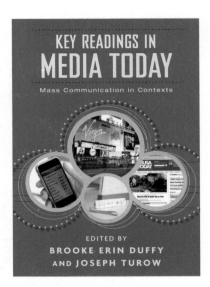

By combining classic studies of mass communication with contemporary research on media, technology, and culture, *Key Readings in Media Today* will help students to make sense of the rapidly changing media environment. The reader is designed to supplement the 3rd edition of *Media Today: An Introduction to Mass Communication*, but it can also be used independently.

Key Readings in Media Today includes 31 articles that will enable students to understand the role of media in the 21st century and the implications for society and each article is framed with a brief introduction designed to orient the reader and weave together the readings.

Key Readings in Media Today incorporates:

- Essential classic and contemporary scholarly articles, as well as recent articles from the trade and mainstream presses selected to provide an in-depth look at the changing nature of media production, distribution, and exhibition.
- Historical and contemporary analyses of each of the major media industries: book, newspaper, magazine, sound recording/radio, motion picture, television, and the internet.
- A concluding section with a selection of essays on the social implications of an increasingly convergent media world, where the boundaries between these media industries are blurring and combining in surprising new ways.
- Questions for discussion at the end of each section.
- Additional student and instructor resources available on a companion website to spark classroom discussion and connect the readings to the latest contemporary media issues and controversies.

Key Readings in Media Today
HB 978-0-415-99204-6
PB 978-0-415-99205-3

Available at all good bookshops
For ordering and further information please visit:
www.routledge.com